Ex Líbris

Randy Manning

© APCo

The Gettysburg Campaign

EDWIN B. CODDINGTON

THE GETTYSBURG CAMPAIGN

A Study in Command

Morningside Press

DAYTON, OHIO
1994

MAPS BY SAMUEL H. BRYANT
based on research and draft maps
prepared by Mrs. James R. Vitelli

This edition is a reprint of the Morningside Bookshop hardcover
edition; Copyright © 1979 by Morningside Bookshop

Substantial parts of Chapters VI and VII were first
published in *Pennsylvania History,* a quarterly journal
of the Pennsylvania Historical Association.
Copyright © 1963, 1964 Edwin B. Coddington.

A-3.68[V]

Printed in the United States of America

Library of Congress Catalog Card Number 68-11538

ISBN-089029-049X

THIS EDITION PUBLISHED BY ARRANGEMENT
WITH CHARLES SCRIBNER'S SONS

ILLUSTRATION ACKNOWLEDGMENTS

Battles and Leaders of the Civil War, Vol. III, edited by Johnson and Buel. The Century Company, New York, 1888: 18, 30, 38; Culver Pictures, Inc.: 4; Library of Congress: 2, 10, 16, 20, 21, 23, 25, 27, 31, 32, 37, 39, 40; Courtesy of Francis C. Carleton of Belmont, Massachusetts: 11, 24, 33, 34, 35 (all from the Bachelder Scrapbook), 36 (from the Bachelder Sketch Book); The National Archives: 1 (U. S. Signal Corps Photo, Brady Collection), 26, 29 (National Park Service Photos), 41 (U. S. War Department General Staff Photo); Princeton University Library: 28 (from Charles W. Reed Collection); Scribner Art Files: 3, 5, 6, 7, 8, 9 (by Brady), 12 (by F. B. Johnston), 13, 14 (by Cook), 15, 17 (by Cook), 22; Valentine Museum: 19 (from Cook Collection)

TO CAROLINE

Facsimile
49
Reprinted April, 1994

This book is printed on
Glatfelter acid-free paper

Printed in the United States of America

EDWIN B. CODDINGTON

INTRODUCTION TO
THE MORNINGSIDE EDITION

Outstanding historians of successive generations produce books that endure either because of the research and writing they subsequently promote or their definitive treatment of a consequential subject. In thinking of the first category, the works of historians like Frederick J. Turner and Charles A. Beard immediately come to mind; on pondering the second group, one promptly recalls books like B. F. Lossing's **Pictorial Field-Book of the American Revolution** (published in the 1850s and still relied on more than its users acknowledge) and Edwin B. Coddington's magisterial **The Battle of Gettysburg.**

Coddington's treatise is not just one more commonplace addition to the many volumes on the Civil War that are perennially published to appease the appetite of Civil War enthusiasts. It is rather a monument to exacting scholarship, a study so exhaustively thorough that it need not be done again, at least for the foreseeable future. And that remark, obviously enough, applies to an antonishingly small number of history books.

A native of Wisconsin, Coddington received his undergraduate education at Dartmouth College and his graduate training at Clark University. An academic career that began in 1937 culminated in an appointment as head of the history department at Lafayette College, a position that he held for two decades and that he filled with distinction, both as an able administrator and outstanding teacher.

In addition to his strictly professorial duties, Coddington happily shouldered many and varied professional responsibilities. They reflected his abiding concern with the study and writing of history and were expressed by his contributions to historical societies and associations — local, state, and national. Among those in whose activities he played a prominent part were the Pennsylvania Historical Association of which he became president in 1966, the Pennsylvania Historical and Museum Commission to which he was appointed in 1963, and Phi Alpha Theta, the national history honorary society, of which he was a council member and for two years president.

From these myriad professional commitments, Dr. Coddington found time to indulge his abiding absorption in the history of the Civil War. The subject of his doctoral dissertation was the social and economic history of the seaboard states of the Confederacy, and on this and other aspects of Civil War history he continued to focus his scholarly interest. The result was a number of first-rate articles that enhanced our knowledge of this turbulent and critical era. But Coddington's overarching interest, and the field of his unique expertness, was the military history of the war. The ripe harvest of his unflagging cultivation was **The Battle of Gettysburg: A Study in Command,** published in 1968 just following his death.

Ten years (to Coddington, joyous ones all) went into the research and preparation of **The Battle of Gettysburg.** He overlooked no possible historical source, consequential or only marginally relevant; he omitted from his peripatetic research no historical society that might afford a nugget of data, no manuscript collection that might include a germane document on the famous military engagement that he intended to recount. He did so in rich historical detail. More impressively yet, he also contrived in the process of research and writing to vicariously relive and thus to compellingly recreate for his readers a memorably engaging story of the battle that more than any other determined the outcome of the American Civil War.

The subtitle of Coddington's work ("a study in command") cryptically describes his approach and intent: a fresh assessment of the nature and quality of leadership displayed by the high-ranking Union and Confederate officers who confronted each other at Gettysburg and an innovative interpretation of the success or failure of the commanders' crucial decisions. Coddington's original thesis is that Northern victory was due as much to the hitherto unappreciated talents of Union generals as to the mistaken strategy and tactics of General Robert E. Lee. This thesis is embedded in a narrative that also dispels many of the myths surrounding a kaleidoscopic battle that was also a decisive one.

Coddington's many friends and professional colleagues, nonspecialist readers of history books, and particularly Civil War scholars should applaud the Morningside Bookshop's reissue of this important monograph. **The Battle of Gettysburg** will endure as long as Americans continue to be fascinated by the war in which American nationality was finally forged.

Jacob E. Cooke
MacCracken Professor of History
Lafayette College
February 26, 1979

Acknowledgments

IN WRITING this book many people have aided me in countless ways, and some have gone far beyond the call of duty in giving of their time and effort. Of these I wish to thank particularly my wife, Caroline Quarles Coddington. As research assistant she accompanied me on my jaunts along the Eastern Seaboard and to the West Coast in search of material; as literary critic she improved my style and corrected errors; and as secretary she typed and retyped the manuscript and its many revisions. My thanks go also to our daughter, Louise, who was of immense help as an eagle-eyed reader of proof.

Two of the primary requisites for writing this book, time and money, were in large measure made possible by the generosity of President K. Roald Bergethon and the Board of Trustees of Lafayette College. For two consecutive years they granted me leaves of absence from my regular duties and paid part of my salary during that time, as well as advancing funds for travel and research. Needless to say, I am deeply grateful.

I wish also to express my appreciation to Mrs. James R. Vitelli, wife of one of my colleagues at Lafayette College, for her skill and dedication in drawing the maps. They are based upon various sources: the maps of the United States Geological Survey which were kindly furnished me by the late Dr. James L. Dyson, for many years Professor of Geology and Head of the Department of Geology at Lafayette College; the Atlas of the *Official Records;* the battle maps of General G. K. Warren; and those of Colonel John B. Bachelder. In view of my own supervision of their preparation I take full responsibility for any mistakes.

Research at certain libraries and depositories proved especially rewarding because members of their staffs showed unusual interest in my project and diligently dug up new material or were helpful in other ways. I wish particularly to thank Dr. James W. Patton, Director, and the staff of the Southern Historical Collection, University of North Carolina Library; Dr. Mattie Russell and Mrs. Virginia R. Gray, Manuscripts Department, Duke University Library; William Work, Archivist, and Dr.

ACKNOWLEDGMENTS

Frank Evans and the late Henry Eddy, former Archivists, Division of Public Records, Pennsylvania Historical and Museum Commission; Dr. Howard B. Gotlieb, formerly Librarian of Historical Manuscripts, Yale University Library; Dr. Stephen T. Riley, Director, Massachusetts Historical Society; Mrs. Sarah Jackson, National Archives; Roger Preston, Manuscripts Division, Library of Congress; Miss Mary C. Shafer, formerly Reference Librarian, Lafayette College Library; Richard B. Harwell, Librarian, Bowdoin College; and Dr. Clifford K. Shipton, formerly Director, American Antiquarian Society.

In seeking new sources of information about the battle of Gettysburg my attention early turned to one Colonel John B. Bachelder whose name was occasionally mentioned in the correspondence of participants as an authority on the engagement. Very few twentieth century scholars cited him, and those who did seemed to have no idea of who he really was; as late as 1962 the historians at the Gettysburg National Military Park had only vague notions about him. For reasons unknown he had disappeared into obscurity after his death in 1894. Under the circumstances, learning more about Bachelder proved to be difficult, but I finally tracked him down at the New Hampshire Historical Society. There I not only discovered his identity, but I also unearthed his sizeable collection of letters, diaries, memoirs, statements by participants in the battle both Union and Confederate, and a variety of other documents. The manuscript of Bachelder's own history of the campaign and battle was also there; although he collected material for it for thirty-one years, it was not published, probably because it never measured up to his standards of complete accuracy in each detail.

Bachelder, a native of New Hampshire, was working as a lithographer and printer in Boston when the Civil War broke out. In 1862 he attached himself to the Army of the Potomac as an observer and artist in search of scenes to be recorded for posterity. Although many years earlier the Governor of Pennsylvania had conferred on him the courtesy title of Lieutenant Colonel of the Pennsylvania Militia, Bachelder remained a civilian even while accompanying the army on its various campaigns. For some reason he was not on hand during the battle of Gettysburg; but he reached the field a few days later and stayed there for over three months, interviewing many of the thousands of wounded of both armies who were hospitalized in the town and surrounding countryside, and taking notes on what they said. Armed with this voluminous first-hand information, Bachelder set to work producing a colored isometrical drawing of the battlefield, on which he indicated the position of every Northern and Southern infantry regiment at the beginning of each of the three days' fighting. From then on the study of the battle became his major concern, amounting almost to an obsession, as his enormous correspondence reveals. Soon he had established himself as *the* authority to whom veterans of both camps, from generals to privates, could—and did —turn for assistance in checking their recollections. He helped organize reunions at the battlefield, to which participants of both sides were invited, and at which he acted as guide.

Because of his great knowledge of the battle Bachelder was named Superintendent of Tablets and Legends of the Gettysburg Battlefield Memorial Association, a private organization dedicated to preserving the field as it was in 1863. It was his responsibility to work with survivors of various military units and approve the location of their plaques and monuments, a task which he carried out with tact and firmness in the face of conflicting claims. The War Department also used his services to indicate troop positions and movements on a set of battle maps which it published in 1876. Sometime later Congress named him Government Historian of the Battle of Gettysburg, a high-sounding title which seems to have entailed more wind than substance. Nevertheless, it testified to Bachelder's stature and to the authority of his findings on Gettysburg. His papers contain much information not to be found elsewhere and thus fill in serious gaps in the story.

Not all of Bachelder's papers have been preserved, but of those extant the New Hampshire Historical Society has by far the greatest number. In this connection I wish to thank Mrs. Russell B. Tobey, the society's librarian, for her diligence in locating them, box after box. A few of Bachelder's notes are at the Henry E. Huntington Library, and a number of his letters and some documents belong to his grandnephew, Francis C. Carleton of Belmont, Massachusetts. Thanks to the efforts of Philip N. Guyol, formerly Director of the New Hampshire Historical Society, I was able to meet Mr. Carleton at the old family homestead in Nottingham, New Hampshire. I am deeply grateful to that gentleman for his warm hospitality, his generous gifts of Bachelder mementos, and permission to obtain microfilms of the Bachelder papers in his possession. To Dr. Malcolm Freiberg, Editor of Publications of the Massachusetts Historical Society, I extend my appreciation for his efforts in having the papers microfilmed.

Various people have liberally given of their time and shared their knowledge with me. My former professor, Dr. Ray A. Billington, presently Research Associate at the Huntington Library, kindly read parts of my first draft and offered me sound advice about how best to approach the subject. Dr. Frederick Tilberg, Senior Historian Emeritus, and Dr. Harry W. Pfanz, formerly Supervisory Historian of the Gettysburg National Military Park, spent long hours with me discussing the battle and studying the terrain on my visits to Gettysburg. They made my trips there a source of pleasure and knowledge. I am under deep obligation to Dr. Robert L. Bloom, Professor of History and Head of the Department, Gettysburg College, for reading my manuscript, appraising its contents, and making suggestions. Robert J. Jurgen of New York City furnished me with valuable information he had gathered in his studies of General John Sedgwick and the Sixth Corps. I owe much to Dr. Frederic S. Klein, Professor of History at Franklin and Marshall College, for his help in tracing the route of the Sixth Corps in its march from Manchester, Maryland, to Gettysburg, and for his gift of copies of family letters written during the campaign and battle. Dr. John Bakeless of Seymour, Connecticut, in generously sharing with me his knowledge of Civil War espionage revealed the identity of Harrison, the Confederate spy. Miss Lee Bacon of Milwaukee, Wisconsin, graciously turned over for my use typescripts of the Civil War letters of her grandfather, Colonel Lucius Fairchild of the 2nd Wisconsin regiment, and of his brother Charles. Morton C. Jaquith of Worcester, Massachusetts, kindly allowed me to use material from letters written by his great-uncle, Captain Henry N. Comey of the 2nd Massachusetts regiment. Last, but certainly not least, I give much credit for what I have been able to accomplish in my Civil War studies to the late Percy H. Batten of Racine, Wisconsin, an uncle by marriage and a friend of long standing. He gave me as many books as I wished to have from his fine Civil War library. These volumes proved invaluable and greatly aided in my research.

Dr. Russell F. Weigley, formerly editor of *Pennsylvania History*, has kindly permitted me to use two of my articles which appeared in the April, 1963, and April, 1964, issues of the magazine as parts of Chapters VI and VII of the book. I wish also to thank Mrs. Lindley Murray Winston of Altavista, Virginia, for allowing me to quote a long passage from a letter written by Major James Dearing, C.S.A., on July 26, 1863.

Preface

THE CAMPAIGN and battle of Gettysburg have great significance in themselves, but they gain in dimension when viewed in the overall context of the American Civil War. The campaign of many weeks duration occurred almost midway in the course of the war. It began with a period of preparation in the middle of May, 1863, and for the purposes of this book ended when the last Confederate brigade slipped across the Potomac River on July 14. The battle itself was fought on July 1, 2, and 3, just as General Ulysses S. Grant was forcing the capitulation of the mighty Mississippi River fortress of Vicksburg. In retrospect the battle of Gettysburg seemed to have been a turning point in the course of the conflict, and it became popularly known as the place where the Confederacy reached its High Water Mark. This interpretation has validity, however, only if the history of the war is confined to a study of military and political events and developments.

Certainly by late spring of 1863 the struggle between the two sections of the country had assumed many of the earmarks of a frustrating military stalemate. The Confederacy still retained viability as a political, economic, and geographic entity. It had achieved an organization of its slim supply of manpower and material resources sufficient to withstand increasing pressure on all sides while mounting its greatest military offensive of the conflict. Only after a bloody three day battle—the bloodiest of the war—in which veteran armies fought with skill and determination, did this Southern surge of power sullenly recede to its homeland. A Confederate victory might well have brought results favorable to the South almost immediately. The triumph of Federal arms, on the other hand, though it was hailed by Northerners as cause for rejoicing, was really not appreciated by most observers until after the war. At the time, the successful retreat of Lee's army into Virginia placed a damper upon elation in the North. There was still danger that if Southern resistance persisted the federal government would give up its efforts to conquer the Confederacy and the South would gain independence by default.

The real question in 1863 was the Northern will to fight. Should the people support Lincoln in his determination to defeat the Confederacy, victory was a foregone conclusion, largely because of fundamental developments which were becoming evident. The North had organized its sprawling, loose-jointed economy efficiently enough to sustain the material well-being of its civilians while prosecuting the war on an ever vaster scale. In contrast the Confederate economy, undermined by external and internal forces, had begun a rapid decline in many areas from scarcity to real want. Commodities which at one time had filled the pantries of well regulated Southern households or lined the shelves of well run stores had long since disappeared, to be replaced in some instances by unsatisfactory substitutes. Blockade-running could satisfy only the pressing needs of the military. Runaway inflation and the army's drain on Southern manpower had already stopped industrial growth and seriously hindered agricultural production which was needed to meet the demand for foodstuffs. As Northern armies edged deeper into the South, the old plantation economy, and with it a way of life, began to crumble when Negroes in increasing hordes flocked to the military camps or followed in the wake of advancing forces. The federal government was thus compelled to lift its sights and place its war aims on a loftier level. The struggle to save the Union became the fight for freedom. Ironically, if Meade had destroyed Lee's army at Gettysburg and brought hostilities to a successful close, as Lincoln had fervently hoped and expected, the movement toward abolition of slavery would very likely have sputtered to a halt.

As Lee brought his army back safely to Virginia in July of 1863, a sense of failure began to creep over Northerners, especially after they heard of Grant's great triumph at Vicksburg, when he wiped out an entire Confederate army through capture. By comparison Meade's victory at Gettysburg seemed like unfinished business, in view of what many critics termed Lee's "escape." People in the North immediately asked "Why," while those in the South shook their heads in shock and disbelief at their hero's defeat. Over the years this feeling of dissatisfaction with the results of the battle led to an outpouring of books, articles, pamphlets, and orations, in which writers both Northern and Southern overindulged in the use of the word "if." The volume of this literature became so vast that as early as 1900 one historian timidly suggested that "another history of Gettysburg may seem superfluous and presumptuous," especially, he should have added, if traditional interpretations were accepted. In most of these accounts Meade as a general was reduced to a cipher. Sometimes he was depicted as lost in the smoke of battle and furnishing no overall direction to the men, who nonetheless fought more brilliantly than ever; sometimes as not possessing enough ability to realize the advantages of his position at Gettysburg and wanting to get out, until his more stouthearted generals such as Dan Sickles forced him to stay and fight. Most authors, regardless of their sympathies, agreed that Meade missed golden opportunities to crush Lee during the retreat. Confederate writers, generally overlooking Northern mistakes, almost consistently blamed General James Longstreet for their defeat, while they damned the delinquencies of Generals "Jeb" Stuart and Richard S. Ewell with only slightly less fervor.

Because these traditional interpretations have become threadbare and somewhat frayed around the edges, another account of the battle seems to be needed, even at the risk of its being considered by some "superfluous and presumptuous." To achieve better focus and deeper perspective this study emphasizes Northern and Southern problems of command in the broader setting of the whole campaign. By using many new sources of information and concentrating on questions of command, it is hoped this book will dust off a few of the older explanations for its outcome, alter some, and discard others.

If this justification for another volume on Gettysburg is not enough, it should be pointed out that the unique features of this campaign and battle have always had a fatal attraction for historians. The unusual duration of the campaign and the long, hard marches in torrid summer weather made an indelible impression upon soldiers in both camps. Never before had they gone so far—nor would they again—to grab at each others' throats. Furthermore, in the great encounter at Gettysburg the Army of the Potomac gained new confidence in itself which was to carry it through the agonizing months ahead and eventually to victory. One tough Northern general, A. A. Humphreys, described the experiences of many soldiers when in August of 1863 he wrote:

> What a campaign we have had. . . . The immense marches—the extraordinary fatigue—the nights of no sleep, of lying in the rain— of watching the enemy—of marching to meet him—of maneuvering —of fighting—marching again in pursuit, of attacks & hopes of other battles—we have marched not less than 500 miles—fought the heaviest battle of the war . . . & tried twice in attacking the enemy to bring on another great battle & break up his army. The army has never before done so much—never moved so rapidly— never been so *offensive* in its operations. . . .

But the uncompleted task at Gettysburg forced the Army of the Potomac to return unhappily to old haunts in Virginia. Meade continued as commander of the Army of the Potomac and would remain so until Lee's surrender, despite Lincoln's disappointment with his performance immediately after Gettysburg. In the remaining months of 1863 Lee and Meade maneuvered their armies in futile efforts to catch each other off balance. They had some sharp encounters, but no pitched battles. Meanwhile the Eleventh and Twelfth Corps left Meade's army and became the Twentieth Corps in General William T. Sherman's forces in the West. Then in March of 1864 when the new General in Chief, U. S. Grant, came east to direct operations, the Army of the Potomac was reorganized and given substantial reinforcements. Patterned after its Southern adversary, it now had but three infantry and one cavalry corps. In the rearrangement the famous First and Third Corps, which the fighting at Gettysburg had shattered, were broken up and their divisions distributed among the Second, Fifth, and Sixth Corps. Though Grant accompanied the army, he and Meade maintained separate headquarters. Under the circumstances it was a trying situation for Meade, but the two generals got along well because of their mutual admiration for each other as highly competent officers. In the long struggle to subdue Lee, Grant depended largely upon the Army of the Potomac to carry out his plans, though he had other forces in the East at his disposal.

During this period the vicissitudes of war brought about important changes in the top command of the Army of the Potomac.

General A. A. Humphreys succeeded General Winfield S. Hancock, who had not fully recovered from his wound at Gettysburg, as commander of the Second Corps. General Horatio G. Wright took the Sixth Corps in place of General John Sedgwick, who had been picked off by a sniper, and General Alexander S. Webb became Meade's chief of staff. Shortly before the Appomattox campaign Grant brought in General Philip Sheridan and his cavalry to help in the final effort to surround Lee's army. Meade, Humphreys, and Wright contributed as much as anyone—and more than most—to the desperate pursuit, but Sheridan grabbed the glory. Meade was not even accorded the honor of being present at the surrender ceremonies at Appomattox.

Meade ignored the slight, and when he heard of the surrender he went through the Confederate lines, unescorted except for two aides, and sought out Lee in an effort to ease the pain of his defeat. In the same spirit General Webb visited with old friends four days after the surrender and received greetings to be sent on to his wife:

> Last night E. P. Alexander Brig. Genl C.S.A. sent his kindest regards to you. Maj. Webb & Genl Field and Genl Wilcox do the same—I took them a bottle of whiskey a candle a candle stick & box of matches & they were very jolly over it. We had a lively time of it. . . . I find that I had fought them all at times & they give me credit of doing it well.

It was a strange and tragic war, the bloodiest in our history; yet often the participants seemed to treat it as nothing but a rough game played according to established rules. Therein lies at least part of the fascination of the story.

Contents

ILLUSTRATIONS

Between pages 198 and 199

AND

Between pages 380 and 381

LIST OF MAPS

The Gettysburg Campaign

I

LEE PREPARES FOR A SUMMER CAMPAIGN, 1863

THE MONTH of April, 1863, marked in the pages of history the midway point of the Civil War in the United States, but to the people of the North and the South living at that time it had a different meaning. It signified for them the opening of another season when the thunder of battle would once more roll across the land and the casualty lists stretch out endlessly. They could not know how much longer the war would last, but by 1863 they felt it had been with them forever and might go on forever.

After two years of struggle the South still bristled defiance and vigorously fought off the invaders who continued to pound against her defenses in the major military theaters. Northern forces for months had been striving to seize control of the Mississippi River and cut the Confederacy in two, but since their early successes in 1862 when New Orleans and Memphis were captured they had made little progress, for the remaining section of the river was guarded by the formidable defenses of Vicksburg on the north and Port Hudson 300 miles to the south. In central Tennessee not far from the western edge of the Appalachians the armies of the Union general, William S. Rosecrans, and the Confederate general, Braxton Bragg, stood glaring at each other after having fought themselves to a standstill at the battle of Murfreesboro many weeks earlier. Rosecrans was no closer to capturing Chattanooga, a railroad center and gateway to the lower South, than he had been at the beginning of the year. Along the Atlantic seaboard the experience of

Federal generals, especially those operating between Washington, D. C., and Richmond, Virginia, was proving even more frustrating and humiliating. Ever since the start of the war one of their major goals had been the capture of the Confederate capital, but only General George B. McClellan could boast of having come close enough to see the church spires of the city. Now in April, 1863, a new general, Joseph Hooker, stood ready in burnished armor to try his luck and skill against the fearsome, wily Confederate general, Robert E. Lee.

Hooker's powerful Army of the Potomac was at peak strength as he began a series of complicated maneuvers near Fredericksburg, Virginia, which were designed to crush his foe in one mighty blow and open up the road to Richmond. With the Union army once more on the prowl, people in the North from President Abraham Lincoln to the most humble citizen during the first few days of May hopefully awaited news of a great and final victory. What they finally heard with aching hearts was the same old refrain: Lee had again escaped a trap near the little crossroads hamlet of Chancellorsville and in one of his most brilliant displays of generalship had inflicted ignominious defeat upon a force twice the size of his own. While many people in both the North and the South saw in Chancellorsville further evidence of the Confederacy's invincibility, they overlooked certain realities.

Lee, it is true, had prevented Hooker from accomplishing his objective and had forced him to retreat to his winter quarters. Although the Northern army had suffered heavy losses, it still was intact and could renew the offensive if given a breathing spell. The Confederates, however, could not afford to wait. Lee and other Southern leaders felt they had to gain a decisive victory that summer, as time was running out and never again would the South be so strong. Even as they celebrated the glorious triumph at Chancellorsville they saw ominous developments unfolding in the Mississippi Valley. General U. S. Grant had finally solved a difficult strategic problem and on April 30 had gotten his army on the same side of the river as the defenders of Vicksburg. In a series of swift moves and skillfully fought engagements he had defeated one Confederate force and then turned to pin down a larger one in the elaborate defenses protecting Vicksburg. Grant's siege of the city could have but one result unless the Southerners could think of some way to divert his attention and loosen his grip. Some of them clearly recognized the danger, as did an important official in the Confederate War Department who wrote: "The crisis there is of the greatest moment. The loss of Vicksburg and the Mississippi river . . . would wound us very deeply in a political as well as a military point of view." [1]

These developments during early May forced Southern leaders to take a hard look at the overall military picture and come to some vital decisions. At this stage of the war President Jefferson Davis, Secretary of War James A. Seddon, and General Lee were acting as an informal board which had final say in all major questions of Confederate strategy. Seddon, who had definite ideas of his own about military affairs, was usually but not always a party to Davis' discussions with Lee. From time to time other important political and military figures were invited to join these sessions, but Davis invariably dominated them by virtue of his temperament, his position as President, and his West Point training. In contrast to the Northern command organization, the South had no general in chief. If anyone fulfilled his functions, it was the President.

For some time Davis and Seddon had been worrying about affairs in the West. During the winter of 1862–63 they had suggested to Lee the possibility of shifting some units of his Army of Northern Virginia to reinforce either General Bragg's forces in central Tennessee or General John C. Pemberton's men in Mississippi. Lee always found good reasons for opposing the idea. He questioned whether additional troops there would redress the balance in favor of the Confederacy, and he wondered how with reduced forces he would be able to cope with the powerful Army of the Potomac. Although these arguments had some of the earmarks of special pleading, nevertheless they were essentially sound.[2] To Lee the real solution to the strategic problem was a vigorous counteroffensive in the East. Rather than weaken his magnificent army he proposed that it be strengthened so that he would be able to seize the initiative from the enemy. Long before the Chancellorsville campaign he had contemplated a move toward the Shenandoah Valley to crush Federal forces there and go on to an invasion of the North, but by the time the weather had improved and the roads dried up after the spring rains, Hooker's army was already on the move.[3] Any hopes of an

5

offensive had to be deferred until the outcome of the campaign was determined. The Confederate victory at Chancellorsville encouraged Lee to renew his plans.

He at once took steps to recondition and strengthen his army before the enemy could recover from his defeat. In spite of his heavy losses in general officers, including "Stonewall" Jackson, Lee had gained many advantages, not the least of which were time and the freedom to maneuver. The Confederates had also gained psychologically, and their confidence in the military prowess of the Army of Northern Virginia under Lee soared to new heights. They had won two major battles, Fredericksburg and Chancellorsville, within a period of five months. Particularly impressive was the way in which they had beaten the Federal army in the second engagement. At Fredericksburg they had fought defensively and allowed the enemy to exhaust himself in headlong attacks against a sunken road; at Chancellorsville with forces approximately half the size of those of the enemy they had wrested the initiative from Hooker, gone on the offensive, and forced their opponents to give up the fight. If a fraction of the Army of Northern Virginia could accomplish so much, what could it not do once it had been refurbished and reinforced? The answer depended on Davis and Seddon. Lee had to get their approval and cooperation before he could proceed with his preparations.

While working out his plans Lee kept in constant touch with these men, usually by letter or dispatch but occasionally by personal conference. Their decisions were generally kept secret, much to the annoyance of some of the more important subordinates in the War Department. Insistence upon secrecy was typical of Lee; he was extremely reticent about revealing his plans to anyone except the Secretary of War, the President, and now and then a few of his intimates in the army such as Lieutenant General James Longstreet or certain members of his staff. Newspaper correspondents were never told anything of importance, and it annoyed Lee when they were guilty of security leaks.[4]

Lee had to go to Richmond twice in May for meetings with Davis and Seddon before his summer offensive received final approval. The first conference resulted from Lee's desire to consult with Davis shortly after Chancellorsville. He had suggested that the President visit him at army headquarters, but in the end he went to Richmond

6

himself. He was there several days, from May 14 to 17, and during that time he discussed his plans with the two officials. No minutes were kept—at least none have been found—so there is no way of knowing exactly what Lee said in favor of his proposal or what questions were asked of him. The three men agreed upon an invasion of the North by Lee's army as a means of drawing Grant away from the lower Mississippi Valley before he could do any real harm. A few days later they learned the worst: Grant had finally cornered General Pemberton's army in Vicksburg and laid siege to the city. The news resulted in another conference on May 26. This time Davis, Seddon, and Lee met with the Cabinet to review Confederate grand strategy and decide what measures should be taken to force Grant to lift the siege. Davis now expressed doubts about the wisdom of invading Pennsylvania instead of detaching troops from Lee's army for the relief of Pemberton. Postmaster General John H. Reagan supported his position, but in the end both men yielded to the majority opinion and it was decided that the invasion should take place.[5]

Although the officials had settled the big question, they left many others unresolved, if indeed they considered them at all. How extensive would be Lee's invasion of the North? How many troops would he need? Where would he get them? Would he be allowed to strip the seaboard of all forces except the few required to guard against minor enemy raids? Lee seemed to assume that he and Davis, if not the others, had come to an understanding on these matters. If so, he was soon disillusioned for on May 31, five days after the meeting, Davis made the amazing statement that he had "never fairly comprehended" Lee's "views and purposes" until he received a letter and a dispatch from the general that day.[6] Lee had sent them in reply to a telegram from Davis overruling his efforts to obtain reinforcements from the seaboard. In great detail Lee described his frustrations in trying to get his offensive under way before the enemy could anticipate him. Perhaps it was already too late, he said, for him to accomplish his objectives.[7] Lee's statements seem to have surprised and upset Davis, and he expressed regret that he had "misunderstood" the general; he would have been glad to "second" his wishes if he had known about them sooner.[8] This exchange is hard to understand and makes one wonder what in fact the two men did discuss during Lee's several visits to Richmond.

7

Although Lee's more distant goals might not have been clear, following his victory in May he had a very definite idea of his immediate objectives. First of all he wanted to break up the enemy's plan for a summer campaign in Virginia. He knew that the Union position on the north bank of the Rappahannock opposite Fredericksburg was too strong for him to attack to his "advantage," but he hoped to draw Hooker's army away from the area by moving his own forces toward the Shenandoah Valley and the Potomac River. On the way he would crush Federal troops which, to the annoyance of the Virginians, had been occupying the lower end of the valley during the winter and spring. These maneuvers would force the enemy to make a countermove and might give the Confederates "a fair opportunity to strike a blow." Once arrived on the banks of the Potomac, he would cross the river if such a move seemed "practicable." Lee felt that the presence of Southern forces north of the Potomac would bring to Hooker's support "troops designed to operate against other parts of the country," [9] and whatever military success he might gain there would have much greater impact on enemy morale and plans than a similar achievement in Virginia. Furthermore, by luring the Army of the Potomac out of Virginia Lee would give his people a respite from the ravages of war and a chance to harvest their crops free from interruption by military operations.[10]

It is very probable that Lee had in mind an invasion not only of Maryland but of Pennsylvania as well, for this was a prospect which had long attracted his attention. During the previous winter he had undoubtedly discussed the possibility of such a move with General Jackson, who always ardently seconded any plans for taking the offensive. In February, 1863, the two men had gone so far in their thinking as to direct Jedediah Hotchkiss, Jackson's chief engineer, to draw up a map of the Valley of Virginia "extended to Harrisburg Pa. and then on to Philadelphia—wishing the preparation to be kept a profound secret." [11] Events had forced Lee to lay aside any plans he might have formulated until a more propitious time. With the improvement of his military fortunes in May the moment had come for him to attempt this ambitious enterprise. If he did succeed in getting into Pennsylvania, his subsequent moves would depend upon hoped-for but unpredictable developments. Only a commander who had supreme confidence in himself and his army would dare be so opportunistic. Whatever else he might accomplish, he wanted above all to spend the summer in lower Pennsylvania maneuvering his forces so as to pose threats to the vital centers of Washington, Baltimore, and Philadelphia, while stripping the country of greatly needed supplies. Certainly he had no wish to repeat the campaign of nine months ago, when he had forced the enemy to fight him on the old battleground of Bull Run, not far from Washington. Though badly defeated, the Federal forces had retreated to the elaborate defenses of the capital, regrouped, and emerged ready for another engagement. The Army of Northern Virginia was surfeited with such victories which gained for it fame, but no decisive results. Although Lee was not seeking a "general" or pitched battle with the Union army, he would try to catch it off balance and destroy it bit by bit.

According to Colonel (later General) A. L. Long, his one-time military secretary, Lee foresaw the possibility of being forced to give battle somewhere near Chambersburg, York, or Gettysburg. Should that occur, he would prefer fighting it out in the vicinity of Gettysburg as "much to the point," since it was less distant from his base on the Potomac and close to the passes of South Mountain, which he would have to hold in order to safeguard his lines of communication to Virginia. Apparently there was no question in his mind of driving specifically for some big city, Philadelphia for instance, as many Northern alarmists predicted, because this was not his true military objective. All such rich prizes would fall like ripe plums should he whip the Army of the Potomac. A disaster of such proportions would encourage the Peace Democrats in the North to step up their agitation against continued prosecution of the war; they might even gather enough political power to force the Lincoln administration into a negotiated peace with the South. At this stage of the war a major victory in the East would go further toward solving the strategic dilemma of the Confederacy than any other event, and Lee's army had the best chance of achieving that goal. His move across the Potomac was a big gamble, but it was well worth the risk.[12] Major Charles Marshall, a member of Lee's staff, summed up the situation neatly when he wrote: "So, if General Lee remained inactive, both Vicksburg and Richmond would be imperilled, whereas if he were successful north of the Potomac, both would be saved."[13]

Just as Lee's long-range objectives seemed uncertain to some of his critics, so too his tactics became subject to question in later years. The controversy began when Longstreet, Lee's chief lieutenant, in his postwar writing put forth the doubtful thesis that Lee had agreed to confine himself to fighting defensive battles while he was on his offensive campaign in the North. By this time Longstreet's record in the Gettysburg campaign had become the object of severe and sometimes unfair criticism, and in striking back at his detractors he tried to justify his role by picturing himself as the great strategist whose advice Lee did not appreciate and did not follow. It was he who had "first suggested" to General Lee "the idea of an offensive campaign" of some sort, he said. As for the invasion of Maryland and Pennsylvania, Longstreet declared that he was "never persuaded" to accept the plan "except with the understanding that we were not to deliver an offensive battle . . . , that our campaign should be one of offensive strategy, but defensive tactics." All would have been well, he continued, if the Confederate army had reenacted the battle of Fredericksburg of the previous December, when it held a strong defensive position against which Federal troops vainly hurled themselves in a succession of massive assaults. Lee had suffered defeat in Pennsylvania, he insisted, because he broke his promise to fight in the manner of Fredericksburg.[14] (Apparently it never occurred to Longstreet that Union commanders would certainly have tried to avoid a repetition of their performance in this battle.)

Such then was Longstreet's contention, but there is every reason to doubt its validity. Very possibly in reviewing the campaign he conceived the idea that if he had exacted such a promise from Lee, the outcome might have been different. The more he thought of this possibility, the more his conviction grew that he had suggested defensive tactics when in fact he had not done so. On the contrary, Longstreet himself furnished evidence that he had enthusiastically endorsed a northern offensive by Lee's army without any qualifications. In a letter to a friend written on May 13, 1863, he revealed his thinking as a result of discussions he had had with Lee following his return to the Army of Northern Virginia early in May. Lee was glad to see "Pete" Longstreet, for now that Jackson was gone he needed the comfort of his presence and his observations on military matters. The two generals spent considerable time exploring the possibilities of offensive operations by the Army of Northern Virginia with particular reference to their impact upon the military situation in the West. It is clear that Longstreet agreed with Lee's plans for he wrote, "We should make a grand effort against the Yankees this summer," and then he added, "Every available man and means should be brought to bear against them. . . ." He had urged that Lee's army should make a "forward movement," he said, instead of remaining on the defensive and sending troops to reinforce Pemberton, who might do nothing with them but let them lie idle. In the event of an offensive by the Army of Northern Virginia, Longstreet observed, "We should want everything that we had and all that we could get." Aware of Lee's intentions to meet with Davis and Seddon in Richmond, he had prepared a memorandum of his views which he hoped would help these leaders to "settle upon something at once." Longstreet's letter contained no mention of any condition for his approval of an offensive campaign. Although this fact proves nothing, the tone of the communication in contrast to his postwar recollections suggests complete harmony with Lee and no disposition to urge caution.[15]

With the help of Longstreet and the other top officers Lee proceeded to plan his military operations for the months ahead and get his army in shape. He had paid the price of beating his old adversary by incurring unusually heavy losses in high-ranking officers. Even before operations had ceased in the Chancellorsville campaign Lee sent a hurried call to Davis for two major generals as replacements for two division commanders. On May 6 he appointed Major General A. P. Hill to temporary command of the Second Corps to replace the wounded Jackson.[16] The death of Jackson a few days later led him to propose to Davis a drastic change that for the past year he had considered desirable in the organization of the corps. The Army of Northern Virginia had always contained two infantry corps of about 30,000 men each, the First commanded by Longstreet and the Second by Jackson. Lee felt a corps of that size was too large for one man to handle, especially in heavily wooded country where the various units were "always beyond the range of his vision, and frequently beyond his reach." Until then he had held back from considering any change in organization for want of good commanders.[17] The lack of capable officers had always been one of his major problems. Lee wrote to one of his major generals, John B.

Hood, that the army would be "invincible if it could be properly organized and officered. There never were such men in an Army before. They will go anywhere and do anything if properly led. But there is the difficulty—proper commanders—where can they be obtained?" [18] Now the force of circumstances and the development in recent weeks of the command capabilities of several officers persuaded Lee that the time had come to divide the army into three infantry corps of three divisions each. He took great care in dismissing and appointing officers to obtain the best leaders possible. In the end Longstreet retained command of the First Corps. Richard S. Ewell was promoted to the rank of lieutenant general and appointed to succeed Jackson as head of the Second Corps, while A. P. Hill, who also became a lieutenant general, was made commander of the newly organized Third Corps. It was composed of one division each from the two old corps and a third still to be formed.[19]

For all of his efforts Lee could claim but partial success. There were only so many experienced officers available, and the Army of Northern Virginia ventured forth on the Gettysburg campaign with a high percentage of its commanders new to their posts and to larger responsibilities. Among them was Major General George E. Pickett, who previous to July 3·on the slopes of Cemetery Ridge had never led his division in combat. The capabilities of two of its three corps commanders, Hill and Ewell, to handle more than a single division remained to be tested.[20] If some of these newcomers failed to live up to expectations, Lee could not be charged with negligence or faulty standards in choosing them. He collaborated closely with President Davis in picking his leaders, and Davis apparently accepted without question his judgment of men, which was based upon a careful study of their military records. Though he tried to disregard political considerations, Lee sometimes had to make concessions where local pride demanded that a brigadier be from the same state as the majority of his men.[21]

As part of his program to increase the efficiency of his army Lee decided to complete certain organizational changes in the artillery which he had started during the winter. In February in an effort to achieve greater flexibility and concentration of fire power he had adopted a plan which abolished the system of attaching batteries to certain brigades. Most batteries contained four or six guns, though several had as few as three and others as many as eight. The old system had had many disadvantages because brigade and division commanders had enough to do in handling the infantry without having to give time and attention to one or more batteries. By custom batteries became attached to certain units, and even in an emergency it would take the force of highest authority to pry them loose. By the time they became available for action, it was often too late. Under the new organization the artillery of each corps was divided into battalions, usually of four batteries each. A battalion was assigned to each division, subject to the orders of the division commander, though it was liable to be divided, detached, or used in any other way considered desirable by the general of the army or the corps commanders. As first adopted the plan gave each of the two corps six battalions and held two in a general reserve under the direction of Brigadier General W. N. Pendleton, who was chief of artillery. A field officer with the rank of colonel, lieutenant colonel, or major commanded a battalion, while a captain led a battery with its complement of, on the average, a hundred men.[22] The new scheme had its first real test at Chancellorsville, when rapid concentration of guns enabled Confederate artillerists to overwhelm Union batteries at Fairview, a key point in the battle on May 3. Possessing better ammunition, improved guns, and superior organization to those they had had previously, the Confederates for the first time fought their adversaries on "equal terms." [23]

Lee completed the reorganization of his artillery on June 2.[24] The most significant change was the breaking up of the reserve or pool of guns for use by the army as a whole. The new arrangement actually meant a demotion for General Pendleton, a "well-meaning" but not particularly capable officer,[25] who though still chief of artillery acted henceforth only in an advisory capacity. As such he became the liaison officer for army headquarters in its dealings with corps artillery. Subject to orders of the corps commanders, tactical control of the guns now became the responsibility of the chief of artillery of each corps, who had under him five battalions, one for each infantry division and two in reserve. Not only did this plan secure greater concentration of fire power, but it provided an inducement for able and ambitious officers to remain in the service, since more of them could become field officers. The three corps chiefs of artillery had at least the rank of colonel. Promotions still came more slowly in this branch of the Confederate service than in the others, but they were faster than in the Federal army. This plan of organization for the artillery proved more enduring than the Confederacy itself, for within a few years after the Civil War Prussia, Austria, France, and Great Britain adopted it for their own armies.[26]

Reorganization went only part way, however, toward increasing the efficiency of the artillery, and much more had to be done to get ready for the forthcoming campaign. Lee instructed Pendleton to direct the refitting of batteries as soon as possible. The shortage of horses created the greatest problem, and the corps chiefs of artillery scoured the countryside so they could get the wheels rolling. Much of the equipment too stood in need of repair or replacement. In the Second Corps the unusually able chief of ordnance, Colonel William Allan, had created a field repair shop the previous January for the purpose of keeping guns, rifles, harness, and other equipment in good shape. After Chancellorsville he made several thousand stand of rifles and muskets serviceable again without sending them back to Richmond, and he also repaired quantities of artillery harness. When at the beginning of the Gettysburg campaign the Second Corps defeated the Yankees under Major General Robert H. Milroy at Winchester, Allan obtained over twenty pieces of artillery which had been spiked by the enemy, and his efficient workmen rendered them fit for service within a day. Meanwhile Lee's artillery received additional strength from fourteen guns captured in the battle of Chancellorsville, as well as a fresh consignment of fourteen 12-pounder Napoleons from Colonel Josiah Gorgas, Confederate chief of ordnance, which he had had manufactured to replace the unsatisfactory lighter 6-pounder cannon used earlier in the war.[27]

As it entered the Gettysburg campaign the artillery of the Army of Northern Virginia compared favorably in organization, personnel, and equipment with its rival in the Federal service. Its officers and men had no superiors in ability and experience.[28] Nevertheless in two respects the Confederate batteries were less efficient than their Northern antagonists: the "distressing lack of uniformity" in the types of guns in their batteries, and the excessive amount of their defective ammunition. Although both sides suffered from "duds," the proportion among shells of Confederate manufacture ran as large as 50 percent, "a high figure even by contemporary performance."[29]

While Lee's artillery was being reorganized, his cavalry arm was also undergoing certain changes, although structurally it remained untouched. Early in the war it had been set up as a separate division of two or more brigades of horsemen with accompanying batteries of horse artillery. The redoubtable, flamboyant Major General J. E. B. Stuart commanded it, while his brigadiers were Generals Wade Hampton, Fitzhugh Lee, and W. H. F. Lee. After months of hard campaigning the division needed reinforcements and certain other improvements to bring its regiments up to strength. The questions were how many new units could be obtained, and how good would they and their leaders be. Soon after Chancellorsville Lee informed Stuart of his intention to order in Brigadier General W. E. ("Grumble") Jones's cavalry brigade of four regiments and a battalion which had been operating in the Shenandoah Valley. Obviously pressed for more men, Lee thus reversed a previous decision to keep Jones and Stuart separated. The two did not get along together, for Jones though an able commander had a hatred for Stuart which bordered on the pathological. Stuart, unhappy at the thought of having Jones with him, suggested that Lee peremptorily transfer Jones to the infantry, but Lee refused to do so without Jones's consent. Lee told Stuart that for the good of the cause he must not let his "judgment be warped." To replace Jones in the valley Lee directed that Brigadier General A. G. Jenkins' body of cavalry be sent to Staunton or some other convenient place in the region. While these men lacked the training, experience, and discipline of Stuart's troopers, they did contribute substantially to the size of the cavalry and could be whipped into shape, whether under Jenkins' continued leadership Lee was not sure at the time. Often referred to as Jenkins' Mounted Infantry, they accompanied Ewell's corps into Pennsylvania and gave him assistance as foragers, scouts, and a cavalry screen. Probably they were better foragers than anything else; yet on the third day of the battle of Gettysburg they went into action under Stuart against Union cavalry and retired before the fighting ended only for want of ammunition.

Further strength, such as it was, came from Brigadier General Beverly Robertson's small command of two cavalry regiments which had been serving in North Carolina. Robertson apparently did not endear himself to the sometimes irascible Major General D. H. Hill, who felt the heavy responsibility of protecting eastern North Carolina against the incursions of the enemy with what appeared to him as insufficient forces. While Hill considered losing Robertson good riddance, Lee welcomed him for the little help that he could contribute.

Stuart and Lee did weigh the possibility of creating new brigades by shifting regiments about so as to promote deserving subordinates and to equalize the strength of various commands. Lee decided against the idea because most of the regiments were badly undermanned and under such a scheme the cavalry would end up with more general officers than necessary.[30] Though sorry to disappoint certain men who deserved promotion, Lee's real worry was about the condition of his depleted regiments. For one reason or another an unusually large number of troopers were dismounted or were absent without leave. Battle casualties and the war weariness of the less stout-hearted soldiers partially explained the situation. There were some desertions, although they occurred less frequently in cavalry than infantry units, and some men were away seeking new mounts. Here was another cause of concern to Lee: the growing scarcity of horseflesh which exemplified the general erosion of Southern resources so obvious by 1863. Not only did many horses become worn out and useless from the hardships of campaigning, but lack of fodder in areas close to the army, due to inadequacies in rail transportation, forced the military to keep large numbers at distant places. Other branches of the service as well as the cavalry suffered for want of draft animals. As Lee pointed out, there were not enough teams for the medical wagons, ambulances, and ammunition wagons. He warned that the army faced the question of whether it should not reduce the number of guns rather than increasing them, as Stuart had done in the horse artillery. For the present he thought that four guns to a battery of horse artillery were all they could "horse and maintain." [31]

The difficulty of securing new mounts was compounded by the government's failure to set up a centralized replacement service. Ever since the beginning of the war its policy had been one of requiring each cavalryman to furnish his own horse. The government paid the owner forty cents a day for its use and assumed the cost of feeding and shoeing the animal. Should a horse be killed in action, the trooper would be reimbursed for the estimated value of the animal at the time it entered the service; should he lose it in any other way, he himself would have to assume the loss and would have to get another horse if he wanted to stay in the service. It was a wonderful arrangement for keeping the strength of the cavalry below par, much more so than enemy bullets, for it encouraged absenteeism. Whenever a trooper found himself dismounted, he had to go home to procure a new horse. If he were a Virginian he needed from thirty to sixty days to accomplish his purpose, and a much longer time should he have come from the deeper South. Thus Fitz Lee's brigade, which normally numbered at least 2,500 troopers, was reduced to less than eight hundred in the engagement at Kelly's Ford on March 17, 1863. At the time of Chancellorsville, when many absentees had returned, it still had fewer than 1,500 men, and a few weeks later it was very little stronger. Many men, it seems, never did get back.[32]

In spite of these problems Lee's efforts to strengthen his cavalry resulted in the addition of three fairly efficient brigades and some improvement in equipment. With Stuart's division now about double its former strength it could expect to win glory in the coming campaign. In addition to the regular cavalry Lee ordered another mounted force under Brigadier General John D. Imboden to be ready to accompany the Confederate drive to the north. Imboden had under him an assortment of armed riders even more unruly and untrained than Jenkins' and possessing a well-developed proclivity to rob civilians, especially of their horses. Operating as a rule in the Shenandoah Valley, in the spring with some help from "Grumble" Jones Imboden had raided Yankee-held territory in western Virginia. Militarily the affair had not amounted to much, but it did result in the seizure of supplies highly cherished in the Southern economy of scarcity. In pitched battles with veteran enemy cavalry Imboden's force was of questionable value, but his men could ride and shoot. These skills were highly useful for widespread foraging in poorly defended regions of the North and for guarding supply bases and wagon trains. In its semi-independent status the command served in an auxiliary capacity during the Gettysburg campaign.[33]

At the same time as he was strengthening the cavalry Lee devoted great attention to a task which he had started just before Chancellorsville, that of building up the size of his infantry force without reducing its quality. In response to the exigencies of the war over the past months he had permitted some units to be detached from his army for service elsewhere on the Atlantic seaboard. Late in the winter under Longstreet, their regular commander, Hood's and Pickett's divisions had gone on a separate expedition to drive Yankees out of the area of Suffolk, Virginia, and to gather food for Lee's army. Lee had no trouble in securing their return, for they had obviously been on loan from the First Corps. Though their efforts had been disappointing, he welcomed these veterans back to swell his ranks. He ran into serious difficulties, however, in his attempts to recall other units he considered as belonging to his army. When he tried to get even more troops by scouring the Atlantic seaboard for odds and ends of soldiers and virtually stripping South Carolina, Georgia, and Florida of serviceable men,[34] departmental commanders cried out in alarm and predicted dire consequences. Although Lee might not have thought so, their fears were not entirely imaginary, for Yankee forces occupied strategic positions along the coast from which they could move to threaten important agricultural and manufacturing areas and cut supply lines between the Virginia Peninsula and Charleston, South Carolina. The hard and inescapable fact which confronted Lee and other Confederate leaders was the shortage of first-rate soldiers. With military requirements far greater than its resources, the Confederacy needed an agency comparable to the modern general staff to act as a clearing house for ideas and information, as well as an office to coordinate military movements and apportion troops. The North had taken halting steps in this direction, but in the South there was not even the semblance of such an organization. A busy President, aided of course by his Secretary of War, exercised personal control over such matters. It was an informal and unsatisfactory arrangement to say the least.

Partly for this reason friction developed between Lee and General D. H. Hill. Hill was worried about his ability to defend eastern North Carolina against Federal troops based at New Berne under Major General John G. Foster. He considered his forces barely adequate to the task, and he was convinced he needed greater military strength if he were to protect the railroad between Wilmington, North Carolina, and Petersburg, Virginia. He also wanted to overawe noisy and actively disloyal elements in the state and impress them with the magnitude of Confederate power. Hill was a man to admire as a fighter, but he had a prickly personality and he was not one of Lee's warmest admirers, a fact that perhaps had some bearing on the issue which arose between them. Lee thought Hill had troops to spare, especially the brigades of Brigadier Generals Robert Ransom, Jr., Micah Jenkins, and John Rogers Cooke, all of which had once been with the Army of Northern Virginia. Lee wished them back, not for sentimental reasons but because the generals were all topnotch brigadiers in command of experienced soldiers. Hill did not want to lose these men, even if their ranks were greatly below their authorized strength. He suggested that he keep them and send Lee some of his newer and less experienced brigades which had the advantage of being much larger. He would be willing, he said, to take any of Lee's "reduced brigades" in exchange for his "full" ones. Lee did not think much of this offer and saw little advantage in replacing any of his veteran units with "fresh men and uninstructed commanders," who would give him only "more to feed but less to depend on." [35]

Another source of misunderstanding between Lee, Hill, and others was the lack of carefully appraised intelligence of enemy movements and intentions. Each district or army commander, including the authorities in Richmond, seemed to have his own means of acquiring information. Of course there were the Northern newspapers, quite easily available to all, but they were a mixed blessing. While they gave away military secrets of use to the Confederates, they also indulged in wild speculation and guesses which served only to obfuscate and confuse. Without a central agency to resolve conflicting evidence each commander assumed the correctness of his own knowledge of enemy plans. Lee was in a position to have a better view of the military picture and grasp of strategical possibilities than Hill, yet upon the basis of his information he came to certain conclusions which were not completely warranted. The enemy, he decided, was planning to "concentrate as large a force as possible in Virginia . . . [and] is withdrawing troops from South Carolina and the country south of James River." [36] A short while later he wrote he had heard that the federal government was going to send Major General Samuel P. Heintzelman's corps, which was manning the Washington defenses, to reinforce Hooker on the Rappahannock. Governor Andrew G. Curtin had agreed, he said, to lend 20,000 Pennsylvania state troops as replacements for Heintzelman's men. On the face of it this report made little sense, and it is hard to believe that Lee really thought that official Washington, so sensitive about its protection, would place total reliance upon raw state militia.[37] Nevertheless he passed the story on to Seddon without expressing any reservations as to its truth. Apparently on the basis of such information Lee urged Hill to keep only enough regular troops as were necessary to help the local militia guard the railroads and the rich farms of eastern North Carolina from enemy raids, and to send the rest to Virginia. Late in May, after Hill upon Lee's recommendation had become commander of the department between the James River and Cape Fear, Lee gave him "discretionary instructions . . . to apportion his force to the strength of the enemy, and send . . . every man he could spare." [38] Hill refused to act unless he received positive orders. When Lee sent them, he objected to obeying them because he felt that removal of Ransom's, Jenkins', and Cooke's brigades would allow the enemy to take over the abandoned area. Contrary to Lee's impression that the enemy was gradually withdrawing his forces from the coast, Hill reported that Foster was still in New Berne with a greater number of troops than ever. Hill was right about Foster's location, but he exaggerated the size of his forces.[39]

At this stage Davis became involved in the controversy. Hill had appealed Lee's orders to him to the President, and Lee, thoroughly irritated by Hill's intransigence, asked to be relieved from "any control" of his department. He requested that from now on Davis give Hill his orders directly. Depressed by this turn of events, Lee despaired of being able to start his offensive before the enemy had time to prepare to meet it. On the other hand, should Hooker get the jump on him and move first, as signs indicated he might do, Lee feared he would have no alternative but to fall back.[40] Davis tried to relieve him of his gloom and adjudicate fairly between the contending parties. He took a less serious view than Lee of enemy threats to Richmond by way of the Peninsula and accepted at not quite face value Hill's estimate of the situation in North Carolina. His letter to Lee was cordial, but he had decided that of the brigades Lee wanted returned to him he would get only Cooke's. Jenkins, because of his knowledge of Blackwater country in southeastern Virginia and for other reasons, would remain where he was for the time being, and Brigadier General Joseph R. Davis, a nephew of the President, would go in his place to the Army of Northern Virginia with his brigade of Mississippians. Unfortunately

General Davis had had no previous battle experience, although the President made no mention of that fact. As for Ransom and his brigade, Davis merely said that they would be used to guard the approaches to Richmond from the direction of Norfolk. Obviously he assumed that Lee understood, from previous correspondence, why they would not be returned to his command.

Writing on the eve of Lee's departure on a venture conceived at the flood tide of Confederate hopes, Davis fully appreciated the need for a concentration of strength in the Army of Northern Virginia, and he expressed regret that he could not furnish Lee "the means which would make it quite safe to attempt all that we desire." Nonetheless it is obvious that Davis was conscious of some of the dangers inherent in a Confederate invasion of enemy territory and that they made him and other leaders in Richmond nervous. As Lee moved north and west, the capital and its long line of communication with the blockade-running port of Wilmington would become exposed to enemy attacks from along the seaboard. Should one able and aggressive Yankee general have organized a vigorous drive at this time from the eastern coast of Virginia—and there were enough troops available for such a project—the inadequate nature of the forces left to defend Richmond would have become readily apparent. In North Carolina there was the additional danger from disloyal groups who would have become increasingly bold at signs of Confederate or state military impotence. Despite the danger of exposing the long flank of the Southern seaboard, Davis did force Hill to make some concessions so as to reinforce Lee.[41]

Lee probably gained more than he lost by the furious negotiations which he, Davis, Seddon, Adjutant General Samuel Cooper, D. H. Hill, and others carried on by means of dispatches, letters, and conferences over a period of several weeks. In place of the battle-hardened brigades of Generals Ransom, Jenkins, and A. H. Colquitt who also had been on detached service, he received those of Brigadier Generals Davis, Junius Daniel, and James J. Pettigrew, which if not completely innocent of combat experience were strange to the fighting methods of the Army of Northern Virginia. The possible exception was Pettigrew himself, who had served with the army on the Peninsula and was well thought of by many officers.[42] Daniel and Davis were unknowns, but the former proved himself a valiant soldier and capable leader at Gettysburg. Davis did not distinguish himself there, but he had the misfortune of running into some of the toughest fighting units of the Federal army. Numerically these brigades represented a gain in strength for Lee and almost made up for the permanent loss of General N. G. Evans' brigade which had left the army in the fall of 1862.[43] Cooke's brigade did not replace any other; it had been on special assignment and merely returned to the fold, only to be detached again to guard the approaches to Richmond while the main body of the army set out for Pennsylvania.[44]

On the whole Lee's hard-shooting infantrymen were as well, if not better armed than their Northern foes. The Confederate Ordnance Bureau under the able Colonel Gorgas had made great efforts to secure improved weapons through imports and domestic manufacture, and by June 1 its efforts had begun to bear fruit. In other respects the troops were not so well equipped, although improvements had been made. Some units were better off than others, for they had acquired an abundance of camp equipment such as tents and blankets left behind at Chancellorsville by the retreating Yankees. While on the march more often than not the men had no tents, as they did not want to "tote" them. When it rained two men would share their woolen blankets and a "gumblanket" carried by one of them. The most general complaint was the lack of good shoes; many men were "indifferently shod," and some went barefoot. Their clothes were of all cuts and colors, with blue pants particularly in evidence, reflecting a great shortage of regular issue uniforms. By and large the Confederate soldier travelled lighter than his Yankee counterpart. His woolen blanket, haversack, and cartridge box altogether weighed not more than twelve to fourteen pounds.[45]

Even an army as lean as Lee's and stripped of non-essentials required vast trains of supply and ordnance wagons. Compared with the "sumptuous trains and countless sutlers" accompanying the Federal army, the Confederates seemed to carry little. Yet the wagons needed to supply them would have made an imposing column over sixty miles long if they had been kept together. During the Gettysburg campaign, however, the trains were broken up into at least three groups, as each of the three corps travelled over a different route and at a different time. The problems of protecting the wagons and keeping them on the move were immense. Sometimes one balky horse would make a gap in the line of half a mile, and of course an enemy raid could wreck a whole train.[46]

Despite their great size Lee's supply trains barely kept up with his needs. However, by choosing to invade Pennsylvania by way of the Shenandoah and Cumberland Valleys he had at his disposal the resources of one of the richest agricultural regions in the East. His men could live very well off the country, and they did. The great disadvantage of the route was the lack of direct rail connections with the Confederacy. When the army left Culpeper Court House about the middle of June to move into the valley, it lost the benefits of a location near a railhead. Winchester after its capture by General Ewell became Lee's most advanced base in friendly territory, but it was more than fifty miles from Culpeper and over ninety from Staunton, the only available railroad terminals. Though the Virginia railroads were maddeningly inadequate for military use, supply officers could usually count on them to meet the barest needs of the army from day to day. Dependence upon the purchase or seizure of supplies far from a railhead often meant a situation where the army either feasted or starved. Less obvious but just as important were shortages of more humble and prosaic items such as horseshoes and portable forges for smithies. With over 20,000 horses in the army a lack of shoes or the means to put them on the animals was a serious matter.[47] One officer spelled out the problem when he noted that as soon as a horse lost a shoe and had to go barefoot on the "macadamized" roads of which there were plenty in Pennsylvania, he would become lame and would have to be abandoned unless shod very quickly. Then he added: "I picked up a very fine large horse near Chambersburg and intended substituting him for one of our wagon horses, but he cast a shoe and within five miles became so utterly useless I had to give him to a Maryland farmer." [48]

Not personally concerned with the problems of command or the cares of supply, Lee's famed veterans marched off jauntily to do battle with their Yankee foe in what they hoped would be his own backyard. Always good marchers in an "irregular & careless" manner, they were now doing better than ever according to observers. Major General William D. Pender wrote that he "never saw troops which march as ours do; they will go 15 or 20 miles a day without having a straggler & whoop & yell on all occasions." In similar vein Colonel C. M. Blackford of Longstreet's staff told his wife that he had never seen the army in such fine condition. "We marched from Berryville . . . with scarcely a straggler and the report from every division is the same." [49] General Long, who as a Colonel had been Lee's military secretary, years after the war still recalled that as the Army of Northern Virginia started out on its Pennsylvania campaign it appeared "the best disciplined, the most high-spirited, and enthusiastic army on the continent." [50] Another writer described the main body of troops as presenting a "more imposing appearance than was ever before exhibited by any Southern Army," [51] and still another said that "confidence & good spirits seem to possess every one." [52]

Northern participants eloquently testified to the truth of these estimates of Lee's army. Charles Francis Adams, captain of the 1st Massachusetts Cavalry, writing soon after Gettysburg said that he was struck by its great improvement since Antietam. He had had a chance to observe the condition of the Confederate soldiers while guarding a group of 500 prisoners from every Southern state, and he went so far as to claim for Lee's men superiority in every respect to the Army of the Potomac. In his words, they were "superior in numbers, better officered, a better fighting material, as well armed, better clothed and as well fed. The spirit of his army was much better than that of ours, and I saw no evidence of their ever having been on short rations or demoralized by want or misfortune. Their tone was the very best." [53] The Union Brigadier General Francis C. Barlow, who saw a great many men and officers of Ewell's corps while he lay wounded in Gettysburg after the first day's fight, agreed with Adams' opinion of Confederate morale. "They are more heroic, more modest and more in earnest than we are," he wrote. "Their whole tone is much finer than ours. Except among those on our side who are fighting this war upon anti-slavery grounds, there is not much earnestness nor are there many noble feelings and sentiments involved." [54] Other Northern officers and men, especially those who had fought in both the East and West, testified that no better soldiers could be found anywhere than in the Army of Northern Virginia and that they were the toughest of the Confederate foes.[55] Material want might handicap these "sinewy, tawny, formidable-looking men," but it did not impair their "stoical manliness." [56]

A discerning observation which perhaps best explains their fearsome reputation came from General Hooker. He said that what impressed him most about Lee's men was their "vigorous" and "vehement" mode of assault. Their attacks, he said, were "*blows . . .* and the shock seemed to make the earth tremble on which we stood. With whom this mode of attacking originated I have never been informed, and but from its being confined generally to the Armies in the East I should think it was a concentrated expression of their unity, [and] bitterness of feeling towards their adversaries." [57]

As the long columns wound their way over the roads toward Pennsylvania the Army of Northern Virginia, victorious, powerful, and stronger numerically than it had been for some time, anticipated another smashing success which could easily end the war. Under a beloved and respected leader it had become convinced of its invincibility and supremely confident of its ability to annihilate the despicable enemy. Here perhaps was the fatal defect, the attitude that breeds overconfidence, which in turn leads to mistakes when the foe proves worthy of his mettle.[58]

II

HOOKER MARKS TIME

FOR THE North the Chancellorsville campaign was one of the most frustrating experiences of the war. It started out with the assurance of a quick and decisive victory and ended in ignominious defeat. For the second time in six months the Army of the Potomac had gone on the offensive with high hopes, only to have them completely crushed.

Following the debacle at Fredericksburg in December of 1862 the Army of the Potomac lay prostrate, physically exhausted and utterly dejected by defeat. Then the ambitious and able Major General Joseph Hooker replaced the disgraced Ambrose E. Burnside and became the army's new commander. He seemed to possess the same genius for organization as General McClellan, and immediately upon his appointment he took a firm grip on the army and infused new life into it by introducing some badly needed changes. Hooker was the kind of person who at first meeting inspired confidence. His combat record was impressive, and he had the attractive personality of a good companion and a fluent talker. Dashing and handsome, he looked and acted the great soldier, and whenever he rode smartly along the lines, his men would break into cheers. Under his direction an able staff, headed by Major General Daniel Butterfield, effected various reforms to improve the efficiency of the troops.[1]

Of major concern to Hooker was the physical condition of his men, whose health he knew was not what it should have been as a result of poor diet, inadequate sanitary arrangements, and bad personal habits. Hooker was fortunate in having as his medical director Dr. Jonathan Letterman, a man of great ability and persuasiveness, who, since assuming his position in July, 1862, had worked hard to improve conditions among the soldiers. Letterman appreciated the importance of preventive medicine, and he had gradually converted many of the army surgeons to his ideas. Hooker had great respect for Letterman's devotion to the welfare of the men, his professional knowledge, and administrative skill, and when he took command of the army he did all he could to support him in his work.[2] As a result in May of 1863 Letterman drew up and put into effect certain rules and regulations for the promotion of sanitary conditions which were to become a model for other Union armies. The new regulations covered such matters as periodic relocation of camps, the number and depth of drainage ditches, the airing of tents and their contents, methods of preparing food, rubbish and garbage disposal, toilet facilities, and personal hygiene. Letterman's program succeeded in bringing about a general improvement in army health, while sharply reducing the number of cases of camp fever and the mortality rate of the sick and wounded. Although some sanitary abuses continued, the standards which he established were followed faithfully by veteran regiments for the remainder of the war.[3]

In view of the agricultural wealth of the North it is startling to learn that many a Northern soldier suffered from a poor and unbalanced diet. While food was usually plentiful in supply, it was often of inferior quality, sometimes "nauseatingly bad," and of the wrong sort. There was too much emphasis upon salted meats and starches and not enough on vegetables, and frequently the rations were poorly cooked. As a result scurvy broke out in some units, especially when the men were on long and arduous campaigns where the foraging was slim and they had to depend upon their field rations. Even when they were located near the main supply bases, the diet was little better. Some soldiers developed a yearning for vegetables which "amounted almost to mania," and they resorted to all kinds of schemes to obtain them. If the foraging—that is, stealing—was good, they might also get milk and other delicacies at the expense of the local inhabitants. Those with money could go to a sutler, who was a private businessman running a general store in the camp with army permission. From him they might buy pies, cakes, cheeses, canned milk, or butter, all at exorbitant prices. In addition there was always the chance of receiving a box of foodstuffs from home, but all too often it turned out that the contents had spoiled along the way.[4]

The dishonesty of commissary officers often hampered the efforts of army authorities to improve the diet of the private soldiers. Anxious to make a quick dollar, many of them developed schemes of selling fresh and desiccated vegetables to the troops, while issuing them only salt pork, hardtack, and coffee. Hooker put an immediate stop to this practice and gave strict orders for the distribution of flour or soft bread and vegetables at stated times each week.[5] As a result of this directive and the measures taken by Dr. Letterman, the health of the army greatly improved almost overnight. Symptoms of scurvy that in January had begun to assume serious proportions disappeared by March, and other diseases as well showed a marked decline.[6]

Hooker adopted other important measures to maintain the well-being of the men and strengthen the army. In an effort to cut down straggling along the march and to develop within the soldier a feeling of pride and proprietary interest in a unit larger than his own regiment, Hooker in March assigned to each corps its own special insignia or identification mark, such as a star, a Greek cross, or a crescent. In each corps the badge of the first division was the corps insignia in red, the second in white, and the third in blue, and the soldier wore it on his fatigue cap. Armies in the West as well as the East soon heard about this system of identification and adopted it too. It had, Hooker afterwards asserted, a *"magical"* effect on the discipline and conduct of the troops, for the badges became "very precious" to them and remained so even after the war.[7]

A greater problem than straggling at this time was that of desertions. Though in general one often led to the other, in the winter of 1862–63 there were other more fundamental reasons for the number of men who kept disappearing from the ranks. A wave of despair seemed to have swept over the Army of the Potomac following its defeat at Fredericksburg, and thousands of men lost faith in their cause and their leaders. The temptation to escape the hardships of military life had always been present for many men, but it became stronger in a time of general discouragement such as then prevailed not only in the army but throughout much of the country. The rate of desertions became alarmingly high, and Hooker soon realized that the problem could no longer be met by palliatives if there was to be any kind of an army at all. To his everlasting credit, he reduced desertions to a trickle and induced many men absent without leave to return to their posts. The granting of leaves to officers and furloughs to privates was put on an orderly, systematic basis so that everyone knew what to expect—and when. Previously no one had been able to get a leave or furlough while on field duty "except to prevent death or permanent disability," a standard that left matters pretty much to chance or political pull. For most men the new system of periodic leaves afforded relief from homesickness and the boredom of camp life, which had been the main causes of desertions. Hooker also used the new arrangement as a way of rewarding or penalizing regiments for their efficiency ratings, so that as a result of greater effort on duty the troops might hope for more frequent furloughs.

Hooker supplemented this indirect method of coping with desertions by using more drastic measures. He issued orders prohibiting packages from home which contained the outer garments of civilian dress, he punished local inhabitants who furnished civilian clothing to soldiers, and he blocked the routes commonly used by deserters going north. The arm of his authority reached out as far as Washington and Baltimore in an effort to apprehend deserters before they could go far, for he knew that once soldiers got home it was hard to make them return to the ranks. President Lincoln helped Hooker by issuing a proclamation on March 10, 1863, which offered deserters or soldiers who had overstayed their leaves a chance to get back into the good graces of the army with no other punishment than loss of pay. This pardon was good only until April 1, by which time the men had to be back with their regiments or at a rendezvous designated by the government in each state. The appeal had gratifying results.[8]

While working to keep the ranks filled with healthy men, Hooker effected certain organizational changes in the Army of the Potomac. A very important but controversial one was the abolition of the grand division, which his predecessor, General Burnside, had introduced, and the reestablishment of the corps organization. Under the new system the seven infantry corps commanders, most of whom had major general rank, all reported directly to Hooker, instead of to one of the three generals in command of the grand divisions. Hooker and some other officers had thought poorly of the grand division as "impeding rather than facilitating the dispatch of . . . business." [9] Although no one said so, they may have objected because it superimposed another general with his staff upon two or more corps, thus lengthening the chain of command from the corps to army headquarters. Critics of the Army of the Potomac have felt that Burnside had the right idea when he reduced the number of his immediate subordinates, while increasing their responsibilities. Nevertheless by scrapping the grand division without reducing the number of corps Hooker brought about no real improvement in the efficiency of the army. Brigadier General Henry J. Hunt, chief of artillery of the Army of the Potomac, felt Hooker's organization was in "every way inferior" to that of Lee's army, for the corps and divisions were "too numerous and too weak" and they required "too many commanders and staffs." With so many separate units to look after, as Hunt said, the general of the army in time of an emergency had to place several corps temporarily under a senior major general, an arrangement which was clumsy at best and often caused confusion in the chain of command. [10] A reorganization reducing the number of corps and increasing the size of the remaining ones finally took place, but not until March of 1864.

At the same time that he abolished the grand division Hooker made another major organizational change which was long overdue by consolidating the cavalry into one corps under Major General George Stoneman. Prior to his appointment as head of the Army of the Potomac the cavalry had had no unit of organization larger than a division. Its divisions and brigades had been scattered among the various grand divisions, and subject to the orders of their commanders. Although the new system compounded Hooker's administrative problems by adding to his list of corps commanders, it received universal approval because it gave the cavalry greater cohesiveness and strength to cope with the famous Confederate horsemen united under "Jeb" Stuart. From that time on the Union cavalry in the Army of the Potomac was an effective fighting force. [11]

In this reshuffling of commands, responsibilities, and tables of organization Hooker accomplished much good, but he made one serious mistake. Late in March he decided to strip General Hunt of command of the artillery and restrict him to purely administrative duties. Hunt was a splendid soldier who had won great fame as an artillerist at Malvern Hill, Antietam, and Fredericksburg, and he well merited the position of chief of artillery.[12] Hooker's explanation years later for the demotion of Hunt proved to be a weird mixture of irrelevancies and petty spite. He tried to make Hunt the real culprit, saying that Hunt had wanted the artillery organized into a corps with himself in command. Hooker had "demurred," and besides, he added, "in my old Brigade and Division I found that my men had learned to regard their batteries, with a feeling of devotion which I considered contributed greatly to our success, and presumed, that the same feeling existed in other bodies of the troops and was, therefore unwilling to make the change proposed by him [Hunt]. In this he showed so much ill feeling that I was unwilling to place my artillery in his charge at Chancellorsville. . . ."[13] Hooker forgot to add that he had restored Hunt to command the night of May 3 after the Confederates had driven him out of Chancellorsville and back to within a short distance of the Rappahannock River. The advantages traditionally possessed by the Union artillery in the quality of its materiel and cannon disappeared in this battle through Hooker's inept handling of his forces.[14]

General Hunt, still smarting from Hooker's treatment, nevertheless had the final word after Hooker had ceased to command the Army of the Potomac. An expert duellist with pen as well as cannon, he said sharply that he doubted whether "the history of modern armies can exhibit a parallel instance of such palpable crippling of a great arm of the service in the very presence of a powerful enemy. . . . It is not, therefore, to be wondered at that confusion and mismanagement ensued. . . ."[15] This is pretty strong language; but Hunt's war record demands respect for his opinions, and what happened at Chancellorsville substantiates his indictment of Hooker.

Whatever his mistakes, Hooker's record as a military administrator ranks him near the top, for he refashioned the army into an effective fighting machine. He saved it from disintegration, gradually filled its ranks to peak strength, inflated its morale, and put it in superb condition for the start of the spring campaign. As the season opened, the North waited with bated breath to see what he could do, fully expecting him to crush Lee. Finally the weather improved enough for him to start operations. During the last week in April he maneuvered his army so as to confront Lee with large forces on his front and rear; if they were brought together they would crush him like huge pincers. Keeping his poise, Lee turned the tables on his adversary and gained a spectacular victory at Chancellorsville. Though losses were heavy, the damage to the Union army was more psychological than physical. Comments among both officers and men indicated disgust and exasperation over the performance of the army and its leaders. One bitter observer in the Second Corps said: "There is only one real reason [for our defeat], and that the simplest possible,—our army didn't fight as well as that of our enemies. We had every possible advantage. . . . They beat us easily." [16]

Feeling ran high in particular against Major General O. O. Howard's Eleventh Corps, which had the misfortune of being in "Stonewall" Jackson's way when he crashed into the Union right flank late in the afternoon of May 2. It had been a rather unhappy corps before the battle, but it was even more unhappy when it suddenly found itself being overwhelmed by an irresistible force. The men did what came naturally to most soldiers under similar circumstances—they ran! They saved their lives, but in so doing they lost their reputations and became the scapegoats of the Northern army. It so happened that an unusually large number of the officers and men of the Eleventh Corps were German-born or of German background. Many native Americans both in and out of the corps had a strong prejudice against foreigners and considered the Germans to blame for the disaster. As a result dissension broke out in the corps and reduced morale to a low point. The German element had an articulate champion in the person of Major General Carl Schurz, one of Lincoln's good Republican friends, who commanded the Third Division of the Eleventh Corps in the battle. He complained bitterly of the "abuse and insult" suffered by the corps and blamed Howard's negligence and improper handling of the troops for what happened.[17] The bickering was slow to die down. Almost a month after the event Brigadier General Francis C. Barlow, commander of the First Division of the corps, wrote: "The Corps is in a state of continual excitement & quarreling—one Dutchman accuses another of misconduct in the late battle & the Dutch accuse the Americans & vice versa—I think Schurz is intriguing to get command of the Corps & is trying insidiously to injure Gen. Howard. I do not fear that he will succeed." [18] General Howard expressed great unhappiness over the state of affairs, saying that "everybody who is to blame tries to shift the responsibility upon somebody's else shoulders." [19]

Although the black mark against the Eleventh Corps left an indelible impression, the general opinion in the army, especially among the officers, was that General Hooker himself was responsible for the fiasco at Chancellorsville. They felt that the army had suffered an ignominious and unnecessary defeat, and that Hooker could not escape the blame for it. Brigadier General Alpheus S. Williams of the Twelfth Corps made a remark typical of many when he said: "I think this last [battle] has been the greatest of bunglings in this war. I despair of ever accomplishing anything so long as generals are made as they have been." [20] An officer on Major General John Sedgwick's staff felt that the outcome would have been different if the Sixth Corps had had the "cooperation of even a small part of the immense forces with Fighting Joe Hooker." [21] To Colonel (later General) Alexander S. Webb losing the battle was "incredible." He observed that "Fighting Joe lost himself very suddenly . . . and we . . . [retreated] without sufficient reason." [22] With a bluntness characteristic of his family Captain Charles Francis Adams of the 1st Massachusetts Cavalry expressed the extreme bitterness felt by a good many officers who disapproved not only of Hooker's conduct in the battle but of everything else about him. Adams claimed that Hooker stood "lower in the estimation of the Army than ever did the redoubtable John Pope. . . ." He characterized Hooker and his two cronies, Major Generals Daniel E. Sickles and Daniel Butterfield, as "the disgrace and bane of this army; they are our three humbugs, intriguers and demagogues." [23]

Close examination of Hooker's generalship at Chancellorsville shows that these comments and many others of similar nature were well warranted. It was generally agreed that Hooker lost his nerve when he met stiff enemy resistance for the first time on May 1. Whatever the reason, he suddenly retreated into the wilderness and assumed the defensive in a position poorly adapted for it. After that, as the old song goes, he never did get out of the wilderness, either literally or figuratively. He compounded his difficulties with serious errors in judgment. Instead of using his cavalry as a screen for his advance, he sent most of it off on a wild goose chase to cut Lee's line of communication many miles from the scene of operations.

Hooker's misuse of his artillery too was unforgivable. More unfortunate than anything else, at least from Lincoln's point of view, was his failure to use two of his finest corps, the First and the Fifth, which were commanded by the fighting generals, John F. Reynolds and George G. Meade. They stood virtually idle when they were in fact available for immediate use.[24]

Hooker's reaction to Chancellorsville was strange and disturbing in its lack of realism. Before the battle when he withdrew from his most advanced position and returned to Chancellorsville, thus forfeiting the initiative to Lee, he talked as if he had the enemy on the run and victory well within his grasp. After the fight and his retreat across the Rappahannock he refused to admit the outcome either as a defeat or a reflection on his generalship.[25] In writing to President Lincoln he was naive or disingenuous enough to refer to the battle as a "reverse," attributable to a "cause which could not be foreseen, and not be provided against." [26] Later he claimed that "no general battle was fought at Chancellorsville, I was unwilling to give battle with such great odds against me. . . . We lost no honor at Chancellorsville." [27] So it seems there was no battle there, and ergo, no defeat! [28]

Once across the Rappahannock River and back to the old encampment north and east of Fredericksburg, Hooker's buoyancy partially returned, and he murmured something about resuming the offensive after a short breathing spell. Whether he really meant to make another move forward, or whether he mentioned it just to impress Lincoln, is not clear. Regardless of his intentions Lincoln on May 14 advised against an "early renewal" of an attempt to cross the Rappahannock, since it did not "appear probable" to him that Hooker would gain anything by it. He added that he would not "complain" if Hooker did nothing more for a time than to "keep the enemy at bay, and out of other mischief by menaces and occasional cavalry raids, if practicable, and to put your own army in good condition again." Lincoln made it clear that he was only advising and not ordering Hooker to adopt this policy.[29] Hooker accepted the President's suggestions, a wise course in view of the condition of the Army of the Potomac at the time. But even as Hooker's forces remained comparatively quiet, Lee was busily preparing for a major offensive. The very day after Lincoln advised Hooker to restrict himself to defensive measures, Lee was in Richmond conferring with Davis and Seddon on matters of grand strategy and convincing them of the advantages of a northern invasion by his army.

Lincoln's advice to Hooker was sensible, but putting the forces in condition for another advance against the Confederates was more easily said than done. While the Army of the Potomac was fundamentally sound and still had faith in itself, it was discouraged. Many officers tried to analyze the situation. When Colonel Lucius Fairchild of the 2nd Wisconsin exclaimed, "What an unfortunate set of fellows we are, and have been," he was only saying what many others thought. The army, he maintained, was not to blame for "its reverses, its repulses, its defeats," nor was it demoralized by them. There was no "better disciplined, better equipped, better behaved army in the world," and "when it has a fair fight you will hear a good account of it." [30] Another officer referred to the troops as possessing "something of the English bulldog. . . . You can whip them time and again, but the next fight they go into, they are in good spirits, and as full of pluck as ever. They are used to being whipped, and no longer mind it. Some day or other we shall have our turn." [31] What the army needed, everyone seemed to agree, was better leadership, from the commanding general down to many of the corps, division, and brigade commanders. Brigadier General John Gibbon thought that while the volunteer army was not well disciplined according to European military standards, most of the men possessed "bravery, enthusiasm, coolness, dash and above all, intelligence." By 1863 they had learned through experience how to size up their leaders and to place "utmost confidence" in the able and successful officer, not necessarily the most popular one.[32] Webb commented that once the soldiers felt themselves to be under a "fighting man" who kept near them, "*directing* all things," they became the "best fighting men in the world. But they . . . [were] too intelligent to fight under *fools*." [33] Whether fools or not, it was Brigadier General G. K. Warren's opinion that too many officers in the Army of the Potomac after two years of war still did not know how to "manage and fight troops." [34]

Of utmost concern to everyone was the lack of confidence in General Hooker. Once good will toward him had evaporated and he had fallen in the esteem of the army, the camp began to seethe with rumors, charges, and countercharges. Under the circumstances many officers felt ready to give up and resign; others worked against

the general to get rid of him. Some of the corps commanders conferred with Lincoln when he and General in Chief Henry W.
Halleck suddenly appeared at Hooker's headquarters late on May 6,
the day the army retreated across the Rappahannock. One of them,
Major General Darius N. Couch, commander of the Second Corps,
told the President that he would not serve any longer under Hooker.
He went so far as to recommend Hooker's removal and Meade's
appointment as commander of the army. A few days later three of
the corps commanders, Major Generals Couch, Henry W. Slocum,
and John Sedgwick, who were Meade's seniors in rank, sent him word
that they were willing to serve under him, a most unusual procedure
to say the least. Though flattered by these expressions of confidence,
Meade wisely refused to join Couch and Slocum in their actions
against Hooker. He did speak freely to Governor Andrew G. Curtin
of Pennsylvania in answer to some pointed questions.[35] Hooker
heard about the conversation and confronted Meade with it. Meade
assured him that his unfavorable remarks had been for Curtin's ears
only and that he was not seeking the command of the army. After
this slight flare-up relations between the two men remained unbroken, though somewhat strained.[36]

After Lincoln's visit to the army there seemed to be a constant
stream of general officers going to Washington either of their own
volition or upon invitation. In most instances they went to discuss
Hooker's shortcomings and to advise as to who might take his place
in case the President decided to relieve him of his command. Unfortunately replacement was not a simple case of pointing to the
ablest general and saying, "You are it." Politically powerful groups,
especially the Radical Republicans, wanted to have a say in the
matter and help Lincoln choose the right man. They were convinced
that otherwise the war would not be fought in a way to bring about
the destruction of slavery and the South. Although representing minority opinion in the country, certain leaders of the Radicals such as
Charles Sumner of Massachusetts, Ben Wade of Ohio, Zachariah
Chandler of Michigan, and Thaddeus Stevens of Pennsylvania were
influential figures in Congress. They dominated the important Congressional Joint Committee on the Conduct of the War, which had
assumed full investigative powers over the government's prosecution of the conflict. The committee made life miserable for officers
who did not agree that the primary objective of the war was the

merciless subjugation of the South. Furthermore they judged military leaders by the purity of their political principles rather than by their prowess as warriors. They had an important ally in Secretary of the Treasury Salmon P. Chase, a perennial presidential aspirant, who worked to undermine Lincoln's authority. Only a person with Lincoln's political abilities and statesmanlike qualities could have kept the Radicals in check, and even he had to reckon with them constantly. They were not going to let the President oust their man Hooker from command of a powerful army without strenuous objections. To complicate matters, about this time friends of General McClellan began to urge his reappointment. Mere mention of his name immediately aroused the apprehension of the Radicals and made them even more importunate in their demands to keep Hooker. Anxiety mounted both in Washington and in the army as all sorts of stories became bruited about, some of them wild, others more authentic.[37]

When General Howard heard a rumor that General Sickles was being considered for Hooker's position he raised his pious hands in horror and exclaimed: "If God gives us Sickles to lead us I shall cry with vexation & sorrow and plead to be delivered."[38] Likely candidates in addition to Meade were Generals Winfield S. Hancock, John Sedgwick, Darius N. Couch, and John F. Reynolds, all of whom were reliably mentioned as under consideration.[39] Of these officers Reynolds is definitely known to have received an offer at this time to assume command of the Army of the Potomac. He was an excellent choice for the position, well qualified in every respect. A graduate of West Point and "regular army" to the core, since September, 1862, he had been in command of the First Corps and had succeeded in hammering it into a well-disciplined and hard-hitting outfit. In spite of his high standards Reynolds had a way with volunteers; he took good care of their creature comforts and treated them as human beings. He was a first-class fighting man, universally respected and admired. If the fates had decreed other than they did, he might have gone down in history as one of the greatest generals of the Civil War. But Reynolds must share some of the responsibility with the fates; he turned down the offer of the command because, he said, Washington authorities would not promise him a "free hand" with the army.

The question of Hooker's removal seems to have reached a crisis when Reynolds received his offer of the command on June 2. Immediately thereafter Lee initiated the first phases of the Gettysburg campaign and momentarily distracted the attention of official Washington from its problem child.[40] Meanwhile the army's lack of faith in Hooker's generalship and the various developments arising from it precluded any offensive operations. Under any circumstances it is doubtful whether Hooker could have regrouped his forces for another try at Lee within a month after the serious setback at Chancellorsville. To compound its difficulties, the army was losing many valuable men whose terms of enlistment had expired.

The ill-conceived and politically expedient recruitment policies of the government were beginning to bear fruit at a most inopportune moment. Although the backbone of the army was made up of men who had enlisted in 1861 for three years, there were others who had enlisted at the same time for only two years. Usually these men were grouped in separate regiments, but some two-year companies had been combined with three-year units, and in some instances individual soldiers who had agreed to serve for two years were scattered throughout companies of three-year men. As a further complication many regiments were composed of men who, in response to an emergency call for troops during the summer of 1862, had signed up for nine months. The terms of enlistment of all of these regiments began to expire early in the spring of 1863. Prior to Chancellorsville some nine-month and two-year regiments had begun to leave the army, and the pace increased in the latter part of May. Between the last of April and the middle of June about 23,000 men left the army, and few if any of them reenlisted when their regiments were disbanded. There were two main reasons for their reluctance to continue in service: the vicious system of bounties offered by the local, state, and federal governments, and a serious loophole in the Enrollment Act of March 3, 1863, which had instituted compulsory military service. Under the act a draftee could escape service if he furnished a substitute or paid a three-hundred-dollar commutation fee to the federal government. A veteran recently discharged from the army who might otherwise have immediately reenlisted would realize that if he waited until compulsory service was put into effect he could make three hundred dollars by substituting for a conscript. As three hundred dollars was the average annual wage for a day laborer at the time, it was well worth waiting for. In addition there was a possibility of receiving a larger bounty by delaying, for the amounts paid seemed to increase as patriotic feeling declined. The monetary incentives thus postponed rather than hastened reenlistment.[41]

The numerical strength of the army fell about 20 percent in May and June as terms of enlistment expired. This loss, in addition to the 12 percent casualty rate suffered at Chancellorsville, produced more serious consequences, however, than a mere reduction in numbers. Many of those who left were veterans of two years' service.[42] Another group, the nine-month volunteers, whom many people had regarded as not much better than the three-month militia called up at the beginning of the war, were leaving just as they were becoming experienced and useful.[43] The departure of thousands of trained troops necessitated considerable reshuffling of enlisted men and officers among the various army units. In some instances groups which had been together for months, if not years, disappeared and became matters of history. The bonds of friendship between individuals and the efficient cooperation of units created through close association were destroyed, not as a result of combat but through lack of planning in raising the army.

Anticipating the need for reorganization, army headquarters late in April provided that three-year men in two-year regiments would be transferred to three-year units should their departing comrades refuse to sign up again. The men who remained perforce had to adjust to new associates and new surroundings, sometimes an unpleasant and demoralizing experience. A case in point occurred after Chancellorsville when General Sedgwick, commander of the Sixth Corps, broke up the Light Brigade, a famous outfit, and assigned its infantry regiments to the First and Second Divisions and its battery to the Third Division. Similarly in the Fifth Corps General Meade lost nearly a division by the termination of the service of his two-year and nine-month men, so that he had to break up Brigadier General A. A. Humphreys' division. Fortunately the army did not lose Humphreys; he was ordered to fill a vacancy created by the death at Chancellorsville of Major General Hiram G. Berry, commander of the Second Division, Third Corps, under General Sickles.[44] Meade considered that his loss was Sickles' gain for Humphreys was a topnotch soldier and a "splendid man."[45]

One of the gravest errors committed by Union authorities in their recruitment program was their failure to adopt a systematic method of filling up the depleted ranks of veteran regiments. If recruits had been sent regularly to the old regiments, they would quickly have acquired the good habits of the men, as well as some of their spirit and daring. According to General Alpheus S. Williams, it was "wonderful" how soon a recruit became a "good soldier" when placed among old troops. The size and effectiveness of the army, he said, could be maintained only by a constant stream of individual recruits to be used as replacements. When a regiment fell below a certain size, its efficiency and morale were impaired and the men became oppressed by the frequency of special assignments and "daily duty" work.[46]

In addition to the demobilization of thousands of its troops the army had incurred the loss of 17,287 men in killed, wounded, or captured at Chancellorsville.[47] Although some of the wounded and captured undoubtedly returned to the ranks before Gettysburg, their number is not known. Official estimates on April 30 indicated a force of 111,650 infantry ready for front-line duty. Hooker wrote two weeks later, however, that his "marching force" of infantry was down to about 80,000 men. Presumably by "marching force" he meant those troops ready for action.[48] The cavalry was in even worse shape. The wear and tear of the campaign, which was particularly hard on the horses, and special assignments for certain units had reduced the number of cavalrymen ready for active duty from 11,542 on April 30 to 4,677 on May 27, a decrease of almost 60 percent.[49]

Reductions in the numerical strength of these two branches of the service and especially of the infantry furnished Hooker with plausible reasons for reorganizing his third branch, the artillery. Even when the army was stronger he had considered the proportion of artillery too great, since most of the fighting was done in heavily wooded country. He wrote Lincoln on May 13 that in view of the present size of the infantry corps and for the sake of efficiency he had decided he ought to store half the guns in army depots. Here he was indulging in his usual tendency to exaggerate while telling only part of the truth. As it turned out, Hooker cut the number of cannon by about 10 percent; there were 366 at Gettysburg compared to 411 at Chancellorsville. Perhaps it had occurred to him that the army might sometime campaign in more open country where artillery could be used to greater advantage. Actually much of the reduction in the strength of the artillery was due to forces beyond his control. Seven batteries were mustered out of the service, and eight others because of a high rate of attrition had to be consolidated to make four complete units. The loss in guns was partly made up before Gettysburg, however, by the addition of four new batteries.[50]

Besides trying to cut the number of his batteries Hooker on May 12 ordered a complete reorganization of the artillery. The ostensible reason for the change, as stated in his orders, was the "reduction of the strength of the infantry." Probably the real cause was his unfortunate experience at Chancellorsville when he learned (though he never admitted so publicly) that the Union artillery had suffered from poor management. As in the case of the Confederate artillery prior to its overhauling during the winter of 1863, the fire power of Union guns had been dissipated by the distribution of batteries among the divisions, to which they were more or less permanently attached. Hooker realized too that the Artillery Reserve of only twelve batteries for the entire army was much too small. He and General Hunt worked out a new plan under which the batteries were assigned to the various corps. The brigade, under the command of an artilleryman, became the coordinating unit for the batteries, each of which usually had six guns. Most brigades consisted of five batteries; four had only four batteries, and one had eight. There were fourteen brigades of artillery in the entire Army of the Potomac, and they were distributed so as to give each infantry corps one and the cavalry corps two. The remaining five brigades, under Brigadier General Robert O. Tyler, made up the Artillery Reserve, which thus became almost twice the size it had been at Chancellorsville. This new arrangement increased the effectiveness of the artillery through centralized control. Guns could be rushed to critical areas as they were needed to give the Union forces greater concentration of fire power.

The newly organized artillery of the Army of the Potomac under the personal direction of General Hunt compared very favorably with its rival in the Army of Northern Virginia. Whereas the brigade corresponded to the Confederate artillery battalion in size and function, the big difference between the two organizations was in the Artillery Reserve. In the Union army it consisted of twenty-one batteries mounting 118 guns, while the Confederates had a smaller reserve of eight to ten batteries for each of their three infantry corps. Most of the Confederate battalion commanders had higher rank than their counterparts in the Federal army, for promotions did not accompany the increased responsibilities of corps chiefs of artillery in the Union army, much to Hunt's disappointment. All during the war he had lost competent artillerymen because they could obtain higher rank by transferring to the infantry or cavalry. On the whole, however, Hunt was satisfied with the changes in organization.

One in particular pleased him for it solved a longstanding problem, that of supplying ammunition for the artillery. Previous to the reorganization all reserve ammunition for a division, whether infantry or artillery, had been dumped in its supply train and placed under the control of either an infantry officer, a staff officer detailed to the job, or a quartermaster. Hunt never trusted this arrangement, for he was convinced that these officers possessed no real understanding of artillery needs. There was no guarantee that they would have their trains available where most needed in the heat of battle, or that their chests would be well filled with the right kind of ammunition. The new system placed the artillery ammunition train of each corps under the direction of the chief of artillery of that corps. The Artillery Reserve had its own supply train, which was controlled by Hunt's immediate subordinate, General Tyler. More important than any of the new arrangements was the presence of General Hunt to make them work. Among his attributes as a commander was his ability to allow for the shortcomings of others and anticipate the unexpected. The Army of Northern Virginia had no one who could compare with him as an administrator and artillery expert except possibly Colonel E. P. Alexander, and he did not hold a position of similar authority. In organization and equipment the artillery of the Army of the Potomac was fully prepared for a new campaign.[51]

Aside from these improvements in the artillery, Hooker and the high command in Washington took little advantage of the month's respite between the Chancellorsville and Gettysburg campaigns to get military forces in the East ready for further operations, which everyone knew were bound to occur soon.[52] One important obstacle developed from the lack of proper coordination between movements of the Army of the Potomac and other Union forces in the East. The person immediately responsible for this sad state of affairs was General in Chief H. W. Halleck, who had the duty of securing cooperation between the various Union armies and departments. Although professionally competent, there was a fatal flaw in his makeup. He would make suggestions to his subordinates and even criticize them, but he would not give an order if he could help it. A further difficulty was the intense dislike he and Hooker had for each other, a feeling which dated back to a time before the war when both of them lived in California. Lincoln and Hooker were jointly responsible for the confused situation. Hooker was Halleck's subordinate, but he refused to report information or exchange thoughts with his chief. Instead he communicated directly with Lincoln and received instructions directly from him. How well Lincoln kept Halleck informed of what went on between him and Hooker is not clear, but Halleck often professed ignorance of Hooker's situation and plans. It was a clumsy arrangement at best. Either Lincoln should have told Hooker to go through channels, or he should have removed Halleck. Apparently under prodding from Secretary of War Edwin M. Stanton, on June 16 Lincoln finally ordered Hooker to report directly to Halleck, but by that time the Gettysburg campaign was well under way and much of the harm had been done.[53]

During the critical month before Lee started his invasion of the North Hooker and Halleck seemed to be pretty much in the dark about each other's thoughts and intentions on questions of strategy. Hooker did make some effort to keep Lincoln informed, as when on May 13 he wrote the President about the condition of his army, the possibility of resuming the offensive, and the disposition of Federal forces along the Virginia seaboard. He would like to know, he said, whether Washington authorities thought the Union general, John J. Peck, could keep General Longstreet pinned down near Richmond and prevent him from joining Lee. If not, Hooker suggested vaguely that a "reserve infantry force of 25,000" might be placed at his disposal, presumably near Fredericksburg.[54] If he was asking for infantry reinforcements, he was doing it in a left-handed way.

A few days later Secretary Stanton, who was worried about the "condition of affairs on the Rappahannock," asked Halleck to make a "detailed report" about the size, location, and nature of the forces around Washington. It was the kind of assignment that Halleck's scholarly soul dearly loved, and he made a careful analysis of the

43

situation on May 18. In so doing he had to refer to possible moves by the Army of the Potomac. What information he possessed was based entirely upon conversations he had had with Hooker when he and the President had visited the army some two weeks previously. Since then Hooker had not seen fit to keep Halleck posted on developments. Halleck in turn neglected to make the courteous and sensible gesture of sending Hooker a copy of his report, so that in truth the left hand did not know what the right hand was doing and vice versa. It would have been helpful for Hooker to know what Halleck thought about the military situation in the East, particularly as Halleck advised against weakening the inadequate forces defending Washington to reinforce the Army of the Potomac, and he seemed to have no ideas about getting troops anywhere else in the East.[55] While these efforts at strategic planning, if they could be called that, came to naught, the Army of the Potomac except for the artillery was no better prepared for a new campaign than it had been immediately after the battle of Chancellorsville.

Much remained to be done to get the other two branches of the service in shape for combat. The equipment of the cavalry remained superior to that of the enemy and would continue to be so, but in numbers it had not recovered its former strength. Furthermore, the attrition in horseflesh resulting from a hard campaign had reduced very considerably the effectiveness of the troopers. The corps too had a new chief, Brigadier General Alfred Pleasonton, who replaced General Stoneman on May 22. Stoneman had incurred Hooker's extreme displeasure by failing to employ his cavalry more effectively when striking at Lee's lines of communication.[56] Whether deserved or not, Pleasonton had gained a reputation for resourcefulness and boldness during the frantic efforts of Union officers to stop Jackson's flanking attack at Chancellorsville late in the evening of May 2. Nevertheless it is questionable whether Pleasonton was any great improvement over Stoneman. In later years General Hooker agreed that Brigadier General John Buford, commander of the First Cavalry Division, would have been a better man for the position of chief, but Pleasonton's commission antedated Buford's by eleven days and for this reason Hooker felt he had to be appointed.[57]

The third branch of the army, the infantry, caused Hooker his greatest concern, for he realized that while Lee's infantry corps were growing larger, those of the Army of the Potomac were becoming smaller. In materiel also the Union soldier did not possess the great advantage that has been traditionally assumed. No doubt he was better clad, shod, and fed than the Confederate, but in the things that count in battle, arms and ammunition, he did not have an edge. As for experience, all of the corps had been tested thoroughly by the enemy's fire and had established traditions of military success. The one exception was the Eleventh Corps, which together with its commander, General Howard, was under a cloud and suffering from an angry sense of inferiority. There were no doubts about General Reynolds of the First Corps or General Meade of the Fifth. They and their commands could be depended upon to do the right thing at the right time. The same could be said of General Sedgwick commanding the Sixth Corps, despite Hooker's accusation that he was slow at Chancellorsville. The Sixth Corps had a proud record, and it loved John Sedgwick well enough to march its legs off should he ask. The Twelfth Corps like the others had a West Pointer to command it, General Henry W. Slocum, one of Phil Sheridan's roommates but in no respect like him. Slocum was careful and able but certainly not dashing. The commander of the Third Corps, General Daniel E. Sickles, was a question mark. One count against him was that he had graduated from the Tammany school of politics rather than from the school of military science at West Point. Flamboyant, impulsive, and brave, some would wonder about his sense of discipline and his military judgment. Last but not least there was a new commander for the famous Second Corps, Major General Winfield S. Hancock. When General Couch left the army in disgust, Hancock, West Point class of '40, was elevated to his post. The change was a promotion for him and a boost for the army. Hancock was just as able as Couch, and in addition he possessed qualities of leadership that made men call him "superb." [58] On the whole Hooker had a very competent set of corps commanders, although some of the generals commanding his divisions and brigades did not measure up to their standard.

The greatest deficiency in the Army of the Potomac at this time was lack of confidence, not so much in itself as in its commander. With all its shortcomings, for which the federal government was much to blame, it was still a magnificent army. Its ranks, though thinner than they had been, were largely comprised of veterans who had endured many months of hard marching and tough fighting.

Most of them were native-born Americans who had volunteered for reasons that ranged from material gain or love of adventure to an ideal of freedom. To call them hirelings, foreign mercenaries, scum of the cities, and the poorer classes of the country, terms used in derision and contempt by the Southern press and some Confederate officers, reveals a fatal delusion.[59] Regardless of what their foes said about the Federal troops, General Hunt did not believe there was any important difference between them and the Southern soldiers. He also knew that "the same army is a different thing under different circumstances—that Napoleon says that in war the moral is to the physical as three to one—that much depends on commanders—much on discipline—much on other things. . . ."[60] According to this formula the Army of the Potomac, despondent and low in spirit, could be said to have started the Gettysburg campaign with a three to one handicap.

III

BRANDY STATION, A DOUBLE SURPRISE

THE TWO mighty armies stood poised on the banks of the Rappahannock River at Fredericksburg, each waiting for the other to make the first move. After the snow, sleet, and muck of the winter months and the endless spring rains they were enjoying midsummer heat in May, but instead of relaxing, the soldiers in both armies were tense, warily watching for some incident that would precipitate another head-on clash of arms.

During the winter lull the common soldier had run the war more or less according to his sense of the fitness of things, contrary to the orders of his officers. Being American, whether from the North or the South, he was eminently practical. There was a time and a place for killing, and that was in formal combat. Otherwise he lived and let live, especially when he had been opposing the same men for months. On picket duty far in advance of the main lines and away from the companionship of his comrades he was in a little world by himself, lonely and isolated. In the dark of the night the slightest noise would cause alarm. The trigger-happy recruit would bang away at the shadow of a stump, but the cool veteran would sing out, "Hey, Johnny," or "Hi, Yank," as the case might be. Such incidents kept the soldier awake and gave him news or some small article of commerce cherished for its scarcity. And so the pickets along the banks of the Rappahannock maintained an informal truce, freely exchanging information and goods. Now those easier days were over; it was harder to learn anything. Something was up.[1]

The Rappahannock River was one of the most important geographic features of northern Virginia. From headwaters in the recesses of the Blue Ridge Mountains it wound in a southeasterly direction through the Virginia piedmont, tumbled across the fall line at Fredericksburg, and flowed gently into Chesapeake Bay. During the war the Rappahannock gained a prominence almost equal to that of the more famous Mississippi, Tennessee, and Potomac Rivers because of its psychological and military significance to the two great Eastern armies. In the spring of 1863 it separated them physically so that regardless of their positions the two opposing generals always had to reckon with it as they planned their moves. To both it acted sometimes as an obstacle and sometimes as a welcome barrier, depending on what they had in mind. For two years Lee had used the Rappahannock to block the way to Richmond, and now as he was about to start offensive maneuvers he hoped it would screen his army while it moved northwest toward the mountains sheltering the Shenandoah and Cumberland Valleys.

The need to guard the main fords against enemy crossings had long been the first consideration of Union and Confederate generals in their cat and mouse game of trying to capture the enemy's capital. Except when its waters were swollen from heavy rains the river could be forded easily at any number of places between Fredericksburg and the Orange and Alexandria Railroad bridge some thirty miles to the northwest. The most important fords along this section of the river were, from south to north, Banks's, United States, Richards', Ellis', Kemper's, Kelly's, and Beverly. Large bodies of infantry, cavalry, or artillery could cross at these places, and smaller groups at many other points when the water was low, as it was in May and June of 1863. The banks were generally steep and high on both sides, making approaches to the river difficult and increasing the importance of the fords to military movements.[2] As Lee at the start of his offensive gradually shifted his forces up the river, Hooker countered by placing more troops at the upper fords. Both armies could be stretched just so far, however, and the question was when and where would one of the generals decide to cross the river and directly confront his opponent.

About two weeks after Chancellorsville warnings had come to Washington that the Confederates were up to something. Predictions ran from a huge cavalry raid by Stuart to a full-scale invasion of Maryland and Pennsylvania by Lee's entire army. The idea of a raid impressed Stanton and other Union leaders as a definite possibility and would continue to obsess them until the realities of the situation became too obvious for anyone to deny.[3]

Among the early estimates of enemy intentions the shrewdest and most accurate came from a man whose name reflected the cast of his abilities and the character of his work: Colonel G. H. Sharpe. As deputy provost marshal general in charge of the Bureau of Information at Hooker's headquarters Sharpe gave his chief an intelligence report on May 27 which clearly revealed that the Confederates were about ready to start a major offensive. From his informants, many of whom were deserters, he had learned definitely that all of Longstreet's men had rejoined Lee, and he pinpointed the location of Hood's and Pickett's divisions, as well as other units. Sharpe warned that Stuart's cavalry, which was concentrated around Culpeper Court House, was getting stronger every day as dismounted men returned with their horses. Soon, he reported, the Confederates expected to enter a campaign of "long marches and hard fighting, in a part of the country where they would have no railroad transportation"; and they would move in a northwesterly direction so as to bring them upon the right flank of the Union army or above it.[4]

This report did not convince Hooker. When he noted, on the day after receiving it, that enemy camps across the river at Fredericksburg appeared as "numerous and as well filled as ever," he decided against any hasty move and kept the bulk of his forces concentrated near Falmouth on the opposite bank.[5] Then came news of the appearance of enemy skirmishers on the north side of the Rappahannock in the vicinity of Warrenton. Considering them a threat to his right flank, Hooker at once ordered General Pleasonton to send General Buford with a force of about nine hundred men from Dumfries to Bealeton to reinforce the Second and Third Cavalry Divisions under Brigadier General D. McM. Gregg, which were already there. Buford was to assume command of the combined forces and with them drive the enemy back across the Rappahannock, then if possible out of Culpeper Court House and across the Rapidan River about ten miles to the south. At the same time Hooker directed General

49

Meade, who commanded the Fifth Corps, to replace the cavalry pickets at all the lower fords with infantry from one of his divisions so the cavalry units could be moved up the river.[6]

Meanwhile on May 27 Hooker had sent a dispatch to General Reynolds, commander of the First Corps, directing him to get his men ready for maneuvers and to report personally to headquarters for "special instructions."[7] Although these orders sounded very secret and important, they probably only reflected Hooker's reaction to the news of Longstreet's return to Lee with his command and his fear that Lee, with his army greatly strengthened, would attempt a surprise attack. Certainly Hooker and his commanders were in no mood to take the offensive at this time in view of the army's weakened condition after Chancellorsville. General Alpheus Williams expressed the thoughts of many Northern officers when he predicted a Confederate offensive; and it was inconceivable, he said, that "with our reduced army we can, with the least prospect of success, cross the Rappahannock just now."[8] Ironically General Lee, assuming that Hooker had been reinforced, thought that the Federals might do just that.

At this time Lee's methods of obtaining news of the enemy were not as effective as those used by his opponent, and he found it hard to get reliable information. For one thing, Hooker had established strict security measures with the help of Colonel Sharpe, his new intelligence officer. The improved efficiency of the Union cavalry in forming a screen around the army also made it difficult for news to filter through the lines.[9] While Lee constantly claimed that he was unable to fathom Hooker's intentions, in the same breath he would contradict himself and assert that Hooker was being reinforced and was getting ready to make another move.[10] Since he did not know what to expect, Lee had to place his troops in positions for an adequate defense while at the same time arranging for offensive operations. To prepare for a possible attack he ordered Stuart to Culpeper where he could "better observe the enemy."[11] This uncertainty no doubt resulted in lost motion and made it difficult for Lee to gather his forces for a rapid forward movement. He was aware too that ignorance of Hooker's movements or a misreading of his intentions might cause official Richmond finally to decide against his campaign.

Of considerable concern to Lee were 32,000 effective Federal troops in Major General John A. Dix's Department of Virginia scattered along the coast at such places as Fortress Monroe, Norfolk, Suffolk, Yorktown, and West Point. Always a potential threat to Richmond, Lee could not be sure whether the Union authorities intended to use them to mount a determined drive against the Confederate capital.[12] If they did, it might delay the start of his campaign or at least deprive him of troops he sorely needed to carry it out. His greatest worry was a Union detachment of 5,000 infantry, 100 cavalry, and two batteries of artillery that Dix had sent during the first week of May to occupy West Point, a town thirty-five miles east of Richmond at the confluence of the Mattaponi and Pamunkey Rivers as they flowed into the York.[13] To his relief Lee heard on June 2 that this force was evacuating West Point and was retiring down the Peninsula and away from Richmond.[14] Simultaneously as a result of a careful reconnaissance of Hooker's line on the Rappahannock by General Wade Hampton's cavalry, Lee came to the conclusion that the enemy was not contemplating any aggressive movement for the present.[15] There was no longer any reason to wait. Lee had completed the task of rebuilding his army for its summer's work, and he had assurance that most of Pickett's division and all of Pettigrew's brigade, which had been guarding the northern approaches to Richmond near Hanover Junction, would soon be able to follow him. Furthermore, once he had started his forward movement he had reason to hope that Cooke's and Jenkins' brigades would join him.[16] His army might not have the numerical strength he wished, but it was about as large as it had ever been and was much better organized than ever before.

Accordingly on Wednesday morning, June 3, Lee commenced to withdraw his army from the vicinity of Fredericksburg for a concentration at Culpeper Court House. The divisions of Major Generals Lafayette McLaws and J. B. Hood, which had been previously advanced to the Rapidan River, were the first to pull out. They were followed by the three divisions of Ewell's corps: that of Major General Robert E. Rodes on Thursday morning, and on Friday those of Major Generals Jubal A. Early and Edward Johnson. On Friday morning the enemy opened with a furious cannonade and sent a small force across the river. Lee halted Ewell's columns, but being satisfied next morning that the enemy threat was no more than a demonstration to upset his timetable, he ordered Ewell to proceed again. That evening Lee moved his headquarters to Culpeper Court House, leaving General A. P. Hill in charge at Fredericksburg. He gave Hill instructions as to what to do in case the enemy should mount an offensive against him or withdraw to follow Lee. As he had promised Davis, Lee moved "cautiously, watching the result" and did not get "beyond recall" until he felt sure Richmond was safe.[17]

Although by June 4 Hooker was aware of Confederate activity, he was uncertain at first of its meaning. The next day he concluded that the enemy was moving up the river for the purpose of crossing the upper Potomac, or of enveloping his right flank and trying to cut him off from Washington. Hoping to force Lee to show his hand, if not to throw him off balance, Hooker at once alerted the commanding officers of the Second, Eleventh, and Twelfth Corps to have their troops ready to move at short notice. He also ordered Buford to make strong moves against enemy forces near Culpeper and push them as far as possible without endangering his command. On the following day, June 6, he ordered General Sedgwick, commander of the Sixth Corps, to make a reconnaissance in force in front of some pontoon bridges which had been thrown across the Rappahannock at Deep Run just south of Fredericksburg.[18]

Meanwhile on the morning of June 5 Hooker wrote Lincoln to inform him of recent developments. In his communication he raised questions of strategy that must have caused amazement in Washington. Influenced as he was by events of the past year, Hooker guessed that Lee would try to repeat the Manassas campaign of 1862, in which the Confederates had soundly thrashed the Federal army in front of the defenses of Washington and had then proceeded to invade Maryland. He assumed that in his present campaign, as in the previous one, Lee would keep east of the mountains. Although, as it turned out, Hooker was wrong about Lee's route, he was right in thinking that in moving toward his objective, wherever it might be, the vanguard of his army would head toward the Potomac by way of Gordonsville or Culpeper, while the rear would stay at Fredericksburg. Acting on this assumption, Hooker told Lincoln that he proposed to "pitch into" Lee's rear, since he realized that the head of the Confederate army would probably reach Warrenton before he could cope with it. He asked the President whether in so doing he would be within the "spirit," if not the letter of Halleck's instruc-

⚛ *Map 1* ⚛

MOVEMENTS OF ARMIES FROM JUNE 1
TO JUNE 28, 1863

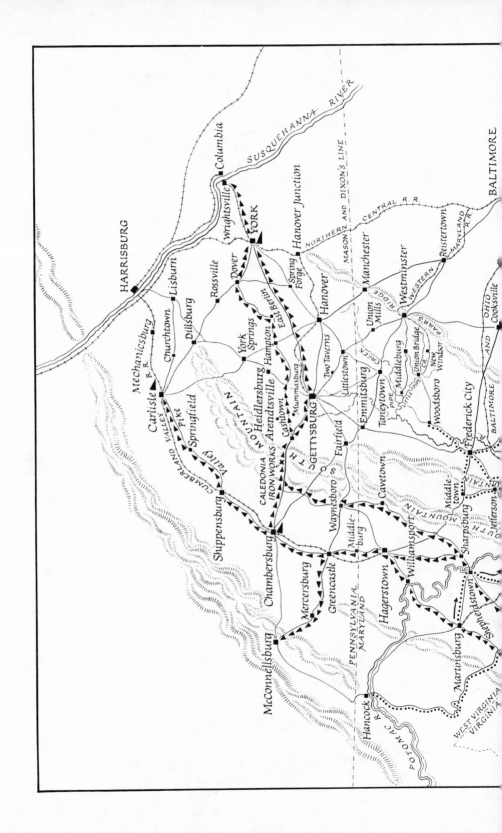

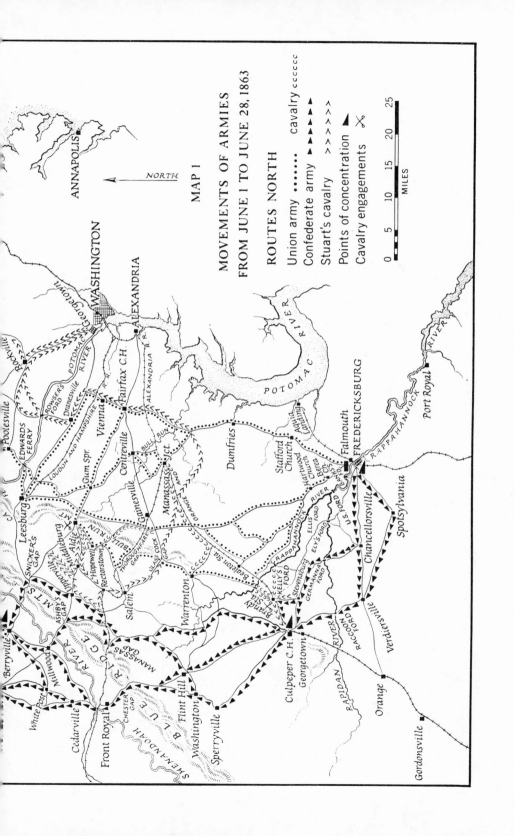

MAP 1

MOVEMENTS OF ARMIES
FROM JUNE 1 TO JUNE 28, 1863

ROUTES NORTH

Union army .... Cavalry ccccccc
Confederate army ▲▲▲ Cavalry c
Stuart's cavalry ▲▲▲▲ >>>>>
Points of concentration ▲
Cavalry engagements ✕

| 0 | 5 | 10 | 15 | 20 | 25 |
MILES

tions of January 31, when the general in chief had told him to keep "in view always the importance of covering Washington and Harpers Ferry, either directly or by so operating as to be able to punish any force of the enemy sent against them." [19]

Lincoln and Halleck greatly disliked Hooker's proposal, and Lincoln lost no time in telling him so. He feared that if Hooker moved against Hill at Fredericksburg he would fall into a trap and be doing what Lee wanted. Hill was a tempting prize, Lincoln admitted, but the strong entrenchments which protected him would place Hooker "man for man" at a disadvantage and would subject him to the risk of being "entangled upon the river, like an ox jumped half over a fence and liable to be torn by dogs front and rear, without a fair chance to gore one way or kick the other." [20] Halleck agreed with the President's objections to Hooker's strategy and suggested that it would be better for him to fight Lee's "movable column" first instead of attacking Hill, since such a maneuver would mean that his own forces would have to be separated by the Rappahannock.[21]

Both Lincoln's and Halleck's fears were well founded. There was real danger that should Hooker cross the river and attack Hill, he would face the likelihood of an envelopment by the forces under Lee near Culpeper. Hill's 15,000 men, well protected by earthworks, could offer stiff and perhaps prolonged resistance. If overpowered they would fall back, according to Lee's instructions, along the line of the railroad running between Fredericksburg and Richmond, where at Hanover Junction, twenty miles south of them, they would be reinforced by Pickett's division and Pettigrew's brigade, about 9,500 men in all. Depending upon how well Hill was handling Hooker with possible aid from Pickett and Pettigrew, Lee would have two alternatives: Either he could continue toward the Potomac and threaten Washington with the main body of his troops, or, what was more likely, he could recall his advanced columns, hammer at Hooker's right flank, and very possibly administer him another defeat even more demoralizing than the one he suffered at Chancellorsville. Thus rather than heading off Lee's invasion of the North, a countermove by Hooker at Fredericksburg might well have produced the opposite effect.[22]

On the same day that Hooker received Lincoln's and Halleck's advice not to attack the enemy at Fredericksburg, he learned from intelligence reports sent him by the vigilant General Buford that

Lee's "movable column" was located near Culpeper Court House and that it consisted of Stuart's three brigades heavily reinforced by Robertson's, "Grumble" Jones's, and Jenkins' brigades.[23] Hooker spent the night digesting the information and advice, and by the afternoon of June 7 he had completed plans for another counter-move. He ordered General Pleasonton to take all of his cavalry, plus a picked body of 3,000 infantrymen [24] who had the reputation of being among the best marchers and fighters in the army,[25] across the upper Rappahannock not far from Brandy Station on the Orange and Alexandria Railroad. Once on the other side he was to seek out the rebel force in the vicinity of Culpeper and "disperse and destroy" it, along with all its trains and supplies.[26] In other words, Hooker was trying to stop a Confederate raid or something even more serious before it could get started. Nowhere in his instructions, which were very detailed and explicit, did he suggest that Pleasonton was to make merely a "reconnaissance in force" for the purpose of securing information, as Pleasonton himself later claimed.[27] Since he wanted Pleasonton to fight and not just scout the enemy, Hooker furnished him with enough infantry supports to compensate for the greatly reduced strength of his cavalry regiments following Chancellorsville.[28] The infantry, Hooker pointed out, would give him the advantage of being able to form a "moving *point d'appui* to rally on at all times" which no cavalry force would be able to shake.[29] Pleasonton's combined force numbered about 11,000 infantry, cavalry, and artillery. As an added precaution Hooker instructed General Meade to have troops in Brigadier General James Barnes's division, which were guarding Kelly's Ford, ready to assist Pleasonton should he need them.[30]

Hooker did not know the exact size of the force under Stuart, but he thought it much less than the estimate of 20,000 given Buford on June 5 by a refugee from Madison County.[31] It would have been better if he had accepted this inflated figure and planned accordingly, for as it turned out, he furnished Pleasonton with sufficient men to make a good showing against the approximately 10,000 troopers under Stuart, but not enough to assure their destruction.[32] Hooker also took an unnecessary risk when he assumed that no large bodies of Confederate infantry were located near Culpeper Court House within supporting distance of Stuart. He had not heard of the arrival there of all of Ewell's corps and two divisions of Longstreet's, but by June 6 he did know that Hood's men had advanced as far west as Raccoon Ford on the Rapidan River, which put them within easy marching distance of Culpeper.[33] This information, though fragmentary, should have been enough to make him suspect hidden dangers and provide for them by sending overwhelming infantry supports for Pleasonton's forces. Had he done so, the battle of Brandy Station would very likely have expanded from an encounter between Stuart's and Pleasonton's cavalry into a major engagement between the two armies, with Hooker having a much better opportunity for success than at Fredericksburg.[34]

Following Hooker's orders, on the night of June 8 Pleasonton quietly drew his forces up to the east bank of the Rappahannock River. He had divided his cavalry with its infantry supports into two groups. General John Buford commanded the right wing, which consisted of the Reserve Brigade (army regulars and the 6th Pennsylvania Cavalry), the First Cavalry Division, and a large detachment of infantry under Brigadier General Adelbert Ames. The left wing, led by General Gregg, included the Second and Third Cavalry Divisions and Brigadier General David A. Russell's force of infantry. Buford's command stood poised at Beverly Ford a mile and a half northwest of the Orange and Alexandria Railroad bridge across the river, while Gregg and his men were gathered around the approaches to Kelly's Ford some four miles southeast of the bridge. Both wings were to cross the river at dawn. With the exception of the Second Cavalry Division under Colonel Alfred N. Duffié which was to go to Stevensburg, the entire force was to unite at Brandy Station four miles southwest of Beverly Ford and about twice that distance from Kelly's Ford. From there Pleasonton planned to push on toward Culpeper six miles farther west.

Pleasonton had undoubtedly been briefed by his scouts about the main geographical features of the region he was about to enter. Although the country near the river was heavily wooded, he knew it became more open toward Brandy Station and would lend itself to rapid movements of large bodies of men on horseback. About half a mile east of the station and just north of the railroad a dominating feature of the landscape was Fleetwood Hill, really a long, partly wooded ridge running north and south, while five miles to the south was Stevensburg, Colonel Duffié's objective point. Occupation of Stevensburg would protect the left flank of the main body of

Pleasonton's force as it advanced from Brandy Station toward Culpeper. It would also form a vantage point to prevent a surprise attack should the enemy cross at Raccoon Ford to the south.[35]

As Pleasonton gathered his troopers for his undertaking, Stuart, oblivious of the threat, was preparing for his role in the coming campaign by displaying his five brigades of cavalry in a brilliant review before his chief. It was a repeat performance, for Lee could not get to the original affair held three days earlier. Although lacking the spontaneity and fanfare of the first review (Lee would not allow the cavalry to gallop nor permit the artillerymen to work their guns), 10,000 troopers passing by in row after row before an admiring crowd of onlookers made an impressive sight. Stuart was pleased to show off the largest number of cavalrymen he had ever commanded,[36] and the review was an excuse to bring them together before they moved across the Rappahannock to screen the infantry marching toward the Shenandoah Valley. At the conclusion of the review Stuart moved his brigades down toward the river and issued orders for an early start the next day. With all his equipment and baggage, except two tent flies, packed and stowed in wagons, Stuart himself camped for the night on Fleetwood Hill. From there he could survey the countryside in every direction except for a narrow strip to the west which was hidden by a somewhat higher hill.[37]

Just before dawn a sleepy picket at Beverly Ford could see nothing but the ghostly white of the mist rising from the river and hear only a slight rustling of leaves. Suddenly there was the crack of a Sharps carbine, the opening shot of one of the most famous cavalry fights of the war. This was followed by the splash of Buford's troopers as they dashed across the river. After a brief exchange of shots with Company A of the 6th Virginia Cavalry, which was stretched along the bank on picket duty, they broke out of the narrow road near the ford and pressed their opponents back to the edge of the woods skirting an open field north of St. James Church. Momentarily checked by another group from the 6th Virginia, the Union cavalrymen advanced surprisingly fast and barely missed seizing four batteries of horse artillery which were parked near the church about two miles from the ford. These Confederate batteries escaped capture only because Captain J. F. Hart managed to wheel two guns into position and open fire in time to cover the withdrawal of the other pieces. The timely arrival of the 7th Virginia Cavalry whose troopers came on pell-mell, many still undressed and riding bare-back, slowed up Buford's men long enough for the rest of "Grumble" Jones's brigade to rush up. They were soon followed by Hampton with four of his regiments and several squadrons of dismounted men from W. H. F. Lee's brigade. Though badly surprised by the Union attack, the Confederates kept their poise and with quick thinking and rapid movements slowed Buford's advance to a walk. Finally about 10:00 A.M. they gathered sufficient strength to mount a coun-terattack in the hope of hurling the Northerners back toward the river. Before they could accomplish their purpose, however, the ad-vance of General Gregg toward Brandy Station seriously threatened their rear. Buford, perceiving the lessening of pressure on his front, immediately urged his men forward.[38]

Gregg had been several hours late in getting started because he had had to wait for Colonel Duffié, who with his division had be-come lost in some remote country lane. Once he had joined Gregg the two forces crossed the river at Kelly's Ford without opposition and took the direct road to Stevensburg. About halfway there Gregg with the Third Division of cavalry and an infantry detach-ment turned off to the right on a road to Brandy Station, while Duffié proceeded to Stevensburg according to plan. In taking this route Gregg unwittingly avoided a clash with Robertson's brigade of two large regiments which had moved at dawn within supporting distance of Confederate pickets at Kelly's Ford. Robertson, in posi-tion south of the railroad, reported the advance of Gregg and his men but did nothing to stop them because he conceived it his duty to protect the right flank of the Confederate forces confronting Bu-ford's men north of the rail line. What Robertson thought would happen to Stuart's right flank should Gregg get behind it is not known. Perhaps he didn't think. Whatever the explanation for Rob-ertson's conduct, Gregg's troopers were unaware of his presence, and they went around him and continued on their way without in-terference.

Imagine the consternation of Major Henry B. McClellan, Stuart's assistant adjutant general, when he looked south from Fleetwood Hill about noon and saw a long column of the enemy filling the road from Kelly's Ford to Brandy Station. When Stuart had gone to the front near St. James Church, he had left his adjutant in charge of the old headquarters. Everyone except some couriers, who were darting here and there with messages, had accompanied Stuart to the scene of the fighting. A rider sent by Robertson had warned McClellan of Gregg's approach, but the adjutant refused to believe it until he saw the Union troops with his own eyes. McClellan did what was expected of him. He sent a hurry-up call to Stuart for aid, while ordering Lieutenant John W. Carter, who was on top of the hill with one little 6-pounder howitzer, to lob a few shells as a show of resistance. The stratagem worked. Gregg, unduly impressed, hesitated and thus lost the opportunity to seize the key to Stuart's entire position and its handful of defenders with one of his cavalry regiments. Within minutes the 12th Virginia Cavalry and the 35th Battalion came thundering to the rescue, and there ensued a wild fracas with charges and countercharges by regiments, squadrons, and companies. Clouds of dust and smoke enveloped the field, and above the confusion could be heard the sound of bugles and of shouted orders, cries of anguish and the whinnying of horses, clash of sabers and bark of revolvers. Here was the cavalry fight as pictured by the romantic artist or the theorist in military tactics. Men on both sides showed determination and skill. The issue was long in doubt.

Meanwhile Duffié, who had been late in starting, reached Stevensburg in time to become involved in a spirited encounter with the 2nd South Carolina and 4th Virginia Cavalry. Though something of a sideshow to the main event several miles to the north, the affair had its share of drama. Duffié overcame the resistance of his opponents, but not soon enough to join in the battle swirling around Fleetwood Hill and Brandy Station.[39]

By late afternoon both forces had had enough. Stuart had concentrated his command and consolidated his hold on Fleetwood Hill. Pleasonton's strength was insufficient to push him off, and when he became aware of the approach of Confederate infantry he decided to withdraw. General Lee, who arrived just in time to see his wounded son carried off the field, did not have to bring up his infantry, although Rodes's division of Ewell's corps was near at hand.[40] Despite claims to the contrary, the Federal forces were able to withdraw gradually across the Rappahannock at Beverly Ford and Rappahannock Station without further molestation from the enemy. The battle of Brandy Station was over. What did it mean?

The engagement had proved a disillusioning experience for many

Confederate officers, although they would never acknowledge it publicly. Stuart's report was remarkable for its restraint and its omissions. He did not admit that the Yankees had surprised him, nor did he claim a great victory; and he suggested that though there had been tight moments, the situation really never got out of hand. True, the performance of certain subordinates, such as General Robertson and Colonel Thomas T. Munford, had not come up to expectations, and two cavalry regiments had broken under the pressure of enemy attacks. But these shortcomings, he implied, had had little effect on the outcome of the engagement, for as was to be expected, the might of his cavalry had finally prevailed. In contrast to the moderation of his report, Stuart in a congratulatory order to his men broke out in the usual Civil War bombast and exaggerated the magnitude of their accomplishments. Though he insisted upon calling the battle a victory, the figures upon which he based his claim were far from impressive. He listed the capture of a few battle flags, three cannon, and several hundred prisoners, but said nothing about crippling the enemy.[41] If this was a victory, it was by a slender margin.

Other Southern officers were not so sure about the victory. One of them, General McLaws of Longstreet's corps, the day after the battle wrote his wife that "our cavalry were surprised yesterday by the enemy and had to do some desperate fighting to retrieve the day. As you will perceive from General Lee's dispatch the enemy were driven across the river again. All this is not true, but it will be better to allow the impression to prevail. The enemy were not however driven back but retired at their leisure, having accomplished I suppose what they intended." [42] Another officer stated the case even more bluntly while taking a side glance at Stuart's generalship. "The cavalry fight at Brandy Station," he wrote, "can hardly be called a *victory*. Stuart was certainly surprised and but for the supreme gallantry of his subordinate officers and the men in his command it would have been a day of disaster and disgrace." [43] Perhaps he got this appraisal of the battle from General Wade Hampton who in his battle report had the temerity to be critical of his commanding officer. For various reasons Hampton was quite disgruntled with the whole affair. Years later in discussing the battle with Major McClellan he was even more outspoken when he said that Stuart had failed to give his—Hampton's—brigade credit for the "only successful fighting . . . of the day." Hampton thought Robertson had not been responsible for the enemy having gotten to Brandy Station and the rear of Stuart's cavalry. After referring to other "blunders & disasters of the day" he concluded: "Stuart managed badly that day, but I would not say so publicly." [44]

Allowing for possible jealousy and a desire to see Lee's favorite cavalry leader humbled, these critics were not far from the mark. Whatever standard is used, the facts barely justified Stuart's claim of victory. The Yankees had given him a rough time of it, and he knew it. Particularly galling was the realization that they had deliberately hunted him out and badly bruised him the very day after he had proudly paraded his troopers with all the pomp of a tournament. Stuart's detractors within the army kept their counsel or restricted their observations to personal letters, but not so those outside military circles. The *Richmond Examiner* called the signal in an article uncomplimentary of the battle and Stuart's management of it, and soon other papers took up the hue and cry. Some writers pointed to his propensity for reviews as an indication of overweening pride, and they noted the ironical juxtaposition of the review with its make-believe war on one day and the battle with its encounter with death the next. What hurt perhaps worst of all was their emphasis on the word "surprise." Stuart was deeply chagrined and humiliated, but what effect the bitter experience may have had upon his conduct in the Gettysburg campaign is impossible to tell. Some people felt that his wounded pride and his anxiety to redeem himself were determining influences on his course of action.[45]

Stuart's opponent, General Pleasonton, had reason to congratulate himself on Brandy Station, but for reasons other than the ones he gave. If he had been honest with himself and his commander he would have had to report, "Mission not accomplished." Of course he did nothing of the sort. Instead over a period of several years he came up with a number of different accounts of the engagement: first in messages to army headquarters during and immediately after the fighting, then in his battle report, later in testimony before the Committee on the Conduct of the War, and finally in a postwar publication. He never told the same story twice, and as he kept going over it certain of its main features, as well as its tone and emphasis, became so changed that there was little resemblance between the earliest and latest versions. He had an unfortunate propensity to exaggerate both his difficulties and his accomplishments, arising perhaps from an excessive ambition and desire for glory which were somewhat reminiscent of Stuart. In his report, for instance, he complained of the enemy's force being superior to his by "at least three to one at every point. . . ." If so, he must have been guilty of bad tactics for the forces were about equal in size. In another passage he strained credibility even more when he said that "the enemy's cavalry would retreat, and their officers were seen to sabre and shoot their men to keep them to the fight." [46]

It is not surprising therefore that at first Pleasonton claimed to have done what Hooker had wanted: "crippled" Stuart so that he could not go on a raid.[47] But he soon stopped talking in this vein as subsequent developments proved him wrong. Instead he began to stress another accomplishment which he had mentioned in several of his messages to Hooker and in his battle report a few days later: the capture of some important papers. He said that as his forces overran the camp of the Confederate horse artillery and Stuart's headquarters they had found documents which revealed Stuart's intention to start a raid into Maryland.[48] As he kept repeating this story and adding embellishments, the disclosures in the papers grew ever more astonishing and important. In his later accounts, which were noticeable for their double-talk and lack of clarity, he said he had learned, apparently from these documents, that on the morning of the Union attack Stuart was to have crossed the river at Beverly Ford and destroyed the railroad to Alexandria, so as to delay the Army of the Potomac in its movement north; and that Lee intended to cross the Potomac east of the Blue Ridge Mountains near Leesburg, Virginia. Hooker, forewarned of Lee's plan of campaign, acted immediately, Pleasonton said, and moved his army toward Maryland, thus forcing Lee to take the more roundabout route along the Shenandoah and Cumberland Valleys into Pennsylvania.[49] The tale of the captured documents also became the basis for Pleasonton's thesis that his expedition was a "reconnaissance in force to gain information." His instructions, he finally claimed, were neither to seek nor to avoid a fight, but to arrange his forces in the best way possible to obtain intelligence about the enemy.[50] He had done that, and therefore his mission was completely successful. Though this version of what Hooker expected of him was a gross perversion of the truth, it became the generally accepted one in other accounts of the battle.[51]

The amazing thing about Pleasonton's story of Stuart's papers was that not once did he give an idea of how many documents he had captured or what their contents were. Some historians have even doubted whether he seized any papers at all. Then recently two of three documents which he had handed over to his commander turned up in a private collection of Hooker's papers. Unfortunately they prove nothing. One was an order of march for General "Grumble" Jones's brigade for the review of Stuart's cavalry on June 8; the other a letter dated June 4 from an unknown Confederate named Bill to his father, containing the typical camp rumors about big doings in store for the Confederate cavalry as the season for campaigning got under way. Bill said Stuart was preparing to make a grand raid into enemy country with a force which had recently grown from 4,000 to 12,000 men.[52] Perhaps from this letter Pleasonton got his figure of 12,000 troopers for the size of Stuart's cavalry, as well as what seemed to him to be confirmation of the gossip bruited about in the North as to the possibility of another Stuart raid.[53]

As a result of this recent discovery there can be little doubt that Pleasonton did in fact capture some papers. Still it is very unlikely they were from Stuart's headquarters because the general stoutly maintained that early in the engagement he had sent all wagons of the division to the rear, including every "vestige" of his own camp. McClellan, Stuart's adjutant and an honest man, vouched for this statement, while admitting the loss of a desk belonging to Major R. F. Beckham, Stuart's chief of artillery, which bounced off a wagon as he was hastily abandoning his own headquarters.[54] Perhaps Pleasonton's men found some documents in the desk drawers. Whatever the contents of these or any other papers picked up on the battlefield, surely none of them contained orders for a raid by Stuart's cavalry into Maryland, for Lee at no time had such an expedition in mind; nor did he consider crossing the Potomac east of the mountains. On the contrary, he wanted to have the cavalry serve as a screen between him and the enemy as he advanced north with his army.

Pleasonton did obtain from other sources as well as from the captured papers information useful but not vital to Hooker. Probably as a result of observations by his subordinates during the battle he learned of the presence of Confederate infantry near Culpeper, but not the identity of the units. He also got a good idea—only slightly exaggerated—of the size of Stuart's force. Then the day after the battle a Negro servant, captured from an officer in Stuart's artillery, furnished him with remarkably reliable intelligence about the location of the various parts of Lee's army. Both Longstreet's and Ewell's corps were in Culpeper, he said, while Hill's was still at Fredericksburg. Other bits of information were equally accurate, but there was nothing credible about what he said of Lee's intentions. Here was an even more fantastic version of Stuart's raid. This time it seems Lee intended to penetrate into Pennsylvania as far as Pittsburgh! Pleasonton dutifully passed his news on to Hooker, but the next day, June 11, he confused him with another dispatch in which he quoted Confederate deserters as saying that Ewell was still at Fredericksburg along with Hill. Hooker chose to accept this latest report as reliable, and he sent it on to Halleck with obvious approval. At that hour Ewell was well on his way toward the Shenandoah Valley.[55] Somehow those valuable documents which Pleasonton so proudly hailed as prizes of war failed to reveal the inner secrets of Confederate strategy after all.

Pleasonton's accomplishments at Brandy Station, though less than he imagined, nevertheless were real ones. What is more, he came within an ace of winning signal success despite poor intelligence work which misled Hooker, as he drew up instructions for Pleasonton's expedition, into thinking that the Confederate cavalry was clustered about Culpeper ten miles or so west of the Rappahannock. Instead to his surprise Pleasonton found it within a short distance of the river and east rather than west of Brandy Station. Hence the hurt tone in a message which he sent to Hooker early in the engagement: "They were aware of our movement, and were prepared." [56] At first glance it would appear that in sending this dispatch he looking for an excuse for an early retreat. Hooker seemed to take it that way and told him to withdraw if necessary,[57] but to his credit Pleasonton went ahead with the attack and gave the Confederates a good scare if not a beating. Actually Hooker's battle plan, though based on a false supposition, had great merit. With Stuart closer to the river than he or Pleasonton had thought, the arrangement for a

double crossing of the river, which was designed to facilitate movement, became converted into a double envelopment of most of the
Confederate cavalry. Pleasonton tried to take advantage of his discovery of the enemy's position and sent couriers to Gregg informing
him of the situation.[58] What had become a two-pronged attack
would have succeeded if—a big if—the movement of the two wings
had been properly coordinated, but good staff work and an efficient
communications system were lacking. Many Civil War battles in
which success depended upon coordinated movements ended in disappointment because somebody failed to get a message straight or
could not get to the appointed place on time. So it was at Brandy
Station, where Duffié lost his way to Kelly's Ford and delayed the
whole left wing. An earlier start by perhaps as little as half an hour
might have given Gregg enough time to seize and hold Fleetwood
Hill against all comers. In that case two brigades of Stuart's division
and most of his artillery would have been squeezed between the
jaws of pincers. Though it did not happen that way, Pleasonton and
his troopers did gain fame for themselves as a result of their try.

For the first time at Brandy Station the cavalry of the Army of the
Potomac acting as a unit fought a pitched battle with Stuart's
cavalry in which the honors were about even. More important, it
took the offensive, which to Stuart and other Confederates was one
of the most discomfiting surprises of all. Under expert handling it
had evolved into a hard-hitting outfit rightfully proud of its vigor
and skill. As leaders it had such men of experience and ability as
John Buford, a Kentuckian who always knew what to do when the
going was rough; Alfred Duffié, truly a *"beau sabreur,"* [59] always
ready for a good fight; David McM. Gregg, modest, able, and beloved by his men; and last but not to be overlooked, Alfred Pleasonton, who if he had let the facts speak for themselves might have
been known as another Phil Sheridan. Pleasonton realized that his
men had done well, and he wired Hooker that they were "entitled to
the highest praise for their distinguished conduct." [60] He also recommended the promotion of Brigadier Generals Buford and Gregg
for the "gallantry and ability" with which they fought their commands.[61]

Pleasonton's appraisal of his cavalry would very likely have been
confirmed by Confederate cavalry leaders if they had known about
it, for they had acquired new respect for their opponents.[62] Years

later Major McClellan, Stuart's adjutant, went so far as to say that "one result of incalculable importance did follow this battle,—it *made* the Federal cavalry." [63]

It would be misleading, however, to attach undue military importance to the battle of Brandy Station. While it represented Hooker's first and last attempt to break up Lee's drive to the North with a counteroffensive and on the whole was well executed, Pleasonton's attack failed completely to achieve its primary objective, the destruction of Stuart's cavalry. Although Stuart and his men received a blow to their pride, they obviously were not crippled physically because less than a week later they crossed the upper Rappahannock and fanned out over the countryside to screen the Confederate infantry from their inquisitive opponents. [64] If Pleasonton's secondary purpose was to gain intelligence of enemy moves and intentions, he obtained precious little. His one real accomplishment was to demonstrate the ability of his cavalry to ride up to and fight Stuart's troopers on equal terms, to the surprise of people in the North as well as the South.

Much of the fighting conformed to classical concepts of cavalry engagements dear to the heart of the European traditionalist, though not to the extent that was generally supposed, for the Americans could not get over their bad habits. For one thing, at Brandy Station as in other Civil War battles both sides dismounted a large proportion of their troopers and fought them as infantry. Every Confederate cavalry brigade had squadrons of sharpshooters armed with rifles, which in action were always placed behind stone walls, if there were any, to protect the flanks of the horsemen. These tactics were very much in evidence at Brandy Station. General Buford too dismounted practically all of his First Division of about 2,100 troopers and put them in a skirmish line on his left to cooperate with General Adelbert Ames's brigade of infantry. He kept the 1,800 men in the Reserve Brigade mounted and used them as the movable end of a flail to beat the enemy. [65] Pleasonton committed the further unforgivable sin of using infantrymen in what was supposed to be a bona fide cavalry fight. In so doing he equalized his smaller cavalry force and Stuart's larger one, and thus he did not need to have as many of his cavalry troopers fight dismounted as did Stuart. The presence of eight infantry regiments, two of them from the famous Iron Brigade and all of them veteran outfits, helps to explain why

Pleasonton had no trouble in withdrawing his force across the river in the face of a formidable foe.[66]

In view of the length of the battle—Buford said they fought for nearly fourteen hours [67]—and the quality of the action which many participants characterized as close and bitter, it is remarkable that the losses were not heavier. As usual it is easier to get reasonably accurate figures for Federal casualties than for Confederate. The Union loss amounted to 866 officers and men; of this number 382 were counted as captured or missing. Since complete returns from all Confederate brigades never became available, their total loss was uncertain, ranging from an estimated minimum of 375 officers and men to a maximum of 485. Of these numbers the Confederates admitted 132 as captured or missing, although Pleasonton claimed to have taken over 200 prisoners.[68] A unique feature of the fight, where masses of horsemen hurled themselves at each other and entered into a general melee involving hand to hand combat, was the number of saber wounds, many more than in previous battles.[69] But after all was said and done Colonel E. P. Alexander of Longstreet's corps with the disdain of a tough artilleryman pronounced the cavalry fight what it probably was: "a great humbug. Twelve or fifteen thousand engaged all day," he wrote, "and loss on our side not four hundred. I rode over the field next day and saw only about twenty dead Yankees—only two killed with the sabre." [70]

The day after the battle Hooker, using what little information Pleasonton had furnished him, tried to make some reasonable conjectures about Lee's moves. He still believed, in spite of Pleasonton's assurances to the contrary, that Stuart would make his raid, and he tried to conjure up some way to stop him. After considerable soul searching he resurrected his previous proposal to President Lincoln to the effect that if Lee withdrew his infantry from Fredericksburg to reinforce Stuart, he would throw a force across the river and compel Hill to abandon his position. Should Lee continue with his invasion, he would march toward Richmond, where he was sure that the defenses were stripped of all troops except 1,500 of the provost guard. Once he had captured the city he would send troops from his own army to unite with any that the authorities in Washington might be able to collect, and together they would stop Lee's advance. He already had two brigades across the Rappahannock, he said, and he was ready to "spring over" the river below Fredericksburg. All he wanted was word from Lincoln before starting out. It took the President no more than an hour and a half to decide that Hooker's suggestion was fantastically bad. He explained the dangers of getting the army entangled in Richmond's defenses, and he reminded the general that Lee's army and not Richmond was his "sure objective point." If Lee moved toward the upper Potomac, Lincoln explained, his line of communication would become longer and his flank more exposed, while Hooker would have a chance to shorten his own line if he kept on the inside track and attacked Lee somewhere along his flank.[71] During this exchange of ideas it apparently never occurred to Hooker to strike Lee again in the vicinity of Culpeper with an even larger force than the one used at Brandy Station. Lincoln on the other hand advised Hooker, if Lee stayed where he was, to "fret him and fret him." [72]

What worried Lee right after the battle was not the threat which Hooker's two brigades posed to Hill's position at Fredericksburg, but rather the problem of how he could bring all of his forces forward to follow after Ewell and Longstreet and at the same time provide Richmond with adequate troops for its defense. The thought of an enemy drive from the coast toward the capital and the Richmond, Fredericksburg, and Potomac Railroad bothered him constantly. He had a genuine concern for the safety of Richmond, and he could see no strategic advantage in swapping a queen for a queen—Richmond for Washington. His problem was to convince Davis and Seddon, who were very sensitive about the security of the Confederate capital, to take a calculated risk and spare him all troops possible from its defenses. Nevertheless he realized that unless he eased their fears by leaving behind some of his best troops, they as his superiors could call a halt and wreck his offensive.[73]

It annoyed him when they seemed to pay undue heed to the representations of Generals D. H. Hill and William H. C. Whiting, who cried out in alarm that the North Carolina seaboard was in serious danger and no more troops could be spared from the area. He wrote Seddon on June 8 that the importunities of these two generals were disrupting his plan to withdraw gradually all of his men from around Richmond and replace them with units from lower down the coast. He still held to the opinion that during the summer, the "sickly season" as he put it, the enemy would reduce the size of his forces in the deep South, and his "predatory excursions" could be handled by local troops aided by small units of the Confederate army. The alternative to his offensive, Lee said, was a defensive policy in which he would attempt to "guard as far as possible all the avenues of approach, and await the time of the enemy. . . ." Should the War Department decide this course to be the better part of wisdom, he was ready to follow it. Tactfully but forcefully Lee urged Davis and Seddon to study well the implications of any decision they might make.[74]

Acting on the assumption that Davis had accepted his views on strategy, Lee sent him a message on June 9 suggesting certain shifts in command. Since Lee had ordered Brigadier General Montgomery D. Corse's brigade to join Pickett's division in Culpeper, he proposed that Corse's place at Hanover Junction be taken by General John R. Cooke and his brigade. At the same time he recommended transferring General Micah Jenkins' brigade to the Chickahominy River to guard the approaches to Richmond from the east and northeast. Davis accepted Lee's proposal about Cooke and ordered him to Hanover Junction, but he referred the suggestion about Jenkins to D. H. Hill for decision.[75] When Lee learned from Seddon on June 13 that Davis had refused to order Jenkins to the Chickahominy, he sharply reminded him that it was useless for the Army of Northern Virginia to attempt an offensive of any kind if it had to be divided to cover Richmond. He implied that fears for the safety of the capital had become groundless, since all reports indicated that Federal forces at Suffolk, Yorktown, Gloucester, and other places had been reduced to reinforce Hooker. As supporting evidence he cited the capture on June 11 of some of General Dix's men at Fredericksburg.[76] Lee's sense of grievance over Seddon's letter was perhaps heightened by the fact that before receiving it he had ordered the return of Corse's brigade to Hanover Junction together with a regiment from A. P. Hill's corps so as to relieve Cooke of the assignment.[77] In light of these measures which he had taken to protect the capital, Seddon's letter made Lee impatient.[78] On June 15 in a message to the President he said he despaired of accomplishing all that he had hoped to in his offensive. Reports of enemy expeditions threatening the coast of North Carolina and the area of Virginia between the Rappahannock and James Rivers had caused delays in the movements of his army and made him hesitate to draw the whole of A. P. Hill's corps away from Fredericksburg.[79]

This issue involving the need to furnish Lee with a maximum number of troops while providing for the protection of Richmond, the railroads to the north and west of it, and the southern seaboard as far as Charleston was never resolved to the satisfaction of those in authority, because they could not agree on what constituted an adequate defense force. Lee himself was not sure of the answer, and partly for this reason he deferred to the judgment of the President, who in this instance cannot be accused of timidity or lack of imagination. He fully appreciated the importance and magnitude of Lee's task, but he could see that the loss of Richmond would nullify any victory Lee might gain. In retrospect it is clear that the Federal threat to Richmond amounted to little, but at the time there was enough substance to it to warrant concern. That Dix's advance ultimately proved an empty gesture was in large part due to the skillful resistance of the few veteran brigades left behind in the area of the capital. Meanwhile, though Lee was still in a quandary about the situation around Richmond, he proceeded with his plans and on June 15 took steps to concentrate all of his army for its northern offensive. In part he was reacting to Hooker's responses to his own sidling movement up the river.[80]

During this time Hooker had finally become convinced of the truth of Pleasonton's claim that enemy infantry was at Culpeper. He was worried about the possibility of Lee turning Pleasonton's right, cutting the Orange and Alexandria Railroad, and getting between him and Washington. He began to take steps to counter the threat, and as a result June 11 turned out to be a very busy day. Previously he had stationed the Fifth Corps between Kelly's and Banks's Fords to extend the army's right flank northward along the river, as well as to furnish some infantry support for the cavalry. Now he shifted the Third Corps to Bealeton, beyond the Fifth Corps, thus giving Pleasonton even more support and strengthening the Federal hold on the stretch of river between Kelly's and Beverly Fords; and he also sent the First Corps to the vicinity of Berea Church to act as a reserve for both the Fifth and Third. Next he ordered Pleasonton to use his whole force to guard the river above Beverly Ford and to check any attempt the enemy might make to ride around the Army of the Potomac and raid the country behind it. Then he sent a circular to all corps commanders warning them to send to the rear all surplus baggage and all camp followers.[81] By the night of June 12, when

Hooker learned definitely that the greater portion of Lee's army had left Fredericksburg, the Army of the Potomac stretched for forty miles from a position immediately south of Fredericksburg all the way to Beverly Ford.

During the process of shifting more and more of his corps to the northwest to check Lee's threat to his right flank Hooker placed General Reynolds in command of the right wing of the army, which was concentrated near Bealeton. Reynolds had under his orders the First, Third, and Fifth Corps; the Eleventh Corps after its arrival at Catlett's Station; and the Cavalry Corps. Hooker warned him to pay particular attention to the protection of Beverly and Rappahannock Fords. As a further precaution he instructed Brigadier General William Birney, in temporary command of the Third Corps, to construct field fortifications at the fords which could be used by the artillery, cavalry, and infantry. At the same time as he was strengthening his extreme right Hooker was preparing for the possible withdrawal of all his forces from Fredericksburg. To this end he ordered General Sedgwick, whose Sixth Corps had effected a foothold south of the Rappahannock below Fredericksburg, to return to the north bank.[82]

Early on June 13 Hooker wrote to Reynolds and Meade that he felt that Lee must be contemplating several alternatives. Either he would pass through the Shenandoah on his way toward Maryland and Pennsylvania, or he would send his cavalry on a raid. Perhaps the infantry was at Culpeper as support for the cavalry. The reverse might also be true; that is, a cavalry raid would be used as a cover for the movement of the bulk of Lee's infantry around the Federal right. Hooker said that he had decided that as soon as he knew definitely that Lee's army was moving to the valley, he would withdraw all of his army from Fredericksburg, join Reynolds, and "marching on the inner circle . . . attack them, if opportunity offers." [83] He did not say what he would do in case a cavalry raid should develop or Lee should attack the Union right flank, nor did he show any concern for the safety of Union forces in the valley under General Milroy. Within a few hours of writing Reynolds and Meade, Hooker heard that Longstreet's and Ewell's corps had passed through Culpeper and Sperryville and were streaming toward the Shenandoah Valley. Now for the first time he had definite information about the enemy's route and could take effective measures to protect his own army.[84] He at once issued detailed instructions for an orderly but speedy withdrawal from the Rappahannock River. By the next day some of the Union corps were well on the way to their new points of concentration, Hooker had transferred his headquarters to Dumfries,[85] and Lee was preparing to follow the vanguard of his army to the valley.

On the night of June 13 Hooker informed General in Chief Halleck of his decision to move his base of operations from Aquia Creek to some point on the Orange and Alexandria Railroad near Washington. He said that Lincoln's and Halleck's instructions had forced him to make this strategic change. This remark was more an ill-natured jibe than an explanation, for Hooker knew (and later admitted) that his real reason, which was a sound one, was to remove the potential threat to his right flank. He told Halleck that after having divided his army into two wings he had ordered the right wing, composed of the First, Third, Fifth, and Eleventh Corps, to rendezvous with the cavalry at Manassas Junction. In reporting these operations he forgot to add that at noon he had directed Pleasonton to hold the important Thoroughfare Gap in the Manassas Mountains with a brigade of cavalry and a battery of artillery. The second wing, which was made up of the Second, Sixth, and Twelfth Corps together with the Reserve Artillery, he said would cover the withdrawal of government property from the depots, especially the main base at Aquia Creek. Here the army had stored supplies between unloading them from ships on the Potomac and sending them by railroad to the camps around Fredericksburg. After completing these tasks these corps would march to Dumfries, about twenty miles north of Fredericksburg and fifteen miles southeast of Manassas Junction. From that point on, Hooker said, the operations of the two wings would be "governed by the movements of the enemy," although he intended to bring them together "as far in advance on that line as the movements of the enemy will justify." [86] Whether he realized it or not, Hooker in these few words admitted his loss of initiative to Lee and his reluctance or inability to suggest any effective countermoves to upset the enemy's plans.

The battle of Brandy Station and its immediate aftermath marked the end of the first phase of the Gettysburg campaign. There Hooker made his one and only bid to regain the initiative from his adversary and frustrate his designs for a summer offensive. When he failed for want of foresight or courage or both, he permitted Lee to force the withdrawal of his army from its old lines on the Rappahannock and to accomplish at small cost the first objective of the Confederate campaign. The two armies moved on to new fields, and the Rappahannock flowed quietly to the sea undisturbed by the sounds of battle.

IV

ARMIES ON THE MOVE

FOR GENERAL Lee the campaign had so far gone quite smoothly. There had been difficulties, but none serious enough to stop him or force him to reshape his strategy. The first threat to his plans occurred on June 5 and 6 when Hooker demonstrated against the Confederate lines at Fredericksburg. Judging these moves to be but a feint, Lee ordered Ewell to resume his march to Culpeper and had Longstreet follow him. Hooker's attack at Brandy Station on June 9 threatened to thwart Lee's designs for an invasion, but the Confederates turned it back without serious loss. Subsequent enemy moves up the Peninsula toward Richmond, though not a direct challenge, worried Lee lest they delay him or dissipate some of the strength of his army. On the whole, however, developments favored him, and with reasonable expectations of success he went ahead with his operations.

On June 10 immediately after Brandy Station Lee sent Ewell's Second Corps on its way from Culpeper to Cedarville, a little valley town four miles north of Front Royal, where General Jenkins' cavalry brigade joined it. In two days his swinging columns covered over forty-five miles, and on June 13 two of his divisions suddenly appeared not far from Winchester.[1] That day Lee's army stretched for a hundred miles from there back to Fredericksburg. Although it seemed dangerously exposed to a flanking attack, Lee by taking advantage of natural barriers had disposed his men so as to threaten the enemy at three vital points: the lower valley, the upper Rappahannock, and Fredericksburg. The Confederate posture at Fredericksburg was more defensive than aggressive in character, but should the Federals have shown signs of weakness there, Hill had instructions to attack. When Hooker withdrew on June 14, as he was almost forced to do, Lee ordered Hill to proceed to Culpeper and Longstreet to go to the mountains, while Stuart's five brigades of cavalry covered the flanks.[2]

For the next few days large masses of men of both armies were on the move, until they formed a new front along a north-south axis bounded by the Blue Ridge Mountains on the west and the Bull Run Mountains on the east. These mountains and the Potomac River became the predominant geographical features of the early phases of the campaign. The Blue Ridge, higher and more rugged than the neighboring mountains to the east, extended as far north as Harpers Ferry on the Potomac River and overlooked the Shenandoah Valley to the west. Since this range could be pierced by large bodies of men at only a few passes, it formed a screen for the movements of the Army of Northern Virginia and protected Lee's lines of communication to Culpeper and to Staunton in the Shenandoah Valley. A similar service was performed for the Army of the Potomac by the Bull Run Mountains. In Virginia the area between the ranges, known as Loudoun Valley, became a "no man's land" where for a period of almost a week units of the contending armies, especially cavalry, skirmished furiously.

By June 17 the first phase of the Gettysburg campaign had ended. The Army of Northern Virginia was largely concentrated in the Shenandoah generally facing east and north, while the Army of the Potomac, strung out along the Orange and Alexandria Railroad, had begun to push west toward the Bull Run Mountains. Hooker had moved his headquarters from Dumfries to Fairfax Station, and the evacuation of Federal forces along the Rappahannock had been completed. Lee's headquarters were still at Culpeper, and from there he watched the last of his infantry, A. P. Hill's Third Corps, go rapidly through town on its way to the valley. The cavalry brigades of "Grumble" Jones and Wade Hampton guarded the line of the Rappahannock and screened Hill's men from the prying eyes of the enemy. Longstreet's First Corps had already moved to occupy Ashby's and Snicker's Gaps in the Blue Ridge, while Stuart covered its front with three brigades. To the north of Longstreet, Ewell's corps in the valley held a line along the Potomac near Williamsport, after having driven the enemy from Winchester and Martinsburg to Maryland Heights overlooking Harpers Ferry.[3]

These movements which resulted in the realignment of the two armies occurred during a heat wave, so typical of the month of June. The weather affected everyone, in some cases disastrously so. At the beginning of the campaign most of the Federal troops had remained in more or less fixed positions while their adversary slyly moved away from them. Almost before anyone knew it, the Army of the Potomac was facing an emergency: It was in danger of being cut off from Washington. To catch up with the enemy one corps after another wheeled into long columns and hour after hour tramped northward over rough roads, though stifled by the broiling sun and blinded by clouds of dust. For the men in blue these forced marches marked the real beginning of a campaign memorable for such hardships, when it was not an unusual occurrence to cover thirty-five miles in twenty-four hours. One member of the 7th Maine thus described his experiences at this time: "We left the Rappahannock Saturday night and have been marching ever since [four days later], hardly stopping to eat or sleep. It has been the hardest march in my experience. It was hot; the roads were dusty and filled with trains and the men fell out by the road-side in scores overcome by the heat and exertion. Numbers died from sunstroke." Although thoroughly exhausted, when the hardy men from Maine read in the Washington papers that they were making forced marches to overtake the enemy, they at once felt rejuvenated and quickened their pace, singing and joking as they went along.[4]

The combination of heat and hard marching caused more than the usual amount of straggling. Fortunately General Hancock's Second Corps formed the rear guard for the left wing as it moved northward from Fredericksburg. Hancock was too good a soldier not to take special pains to round up all stragglers, most of whom were not malingerers but victims of loss of sleep and heat exhaustion. He filled his ambulances with sick men and stopped for awhile at Dumfries to give his cavalry patrol time to bring up all stragglers of the Sixth and Second Corps. By June 17 all the corps were well concentrated in the general area of Centerville, and the men had an opportunity to rest or make only short marches. Heavy thunder showers late on June 18 broke the heat wave and made life more bearable.[5]

Meanwhile in order to maintain his advantage Lee ordered the men of Hill's and Longstreet's corps to travel rapidly during those days of excessive heat. They told the same story as their enemy of their sufferings from "heat, dust, and fatigue, and worst of all—*lack of drinking water*. . . ." There were few streams near the roads, for they were following the ridges, and when they did come to a spring there was "always a wall of men surrounding it—struggling to dip cup or canteen into it. . . ." [6] One average soldier described such a march in ranks for thirty miles. The experience had been a real nightmare, for men were "crowding you at each elbow, stepping on you from behind, and getting in your way in front; like a flock of sheep, frightened and confused—stirring up a tornado of dust, and making one's eyes ache with the constant motion of surrounding figures." To add to his discomfort the soldier had to endure the weight of his gun, knapsack, blankets, bayonet, cartridge and cap boxes, canteen, tin cup, frying pan, and other essentials which chafed his perspiring skin and seemed to choke him. At the end of the thirty miles the "footsore, weary, supperless, and half-sick men . . . [lay] down in their wet clothes and grimy condition to catch seven hours sleep to sustain the same ordeal on the morrow." [7] Suddenly the ordeal changed character, and the Confederates at Ashby's Gap on the night of June 18 found themselves shivering. The cold front which brought heavy rain and relief from the heat to the Federals below on the plains of Manassas pelted the Southerners with hail and sleet.[8] Now there began for the men in both armies a pause in the eternal marching. The time had arrived for another trial by arms.

It all began on the morning of June 17 when Pleasonton upon orders from Hooker sent the three brigades of Gregg's Second Division of cavalry from their camp near Manassas Junction to Aldie, a little town strategically located at the western end of a gap in the Bull Run Mountains and at the fork of two important roads to Winchester, one by way of Snicker's Gap and the other through Ashby's Gap farther south. Once arrived in Aldie the men were instructed to sweep the country between the two mountain ranges in search of the enemy. Before starting out and in line with Pleasonton's orders, Gregg detached Colonel Duffié with his regiment of 275 men and sent him south to Middleburg by a roundabout way through Thoroughfare Gap. As soon as he got to Middleburg, which was only four miles west of Aldie on the Ashby's Gap road, he was to get in touch with Gregg, who presumably by that time would be in Aldie. Pleasonton accompanied Gregg and the rest of the division on their march of twenty-two miles. They got to Aldie around 4:00 P.M., just as Fitz Lee's brigade, temporarily commanded by Colonel Thomas T. Munford, was encamping there for the night. The encounter was a complete surprise to everyone and turned into a spirited affair. Gregg immediately attacked, but as he used only about a third of his force he made little headway. Very possibly the rough character of the terrain and the heavy stone walls and fences which lined the roads made it difficult for him to maneuver his men against Munford's dismounted troopers and take advantage of his numerical superiority.[9] Although the Confederates fought vigorously and gave the larger Union forces a rather hard time of it, after several hours of resistance they withdrew toward Middleburg. Union reports of the engagement gave the impression of a smooth and easy victory, but they were misleading and far from true. Several things went wrong. The 4th New York Cavalry performed badly, and the handling of the 1st Massachusetts was clumsy.[10] Captain Charles Francis Adams grumbled that although his men "behaved nobly," they were "just slaughtered"; he felt that the regiment was a "sacrifice either to incompetence or jealousies of Generals."[11] Stuart called the engagement one of the "most sanguinary" of the war. Refusing to admit defeat, he claimed he had ordered Munford back toward Middleburg only when he learned of Duffié's approach, but Colonel Thomas L. Rosser of the 5th Virginia Cavalry said that they had been "compelled to fall back."[12] Whatever the reason, Munford retreated without being molested by Federal forces.

Duffié got to Middleburg in time to drive out Stuart's rear guard, and if he had known of the fight at Aldie he could have come to Gregg's assistance. But he did not, and his orders specified that he was to remain in Middleburg and get into communication with the headquarters of the Second Cavalry Brigade under Brigadier General Judson Kilpatrick at Aldie. Soon he realized that the enemy was rapidly concentrating against him, so he dismounted half of his force behind stone walls and barricades and sent Captain Frank Allen to Aldie for help.[13] After considerable difficulty Allen got to headquarters about 9:00 P.M. and reported Duffié's predicament to General Kilpatrick. The general went to confer with Gregg about the matter, since he said his own brigade was too worn out to come to Duffié's rescue. As Allen told it: "Returning, he [Kilpatrick] said that General Gregg had gone to state the facts to General Pleasonton, and directed me to remain at Aldie until he heard from General Pleasonton. I remained, but received no further orders." [14]

There are several unanswered questions in connection with this episode. Since Pleasonton was at Aldie during the engagement, had he left before Allen arrived? If not, why did he not at least make a gesture toward saving Duffié's regiment from disaster, for disaster is exactly what happened to it? During the evening Robertson's brigade badly mauled the regiment, but only after it had put up such a stiff fight that it evoked favorable comment even from the Confederates. Duffié retreated down the road whence he had come and camped for the night. Near dawn the next morning, after learning from scouts that the enemy blocked every road, he tried to fight his way out to Aldie. Finding himself completely surrounded, he refused to surrender and told his command to scatter. Exhausted and heartbroken, Duffié with four officers and twenty-seven men reached the Union lines near Centerville at half past one that afternoon, having escaped over the mountains by way of Hopewell. The regiment's loss, though very heavy, was not as great as Duffié at first had feared, for in the next two days five officers and sixty men succeeded in filtering back into the Federal camps. [15] In light of this fiasco the Confederates exacted a high price for any advantage Pleasonton claimed to have gained at Aldie. [16]

When General Hooker heard of the action at Aldie, he instructed Pleasonton, now that a part of Stuart's cavalry had been located, to "find out what was behind them." [17] In obedience to or in anticipation of these orders—it is not clear just when he received them— Pleasonton on June 18 sent more of his men beyond Aldie on the roads to Ashby's and Snicker's Gaps. The constant skirmishing which went on all day turned into more serious fighting when Union troopers attacked the Confederates and drove them out of Middleburg. [18] Similar minor engagements continued for the next two days. Because not all of his brigades were immediately available, Stuart had decided to remain on the defensive and avoid a general engagement. He considered it his duty to mask the movements of Lee's infantry by "checking the enemy's reconnaissance and by continually threatening attack." [19] At the same time Pleasonton became more aggressive as his troopers slowly pushed their adversaries back toward the Blue Ridge.

From information which Pleasonton and Gregg gathered, they came to the conclusion that only Stuart's force was east of the mountains. That being the case, Pleasonton asked Hooker for permission to throw his whole corps, reinforced with brigades of infantry, at Stuart's cavalry on the morning of June 21 and "cripple it up." [20] Hooker at once instructed Meade to rush the three brigades of Barnes's division of the Fifth Corps to cooperate with the drive against Stuart. Leaving two of the brigades at Middleburg to guard his communications, Pleasonton took with him the third brigade under Colonel Strong Vincent and five of his own cavalry brigades. (Vincent's men were fighters and were good to have around to handle Stuart's dismounted troopers.) With these forces he made a two-pronged assault upon Stuart's five brigades and drove them through Upperville into Ashby's Gap. Once there Pleasonton broke off the attack [21] and returned to Aldie, "being satisfied," he said, that he had "accomplished all that the expedition designed." Although he claimed that it had been a "most disastrous day to rebel cavalry," his statements cannot be accepted at face value. [22] Enemy losses as tabulated in Union reports were far from impressive, and the capture of two pieces of artillery—Stuart admitted the loss of only one—and approximately 250 prisoners was a blow hardly heavy enough to cripple the enemy. One important thing Pleasonton did accomplish, which, if he had known it, would have given him cause for gratification and might have suggested to Hooker how sensitive Lee was to a threat to his flank. He pressed Stuart's cavalry so hard that Lee ordered McLaws' division of Longstreet's corps back to hold Ashby's Gap, and he momentarily halted Major General Richard H. Anderson's division of Hill's corps on its way to Shepherdstown. [23]

The four days of continual cavalry action, which broke out at times into furious forays and then subsided to scattered, sporadic scuffles, gained certain other advantages for Union arms. The Federal cavalry had again demonstrated its ability to stand up against its old adversary and give a good account of itself, and its new self-confidence furnished the Army of the Potomac with added strength when it was most needed. At considerable cost, which was perhaps necessary, it had finally secured some reasonably accurate facts about Lee, while keeping Stuart well away from the Bull Run Mountains. Pleasonton's reports of June 21 and 22 provided Hooker with good coverage of news about the Confederates. Ewell's corps, he said, had gone toward Winchester on June 17 (this information was off by four days), Longstreet's men were on their way there to join Lee, and Hill's troops had crossed the mountains into the valley. He also confirmed Hooker's fears that Confederate infantry and artillery held all the gaps in the Blue Ridge so as to cover the movement of Ewell across the Potomac.[24] The tenor of these dispatches agreed with information which Hooker had secured from other quarters and should have removed all doubts about Lee's location if not his intentions.[25]

Up until this time, and despite both positive and negative signs suggesting Lee's objectives, Hooker had appeared unable to fathom the real meaning of the enemy's movements. On June 13 and 14 he had received dispatches from Pleasonton which should have warned him that Lee had sent a substantial portion of his army to "gobble up," as Lincoln put it, Milroy's forces in Winchester and Berryville. Lincoln and Halleck sitting in Washington seemed far more alert than Hooker to the unpleasant implications of some of the news they received. When Halleck on June 14 heard that Longstreet and Ewell had passed through Sperryville, located immediately east of the Blue Ridge, he warned Major General Robert C. Schenck, Milroy's superior, of the danger. Lincoln also became worried and ordered Schenck to get Milroy out of Winchester and, if he could, to Harpers Ferry.[26] At the same time he turned to Hooker and asked whether he thought it possible that 15,000 of Ewell's men were now in Winchester. Hooker at first ventured no opinion; instead he begged the question by referring the President to Pleasonton's latest dispatch.[27] It contained remarkably accurate information obtained from a Negro who on June 12 near Sperryville had seen a long enemy column heading for Harpers Ferry; Lee was in command, he stated, and he had personally seen Longstreet, Early, and Ewell.[28] Hooker gave Lincoln's query some further thought. Then he sent the President another telegram later that evening to say that he had "reason to believe" that Longstreet's and the greater part of Ewell's corps had started on June 7 from Culpeper for the valley and that the rest of the Confederates had followed them on June 11. Therefore he thought the head of the column had had time to reach Winchester. The tone of this message revealed a mind so beset by worry and uncertainty that it was difficult for him to give a straightforward answer to a simple question. In view of his months of experience in fighting the Army of Northern Virginia his unrealistic appraisal of its marching ability was astonishing. In his dispatch he implied it would take Lee's men almost a week to cover the sixty-five miles from Culpeper to Winchester,[29] whereas in reality Ewell required only four days, from June 10 to the evening of June 13, to march all his men from Culpeper, skirmish with the enemy in the valley on June 12, and form a line of battle on the outskirts of Winchester.[30]

A few hours before Hooker sent this telegram to the President, Lincoln had informed him of the opinion held in Washington that the enemy had surrounded General Milroy at Winchester and Brigadier General Daniel Tyler at Martinsburg. He asked whether Hooker could help them if they were able to hold out a few days. Using the metaphor that has since become famous, he said: "If the head of Lee's army is at Martinsburg and the tail of it on the Plank road between Fredericksburg and Chancellorsville, the animal must be very slim somewhere. Could you not break him?"[31] Lincoln's queries troubled Hooker, and plagued as he was by indecision, he tried to pass the burden back to the President. In still another wire sent near midnight June 14 he asked Lincoln whether in *his* opinion Winchester was surrounded by rebel forces. Lincoln had previously said he thought so, but Hooker was so agitated that he had either forgotten the contents of the President's dispatch or had not believed what he read. He clearly remained sceptical about the situation at Winchester, for he added: "I do not feel like making a move for an enemy until I am satisfied as to his whereabouts." The dark forests of Chancellorsville were closing in on him again. He then made a comment that must have disturbed Lincoln as being beside the point, if not absurd. "To proceed to Winchester," Hooker said, "and have him [the enemy] make his appearance elsewhere, would subject me to ridicule." He had therefore decided to move his forces according to the plan he had outlined in a dispatch to Halleck the previous night.[32] He would divide his army into two wings, withdraw them from the Fredericksburg line by two separate routes, and regroup them along the Orange and Fredericksburg Railroad. The salient feature of this plan was its defensive character, for in the disposition of his forces Hooker would be guided by what the enemy did.[33]

Obviously annoyed, Lincoln did not permit Hooker to evade his responsibilities as a commander. Twenty-five minutes after receiving his wire he snapped back an answer. Hooker, he said, had "nearly all the elements for forming an opinion" as to whether Winchester was surrounded that he had, and he himself feared, "almost" believed, it was endangered. Lincoln then gave Hooker a good lesson in logic. "If I could know that Longstreet and Ewell moved in that direction [Berryville and Winchester] so long ago as you stated in your last, then I should feel sure that Winchester is strongly invested. It is quite certain that a considerable force of the enemy is thereabout, and I fear it is an overwhelming one compared to Milroy's. I am unable to give you any more certain opinions." [34] If Hooker needed additional evidence, he got it from Stanton, who dispatched a telegram within five minutes of the President's stating that according to a report sent by Milroy to Schenck, Ewell's corps had arrived before Winchester on the night of June 13.[35]

Still not convinced, Hooker wired Halleck the next morning, June 15, asking that he be notified immediately if information from the upper Potomac was of such character as to warrant a movement in that direction. At that time Hooker knew Hill's forces were beginning to move from Fredericksburg toward Culpeper. Yet he allowed himself to be thrown off the scent by reports received from Pleasonton on June 15. Basing his intelligence on word from his scouts and some Confederate prisoners, Pleasonton said that Stuart was at Upperville and Longstreet's corps was supporting him. He claimed further that Hill and Ewell, still south of the Rappahannock, were planning to cross the river at Banks's and United States Fords and Sulphur Springs and attack Hooker's rear.[36] When Halleck learned of the contents of Pleasonton's reports, he termed them "very contradictory" and "very unsatisfactory." Nevertheless he conceded the bare possibility that some of the intelligence might be reliable. If, as Pleasonton indicated, Longstreet and Stuart were threatening Harpers Ferry, Halleck suggested that Hooker should go after them by way of Leesburg and at the same time guard his rear against a possible attack from Ewell and Hill. He was "entirely free" to operate against Lee as he desired so long as he kept the main Confederate forces away from Washington. Here was a deliberate attempt to free

Hooker's mind from any inhibitions and encourage him to devise effective means for crushing Lee's army.[37]

Early in the evening of June 15 Lincoln wired Hooker that any doubts about Confederate attacks on Winchester and Martinsburg had vanished, for the survivors had fled to Harpers Ferry bringing news of their defeat and their heavy losses. Lincoln wanted to know what Hooker thought about this information. The general's response, conveyed in three separate dispatches, was a mixture of apology and indecision. Lincoln's message, he said, contained more conclusive evidence than any he had received. In view of it he felt that "invasion is . . . [Lee's] settled purpose," and he did not believe it was in his "power to prevent it." Further, he did not know whether his views of what the Army of the Potomac should do in the emergency were wanted. Although he made no definite suggestions, he speculated vaguely on what direction Lee's invasion might take and what the Army of the Potomac could do to oppose it. Why he professed hesitancy in offering his ideas on matters of strategy when the President had specifically asked to hear them is not clear, although there are clues to his behavior.[38]

One of Hooker's difficulties went back to a time shortly after his appointment as commander of the Army of the Potomac in January, when Halleck with the President's approval had outlined the strategic purpose and obligations of his position. His first object was not the capture of Richmond, he explained, but the "defeat or scattering" of Lee's army; he would have a free hand in the operations of his own army as long as he kept "in view always the importance of covering Washington and Harpers Ferry either directly or by so operating as to be able to punish any force the enemy sent against them." [39] The first alternative, that of covering Washington "directly," if left unqualified would have been an impossible assignment, but the second permitted a reasonable interpretation of the meaning of the word "covering." Circumstances might arise when the Army of the Potomac would not have to remain physically between the capital and Lee's army. Before Chancellorsville the enjoinder about covering Washington apparently had not bothered Hooker, but as the Gettysburg campaign unfolded it became an onerous limitation to him and the source of one of his grievances against Halleck. Now on June 15 he felt it explained Lincoln's and Halleck's disapproval of his plans to "pitch" into Lee's rear at Fredericksburg and to strike out for Richmond, and their rejection of his proposals became another cause of difficulty between him and the administration. He never got over the feeling that their opposition had deprived him of an opportunity to make the most effective countermove against Lee, which was "to cross and whip A. P. Hill, while Longstreet and Ewell were moving off through Culpeper and Sperryville. . . ." [40] What Hooker apparently failed to appreciate was that the two officials were even more anxious than he to have him take the offensive, but they thought that an attack on Hill in a prepared position was not worth the risk. They felt that Lee in carrying out a hazardous operation had exposed his moving columns to attack at several places. Hooker's opportunity was to attack at one of those places, not at Fredericksburg. [41]

From then on Hooker seemed to lose his power for constructive thought. In contrast to his earlier show of energy and decisiveness in maneuvering his army, he became apathetic, if not demoralized, and resigned himself to a defensive policy unless Lincoln ordered otherwise. A close observer of him at that time, Brigadier General Marsena R. Patrick, who as provost marshal general was a member of Hooker's staff, made the following comment:

> He acts like a man without a plan and is entirely at a loss what to do, or how to match the enemy, or counteract his movements. Whatever he does is the result of impulse, now, after having failed, so signally, at Chancellorsville. His role now is that of Micawber, "waiting for something to turn up," and when something turns up, he plays like a gambler. . . . We get accurate information, but Hooker will not use it and insults all who differ from him in opinion. He has declared that the enemy are over 100,000 strong—it is his only salvation to make it appear that the enemy's forces are larger than his own, which is all false & he knows it—He knows that Lee is his master & is afraid to meet him in fair battle. [42]

This appraisal reveals in a few sentences Hooker's disturbed state of mind, which can only be inferred from his messages to Halleck and Lincoln. He had an almost abnormal tendency to blame other people or circumstances for his failures, as witness his estimate of the size of the Army of Northern Virginia. Just before the start of the Gettysburg campaign he had made a realistic count, but after the campaign got under way he suddenly magnified its size. If anything went wrong, he had an excuse. Similarly on June 16 Hooker complained to the President about Halleck's lack of confidence in him and cited it as an obstacle to his successful conduct of operations and a possible cause of defeat. If he felt this way about his relations with Halleck, why did he not resign when he made his accusation? [43]

Lincoln's answer to Hooker's message came late that night in the form of an order placing him "in the strict military relation to General Halleck of a commander of one of the armies to the general-in-chief of all the armies." [44] Lincoln thus clearly indicated his continued confidence in Halleck, while taking a step to centralize matters of broad strategy in the hands of a person trained for such work. Theoretically Halleck had held the position all during Hooker's tenure as commander of the Army of the Potomac, but Lincoln now made it official. It was a move long overdue and one which had become imperative. The swirl of events had brought the Army of the Potomac more and more within the bounds of several departments and increased the need for a guiding hand to prevent conflicts in command and confusion in movements. Halleck in the eyes of many of his contemporaries was not the man for the position, but Lincoln appreciated his virtues even while he was aware of his shortcomings. Certainly it was far better to have him than no one at all to coordinate operations of the Federal forces, as had been the case before his appointment, and on paper at least his qualifications were excellent.

Major General Henry W. Halleck, graduate of Union College and the United States Military Academy, Phi Beta Kappa, engineer, lawyer, and writer, was born to advise and counsel, not to command. He received his appointment as general in chief on July 11, 1862, during the despair of Union defeat in McClellan's Peninsular campaign. Up until then Lincoln and Stanton had been pretty much running the show themselves. Lincoln felt they needed the help of a professional soldier in coordinating military operations, so he brought Halleck from the West where as a department commander he had gained the reputation of being an efficient administrator and had surrounded himself with an aura of military success as the result of the work of such subordinates as General Ulysses S. Grant. In his new post his record was spotty and in many respects disappointing to Lincoln, largely because Halleck suggested rather than directed. With his bulbous forehead, pop eyes, and dimpled chin

accenting heavy jowls fringed with whiskers, he looked like the so-
briquet his comrades in arms had bestowed upon him, "Old
Brains." [45] In spite of his deficiencies Lincoln kept him in power and
grew to appreciate his worth as chief administrator of top military
personnel and planning rather than general in chief. Lincoln also
found him a competent technical adviser, as well as a useful foil
against importunate generals.[46]

Halleck's first test in the Gettysburg campaign occurred when
Lee achieved spectacular success at the expense of General Milroy's
command in Winchester and Berryville on June 14 and 15. It was a
decisive triumph for the Confederates and represented the accomplishment of one more objective in Lee's strategy. For the Federals
Milroy's defeat was a humiliating fiasco which seemed to furnish
further proof to the world of the irresistible power of the Army of
Northern Virginia. Northern observers felt otherwise and were convinced that it could have been avoided but for the ineptitude of the
Union command. Their concern was shared by Federal military
authorities who in August instituted a Court of Inquiry to find out
who had bungled. The court indicated by its findings that the whole
military system lacked discipline, cohesion, and unity, and that Halleck had to share some of the blame.[47]

The events leading to the debacle at Winchester had been in the
process of development for some time. It all began with General
Schenck's disposition of troops in the Eighth Corps. Schenck commanded the Middle Department with headquarters at Baltimore,
his main responsibility being protection of the Baltimore and Ohio
Railroad in Maryland, Virginia, and West Virginia. During the winter he had stationed his Second Division under General Milroy at
Winchester, except for one brigade which he placed at Berryville.
Large by the standards of the Army of the Potomac at that time,
Milroy's division had the characteristics of a small army, for each of
its three brigades had strong complements of cavalry and artillery.
Altogether it mustered about 9,000 men, of which 7,000 were ef-
fective troops. In addition to Milroy's men Schenck had in his department troops of Brigadier General Benjamin F. Kelley's First
Division which were stationed at various places in the lower Shenandoah and upper Potomac Valleys. Kelley's division of six brigades
was even larger than Milroy's, but it covered a much larger area.
Kelley made Harpers Ferry his headquarters and kept a large pro-

portion of his division there because Halleck considered it strategically important. A force at the ferry, especially if located on Maryland Heights on the north bank of the river, was in a naturally strong position to guard the mountain pass through which flowed the Potomac River, and the important bridge of the Baltimore and Ohio Railroad which there crossed from Maryland into Virginia. Kelley also stationed a force of about 1,300 men at Martinsburg, which was located twenty miles or so to the northwest of Harpers Ferry and was important for its railroad shops and buildings.[48]

If Schenck's duty was to protect the railroad, what was Milroy's large force doing in Winchester over twenty miles away to the south of it? Halleck wondered too and raised objections. On January 5, 1863, he had wired Schenck: "No attempt should be made to hold Winchester against a large force of the enemy, but use it simply as an outpost as advised in our conversation a few days ago. Isolated posts and columns are liable to be cut off." Almost four months elapsed before he sent Schenck another communication. Then on April 30 he telegraphed a further warning about Winchester: "As I have often repeated to you verbally and in writing, that is no place to fight a battle. It is merely an outpost, which should not be exposed to an attack in force." [49] Schenck, a politician without benefit of previous military training, disregarded the advice of his superior and held to his policy of establishing "strong garrisons in a cordon of posts considerably to the south of the [rail]road," instead of stationing guards and pickets near or along the line [50] and heavily concentrating troops at important places like Harpers Ferry. Finally Halleck became so alarmed about Milroy's exposed position that on May 8 he instructed Schenck to withdraw all but a few of the troops from Winchester. Thinking the order just another of Halleck's suggestions, Schenck ignored it. At this point the general in chief made the mistake which became his contribution to the catastrophe at Winchester: He permitted Schenck, his subordinate, to defy the order. There is no record that he ever tried to force Schenck to follow instructions during these weeks by telling him to obey or resign his command. Not until June 14, when it was too late, did Halleck threaten to remove Schenck unless he obeyed orders.[51]

As Halleck suspected, Milroy's large division was relatively isolated in Winchester. It made a tempting prize for Lee, and it was only a matter of time before he would try to claim it. What happened was a story that had become painfully familiar to Lincoln. Lee skillfully maneuvered Ewell's corps and Jenkins' cavalry so as to escape detection until they appeared before Milroy's defenses at Berryville and Winchester. Faulty intelligence work in Federal commands helped to make the surprise a complete one. It is true there had been alerts from Washington warning Schenck of possible enemy attacks in the valley. Milroy had also noticed increased enemy activity, but he attributed it to Stuart's preparations for a raid, which the Union high command seemed sure he would make. Even General Kelley, a Virginian wise in the ways of the valley, was fooled. Either his scouts saw no enemy troops or he interpreted their information erroneously. In spite of skirmishes his men had had with the enemy on June 12 and 13, Milroy did not learn definitely of the approach of Ewell's forces until between 6:00 and 7:00 P.M. on June 13, when he interviewed a prisoner from a Louisiana regiment in Early's division. Then it was too late for him to get permission to evacuate his position.[52] At this point both he and Schenck paid for their mistakes and false pride. Milroy was guilty of "overweening confidence" in the strength of his position and his own ability to defend it. As late as June 14 he wired Schenck that he could hold out against all attacks for five days if necessary before help came, although where it would come from is hard to imagine. On the same day in a burst of optimism he sent Schenck another message assuring him that he could hold his position "in spite of fate." [53] As for Schenck, he had persistently set his judgment against Halleck's. When he at last fully appreciated Milroy's danger and decided to order his withdrawal, there was no way to reach him; the telegraph lines had been cut. Before this breakdown in communications Schenck had ordered Milroy to remain in Winchester until further notice. For that reason Milroy felt duty bound to put up a show of resistance before retreating or until help arrived, even when he knew that he was threatened by all of Ewell's corps.

Any illusions Milroy had about his ability to hold out for long were soon dispelled, for the enemy swiftly and effectively broke through his outer lines. By the night of June 14 with only one day's supply of rations left and the enemy moving in on his inner defenses and almost surrounding him, Milroy's position became untenable. He started his retreat in good order about 2:00 A.M.; then some four miles out of Winchester at Stephenson's Depot he ran into an ambush cleverly laid by Ewell. Though surprised he kept his poise and fought bravely, but lost control of his men because of darkness and the failure of the rear brigade under Colonel Andrew T. McReynolds to come to his support. McReynolds in turn blamed teamsters and camp followers in their frenzy to escape Confederate shells for riding down and scattering his men. Most of Milroy's losses occurred with the collapse of organized resistance at Stephenson's Depot. In the confusion fewer than 4,000 men escaped. One group of about 1,200 led by Milroy himself staggered into Harpers Ferry during the afternoon and evening of June 15 after a grim march of over thirty miles. Another column went in the direction of Bath, crossed the Potomac at Hancock, Maryland, and finally congregated at Bloody Run (Everett), Pennsylvania, 2,700 strong. Milroy's total loss of 4,443 officers and men represented about half of his command; of this number 3,856 were listed as captured or missing. His losses in equipment and horses were too painful for Union authorities to contemplate, since they included such items as 200,000 rounds of small-arms ammunition, four 20-pounder Parrotts, seventeen 3-inch rifles, and two 24-pounder howitzers. Fortunately Milroy had taken the precaution on June 11 of shipping off 114 wagons loaded with quartermaster's stores.[54] In view of his overly optimistic attitude all during the crisis, this was an act of amazing good sense. When Halleck heard the news of the blow he became white with rage. He immediately wired Schenck not to give Milroy any command at Harpers Ferry and added: "We have had enough of that sort of military genius."[55] As for Schenck's military genius, Halleck wisely refrained from comment.

The Army of Northern Virginia had reason to rejoice over its exploits in the lower valley. After a rather dubious beginning at Brandy Station it demonstrated at Winchester the finesse and skill for which it was justly famous. The manner in which General Ewell conducted operations removed lingering doubts about his ability to carry on in the tradition of "Stonewall" Jackson, as well as about his physical capacity, after the loss of a leg, to endure the rigors of active campaigning. Riding in a buggy when not on horseback, he got about with comparative ease and seemed not at all handicapped. He knew just how to go about attacking Winchester, and after achieving victory he knew exactly what his next move should be.

Having brought his corps across the mountains through Chester

Gap in the vicinity of Front Royal and Cedarville on June 12, Ewell had divided his command into two columns. One under General Robert E. Rodes included his big division of about 8,000 men and also Jenkins' cavalry, over 1,600 troopers strong, which had just joined Ewell. Rodes's instructions were to capture Milroy's third brigade, estimated to be a force of 1,800 men under Colonel McReynolds at Berryville, and then to go on to Martinsburg to seize Colonel B. F. Smith's force of about 1,300 men. He failed to capture either group, however, owing to a combination of circumstances which included the inefficiency of Jenkins' cavalry, the element of luck, and good generalship on the part of the enemy. McReynolds had skillfully evacuated Berryville on June 13 and brought his command back safely to Winchester. Frustrated at Berryville, Rodes hurried his infantry to Martinsburg, but they arrived too late on June 14 to catch either the Yankee infantry, which had escaped by way of Shepherdstown to Harpers Ferry, or their cavalry and artillery, which had fled across the Potomac to Williamsport. Nevertheless, he had the satisfaction of securing supplies at Berryville and an even richer haul at Martinsburg. There he captured five pieces of artillery with their caissons and most of their horses, about 6,000 bushels of fine grain, some commissary stores, about 400 rounds of rifled artillery ammunition, a quantity of small arms and ammunition, and last but not least, two excellent ambulances. These additions to the larder and ordnance of the Army of Northern Virginia were consolation prizes worthy of notice.[56]

The second column under the personal direction of General Ewell put on the big show, for it attacked the main forces of the enemy in the valley. Consisting of two infantry divisions, about 12,000 men strong, it moved rapidly down the road from Front Royal in the afternoon of June 13 and had several brushes with the Yankees, who pulled back toward Winchester. Ewell had learned beforehand that the only chance of success against the Union fortifications was an approach from a range of hills on the west and northwest overlooking the town, so he used General Edward Johnson's division as a feint and had him threaten an attack from the east. The next morning Ewell and General Early carefully examined the ground from a high point. Early suggested a plan of penetrating Milroy's defenses, to which Ewell immediately assented. While Johnson's division moved in closer from the east and continued to attract the enemy's attention with demonstrations, Early took three of his brigades by a circuitous route of eight or ten miles to a position northwest of the town, from which he could attack a fortified hill overlooking the main works of Milroy's defenses. He arrived undetected about 4:00 P.M. and stationed himself behind a ridge about two-thirds of a mile west of his objective. There his men rested while the general himself reconnoitered and chose the best positions to place his infantry and artillery for the attack.

The enemy on the hill, failing to keep a lookout in Early's direction, was completely surprised when an hour before sunset twenty pieces of Confederate artillery suddenly rolled out into the open and started a furious cannonade. Forty-five minutes later the infantry made its assault. Early handled his men beautifully. One brigade broke the enemy's fortifications with a dashing attack. It was immediately given overwhelming infantry and artillery support, and it soon captured the hill commanding Milroy's main works, as well as a small redoubt to the north of it. By then it was too dark for Early to do anything more,[57] but he had rendered the enemy's main fort untenable and accomplished what Milroy had boasted could not be done.[58] Hearing of Early's success, Ewell anticipated an evacuation of the town by the enemy and quickly ordered Johnson to send two brigades and part of another out onto the Martinsburg Pike to intercept the retreating troops. Just before dawn about 1,200 of Johnson's men met the enemy. Though outnumbered they held up the Yankees long enough for Brigadier General James A. Walker's famous Stonewall Brigade, which had been delayed through a misunderstanding, to arrive just in the nick of time. Two regiments of Brigadier General Francis R. T. Nicholls' brigade which had been held in reserve went into action at almost the same moment.[59] Milroy's men were no match for veterans who fought to the last cartridge and whose officers threw in reinforcements with skill and timing "as perfect as a textbook example." [60]

Although Confederate successes in the lower valley were another blow to the prestige of Federal arms and a stimulus to Southern morale, they did not directly affect the power of the Army of the Potomac. They did eliminate, however, more than 7,000 Union troops from further service at a time when trained soldiers were at a premium and Hooker needed reinforcements. The North paid a heavy price for inept generalship and Halleck's reluctance to assume the full responsibilities of his position.[61] The question was what could he do to repair the damage and prevent similar blunders in the future. For awhile at least following the disaster he took a more active role in military affairs. One of his first steps was to direct Schenck to secure the Federal hold on Harpers Ferry by abandoning all small posts and concentrating his troops there. When Milroy arrived at Harpers Ferry late on June 15, he was the ranking general, but Halleck ordered General Tyler, who had just reached the post that morning after evacuating his position at Martinsburg, to remain in command of the garrison. Although a Military Court of Inquiry was later to declare Tyler guilty of evasion of his responsibilities at Martinsburg, he displayed energy and intelligence in his conduct of affairs at Harpers Ferry. As soon as all stragglers from Winchester had come in and military stores in the town had been removed to a safer place, he concentrated his force of 3,300 men, not including Milroy's survivors, on Maryland Heights, which was a naturally strong position. Noticing the decayed condition of the fortifications, he set about repairing them and adding new ones. During the next ten days he received 3,400 men as reinforcements and had time to whip into shape the 1,500 or so survivors from Milroy's command.[62] By June 19 Tyler reported confidence in his ability to hold out against a force of around 10,000 men and, if given a few more days of preparation, to oppose successfully all of Lee's army.[63] When Lee did not make so much as a feint against Harpers Ferry, these frantic exertions of the Union high command to improve its defenses and strengthen the garrison appeared unnecessary. Nevertheless, in view of Lee's overwhelming attacks on the post in his Maryland invasion of the previous year, the efforts of Halleck and his subordinates were natural and proper, and they would have been remiss in their duties if they had done otherwise.

Federal troops at Harpers Ferry not only guarded a gateway to the valley and Washington, but they also controlled an important lookout from which to watch movements of the enemy. On a clear day they could see fairly well all the country between Martinsburg and Williamsport, a distance of fifteen to twenty miles, and perfectly the area about Shepherdstown some ten miles away.[64] At night campfires revealed the presence of Confederate forces stretching in a wide arc from Charlestown and Berryville north to Sharps-

burg and Antietam.[65] On June 17 officers of the Signal Corps
arrived to set up a station on the heights from which to communicate with other commands. Tyler, however, was not satisfied with
these efforts to secure information, and with commendable zeal and
imagination he adopted other methods. On one occasion he sent a
signal officer with an armed escort to a high point near Sharpsburg,
from which he could observe the enemy with strong field glasses.
Tyler also directed what little cavalry he had at his disposal to scout
the country from Harpers Ferry east to Point of Rocks and west and
northwest to Shepherdstown, Sharpsburg, and Boonsborough. From
time to time he received news of the enemy from loyal natives,
scouts, prisoners, and deserters. As a result between June 17 and 26,
when he was replaced by Major General William H. French, Tyler
was able to send a stream of unusually complete and accurate
information directly to Hooker and Halleck.[66]

Halleck kept Hooker informed of developments in the lower
valley and at Harpers Ferry to the extent that he could understand
them during the confusion following the evacuation of Berryville,
Winchester, and Martinsburg. Early in the afternoon of June 15
Halleck expressed confidence in the ability of the garrison at
Harpers Ferry to hold out for some time with the arrival of the
forces from Martinsburg to strengthen it. What concerned him were
reports from Pleasonton that Longstreet and Stuart intended to
cross the Potomac both above and below Harpers Ferry. He suggested to Hooker that he pursue them, but the question of what
forces should be used he left for the general to decide once he had
learned of the movements of the rest of Lee's army. He did propose
that Hooker's first move under present circumstances should be the
occupation of Leesburg.[67] This suggestion was a sensible one, for
the location of Leesburg was strategically important for various
reasons. The lower fords of the Potomac were nearby; and Conrad's
and Edwards Ferries, where relatively short pontoon bridges were
required to span the river, were within a short distance. The town
was thirty-eight miles from Alexandria and thirty-two from Georgetown by way of "excellent" turnpikes. The railroad, the Loudoun and
Hampshire, was in working order from Alexandria to Vienna and
could be easily repaired from there to Leesburg. Occupation then of
Leesburg with a considerable force was a move which Halleck

thought essential to the pursuit of Lee's army if it penetrated deep into Maryland and Pennsylvania, or to the support of Harpers Ferry if it should come under heavy attack.[68]

On June 16 Halleck became uneasy about the safety of Harpers Ferry. He told Hooker that word from Schenck led him to think that the post was in immediate danger of being surrounded. Since there were fewer troops there than had been previously reported, he feared that it could not withstand an attack for very long. Any help for Tyler, Halleck added, could come only from the Army of the Potomac. When the dispatch reached Hooker he was in a perverse and faultfinding mood, and he chose to interpret it as an order for him to move all of his army to the relief of Harpers Ferry.[69] He was annoyed with Halleck and his own ignorance of affairs in other military departments, and he virtually accused the War Department, in telegrams to Lincoln and Stanton, of withholding information from him.[70] Stanton sent back a tart reply promising to keep Hooker fully informed, but leaving it up to him to use his judgment as to the "credibility" of reports. Grimly he added the warning that "the very demon of lying seems to be about these times, and generals will have to be broken for ignorance before they will take the trouble to find out the truth of reports." [71] Lincoln looked into the matter too and the next day assured Hooker that Major Thomas T. Eckert, superintendent of the telegraph office, had sent the general everything coming into the office and would continue to do so.[72] Just prior to sending this message Lincoln had reacted to Hooker's complaints about the War Department, Halleck, and affairs in general by placing the general directly under Halleck's orders. It was turning out to be a bad day for Hooker. Toward evening Halleck in a spirit of sweet reasonableness told him that he had given no "directions" for the Army of the Potomac to move to Harpers Ferry. Then he made an effort to clarify the relations between himself and the general.

First of all Halleck spelled out what he had meant in his previous messages to Hooker. He had advised the movement of a force on Leesburg, he said, which would be sufficiently strong to meet Longstreet should he appear. Once at Leesburg Hooker could move to the relief of Harpers Ferry or elsewhere as "circumstances might require." Halleck then wanted him to push out the cavalry to "ascertain something definite about the enemy," while keeping the rest of his force within supporting distance. It was this suggestion that led to Hooker's order to Pleasonton to make an extensive reconnaissance of the whole region between the Bull Run and Blue Ridge Mountains and beyond that toward Winchester, Berryville, and Harpers Ferry. Halleck then said in so many words that as his superior he would only indicate the "objects to be aimed at." Within those limitations Hooker as commander of the Army of the Potomac was to make the "particular dispositions" which he deemed proper.[73]

Hooker agreed to dispose his forces so as to comply with the objectives mentioned in Halleck's telegram. As a result he sent orders to his cavalry to search out the enemy, and to some of his infantry corps to advance northward "by easy marches." [74] The next day when he heard of enemy cavalry near Point of Rocks, about twelve miles east of Harpers Ferry on the Maryland side of the Potomac, Hooker immediately hurried the Twelfth Corps to Leesburg. Meanwhile, he told Halleck, he was irked by conflicting reports about enemy movements in the lower valley and Pennsylvania, all of which appeared to be nothing but wild rumors. Halleck in reply made it clear that in spite of all efforts by his office and the departmental commanders, Heintzelman and Schenck, to get accurate information, the person who should know most about the location of Lee's army was Hooker himself—he was the nearest to it. Although Halleck was annoyed, he sincerely wanted to help coordinate the military resources of the threatened area. When Hooker asked that signal officers be posted at Crampton's Gap and South Mountain to observe the enemy in Maryland, Halleck ordered Colonel Albert J. Myer to try to comply with the request. More important, when Hooker told the general in chief that he thought he might have to seize the passes and would like to use some of Schenck's men for that purpose, Halleck replied that Schenck had been notified of the authority given to Hooker to control any forces "within the sphere of . . . [his] operations." This clause was open to interpretation and could cause trouble, but it revealed Halleck's intention to cooperate with Hooker to the extent of breaking down departmental lines. He further authorized Hooker to get into direct touch with Generals Heintzelman and Schenck if he wanted anything of them.[75]

The trend of events seemed to be granting to Hooker his fondest wish, which he had expressed in a letter to Lincoln on June 5: the appointment of a single commander for "all of the troops whose operations can have an influence on those of Lee's army." [76] As the Army of the Potomac followed Lee northward, its movements impinged upon the activities of troops in the Middle Department and the Department of Washington. To avoid duplication of effort, waste motion, and conflict of authority, Halleck did the sensible thing; though Hooker had disclaimed any desire for the appointment himself, Halleck gave him control over forces in the area not normally under him because he was commander of the major field army in the East. Troubled by the vagueness of Halleck's language, Hooker understandably wanted clarification of his new authority over Heintzelman's and Schenck's commands. After discussing the matter with Lincoln, Halleck on June 22 gave Hooker authority over all troops in the Eighth Corps and the Middle Department east of Cumberland, Maryland. As for the Department of Washington, its status remained unchanged, for instead of eliminating the departmental commander as an intermediary Halleck authorized Hooker to give orders directly to Heintzelman. Should Heintzelman consider Hooker's directions in conflict with his "special instructions" for the defense of Washington, the matter would be referred to Halleck. The Lincoln administration considered the safety of the capital so vital that Halleck could not permit a field commander to have a free hand in its defenses.[77] Memories of the misunderstanding between Lincoln and McClellan in 1862 over the defense of Washington were too painful to forget, and Halleck, who knew which side his political bread was buttered on, was not going to have the experience repeated.

Hooker could or would not see that he did not have the same control over Heintzelman's troops as he had over Schenck's. He complained bitterly when Colonel C. R. Lowell, Jr., of the 2nd Massachusetts Cavalry in Poolesville, Maryland, refused to obey an order on the grounds that he was under Heintzelman and subject to his commands.[78] Hooker's anger rose to white heat when Brigadier General John P. Slough would not release the Second Brigade of the Pennsylvania Reserve Corps for service with the Army of the Potomac. Hooker requested Halleck to arrest Slough at once, while he in his own good time would prefer charges against him, and then he added the barbed and officious remark: "You will find, I fear, when it is too late, that the effort to preserve departmental lines will be fatal to the cause of the country." [79] While it is true that Halleck insisted upon maintaining the integrity of the Department of Washington, and indirectly his own control of it, he did have Heintzelman give generously of his best troops to reinforce Hooker's various corps. The remaining units, including the 2nd Massachusetts Cavalry and Second Brigade of the Reserves, were kept directly under Heintzelman. Hooker, who was still dissatisfied with his increased power and suspicious of Halleck's good intentions, on June 24 sent his good friend and chief of staff, General Daniel Butterfield, to go over Halleck's head and present his case for more reinforcements and greater military control to the President. Lincoln did not let him get away with this trick, so typical of Hooker, and refused to undercut Halleck's authority. When Halleck said no more troops were available for Hooker's army from the defenses of Washington, Lincoln accepted his decision.[80]

Hooker added this refusal to the huge stock of grievances he accumulated against Halleck. In his barrage of words when testifying before the Committee on the Conduct of the War in March of 1865, he accused Halleck of thwarting him at every turn while he was commander of the Army of the Potomac. The committee for over a year had been trying to find out why General Hooker had been defeated at Chancellorsville and why the victory at Gettysburg had not been more decisive. If they had had any doubts about Hooker's generalship, he proceeded to disabuse them of their erroneous notions. He wanted them to understand that because of Halleck's unreasonable demands and refusal to cooperate he had not been able to maneuver his own army in a way he thought fit in the presence of the enemy. He had had the impossible task of covering Harpers Ferry and Washington with a force inferior to that of the enemy, for which Halleck was to blame. The few reinforcements he received had come largely from the Middle Department through the prompt and cheerful response of its commander, General Schenck.[81]

In the matter of reinforcements, the facts do not substantiate Hooker's statements before the committee, which were quite misleading. He admitted that he had been reinforced by Brigadier General J. J. Abercrombie's division and two brigades of Brigadier General Samuel W. Crawford's division, both from the Department of Washington. He said, however, that "as the term of service had nearly expired with the greater part of the former [Abercrombie's division], it added no material strength to my command." [82] In view of the prodigious deeds performed by the men of this division on the battlefield of Gettysburg this statement, if not outright prevarication, was at the very least ironical. Abercrombie's division, according to the tri-monthly return ending May 31, 1863, had 7,323 officers and men present for duty. It was composed of three brigades of infantry and four batteries of artillery, of which two brigades and two batteries fought at Gettysburg. The largest of the brigades representing almost half the strength of the division consisted of five full regiments of nine-month men from Vermont under Brigadier General George J. Stannard, which joined the First Corps at Gettysburg. They demonstrated convincingly that nine-month men even within days of being mustered out of service could fight splendidly under able and experienced leaders. The Vermonters helped turn back Longstreet's assault on July 2 and played a prominent role in crushing Pickett's right flank on July 3.[83] The other brigade under Brigadier General Alexander Hays, a first-class fighting man, became attached to the Third Division of the Second Corps, of which Hays was appointed commander.[84] Hays, with the touch of the Irish poet in him, proudly said that his old brigade's record at Gettysburg had been "written in blood." [85] The two batteries from Abercrombie's division, the 2nd Connecticut under Captain John W. Sterling and the 9th Massachusetts under Captain John Bigelow, joined the Artillery Reserve of the Army of the Potomac. Both became engaged at Gettysburg, with the 9th Massachusetts sacrificing itself to check an enemy advance on July 2 long enough for help to arrive.[86]

The other forces which joined Hooker from the Department of Washington were General Crawford's division of two brigades of Pennsylvania Reserves numbering 3,817 officers and men, and Major General Julius Stahel's cavalry division of 3,612 officers and troopers. Crawford's veteran division, assigned to the Fifth Corps, gained further distinction when one of its brigades charged at Plum Run on July 2. Stahel's division after joining Pleasonton's Cavalry Corps was reorganized and emerged under the leadership of General Judson Kilpatrick. Its two brigades, one under Brigadier General Elon J. Farnsworth and the other commanded by Brigadier General George A. Custer, made names for themselves on different parts of the Gettysburg battlefield on July 3.[87] Yet all of these were the troops which Hooker dismissed as adding "no material strength" to his command!

There is no doubt that reinforcements for the Army of the Potomac stripped the defenses of Washington of practically all of their mobile units, which were composed largely of veteran troops. What Hooker did not know was that before his army withdrew from the Rappahannock, more than 10,000 troops from the Department of Washington had been turned over to General Dix. By June 25 General J. G. Barnard, chief engineer for the defenses, reported that there were "no troops left to man the rifle pits and to support the artillerymen of the forts. . . ." [88] In addition the batteries on garrison duty did not have their normal complement of cannoneers. The June 30 roster of troop units in the department showed at the most two brigades of infantry known as the City Guards, the equivalent of a regiment of cavalry, seven brigades of heavy artillery, twelve batteries of light artillery in the Artillery Camp of Instruction, and such odds and ends as camp convalescents and paroled prisoners. To replace the troops sent to Hooker and Dix, Heintzelman had organized the employees of the Quartermaster's and Commissary Departments. Their fighting qualities were dubious to say the least. Heintzelman's forces in June, 1863, fell far below the number of troops which, at a meeting in March of 1862, the corps commanders of the Army of the Potomac had decided were necessary for the defense of Washington.[89]

According to a conservative estimate Hooker received from the two departments about 25,000 troops, including the force of 10,000 men at Harpers Ferry which did not fight at Gettysburg but performed important rearguard duties. The 15,000 reinforcements available for battle duty were equivalent in size to the largest corps in the Army of the Potomac. Over two-thirds of them were veterans, and those not in this category fought like veterans. Except for the 2,100 to 2,500 men in Brigadier General Henry H. Lockwood's brigade which came from Schenck's Middle Department, all of these top quality troops had been in the Department of Washington. Perhaps it was Meade, though the records do not say, who distributed them wisely where they were most needed among the various corps.[90] Still on June 27 Hooker in a hurt tone told Halleck that including the portions of Heintzelman's and Schenck's commands sent him, his "whole force of enlisted men for duty . . . [would] not exceed 105,000." [91] Whatever his shortcomings, Halleck had not held back the best available troops for Hooker's army. He had wiped out the lines of one department and blurred those of another in order to coordinate better the operations of all Federal forces in the area immediately threatened by Lee's corps. As new units came within Hooker's province, he often sought changes in their commanding officers, presumably to increase their effectiveness. Halleck seems to have agreed to these requests without question. As a result General French assumed command of Tyler's men, Kilpatrick took over Stahel's division, and Abercrombie lost his division, which was broken up and distributed among the various corps.[92] Hooker's indictment of Halleck before the Committee on the Conduct of the War failed in its poorly drawn and unconvincing bill of particulars.

One of Halleck's prime functions as general in chief, besides that of coordinating military operations, was overall planning or grand strategy. As the nature of Lee's offense began to unfold he had to consider the military resources at his disposal and their use in thwarting the Confederates. An obvious countermove would be to mount a threat against the most sensitive strategic point in the South, the Confederate capital, when Lee's army was no longer nearby to cover it. Hooker thought of this possibility and so did Halleck. Where he and Lincoln differed from Hooker was in the way the move might be made and who might make it. After giving Hooker his instructions to keep his eye on Lee, Halleck turned the Richmond job over to the two army corps in General John Dix's Department of Virginia, which were the only forces immediately available. Unfortunately Dix, a much respected politician and staunch War Democrat, was not the most aggressive of the generals. He had some good men under him, however, and they might, Halleck hoped, cause serious trouble for the Confederates responsible for the safety of the capital and the area about it.

In May and early June one part of Dix's forces was on the Peninsula in the neighborhood of Yorktown and Williamsburg, while another part covered the area west of Norfolk and around Suffolk. For a month or so after Chancellorsville Dix had been frittering away his energies in the Peninsula not accomplishing much. He had sent troops to West Point, which had caused concern in Confederate quarters and perhaps delayed Lee's departure for a few days.[93]

Thinking his small force too exposed at West Point, he withdrew it
and decided to start all over again in a drive toward Richmond and
the railroads feeding into it and Petersburg. On June 4 he warned
Hooker not to expect too much of him because he did not have
enough men to create anything more than a diversion. Two days
later he told of an expedition by General E. D. Keyes which had
gone from Yorktown up the Mattaponi River to Walkerton, above
West Point, and destroyed a large amount of property and stores,
after which it withdrew to its point of departure. On June 9 Dix
announced to Hooker that he was on the point of making two
moves, one up the Peninsula from Williamsburg and the other on
the Blackwater River from Suffolk.[94] During all this time he kept
using the small size of his forces as an excuse for not doing more. He
failed to see that he was dissipating the strength of an army of
more than 32,000 men [95] by making fruitless raids on enemy people
and property, rather than against their armed forces, and by conducting an offense simultaneously on two fronts.[96]

Halleck apparently made no effort to correct these errors in Dix's
strategy until he was assured on June 14 of Lee's movements toward
the Shenandoah Valley. He then told Dix that since there was no
longer any serious danger of an attack on Norfolk, he should concentrate his forces on the Peninsula and set them in motion toward
Richmond. If he had wanted Dix to take Richmond, he made the
mistake of not saying so bluntly. When Dix was called upon to give
an accounting of his offensive, he could—and did—in good conscience claim that he had never been ordered to attack the capital.
All Halleck had actually asked him to do was to "threaten Richmond, by seizing and destroying their railroad bridges over the
South and North Anna Rivers, and do them all the damage possible." If Dix could not accomplish this, Halleck had said vaguely,
he could "at least find occupation for a large force of the enemy." [97]
But when Halleck made his annual report he implied he had
ordered Dix to attack, not just threaten, Richmond and cut Lee's
lines of communication with the city. Dix took him to task for the
implication and rightly so.[98] Halleck, the master of indirection, had
outdone himself in this instance, for he could expect only the most
rash and headstrong general to attack a major objective without
having received clear-cut orders to do so. His fatal inability or
refusal to give orders ruined whatever chances of success Dix's move

up the Peninsula might have had. The tragic aspect of this whole operation is that Halleck had correctly diagnosed Dix's troubles, suggested the right moves, and then failed to give precise directions.

In spite of the vagueness of Halleck's instructions, Dix did in fact consider attacking Richmond. After a council of war on June 29 he and his chief subordinates, thinking their force too small for such an ambitious project, decided to confine themselves to threatening gestures which proved feeble, if not empty.[99] Sardonically General D. H. Hill characterized the Federal advance on Richmond as "not a feint but a faint." [100] In a way Hill's humor was misplaced for Dix's offensive against Richmond, if it could be called that, was not barren of results. He had enough men to create the illusion of a real threat, and he started out well by making a successful cavalry raid on Hanover Junction on June 27. Colonel Samuel P. Spear's troopers defeated the Confederate regiment guarding the junction, destroyed the railroad bridge over the South Anna River and the quartermaster's depot there, and took away 35 army wagons, 700 horses and mules, and 100 prisoners including Lee's son, General W. H. F. Lee who was recuperating from a wound received at Brandy Station. The psychological impact of this operation on Confederate leaders was greater than the actual losses. The raid and the mere presence of Dix's army on the Peninsula heightened their fears for the safety of the capital and impelled them to hold back troops that otherwise would have gone with Lee in his quest for victory in Pennsylvania.[101] This result took some of the stigma from Dix's expedition, of which it could be said that it was conceived in sound strategy but died aborning for want of a good midwife.[102] Again Halleck should receive a mixture of praise and blame for what happened.

V

HOOKER BOWS OUT

THE NEWS of the concentration of Dix's army at Yorktown and consequent mounting pressure on Richmond reached Confederate leaders on June 27 at a critical moment in Lee's offensive.[1] By that time all of the Army of Northern Virginia had crossed the Potomac River into Maryland except "Grumble" Jones's and Robertson's brigades of cavalry and a few regiments of infantry.[2] Within a little less than a week after the encounter on June 21 between Pleasonton and Stuart at Upperville, Lee's operations, so long cloaked in obscurity to anxious watchers in the North, had emerged into an invasion of major proportions. Though he had enjoyed unimpeded progress since that time, Lee knew that the moment of reckoning was approaching when somewhere he might have to fight a major battle with his old adversary. He would then have need of all his forces, including the units left behind to guard his rear and Richmond.

Prior to the engagement at Aldie on June 17 everything for Lee had gone pretty much according to plan. On June 15 Rodes's division of Ewell's corps, after having driven General Tyler's Yankees out of Martinsburg the day before, arrived at Williamsport on the Potomac and crossed the river. Jenkins' cavalry pressed ahead into Pennsylvania as far as Chambersburg, where its appearance on June 15 [3] raised the hue and cry of an invasion. Its early withdrawal, plus rumors of other Confederate movements, confused Northern intelligence about Lee's real intentions.[4] As for the rest of Ewell's corps, after defeating Milroy at Winchester Johnson's division stayed outside of town until June 16, when it left for Shepherdstown; Early's division tarried a few days longer.[5]

Meanwhile during all of these operations Lee kept his headquarters at Culpeper. From there he directed the movements of
Hill's corps as it gradually marched away from Fredericksburg.
Longstreet's corps had already left for the valley, taking a route on
the east side of the Blue Ridge Mountains which would furnish good
grazing and "tend to deceive the enemy as to . . . [Lee's] ultimate
destination, at least for a time." [6] It was an unnecessary precaution
on Lee's part, for until Pleasonton began battling Stuart again on
June 17 Hooker was oblivious of Longstreet's imminence on his
flank. Some of Lee's ruses to confuse Hooker seem to have been
wasted effort, for he was either unaware of them or gave them a
false interpretation. One such device was his order to Ewell to move
up to the Potomac in the hope that Hooker would follow him and
enable Hill's corps to withdraw from Fredericksburg. The plan had
no effect on Hooker, however, for by the time it was put into operation he had already left the Rappahannock.[7]

On June 16 Lee left Culpeper and followed after Longstreet's
corps. When he reached Markham in Manassas Gap the next day, he
ordered Ewell to have Rodes's division move forward as far as Hagerstown and "operate in the enemy's country according to the plan
proposed." [8] Still uncertain about Hooker's movements, Lee continued to advance the segments of his army cautiously so that he
would not be outmaneuvered and would be in a position to benefit
from any slip the enemy might make. When on June 18 he heard of
Pleasonton's menacing activities around Aldie and Middleburg, his
foresight was rewarded. He had kept Longstreet's corps near the
mountain passes to cover A. P. Hill's advance into the valley; as a
result it was also in a position to support Stuart. To prevent the
enemy from forcing passage of the gaps and separating Ewell from
the rest of the army Lee rerouted Hood's division of Longstreet's
corps, on its way to replace Early at Shepherdstown, and posted it
at Snicker's Gap. During the emergency Early was ordered to
remain where he was until one of Hill's divisions could relieve him.
Lee then instructed Ewell to go forward with two divisions of his
corps and carry out his plans north of the river. Should all or part of
Hooker's army follow him, Lee said he would send Longstreet's
corps as reinforcement. He regretted that Ewell did not have the use
of all his own corps, but should the Confederates be able to prevent the Northern army from crossing the river, Ewell, he felt,

"would be able to accomplish as much, unmolested, as the whole army could perform with General Hooker in its front." [9] Lee was indulging in the fond hope of gathering all the fruits of an invasion, particularly supplies and horses which were desperately needed, without incurring the cost of a heavy encounter with the enemy. This dream soon faded in the light of rapid changes.

During a pause of almost a week Lee in the valley watched developments on Longstreet's and Stuart's front and awaited the arrival of Hill's corps. He kept busy planning, directing, and corresponding with President Davis, the Confederate War Department, and his subordinates about the problem of conducting an offensive against the North. The demands of a major campaign with its calculated risks and daring strokes acted as a tonic to him. With affairs in full swing he appeared at his best—vigorous, alert, and in good spirits. General Pender reported that Lee was in a relaxed mood and had joshingly said that "he was going to shoot us if we did not keep our men from straggling. . . ." Pender replied that if Lee gave his generals "authority to shoot those under us he might take the same privilege with us." [10] Nothing escaped Lee's attention. He was gratified to hear that General Imboden had caused considerable destruction to the Baltimore and Ohio Railroad and the Chesapeake and Ohio Canal near Cumberland, Maryland, while gathering in large numbers of cattle and horses. There was more for Imboden to do, and Lee urged him to advance north of the Potomac but to keep to the left of the army. Obviously Lee had in mind the double advantage of this move which would enable him to tap other parts of enemy country for supplies and at the same time broaden the front of his invasion. As a further distraction to the enemy he suggested to Major General Samuel Jones, commander of the Department of Western Virginia, that now was the time for him to threaten Federal garrisons in that area and if circumstances favored him, he might "convert the threat into a real attack." [11]

The activities of Imboden's and Jones's forces were incidental, however, to those of the Army of Northern Virginia. Its forward movement depended upon Lee's solution of the problems of logistics. A long way from its railheads at Staunton and Culpeper, the army had to subsist upon the country. Lee realized that a large body of men exhausted supplies in an area within a short time, so he directed his foraging parties to roam widely and purchase foodstuffs throughout Fauquier and Loudoun Counties, the Shenandoah Valley, and the country west of the Allegheny Mountains in Virginia. The greatest scarcity was forage. The army had to depend upon grass for its cavalry horses and draft animals,[12] but fortunately it was in country where good grass was plentiful. Although Lee succeeded in collecting enough food for his army's needs, he realized that the best prospects for subsistence were north of the Potomac. The Cumberland Valley in Maryland and Pennsylvania was so rich in agricultural produce that by June 23, within a week after the first units of Ewell's corps had crossed the Potomac, they had accumulated enough supplies to feed all of his corps until June 30, as well as 1,700 barrels of flour for the rest of the army. One of the important items in that day and age of no refrigeration was salt, of which there was a great lack in the Confederacy. Lee's men found that north of the Potomac they could obtain all the salt they needed at 75¢ a barrel. They bought it liberally, using Confederate money for all payments, and they also purchased flour in Maryland at $6.50 per barrel and beef at $5.00 per hundred weight gross. Confederate policy was to buy all stores in enemy country, impressing only when necessary.[13]

But back in Virginia the great difficulty in procuring supplies, Lee felt, retarded and rendered more uncertain his future movements.[14] As he waited for his men to scour the countryside, the first of A. P. Hill's divisions arrived at Berryville on June 21, and the rest of the corps was not far behind.[15] Under no circumstances would Lee have followed Ewell across the Potomac before all of Hill's men had come up, so the problem of supplies caused but slight delay, if any, Lee's statement to the contrary notwithstanding. Fortunately the cavalry engagements between Stuart and Pleasonton, which had caused him increasing concern, ceased about the time he was ready for further maneuvers. Uncertain about the outcome of the fight at Upperville on June 21, he had sent McLaws' division back to Ashby's Gap as support for the cavalry. Stuart at the time could not tell whether the enemy was attempting an advance toward the valley or was only feeling out Lee's position.[16]

Upon learning next morning of Pleasonton's retirement to Aldie, Lee accelerated the movement of his army northward. Earlier that day he had given Ewell instructions to march with two of his divisions and Jenkins' cavalry toward the Susquehanna River by several routes: one through Emmitsburg, another by way of Chambersburg, and the last through McConnellsburg. Ewell's main task was to collect supplies for the army, particularly breadstuffs. Ever the opportunist in military operations, Lee suggested that Ewell's "progress and direction" should depend upon the "development of circumstances." If Harrisburg should come within his "means," he was directed to capture it.[17] When Lee heard that Pleasonton was no longer threatening his flank, he sent Ewell a second letter that same day, June 22, telling him that the pace and scope of the invasion across the Potomac were to be increased. Anderson's division of Hill's corps would relieve Early at Shepherdstown, thus releasing the third of Ewell's divisions for his own use. In addition Lee had instructed Stuart that, if the enemy threat on his front had subsided, he was to march with three of his brigades across the Potomac and place himself on Ewell's right, where he could guard his flank, watch enemy movements, and help gather food and forage. Lee also told Ewell there was a possibility that Imboden would cross the Potomac and perform the same services on his left as Stuart was to do on his right. It was a well thought out scheme, for it would give Ewell a highly mobile force of over 30,000 infantry and cavalry which could scoop up supplies at a furious pace and perhaps cause even more serious damage to the North should the Army of the Potomac be slow in reacting to the raid. Whether, as Lee hoped, Ewell would have all the cavalry he needed would depend upon two developments. Imboden had been ordered to cross the Potomac and join him "if opportunity offered." Who but Imboden was to tell whether he would have the opportunity? He decided that he did not. Stuart was given similar discretion. He was instructed to catch up with Ewell immediately "should the enemy have so far retired from his front as to permit of the departure of a portion of the cavalry. . . ."[18] Stuart did not reach Ewell either, but for other reasons.

In seeking causes for Stuart's failure two important considerations must be stressed. Without question Lee wanted him to take three of his five brigades, move ahead of the rest of the army, and align himself with Ewell in the vanguard, for if Stuart were personally directing all cavalry, including Jenkins', in a hazardous enterprise that required close cooperation with the infantry and the most efficient use of the mounted forces, Lee would have greater assurance of success. Although Lee of course did not know Hooker's intentions, he strongly suspected what they were, and he based his orders upon certain eventualities. He had so much faith in Stuart's judgment and ability to make the right moves that after indicating his wishes he gave him considerable latitude in carrying them out. His orders were more in the nature of suggestions than commands. In military affairs very few subordinates can be entrusted with so much discretionary power and even fewer care to assume the responsibilities that go with it. Stuart, however, was sanguine in temperament and experienced in semi-independent command, and he did not mind responsibility. On the contrary, he sought it. Regardless of the merits and shortcomings of this system of command, if orders or suggestions are conditional, the conditions upon which they are based should be made clear.

Lee's orders to Stuart did not meet this standard. His first letter written on June 22 gave Stuart permission to join Ewell "if you find that he [the enemy] is moving northward. . . ."[19] In a second letter sent at 5:00 P.M., June 23, the conditions Lee laid down were just the reverse. Stuart could move, presumably somewhere across the Potomac, "if General Hooker's army remains inactive . . . ," but "should he not appear to be moving northward" Lee thought it better for his cavalry leader to withdraw west of the Blue Ridge the next night, and the following day cross at Shepherdstown and proceed to Frederick, Maryland.[20] What Lee meant by the second proviso is not clear. Perhaps he considered it possible that Hooker would move southward to threaten Richmond, in which case Stuart's occupation of Frederick, a town equidistant from Baltimore and Washington, would be an effective deterrent. Without qualification, however, Lee pointed out Stuart's ultimate objective. Once across the Potomac "he must move on and feel the right of Ewell's troops. . . ."[21] The hour at which Stuart was to move Lee left to his discretion.

Once Stuart had decided conditions were right for him to move, there was still the fateful question of his route. Judging by Lee's silence on the matter in his first letter and in the light of other evidence, Lee undoubtedly expected Stuart to follow Ewell by way of the Shenandoah and Cumberland Valleys. But Stuart had something else in mind. He had been in constant touch with Major John S. Mosby, who with his band of twenty or thirty partisan rangers had been making life miserable for Northern soldiers and officers. Highly resourceful and intelligent, he had been flitting back and forth across Union lines bringing Stuart prisoners, booty, and most important of all, accurate news of the enemy. He pointed out to Stuart on June 23 the opportunity of striking Hooker a "damaging blow." Mosby had located the position of each corps of the Army of the Potomac on a twenty-five-mile front stretching from Leesburg south to Thoroughfare Gap. They were so widely separated, he claimed, that a column of cavalry could easily get between them. He suggested that Stuart could slip through Hooker's army by way of Hopewell Gap, which was lightly guarded by a cavalry picket, then head in a northeasterly direction, and cross the Potomac at Seneca Ford about twenty miles above Washington. The element of surprise practically guaranteed a safe march through the opposing lines, while Stuart's column as it went along could cause the enemy considerable trouble. Mosby drew a glowing picture of what Stuart could accomplish by taking this route. He could sever communications between Hooker and Pleasonton, destroy a "large portion" of Hooker's transportation, and take some of the pressure off Lee by creating a diversion for the Union cavalry. Once he had crossed the river into Maryland Stuart could wreck the Chesapeake and Ohio Canal, one of the main arteries in Hooker's supply line, and railroad communications with Washington. Mosby also predicted that the sudden appearance of Stuart's cavalry in such a sensitive area would create panic in Washington and probably cause Hooker's army to fall back to give the capital greater protection.[22]

Here was a scheme befitting the Lochinvar of the South—the bold, dashing, gay warrior in the tradition of Sir Walter Scott, dear to the heart of his Southern admirers. A quick thrust, a clever parry, and away he would ride from his slow-footed foe with peals of mocking laughter. Stuart and his cavalry, once more confounding his enemies and confusing his detractors, would redeem the setbacks at Brandy Station and Upperville. But it was serious business too and brought to mind the constant pressure on the Confederate leaders to achieve the extraordinary with limited resources. There was the danger that in daring too much Stuart would accomplish nothing. According to tradition, he discussed the matter with Lee and Longstreet.[23] Undoubtedly they weighed the ponderables and imponderables and sought ways to cut the risks of the venture to a minimum. They decided that rather than attempting to penetrate enemy lines, it would be safer for him to go around them by way of Glasscock Gap to the south. Stuart considered his ultimate destination to be York, Pennsylvania, where he expected to find Ewell's right. Going by way of Glasscock Gap meant adding many miles to the Seneca Ford route which Mosby had suggested and Stuart wanted to take. There was also the chance that by the time Stuart got started Hooker's army would be on the move and he might accidentally run into one or two of the Union corps. Beyond the Potomac there might be hidden dangers to delay or even cripple him. In spite of these objections he was lured by the prospects of a brilliant and dramatic stroke against the heavy, unimaginative, and oafish enemy. Assuming that he could ride "around their army without hindrance," Lee finally gave Stuart a free hand in choosing his route; he could cross the river either west or east of the Blue Ridge Mountains as he saw fit. Lee made it clear that before Stuart started he was to instruct the commander of the brigades left behind to watch the flank and rear of his army. Should the enemy move northward, the commanders of these brigades after leaving pickets to guard the passes should withdraw west of the mountains, bring "everything clean along the Valley," and catch up with the rear of the Confederate army.[24]

Whether Lee's approval of the Seneca Ford route was wise depends upon what he really had in mind for Stuart to do. If his purpose was to have him make a raid on the enemy's rear, causing as much damage as possible while going in the direction of Ewell's corps in Pennsylvania, the results of the ride should be judged in the light of that objective. But if Lee wanted primarily to get Stuart into Pennsylvania, as the tenor of his messages suggested, and incidentally use the march to confuse and harm the enemy, then another standard should be used in appraising the move. In the first instance Stuart and his troopers would be expected to roam in the enemy's rear for an unpredictable period of time, raising havoc with his communications, supplies, and isolated commands. Then they would seek out Ewell's corps and use it as a place of refuge and escape from an aroused enemy. Under such circumstances there could be no complaint if they did not arrive soon enough to take part in a major engagement. But if Lee's objective was to get Stuart's men into Pennsylvania in time to operate in conjunction with Ewell's men, this route was deceptive in the advantages it seemed to offer. One of them was the opportunity, as Lee put it, of doing the enemy "all the damage" they could on the way.[25] This directive was an invitation for Stuart to delay, since any blow against the enemy would take time and would divert him from his real purpose. The question was whether the amount of damage he could do to the enemy would be worth the risk of wearing out three brigades of cavalry and preventing their timely arrival on Ewell's flank. Cavalry raids on enemy communications usually had nuisance value only.

Another possible advantage in having Stuart pass between Hooker's army and Washington was suggested by Longstreet. He thought that Stuart would be "less likely to indicate what our plans are" than if he should cross "by passing to our rear." [26] Whatever its merits, this precaution became unnecessary when Union signal officers on Maryland Heights observed the movements of Longstreet's and Hill's corps as they approached and crossed the Potomac River on June 23, 24, and 25, just as Stuart was starting on his ride.[27] Besides the risks involved and the chances of delay, the greatest drawback to the route east of the mountains was its greater distance to York from Stuart's center of operations near Upperville and Middleburg. A difference of approximately thirty miles was a serious matter when time was at a premium, for it took cavalry accompanied by artillery most of a day to cover that much ground.[28]

Stuart, having the choice of routes, apparently decided to go around the Federal army on his way to Pennsylvania after Major Mosby reported to him on the morning of June 24 that Hooker showed no signs of moving. He took with him his three most experienced brigades commanded by Generals Wade Hampton and Fitz Lee and Colonel John R. Chambliss, Jr., which together had a numerical strength of about half of his total forces. He left the two remaining brigades in charge of General Robertson, since he was senior to General "Grumble" Jones who commanded one of the brigades. Presumably Stuart had several things in mind when he disposed his forces in this manner. In a hazardous enterprise it was natural for him to take with him the troopers and subordinates in whom he had complete confidence. He wanted neither Jones nor Robertson. For one thing, he and Jones did not get along well together. Since Jones had the biggest brigade in the division and the reputation of being the "best outpost officer," Stuart neatly avoided taking him while at the same time making adequate provisions for safeguarding the army's rear. In a way Robertson was a bigger problem.[29] If Stuart seriously considered leaving Hampton behind, as Longstreet had wanted and expected him to do,[30] then he would have had to take Robertson with him. But that was out of the question. Having neither the initiative nor the enterprise expected of a cavalry officer in the Army of Northern Virginia, Robertson could only be used for routine work, such as guarding the mountain passes. He was a conscientious disciplinarian who would obey orders, so it seemed safe to leave him in charge of rearguard duties.[31] Recognizing Robertson's shortcomings, Stuart gave him explicit instructions to watch and harass the enemy, guard the passes, and follow the Confederate army on its right and rear after Hooker had moved beyond his reach. As a further precaution because Jones was the more able officer of the two, Stuart sent an open letter of instructions to him through Robertson.[32] Nevertheless in view of the criticism to which Stuart was subsequently subjected he might have done better if he had put Hampton in command of the brigades which remained behind.

It took Stuart a day to issue three days' rations, send back all wagons and other vehicles except six pieces of artillery, caissons, and ambulances, and bring his brigades together for the rendezvous near Salem Depot. At one o'clock on the morning of June 25 he departed for Hay Market by way of Glasscock Gap. Hoping to meet Mosby near Gum Springs that day, he ran into his first obstacle, a formidable one at that: General Hancock's Second Corps which was on its way to the same place Stuart had hoped to reach. Stuart made known his presence by firing a few shells at the enemy, an act of questionable judgment. With a touch of humor Stuart remarked: "As Hancock had the right of way on my road, I sent Fitz. Lee's brigade to Gainesville to reconnoiter. . . ."[33] The rest of the day he spent grazing his horses, as he had no forage, and trying to locate other units of the enemy. He also sent Lee a dispatch concerning Hancock's movements. Then his brigades retraced their steps six miles to Buckland, as Stuart explained it, "to deceive the enemy," but really to take a detour. Despite this setback Stuart persisted in his plan to go around the Federal army. It was a crucial decision, for he still could have turned back without losing any more time. From Buckland the distances northwest to Shepherdstown and northeast to Rowser's Ford by way of Wolf Run Shoals were about the same. Shepherdstown was a few miles closer to York than Rowser's Ford.[34] According to Mosby's timetable Stuart was already one day behind schedule.

The next day he did better. After a march of twenty-five miles he reached Wolf Run Shoals on the Occoquan River. Although he had met no Federal forces, he had to halt again in order to graze his horses, since "hard marching without grain was fast breaking [them] down." [35] On the 27th he crossed the Occoquan at Wolf Run Shoals to Fairfax Station, where Hampton had a skirmish with a detachment of Union cavalry. After a rest of several hours at Fairfax Court House Stuart pushed on to Dranesville and discovered the dying embers of some campfires of Sedgwick's Sixth Corps, which unit had gone west toward Leesburg that morning. Although it was late in the afternoon, he decided to go on a few miles more and cross the Potomac that night at Rowser's Ford. With the water level two feet higher than normal he had considerable difficulty in getting his command, especially the artillery, over to the other side. Not until 3:00 A.M. did he succeed in accomplishing this task.[36] It had been a long and tiring day, in which Stuart and his men had travelled almost thirty miles in reaching the river. Before turning in for a few hours of sleep they broke a lockgate and captured a dozen or so canal boats loaded with soldiers, Negroes, and stores. From the prisoners Stuart learned that the Army of the Potomac was moving toward Frederick and that Hooker had set up his headquarters at Poolesville the day before. Upon hearing this news Stuart realized the importance of joining Ewell as soon as possible, and he continued his march northward early on the 28th,[37] a day of fateful consequences for both armies.

Before Stuart departed on his venture Lee ordered Hill's and Longstreet's corps to move northward. He brought Hill up to the Potomac on June 22 and at the same time withdrew Longstreet from the mountains west of the Shenandoah River when it became clear that the Federal army did not seem "disposed" to penetrate the passes. Anderson's division, followed by Pender's and Brigadier General Henry Heth's of Hill's corps, reached Shepherdstown on June 23 and crossed the Potomac the next day. Longstreet started toward Williamsport at dawn on June 24 with Pickett's division in the lead, followed by the Reserve Artillery battalions, Hood's division, and McLaws' division in that order. After a long march by way of Berryville and Martinsburg the first two units of his command crossed the Potomac on June 25 and the others the next day. Both Hill's and Longstreet's corps continued north and concentrated in the vicinity of Chambersburg, Pennsylvania, on June 27.[38]

Wherever Confederate troops crossed the Potomac they displayed great enthusiasm despite their fatigue. At Shepherdstown Brigadier General William Mahone sent the brigade band ahead to the other side. After a short rest he ordered his men to fall in; with dressed ranks they moved forward, the general and his staff leading the way. As they entered the water which was waist deep, the band played "Maryland, My Maryland," and the men broke out in the rebel yell.[39] The crossing at Williamsport where the water of the ford stood shoulder high was even more colorful. According to one participant, as they crossed the men sang "The Bonnie Blue Flag" and "Maryland, My Maryland," while the bands "played their liveliest airs;—the musicians, nude as Adam, each with a bundle of clothes on top of his head (to keep them dry) tooting with 'might and main' at their brass horns. . . ." At one point several columns crossed together, and the scene was brilliant with "colonels on horseback, flags fluttering, and the forest of bright bayonets glistening in the afternoon sun. . . ." The writer further noted that "many citizens, including women, and negroes of all ages and sexes, occupied the high ground near the river watching us come over. Perhaps they thought the 'ragged Rebels' best dressed when entirely undressed. . . ."[40] To warm the men after their immersion in the chilly waters of the river General McLaws, who had discovered a "quantity of whiskey" in Williamsport, gave each soldier who wanted it a gill (four ounces) of spirits. The general later asserted that he never heard of anyone refusing it, and as a result all the men were in very good humor.[41] His description of the condition of his men after these libations seems to have been something of an understatement. According to a lowly private, some of the soldiers who did not want their shares of spirits for themselves passed them on to others, so that "with empty stomachs, standing around the fire, it was soon showing its effects—some cutting antics, halloaing, or singing; and from appearances, the larger part fighting and parting combatants." In the confusion some careless or perhaps vengeful soul struck an officer in the cheek with a bayonet. The private concluded: "I guess our officers learned a lesson, as they never after that offered drink." [42]

Lee gave Ewell's progress in Pennsylvania as the reason for sending Longstreet and Hill across the Potomac; he wanted them within supporting distance of the leading corps. He also indicated another purpose when he said that General Jenkins' penetration of Pennsylvania as far as Chambersburg did not have the desired effect of "causing the Federal Army to leave Virginia. . . ." [43] If a cavalry brigade, even though a large one, could not induce Hooker to cross the Potomac, perhaps the entire Army of Northern Virginia could do so. What worried Lee during these critical days was not so much a movement by Hooker across the river as the timing of it. Lee wanted to be there to greet him, and on June 22 he expressed a fear to Stuart that Hooker would "steal a march on us, and get across the Potomac before we are aware." [44] The next day he wrote Davis of a report he had received of a pontoon bridge at Edwards Ferry, about three miles east of Leesburg, and signs of Hooker's withdrawal from that town and from the foot of the Blue Ridge Mountains. There is good evidence that Lee hoped and expected to have Hooker follow him into Maryland. [45]

Once he had committed all of his army to the invasion of the country north of the Potomac, Lee tried again to recall from the South all the units he considered as belonging to him. On June 23 he asked Adjutant General Samuel Cooper to send the brigades of Generals Corse and Cooke from Hanover Junction to Winchester, where they would receive instructions about joining the rest of the army. Corse's brigade was to have been relieved at the junction by the 44th North Carolina regiment from Pettigrew's brigade so as to permit it to rejoin Pickett's division. Subsequently the order was rescinded and Corse remained at Hanover Junction. Lee wondered whether he was still there. Confident that the 44th North Carolina would afford sufficient protection for the place, he requested Cooper to give Corse orders to march as soon as possible. He also asked Cooper to send him Cooke's brigade which was guarding Richmond, since he felt that large numbers of men were no longer necessary in the capital area and he himself needed every man he could get. [46]

In anticipation of possible objections to his request Lee at the same time wrote to Davis outlining in detail a new but well thought out idea of strategy at which he had hinted in previous correspondence. His plan was to create a new force in northern Virginia under

General Pierre G. T. Beauregard. In answer to the basic question of where the troops were to be obtained, he said a part of them could come from North Carolina and the remainder from Beauregard's forces in South Carolina and Georgia. A careful reading of Northern newspapers, he argued, had confirmed his impression of a slowing down of operations by the enemy along the Carolina and Georgia coast during the summer months. He repeated his favorite thesis that during the unhealthy months of summer and early autumn no benefit could be derived from maintaining a large force on the southern coast. It seemed good sense to him for both sides to agree tacitly upon a cessation of active military operations in those parts of the South where outbreaks of yellow fever and malaria were most likely to occur. Should Davis not agree and think it "imprudent" to withdraw a part of Beauregard's army from South Carolina, Lee suggested using "such of the troops about Richmond and in North Carolina as could be spared for a short time." [47]

Whatever troops were used, he wanted Beauregard given command over them, as well as the Department of North Carolina and Virginia, because "his presence would give magnitude to even a small demonstration, and tend greatly to perplex and confound the enemy." Once organized, this new army would advance to Culpeper Court House and threaten Washington from that direction. Lee pointed out that the "well known anxiety of the Northern Government for the safety of its capital" would cause it to react in a manner in many ways favorable to Southern arms. He predicted that the Federal high command would call in troops from all directions, even the West, to man the defenses of Washington. This action, he thought, would divert pressure from his own army, relieve Richmond of danger, free the seaboard of invaders, and perhaps ease the situation in the Mississippi Valley. [48]

The whole idea glittered with appeal for it offered so much for so little. There was one flaw to mar its bright surface, however, and that was its timing. Lee had had the scheme in the back of his mind for some weeks, and it is hard to understand why he did not broach it to Davis in its well-developed form earlier in the campaign. Since the main purpose of this plan was to ensure the success of his offense, which by June 23 was approaching a crisis he himself had precipitated, he did not allow much time for the organization of even a scratch force to divert the enemy's attention. Lee sensed this weakness, for in pursuing the subject with Davis two days later he said that, if nothing else could be done, even an army in "effigy" at Culpeper under Beauregard would afford "much relief." Revealing both his remoteness from affairs at Richmond and his annoyance with General D. H. Hill and Major General Arnold Elzey, who was commander of the Department of Richmond, Lee wrote: "If even the brigades in Virginia and North Carolina, which Generals Hill and Elzey think cannot be spared, were ordered there [Culpeper] at once, and General Beauregard were sent there, . . . it would do more to protect both States from marauding expeditions of the enemy than anything else." [49] If it had not been for the threat posed to Richmond by Dix's army concentrated on the lower Peninsula, Davis' refusal to accept Lee's proposal of a diversionary force would have been inexcusable. But the danger created by Dix's army was no figment of Davis' imagination. The Northern press, reflecting the excitement caused by Lee's advance, filled their columns with news, rumors, and the prognostications of armchair strategists about the invasion to the exclusion of almost anything else. As a result Lee was misled into thinking the danger to Richmond had evaporated.

When Lee's letter of June 23 got to Richmond five days later, Cooper proceeded to disabuse him of any false notions about the security of the Confederate capital. Quite irritated, he said Lee had been wrong in assuming that a regiment was large enough to protect the area around Hanover Junction. On June 25, in response to Lee's urgings, he had sent Corse's brigade to Gordonsville on the first leg of its journey to join the Army of Northern Virginia. Two days later about 1,200 Yankee cavalry suddenly appeared; they wrecked the railroad and burned a bridge, some buildings, and public stores. Rather than sending any troops to the army, Cooper suggested that under the circumstances it might be well for Lee to assign a portion of his own forces to the task of protecting his line of communications against enemy raids. Cooper stated also that the President had been "embarrassed" to learn of Lee's plan for a new army at Culpeper, for two reasons: It was the first intimation he had received of such an idea, and he could not see how it could be carried out.[50]

Davis' letter, which was carried in the same mail pouch as Cooper's, was kinder and more understanding in tone, though he also rejected Lee's plan as out of the question. The danger to Richmond and its communications, he said, was "materially greater" than it had been when Lee was there. Now that Corse had gone to join Lee, no more men were available; and during the emergency he was under pressure to recall troops to protect the city and the railroads serving Lee's army. With the exception of Brigadier General Henry A. Wise's brigade, which he had left behind to guard Richmond, Lee had all the units which were regularly assigned to his army. Cooke's brigade no longer belonged to it, for Davis' brigade had been sent to Lee as a replacement.[51] At this point the President forgot that a month earlier he had said that Davis' brigade would be exchanged for Jenkins' men and Cooke's place in North Carolina would be filled by a temporary force to be organized by Hill.[52] Apparently Hill had not succeeded in doing so. Davis was very apologetic and told Lee not to misunderstand him or think that he was "balancing accounts in the matter of brigades. . . ." He stressed his inability to reinforce Lee and form an army at Culpeper at the same time.[53] Actually he did neither. Davis had perennially faced the perplexing problem of meeting all needs with not enough troops, which was compounded by the threat of Dix's forces at a most inopportune time. He suspected that the situation might not be as serious as it appeared, but who could tell? Consequently on June 28, immediately after the Yankee raid on Hanover Junction, Davis had Seddon recall Corse from Gordonsville.[54] His decision at such a late date made no difference in the outcome of the campaign, for any reinforcements he might have been willing to send Lee would have arrived too late for the battle.[55]

This letter from Davis revealed the basic difference in temperament and sense of military values between him and Lee. Whereas the President tried to cover all strategic areas with a limited number of troops, Lee was willing to take the chance of concentrating them at what he considered the vital point. While Davis was worrying about the defense of Richmond and Lee's lines of communication, Lee realized he could not maintain them if he wanted to continue with his offensive, and he deliberately outran them.[56] Such willingness to take risks was typical of the whole campaign. Of this characteristic Colonel E. P. Alexander astutely observed: "It is certainly very bold & hazardous to separate our forces so far, but the enemy are so demoralized that I feel little anxiety about it."[57] He was wrong about the demoralization of the enemy army, but right about its commander.

During the week of June 17 to 24 while waiting "until the enemy develops his intention or force," [58] Hooker made no major moves. At Halleck's suggestion he did order Pleasonton to make vigorous use of his cavalry in an effort to locate Lee's whereabouts, which resulted in some heavy clashes of arms between the troopers of both sides. Until he could learn the outcome of Pleasonton's engagements Hooker shifted his corps around to consolidate his position just east of the Bull Run Mountains. Whether fortuitous or planned, by June 21 Hooker had first-class generals holding both ends and the center of his front: Hancock with two divisions of his Second Corps at Thoroughfare Gap, Meade and his Fifth Corps near Aldie Gap, and in accordance with a suggestion from Halleck, Slocum's Twelfth Corps at Leesburg,[59] which in relation to the general trend in Lee's movements was a key point. Once in firm control there Hooker could guard the fords for miles around and maintain his communications with Harpers Ferry.

Slocum, who was a very good man, had arrived in Leesburg late in the afternoon of June 18 after a most uncomfortable march from Dranesville. The day was the hottest his men had endured, and the pike was strewn with unbroken stones, which were very hard on the feet of the men and animals accustomed to soft dirt roads. About 1:00 P.M. a brisk shower relieved them. When they got to Goose Creek three and a half miles from Leesburg they found the bridge gone, and at least one division plunged into the waist-deep ford with yells and jokes.[60] They found no enemy at Leesburg, and Slocum immediately took steps to protect his position. He discovered three old Confederate redoubts; although they were not within easy supporting distance of one another and were in a dilapidated condition, he thought them better than nothing and put his men to work strengthening them. Slocum considered his position a strong one, but General Alpheus Williams did not share his opinion, as there were no works to protect the approaches to the town from the west.[61]

After looking over the area Slocum recommended that if they were to stay there for any length of time a pontoon bridge should be thrown across the Potomac near Edwards Ferry. When army headquarters asked why there and not somewhere else, Slocum explained that the approaches to the ferry on the Virginia side were already covered by a strong redoubt. A bridge there would have the additional advantage of connecting him with the Chesapeake and Ohio Canal on the north bank of the river. His supplies could come more safely by boat from Georgetown than overland from Vienna, Virginia, through country infested with guerrillas.[62] Slocum's arguments finally convinced Hooker, and he ordered the laying of one bridge and subsequently a second one. It took almost a week before both were ready, but by the middle of the afternoon of June 25 Hooker could march his whole army with its long supply trains across the river in a very short time.[63] Being forehanded, Slocum had parked his own wagons near the bridges so that they could be run across without delay.[64]

It was only a matter of time before the Union army would have to move into Maryland, but Hooker was slow to recognize the signs. Reports of enemy activities in Maryland and Pennsylvania three or four days after the Union defeat at Winchester on June 15 confused everyone, but instead of sniffing the air suspiciously Hooker became annoyed and contemptuously dismissed them as the work of alarmists. Butterfield in a message to Meade, commander of the Fifth Corps, on June 18 said the people of Pennsylvania were getting "sufficiently over their stampede to speak collectedly and coolly. . . ."[65] General Patrick confided to his diary that "the movements of Gen. Lee are not at all understood, apparently—no one is acquainted with, or even conjectures his plans of Campaign."[66] Although Hooker had taken the precaution of sending Slocum's Twelfth Corps to Leesburg to anchor his right wing on the Potomac, he seemed unduly deliberate and hesitant about strengthening the position there and deciding where to cross his army if it should become necessary. Slocum had rather optimistically reported his position as strong, but on June 21 he admitted the need for more artillery. His request evoked no response, and three days later he repeated it. In spite of Slocum's suggestion that some of the reserve units be moved to Leesburg so that they would be in position to spring across the Potomac when necessary, nothing was done. He felt that since the occupation of Leesburg secured all the fords below the town, including Edwards Ferry, the position should be held at "all hazards."[67] Hooker, however, continued to keep the bulk of his army concentrated at the center and left wing of his line.[68] Whereas he ordered Pleasonton to exert himself to penetrate Stuart's cavalry screen for information, he failed to provide either Slocum or Tyler with mounted units to scout the enemy. Both generals were well placed to find out what was going on, and Slocum possessed the right amount of scepticism and good sense for intelligence work.[69]

By June 22 Hooker knew definitely from Pleasonton's reports that two of Lee's corps were or would very shortly be concentrated in the valley between Winchester and the mountains. Having heard from Tyler of Ewell's crossing of the Potomac, Hooker feared that Lee held the gaps in the Blue Ridge to cover Ewell's movement. He asked Pleasonton to find out whether Longstreet had gone through the mountains into the valley. Pleasonton gave him an affirmative answer.[70] Signs of a major movement of the enemy into Maryland and Pennsylvania suddenly grew stronger. On June 23 and 24 the alarm bells rang loudly enough for even Hooker to hear, and he began to consider countermeasures.[71] He informed Halleck that as soon as he knew whether enemy troops which had arrived at Shepherdstown the day before had crossed the Potomac, he himself would commence moving. Previously he had taken several important steps preparatory to following Lee. He had replaced Tyler at Harpers Ferry with General French, in whom he apparently had greater confidence, and he had ordered General Stahel's cavalry division and a small force at Poolesville to report to French. He had instructed French to use the cavalry, if and when it arrived—it never did—to drive away and destroy any rebel cavalry on the north side of the river. What was more important, Hooker said that if he could do so "without attracting observation," he planned to send over a corps or two "in order, if possible, to sever Ewell from the balance of the rebel army, in case he should make a protracted sojourn with his Pennsylvania neighbors." [72]

Although he did not tell Halleck so in his dispatch, Hooker had already initiated that move late on the night of June 23, when he ordered General Howard with the Eleventh Corps to start his command at daylight on a march to Harpers Ferry with instructions to make the distance in two days.[73] Then Hooker reversed himself, and when Howard got near Edwards Ferry in the afternoon of June 24, he ordered him to stay there as support for Slocum. Early that evening he had another idea and had Howard cross the Potomac for the purpose of guarding the bridge and depots on the north bank. Several hours later Hooker again changed his mind and directed the corps to march to Sandy Hook near Harpers Ferry. In good faith

Howard started off, but he never got to Harpers Ferry or even near it because Hooker had still another change of thought.[74] If his orders to the Eleventh Corps were any indication, it would seem that for twenty-four hours he was completely undecided about what to do with his army.

On June 25 events forced Hooker to revise his overall plans. He realized at last that it was too late for him to attempt his scheme of using part of his army to cut off Ewell north of the Potomac, because by that time almost all of Lee's forces were across the river and some of them had penetrated as far as Chambersburg and Greenwood, Pennsylvania. Lee had stolen a two-day march on Hooker, who had waited too long before acting. He knew beyond doubt by midafternoon of June 24 that Lee's invasion of the country north of the Potomac was a sure thing, and that the force at Shepherdstown, about which he had worried, had crossed the river. After receiving this information, however, he let hours go by without taking any action. Finally on June 25 he issued orders for the army to move.[75] Once he had overcome his irresolution he acted with dispatch, but his men had to make forced marches in an effort to catch up with the Confederates.

To assist him during the ensuing period of rapid maneuvers Hooker on June 25 wisely appointed General Reynolds commander of the advanced wing of the army, as he had done at Fredericksburg, and gave him the task of moving the First, Third, and Eleventh Corps and Stahel's cavalry to Middletown, just east of South Mountain, to occupy Crampton's and Turner's Gaps. Thus as the rest of the army moved north toward Frederick, Hooker's left flank would be secured against surprise attack. Because Lee sent his army straight up the Cumberland Valley and did not turn any portion of it east of the mountains until it reached Chambersburg, Reynolds' assignment in retrospect seemed unnecessary, but Hooker at the time could not know where Lee would turn east, and if he had not taken the precaution of seizing the passes he would have been guilty of negligence. Hooker did not give Reynolds much time to get to his destination; he hoped the cavalry would reach the gaps that same night and would be "closely followed" by infantry and artillery.[76] It was a tall order and would put commanders and troops under a severe strain. To expedite matters the efficient and aggressive Reynolds took his staff early in the morning to a point near Poolesville, where it would be more centrally located to carry out his orders. He himself rode back and forth over the six miles between Edwards Ferry and Poolesville supervising operations.[77]

The Eleventh Corps was the only unit in Reynolds' temporary command readily available for Hooker's purposes. Howard's columns had gotten off to a good start from Edwards Ferry at 3:45 A.M. on June 25, but they pushed rather slowly toward Sandy Hook. Riding ahead of his men, Howard reached Point of Rocks an hour before noon, when he received word of a change of orders and destination. He at once instructed his men to turn off the river road and head for Jefferson, which was six miles from Middletown. It was a hard march of between twenty-five and thirty miles. The men had to cross the Monocacy River on a rickety and unsafe bridge and tramp over very bad roads in the Catoctins.[78]

The other two corps in the advanced wing, the First and Third, and Stahel's cavalry were located at greater distances from Edwards Ferry or any of the fords so it took them longer to get across the river. Stahel's cavalry crossed at Young's Island Ford, thus relieving somewhat the traffic on the bridges at Edwards Ferry, but because of high water they had to leave their trains behind at the ferry. By the time the division got to South Mountain it had exhausted its rations and had to borrow from Howard.[79] As for the First Corps, it was located at Guilford Station, closer to the river than the Third, and had less distance to go to its objective. Reynolds ordered it to march to Middletown by way of Barnesville, Adamstown, and Jefferson.[80] The Third Corps, which was encamped at Gum Springs, tramped fifteen miles up and down hill over sandy and gravelly roads, and finally reached Edwards Ferry about half past five in the afternoon. There the men looked forward to settling down for the night. Before they had time to do so, an order reached them to press on to the mouth of the Monocacy River, a good twelve miles farther to the northwest. The exhausted soldiers, not understanding the situation, of course blamed their commanders for the order, but at least one old veteran, Brigadier General A. A. Humphreys, commander of the Second Division, was too wise in the ways of hard campaigning to be bothered by uncomplimentary remarks as he urged his men on in the dark. He worried about their fatigue as they stumbled along the towpath of the Chesapeake and Ohio Canal, laden down with full equipment and three days' rations.

Large numbers could not keep up with their commands, and when the division finally arrived at the Monocacy about 12:30 A.M. many of the units were greatly depleted. In the 1st Massachusetts regiment, for example, only twenty-nine men lined up before striking arms for the night, and nearly a third of the men in the command had lost their shoes or had worn them out. Nevertheless by ten-thirty next morning nearly all of the stragglers had caught up with the regiment, and most of them were in condition to make the march of only seven miles to Point of Rocks, which was prescribed for the day.[81]

June 25 had been a busy day for Reynolds He had taken hold of affairs with a sure hand, and when operations became snarled he was there to straighten things out. But he felt that the commanding general should be at Edwards Ferry or Poolesville to supervise the crossing of the army, and he bluntly told him so. Late that night Reynolds reported with satisfaction the occupation of Crampton's Gap by Colonel Othneil De Forest's brigade of cavalry from Stahel's division, which was shortly to be reinforced by a brigade of infantry from the Eleventh Corps.[82] The next day, as Hooker had directed, the three corps under Reynolds remained pretty well concentrated near Middletown and in position to support the small infantry and cavalry forces guarding the passes. Reynolds seemed pleased with the performance of his troops except for Stahel's cavalry, which he said did nothing.[83] Apparently some of the troopers obtained a quantity of good Maryland rye, for two of them at Crampton's Gap became intoxicated and went riding around at full speed brandishing their sabers recklessly. The boys of Colonel Leopold von Gilsa's brigade charged them with bayonets and took them to headquarters.[84] Later Reynolds complained again of Stahel's inefficiency, noting that he had stayed in Frederick when he should have been in Middletown pushing his cavalrymen out aggressively toward Sharpsburg and Williamsport, and that he had failed to follow directions in reporting intelligence of enemy movements to army headquarters. It seems to be more than sheer coincidence that late on the night of June 26 Hooker asked Stanton to assign Stahel to Couch on the grounds that his presence with the Army of the Potomac would "much embarrass me and retard my movements." [85] Two days later Stahel received orders to report to Couch, although his command stayed with Pleasonton.[86]

The rest of the army followed Reynolds' wing and began its crossing of the Potomac on June 26. Hooker planned to concentrate his army at Middletown and Frederick, the two towns being only seven miles apart. He ordered all of the infantry except Slocum's Twelfth Corps to proceed toward Frederick; Slocum he instructed to go to Point of Rocks and then on to Middletown unless otherwise ordered. Pleasonton received directions to send one of his divisions to Middletown and presumably the other to Frederick. Hooker carefully drew up a schedule for the units to cross the river, beginning with the Twelfth Corps at 3:00 A.M. on June 26 and ending with the Cavalry Corps at an undesignated time but as soon as possible.[87] Although there were two bridges, they were fairly close together, and their approaches unless carefully policed would become choked with the long and slow moving trains. In crossing the Potomac Hooker had none of the geographical advantages enjoyed by Lee, who had used the fords at Shepherdstown and Williamsport where the water was much shallower. The fords used by Lee were many miles apart, so his long columns had been able to march on roughly parallel roads without interfering with one another. Once across the river the roads from the two fords converged at Hagerstown, thus facilitating easy concentration of the Southern forces. Hooker on the other hand had to bring his army together at a bottleneck, although beyond the bridgehead he could use many different roads which insured rapid marching through the Maryland countryside. At the same time he watched to see that his troops did not become too widely scattered. In spite of efforts at army headquarters to reduce the size of the trains from what they had been at Fredericksburg,[88] they still interfered with the marching infantry, and at times traffic became badly snarled. There was always some officer who failed to obey orders or pushed ahead when he should not, so that a difficult situation would become worse. Bad weather increased the confusion. June 26 started with a drizzling rain which persisted until dark. The effect of this precipitation on unpaved and heavily travelled roads can be easily imagined. When General Patrick, the provost marshal general, reached Edwards Ferry after a twenty-three-mile ride from Fairfax Station, he found a "deal of trouble." He spotted two young officers whom he knew and put them to work clearing the roads and bridges with a detail from the 20th New York regiment. He or someone with equal authority should have been there from the beginning to direct traffic. No wonder that at the end of the day he wrote: "I am fatigued, feel very much disgusted and satisfied that there is great want of a Commander." [89]

Despite the attending confusion the Union army crossed the river without any major mishaps. In contrast to their Confederate adversaries, the Northern soldiers did not mark the occasion with whooping and hollering. Most were not dejected by their move backwards, so to speak—many in fact felt relief at getting back to friendly country where Marylanders greeted them enthusiastically and plied them with refreshments—but there is something more prosaic about walking over a bridge than wading through a ford. Furthermore the last troops to leave Virginia had the rather unhappy task of burning government buildings and supplies at Centerville, Union Mills, and Fairfax Station, a job which must have had a sobering effect. [90] All of Hooker's army had reached Maryland by the evening of June 27 and by midnight had taken up the bridges. With both armies north of the Potomac the hour of combat was at hand.

Very cleverly Hooker had arranged that after two days of marching most of his forces would be in position well to the west of Frederick. By the night of June 27 five infantry corps, three cavalry divisions, and the Artillery Reserve were just east of the South Mountain passes, most of them concentrated between Middletown and Frederick. [91] While Hooker deserved credit for this accomplishment, his men did even more so. They had grumbled at long marches in the dark of a rainy night, but they were essentially in good spirits and in fighting trim. Their only important needs were shoes and clothing. [92] Officers and men alike had demonstrated amazing energy, and the rapidity of their movements was unprecedented in the East. In 1862 the army had moved with irritating deliberation at an average rate of six miles per day, whereas in 1863 it shifted its base of operations forty-five miles in two days. In an effort to accelerate its advance Hooker's assistant adjutant general and workhorse of the staff, Brigadier General Seth Williams, rode beside the marching columns and covered fifty miles without leaving the saddle. [93]

In his new location at Frederick Hooker had good roads, a railroad, and a canal to connect him with his main base of supplies at

Washington, forty-five miles away. The river protected the army's left flank and South Mountain its front. There was only one flaw in a picture that otherwise seemed perfect. General Lee on the 27th had the main body of his army at Chambersburg, forty-two miles almost due north of Middletown, and two strong arms of it stretched out toward the Susquehanna in the directions of Harrisburg and York. And the Governor of Pennsylvania was screaming out in wild alarm.

Because the curtain dropped before the end of the drama it is impossible to tell how Hooker would have played his role as commander of the Army of the Potomac in the last act, though there are strong hints of what he might have done. The documentary evidence is missing, if it ever existed, that he planned an immediate pursuit of Lee. He did wire Butterfield the following message at 10:00 A.M. on June 27 from Point of Rocks while he was on his way to Harpers Ferry: "Direct that the cavalry be sent well to the advance of Frederick, in the direction of Gettysburg and Emmitsburg, and see what they can of the movements of the enemy." [94] Years later Hooker claimed this order resulted in advancing Buford to Gettysburg even though the general's name was not mentioned in the dispatch. If Hooker had had in mind sending all of the cavalry, then of course Buford's command would have been included, and one might agree that Hooker was right in saying he had sent Buford to Gettysburg. The message was much too cryptic and ambiguous, however, for such a claim to stand up. Two regiments of Stahel's division under Brigadier General Joseph T. Copeland were already scouting in the immediate vicinity of Hagerstown, Emmitsburg, and Gettysburg when the wire was sent, and Copeland expected to be in Gettysburg the morning of June 28. Stahel evidently did not understand the message which Butterfield passed on to him, and in midafternoon of June 27 he inquired whether Hooker wanted him to withdraw the rest of his cavalry from Middletown to reinforce Copeland's regiments. [95] In view of Hooker's plans and commitments it is unbelievable that he intended to send all of his cavalry out into the country north of Frederick, but the wording of the message could lead to that conclusion. The question is how far did he mean by "well to the advance of Frederick?" In the thirty-five miles between Frederick and Gettysburg there was considerable room to maneuver.

After the war in an effort to find a copy of this message so as to substantiate his claim of having had the foresight to send Buford to Gettysburg, Hooker got in touch with Pleasonton. His inquiry gave Pleasonton a chance to blow his own horn and to claim that it was he who had ordered Buford's division to Gettysburg. "I considered it would be a point . . . which Gen. Lee would seek to occupy," Pleasonton wrote. "My authority was my own good sense in the matter, as I was thoroughly acquainted with all of that country & had occupied it the year before, the year of Antietam." Hooker snorted when he read Pleasonton's letter and branded his claim as "simply preposterous"; [96] and considering Pleasonton's penchant for attaching the wrong meaning to intelligence reports, his gift of second sight in the case of Gettysburg was truly amazing. Pleasonton did in fact order Buford to Gettysburg but for more prosaic reasons than the ones he gave. General Meade in his orders for the whole army to begin its march toward Pennsylvania stipulated that the cavalry should guard the right and left flanks and the rear. In response to these instructions Pleasonton early on June 29 tapped Kilpatrick to cover the right flank and Buford the left, which included the towns of Emmitsburg and Gettysburg. [97] Both Hooker and Pleasonton, however, were guilty of the same error: attaching a meaning to Gettysburg before the fact. Prior to the battle this little town had no more importance than a point on the map where many roads happened to intersect. But a great victory was won there, and Buford was one of the heroes. If his commanding general couldn't be a hero, he could at least try to bask in reflected glory.

As further evidence of his intention to go after Lee in Pennsylvania Hooker asserted to the Committee on the Conduct of the War that when he relinquished his command to Meade he gave him information about Lee and the position of the Army of the Potomac, as well as his ideas on when, how, and where the troops should march. Previously Butterfield had told the committee substantially the same thing, but in greater detail. He also claimed that Hooker had intended to move the army on June 29, after allowing it to rest at Frederick on Sunday, June 28. [98] Meade categorically denied having received any plans from Hooker. [99]

Actually just before Hooker resigned, instead of planning a move to Gettysburg he had in mind quite a different scheme on which he pinned his hopes of halting Lee's invasion. He told the committee that he had intended to organize the Harpers Ferry garrison and the Twelfth Corps into an expeditionary force of 25,000 men, and "throw them rapidly in rear of General Lee's army, cut his communications, destroy the bridges and capture his trains, and then reunite with the main army for the battle." [100] One might ask, "What battle?" How was Hooker so sure one would take place? The three corps at Middletown under Reynolds, according to Hooker and Butterfield, had been assembled with this movement in mind. Should Lee turn back to attack the force in his rear, the corps in Middletown could fall on his flank.[101] There is no doubt that Hooker was contemplating some such operation, for early in the evening of June 25 he ordered General French at Harpers Ferry to have his men prepared to march at a moment's notice. In marching orders to Slocum on the same day he intimated that he might change the destination of the Twelfth Corps. Two days later at 8:00 P.M. he sent a dispatch to Slocum, who was then at Knoxville, ordering him to pick up two brigades of French's command at Harpers Ferry early the next morning and then proceed from there toward Williamsport. Slocum would also have at his disposal a regiment of cavalry under Colonel Charles R. Lowell, Jr. The command would travel light, taking with it ambulances but no supply trains. Slocum would receive notice of his objective during the night.[102] In the light of these orders Hooker's poorly drawn directive to Butterfield about the cavalry gains a different connotation. Hooker hoped to trap Lee, and while doing so he wanted to protect his own right flank or front, depending upon which way the army faced, by throwing out a cavalry screen.

Several features of Hooker's strategy should be stressed. Butterfield talked about 25,000 men being used for the raid on Lee's supply line. A more careful count of the numerical strength of the Twelfth Corps, the garrison at Harpers Ferry, and Lowell's cavalry would reveal a combined force of no more than 17,000 men, of whom only half were veteran troops.[103] Hooker was asking some of his infantry to march to Williamsport and back, a round trip of forty miles, and to wreck Lee's supply line along the way. Such use of infantrymen was questionable, for it would take them at least two days to make the round trip without allowing any time for delays due to skirmishing or for rest. In organizing this expedition

Hooker made two assumptions: that Lee had a supply line in the strictest sense and was trying to maintain it; and that he would react to the threat to his communications in the way Hooker expected him to do. That these assumptions were erroneous is beside the point.[104] In planning this countermove Hooker's thoughts obviously were not on a pursuit of Lee, but on forcing him back toward the Potomac. By the time he had called off the project because of his quarrel with Halleck over the fate of Harpers Ferry, and as a result had ordered Slocum to Frederick, it was eight-thirty on the night of June 27. Very possibly Hooker had just received an acknowledgment of his resignation from Halleck. It had been referred to the President, Halleck said, and Hooker realized it might well be accepted.[105] Under the circumstances it is difficult to imagine him calmly sitting down and planning the moves he later claimed to have passed on to Meade.

Because of his desire to use the Harpers Ferry garrison for his countermoves against Lee Hooker had become involved in a quarrel with Halleck which led to his resignation. It had started with Hooker's suggestion that military occupation of Maryland Heights, which was the key to Harpers Ferry, no longer served a useful function and that the men in the garrison should be sent to reinforce the Army of the Potomac. He claimed he had a force "inferior in numbers to that of the enemy," and he therefore needed "every available man to use on the field." He asked Halleck whether there was any reason for holding on to the position.[106] On June 27 Hooker went to Harpers Ferry to investigate the situation personally, and while he was there he received Halleck's reply. Maryland Heights had always been regarded as important, Halleck said, and he would not approve their abandonment "except in case of absolute necessity." Hooker in turn answered his chief with some heat, marshalling all the arguments he could for his point of view. He asked that his case be presented to Stanton and Lincoln. Then apparently without waiting for an answer, he sent in his resignation on the grounds that with the military means at his disposal he could not comply with his original instructions to cover both Harpers Ferry and Washington.[107]

It could be argued that Halleck had deliberately taken an unreasonable stand in the matter so as to force Hooker's resignation. The two men had always been at odds, and Halleck's own chief of staff,

General G. W. Cullum, admitted that he had worked hard to get rid of Hooker.[108] In addition Stanton and possibly Lincoln had their own doubts about Hooker's ability and willingness to face Lee in battle again. Some evidence thus seems to substantiate the popularly accepted belief that the administration maneuvered to get rid of a man in whom it had lost confidence.

A closer examination of the episode, however, leads to the suspicion that Hooker used his resignation as a club to bully Halleck into giving him a free hand in questions of strategy. At this stage of the campaign he did not expect the general in chief to take him so seriously as to refer the issue to Lincoln. The timing of his resignation, his orders to Slocum, and Halleck's response to the resignation suggest this explanation.[109] Hooker's sudden impulse to resign also revealed his feeling of insecurity at the thought of facing Lee again in a head-on collision. All during the campaign he had evinced a tendency to let someone else cope with Lee, while he sought an easy way out of his dilemma by some spectacular achievement, such as the capture of Richmond.[110] He was particularly reluctant to confront Lee without having overwhelming numerical strength. Hence he exaggerated the size of Lee's army and complained that the government gave him grudging support while expecting the impossible of him. Under the circumstances he felt that he could do no less than resign in view of Halleck's lack of cooperation. Whatever his motives, it is questionable whether he expected Lincoln to accept his resignation. Imagine his surprise when he did!

In the controversy over the garrison at Maryland Heights Halleck has been accused of having been thoroughly inconsistent because of his dislike for Hooker. It was charged that whereas he stubbornly refused even to consider Hooker's evacuation of the post, he accepted Meade's proposal to abandon it without argument. In defense of Halleck it should be recalled, however, that Hooker had really never accepted him as his superior officer. Although not guilty of downright insubordination, he had refused to take Halleck into his confidence and explain fully what he hoped to accomplish in his operations. Halleck, being somewhat in the dark, did not flatly turn down Hooker's request to evacuate the heights; instead he asked obliquely for convincing arguments for their abandonment. Nor did Halleck give Meade a free hand when he took over. Meade requested permission to withdraw a large part of the garrison, for with the bulk of Lee's forces north of the Potomac he said he had better use for the men elsewhere.[111] Halleck's response gave him authority to "diminish or increase" the garrison as he saw fit, but nothing more.[112] When Meade informed Halleck the next day that he had to abandon Harpers Ferry outright, he carefully and tactfully explained his reasons for doing so.[113] In contrast, when Hooker wanted to do the same thing he revealed an uncompromising attitude and a marked unwillingness to discuss the matter, thus reducing the issue to one of two choices: Either Halleck would accept his proposal without question, or he would resign. The whole affair well illustrated the difference in tone in the relations between Halleck and the two commanding generals.

Hooker's justification for resigning depended considerably upon the merits of his appraisal of Harpers Ferry as a strategic point. Because of its location where the river, the railroad, and the canal converged at a mountain pass, the post possessed great value. Abandonment of it at any time during the war was questionable, but for Hooker to recommend evacuation while he was holding the South Mountain passes to the north and was planning operations along the Potomac seems incomprehensible. Meade's subsequent withdrawal of forces from Maryland Heights was by no means a confirmation of Hooker's judgment. Meade considered Harpers Ferry important as a base of operations, a "debouchée," as he called it, into the Cumberland and Shenandoah Valleys. He abandoned it reluctantly and only upon advice and information furnished him by Butterfield.[114]

Coming when it did Hooker's resignation both embarrassed and relieved the Lincoln administration. A change of command always requires a period of adjustment on the part of the new general, who wants time to appoint his own staff, become familiar with the organization, and introduce his own innovations and reforms. At best it is an awkward period in the life of an army and particularly so when the enemy has gained an advantage which, unless quickly nullified, can result in catastrophe. Despite their prejudices contemporary observers were right when they criticized the replacement of Hooker during the emergency as being singularly inappropriate. What they did not know or overlooked was Hooker's responsibility for creating the crisis which led to his removal.[115] The charge that Lincoln and his advisers contrived in some mysterious fashion to force his resignation gained credence when people heard of the manner in which the change of commanders occurred. Perhaps the administration effected the transfer too much in the manner of a cloak and dagger thriller, but it is easy to understand why it did so.[116] A decision to replace Hooker having been made, it was imperative to carry it out as quickly and smoothly as possible and without any fanfare. Lincoln for very good reasons did not discuss the matter with the Cabinet until after the deed was done.[117]

It should not be forgotten that Hooker, not the administration, asked for the change. Lincoln, Stanton, and Halleck may have been looking for an excuse to get rid of him, but he, and no one else, gave it to them. What little confidence they still had in him was shattered when he asked to be relieved at a critical moment in the campaign, for he had no just cause to resign. Until then Hooker's conduct of operations had been adequate, if not brilliant. He had done the obvious and kept his army between Lee and Washington, an accomplishment which was to his credit. But when it came to devising countermeasures, he was plagued with uncertainty as to what he should do and what were his true military objectives. The tone of his correspondence with Washington authorities was continually querulous and angry, and he seemed to worry more about getting reinforcements for his army than about how to use the men he had. Part of his ill-temper was due to his dislike for Halleck and a refusal to serve under him gracefully. With all his shortcomings, however, Hooker deserved the country's gratitude for having maintained an army in good fighting trim and not squandering its strength in futile and ill-conceived assaults on the enemy. Nevertheless it would have been better if he and the high command in Washington had parted company long before they did.[118]

VI

PENNSYLVANIA PREPARES
FOR INVASION

ON JUNE 12, 1863, the people of Pennsylvania read a proclamation from Governor Andrew G. Curtin in which he officially confirmed the truth of rumors that the state was in danger of an invasion by a "large rebel force." He called upon the men to enlist for the defense of their "own homes, firesides, and property" in a new corps of home guards to be organized by the War Department.[1]

Curtin's announcement came as a result of a meeting he had had in Washington late in May with President Lincoln and Secretary of War Edwin M. Stanton. With signs of a major enemy raid becoming stronger every day, he had gone there to discuss ways of protecting the border areas of the North, particularly the southern counties of Pennsylvania which were of vital concern to him.[2] All agreed that Hooker's army must be reinforced, but aside from stripping Washington of its defenses the only recourse was to raise a force of emergency troops to be made up largely of Pennsylvanians. Since Stanton had little faith in the efficiency of the traditional state militia system, he decided this time to try something new: raise a force of militia which would be recruited, maintained, and controlled by the national government. It would be composed of volunteers between the ages of eighteen and sixty who would serve during "the pleasure of the President or the continuance of the war." They would be kept on a standby basis and during an emergency would go on active duty in the military department in which they lived. After it was over they could return home but would remain subject to call at any time. Curtin was struck by the many unique features of Stanton's plan, and he accepted it reluctantly and with premonitions that the people of Pennsylvania would not support it.

As reports about the enemy threat became ever more ominous, the War Department finally decided to put its new scheme into operation. On June 9 and 10 it announced its plans for the new federal militia and the creation of two new military departments with their commanding officers. The Department of the Monongahela, under Major General W.T. H. Brooks with headquarters in Pittsburgh, embraced all of Pennsylvania west of Johnstown and Laurel Hill, as well as some northern counties of West Virginia and certain eastern ones in Ohio. More important in the history of the Gettysburg campaign, however, was the Department of the Susquehanna, which had its base of operations in Harrisburg and included all the rest of Pennsylvania not under General Brooks. For the position of commander Stanton fortunately had at his disposal the able and level-headed Major General Darius N. Couch,[3] who after distinguishing himself at Chancellorsville had given up his command of the Second Corps rather than serve any longer under General Hooker.

Despite Curtin's call to arms, the departmental commanders found men reluctant to enlist in the new corps.[4] There were many objections to the conditions of service. First of all, volunteers would receive no bounty for enlisting. Federal officials had reasoned that since members of the corps would not serve in any of the field armies but would be used mainly for the defense of their own states, they were not entitled to a bounty.[5] Even more upsetting, the volunteers feared they would not be paid until Congress got around to appropriating funds the next time it met. (For some reason it had not earmarked money for a federal reserve force of this type.) To take care of the men during the interim Colonel Thomas A. Scott, a leading railroader and powerful political figure in Pennsylvania, felt confident of his ability to get a sufficient loan from "corporate and other moneyed interests."[6] Though they were thus guaranteed of payment, many men still remained unwilling to enlist because of the "indefiniteness of the length of service," or because of a suspicion that they might end up serving outside the state.[7] In spite of these reservations the War Department and state officials might have succeeded in recruiting two corps of respectable size if they had had enough time. The Confederates, however, did not cooperate, and by appearing suddenly at Winchester and Martinsburg on June 13 and 14 respectively they forced the Union authorities to adopt a more expeditious arrangement for raising troops.

As Curtin's personal emissary Scott made a hurried trip to Washington on June 14. He appeared in Stanton's office in the dead of night to present the Governor's proposal for the immediate enlistment of 50,000 men.[8] After conferring for an hour and a half with the Secretary of War, the Secretary of State, and the solicitor of the War Department Scott agreed to a new scheme which, though not exactly in accord with Curtin's ideas, he nevertheless felt might hasten the mobilization of emergency troops. According to the plan the President would immediately issue a proclamation calling for 100,000 volunteer militia from Pennsylvania, Ohio, Maryland, and West Virginia. Pennsylvania's quota would be 50,000. The terms of enlistment would be more specific than under the previous scheme. The men would enter the federal militia without receiving a bounty and would serve for a maximum of six months; but should the emergency end before that time, they would be discharged. Furthermore there would be no problem of paying them, for troops enlisted under Presidential proclamation were entitled to money already appropriated by Congress.[9] Scott just before dawn on June 15 wired Curtin the details of the new plan and urged him to "get up a strong proclamation, calling upon our people to rise at once. There is not a moment to be lost. The rebels are moving in large force, and invasion cannot be checked excepting by immediate action."[10]

The President issued his proclamation early on June 15, and Curtin's followed later in the day,[11] even though he was then having second thoughts about the terms of enlistment. He wondered whether it would not be better if he appealed to the people "to meet the emergency without regard to time of service."[12] In response Stanton shrugged his shoulders and said it was up to Curtin to decide what appeal would "operate most effectually on the people of the State." Rather cryptically he added: "All the facilities in the power of this Department to meet the case have been and will continue to be afforded."[13] This statement furnished Curtin with a convenient excuse to change the terms of enlistment. When

Philadelphia did not respond to his second proclamation, he announced on June 16 that the state would "accept men without reference to the six months [service]." [14] The next day Stanton indirectly approved of this move when he advised Couch to secure men in any way he could.[15]

Stanton soon found that reluctance to enlist in the federal service for six months prevailed in other states as well as in Pennsylvania. On June 16 he sent messages to all Northern governors about the need for emergency troops. He wanted to know how many volunteers they could get to serve for a maximum of six months without the inducement of a bounty. Any troops they could furnish would be credited to their state quotas in the draft. Replies were not encouraging except from New York and Rhode Island.[16] New York had a well-organized militia, and in response to a special request from Stanton for 20,000 volunteers it offered 8,000 to 10,000 men from New York City to serve immediately but for three months only. In his eagerness to get troops Stanton gladly agreed to take the city regiments for "any term of service" and furnish them arms.[17] These concessions about terms of enlistment still did not produce the desired results. With the military situation becoming ever more critical Stanton, Couch, and Curtin were forced to improvise. After another conference with Colonel Scott, who represented Curtin, Stanton authorized Couch on June 25 to furnish arms, ammunition, subsistence, transportation, and all needful supplies to any troops which might be placed under his command whether sworn into the service of the United States or that of a state. As long as Couch commanded the emergency troops the United States government would assume the cost of maintaining them regardless of their status. But Stanton drew the line on uniforms; they could be furnished only to federal troops.[18]

The way was now clear for adoption of what seemed to Curtin and Couch the only practical means of raising a large force quickly enough to resist the invaders: an independent call for troops to serve within the state. Before making the appeal, however, Curtin sought Lincoln's approval.[19] The President gave his consent, and on June 26 Curtin issued his third and most stirring proclamation. He called for 60,000 men to come "promptly forward" to defend the state for ninety days. He promised to keep them only as long as necessary.[20] This appeal met with a more favorable response than the previous ones for a variety of reasons. In the first place, men were to be mustered into state, not federal service, thus removing from their suspicious minds the fear of being placed in one of the national armies in the field by way of the back door, so to speak. In addition the states rightists of the more die-hard variety would be willing to enlist in state forces when they would not consider entering the Union army. The contract to serve only ninety days was an advantage to the man on the street who saw affairs through the eyes of a private. Should the Governor break his promise to keep them only as long as the emergency lasted, he would be forced to let them go at the end of the period.

In calling for volunteers to serve in the state militia for a certain length of time the Governor avoided some mistakes of the previous year, when, during the crisis caused by Lee's invasion of Maryland and his threat to Pennsylvania, many men had been armed without being sworn into either federal or state forces. The result had been confusion, poor discipline, and controversies in adjusting service pay.[21] Now in 1863 the reluctance of civilians to accept any radically new system forced Curtin, Stanton, and Lincoln as practical Americans to devise an ingenious compromise. Pennsylvania lacked the money and the equipment to organize its own state forces, so during the crisis of the Gettysburg campaign the national government agreed to foot the bill if it exercised command over the troops. Although Stanton had balked at the idea of clothing state troops with United States uniforms, at Lincoln's suggestion that the "Secretary of War better let them have the clothes," [22] he found a way to grant Curtin's request for these items.[23] Aside from his momentary stubbornness about the uniforms, Stanton did not insist that his ideas be blindly followed. He departed from his blueprints and made concessions in face of the growing danger, although perhaps not rapidly enough. He was adamant, however, in maintaining the authority of federal officers over the militia and his own control over them.[24]

The department commanders in the critical area, Generals Brooks and Couch, were both able and sensible men who did the best they could under trying circumstances. Couch with his distinguished military career brought prestige to his position in Pennsylvania. Nevertheless, many prominent citizens and politicians of both parties in the North were worried about popular apathy and the mounting threat of invasion, and they felt that a more impressive leader was needed. To them the man of the hour was General George B. McClellan. The deeper Lee's army penetrated into Pennsylvania, the louder became the clamor for McClellan's recall to active duty in some capacity. Many people wanted him to organize and lead the emergency troops if the administration did not see fit to place him again in command of the Army of the Potomac. Stanton was well aware of this demand and perhaps suspected that putting the Pennsylvania militia in the service of the state was a way of bringing pressure on Lincoln to name McClellan as its commanding general.[25] He must have realized, however, that with the federal government paying the cost of the militia, he himself exercised control over the appointment of commanding officers unless the President failed to support him. Whatever may have been the threat to Stanton's authority, it evaporated when Lincoln tactfully but firmly turned down pleas to give McClellan command of the emergency troops. These requests had come from such important politicians as Governor Joel Parker of New Jersey and Colonel A. K. McClure, a Pennsylvania Republican from Chambersburg.[26]

It is doubtful whether under the circumstances McClellan could have improved upon Couch's performance. Couch did not have much to work with, but he never whined about his predicament [27] or demanded more authority.[28] Because of the difficulties in raising troops his position as department commander soon became somewhat of an anomaly. In reality he was working for two masters: Governor Curtin who had called for volunteers, and Secretary Stanton who equipped and maintained them. Through it all Couch remained calm and worked harmoniously with both gentlemen, who on occasion could be difficult.[29]

Perhaps one of Couch's greatest services was his ability to gather accurate and reliable information about the enemy, which he faithfully passed on to the War Department and the Army of the Potomac. News naturally gravitated toward Harrisburg, and he was there to give it his calm appraisal. In addition to his own sources, Couch received information from three different intelligence systems organized by civilians. One of these was under the direction of Colonel Scott, who when Lee's army crossed the Potomac into Maryland in 1862 had developed an intelligence agency to safeguard the Pennsylvania Central Railroad, today the Pennsylvania Railroad.

When he received intimations of Lee's second invasion of the North, he employed the same methods as previously to get news of the Confederates. Again he sent his chief operator, William Bender Wilson, to Williamsport. Wilson established headquarters there and directed a whole company of scouts who dogged Lee's trail all the way from the Potomac to the Susquehanna. Another guiding figure in this work was Colonel McClure, who had his friends and neighbors in Chambersburg act as agents in gathering reports of enemy movements. The organizer of the third group was Alexander Lloyd of Hollidaysburg. In the country west of the Cumberland Valley Lloyd commanded a force of twelve men to guard the railroad property at Mount Union and try to learn of enemy activities so as to be forewarned of raids. All of these people kept Couch informed, and their contribution to Union success in the campaign proved invaluable. When civil and military authorities wanted reliable knowledge, they would turn to Couch.[30]

Stanton undoubtedly established the command post for the Department of the Susquehanna at Harrisburg because of the city's strategic importance as a political and communications center. It was located at the crossroads of the Cumberland and Susquehanna Valleys on the natural invasion route to the heart of Pennsylvania and the cities of the northeast. Widespread rail connections furnished Couch with excellent facilities for gathering news and organizing an army. He also had at his disposal the machinery and personnel of the state government to help him in his activities. The features which gave Harrisburg importance to the North of course made it an attractive military objective to the invading Confederates, and Couch was well aware of the danger.

So long as men responded feebly to the calls to arms he could do little to protect the state should the enemy get there ahead of the Army of the Potomac. A newspaper reporter who visited Pennsylvania at this time considered the people to be "strangely apathetic." He wrote that in 1862 when Lee threatened the state the people had rushed to arms and cried, " 'Drive the enemy from our soil!' " but now they seemed to have lost the will to resist, and their cry had become one of " 'Where shall we hide our goods?' "[31] Though somewhat exaggerated, this indictment was essentially just, for during the year many people had grown weary of the war and distrustful of the Lincoln administration. The Democratic majority in the

Pennsylvania General Assembly reflected the strong peace sentiment throughout the state when in the spring it passed a series of resolutions condemning Lincoln's prosecution of the war and calling for a constitutional convention as a way of restoring the Union.[32] Many Democrats pretended to believe that the report of an invasion was so much Republican propaganda, possibly dreamed up as a way to get men into the service so they could not vote in the coming election. If there was some basis of fact to the rumor of an invasion, the Democrats confidently predicted that it would turn out to be nothing more than a cavalry raid, and no large force would therefore be needed to cope with it.[33]

When the invaders actually came into Pennsylvania, a few Democrats—how many is not known—whether out of blind hatred for the Republicans or real sympathy for the South welcomed and aided them. Others feigned support of the rebel cause as a means of saving their property from confiscation or destruction. Though charges abounded that the inhabitants of southern Pennsylvania were generally Copperheads and disloyal to the Union,[34] very few cases of actual subversion were recorded. One famous incident was described after the war by General John B. Gordon, a brigadier in General Early's division. As his brigade moved down the street in York a twelve-year-old girl ran up to Gordon's horse and handed him a bouquet of flowers; in it was hidden a note containing information about the strength and position of Union forces at Wrightsville.[35] General Patrick, provost marshal general of the Army of the Potomac, mentioned in his diary that there were large numbers of Copperheads in and around Gettysburg, but he gave the name of only one person, an editor in town, who had been brought before him on charges of aiding the enemy. Convinced by the testimony that the man had pointed out to Confederate officers the hiding places of some Union soldiers, Patrick had shipped him off to prison in Baltimore.[36]

Overwhelming evidence suggests that many Pennsylvanians, especially those known as the "Dutch," had a "plague on both your houses" attitude toward all combatants. They abhorred the war and would have none of it. When the armies came, their only concern was the security of their property and the safety of their persons. They maintained complete indifference to the many calls from their government to rise up and smite the invader. One foreign observer with the Confederate army was amazed at the "large number of young fellows loafing" about Chambersburg. Though a Southern sympathizer, it offended his sense of propriety that they were not in the Union army or at least the state militia. The rationale for their conduct was well expressed by an innkeeper who professed "entire neutrality," and asserted that, as the administration at Washington had done nothing to defend his state, he could see no obligation to turn out to defend the government.[37]

Many Pennsylvanians who avowed ardent support of the war had no better records during the emergency than the Peace Democrats and Copperheads. Most of them were farmers, and they greatly disliked committing themselves to serve, especially at a season of the year when every able hand was needed to harvest the maturing crops. There were other less understandable reasons for their reluctance to join. When the people in the Gettysburg area heard that military authorities in Harrisburg wanted to do the obvious and sensible thing and draw the main defensive line along the Susquehanna River, thus leaving the border region unprotected, many of them refused to enlist. They excused themselves on the grounds of wanting to stay home with their families in the hour of danger instead of going off to defend less exposed places.[38] Even after state authorities succumbed to popular pressure and restored the old-time militia system with the limit of three months service, many citizens still would not join. If they fought at all, it must be on their own terms. At Johnstown a German artillery company refused to be mustered in unless the Governor promised not to have them taken out of the state. More than once arms were requested for groups of minutemen who had no legal or formal organization, and the state adjutant general had to send a reminder that weapons would go only to the regular militia. When some state official made the mistake of allowing nearly all the men in Mercer and Crawford Counties to enlist for only sixty days, it proved impossible to get many to agree to a ninety-day term of service. The assistant adjutant general in Pittsburgh asked Curtin helplessly: "What shall I do?" [39]

The idea of bushwhacking, or guerrilla warfare, appealed to some people who were romantically inclined and wanted to engage in the dangerous but exciting sport of taking pot shots at the enemy. One writer proposed that the government send two thousand troops to the Cumberland Valley—where it would get them he did not say—

and call on the local men to rise up and join in the fun. He guaranteed that nearly every man who could carry a gun would turn out, for "all they want is the chance to act and the government to lead." [40] Another correspondent asked Curtin if he would accept one hundred or more good men for the purpose of "bushwackering," as he called it, and harrying the rebels. He felt sure he could get them if they were wanted. Another claimed that whereas Curtin could not find ten men to enlist in regular militia companies, he would have no trouble getting 1,000 to fight as bushwhackers. Each would use his own rifle and fight without pay. With such a force, he said, the Governor could defy the whole rebel army and clear the state in three weeks. [41]

Without asking for official permission some Pennsylvanians did in fact engage in bushwhacking. They were civilians armed with their own rifles, and they would hide in bushes or behind rocks and waylay Confederate detachments. It was risky business because there was a question of whether they would be protected by the rules of war if captured. Most of them, perhaps as many as 5,000, gathered in the counties of the Juniata River Valley, west of the Cumberland Valley, where under the command of ex-officers they guarded the mountain passes leading to their homes. Bushwhackers appeared in other parts of the state as well, although in fewer numbers. Some hid in the recesses of South Mountain near Greenwood, which was on the route taken by the invading army, and made it dangerous for Confederates to travel in small groups. [42] Because the bushwhackers were not well organized or expertly led they accomplished little of military value.

To defend the state the authorities in Harrisburg depended upon groups organized and trained according to traditional practices, but because of the lethargy of the Pennsylvanians they were slow to materialize. If New York had not had a large number of militia ready and willing to serve in the Department of the Susquehanna, General Couch would have been without any kind of force on June 22 when Lee stood poised to cross the Potomac with the main body of his army. Couch had under his immediate control near Harrisburg at the very outside 11,500 men, of whom a little over 8,000 were from the state of New York. [43] To the west near Bedford was General Milroy with perhaps 2,800 of his old force and 1,000 newly enlisted militia. Speaking to Stanton of the quality of his troops Couch said:

"You will readily understand what kind of a force I have, when a few regiments, with a sprinkling of nine-months' men in them, are veterans." [44] He soon found out that the men with Milroy were not in fighting trim either and were much fewer in number than he had thought. As for the Pennsylvania militiamen who were supposed to be with them, they were not mustered in and never would be, for shortly after their enlistment Couch reported that they had gone home.[45] Reinforcements for his small army arrived in driblets. On June 29, at the time of the greatest threat to Harrisburg, Couch estimated his whole organized force, including Milroy's men, to be perhaps 16,000. Their quality had not improved since June 22, and Couch stated that "five thousand regulars will whip them all to pieces in an open field." [46] Confederate comments on the emergency troops were even less complimentary. General Early observed caustically that his march to the bank of the Susquehanna and back had been "without resistance, the performance of the militia force at Gettysburg and Wrightsville amounting to no resistance at all, but being merely a source of amusement to my troops." [47]

The appearance on Pennsylvania soil of the entire Army of Northern Virginia, not just a part of it, convinced even the most sceptical that the Confederates meant business. Indifference changed to alarm, and a rush to the colors began. In Philadelphia where apathy had been particularly noticeable, the people became thoroughly aroused and eagerly sought to cooperate with the military authorities. Couch had appointed to command the city's emergency troops a major general of the Army of the Potomac who was still recovering from a wound at Antietam. He had the wonderful name of Napoleon Jackson Tecumseh Dana,[48] surely formidable enough to stop any enemy army. The City Council at a special meeting voted $500,000 to recruit, equip, and pay volunteers. A military organization known as the Blue and Gray Reserves became activated, while the police formed a company from their own force. To stimulate recruiting, which appropriately was being carried on in Independence Square,[49] the mayor made a stirring appeal for enlistments in the "name of duty and of manhood." With the rebels at the "gates" of the capital, he urged the men to close their factories, workshops, and stores and assemble for organization and drill for the protection of their homes.[50]

Similar scenes took place in other Pennsylvania cities, and almost

24,000 men volunteered for service within a period of three weeks. To try to recruit, muster in, equip, and send to the front such numbers in a short time caused boundless confusion. Neither Couch nor Curtin had a large enough staff of administrators trained in military affairs to keep matters from getting into a tangle. A steady stream of dispatches swamped Curtin with demands to straighten out all sorts of difficulties. Everyone was impatient and could hardly wait for a reply. One particularly irascible recruiter wired Curtin: "Why in hell don't you answer. Will you or will you not accept us ready to leave tonight." [51] After waiting so long for any volunteers the Governor was not ready for the rush, but he and Couch tried valiantly to handle problems as they arose.

To get the volunteers quickly to Reading, the rendezvous for the area east of Harrisburg, Couch instructed the railroads to carry regiments, companies, and squads to their destination, even though they had no regular orders for transportation, and to charge the fare to the United States government. The railroads cooperated, but where the conductors knew a man was an impostor getting a free ride by saying he was going to join the militia, they refused him passage. One man boasted that he went to Harrisburg three or four times without paying for the trips.[52] When the recruits got to Reading they found things in confusion. On the 1st of July 5,000 men had assembled there without tents or camp equipment of any kind, even kettles, plates, or cups with which to prepare and eat their rations. The commandant of the camp wired Harrisburg for arms so that his guards could enforce discipline in camp and prevent trouble in town.[53] A similar situation existed at Huntingdon where seven full companies and several squads had gathered and were without tents and cooking utensils. The civilians had done what they could, but they were unable to take care of any more men, and the quartermaster had disappeared somewhere and was not to be found.[54] Unfortunately the same shortages persisted when the emergency troops went on active duty and marched out looking for the enemy. One private in the 43rd Pennsylvania Militia, who like many was thoroughly disillusioned with the realities of campaigning, plaintively asked Curtin for permission to go home, for he had "not received but half rations" during the whole period of his service.[55]

Even after the Confederates withdrew from the outskirts of Harrisburg Governor Curtin wisely continued his mobilization of emergency troops. At the same time he urged the governors of neighboring states to dip deeply into their reservoirs of manpower and send on whatever organized forces they had available.[56] Curtin perhaps placed too much faith in the military effectiveness of the militia, but any force was obviously better than none at all, and should the Army of the Potomac have been defeated, remnants of it could have combined with the emergency troops and offered continued resistance.

While military and civilian authorities were thus busy organizing a force of militia, they were at the same time inventing ways to obstruct the invaders and slow them down until the Union army could overtake them. Couch had barely arrived in Harrisburg when he received word of Ewell's attacks on Winchester and Martinsburg and the retreat of part of Milroy's forces to Maryland Heights,[57] which opened the Cumberland Valley and Pennsylvania to invasion. The first barrier to the Confederate advance was the Susquehanna River, and though it was not a very formidable stream Couch decided to establish his main line of defense along its banks from its confluence with the Juniata River fifteen miles north of Harrisburg down to the Maryland border. Later he extended the line to the Conowingo bridge eight miles farther south. In spite of the low level of the water, Couch expressed confidence in his ability to put up a good defense at the few bridges and fords along the river and prevent the rebels from crossing.[58]

The weakest and most accessible point in Couch's defensive line was at Harrisburg. It was connected with the southwest bank of the Susquehanna by the Cumberland Valley Railroad bridge and the Theodore Burr bridge for vehicular and pedestrian traffic. Couch placed guards at these bridges and arranged to have them burned should the rebels threaten to seize them. As further protection he enlisted citizens and soldiers to build rather elaborate fortifications on the west bank directly opposite the city. Here they dug trenches, threw up earthworks, and prepared artillery positions. As the militia trickled into Harrisburg, Couch sent them to man the forts under the command of Brigadier General William F. Smith, a veteran officer of great ability.[59]

Meanwhile the region along the river southeast of Harrisburg was put in charge of another experienced officer, Colonel J. G. Frick.[60] Under his direction local men turned out en masse equipped with their own guns, three days rations, and trench tools (ax, pick, or shovel), and in short order they dug rifle pits and built breastworks along the whole length of Lancaster County facing the Susquehanna.[61] Couch ordered the Pennsylvania and Union Canals drained, all canal boats removed to places of safety, and a constant guard maintained at the bridges and fords.[62] On the northeast side of the river at Wrightsville carpenters and mechanics were hired to weaken a section of the mile-and-a-quarter-long bridge to Columbia and prepare it for partial destruction. If the rebels came, one of the twenty-eight spans was to be dumped into the river by blowing up its braces and arches. As it turned out, the arrangements proved ineffective, and at the crucial moment to prevent Gordon's brigade from seizing the bridge Colonel Frick ordered it totally destroyed by fire.[63]

While these defensive measures were for the most part warranted, there was less justification for the hysterical actions of people in several of the large cities. To be sure, throughout the ages the tried and true method of getting ready for an enemy attack has been to get the inhabitants to erect fortifications, whether needed or not. If nothing more, the exercise relieves their anxieties and frustrations. So it was now in Pittsburgh, Philadelphia, and Baltimore, where the people suddenly became panicky and felt they must do something —anything—to meet the danger. In Baltimore where there was a real threat of invasion the authorities impressed all Negroes, whether free or slave, to construct lines of entrenchments and redoubts for many miles so that the city was completely enclosed on the land side.[64] Philadelphia and Pittsburgh on the other hand were well removed from the possibility of attack, each being about 135 miles from Chambersburg where Lee first concentrated his army in Pennsylvania. Nevertheless the citizens in both cities acted as if they were already in the line of fire. In Pittsburgh thousands of people fell to work constructing forts which had been staked out by engineers. Although the Philadelphians were slower to awake to their danger, when they did they put on quite a show of patriotic effort. Among their various projects was a system of earthworks and trenches for which they paid $51,537.37 for labor and materials. With the retreat of the Confederates they regained their sense of proportion and felt free to laugh at their "pretty little redoubts." [65]

During all these frantic preparations to meet the invasion an unusual and ironic development occurred among civilian leaders. In an effort to shake the people out of their lethargy, to force their active participation in the defense of the state, and to control subversive elements, prominent citizens made strong appeals to the President and the Governor to declare martial law in their respective cities. In answer to inquiries from Lincoln, both General Brooks in Pittsburgh and General Dana in Philadelphia, contrary to the stereotype of the military mind, opposed its imposition. Brooks said that although many "nervous" men were constantly besetting him to declare martial law, he considered the idea "unwise, unnecessary, and not to be thought of for an instant." Dana saw no more reason to declare it in Philadelphia than any other place in the state, and he would recommend it only if the enemy should immediately threaten the city.[66] In contrast to his confreres in Pennsylvania the commanding general in Baltimore was understandably worried about the great number of Southern sympathizers in Maryland who, with the Confederate army so close, might rise up against constituted authority. As a precaution he declared martial law in Baltimore and the western counties of Maryland on June 30, and in the whole state of Delaware on July 3.[67]

Officials of the railroads, realizing how essential they were to the economy and military operations of the North, were among the most efficient in arranging to protect their property in case of invasion. Colonel Scott of the Pennsylvania Central suspended all work upon the roadbed and used his workers at Columbia, Harrisburg, Mifflin, and Altoona to build blockhouses as defense for the important bridges because they were so vulnerable to attack and difficult to replace. Any property that could be carried away, such as shop machinery and shafting, was loaded up and shipped to places of safety. The more valuable locomotives and the newer freight and passenger cars were sent to Philadelphia or Pittsburgh. Much of this work required careful timing. Scott did not wish to strip the road of its rolling stock until the very last moment, since there was much for the line to do in bringing emergency troops to threatened areas, as well as carrying on its regular business.[68]

Preparations to meet the invasion were by no means confined to the large cities, and people in the rural areas of Pennsylvania also took measures to protect their property if and when the rebels should come their way. As early as June 15 Couch had warned the residents of the Cumberland Valley of the possibility of a Confederate advance, and he advised the farmers to run off their horses to places of safety.[69] Many banded together and sent hundreds of their best animals to the mountains or across the Susquehanna. Others hid them in obscure nooks on their property. In desperation one farmer sought to save his big gray from seizure by putting him in the basement of his house, which was quite a feat. Other livestock, food supplies, harness, wagons, and similar items were secreted in lofts and haystacks, for everyone feared the rebels would appropriate all they saw for their own use, and what they could not use they would destroy. Shopkeepers in the small towns, equally worried about what the Confederates would do, began to ship their most valuable merchandise to Harrisburg and other cities farther east.[70]

Before the people living near the Maryland border could heed Couch's warning, however, the invasion had begun. Milroy's wagon train suddenly appeared near Chambersburg fleeing wildly before Jenkins' Confederate cavalry. The teamsters were greatly frightened; their fright proved contagious, and soon panic spread throughout the valley. Everyone wanted to leave at once, not realizing that by abandoning their homes they were exposing them to the depredations of friend and foe alike. An army of refugees, both Negro and white, streamed into the road and formed an endless column behind the heavy four-horse army wagons.[71] In clouds of dust which could be seen for miles the procession approached Harrisburg.[72] When it entered the great covered bridge there arose a "deep tremulous, rumbling sound, as of the voice of many waters." Then came the farmers of the Cumberland Valley with their household goods piled high on their wagons; "bedding, tables, chairs, their wives and children perched on the top; kettles and pails dangling beneath." Bringing up the rear were their sons driving cattle and horses. Their arrival in Harrisburg increased the pitch of excitement there. In terror men, women, and children swarmed to the railroad station and sought to leave the city. "With trunks, boxes, bundles; packages tied up in bed-blankets and quilts; mountains of baggage," they scrambled onto the trains, "rushing here and there in a frantic manner; shouting, screaming, as if the Rebels were about to dash into the town and lay it in ashes." [73]

The panic subsided somewhat with the retirement of Jenkins'

cavalry down the valley, only to revive about ten days later when two large columns of Ewell's corps drove north, one toward Wrightsville by way of Gettysburg and York, the other toward Harrisburg through Carlisle.[74] News of the appearance of the Confederates before York and the surrender of the town filled the people with dismay. At Wrightsville the rush of farmers, burgers, teamsters, and railroad men to get themselves and their property across the multipurpose bridge presented a scene of great confusion. Despite the need for haste the keepers of the bridge increased the traffic jam and slowed passage to a trickle by stubbornly demanding payment of the regular toll. Fortunately an aide of General Couch who was nearby persuaded the president of the company to waive all charges during the crisis.[75] In Carlisle the situation was hardly less frantic. One of the first Confederates to arrive on the scene, Brigadier General Stephen D. Ramseur of Rodes's division, wrote: "So hurried was the flight of the Yanks that many household ornaments & luxuries were left behind. This morning I breakfasted on salmon left in ice."[76] In Harrisburg hundreds of people continued to flee, and Colonel Scott offered free transportation to women and children on the Pennsylvania Central. One of the most pitiful sights was the "thousands" of free Negroes from the Cumberland Valley swarming through the city. They rightly feared that if they were caught they would be returned to slavery in the South, and they were desperately seeking any refuge they could find.[77]

With the approach of the Confederates toward Carlisle state officials made hurried preparations to move the seat of government farther east. Men in their shirtsleeves worked all night at the State House packing records and papers, as well as 28,000 volumes of the State Library and fine old portraits of the governors. Everything was ordered sent to Patterson's Warehouse in Philadelphia. The Philadelphians at the same moment were getting ready to ship their specie and valuables east of the Hudson River.[78]

The rumor of a Confederate shelling of Harrisburg reached Philadelphia the evening of June 28 and packed Chestnut and Market Streets with people milling about aimlessly, wondering what to do.[79] Next day two prominent citizens solemnly declared to Secretary of War Stanton that the rebels were marching on their city in large numbers and were threatening the Philadelphia, Wilmington and Baltimore Railroad. It behooved him therefore to get fifty pieces of artillery and 20,000 veterans onto the railroad and to the city as soon as possible; 10,000 must move at once.[80] Just how in their unbounded wisdom the citizens arrived at these precise figures and how they thought Stanton could get that number of veteran troops by the snap of his fingers they failed to make clear. This ill-advised and ill-considered message meant one thing: Those who wrote it were thoroughly frightened men. Perhaps if they and others had given more active support to recruitment efforts earlier in the war, the Army of the Potomac would have been stronger and they would have had fewer worries about their own safety.

In the reckoning that followed the crisis of the invasion Pennsylvanians had little cause either to congratulate themselves or indulge in bitter recriminations for the part they had played. During this time a total of 36,727 men gathered around the state and national emblems. Of the 12,920 who entered the federal service only 5,459 agreed to serve six months; the rest enlisted only for the duration of the emergency. The vast bulk of these troops were not mustered in until after the Army of the Potomac had already forced Lee to retreat, and they became a form of insurance against possible serious reverses to Meade's army. To that extent and for other minor contributions to the success of the campaign they deserved some recognition. This record, however, did not still the critics of Pennsylvania, who were numerous and widespread. They pointed out that but for the prompt cooperation of Governor Horatio Seymour of New York, Couch would have had practically no troops with which to oppose the vanguard of the Confederate army from June 27 to June 29. By then almost all of the 13,500 troops from New York had gotten to Pennsylvania. They were armed, equipped, and ready for field service, and their arrival "brought confidence." When they agreed to enter federal service, even though it was for only thirty days, they set a good example to the local volunteers. New York, however, was the only state in the northeast to send any large number of troops to the threatened area. For various reasons that are not clear few New Jersey men came to the aid of their neighbors. One regiment which made its appearance stayed for only three days. In contrast several independent companies served apparently throughout the emergency.[81]

Critics of Pennsylvania's record also complained loudly of the treatment accorded the soldiers of the Army of the Potomac by people of the state. Of course the experiences of individuals and groups varied; they depended upon who met whom and when. Nevertheless there is no doubt that all too many citizens watched with indifference as the regiments filed past in the sultry heat. Few offered them food or drink, and those who did often demanded excessive payment. In contrast the people of Maryland went out of their way to demonstrate their loyalty to the Union and to welcome the tired and thirsty men of Meade's army as they trudged sturdily toward their rendezvous at Gettysburg.[82]

The emergency also demonstrated that in the realm of high command American leaders, whether national or state officials, showed a remarkable freedom from political dogma in coping with a difficult situation. Their differences over methods of raising troops and their failure to receive overwhelming popular support might be considered another manifestation of the fundamental cleavage between the states rights and national schools of political thought. This explanation seems adequate, but it is a little too glib.

What hampered the political leaders was not a controversy over the nature of the federal union, but a massive reluctance of the people to volunteer for any kind of military service.[83] This revelation was the most disillusioning of all. Contrary to the fears of some Confederate strategists and Southern sympathizers, the invasion of Pennsylvania failed to spur the people of the North to new heights of patriotic devotion and sacrifice.[84] Their response to the challenge was barely adequate and certainly uninspiring.

VII

THE CONFEDERATES PLUNDER
PENNSYLVANIA

WHEN GENERAL Lee crossed the Mason and Dixon Line into Pennsylvania on June 27, 1863, for the first time in his distinguished military career he played the part of the commander of a conquering army. The year before he had entered Maryland as the savior of the state from the oppressor's heel, but in his second venture north of the Potomac he reversed himself and emerged as the bold, proud aggressor. In the general context of his life, however, this role does not become him. Although one of the greatest warriors of all time, he was preeminently a man of honor, iron self-discipline, and deep piety who adhered to a concept of limited war. In contrast to other famous conquerors he believed in crushing the opposing forces only by the most direct and honorable methods, and in sparing women, children, and the aged from unnecessary suffering. This attitude ruled out any attempts to break the will of the enemy by deliberately attacking defenseless civilians. Even to some of his contemporaries such ideas seemed unduly chivalrous and unrealistic; to today's proponents of total warfare they appear wholly quixotic.

The people of Pennsylvania were fortunate that it was Lee and not someone like General Early who led the invaders. Early's concepts of war were perhaps not unlike Lee's, but there was acid in his makeup and he felt impelled to resort to harsh retaliatory measures to repay the hated Yankees for their alleged acts of vandalism. While Lee refrained from a deliberate program of terror, he adopted and carried out policies which gained for the occupying forces legitimate military advantages but at the same time caused hardships among the conquered people. Nevertheless the whole experience for them could have been much worse, and it was a good deal less terrifying than they had imagined it would be. Confederate officers and privates were justly proud of their conduct as invaders, but many of them overstated their case. One was General John B. Gordon who years after the war wrote: "The citizens . . . will bear me out in the assertion that we marched into that delightful region, and then marched out of it, without leaving any scars to mar its beauty or lessen its value." He reluctantly admitted two exceptions: the wholesale appropriation of fence railings for campfires, and the seizure of Pennsylvania horses for transportation purposes.[1] As a Georgian he naturally went to extremes to show the difference between the wide smoky swath of destruction wrought by Sherman's men in their famous march to the sea and the comparatively slight damage done to permanent structures by Lee's army.

In spite of what Gordon and others might say, some scars did remain in the paths taken by the Confederates, and their actions along the way decreased the value of private property, according to conservative estimates, by two and a half million dollars.[2] This damage was largely unintentional, though it was almost bound to occur because in reality Lee's whole army was on a huge raid to get supplies for its immediate and future needs. Since Lee did not know how long he would be able to stay in enemy territory, he had his columns cover as wide an area as possible. He concentrated the bulk of his forces in Franklin and Adams Counties, while detachments ranged through York, Cumberland, Fulton, Bedford, and Somerset Counties. Most of his loot, however, came from an area roughly one hundred miles east and west by forty miles north and south.

Preparatory to the movement of his main forces across the Potomac Lee issued General Orders No. 72 for the twofold purpose of prohibiting damage or destruction of private property and authorizing only certain officers to seize it. The orders gave detailed instructions to the chiefs of the commissary, quartermaster's, ordnance, and medical departments on procedures for acquiring supplies from enemy civil officers and private citizens. Lee empowered them to make requisitions upon "local authorities or inhabitants" and to pay the market price for whatever they took. Should the people in a locality refuse to honor these requisitions or fail to meet their quotas, the chiefs could seize necessary supplies from the nearest inhabitants without payment of cash. In such cases they would give the owners a receipt specifying the kind, amount, and market price of the property taken. The supply officers had the power to use the same procedures with anyone who concealed his property.[3]

Although these regulations were designed to prevent lawless confiscation of property, they naturally gave civilians no real choice in the matter of seizures. Whether articles were for sale or not, Lee's supply officers could force owners to dispose of them at prices they decided were the prevailing ones in the markets. The orders did not indicate which markets, but presumably they referred to the local ones. For compensation the officers were to offer payment in Confederate paper currency, which was greatly depreciated in the South and nearly worthless in the North, or as an alternative, a claim on the Confederate government to be honored in the future. For the farmer or merchant such unprofitable transactions were to be avoided by all means; hence their anxiety to hide their valuables. The only difference between illegal and legal confiscation was that the latter gave civilians the possibility of recovering some of their losses should the Confederacy win the war.

Under the circumstances the citizens of Pennsylvania could not have had a fairer arrangement to compensate them; nevertheless the primary purpose of these regulations was not a humanitarian one. Lee wanted to make sure that seizure of the region's movable wealth was done efficiently and for the benefit of the whole army. He also knew that wanton and indiscriminate pillaging and destruction of property by individual soldiers would break down discipline and reduce the effectiveness of the army. For this reason his general officers cooperated in enforcing his orders, and not because they were kindly disposed toward the inhabitants.[4] Lee's regulations were perhaps designed to encourage the Northern peace movement by inducing respect for Southerners instead of hatred. If so, this objective was never stated, and it appeared to be incidental at best to his real purposes and principles.[5] Lee's primary task was a military one, but if in the process of carrying it out the behavior of his men promoted a political end, so much the better.

Basically the regulations demanded the impossible, since they resulted from certain questionable assumptions in their formulation.

A correspondent of the *Richmond Sentinel* saw some of their inherent difficulties when he said that "the doctrine of not using or destroying some of the private property of an enemy while in his country is a pure abstraction. You cannot possibly introduce an army for one hour into an enemy's country without damaging private property, and in a way often in which compensation cannot be made. . . . Yet if a man takes an onion, or climbs a cherry tree, he is, by this order, to be punished." [6] He might have said also that any large body of men, such as an army on the move, can unintentionally cause great damage. Colonel Alexander recalled that in the march of the First Corps on June 30 from Chambersburg toward Gettysburg rain had made the roads very muddy, so that the infantry seldom used them. Instead they marched in the fields and trampled broad paths in the wheat, which was nearly ripe. It was a clear, hot day, and Alexander, seeing a house with a pump on the front porch, rode up to see if he could get a drink. The "Dutch" owner came forward in a "state of abject despair," for as the Colonel explained, "the infantry ahead of us had not only made a path along the edge of his wheatfield, but in trying to pump their canteens full of water at his well had pumped the well dry, & [made] the porch very wet & very muddy." [7]

Another difficulty was that a literal interpretation of the regulations prohibited the supply chiefs from delegating authority in the matter of seizures. They themselves could not cover an area large enough to secure all they needed, yet when underlings took over the job there were many more opportunities for abuse of power and unwarranted confiscations of property. Such instances occurred.[8]

When General Lee warned his men to be on their good behavior and act as invited guests in an enemy land, he gave them no inkling of the rich and strange country they were about to enter. They had never seen anything like it before. General Pender summed up the feelings of many of them when he wrote: "This is a most magnificent country to look at; but the most miserable people. I have yet to see a nice looking lady. . . . And such barns I never dreamt of. Their dwelling houses are large & comfortable looking . . . but such louts that live in them." [9] Reflecting their own provincialism and the great differences in culture in various parts of the United States, he and other Southerners from all ranks could not get over the fact that women went barefoot, worked in the fields, and did all their own cooking, washing, and household chores. One highly illiterate soldier wrote indignantly to his sister that the girls in "pinsyllvania" were "nothing but Dutch and Irish and the dirty and . . . menest looking creaturs that I ever saw for to call themselves white girls." Besides going barefooted, they wore no bonnets while weeding corn or "picking up wheat." He concluded with the observation that "them is the girls that is writing to their husbands and sweethearts and brothers to fight on and restore the union again and then they will make our Southern girls maids for them and our men butlers for them and then have their large farms and everry thing to suit them and say evry Southern man wil not fight on them terms they ought to be shot on the spot." [10]

Though contemptuous of their Pennsylvania hosts, the Southerners entered the country in a spirit of high adventure and good humor. These feelings acted as a release and helped to counteract the desire to avenge the depredations they claimed the Yankees had committed in their homeland. As was to be expected, the people were often sullen and looked glum and sour, particularly so in Greencastle and Chambersburg where some of them made unfavorable comments on the ragged appearance of the Confederates. Such unfriendly manifestations only amused the soldiers, and as they marched gayly past to the tune of "Dixie" they retorted by reminding their critics of Yankee defeats and inquiring about distances to Philadelphia, Baltimore, and other cities.[11] General Hood's men, who were "a queer lot to look at," answered the taunts of the Chambersburg women with cheers and laughter. A story went the rounds concerning a woman who stood looking defiantly at the Texans as they streamed past the door of her house. She had a huge American flag pinned to her "ample" bosom. One of the men with a straight face called out, "Take care, Madam, for Hood's boys are great at storming breastworks when the Yankee colors is on them." [12]

It was not the defiance of some people which impressed the Confederates so much as the more prevailing attitude of submissiveness. Many Pennsylvanians had conjured up all sorts of horrible thoughts about what the Confederates would do to them. When they found that the invaders did not burn their houses and barns, they willingly cooperated with the requests of polite officers to furnish food, horses, wagons, leather, saddles, and similar articles. One old man more stubborn than most steadfastly refused to surrender his horses.

When the requisitioning party insisted, he grabbed a gun and succeeded in killing five soldiers before they could shoot him.[13] But such occurrences were rare, and for the most part supplies were obtained without incident. One officer said: "It was one of the most amusing sights I ever saw to see the broad-clothed gentry coming in and bringing saddles, bridles, etc., and making a pile of them in the square for use of the Rebels. . . ." [14] Another Southerner wished that his sister could have seen the "Dutch people in York Co. turning out with water and milk and bread and butter and 'apple-butter' for the 'rugged rebels.'" Amused at their naiveté, he observed that the people "generally seemed not to know exactly what to expect and I don't think would have been at all astonished if every building had been set on fire by us as we reached it, nor would a great many have been surprised if we had concluded the business by massacreing the women and children." He went on to tell that he had stopped at a farm near Petersburg in Adams County and almost the first question the daughter of the house asked him was whether the Confederates would molest the women. This same girl, he continued, had said "in all seriousness that she had heard, and believed it, that *the Southern women all wore revolvers.*" [15]

Some of the Confederates were puzzled by mysterious signs which the farmers made with their hands as they marched by. A slick huckster, it seems, had instructed them—for a price—in this hocus-pocus as a way of warding off any evil the invaders might bring them.[16] Less humorous was the refusal of citizens to furnish Union commanders information about Confederate movements out of fear of enemy reprisals. General Buford on his way toward Gettysburg on June 29 snorted with disgust when he learned that he had lost a chance near Fairfield to gobble up two detached Mississippi regiments which the farmers knew about but did not report.[17]

Although the Confederates were pleased that people in the Cumberland Valley, except for a few bushwhackers, offered little open resistance, they noticed certain ways in which they were quietly opposed. When General Gordon tried to put out the fire on the Wrightsville bridge which Union forces had set, he appealed to the residents for buckets and pails. None were to be found. Flames from the burning bridge finally jumped to the lumberyard and then to some buildings, whereupon buckets, tubs, pails, and pans without number suddenly appeared on the scene. They were used by

Southern soldiers who labored far into the night to put out the raging fire which threatened the whole community.[18] The Confederates also found that upon their arrival the valley towns looked deserted; streets were empty, shops remained closed, and people stayed at home. They were very much annoyed to learn that many of the "rascals" had taken the precaution to "run off most of their stock & goods." [19]

But the Southerners really had nothing to complain about, because for the first time in many months they were living off the fat of the land. They had an abundance of everything good to eat: milk, butter, eggs, beef, fresh pork, bacon, chicken, and New Orleans syrup, as they called molasses. General Ewell remarked that if this kept up they would all get fat.[20] In Carlisle General Rodes and some members of his staff found that Pennsylvania lager beer was good but strong. They plied themselves liberally with the brew in honor of a Confederate flag-raising ceremony, with the result that one member of Rodes's staff became incoherent and had to be pulled down twice from the speakers' platform and finally put to bed. Another officer said it was the strongest beer he had ever tasted, and then he added knowingly that it was "probably mixed with whiskey." [21]

What delighted the rebels as much as anything was the chance to buy goods which had long disappeared from the shelves of most stores in the South. Although the merchants in Chambersburg had sent away their more valuable articles, what they had left was to Confederate eyes "something superb." They bought calicoes, bleached cotton, ginghams, woolens, hoops, gloves, thread, china buttons, flavoring essences, and the like, all of which would be greatly appreciated by their wives, sweethearts, and mothers.[22] One officer wrote with feeling: "[Our] army likes this country very well,—and O! what a relief it will be to our country to be rid of our army for some time. I hope we may keep away for some time and so relieve the calls for supplies that have been so long made upon our people." [23]

The Confederate army at first came to Pennsylvania in driblets; the stream broadened, and then came the flood. The initial movement had the appearance of a small and cautious group of ants sent ahead as a task force to make a survey and if conditions proved propitious, to wave the others on. The advance also depended upon what Hooker would do, for Lee hesitated to cross the Potomac until he became convinced that the Union army would not attack him in Virginia. The effects of a piecemeal invasion were to increase the hardships for Pennsylvanians living in the path of the main stream because each contingent made its own demands upon the wealth of the community.

The town hardest hit of all was Chambersburg; it was visited by successive waves of rebels, and finally it became the headquarters for Lee's mighty hosts. Mercersburg too was heavily raided many times, but its economy did not get the full impact of being visited by the main body of the Confederate army.[24] Chambersburg had the additional dubious honor of being the first and most important testing place for Lee's occupation policies in a territory that the Confederates considered completely alien. Their feelings about Maryland were mixed; she was still regarded in 1863, only less so than in 1862, as an erring sister who somehow had become compromised into making an unhappy marriage. If some of the Southerners had hopes of bringing her back into the fold, they had no illusions about Pennsylvania. The people there were going to pay and many times over if possible for their loyalty to the Union.

The first elements to appear in Chambersburg were Jenkins' cavalry. General Jenkins had obviously been properly instructed by Lee, and he set the pattern, if not quite the elevated tone, for Confederate occupation of the town and the surrounding countryside. His first visit was rather a short one, but it was amazing what he accomplished in stripping the people of their first layer of wealth without being unduly offensive about it. Arriving late on the night of June 15, he disposed his forces four miles north of town, on a hill which commanded the approaches in that direction. The next morning while some detachments scoured the country for supplies and horses, Jenkins and his staff rode into Chambersburg and set up headquarters at the Montgomery House. One of his first acts was to order private citizens to surrender all arms in their possession within two hours; otherwise their homes would be searched and plundered. Enough of the citizens obeyed the order to satisfy the general's demand. The next day he ordered all stores and shops to be opened for two hours to enable his men to purchase articles they personally needed. He insisted that the soldiers pay for what they got but was not particular about what they used for money. As a result the men offered not only Confederate currency but worthless "shin-plasters" issued by the city of Richmond and other Southern corporations. Although the accounts are not entirely clear, Jenkins apparently forced the people to feed his troops. He also requisitioned goods from storekeepers, especially drugs, for which he paid generously in Confederate money. The merchants appreciated the fact that he did not stop to haggle but told them to guess at the value of the goods taken.[25] Reports that a large force of Yankees was coming suddenly interrupted this thriving business, and the Confederates took to their horses. Before leaving, Jenkins' rear guard for some reason set fire to a large warehouse on the north side of town, but the citizens speedily put out the blaze. The attempt to burn this building and the destruction of the Scotland railroad bridge were the only acts of vandalism committed in town at this time.[26]

More reprehensible than any destruction of property was the search for Negroes by Jenkins and other semi-independent cavalry commands. Any that were found were seized and sent South into slavery. The Confederates carried on this practice in many sections of the state, but particularly around Mercersburg where they took free Negroes who had been born and raised in Pennsylvania. Jenkins captured "quite a number" and started them South. Fortunately many escaped, and one group was released by some people in Greencastle after capturing their guards. According to one account, at least fifty Negroes were sent into slavery in this way. Under no circumstances could the Confederates justify the hunt on grounds of military necessity. Even members of the high command were not above engaging in this practice. Longstreet instructed Pickett, who was in Chambersburg, to bring along the "captured contrabands" (a military term for Negroes) when his division rejoined the First Corps on the road to Gettysburg.[27]

Jenkins' withdrawal on June 17 gave Chambersburg a slight respite, but the rest of lower Franklin County and parts of Fulton and Adams Counties were not so fortunate. Retiring to the vicinity of Greencastle for the next five days, Jenkins continued the practice of sending out detachments from his main body to raid the countryside and the communities of Greencastle, Waynesboro, Welsh Run, and Fairfield. About two hundred of his men under Colonel M. J. Ferguson went to Mercersburg on their way to Cove Mountain and McConnellsburg. They were a fierce and hard-bitten lot of warriors who rode with pointed pistols and drawn sabers, looking and hoping for trouble. During the week of his operations in this part of Pennsylvania Jenkins succeeded in taking from farmers large numbers of horses and cattle without compensation. Before his arrival many had sent their horses, flocks, and herds to the mountains or across the Susquehanna; otherwise their losses would have been heavier. Taking every road and byway, the Confederates were very adept at ferreting out livestock and horses hidden in obscure corners of the farm or some valley not too deep in the mountains. Jenkins turned the results of his searches over to General Rodes at Williamsport and later at Hagerstown. The value of the property he took on this extensive raid was estimated to have been between $100,000 and $250,000. The direct financial loss in the seizure of valuable horses and stock was compounded by its timing. With the harvest season just days away farmers deprived of their draft animals faced the ruin of their crops for want of the means to reap them. Some of them whose wealth consisted entirely of livestock went bankrupt.[28]

By June 22 the raid had ended, after the various detachments reported to the main body of Jenkins' cavalry then stationed between Greencastle and Hagerstown. On that day Rodes's division of infantry moved up to join Jenkins and begin the real invasion of Pennsylvania.[29] His division on June 19 had started to march from Williamsport toward Hagerstown, when he received instructions to head in the direction of Boonsboro, as if he were threatening Harpers Ferry. He stayed two miles outside of Hagerstown for two days waiting for General Edward Johnson to cross the Potomac. On June 22 he resumed his march, and the head of his column reached Greencastle by midmorning.[30]

With the appearance of Rodes's infantry Jenkins sent a scouting force on the road to Chambersburg. On their way they met Captain William H. Boyd's company of the 1st New York Cavalry, which after escorting Milroy's supply train safely to Harrisburg had returned to the valley to watch the enemy advance. Boyd, a bold and dashing leader, immediately attacked the Confederate detachment and pushed it back to within a mile of Greencastle, where Jenkins, slightly forewarned, had hastily established a battle line. Boyd prudently withdrew before this display of force, but not before a fusillade had caused two Union casualties, one killed and one wounded. In the meantime a force of raw Pennsylvania and New

York militia had been sent to Chambersburg under Brigadier General Joseph F. Knipe, a veteran who was still recovering from a wound received at Chancellorsville. When they heard of Rodes's approach, they hastily boarded a train for Harrisburg, thus abandoning the lower valley to the Confederates.[31]

Immediately upon his arrival in Greencastle Rodes appointed Colonel Edward Willis, of the 12th Georgia regiment, provost marshal and gave him a detachment of men to maintain order in the town. In so doing Rodes was carrying out general orders which Ewell had issued that day; they officially proclaimed the policies of his corps while occupying enemy territory. Ewell had anticipated Lee in this matter, but his purposes were no different from those of his commander. Although not so detailed and specific, in essence his orders were the same as Lee's.[32]

After getting his division comfortably ensconced in Greencastle, Rodes retraced his steps to Beaver Creek, located between Boonsboro and Hagerstown, to consult with Ewell and Early. By this time all three of Ewell's divisions were moving toward Chambersburg. Johnson had been at Sharpsburg and was behind Rodes near Greencastle. Early, having crossed the Potomac at Shepherdstown on June 22, had marched to a point three miles beyond Boonsboro on the Hagerstown road. After the conference Ewell accompanied Rodes to Greencastle and from there to Chambersburg. Before leaving Greencastle Rodes's officers made heavy demands upon the people for fresh vegetables and sauerkraut, an item which the Southerners thought the "Dutch" would have in great supply even in summer. Their requisitions for durable goods such as saddles and bridles, pistols, lead, and leather were so excessive that the town council made no attempt to meet them. Being reasonable, the Confederates took what they could get without causing trouble.

Jenkins' cavalry arrived in Chambersburg one day ahead of Rodes's division. Jenkins' chief of staff, a Captain Fitzhugh, promptly ordered the people to furnish large amounts of provisions for his command which were to be brought to the front of the court house by a specified time. Should they refuse, he would institute a general search of the houses for food. The next morning, June 24, at nine o'clock Rodes's division, preceded by a band playing "The Bonnie Blue Flag," appeared on the brow of the hill near the Reformed Church. It was the beginning of a long and impressive column of infantry and artillery, accompanied by immense wagon trains, droves of cattle, and ambulances, which took all day to pass through the streets to a strong position on Shirk's Hill north of town.

Preparing for an extended sojourn, Ewell took several important steps to provide for the comfort and safety of his troops. Colonel Willis again acted as provost marshal and established headquarters in the court house. Following Ewell's orders, he set up a hospital in the public school and equipped it with mattresses and bed clothing obtained from several hotels. One measure which Ewell adopted perhaps benefited the town as much as the army. He prohibited the sale of intoxicating liquors without his permission and ordered a declaration of possession from everyone so that guards could be placed over all supplies against the thirst of the soldiers. Next he called a meeting of the businessmen to place before them requisitions for enormous quantities of clothing, harness, horseshoes, lead, rope, leather, Neat's foot oil, grain, bread, salt, molasses, flour, beans, sauerkraut, potatoes, coffee, sugar, and many other things. It was an impossible demand, for many businessmen in fleeing from town had taken much of their movable property with them. Those who stayed behind had sent away large quantities of goods after Jenkins' first visit to Chambersburg on June 17. As a result the boots, hats, and other articles of apparel which Rodes expected to find for his men were to his annoyance not available. Nevertheless the Confederates did obtain large amounts of other goods they needed, for which they paid in their own money.[33]

General Johnson, on his way to join Ewell and Rodes in Chambersburg, on June 23 ordered Brigadier General George H. Steuart to leave the main column at Greencastle and take his infantry brigade of about 2,500 men, some three hundred cavalry, and a battery of six guns on a huge horse and cattle raid to Mercersburg and McConnellsburg. Upon his arrival in Mercersburg the next day Steuart called a meeting of the few leading citizens who had remained in town and read them Lee's proclamation about the treatment of property. He then ordered the merchants to open their stores to his men so they could buy what goods were left with Confederate money. There was no pillaging, and no one was hurt. Upon the whole the people were "thankful that they behaved no worse," but it was the third and most formidable visitation of the invaders within less than a week, and more were to come. The community had begun to feel pinched for food; no fresh meat was available, scarcely any flour or groceries, and no wood. The harvest was ripe for cutting, but there was no one to cut it. The loss to farmers in hay and grain which rotted in the fields was "incalculable." [34] Steuart went on to McConnellsburg and rejoined his division at Carlisle, bringing with him only a fair haul of horses, cattle, and supplies.[35]

By sending Steuart to Mercersburg and McConnellsburg Ewell had broadened the front of his advance by twenty or so miles. He widened it even more by ordering all of Early's division east over South Mountain as far as York; one brigade was directed to march even farther, to Wrightsville on the Susquehanna River. York is fifty-two miles from Chambersburg by way of the main road through Gettysburg, and Wrightsville is another eleven miles beyond. In sending Early so far east Ewell temporarily created a wide gap between Early's division and the forces in Chambersburg; but there was little danger in the move since no units of the Army of the Potomac had as yet made an appearance. Furthermore, as Ewell moved down the valley toward Carlisle and Harrisburg, he took a northeasterly direction which drew him closer to Early.

While Rodes's and Johnson's divisions were moving on June 23 toward Chambersburg through Greencastle and Marion, Early was taking a parallel route eight to ten miles east, hugging the western face of South Mountain. Starting from a point three miles northeast of Boonsboro, in two days he went some thirty miles directly north through Cavetown, Smithsburg, Ringgold, Waynesboro, Quincy, and Altodale to Greenwood, which is on the turnpike between Chambersburg and Gettysburg.[36] On June 25 while his division gathered supplies from the farmers in the area, Early rode over to Chambersburg to visit with Ewell, who instructed him to march to York by way of Gettysburg. Possibly as a way of isolating Harrisburg from Federal forces to the south, he was directed to cut the Northern Central Railroad connecting Baltimore with Harrisburg and destroy the Wrightsville-Columbia bridge across the Susquehanna, after which he would take the road through Dillsburg and rejoin Ewell at Carlisle.[37]

In preparing for this expedition Early stripped his column of unnecessary encumbrances and sent all his trains to Chambersburg except ambulances and a few medical, ordnance, and general utility wagons. He also took care to include fifteen empty wagons to carry supplies which he planned to garner along the way from civilians. For escort he had Colonel William H. French's 17th Virginia Cavalry from Jenkins' brigade and Colonel E. V. White's 35th Virginia Cavalry Battalion of General "Grumble" Jones's brigade.[38]

On his way over the mountain on the morning of June 26 Early stopped long enough to put to the torch all the buildings of the Caledonia Iron Works, an enterprise which belonged to Congressman Thaddeus H. Stevens, the famous Radical Republican. In this action Early revealed himself as a headstrong and independent leader who had the temerity to defy orders whenever he thought fit. He justified his act on two grounds: retaliation for the "various deeds of barbarity perpetrated by Federal troops in some of the southern states," and repayment to Stevens for "a most vindictive spirit toward the people of the South."[39] Though the works had recently been profitable for the first time since their founding in 1837 and represented an investment of $65,000, Stevens took their destruction philosophically, saying that everyone must expect to suffer from this war. Perhaps the heaviest burden of loss fell on the more than two hundred workers whose means of livelihood were destroyed. Early's men and other Confederates at different times during the campaign ran off with forty horses and mules belonging to Stevens at Caledonia, seized about $10,000 worth of provisions and goods from the company stores, as well as large quantities of corn and grain in the mills, hauled away his bar iron valued at $4,000, destroyed all his fence rails, used up eighty tons of grass, and finally broke the windows of the houses of the workingmen. In an ironical vein Stevens commended them for doing such a thorough job in cleaning him out. In view of Lee's occupation policies so clearly spelled out in General Orders No. 72, Early's conduct in burning the furnace, saw mill, two forges, and a rolling mill at Caledonia was rank insubordination.[40]

After this auspicious beginning Early continued his march to Gettysburg. Learning of the presence of an enemy force of indeterminate size near the town, he decided to split his division into two wings at a fork in the road about a mile and a half from Cashtown. He sent Gordon's brigade and White's battalion on the main pike, and with the rest of his command he himself took the road to the left through Hilltown to Mummasburg. His purpose was to threaten the enemy's flank and rear, while Gordon kept him busy on his front.

At Mummasburg Early discovered that Gordon and White had encountered the 26th Pennsylvania Militia numbering about 750 officers and men. They had just been mustered into the United States service four days earlier and were a splendid looking outfit, clothed, equipped, and armed according to regulations. The trouble was they had had no training and were "raw and undisciplined." Their commander, Colonel William W. Jennings, a friend of Governor Curtin and the manager of a factory at Harrisburg, evidently had had no previous military experience. One of his men later confessed that as a private he was so green he did not even know how to affix a bayonet to a gun. Undoubtedly others were just as ignorant. They had arrived in Gettysburg the night before and started out on the pike in the morning for the purpose of occupying Cashtown Gap. About three miles out of Gettysburg they saw Gordon's and White's men. One glance was enough, and they were off in the opposite direction.[41] In his report Early cackled: "It was well that the regiment took to its heels so quickly, or some of its members might have been hurt, and all would have been captured." [42] He was right. Their retreat amounted to a rout, and there was utter confusion. As one member of the group described it: "The officers were running around waving their swords, shouting and swearing, but no one dreamed of obeying them; the men . . . were separated from their companies, and each fellow did as he thought proper. . . . The commands from half crazy Captains and Lieutenants were often unintelligible, and perfectly contradictory. . . . Some [men] were falling in behind the fences, and others streaking off over the fields." [43] If they could not do anything else, they could run fast enough to escape Early's trap. He claimed to have taken 175 prisoners, only to parole them the next day.[44] The affair affords another example of how the myth of the untrained minuteman rushing to the defense of his hearth and hurling back the invader can become a cruel joke.

Upon his arrival in Gettysburg Early requisitioned from the town fathers large amounts of provisions, 1,000 pairs of shoes, and 500 hats, or as an alternative $10,000 in cash. The authorities, pleading poverty and an inability to meet any of his demands, agreed to request merchants to open their stores and citizens to furnish provisions. Early searched the shops and found very few supplies for his commissary, but he did succeed in practically stripping the community of the horseshoes and nails usually kept on hand. Convinced of the town's inability to meet his demands and pressed for time, he did not try to force compliance. Some of his men robbed a few houses and took some articles that Gettysburg merchants had not sent away to Philadelphia.[45] The officers issued rations of liquor found in taverns and warehouses,[46] with the result that all of Brigadier General Harry T. Hays's brigade got drunk. One writer said, "I never saw such a set in my life." [47] Early discovered about 2,000 food rations in a train of ten or twelve cars and after distributing them to Gordon's brigade proceeded to burn the cars and a small railroad bridge nearby. On the whole the "pickings" were pretty slim in Gettysburg.[48]

The next day, June 27, Early's division marched at a deliberate pace toward York, twenty-seven miles away. Gordon took the main road to the town, while Early marched on a parallel route to the north.[49] He sent White on a special assignment to wreck the Northern Central Railroad from south of Hanover Junction to York, a distance of ten miles.[50] Since Early and Gordon were somewhat uncertain as to whether or not Union forces were in York in large numbers, they halted and camped for the night a few miles away. While making their plans for the next day a deputation from York led by the burgess appeared at Gordon's camp and surrendered the town, in the hope of obtaining special protection for their private property.

The 28th was the beginning of a busy and momentous two days for Early and his command. Colonel French with his cavalry rode to the mouth of the Conewago Creek to burn two railroad bridges at that point and all others between there and York, while the rest of Early's men with Gordon leading the way gradually moved into York. Early himself joined Gordon in town and ignoring the surrender, immediately requisitioned large numbers of hats, shoes, and socks, enough supplies to last his division for three days, and $100,000 in cash. If the people complied he promised to protect private property; otherwise he would turn his men loose and allow them to sack the town. A committee of citizens appointed to obtain the articles and raise the money met all of Early's demands except those for shoes and cash. Instead of 2,000 pairs of shoes they could give him only 1,500, and of the $100,000 demanded they could turn over but $28,600. Convinced of their inability to get more money because the banks had sent their funds away for safekeeping, Early expressed his satisfaction with their efforts and considered the requisition as having been met. The shoes, hats, and socks were issued to the men, who stood very much in need of them. The commissary general used part of the money to buy beef cattle, because farmers he found were far more willing to part with their goods in exchange for United States paper money than Confederate receipts of purchase. The remainder of the money Early turned over to the quartermaster general of the army.[51] In return for their compliance with most of his demands Early kept his word and respected private property. Nothing belonging to any citizen in town was touched, and guards protected hotels, stores, and other important buildings in the community against plunder. Upon request many stores opened to give soldiers and officers a chance to buy goods with Confederate money. People came and went freely within the limits of the town, but they had to get military passes should they want to go into the country. The farmers in the area did not fare so well as their neighbors in York, however, for Early's promises about private property did not include them. He made no effort to prevent his troops from visiting farms and taking horses and mules, as well as various kinds of food. Though some farmers received payment in United States money, probably greenbacks, and others saved droves of livestock by sending them across the river, nevertheless many unhappily reported heavy losses.[52]

Early had other important objectives in mind besides levying a tribute on York. Here again he showed his disposition to follow his own concepts of strategy without authority to do so. He ordered Gordon to take his brigade and some cavalry to Wrightsville to seize and hold the bridge across the Susquehanna, instead of burning it as Ewell had instructed. He had perceived the defenseless nature of the country and the feeble opposition offered by the militia, and he had therefore decided that there would be little risk and many advantages should he take the bridge intact. He would then cross the river with his whole division, cut the Pennsylvania Central Railroad, march upon Lancaster, exact a heavy requisition there, and attack Harrisburg in the rear while the rest of Ewell's corps would threaten it from the front. Should he run into unforeseen obstacles, he would corral the immense number of horses that had been driven across the river and mount all his men. Although he did not say how, in some manner he would then recross to the west bank, destroying the railroad and canals on the way. It was a boldly conceived scheme which held promise of rich rewards for Confederate arms; and it could very well have succeeded without endangering the rest of Lee's army, had it not been for the rapid advance of Federal forces into Pennsylvania. But Early's dreams of conquest went up with the smoke of the burning bridge, for the river at that point was too wide and deep to be forded.[53]

Whatever may have been the reasons for Gordon's failure to capture the bridge before its destruction, Early in no way blamed him. The forces guarding the western approaches to the bridge numbered around 1,000, mostly untrained and untested militia who, although they were entrenched, had no artillery support. They were opposed by Gordon's veterans who were greater in number and who had artillery. The amount of resistance which the militia offered was later a subject of dispute,[54] but Early, who was given to the use of hyperbole, claimed that because Gordon's men had marched "a little over 20 miles, on a very warm day, the enemy beat him running." [55] Whatever their shortcomings as warriors, the militia gave Colonel Frick enough time to set such a large fire on the wooden structure that hundreds of Confederates could not put it out. When the blaze got out of control and spread to Wrightsville, to their everlasting credit Gordon's men worked feverishly and succeeded in saving the town from total ruin.[56]

Early confined his deliberate destruction of private property to railroads. His cavalry did an efficient job of burning bridges, railroad cars, and depots on the Northern Central Railroad from Hanover Junction almost to Harrisburg, while Gordon did similar work on the line running between Wrightsville and York. For reasons not entirely clear Early refrained from burning the railroad buildings and two railroad car manufacturing plants in York. When he left there on June 30 the physical appearance of the town was unaltered except for charred remains of railroad cars, torn up sections of track, and broken switches.[57] Another reminder of his visitation was the presence of some stragglers, the debris of every Civil War army, who purposely stayed behind or were too drunk to go with their commands.[58]

Before Early began his junket to York, Ewell had already started the movement of the rest of his corps toward Carlisle. General

Junius Daniel's brigade of Rodes's division got on the road about 1:00 A.M. on June 25, and four hours later it arrived at Shippensburg to reinforce Jenkins, who again had visions of an enemy attack. The next day the other brigades of the division joined Daniel, and the whole division reached Carlisle on June 27.[59] Most of Johnson's division kept up with Rodes and arrived at Carlisle on the same day.[60] Feeling fit and confident, Ewell's men marched jauntily into town singing "Dixie" at the top of their lungs. At Shippensburg and Carlisle Ewell made out requisitions for the people to fill. In Carlisle he obtained $50,000 worth of medicines, and provisions in sufficient quantities to feed the two divisions, as well as to send large amounts back to Virginia. He also fell heir to large quantities of food, uniforms, arms, saddles, bridles, and articles of every description which Couch's men had left behind. Ewell's troops, who were under strict orders to leave private dwellings untouched, nevertheless stripped the stores. They treated the civilians, especially the ladies, with great courtesy and politeness.[61] On Sunday, June 28, Ewell sent word to the clergy to hold services as usual, for no one would disturb them. Some of the churches opened, and the "preachers, though nervous, prayed for their country in peril and their friends in danger;—they also prayed for the strangers that were among them; some of them prayed for peace." [62] The Confederates took exceptional care of the campus of Dickinson College, since a few of them said they or their fathers had graduated there.[63] Even more surprising was the fact that Ewell, out of respect for the wishes of his commander, did not burn the Carlisle barracks of the United States Army, which normally would have been marked for destruction. He even went so far as to stop the looting of abandoned army buildings by a mob of civilians.[64]

As usual the farmers suffered most from the exactions which the rebels levied upon the country around Carlisle. There were instances where Ewell's men paid the farmers in gold, but ordinarily they offered Confederate scrip. Some of the shrewder farmers got rid of part of this money by selling it to Yankee militia as mementos at the extraordinarily high rate of one United States dollar for two Confederate ones. Occasionally a farmer was so badly stripped of provisions by the forced purchases of Southerners that he had nothing left for his family.[65]

Ewell, who did not believe in "houseburning or anything of that sort," [66] was thorough in his destruction of railroads. In the area of Carlisle he broke down a bridge and a six-hundred-foot trestle of the Cumberland Valley Railroad; he warped the rails by heating them in the fire of burning ties; and he chopped down the poles and cut the wire of the telegraph line. The work of demolition for twenty-eight miles from Scotland, Pennsylvania, to Hagerstown, Maryland, was so complete that the company hesitated about incurring the cost of rebuilding the line even as far as Chambersburg.[67] What railroad property Ewell neglected to destroy in Chambersburg General Pickett effectively demolished a few days later.[68] Thus as one of the chief lieutenants of Lee, Ewell faithfully executed his commander's occupation policies, keeping true to the spirit as well as the letter of his instructions.

General A. P. Hill's men with the division of General Henry Heth in the lead entered Chambersburg on the morning of June 26, at almost the same time that Rodes's and Johnson's divisions were leaving it to march north on the Harrisburg road. Instead of going to the old camping ground of Ewell's corps on the north end of town, Hill's divisions one by one turned east in the diamond, or public square, tramped out on the Gettysburg Pike, and stopped near Fayetteville. Longstreet's corps was almost a day's march behind Hill. Most of his men camped on the night of June 26 about four miles south of Greencastle, and next day marched to within a few miles of Chambersburg. On the 29th Longstreet's corps, except Pickett's division which remained behind to hold the town, moved out to Greenwood on the Gettysburg Pike. Lee had preceded them, accompanying Hill's corps to the eastern edge of Chambersburg where he set up headquarters in Messersmith's Woods. Here he stayed for four days, until Tuesday morning, June 30.[69]

Lee maintained tight control over the activities of his troops in the town. He placed sentries at the homes of all leading citizens and allowed no one to take up quarters in town or visit it without a permit from him. The residents felt free to come to him with complaints of wrongdoing. In some instances they trumped up charges as an excuse to visit headquarters and catch a glimpse of the great Lee or Longstreet.[70] As a precaution against outbreaks of disorder on the part of his troops Lee had his men empty barrels of whiskey and bottles of rum and brandy into the streets, after the army doctors had first replenished their stocks for medicinal purposes. A

German officer, a guest of the army, made the amazing statement that Lee had ordered this destruction "since the entire *army had voluntarily abjured spirituous alcohol. . . .*" [71] If so, it was one of the most astounding conversions to the cold-water brigade in history!

On June 27 Lee issued General Orders No. 73, congratulating his men upon their general good behavior and urging them to continue it. In this document he reiterated his adherence to a doctrine of war upon armed men only, and denounced "barbarous outrages upon the unarmed and defenceless, and the wanton destruction of private property, that have marked the course of the enemy in our own country." [72]

With Lee near at hand to supervise affairs, the gathering of supplies in Chambersburg proceeded in the orderly but determined fashion he had prescribed. Because officials of the borough had skipped town and were not available to meet requisitions against the people, the rebels forcibly entered stores and warehouses to seize goods, for which they later paid with Confederate money. In spite of these draconian measures the haul was not rich, for most supplies had been taken by the vanguard of Lee's army. By this time there was no longer enough food in town for all the people. When a prominent and courageous woman, Mrs. Ellen McLellan, told Lee of the needy condition of many families in Chambersburg, he agreed to furnish them with some flour.[73] Apparently other women successfully appealed to the gallantry of Confederate officers and saved their supplies from seizure. Though the levies of a huge army on a borough the size of Chambersburg caused severe financial hardship and inconvenience, prominent Union leaders privately admitted that there was no physical suffering and "little damage beyond the stealing," as they put it.[74]

During Lee's occupation of Chambersburg General Imboden and his command appeared on June 29 at Mercersburg, having come from Cumberland and Hancock, Maryland. They represented the fifth and in some respects the harshest visitation of the rebels to this community. They cleaned out all the surrounding farm houses and discovered most of the hiding places of the horses in the mountains, rounding up at least 400 of them. The next day Imboden demanded of the town 5,000 pounds of bacon, 35 barrels of flour, and quantities of shoes, hats, and other articles of clothing to be furnished by

11:00 A.M. Failure to meet the requisition, he threatened, would result in having his soldiers quartered in private homes. The penalty was not imposed because the citizens met most of his demands for provisions, for which he gave them a worthless "sort of receipt." Imboden frankly expressed regret at his lack of authority to burn every town and lay waste every farm in Pennsylvania. He justified his harsh manner toward the people and his desire to wreak destruction as retaliation for Yankee depredations.[75]

This systematic and thorough levy on the wealth of the invaded areas permitted the Army of Northern Virginia to live well off the country, to clothe itself in better fashion, and to improve its means of transportation. The big disappointment was the failure to get replacements for worn-out cavalry mounts. According to one disgusted Confederate, the horses from Pennsylvania proved "utterly unserviceable, and seemingly have as little taste or talent for war as their fat dutch proprietors."[76] It is impossible to determine, however, how much surplus in raw materials, finished goods, drugs, provisions, vehicles, and draft horses Lee was able to accumulate for the future needs of the army. Official reports of the campaign give the impression that he was quite successful in this respect, but neither he nor anyone else offered overall figures. Ewell reported his corps as having collected 3,000 head of cattle, which were sent to the rear. He also said that at Chambersburg he loaded a wagon train with ordnance and medical stores for shipment presumably to Virginia, but he gave no idea of the size of the train. General Rodes vaguely mentioned large quantities of articles suitable for government use which he had obtained in Williamsport, Hagerstown, Chambersburg, and elsewhere. As for horses, he complained that almost all of them were seized by Jenkins' cavalry and were "rarely accounted for."[77] One foreign observer accompanying the army noted that beyond Williamsport the road was crowded with wagons, horses, and droves of cattle and sheep going south from Pennsylvania. He was amazed by the wagons and referred to them as of the "most extraordinary size, drawn by six or eight horses."[78] Another foreign observer noted in his diary on June 27 that Ewell had already sent back "great quantities of horses, mules, wagons, beefs, and other necessaries;—he is now at or beyond Carlisle, laying the country under contribution, and making Pennsylvania support the war, instead of poor, used-up and worn-out Virginia." Immediately after the battle on July 4 the same writer said that the booty in wagons and on the hoof made a train "so interminable" that it was winding its way along the Fairfield road all day, and for this reason he doubted whether the army could start its retreat till late at night.[79]

The most definite and impressive figures about booty, however, were given by a soldier of Gordon's brigade in his recollections written many years after the war. At a big horseshoe bend in the Shenandoah River near Mount Jackson, Virginia, he remembered having seen the two or three thousand acres of bottomland filled with cattle and sheep. Upon inquiry one of the herdsmen told him that approximately 26,000 head of cattle and 22,000 head of sheep taken in Maryland and Pennsylvania were gathered there.[80] These numbers may read like the exaggerations of an old soldier's yarn; yet a remark made soon after the battle by a Confederate surgeon seems to substantiate them. He wrote: "We gathered up thousands of beeves in Pennsylvania—enough to feed our army until cold weather." [81]

Judging by all this evidence it would appear that the regulations in General Orders No. 72 as interpreted by Lee's subordinates facilitated rather than obstructed the efficient collection of supplies, for they reduced the amount of indiscriminate seizures by unauthorized personnel. Because it was based upon orderly procedure rather than arbitrary acts, the confiscation of private property may have been less shocking to the victims, but the losses were just as real. To Greenwalt S. Barr, a miller of Franklin County, the visits of some Confederate officers meant that between June 24 and July 1 the following items were taken from his mill: 1,100 bushels of wheat, 400 bushels of "mills stuff," 175 empty flour barrels, 100 bushels of corn, 100 bushels of oats, and 391 barrels of flour. After that clean sweep it is possible that Barr had nothing left with which to face his creditors and avoid bankruptcy. Another miller, Jacob Hargbroad, who was also a distiller, suffered even greater loss. He owned two mills and two warehouses, from which the Southerners took large quantities of flour, shelled corn, rye, and oats. They also poured into the gutters 3,010 gallons of his whiskey. An example of what happened to retailers was given by Eyster and Brothers, who ran a big dry goods and grocery store in Chambersburg. They claimed to have made "compulsory sales" of dry goods to different units of

Lee's army as they appeared in town, for which they received $6,300 in Confederate money. They sold this currency for $320, about five cents on the dollar. The rebels, they said, also "stole" $1,200 worth of goods. Deducting the amount of United States money which they obtained in exchange for Confederate, their total loss was almost $7,200. Among the farmers a typical experience was that of Christian Bitner, whose farm in Franklin County stood directly in the path of the invaders. He reported that they took from him nineteen horses, two cows, a heifer and a bull, as well as quantities of food, ten tons of straw, harnesses, and tools of all kinds. While camping on his property the Confederates also used 12,550 of his fence rails for firewood, tent poles, and other purposes. They in addition cut down 379 trees and saplings which would take years to replace.[82]

There is still the question of how effective were Lee's regulations in controlling the conduct of the Confederate soldier. For most men the command to avoid bullying and vandalism by a general as revered and respected as Lee was enough to discourage misbehavior. In spite of his efforts, however, some soldiers did go off limits and commit depredations. Even Lee admitted derelictions from good behavior when in General Orders No. 73 he observed euphemistically that there had been "instances of forgetfulness." [83] This reproof, though unduly mild, showed that a soldier, whether his uniform were blue or gray, was more impressed by stern discipline than exhortations. And strict control was not always possible.

Confederate officers policed the activities of their men effectively in town, but not so well in the country. The infantry, easier to restrain than the cavalry, were "kept close in ranks and marched slowly," and when camped near a town they could not get in without a pass. On the march the cavalry kept in front and on the flanks and thus had better opportunities for plunder of property and seizure of horses.[84] Some of the troopers travelled in small detachments, scouring the byways and back roads and visiting isolated farms,[85] while bands of independent and irregular horsemen rode through the country "taking what they wanted and wantonly destroying a good deal." [86]

The worst malefactor, a disgrace to his uniform and flag and destroyer of his army's reputation, was the so-called straggler. A better name for him was skulker or bummer because often there were legitimate stragglers, soldiers who because of illness or exhaustion had to "fall out" during a long hard march. After a rest they would try to catch up with their commands as soon as possible. The skulker on the other hand never kept up with his comrades if he could avoid it. He was a professional shirker and troublemaker who represented the scum of both Civil War armies. In the Gettysburg campaign skulkers spread like a blight over the Maryland and Pennsylvania countryside. Although the majority wore the blue uniform, the Confederate gray was also much in evidence, in spite of better discipline in Lee's army.[87]

The offenses of the rebel soldier as a rule were committed against property rather than persons. In the vast literature of the campaign not once has a case of rape been mentioned. Other acts of violence against persons were rare, although one or two cases of murder did occur.[88] Petty theft was widespread, and reports of it came from every corner of the invaded area. Observers noted that as the Confederates marched along roads lined with cherry trees they could not resist stripping them of their ripened fruit, but in this respect they were no worse than the Union troops.[89] The Southern soldier was very adept, when an officer's back was turned, at forcing an exchange of hats with a surprised native. At times he even got a better pair of boots that way.[90]

Such incidents were more annoying than harmful, but horse stealing in those days was a serious crime. Colonel James A. L. Fremantle, an observer from the British army, for all his bias in favor of the South admitted that the "Confederate soldier, in spite of his many virtues, is as a rule, the most incorrigible horse stealer in the world." [91] Writing confidentially in their letters or diaries and later in memoirs, Southerners mentioned not only thefts of horses, but of other kinds of property as well. In looking for food and fuel privates often ignored Lee's orders and took fence rails, whiskey, chickens, and other kinds of supplies in large quantities.[92] One soldier noted in his diary that nearly half the men in his regiment were out foraging, and they could get almost anything at their own prices.[93] And General Pender observed: "Until we crossed the Md. line our men behaved as well as troops could but here [in Pennsylvania] it will be hard to restrain them for they have an idea that they are to indulge in unlicensed plunder." [94] Considering the great scarcity of the necessities of life in the Confederacy, such depredations by hungry,

177

footsore soldiers were understandable. Less justifiable were forced sales of goods in stores without any pretense of payment, as well as the appropriation from private dwellings of household furnishings, clothing for men, women, and children, cooking utensils, tableware, watches and jewelry, cash, and last but not least, sleigh bells.[95] A chaplain of a North Carolina regiment learned to his sorrow that the men "committed many depredations yesterday afternoon and last night, going to houses and taking whatever they could lay their hands upon." [96] Later a Yankee bugler charged that "large quantities of greenbacks and gold and silver were found on the bodies of Rebs after the fight, gold and silver watches, etc." [97]

The amount of vandalism and robbery seemed to increase as the campaign progressed, especially during the heat of battle and the confusion of retreat when Confederate officers were preoccupied with more pressing duties than the protection of civilian belongings. Some of the farmers who lived on or near the battlefield suffered great losses. There were instances where houses and barns were wantonly burned, although there was no military reason for their destruction.[98] Property left vacant and unprotected by terror-stricken owners fleeing before the invaders was often thoroughly ransacked. The more stouthearted citizens who stayed at home usually stood to lose only a part of their property in forced sales.[99]

Although many a rebel plundered and stole with great efficiency, the army as a whole never got out of hand. Most Southern soldiers would have liked to have indulged themselves at the expense of their rich and hated enemy, but nevertheless they exercised restraint out of respect for their commander and the code of the times. Products of a more romantic age with its antiquated notions of chivalry and Christian ethics, General Lee, as well as most other Confederate and Union commanders, waged an old-fashioned kind of war with none of the refinements of the twentieth century: indiscriminate use of the torch, rape, mass murder, holding of hostages, and employment of fifth columns and Quislings. Yet the Confederate invasion left its mark. It was "heartrending" to observers to visit Pennsylvania at the end of the campaign, and they were appalled by the scenes of desolation that marked the footsteps of the armies: fences destroyed, ripe grain trodden and ground into the rain-soaked soil, no signs of life except for an occasional dilapidated wagon creeping along cautiously or a little caravan of refugees on its way home.[100] Considering the accusations Southerners constantly hurled at Yankee "vandals," it was ironic that soldiers of the Army of the Potomac in their turn "felt inclined to retaliate [for] the losses of Pennsylvania"; [101] the rebels, they said, had acted like a "set of demons . . . destroying and stealing property whenever they could lay their hands upon it. . . ." [102] Because of the North's greater wealth and more efficient transportation facilities the Army of the Potomac had not made it a practice to live off occupied territory, so that a systematic and thorough stripping of an area's resources to support an army was a strange and horrifying experience to the Union soldier. His unsophisticated mind could see little if any difference between legal seizure of goods by duly constituted military authorities, who paid for their confiscations with worthless money, and brazen theft with no pretense of legality. For that matter, neither could the storekeepers and farmers in Pennsylvania.

Favorable comment on the humaneness of General Lee should not obscure the fact that the Confederates were waging war against the United States, and in June of 1863 they extended it to Pennsylvania. For many Pennsylvanians the war now attained the same dimensions of senseless cruelty as it had come to have for their former compatriots in Virginia.

VIII

THE CONFEDERATES MOVE
TO BATTLE

WITH THE advantage of hindsight the historian can ponder over the records, point his finger, and say: "This day was the turning point." In the history of the Gettysburg campaign Sunday, June 28, may perhaps be given this distinction, even though on this day neither army made any major moves. They had lost direct touch with one another, and a greater distance separated them than previously in the campaign. Too, their customary positions with respect to each other were reversed. Except for Stuart's cavalry Lee's army was concentrated around Chambersburg, Pennsylvania, with columns in Carlisle and York, while Meade's forces were gathered many miles to the south near Frederick and Middletown in Maryland. As for the whereabouts of Stuart, it was anybody's guess.

Although Sunday, June 28, was uneventful for the men in the ranks, it represented a crisis in the lives of three generals, Meade, Stuart, and Lee. In the early morning hours Meade had been ordered to replace Hooker as commander of the Army of the Potomac, and as the day wore on he learned that the last of the Confederate columns had marched through Hagerstown the day before, presumably on their way to Chambersburg and who knew how far beyond. Stuart on the morning of June 28 found out to his amazement that the Union army was moving toward Frederick and that Hooker himself had reached Poolesville the day before. And Lee late that Sunday night was startled to learn from a spy that Hooker was north of the Potomac with his entire army and well on his way

❦ *Map 2* ❦

TROOP MOVEMENTS FROM JUNE 28
TO MORNING OF JULY 1

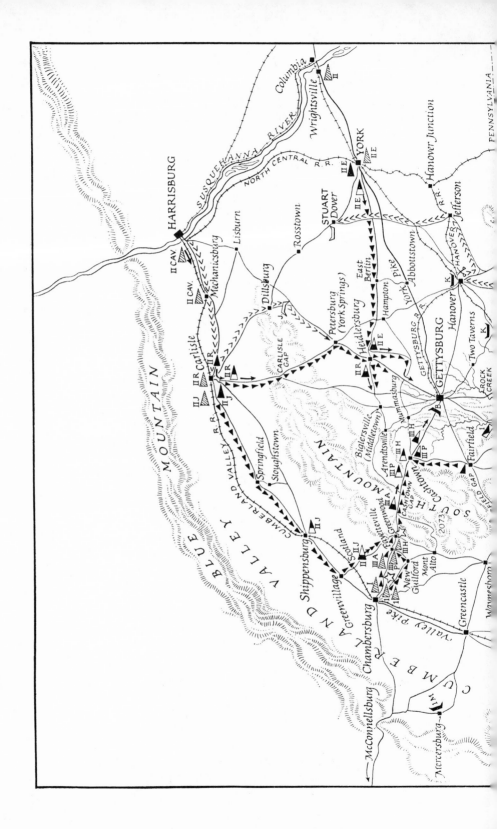

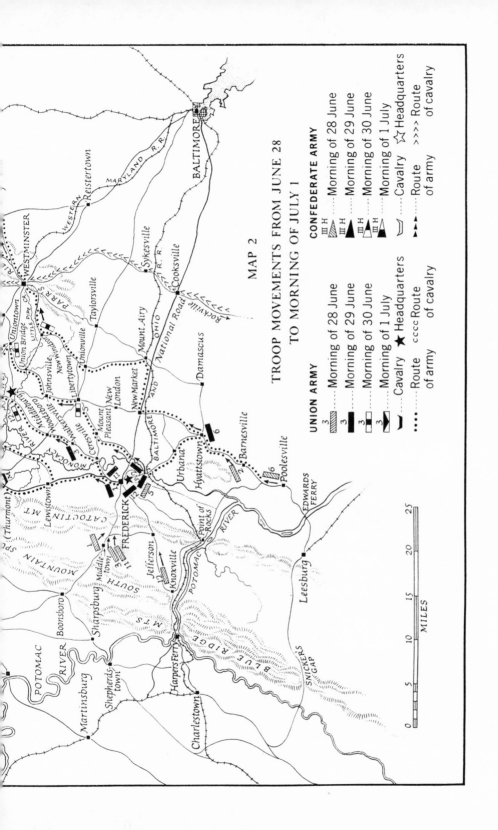

MAP 2

TROOP MOVEMENTS FROM JUNE 28
TO MORNING OF JULY 1

UNION ARMY

⬛ Morning of 28 June
⬛ Morning of 29 June
⬛ Morning of 30 June
⬛ Morning of 1 July
⌐ Cavalry   ★ Headquarters
Route ⊂⊂⊂⊂ Route
of army   of cavalry

CONFEDERATE ARMY

III H Morning of 28 June
III H Morning of 29 June
III H Morning of 30 June
III H Morning of 1 July
Cavalry   ☆ Headquarters
Route   >>>> Route
of army   of cavalry

to South Mountain,[1] from where he would threaten Confederate communications in the Cumberland Valley.

The contents, timing, and source of the spy's report bothered Lee. He had been in the dark for almost a week about any major moves of the enemy, and now upsetting news reached him without any advance warning. Instead of coming from Stuart, upon whom Lee was depending for reliable information, the intelligence was brought by a person unknown to him whose word had to be taken on faith. True, before the army left Culpeper General Longstreet, Lee's senior corps commander, had hired the spy who was known at the time only as Harrison, although later investigation revealed that his given name was James and he made his living as an actor. Longstreet vouched for the man's integrity, but nevertheless Lee disliked receiving important intelligence in such an irregular manner.[2] Ironically Stuart, who still possessed a keen nose for news, could have told Lee the same thing as Harrison if he had been able to communicate with him, but his cavalry brigades were near Rockville, Maryland, and seventy-five long miles and the whole Army of the Potomac lay between him and his commander.

The dramatic incident of the spy is one of the many episodes and names which have become imperishably linked with the Gettysburg story and make it distinctive. The battle would lose some of its fascination for Americans without such places as Little Round Top, Devil's Den, the Wheatfield, and Spangler's Spring; such vignettes as that of General Pettigrew and his shoeless brigade starting the battle, General Gordon giving succor to the wounded General Barlow, General Hooker being removed under strange circumstances, and the spy, Harrison, finding the Army of the Potomac for Lee. Though a mixture of truth and fiction, these stories are usually accepted without question and are recited over and over almost as a litany of the battle.

Official versions of the spy incident, bringing out its main features and meaning, appeared in both of Lee's reports of the campaign. The accounts, however, were somewhat contradictory; they both suffered from ambiguity and left certain questions unanswered. With respect to his movements the week before the battle Lee stated that the "absence" of cavalry had "embarrassed" him, and the timely appearance of Harrison gave him a chance to call in his scattered forces. Although Lee admitted he had given Stuart discretion in conducting operations against the enemy and choosing the site for crossing the Potomac to join Ewell, nevertheless he held him responsible for failing to report Hooker's movements. "It was expected," he said, "that as soon as the Federal Army should cross the Potomac, General Stuart would give notice of its movement, and nothing having been heard from him since our entrance into Maryland, it was inferred that the enemy had not left Virginia." [3] Lee could reasonably have made this inference only if he had told Stuart precisely and clearly to withdraw to the west side of the Blue Ridge on the night of June 24, cross at Shepherdstown on June 25, and move to Frederick before proceeding on his way to join Ewell. Stuart could easily have travelled the twenty-one miles between Shepherdstown and Frederick by the longest but best route and arrived late in the afternoon or early in the evening of June 25. By that hour movements of the Army of the Potomac across the river were so extensive that news of them would surely have spread among the natives in Frederick and have come to Stuart's ears by the next morning, if not earlier. When the Eleventh Corps reached Jefferson around midnight on June 25, it was only eight miles from Frederick;[4] if Stuart had been there his opportunities for getting information about Hooker would have been exceptionally good. In that case Lee would have known of the Union army's crossing as early as June 26. However, since Lee had given Stuart a choice of routes without carefully defining the conditions, he should have faced the possibility that his cavalry leader would be out of touch with him for two or three days.

Lee's surprise upon hearing of Hooker's crossing is therefore puzzling. For over a week prior to the appearance of Harrison he had been aware that the movement of the main body of the enemy was toward the Potomac. Although he did not know Hooker's "real destination," [5] he worried that the Union army might get across the river without his finding out about it.[6] On June 23 he learned of the first pontoon bridge at Edwards Ferry and that some of the enemy were withdrawing from the foot of the mountains near Leesburg. This information led Lee to believe that a crossing was imminent.[7] He had considered, although not very seriously, certain other alternatives which the enemy might follow. For one thing, Hooker might remain inactive, but Lee thought this course was not very likely, especially if he himself made any important moves. There was a chance too that the enemy might withdraw to the east toward the fortifications of Washington, or to the south to threaten the Confederates' communications with Richmond. However, in view of the pattern of Hooker's countermoves throughout the campaign Lee logically should have expected the enemy to follow him across the Potomac. From the beginning he had been confident he could induce Hooker to pursue him,[8] and with this certainty in mind he had carried out his plan of marching all of his army to Maryland and Pennsylvania.[9] Why then did knowledge of his success in drawing Hooker after him cause Lee surprise and consternation? The answer can perhaps be found in his complaint about the absence of cavalry which, he said, made it "impossible to obtain accurate information" or to "ascertain . . . [the enemy's] intentions." [10]

These statements about the cavalry were misleading for they implied that no troopers were available to keep close watch on the enemy, whereas in fact two brigades were at hand. It is true, Stuart himself and three of his brigades had ridden out of the main theater of operations, but this development should have been no surprise to Lee. When he did not hear from his cavalry leader, he should have concluded that he had passed around the enemy and become temporarily incommunicado. Instead he inferred from Stuart's silence that Hooker had not crossed the Potomac.[11] Lee's apparent assumption that only Stuart would be in a position to know when this move had occurred suggests his lack of confidence in Robertson and the two brigades under him. For all the use he made of them, they might as well not have been around. Stuart made a serious if not fatal mistake, for which Lee must share the blame, when he did not place the able and aggressive Wade Hampton in command of the cavalry units which he left to guard the rear of the army. Lee had planned from the beginning that Stuart was to take with him only three of his five brigades. If he had any preferences, he kept them to himself, for as in other matters he gave Stuart a free hand in picking out the units to go with him. It was Longstreet, not Lee, who suggested Hampton as commander of the remaining brigades.[12] Robertson had shown some serious shortcomings as a leader at Brandy Station, of which Stuart was aware, and only his seniority over Jones entitled him to the command. Stuart sought to overcome Robertson's inadequacies by leaving careful instructions for all conceivable contingencies and by tactfully placing Jones in the position of a guardian angel. He also urged Robertson to keep in close touch with Longstreet by relays of couriers. These arrangements were at best makeshifts and poor substitutes for the presence of Stuart himself or of Wade Hampton. Nevertheless the fact remains that Lee did have for his immediate use more than half of the troopers in Stuart's division.

If Robertson had followed Stuart's orders, Lee would not have felt the want of adequate cavalry support. Stuart had been most explicit in giving his instructions.[13] Robertson in guarding Ashby's and Snicker's Gaps was to patrol the area between the Blue Ridge and Bull Run Mountains so as to keep constant pressure on enemy outposts. Only in that way could he know whether the enemy remained in force on his front. A very alert officer, which Robertson apparently was not, might have gotten wind of massive movements across the Potomac near Leesburg as early as June 25. If not Robertson, why did not Jones, an outstanding outpost officer whose brigade was near Snickersville, keep an eye on Union activities around Edwards Ferry? General Lee learned about the first pontoon bridge there within forty-eight hours after it was built,[14] but not from his cavalrymen. If, as is reasonably supposed, Robertson and Jones possessed the same information, they should have focused their attention on the area around Leesburg and the bridge and watched for developments. Certainly the noise and confusion caused by the herding together of thousands of troops with their long wagon and artillery trains, all waiting to cross the narrow pontoon bridges at one place on the river, should have made even the most incurious native suspect that the Federal army was carrying out an important maneuver. Somehow this news should have filtered through the lines to Confederate cavalry patrols, assuming there were any.[15] If there were none, then why not? [16]

When Gregg's and Buford's divisions of Pleasonton's cavalry pulled out of Aldie on June 26 to cover the rear of the Union army at Edwards Ferry,[17] Robertson, who supposedly was watching them, should have concluded that one of the conditions laid down by Stuart upon which his own movements depended had been met. The enemy had retired from his front and moved beyond his reach. Stuart had specifically told him what to do should that happen. He was to leave sufficient pickets in the mountains, withdraw to the valley, and follow the Confederate army, keeping on its right and rear. If he was still uncertain about how to proceed, he had only to refer the matter to General Longstreet, as Stuart had instructed him to do. Whatever the reasons, Robertson did not act according to Stuart's orders, and he and Jones remained at their posts at Ashby's and Snicker's Gaps until Lee ordered them on June 29 to join him in Pennsylvania. There is no evidence to suggest that they did anything more than guard the passes and keep their men on picket duty near them. General Jones did assign one of his regiments, the 12th Virginia, the task of observing the enemy at Harpers Ferry, and on June 30 some of the troopers broke their dull routine by surprising and capturing a party of Union pickets on Bolivar Heights overlooking the town.[18] General Howard reported in the afternoon of June 26 that fifteen cavalrymen attached to his headquarters had dashed into Boonsboro and chased out a squad of rebel cavalry.[19] They might have been a group of scouts from the 12th Virginia. Aside from these signs of life Robertson's cavalry apparently confined itself to limited activity for a period of five days.

Why Lee permitted this situation causes wonder. Either Robertson misunderstood Stuart's instructions, or Lee, who was in constant touch with him,[20] ordered him to remain on the defensive so as not to uncover the passes prematurely. It was an unnecessary precaution after June 26, when the Federal cavalry moved north from Aldie on its way to Maryland. If Lee was concerned about the passes in the Blue Ridge, why was he not equally worried about the gaps in South Mountain which led to the routes his army took in Maryland? Control of these points afforded lookouts from which to observe enemy movements in the direction of Jefferson, Middletown, and Frederick. Instead of keeping two brigades behind in Virginia it would have been better for Lee to have had some of the cavalry accompany his infantry on his right and rear so as to skirt the western face of South Mountain and if need be seize the passes. Hooker feared such a move and rushed his men to get to the mountain first. They found no Confederates.[21] On June 26, the day when the rear columns of Lee's infantry waded across the Potomac, an energetic cavalry officer roaming over the top ridges of South Mountain might easily have seen enough blue-coated soldiers of Howard's Eleventh Corps in Middletown to have convinced Lee of Hooker's growing presence in Maryland. On that same day General Lee as he rode through Maryland on his way to Pennsylvania was not far from South Mountain. The conclusion must be drawn that while Stuart's vainglorious ride around the Union army was a gross misuse of horseflesh and manpower, it neither stripped Lee of cavalry nor deprived him of all opportunities to learn Hooker's whereabouts. There are no indications that Lee ordered the troopers still available to him to look for the enemy at the obvious places. Robertson was not an enterprising officer, and Lee was not the kind of commander to force him to be one.[22]

Whatever else the appearance of Longstreet's spy may have accomplished, it forced Lee to modify his plan of operations for the next few days. He could no longer keep his forces scattered over the Pennsylvania countryside happily enjoying the fruits of a rich land, nor could he push them on toward Harrisburg. His expedition, which up until then had had all the aspects of a huge raid, now took on a more ominous character and developed into a maneuver for advantage prior to a major engagement. Lee ordered a concentration of his army around Cashtown on the east flank of South Mountain, so as to "deter . . . [the enemy] from advancing farther west, and intercepting our communication with Virginia. . . ."[23]

The importance of this explanation should not be exaggerated, however, for in this campaign Lee's fears for his communications were not as all-absorbing as they ordinarily would have been, and should the Union army have got athwart them, the effect would have been inconvenient rather than fatal. To intercept Lee's communications effectively, Union forces would have had to stretch across the width of either the Shenandoah or Cumberland Valley for a distance of fifteen to twenty-five miles. There were no railroads to cut or bridges to destroy, except for one built on pontoons near Falling Waters, a few miles down the river from Williamsport. Since the Potomac was fordable at many places, especially during the summer months, Lee did not consider it an obstacle, and he used the valleys as broad highways to connect him with his railheads many miles away at Staunton in the valley and Culpeper in the piedmont. Aside from ammunition, of which he had enough for one major engagement, he did not have to depend upon Virginia for his supplies. Food and other necessities he had obtained in bountiful amounts in Maryland and Pennsylvania. Surprisingly enough, the only article which he did not find in large quantity was horseshoes, so desperately needed during the campaign.[24] Reinforcements, if any, also came from Virginia. Lee had left orders for men who had recovered from illness or wounds and were returning to their commands singly or in groups to travel by way of Staunton.[25] The bulk of his army traffic, however, went south from Pennsylvania. Should the Federals have seized many trains on their way back to Virginia laden with goods and driving livestock, they would have wrecked one of Lee's important long-range objectives in making the invasion, the accumulation of food and supplies for future needs. Such operations would have threatened the ultimate security of his army but not its immediate position. If the Confederates were not forced into a major engagement, they could stay in Pennsylvania for some time even if their communications with Virginia were cut off.[26]

When Lee in his battle report told how he had recalled his advance units so as to regroup his forces and set them in motion toward the east, instead of having them continue north from Chambersburg, he failed to explain what he had hoped to accomplish in a movement on Harrisburg. It is doubtful whether he himself could have calculated the advantages of capturing the capital, other than the obvious ones of delivering a severe blow to Northern morale, causing destruction, and carrying off plunder. Nevertheless, the move toward this key point showed signs of careful planning on the part of Lee, although some of the preparations were due to the initiative of Ewell. Lee reported that he had ordered Ewell to send Early to York with the idea of keeping the Federal army east of the mountains should it enter Maryland. Ewell's move to Carlisle, on the other hand, would have had the same effect upon the disposition of the Union forces, although Lee did not say so. With Early in York, Lee also pictured him as being in a position to prepare the way for the movement of the whole army on the state capital. He could cut the railroad between Harrisburg and Baltimore and seize the Wrightsville bridge, thus severing direct rail connections between Harrisburg and the Army of the Potomac.[27] The reference to seizure of the bridge must have surprised Early when he read Lee's report, for according to his own account his immediate superior, General Ewell, had ordered him to burn the bridge. The mix-up of orders perhaps was another illustration of the slovenly staff work which plagued the Confederate high command during the campaign, and for that reason it has importance. If Lee sent Ewell orders to have Early seize the bridge, either the commander of the

Second Corps did not get them or he misunderstood them, for there is evidence in addition to Early's report to show that Ewell told him to burn the structure. After Early had completed his work in York, the plans called for his division to march and rejoin the rest of the corps at Carlisle.[28]

During Early's absence Ewell reached Carlisle and used it as a base from which Jenkins' cavalry probed the Harrisburg defenses on the west bank of the Susquehanna. On the morning of June 28 Jenkins rode to the outskirts of Mechanicsburg and occupied the town after a skirmish with some of Couch's cavalry. Upon his demand for food for his men the frightened people hastily prepared a fine meal for them. The troopers then moved to a position on a "dominating hill" about four miles southwest of Harrisburg. There a battery of the brigade exchanged artillery fire with the enemy until dark, after which the men encamped for the night. The next morning, accompanied by a cavalry detachment, Jenkins and Captain H. B. Richardson, an engineer on Ewell's staff, reconnoitered to the right of the Harrisburg-Carlisle Turnpike, charged on some Union outposts, and took a long look at the city and its defenses. The Confederates here reached the farthest point on their invasion of Pennsylvania. Some of Jenkins' command remained in the vicinity of Mechanicsburg that night and all the next day, spending their time demolishing the railroad tracks and skirmishing with Union forces.[29]

Ewell also sent scouts through Couch's lines to make a thorough examination of the area. Of these three were captured, one while he was making soundings of the river's depths from a rowboat.[30] Disloyal Pennsylvanians furnished Ewell with maps of the Harrisburg defenses and "full and accurate" information about the number and condition of the militia and the location of the river fords.[31] Although Ewell was still uncertain about Lee's plans as late as the afternoon of June 28,[32] he had confidence in his ability to take Harrisburg without great difficulty, and he decided to advance on the city the next morning. According to one account, his men were "actually in the road about to start" when an order came from General Lee withdrawing the Second Corps from Carlisle and instructing it to rejoin the rest of the army.[33]

Lee sent two messages to Carlisle recalling Ewell, but no one knows exactly when they were sent or when they arrived. There is even some question of just when Lee received word from Harrison that the Army of the Potomac had crossed the river. This uncertainty comes from the fact that Colonel Charles Venable of Lee's staff entered in the headquarters letter book 7:30 A.M., June 28, 1863, as the hour when Lee wrote his second dispatch to Ewell. If this time was correct, then Lee's first dispatch must have been written the previous night, June 27, and either Harrison reached Lee the night of the 27th instead of the 28th or Lee had heard the news from someone else before his arrival. Neither possibility seems likely, as both Lee's and Longstreet's official reports of the campaign categorically state that Harrison arrived in Chambersburg on the night of June 28.[34] Another explanation of the discrepancy in dates is the possibility that Venable made a clerical error. He noted in the letter book that he had copied the message from memory,[35] and he could easily have entered the wrong date, especially the one preceding the correct one.

The best evidence indicates that Lee's first message to Ewell was written on the night of the 28th soon after his interview with Harrison, and it probably reached him the next morning. It informed Ewell that Hooker had crossed the Potomac and directed him to return with his forces to Chambersburg.[36] During the night Lee had further thoughts about the movements of Ewell's corps, and about 7:30 A.M. on June 29 he sent off a second dispatch. He had decided that instead of having the Second Corps concentrate at Chambersburg with the others, he would keep it east of South Mountain and effect a reunion of its divisions at Heidlersburg, ten miles north of Gettysburg on the Harrisburg Pike. According to the new orders, once Ewell reached Heidlersburg he would have the choice of moving directly toward Gettysburg or turning off to Cashtown. Lee did not explain why he made this change in Ewell's destination, other than to say that the Second Corps would have the advantage of travelling over turnpike most of the way and that he thought it "preferable to keep on the east side of the mountains." [37] Although he made no mention of it, Lee in concentrating his army undoubtedly saw the wisdom of marching part of it over other roads than the Chambersburg-Cashtown Turnpike so as to relieve some of the congestion.

If he had that purpose in mind, he was only partially successful in accomplishing it, because by the time Ewell got the second message late in the afternoon he had already started General Edward Johnson's division, together with the Second Corps wagon train and two battalions of its Artillery Reserve, on the valley road toward Chambersburg. They left Carlisle at 1:00 P.M. and spent the night outside of Shippensburg.[38] On the 30th Johnson led his infantry and the artillery to Green Village, where he turned off to camp at Scotland about five miles from Fayetteville, while the wagons lumbered on to Chambersburg. He still could not avoid using the main road to Cashtown and running into part of Longstreet's corps near Greenwood. Johnson's fourteen-mile wagon train apparently caught up with him on July 1 and added to the confusion of too much traffic on a single road. The tangle delayed the march of most of Longstreet's corps, as well as Johnson's division, to the annoyance of both generals, each of whom accused the other of holding him up. The truth was that Longstreet halted his leading division, McLaws', until Johnson's division and Ewell's wagon train could move ahead over the mountain.[39]

Although Lee's second message to Ewell arrived too late to change Johnson's route, it came in time to divert Rodes to Heidlersburg. He started out on the morning of the 30th and had a "very fatiguing march through rain and mud,"[40] twenty-two miles by way of Petersburg (York Springs).[41] Meanwhile Early, who was still in York with his division of the Second Corps, received word of the change in plans late on June 29. Captain Elliott Johnston of Ewell's staff brought him what was obviously a copy of Lee's first note and verbal instructions to rejoin the rest of the corps on the "western side of the South Mountain," instead of near Carlisle as he had been previously instructed to do. The next morning Early started his command on the Weigelstown and East Berlin road leading to Heidlersburg. He expected to go to Arendtsville and thence either to Shippensburg or to Greenwood "as circumstances might require." On the march he received another dispatch from Ewell and as directed encamped his men three miles east of Heidlersburg on the road to East Berlin. Then he himself rode to Heidlersburg to confer with Ewell, who had accompanied Rodes's division down from Carlisle. It was there that Early learned of Lee's second message to Ewell ordering his division to a rendezvous with Rodes at Heidlersburg.[42]

This message had an important result which Lee perhaps anticipated but did not mention. With the Second Corps, or a major portion of it, at Heidlersburg the Confederates would be able to approach Gettysburg from two directions should an engagement occur in that area. Lee considered this development very possible, for he knew that on June 28 the Union army was nearing South Mountain somewhere between Maryland Heights and Frederick. Even without benefit of cavalry he could tell by looking at his maps of southern Pennsylvania and western Maryland that the Federal troops were almost bound to march north from Frederick in their pursuit of the invaders and that some would undoubtedly be in the vicinity of Cashtown or Gettysburg by June 30 or July 1.[43] From Heidlersburg Ewell could reach either place without much difficulty by marching fourteen miles west to Cashtown or ten south to Gettysburg. Presumably Lee gave him the choice of destination so he would be prepared for any eventuality.[44]

Ewell's response to Lee's directives was prompt and efficient.[45] In one day he brought together two of his divisions, which were miles apart, without a hitch. Rodes's division numbered over 8,000 officers and men; together with Early's division it made up a formidable force of between 13,500 and 14,000 infantrymen which Ewell had at his immediate disposal.[46] His greatest handicap was his lack of effective cavalry. Although he had at least 2,000 troopers assigned to him,[47] most of them were in Jenkins' command, and instead of leading the way and guarding the flanks, for some reason they lagged behind. Perhaps Ewell wanted them to protect the rear of his advancing columns, bring up straggling soldiers and wagons, and discourage any venturesome Union forces under Couch from becoming too bold. It is hard to believe though that Yankee militia gave Ewell much concern or that he assigned some 1,600 troopers to act as a screen for his rear columns. More likely this was another instance of Jenkins' cavalry not reaching the usual standard of performance of the Army of Northern Virginia. There are indications that Jenkins was slow in bringing his command together for its march to Heidlersburg.[48] One of his cavalry companies and half a section of a battery wasted all of June 30 in Mechanicsburg carrying out what had become nonessential tasks. At sunset a courier ordered them back to Carlisle. From there the entire command marched to Petersburg, reaching it about 2:00 A.M. The men and horses got little rest that night, for the jittery general, expecting an enemy attack, kept the troopers under arms and their mounts saddled. At daybreak they were again on the road to Gettysburg, but not in the best of shape to do battle with the enemy.[49] On the march from Carlisle to Gettysburg Jenkins' men had been absolutely worthless to Ewell.

In contrast Early, who had about five hundred troopers of Ewell's cavalry with him, made good use of some of his mounted force during the march to Heidlersburg. He sent Colonel E. V. White's battalion on the pike from York to Gettysburg with instructions to scout the area between Gettysburg and Heidlersburg. He also told White to picket Mummasburg and Hunterstown, while sending parties out in the direction of Gettysburg to find out who was there, and to report the information to Ewell. White kept his small force busy. At East Berlin he pursued a small squad of enemy horsemen, and at Abbott's Ford he saw a mixed force of enemy cavalry and infantry moving south toward Hanover. Although he obtained very little precise information because of the thick cavalry screen General Buford had established late on June 30 west and north of Gettysburg, White did find strong signs of enemy activity. A battle-wise trooper such as he probably suspected that the Army of the Potomac was not very far away.[50]

Ewell had carried out Lee's orders to withdraw from his advanced position conscientiously and quickly, but with a heavy heart. Having set his sights on Harrisburg, he was bitterly disappointed that circumstances forced him to abandon a chance to seize a glittering prize of war. The capture of the capital of the second most powerful state in the North would have been no mean trophy. Members of his staff were well aware of his disappointment, for he became "quite testy" and "hard to please," and he made them "fly around" in preparation for the move to Heidlersburg.[51] Lee's message of June 29 left no doubt in Ewell's mind about what he was to do on the first leg of his journey to rejoin the main forces, but he seemed to be bothered by the necessity of having to make the choice of whether to "move directly on Gettysburg or turn down to Cashtown." [52] When he reached Heidlersburg he apparently received another order from Lee about choosing his destination, but this time a qualifying clause had been added: "as circumstances might dictate." [53] Ewell was more than ever upset, for he did not know what "circumstances" Lee had in mind. He thought that possibly Lee was aware of some movements of the enemy which would become the controlling factors in his decision. Ewell remembered that Lee had predicted a battle near Frederick or Gettysburg,[54] but this knowledge was of little help to him in choosing where to go. If he was irritated over the vagueness of Lee's messages it might have been nothing more than the understandable reaction of one who liked his orders clear, crisp, and to the point. On the other hand his annoyance could be regarded as a cover-up for a man who suddenly sensed his own inadequacies and sought a way to escape his responsibilities. In the light of adverse comments on Ewell's generalship on July 1 any hesitation on his part as to whether he should go to Gettysburg or Cashtown might be interpreted as proof that his will to act decisively had already become weakened before the battle.[55] Such an interpretation, however, ignores the gross lack of precision in Lee's orders and exaggerates the importance of the discretion given Ewell. It really did not make much difference which town he started for, because Cashtown and Gettysburg were only eight miles apart and there were enough back roads so that if he decided to shift his destination, he could do so without losing much time during the march. That is exactly what happened on July 1.

While at Heidlersburg on June 30 Ewell heard from A. P. Hill that the Third Corps was at Cashtown, and he decided to move toward it. The next morning, not aware of any emergency, he got both divisions off to a reasonably early start,[56] on two different routes so as to avoid overcrowding the roads. Rodes went almost directly west by way of Middletown (Biglerville), and Early, since he was three miles east of Heidlersburg, was ordered to go south to Hunterstown on a road parallel to the Harrisburg Pike and then turn west toward Mummasburg and Cashtown. By going to Hunterstown, which was a little more than half the distance from Heidlersburg to Gettysburg, Early could come within four miles of Gettysburg before turning west for Cashtown. Should "circumstances dictate" he could proceed to Gettysburg without a hitch. Ewell had cleverly chosen roads which would enable his divisions to go either to Cashtown or Gettysburg in the quickest possible time. Early improved upon his route by moving at once to Heidlersburg so as to take advantage of the pike which was smoother and straighter than the direct road from his division's campground to Hunterstown. Before Ewell, who accompanied Rodes, reached Middletown, a courier brought him a note from Hill, saying that the

Third Corps was advancing upon Gettysburg. Thereupon Ewell changed the direction of Rodes's marching columns without causing them to miss a step and sent Early word to continue on his present course.[57] At a crucial moment in the campaign Ewell could not have had his two divisions in a better position to cause the Yankee forces mortification and pain.

During the two days it took to bring Ewell's corps back within supporting distance of the army, Longstreet's and Hill's infantry and artillery rested in camps, most of them along the Gettysburg Pike east of Chambersburg. The men later recalled these few days as a very pleasant interlude when they were "quietly bivouacing in a shady grove . . . [with] not a ripple of excitement crossing the surface of the camp, lulled by the sound of distant music of brass bands, the nearer murmur of many voices amid the green thickets. . . ."[58] Yet they were poised for they knew not what, and their unusual situation made them uneasy. One soldier probably reflected the feelings of many others when he wrote: "Indeed it is an incomprehensible mystery to me—this sudden pause and inaction at the distance of a day's march from the borders of the invaded state!"[59] Gradually, however, in those two days of rest the weight of Lee's army shifted toward Cashtown with Hill's men in the lead. Until reliable word of enemy advances came in, Lee saw no need to wear out the troops by forcing them to move rapidly when the weather was so warm, rainy, and muggy.[60]

In carrying out his design to concentrate his forces near Cashtown, Lee on June 29, the day he sent his second message to Ewell, ordered Hill's corps to proceed from Fayetteville to Cashtown. Longstreet's corps was to follow the next day, leaving Pickett's division at Chambersburg until Imboden's cavalry could come over the mountain from Mercersburg to relieve it. Heth's division of Hill's corps reached Cashtown on the 29th, and Pender's division, together with Hill and his staff, came up on the 30th. Hill had ordered Anderson to remain at Fayetteville until July 1, when he would join the rest of the corps at Cashtown. On June 30 Longstreet also moved along leisurely with McLaws' and Hood's divisions from their camps a mile or so east of Chambersburg to Greenwood, six miles farther east. Brigadier General Joseph B. Kershaw's brigade of McLaws' division camped nearby at Fayetteville, and Brigadier General E. M. Law's brigade of Hood's division with a battery of artillery relieved two regiments of McLaws' division and went on picket duty at New Guilford to watch the mountain road leading to Emmitsburg. As a further protection to Lee's right flank against a surprise attack from Maryland, two Mississippi regiments reinforced by a section of artillery were posted near Fairfield, which was six miles directly south of Cashtown.[61]

On the night of June 30 Lee thus had four of his nine infantry divisions east of South Mountain. The two at Heidlersburg and the two at Cashtown were within less than a day's march of each other and so located that they could easily converge on Gettysburg and entrap any force the enemy might move there. One grave disadvantage of Lee's location that night arose from the disposition of the rest of his army on the western flank of South Mountain. Should he need to get the remaining divisions to the other side of the mountain in a hurry, he would have to crowd them and their long artillery and wagon trains onto a single road, up steep grades for a distance of nine or ten miles and through Cashtown Pass, from where they could take alternate routes to Gettysburg. With its hard limestone surface [62] the road through the pass could withstand the severe pounding of hundreds of cannon with their limbers and caissons and countless heavy, lumbering supply wagons, but it could not accommodate over half of Lee's army at one time during an emergency such as occurred on July 1. As a consequence none of the divisions in the Cumberland Valley which appeared to be within easy supporting distance of Hill and Ewell arrived soon enough to take part in the battle of July 1. Some of the congestion could have been avoided if Anderson's division had moved with Pender's on June 30. In that case Hill would have had all of his corps at hand ready for operations the next day. One fresh division immediately available for action might have ended the battle of Gettysburg on July 1 with another conclusive triumph for Confederate arms.[63]

In his anxiety to keep the Federal army out of the Cumberland Valley, Lee tried to attract the attention of the Union commander to his movements. In so doing he gave away his exact location, but he was willing to pay this price in order to hold the enemy east of the mountains. By June 29 the approach of the Confederate army was evident to the people of Gettysburg. That night they could see the eastern side of the mountain eight miles away ablaze with the lights of hundreds of campfires cooking the meals of Henry Heth's men.

They also became aware that the country to the west of them swarmed with enemy foraging parties.[64]

But even as Lee seemed to wave his hat vigorously so the Union commander could easily find him, he himself had but a vague notion of the whereabouts of the Northern army. The time had come when the lack of effective cavalry support to screen his advance and to pinpoint the location of enemy forces was impairing Lee's efficiency. If the 2,000 or so cavalry troopers accompanying Ewell had been guided by such wily warriors as Stuart, Wade Hampton, Fitz Lee, or "Grumble" Jones, they might have served the purpose, but under Jenkins they could not cope with tough, aggressive John Buford, who easily kept them from spying on the Union forces advancing south of Gettysburg. To get information about the Army of the Potomac Lee and his corps commanders did the next best thing: They sent out scouts.[65] Most of what Lee learned about the Federal army on June 30, though useful and in some respects significant, was negative in character. He found out that it was somewhere in northern Maryland near Middleburg and not in the Cumberland Valley, which information should have relieved him of one of his fears.[66] As confirmation he heard through Hill that General James J. Pettigrew had discovered Federal cavalry and perhaps some infantry at Gettysburg in sufficient force to induce him to withdraw his large brigade without issuing a challenge to them. In sending Pettigrew with most of his brigade to Gettysburg on another errand, Henry Heth, the commander of the division, had through sheer chance located a considerable enemy force, but he had no definite idea of its size, composition, or quality. For all he knew Buford's men could have been only an unusually large contingent of the much despised militia.[67]

Sometime between June 28 and July 1 Lee received word of the change in commanders of the Army of the Potomac; quite likely he got the information from Longstreet on the eve of the battle.[68] Although Lee evidently thought better of Meade as a general than he did of Hooker, the news of the replacement in no way affected his plans. Then or a little later he was reported to have remarked that "General Meade will commit no blunder in my front, and if I make one he will make haste to take advantage of it." [69] Any benefits the Union army might have gained from the promotion of Meade, Lee felt were offset by the timing of the move. A major change of this

sort usually required a period of adjustment for the new commander, in which waste motion occurred with a corresponding
reduction in the army's efficiency. Lee expected such a development
with the advent of Meade and regarded the change in Union
commanders as beneficial to him.[70]

If by June 30 Lee could not point to a map and say, "Here is the
Army of the Potomac; we must do such and such to get ready for it,"
he did sense with supreme confidence that a battle was imminent
somewhere along the Chambersburg-Gettysburg Pike instead of in
the direction of Harrisburg.[71] Whatever qualms Lee may have felt
about entering an engagement without effective cavalry support he
kept pretty well to himself, and he maintained the calm and poised
exterior which impressed so many people. In the eyes of foreign
visitors Lee stood in appearance, manners, and ability the perfect
general. His modest but neat dress, consisting of a well-worn long
gray jacket with three stars on the collar, a high-crowned black felt
hat, and blue trousers tucked into Wellington boots, set off his fine
physique.[72] One observer said he was the "handsomest" man of
middle age he had ever seen. Courteous, dignified, and without
bluster, he was a "gentleman in every respect." [73] During the few
days of quiet waiting at Chambersburg Lee kept himself busy
planning operations and constantly meeting with Longstreet to
exchange views and possibly pleasantries.[74] General Hood, who
paid Lee a visit during this period, found him in the "same buoyant
spirits which pervaded his magnificent army." Lee had exclaimed to
him, "Ah! General, the enemy is a long time finding us; if he does
not succeed soon, we must go in search of him," and Hood had
replied that he himself was "never so well prepared or more willing." [75] Such remarks should not be taken at face value, for they
were often in the category of just so much conversation. Other
evidence suggests too that though Lee spoke lightly and perhaps in
jest, he had a feeling of impatience which he could not entirely
repress.

When Lee decided to concentrate his army at Cashtown, Imboden and Robertson had not yet made their appearances at Chambersburg. Consequently Lee was forced to leave behind strong
detachments of his infantry to do the work of the cavalry in guarding his immediate rear. On July 1 Pickett's division still occupied
Chambersburg and Law's brigade of Hood's division remained at

New Guilford. If Imboden were to come up as Lee had ordered, he could release Pickett for the front line and establish a watch over all the roads converging on the Chambersburg-Gettysburg Pike near Greenwood.[76] What troubled Lee more than anything else was the absence of Stuart and his veteran brigades, for the time had come when they could be most useful, if not indispensable. Lee kept asking the same questions over and over: Where was Stuart, and why had he not rejoined the army?[77] Well might Lee wonder, for Stuart was long overdue.

News of the presence of the Union army in Maryland on June 28 had made Stuart realize the importance of uniting with his compatriots in Pennsylvania, and he apparently resolved to move directly there. His proclivity for the spectacular soon broke down his good intentions, however, and he succumbed to the temptation of capturing a beautifully equipped and heavily laden Union supply train near Rockville, Maryland, at the cost of exhausting his cavalry and wasting precious time.[78] In this escapade if he did not disobey Lee's orders, he at least went contrary to his commander's intentions, because in his last letter to Stuart on June 23 Lee had specifically told him that once across the Potomac he "must move on and feel the right of Ewell's troops, collecting information, provisions, etc."[79] Unfortunately the force of the order had been weakened when Lee added the last phrase. It was no longer a straightforward and unequivocal directive, and Stuart was furnished with a convenient excuse for delay.

If Stuart had been on just another cavalry raid, he would have had good reason to boast of his rich haul at the expense of the enemy. Brigadier General M. C. Meigs, the efficient quartermaster general of the Union army, was greatly annoyed when for want of a cavalry escort he lost to Colonel Chambliss' brigade an eight-mile-long train of 900 sleek mules and 150 well-appointed wagons carrying oats, corn, ham, and whiskey for Hooker's army. In trying to escape from the Confederates the teamsters upset and wrecked many of the wagons, but Stuart was able to take 125 of them away with him.[80] Usually the rebel forces stood in great need of everything Stuart captured, but at this time the booty they were obtaining in Pennsylvania without help from Stuart was supplying their wants for the present and for some months to come.[81] It took Stuart several hours to burn the wrecked wagons, await the return of Fitz

1. Major General George Gordon Meade.

2. Major General John F. Reynolds.

3. General Meade and his staff.

4. Brigadier General John Buford.

5. Major General Oliver O. Howard.

6. Major General Joseph Hooker.

7. Major General Abner Doubleday.

8. Major General Daniel E. Sickles.

9. Major General Henry W. Slocum.

10. Brigadier General James S. Wadsworth.

11. Lieutenant Colonel Freeman McGilvery.

12. Major General Winfield S. Hancock and other officers. The man leaning against the tree is Brigadier General Francis C. Barlow, and to General Hancock's right are Major General David B. Birney, and (front row) Brigadier General John Gibbon.

❧ Confederate Commanders ❧

13. General Robert E. Lee.

14. Major General J. E. B. Stuart

15. Lieutenant General
James Longstreet.

18. Major General George E. Pickett.

16. Major General Jubal A. Early.

19. Lieutenant General Richard S. Ewell.

17. Lieutenant General
Ambrose P. Hill.

20. Gettysburg from Cemetery Hill, showing a Union camp. The photograph was probably taken after the battle.

21. Southern approach to Gettysburg, the route used by Union troops.

22. Culp's Hill as seen from Cemetery Hill.

23. McPherson's Ridge and the woods where General Reynolds was killed. The man wearing the straw hat may be the photographer Matthew Brady.

24. Attack of McGowan's South Carolina Brigade on the 151st Pennsylvania Volunteers, July 1. The sketch from which the engraving was made may have been drawn by A. R. Waud.

25. Gateway of Evergreen Cemetery at Gettysburg.

Lee's brigade which had become widely scattered while whooping after the train, and finally start parolling the four hundred or so prisoners. A more unfortunate result and one of longer duration was Stuart's decision to take the train with him, for it cut down the pace of his whole column to the slower one of the wagons.

The fracas over the wagon train occurred early in the afternoon of the 28th soon after Stuart's arrival in Rockville. After securing the train Stuart turned north and went on to Brookeville about ten miles beyond. He made twenty miles that day. At Brookeville he and his staff spent much of the night parolling the prisoners, an arrangement which Halleck churlishly refused to accept as binding. Since Stuart recognized the prisoners as another encumbrance,[82] there was nothing else he could have done with them unless he had turned his back and allowed them to wander off, or had shot them down in cold blood, a solution which Civil War military ethics would never have condoned. Next morning, after a march of ten miles and a brush with a small force of enemy cavalry, Stuart and his men came to Cooksville. In the meantime Fitz Lee with his brigade had marched all night to reach Hood's Mill at daylight. There they proceeded to tear up the track of the main line of the Baltimore and Ohio Railroad and burn the bridge at Sykesville three miles to the east. They also cut telegraph lines in the area so as to sever communications between Washington and points north and west. Maintaining possession of the railroad nearly all day, they tried to intercept trains, but the engineers were too wily and quickly backed up as soon as they saw the obstructions on the tracks.[83]

Stuart and the other brigades with the wagons finally caught up with Fitz Lee. They all went on to Westminster, twenty-five miles from Brookeville and fifteen from Hood's Mill, getting there around 5:00 P.M. on June 29. Just outside of Westminster Stuart's vanguard met two companies of the 1st Delaware Cavalry under Major N. B. Knight and overwhelmed them after a brief but fierce encounter.[84] Out of sheer exuberance some of the men pursued the fleeing enemy a "long distance on the Baltimore road," for which caper Stuart half apologized though claiming that they had "created a great panic" in Baltimore.[85] After mourning the loss in the engagement of two lieutenants of the 4th Virginia Cavalry, Stuart in a sentimental gesture acceded to the request of the ladies of Westminster and allowed them to bury the "young heroes."[86] Then he got down to the important business of securing food for the men and fodder for the horses, of which there seemed to be an abundance around Westminster. Once the foraging parties had returned to their camps, which were strung along the road to Union Mills, everyone had enough to eat for the first time since June 24. Plenty of food and a little rest were more than welcome after the day's march of twenty-five to thirty miles.[87]

If there had not been such a need to hurry June 29 could have counted as a good day for Stuart, but a gnawing sense of urgency deprived him of any real satisfaction in his accomplishments. When news came to him of the enemy movement "through Frederick City northward," he was a good twenty miles east of Frederick. Transmission of this intelligence was amazingly rapid, for the Federal advance had started only that morning. The effect of this information was to make Stuart realize with a jolt how important it was for him to march his column with as "little delay as possible," so that he could "acquaint the commanding general with the nature of the enemy's movements" and also join his force to the main body of the army.[88] A fine resolution and made by a general who clearly knew his duty, but it was not strong enough to force him to forego pleasures dear to the heart of a cavalry raider. If Stuart had really meant what he said, he could have relieved himself of the captured wagon train by destroying it immediately and have somehow gotten rid of the approximately four hundred prisoners taken since Cooksville.[89] With them out of the way he might have recovered a few precious hours on June 30 by starting out earlier and proceeding at a faster pace. He would then have avoided the time-consuming clash with General Kilpatrick at Hanover and perhaps have crossed Early's trail from York to Heidlersburg before it got cold.[90]

Instead June 30 became a day of frustration if not catastrophe for Stuart. Kilpatrick, whose camp at Littlestown the previous night was a few miles nearer to Hanover than Stuart's, arrived in town ahead of his adversary. When late in the morning the head of Stuart's column suddenly hit the rear of Kilpatrick's division on its way through Hanover and caused it to scatter, Stuart could not follow up his advantage because, with Fitz Lee's brigade off to the west guarding his left flank against possible attack from Littlestown and Hampton's brigade bringing up the rear, Stuart's cavalry was in better position to protect a long wagon train than to fight an engagement. Recovering from their surprise, Kilpatrick's troopers drove the Confederates out of the town and retained possession of it.[91] The encounter in the end proved to be a standoff affair, in which Stuart had understandably found his wagons and prisoners a great nuisance. To save them he made a detour around Hanover by way of Jefferson to the east, thereby lengthening his march forward by five miles, but because Kilpatrick continued to threaten his left flank Stuart did not dare resume his march until nightfall. Then to get away from the enemy he made his exhausted men plod on hour after hour for twenty miles in the dark.[92] In his report Stuart described the agonies of that ride: "Whole regiments slept in the saddle, their faithful animals keeping the road unguided. In some instances they fell from their horses, overcome with physical fatigue and sleepiness." [93] Upon reaching Dover in the morning they stopped for a welcome but all too short rest. It was July 1; Ewell and Early had kept their appointment at Gettysburg as decreed by the fates, but proud Stuart had missed it. The rest of his ride was an anticlimax.

Fitz Lee, while crossing the main road from York to Gettysburg, learned that Early had withdrawn from his advanced position near the Susquehanna and marched to the west. Further inquiries led Stuart to believe that the Confederate army was concentrating around Shippensburg. Instead of going in that direction, however, he headed for Carlisle, where he expected to find desperately needed provisions and a part of the army. At the same time he sent out Major Andrew R. Venable of his staff with instructions to locate Early. Instead Venable found Ewell and the commanding general himself near Gettysburg.[94] There is no real reason why Stuart could not have done so too. If he had taken the tip from Fitz Lee and tried to follow Early's route, he might have saved himself a day and perhaps some of his reputation. Instead he undertook the move to Carlisle, which put an added strain on the fading endurance of his men and their mounts without any compensating military advantages. When he got there he could not even fill his empty saddle and feed bags because he found the town was in possession of Union troops. Upon its evacuation by Ewell, Brigadier General William F. Smith had moved in with two brigades of militia, supported by artillery and a detachment of cavalry. Frustrated in his design to get provisions through a levy on the inhabitants, Stuart summoned Smith to surrender. The Union general refused, whereupon Stuart burned a lumber yard and the gas works, as well as the government barracks, and then shelled the town, causing more noise than harm. The valor of Smith's men remained untested, for Stuart ceased his demonstrations when he received a dispatch from Lee telling him to take a position on the left of the Confederate infantry at Gettysburg.[95] Lee had at last learned of his whereabouts from Venable. With this order in his pocket Stuart early on July 2 rode back into the Gettysburg campaign, trailing his captured wagon train behind him.

To those who participated, Stuart's expedition around the Army of the Potomac was a horrible experience with the nightmarish qualities of a bad dream. As they frantically went through the motions of hurrying, their appointed destination seemed to fade farther and farther into the distance. The frustrations and the meager results of the venture would perhaps have been overlooked in the glow of a victorious campaign, but the shock of defeat at Gettysburg made Confederates weigh carefully the worth of various command decisions and operations before, during, and after the battle. Since it was impossible to conceive of defeat as the accomplishment of the despised Yankees, the rebels looked inward and sought the explanation in some fatal weakness on their own part. Among those commanders found wanting Stuart received more widespread and unfavorable comments than anyone else, ranging from gentle reproof by his friends to bitter indictment by his enemies.

Stuart pleaded his case in the longest and in some respects the most detailed battle report of all those published in the official records of the campaign. It was a strange document, more of an apology than a report, in which he tried to prove the virtues of his venture. According to him, its strategy was sound, its execution was as good as could be expected, and its achievements justified the trials and tribulations of his men and their mounts. But Stuart wrote too much, and he made certain statements which had the opposite effect from the one he intended. His self-righteous attitude and tendency to complain of the failures of others also reduced the effectiveness of his report.[96]

While stressing the immediate as well as the ultimate importance of his operations to the success of the campaign, Stuart refused to admit that he himself was responsible for his delay in reaching the army. He implied that military necessity dictated his conduct and as a result he had no alternatives. Stuart himself unwittingly repudiated this thesis when he explained why he had resisted a momentary impulse to organize an attack against Washington after Chambliss' brigade had chased the supply train within three or four miles of the city. He offered the following reasons for this fine show of restraint: "To attack at night with cavalry, particularly unless certain of surprise, would have been extremely hazardous; to wait till morning, would have lost much time from my march to join General Lee, without the probability of compensating results." [97] This comment, which had its ironic twist because he had already delayed his march for a wagon train, clearly revealed the cast of his thinking. If any move would result in what he considered to be a military advantage, he felt himself justified in making it, even if he then needed a longer time to carry out Lee's order to join Ewell.

What were the "compensating results" of which he was so proud, and how valid were his claims? In listing his accomplishments he stressed the "serious loss" his expedition caused the enemy in "men and *matériel* (over 1,000 prisoners having been captured)" as well as the "terror and consternation" it brought to the "very gates of the capital" and Baltimore. According to Stuart, Meade with his supply lines and communications with Washington cut had withdrawn his cavalry from the Cumberland Valley and sent it together with the entire Sixth Corps to intercept him. Fear of cavalry attacks on his rear, he said, caused Meade to weaken his army even more by diverting 4,000 troops under General French from Maryland Heights to escort government property from Frederick to Washington. The result of these moves, Stuart boasted, was to free Lee's communications in the valley from enemy threats, to slow up the advance of Meade's army, and to prevent the participation of the Sixth Corps in the first two days of the battle.[98] This account of his achievements with approximately 4,000 cavalrymen looked very impressive, if only it were true.

The Union loss in materiel with the capture or destruction of a dozen or so canal boats and 150 supply wagons and their 900 mules was very distressing to General Meigs, but it inconvenienced the Army of the Potomac rather than crippling it.[99] Once Stuart moved on and was no longer a threat these losses were readily replaced by new supply trains filled with provisions and equipment from the vast resources of the North. Cutting Meade's communications with Washington was a meaningless effort, because as the Union army moved north, Meade shifted his supply base from Frederick to Westminster, where he had the use of an inadequate but still intact railroad to Baltimore.[100] Stuart had not touched the rail connections between Washington and Baltimore. In certain respects the loss to the North of 1,000 men taken prisoner was a more serious matter, especially if they were trained soldiers. As far as can be determined, about 600 of the prisoners were cavalrymen. In the summation of his achievements Stuart forgot to mention that the rest were teamsters.[101]

The panic which Stuart claimed to have created in Washington and Baltimore in no way affected Meade's thinking or actions. Meade knew that Lee's army, stretched out between the Cumberland and Susquehanna Valleys, was his true objective, and he arranged his forces accordingly. He advanced them on a broad front as a foil against a flanking movement which might force him to uncover Baltimore or Washington. As part of his strategy on June 30 he sent the Sixth Corps eastward through Westminster to Manchester to guard his right flank against Lee's infantry, not Stuart's troopers.[102] Stuart's report notwithstanding, the Sixth Corps arrived at Gettysburg late in the afternoon of July 2—and not on July 3—in time to help stop the Confederate attack on the Union left.[103] Meade said he would "submit to the cavalry raid around . . . [him] in some measure," because he did not intend to waste his forces by "useless movements." [104] He expected to use cavalry and not infantry to fight Stuart, and for that purpose he diverted only a portion of his troopers. The two brigades and a battery from General Gregg's division, which he sent out under Colonel John B. McIntosh, found the roads blocked by Union infantry, and they never did locate their quarry.[105] It was Kilpatrick's division, while covering Meade's right front and trying to find the main body of Lee's army, that accidentally clashed with Stuart at Hanover.[106]

Meade for reasons quite different from those claimed by Stuart sent an escort of 3,000—not 4,000—men to guard government supplies, arms, and equipment shipped to Washington on the Chesapeake and Ohio Canal from the abandoned post on Maryland Heights. He knew that the north bank of the Potomac from Harpers

Ferry to the capital had been practically stripped of cavalry pickets during the emergency of Lee's invasion, and there was danger of incursions by guerrillas roaming through northern Virginia. Halleck also believed that some of Lee's cavalry remained south of the Potomac and was a threat to the Maryland side of the river. The escort would perform a dual role: as guard for government property in transit, and as reinforcement for the units protecting the capital.[107] Although he did not say so, Meade probably suspected that these men would be of little use to him in the field, for after garrison duty newcomers to the army had trouble keeping up with the fast pace maintained by veterans on the march.[108]

General Stuart may have convinced himself and his friends that the military advantages gained in attacking the communications and supply lines of the Army of the Potomac were worth the delay in joining Lee, but no one else in either army believed it. The Union General Henry Hunt neatly summed up Stuart's exploit by saying: "It is a good lesson on cavalry raids around armies, a thing easily done but of no particular use." [109]

Although it was natural and understandable for a proud man such as Stuart to try to exalt his accomplishments and minimize his shortcomings, it was poor grace and unforgivable for him to try to find excuses at the expense of others. His complaint about the army not being where he thought it would be seemed to imply that all its movements should have been conditioned by what he chose to do. When near Hanover he had learned of the arrival of Meade's army at Taneytown. From this information he came to the unwarranted conclusion that Lee's army was already in York or Harrisburg. Annoyed that his own presuppositions had misled him, he accused two of his colleagues of tardiness and in so doing unwittingly questioned the soundness of Lee's strategy. "It is believed," he wrote, "that, had the corps of Hill and Longstreet moved on instead of halting near Chambersburg, York could have been the place of concentration instead of Gettysburg." [110] After Hill and Longstreet, Stuart's next culprit was Early, who had had the effrontery to depart from York without leaving word or a guide to direct Stuart to him. Early, Stuart charged, had "reason to expect me, and had been directed to look out for me. He heard my guns at Hanover, and correctly conjectured whose they were, but left me no clew [sic] to his destination on leaving York, which would have saved me a long and tedious march to Carlisle and thence back to Gettysburg." [111] Now who was derelict in the performance of his duties? Certainly not "Jeb" Stuart! By a neat sleight of hand he shifted the blame. Early's reaction when confronted with the charge after the war was surprisingly mild, though he emphatically denied having received instructions to "co-operate" with Stuart or "to send out scouts to endeavor to establish communications" with him.[112] Early had discussed the matter, he said, with Colonel Charles S. Venable, formerly of Lee's staff, who had agreed it was "absurd to suppose that I was to look out for the Cavalry and keep it informed of the movements of the army—that, in fact, I was to play the part of a sort of wet-nurse for the cavalry." [113] Beyond Stuart's report and the recollections of Major Henry B. McClellan there is no evidence to indicate that Lee or Ewell told Early to watch for Stuart.[114]

In answer to his critics who complained of the lack of cavalry on July 1 Stuart rightly pointed to the availability of Jenkins' forces. He then observed that if the army had still felt the absence of his three brigades, Jenkins' cavalry had not been "as efficient as it ought to have been." [115] Though this was a just criticism, Stuart forgot to mention that Lee had long worried about Jenkins' effectiveness as a cavalry leader and had wanted Stuart to direct him once he got to Pennsylvania.[116]

If Stuart had been willing to arrive empty-handed, he could have joined Early before the battle and weakened the adverse comments of his critics. He had learned of Hooker's whereabouts in Maryland just after crossing his cavalry at Rowser's Ford early on June 28. Between then and late afternoon of June 29 his force had marched about forty-five miles to Westminster, and a part of it had gone to Union Mills five miles farther north. They had spent many hours and gone many extra miles wrecking and seizing enemy property. If Stuart had decided to head straight north for Ewell's right wing without loitering along the way, he could have made Hanover instead of Westminster at a reasonable hour on June 29 without unduly taxing the energies of his men. There they could have obtained food and rest before an early start the next morning for a march of no more than fifteen miles to meet Early's column on its way from York to a point near Heidlersburg. There was a chance too that before coming up to Early, Stuart might have encountered Colonel White's troopers riding southwest on the York-Gettysburg

Pike on the lookout for the enemy.[117] But instead of this happy ending Stuart finally returned to the army at Gettysburg on the afternoon of July 2, over sixty hours late, and found himself, rightly or wrongly, in the position of a person who had betrayed a sacred trust.[118]

Stuart's personal enemies never let him forget his performance, and over the years they made him the scapegoat for Confederate failure at Gettysburg. As a result his role in the campaign became an object of scorn and derision, as well as the most generally accepted explanation for what went wrong for the rebels.[119] To say that Stuart's late arrival was a major cause of Lee's defeat is a little too pat an answer to the question of why the Confederates lost the battle. There is no doubt that when he was riding around Meade's army he was of little help to his commander. Who can say though what difference it would have made if he had met Early on June 30? He might have discovered the composition of the Federal force at Gettysburg, and Heth with his strong infantry division might have pushed boldly ahead to sweep Buford out of town before Reynolds could arrive with his corps, thus depriving this Pennsylvania community of its claim to fame. With Stuart there at the opening of the battle Lee might have decided upon a turning movement on July 2 to force Meade out of his position, instead of ordering Longstreet to attack the Federal left flank and Ewell the right. Such speculations are needed in appraising historical situations, but unless used with restraint they can lead to fruitless controversy.

One thing is sure. On the eve of July 1 Lee had his forces in splendid shape to carry out his strategy of defeating the Army of the Potomac "in detail," that is, one part of it at a time.[120] If, as Stuart's accusers insisted, the absence of cavalry permitted Lee to be surprised into an unfortunate encounter of major proportions at Gettysburg,[121] they overlooked two important elements in the situation. Meade was just as surprised, and the initial advantage lay with Lee.

Lee's favorable position was largely due to his good judgment aided somewhat by luck. On June 28, the day of decision for three generals, he became convinced that the Union army was following him and made on the whole skillful arrangements to meet it. Stuart on that day received the same warning of the approaching conflict, but he failed to see his duty clearly enough to prepare for it and thus lost the chance to redeem himself. General Fitz Lee raised the question of "whether Stuart exercised the discretion *undoubtedly given to him, judiciously,*" [122] and the answer is no. Therein lies the tragedy of "Jeb" Stuart in the Gettysburg campaign.

IX

MEADE TAKES OVER

JUNE 28 was a long day of excitement and change for the Army of the Potomac, but particularly so for one man, Major General George Gordon Meade. When he turned in for the night on June 27 he was just another corps commander who had conscientiously and expeditiously completed one more day's march and patiently awaited orders for tomorrow's maneuvers. His corps, the first to arrive just outside of Frederick, had come that day about sixteen miles from a bivouac four miles east of the mouth of the Monocacy River. After making arrangements for the encampment of his men, Meade with one or two of his staff rode into town for a visit with Hooker, whom he had not seen since leaving the Rappahannock on June 13. Hooker had not yet arrived, so Meade returned to his quarters still ignorant of his commander's plans and the whereabouts of the enemy.[1] At three o'clock in the morning of June 28, the quietest hour before dawn when the slightest noise could be heard at a distance, voices outside his tent woke him up. Sleepily he received Colonel James A. Hardie of the staff of General in Chief Halleck, who said he came to Meade as a bearer of "trouble." The general, whose sense of irony was no more awake at that hour than he was, promptly interpreted the declaration to mean his arrest or dismissal from command, and he exclaimed that his conscience was clear of any sense of wrongdoing.[2] Hardie then handed him a communication from the adjutant general's office which was not a request, but an order, from the President placing him in command of the Army of the Potomac.[3] Being a good soldier, Meade had no recourse except to bow to the inevitable and obey.[4]

News of this dramatic encounter spread rapidly through the army, to the complete surprise of everybody except possibly Hooker and Butterfield. The feelings of the men in the ranks were mixed. Many regarded the event as nothing very unusual—it was the fourth change in command within the last eight months—and they shrugged their shoulders in indifference. Others would have preferred one of their own favorites among the generals, especially McClellan who topped everyone else in popularity. Most of the men knew nothing about Meade, and what they saw did not impress them much,[5] for in no way did he fit the popular stereotype of the general of an army. Possessing little flair for the theatrical, he had about as much appeal as a scholarly circuit judge awkwardly and sedately riding his horse to court. The very qualities, however, which endeared him to his intimates, modesty and a dislike for publicity, made him a drab figure to his soldiers.[6] They saw a "tall, slim, gray-bearded man" who wore glasses and "an old slouched hat, a blue blouse, with corduroy pants tucked into his long jack boots," a combination of physical characteristics and attire which made him "ungainly in looks and actions."[7]

Nevertheless more thoughtful and discerning observers saw beneath the surface certain qualities which explained why Meade's appointment to the top post in the army was not a case of the lesser of many evils for the Lincoln administration. True, unless Lincoln had wanted to reach out beyond the Army of the Potomac and pick a Western general, an impossible move at this stage of the campaign, there was no one available but Meade, and without him the President for better or worse would have had to put up with Hooker. Except for those closely associated with Hooker and his friends, Butterfield and Sickles, most general officers were gratified and relieved at the change in command, and they considered Meade the best choice of all the generals in the army. One of them observed that the government had "at length found the general equal to the crisis,"[8] and another expressed renewed confidence in the capacity of the army to "preserve . . . [its] honor and the safety of the Republic."[9]

People who worked with Meade and knew him well overlooked some of his less prepossessing characteristics and saw, as did Frederick Law Olmsted of the United States Sanitary Commission, a man with a "most soldierly and veteran-like appearance; a grave, stern countenance—somewhat Oriental in its dignified expression, yet American in its race horse gauntness. He is simple, direct, deliberate and thoughtful in manner of speech and general address. . . . He is a gentleman and an old soldier." [10] A long-time friend and member of his staff, Colonel Theodore Lyman, called Meade a "thorough soldier, and a mighty clear-headed man; and one who does not move unless he knows where and how many his men are; where and how many his enemy's men are; and what sort of country he has to go through. I never saw a man in my life who was so characterized by straightforward truthfulness as he is. He will pitch into himself in a moment, if he thinks he had done wrong; and woe to those, no matter who they are, who do not do it right!" [11]

Meade's love of truth, strong sense of the fitness of things, and dedication to duty explain the quality of his temper, which was an element in his makeup that caused universal comment among his contemporaries. A quick, active, energetic, masterful man, he had the violent impatience of a perfectionist with stupidity, negligence, or laziness. His temper would erupt easily in bursts of rage or annoyance when he felt the pressures of his position during large-scale movements or major engagements. As Lyman described it: "I don't know any thin old gentleman, with a hooked nose and cold blue eye, who, when he is wrathy, exercises less of Christian charity than my well-beloved chief!" [12] But in matters involving the safety of the army or the lives of thousands of men he exercised self-control and showed great moral courage in his decisions, as for example in the Mine Run campaign in the fall of 1863 when because of the mistakes of his subordinates he called off a flanking attack toward which he had maneuvered for days, to prevent the senseless slaughter of his men. He made this decision at the risk of his position as commanding general and his reputation. The nagging of his superiors never moved him to act in a manner contrary to his own good judgment.[13]

Less sympathetic observers have given to posterity a distorted picture of the general. One of these was Charles A. Dana who as Assistant Secretary of War from 1863 to 1865 frequently visited the battlefronts and had occasion to observe Meade. He exaggerated the less attractive features of the general's temperament and their unfortunate effects on his relations with others. Dana accused Meade of having the "worst possible temper, especially toward his subordinates. I think he had not a friend in the whole army." He went on to say that no one could approach the general regardless of his business without being insulted, and that Meade sneered at his staff officers and cursed them violently "without occasion and without reason." In this portrayal Dana made Meade out to be an unreasonable boor completely bereft of friends, who lacked "self-confidence and tenacity of purpose" as well as "moral authority." [14] Obviously this characterization was a cruel caricature, for it is impossible to imagine such an unsuitable person as he described remaining long in a position of authority.

The general's friends, and he had many, would have been among the first to admit that when under tension during important maneuvers or in an engagement he would become irascible and peppery, but his decisions were "always founded in good reason." [15] In such moments when "his severity . . . [was] not exactly ungentlemanly but a little tough," [16] his subordinates knew enough to get things done right or scurry for cover. Though a hard taskmaster, he had a "tremendous nervous system" that held him up "through everything." [17] After a violent outburst against some unfortunate underling Meade always was full of regret and had a "cordial desire, if he had been wrong, to make amends." [18] Although his manner was hard on people, it brought results. Lyman noted that Meade was "always stirring up somebody. This morning it was the cavalry picket line, which extends for miles, and which he declared was ridiculously placed. But, by worrying, and flaring out unexpectedly on various officers, he does manage to have things pretty shipshape. . . ." [19]

When not absorbed in military operations Meade was a different person, cracking jokes and relating stories [20] with "great fluency and . . . elegant language," [21] and on rare occasions he would sit by the campfire "talking familiarly with all the aides." [22] There were other manifestations of a pleasanter side. The sight of unfortunate women and children in enemy country often moved him to acts of charity. Though too sparing in his praise of the work and deeds [23] of his subordinates, perhaps out of a reluctance to show his feelings, he was not unaware of their merits. A case in point occurred after the war when the Union League of Philadelphia awarded him a gold medal in "commemoration of the Battle of Gettysburg." Several copies were struck off in bronze, and Meade gave one of them to Brigadier General Alexander S. Webb in recognition of his "distinguished personal gallantry on that ever memorable field" and in appreciation of his "cordial, warm, & generous sympathy and support so grateful for a commanding General to receive from his Subordinates." [24]

Outsiders rarely if ever saw this side of Meade. Not naturally genial or easygoing in his manner, he usually kept aloof and made no effort to make himself popular. As a rule he would not even speak to a member of the press, and reporters in turn did not dare to address him. They exacted a toll for this treatment, and as a result Meade's reputation suffered from a poor press.[25] Yet this man with the prickly personality, who was so graceless to so many people, years later received the highest tribute possible from one of his subordinates and himself a Gettysburg hero, General G. K. Warren. Although he had not always been on the best of terms with his commander,[26] in looking back over the years Warren concluded that at Gettysburg Meade's "moral character was a tower of strength to us and gave hope to the hearts of those who sought the favor of Providence and believed in the success of a just cause." He did not know another man who could "so thoroughly have inspired the Army of the Potomac to meet with confidence the great trial it was about to make. . . ." [27]

The high opinion many people had of Meade as an officer and a gentleman had become well enough known to Lincoln and Stanton to convince them that he was worth the great risk of changing commanders at a crucial moment in the campaign. They had no qualms about his professional competence. A graduate of West Point in 1835, he had become a captain in the engineers. With the outbreak of war he sought an appointment from Secretary of War Simon Cameron as an officer in one of the new regiments of volunteers. After considerable delay the War Department on August 31, 1861, commissioned him brigadier general of volunteers and assigned him to a division recently organized in his home state and known as the Pennsylvania Reserves. Serving in the Peninsular campaign where he was wounded at White Oak Swamp, and in the battles of Antietam, Fredericksburg, and Chancellorsville, he gained increasing distinction as a highly competent and skillful officer. At Fredericksburg his division was the only unit to achieve any kind of success in a battle that otherwise was known as the worst fiasco in the history of the Army of the Potomac. In command of the Fifth Corps at Chancellorsville, he saw little action but attracted the attention of his fellow officers by his pleas to Hooker to resume the offensive.[28] He was the kind of officer who tended strictly to business and kept himself free of military intrigues and cabals, a characteristic that must have pleased his superiors who had been constantly subjected to the importunities and machinations of overly ambitious generals. Lincoln and Stanton also were aware of Meade's political availability in a larger sense, for though no powerful faction in the country advocated his appointment, neither did any important group oppose it.[29] Conscious of the growing likelihood of a major engagement between the two armies, they knew no time must be lost in the actual transfer of command. Probably for that reason they placed him in a position where a man of his character could do nothing but obey immediately and without question.[30] They realized his dilemma and the difficulties he faced in assuming such an immense burden upon short notice and did what they could to furnish him with the power and means to make his command effective.[31]

Halleck carried out their wishes by sending an explanatory letter to accompany the order from the adjutant general's office, which was only a simple transfer of authority from one person to another. Halleck's letter, however, was an important document because it contained a statement of the extent of Meade's control over the Army of the Potomac and forces immediately outside of it, as well as a definition of his relations with the general in chief. He carefully outlined the dual role of the army according to the strategical concepts of Lincoln and the War Department. They perceived its function to be that of "the covering army of Washington as well as the army of operation against the invading forces of the rebels." Halleck enjoined Meade to "maneuver and fight in such manner as to cover the capital and also Baltimore, as far as circumstances will admit. Should General Lee move upon either of these places, it is expected that you will either anticipate him or arrive with him so as to give him battle." Within these limits Meade was "free to act" as he deemed proper. Beyond the immediate resources of the Army of the Potomac, Meade had subject to his orders the stronghold at Maryland Heights and its garrison, together with all forces "within the sphere of . . . [his] operations." The President, the Secretary of

War, and the general in chief entrusted him with "all the power and authority" they could legally confer upon him, including the right to remove, as he saw fit, any officer from command and dismiss him from the army. Not only officers but any other persons could also be sent away. He also had authority to appoint anyone to a command regardless of seniority, a power which was to prove of immense value to him. Although Halleck said he would confine his control over Meade to advice and would not "hamper" him with "any minute instructions," he expected to be kept "fully informed" of all movements and the positions of both armies so far as possible.[32]

Except for the authority to remove and appoint subordinates Meade's powers, duties, and resources as a commander were neither greater nor less than Hooker's. Halleck would supervise Meade no more closely than he did Hooker, and restrictions on the movements of the army would remain about the same, possibly a bit tighter. The constant obligation to "cover" Washington would set limits on his freedom to maneuver, as it had with Hooker. The concern of the Lincoln administration over the safety of the capital might seem excessive and shortsighted from the standpoint of sound military strategy, but it was understandable because Washington was not only the political but the administrative center of the national government, where the nation's archives were kept. Foreign ministers who reflected and helped to mold world opinion resided there. Washington was the symbol of national prestige and the home of the original Declaration of Independence and the Constitution, sacred records of the nation's hopes, aspirations, and accomplishments. For these reasons General Ethan Allen Hitchcock, the scholarly and venerable military adviser to the War Department, felt its "possession by the enemy [even] for a short time, would injure the cause of the country more than the loss of many battles. . . ."[33]

But the instructions to "cover" Washington were ambiguous. The War Department could have interpreted them as setting up a zone of operations beyond which the Army of the Potomac could not go, thus converting it virtually into a garrison force and reducing its effectiveness as a field army almost to zero. Fortunately in practice Halleck did not give the requirement such a strict interpretation, but he did demand that the safety of Washington and Baltimore (which had just been added to the list of sacred cows) be a foremost consideration in Meade's strategy. Whether Halleck expected

Meade to keep his army always physically interposed between the enemy and Washington is not certain. Meade probably knew without being told that should he leave the approaches to the capital open, even though there was no actual danger the authorities would raise a storm of protest strong enough to blast him from command. If the Washington defenses had been properly manned it might have been the better part of good strategy to catch the enemy between them and the Union army, but in the Gettysburg campaign with total manpower in the East at its lowest ebb, Halleck had reduced the Washington garrison below the limits of safety in order to bolster the diminished ranks of the Army of the Potomac. An attempt therefore to get Lee's army between a hammer and an anvil was not possible. Although Halleck tried to give Meade all the latitude he could, his instructions about the protection of Washington did to a certain extent fetter Meade's strategy because to a conscientious soldier the obvious and safe way to conduct a covering operation is to assume the defensive, which is not usually conducive to destruction of the enemy's army.[34]

While Halleck's letter gave Meade direct control over Harpers Ferry and its garrison to use in conjunction with operations of his army, it did not authorize him to abandon the post or merge its troops with his own forces. That development would come later, after Meade requested permission to do so. With respect to troops in the various military departments, Halleck's instructions to Meade were similar to those he had given Hooker.[35] If Meade's movements should bring him into Pennsylvania and within the jurisdiction of the Department of the Susquehanna, he could assume control over Couch and his forces. As the army approached Frederick, Maryland, Halleck apparently thought it was close enough to Pennsylvania for Couch's command to be considered within Meade's sphere of operations. Accordingly, and to remove any chance of a misunderstanding, he wired Couch to that effect at noon on June 28, while taking the occasion to announce the change in command, a development which must have pleased Couch as the achievement of a long-cherished goal.[36]

Possibly the most valuable of Meade's powers was the unusual authority granted him over anyone directly or indirectly connected with the army. This gave him a tremendous advantage which Hooker did not enjoy. In those days it was the rule that even the general of an army could not make changes in command without preferring charges and paying strict attention to seniority, and any major change had to receive the approval of army headquarters in Washington. Lincoln and Stanton authorized Meade to ignore this practice and make promotions as he saw fit. For greater effectiveness in his military operations he could thus appoint a junior officer in whom he had confidence to a position of authority over his seniors, and he could dismiss from the army not only officers but anyone else he wanted to be rid of, such as newspapermen, volunteer aides, and the like. While his use of this power in the case of Hancock on July 1 and in other instances during the battle increased the efficiency of the army, it caused unfavorable comment and opened him to heavy criticism, for few knew of his unusual authority.

During the four hours between Hardie's arrival at 3:00 A.M. and Meade's reply to Halleck's letter [37] the new commander was busily engaged in observing certain amenities, receiving a briefing of sorts on the military situation, and deciding on the direction of his moves. To this end shortly before dawn he and his son George, who was a captain on his staff, rode with Hardie to Hooker's headquarters some distance away, which they reached just before daylight. Hooker, who had intimations that an important visitor was in camp, was waiting for them fully dressed. Hardie handed him the message from the War Department relieving him of command, and Hooker accepted it with good grace and courtesy. With his usual charm he helped to ease the tenseness and embarrassment of the moment for Meade. The two generals then sat down for a rather lengthy discussion, in which Butterfield soon joined them.[38] Finally Meade emerged from the interview still looking very grave. Then he spotted his son, and with a slight "twinkle of the eye" he said to him, " 'Well, George, I am in command of the Army of the Potomac.' " [39]

What the three generals talked about in their conference can be determined to a certain extent. Undoubtedly Hooker gave Meade his side of the story about the quarrel with Halleck over Harpers Ferry and his reasons for wanting to abandon it. Meade was to use this information, as well as some he received later from Butterfield, in coming to his own conclusions about the post and its garrison.[40] Meade must also have learned where the various units of the army were located, although he later said that he had obtained no "exact information about the condition of the troops and the position of the enemy." [41] If Hooker had any plans for the campaign Meade must have considered them either too vague or completely worthless, for when asked about them sometime after the battle he swore that Hooker had given him "no intimation of any plan, or any views that he may have had up to that moment." Meade said he thought Hooker expected to improvise as he went along according to the exigencies of the situation, just as he himself did during much of the Gettysburg campaign.[42] Actually Meade was unfair to himself in this statement, because he did try to formulate a plan of action in which he could anticipate and not simply follow Lee. His denial of Hooker's assistance in determining his moves for the next few days is borne out by contemporary evidence.[43]

After his interview with Hooker, Meade formally accepted command of the Army of the Potomac in a message sent to Halleck at 7:00 A.M. From that moment it could be said that he was officially in charge of the army, although Hooker remained in Frederick until around 6:00 P.M., when he left for Baltimore to await further orders. Colonel Hardie did not return to Washington until that night, because before he left he wanted to hear Hooker's farewell order to the army, which came out in the afternoon, and as it were to feel its pulse. He pronounced it good.[44] For the time being Butterfield was to continue as chief of staff, until Meade, as was the custom, could appoint his successor. During the day he interviewed three highly desirable candidates, Generals Seth Williams, G. K. Warren, and Andrew A. Humphreys, all of whom for various reasons turned him down. Neither Williams, the adjutant general of the army, nor Warren, the chief of engineers, wanted to take on the work of chief of staff in addition to his regular duties. Humphreys, who finally assumed the position after the battle, spent considerable time in headquarters discussing the matter and decided not to accept then. A topnotch engineer and an excellent administrator, he did not relish giving up combat duty for a desk job, preferring to continue as commander of the Second Division, Third Corps.[45] Under the circumstances Meade had no recourse but to ask Butterfield to remain in his present capacity for an indefinite period.[46] Considering the emergency it was perhaps for the best, since he was familiar with the machinery of the army and was reasonably efficient. A new man might have lost precious hours in becoming accustomed to the duties and responsibilities of this pivotal position in the echelon of command.

Butterfield unfortunately was a controversial figure and later on proved to be no friend of Meade's, though he apparently served him loyally during the Gettysburg campaign. He, Hooker, and Sickles formed an intimate trio in army circles which had powerful connections in the area of national politics and good relations with certain outstanding newspapers.[47] While he counted among his friends such important politicians as Secretary of the Treasury Salmon P. Chase and Senator Henry Wilson, chairman of the Senate Committee on Military Affairs,[48] many able and prominent officers in the army disliked and distrusted him. General Patrick considered him a busybody who "seems to be held in universal contempt yet is regarded with more than loathing by those who feel his power."[49] General Humphreys fully agreed with this appraisal and added his own epithets of "false, treacherous, and cowardly" to characterize him.[50] Yet Meade, who once thought Butterfield a bad influence on Hooker, to all appearances got along with him and expressed appreciation for his help during the week they worked together in army headquarters.[51]

Even before Meade had made arrangements for Butterfield to remain, he started to work "with a will"[52] on the many other problems confronting him. He was much too busy to call his important officers together and meet them formally or to seek major changes other than in the position of chief of staff. Without bothering to publish a list of his general staff Meade apparently asked such specialists as Brigadier Generals Henry J. Hunt, chief of artillery, Marsena R. Patrick, provost marshal general, and Rufus Ingalls, chief quartermaster, to continue in their present capacities. They were all good men, and by retaining them he avoided a huge turnover of personnel in army headquarters and consequent waste motion because each general had his own personal staff.[53] Meade as commander of the Fifth Corps of course had his own aides whom he brought with him.

By the time Meade wired his obedience to the order to assume command of the army, he had already decided upon a general course of action. He told Halleck that he would "move toward the Susquehanna, keeping Washington and Baltimore well covered, and if the enemy is checked in his attempt to cross the Susquehanna or if he turns toward Baltimore, to give him battle." [54] In preparation for a general advance the next day Meade began pulling in the loose ends of his army toward Frederick. The infantry and the cavalry were well scattered between Middletown and Poolesville, Maryland, twenty miles away to the southeast. The Twelfth Corps at Knoxville, having received orders from Hooker the night before, had marched to Frederick on the morning of the 28th and reached its destination about noon.[55] One of Meade's first orders went out at 7:30 A.M. to General Sedgwick near Poolesville, directing him to move the Sixth Corps straight north to New Market, a town six or seven miles east of Frederick on the main road to Baltimore.[56] Later in the morning he called in Reynolds and the three corps under him from Middletown to Frederick. The Third Corps went beyond Frederick to encamp near Woodsborough. ten miles to the northeast.[57] At the same time the Second Corps moved up from Barnesville to Monocacy Junction, three miles south of Frederick.[58] By the end of the day Meade had concentrated the bulk of his infantry in or near Frederick and pushed one corps well in advance. The Sixth Corps was the only one that did not reach its destination that night; it stopped at Hyattstown, nine miles southeast of Frederick.[59]

As part of his preparations for his forward movement Meade shook up the command of the cavalry in the hope of improving its efficiency. After consulting General Pleasonton and accepting his recommendations, Meade wired Halleck an unheard-of request: to promote in one jump three brilliant young officers from the rank of captain to that of brigadier general. They were Elon J. Farnsworth of the 8th Illinois Cavalry, George A. Custer of the 5th United States Cavalry, and Wesley Merritt of the 2nd United States Cavalry. Either Halleck approved in record time, or else Meade went ahead without his permission, for within a matter of hours Pleasonton had three new generals who could be assigned to commands in the reorganization of the cavalry he made that day. Pleasonton converted Stahel's division, which had just joined his command, into the Third Division of his corps and assigned to it Brigadier General Judson Kilpatrick, who was known more for his reckless bravery than his brains. Farnsworth and Custer took over the two brigades of the division. Merritt reported to Buford, who put him in charge of the Reserve Brigade of the First Division. The horse artillery received reinforcements and was organized into two brigades: the First under Captain James M. Robertson consisting of five batteries, and the Second under Captain John C. Tidball which had four batteries.[60] Strengthened in numbers, reinvigorated by the addition of aggressive leaders, and divided into three equally strong divisions, the Cavalry Corps stood ready to meet the increased rigors of the campaign. Two of its divisional commanders, Buford and Gregg, had been tried and found capable of meeting the responsibilities of their positions. Kilpatrick remained to be tested.

The tempo of Meade's preparations seemed to increase as the day went on. Early in the afternoon Halleck sent him a cordial message approving of his "general views" on strategy and offering to assist him in every way possible. He told Meade that those of Schenck's troops in the Baltimore area which were not on garrison duty and all of Couch's men were subject to his orders. Halleck also informed Meade of a policy of the government requiring military commanders to take possession of military supplies which were likely to fall into enemy hands, even though at the time they were not needed by their own troops. He was particularly anxious to prevent the enemy from seizing horses and beef cattle, he said. He also gave Meade the unwelcome news of Stuart's raid, but he refrained from offering any suggestions for countermeasures other than to say that General Heintzelman, who was in charge of the Washington defenses, had no cavalry at his disposal. Meade immediately assigned two brigades and a battery of Gregg's division to go out after Stuart, but otherwise he showed no undue concern over the threat to his communications.[61] He took the precaution, however, of suggesting to Halleck that he have Schenck increase the force at Ellicott's Mills, with orders to hold the bridge there at "all hazards," and to guard Relay Junction, a key point on the Baltimore and Ohio Railroad between Washington and Baltimore. Meade informed Halleck that he had previously ordered the 6th New York Militia and a section of artillery to leave Monocacy Bridge and rejoin Schenck, and that these men could be used to strengthen the forces at the places mentioned. Halleck was worried about the safety of unprotected government property while it was being transported by canal from Edwards Ferry to Washington, so Meade instructed Pleasonton to have Gregg detail a regiment for escort duty.[62]

The question of what to do about Maryland Heights and the force there under General French bothered Meade all day, apparently as a result of some needling suggestions from Butterfield. Meade and his chief of staff discussed the matter after Butterfield asked him whether he intended to keep the troops there. When Meade answered in the affirmative, Butterfield, taking advantage of his greater familiarity with problems of strategy, presented convincing reasons for removing the garrison and ordering the men to join the rest of the army. Meade, he pointed out, had the authority to do what he wished with them. The supply lines between Washington and Harpers Ferry were exposed and difficult to protect; once cut, the garrison which had limited rations on hand would have to evacuate the post anyway. What worried Butterfield more than anything was the size of Lee's army, which he obviously considered to be as big as Meade's. Under these circumstances it would be the better part of wisdom in his opinion for Meade to reinforce the Army of the Potomac with French's men; otherwise he might end up with fewer infantry than the enemy. Butterfield undoubtedly was genuinely concerned about the need to bolster the ranks of the Union army, but there is the suspicion that in presenting his arguments he also saw an opportunity to vindicate his friend, Joe Hooker. If he could persuade Meade to abandon Harpers Ferry, it would serve to confirm the soundness of Hooker's strategy while repudiating Halleck's.

Meade was not sure about giving up the post, for while he agreed with Hooker's analysis that Harpers Ferry was of no importance as a "crossing-place" of the Potomac River, he did think it extremely useful as a base from which to conduct operations in the Cumberland Valley. Rather diffident about making a decision without consulting Halleck, Meade asked approval of a compromise arrangement allowing him to withdraw a portion of the garrison and leave a force just strong enough to hold out against a surprise attack. Upon receiving Halleck's permission, Meade proposed to keep 4,000 men at the post and order the remainder, estimated to be 7,000, to Frederick to guard the Baltimore and Ohio Railroad.[63] Before executing the plan he decided to ask French how many troops he thought were needed to hold Maryland Heights. French's response was like a dash of cold water to Meade's scheme, for he clearly indicated he could not hope to protect the post with less than his present force of between 10,000 and 11,000 men, since they were of such poor quality as to be worth only half the same number of veterans.[64]

After getting this unfavorable report Meade yielded to further arguments from Butterfield, and late on the night of the 28th [65] he ordered French to abandon Maryland Heights and send all government property with an escort of not over 3,000 men by canal to Washington. This detachment would join General Heintzelman to help protect the capital against any cavalry raid, while French with the bulk of his force would set out to catch up with the Army of the Potomac. In a long dispatch Meade made it clear to Halleck that the decision to give up Maryland Heights fitted into an elaborate scheme of operations he had worked out in hopes of finding and fighting the enemy. Since Stuart's cavalry had cut off telegraphic communications between him and Washington, he said he had to go ahead with his movements without waiting to hear Halleck's reactions to his plans. Halleck finally approved of Meade's strategy, including abandonment of the heights, only to point out to Meade some of the practical difficulties in vacating the position. He wanted none of the ordnance stores destroyed unless absolutely necessary; yet with the canal greatly damaged there would be difficulty in transporting them to Washington. French too wondered how he could obey Meade's orders virtually on a minute's notice without resorting to a wholesale destruction of government property. Finally French decided to ignore Halleck's warning not to destroy ammunition and supplies, and he left Brigadier General W. L. Elliott behind with 4,000 men to do the task. French himself marched with 6,000 troops to Frederick, which he reached on the afternoon of July 1. Early that night he received new directions from Meade to establish his command near Frederick for the purpose of holding the town and protecting the communications between it and Baltimore to the east and the Army of the Potomac to the north. It was a fortunate assignment because French's inexperienced troops were given an important task, for which nevertheless they were well suited, that of guarding the rear of the army from the Potomac River northward. Should the army meet disaster, Meade instructed French to fall back and add his forces to the defenses of Washington.[66]

As it turned out, the remainder of French's command left Maryland Heights on July 2. Some of the men joined him and the others went to Washington, thus leaving the post in splendid isolation. The evacuation had no sooner been accomplished than the course of the battle became more favorable to Northern arms, and Meade sent messages to French about the possibility of reoccupying Harpers Ferry.[67] The unforeseen twist of events showed that Meade's original idea of holding the place with reduced forces while using the bulk of the garrison for other purposes had been the right one.

The fate of an outpost at Harpers Ferry was a matter of little consequence compared with the complex problems involved in moving a huge army made up of seven infantry corps, each with its own batteries and wagon trains, one cavalry corps, and an Artillery Reserve of over one hundred guns. At best such a march would be slow going, and there was always the danger of it becoming slower due to traffic jams caused by the trains. A corps of 11,000 men marching four abreast, closed up and without the wagons and artillery, would make a column from two to three miles long. If the marchers were accompanied by a train conservatively estimated to include 222 team-drawn army wagons, some two-horse lighter vehicles, 50 ambulances, and about 26 guns with their limbers and caissons, the column would become five or six times longer, or between ten and eighteen miles.[68] If not properly managed such a large-scale movement by thousands of men and horse-drawn vehicles could easily get into a snarl that would take hours to untangle. The cavalry was less of a problem because it was more mobile and moved at about twice the rate of the infantry, though not nearly as fast as was generally thought. The horsemen rarely went beyond a walk, and it usually took them almost fifteen hours to cover what was considered their maximum for one day, forty miles—and this at the cost of exhausting and laming many of the horses.[69]

Keeping in mind the marching capabilities of his army and the general location of enemy forces, Meade on June 28 carefully planned the advance of each corps and cavalry division so as to bring them close to the Pennsylvania state line twenty-five miles due north of Frederick. Ordinarily he would have allowed two days for such a movement, but in the emergency he realized he had to make it in half the time. To avoid delays and congestion he arranged to have the various units use different roads which went generally in the same direction and more or less parallel to each other, and he carefully designated the time of departure, as well as the route for each infantry corps to follow.[70] By the night of June 28 he knew definitely that the main body of Lee's infantry was in the Cumberland Valley north of Hagerstown and going in the direction of Pennsylvania; that Early's division or a part of it had moved through Gettysburg toward Hanover Junction and York; and that Confederate cavalry, reported to be 3,000 troopers strong, was between him and Washington.[71] His greatest worry was the possibility that Lee was already crossing the Susquehanna.[72] The only hope then would be for Couch to hold him long enough for Meade to "fall upon his rear and give him battle. . . ." If Lee struck out for Baltimore, he would have to intercept him.[73] Meade expected that by nightfall of June 29 he would have his army encamped near his first objective, a front extending between Emmitsburg and Westminster twenty miles to the east.[74] With his men there he would control the main road which ran from Baltimore west through Westminster, Taneytown, and Emmitsburg, and then across the mountain near Fountaindale to Waynesboro, Greencastle, and beyond.

During the period of a little more than twenty-four hours after Hardie tapped him General Meade concentrated his army about Frederick, worked out arrangements for a general advance of over twenty miles, and got his men off to an early start on June 29. It was no mean achievement, and General A. A. Humphreys, a veteran of many campaigns and one of the more astute military critics of his day, fully appreciated it. "I don't know that anyone has an idea of the vast labor connected with the movement of a great Army," he wrote, "unless it is those few that have had experience in moving such an Army." Then he added: "I take it too that this Army has never been moved so skillfully before as it has been during Meade's command." [75]

In spite of Meade's best efforts and his administrative skill unforeseen difficulties arose to hamper operations and to cause tempers to flare. Many of the men were fagged out, some of them completely so, from the fast clip maintained by the army during the three days before Meade took command. Upon reaching Frederick they somehow got the notion that they could rest and relax for a day or so. It came as a shock when almost immediately they were ordered to be up and moving again, as word had been received that the rebels were already in Pennsylvania. At the call to fall in most of them loyally and grimly picked up their belongings and trudged off down the dusty roads with their units.[76] But many of their comrades after months of campaigning in the battle-scarred sections of Virginia found the temptations of Frederick irresistible, and they succumbed happily to the fleshpots of the fair city. Regardless of "stringent orders" and the vigilance of camp guards, they wound up in the bars where good Maryland rye whiskey was plentiful and "made merry with the townsfolk." [77] The people of Frederick had greeted the soldiers with open arms, and Sunday, June 28, became a festive and memorable occasion when business in stores and saloons went on as usual even while the churches were open for worship. Some of the officers and soldiers attended service, but the vast majority crowded into the stores and bought up all the available boots, shoes, needles, pins, tobacco, pipes, paper, pencils, and "other trifles which add to a soldier's comfort." [78] At the moment when his authority was most needed to maintain military discipline, the office of the provost marshal general became singularly ineffective. Owing perhaps to the confusion attending a change in commanders General Patrick had no cavalry detachment at his disposal with which to enforce discipline in camp or on the march. Without it he could not hope to operate efficiently, and as a result he did nothing.[79] One critical newspaperman suggested that Patrick should have followed the example General Ewell set in Chambersburg by issuing an order to close the liquor stores,[80] but if he had done so it is questionable whether he would have had the means to enforce it.

According to one observer, with nobody to maintain order Frederick witnessed "pandemonium" for several days; scores of inebriated officers and soldiers made the nights hideous, reeling down the streets, trying to steal horses or break into houses, and "filling the air with the blasphemy of their drunken brawls." [81] During the day "hundreds" of men were sleeping it off, "lying about the streets, on the door steps, under fences, in the mud, dead drunk. . . ." [82] The attractions of Frederick produced an undue amount of straggling in every corps of the army.[83] From there on north the road was said to be "lined" with stragglers, and every farm was overrun with drunken soldiers, who swarmed around the stables and stole horses whenever they could to avoid walking. Others wheedled or frightened women into giving them food and lodging. In fence corners along the road groups lay too drunk to get up. The few mounted patrols sent out to gather up the stragglers were "ineffective," and many of them were drunk too.[84] Even some usually conscientious soldiers who after days of hard marching had sought a little relaxation and indulged too heavily in the bottle could not keep up with their regiments and fell by the wayside.[85]

Early in the evening of June 29 General Slocum apprised Meade of the situation in Frederick, and he in turn ordered General Patrick to take drastic measures. Stirred up by his commanding officer and finally assigned two squadrons of the 2nd Pennsylvania Cavalry, Patrick sent them back to Frederick to clean out the town, and he also took steps to round up stragglers along the line of march, especially in Middleburg.[86] It was too much to expect the provost marshal general and his assistants without outside help to keep the men away from liquor. Commanding officers of the various units did much themselves to curb the evil when they found that whiskey was abundant along the way as well as in Frederick. The chief of artillery of the First Corps, Colonel Charles S. Wainwright, upon finding several of his men drunk, as punishment tied them by the hand to the rear of a gun and forced them to keep up with the column. After that he rode ahead as they approached each village and emptied out all the liquor he could find in the taverns and shops.[87]

With the difficulties created by drunken soldiers and officers, rainy and drizzly weather which made heavy going on the dirt roads,[88] and the failures of some people to carry out orders, it was a wonder that the army made any progress at all on June 29. Apparently the most serious delay occurred on the road from Frederick to Middleburg. General Slocum, finding his way blocked by the trains of the Third Corps, was held up so many hours that only a part of his Twelfth Corps reached its destination, which was Taneytown; the rest got only as far as Bruceville, five miles to the south. Trains and troops kept coming into Middleburg until late at night.[89] One of the most reprehensible mistakes was made by an "irresponsible" clerk in General Hancock's headquarters who, by failing to deliver Meade's marching orders to the general, delayed the departure of the Second Corps by three hours. It in turn held up the Fifth Corps, which according to Meade's marching schedule could not leave until the Second Corps had cleared the road over which it was to follow. Consequently the Fifth Corps got only as far as Liberty, which was fifteen miles or so from Uniontown, its destination for the day. Both Meade and Hancock were furious. Hancock immediately punished the culprit, but the real sufferers were the men in the ranks. Come what may, Hancock was determined to reach Frizzelburg, the day's objective, or get mighty close to it. Under his stirring leadership and strict discipline which prevented drinking, marauding, and straggling, the men trudged along mile after mile cheerfully and at a good clip though laden with fifty-seven pounds of musket, ammunition, knapsack, cartridge box, shelter tent, blanket, canteen, and rations. As they splashed along the muddy roads the sight of friendly faces and offers of food from kindhearted people cheered them on. The corps made Uniontown that night, just two miles from Frizzelburg, having marched thirty-two miles, much of it in the dark. Its eight-mile-long wagon train had kept up all the way. Upon their arrival the men were greeted warmly by people in the town who furnished them with water, cookies, and in many instances full meals free of charge.[90]

Hancock had no sooner arrived in Uniontown than he got the startling news from some natives that Stuart was in Westminister about four miles away. He at once sent word to army headquarters by special messenger. Meade referred the matter to Pleasonton, who assured him that the "country people" must have mistaken Union cavalry for the enemy's because he knew positively that two brigades under Gregg were at Westminster. Pleasonton could not have been more wrong, for Gregg was nowhere near Westminster, and Stuart's men were there pleasantly engaged in surfeiting themselves with food for the first time in days at the expense of the Marylanders. There is no telling what would have happened if Kilpatrick at Littlestown and Hancock at Uniontown had been told to go after Stuart. Instead of a misadventure Stuart's ride might have turned into a catastrophe.[91]

Meanwhile the First Corps commanded by Major General John F. Reynolds had gone along "swimmingly" all day and reached Emmitsburg a couple of hours before dark. The men were in "fine spirits, marched lively, and behave[d] themselves quite well. . . ." Although some people along the road sold foodstuffs to the men at very high prices, others gave them all they could and encouraged them with smiles and good wishes.[92] The route Reynolds took was a good one; one half of the way the road was turnpike and ran along not far from the eastern edge of the Catoctins. At the same time about ten miles to the west of him Buford with two brigades of his division marched from Middletown to Fairfield by way of the valley towns of Boonsboro and Cavetown. He took the road from Waynesboro through Monterey Pass to cross South Mountain, where he found signs of Confederate cavalry (probably Jenkins') having gone by sometime previously, but no Confederates. The Southerners and the local emergency troops who had tried to delay and annoy them had left a trail of dead horses, barricades, destroyed and abandoned property, and refugees. Buford covered at least thirty-five miles that day to get into a good position to screen Reynolds' advance. Before he left Middletown, according to orders, he sent his reserve brigade under Merritt to Mechanicstown about eight miles southwest of Emmitsburg and near the mountain to protect the rear of the First and Eleventh Corps and bring up all stragglers.[93]

It had been a long day for everybody, but in spite of frustrating delays the results had been satisfactory. Meade, who was "determined," as Colonel Wainwright observed, "not to let the grass grow under his feet,"[94] had demonstrated his ability to move an army quickly. The general advance beyond Frederick had been a good twenty miles, and the only units not to have come close to their objectives were the Fifth Corps and Gregg's cavalry division.[95] Meade kept in close touch with affairs, sending out orders and instructions designed to spur rapid progress. In reply to General Sedgwick, who said he could not reach New Windsor that night, Meade directed him to make an early start in the morning because it was of the "utmost importance" for him to occupy the railroad terminal at Westminster with part of his corps.[96] Apparently this implied rebuke made Sedgwick decide to keep on, for his troops got nearly to New Windsor after all.[97] When Major General George Sykes, who replaced Meade as commander of the Fifth Corps, expressed unhappiness over his progress because of delays beyond his control, Meade reassured him and told him to get over as much ground as he could without fatiguing his men.[98] The Meade temper flashed out when he severely reprimanded General Sickles for the poor performance of the Third Corps on its march to Taneytown. Either he had gotten it off to a late start, or Sickles had failed to keep his command moving at a good pace; whatever the reason, the rear of his column did not clear Middleburg until 6:00 P.M. and seriously delayed the trains and troops following behind. Thoroughly annoyed, Meade told Sickles bluntly and bitingly that the weather and condition of the road did not excuse the bad showing of his corps, which in the same length of time had marched only about half the distance of the Second Corps. He admonished Sickles that he must be ready to move rapidly at any moment.[99]

With the Second Corps at Uniontown, the First and Eleventh at Emmitsburg, and two cavalry divisions out in front, one near Fairfield and the other at Littlestown, Meade on the night of June 29 had both his wings secure.[100] Not knowing the exact location of the enemy and fearing the worst, which would have been an attack on Harrisburg and other important points east of it, he had extended his flanks as far as he could consistent with the "safety and rapid concentration" of the army.[101] He had also kept a slightly greater part of his strength on the left wing as a precaution against a possible sidling movement by the enemy through the mountain passes leading to Frederick.[102] He had set up headquarters at Middleburg, Maryland, which placed him a few miles south of the Emmitsburg-Westminster line and midway between the outer edges of his command.[103] Should the need arise, he could effectively direct a speedy concentration of his forces by using the main road from Baltimore as the axis of his movements.

At Middleburg Meade wrote Halleck a long dispatch giving him a full review of the military situation and what he planned and hoped to do. Satisfied that all of Lee's men had passed through Hagerstown on their way to Chambersburg, Meade said he had decided to shift the weight of his own army somewhat to the right toward the Baltimore and Harrisburg road. The road he probably had in mind went from Baltimore in a northwesterly direction through Reistertown, Manchester, and Hanover to York Springs, where it changed to a northeasterly direction and continued to Harrisburg. This move would permit him to cover the road and use it as a main supply line. Although he did not say so, judging from his orders and other communications he probably felt it would put the army in a good position to meet all eventualities: threats either to Harrisburg, Baltimore, or Washington. He also told Halleck that he would try to keep his forces together with the hope of "falling upon some portion of Lee's army in detail." [104] His order of march for June 30 was designed to carry out this purpose. In its advance the army would tend to move toward the right in the direction of York, but would go less than half the distance of the previous day, thus giving the men in most corps a rest or requiring them to march but a few miles. Army headquarters would move only to Taneytown, six miles by road to the northeast of Middleburg. The Sixth Corps would advance from near New Windsor to Manchester about twenty-two miles to the northeast and thus would increase its distance from the left wing of the army which was at Emmitsburg. Nevertheless, this increased separation of the corps was more apparent than real. Except for the Sixth, all of them, as well as the Artillery Reserve, would be located within a radius of ten miles of Taneytown, and each would have one or two others within supporting distance.[105]

June 30 turned out to be quite different from what Meade probably anticipated when he planned the movements of the various parts of his army. More precise knowledge of the enemy's location forced him to change the emphasis if not actually the direction of the advance. Longstreet and Hill, he learned, were at Chambersburg, pointing toward Gettysburg, and Ewell was at Carlisle and York. Concluding from this information an enemy "disposition" to advance to Gettysburg, he decided to strengthen his left flank by moving the Second Corps to Taneytown and the Third Corps to Emmitsburg to reinforce the two already near there under command of General Reynolds. By giving Reynolds authority to coordinate the operations of the three corps Meade greatly increased their effectiveness. Although Meade had full confidence in Reynolds' judgment, he nevertheless expected him to keep in close touch with headquarters.

Judging from some directions which Meade gave Sickles, however, the lines of Reynolds' authority as commander of the left wing were fuzzier than the orders appointing him to the position seemed to indicate. Early in the afternoon Meade sent Sickles a message directing him to take the Third Corps and report to Reynolds at Emmitsburg, and at the same time he gave him specific instructions about the disposition of his troops when he got there. While on the march Sickles received a verbal order from Meade which countermanded the previous written one and stopped all forward movement of the corps. Meanwhile Reynolds sent his own instructions to Sickles about the location of his troops upon his arrival in Emmitsburg. Sickles wisely referred the conflict of orders to army headquarters, and when the day ended his corps was encamped between Bridgeport and Emmitsburg.[106] Although this administrative confusion may have been due to poor staff work in Meade's headquarters, there is a more likely explanation. As the day wore on with reports of enemy activities pouring in, Meade became ever more anxious about the situation in the area from Gettysburg to Emmitsburg and could not resist issuing direct orders to Sickles and also to Howard without going through Reynolds.[17] Meade's interference apparently caused no difficulties, for there was full and frank exchange of views between him and Reynolds during the day. There is then the question of why Meade bothered to give Reynolds temporary command of at least a third of the army if he was not going to let him exercise it. The answer is perhaps found in what happened on July 1. Once several of his corps were beyond easy reach of his own authority, Meade wanted someone whom he trusted to act in his stead. When Reynolds was killed, Meade deputized Hancock with virtually the same powers.

The presence of Reynolds in Emmitsburg assured Meade that an aggressive and intelligent leader watched over the army's left flank, which was becoming the point of greatest danger. Fortunately Reynolds had the able assistance of Buford.[108] While exercising vigilance and a prowling persistence in scouting the enemy, Buford at the same time protected the Union forces against the prying activities of Lee's men. Pleasonton on the 29th had ordered Buford to proceed to Gettysburg by way of Boonsboro, Fairfield, and Emmitsburg.[109] He very likely stopped on the 30th to consult with Reynolds in Emmitsburg and tell him about two Mississippi infantry regiments with a battery which he had discovered near Fairfield. Because the people in the community out of fear of the enemy had given him not a "particle of information" about them the night before, he unexpectedly had run into the detachments early in the morning. Resisting an impulse to pitch into them because he thought an attack might upset Meade's strategy, he had gone ahead to Gettysburg according to orders.[110] Arriving there at 11:00 A.M. he found "everybody in a terrible state of excitement" because of Pettigrew's advance on the town. Buford's men and horses were, as he said, "fagged out," their rations and forage were exhausted, and none could be found in town. Buford commented disgustedly that "the people talk instead of working." [111] In spite of the poor condition of his command he continued his practice of the previous night of sending parties of troopers throughout the country north, northwest, and northeast of Gettysburg. His reports to Pleasonton and Reynolds were models of accuracy and succinctness, revealing a man dedicated to his work and intolerant of any nonsense. He was all business. [112]

Warned by Buford of the mounting enemy threat, Reynolds took steps to guard the approaches to Emmitsburg from several directions. With two of Buford's brigades at Gettysburg, one of his regiments at Fairfield, and his third brigade at Mechanicstown, Reynolds felt confident that should the enemy advance through the mountains against him he would get prior notice. After he had moved the First Corps along the Emmitsburg road to the bridge across Marsh Creek some five miles south of Gettysburg, he placed two of his divisions to block the roads from Fairfield and Gettysburg and kept one in reserve. Should Lee advance with the bulk of his army from Gettysburg, Reynolds greatly feared he might also send a force from Fairfield to turn the Union left near Emmitsburg. As a precaution he directed Howard to move his corps there and arrange his troops so as to command the roads from Fairfield to Emmitsburg, as well as the pike to Frederick.

While passing on to army headquarters his own appraisal of the situation as it seemed to be developing, Reynolds suggested that if Meade expected to fight a defensive battle he should establish a defensive line just north of Emmitsburg in anticipation of a Confederate advance from Gettysburg. Although he admitted he was indulging in surmise, he felt it would be wise to have an engineer sent out to reconnoiter the position around Emmitsburg. [113] In response to Reynolds' views and suggestions Meade agreed that with the enemy concentrated around Chambersburg an attack on Emmitsburg was possible. He was not sure, however, "whether the holding of the Cashtown gap is to prevent our entrance, or is [to facilitate] their advance against us. . . ." [114] In case of an enemy advance on Reynolds near Marsh Creek or Howard on the Fairfield road, Meade instructed Reynolds to have both corps fall back on Emmitsburg, where he would reinforce them. Reynolds, Meade added, need not await the threat of an enemy attack before retiring from his position if in his judgment one at Emmitsburg were better. He said he regarded Reynolds' location at Marsh Creek as a stepping stone to an advance on Gettysburg rather than as a place to defend.[115]

During the day while waiting for further news and developments Reynolds and Howard under Reynolds' direction worked smoothly together preparing for all eventualities.[116] They looked forward to the morrow with considerable anticipation. Less than a year after the event Howard recalled with affection the last hours he and Reynolds had spent together on the eve of the battle. Ten years Reynolds' junior, Howard had known and admired him since the days just before the war when he had served as instructor of mathematics at West Point and Reynolds held the more exalted position of Commandant of Cadets.[117] On the evening of June 30 at Reynolds' behest Howard rode out from Emmitsburg to First Corps headquarters at Moritz Tavern near Marsh Creek. "I was just in time for supper," Howard wrote, "and sat down with himself and staff in the front room of the house. . . . We had cheerful conversation on ordinary topics during the meal, and then retired to a back room, where the General read me some communication he had received from Gen. Meade, requesting us to animate our troops in view of the struggle soon to transpire. . . . General Reynolds treated me with the most marked confidence," Howard continued, "and we conversed together till a late hour, being in momentarily [sic] expectation of orders from Gen. Meade for the next day. . . . The orders did not arrive by 11 P.M. and I returned to Emmitsburg." [118]

Meade too wondered about what the next day would bring. His perplexity seemed to increase as the pressure on him to make decisions mounted. He knew the Confederates were near at hand, and he worried about precisely where they would strike. An engagement, he sensed, was imminent and would occur within hours. Although he was not unwilling to be decisive, he realized that with so much at stake he could not afford to make an error. A letter to his wife from Taneytown reflected his emotional condition and the slant of his thinking. "All is going on well," he wrote. "I think I have relieved Harrisburg and Philadelphia, and that Lee has now come to the conclusion that he must attend to other matters. I continue well, but much oppressed with a sense of responsibility and the magnitude of the great interests entrusted me. Of course, in time I will become accustomed to this." [119]

Meade's belief in the effect of his advance upon Lee's strategy, though wrong, offers a key to his thoughts, plans, and actions just before the battle. During the day intelligence reports had convinced him that he had achieved the first goal of his campaign, the removal of Confederate threats to Harrisburg. Though he had no way of knowing that Lee had already ordered the withdrawal of his forces from the Susquehanna before he learned of the Federal army's march north of Frederick, Meade's mistaken assumption had certain important effects upon his strategy. It gave him a sense of accomplishment which was good for his morale and that of the army, and it induced him to slow down the furious pace of his march from Frederick just when he was beginning to worry about the need of his men for rest.[120]

Although not sure as yet about his next move, he did know that the time had come for him to get his men physically and mentally ready for battle. He issued a circular requesting all commanding officers to address their troops "explaining to them briefly the immense issues involved in the struggle," and also authorizing them to "order the instant death of any soldier who fails in his duty at this hour."[121] Corps commanders received warnings not to wear the troops out by excessive marching which would "unfit them for the work they will be called upon to perform." To facilitate rapid movement Meade ordered them to give special attention to the reduction of "impedimenta,"[122] arrange to leave empty wagons, surplus baggage, useless animals, and all other unnecessary articles behind, and get their commands ready to move at a moment's notice. Only ammunition wagons and ambulances should accompany the troops, who would carry on their persons three days' rations in haversacks and sixty rounds of ammunition. Meade also directed his corps commanders to familiarize themselves with roads connecting the different corps. For instance, he told Slocum at Littlestown to become thoroughly acquainted with roads, lanes, and bypaths between his position and Gettysburg, and between him and General Reynolds ten miles to his left at Marsh Creek.[123] Meade kept his corps commanders informed on the current military situation, including what he knew about enemy movements, what his army had accomplished so far, and what it would have to do in the immediate future. Treating them as colleagues with common problems rather than as subordinates, his policy was quite the opposite of Hooker's, who had

kept the commanders completely in the dark. Meade had objected
to Hooker's way because, as he said, "important plans may be frustrated by subordinates, from their ignorance of how much depended
on their share of the work." [124] Meade told his commanders that
since Harrisburg and Philadelphia were now relieved of danger, the
army's next moves would depend upon the enemy. His greatest need
was for complete and accurate information, and although it was
mainly a task for Pleasonton's cavalry, he asked for the cooperation
of all corps commanders in securing it.[125]

To Pleasonton Meade explained in detail the nature of his strategic problem as he saw it and what he expected of the cavalry. Because the people in the country were too frightened to pass information along, Meade said that he was largely dependent upon the
cavalry for news. The projected movement of the army, he said, was
toward the main road connecting Baltimore and Harrisburg, and the
"great object" was to find out whether the Confederate army was
divided. He was particularly anxious to prevent any force from concentrating on his right near York, which could get between him and
the Susquehanna, or any on his left, which could move "toward
Hagerstown and the passes below Cashtown." [126] Speaking like a
good infantry officer, Meade emphatically reminded Pleasonton that
obtaining reliable information was the primary duty of the cavalry,
and fighting battles was of secondary importance.[127] Pleasonton
apparently did not agree with Meade's views on the functions of the
cavalry, as witness his comments on two reports which came into
cavalry headquarters late that night. One from Kilpatrick told of his
inconclusive engagement with Stuart and gave information about
the enemy, some of it very inaccurate. The other from Buford was
the culmination of many similar messages from him representing the
work of two days of intensive and superb reconnaissance of enemy
movements. Pleasonton sent them on to army headquarters with the
following endorsement: "Respectfully forwarded. A report from
General Buford and one from General Kilpatrick. Kilpatrick has
done very well." [128]

Messages from various people such as Buford, Couch, Secretary
Stanton, and others, giving ever more definite information about the
enemy, increased in volume during the night. Before many of them
reached headquarters and before Meade could determine the point
of Lee's concentration for an attack and the nature of the country in

✄ *Map 3* ✄

MOVEMENT OF ARMIES,
JULY 1

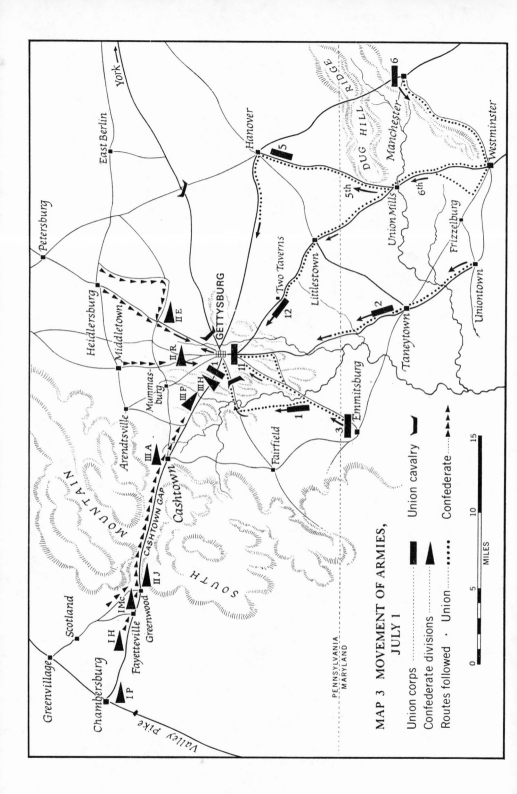

MAP 3 MOVEMENT OF ARMIES, JULY 1

Union corps ━━━   Union cavalry ⊐

Confederate divisions ━━━

Routes followed ┄┄┄ Union ••••   Confederate ▲▲▲

0   5   10   15

MILES

which it would take place, he made two important decisions.[129] One resulted in orders for the army's advance on July 1, and the other produced the famous Pipe Creek Circular providing for a possible withdrawal to a predetermined defensive position. Issued within hours of each other sometime early in the morning of July 1,[130] at first glance these directives appear not only antithetical but irreconcilable. They also seem to reveal extreme vacillation, if not a collapse of "moral courage," on the part of Meade.[131]

Meade's orders were for a general advance in the direction of Gettysburg, which was anywhere from five to twenty-five miles distant from the various corps. Headquarters were to remain at Taneytown. Holding the Sixth Corps at Manchester, Maryland, he instructed the other corps to advance as follows: the First to Gettysburg and the Eleventh to follow within supporting distance; the Second to Taneytown or on to Gettysburg or Emmitsburg as circumstances might prescribe; the Third to Emmitsburg; the Fifth to Hanover; and the Twelfth to Two Taverns.[132] A look at an area map will show that Meade thus placed two corps at or near Gettysburg and four others on main roads converging on the town. Three of the latter were from eleven to thirteen miles away from the center of the borough or about six hours marching time and perhaps considerably less if pushed, since they were supposed to have cut their trains down to ambulances and ammunition wagons. The Twelfth at Two Taverns on the Baltimore Pike was a bare five miles from Gettysburg and could be considered to be almost within supporting distance of the First and Eleventh. One fault with Meade's arrangements was the retention of army headquarters at Taneytown. The movement of most of the corps away from it increased the problem of rapid communication and weakened his personal control of operations. However, since Meade kept the weight of his forces left of center, it is questionable whether any other place would have been better for his headquarters. To compensate for the lessening of his direct control of affairs in the outer perimeter, where he felt there was the greatest danger, he had delegated authority to General Reynolds to command three corps.

To challenge the enemy without recklessly exposing his army Meade had worked out a beautiful strategic pattern based upon a realistic appraisal of geographical factors and intelligence reports. He boldly thrust out two infantry corps under perhaps his ablest general to a place where the greatest enemy strength seemed to be concentrating. Together with Buford's cavalry of about 2,900 troopers Reynolds had a force at his disposal of between 21,000 and 24,000 men.[133] If skillfully handled they could successfully attack the enemy or hold him in check until help arrived. In case the Confederates tried to turn Reynolds out of his position near Gettysburg by marching in the direction of Emmitsburg, the Third Corps would be there to meet them and could call upon the Second for help. Should an enemy force at York start out for Baltimore, Meade had the Sixth Corps at Manchester and the Fifth at Hanover with which to check them. On both flanks he had set up a dense cavalry screen. To the perfectionist the flaw in this scheme of things was the location of the Sixth Corps, which in relation to a possible engagement at Gettysburg was too far away.[134]

The position of this corps had greater meaning with respect to another possible battleground which Meade had chosen with the help of his engineers and described in his Pipe Creek Circular.[135] He had planned a line of battle to which his army could withdraw in the event it was unable to fight the enemy on its "own terms" elsewhere,[136] and he had outlined the manner and direction of such a withdrawal, as well as the general positions to be taken by the various corps. Its timing would depend upon the nature of the enemy's movements. Retirement to this line might not take place at all, Meade said in so many words, for he might find it to his advantage to take the offensive himself from the positions his corps would assume on July 1.[137]

It is obvious from this long and detailed directive that Meade was preparing his corps commanders for various contingencies, since he was not sure of the soundness of his move toward Gettysburg and he still remained uncertain about the enemy's intentions. Above all he wanted his commanders ready to make an orderly withdrawal to a prepared position, from which he could defend himself to advantage and move to a counteroffensive. He told his subordinates that since he had achieved his first objective of preventing an enemy invasion beyond the Susquehanna, he would suspend further forward movement "until the enemy's movements or position should render such an operation certain of success." As he saw affairs at the time he wrote the circular, if the enemy assumed the offensive and attacked, his army after holding operations would withdraw to the

Pipe Creek line unless unforeseen developments should occur to change the picture.[138]

The line Meade selected had many advantages. Between fifteen and twenty miles by road south and southeast of Gettysburg, it stretched some twenty miles from Manchester to Middleburg south of Pipe Creek. The creek flowed from the northeast into the Monocacy River about three miles west of Middleburg. Although it would not have been a formidable barrier, the important geological feature of the area with real military significance was Parr Ridge, extending northeast and southwest through Westminster at elevations of 800 to 1,000 feet and widths of four to ten miles. Entrenched on this high ground, the army would have positions almost impossible to storm in frontal attacks or to turn, so that it could effectively cover the approaches to Baltimore and Washington. The line would also be close to the main supply base at Westminster, which was served after a fashion by the Western Maryland Railroad coming from Baltimore. Should the army fall back to the line, the Sixth Corps, the largest in the army, was already in position, and the Second and Third Corps had but a short march to reach it.[139]

Although this plan possessed many of the virtues of a carefully worked out blueprint, which might be expected of Meade with his engineer's mind and temperament, it had several serious drawbacks. Perhaps the general did not give enough consideration to certain intangibles in the situation. For one thing, Meade assumed that he could entice his wily opponent, General Lee, to attack a prepared position inherently stronger than the one at Gettysburg. Lee might well refuse to attack at all and decide to evacuate Pennsylvania and Maryland with all his loot and without offering battle. Should he get his army back to Virginia unpunished, the loss to Northern morale and prestige would be incalculable.[140] The plan also called not only for defensive tactics but defensive strategy as well. If challenged by the enemy, Meade would resort to holding actions while most of the corps retreated for a good many miles to designated spots. Though perhaps militarily sound, such strategy was psychologically undesirable and might demoralize the army. Meade had in mind fighting at Pipe Creek the kind of battle he was to fight at Gettysburg, but there was one important difference. He advanced to Gettysburg to engage the enemy, whereas he proposed to retire to Pipe Creek and wait for the enemy to engage him.

239

On the whole Meade's reasons and motives for issuing the circular were sound, but it proved costly to his reputation as a general. The accent of the paper was on withdrawal and a defensive posture, despite allowances made in fine print, so to speak, for an opposite policy. Taken out of the context of what he did during the critical two days before the battle, the document can easily be interpreted by an unfriendly critic as a confession of Meade's confusion and paralysis. When considered as part of a larger scheme of things, however, it can be seen that Meade's commitment to the plan was only tentative and that he had devised it as a hedge against certain contingencies.[141]

About the time that Meade dispatched the circular to Reynolds on July 1 he sent him a long and revealing message.[142] In it he said he could not decide whether to attack until he learned more definitely at which point the enemy was concentrating. He hoped to get the necessary information during the day. Meanwhile since Reynolds knew more about the condition of the troops in his area than he did, Meade wanted his advice on whether Gettysburg was a good place for either defensive or offensive operations.[143] Thus he left the question of a general engagement at Gettysburg to the able and aggressive Reynolds. In this message Meade resolved the contradiction between the order for a general advance and the instructions for withdrawal contained in the Pipe Creek Circular. When studied in reference to each other the three papers demonstrate Meade's willingness to fight Lee at any time and any place as long as it was to his advantage to do so.

Without missing a beat in tempo, in a little over two days after assuming command Meade had made a general advance of thirty miles and put his army in a good position to meet a challenge from the enemy. Considering the nature of his instructions and his uncertainty about the concentration of Lee's army, his own forces were not unduly scattered. Halleck, with whom Meade kept in touch as much as possible, approved of his dispositions with one reservation. Not getting the complete picture from Meade's messages, the general in chief expressed fear that the enemy was drawing Meade too far to the east of the mountains.[144] He should not have worried, for Meade kept a sharper eye on his left than his dispatches indicated.

When Meade sent two corps to Gettysburg on July 1, he probably did not anticipate real trouble, but neither did he try to avoid it.

John C. Ropes, the distinguished military historian, had the rare opportunity in April, 1864, of discussing the Gettysburg campaign with Meade. His cautious comments offer a fair appraisal of Meade's generalship up to the time of the battle. "In all this," Ropes wrote, "it seems to me that Meade acted with great prudence, and with sufficient boldness. I don't see any objections to his plan, so far." [145]

X

ARMS AND MEN

By the time the two armies became locked in bloody combat at Gettysburg after days of groping blindly for each other, both generals knew they were beyond easy reach of their bases of supply and they would have to fight with the men and materiel they had on hand. Both forces already included most of the first-class soldiers readily available in the eastern theater of the war, and before any more could be gathered the issue would be decided in battle. According to tradition, the Northern army had a decided advantage over its Southern opponent in manpower and equipment. A typical comment on the greater strength of the Army of the Potomac was made by General Longstreet, who in his memoirs waxed truly lyrical about Northern arms and munitions. With considerable exaggeration he said that Federal artillery appointments were so "superior" that Confederate officers "sometimes felt humiliated" when forced to face them in "unequal" combat. In small arms he maintained Union troops had the "most improved styles." [1] Though the testimony of such an outstanding soldier deserves respect, the extent of Northern superiority in arms and men in the Gettysburg campaign to this day remains a matter of speculation.

In preparing for the campaign General Lee had assumed on the basis of fragmentary information that the Union army under General Hooker considerably outnumbered his own. It is doubtful, however, whether he ever learned the exact number of brigades in the Army of the Potomac or their identities. At least in his correspondence and reports he never gave any indication that he had such knowledge, though he faithfully read the Northern newspapers to obtain any facts and figures they might obligingly publish just, it would seem, for his special benefit. Such information was often unreliable and out of date, but at times it was all he could get. Early in May, for example, immediately after the battle of Chancellorsville, he saw a report of Dr. Jonathan Letterman, Hooker's medical director, which some careless official in the War Department had allowed to be printed in the Washington *Morning Chronicle,* and from it he concluded that late in April the Army of the Potomac had numbered more than 159,000 troops. At the same time he read a false report in the *New York Herald* about reinforcements being sent to Hooker, presumably to make up for losses he had incurred in the recent engagement at Chancellorsville.

Using these figures as a basis for his calculations, Lee estimated the odds to be more than two to one against him. He seemed completely unaware that with thousands of Hooker's men leaving the service as their terms of enlistment expired, the Army of the Potomac was rapidly declining to the nadir of its strength during the war. As the Gettysburg campaign unfolded and Lee planned his moves, he continued to assume the enemy still possessed vast numerical superiority.[2] This state of affairs did not bother him—he had grown accustomed to it—if only he would be able to concentrate all of his own forces against Hooker. His greatest concern was the possibility that General John A. Dix would organize a drive against Richmond from the east and force him to divert some of his brigades to protect the capital while the main body of the Army of Northern Virginia was confronting Hooker at Fredericksburg.[3] Should that threat evaporate and he could have all his men with him, Lee felt perfectly confident of being able to wage a successful offensive against what he thought was a much larger army, because man for man he considered his own forces infinitely superior to those of the Army of the Potomac.

In contrast to Lee's views Generals Hooker and Meade guessed the two armies to be quite evenly matched. Hooker thought there could not be a difference of 2,000 men one way or the other between the two forces, while Meade went so far as to give the balance to the Confederates by more than 11,000 men.[4] Neither general estimated his opponent's strength correctly, and it is doubtful whether Meade even knew how many men he himself had at the beginning of the battle.[5]

Ever since then students of the engagement have been unable to agree about the size of either army, although for what the figures are worth, it is known that Lee had thirty-seven infantry brigades and Meade fifty-one. If this number seemed to give Meade a decided advantage, it was nothing compared to Hooker's at Chancellorsville when he had fifty-seven brigades of foot soldiers to Lee's twenty-eight. With respect to cavalry at Gettysburg, the Federals could pit eight brigades against the six of the Confederates, plus Imboden's semi-independent command of mounted men.[6] Northern advantage in this auxiliary service apparently was only slight, although information about the number and condition of the troopers and their mounts on both sides is irritatingly vague. As for artillery, the Confederates could boast of sixty-nine batteries to the sixty-five brought up by the Union army, but thereby hangs a tale. Because a Confederate battery had a normal complement of four guns, while its Union counterpart had six, Lee possessed 272 or 281 pieces as against Meade's 362, 364, 366, 370, or 374, depending upon who counted.[7] Theoretically the Federals could smother the Southerners with the greater weight of their metal, but whether this would happen depended upon such unforeseen circumstances as gun emplacements, location of the battle lines, and tactics.

The Army of the Potomac, mustering fourteen more infantry brigades than its adversary, seemed to have overwhelming superiority where it counted most, for in Civil War tactics the chief fighting unit was the infantry brigade. The regiment, having an authorized strength of between 900 and 1,000 men, was its basic component for purposes of recruitment and the distribution of supplies, equipment, and ordnance. The center of the soldier's universe was the regiment, but the real concern of the commanding general was the number and strength of his brigades. The brigade had at least two regiments, and at the beginning of the war it numbered about 2,000 officers and men, but after two years of hard campaigning most brigades had fallen way below their normal complement unless more regiments had been added to them. By 1863 the average brigade was composed of four or five regiments, yet few of them could muster as many as 2,000 troops because their reinforcement did not keep pace with the rate of attrition in their regiments. Both the Federal and Confederate governments had not maintained the authorized strength of their regiments, although for somewhat different reasons. The South understandably had greater difficulty in keeping the ranks filled because of its much smaller white population and the fact that many men had to stay home to work in the factories, run the railroads, and maintain the food-producing farms. In the name of states' rights and constitutional freedom many Southern governors vigorously opposed the Confederate Conscription Act of 1862 and impaired its effectiveness.[8] The Northern government had less excuse for its shortcomings in mobilizing its manpower. At first it had no well-designed program to replace losses in its older regiments. Finally it adopted one with the passage of the Conscription Act of March, 1863, only to eviscerate it by disbanding undermanned regiments at the same time as it was accepting new ones sponsored by state governors.[9] By the summer of 1863 most Union regiments which had entered service during the early months of the war had dwindled to a fraction of their original strength. In the Peninsular campaign the average size was already down to 650 officers and men; at Chancellorsville this figure had fallen to 530, and at Gettysburg to 375.[10] In many regiments the reduction was even more drastic, with certain units being able to present for duty only 100 officers and men and in some cases even fewer.[11]

At Gettysburg out of the total of eighty-eight infantry brigades which both armies brought on the field sixty-eight had four or five regiments. Yet as far as can be determined most of them mustered only somewhere between 1,000 and 2,000 officers and men.[12] Because of this great variation in the size of these units and the impossibility of getting their exact numbers, merely counting brigades in each army does not afford a fair comparison of their respective strength. It is misleading therefore to say that Meade, because he had fourteen more infantry brigades than Lee, had a decided advantage over him.

General Henry J. Hunt, the grizzled Union artillerist who years later wrote his own history of the battle, complained in irritation that there was no subject on which everyone was so much "at sea" as on the question of relative numbers. All through the war, he said, both sides were guilty of "absurd exaggeration" about the strength of the enemy.[13] As for the various tabulations made in June of 1863 of the size of the major units in the Army of the Potomac, he wrote emphatically that he would not give a "bawbee" for them. The one computed for June 20 he adjudged to be probably a field return, "a count of noses—with most commands." That of June 30 was a regular return such as an adjutant general "delights in and swears by," but it was "pretty much guesswork," having been made out "long after that date when the army was on the move." The reports of Hooker and Meade, he said, were simply "signed aggregates of the returns however made out," and most such reports he considered "unreliable."

For one thing, many of the returns were padded, Hunt said, whether consciously or not, although the Union commanders seemed unaware of the unreliability of their returns. At the battle of Antietam, for example, 400 cavalrymen had been detached from their regiments to serve in several batteries of horse artillery under his command, but through some error the 400 men had been counted as 1,200 in the army tabulation. Again, Hunt pointed out, when Hooker appeared before the Committee on the Conduct of the War, he testified that at the time Stahel's cavalry joined the Army of the Potomac it numbered 6,100 sabers. But when this force became the Third Division of Pleasonton's cavalry on June 28, its strength was reported to be between 4,000 and 5,000 troopers. The next day, according to Hunt, its new commander, General Judson Kilpatrick, made another check of the figures and found the unit had an effective strength of only 3,500 men.[14]

In many instances a glance at the muster rolls of a regiment would not reveal its actual strength, particularly in the Federal service, for the number of men present for duty might be far less than the total listed. Sometimes the proportion was less than a third of those reported, as in the case of one regiment in the Army of the Potomac in the summer of 1863 which on the books had a strength of 525 men but only 172 officers and men were present for duty. The rest of the members were on special duty, detached duty, or in the hospital. Only a few were absent without leave.[15] To make matters worse, the classification "present for duty" often did not reflect the real situation, since certain essential services behind the lines had to go on. Sometimes such assignments cut down the number of men to a point where there was practically no one available for the front line. One company in the 12th Massachusetts, which was perhaps typical of many, reported thirty-four men present for duty on July 1, 1863; yet only seventeen rifles appeared on the crest of Seminary Ridge. Of the rest one had been assigned as color guard, two as drummers, two as provost guards, and one each for the following duties: bugler, wagonmaster, teamster, ambulance driver, headquarters aide, hospital cook, brigade butcher, brigade engineering worker, brigade cattle guard. As if these details had not weakened the company sufficiently, three men who might otherwise have strengthened the battle line had straggled during the march to Gettysburg.[16]

Once an army began active campaigning it became almost impossible to know its numerical strength. During these periods of marching, countermarching, halting, and fighting, the old routine of camp disappeared, many extra new duties came into being, and the "curse of straggling" set in, some of it necessary but much of it willful. Under these circumstances the regimental morning reports were apt to be slurred over or suspended; even if they were made according to regulations they were liable to be untrustworthy as to the number of men who could be placed in line of battle.[17] What falsified the records even more was the practice of leaving large numbers of stragglers on the rolls as present for duty because their officers expected them to catch up with the marching columns.[18] In the Gettysburg campaign where many regiments made forced marches day after day this method of covering up for responsible but exhausted men undoubtedly became widespread. For these reasons there is no way of knowing the exact strength of the two armies on the eve of the battle. The figures in Union reports made in June, especially the one of the 30th, are highly suspect, while the Confederates attempted no reckoning of their numbers after May 31; at least no such report has been found. Therefore it is not surprising that estimates of effective strength in both forces fluctuated from the fantastic to the plausible.

Among the many attempts made after the war to ascertain the exact strength of the opposing forces at Gettysburg two are noteworthy. A group of Union officers in search of more accurate figures for the size of the Army of the Potomac proposed to return to "first principles" and go to the same men for information from whom the consolidated morning reports had been primarily received, that is, the commanding officers of regiments and batteries. They assumed that an officer despite the "turmoil and confusion" of a campaign would in most cases accurately remember the number of men he had carried into battle. If by correspondence they could tap the memories of enough officers to fix the number of men in one corps, they could then compare it with the consolidated reports in the War Office and strike a fair average for the strength of the other corps and the whole army.[19] Unfortunately the outcome of the study is not known, but whether these officers realized it or not, they were imitating the Confederate practice of determining the strength of their forces by counting the number of muskets actually carried into battle instead of the names found on the rolls.[20] Such different methods of computing the sizes of the opposing forces explain why a Confederate division of 6,000 officers and men could very well have had as many troops in the battle line as a Union corps reported to be half again as large.

Another study of comparative strength at Gettysburg was made in November, 1886, by the War Records Office of the United States War Department while it was in the process of compiling the famous *Official Records of the Union and Confederate Armies*. It came to the conclusion that the effective strength of Union forces was 93,500 and of Confederate 70,000. Despite its shortcomings this estimate is more realistic than any of the others, for it took into consideration certain known facts.[21] It rightly assumed that Lee started out from Virginia with a force of 77,518, which was over 2,000 men stronger than the 75,268 officers and men reported to be at Fredericksburg on May 31. Those who made the study noted that while Lee received reinforcements after that date, he also dropped off some units along the way: Corse's brigade of Pickett's division and one regiment of Pettigrew's brigade at Hanover Court House; three regiments of Early's division at Winchester; and one regiment of Stuart's cavalry division somewhere in Virginia. The mistake they made was in not including all additions to Lee's army, as well as in generally underestimating the strength of these units. The study then compounded the error by making an overly generous allowance of almost 10 percent for losses from sickness, straggling, guard duty, and casualties incurred in various encounters between June 1 and June 30. In this manner it reduced the size of Lee's army to a questionable total of 70,000 troops of all arms as it approached Gettysburg on July 1.[22] It would have been better if the study had avoided such slippery subjects as the extent of sickness and straggling while the army was on the march because information about them is frustratingly elusive. But since it did raise these questions it should be pointed out that according to strong evidence, Lee's army on its way to Pennsylvania suffered little from straggling, while it enjoyed better health than ever before.[23] It seems fair to assume then that losses from these causes were more than offset by the large number of reinforcements which it received. The only legitimate deduction from the 77,518 officers and men who started out on the campaign would be the 1,680 casualties in minor but nameless skirmishes and in the engagements at Brandy Station, Winchester, Aldie, Upperville, and Hanover. Thus it appears likely that Lee brought at least 75,000 troops to Gettysburg, truly a formidable force.[24]

The War Records Office study used a different and perhaps sounder approach in arriving at the figure of 93,500 officers and men for Meade's army, after it had at first estimated his force to have been as much as 101,679 effectives of all arms. This larger total resulted from adding 4,310 reinforcements received between June 30 and July 3 to the 97,369 officers and men reported on June 30. In the study no attempt was made to estimate the amount of straggling after June 30, which was considerable, and deduct it from the figure of 101,679. For reasons not given, the War Records Office apparently thought this total was unrealistic and decided to get at the problem in a different way. Fortunately it had available the consolidated field return of the Army of the Potomac, which was based upon roll calls made on July 4 by all batteries except the Artillery Reserve and all corps except the cavalry. To the 56,138 officers and men who answered the roll call it added the 21,895 casualties sustained by the seven infantry corps and their artillery during the battle; 13,000 men in the cavalry; and 2,500 in the Artillery Reserve as shown by the return for June 30. Thus it came up with the figure of 93,500.[25] This total represented a more accurate calculation of Union strength than did the first estimate, because it was based upon roll calls taken after the battle when the army was resting, many stragglers had been rounded up, and medical authorities had obtained a fairly complete count of the wounded with the reoccupation of Gettysburg on the 4th. Nevertheless the more conservative figure of 93,500 in all probability still reflected an inflated picture of the actual fighting strength of the Union army, if for no other reason than the fact that four of the corps included in their field returns for July 4 anyone who could report for duty whether or not he carried a rifle.[26]

If the estimates of 75,000 troops for Lee and 93,500 for Meade are accepted at face value, it must be admitted that the disparity in favor of the Union army gave the Northern commander an advantage, although not an overpowering one because he was opposing a superbly led force possessing tremendous confidence and cohesion. A close study of action during the three-day battle, however, increases the suspicion that the difference in strength between the two armies instead of being greater than 18,500 troops, as many Confederate officers maintained, was considerably less.[27] Tangible evidence to support this contention is found in a roll call of the Union infantry and cavalry which was taken on July 5. This time all the corps seem to have reported only their effective strength because the infantry units listed almost 2,500 fewer officers and men than they did the previous day. If these figures for the strength of the infantry and cavalry on July 5 are added to those for the artillery on July 4 and to the battle casualties, it appears that Meade's army had only about 85,500 effectives at Gettysburg.[28] This lower estimate bears out the impression prevailing among Union officers at the time that the "forces engaged were very nearly equal." [29]

Thus the advantage which Federal forces possessed in numbers was probably much smaller than is commonly supposed. As for the arms and equipment used by both armies, despite the claims of General Longstreet and his fellow officers there was little to choose between them. The superiority of Meade's artillery lay in a larger number of guns, somewhat better ammunition, and greater uniformity of equipment in many batteries. General Hunt had from eighty to ninety more guns than General Pendleton, chief of Confederate artillery, and could expect a higher proportion of his shells to explode than could his opponent. Hunt's batteries always contained the same type of gun, such as four to six 3-inch rifles or the same number of 12-pounder smoothbores, whereas the Confederates might have two of one kind and two or four of another in one battery. This arrangement increased the problems of supply in a battery and impaired its general efficiency. The Confederates had resorted to this makeshift in the early months of the war because of a shortage of guns of all kinds. By May of 1863, however, the scarcity of cannon had been greatly eased, and only the reluctance of Pendleton to force his artillerists to break old habits and work with unfamiliar equipment prevented the adoption of a rule of uniformity.[30]

Despite these differences Lee's and Meade's artillery were basically the same; both sides relied primarily on identical types of guns and used them in almost the same proportion. Over 40 percent of the cannon hauled to Gettysburg were Napoleons or guns similar to them,[31] for these smoothbore muzzle-loading weapons, designed during the reign of Napoleon III of France, had become the favorite light fieldpieces of both Northern and Southern armies. Sometimes referred to as "the 12-pounder gun-howitzers," with a bore diameter of 4.62 inches, they had when using 12-pound solid shot a maximum range of 1,680 yards and an effective range of around 1,200 yards. Served by a crew of five or six men, as in the case of most other field guns, they could fire two "aimed shots" a minute with shells or solid balls, or four charges of canister at "point-blank range" as an enemy attacked.[32] No other gun could match it for effectiveness against infantry at close range. Placed on the battle line or immediately behind it, and firing canister, which was nothing more than a tin can jammed with between twenty-five and seventy-six pellets from a half to one and a half inches in diameter, it could blow huge holes in the close formations of attacking forces.[33] For them the shouted command, "double canister," had an ominous sound and spelled disaster unless the gunners could be picked off.

The bulk of the other field guns in both armies, although muzzle-loaders, had rifled barrels, usually three inches in diameter, and could hurtle a smaller projectile much farther with greater accuracy than could the Napoleons. Of this class were the 3-inch Ordnance and the 10-pounder Parrotts. Although both used explosive shells, solid shot, and canister, they proved more useful in silencing enemy batteries than in stopping infantry. Of breech-loading rifled cannon the Confederates at Gettysburg had two of the British-made Whitworths, which had exceptional range and accuracy. Stationed on Oak Ridge to the northwest of the town, they were beyond the range of even the nearest Union guns, but could send their own "bolts" screaming down to Little Round Top, a distance of over three miles. The effect of these guns was more psychological than real, for long-range artillery fire did not cause many casualties. Aside from small-arms fire the efficient killers of troops all during the war were the Napoleons at close range.[34]

When Longstreet wrote that Union troops at Gettysburg had small arms of the "most improved styles," veterans of infantry regiments were glad to read about it for they had not been aware of it at the time.[35] They had all heard of fancy new breech-loaders of latest design, but few had seen any and fewer still had used one. Most infantrymen considered themselves fortunate if they were equipped with a recent model of the muzzle-loading British-made rifled musket, the Enfield, or its counterpart, the faithful Springfield, a product of the United States Arsenal at Springfield, Massachusetts. Soldiers in Lee's army had the same high regard for both of these arms, and most of them carried one or the other into battle. At Gettysburg the standard weapon of both Northern and Southern infantry was a muzzle-loader of some sort, whether a Springfield, Enfield, or a less desirable make.[36] In the hands of trained and experienced troops they could kill and maim a tremendous number of men.

To fire a Springfield or an Enfield a soldier had to bite off the end of the cartridge, pour the powder down the barrel, and ram the bullet on top of it. He then affixed the percussion cap to a nipple, against which the hammer struck when he pulled the trigger and made the spark ignite the powder. A veteran could blaze away four times a minute, but only for a short while before his barrel would become foul. Usually he maintained a rate of fire of between two and three shots a minute. He could easily hit a small object up to two hundred yards, and a much larger one up to five hundred yards. At these distances the muzzle-loading rifled musket was a deadly weapon, and using the .58 caliber soft lead bullet, almost half an inch in diameter, it inflicted an ugly wound.

The bullets of the .577 caliber Enfields and the .58 caliber Springfields could be used interchangeably, but at the risk of jamming the gun with the slightly smaller bore after several shots. The ammunition most popular with the soldiers was the "minnie" ball which was misnamed, for actually it was not a ball but a conical-shaped bullet invented by Captain C. E. Minié of the French army. The important feature of its design was the hollow base which the gases of the exploding gunpowder expanded to press the bullet snugly against the rifling of the barrel. The greater spin thus given the bullet increased the range and accuracy of the gun. A paper cartridge contained both the powder charge and the bullet.[37]

By the time the Army of Northern Virginia entered Pennsylvania most of its infantrymen were armed with Springfields or Enfields.[38] The Confederate government's efforts through imports and domestic manufacture to replace the smoothbores carried by nine-tenths of its soldiers at the start of the war had brought results. In addition Southern soldiers and officers gathered thousands of excellent rifles and rifled muskets from battlefield debris left by fleeing Yankees. Colonel William Allan, chief of ordnance of Ewell's Second Corps, recalled that after Chancellorsville as a result of such scavenging he had furnished all the regiments of his corps with rifled muskets, caliber .58. In this instance his memory tripped him up, for it seems he forgot that two of General Early's brigades completely re-outfitted themselves from a sizeable cache of small arms which General Milroy thoughtfully left behind in his retreat from Winchester on June 15. Very possibly the weapons these brigades took were of the same caliber as the ones picked up after Chancellorsville. If so, Allan was right in saying that his work in supplying ammunition for the infantry in the Second Corps had been greatly simplified.[39]

No chief of ordnance in any corps of the Army of the Potomac enjoyed Allan's enviable position. After two years of war the federal government despite its tremendous industrial and financial resources had not succeeded in issuing a standard shoulder arm in sufficient quantity to equip all of its infantry. It had developed the best muzzle-loading rifled musket of the day, the Springfield, and could get the equally good Enfield from England, but still there were not nearly enough of either weapon to go around. What is more, in many instances the problems of maintaining proper inventories of ammunition had increased instead of growing less by 1863 as a greater variety of shoulder arms was placed in the hands of the infantry. The explanation for the situation can be traced to a combination of circumstances: lethargic and inadequate mobilization for a prolonged conflict, unimaginative and shortsighted leadership in the War Department, and administrative inertia.

The butt of criticism for the failures and shortcomings of the government's arms procurement program was Brigadier General James W. Ripley, the Union chief of ordnance. The main complaint against him was that at the beginning of the war when he had the rare opportunity of adopting a breech-loading single-shot rifle, or even a more modern repeater, as the standard firearm for the infantry, he chose instead the outmoded muzzle-loader. Since the government had not nearly enough first-class muzzle-loading rifles or rifled muskets on hand to fight even a short war and he had to start from scratch anyway, he would have lost little or no time if he had gotten private and government arms producers to retool and manufacture a breech-loader rather than the tried and true but obsolete Springfield.[40]

Critics who harshly judged Ripley's performance as chief of ordnance were largely justified, though it was unfair to place on him the onus for all the deficiencies in the Union arms program. Ripley possessed the capacity to handle routine matters, but in an emergency the office needed someone with fewer allergies to innovation and with the ability and energy to organize the work of the bureau more efficiently. His aversion to adopting one of the newfangled repeating rifles without thorough laboratory and field testing is understandable; less so is the case of single-shot breech-loaders such as the well-known Sharps, for they had been manufactured since the 1850's. Ripley's worst failure was his refusal to devise a system for testing new weapons and his tendency to argue against their adoption on theoretical grounds before trying them out. To a person of his conservative temperament and training it seemed obvious and sensible to pick out a shoulder arm which needed no testing to show that it could perform well even when subject to the abuse of hard campaigning, and which because of its simple design could be manufactured in large quantities rather quickly. The relatively slow-firing but rugged muzzle-loading Springfield rifled musket seemed to fill the bill, and he decided in its favor.[41]

The effect of Ripley's shortsighted policy on the course of the war should not be overemphasized. Some critics have implied that the war would have been greatly shortened if Union soldiers had carried arms of the latest design into battle. Were these ideas correct, it would be relatively easy to say why this or that engagement was won or lost; but on the contrary, the men who fought in them became efficient killers for a variety of reasons, not because they happened to have a certain kind of rifle. Just as clothes don't make the man, it can be shown that weapons don't make the soldier. One of the more lethal shoulder arms developed during the war was the 12-shot Henry repeating rifle. In the spring of 1863 some of the regiments in General Milroy's command in Winchester at their own expense armed picked men from different companies with these rifles.[42] Although a few men so equipped could not be expected to make much impression on the enemy, they ought to have made some. Nevertheless when Ewell's corps attacked Winchester in the middle of June, Milroy's men did not distinguish themselves either for the heavy losses they inflicted upon the enemy or for their own die-hard resistance against great odds. In contrast, a crack regiment in the famous Iron Brigade, the 2nd Wisconsin, went into battle at Gettysburg carrying Austrian rifled muskets, a most inferior weapon.[43] If this poor rifle interfered in any way with the fine showing of the regiment on July 1, there is nothing in the records to indicate it.

Ripley's insistence upon making the Springfield rifled muskets standard equipment for the Union soldier would perhaps have been subject to less criticism if by the summer of 1863 they had been issued to all infantry regiments in the major armies. The fact that they were not shows it was one thing to adopt a standard weapon and another to purchase and distribute it. For this breakdown in the procurement program the Secretary of War, Simon Cameron, and Edwin M. Stanton who succeeded him, as well as Lincoln as the final authority, must share much of the blame with Ripley. It was Cameron, an unusually inept administrator, who sent purchasing agents abroad at the outbreak of hostilities to scour European arsenals and markets for any available weapons. The government had not enough first-class muzzle-loading rifles or rifled muskets on hand to equip its first group of volunteers and could not wait for its armories and domestic manufacturers to ease the shortage. Through bungling and incompetence the War Department acquired many relics, some of them practically unusable, and at best generally inferior arms.[44] Once these weapons became a part of the Ordnance Department inventories, Ripley faithfully kept them as part of the regular issue of equipment, though they should have been scrapped as soon as the better Springfields became available.

These estimable muskets remained scarce longer than necessary because in the early months of the war the Ordnance Department delayed in arranging for their manufacture on a large scale by private industry, partly because Cameron and Stanton miscalculated the length of the war and partly because of the department's policy of depending as much as possible upon government arsenals and armories for their ordnance and ordnance stores. When the demands of war increased more rapidly than the expansion of facilities at the principal arsenals,[45] the department at length turned to a few private manufacturers. Of the twenty-two companies capable of turning out United States army rifles or Springfields in large numbers, only four received orders in the summer of 1861, and even they did not get into large-scale production until months later. More revealing, the largest number of orders ever made at one time, twelve in all, were dated June, 1862. By then official Washington had at last begun to realize that it would probably be a long war. The remaining orders went out later in 1862 and in 1863. In most instances it took the companies several months to start deliveries. As for Enfield muskets, the department obtained some from domestic manufacturers, as well as by import. The largest producer was Naylor and Company of New York City, which did not make its first delivery until December, 1861. And as might be expected, its biggest order came late in 1862.[46]

The procurement policies of the Ordnance Department and the Lincoln administration as a whole during the first years of the conflict bore fruit in the oddest collection imaginable of shoulder arms. According to the inventory of infantry small arms for the second quarter of 1863 ending June 30, the department had on hand three classes of weapons. Under the heading of "First-Class Arms" there were ten different designs and four different calibers, all but two of which were muzzle-loaders. These included Springfield rifled muskets, models '55 and '61, .58 caliber; United States rifles, models '40 and '45, .58 and .54 calibers; Enfield rifles and rifled muskets, .58 and .577 calibers; French rifled muskets, .58 caliber; French light or "Liege" rifles, .577 caliber; and finally "Dresden" and "Suhl" rifled muskets, .58 caliber. The breech-loaders were .52 caliber Sharps and Merrill rifles. The "Second-Class Arms" included nine different designs, varying in caliber from .54 to .71 with most of them either .69 or .71. All of them were muzzle-loading rifled muskets or rifles, mostly imports of rather ancient vintage from France, Austria, and Belgium. Real antiques made up the list of the five different designs of "Third-Class Arms." Most of them were smoothbore muskets of American, English, Austrian, Prussian, and French manufacture. They all threw out a tremendous slug of lead that would fit in a barrel ranging in size from .69 to .72 caliber. The only rifled muskets rated as third-class arms were the inferior ones of Austrian, Prussian, or Saxon make. During the remainder of 1863 the department increased the size of its inventory without removing any outmoded weapons from its list when it purchased the up-to-date Spencer, Henry, and Colt repeating rifles.[47]

Under the circumstances it is not surprising that only about two-thirds of the Union infantry regiments at Gettysburg were uniformly equipped with either Springfield or Enfield rifled muskets. In a little over a fifth of the regiments the companies had different types of arms. Most of them reported having either Springfields or Enfields, between which there was little to choose, although the men seemed to prefer the Springfields because they were easier to keep in condition. In some regiments, however, the mixture of arms was more unusual. In a few instances there were three different kinds of shoulder arms, as for example the Enfield, Springfield, and Austrian; or the Enfield, Springfield, and Light French. Where the caliber and quality were approximately the same, as in the case of the .577 Enfield and the .58 caliber Springfield, differences in manufacture had little or no effect on the efficiency of the regiment, but it must have been quite disconcerting to ordnance officers in several regiments to find .69 caliber smoothbore muskets being used side by side with .58 caliber Springfield rifled muskets.[48]

In eight regiments apparently all the men had smoothbore muskets as shoulder arms. Whether by design or not, it was probably useful to have a few regiments so equipped, because when loaded with buck (three fair-sized pellets) and ball this musket was deadly in close fighting. The most unsatisfactory rifle, and one which aroused much unfavorable comment, was the Austrian. The springs of the hammer lock were so badly tempered that in many pieces the trigger had to be pulled three or four times before the percussion cap exploded. When the gun finally went off, it had the kick of a mule. These rifles should never have been bought in the first place; yet eighteen regiments carried them into battle at Gettysburg, including three crack Wisconsin regiments.[49] When dissatisfied with their arms and unable to get relief from the Ordnance Department, the men often took matters into their own hands and after a big battle scoured the field for better weapons to replace the ones they wanted to discard.[50] The Confederate soldiers were not the only good scavengers in the war!

Very few Union infantrymen at Gettysburg could boast of having the more modern breech-loading rifle. The possessors of these arms usually belonged to special or *élite* units such as the 1st United States Sharpshooters commanded by Colonel Hiram Berdan of the Third Corps, who had equipped his men with the single-shot Sharps. A similar group, the 1st Company of Massachusetts Sharpshooters, had both Sharps and Merrill breech-loading target rifles. One company in the 1st Minnesota regiment carried Sharps rifles. Another famous outfit, the 13th Pennsylvania Reserve Regiment, known as the Bucktailed Wildcats, apparently had them too. As far as can be determined, no infantryman, unless he had bought one for himself, used at Gettysburg a Spencer or a Henry repeater, about which so much has been written in recent years. Possession of the less esteemed Sharps would have made most Union soldiers happy, for they readily appreciated the advantages of this single-action breech-loader over the best muzzle-loader. In using the Sharps the men could fire more often, while keeping well under cover as they reloaded. In contrast many of those who used muzzle-loaders were hit in the process of getting them ready to fire.[51]

Whereas only a few of the infantry enjoyed the benefits of breech-loading shoulder arms, the entire Cavalry Corps was equipped with them. The Ordnance Department was very generous in supplying troopers with the latest models of carbine, probably because even the unimaginative Ripley must have realized how virtually impossible it would be for a trooper on a horse to get a muzzle-loading carbine ready to fire. The contrast in the department's program for equipping infantry and cavalry units is well illustrated in its purchase during the war of a total of 8,020 breech-loading rifles as against 76,430 breech-loading carbines from the Sharps Rifle Manufacturing Company.[52] It pursued the same policy in buying Spencer repeating rifles and carbines. Although the Spencer Repeating Rifle Company did not start production of its carbine until the summer of 1863, after it had been manufacturing the rifle for some time, the bureau ordered a total of 64,685 carbines but only 11,471 rifles.[53]

Cavalry regiments of Meade's army with a few exceptions went into the Gettysburg campaign with the finest equipment and arms obtainable. The troopers in almost every unit carried breech-loading carbines (usually Sharps single-shot) hitched to their belts; they also carried revolvers (usually Colt army) and cavalry sabers. The exceptions were the men in the 5th Michigan and in at least two companies of the 6th Michigan who were equipped with Spencer repeating rifles instead of carbines. Of all the makes the Sharps carbine was preferred, although the Burnside was also considered acceptable. Troopers in some regiments carried Merrills, Smiths, Lindners, or Gallaghers. In some companies there was no uniformity, and the men might be equipped with two or three different makes, with the caliber varying anywhere from .50 to .54.[54] In the matter of equipment and arms the Cavalry Corps had few complaints while possessing definite superiority over its Confederate adversary.

Stuart could well boast of the verve, the dash, and the skill of his riders, for as expert cavalrymen they had no peers. Their disadvantage lay in mediocre equipment and inadequate arms, in spite of some improvements before the start of the Gettysburg campaign. Above all his troopers detested the Confederate saddle which was unsightly and uncomfortable, and they always sought the chance to exchange it for one made in the North. They suffered their greatest handicap in arms, for with only pistols, revolvers, and sabers they had difficulty in coping with Yankees armed with breech-loading carbines. By 1863 a few of these carbines had become available, even a Southern version of the famous Sharps, but there were never enough to arm more than one, or at the most, two squadrons in a regiment. Carbines of any sort, muzzle-loaders or breech-loaders, were very scarce, and General Lee put pressure on the Confederate Ordnance Bureau to secure some for Stuart. The able Colonel Josiah Gorgas, chief of the bureau, promised in May to send Stuart 1,000 marine carbines, and Colonel B. G. Baldwin, chief of ordnance of the Army of Northern Virginia, strangely enough thought he could round up for the cavalry five hundred of them scattered throughout the other branches of the army. Lacking carbines, some units equipped themselves with rifles, as was the case with Robertson's two North Carolina regiments which joined Stuart armed with sabers and Enfields.[55] At best Stuart confronted his opponents with a motley collection of arms.

Everything considered, the two armies were quite well matched. Never again would General Lee have as good an opportunity to defeat his old foe under conditions which might bring about the decisive military and political results he so eagerly sought.

XI

REYNOLDS ACCEPTS
A CHALLENGE

FOR SEVERAL days the opposing armies had been on a course where a head-on collision seemed inevitable to everyone except those who were to do the fighting. Years later when the passing of time had put the battle in better perspective and highlighted its importance, some people sought to divert glory to themselves by claiming they had known all along that it would happen where it did. Among these were Generals Hooker and Pleasonton, both of whom clamored for recognition of their remarkable prescience.[1] To them Gettysburg had obviously been the place to fight by virtue of its geography and network of roads. Any Union general not immediately seeing its advantages had been either blind or afraid. Basing their interpretation upon the certainty of hindsight, they refused to admit that the battle could have been fought elsewhere or that it might have resulted in an even greater victory for the North. To do so would have proved embarrassing and upset their appraisal of the campaign.

The theory of the inevitability of a battle at Gettysburg is challenged by a contrary tradition which has become an axiom: that the engagement was an accident. Although this interpretation needs qualification, it comes close to the truth for there is no convincing evidence that any commanding officer of either side sat down before a map, pointed to Gettysburg, and said, "Here is where we shall fight. We must plan accordingly." On the other hand, by the night of June 30 both Lee and Meade, judging by what each knew about the other and the disposition of his forces, must have suspected that an early clash of arms in the vicinity of Gettysburg was very possible. Each commander was still feeling his way, however, and neither had as yet decided just where or how he would try to meet his foe.[2]

For General John F. Reynolds, commander of Meade's vanguard, the war had become a very personal affair, because it had brought him close to Lancaster, his birthplace and the home of his youth. He now stood in familiar country, over much of which he had tramped in search of game or fish. The rebel invasion had caused him deep anxiety, and he eagerly sought another encounter with the enemy. Fully appreciative of the importance of Gettysburg in the general scheme of things, he had been well posted by General John Buford on the approaching danger.[3] Nevertheless Reynolds did not anticipate a fight on the morning of July 1.[4] He had spent much of the previous night at Moritz Tavern studying the military situation with Howard and keeping in touch with army headquarters. Finally at midnight, not bothering to get undressed, he had wrapped himself in a blanket and lain down on the floor for a few hours rest. At 4:00 A.M. his aide, Major William Riddle, had returned from Taneytown with Meade's order to advance the First and Eleventh Corps toward Gettysburg. Alert and vigorous as ever, Reynolds studied the order for awhile before going in to wake his aides, as was often his custom.[5]

Although the men breakfasted soon after sunrise and made preparations for the advance, there seemed to be no sense of urgency in their movements. Colonel Wainwright thought that it "rather promised then to be a quiet day for us," but to make sure he asked Reynolds about the "prospects of a fight." In reply the general said he expected none and was "only moving up so as to be within supporting distance to Buford, who was to push out further." [6] Reynolds gave Howard his marching orders and instructed Sickles where to place his corps near Emmitsburg. Major General Abner Doubleday, in temporary command of the First Corps while Reynolds acted as commander of the left wing, issued directions for the order of march, which placed the Third Division in the lead and the First at the rear, but to save time Reynolds reversed it. When the Third Division reached the crossroads at Moritz Tavern he turned it off on a road to the left. He then rode ahead to the First Division, which with Captain James A. Hall's 2nd Maine Battery had camped three miles in advance of the rest of the corps on the Gettysburg road, and ordered it to move immediately without waiting for the Third Division.[7] Because of this switch all units were on the road probably between 8:00 and 9:30 A.M.,[8] and the First Division, which had a considerable headstart, now took the lead.

Composed of two brigades, the division was a first-class fighting outfit and was led by Brigadier General James S. Wadsworth, a distinguished New York State politico turned ardent warrior. The First Brigade of the First Division of the First Corps—to its members sporting their black hats it was first in everything—was made up of Westerners: three regiments from Wisconsin, the 2nd, 6th, and 7th; one from Indiana, the 19th; and one from Michigan, the 24th. Led by a Hoosier, Brigadier General Solomon Meredith, and schooled in the art of warfare by Brigadier General John Gibbon, a West Pointer from North Carolina who had remained loyal to the Union, the unit by its dash and steadfastness at South Mountain in 1862 had earned the proud title of "Iron Brigade."[9] Gibbon had been transferred to a different command in the fall of '62 and at Gettysburg led the Second Division of the Second Corps.[10] He would have cause to be proud of his old brigade on that first day of July, 1863.

With Reynolds and his staff in the lead, the First Division marched along at a good but unhurried pace, for it had only about five miles to go to its destination and the weather was disagreeably hot and muggy.[11] The Second Brigade, which was commanded by the rugged former "Down Mainer," Brigadier General Lysander Cutler, and Hall's battery preceded the First Brigade in the order of march. The 6th Wisconsin and a brigade guard of twenty men from each regiment brought up the rear of the division.[12] Lieutenant Colonel Rufus R. Dawes of the 6th recalled that he had his drum corps in front, and as he approached Gettysburg he had just unfurled the colors, closed up the ranks, and "taken the step to the 'Campbells Are Coming'" to march into town, when he heard the boom of artillery.[13]

Reynolds had had warning of trouble a little earlier when about two miles from Gettysburg a messenger from Buford had brought him word of an enemy advance on the Chambersburg Pike (Cashtown road). Sending an aide to Wadsworth with orders to close up the division and hurry ahead, Reynolds went to the front of the column. Within half a mile of town he met a frightened citizen on horseback who told him that Buford's cavalry was engaged in a fight. After stopping at a house to ask the way, Reynolds galloped into town and out to the west side, where a little after ten o'clock he found Buford on McPherson's Ridge.[14] What Buford ever since daylight had feared would happen was already very evident: Enemy forces were putting pressure on positions his troopers held west of town.

When Buford entered Gettysburg the day before he had found the people greatly excited over the appearance of a column of Confederate infantry on the outskirts of town. He reported to Pleasonton that as he "pushed" the rebels back toward Cashtown, he perceived the force to be less formidable than what wild-eyed civilians had suggested, but he suspected it was a promise of a major thrust toward Gettysburg. "Push" was not quite the right word for Buford to have used, for Pettigrew's North Carolinians retired peacefully only because they chose to do so. It would have been more accurate for Buford to have said that his tough and battle-wise troopers just followed and observed. Nobody was fooled, but the time had not yet arrived for a showdown.[15] The question was how did General James J. Pettigrew with three-fourths of his brigade happen to be going to Gettysburg in the first place?

The story is—Henry Heth said so himself—that he had ordered Pettigrew to take his brigade to Gettysburg, "search the town for army supplies (shoes especially), and return the same day." [16] In other words, he used up the shoe leather of approximately 2,400 of his infantrymen on a foraging expedition which involved a round trip of sixteen miles or more in weather Lee felt was almost too enervating for men on the move. General Heth should have realized that there was little likelihood of finding worthwhile supplies of any kind and shoes in particular in a town through which Early's men had swept four days earlier. Even if he did not know about Early, Heth's objectives hardly justified using so many men on a long, tiring march, especially as without a cavalry escort he took the added risk of sending them into a trap.[17] Fortunately for him, however, Pettigrew discovered the Federal force in time, and he retired without disputing Buford's possession of the town.[18]

An unforseen bonus of Pettigrew's excursion was the useful information he obtained about the enemy. He told Hill and Heth that he was sure the force occupying Gettysburg was a part of the Army of the Potomac, but the two generals were sceptical. Then he called in a member of his staff, Captain Louis G. Young, who had remained in the rear of the brigade as it retired to Cashtown to observe the Union cavalry following them. Young testified that "their movements were those of well-trained troops" rather than of a home guard unit, but Hill still refused to believe that any portion of the Union army was up.[19] He had just come from a conference with General Lee, where both generals had concluded from intelligence reports that the enemy army was still at Middleburg. As for the cavalry Pettigrew had discovered at Gettysburg, Hill was of the opinion that it was probably a "detachment of observation." Heth then spoke up and asked, since that was the case, whether Hill would have any objection to his taking his division to Gettysburg again the next day to get those shoes. Hill replied: " 'None in the world.' " [20]

According to Captain Young, this "spirit of unbelief" seemed to have clouded the thinking of most, if not all of the commanding officers in Hill's corps and left them unprepared for what happened. Pettigrew had noted the topography of the country between Cashtown and Gettysburg and passed on his observations to Brigadier General James J. Archer, whose brigade would take the lead in the morning.[21] He warned Archer about a certain road intersecting the pike which the Yankees might use to hit his flank, and the dangers of McPherson's Ridge. Archer "listened, believed not, marched on unprepared. . . ." [22]

Hill sent word to General Lee at his headquarters in Greenwood that an unknown number of enemy cavalry was at Gettysburg and that he intended to march there in the morning and find out who was in his front.[23] The announcement seemed not to have disturbed the commanding general, since he expected to move his headquarters only as far as Cashtown the next day.[24] Colonel E. P. Alexander remembered going to Lee's headquarters late on June 30 and having a "long visit" with his "old comrades" on the general's staff. Everyone was relaxed, and the conversation was "unusually careless & jolly. Certainly there was no premonition that the next morning was to open the great battle of the campaign." [25]

McPherson's Ridge, which Buford had chosen as a good defensive position to oppose Heth's division, was a typical feature of the country west of Gettysburg. The town itself lay in the center of a

꧁ *Map 4* ꧂

THE INFANTRY ENGAGEMENT,
MORNING OF JULY 1

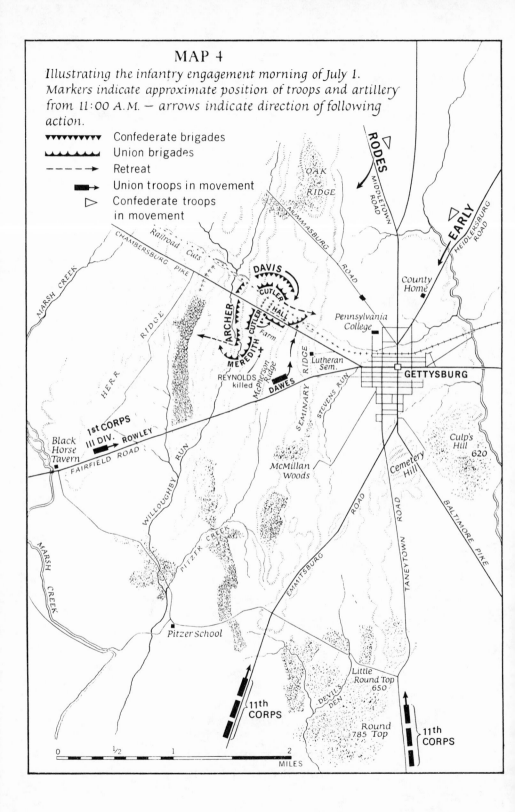

MAP 4

*Illustrating the infantry engagement morning of July 1.
Markers indicate approximate position of troops and artillery
from 11:00 A.M. — arrows indicate direction of following
action.*

vvvvvvvvvvvv Confederate brigades
⌄⌄⌄⌄⌄⌄⌄⌄ Union brigades
– – – –→ Retreat
▬▬▬→ Union troops in movement
▷ Confederate troops
in movement

RODES

EARLY

MIDDLETOWN ROAD

HEIDLERSBURG ROAD

OAK RIDGE

NUMMASBURG ROAD

CHAMBERSBURG PIKE

Railroad Cuts

MARSH CREEK

HERR RIDGE

DAVIS

CUTLER

HALL

ARCHER

CUTLER

Farm

MEREDITH

REYNOLDS killed

DAWES

McPherson Ridge

SEMINARY RIDGE

County Home

Pennsylvania College

Lutheran Sem.

STEVENS RUN

GETTYSBURG

1st CORPS
III DIV. ROWLEY

Black Horse Tavern

FAIRFIELD ROAD

WILLOUGHBY RUN

McMillan Woods

Culp's Hill
620

Cemetery Hill

EMMITSBURG ROAD

TANEYTOWN ROAD

BALTIMORE PIKE

PITZER CREEK

MARSH CREEK

Pitzer School

DEVIL'S DEN

Little Round Top
650

Round Top
785

11th CORPS

11th CORPS

0   ½   1   2
MILES

basin, squeezed from the east and west by a series of long, rather flat hills and ridges, between which stretched fertile fields and lush meadows and pastures. In 1863 the countryside was much more open than it is today. Even the woods were comparatively open, for their fine tall trees kept them free of underbrush. Out of keeping with the rest of the landscape were such rocky and rugged prominences to the east and south as Culp's Hill, Little and Big Round Top, and Devil's Den, which seemed to have a New England cast about them.[26] Although Gettysburg was the seat of Adams County with a population of about 2,400,[27] in appearance it had nothing to distinguish it from many other towns in that part of the state. The streets followed the usual gridiron pattern pretty faithfully, and the main thoroughfares connecting it with the outside world came together at the square in the center of town. The most unusual feature of the place was the large number of roads converging there, all of which had lateral connections so that the town formed the center of a weblike complex of highways. Three of these were the turnpikes to Chambersburg, Baltimore, and York, which because of their improved surfaces could be used in all weather for heavy transportation.[28] This network of roads and the open nature of the country would lend themselves to rapid military maneuvers for offensive operations, while the hills and ridges would afford many fine positions for an army on the defensive.

Of the landmarks destined to figure prominently in the battle the first was the Lutheran Theological Seminary which stood on Seminary Ridge about three-quarters of a mile west of Gettysburg. It was beautifully located in a grove of trees about a quarter of a mile south of the Chambersburg Pike and the same distance north of the Fairfield road. The ridge ran north and south for about two miles at an elevation of approximately forty feet above the town. A belt of trees crowned it for most of its length. In the estimation of Colonel Wainwright, who had the artillerist's good eye for such things, the position at the seminary, "though wanting in depth, was not a bad one on which to resist a front attack, if we should not be outflanked." [29]

Less than half a mile west of Seminary Ridge and separated from it by low, moist ground covered with swale rose the wider and more open McPherson's Ridge. It stretched north from the Fairfield road to a point beyond an unfinished railroad cut, where it veered to the

northeast to merge with Oak Ridge, which was really an extension
of Seminary Ridge. The cut ran almost parallel to the pike and
about four hundred feet north of it. South of the cut McPherson's
Ridge had two crests about a fifth of a mile apart, which gradually
came together in woodland of a little over seventeen acres in area.
In the depression between them and just north of the wooded area
were McPherson's barns and large farmhouse. Willoughby Run
meandered south along the western side of McPherson's Ridge, and
beyond it the ground rose to Herr Ridge, an even higher elevation.[30]
It was from here that the Confederates launched their first major
attack.

Heth had started his division and Major W. J. Pegram's battalion
of artillery for Gettysburg at 5:00 A.M. on July 1.[31] General Buford
was ready for him. Having gained "positive information of the
enemy's position and movements," he wryly reported that he had
made his "arrangements" for "entertaining him until General Reynolds could reach the scene." [32] During the night of June 30 Buford
had placed videttes on the Chambersburg Pike about four miles
from Gettysburg to keep an eye on the enemy skirmish line half a
mile farther west. They received the first intimation of a general
movement when Heth's skirmishers, stretched out for a mile and a
half, advanced slowly but steadily. In the rear of the line, columns
of Heth's infantry deployed into the woods. Buford's pickets used delaying tactics by scattering themselves at intervals of thirty feet behind post and rail fences and throwing up a rapid fire with their
Sharps carbines. The Confederates, sensing that only a small force
was opposing them, resorted to frontal and flanking moves. Gradually their pressure increased. About 8:00 A.M. Colonel William
Gamble, commander of Buford's First Cavalry Brigade, received a
report at his headquarters in the seminary building that a strong
enemy force was driving in his pickets.[33] He at once informed
Buford of the situation, and he in turn ordered Gamble's 1,600
troopers to form a battle line on Herr Ridge a mile west of the seminary, the right resting on the railroad cut and the left near the Fairfield road about a mile to the south. Lieutenant John H. Calef took a
battery of six 3-inch guns of the Horse Artillery (Battery A, 2nd
United States) and placed one section on each side of the Chambersburg Pike, covering the approaches of the enemy, and a third section
considerably to the left.[34] The Confederates advanced cautiously in

column on the road, with three extended lines on each flank. Soon they opened on Gamble's men and Calef's battery with two batteries judged to have had four guns each. Calef held his own and Gamble's troopers kept the enemy in check, but the pressure became so great that the Union line moved back to McPherson's Ridge, where the men continued to make a stand.[35]

Reynolds found Buford shortly after 10:00 A.M. When he saw the strength of the cavalryman's position he ordered him to hold back the enemy as long as possible,[36] for the First Division with its 3,500 veteran soldiers[37] was still some distance off.[38] To hurry up reinforcements for the hard-pressed Buford, Reynolds rode back through town and out about half a mile on the Emmitsburg road. Here he ordered his escort to tear down all fences and make way for his men to cut across the fields to Seminary Ridge. Meanwhile he rushed off several messages. One went to Howard urging him to hurry, and another to Meade, informing him that the situation was serious and that the rebels were coming on in large numbers and might seize the heights on the other side of the town before he himself could occupy them in force. He promised Meade that if he were driven into town, he would fight step by step behind barricades until help arrived.[39]

Reynolds had good reason for wanting to hold McPherson's Ridge in spite of certain weaknesses in the position. As long as the enemy came from the west it adequately covered the approaches to the town. The stand of timber in approximately the center of the ridge afforded protection for occupying forces because they could send an enfilading fire on enemy columns moving along either the Chambersburg Pike or the Fairfield road or both at once. The greatest defect of the position was the exposure of its right flank to artillery fire from Oak Hill to the north and attacks from infantry which could use nearby fields of tall wheat as a cover for their movements.[40] The railroad cut, which was ten to twenty feet deep, partly offset this weakness because it would prevent a sudden assault on the right flank of a line facing west, but if not watched it could also be used as a hidden passage for a flanking column.

Reynolds did not have long to wait at the Emmitsburg road for Cutler's Second Brigade, which was in the lead, followed immediately by Hall's 2nd Maine Battery of six 3-inch guns. As the infantry dropped off noncombatants and useless luggage and hurried at "double-quick" across the fields around McMillan's and Dr. Schumacher's homes to Seminary Ridge, Reynolds himself escorted Hall to a position previously occupied by a section of Calef's horse artillery.[41] The cavalry had started to give way before the mounting pressure of Archer's brigade attacking south of the pike and General Joseph R. Davis' brigade north of it, so Buford had ordered Calef to pull out before it was too late.[42] When Reynolds placed Hall's battery between the pike and the railroad cut, he fully appreciated the hazards of the move, for the Confederates were beginning to swarm through the cut and appear on Hall's flank. Reynolds and Wadsworth both came up to Hall and briefly discussed the situation with him. Reynolds, who was extremely concerned, turned to Wadsworth and ordered him to move strong infantry support to Hall's right until he himself could bring up the other troops who were just arriving. Then, speaking as an old artilleryman, he explained to Hall that he had put him in an exposed position because he wanted him to smother the enemy battery on his front and prevent it from firing on Union infantry while it was being deployed. Reynolds promised to pull Hall back as soon as he could because he was too far in advance of the general line. Reynolds' tactics were successful, for at 10:45 Hall started firing at the enemy battery 1,300 yards away, and after six shots caused its commander to place two of his guns under cover behind a barn.[43]

Cutler's brigade was the first to get into line. Two regiments, the 84th and 95th New York, at Reynolds' direction were placed south of the pike near McPherson's farm to protect Hall's left flank, while three regiments, the 76th and 147th New York and the 56th Pennsylvania, under Cutler moved across the railroad cut to the right of the battery. When Reynolds left Hall he rode to the left of the Union position to hurry the Iron Brigade to the front. Captain Daniel Hall of Howard's staff, who had left his superior three or four miles from Gettysburg on the Emmitsburg road and had galloped ahead, found Reynolds with his staff riding rapidly across the open fields west of the seminary. Spurring forward, Hall overtook Reynolds almost at the skirmish line, reported to him, and asked for orders. Reynolds directed him to order Howard to move up with his corps as rapidly as possible and "join him at the scene of action." [44] He had previously sent his aide, Major William Riddle, to Howard with orders to have the Eleventh Corps camp on the right of the

Emmitsburg road south of Gettysburg.[45] Now he was most anxious to change these instructions and hurry Howard forward. His order revealed Reynolds' increasing concern about the strength of the enemy attack and his determination to force an immediate show-down.

The first crisis of the battle had developed, and it was questionable whether Reynolds could hold on alone. The three right regiments of Cutler's brigade barely had time to deploy in their line of battle before the enemy advanced within easy musket range. Although some good Wisconsin men in later years vehemently disputed its right to the honor, General Cutler accorded to the 56th Pennsylvania regiment under Colonel J. William Hofmann the distinction of being the infantry unit which fired the first volley in the battle of Gettysburg.[46] At this moment the Iron Brigade was pouring into the depression just west of the seminary. Officers from General Wadsworth's staff ordered the men forward. Then Captain Craig Wadsworth of Reynolds' staff galloped over to the brigade and, pointing to the Chambersburg Pike, yelled that the enemy was advancing on both sides of it; Reynolds wanted them to hurry up and get to the ridge [47] for Archer's brigade was rushing up its western slope.[48] Immediately the 2nd Wisconsin, which was the lead regiment under the highly esteemed Colonel Lucius Fairchild, dashed forward.[49] Near the ridge they met Reynolds, who shouted, " 'Forward men, forward for God's sake and drive those fellows out of those woods. . . .' " [50] The men loaded their guns as they ran up the slope, to be greeted at the crest by a volley of musketry which brought many of them down. Without breaking step they followed their determined colonel and advanced steadily into the timber.[51] As Reynolds, at the rear of the regiment, turned in his saddle to look for supports, there was a heavy exchange of volleys between the enemy and the 2nd Wisconsin. Reynolds suddenly swayed and fell to the ground. Veil, his devoted orderly who was nearest to him, leaped down, raised the general's head, and held it in his lap for a moment until members of his staff joined him. But Reynolds was dead, killed by a ball which had struck him behind the right ear.[52] With his death Doubleday, who was next in rank, took over as commander of the corps.

At this stage of the engagement the movements of the contending forces had the appearance of two swinging doors hinged together on the pike. Davis' brigade, largely concentrated north of the cut, swung east and south to hit Cutler's three right regiments head on, while the 55th North Carolina regiment, taking advantage of the peculiar topography, worked itself around and attacked them on the right flank.[53] They fought back, but soon, upon orders from Wadsworth, the 56th Pennsylvania and the 76th New York retired hastily to the cover of the woods on Seminary Ridge, leaving the 147th New York, which had not received the order, to stand alone.[54] This movement of Davis' brigade at the same time threatened the position of Cutler's two regiments, the 84th and 95th New York, which were south of the road, and caused them to pull back and change front to the north.[55] In this realignment Captain Hall saw his infantry supports suddenly leave him just after he had broken a charge on his right and left with double canister. Thoroughly annoyed, he ordered the battery to retire "by sections," although he had no instructions to do so, because he felt that "if the position was too advanced for infantry it was equally so for artillery." After some difficulty Hall got all of his battery safely off except for one piece.[56]

Hall and Wadsworth proceeded to have words of "rather an animated nature" about the affair. Hall, who was very angry, bluntly characterized the "forsaking" of his right by the infantry as a "cowardly operation." Later Wadsworth said it had been an unfortunate mistake. Unaware of Reynolds' death, he knew Hall had been given a special assignment, and he supposed the commanding officer was looking out for him. Hall thought this was a pretty lame excuse.[57] Here was an instance of a conflict in judgment between two good officers, one an infantryman and the other an artilleryman. Reynolds had knowingly put Hall in what proved to be a hot corner to meet an emergency. Wadsworth, with little professional experience, did not fully appreciate the hazards of the exposed position for artillery, especially without proper infantry support. When Hall later in the engagement wanted to return to his original position, Colonel Wainwright, his superior officer, to Wadsworth's annoyance refused to give his permission unless he knew there were troops on hand to guard his right flank.[58]

Whereas the swinging door pushed by Davis' brigade had swept Cutler's men back a quarter of a mile, its counterpart on the other side of the pike brought disaster to Archer's brigade. The timely charge of the 2nd Wisconsin had checked the advance of Archer's men, and at the moment of Reynolds' death the other regiments of the Iron Brigade, except the 6th Wisconsin, were rushing up to lend their strength to the attack. They had quickly changed from a marching formation to a battle line, and each regiment followed the next from right to left in echelon so that the enemy felt the force of successive sledgehammer blows. The Westerners used the same hard-hitting tactics as the Confederates, and the results were devastating to Archer. His men hurriedly backed down the hill, and as they splashed across Willoughby Run the 19th Indiana and the 24th Michigan came sweeping in on their right flank.[59] It was a bad moment for the Army of Northern Virginia, and Archer gained the unenviable distinction of being the first of its general officers to be captured after Lee took command.[60] A good many of Archer's men—the actual number is not known—accompanied him to the rear of the Union line as prisoners of war.[61] The remainder of his brigade under the command of Colonel B. D. Fry fell back to a grove on Herr Ridge about a thousand feet away. The Iron Brigade returned to the west of McPherson's Ridge, where most of it concentrated in the timber tract.[62]

Success for Union arms was not assured, however, as long as Davis' brigade continued unchecked. Cutler's brigade was in serious difficulty. Should its resistance collapse, the rest of the First Division would be in danger, for then the Confederates could move against its right rear. Cutler needed help badly, but where could it be found? Fortunately General Doubleday had available the 6th Wisconsin and the brigade guard of one hundred men which had been attached to it.[63] Together these units totalled 450 officers and men under the command of Lieutenant Colonel Dawes of the 6th Wisconsin.[64] As the fury of the combat increased Dawes did not have long to wait before two staff officers came with orders for him to " 'move to the right' and 'go like hell.' " This was enough for a veteran like Dawes, and he knew at once what to do. Starting from the extreme left flank of the Iron Brigade near the Fairfield road, Dawes turned his regiment ninety degrees and moved it on the run along the depression between Seminary and McPherson's Ridges toward the Chambersburg Pike. As he approached the road he saw a scattered but strong line of rebels at right angles to his line pursuing the two regiments of Cutler's brigade, which were falling back toward town. His line reached a fence at the pike, halted, and opened an enfilading fire which immediately checked the enemy advance. The Confederates, not easily scared, did the obvious thing: They ran to the railroad cut for cover, and from there they mounted a "murderous" fire. Against a less determined foe their maneuver might well have ended in another victory for the Southerners, but instead it proved disastrous. The 95th New York regiment of Cutler's brigade, which had been retiring south of the pike toward Gettysburg, quickly formed on Dawes's left, and the 84th New York, which was farther away, joined it afterward. Dawes ordered his men over the fence, a move which was a "sure test of metal and discipline," and once on the other side he shouted his command as loudly as he could: " 'Forward double quick charge, align on the Color.' " [65] With the 6th Wisconsin and the brigade guard in the lead the men of the various regiments formed a -shaped line and moved firmly and rapidly forward in the face of heavy fire.[66] Finally a number of 6th Wisconsin men got astride the cut at a place where the grading was on nearly the same level as the surrounding fields and laid a heavy cross fire on the Confederates. With one end closed off, hundreds of rebels found themselves trapped in the steep, narrow cut where in places the sides rose as high as twenty feet.[67] All of the 2nd Mississippi regiment and many men of the 42nd Mississippi and 55th North Carolina regiments threw down their arms in token of surrender. Major John A. Blair, then commanding the 2nd Mississippi, and six other officers handed their swords to Dawes and marched off with two or three hundred of their men as prisoners of war.[68]

The rest of Davis' brigade withdrew over the ridge or through the cut, thus removing the threat to the right rear of the Iron Brigade. This counterblow also saved what was left of the 147th New York regiment, which had been cut off, and permitted Cutler to advance some of his regiments to their original positions along the ridge. After these furious engagements on both sides of the pike serious fighting ceased for the next two hours.[69] It was about noon.

The day had started out very badly for General Heth, who had gone on what he thought was a routine mission in search of shoes and information and instead got a fight. Whether his primary objective was footwear or facts Heth did not make clear in his various accounts. Neither did he explain how such an experienced soldier as he had "stumbled" into a major engagement. Whereas years after the battle he claimed he had gone "to get shoes, not to fight," [70] in his battle report he talked about "feeling the enemy" and making a "forced reconnaissance"—whatever that may be—with the object of determining the size and nature of the Union forces in the area.[71] Although he described bitter fighting in which Union soldiers mercilessly mauled two of his brigades, he seemed unwilling to admit what had happened and reported with unconscious irony that "the enemy had now been felt, and found to be in heavy force in and around Gettysburg." [72] Before he decided to commit two of his four brigades to the so-called "forced reconnaissance," he had had warning of danger ahead. He himself had seen from Herr Ridge signs of infantry, cavalry, and artillery in and around the town, but he still assumed that the forces consisted only of cavalry, supported by a brigade or two of infantry at the most.[73] Buford's resistance to his advance seemed to have made little impression on him, for in one of his later accounts he made the amazing denial that he had had "so much as a skirmish with General Buford's cavalry or with any other cavalry." [74]

It may be that Buford's tactics fooled Heth into thinking he had not fought cavalry and instead had engaged a relatively weak infantry force. The Union general had dismounted about three-quarters of his troopers—the others held the horses to the rear—and deployed them in a heavy skirmish line stretching on Colonel William Gamble's front from the Fairfield road to the railroad cut and thence northward on Colonel Thomas C. Devin's front to the Mummasburg road. From his position Devin used skirmishers and videttes to connect with pickets on all roads coming into Gettysburg from York, Harrisburg, and Carlisle.[75] With the limited number of men at his disposal Buford could not establish the kind of battle line ordinarily held by infantry. Therefore Archer and Davis in their advance at first found opposition of not too formidable a nature, and apparently they were overconfident. They pushed ahead too fast, and before they knew it they became fully engaged with infantry and not cavalry. After his initial advantage over Cutler's brigade Davis, flushed with success, lost sight of his objective, which was to feel out the enemy, and plunged to disaster. Archer's sins were of a similar nature, and a foe just as aggressive and skillful as he caught him in the woods.

This explanation loses sight of the fact that Heth possibly had something more on his mind than shoes and information when he made his advance toward Gettysburg. Major John S. Mosby, brilliant Confederate guerrilla fighter and defender of "Jeb" Stuart's reputation, may have been right when he charged Hill with planning a "foray" and calling it a "reconnaissance." Both Hill and Heth, Mosby asserted, "evidently expected to bag a few thousand Yankees, return to Cashtown, and present them to General Lee that evening. But . . . 'they bit off more than they could chew.' "[76] Whatever their reasons for the advance to Gettysburg, now that they had a real fight on their hands Hill and Heth felt compelled to throw in fresh troops, and willy-nilly they committed Lee to a battle without prior notice. Heth refused to concede that he and Hill because of recklessness and poor judgment were largely responsible for this development. Instead he tried to shift the entire blame onto Stuart for not being on hand to perform for Lee the same service that Buford had given to Meade.[77]

The stock Confederate explanation for Heth's unexpected repulse was the appearance of "overwhelming forces" or "greatly superior numbers" of the enemy,[78] but a close examination of the figures does not bear out this contention. When the Iron Brigade attacked Archer on McPherson's Ridge, it went into action without the 6th Wisconsin and the brigade guard. A little more than 1,400 officers and soldiers, aided by a few of Buford's more combative cavalrymen, made up the "overwhelming force" which hurled back Archer's brigade of approximately 1,130 officers and men.[79] On the other side of the Chambersburg Pike the ratio of strength was in favor of Davis' brigade, which had between 2,400 and 2,600 officers and men against a little over 1,600 under Cutler.[80] With the size and quality of the opposing forces approximately the same, the outcome of the morning's engagement may be explained by the greater tactical skill of the Northern generals. When they created a reserve force they took a calculated risk that four-fifths of the Iron Brigade could handle Archer effectively. This reserve permitted them to take full advantage of their interior lines, shift their strength about, and apply it where most needed. The rather intricate movements involved in achieving success were only possible with highly trained soldiers and quick-thinking officers. Heth had the misfortune of meeting one of the crack divisions of the Army of the Potomac, led at the beginning by one of the Union's most outstanding generals. It was here that the element of chance, which often determines the results of an engagement, played its role on July 1. It also entered the situation when Reynolds and his men arrived just in time to replace Buford's troopers as they began to sag under Heth's pressure. Again the attack of the 6th Wisconsin and the brigade guard in conjunction with the 84th and 95th New York regiments must be regarded as an "accidental meeting and voluntary union of two gallant commands from different brigades. . . ." [81]

The question of who among the general officers deserved credit for the decided advantage gained by Union arms in the morning is a difficult one, since the answer depends largely on what was the military situation at the moment of Reynolds' death and where Doubleday, his successor, was at the time. In what was by far the longest battle report of the Union army Doubleday gave a fascinating account of his activities on July 1—if only it were reliable! Since Meade, who had little confidence in him, early on July 2 removed him as commander of the First Corps and appointed in his place Major General John Newton, his junior in rank, Doubleday apparently felt the need to offer lengthy explanations to vindicate himself.[82] Under the circumstances his performance as commander, if not brilliant, was very creditable, and he would have been wiser not to have written quite so much. The element of second-guessing was very strong in his report, and he claimed to have said and done things which are open to question.[83]

If Doubleday, as he asserted, arrived on the field while Reynolds was still alive, then his description of operations and the role he played at the opening of the engagement bears the stamp of authenticity. Doubleday told how he overtook Wadsworth's division as it was approaching the battle line and how he pleaded with the men of the Iron Brigade to hold McPherson's Ridge to the "last extremity." Their response, he said, was, " 'If we can't hold it, where will you find men who can?' " [84] Although they might have said something like this later in the day when the Confederates were making their final and successful attack, it is inconceivable that they did at this time. Regimental reports show that the brigade advanced quickly without a pause from the Emmitsburg road to the depression between the ridges, and that Wadsworth ordered the charge before the men had time to load their guns, much less listen to exhortations from anyone.[85]

Contrary to Doubleday's assertions, there is strong evidence that he came up after, rather than before the action started. According to Wainwright's account, Doubleday rode with him toward Gettysburg at the head of the artillery brigade. When they were about two miles from the town, between 10:30 and 11:00 A.M., they were discussing Meade's promotion, and Doubleday, who was very sensitive about such matters, was complaining about General George Sykes, his junior in rank, having been given command of the Fifth Corps to replace Meade. At that moment someone called Wainwright's attention to the smoke of bursting shells. Upon stopping to listen, they could hear the rumble of cannon apparently three or four miles off, which they thought was from Buford's cavalry. In a few minutes an officer came with orders for them to hurry on, as Reynolds was already fighting. Doubleday and Wainwright then went their separate ways. Wainwright at once spurred on his three reserve batteries, and after going half a mile he turned them off to the left across the fields where earlier in the morning the troops had marched toward the seminary. Halfway there he met Craig Wadsworth, who told him that Reynolds was dead. Shortly afterward the general's body was carried by. Wainwright halted, uncovered, and then went on to the seminary, where he learned that Cutler's brigade had reoccupied its section of McPherson's Ridge.[86] In the meantime Doubleday, who was not encumbered with an artillery train, had ridden ahead of Wainwright and reached the field in time to order the 6th Wisconsin and the brigade guard to the relief of Cutler's men.

Although the accounts are not clear, it seems pretty certain that it was General Meredith who had halted the 6th Wisconsin, which was the rear regiment in the brigade, in order to hold it in reserve along with the brigade guard. After placing the guard under Colonel Dawes's command, he or someone else ordered the combined force forward to join the rest of the Iron Brigade, which was successfully attacking Archer's men. By this time the battle was raging along the entire front of the division. Before Dawes could carry out the order, Doubleday halted him again and detached him from Meredith's brigade to act as a reserve for the whole division. Shortly afterwards staff officers from both Doubleday and Meredith sent Dawes to Cutler's aid.[87] Coming on the field when he did, Doubleday had quickly sized up the situation. He ordered his reserves to make the right moves and they gained a decided advantage for the

division. This measure of praise is due him, but it is very questionable that he organized the attack of the Iron Brigade on Archer's
men, as his report claimed.

Until noon of July 1 the battle really belonged to Buford and
Reynolds. Knowing fairly well what was in store for him, Buford
with cool deliberation had decided to resist the enemy as long as he
was able. He had had time to study the terrain and select his battleground. Apparently without any hesitation Reynolds had accepted
his choice of position to halt the enemy advance.[88] What impressed
Reynolds' aides, especially in retrospect, was the feeling that they
had "come there to stay" and were fighting against time until the
rest of the army could concentrate.[89] Reynolds' actions in the last
moments of his life and his message to Meade showed his determination to force a major engagement at Gettysburg. With barely a
third of his corps immediately available, and confronting a force of
unknown size, he had put himself at the head of his troops to lead
them in a vigorous attack. Personal leadership of this kind, though
considered unduly rash by many people, conformed to Reynolds'
temperament and his philosophy of command. Volunteer troops, he
felt, were better led than driven.[90] Though his death was an excessively high price for any advantages the army might have gained,
his aggressive tactics gave the First Corps room to maneuver in
front of Gettysburg on the west and upset General Hill's timetable.
General Howard expressed the conviction that had General Reynolds "exhibited a less bold front," the Union forces might have been
crushed. "The very energy of Reynolds' attack deceived the Rebel
general," he continued, "and made him cautious in his approaches
. . . before he attacked us." Even after their attack the Confederates did not follow up their advantage, he said, because they were
uncertain of the Union strength and wary of assaulting a strong
position.[91]

Although Howard did not mention the point, if Reynolds had
chosen to be less aggressive in his holding operations he could have
placed his troops on Seminary Ridge and used them to cover Buford's withdrawal from McPherson's Ridge. In that case should the
Confederates have persisted in their advance, the opening phases of
the engagement would have occurred closer to town and Reynolds
would have been deprived of a defense in depth. But because Reynolds decided to fight on McPherson's Ridge, there is no reason to

suppose that he would have continued to maintain the line there indefinitely. The position was strong only if the enemy confined the bulk of his attack to the area between the Chambersburg Pike and the Fairfield road. The weaknesses of the line became apparent in the early afternoon when the weight of the Confederate attack shifted north of the pike and railroad cut. To counteract this move Union officers adjusted the line so that it ran diagonally in a north-easterly direction from McPherson's farm across the pike and cut to Oak Ridge. The farm buildings formed the apex of a salient, so that the Union troops holding the position had to fight on two fronts. To make matters worse, Confederate artillery fire from Oak Hill enfiladed the whole length of the line along McPherson's Ridge.[92]

What Reynolds would have done under these circumstances is impossible to tell because other than informing Meade of his determination to resort to rearguard action by barricading the streets of the town if forced to retreat, he revealed no plans to anyone. Now that he was gone, what would the new senior commander on the field of battle decide to do? As fate would have it, command at Gettysburg devolved upon General O. O. Howard, a good man as his military record during the war demonstrated, but one whose reputation at the time of the battle was suspect because of the poor showing of his Eleventh Corps at Chancellorsville. Suddenly he was on his own many miles from the commanding general, with whom he was on correct if distant terms.

Howard had started his corps from near Emmitsburg after receiving his orders from Reynolds at eight that morning. The First Division under Brigadier General Francis C. Barlow took the direct route of ten or eleven miles to Gettysburg. The Second Division under Brigadier General Adolph von Steinwehr and the Third under Major General Carl Schurz followed the somewhat parallel but two-mile-longer route through Horner's Mills and entered Gettysburg on the Taneytown road. Howard with his staff and a small escort of horsemen rode rapidly to the front through the fields and woods bordering the Emmitsburg road so as to avoid the columns of marching men and the artillery and wagon trains. According to Howard's watch, it was 10:30 A.M. and he was within sight of Gettysburg when a staff officer from Reynolds brought him news that the battle had started. He at once sent an aide, Captain Daniel Hall, in search of Reynolds for further orders, while he himself went forward to see what was going on and to learn something about the country. He noticed Cemetery Hill and immediately saw its advantages as a military position. Riding down into the village to find a vantage point from which to watch the battle, a town resident told him about Fahnestock's Observatory across the street from the courthouse. There he saw the last stages of the morning's fight as Confederate prisoners passed down the street in front of him.[93] About 11:30 Major William Riddle brought him word of Reynolds' death, which had occurred between a half and three-quarters of an hour earlier.[94]

Since he was the ranking officer and now in charge of all the forces on the field, Howard returned to Cemetery Hill for the purpose of establishing his headquarters there and selecting a strong point for his reserves, which he designated to be the Second Division under von Steinwehr and three batteries of artillery under the corps chief Major Thomas W. Osborn. When General Schurz and his staff arrived around noon, Howard turned command of the Eleventh Corps over to him. Schurz's Third Division came up about 1:00 P.M., the men "much out of breath," and moved briskly through town to their positions. Howard rode to town with two or three of his staff in time to meet the head of Barlow's division and accompanied it as it passed along the silent, almost deserted streets on its way to join the preceding division. Barlow sent the four 3-inch guns of Lieutenant William Wheeler's 13th Battery, New York Light, ahead of the column at a fast trot to reinforce the six 12-pounders of Captain Hubert Dilger's Battery I, 1st Ohio Light. Meanwhile the infantry marched more slowly to keep itself fresh for battle. There was little excitement at this hour, and only an occasional outburst of firing beyond the seminary broke the calm.[95]

Between 11:30 A.M. and early afternoon both armies brought up more men and regrouped their forces. The first of the Northern reinforcements to arrive on the scene were the Second and Third Divisions of the First Corps, which had not as yet been in action. They joined their comrades on McPherson's and Seminary Ridges. The Third Division, temporarily under Brigadier General Thomas A. Rowley in place of Doubleday, had taken a route west of the Emmitsburg road and arrived at a point on the Fairfield road south and west of the Union line sometime between 11:00 A.M. and noon. It is probably safe to say that, despite wide disagreements in the reports, the Third Division got in a little ahead of the Second Division of Brigadier General John C. Robinson.[96] An hour or so later Barlow's First Division and Schurz's Third Division of the Eleventh Corps appeared at almost the same time. The last of the Eleventh Corps divisions to arrive was von Steinwehr's, which he reported got there about 2:00 P.M.[97] Although Howard had many more men at his disposal than Reynolds did, he still had less numerical strength than his opponent.

Heth too reorganized his line during the lull in the fighting. After breaking off action with the First Corps he withdrew some distance west of the Union line to re-form his division. He brought his two fresh brigades forward, those of General Pettigrew and of Colonel J. M. Brockenbrough, and placed them in the part of the line which he expected would bear the brunt of a new attack. Archer's and Davis' shattered brigades he assigned secondary rôles. Archer's was placed far to the right to guard the flank, and Davis' to the left of the road where it might collect stragglers. While his artillery and skirmishers maintained pressure on the enemy, Heth gave his men a rest.[98] No doubt he informed Hill of his unfortunate encounter with a tough lot of Federal troops, for before long he received word that he was to attack the enemy once more and that General Pender's division would come to his support.[99]

It is not certain at what hour General Hill, who was ailing and not in the best of form that day, learned about what was going on, or how well he kept General Lee informed of developments. In all probability Lee knew nothing of the engagement until he heard the sound of cannon fire as he was riding along the road to Cashtown.[100] He was visibly disturbed by what it might mean and could barely hide his impatience. To him matters seemed to have gotten out of hand; evidently without his sanction Confederate troops were plunging ahead to battle a foe of undetermined strength and quality. Although Hill doubtless knew of Lee's desire to avoid a general engagement before the army had been fully concentrated, he decided to renew the attack on a much larger scale. There is no record that Hill cleared this operation with Lee or that he sent him a report of Heth's findings from his so-called reconnaissance. If he did, Lee must have had little confidence in Heth's work as an intelligence officer or else he considered the information insufficient as a basis for action. At this moment Lee missed Stuart more than ever. for at the start of every battle it was his custom to send Lee a complete appraisal of the situation.[101] According to General Richard H. Anderson, Lee aired his concern and perplexity half to himself and half to Anderson, saying:

> I cannot think what has become of Stuart; I ought to have heard from him long before now. He may have met with disaster, but I hope not. In the absence of reports from him, I am in ignorance as to what we have in front of us here. It may be the whole Federal army, or it may be only a detachment. If it is the whole Federal force we must fight a battle here; if we do not gain a victory, those defiles and gorges through which we passed this morning will shelter us from disaster.[102]

Though Lee fretted over the absence of Stuart, the knowledge of Ewell's imminence on the enemy's right flank and rear must have been of some comfort to him. His foresight was about to pay off. He had ordered Ewell to Heidlersburg and then given him the option, depending upon circumstances, of going either to Gettysburg or to Cashtown. The time had come for him to make his choice. Whatever Hill's shortcomings in keeping Lee informed, early that morning he had notified Ewell of his intention to advance on Gettysburg. Perhaps he had a premonition of something serious growing out of his expedition. Ewell received the message sometime between 8:00 and 9:00 A.M. before he reached Middletown. He at once turned Rodes's column onto the Middletown-Gettysburg road and instructed Early to march directly toward Gettysburg on the Heidlersburg road. At the same time he very properly sent word to Lee of his movements.[103] The commanding general sent back a warning that if Ewell "found the enemy's force very large, he did not want a general engagement brought on till the rest of the army came up." [104] In a way this was the counsel of perfection, for unless his cavalry could effectively penetrate Buford's screen, Ewell had no way of knowing the strength of the enemy until he tested it himself. As far as can be determined, his cavalrymen seemed singularly ineffective in obtaining information and transmitting it to him. If they were aware of heavy fighting at Gettysburg, they failed to get word to Rodes because, until he got within four miles of the town and heard the sound of a "sharp cannonade," he was completely ignorant of the presence of strong enemy forces.[105]

In contrast Buford's efficiency looms large. About 12:30 P.M. he warned Howard of enemy units massing three or four miles north between the Heidlersburg and York roads. This notice gave Howard time to change the dispositions he had planned for his corps. Instead of prolonging Doubleday's line along Seminary and Oak Ridges north of the railroad cut to a point beyond the Mummasburg road, he had Schurz place the First and Third Divisions, each with a battery of artillery, in the open and relatively flat valley immediately north of town so as to face any enemy force which might come from the direction of Heidlersburg and Middletown. Schurz completed his deployment of the troops about 2:00 P.M. in positions roughly at right angles to Doubleday's front.[106]

A little after 2:00 P.M. Howard, who had previously been in communication with Doubleday by messenger, went to have a look at the part of the battlefield held by the First Corps and to get a better idea of its topography. He met Doubleday on McPherson's Ridge. What the two generals actually said was not recorded, though their reports and correspondence offer clues. Howard undoubtedly told Doubleday about the arrival of the Eleventh Corps, the location of his headquarters, and the disposition of his three divisions: one in reserve on Cemetery Hill, and the other two north of the town. He asked Doubleday to continue his work of protecting the left of the Union position, while he would take care of the right. During their talk Howard expressed concern over the strength of the left of the First Corps line. Doubleday assured him that it was not likely to be turned, particularly since he held McPherson's Woods which he felt possessed the advantages of a redoubt. Howard then decided not to change the position of the First Corps. If Doubleday had any thought about the desirability of retreating to another position, either he did not voice it or Howard did not agree with the suggestion, for neither man mentioned in his writings having had the idea at the time. Before leaving, Howard repeated the instructions he had given Wadsworth, to hold the position as long as he could and then retire.[107]

Prior to his meeting with Doubleday Howard had sent several important messages. The first dispatches, sent at 1:00 P.M., informed both Sickles and Slocum of the fight with Hill and the advance of Ewell on Gettysburg. They made no mention of Reynolds' death or the need for reinforcements. Upon second thought, half an hour later Howard decided to call upon Sickles for help, and he sent him another message. The time at which he sent Slocum a similar one is not known. At 2:00 P.M. he dispatched a very brief report of the situation to Meade at Taneytown with the information that he had ordered Sickles to push forward.[108]

The sleepy little Maryland hamlet of Taneytown had already seen much activity that morning. When the two couriers from Reynolds and Buford reached it, probably within minutes of each other, it was considerably after 11:00 A.M. From Seminary Ridge to Taneytown it had been a hard pounding ride of thirteen miles by the most direct route. Working their way through the main street which was blocked by army trains and filled with bustling quartermasters and commissaries, the messengers found the headquarters of the Army of the Potomac located half a mile farther east in an "unpretending camp, looking very much like that of a battalion of cavalry. . . ." Here the commanding general slept and kept his office in a "plain little wall tent." [109] It is not certain whose dispatch reached Meade first, but for what it is worth, the accounts seem to agree that Reynolds' aide, Captain Stephen M. Weld, got there ahead of Buford's messenger.[110] Meade probably appreciated hearing directly from Reynolds, though it disturbed him to learn that his friend feared an enemy seizure of the "heights on the other side of town" before he could occupy them himself. Weld said that Meade exclaimed, " 'Good God! if the enemy get Gettysburg, we are lost!' " and then he "roundly damned the Chief of Staff . . . for his slowness in getting out orders." When Weld reported that Reynolds had talked about barricading the streets at Gettysburg if it were necessary to stop the enemy, Meade said, " 'Good! That is just like Reynolds.' " Then the general sent all of his aides to "hurry up Hancock and all the other commands." [111]

Other than his indiscreet outburst against Butterfield Meade said nothing about his concern over affairs in Gettysburg. In view of his uncertainty about how the place fitted into his strategy, as explained in his message to Reynolds earlier in the day, his reaction to Reynolds' fears is puzzling. The clue to his behavior perhaps lies in a directive he sent Hancock at 12:30 P.M. about possible movements of the Second Corps in case Reynolds had not received the Pipe Creek Circular. According to instructions in the circular, if Reynolds retired from Gettysburg he was to move down the Taneytown road to cover the center of Meade's position. But if he had not received the circular or was forced to take the Emmitsburg road, Hancock was to advance on the "direct road" to Gettysburg from Taneytown. Seizure of the heights south and east of the town by the Confederates would give them control of the Taneytown road exit from Gettysburg, thus exposing the center of Meade's position and possibly cutting off the two corps under Reynolds from the rest of the army. Furthermore, if no sizeable force stood in their way, Lee's soldiers might swoop down, take Taneytown, and cut the Union army in two. Having complete faith in Reynolds' generalship, it relieved Meade to know that the commander of the left wing was determined to take extreme measures to keep the heights out of the hands of the enemy.[112]

Half an hour prior to dispatching his message to Hancock, Meade in his anxiety to help Reynolds had sent Couch a request to throw a force in Ewell's rear as a threat. Although theoretically the suggestion was well conceived, it was in fact a forlorn hope, since with Couch's main forces thirty miles away at Carlisle and Harrisburg, his intervention could not possibly have influenced events for at least twelve hours after receipt of the dispatch.[113]

The tempo of affairs at headquarters rapidly increased soon after the noon hour. It was then that Meade heard of Reynolds' death.[114] It was a bitter blow, for he lost a friend as well as an officer in whom he had the fullest confidence.[115] Meade had sent Reynolds to Gettysburg partly for the purpose of looking it over as a place to fight. Death cut off his final report, so Meade still faced unanswered questions. Fortunately he had an equally active and energetic friend and subordinate in General Hancock, to whom he could turn to complete Reynolds' work.[116] Hancock had marched his Second Corps into Taneytown from Uniontown that morning. After arranging for it to go into bivouac about 11:00 A.M., he had ridden over to make Meade a courtesy call and to find out what was going on. After exchanging pleasantries, as is the way with old friends, the two generals got down to business and discussed Reynolds' advance to Gettysburg, Meade's plan to fight somewhere along Pipe Creek, and the orders he was preparing to carry out his intentions. Hancock returned to his quarters and had not been there long when Meade appeared at his tent with the announcement of fighting at Gettysburg and the death of Reynolds. He wanted Hancock, he said, to transfer command of the Second Corps to General John Gibbon and himself to depart immediately for Gettysburg, where he would take command of the First and Eleventh Corps and also of the Third which was at Emmitsburg. Knowing Meade's views, Hancock was also to decide whether Gettysburg was a good place to fight, considering the terrain, the positions of Union troops, and other circumstances. Should the report be in the affirmative, Meade would scrap his present plans and order a concentration of the army there. When Hancock pointed out that he was junior in rank to Sickles and Howard and that Gibbon was not the senior brigadier in the Second Corps, Meade assured him that Stanton had authorized him to make whatever changes he saw fit among his commanders. The emergency was so great, Meade explained, that he had to use Hancock, the one able and available officer who had just received a complete review of his plans. Although Hancock had his reservations about the legality of such a procedure and the acquiescence of his seniors to his temporary command, he accepted the assignment without further question and about 1:30 P.M. set out for Gettysburg.[117]

XII

THE FRUITS OF VICTORY
ELUDE LEE

ABOUT 2:30 P.M. General Rodes's long lines of infantry emerged
from the cover of the woods on Oak Hill, and the fighting broke out
with renewed fury.[1] Rodes had ridden ahead of his men to look over
the field and plan how best to strike the right flank of the First
Corps, which at that moment extended about a quarter of a mile
north of the railroad cut. He perceived that if he moved his men
south along Oak Ridge, which was heavily wooded, he would have
the advantages of concealment and of position for a surprise flanking
attack. However, before he could advance his division and deploy it
along the ridge the First Corps generals had made preparations to
oppose him.

Warned of Rodes's approach by Buford's cavalry, Doubleday had
used his reserve division, Robinson's Second, to extend his line north
about half a mile on Oak Ridge to its final position near the Mummasburg road. Farther south other units of the First Corps on
McPherson's Ridge were preoccupied with Hill's men. All at once
they became painfully aware of impending blows from another
quarter when two batteries of Lieutenant Colonel Thomas H.
Carter's Artillery Battalion moved into position on Oak Hill and
opened an enfilading fire all along the line to the Fairfield road. Because Cutler's brigade was particularly vulnerable to an attack from
that direction, General Wadsworth pulled some of its regiments
back to Seminary Ridge and formed a line diagonal to the Chambersburg Pike facing northwest and connecting with Robinson's di-

✖ *Map 5* ✖

AFTERNOON BATTLE,
2:30–3:30 P.M., JULY 1

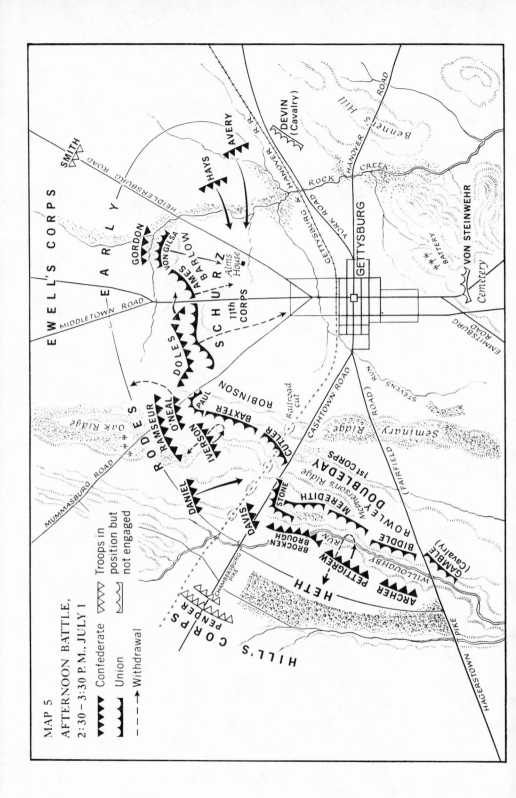

MAP 5

AFTERNOON BATTLE,
2:30 – 3:30 P.M., JULY 1

▼▼▼ Confederate   〜〜〜 Troops in
position but
not engaged

△△△ Union

---→ Withdrawal

vision.[2] This readjustment left McPherson's Ridge in the hands of three brigades of the First Corps, numbering altogether 4,586 officers and men. The First Brigade of General Rowley's Third Division under Colonel Chapman Biddle filled in the gap between the Fairfield road and McPherson's Woods. The Iron Brigade, still without the help of the 6th Wisconsin regiment, occupied the woods. Between it and the pike the Second Brigade of Rowley's division under Colonel Roy Stone occupied an important salient which was centered at McPherson's stone barn and house. During most of the heavy fighting two of its regiments held a position parallel to the pike and facing north and northeast. Several times they pushed their line out into the railroad cut, only to return to their former position.[3]

Between the right flank of these regiments and the left of the First Corps line on Seminary and Oak Ridges there was a gap of some six hundred feet along the pike. The ridges were ultimately held, from left to right, by Cutler's brigade, the 6th Wisconsin regiment, and two brigades of Robinson's division, Brigadier General Gabriel Paul's First and Brigadier General Henry Baxter's Second. At the beginning of the fighting in the afternoon Doubleday had Robinson post only Baxter's brigade on the right, but when the going got heavy he sent Paul's as well. Altogether these units numbered about 3,800 officers and men. The right flank of this line at times was refused by the length of a regiment along the Mummasburg road down the east side of the ridge and almost to the floor of the valley north of town.[4]

In the valley the First and Third Divisions of Howard's Eleventh Corps prolonged the Union line from the Mummasburg road east to the Heidlersburg (Harrisburg) road. Tradition has it that the line faced north and ran without a break at right angles to the First Corps line. In actual fact with its left flank resting on the Mummasburg road about a quarter of a mile east of the First Corps position on Oak Ridge, the Eleventh Corps line extended some three-quarters of a mile northeast to a knoll just west of Rock Creek and the Heidlersburg road. Most of the regiments in the corps faced northwest, and thus their positions were generally at an obtuse angle to the line of the First Corps. The Third Division held the left of the line. It was commanded temporarily by Brigadier General Alexander Schimmelfennig in place of General Schurz and consisted of two brigades, the First under Colonel George von Amsberg and the Second under Colonel Wladimir Krzyzanowski. To its right was the First Division under General Francis C. Barlow. It also had but two brigades, the First commanded by Colonel Leopold von Gilsa and the Second by General Adelbert Ames.[5] Schurz reported that his two small divisions numbered "hardly over 6,000 effective men when going into battle. . . ."[6]

None of the brigades of either corps remained in fixed positions within their parts of the line even before the general retreat. Whenever necessary and depending upon the direction of the attack, their commanders changed the fronts of the regiments, usually with consummate skill. The need for rapid maneuvers of regiments and brigades was especially great on Seminary and Oak Ridges because the enemy greatly outnumbered the First Corps forces there and often threatened them from two sides at once. On Oak Ridge, for instance, Paul's brigade in confronting superior forces which attacked it from several directions went into action by regiments with great intervals between them in order to cover as much ground as possible. On McPherson's Ridge the regiments in Stone's brigade holding the salient at the farm had a lively time shifting positions during the course of the fighting, while Biddle's brigade in open fields on the extreme left of the First Corps line kept busy protecting itself from enemy gunfire on Oak Hill. At certain times it supported Union batteries trying to silence the Confederate cannon, and at others it sought shelter behind the banks and stone walls along the Fairfield road, until it finally had to make a complete change of front when rebel brigades renewed their attacks from the west.[7]

Buford's cavalry force of approximately 2,900 officers and men guarded the flanks of the infantry; Gamble's brigade was on the left of the First Corps and Devin's on the right of the Eleventh. All five of the First Corps batteries, having a total of twenty-eight guns, served at the front and were aided by Calef's horse artillery with its six 3-inch cannon. The Eleventh Corps had the same number of batteries but only twenty-six guns. Three of the batteries worked with the infantry in positions north of the town, while two remained in reserve on Cemetery Hill.[8] Howard could easily have used twice their number.

When Rodes made final preparations for his attack, he had to rearrange his forces to conform to changes in the Yankee positions.

His division of 8,000 officers and men, almost the size of the Union First Corps, was composed of five brigades.[9] They were led by four brigadier generals, Junius Daniel, George P. Doles, Alfred Iverson, Jr., and Stephen D. Ramseur, and by Colonel Edward A. O'Neal. All had had battlefield experience as commanding officers, and three of them, Daniel, Doles, and Ramseur, had the reputation of being hard fighters.[10] The men matched their officers in experience and aggressiveness so that in quality and size Rodes commanded a truly outstanding division.

To meet the Yankee threat and keep Schurz's men in check until Early arrived, Rodes placed Doles's brigade to the right of the Middletown road in the valley. The gap between Doles and the rest of the division, which was on Oak Hill, he filled with the 5th Alabama regiment. Ramseur's men he kept in reserve. Then, as Rodes arrogantly wrote in his battle report, "finding that the enemy was rash enough to come out from the woods" on Oak Ridge to attack him, he ordered Iverson's and O'Neal's brigades forward with Daniel's brigade in supporting position on the right of Iverson. Moving from the north he had O'Neal's men keep straight ahead so as to hit the Union line at right angles to its flank, while Iverson's brigade on the right would strike it obliquely.[11]

In "gallant style" Rodes's brigades marched proudly against the enemy,[12] but almost immediately things went wrong and the attack soon fell apart. The explanation is not hard to find. Rodes for reasons never given had assigned leading roles in his assault to officers with undistinguished records.[13] Against ordinary troops their shortcomings might have been of little importance, but they were fighting against men who would take advantage of any mistakes they might make. A fatal error was that neither Iverson nor O'Neal led his troops in person.[14] Furthermore, because of a misunderstanding O'Neal used only three instead of four regiments; he failed to strike the enemy at the point Rodes had carefully indicated, and he attacked on too narrow a front. The Yankees under Robinson's watchful eye quickly changed front and hurled O'Neal's Alabamians back in confusion, thus exposing Iverson's left flank.[15] His brigade, about 1,450 strong, kept on under artillery fire through the open field "as evenly as if on parade." [16] Then its alignment became faulty, and without Iverson on hand to correct it, the brigade with strange fatality began to bear to the left toward a stone wall, behind which

Yankee soldiers lay concealed. At just the right moment they raised their rifles and with deadly aim mowed down five hundred North Carolinians on a "line as straight as a dress parade." [17] With O'Neal in retreat some of the regiments in Robinson's division changed front again, charged, and captured nearly all of the men who were left unhurt in three of Iverson's regiments. At about the same moment Cutler swung his brigade around from west to north, and his men blazed away at Daniel's and Iverson's men. Two regiments in Stone's brigade, aligned along the south edge of the Chambersburg Pike facing north, also contributed the fire of their muskets at long range.[18] All of this was too much for Iverson. To watch the relentless destruction of his own command was unnerving enough, but the disaster was compounded by the disgraceful sight of white handkerchiefs being waved by seemingly able-bodied men lying on the ground in battle formation. The general went to pieces and became unfit for further command, even though he learned later that he had made a ghastly mistake. The men in line whom he had thought alive were dead or badly wounded, and the white handkerchiefs had been waved by a few survivors who found themselves surrounded and about to be slaughtered.[19]

With one brigade practically destroyed and another badly mauled, Rodes's attack so far was a dismal failure. Though his center was crushed and Doles's brigade temporarily isolated, he had Ramseur in reserve and Daniel's large brigade out in the field to the right just beginning to fight. With Early momentarily expected to relieve the mounting pressure on Doles, Rodes still had on hand his ablest officers and enough troops to try to retrieve his fortunes and save his reputation.[20] With help from the capable Ramseur Rodes regrouped the regiments in his center and prepared to renew the attack on Robinson. Ramseur's small force of 1,100 officers and men was strengthened by remnants of Iverson's brigade, led by his assistant adjutant general, Captain D. P. Halsey, and the 3rd Alabama regiment under the brilliant Colonel C. A. Battle.[21]

During the fierce action on the ridge Doles in the valley below had been holding his own, but with increasing difficulty. Aided by Major Eugene Blackford's battalion of sharpshooters of the 5th Alabama regiment, he gradually pushed back Devin's skirmishers, who had a line stretching from the ridge to the Heidlersburg road. Federal infantry then moved forward and drove Doles's skirmishers from the high ground he had taken on his left. In trying to regain what he had lost Doles discovered the enemy strongly posted with infantry and artillery. Howard's men then undertook to drive a column between Doles and O'Neal, but Doles changed front with his two right regiments and counterattacked. Nevertheless his situation was critical, for the Federals were too much for his brigade of 1,400 men to handle, though they were bolstered by the entire 5th Alabama regiment.[22]

Suddenly Howard's battle lines were subjected to heavy cross fire from twelve guns placed on the east side of the Heidlersburg road under Lieutenant Colonel H. P. Jones, commanding Early's Artillery Battalion.[23] A prominent member of Ewell's staff later said he had never seen guns "better served than Jones' were on this occasion."[24] Once more the timing of the Confederate commanders under Ewell had proved perfect. Early had planned the cannonade as preparation for an attack on the extreme right flank of the Union line. On his way from Heidlersburg and while still some distance from the front he had deployed Gordon's brigade on the right of the road, Hoke's brigade under Colonel Isaac E. Avery on the left, General Harry T. Hays's brigade in the center, and Brigadier General William ("Extra Billy") Smith's in the rear of Hoke's. The Heidlersburg road was wooded nearly to within cannon shot of the enemy, so that Early's movements were well concealed and his men could remain hidden until the last moment before attacking.[25]

Gordon's brigade of about 1,200 Georgians, which was in the lead, was ordered by Early to go to the support of Doles whose men were retreating before an enemy attack on their left flank. Not wanting to wind his men who were tired out from long marches, Gordon moved them forward slowly until within nine hundred feet of the enemy line. There he found that the right flank of the forces attacking Doles was protected by what proved to be von Gilsa's First Brigade of Barlow's division, 1,300 strong.[26] It occupied the crest of a partly wooded knoll northwest of the road and curled around its lower edges.[27] This was a strong position if the enemy attacked it directly, but it could easily be turned by a movement sweeping wide from the east across Rock Creek and the road. The front of the brigade generally faced north, while Ames's Second Brigade stood roughly at right angles to it looking west.[28] Should the Confederates crush von Gilsa they could easily roll up Ames's right flank; and that is exactly what happened. Gordon's assault was a beautiful example of the effectiveness of shock tactics. Putting on a most "warlike" and "animated" spectacle,[29] his men under heavy fire charged over rail and plank fences, scrambled across the creek, and overran the knoll.[30] The attack hit the First Brigade on its front somewhat toward the left. At the same time all or part of Doles's brigade and sharpshooters from O'Neal's brigade cooperated by putting pressure on Ames's brigade to the left rear of the First.[31] Barlow, right in the thick of things, with the "most praiseworthy coolness and intrepidity," as Schurz put it, fell seriously wounded while trying to rally his men.[32] Ames, a brave and able leader, assumed command and had just succeeded in slowing up the retreat and establishing a second line when Avery's and Hays's brigades came crashing in on the right. Their attack completely unhinged the end of the long Union line and destroyed any opportunities for further resistance on that part of the field. Only retreat through the town and up Cemetery Hill to von Steinwehr's prepared position could save the remnants of the division.[33]

General Early's appearance and Gordon's attack seemed to be a signal for all Confederate forces to close in on Federal positions stretching from the Fairfield to the Heidlersburg road. The advance could not have been better synchronized if Lee had been in position to issue orders to all his commanders at once. Immediately to the right of Early's men Doles, having been relieved of enemy pressure, seized the initiative and without waiting for orders from Rodes boldly mounted a counterattack against forces which outnumbered his own.[34] On his left Early's three brigades were sweeping everything before them. The rest of Rodes's division now got into the act with Daniel on the right taking the lead. After Iverson's debacle Daniel had pushed ahead against Stone's brigade, which was operating from McPherson's farm buildings, the pike, and the railroad cut. Daniel also struck at Cutler's brigade. These Yankees fought him savagely and skillfully, inflicting heavy losses and forcing him to withdraw and regroup his men for a renewed attack. In spite of Daniel's courageous persistence and ingenuity in overcoming the obstacle of the railroad cut, it is doubtful whether his drive would have succeeded alone. As he was making his final effort he received unexpected relief when General Ramseur renewed with increased fury the attack on Robinson's division to the north of where he was

☙ Map 6 ☙

**ACTION FROM 3:30
TO 4:00 P.M., JULY 1**

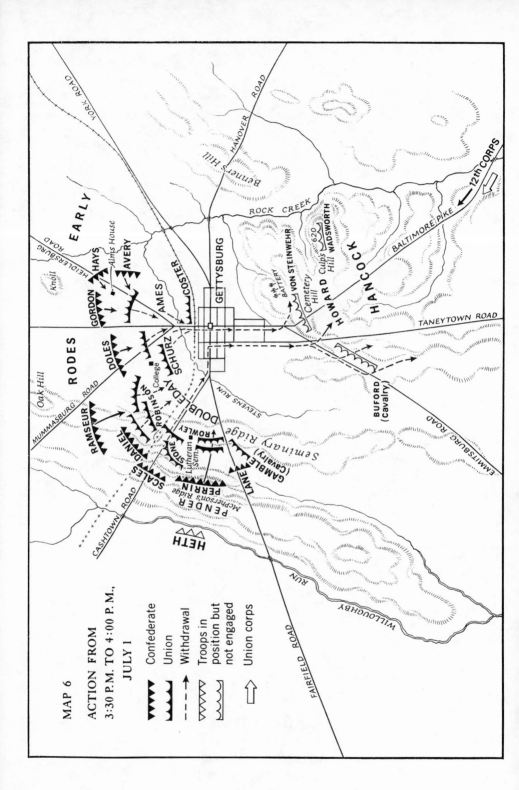

MAP 6

ACTION FROM
3:30 P.M. TO 4:00 P.M.,
JULY 1

Confederate

Union

Withdrawal

Troops in
position but
not engaged

Union corps

fighting. Ramseur was a much more skillful commander than Iverson or O'Neal, and he was helped by the growing inability of the exhausted Federals to continue their resistance.[35]

More important to Daniel's purposes, however, was the commitment of the eight brigades of Heth's and Pender's divisions to a grand assault on three First Corps brigades defending McPherson's Ridge.[36] The brunt of the attack was at first assumed by Pettigrew's strong brigade and Brockenbrough's weak one on its left immediately south of the Chambersburg Pike. Archer's brigade guarded Pettigrew's right flank against Gamble's cavalry,[37] and Davis' disorganized brigade aided Brockenbrough's men to some extent.[38] The left of Heth's line near the pike and the railroad cut received important help from Daniel's brigade which was bearing down on the Union line from the north and northwest.[39] Pettigrew's brigade advanced in perfect alignment over an open field west and southwest of McPherson's Ridge against Union troops partly hidden by woods and growing wheat. The North Carolinians made a magnificent spectacle, but the fire of Union batteries, followed by volleys from the infantry, blew holes in their ranks. Despite heavy losses they kept on and forced troops of the First Brigade of Rowley's Third Division to give way, thus uncovering the left flank of the Iron Brigade. The left of Pettigrew's line, which was composed of the 26th and 11th North Carolina regiments, had the misfortune to clash with the Westerners of the Iron Brigade, who fought so desperately and inflicted such heavy losses on the Confederates that there were not enough men left even for a successful bayonet charge.[40] To the right of Meredith's men Stone's brigade, constantly shifting its front and maneuvering with consummate skill, held off Brockenbrough's men until Daniel's troops added their strength to the attack.[41] Under such great pressure the Union infantry on McPherson's Ridge began gradually to withdraw to positions on Seminary Ridge. The regiments nearest the Fairfield road were the first to go; the last were the 143rd, 149th, and 150th Pennsylvania which comprised Stone's brigade.[42] Hill quickly followed up the advantage that Heth's thoroughly exhausted troops had gained by advancing Pender's fresh division to the front, where he formed a battle line almost a mile wide from the Chambersburg Pike to the Fairfield road. Brigadier General A. M. Scales's brigade advanced on the left, Colonel Abner Perrin's in the center, and Brigadier General James H.

Lane's on the right.[43] Perrin afterwards recalled that his men moved as "bravely forward as any troops ever did on earth," and when they overtook and charged beyond Pettigrew's brigade, "the poor fellows could scarcely raise a cheer for us as we passed." [44] Having paused long enough to reform his line, Perrin pushed his men on, in an alignment with Scales's brigade, to Seminary Ridge.[45] As he approached it, he was met with the "most destructive fire of musketry, grape & canister" he had ever experienced. "It was however but a volley," he continued. "Under this volley Scales Brigade came to a dead halt. The men lay down attempting to return the enemy's fire." [46]

Here on Seminary Ridge the First Corps made its last stand before the retreat through town to Cemetery Hill. Reduced to a shadow of its strength before the engagement, the corps continued to resist stoutly. Immediately west of the seminary the men took advantage of a barricade of fence railings; elsewhere they lay on their stomachs and made themselves as inconspicuous as possible while blazing away at the enemy. They could not help admiring the magnificent bearing of Hill's veterans as they maintained their alignments with great precision in face of the heavy fire. Many of his regiments retained the classic formations of the 19th-century parade ground and kept their colors several paces in advance of the line. In an effort to guard the entrance to the town by way of the pike eighteen pieces of Wainwright's First Corps artillery were concentrated almost hub to hub on a front of not over six hundred feet. South of where the Fairfield road crossed Seminary Ridge about half of Gamble's men dismounted and took up positions behind a stone wall. The fire from their Sharps carbines kept Lane's brigade at bay,[47] but Perrin's men "with a yell and without firing a gun" broke through the Yankee line just south of the seminary building. Once Perrin had penetrated it, he neatly fanned out his regiments to the left and right so as to attack his opponent on the flanks.[48] Meanwhile north of the railroad cut Daniel's and Ramseur's forces soon crushed further Yankee resistance along that part of the ridge,[49] and all the regiments of the First Corps began streaming through town. Many of them followed the cut and the pike to the square, from where they went out the main street to the south and thence up the Baltimore Pike to Cemetery Hill. Among the very last units to leave were the eighteen guns and six caissons of Wainwright's artillery which galloped to safety down the Chambersburg Pike. Before they could get out of range, however, they lost three caissons and one gun to Confederate fire.[50]

The collapse of the Union line along Seminary and Oak Ridges and in the fields north of the town was described as a rout by General Hill and as an orderly withdrawal by General Howard. Hill and Lee talked about having driven the enemy through Gettysburg,[51] thus giving the impression that the Yankees had fled pell-mell,[52] but Howard would admit little if any loss in his control of affairs. Finding it impossible to hold out any longer, for the men were already giving way, he said that he had sent "positive" orders to the commanders of the two corps to fall back gradually, "disputing every inch of ground," and to form near his position on Cemetery Hill, the Eleventh Corps on the right and the First on the left of the Baltimore Pike. The movement was carried out as ordered, Howard insisted, though with "considerable confusion" because both corps went through town at the same time.[53] Quite understandably his picture of conditions at that hour omitted many distressing features, although it did keep fairly close to reality.

The truth is that the Yankees did not suddenly become panic-stricken and abandon their original positions all at once, as Confederate accounts suggested, nor on the other hand was their retirement as orderly as Howard implied. The line at first became frayed at the extreme flanks and then gradually unravelled in its entire length. After leaving their original positions both corps continued organized resistance for a time, the First on Seminary Ridge and the Eleventh along the north edge of town. Once they gave up their final positions most of the troops became disorganized but not demoralized. Wainwright noted no panic among the men he saw; most of them, he said, were "talking and joking" as they hurried along.[54] Some units retained cohesion, as for example the 6th Wisconsin regiment which reflected the high morale of the Iron Brigade. During the retreat these men were exposed to the fire of Ewell's sharpshooters coming from the left, but they maintained their poise and paused in the streets long enough to rally round their colors and give a cheer for the "old Sixth and the good cause."[55] They joined with soldiers from other regiments to form pockets of resistance and continue fighting as they gradually withdrew through town.[56] Brigades and divisions got pretty well mixed up, and there was little order among them except for an arrangement the men themselves seemed instinctively to have worked out, of keeping soldiers of the First Corps on one side of the street and those of the Eleventh on the other.[57] The greatest contributors to disorder and demoralization were the stragglers and skulkers. Some of them had faded away from the battle line and huddled in barns and sheds near town, ripe for capture, while others wandered aimlessly in the streets. Large numbers of them, mostly from the Eleventh Corps, followed frightened civilians down the Taneytown road and Baltimore Pike, to be rounded up finally by the provost guard of the Twelfth Corps.[58] Army and civilian vehicles of every description which were being hauled through town added to the confusion and turned into troublesome obstructions.

Many officers and men got lost in cross streets and blind alleys, so that the town became for them a trap rather than a shield. Before they could work their way out of the tangle or from traffic jams, advanced elements of the enemy came up and seized them. In some instances the Confederates took almost entire regiments as captives. Though the town became the means by which the rebels caught most of their prisoners during the three-day battle,[59] its dwellings and byways furnished the cover under which many Yankees escaped to fight again. Troops in Ewell's corps hotly pursued their quarry through the streets, but they were not in a good position to close off the southeast exit to Cemetery Hill. If Hill's divisions, which had attacked the First Corps from the west and southwest, had not been so badly mauled, they might have been able to thrust enough men straight ahead through the southern edge of town and block the streets leading to the Baltimore Pike. Perrin's brigade, which had broken the line just south of the seminary and occupied the area south of the pike,[60] found itself without support from Hill's other brigades. In the struggle its losses had been heavy, and without the help of Lane's brigade, whose advance Gamble's cavalry had checked, it lacked the strength to encircle the enemy on the south.[61]

Cemetery Hill gave to the defeated corps a reprieve from the consequences of a bitter defeat. As the hot, thirsty, exhausted Yankees trudged up the pike, the sight of Colonel Orland Smith's brigade of about 2,000 fresh veteran troops massed on the crest and of Captain Michael Wiedrich's battery of six 3-inch guns (Battery I, 1st New York Light) firing on the Confederates below relieved some of their gloom. Out on the open west slope of Cemetery Ridge Buford's faithful troopers stood in an imposing line of battle awaiting further attacks of the enemy.[62] Perhaps even more welcome was the presence on the hill of General Hancock riding about giving orders. A member of the 5th Maine Battery never forgot the "inspiration of his commanding, controlling presence, nor the fresh courage he imparted. . . ." Against the blood and grime of the battle-weary soldiers his clean white linen shirt, open at the neck and with sleeves rolled back, made a striking contrast.[63] Hancock had arrived probably between 4:00 and 4:30 P.M., just as the Union troops began streaming through town to the hill.[64] He had ridden in a slow-moving ambulance for awhile to study the maps of the area laid out before him. Finished with this task and becoming impatient, he had taken to his horse and urged him forward as much as he dared on a very hot day.[65]

Hancock had found Howard near the Baltimore Pike on the top of Cemetery Hill and informed the surprised general of his authorization from Meade to assume command of all the troops at Gettysburg. Mortified and sure that he had been disgraced, Howard accepted the written order without asking to read it and loyally cooperated with Hancock in arranging the troops in their new positions.[66] Howard acknowledged Hancock's "courtesy of deportment and gallantry of action" in helping restore order. Hancock, he said, had moved "personally from point to point, encouraging the men, locating regiments and batteries," and had then suggested that Wadsworth's division be sent to occupy Culp's Hill.[67] When Doubleday raised objections to the plan, Hancock roared out the order for Wadsworth to go there in no uncertain terms.[68] Buford in his report made special note of Hancock's "superb disposition[s] to resist any attack." [69] But perhaps Hancock's greatest contribution at this moment in the battle was psychological. He looked and acted like the magnificent general that he was. His presence gave everyone who saw him renewed confidence and offered tangible evidence that his redoubtable Second Corps was not far away.

While quite honestly acknowledging Hancock's assistance, Howard, perhaps as salve for his pride, later insisted that he and Hancock had agreed to a geographical division of their authority: Hancock was to "arrange the troops, and place the batteries upon the left of the Baltimore pike," while Howard should "take the right of the same." [70] Hancock denied any such agreement and maintained that he had exercised "positive and vigorous" command over all the troops. As far as he knew, he said, Howard had given no orders save to the men of his own corps.[71] Neither general was completely right in his recollection of who gave orders to whom, for Colonel Wainwright recorded in his diary that as he reached the top of the hill Howard asked him to take charge of all artillery and place it in position. With Howard's assurance that Major Thomas W. Osborn would take orders from him, Wainwright went ahead and arranged all batteries in the best manner possible to repel an attack. It was he who put the 5th Maine Battery on a neck of land (later known as Stevens' Knoll) between Cemetery and Culp's Hills so it could cover the north side of Cemetery Hill with a cross fire if need be. He also instructed his subordinates not to waste ammunition, nor were they to take orders from just any man with "a star on his shoulders who might choose to give them." [72] Neither Hancock, Howard, nor Wainwright, for that matter, mentioned in his official report this temporary enlargement of Wainwright's command. There is no reason to doubt the reliability of his story, however, for he was the ranking artillery officer on the field and had an unusually keen understanding of the proper use of guns, which Howard apparently appreciated.[73]

Whatever the actual relationship between Howard and Hancock, they, together with Buford and General G. K. Warren, chief engineer of the Army of the Potomac who had arrived meanwhile, quickly prepared the survivors of the two corps for further action. Rather than changing what Howard had accomplished, Hancock gave whole-hearted assistance in supplementing it. In his report to Meade he accepted Howard's judgment of Cemetery Hill as a place to make a stand, at least for awhile. Whether it would serve in a more permanent capacity would depend upon circumstances, such as the timely arrival of reinforcements. About 5:30 P.M. as the Twelfth Corps approached on the right he felt satisfied the hill could not be easily turned in that direction. Until the Third Corps arrived on the Emmitsburg road and prolonged the Union line on Cemetery Ridge he worried about the exposure of the left flank to a turning movement, but he concluded that the position would be safe until night, when Meade could decide whether to fight there or retire. As a precaution Hancock sent back all trains and recommended that General Gibbon with the Second Corps be ordered forward.[74] Before Hancock completed his work and returned to Taneytown, General Slocum agreed to place the First Division of the Twelfth Corps under General Alpheus Williams in a position east of Rock Creek and to the right and rear of Wadsworth, who by this time was on Culp's Hill. When Brigadier General John W. Geary's Second Division of the same corps arrived near Cemetery Hill, Hancock, not being able to reach Slocum, took it upon himself to place it on the high ground to the right of Little Round Top, commanding the Emmitsburg road to the front and the Taneytown road to the rear.[75]

Though Hancock by implication approved of Howard's decision to hold Cemetery Hill and even accepted his preliminary dispositions of the troops with but few changes,[76] he never commented on the way Howard had fought the battle.[77] Howard on the other hand through the years made many observations about the engagement largely as a result of attacks upon his record, many of which were unfair.[78] It was—and is—rather presumptuous to say categorically that if Howard had done this or that, certain developments would have occurred. From the very first he himself had recognized grave faults in the Union position which, unless corrected, would lead to disaster. In a bitter note to Meade on the night of July 1 he protested the fact that he had been superseded by Hancock, and he claimed that none of the corps commanders could have done better than he under the circumstances. In an effort to justify his generalship he wrote:

> Had we received re-enforcements a little sooner, the first position assumed by General Reynolds, and held by General Doubleday till my corps came up, might have been maintained; but the position was not a good one, because both flanks were exposed, and a heavy force approaching from the northern roads rendered it untenable, being already turned, so that I was forced to retire the command to the position now occupied, which I regard as a very strong one.[79]

Fortunately for Howard none of his critics saw this message, for they would have enjoyed pointing out its errors, though perhaps acknowledging the accuracy of his appraisal of the position on McPherson's Ridge. Howard obviously perceived some of its undesirable features for, after going over the line in the afternoon with Doubleday, he had expressed concern about the strength of the left flank of the First Corps. At the time he saw no reason to modify or change Doubleday's position. He felt his mission was to use the left wing, which even with his own "small corps" amounted only to an "advanced guard," to hold the position till the rest of the army could come up.[80] A plausible explanation, it still did not excuse his failure to correct faulty tactical arrangements when he saw them. In a holding operation the main duty is to defend a position as long as possible, while keeping losses to a minimum. Such a situation calls for expert timing in maneuvers and careful choice of sites in placing the troops.

McPherson's Ridge did not meet such requirements. There was nothing sacred about the line Reynolds had established there, although Howard and Doubleday seemed to act as if there were. Both flanks were weak for several reasons: the left because the open fields furnished little cover for infantry; the right because it was a salient open to fire from two directions and was an impossible position for artillery. A force holding the wooded area in the center, which Doubleday prized so highly for its tactical possibilities, could easily have been surrounded once the enemy reached the depression separating McPherson's and Seminary Ridges. Its abandonment for prepared positions on Seminary Ridge would have straightened the First Corps line, and it would have given the infantry the protection of the wooded areas covering most of the ridge and the artillery an excellent field of fire across the depression. Doubleday had considered withdrawal to Seminary Ridge but decided against it because he said it was "open ground, and could have been, as it was afterward, enfiladed by Ewell's batteries throughout its whole extent." [81] This observation was true of McPherson's but not of Seminary Ridge. If he and Howard had straightened this part of the line before the final Confederate assault forced the retreat of both corps to Cemetery Hill, the heavy casualties incurred by brigades of the First Corps in their withdrawal from McPherson's Ridge might have been avoided. During the respite from heavy fighting Doubleday could have built breastworks more formidable than the ones he did put up on Seminary Ridge, and he could have brought his main battle line back to it. A skirmish line, perhaps of brigade strength, could have continued to hold McPherson's Ridge with the purpose of slowing down a Confederate assault.[82] Doubleday and Howard were both guilty of negligence in not modifying and strengthening their line to the west of Gettysburg.

Heaviest criticism of Howard's generalship centered on the location of the two Eleventh Corps divisions north of town. Assuming they had to be placed there to cover the right rear of the First Corps, their dispositions were generally poor, with the right flank being particularly vulnerable to an envelopment. A line could have been drawn at right angles to Seminary Ridge along Stevens Run, about six hundred feet north and parallel to the railroad line and cut. This line would have been almost a mile closer to town than the one that was formed and would have had the advantage of not being easily flanked by a force coming down the Heidlersburg road. The open fields and swale would have offered the enemy little cover against heavy artillery fire,[83] and in case of retreat Howard's men would have had less distance to travel to Cemetery Hill. If Howard had had any qualms about establishing a position so close to town, he could have chosen one farther out near the County Home, which was approximately half the distance to the knoll where the end of the line was finally anchored. General Schurz implied that General Barlow had acted without orders when he stretched his division to the knoll,[84] but there is evidence to indicate that he did so with Howard's approval.[85] One veteran of the campaign called the entire advance of Howard's line by the right flank an "act of unspeakable folly." Then he continued:

> Instead of advancing we should have fallen back as soon as the approach of the enemy from the right was developed, and should have reformed, and barricaded the line with our right well refused upon the town, and our left connecting, as well as might be, with the right of the First Corps. We could then have punished the enemy more severely, and, perhaps, have held the town until dark. I do not know who is responsible for the advance, but whoever ordered it deserves the severest censure.[86]

Howard claimed that if he had followed his own instincts he would not have advanced beyond the eastern edge of town; he did so only because Reynolds had already commenced to fight on the western slopes.[87] Even so there was no reason for him to have maintained Reynolds' lines, much less extended them. He had had an opportunity around noon to withdraw the First Corps without serious harassment from the enemy, and in retrospect Doubleday thought such a move then would have had much to recommend it.[88] Howard undoubtedly expected reinforcements to arrive in time for him to maintain the original position of the First Corps, but his hope was both unrealistic and unfair to the commanders of the other corps. The Twelfth, which was on its way to Two Taverns, was coming within supporting distance, but it is questionable whether Slocum could have pushed on to Gettysburg in time to affect the outcome of the battle on July 1 even if he had not hesitated in his movements. Sickles could do even less to help, for he was over twice as far away as Slocum and did not hear of Howard's plight until midafternoon. It would have been better then for Howard to have based his strategy on the supposition that the only infantry available to him would be the First and Eleventh Corps.

When Howard hedged against a retreat and possible disaster by planting one division of his corps on Cemetery Hill, he won for himself a Congressional Resolution thanking him for his services at Gettysburg.[89] Friends and admirers of General Reynolds tried to deny Howard's claim to fame when they insisted upon giving credit for occupation of the hill to the dead general. Reynolds, they said, had ordered Howard to place troops there. Their contention became the subject of considerable correspondence after the war, and the evidence, though flimsy, convinced those who were unwilling to think anything good of a man they considered a pious nincompoop.[90] It was a silly argument, arising to some extent from partisan feelings in a war in which too many generals were politically minded and too often Congress judged the excellence of commanders by their political coloration. Certainly it did not add to the luster of Reynolds' reputation to deprive Howard of the credit he deserved. Howard could have learned about the strategic possibilities of Cemetery Hill in various ways: from one of Reynolds' aides, from Buford, or most likely from his own observation, as he himself claimed. Before the arrival of his corps and the death of Reynolds he had had time to reconnoiter, and as mentioned before, he was surveying the countryside from Fahnestock's Observatory when he received word that he was in charge of operations. If nothing else did, the appearance of two divisions of his corps over the Taneytown road must have brought the hill to his attention, for the road rose to the western edge of its crest before descending into town. More important, it was Howard—and it could have been no one else—who decided to keep his reserve force there and prepare it for occupation by an even larger number of men.[91] The size of the force was also his decision; it could have been one brigade, one division, two divisions, or the whole corps. The placing of the reserves on Cemetery Hill, and not in the town or some other place, testified to the importance he attached to it as a possible stronghold and to his lack of confidence in the Union position.

Having committed the bulk of his forces to the outer perimeter, so to speak, of his defensive position, and as enemy strength increased, withdrawal to his inner lines on the hill became a matter of timing. This movement in turn depended upon the effectiveness of his control over the two corps. In Buford's judgment Howard exercised none at all, and for that matter he felt that no one else did either.[92] After the war when someone called Howard's attention to the remark, he dismissed it as mere opinion.[93] It was, however, the appraisal of one of the ablest officers of the war, and events that afternoon seemed to substantiate him.

To be fair to Howard, he had to improvise under conditions which gave him little time to think and act. Another very likely handicap was a staff quite inadequate to meet the requirements of his additional responsibilities.[94] Although he ordered Doubleday and presumably Schurz to retreat to Cemetery Hill if necessary,[95] he apparently failed to give either commander explicit instructions on the route his corps should take through town. If he had done so, much of the confusion and resulting loss in prisoners might have been avoided. Furthermore there is no indication that during the actual fighting Howard personally supervised affairs at any place closer to the battle front than his headquarters on Cemetery Hill, which was almost two miles to the rear.[96] Nearer at hand he could have sensed developments more quickly and increased the efficiency of his aides by cutting down the distances they had to travel to carry out orders and receive information. Cemetery Hill was a good vantage point, but even with field glasses it is doubtful whether Howard could have determined accurately what was going on because of the clouds of smoke and the screen of trees. Before he knew it, his whole front seemed to crumble, and his orders to retreat were meaningless.[97] The enemy had already made the decision.

Howard did try to cover the retreat of the Eleventh Corps by sending Colonel Charles R. Coster's brigade of about 1,400 officers and men out on the east side of Harrisburg Street just beyond the railroad station, but they were too little and too late to stem the tide.[98] Only the steadiness of the veteran troops themselves saved Howard from catastrophe.

A general may make many mistakes which will never be noticed so long as his soldiers fight well, and rarely will a commander openly admit a poor performance by his men. It is always the unit to the left or to the right which gives way and makes his own position untenable, never the opposite. So it was that in reviewing the results of the first day's battle soldiers and officers of the First and Eleventh Corps almost immediately began to indulge in recriminations. Each group charged the other with poor fighting and being the first to break its lines. If the criterion for judging the records of the two corps was the time its front broke, then it would be impossible to choose between them, because the whole Union line seemed to collapse at once, and First and Eleventh Corps troops began to fill the streets at about the same moment. Yet Howard reported to Hancock, who passed it on to Meade, that "Doubleday's command gave way." [99] An unfortunate and presumptous observation, this statement became gall and wormwood to members of the First Corps and did anything but endear Howard to them. There are various ways of determining how well the corps fought. They include such considerations as impressions of eye witnesses, the relative strength of the opposing forces, and the kind and number of losses inflicted on both sides. By these standards the First Corps did supremely well, and the Eleventh Corps showed up badly.

No one was more bitterly disappointed with his men than General Barlow, although he never said so publicly. In a letter to his mother, however, he insisted that he had had an "admirable" position. Then he went on to say: "We ought to have held the place easily, for I had my entire force at the very point where the attack was made. But the enemies [sic] skirmishers had hardly attacked us before my men began to run. No fight at all was made. Finding that they were going I started to get ahead of them to try to rally them and form another line in the rear." At that moment a shot in the left side forced him to dismount from his horse, and he tried to walk off the field. "Everybody was then running to the rear," Barlow continued, "and the enemy were approaching rapidly." [100] In contrast to such testimony Howard kept expressing his satisfaction with the entire corps,[101] but his brother Charles, who was a member of his staff, privately admitted that Barlow's division "did not fight *very well* the first day." [102] Although General Gordon, whose brigade broke Barlow's line, said that the "enemy made a most obstinate resistance," [103] the opinion about the Eleventh Corps which apparently prevailed in the Confederate army was expressed by a London correspondent who reported: "Again the Germans broke and fled." [104]

The old hue and cry about "heavy masses" of the enemy overwhelming the thin lines of the two small divisions of the Eleventh Corps makes better rhetoric than historical truth.[105] Actually the odds were slightly in favor of the corps. When Schurz established his position north of the town he had four brigades amounting to little more than 6,000 officers and men; they struggled against four enemy brigades of almost the same size, about 5,800 officers and men.[106] Coster's brigade of 1,400 came too late to bolster the sagging lines and could only help to cover the retreat. Schurz's complaint that its delayed arrival deprived him of an opportunity to mount an offensive counterattack was justified.[107] In a comparison of the losses of the contending forces the Eleventh Corps showed up in even poorer light. Of the total force of 7,500 ultimately used by Schurz, 3,000 became casualties, or almost 40 percent. In turn these men inflicted losses on the enemy of about 14 percent. Ninety percent of the Confederate casualties were listed as killed or wounded, and only 10 percent as captured or missing, whereas 50 percent of the Union losses were counted in the latter category. Gordon's brigade suffered more than any of the other Confederate units, about 30 percent of its number, probably because it made a frontal attack on the knoll. Hays's and Hoke's brigades attacked from the right after the line had been broken and before the Union troops had time to get set for a determined stand. Hence their losses were slight.[108] It is possible that Barlow's men opposing them fought better than he said, but still it was not good enough.

The poor record of the Eleventh Corps is a puzzle. Barlow and other native American officers, especially those of English antecedents, scornfully blamed the corps' performance on the preponderance of German regiments, which they said marched well but fought badly.[109] Such statements revealed more prejudice than truth because almost 50 percent of the men in the corps were of so-called old Yankee stock. General Carl Schurz, an *émigré* of the Revolution of 1848 and rightfully proud of his liberal tradition, loudly denounced the aspersions the Americans cast upon the German soldiers. As self-appointed spokesman for the German element in the Eleventh Corps, Schurz's self-righteous attitude irritated his fellow officers and caused them to suspect his motives. The stubborn and defiant loyalty of the Germans to the language, customs, and leaders of the Old Country became another source of trouble. They keenly resented the replacement of their beloved but inept Major General Franz Sigel by a Maine Yankee, O. O. Howard, and their bitterness increased when they became the scapegoats for Hooker's failure at Chancellorsville. They seemed never to have recovered from the nightmarish experience of having "Stonewall" Jackson's men in overwhelming numbers suddenly emerge from the lengthening shadows of the wilderness and with eerie yells break the peace as they placidly cooked their evening meal.[110]

The Eleventh Corps had more than the usual complement of good general officers. Howard had his shortcomings, but he was above average in competence. There was nothing wrong with Schurz, although perhaps he did not deserve the rank of major general when his record is compared to those of officers of greater experience and ability. The other officers with foreign names, Leopold von Gilsa, Alexander Schimmelfennig, Wladimir Krzyzanowski, and Adolf von Steinwehr stood well in the estimation of their American colleagues.[111] Adelbert Ames and Francis Barlow had excellent records. Of the latter Captain Charles Francis Adams wrote: "I am more disposed to regard Barlow as a military genius than any man I have yet seen."[112] The troubles of the corps did not arise from a want of competent leaders, whether native or foreign born, but from the prejudice of the Americans[113] and the defensive attitude of the Germans. As a result the men had little pride or confidence in their outfits, and the corps lacked that indefinable something called morale. In contrast the First Corps was suffused with it.[114]

The Confederates noticed the difference and commented on it as quite remarkable. In speaking of the experiences of Hill's men on July 1 they said the engagement with the First Corps was fierce, for the Yankees fought with a determination unusual for them.[115] What the Confederates did not know or had forgotten was that every time they had encountered this corps in the past they had had a real battle. At Chancellorsville the First had played a minor role and had had only slight brushes with the enemy. Although other able commanders such as Hooker and Meade had shared in its development, the First Corps was the creation of Reynolds, who had molded it into an efficient fighting machine. He was proud of it, and his pride rubbed off onto his men. They would carry on after he was gone.[116] Consequently on July 1 the stubborn and skillful opposition of the 8,500 men of the First Corps came as a shock to the Confederates of Heth's, Pender's, and Rodes's divisions who met them head-on.[117] Constantly increasing the strength of their forces during the five or six hours of fighting, the Confederates with almost 16,000 men finally shattered the corps, but only at the cost of extraordinary losses to themselves. Seven of the ten Southern brigades incurred casualties of from 35 to 50 percent, and the total for all brigades came to an estimated 6,300 officers and men, or about 40 percent of their strength. Four brigades lost fairly heavily in prisoners, a total of 850 men in all.[118] But the six brigades of the First Corps paid a prohibitive price for their determined stand and never recovered from it. As the survivors painfully re-formed on the slopes of Cemetery and Culp's Hills late in the afternoon, they represented only 35 percent of the corps as it went into action that morning. The rest of their comrades lay in the fields and woods west of the town or had begun the long march to the prison camps down South. Of the approximately 5,500 men lost to the corps about 2,000 were captured during the retreat. Robinson's division suffered the most in this respect because the enemy, coming against its position from both the north and the west, cut off many of the men trying to escape through town.[119]

The advantages the First had over the Eleventh Corps in a better defensive position and higher morale were offset somewhat by its longer battle line and the loss of its commanding general at the beginning of the engagement. In place of the dead Reynolds, Doubleday with dogged determination kept the corps together and apparently worked it well against the enemy. Of his three division commanders, Robinson handled his two brigades masterfully and deserved the highest commendation. Wadsworth made up in courage what he lacked in skill, and he fought to the bitter end.[120] In contrast Rowley's conduct was questionable in the extreme; it led to charges of drunkenness on duty on the battlefield, conduct prejudicial to good order and military discipline, conduct unbecoming an officer and a gentleman, and disobedience of orders. Although declared guilty by a court-martial of all accusations except the last,[121] at least one colleague, Colonel Wainwright, doubted whether Rowley would have handled his division any better had he been sober. One of his worst blunders occurred just before the final Confederate assault on McPherson's Ridge, when the First Brigade of his division under Colonel Chapman Biddle was sent in support of two sections of Lieutenant George Breck's battery and through improper management persisted in getting in front of the guns and obstructing their fire.[122] Whatever mistakes Colonel Biddle may have made, Rowley was in large measure responsible by virtue of his position. Evidently he gave little attention to his duties as division commander, although he did devote some time to the First Brigade which normally was his command. Neither he nor anyone else mentioned his supervision of the Second Brigade under Colonel Roy Stone, which was fighting valiantly in McPherson's farmyard north of the woods. Even his control over the First Brigade seemed feeble, because during the engagement Colonels Biddle and Theodore B. Gates of the 80th New York seem to have divided direction of affairs between them without referring matters to Rowley.[123] Testimony at the court-martial suggested that strong drink fortified his natural tendencies toward brave if erratic conduct. Doubleday rightly cited him for gallantry in action, though the court-martial later found him guilty of questionable generalship.

Just how much personal control Doubleday maintained over the operations of his divisions is impossible to tell, for the accounts are both confusing and contradictory. From them it would seem that he failed to notice Rowley's condition until the corps had retreated to Cemetery Hill.[124] Either he did not keep a sharp eye on affairs or Rowley covered up his intoxicated state quite well. In any case, since one of his own generals got out of hand Doubleday's critical attitude toward Howard's management of the battle was in rather bad taste.[125]

When the battle ended late in the afternoon the Confederates had brought into action at least 23,000 of their infantry to overcome the resistance of a combined force of 18,800 Union cavalry and infantry.[126] Although the Confederates suffered losses heavy enough to reduce seriously the striking power of three divisions, they took as compensation an excessive number of Union prisoners. The total of 3,655 officers and men captured was not as large as the Southerners claimed, but it still amounted to the equivalent of a sizeable division in the Northern army at that period of the war.[127] The Southerners in addition to their superiority in infantry had a greater number of guns, although for various reasons not all of them were used.[128]

Greater numbers of men and cannon, however, did not tell the whole story of the victory of the Confederates. The explanation lay in their well-coordinated attack on two fronts and their judicious use of reserves at just the right moment. Some planning, some luck, and an almost instinctive sense of timing possessed by veteran troops all played a part in determining the outcome. In their fighting the Southerners, showing *élan* as well as contempt for the foe, usually hit the Union lines head-on and with a wild abandon that was truly magnificent but costly. Without enough cavalry to neutralize the skillfully handled forces under Buford, they made no effort to turn the Yankees out of their positions by means of wide sweeping movements or cut them off in their retreat. Even if they had had the cavalry it is questionable whether they would have had enough time to employ such measures without previous planning and a better knowledge of the terrain around Gettysburg. With the forces then at their disposal they could not in all likelihood have obtained a greater triumph than they did in one day of fighting.

Because Lee was ignorant of the strength of the forces opposed to him and had only a part of his own army immediately available, he had mixed feelings about this fight which willy-nilly had become a real battle. At first Lee had tried to slow down its tempo and had given his generals vague warnings about not wanting a "general engagement brought on till the rest of the army came up." [129] But then Heth saw Rodes's division become heavily engaged, and he took the trouble to find Lee and seek his permission to attack in co-ordination with Rodes. Lee refused the request on the grounds that Longstreet was not up. Returning to his division, Heth saw the enemy shifting his weight to meet Rodes's attack. He again sought Lee's consent to give assistance, and this time received it. These meetings of the two generals occurred before the grand assault all along the Union line.[130] Although the account seems to contradict the statement in Lee's report that Hill ordered Heth to advance once

Pender had come up to support him, it has the ring of authenticity about it.[131] Lee did hesitate to permit the attack to be pressed, and for that reason went contrary to his usual practice of leaving control of operations to his generals once he had formulated battle strategy and tactics. It is also possible that Hill, having been warned not to bring on a general engagement and learning of Lee's presence on the battlefield, had had Heth refer the matter of a combined assault to the commanding general himself. Otherwise it was extraordinary even for Henry Heth, one of the few generals whom Lee called by his first name, not to have gone through channels.[132]

While Heth's persistence undoubtedly helped to induce Lee to reverse himself and decide to press the attack, a stronger influence was probably at work to cause him to change his mind. Having arrived on the field around 2:00 P.M., Lee perceived, as did Ewell, that the determined resistance of the enemy gave him no alternative but to continue a vigorous attack.[133] He watched with admiration as Rodes's men drove home their final assault, and afterwards he told Rodes he was proud of his division.[134] At 4:30 P.M. he and Hill stood on Seminary Ridge and saw the enemy retreating up Cemetery Hill pursued by the shouting Confederates. It was a stirring sight, but the new enemy position gave him pause because it appeared to be a strong one.[135] Hill's impression that the Yankees were "entirely routed" [136] was false and Lee knew it, for they seemed to be preparing for another stand, probably as soon as fresh troops could arrive on the scene.

Although Howard could hardly have expected reinforcements in time to save the corps from a costly retreat, he had a justifiable grievance against General Henry W. Slocum, who was unnecessarily slow in responding to calls for help. When Howard assumed command late in the morning, the Twelfth Corps, led by Slocum who was the ranking major general in the army,[137] was either in or near Two Taverns, a little hamlet on the Baltimore Pike only five miles southeast of Gettysburg. This corps seemed to be the most obvious and immediate source of relief because it was marching on a hard surfaced road leading directly to the rear of the Union lines, whether they were on the far side of Gettysburg or stretched along Cemetery and Culp's Hills.

With the First Division leading, the Twelfth Corps had begun filing into Two Taverns an hour or so before noon after a leisurely march of six miles from Littlestown.[138] Quite innocent of events not far away, the men made preparations for the midday meal, while keeping on the alert for a resumption of the march at a moment's notice. Slocum later admitted they had heard firing on their way to Two Taverns and after they got there, but he explained that it had sounded more like cavalry carbines accompanied occasionally by the roar of cannon than like a general engagement. Some time after their arrival—Slocum did not say when—a civilian came down the road from Gettysburg and said a battle was being fought. Slocum sent a member of his staff, Major E. W. Guindon, to investigate. Guindon rode ahead, and upon reaching a high point on the way heard very distinctly the sound of heavy cannonading, which to his trained ear indicated an engagement involving a large number of infantry. He realized that the hills between Two Taverns and Gettysburg had probably muffled the rattle of musketry and the sustained boom of artillery. The major reported his findings to Slocum, and soon the Twelfth Corps began to move forward. It arrived near Gettysburg about 5:00 P.M.[139]

Both this account by Slocum and his official report left a great deal unsaid. Although the general denied having heard the noise of battle, other officers reported that about 1:00 P.M., while the men were snoozing or making coffee, the sound of cannon suddenly attracted their attention. Later it became a steady roar with overtones of heavy musketry fire. Looking to the northwest, they could see smoke rising high over the hills and the bursting of shells.[140] Slocum's failure to hear convincing sounds of fighting might have been caused by an acoustical freak connected with the location of his headquarters, or perhaps by the coincidence of his appearance in Two Taverns at the time of the lull in the battle. Guindon then might have ridden to the top of a hill just as the engagement broke out with renewed fury. Whatever the explanation of Slocum's delay in learning of the engagement from the noise, he overlooked in his account the messages Howard claimed to have sent him, which were more reliable as a source of information than sound waves.

The first dispatch, which left Eleventh Corps headquarters at 1:00 P.M., did not specifically ask for reinforcements, but the inference was obvious. It said that Ewell's corps was advancing from York, and the left wing of the Army of the Potomac was engaged with A. P. Hill's corps. The term "left wing" was ambiguous, it is

311

true, for it could have meant that the First, Third, and Eleventh Corps were all together; but having received a copy of the order of march for all corps on July 1,[141] an officer of Slocum's experience should have known there was little likelihood that the Third Corps had arrived at Gettysburg at such an early hour in the afternoon. He should also have perceived that the First and Eleventh Corps were in for serious trouble with two enemy corps converging upon them. The exact time at which Slocum received Howard's dispatch is uncertain, but assuming the courier left headquarters promptly he should have delivered it to Slocum four or five miles away between 1:30 and 2:00 P.M. Slocum apparently had to get more explicit pleas for help before he would decide to move his corps. Despite Geary's report of the departure of his division from Two Taverns "at about 2 p.m.," it seems clear that the corps did not get under way until at least an hour later, or around 3:00 P.M.[142] The real difficulty was with Slocum himself; he was plagued by doubts, and it took time for him to resolve them.

In seeking an explanation for Slocum's indecision some students of the battle have placed the onus on the Pipe Creek Circular, saying that it misled him into thinking that Meade wished to avoid a general engagement at Gettysburg.[143] They failed to point out, however, that the circular, and more especially Meade's supplementary order to Slocum placing the Fifth Corps as well as the Twelfth under his direction, made any retrograde movement depend upon what Reynolds did. Should Reynolds inform Slocum of his intention to retreat, then and only then would the Fifth and Twelfth Corps retire from their advanced positions at Hanover and Two Taverns respectively.[144] But Reynolds was dead—though Slocum did not know it as soon as he should have because of Howard's oversight —and the First and Eleventh Corps instead of retreating were engaged in a deadly struggle with the enemy. Clearly events which Meade had thought possible had already occurred and had outmoded the strategy of the Pipe Creek Circular. Upon receiving official word of fighting from Howard, Slocum should have turned command of the corps over to General Alpheus Williams and himself have hurried ahead to Gettysburg for first-hand information on the situation. After consultation with Howard he could then have decided where best to dispose his men, who by then would have been well on their way to join him.

Instead Slocum started his corps for Gettysburg, but refused to make his appearance in spite of "urgent" requests from Howard for his aid and counsel. Sometime in midafternoon Slocum learned from a courier sent by Meade about Reynolds' death and Hancock's assignment at Gettysburg. The message also included orders for all corps commanders to hurry their troops forward. What Meade failed to do until later was to give Slocum explicit instructions to take command of all troops at Gettysburg by virtue of his seniority in rank once he had arrived on the field. Meade apparently assumed Slocum would get there as soon as possible and take over without having to be told to do so. This careless oversight turned out to be one of the causes for Slocum's hesitation.[145] Finally around 4:00 P.M., just as the Union line was collapsing, Howard in desperation sent his brother Charles to urge Slocum to hurry his men and to come himself to Cemetery Hill. Major Howard found Slocum on the Baltimore Pike about a mile from General Howard's headquarters. Saying he had already ordered one division to the right, Slocum agreed to send the other, as Howard suggested, to the left,[146] but he said he could not "assume the responsibility of that day's fighting & of those two corps." [147] When Geary's division approached Cemetery Hill about 5:00 P.M. Hancock sent his inspector general and chief of staff, Lieutenant Colonel C. H. Morgan, to locate the other division of the Twelfth Corps. On the way Morgan met Slocum and asked why he did not take command. Slocum again refused for the same reason he had given Major Howard and offered an additional excuse. Since Hancock had been "specially selected" over his head to command the troops, he did not wish to interfere. Mollified by Morgan's assurance that Hancock had been instructed to turn over the control of affairs to him when he appeared on the scene, Slocum made no further objections. He relieved Hancock between 5:30 and 6:00 P.M.,[148] but the question of who commanded the forces at Gettysburg was not finally settled until Howard personally submitted to Slocum's authority at 7:00 P.M. Unbending in his insistence upon military protocol, Slocum, a graduate of West Point though a lawyer by profession, had demonstrated the spirit that wins cases at the bar, not battles.[149]

Meanwhile without consulting his colleagues so as to coordinate their efforts Slocum had decided upon a bit of strategy which promised either brilliant success for Union arms or abysmal failure. It proved to be neither. At 3:35 P.M. he sent a message to "General Hancock or General Howard," saying that he was moving the Twelfth Corps "so as to come in about 1 mile to the right of Gettysburg." It was a vague communication at best, and the phrase "to the right" of the town depended upon where one stood. Since it was delivered to generals standing on Cemetery Hill, presumably Slocum meant he was bringing his corps somewhere toward the eastern edge of Gettysburg, probably by way of the Hanover road. As it turned out, that is just what he did.[150] Before the First Division crossed Rock Creek about two miles from town on its way to Cemetery Hill, one of Slocum's staff officers met General Alpheus Williams, commander of the division, with orders for him to take a crossroad to the Hanover road. Williams was instructed to have as his objective a high bald hill overlooking the town about a mile away. Although he did not know its name, it proved to be Benner's Hill, which the Confederates were to use for their artillery the next day against Cemetery and Culp's Hills to the south of them. Judging from his dispatch Slocum intended to have the Second Division follow the First, but Howard's request for support on the left of Gettysburg came in the meantime, and the Second was diverted elsewhere. Williams pressed his men over a "narrow, winding path or country road" which was very "muddy and slippery." After a few miles they reached some dense woods, at the bottom of which was a ravine. The ascent of Benner's Hill began from there. Just as they were starting to climb Williams learned of the presence of Confederate cavalry on the hill, so he prepared to assault it. By then it was between 5:30 and 6:00 P.M. Before he could attack, one of Slocum's staff officers rushed up with orders for him to withdraw, as Union troops had retreated from town and Williams and his men were in danger of being cut off. Retracing their steps, they bivouacked for the night near the place where they had turned off from the Baltimore Pike. Before long Williams received notice that with Slocum in charge of the right wing he had been put in command of the Twelfth Corps. In complete ignorance of the condition of the First and Eleventh Corps, the location of Geary's division, and the nature of the terrain, Williams felt very uncomfortable about his situation.[151]

In an analysis of the battle the question arises as to whether it would have been better for Slocum to have ordered all of his men to

Gettysburg by way of the Baltimore Pike, the most direct route from Two Taverns. Assuming that the corps was well on its way when he dispatched his message to Hancock or Howard at 3:35 P.M., it is barely possible that a brigade or more by following the pike might have reached the town in time to protect the First and Eleventh Corps in their retreat. If he had responded quickly to Howard's first message and started his men around 2:00 P.M., perhaps at least a division could have marched to Gettysburg before the left wing gave way. It is highly doubtful, however, whether they could have deployed beyond the town in time to mount a counter-attack. Howard's delay in informing Slocum about the fight was compounded by Slocum's sluggishness in sending help. In spite of his strange behavior Slocum did finally succeed in bringing his corps within supporting distance of the new Union positions on Cemetery and Culp's Hills should the Confederates renew the offensive.

The Federal forces had yet to be thoroughly crushed, though the Southerners had gained a substantial victory. With approximately four hours of daylight remaining Lee was unsure in his own mind about what the next step should be. Instead of the comparatively simple task of pursuing a fleeing enemy, he had the more complex one of organizing a new attack. Five of his infantry divisions had yet to appear, and he remained uncertain about the location of those of Meade's army which had not yet arrived. For these reasons Lee still wished to avoid a general engagement, while at the same time he decided he should make an effort to carry Cemetery Hill.[152] His military judgment told him he had to attempt the move, though his resources for the present were rather slim. Having followed Hill's two divisions to the outskirts of town, he knew how exhausted and disorganized most of their brigades were after hours of fighting.[153] He had not had an opportunity of learning at first hand the condition of Ewell's troops, and his only recourse was to suggest, not order, that Ewell should storm Cemetery Hill if he thought it "practicable."[154] For various reasons Ewell decided such an attack was not "practicable," so the first day's fighting, except for some desultory outbursts of artillery and rifle fire, ended when the survivors of the First and Eleventh Corps finally became ensconced on Cemetery Hill.

In the weeks following the battle the Confederates began to have second thoughts about events and to discover lost opportunities. At first their comments were general in character and made no allusions to the performance of anyone in particular. The correspondent of the London *Times* remarked only that the engagement was premature and the Confederates did not take advantage of their tremendous gains.[155] But when sometime later Colonel Perrin wrote to his friend, Governor Luke Bonham of South Carolina, his criticisms were harsher and more specific. While complaining of Lee's failure to concentrate his army in time to overwhelm the First and Eleventh Corps, he reserved his sharpest barbs for Major General Richard H. Anderson of South Carolina, in command of a division in Hill's corps. Perrin said that after he (Perrin) had driven the enemy from Seminary Ridge, Pender told him to collect his scattered brigade and rest it, for he had sent back for Anderson's division to come up. "But neither Anderson nor his Division was anywhere to be found," he wrote. Meanwhile, much to Perrin's annoyance, "the very batteries which we had run off & which we saw them take off through Gettysburg, were the first to fire a shot from their new position. . . . The first shell fired by them . . . was aimed at my Brigade. . . . The very infantry that we had run from the stone walls that surround Gettysburg, were the first to fire a shot from their new position." Though admitting he did not know whether Hill or Anderson was responsible, he bluntly pronounced Anderson's failure to be up as *"the cause of the failure of the campaign."* [156] Revealing more righteous anger than sound judgment, Perrin's analysis nevertheless raised the pertinent question of why Anderson was not available or why he was not used.

Anderson's division had started from Fayetteville early in the morning of July 1 to clear the way for Johnson's division and Ewell's wagon train. He halted in Cashtown early in the afternoon and after a wait of an hour or so received orders from Hill to proceed along the Chambersburg Pike. Both Lee and Hill in their reports referred vaguely to Anderson's arrival near Gettysburg after the start of the engagement, but did not give the hour.[157] Hill said the division bivouacked "some 2 miles in rear of the battleground." [158] According to Brigadier General A. R. Wright of Anderson's division, his brigade, following immediately behind Brigadier General William Mahone's, came to a position three-quarters of a mile south of the pike and about three miles from Gettysburg between 4:00 and 5:00 P.M.[159] Lee perhaps figured that by that time it was too late to throw in fresh troops, although several hours of daylight remained. Neither he nor Hill mentioned the possibility of using Anderson late in the afternoon or early in the evening of July 1. The records do not explain why it took the division so long to march from Fayetteville to Cashtown, a distance of eleven miles, or why he was kept waiting there for a considerable time, thus delaying his arrival at Gettysburg.[160] Apparently no one but Perrin noticed any shortcomings in his performance on July 1, and it never became a subject of discussion after the battle. After the war Anderson told a story which, though unreliable in some details, suggests a possible explanation for his inactive role on July 1. When his division, hastening to join the other units, was only two miles away, he said, a messenger from Lee ordered him to halt and go into camp. Completely puzzled, he obeyed and then later sought out his commander to see whether the courier had given the order correctly. Lee said there had been no mistake and then offered an explanation. With his army still not concentrated and ignorant of the enemy's strength, Anderson's troops were the only fresh ones present and he wanted to keep them as a reserve in case of disaster.[161]

Through the years critics of Confederate fighting on July 1 have asserted that the Southerners should have advanced on Cemetery Hill immediately after the Union retreat. It could then have been taken, they claimed, with comparatively little loss, and the enemy would have been deprived of his immense advantage of position which was afterwards an important element in his success.[162] The object of their scorn in time came to be General Ewell, who they said had suddenly become confused and indecisive and had fumbled away an opportunity to attack Cemetery Hill when the Yankees could have been easily overwhelmed. He should at least have taken immediate steps to seize Culp's Hill, they continued, because it was unoccupied at the time, and its capture would have rendered untenable the Union position on Cemetery Hill half a mile away. These statements raise some important questions which have never been satisfactorily answered. What troops did Ewell have at his disposal for an immediate attack? Was Culp's Hill in fact unoccupied for a considerable period, as his critics have assumed? And why was the onus placed upon Ewell for Confederate failure to move against the Yankees after their retreat through town?

It so happened that Ewell's corps had a number of highly articulate and intelligent officers such as Brigadier General Gordon, Major Generals Early and Isaac R. Trimble, and a number of lesser officers, all of whom wrote lengthy recollections of the events of that memorable afternoon. Some of the lesser lights had been members of "Stonewall" Jackson's staff, and they watched the great man's successor with a critical eye. Since Ewell obviously lacked many of Jackson's qualities, he often came out second best in their estimation. All of them had been personally involved in affairs of the Second Corps, so in their writings they concentrated their attention on Ewell's activities in an effort to find out what had gone wrong at Gettysburg.[163] Neither they nor anyone else sought to investigate Hill's conduct with similar intensity, for with Lee present on Seminary Ridge and in a position to supervise Hill's corps everyone assumed its movements were subject to his approval. Any criticism of Hill would then have become a reproach to Lee, an unthinkable gaffe. Confederate literature about the first day of the battle therefore publicized what Ewell did and did not do, to the neglect of Hill's record.

The severest critics of Ewell, Generals Gordon and Trimble, wrote years after the event when in retrospect it seemed relatively easy to have organized a rapid pursuit of the Yankees and driven them off the hill.[164] They forgot, however, the exact circumstances that kept the move from being "practicable" at the time.[165] The extravagance of their own language and that of other Confederates in describing the defeat of the enemy trapped them into believing the Yankees were completely demoralized.[166] To back up their claims they could point to General Hancock's letter written after the war to General Fitzhugh Lee, in which he expressed the opinion that if the Confederates had continued the pursuit of Howard they would have driven him "over and beyond Cemetery Hill." [167] Though impressive because of the source, this document really proved nothing except to indicate one thing: To achieve complete success after smashing the Union positions north and west of the town the Confederates would have had to continue their drive through the streets and up Cemetery Hill without a letup.

The fact is that the Southern assault lost its momentum after the Federal lines were crushed. Whereas the town became an obstacle to swift movement by the retreating Northerners and trapped many of them in its streets, in similar fashion it retarded the forward progress of the pursuing Confederates. Near Cemetery Hill Yankee sharpshooters and skirmishers used buildings as barriers to slow down or stop the further progress of the enemy.[168] Many Confederate units became thoroughly disorganized as a result of fighting their opponents for hours and then driving them through narrow streets and lanes. Heavy casualties and general fatigue, which were accentuated by the heat of the day and the lack of water, seriously reduced the effectiveness of many regiments,[169] while the mere physical task of rounding up and guarding thousands of prisoners further depleted manpower otherwise available for fighting.[170]

These problems upset Ewell, for he was faced with the prospect of organizing a new attack with tired men even while he felt constrained by Lee's injunction not to open a full-fledged battle. No wonder he seemed perplexed and uncertain! He was annoyed too by the gratuitous advice of General Trimble, who was a supernumerary at the time—an officer without a command—and Ewell's negative reaction to his suggestions may have contributed to the tradition that he had become paralyzed by indecision.[171] The Union position, from what he could see of it, looked formidable, especially if it were attacked from the town, and good positions for his artillery were scarce.[172] Naturally he turned to his senior major general, Jubal A. Early, who had led three brigades brilliantly against the Eleventh Corps, for his estimate of the situation.[173] Early urged him to move against Cemetery Hill or more importantly, Culp's Hill, saying he could count on the use of Gordon's, Hays's, and Hoke's brigades because their losses had been slight, and possibly on "Extra Billy" Smith's brigade which was to the rear on the York Turnpike. Of Rodes's division, Dole's brigade was also available, since it had suffered few casualties. In given time Ewell could organize an attacking column of 6,000 to 7,000 men.[174] To assure their chances of success he sent Lieutenant J. P. Smith to inquire of Lee what help might be forthcoming from Hill. The commanding general apparently ruled out the possibility of using Anderson's division, as well as Lane's brigade and that of Brigadier General Edward L. Thomas of Pender's division which were relatively unscathed, for he told Ewell that he was on his own. A few minutes previously Lee had sent Major Walter Taylor to Ewell with the suggestion that he try to seize Cemetery Hill. The two messengers evidently passed each other on the way.[175]

During this period of uncertainty Early received an alarm from General Smith that the enemy was approaching on the York Pike. Although Early believed it to be false, he took the precaution of sending Gordon with his brigade to the threatened point. Thus temporarily deprived of the use of two brigades and without any support on his right from Hill should he attack, Ewell decided to postpone any action until Johnson's strong division arrived. He planned that when it came up he would deploy it on his extreme left for an attack on Culp's Hill.[176]

Meanwhile cavalrymen brought new rumors of an approaching Federal force, and Ewell joined Early and Rodes on the east side of town to see whether the threat to their left was more than the figment of somebody's imagination. From a vantage point overlooking Rock Creek they could see a considerable distance down the York Pike. With the appearance of skirmishers to the south of the pike, a dispute arose between the three generals over their identity. Early vehemently insisted no Yankees were on that flank.[177] He proved to be right about the skirmishers, for they were Confederates, but he was wrong in his denial that there had been a Federal threat to his flank an hour or so earlier. Somehow some troops, maybe a few of Jenkins' cavalrymen untrained in reconnaissance work, had got wind of Williams' division on its way to Benner's Hill, but they gave confused reports which did more harm than good. Whatever the reason, the Confederate generals kept looking for Yankees on the wrong road. Why Early was so cocksure in his estimate of the danger and why no one thought to reconnoiter along the Hanover road are questions to be listed among the mysteries of the campaign. If Ewell had decided earlier to dismiss the reports as empty rumors and had proceeded to attack, he could very well have found himself suddenly ambushed by Williams. By the time Ewell returned to his temporary headquarters north of town from the investigation of the scare on the left, it was close to sunset and Johnson's division was just beginning to stream in toward Seminary Ridge. Before it could get into position on the eastern outskirts of town darkness had fallen, and the men, thoroughly weary after a march of twenty-five miles, were ready to turn in for the night. All thought of renewing the struggle that day was abandoned.[178]

Responsibility for the failure of the Confederates to make an all-out assault on Cemetery Hill on July 1 must rest with Lee. If Ewell had been a Jackson he might have been able to regroup his forces quickly enough to attack within an hour after the Yankees had started to retreat through the town. The likelihood of success decreased rapidly after that time unless Lee were willing to risk everything.[179] The Federal retreat had started around 4:00 P.M.,[180] and at 5:25 P.M. Hancock pronounced the Union position as one that "cannot well be taken." His only concern was about the unprotected condition of his left flank along Cemetery Ridge south to the Round Tops.[181] There was no danger on his immediate front as long as Hill did not move and Longstreet was not up, although Hancock of course did not know that. As for his right, Slocum was in the offing just beyond Rock Creek, and Wadsworth's division was on Culp's Hill.

About 5:00 P.M. the 12,000 Union officers and men who had survived the day's fighting began to receive substantial reinforcements. Scattered units of the First and Eleventh Corps, amounting to about eight hundred men who had been on guard duty at Emmitsburg, rejoined their commands.[182] Shortly afterwards three big regiments of General Stannard's brigade, over 2,100 men in all, finally reached Gettysburg and were attached to the Third Division of the First Corps,[183] while two brigades of Geary's division of the Twelfth Corps took positions on Cemetery Ridge just to the north of Little Round Top.[184] By 6:00 P.M. these reinforcements had brought the strength of Union forces up to 20,000, and more troops kept pouring in. At dusk two brigades of the Third Corps under General David B. Birney began to arrive and were placed just north of Geary.[185] Williams' division of the Twelfth Corps had meanwhile returned from its junket to Benner's Hill and had bivouacked for the night near the Baltimore Pike.[186] General Slocum, who was now in charge of all the Union forces, had over 27,000 officers and men at his disposal to repulse any attack. These troops had considerable artillery support. They were backed by forty-one guns of the First and Eleventh Corps, twenty of the Twelfth Corps, eighteen attached to Birney's two brigades, and six with Buford's cavalry, making eighty-five in all.[187] Though still outnumbered in men and guns, Slocum had a large enough force to hold his strong position until the rest of the army could come up.

The Army of the Potomac had again displayed its resiliency under extreme adversity. The men of the First and Eleventh Corps and

Buford's cavalry, though defeated, were able to regroup and turn once more to face the foe. They had forced the enemy to pay such a heavy price for his victory that he hesitated until it was too late to renew the contest.[188] Meade's skillful distribution of his corps during his maneuvers to stop Lee and the marching abilities of his hardy veterans had brought rich rewards.

XIII

MEADE PREPARES FOR BATTLE

SOMETIME BEFORE dawn on July 2 General Meade, accompanied by
some of his staff and General Hunt, rode up to the gatekeeper's
cottage [1] at the entrance to the Gettysburg cemetery on the Baltimore Pike and dismounted rather stiffly after his uncomfortable ride
of a dozen miles in the dark from Taneytown.[2] Meade, not given to
histrionics, was simple, direct, and businesslike in his manner as he
greeted Slocum, Howard, Sickles, and other officers who gathered
there to meet him.[3] Looking about him, Meade asked for opinions
about the army's position. When assured that it was a good one, he
remarked drily that he was glad to hear it for "it was too late to
leave it." [4] This incident served as a fitting end to the uncertainty
confronting him upon his assumption of command. Having finally
pinned down the location of his quarry, Meade had come to Gettysburg to fight it out with him.

Upon learning of the outbreak of serious fighting and the death of
Reynolds, Meade may have restrained a natural impulse to rush off
to the battleground and take over control of affairs himself. Instead
he delegated authority to a highly competent subordinate, while he
himself stayed close to the center of operations at army headquarters. Here he could better supervise all his forces until he determined whether to advance to Gettysburg or follow through with his
previous plans. It was a wise decision, for if he had dropped everything and gone to Gettysburg after hearing about Reynolds' death,
he would not have arrived until the contest was almost over. It is
doubtful too whether he could have improved upon Hancock as a tac-
tician or as an inspiration for dispirited troops.[5]

Hancock deserved great praise for the manner in which he carried out his double assignment. He took command of defeated troops, placed them and their reinforcements on Cemetery and Culp's Hills as judiciously as possible, and decided to hold on until nightfall so as to give his commander time to make up his mind about the next step. To clear the way for any troops that might be advanced, he sent all trains to the rear.[6] Then in line with instructions from Meade he set down his considered judgment about the possibilities of Gettysburg as a battleground. Sometime after 4:00 P.M. he had an aide, Major William G. Mitchell, carry word to Meade about the situation, together with the assurance that he could maintain the new position for the rest of the day. At 5:25 P.M. he sent another aide, Captain I. B. Parker, with a written analysis of the advantages and disadvantages of making a stand at Gettysburg. In both messages he was careful to inform Meade but not to advise him. Then after all signs of further Confederate activity had ceased, Hancock turned his command over to Slocum and about dark started out to report to Meade in person. Arriving in Taneytown between 9:00 and 10:00 P.M., he found that Meade had already ordered the rest of the army to advance at once to Gettysburg. Hancock seemed surprised at the general's decision, so evidently he had not received a message Meade sent to him and Doubleday at 6:00 P.M. announcing his plans.[7]

During the afternoon Meade had become convinced by information arriving from various sources that Lee was bringing up the rest of his army. Thus he made his decision to fight at Gettysburg.[8] Hancock's report, delivered verbally by Major Mitchell, affirmed his judgment, for it probably arrived just after he had sent off his own dispatch at 6:00 P.M. Mitchell was a "most intelligent and reliable officer, greatly trusted by Hancock and highly thought of by Meade." Thoroughly briefing the general on the state of affairs on the field, he told him that in Hancock's opinion Gettysburg was the place to fight a battle.[9] Once Meade had made up his mind to challenge Lee there, he abandoned all thought of the provisional line along Pipe Creek. What information he received during the evening from Hancock, Warren, and others about the situation at Gettysburg and the character of the surrounding country helped him in effecting a rapid concentration of his army at the threatened point.[10]

Earlier in the day, even before receiving word of the morning's engagement, Meade had already taken the first step toward that end when he alerted General Sedgwick, whose big Sixth Corps was in the outer periphery of operations near Manchester, to be ready to move in any direction at a moment's notice. After news of the fighting reached headquarters the tempo of his operations increased. At 4:30 P.M. he ordered Sedgwick to march the corps to Taneytown that night, after sending his trains, except for ambulances and ammunition wagons, to Westminster.[11] Fifteen minutes later Meade received a copy of Howard's message to Sickles, ordering him to advance his corps to Gettysburg. Since he had placed Hancock in temporary command of the First, Third, and Eleventh Corps, Meade sent a dispatch to Sickles suggesting that he await word from Hancock before moving. Should Hancock ask for the Third Corps, Meade wanted a division left behind to guard the army's left and rear at Emmitsburg. Sickles, as it turned out, had already started his corps for Gettysburg before receiving these instructions, but he had taken the wise precaution of keeping two brigades and two batteries at Emmitsburg under one of his senior officers, Brigadier General Charles K. Graham. Sickles had worried about what he should do, for he had felt that he was subjected to conflicting orders, first those from Meade placing his corps at Emmitsburg and then later ones from Howard directing him to Gettysburg. Considering the emergency too great for him to delay his departure until he received clearance from headquarters at Taneytown nine miles away, he hurried to the battlefield with the hope that Meade would give him his blessing, which he ultimately did.[12]

Sometime during the afternoon and probably before sending his messages to Sickles and Sedgwick Meade had ordered General Gibbon, in temporary command of the Second Corps, to advance his men up the Taneytown road. When Gibbon got within three miles of Gettysburg, he received orders from General Hancock to halt because with the cessation of fighting there was no pressing need for his corps in the line. Hancock was just as worried as Meade about the possibility of a turning movement by the Confederates somewhere along the Union flank between Gettysburg and Emmitsburg. By keeping the Second Corps three miles or so to the rear of the Union position he placed it where it could take one of several crossroads connecting the Emmitsburg and Taneytown roads and could thus intercept any force threatening either of these towns.[13]

Shortly after his 6:00 P.M. message to Hancock and Doubleday Meade ordered Sykes and his Fifth Corps to start that night from Hanover for Gettysburg, and he directed the two brigades of the Third Corps left at Emmitsburg to join their divisions at Gettysburg by daylight next morning. He also got "about eight batteries" of the Artillery Reserve under General Robert O. Tyler on their way near sundown with instructions to report to General Hancock upon their arrival at Gettysburg. Tyler, apparently not understanding the nature of Hancock's temporary assignment during the day, stopped his column when he came to Second Corps headquarters around 10:30 P.M. There he found Gibbon, not Hancock, so he moved on for a short distance and camped for the night.[14]

Meanwhile the orders to Sedgwick had been changed. Instead of marching his Sixth Corps to Taneytown, Meade instructed him to head immediately for Gettysburg by the shortest route because without these men he felt the enemy would outnumber him considerably. Sedgwick himself was to proceed to Taneytown for a conference with Meade.[15] To hasten the movements of the corps Meade authorized Sedgwick to stop all trains which might be in his way or force them off the road. Whereas the first order to Sedgwick, sent at 4:30 P.M., had called for a stiff tramp of twenty miles from Manchester to Taneytown by way of Westminster, the second one demanded a forced march over half again as long. Since to deliver the message the courier had to ride from Taneytown to Sixth Corps headquarters in Manchester,[16] Sedgwick did not receive the first order until approximately 8:00 P.M. He got his corps started within the hour.[17] While on the way he received the second order, and since it gave him discretion about routes, he continued as he had started. Some three hours later, while Sedgwick was riding ahead of his men with General Newton, a third message came to him from Meade, directing him to march his men to Gettysburg by way of the Baltimore Pike. Although he and Newton were already beyond Westminster on the road to Taneytown, he turned back and led his men by way of a crossroad to the pike.[18] At this point he would have saved distance if he had pushed ahead to Taneytown and proceeded from there to Gettysburg; but he agreed with Meade that the pike was better for fast marching, and he decided it was worth the extra distance to get on it.[19] As for Meade's directive for him to come personally to Taneytown, either Sedgwick did not understand the message or he considered it better for him to remain with his corps; in any event he did not go to see Meade. The general meanwhile decided not to wait for Sedgwick any later than midnight, and shortly thereafter he started out for Gettysburg. Butterfield stayed behind in Taneytown, and when neither the headquarters messenger nor Sedgwick had made his appearance by 2:40 A.M. he had visions of rebel cavalry having cut his communications with the Sixth Corps. Should that have been the case, he would have been helpless, for the cavalry detachment left at headquarters was too small to fight its way through any large force in order to carry a message to Sedgwick.[20] In company with many other Union generals Butterfield enjoyed very little if any sleep that night.

At 5:30 A.M. he dispatched a long message to Sedgwick. Assuming by then that the commander of the Sixth Corps must have gone with his men to Gettysburg by way of the Baltimore Pike, Butterfield enclosed a memorandum which Meade had dictated to him before leaving headquarters. This document explained why Meade was so anxious to talk to his friend John Sedgwick, whom he had not seen since taking command of the army. He had a certain role in mind for his largest corps, and he wanted first-hand information about its condition from its commanding officer. He wrote Sedgwick that he proposed to make a vigorous attack on the enemy on July 2. Assuming that after a long march the Sixth Corps would be in no condition to go into action immediately, he suggested that following a rest only long enough to revive the men, Sedgwick should push on as far as possible and form a line of battle at some strong point. This position could be used to cover a retreat in case Meade should meet with disaster, or it could act as a springboard for an advance to follow up a successful attack. Though fuzzy in its details because Meade still had to learn about actual conditions in Gettysburg, the memo brought out his intention to take the offensive and to use the Sixth Corps as a reserve force in order to achieve decisive results.[21]

Before Meade left headquarters at Taneytown with orders for the general staff to follow him as soon as possible, he felt fairly sure that all units of his army were in motion toward their appointed places. Though there was some question about the Sixth Corps, he could not wait to find out because he was needed in Gettysburg if he expected to accomplish anything the next day. On his way he stopped off to see his friend General John Gibbon; he awakened him, talked to him for fifteen minutes, and then gave orders for the Second Corps to move forward at daylight. In later years Gibbon recalled, in answer to critics, that there seemed to be no doubt in Meade's mind about where the battle should be fought.[22]

Meade's assurance that concentration of his forces was going along about as well as could be expected might have been shaken if he had known of the difficulties being encountered by the Second Division of the Third Corps. What was happening to it was the sort of thing that would have put him in a towering rage. Fortunately the extremely capable General A. A. Humphreys was in command, and his cool head and iron discipline prevented possible disaster or a premature struggle with the enemy. When Humphreys received Sickles' message of 3:15 P.M. ordering him to march his First and Second Brigades immediately to Gettysburg, his division was occupying a position one mile from Emmitsburg on the road to Fairfield.[23] Since Birney's division would take the Emmitsburg road, Humphreys' men were directed to use a parallel one two miles to the west. Lieutenant Colonel Julius Hayden, assistant inspector general of the corps, headed a party of guides for the division. About halfway to their destination Humphreys received a copy of a dispatch from Howard to Sickles warning him, as he came up the main road near Gettysburg, to beware of enemy forces on his left. Shortly thereafter a native who had guided a part of the First Corps gave him the latest word about the battle. He said the Confederates had driven the Federals to the east of Gettysburg and the main road from Emmitsburg.

Upon hearing this news and coming to a fork, Humphreys wanted to take the right one which led directly to the Emmitsburg road about two miles south of Gettysburg.[24] But Hayden, who was noted more for "froth and foam" than common sense,[25] insisted that in spite of the changes in the opposing lines the column should follow the route he thought Sickles had indicated. They were to take the left fork, he said, and proceed to the Black Horse Tavern on the Fairfield road before turning right for Gettysburg. Though Humphreys had misgivings, he obeyed the order because Sickles had placed the division in Hayden's charge. It was dark when they crossed Marsh Creek and approached the tavern. Sensing danger, Humphreys halted his command and ordered "perfect silence" while Hayden and one or two guides went ahead to the tavern about a quarter of a mile away. His caution paid off, for Hayden found the tavern swarming with rebels. Humphreys would have been willing to pitch into them except that it was dark, the strength of the enemy was unknown, and the rest of the army was too far away to send help in case he needed it. So his division turned around and tiptoed off into the darkness, retracing its steps and finally groping its way about midnight to the safety of the Army of the Potomac. The incompetence of one man had delayed the arrival of the division by four hours. Humphreys commented later: "You see how things were managed in the Third Corps!" [26]

Despite their unfamiliarity with the sections of Maryland and Pennsylvania through which they marched and the scarcity of good maps, most commanding officers reached their objectives efficiently and without going through Humphreys' disconcerting experience of a chance meeting with the enemy. General Warren, chief of engineers, said that though they had "decent" maps of some of the counties, they possessed none of Carroll County, Maryland, through which most of the corps had to come.[27] Here were located such towns as Manchester, Westminster, Union Mills, and Taneytown, all of which figured prominently in the campaign. General Butterfield, who as chief of staff was concerned with such matters, expressed amazement when he learned of an extension of the Western Maryland Railroad from Westminster to Union Bridge which he never knew existed. Army headquarters, having no maps to distribute, instructed corps commanders to obtain them whenever possible from local inhabitants.[28] In this respect General Howard apparently had trouble too, for he asked General Reynolds before going into Pennsylvania whether he had an extra map of Adams County.[29]

Meade was too good an engineer not to be aware of the need to know the geography of an area, and he took particular pains to become familiar with roads and topography. Under his direction members of the general staff, including Generals Warren and Hunt, spent hours locating good positions along the Little Pipe Creek line and examining the country between it and Gettysburg.[30] Meade gave his commanders special instructions to learn about the roads connecting the locations of the different corps on July 1.[31] To supplement their maps or to make up for the lack of them, his generals obtained information from loyal citizens and sometimes enlisted them as guides. They also detailed certain of their staff officers to ride about and become acquainted with the countryside.[32] They could thus use parallel or connecting routes, which prevented overtaxing the capacity of the main highways and enabled Meade to move his army with greater speed than would otherwise have been possible.[33]

Characteristically one of the first things Meade did after he got to Gettysburg was to make a survey of the Union position. He had never been there before, and he wanted to get a first-hand impression of the terrain as soon as possible. Accompanied by one or two officers, he walked out beyond the Baltimore Pike among the batteries posted on the crest and higher slopes of Cemetery Hill. It was still dark, and looking to the west and north all he could see were campfires outlining the Confederate position. He returned to Howard's headquarters in the cemetery to attend to other matters in preparation for the day. Just before dawn he started out with Generals Howard and Hunt and Captain W. H. Paine of the engineer staff for an extensive examination of the area. They rode south along Cemetery Ridge, gradually perceiving its salient features more sharply as the glow in the east grew stronger. When within a short distance of Little Round Top, they turned around and went north to Culp's Hill before riding back to headquarters. During the inspection Captain Paine made a sketch of the terrain, and Meade indicated on it the positions to be held by each corps. He then had Paine send copies of the plan to the corps commanders. Having decided upon the location of the infantry, Meade instructed Hunt to examine the lines more thoroughly and supervise the placing of artillery batteries.[34]

If Meade had by then picked as his permanent headquarters the little white farmhouse of the Widow Leister on the west side of the Taneytown road,[35] Hunt had merely to ride eight hundred feet from it to get to the top of Cemetery Ridge. By the time he got there it was broad daylight, and he could see Union troops occupying the hills and ridges to his right. They were astride the Baltimore Pike coming in from the southeast and the Taneytown road from the south, and from their positions they could overlook and dominate the Emmitsburg road as it converged from the southwest to join the other two highways on the edge of town. Their right flank was protected by forces occupying Culp's Hill, which was a rocky and heavily wooded promontory to the northeast. From it the lines as finally formed extended for about a mile southward and generally parallel to the Baltimore Pike as far as Rock Creek. At this point there was a gap in the lines of five hundred feet caused by low swampy ground surrounding Spangler's Spring, beyond which higher land rose to the southeast. Immediately west of Culp's Hill was a knoll, ultimately named for Captain Greenleaf T. Stevens of the 5th Maine Battery, which partly bridged the depression separating Culp's from Cemetery Hill. Both hills were of the same height, but Cemetery had the advantage of a flat top which acted as a superb platform for a concentration of artillery. At its south end Cemetery Hill tapered off into Cemetery Ridge, which continued for about a mile and a half until it lost its identity in lower and flatter ground leading to the northern shoulder of Little Round Top. The shallow valley west of the ridge and Cemetery Hill contained fields and pastures crisscrossed by stout fences of various types.

South of the ridge the country became extremely rough, its surface strewn with huge boulders or broken by outcroppings of rock, the largest of which was Devil's Den. The most prominent feature of this area was Little Round Top. About a quarter of a mile southwest of it stood the considerably higher hill, Big Round Top. The military advantage of its greater elevation was nullified by its steep slopes and heavily wooded crest which made it practically useless for artillery. Although the two hills were separated by a gap which was greater in width than the effective range of most Civil War shoulder arms, occupation of Big Round Top by Union infantry was desirable to protect the Taneytown road. The real key to the southern section of the Federal position, however, was Little Round Top, for it was accessible to artillery and it guarded the left flank and rear of the line on Cemetery Ridge. On the west its open face dominated a narrow, rocky, and sharply defined valley, through which meandered the little stream of Plum Run. A thousand feet from its base Devil's Den suddenly rose sixty feet above the valley. Except for one large wheat field just beyond this spot the rugged, wooded area continued west without a break for half a mile almost to the Emmitsburg road.

Most of the Union positions were between twenty and thirty feet higher than the areas immediately around them. The exceptions were the four prominent hills: Big Round Top which towered 305 feet above its base, Little Round Top 170 feet, Cemetery Hill from

60 to 80 feet, and Culp's Hill 140 feet. By no stretch of the imagination could any of these heights be called mountains, as they were depicted in some accounts; nor were Cemetery Hill and Ridge as precipitous and formidable as the bravely charging Confederates afterwards remembered them. Though not to be exaggerated, Union positions did offer some real advantages to determined and trained troops who were willing to improve them by building stone walls or throwing up breastworks. They also afforded Federal artillery excellent fields of fire, especially along Cemetery Ridge which overlooked open and cultivated country.

The convex character of the Union line facilitated the rapid movement of troops to reinforce any threatened section. The men never had to march more than two and a half miles and usually less. For example, those on the extreme right flank of Culp's Hill had to go little more than a mile to bring relief to their hard-pressed comrades on Cemetery Ridge. The formation of the Union line was an advantage too to Meade in his supervision of affairs. Though his headquarters was located toward the northern end of the line, it was within an easy canter of any section except the area of the Round Tops and was readily accessible to officers and soldiers having to do business there.[36]

Once established early in the morning of July 2, army headquarters became the center of activities, and Meade remained close by except when some matter arose requiring his personal scrutiny. One by one members of the general staff arrived from Taneytown until by midmorning they were all there, including Butterfield and Patrick.[37] Meade had need of their services for there was much to be done in preparation for a renewal of fighting, which he anticipated might occur at almost any moment. He instructed Butterfield, in addition to his regular duties of coordinating the administrative work of the army, to familiarize himself with the countryside and the location of the various corps. General Patrick as provost marshal general had the task of establishing a compound for prisoners and placing a cordon of provost guards behind the lines to maintain order and to stop fugitives from the front. General Warren's calm, absorbed, and earnest manner, his professional skill and sound judgment pleased Meade, and he consulted with him constantly at headquarters or sent him off on errands of highest military importance.[38] All questions involving administrative detail or military protocol he

*** *Map 7* ***

MOVEMENTS AND POSITIONS OF ARMIES
TO 4:00 P.M., JULY 2

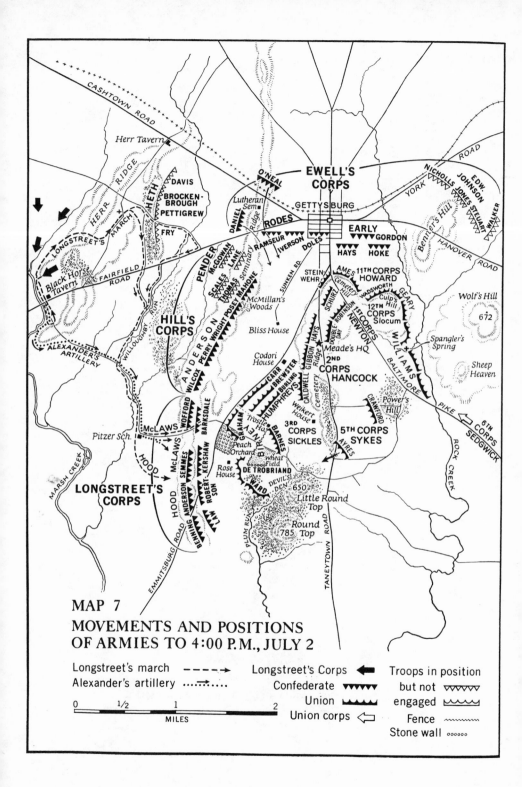

MAP 7

MOVEMENTS AND POSITIONS
OF ARMIES TO 4:00 P.M., JULY 2

Longstreet's march	----→	Longstreet's Corps ◄■■
Alexander's artillery	‥‥▷‥‥	Confederate ▼▼▼▼▼
		Union ◣◣◣◣◣
		Union corps ◁■

Troops in position
but not ∧∧∧∧∧
engaged ∿∿∿∿∿
Fence ∿∿∿∿∿∿
Stone wall ∘∘∘∘∘∘

0   1/2   1   2
MILES

referred to General Seth Williams or Major S. F. Barstow, who seemed to possess encyclopedic knowledge of such matters. While Meade was formulating his plans an eyewitness reported there was a regular flow of orderlies and aides "dashing up with reports and off with orders; the signal officers were bringing in the reports telegraphed by the signal flags from the different crests that overlooked the fight. The rest of the staff stood ready for any duty, and outside the little garden fence a great group of horses stood hitched." [39] The noise, the confusion, and the sense of pressure attending hurried preparations for a great battle can only be imagined. Much of the record has been lost because many orders were delivered orally or placed on slips of paper with no copies being made.[40] Sometimes the commanding general would give his assent or indicate his decisions merely by nodding or shaking his head.

Though fragmentary, the records do show that Meade despite lack of sleep seemed mentally alert and firm but pleasant in his manner. He was pleased with the responsiveness of his officers and men to his directives.[41] By noon all major units had arrived on the battlefield except the Sixth Corps, and Meade had learned from General Newton, who had left Sedgwick early in the morning, that it was pounding along the Baltimore Pike. The Second Corps had arrived between 5:30 and 6:30 A.M., but it took some time before it got into position. Heavy skirmishing between Ewell's corps and Union troops on Cemetery Hill induced Meade to believe that a major assault was imminent, and therefore he had Hancock arrange his men behind Cemetery Hill so that they could be moved quickly in support of the right. Between 7:00 and 8:00 A.M. the firing subsided, and Meade then directed the corps to the position on Cemetery Ridge which it was to hold during the battle. It connected with the Eleventh Corps on its right and covered the front from the Taneytown road south for about a mile, replacing the Second and Third Divisions of the First Corps which were put in reserve behind Cemetery Hill.[42] Having marched the day before to within a short distance of Gettysburg, most of the men of the Second Corps had got a fair amount of rest during the night and were in better shape than those in other units.

The Fifth Corps was not so fortunate and had a grim time in keeping its rendezvous at Gettysburg. It well illustrated the hardihood of the common soldier who was forced day after day to endure hours of tramping through clouds of dust in ninety-degree heat, or of wading through mile after mile of slippery mud. Constant marching began to exact its toll, and the men became increasingly weary. On June 30 they reached Union Mills, Maryland, after a march of twenty-three miles from their bivouac near Liberty. The next day they went on to Hanover twelve miles away, arriving late in the afternoon. There they found the town in a state of excitement over a sharp skirmish between Kilpatrick and Stuart, but that did not prevent the men from looking forward to some food and relaxation before a night's rest. A member of the 140th New York regiment recalled that as they were receiving their ration of fresh meat, submitting their arms for inspection, and performing other routine chores, the "general" was sounded. Their colonel, Patrick H. O'Rorke, a graduate of West Point whose promising army career was to end heroically next day on the slopes of Little Round Top, went to division headquarters to learn the cause of the sudden order to break camp. He came back with news of the desperate fighting between the vanguard of the army and the Confederates, which everyone thought would be renewed early in the morning.[43] The day's march was not over after all. The men quickly gathered up their belongings, seized their rifles, and again fell into marching formation.[44] By 7:00 P.M. they were swinging along the Hanover road toward Bonaughtown (Bonneauville) eight miles farther on. After a five-hour tramp they finally pulled into camp and caught a little sleep before reveille was sounded at 3:30 A.M. Within the hour they were on a road which brought them to the right of the Twelfth Corps near Wolf's Hill.[45] After several changes in their position they finally crossed Rock Creek on the Baltimore Pike about 8:00 A.M. and went into mass formation near Power's Hill, where they were well located to reinforce quickly any part of the main line.[46]

The Third Division of the Fifth Corps, consisting of two brigades of the Pennsylvania Reserves under General Samuel W. Crawford, had an even harder time of it. Assigned from the Washington defenses to reinforce the corps, the division joined it in Frederick but fell behind on the march to Pennsylvania. General Sykes was hard pressed to meet his daily objectives; he dared not wait for Crawford but sent him guides and messages to keep him on the right route.[47] Crawford did his best to catch up. He marched his men throughout most of the night of June 30, and next day after a short rest they continued some twenty-five miles more. That night the division staggered into camp near McSherryville about two miles west of Hanover. The rest of the corps was still ahead of them. They got up at daylight after three hours' sleep, pressed on without letup, and arrived in Gettysburg around noon. Here for the first time they learned about the battle of the preceding day and mourned the loss of one of their favorite generals, John F. Reynolds, a former commander of the Pennsylvania Reserves.[48]

Meanwhile from another direction units of the Third Corps which had been left at Emmitsburg were also moving to join the main body of their command. The two brigades and two batteries finally reached Gettysburg between 9:00 and 10:00 A.M. instead of at daylight as Meade had directed.[49] Unaccountably the dispatch ordering the advance to Gettysburg, which was written by Butterfield at 7:30 P.M., July 1, did not reach the brigade commanders, Colonels George C. Burling and P. Regis De Trobriand, until 1:30 and 2:00 A.M. respectively.[50] It is not known when their superior, General Graham, received the order, since he was captured during the engagement on July 2 and did not write a report;[51] but even assuming it reached him as early as 1:00 A.M., it took the courier between five and five and a half hours to ride the nine miles from Taneytown to Emmitsburg. He could have made better time if he had walked! Graham and the two colonels apparently consulted with one another about what to do after receiving the order at such a late hour, and Graham must have accepted Burling's argument against moving the brigades before daylight because of the "night being so very dark" and his command "covering so much ground." [52] It is not clear whether by this ambiguous statement Burling meant that his men were tired out from marching so many miles, or that they were unduly scattered over the countryside doing picket duty. Whatever Burling's excuses, Meade had not given him, De Trobriand, or Graham authority to delay departure of the brigades. Meade had also warned them against continuing on the Emmitsburg road beyond Marsh Creek because of the danger of running into Confederate troops, and he had directed them to turn right at Greenmount on a road connecting with the Taneytown road near Barlow. They ignored these instructions and proceeded on the main highway from Emmitsburg until they were two and a quarter miles from the center of Gettysburg, when they turned east on the crossroads at the famous Peach Orchard. Starting around 4:00 A.M., they took between five and six hours to march about nine miles, not a particularly impressive record in view of the emergency.[53] Fortunately the Confederates had not yet extended their lines to the Emmitsburg road, and the tardy arrival of this detachment had no ill effects on Meade's strategy.

The performance of these brigades exemplified the undistinguished record of the whole Third Corps in its march from Frederick to Gettysburg. On the first day out of Frederick despite its headstart the corps delayed the progress of other units following it on the road to Middleburg. Then because of the wrongheadedness of a staff officer from corps headquarters, the Second Division strayed too close to enemy lines, arrived hours late at the battlefield, and in the dark lost many stragglers to Confederate pickets.[54] Finally cavalier treatment of Meade's orders contributed to the delinquency of two brigades. Although bad luck might explain some of the corps' difficulties, it seems significant that professionally trained soldiers played a smaller role in this corps than in any of the others. Of its general officers only A. A. Humphreys, in command of the Second Division, was a graduate of West Point and had made the army his career.[55] Though personally brave and full of fight, the other officers had not become imbued with the concepts of discipline and efficiency of the military profession. Such men are apt to be slovenly in their habits of command, sometimes with fatal results.

In contrast the efficient General Henry Hunt had four out of five of his artillery brigades on hand early in the morning of July 2. After camping near the Second Corps during the night of July 1, General Tyler, Hunt's immediate subordinate, moved the reserve batteries up the Taneytown road and parked them about half a mile south of Meade's headquarters. The remainder of the reserve batteries under Major Freeman McGilvery, together with the ammunition train, left Taneytown at dawn and reported to Tyler about 10:30 A.M. Much to Tyler's regret two batteries, B and M of the First Connecticut Artillery, each with four big 4½-inch rifles, had been ordered to Westminster to remain with the army's supply train. Tyler expressed confidence that had the weapons been brought to Gettysburg, they could have demonstrated their "extreme mobility and usefulness" as field guns, in addition to their proved excellence as siege guns.[56] Though deprived of these batteries, Hunt still had 108 cannon for his use in the Artillery Reserve, over a third of the total number brought to the battlefield by the Confederates. He had also taken the precaution of bringing an extra amount of ammunition in the train of the Artillery Reserve, which would make up for all the losses caused by explosions of caissons and limbers from enemy fire and accidents. It would also take care of shortages of ammunition in the artillery of some of the corps occasioned by their commanders, contrary to Meade's orders, leaving their own trains or parts of them behind. Despite its unusually heavy expenditure of ammunition, the army had enough rounds on hand after the battle to fight another engagement of similar length and severity.[57]

As units of the army streamed in toward the battlefield from various directions, Meade's plan of action began to crystallize. He first thought of the possibility of taking the offense from his right flank against Ewell's corps. A dispatch from Slocum the night before may have drawn his attention to this part of the line as a base from which to mount such a movement. Slocum said that if Meade decided to fight at Gettysburg, the Fifth and Sixth Corps could be used to extend the Union right. It was 9:20 P.M. when he wrote the message,[58] and at that time the Second Division of his corps was east of Rock Creek and north of the Baltimore Pike, the extreme right flank of the Union position. The Fifth Corps was already on its way toward Gettysburg on the Hanover road, and the Sixth was just leaving Manchester. It was natural therefore for Slocum to think of these two corps as admirably located to join the army on its right and to increase its strength there. Meade also saw the advantages of a heavy concentration of troops on his right from the standpoint of logistics if for no other reason. About the middle of the morning he directed Slocum and Warren to examine the area around Culp's Hill for the purpose of determining whether it was a desirable place from which to attack the enemy. Whether he would start his offense from there with the Fifth and Twelfth Corps would depend upon their report and the time of the arrival of the Sixth Corps, which he wanted near at hand to participate in the movement. If Slocum on the night of July 1 toyed with the idea of an attack from the Union right, he had second thoughts next day when he could more readily perceive the rugged nature of the terrain along his front. Both he and Warren late in the morning expressed their disapproval of an assault from this position.[59]

Their adverse report confirmed Meade's inclination to remain on the defensive at least until the enemy's dispositions became more apparent. Although concentration of the Union army was progressing satisfactorily, the Sixth Corps still had not made its appearance by noon. Meade also knew his men were worn out from hard marching and might not be able to endure the strain of extensive offensive operations. Recognizing the strength of his position for the defense, he thought it the better part of wisdom to take advantage of it, at least until the Sixth Corps arrived, by waiting for the enemy to attack him.[60]

During this pause Meade prepared for any eventualities by arranging his army so as to be able to maneuver it quickly and efficiently. As part of this program he issued important orders at 11:00 A.M., which revealed how necessary it was to his well-disciplined mind to accumulate all possible data before coming to a decision. He directed the corps commanders to send to headquarters without delay "a sketch of their positions with a view to the roads to the front and rear —with the position and apparent strength of the enemy in their front."[61] To make sure that this work was done effectively and to supplement the information he would thus obtain, he assigned one general staff officer to each corps. Each officer was to learn the location of the corps headquarters and the positions of its artillery, infantry, and trains, particularly with respect to nearby roads which could be used for movements in any direction.[62]

In conformity to his desire to keep fully informed and be ready for any emergency, Meade made a suggestion to Butterfield about this time which was to become a source of annoyance and embarrassment to him. His chief of staff, having just come up from Taneytown, probably bustled into headquarters and asked Meade what he could do. Although later Meade did not remember any such incident, he thought it logical that he might have instructed Butterfield to become thoroughly familiar with the position of the army and the whole complex of roads leading up to it. In the event of "any contingency" Butterfield could then "without any order, be ready to meet it."[63] Whether maliciously or not, Butterfield construed this precautionary measure as an assignment for him to draw up formal orders for a retreat of the army from Gettysburg. According to his own account, he must have spent hours working on this project, when it would have been more profitable for him to have done any number of other things. When he had completed the job, he showed his handiwork for corrections to some of the generals who had come to headquarters on other business. One of them was John Gibbon, a friend of Meade's, who later recalled having met Butterfield as he came out of the little room which he used as his office. The chief of staff asked Gibbon to read over a draft of an order he had in his hand and compare it with a map. Being curious, Gibbon asked him what it was, and Butterfield answered that it was an order for the army to retreat. Gibbon exclaimed with astonishment: " 'Great God! General Meade does not intend to leave this position?' " As Gibbon remembered the incident, Butterfield did not say Meade intended to retreat, but "merely said something to the effect that it was necessary to be prepared, in case it should be necessary to leave, or some remark of that kind." Gibbon was "firmly convinced" at the time that General Meade had no notion of falling back from his position, so it struck him as "very remarkable that his chief of staff should be making out an order to retreat," and he still thought so months after the incident.[64]

Meade knew nothing at all about the affair until eight months later, when the Committee on the Conduct of the War started its investigation of the records of Generals Hooker and Meade as commanders of the Army of the Potomac. The first officer to testify was General Sickles, who accused Meade of wanting to retreat from Gettysburg before the fighting started on July 2. Of course he got the information upon which to base his charge from his good friend, Daniel Butterfield.[65] Meade was astounded. When he appeared before the committee on March 11 he swore that he had no recollection of "ever having directed such an order to be issued, or ever having contemplated the isuing of such an order. . . ."[66] He was finally convinced that a document of this sort had actually existed, for Seth Williams, Meade's adjutant general, as well as Gibbon had seen it. Williams remembered that Butterfield had given him or his clerk a draft of the order. He did not know whether Meade had directed Butterfield to prepare it, nor did he recall whether copies of it had been made. Since it had never been issued and no "vestige" of it remained among his office records, he assumed it must have been destroyed within a day or so after its preparation.[67] Meade ordered his own search but could find no such order or paper in the files of the adjutant general, nor did any of the headquarters clerks recollect it; "tho they remember," he admitted to Mrs. Meade, "something of the kind for a shorter time was done, but it not being required all the papers were destroyed as worthless." [68] What bothered Meade most was that the mere existence of a document of this type was enough to make people suspicious of his intentions, even though in the history of the battle it had as much substance and meaning as a piece of paper with doodling on it.

There is every reason to doubt that Meade ever contemplated issuing the order. In view of his exertions to mass his army at Gettysburg it made no more sense for him to direct a retreat before doing battle than, as in the old rhyme, for the French king and his twenty thousand men to have marched up the hill and marched down again. General Hunt swore he neither saw nor heard of an order for a retreat. If Meade had planned such action, Hunt by virtue of his position as chief of artillery would naturally have been the first to hear about it because, before Meade could withdraw his infantry, he would have had to arrange with Hunt to remove his long artillery trains.[69] Such considerations, however, made little impression on most people who heard Butterfield state categorically that Meade had directed him to prepare such an order. Meade's chief of staff, if anyone, should know about it, they would argue. Butterfield became even more convincing when he put on a show of restraint in telling his story. No, he did not know whether or not Meade had intended to execute the order; it was not for him but for Meade to say. But he would guess that Meade "may have desired it prepared for an emergency, without any view of executing it then, or he may have had it prepared with a full view of its execution." [70] That did it. These statements were used to substantiate the charge that Meade intended to issue an order withdrawing the army from Gettysburg before the enemy forced him to do so.[71] Regardless of the tenuous nature of the evidence this story had amazing vitality and persisted for many years.

It was still a matter of dispute when near the turn of the century the State of New York established the New York Monuments Commission for the Battlefields of Gettysburg and Chattanooga and authorized the publication of a report on the battles. The commission had ten members, including such bigwigs as Major General Daniel E. Sickles, Chairman, Major General Daniel Butterfield, and Brevet Major General Alexander S. Webb. The editor and historian of the three-volume report on Gettysburg was Lieutenant Colonel William F. Fox, formerly of the 107th New York regiment of the Twelfth Corps. In November, 1898, about a year before the report came out, General Webb, who was then President of the College of the City of New York, sent Fox some memoranda in hopes of persuading him to remove from his account of the battle "those few lines found on pages 35–36, etc., which touch upon questions in dispute." He then warned:

> My dear Fox it is well for me to state, here, that you cannot have peace when you bring up those questions again for discussion, in a Board constituted as is our Gettysburg Commission. I cannot sign a report giving some one person's opinion as to what General Meade intended to do on July 2d 1863. When General Meade, a Christian gentlemen [sic], has stated under oath that the charges made against him are absolutely false, I would be condemned by every officer of the Army of the Potomac who knew General Meade, if I were to sign a report stating that he issued an order for the army to leave Gettysburg.[72]

Webb's protest had its effect, for the report as finally published did not include the obnoxious passages.

In expressing righteous anger at Fox's attempt to repeat a worn-out yarn, Webb failed to point out the major flaw in the thesis: that all of Meade's actions and messages from the time of his knowledge of Reynolds' death on July 1 until the Confederate attack in the afternoon of July 2 were clearly aimed at fighting at Gettysburg. Butterfield's absurd story cannot be accepted unless one also accepts the premise that Meade was incompetent and had no idea what to do.[73] It was just this notion that Meade's detractors wanted to have inscribed upon the pages of history. They tried to strengthen it by saying that the redoubtable General Sickles prevented Meade from carrying out his intention to retreat by moving his corps forward and precipitating the Confederate attack.[74] There is something strange, if not uncanny, about the way Meade got into difficulty with those two cronies of Hooker, Generals Butterfield and Sickles.

In the morning of July 2 Meade had no reason to suppose that a misunderstanding about how he wanted things done would arise between him and General Sickles. Not only were his orders for a gathering of his forces being carried out with reasonable dispatch, but other preparations were progressing equally well. General Newton, whom Meade had called up from the Sixth Corps to take over the First Corps in place of Doubleday, reported to his commander at the Cemetery gate early in the morning.[75] At 8:00 A.M. General Alpheus Williams of the Twelfth Corps was pleased to welcome General Henry H. Lockwood, who brought two of the three regiments of his unattached brigade, about 1,100 officers and men, as reinforcements for the First Division of the corps.[76] Although Lockwood, of whom Williams knew very little, appeared to be a very "pleasant gentleman," [77] Williams was embarrassed to discover that he outranked the extremely competent Brigadier General Thomas H. Ruger, who also commanded a brigade in the First Division. When Williams was placed in temporary command of the corps, he wanted Ruger to take charge of his old division. To avoid any questions of rank and to keep the division in trusted hands, Williams told Lockwood to regard his command as an "unattached brigade pending the existing operations," and that he would receive orders directly from him.[78]

At about the same time as Lockwood's arrival Meade completed the final disposition of his troops on the right, which he had been directing for several hours. As early as 5:00 A.M. he had ordered Geary's division of the Twelfth Corps to move from the position it held on Little Round Top and north of it, and to form a line to the right of Wadsworth's division of the First Corps, which occupied the crest of Culp's Hill. At 8:00 A.M. he gave orders to pull Williams' First Division across Rock Creek and extend the line of the Twelfth Corps along the southeast shoulder and spur of the hill down to the point where the pike bridged the creek. The men of the corps followed the example of their comrades in Wadsworth's brigades and in short order built formidable breastworks of logs, earth, and stones. With the Fifth Corps brought from the east to the west bank of the creek to act as a reserve, Meade had his right flank well secured. He kept the Eleventh Corps in line on East Cemetery and Cemetery Hills, to which it had fallen back the previous afternoon. Having put the strong Second Corps in position on Cemetery Ridge around 8:00 A.M., and with two divisions of the First Corps in reserve on the hill, he had little fears for the center of his line. As the Second Corps went into its defensive formation Meade directed Hancock to extend it south along the ridge about halfway from the

Taneytown road to Big Round Top, which could be seen plainly from all parts of the field.[79] As Meade planned it, the Third Corps was to continue the main battle line from the left flank of the Second Corps more or less straight toward Big Round Top.

Between 8:00 and 9:00 A.M. Meade decided to make a routine check of the left flank and find out what Sickles had done to get his troops ready for battle. He also wanted to make sure that the commander of the Third Corps knew the location of army headquarters. Up until then everything had seemed quiet on that part of the Union position in contrast to the right, but Meade was well aware of its potential importance. Hancock, if no one else, had called attention to it in his message of 5:25 P.M. the day before. When Meade came out of his headquarters, he saw his son, Captain George Meade, waiting to be of service. Most of the other aides were away on errands. After chatting with him pleasantly for a few minutes, Meade sent the captain to Sickles to inquire about the position of his troops. In the light of what happened subsequently it would have been better if the general had gone himself to inspect conditions on the left. Young Meade found the temporary headquarters of the Third Corps a little less than half a mile south in a patch of woods on the west side of the Taneytown road. Captain George E. Randolph, chief of artillery of the corps, seemed to be the only one about. He said Sickles was resting in a nearby tent, having been up all night after a hard day's work on July 1. Captain Meade gave the message to Randolph, who delivered it to Sickles and came back with the word that the Third Corps was not in position because its commander was in "some doubt as to where he should go." [80] The nature of General Meade's question and Sickles' reply seem to indicate that the commander of the Third Corps had received previous instructions about his position. Captain Meade, knowing nothing about them, told Randolph he would report back to headquarters immediately and get the matter straightened out. By riding hard it took him only a few minutes to return to the little white house, where he found his father still out in the yard talking to a group of officers. Upon hearing of Sickles' uncertainty, the general told the captain in his "sharp, decisive way" to get back quickly to Third Corps headquarters and to say to Sickles that "his instructions were to go into position on the left of the Second Corps; that his right was to connect with the left of the Second Corps; that he was to prolong with his line the line of that corps, occupying the position that General Geary had held the night before." [81]

A short time after Captain Meade had delivered his second message Sickles did the sensible thing by coming personally to see Meade. He repeated his instructions and again said that Sickles was to occupy the position which he understood Hancock had designated for Geary the previous night. When Sickles claimed Geary had had no position, "as far as he could understand," [82] Meade should have gone with him and pointed it out or even better have asked Hancock to do so. However, the matter was apparently dropped, and Sickles requested help from a member of Meade's staff in posting artillery on some good ground he had noticed in the neighborhood of his corps. When Meade agreed to send Hunt, Sickles asked whether he, Sickles, had authority to place his corps "in such a manner as, in his judgment, he should deem most suitable." Meade replied, " 'Certainly, within the limits of the general instructions I have given to you; any ground within those limits you choose to occupy I leave to you.' " [83] After Hunt and Sickles left the room where they had conferred with Meade, Hunt discovered that Sickles wanted to place his corps well in advance of the position in which it was then located "where it was covered in its front by woods and rock, with a view to cover the Emmitsburg road." Hunt, having no idea then of Meade's battle plans, made no comment about Sickles' proposal. The two generals rode out to the Emmitsburg road and examined the position, with Hunt making observations and offering advice. When a heavy cannonade broke out on Cemetery Hill and showed no signs of slackening, Hunt became anxious to go back and see what was happening. On his way he said he would ride along the proposed line from the famous Peach Orchard to Big Round Top and give his opinion of it to Meade. Before Hunt left, Sickles asked his approval to move the Third Corps to this line. Having no authority in the matter, Hunt naturally told Sickles to await orders from General Meade.

On his way to Cemetery Hill Hunt stopped off at headquarters long enough to tell Meade that the new line Sickles proposed for the Third Corps "taken by itself" was a very good one. He advised Meade, however, to see it for himself before Sickles occupied it with troops. He then left for Cemetery Hill and stayed there long enough to satisfy himself that the exchange of shots had not developed into a major engagement. Uneasy about affairs on the left flank, Hunt returned to find Randolph looking for good locations for his batteries near the Peach Orchard at the intersection of the Emmitsburg road and a crossroad from the Taneytown road. Sickles by then had advanced his troops almost to the Emmitsburg road. Looking for Sickles, Hunt saw him engaged in conversation with Meade and assumed Meade had approved of the line. He did not disturb them but went back to the business of getting the artillery ready for an attack.[84]

After Hunt had reported to Meade at headquarters and ridden on to see what was happening on Cemetery Hill, Meade stayed there awaiting the arrival of the Sixth Corps, which began coming in between two and three in the afternoon.[85] At 3:00 P.M. he sent a message to Halleck saying he had a "strong position for defensive [operations]." The enemy, he said, though moving on both Union flanks without revealing his real intentions, had not attacked so far. If these threats amounted to nothing, he himself would take the offensive provided he could pinpoint the Confederate positions. Meade also expressed fear of a turning movement which would place the enemy forces between him and Washington and Baltimore.[86] At the time he sent the dispatch to Halleck he also called in his corps commanders to discuss the situation and give them some idea of his plans.[87] He had already ordered the Fifth Corps to the left and arranged to have the Sixth take its place in reserve on the right. Shortly before 4:00 P.M. he finally arrived at the left flank to supervise posting of the Fifth Corps and inspect Sickles' position.[88] A growing uneasiness in headquarters arising from reports by Hunt and some engineering officers about the situation on the left might have been an added inducement for Meade to go there.[89] He was astounded by what he saw, for Sickles had assumed a position "very much in advance" of what it had been Meade's intention for him to take. Meade sent for Sickles and asked him to point out roughly the line of the Third Corps. Sickles did so, and Meade in no uncertain terms made clear that Sickles had greatly upset his plans. In placing his corps completely outside the main battle line and beyond ready support of the rest of the army he was forcing Meade to fight on grounds he had not chosen and did not think suitable. Turning around, Meade pointed to the ridge he had wanted Sickles to occupy. Apologizing,

Sickles offered to withdraw to it promptly,[90] but Meade upon hearing the boom of Confederate cannon exclaimed, "'I wish to God you could, but the enemy won't let you!'"[91]

Sickles of course had his own version of the affair and being a smart lawyer knew what to stress and what to omit in making out a plausible case for himself. His account agreed with Meade's and those of more neutral observers in three respects: his early instructions to relieve Geary's division, his visit to army headquarters, and his survey with Henry Hunt of the line finally occupied by the Third Corps later in the afternoon. Admitting that he had received a directive to take the position held by Geary, he claimed the order was not applicable because Geary had only massed his troops and not gotten them ready for action. This contention had the earmarks of a lawyer's quibble. The main thesis around which he built his argument was a denial of ever having received "any order in reference to. . .[his] position. . . ." Feeling bereft and becoming convinced by increased enemy activity that his front was to be the object of a major attack, he had hurried to headquarters to report his fears and receive orders. To his disgust nobody seemed to share his concern or offer him sympathetic advice. This attitude he felt arose from a loss of a will to fight at Gettysburg, and he was satisfied from information he received that "it was intended to retreat from Gettysburg."[92] Failing to persuade Meade or Warren to join him in an examination of the ground on the left flank, he finally secured Hunt's services. While admitting Hunt's refusal to sanction in Meade's name his occupation of a line on the Emmitsburg road, Sickles insisted that Hunt had approved the proposed position as a good one. Before making his dispositions on the line as outlined to Hunt, he had waited some time for orders from Meade, which despite Hunt's assurances never came. To add to his woes, enemy demonstrations became more vigorous, and Buford's cavalry, which had been covering his left, withdrew from the area. He complained to headquarters about this move and received word that a portion of Buford's troopers would return. They never did. When his outposts retired to their supports because of enemy pressure, Sickles said he could not endure the situation any longer. Taking the initiative, he advanced his men promptly toward the Emmitsburg road. While carrying on this work, much to his annoyance he received notice of a meeting of corps commanders at headquarters. Through a courier he begged to be excused, but Meade insisted that he attend. Turning the command over to Birney, he rode rapidly to headquarters, but before he got there the boom of cannon announced the beginning of an attack. As he galloped up to the little house, Meade met him just outside and courteously told him not to dismount, for the sound of firing indicated he was needed at the front. Meade soon followed him and pointed out the weakness of the line. Sickles agreed with his opinion but said he could hold it if he had support. However, if Meade insisted, he would retire to any position the general indicated. Meade told him to hold the line and he would send up the Fifth Corps to support him.[93]

In trying to justify what he had done Sickles denied that he had misinterpreted orders, as Halleck and Meade said when referring to the incident in their reports.[94] On the contrary, there were no orders to misinterpret. For better or worse, he asserted, "I took it [the line] on my own responsibility, except so far. . .[as] it was approved of in general terms by General Hunt. . . ."[95] General Sickles apparently preferred to be guilty of willful insubordination than of stupidity—and he got away with it because even the most stiff-necked military man would hesitate to court-martial a general who had incurred a severe wound while fighting valiantly for the cause. As a cynic might explain it, when Sickles lost his leg at Gettysburg, he saved his reputation.

Dan Sickles was attractive, able, and aggressive, but as a leader his weakness was his inability to take advice or consider other points of view. He had powerful political connections and friends in the army, Congress, and the White House whom he skillfully manipulated to his own advantage.[96] By an artful blending of fact, fancy, and innuendo he conjured up an interpretation of the battle which many historians have taken seriously or accepted outright. His story first received a hearing in February, 1864, before the Committee on the Conduct of the War, some members of which were still mighty displeased by what they considered to have been the arbitrary removal of their favorite, Joe Hooker, from command of the Army of the Potomac. By starting an investigation of the Chancellorsville and Gettysburg campaigns Sickles hoped to enhance his friend Hooker's reputation as well as his own and secure the dismissal of his enemy, George Gordon Meade, from command. He failed to achieve his immediate goal, the removal of Meade, but had more

347

success in realizing his other purposes.[97] There is strong evidence that Sickles, not waiting for publication of the committee report which would include the verbatim statements of witnesses, secretly arranged for the printing of his own account in the *New York Herald* on March 12, 1864, under the pseudonym "Historicus." When two officers of the Fifth Corps took offense at his version of events on July 2, he joyously entered into the fray and, still anonymously, wrote what amounted to a lawyer's brief in an effort to refute their statements.[98] But this was just the beginning. All through his long life he continued to beat out the story of his day of glory at Gettysburg and the valorous deeds of the Third Corps. In his speeches at Gettysburg reunions and other gatherings of veterans and in his correspondence and articles he added embellishments, but basically the account remained the same. It stressed Meade's incompetence and irresolution in contrast to Sickles' foresight and combativeness. Meade had intended to retreat to Pipe Creek, but Sickles seized the initiative from him and moved out to meet the enemy. This advance precipitated a battle which otherwise might never have been fought. The engagement brought victory to Union arms. Therefore in the final analysis Sickles won the battle of Gettysburg.[99]

Sickles' persistence served to obscure the essential fact which he proudly admitted to the committee and which made everything else seem irrelevant. He had acted on his own and arranged his corps for battle as if he had an independent command. Furthermore he failed to notify headquarters or his neighbor, General Hancock, of what he was about to do.[100] When he moved his forces without reference to the others, even if the position were the best in the world, Sickles put the safety of the whole army in jeopardy. Whether his judgment was better than Meade's was not the point. For better or worse, Meade was commander of the Army of the Potomac, and it was his responsibility to coordinate its various parts to gain victory. Unless he could get them to mesh properly, the best-laid plans would be ruined and with them the army. Though Meade and Halleck were willing to give Sickles the benefit of the doubt and conclude he had misunderstood orders, Sickles would have none of it.

In extenuation of his deed Sickles claimed before the committee that Meade had no plans and exercised no leadership. How valid were those charges? Despite errors in the testimony of Meade and other witnesses, the weight of the evidence and the logic of events were against Sickles' account. Meade did have a plan. He proposed to take advantage of the natural strength of his position and fight defensively unless some development should occur which would promise victory if he took the opposite course. While he personally ordered his commanders to take positions in certain areas, he assumed they were competent enough to arrange their troops in the best manner possible within those areas. Whether the line went a few hundred feet this way or that to follow configurations was not his concern. Meade, for instance, told Slocum to place his corps in the "woods east of the turnpike, between Rock Creek and the crest of the hill held by the troops under Brigadier General Wadsworth." [101] When Slocum found it impossible to make a continuous line because of low marshy ground between 450 and 600 feet wide at Spangler's Spring, he arranged his troops in a way to cover the gap with a cross fire. Thus the line as finally formed was the work not of Meade but of Slocum and his able subordinates.[102]

There is no reason to suppose that Meade's orders to Sickles for the placing of his troops were any less definite than those he gave Slocum and Hancock. His first instructions to Sickles, instead of vaguely directing him, as Sickles said, to take the position previously held by Geary, on the contrary ordered him specifically to form a line from Hancock's left to Little Round Top. If he had enough men to occupy the hill, he should do so. Sickles kept insisting that Geary never had a position, which was not true. Geary subsequently told Meade that he had offered the services of one of his aides to show Sickles or a member of his staff the position his division had occupied during the night, for he considered it imperative for the Third Corps to hold on to Little Round Top. Sickles replied that he would "attend to it in due time," but he never did.[103]

By persisting with the claim that he did not know where to go, Sickles developed the thesis of never having received an order directing him to a position. In the light of Meade's testimony and General Birney's battle report, this is another of Sickles' questionable claims. In his report Birney wrote: "At 7 A.M., under orders from Major-General Sickles, I relieved Geary's division, and formed a line, resting its left on the Sugar Loaf Mountain [Big Round Top] and the right thrown in a direct line toward the cemetery, connecting on the right with the Second Division of this corps." [104] Yet an hour or so later Sickles told Captain Meade that his troops were not as yet in position, and he implied that he did not know where they should go. He was partly right in the case of the Second Division, for Humphreys said his men were massed in the vicinity of their bivouac near the crest of Cemetery Ridge. Though not formed in line, they were just about where Meade wanted them.[105] Something was bothering Sickles. Either he was in a difficult and quibbling mood, or else he was playing for bigger stakes, a possibility suggested by the fact that he told Hunt but not Meade about the line he wished to establish.

Less than frank with Meade, he was only a little more so with Hunt. As a reason for wanting to move his men forward he alluded vaguely to woods and rocks complicating his position. Hunt thought too that probably Sickles wished to control the road until the arrival of his ammunition train, which he had not brought up.[106] But his real reason for wanting the advanced line was undoubtedly contained in a letter which his senior aide, Major H. E. Tremain, wrote home soon after the battle. He said:

Our Corps opened the fight. We knew where the battle would begin. *I felt certain, for I told General Sickles on Wednesday night* (as I had been over the ground more and had therefore better opportunities for knowing) *that if the enemy attacked the army at all in its present position, it would be in certain localities on the left, which I designated;* and Thursday morning he examined the topography and agreed with me. It was then he pressed on General Meade the necessity for changing his lines to meet such an anticipated attack. *It was in that very locality, and by the roads I designated that the enemy did come and hurl upon us their tremendous force.*[107]

The self-congratulatory tone of the letter for having possessed such foresight is pure bombast. The important thing is that Sickles and Tremain set themselves up as better tacticians than Meade. Before the Confederates began to threaten their front they had decided to meet a possible attack from positions considerably west and in advance of Meade's line. Sickles knew what Meade wanted, but he gave his commanding officer only hints of his dissatisfaction with his position. For one thing, he could not furnish evidence in the morning that an enemy attack was in the offing. Two of his brigades had just come in over the Emmitsburg road unmolested by anyone except a few enemy skirmishers, and furthermore, after leaving Meade before noon, he and Hunt had ridden out to the road and encountered no trouble. In recounting to members of the committee this phase of his experience on July 2, Sickles covered up the premeditated character of his act of insubordination. He feigned ignorance of the line Meade had instructed him to take and gave the impression that he had been threatened by an assault very early in the day. He led them to believe that he had been forced by circumstances to take matters into his own hands and form his own battle line. Thus he manipulated the facts so that he, not Meade, became the aggrieved party.

Sickles made one complaint which was completely justified, but he expressed it in such a way as to put the entire blame on Meade, whereas in fact he was only partly responsible, if at all. Early in the morning Sickles had had the comfortable feeling of knowing that two brigades of Buford's cavalry were operating south and west of his left flank. Suddenly toward noon they trotted off to Westminster [108] on orders from General Pleasonton, who had cleared the move with Meade. Pleasonton, upon learning from Buford that his men were worn out from days of marching, reconnaissance work, and fighting, had decided to send them back to guard the army's main supply depot and incidentally get a rest.[109] Meade made no objection because he somehow had the idea that all of the cavalry except for a few scattered detachments had arrived at the battlefield.[110] He naturally assumed that Pleasonton would replace Buford's men with another force, for his general instructions to his cavalry leader were to maintain a constant guard over the army's flanks and front. How he did so was up to him.[111] In this instance Pleasonton violated his instructions. It was a serious oversight, and Meade was exceedingly annoyed when he learned of it, probably as a result of Sickles' protests. He ordered Pleasonton to send replacements immediately. The dispatch left headquarters at 12:55 P.M., and fifty minutes later Pleasonton ordered General Gregg, who was protecting the army's right flank near the Hanover road, to send one regiment to the left flank, which was four miles away in a direct line and much farther by road. The regiment unfortunately did not get there before the Confederate attack began.[112]

When Pleasonton pulled the efficient John Buford and his two splendid cavalry brigades away from the scene of battle for reasons that would have made any good infantryman in the First or Eleventh Corps guffaw derisively, he committed one of the sizeable blunders of the campaign. Of course the men were tired and their horses worn out, but so were all the others. The skillful fighting of Buford's men on July 1 earned the eternal gratitude of the infantry, but Pleasanton exaggerated, to say the least, when he claimed they had been "severely handled." [113] Out of 2,800 to 2,900 officers and men Buford lost 127. Compared to the long casualty lists of the First and Eleventh his figures were insignificant.[114]

The immediate and most serious consequence of the removal of Buford was to reduce substantially the size of the Union forces at a key point in the line and to expose the left and rear to a flanking attack. Although there were signal stations on Little Round Top and other high points, the lack of cavalry to scout over wide areas south and west of the Union lines greatly increased the danger of an undetected wide sweep by the enemy for the purpose of turning Meade out of his position,[115] a move he greatly feared. Furthermore, in the bitter and close fighting which broke out amid the rocks and woods of the Round Tops and Devil's Den, Buford's men with their breech-loading Sharps carbines could have rendered useful service and relieved infantrymen needed elsewhere. Pleasonton inadvertently timed the withdrawal of Buford with the arrival of Stuart's cavalry, jaded to be sure but still formidable.[116] Kilpatrick's division of 3,500 officers and men was still miles away to the northeast of Gettysburg hurrying from East Berlin to join the other forces. When it arrived near Gettysburg about 2:00 P.M. Gregg, who was temporarily in command of it as well as his own division, kept it in the area north and east of town. Around sundown Kilpatrick fought Stuart's three brigades at Hunterstown, thus leaving Gregg to guard the Union right flank with two small brigades numbering altogether 2,500 officers and men. Gregg had left his Second Brigade under Colonel Pennock Huey at Manchester to protect the distant rear of the army. With Buford's largest brigade, Merritt's Third, still carrying on reconnaissance work and doing picket duty around Mechanicsburg, Maryland, Pleasanton had available no force of comparable size to replace Buford's other brigades.[117]

Without cavalry Sickles had to depend more than ever upon the nearby signal station and his own infantry for intelligence of enemy activities. In addition to the regular skirmish companies from various regiments he employed two special regiments of sharpshooters, the First and Second United States Sharpshooters, under Colonel Hiram Berdan, to feel out the enemy lines and cover his front. The men in these regiments came from many states and were chosen for their marksmanship. Equipped with Sharps breech-loading rifles and clothed in a special green uniform, they were efficient skirmishers and pickets.[118] They had worked with detachments of Buford's cavalry until the troopers were withdrawn, after which Berdan fanned them out on Sickles' left and front. Berdan also sent out special details to penetrate beyond his skirmish line in search of information. Standing at the Peach Orchard and looking west, he observed a heavily wooded area along Warfield Ridge which extended south of Seminary Ridge, and he wondered about it.[119] Hunt had noticed it too and called Sickles' attention to it.[120] About 11:00 A.M. upon orders from Birney, Berdan with 100 men under Lieutenant Colonel Casper Trepp started out to investigate and flush out any Confederates who might be lurking in the woods.[121] Reinforced by 210 officers and men of the 3rd Maine regiment, Berdan took his little force to the strip of timber, formed a skirmish line running east and west, and advanced north along the ridge. Suddenly he struck the 10th Alabama regiment of General Cadmus Wilcox' brigade which was just getting into position on what was then the extreme right flank of the Confederate line. A lively skirmish broke out and continued until the Confederates finally forced Berdan to back out and return to the Union lines. He reported the affair and his observations to General Birney about 2:00 P.M. The enemy, he said, had three columns in motion in the rear of the woods and showed signs of heading toward the Union left.[122] Birney passed this inconclusive information on to his commanding officer, and Sickles, at last having an excuse, acted on it and ordered Birney and the First Division forward to form on the new line which he had been considering all day. The Second Division under General Humphreys moved out to the Emmitsburg road about an hour later.[123]

When Sickles testified that Hunt had expressed approval of the line, he neglected to add Hunt's reservations,[124] for he was more impressed with the many advantages Hunt's practiced eye had readily noted. He and Sickles had surveyed the position from a high spot a mile northwest of Little Round Top, where the Emmitsburg road was intersected by a lane from the Taneytown road. Immediately south of the intersection lay a tract of land of over three and a half acres, on which there was an orchard of peach trees. From here a broken ridge ran southeast as far as Devil's Den. The line as finally formed by Sickles was anchored at the den; it then extended to the orchard, bent toward the right, and went up the Emmitsburg road toward Gettysburg. The obtuse angle at the orchard formed the famous salient in the Third Corps line.

From where he stood with Hunt Sickles had noted with approval that the ground seemed considerably higher than it was on the southern end of Cemetery Ridge about three-quarters of a mile to the rear. Actually the difference in elevation between any point in the two lines was no more than forty feet. This superiority in height in no way compensated for Sickles' failure to hold on to Little Round Top, a key position in any line. Sickles had also liked the open character of much of the country in which he formed his line, for it reduced the danger of a Confederate surprise attack.[125] He and other Union soldiers could not forget the gloom of the Chancellorsville wilderness when thousands of Confederates, screened by dense underbrush, had suddenly burst upon the startled Yankees screaming like banshees. It was enough to unnerve even the toughest veterans, and Sickles was not going to have his men suffer the fate of the Eleventh Corps. Meade, he felt, had assigned his corps to low ground which seemed to be hemmed in by dark woods on all sides, and he could not wait to break out of these bounds into bright sunlight.[126] In seeking to avoid another Chancellorsville Sickles either overlooked or underestimated the possibilities of Little Round Top, where troops on its open slopes could detect the approach of enemy columns in time to get set for an attack.

Hunt as a good artilleryman had been happy to see that the area around the Emmitsburg road furnished many positions with wide fields of fire on which to post his guns, but he had noticed something more significant. By protruding considerably toward the Confederate right flank the line provided the necessary room from which to launch an offensive, as well as furnish defense in depth, whereas a line extending straight along Cemetery Ridge to the Round Tops would be purely defensive in nature. There was no place in the main battle line of the Army of the Potomac better adapted for offensive operations, provided the Sixth Corps had arrived and was ready for action.[127] Any Union thrust from this direction would cause Lee to react violently, for it would threaten to cut him off from South Mountain, the best place for him to find shelter in case of disaster.

In spite of the virtues of the line Hunt had warned Sickles that his corps was not large enough to occupy it in sufficient strength and also secure its flanks. Hunt had further recognized the woods where Berdan had fought some of Wilcox' men as a serious threat to Sickles' position because it screened Confederate moves toward the Union left. By ignoring this advice and pushing his line forward Sickles put his corps completely out of proper alignment with the rest of the army and exposed both of his flanks. His left, held by Birney's division, instead of resting on Little Round Top was 1,500 feet in advance of it, and separated by the low ground of Plum Run Valley through which Confederate columns could pour. His right, which was secured by Humphreys' division, stretched along the Emmitsburg road, and instead of connecting with Hancock's left, as it had been ordered to do, it ended about half a mile in front of the Second Corps line.[128] The heavy foliage of the orchard on Humphreys' front and right made the gap between him and Brigadier General John C. Caldwell, whose division occupied Hancock's left, even more dangerous, as it furnished a screen for enemy skirmishers trying to infiltrate the lines.[129] The salient at the Peach Orchard was another objectionable feature of the position, for troops and artillery posted there were subject to an enfilading fire from both south and west.[130]

Still the position Sickles chose was a good one as long as there were enough soldiers to man it. But if the Third Corps was considered too weak to hold the line Meade drew for it, how did Sickles expect it to do better on one a quarter of a mile longer?[131] Actually the assignment Meade gave it was a difficult but not an impossible one. To cover the ravine separating the Round Tops Sickles would have had to stretch his men out for a mile and a quarter, whereas the slightly larger Second Corps had a front of only about a mile in length.[132] But then if Sickles had stayed where he had been ordered, Meade could have reinforced him more quickly and effectively.[133]

By upsetting Meade's battle plans just before Longstreet's men started their assault, Sickles gave him little time to adjust to the change.[134] Forced to improvise in response to unexpected needs, Meade had to send in his troops piecemeal, as they came up, to help the hard-pressed Third Corps. In this fashion he used up far more men than would otherwise have been necessary to stop the Confederate attack once it had gained momentum. General Humphreys later commented that if all the troops of the Third, Fifth, and Second Corps engaged on the Union left flank had been in position at the beginning of the battle on July 2, or if all the reinforcements had been sent in in one body, the result would have been different. Any attempt, he asserted, to maintain by successive reinforcements a position which was originally held by inadequate numbers of men and was about to give way, was bound to be unsuccessful. It was so with the Third Corps.[135] Meade bitterly recalled that of the 18,000 men who were killed or wounded on the field during the battle, more than two-thirds were lost on the second day, the greatest number on the left flank.[136] Actually the figure was a little less than half of the total, which was bad enough.[137]

The problems which Sickles' unauthorized move created for Meade might easily have been less formidable if the Fifth Corps had been ready for action when the Confederates struck the Union left flank. Its availability in turn depended upon the arrival of Segdwick's Sixth Corps. The key to all of Meade's battle plans for July 2 both defensive and offensive was this splendid body of men who represented about a fifth of his infantry strength.[138] He would probably have had them near the battlefield in the morning of the 2nd but for an error in judgment in the disposition of his troops before the battle opened. In his anxiety to prevent Lee from getting between him and Washington Meade had advanced his corps on a wide front, and to protect his right flank on June 30 he had instructed the Sixth Corps to march off to Manchester, a relatively inaccessible place eight miles to the northeast of Westminster. By the morning of the 30th Meade should have realized that the signs were already pointing to an enemy concentration in the vicinity of Gettysburg, and he should have kept the Sixth Corps at Westminster and covered the area around Manchester with Gregg's cavalry division, part of which was already there, and perhaps one or two of Sedgwick's brigades.[139] He would thus have saved the corps distance and time in its march to Gettysburg. Instead of floundering over rough and muddy country roads it could have gotten into its stride immediately on the hard-surfaced and relatively smooth pike running through Westminster. By arriving sooner in Gettysburg the men of the Sixth might have thrown the balance in favor of Meade earlier in the day and perhaps have changed the whole course of events.

On the other hand a shorter and less agonizing march would have deprived the story of the battle of one of its more stirring and romantic episodes. Though other corps made marches during the campaign which may have been equally as gruelling, the circumstances attending that of the Sixth Corps made it famous. The word came that they were needed, and needed in a hurry, so they marched from ten at night until five the next afternoon with only a few breaks for coffee or now and then a short rest. On and on they trudged, endlessly it seemed, at first through darkness and then in the glare of the July sun, thirty-four long miles to Gettysburg.[140] One veteran remembered hearing strains of band music. Catching the beat of "Old John Brown's Body," he noted that the men immediately strode along more briskly as first a score, a hundred, a thousand, and then ten thousand voices sang out the battle cry of "Glory, Glory, Hallelujah, His Soul is marching on." All night long they marched at a remarkable pace to the sound of bands which alternated with the shrill of fifes and the roll of drums. Never before had their bands played on the march except when they entered a town, and their performance this time was a "happy inspiration." By mid-morning the heat of the day had wilted the men into complete silence except for the rhythmic slap, slap of their feet on the stony pike. Some reeled and staggered as if drunk. Every now and then someone would collapse in his tracks. His comrades would quickly drag him to the grass along the roadside, place his musket beside him, and then resume their places in the ranks. Thoughtful farmers and their families kept others from dropping out by bringing out to the roadside tubs and pails of cool well water.[141] Some were more generous and fed the men with cherries, milk, and a great variety of cooked food.[142]

Finally they could hear the distant boom of cannon which, as they came closer, became a guide for them to follow. When General Sedgwick arrived with the first division of the corps, without giving it any rest he headed right for the heavy firing, and arrived in time to help turn back the last desperate attack of Longstreet's men.[143] Meade's rapid and efficient concentration of his army took the enemy by surprise. He had planned carefully, and the Union soldier had marched well.[144]

XIV

LEE PLANS AN OFFENSIVE

DESPITE THE misgivings of a few sceptics, most Confederates expressed deep satisfaction at the outcome of the day's work on July 1. Although some slightingly considered the battle as only a "brisk little scurry," [1] many more referred to it as a "stubborn fight" and a great victory for Ewell and Hill. The reports said they had "routed" the opposing forces, "driven" them through Gettysburg, taken from five to seven thousand prisoners, and killed General Reynolds.[2] In town many Confederates, bursting with pride and greatly elated with their success, boasted to the inhabitants about themselves, their cause, and the skill of their officers.[3] Though anticipating a big battle the following day, they were confident of being able to cut up the Union army bit by bit with perfect ease, since it was tired out by long marches and still scattered about the countryside.[4] Neither the hard fighting of the day nor their own heavy losses seem to have impressed them, and they had nothing but contempt for the enemy whom they had so often beaten.[5]

Though sharing this confidence, Lee and his immediate subordinates realized that the task of finishing a job well started was not quite so simple as it appeared. Except for the two infantry corps and some cavalry which his men had fought, he did not know how many Federal soldiers had arrived at Gettysburg or how soon Meade could concentrate the rest of his army. These imponderables and the obvious strength of the enemy's position nevertheless failed to daunt him. The question which concerned him most was how and where to attack with best chances of success. The answer would depend upon the nature of the battleground and the rapidity with which he could bring up all of his troops.

As the last of the Federal troops retreated to Cemetery Hill General Lee stood on Seminary Ridge and watched them intently. Here about 5:00 P.M. he was joined by his chief lieutenant, General James Longstreet, who himself had followed Hill's men as they pursued the Northerners through town and had then sought out his commanding general for an exchange of views. Longstreet studied the new enemy position with his field glasses for five or ten minutes before making his comments. Then turning to Lee, he said that he disliked the look of things, and he urged quite vehemently that the Confederates avoid any attack on the Union position at Gettysburg. Instead he suggested that Lee make a sweeping movement southward along the Confederate right and then veer toward the east so as to get around the left of Meade's army and between it and Washington. In this way, he said, Lee could force Meade to attack him in a place of his own choosing. Longstreet's proposal, as he later wrote about it, was vague in many respects, and he did not make clear whether he meant the turning movement to be strategic or tactical. He might have intended it to be a wide sweep of many miles, necessitating a complete shift in the base of operations of both armies; or perhaps he had in mind an envelopment which would keep his army closer to the left flank of the Union lines and possibly involve an attack on them, once Meade's position had been determined. Judging by Lee's reaction to his views it seems likely that Longstreet was suggesting a strategic turning movement rather than an envelopment, for in this way he thought the Confederates could more readily maneuver Meade into attacking them in well-prepared positions. Such was in fact Longstreet's main objective, and if he could bring it about he anticipated another slaughter such as the one they had perpetrated at Fredericksburg. Before leaving for Pennsylvania it had been his understanding, he said, that Lee would maneuver offensively but fight defensively, as he himself had suggested;[6] now was the time for him to act according to his agreement.

Though not explicitly stated, Longstreet's strategic and tactical concepts grew out of an appreciation of the advantages Civil War military technology gave to the side having strong defensive positions. There is no doubt that General Meade tacitly accepted the soundness of such views, for his operations during the campaign followed the pattern Longstreet had suggested for Lee. But Meade would never, any more than Lee, have agreed to conduct himself in a certain way before the campaign had even started. Longstreet's mistake was to take a pragmatic observation and mold it into dogma, within the limits of which he expected to confine as brilliant and audacious a commander as Lee.[7]

In response to Longstreet's arguments in favor of a turning movement, Lee said emphatically, "If the enemy is there tomorrow, we must attack him." [8] When Longstreet saw that his protests had no effect, he decided to drop the discussion for the time being, although in his estimation there were no good reasons for Lee's rejection of his plan. Later he gave another explanation when in his memoirs he made the astounding statement: "That he [Lee] was excited and off his balance was evident on the afternoon of the 1st, and he labored under that oppression until enough blood was shed to appease him." [9] This charge of bloodthirsty irrationality outraged the admirers of Lee, and they never forgave Longstreet for it. In a clumsy attempt to hit back at those Confederates who had made him the butt of all their own failures at Gettysburg, Longstreet was guilty of bad taste and unfairness.[10] Other observers, it is true, had noted that at Gettysburg Lee's "quiet self-possessed calmness was wanting." Looking "careworn," he seemed uneasy, they said, and kept riding to and fro, frequently changing his position and making inquiries here and there.[11] Anxiety, probably resulting from the loss of Jackson and the absence of Stuart, and uncertainty about Meade's intentions [12] were quite another thing than unreasoning rashness, which Longstreet charged had taken possession of Lee. Much of Lee's uneasiness undoubtedly rose from Longstreet's rather truculent attitude and obvious unwillingness to attack.[13] Lee had affectionate respect for his most experienced corps commander, and he depended upon him to smash the enemy's position with well-timed blows or effectively smother Union attempts to break the Confederate line. All during the campaign the two generals had freely and constantly consulted each other on the basis of mutual confidence, and although Longstreet in no way replaced the dead Jackson, the close relations between him and Lee frequently attracted notice and favorable comment.[14] Now, as Lee began planning for the next day's operations Longstreet's violent objections to his proposals must have come as a shocking surprise. Although disturbed, the commanding general nevertheless kept his temper.

Rather than arbitrarily rejecting Longstreet's plan, Lee appears to have seriously considered its adoption. Contrary to what Longstreet said, Lee never reached his conclusions by an "instinctive, sudden impulse." Rather he "painfully and studiously" labored in planning all of his battles and campaigns, weighing everything, even the smallest detail.[15] In theory Longstreet's proposal sounded good, but Lee saw practical difficulties in its execution. Uncertain about the location of the various Federal corps, deprived of Stuart's cavalry to scout and to screen his movements, and forced by the mountains to march on roads close to the enemy's position, he felt the maneuver to be too risky.[16] Furthermore with a third of his infantry and artillery not up he would have to delay the movement probably until the middle of the next day, when it might be too late. A turning move would take time to effect, and the army did not have enough supplies at hand to delay for long.

Lee thought of other alternatives to a resumption of the engagement at Gettysburg. A withdrawal through the mountains had its attractions, except for the large trains which might seriously hamper rearguard actions against a bold and aggressive enemy following closely. There were also serious drawbacks to a policy of assuming a defensive posture in his present location and awaiting an attack, for the Northerners might very well not accommodate him. While confronting him with the bulk of their forces they could send out strong detachments to occupy the mountain passes in cooperation with local troops and cut off Lee's foraging parties from the rich Cumberland Valley.[17]

The qualms Lee expressed about the dangers of a withdrawal may have been more in the nature of an excuse than an actuality, for unless he maneuvered in the manner suggested by Longstreet, there was nothing he could do except to strike hard at the enemy before him. Psychologically he and his Confederates were not ready to retreat without cause. They had just achieved a smashing success against a part of the Union army, and now was the time for them to finish the job. The stakes were high, and they might never again have as good an opportunity. It also accorded with the traditions of the Army of Northern Virginia, as well as with Lee's temperament and military concepts, to take the offensive whenever possible.[18] A correspondent of the London *Times* who caught the mood of the moment wrote: "A cry for immediate battle . . . swelled the gale —timid and hesitating counsels were impatiently discarded; and . . . the mature and cautious wisdom of General Lee had no choice but to float with the current, and to trust the enthusiasm of his troops to carry him triumphantly . . . over the heights. . . ."[19] This observation presses a little too hard on the irresistible character of the call for a headlong assault, and thus puts Lee in rather bad light. He heeded the cry for action because he and other Confederate generals were under the impression, as Longstreet himself said right after the battle, that the enemy had not been able to get all of his men to the front. Lee therefore thought it "best to attack at once. And we did attack," Longstreet continued, "before our forces got up and it turned out that the enemy was ready with his whole force, and ours was not."[20]

Having made his decision to stay at Gettysburg and go on the offensive, Lee pondered the best way to carry it out. From the close of the first day's fighting until late that night he discussed battle plans with his generals. He held no council of war, nor did he meet all of them together at one time, even informally. Instead he himself rode out to consult with each corps commander and his chief subordinates, and he saw other officers individually or in groups at his headquarters.[21] The records are not definite about the sequence of these conferences, but it seems clear that his first one was with General Ewell.

After his rather heated discussion with Longstreet Lee went to the Confederate left and arrived at Ewell's headquarters sometime after sunset.[22] Here sitting in the arbor near the house Lee, Ewell, and Rodes sought a little relief from the heat of the day and planned for the morrow. At that late hour any thoughts of continuing the day's fighting were dismissed. Early, who had been off inspecting the positions of Hoke's and Hays's brigades, found them talking about the situation of the Second Corps, the condition of the troops, the strength of the enemy, and all other information useful to the commanding general. As Early described the scene, Lee soon made clear his intention of attacking the Federals as early as possible the next day, and he asked whether the Second Corps could not start off the assault by storming Cemetery Hill at daylight. It was a sensible question, for the arrival of General Edward Johnson's division while they were conferring had completed the concentration of Ewell's splendid body of men. In addition, Ewell's losses for the day had been less than Hill's, and his troops seemed to be in better position to strike first. Before Ewell could respond, Early presumed to speak and give his opinion in a positive manner. Claiming to have a better knowledge of the battleground than anyone by virtue of his previous visit to Gettysburg and his observations during the engagement, he declared that an attack from the Confederate left would run into serious trouble and incur heavy losses. The northeast slope of Cemetery Hill, which Ewell faced, was higher and steeper, Early said, than the part facing west and northwest. He also called Lee's attention to the topography of Cemetery Ridge and more particularly the Round Tops, which if seized would render the enemy's position untenable. In his estimation an attack mounted from the Confederate right against Cemetery Ridge would have far greater chances of success than one on the left, and he therefore recommended it to Lee. How Early knew so much about these landmarks at this stage of the battle is somewhat of a mystery. In a man's recollections knowledge gained from hindsight has a way of creeping in through the back door of his mind and rendering his statements untrustworthy.

Ewell, according to Early's recollections, nodded approval of his suggestion, and Rodes openly expressed agreement with his appraisal of the situation. Upon learning that the Second Corps generals were against making an attack from their quarter, Lee, according to Early, asked whether it would not be wise to pull back the Confederate left, since the enemy might break its long thin line. Somehow the intent of the question as Early remembered it does not seem right. In view of the discussion about possible offensive measures from the Confederate left, it would seem illogical for Lee to have shown concern about the generals' ability to resist a Yankee attack there. It would have been more natural for him to have asked why their troops should not be withdrawn and used with other forces in a massive attack from the Confederate right.

Lee's inquiry about the desirability of withdrawing his left brought again an immediate response from the quick-witted and loquacious Early, with Ewell and Rodes openly agreeing with him. Psychologically it was bad, he said, for troops to give up ground they had won. A withdrawal would mean evacuation of part if not all of Gettysburg, thus forcing him to leave many of his badly wounded men behind, as well as many captured enemy weapons. While the ground on their front made offensive moves difficult, Early assured Lee that it was excellent for purposes of defense.[23]

The attitude of these high-ranking officers as described by Early was strangely out of keeping with the aggressive spirit of the Army of Northern Virginia and revealed to Lee another unforeseen difficulty in the formulation of his plans. Instead of offering their commanding officer hearty cooperation and an eagerness to respond positively to his suggestions, they gave him objections and reasons why they should not do certain things. As for Ewell himself, he made a poor impression in the discussion, not so much for what he said as for what he did not say. It may be true, as has been charged, that he suddenly lost his ability to make decisions. Just as likely an explanation is that he put himself in a false position by allowing Early, who as a lawyer and a politician was more articulate than he, to act as his spokesman in a matter that was difficult to explain. This unsatisfactory conference following the unpleasant scene with Longstreet upset Lee. Longstreet wanted to break off the engagement at Gettysburg and fight elsewhere; Ewell and his generals desired the Second Corps to remain on the defensive or at best play a secondary role in the offense. Like balky horses, they would go neither forward nor backward. At length, bowing to the recommendations of his generals, Lee told them that his main attack would be on the enemy's left.[24] What contributions Ewell's corps would make to the offensive had been only tentatively settled.[25] Lee then rode back to his headquarters to start preparations for the next day's exertions.

Soon after his return Lee began to have second thoughts about keeping the Second Corps in its position northeast of Gettysburg, and he sent Ewell orders to withdraw toward the Confederate right. Word of this change in Lee's plans so upset Ewell that he went to see his commander for the purpose of getting him to reconsider.[26] Subsequent to his first meeting with Lee, Ewell had received a report of a reconnaissance made very late in the afternoon or early in the evening by two of his aides. They said they had reached the summit of Culp's Hill without meeting a Federal soldier, and there they saw stretched out before them the enemy's line of battle. Ewell accepted their appraisal of the strategic importance of Culp's Hill:

that if it were seized by the Confederates it would render the Union position on Cemetery Hill untenable. At his second meeting with Lee Ewell proposed to send a force to seize the heights if Lee would agree to let him remain in his present position. Lee granted the request, but probably for reasons other than the ones Ewell gave.[27] Although he undoubtedly accepted the accuracy of the information brought back by the two aides, Lee must have realized that by the time Ewell passed the intelligence on to him it was hours old, and he must have suspected that during the interval the Northerners, perceiving the threat to their position, had sent a force to occupy the hill. What seems to have impressed Lee and made him come to a decision was Ewell's sudden display of initiative and the aggressive spirit so characteristic of the Southern army.[28]

There are certain aspects of this second conference between Ewell and Lee on the night of July 1 which are beyond satisfactory explanation. Very likely Ewell had received the report of the reconnaissance mission to Culp's Hill before Lee's withdrawal order reached him, but he did nothing about it until the commanding general's message galvanized him into action. There is the suggestion that Ewell's desire to remain where he was arose less from conviction on his part than from compliance with Early's positive assurance that it was the right thing to do.[29] Once Ewell had evinced a renewed disposition to fight, Lee overlooked the defects of the Second Corps' position, for he thought he could accomplish his purposes on the Confederate right if he could put simultaneous pressure on the entire length of the Union line.[30] Lee's decision not to move Ewell's corps was a serious miscalculation in the opinion of Colonel E. P. Alexander, one of the more intelligent and dispassionate of the Confederate critics of the battle. With their line, which was two and a half miles long, "bent around toward the point of the fish hook of the enemy's position," many of Ewell's troops, Alexander felt, were in "an awkward place, far from our line of retreat in case of disaster, & not convenient either for reinforcing others or being reinforced." There was "no reasonable probability of . . . [Ewell] accomplishing any good on the enemy's line in his front" where part of it was "almost unassailable." As it turned out, Ewell's corps, as well as all of his artillery, was "practically paralysed by its position during the last two days of the battle."[31] Furthermore by forming a big hook in the Confederate line and increasing the problems of communication, the location of the Second Corps made it impossible to synchronize the different attacks from the flanks and the center.[32]

After his conference with Lee Ewell returned to his headquarters, and although it was after midnight he ordered General Johnson to take possession of Culp's Hill, "if he had not already done so." [33] Johnson, without waiting for word from Ewell, had gone ahead and made preparations to occupy it, but he found the Yankees already there in great numbers. Then Johnson received disconcerting information from a dispatch found on a captured Federal courier: General Sykes with two divisions of the Fifth Corps was at Bonaughtown, which was less than five miles from Johnson's left and rear, and he would renew his march to Gettysburg at 4:00 A.M. Since Sykes had addressed the dispatch to General Slocum, Johnson could be pretty sure that Slocum's Twelfth Corps was either on the battleground or nearby.[34] With one enemy force in front of him and another approaching his left flank he felt affairs were getting beyond his control and that he had better refer matters to his commanding officer.

It was dawn before Ewell heard of these complications, but he did not have to decide what to do for Lee had already sent him his first instructions for the day. According to these orders, Ewell was to delay Johnson's assault until he heard General Longstreet's guns open on the right. Thereupon Ewell directed Johnson to get ready to attack at an undetermined hour.[35] Later in the morning Lee changed his plans somewhat, and he told Ewell that when Longstreet started his offensive the Second Corps should "make a simultaneous demonstration upon the enemy's right, to be converted into a real attack should opportunity offer." [36] In other words, Lee virtually restored discretionary power to Ewell. Whether he made a full-scale attack on the enemy would depend upon circumstances and his own judgment.

After Lee had revoked his order to withdraw Ewell's corps and send it toward the Confederate right, he made no further effort to change its position. He inspected it some time before noon,[37] at which time Johnson was on the extreme left more or less facing south toward Culp's Hill. Most of Early's division extended along the main street of Gettysburg east from the square to the Hanover road, while Rodes's men prolonged the same line west to a spot near which the Fairfield road crosses Seminary Ridge.

From no matter what part of his line Lee launched his main attack on July 2, he would have to wait until Longstreet brought the bulk of his corps to the battleground. All of the other infantry units of the army had arrived, and the sooner Longstreet's men got there the better, for then Lee would have more time during the day to achieve his objectives, whatever they might be. Longstreet emphasized in his recollections that when he left Lee about 7:00 P.M. on July 1 to return to Cashtown, Lee "had formed no plans beyond that of seizing Culp's Hill as his point from which to engage, nor given any orders for the next day, though his desperate mood was painfully evident, and gave rise to serious apprehensions." [38] Aside from the question of the accuracy of this statement, Longstreet was raising an irrelevant, if not bogus issue in mentioning the tentative nature of Lee's plans at that hour. Regardless of how far Lee had gone in his thinking about operations for the next day, Longstreet's primary function without being told was to press his men and get them to the front as quickly as possible.[39]

Longstreet had sent marching orders to the First Corps as early as ten on the morning of July 1, but it was not until 4:00 P.M.—six hours later—that it finally left its bivouac near Greenwood, sixteen or seventeen miles west of Gettysburg on the Chambersburg Pike. The explanation was that it had been held up by Johnson's division and the Second Corps wagon train. Longstreet had directed that an hour after this column had cleared the road, General McLaws' division, followed by General Hood's, should start marching, proceed through Cashtown Pass, and camp on the east side of the mountain. General Pickett's division had orders to remain in Chambersburg until relieved by General Imboden's command, which was coming in from Mercersburg.[40] After Longstreet had conferred with Lee on Seminary Ridge about 5:00 P.M., he modified his orders and told his subordinates to keep moving on through the night as far as they could without wearing out their men and draft animals.[41] A routine march became a forced one. McLaws' division of approximately 6,500 infantrymen,[42] accompanied by four batteries with sixteen pieces of artillery, was on the road for eight hours, from 4:00 P.M. till midnight. During this time it covered the twelve or thirteen miles from its bivouac to Marsh Creek, four miles from Gettysburg, which was one of the few places where the men could get plenty of water. Hood's division started later and did not reach the camp near Marsh Creek until about 1:00 A.M.[43] The Artillery Reserve, consisting of two battalions under Colonel J. B. Walton, left Greenwood between midnight and 1:00 A.M. and got close to the battleground some eight hours later. It was greatly delayed upon the road by wagon trains.[44] For forced marches the pace set by these units was not impressive, especially as they used the Chambersburg Pike which was in pretty good shape despite its pounding by thousands of feet, hooves, and wheels during wet weather.[45] Lee tried to clear the way by ordering the reserve wagon trains to park to the side of the pike between Greenwood and Cashtown.[46]

During the night General E. M. Law's brigade of Hood's division at New Guilford and Pickett's division at Chambersburg received orders to move on to Gettysburg. Both forces left their respective camps early in the morning and apparently made better time than the rest of the corps. Law's brigade, which was in the lead, arrived within three or four miles of Gettysburg around noon and Pickett's men at the same location late in the afternoon.[47] Because of a later start Pickett's division made much of its march during the middle of the day when the heat was most oppressive. One participant said that as the men approached Cashtown Gap the "vertical rays of the sun seemed like real lances of steel tipped with fire!" The broken rock of the "Mc Adamized" surface of the turnpike and the "broad flat flagstones of mountain slate" reflected the heat until steam rose in their faces and "choking dust" gathered in their throats and eyes. Lack of drinking water made these conditions almost unbearable.[48] When the men reached the Confederate line their thirst remained unquenched, for the wells and pumps in the farmers' yards were beginning to run dry and the nearest brooks and springs were too far away to be available to most units.[49] The bivouac at Marsh Creek for McLaws' and Hood's divisions, where thousands of men could get water, showed good planning on the part of Longstreet.

In view of the crowded condition of the pike, which had to be used by most of the Confederate army, Longstreet probably could not have brought McLaws' and Hood's divisions to Marsh Creek much earlier than he did without wearing them out and causing an excessive amount of straggling. The question arises, however, of why he did not notify Law sooner so that his brigade could have been on hand by 11:00 A.M. Perhaps Longstreet did send him marching orders at 5:30 P.M. If so, the messenger must have lost his way, for Longstreet and Lee agreed that Law did not get the orders until three the next morning. It took the courier as long to complete his errand as it took a brigade of 1,500 to 2,000 men to break camp and march almost the same distance. Law's Alabamians with a battery of guns in tow set a fast pace, and they covered twenty miles over the mountain in nine or ten hours. After rejoining their division near Gettysburg they had farther to go than anyone to get into their place in the line of battle for the attack.[50] As for Pickett, his departure for Gettysburg depended upon the vagaries of the inefficient General Imboden.[51] Under the circumstances he did very well to get to the battleground by midafternoon of the second of July.

The arrival of most of Longstreet's corps at Marsh Creek shortly after midnight placed them about three and a half miles from Lee's headquarters on Seminary Ridge, or a two- or two-and-a-half-hour-march away. It would appear that they had come close enough to the main Confederate battle line to be ready for an assault at an early hour in the day. In reality the time of their attack would depend upon many uncertainties. If Lee ever had the notion of striking the enemy at sunrise, as General Pendleton later claimed, his knowledge of logistics would have quickly dispelled it. Members of Lee's staff in contrast to Pendleton's recollection remembered that the general only expected to make an attack "as early as *practicable*,"[52] an expression of hope which left many questions unsettled.

Lee's decisions, first to take the offensive and then to throw the weight of his attack on the enemy's left flank, were merely the first steps in the development of his strategy. Much work had to be done before his plans could be perfected, and this would take time. Lee had to locate the position of the Union left flank before he could decide how much to extend his own battle line and where to arrange his troops for an attack. He had to settle other questions as well. Would he try to conceal his movements so as to surprise the enemy when he launched the assault? What tactics would he employ? How would he hit the enemy flank, head-on or diagonally?

Since Lee had made Longstreet the key figure in the operations for July 2, it was essential that the two generals not misunderstand each other. Although Longstreet had gone back to his headquarters unhappy over the prospects of an offensive against the Yankees in their position on the east side of Gettysburg,[53] he had worked to expedite the forward movement of his troops as they came through Cashtown during the night.[54] He could not have had much rest, for he was up at 3:30 A.M., had his breakfast, and reached Seminary Ridge by 5:00 A.M. Before long he and Lee were sitting under a tree in conversation with Hill, Hood, and Heth. It was an informal gathering, with Longstreet and Hood thoughtfully whittling on sticks and from time to time making comments.[55] Longstreet renewed his objections to an attack, and Lee quietly but firmly said he was determined to make one.[56] It was probably then that Lee told Longstreet of his intention to launch an assault against the enemy's left flank with two divisions of the First Corps. Hill expressed his disapproval of the plan unless it was carried out early in the day, for otherwise darkness would come and deprive Longstreet of the fruits of his victory.[57] But Lee was adamant about the matter, and the talk turned to a discussion of the probable results of the attack. The generals also examined the position of the Federals from afar and got a good idea of the nature of the ground.[58] Hood remembered Lee "with coat buttoned to the throat, sabre-belt buckled round the waist, and field glasses pending at his side," walking up and down in the shade of the large trees near them and stopping every so often to look at the enemy. "He seemed full of hope," he continued, "yet, at times, buried in deep thought." Lee's anxiety for Longstreet to start the attack in the morning appeared obvious to Hood.[59]

The minutes slipped by, and before long McLaws arrived at the head of his column. Evidently Hood's division had preceded him on the short march to Gettysburg because it started around 3:00 A.M., while McLaws' men did not get off until about sunrise, an hour and a half later. The time of their arrival is uncertain, but even if they had marched at a very leisurely pace it is likely that both divisions were on hand for deployment by 8:30 A.M. As the men reached the western edge of the battleground so bitterly contested the day before they quietly turned off the pike, stacked their arms, got under cover wherever they could from the sun, and rested until further orders.[60] The question of when they got there is immaterial, for until Lee and his officers had completed other preparations they could not be used.

The important tasks facing the commanders were to get a clear idea of the nature of the ground south and east of the Confederate main line, and to probe the area of the Round Tops for the Federal left flank. At a very early hour Lee had instructed Colonel A. L. Long of his staff, who had an artilleryman's eye for terrain, to "examine and verify" the position of the Confederate artillery along the whole line. Long started on the right and visited Hill's headquarters about sunrise. While assisting Colonel R. Lindsay Walker, Hill's chief of artillery, in placing the guns of the corps, Long called his attention to the Emmitsburg road heights, extending in the direction of Big Round Top, as a good location for some batteries. Looking across the fields at the enemy, he noticed additional troops on Cemetery Hill, but he could see none on most of the ridge south of Ziegler's Grove.[61] Appearances though were deceiving. From where he stood on Seminary Ridge not far south of the Fairfield road, the rise in the Emmitsburg road as it approached the Peach Orchard hid the location of Sickles' corps, which was massed on the lower ground at the southern end of Cemetery Ridge.[62] A morning mist also helped to cut down visibility.[63] Long could not be aware of the approach of Hancock's Second Corps because Cemetery Ridge completely screened the Taneytown road.

Soon after sunrise General Pendleton, Lee's chief of artillery, with some of his staff also visited the extreme right and front of the Confederate lines to survey the enemy's position "toward some estimate of the ground," he said, "and the best mode of attack." Colonels Long and Walker and Captain S. R. Johnston, an engineer at Lee's headquarters, went with him, he reported. Although none of these officers confirmed his story, they might have started out with him before going off on their own errands. Pendleton continued to the right and the rear of the Confederate position,[64] crossing the picket line Buford had formed the previous night from the Union left to within a short distance of Fairfield.[65] Following the road along Willoughby Run back toward the Confederate lines, he and his party surprised and captured two of Buford's unwary troopers. One of his important accomplishments during the morning was tracing the route of the Willoughby Run road, over which Longstreet's columns could approach the Union left flank without being seen.[66]

Lee knew that Long's and Pendleton's observations of Union lines, though useful, had been made at too great a distance to be anything but superficial and inconclusive. He wanted a more thorough reconnaissance. About daybreak he sent for Captain Johnston and gave him instructions to reconnoiter along the enemy's left and bring the information back as soon as possible. Johnston knew from long service with Lee that in carrying out his assignment the general expected him to consider every contingency which might come up, including the need to have a route over which troops could move unobserved by the enemy. He took Major J. J. Clarke of Longstreet's engineers and two or three other men with him. Lee had taught him, as a result of his own Mexican War experience, that a small party was best for such work because there was less chance of detection. Starting out shortly before sunrise, Johnston and his men rode down the valley of Willoughby Run possibly in company with General Pendleton and Colonel Long. If so, they left their compatriots when they turned east, crossed the Emmitsburg road near the Peach Orchard, and followed the ridge leading to Little Round Top.[67] When they reached the height, Johnston and Clarke climbed it and looked over the ground carefully. By chance they must have come to that natural stronghold just as there was a change of guard, so to speak, for they saw none of the enemy.[68] Perhaps only a few minutes before they got there around 5:30 A.M.[69] the two brigades of Geary's division, which had covered this part of the Federal front during the night, had left to occupy positions on Culp's Hill.[70] It would be an hour or so before Birney's division would extend its line over Little Round Top to the higher peak to the south,[71] but until that happened anyone standing on Little Round Top and looking north would be unable to see Birney's men massed behind the lower rise of Cemetery Ridge because of the heavy foliage in the woods. Johnston did not go in that direction to determine precisely where the Union left flank rested.[72] Instead he and his party were satisfied with having found no one on Little Round Top, and they turned south and rode considerably beyond Big Round Top before returning to the Confederate lines. They were very cautious in slipping past Union pickets, and they met no enemy until the return trip, when they spied three or four Union troopers riding slowly up the Emmitsburg road toward Gettysburg. Not wishing to risk an encounter, they waited until they disappeared from view. Once Johnston got to Willoughby Run he galloped by the most direct route, across fields and over fences in his haste to report to his general. It was about 9:00 A.M.

After some delay in locating headquarters Johnston found Lee sitting upon a fallen tree near the seminary with a map on his knees. Looking up, he called to Johnston and asked him to sketch the route he had taken on the map. Lee expressed surprise and pleasure at the extent to which the captain had penetrated the enemy position and obtained information so vital to his plans.[73] The reconnaissance seemed to confirm his assumption that the Union line extended only from Cemetery Hill to the upper part of the ridge which he could observe directly. From where Lee stood the ridge became lost to sight in the wooded area north of the Round Tops. It did not seem to worry Lee that Johnston had not gone there to look around. About this time he heard from Pendleton that Sickles' two brigades had arrived near the Peach Orchard and then moved east in the direction of the upper valley of Plum Run and the lower sections of Cemetery Ridge.[74] These movements should have made Lee suspect that the Union line extended farther than he thought. His concern, however, was about the Round Tops. Upon further inquiry Johnston assured him that he had climbed Little Round Top and seen no enemy troops about. Lee was confident of the soundness of his plan for an oblique attack north of the hills. It would envelop the Union left flank and roll it up toward Cemetery Hill. There was another advantage in moving obliquely: Union batteries on Cemetery Hill could not mow down his men with an enfilading fire.[75] Now that he had decided just where to launch the major assault, the sooner he made it the better, Lee felt, before the enemy could receive reinforcements and make changes in the disposition of his troops.

After hearing Captain Johnston's report, Lee turned to Longstreet, who with Hill had been listening carefully, and suggested that he had better get his corps in motion again.[76] Previously Lee, upon learning of McLaws' arrival at the head of his division, had sent for him to explain the plan of attack and to show on a map just where his men were to go. He wanted McLaws to get to his position, which was perpendicular to the Emmitsburg road, if possible without being seen by the enemy. He also told McLaws it was unnecessary for him to have his skirmishers reconnoiter the ground, as Captain Johnston would take him out there and help him do it. Longstreet, who had overheard the conversation, came up and forbade McLaws to ride out and examine the position with Johnston.

Then looking at the map, he indicated with his finger that McLaws' position should be at right angles to the one Lee wanted him to occupy. Lee told Longstreet that he was wrong and repeated his instructions to McLaws. At this moment Longstreet's festering hostility to any offensive move and his annoyance with Lee for having overruled him in the deployment of McLaws' division broke out into the open. He persisted in stubbornly and blindly refusing to give McLaws permission to leave his division and accompany Johnston.[77] Lee chose to overlook his senior lieutenant's ill temper and assigned Johnston to him, presumably to act as a guide for the First Corps columns to their point of attack.[78]

Shortly after this outburst Longstreet regained his poise and seemed more like himself. Lee had the satisfaction of hearing him give orders to Colonel Alexander to take charge of three battalions of the First Corps artillery and get them ready for the assault. Alexander's regular command was a battalion in the corps Artillery Reserve, but for today's battle Longstreet wanted this brilliant young officer to supervise the working of his guns instead of Colonel Walton, his chief of artillery. Upon receiving the summons from Longstreet, Alexander reported to him on Seminary Ridge about 10:00 A.M.[79] In Lee's presence Longstreet pointed out the enemy's position and said the Confederates would attack his left flank. He suggested that Alexander start out at once and get an idea of the ground before bringing up his own battalion. Longstreet warned Alexander to keep all his movements carefully out of view of a signal station whose flags they could see wigwagging on Little Round Top. Ten minutes after reporting Alexander had his orders and was off to examine all the roads leading to the right and front, and to determine the best sites for his guns. He rode fast in company with one or two couriers and found out what he needed to know in a little over an hour. Then he returned to pick up the battalions of Colonel H. C. Cabell and Major M. W. Henry, as well as his own near the Chambersburg Pike, and sent them down Willoughby Run to Pitzer's School House on the Fairfield crossroad, which ran west from the Taneytown road past the Peach Orchard and on to Fairfield. He had come there by a short and direct road, which at one place passed over a high point in full view of the Federal signal station. Having a good bump of direction and a feeling for terrain, he easily avoided exposure by turning out to the right and going through fields and hollows before getting back to the road about a quarter of a mile beyond.[80]

Following the interview in which Longstreet had given Alexander his orders, Lee and Longstreet went their separate ways. Lee rode off to Ewell's headquarters. The records offer conflicting evidence about the purpose and the time of his visit.[81] Very early in the morning Lee had sent Major C. S. Venable of his staff to ask Ewell about the possible advantages of an attack from his position. He also reopened the question of the desirability of withdrawing the Second Corps and placing it on the right to cooperate with Longstreet in an attack on that side. Ewell and Venable spent a long time examining conditions along the Confederate lines, and before they had completed their tour General Lee appeared at Ewell's headquarters.[82] Colonel Long, who had completed his morning's assignment of inspecting artillery positions, found Lee there. After discussing affairs of the Second Corps with Ewell, Venable, Long, and others, Lee became satisfied, if he had had any doubts, that the secondary role he had given Ewell to play that day was the correct one. By then it was too late to pull the Second Corps around to the Confederate right, and it seemed better to have Ewell stay where he was and help Longstreet by putting heavy pressure on the enemy at his end of the line.

With these matters settled, Lee, as Long told the story, momentarily expected to hear the boom of First Corps guns announcing the start of the attack. This account was offered as evidence of Lee's impatience with the slow-moving Longstreet.[83] Doubtless Lee was impatient not only with Longstreet himself but with the unavoidable and annoying delays incidental to getting a large army set for an offensive. Time, he knew, was on the side of the Federals. Assuming they had not yet assembled their army in full strength, he feared they would do so before he could strike. It does not seem possible, however, that within the comparatively short time since he had left Longstreet to see Ewell Lee would have expected the attack to begin. His plans for the assault had taken final form only with the receipt of Captain Johnston's report not long before he rode off to inspect the Second Corps. He knew then that Longstreet's men had not yet started to move. Even with very efficient management it would take several hours to march them a distance of four miles or more to the place where they would be deployed for battle.

Various accounts describing Lee's growing uneasiness and impatience upon his return to Seminary Ridge, however, seem authentic.[84] Even Longstreet admitted that he had accomplished little in Lee's absence. Lukewarm about any attack, he had a strong aversion to one made with less than two of his divisions. He wanted to wait for Pickett, for as he explained to Hood, he "never lik[ed] to go into battle with one boot off." [85] Although Lee was aware of these feelings, he decided it was not practicable to wait any longer, and he instructed Longstreet to "move, with the portion of . . . [his] command that was up, around to gain the Emmitsburg road, on the enemy's left." [86] The meaning of this statement as contained in Longstreet's battle report is obscure. In fact, all of the references to Lee's battle plans for July 2 in Confederate reports are cryptic and misleading. They read as if Lee had designed his operations so as to attack the Federal lines where they were finally located later in the day, instead of where they actually were at the time he formulated his plans. Longstreet, for instance, in admitting that he had disobeyed Lee's instructions by waiting for General Law, offered in extenuation the statement that the enemy had taken a strong position "extending from the hill at the cemetery along the Emmitsburg road," and he dared not attack with his weak force.[87] The Emmitsburg road marked a part of the Union line only after General Humphreys advanced his division to it about 4:00 P.M., more than four hours after Lee issued his order to Longstreet. Until that time the Yankee line conformed pretty closely to the configurations of Cemetery Ridge,[88] and when Lee told Longstreet in the morning to take the heights, Sickles was just surveying their possibilities.[89]

As far as can be determined, Lee's offensive move against the Union left flank was to comprise two steps, one preparatory to the other: first, the seizure of good artillery positions at the Peach Orchard and other high ground three-quarters of a mile west of Big Round Top; and second, an oblique attack on Cemetery Ridge covered by artillery fire from these advanced locations. As Longstreet expressed it in his report, Lee's order directed him to take only the first step in the offensive with the troops of the First Corps then on hand. If he had done so, there would have been no danger of his men encountering resistance worth mentioning until the middle of the afternoon. He therefore had no need to wait for Law's fine brigade.[90] On the other hand, if Lee meant that Longstreet was to take the heights on the Emmitsburg road, which included the Peach Orchard, as a prelude to the main assault, he apparently was willing to expose his movements against the Yankee left flank prematurely. Regardless of whether Lee intended a preliminary move of this sort, Longstreet could have started shifting his infantry toward the Confederate right flank in the morning while Lee was conferring with Ewell. His excuse at first was that he was waiting for Pickett. When that was ruled out, he then insisted upon Law's appearance before starting to move his men to the right. He never explained why Law could not have found the rest of Hood's division just as easily near the Emmitsburg road as on the Chambersburg Pike.

When Lee rejoined Longstreet after eleven o'clock [91] and saw what little had been accomplished in the face of signs of growing enemy strength, he departed from his usual custom of "suggesting" movements to his lieutenants.[92] He gave Longstreet an outright order to place McLaws' and Hood's divisions on the right of Hill, "partially enveloping the enemy's left, which he was to drive in." [93] Longstreet asked permission, which Lee granted, to delay the advance until the arrival of Law, who was expected momentarily.[94] When Longstreet heard that Law had joined Hood about noon, he finally began movement of his corps toward the right with McLaws' division in the lead. This march became a comedy of errors such as one might expect of inexperienced commanders and raw militia, but not of Lee's "War Horse" and his veteran troops.

Explanations have never been satisfactory for the snarl in which Hood's and McLaws' divisions found themselves. To untangle it the men had to trudge over dusty lanes and sunbaked fields at the cost of precious minutes and extra miles. The difficulty started when Lee, anxious to make his attack an unpleasant surprise for the enemy, cautioned Longstreet not to reveal his movements. He then assigned Captain Johnston to guide McLaws along a hidden route. Although Johnston had gone over the ground of the Confederate right and the Union left quite thoroughly, it is not certain whether he was familiar with the country along Herr Ridge between the Chambersburg Pike and the Fairfield road.[95] His problem was to move McLaws' and Hood's divisions, without being seen, from the west side of the ridge to a location near the Emmitsburg road heights four miles away.[96] Longstreet, still in a petulant mood, chose this moment to be more than punctilious in complying with army protocol. Since Lee had ordered Johnston to lead and guide the head of the column, which was McLaws' division, Longstreet decided to regard him as Lee's special representative who during the march possessed greater authority over these troops than he. Through this questionable interpretation of Johnston's role Longstreet temporarily relinquished his position as commander of the corps and rode behind with Hood's division.[97] In this way he probably expected to escape responsibility for any mistakes Johnston might make. The captain saw himself in the more modest role of a guide and did not recall having received any instructions from Lee other than an order to attach himself to Longstreet. With Johnston leading the way the division marched south to the Black Horse Tavern, where it turned onto a road which branched off from the Fairfield road and went in a southeasterly direction toward Willoughby Run. Shortly after the turnoff the column came to a rise which the operators at the signal station on Little Round Top could see. Fearing exposure, the division came to a halt while McLaws, Longstreet, and Johnston consulted. At McLaws' suggestion they decided to countermarch for a way and use an unexposed route he had previously discovered. Back to the Black Horse Tavern they tramped and then north on the west side of Herr Ridge. When near their starting point they began to work their way east. By going through fields and knocking down fences they came to Willoughby Run and followed it south to Pitzer's School House on the Fairfield crossroad. According to McLaws, there was considerable confusion during the countermarch because Hood in his eagerness to get to the battle line pushed into the rear of McLaws' division.[98]

Longstreet, however, had a different story. He claimed the honor of having solved the impasse which he had helped create through a quibble. McLaws, he felt, was under direct orders from Lee, but Hood was not, apparently because he did not happen to be at headquarters when Lee assigned Johnston to guide the head of the column. Assuming the Federals had detected their movements, Longstreet concluded that further efforts to conceal them were a waste of time. Therefore he took over control of Hood's division, pushed it ahead of McLaws, and led it forward by the most direct route.[99] Ironically the Union signalmen did not observe Longstreet's men near the Fairfield road—at least there is no record of it—but at 1:30 P.M. they reported a column of 10,000 men moving

379

north toward Herr's Tavern on the Chambersburg Pike.[100] Out of the ineptitude and confusion of the countermarch emerged an unforeseen consequence; Lee could not have devised a better way to mask his real intentions.

This episode, which revealed a dark moment in Longstreet's career as a general, also demonstrated an inherent weakness in Lee's system of command. Alexander analyzed it very well. He told how in getting his battalions to the schoolhouse in the valley of Willoughby Run he had taken the same short cut which he did in the morning. Riding back for something, he found the head of an infantry division halted in sight of the signal station. It remained there well over an hour, he said, until a guide came with orders to lead it by way of the Black Horse Tavern, a name he never forgot. He estimated that by taking this detour the division marched four miles to go less than one. Here was an example of how time could be lost in handling troops, and how generals needed many competent staff officers. Then he went on:

> Scarcely any of our generals had half of what they needed to keep a *constant & close supervision on the execution of important orders.* . . . An army is like a great machine, and in putting it into battle it is not enough for its commander to merely issue the necessary orders. He should have a staff ample to supervise the execution of each step & to promptly report any difficulty or misunderstanding. There is no telling the value of the hours which were lost by that division. . . . Of course I told the officers at the head of the column of the route my artillery had followed—which was easily seen—but there was no one with authority to vary the orders they were under, & they momentarily expected the new ones for which they had sent & wh[ich] were very explicit when they came after the long—long delay.[101]

Once McLaws' division with the brigade of General J. B. Kershaw in the lead had completed its countermarch and made a fresh start, it moved along easily though the road was not wide enough for company front because of fences.[102] At Pitzer's School House it turned to the left on the crossroad to the Peach Orchard,[103] while Hood's division up ahead continued south toward the Emmitsburg road.[104] As Kershaw approached the Peach Orchard, Longstreet rode up and directed him to attack the enemy there and to turn his flank by using the Emmitsburg road as a pivot and swinging to the left. It would

26. Little Round Top from Devil's Den.

27. Interior of breastworks on Little Round Top.

28. Letter of Charles W. Reed with a sketch of action by his unit, Captain John Bigelow's 9th Massachusetts Battery, part of McGilvery's Artillery Reserve.

29. View from Little Round Top to the northwest, showing the Wheatfield and Trostle farm buildings.

30. The Trostle farmhouse.

31. General Meade's headquarters, the widow Leister's farmhouse, just west of the Taneytown Road.

32. A. R. Waud sketching at Gettysburg.

33. Attack on Colonel Strong Vincent's Brigade: the countercharge by the 20th Maine under Colonel Joshua L. Chamberlain, July 2, 1863.

34. Attack by Brigadier General George J. Stannard's Vermont Brigade on Pickett's flank, July 3, 1863.

35. Attack by Colonel Norman J. Hall's Brigade on Pickett's flank, July 3, 1863. From a drawing by A. R. Waud.

37. "The Angle," where Pickett's Charge culminated.

36. Pencil sketch by
Colonel John B. Bachelder
showing Union positions
during Pickett's Charge.

38. Cemetery Ridge after Pickett's Charge.

39. The Bryan house, near the scene of Pickett's Charge.

40. Confederate prisoners.

41. The dead.

be a simple operation, according to Longstreet, for nothing much was there. At the time Kershaw received the order a grove of trees obscured his view of the orchard. About three o'clock he moved his men to the right of the crossroad into an open field, where he formed his battle line. To his amazement he saw the Peach Orchard swarming with Federal troops, supported by artillery. Their line appeared to extend up and onto a rocky mountain to their left "far beyond the point at which . . . [their] flank had [been] supposed to rest." [105] McLaws was just as startled as Kershaw when he received this information from his brigadier, for the latest intelligence reports said the enemy had "but two regiments of infantry and one battery" at the Peach Orchard. Sending Longstreet word of the great strength of the enemy, McLaws prepared to broaden the field of his attack by deploying two of his brigades and holding the other two back as reserves. Ten or twelve pieces of his artillery rolled up and soon were in position to fire. Longstreet could not believe McLaws' report of heavy enemy concentration, and he sent word that "he was satisfied there was a small force of the enemy in front" and that McLaws must "proceed at once to the assault." [106] A short while later when he heard none of the familiar sounds of a Confederate attack, Longstreet sent Major Osmun Latrobe to see what was the matter. McLaws explained that his division was not on the Union flank and he had to make careful preparations for a frontal attack against a superior force in a strong position. This would take time. Longstreet still pressed him to charge immediately. McLaws promised to do so in five minutes, but at the last minute he received an order from Longstreet to hold off until Hood could get into position.[107] Longstreet's blind insistence that he push ahead before he was ready annoyed McLaws, and he aired his grievances in a letter to his wife. "General Longstreet is to blame for not reconnoitering the ground," he wrote, "and for persisting in ordering the assault when his errors were discovered." He ended with this indictment of Longstreet: "During the engagement he was very excited giving contrary orders to everyone, and was exceedingly overbearing. I consider him a humbug—a man of small capacity, very obstinate, not at all chivalrous, exceedingly conceited, and totally selfish. If I can it is my intention to get away from his command." [108]

Meanwhile Hood was also slow to attack. His delay resulted from his efforts to change his orders, not from a request for more time to get into position. His line was an extension of McLaws' on Warfield Ridge, beyond the south end of Seminary Ridge, crossing the Emmitsburg road at an acute angle. He was appalled by what he could see of the Federal position a half to three-quarters of a mile away, for it seemed to extend to Big Round Top. The prospect of driving toward Gettysburg at right angles to the Emmitsburg road, as he had been ordered to do, made even Hood, a fearless and sometimes a reckless fighter, most unhappy. From his own observations and those of his scouts he concluded that the attack would be futile and result in wanton waste of life. His objections to the direction of the assault were many. If his men swept northward they would hit the enemy line stretching from the Peach Orchard to Devil's Den head-on. The huge boulders strewn over the base and slope of Big Round Top would break up his battle formations and force his men to scatter. He realized too that the concave character of the enemy's line from the north end of Cemetery Ridge to Big Round Top would expose his division to a "destructive fire in flank and rear, as well as in front," if his men attacked it obliquely. Hood thought there was a way of overcoming these objections, and he strongly urged it.

His Texas scouts had reported that the summit of Big Round Top and the area south of its base were clear of enemy troops. They had located the Union wagon trains in the rear and discovered a way through an "open woodland pasture" to seize them.[109] In haste Hood sent an aid to Longstreet requesting permission to move his division to the south and east around Big Round Top and attack the enemy in his flank and rear. Longstreet flatly refused to consider the matter and answered: " 'General Lee's orders are to attack up the Emmitsburg road.' " Firmly convinced of the correctness of his suggestion, Hood repeated his request and again it was denied with the same answer. Longstreet, who never referred the protest to Lee, finally came to Hood in person as his troops were starting to move forward. In response to Hood's expression of concern and regret at not being allowed to modify the nature of his attack, Longstreet only said: " 'We must obey the orders of General Lee.' " Hood turned and rode forward with his line under a heavy fire.[110]

Before Longstreet had completed the deployment of his infantry, Colonel Alexander had his artillery ready for the assault. He sent Major M. W. Henry's battalion to the Confederate right flank with Hood's division, and massing fifty-four guns from his own battalion and that of Colonel H. C. Cabell [111] he formed a line along War-field Ridge west and southwest of the Peach Orchard. Covering a front of about half a mile, they bore directly on the Peach Orchard and could mount a cross fire on the Union lines converging at that point.[112] Alexander boldly ran his batteries within a close range of 1,800 feet [113] to make what he hoped would be "short, sharp and decisive" work of destroying the enemy's artillery. By coming in close he also reduced the disparity the Confederates suffered in the quality of their ammunition. Alexander thought that if ever he could "overwhelm and crush them," this was the time.[114]

As the Confederates finally stood poised and ready at four o'clock to strike at the enemy, their main line stretched from the front of Big Round Top along Warfield and Seminary Ridges to the Cham-bersburg Pike. Then it curved through and beyond the town to con-form to the Union position on Culp's Hill, for a total distance of ap-proximately five and a half miles. The Union line at the same hour was about four miles long. Hood's division occupied the right flank of the Confederate position, and next to it was McLaws'. Hill's corps held the center of the line with General Richard H. Ander-son's division on the right, Pender's on the left, and Heth's in re-serve. Rodes's division of Ewell's corps stood in the streets on the west side of town and Early's on the east side, and out on the Han-over road Johnson's division formed the left flank of Ewell's corps and of the whole army.[115] Lee had thirty infantry brigades ready for action and four in reserve, while Meade had thirty-five in line, eight in reserve, and eight more approaching the battleground.[116] But twelve brigades which Meade kept at the front had been so badly battered in the engagement on the first day that they num-bered only a third to two-thirds of their effective strength when they entered the battle. The brigades in the Confederate army which had suffered the most as a result of the previous day's fight Lee kept in reserve. The disparity in strength in the two armies therefore was not as great as it seemed.

According to the Confederate plan, when Longstreet started the main attack Hill's corps was to play a role similar to Ewell's. Lee ordered him to threaten the Federals' center so as to prevent them from taking advantage of their interior lines and shifting reinforce-ments to either wing. General Anderson, however, was to do more than make a demonstration. Lee directed him and his division to participate actively in the assault. Approximately twenty thousand infantry thus comprised the major attacking force against the Union left flank, while the rest of Lee's army was to make threatening gestures against the enemy. In the case of Ewell's corps, the gestures were to be converted into a real attack if the opportunity developed.[117]

None of the Confederate leaders explained clearly in what order Lee expected to use the three divisions for his offensive. Alexander did not remember having heard of "any conference or discussions among our generals at this time as to the best formations & tactics in making our attacks. . . ." Even then the plans struck Alexander as "peculiar," and he did not think they were of the best.[118] His doubts about a careful consideration of tactics might have been true of Longstreet's divisions, but not of Anderson's. Both Hill and Anderson understood that the latter would put his troops "into action by brigades," [119] which in tactics is called the echelon or progressive type of attack.[120] Anderson knew that Longstreet's line would be nearly at right angles to his and he would not advance his brigades until Longstreet's troops had progressed far enough to connect with his right.[121] Longstreet never said in what order he proposed to move his divisions.[122] As the battle finally evolved, Hood's men hit the enemy first, to be followed by McLaws'. If Longstreet planned it that way, his orders to McLaws to attack the Peach Orchard before Hood's line advanced are inexplicable. Perhaps he wanted to seize this height as the first step in his offensive. Nowhere in his various accounts, however, did he state or even intimate such an intention, nor did anyone else among the Confederates say anything about it.

Lee's offensive, based upon attacks in progression until it developed into a giant pincers squeezing both enemy flanks, required careful coordination and expert timing. If this plan was sound, which is debatable, there was still the question of whether the army was equal to the task.

XV

THE FIGHT FOR LITTLE ROUND TOP
AND THE PEACH ORCHARD

ALL DURING the morning of Thursday, July 2, as both Lee and Meade planned their operations and deployed their troops, advance detachments of both armies kept up a lively fire. Union skirmishers formed a long line stretching to the left and forward of the main position on Cemetery Hill. Keeping well covered, they lay flat on the ground in meadows and cornfields, shooting at will at rebels barely visible in the distance. Now and then some Confederate skirmishers suddenly arose from the ground and with a yell rushed forward, firing as they came. If they approached too close to Union outposts and forced them back, the nearest batteries announced their presence by sending out a warning shot or two to discourage any further advance. Such impetuosity on a hot day seemed a useless waste of energy, but rebel officers did learn the location of some guns, which was probably their real purpose anyway.[1]

These encounters, though tentative in character, were but a prelude to more ominous developments. Early in the afternoon General Sickles, sensing an imminent attack, gradually advanced his Third Corps to the battle line he had delineated to General Hunt in the morning. He got General Birney's division into position first. It faced southwest at a forty-five degree angle to the Emmitsburg road, with Brigadier General Charles K. Graham's brigade holding the angle at the Peach Orchard, Brigadier General J. H. Hobart Ward's protecting Devil's Den, and Colonel P. Regis De Trobriand's filling the space between the two.[2] Birney had just about completed the deployment of the division at 3:30 P.M. when he and the signal-men on Little Round Top detected enemy columns massing to the south of the Union line. Birney immediately ordered a battery at the Peach Orchard and one at Devil's Den to open fire,[3] but Colonel Alexander's artillery refused to be baited and remained silent until the colonel received word about 4:00 P.M. that "all was ready" in Longstreet's corps. Then at his signal fifty-four guns answered the two pesky Union batteries and with a roar raked the entire length of the enemy line.[4] Soon Birney saw Confederate infantry rise up from the grass.[5] Covered by what he termed a "cloud" of skirmishers, they advanced in closed ranks,[6] carefully regaining them whenever stone or rail fences caused them to break. They were the men of Hood's division, led by Law's Alabamians on the right and Brigadier General J. B. Robertson's Texans on the left. Moving briskly, sometimes at "double-quick", the men pulled away, contrary to Long-street's orders, from the Emmitsburg road and headed toward Big Round Top three-quarters of a mile to the east so as to envelop the left flank of Sickles' line, which was resting on the end of the ridge at Devil's Den.[7] As Law's brigade approached Big Round Top it wheeled obliquely to the left; some of the men went up over the west face and the crest of the hill, while the rest poured through the gorge of Plum Run in the rear of Sickles' corps. Robertson's men kept close to Law's left and with loud shouts and yells hit Ward's brigade head-on above the den.[8]

The magnificent advance of Hood's division commenced what Longstreet later pronounced to be the "best three hours' fighting ever done by any troops on any battlefield." [9] It was not, however, a simple matter of his infantrymen making one great charge and sweeping everything before them, as Longstreet implied. Actually the issue was long in doubt and the price of victory excessively high. In seeking explanations Southern writers have dwelt upon mistakes in Confederate generalship without clearly showing the connection between them and the fierce resistance made by Yankee soldiers. The stubbornness of their defense and the accuracy of their fire quickly cut down an unusually large number of commanding officers,[10] as well as forcing errors in Confederate tactics. Yankee officers leading veteran troops and wise in the ways of Civil War fighting took advantage of the rugged terrain and the experience of their men to make every shot count. As an example of these methods,

❧ *Map 8* ❧

THE BATTLE FOR LITTLE ROUND TOP
AND THE PEACH ORCHARD,
4:00–7:00 P.M., JULY 2

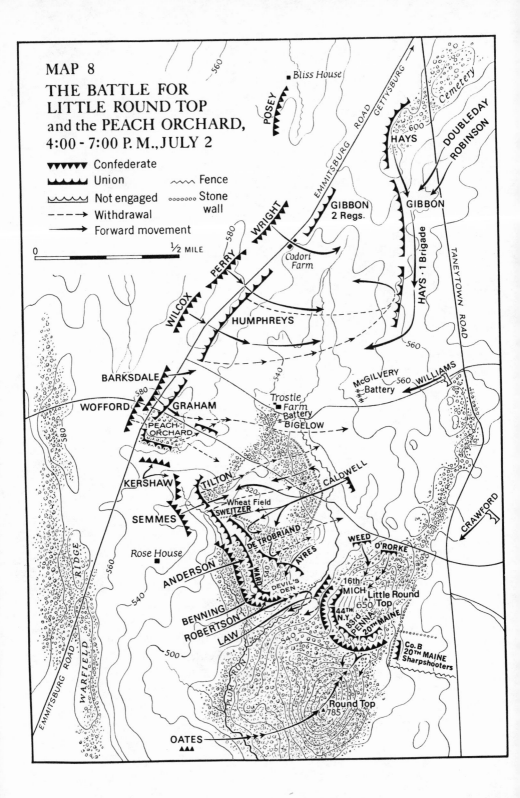

MAP 8

THE BATTLE FOR
LITTLE ROUND TOP
and the PEACH ORCHARD,
4:00 - 7:00 P.M., JULY 2

Confederate
Union   Fence
Not engaged   Stone wall
Withdrawal
Forward movement

0   ½ MILE

General Ward told how he had ordered his men to hold their fire until the enemy came within 600 feet of their positions, 150 feet less than the effective range of a Civil War rifle. Obediently they waited and then in response to his command they fired as a brigade. The volley threw the onrushing enemy into confusion and checked the advance long enough for the Federal soldiers to reload and shoot again. Taking advantage of the enemy's disorder, Ward counterattacked to get possession of a stone wall. When the enemy received reinforcements, his single line recoiled and retreated a short distance, only to attack again. Thus the two forces seesawed back and forth in their fight for the stone wall.[11]

Though in his battle report Ward may have succumbed to the tendency of most commanders to make extravagant claims and exaggerate the prowess of his men, Confederate officers frankly admitted the fierceness of Union resistance along the whole left flank. What impressed General Robertson most was the "heavy and destructive" fire from Union artillery and sharpshooters, to which his men were exposed for half a mile as they advanced across the fields southwest of Devil's Den.[12] Colonel Alexander too was amazed at the enemy's performance. At the start of his cannonade he had had a few more guns than his opponent, some of them of heavier caliber, and the advantage of position which afforded him a better concentration of fire. He had expected to overwhelm the enemy batteries in short order, but they "really surprised" him, he said, both in the "number of guns they developed" and the way in which they "stuck to them."[13] He adjudged the battle to be "the severest & bloodiest artillery fight" he had ever seen; four companies of his battalion lost in forty minutes as much as the whole battalion had lost at Sharpsburg, the "bloodiest of all previous battles."[14] The engagement was described by one reliable Northern reporter as "by all odds the most sanguinary . . . yet chronicled in the annals of war, considering its duration." The armies, he said, fought "at very short range, and for three long hours the . . . [roar] of musketry was incessant." He had heard more noise in other battles, but with both sides moving and deploying troops quickly he never saw or heard of such "desperate tenacious fighting."[15]

Despite the bravery and skill of the veterans of the Third Corps, serious weaknesses in their position and the severity of the Confederate attacks soon made the situation critical. The first crisis and perhaps the most crucial one developed in the sector at the extreme left end of Sickles' line where almost a separate engagement occurred. Very properly it has been called the attack and defense of Little Round Top, and romantic tradition has accorded General G. K. Warren the glory of the main role in the drama enacted on the rocky spur with which his name has become imperishably linked. An admiring newspaperman reported having watched him perform his duties in a "most gallant and heroic manner, riding with the utmost confidence over fields swept by the enemy's fire, seemingly everywhere present, directing, aiding, and cheering the troops." [16] Because Meade and Warren had sized up developments in the engagement in the same way, Meade chose him to act as his alter ego in crucial moments of the battle, and Warren rendered services for which Meade and the country were to be eternally grateful.[17]

The two generals became concerned about the security of the Union left flank when they learned of Sickles' advance toward the Emmitsburg road. Meade directed Warren to ride posthaste to Little Round Top, which he recognized as a key position in the line, and investigate the situation.[18] Accompanied by two lieutenants of engineers and some orderlies, Warren mounted quickly and sped to the hill.[19] To his dismay, except for two or three officers of the signal corps he found no troops there. Looking off to the west about a mile away he could see the Confederate battle lines stretching far enough south along the Emmitsburg road to overlap Sickles' position. There was no time to lose; suddenly messengers seemed to be riding everywhere at once. Warren sent a dispatch to Meade,[20] suggesting that a division occupy the hill immediately, and another one to Sickles asking for help. Sickles replied that he had no troops to spare; he needed all of them to defend his own position.[21] Meade, who had previously told General Sykes to support the Third Corps, ordered him now to bring his whole Fifth Corps to the extreme Union left and be quick about it.[22] Fearful that Sykes would not arrive in time to meet the anticipated attack, Meade overruled Sickles and ordered Humphreys to move his division to the threatened position. At the moment he received the message Humphreys with colors flying was marching his men in line of battle up the slope to the Emmitsburg road; without a hitch he had his division turn and head for Little Round Top to the left. When Meade countermanded the order upon hearing of Sykes's arrival, Humphreys again reversed his division with the "precision of parade" and directed it back to the road. The skill of these troops and their commander in smoothly executing a complicated maneuver while subjected to enemy artillery fire drew admiring comments from their comrades watching them from Cemetery Ridge.[23]

Back on Little Round Top Warren, waiting impatiently for the arrival of reinforcements, decided to go himself and locate Sykes and his Fifth Corps. He found Sykes reconnoitering behind the Third Corps lines in the woods west of the Wheatfield, and he quickly explained to him the need of sending a force immediately to protect Little Round Top. Sykes and General James Barnes had led the First Division, consisting of three brigades, from the Baltimore Pike along a road running past Power's Hill to the Taneytown road. After going south a short way on that road they had cut up over Cemetery Ridge and halted the division in some low ground northeast of the Wheatfield while they rode ahead to examine the battle line. Sykes responded quickly to Warren's call for help by dispatching an order to Barnes, who had gone off to another part of the lines, to send a brigade to Little Round Top. As luck would have it, Colonel Strong Vincent, a Pennsylvania lawyer turned warrior, spied one of Sykes's aides galloping along in search of Barnes. Hailing him, Vincent demanded to know what was up, for he was preparing to go into action with his brigade of four regiments. The messenger said he could not find Barnes and wondered where he was. At Vincent's insistence he reluctantly revealed the contents of the order for one of Barnes's brigades to occupy "yonder hill," the name of which he did not know. Vincent recognized at a glance the strategic importance of the hill and with no further ado said he would hurry there with his men. It was a bold decision, for he risked court-martial by taking his brigade away from the division without Barnes's permission.[24]

Vincent sprang to his saddle, ordered his bugler to sound the advance, waved his sword in the direction of Little Round Top, and went off at a gallop. His brigade followed at "double-quick" across the field to the road leading up the north shoulder of the hill. With Colonel Joshua L. Chamberlain and his hearty men of the 20th Maine regiment in the lead, the brigade dashed over Plum Run, up the ridge, and on to the rocky crest of the hill. They ducked and stepped lively as Confederate shells burst overhead in the treetops, among the rocks beside them, and in their ranks. Even before they reached the top the twenty-six-year-old Vincent with the skill and precision of a professional had reconnoitered and decided how best to place his slim brigade of 1,350 muskets. If he should keep his men on the crest of the hill, he thought the Confederates could easily work themselves around, turn his flank, and come in on his rear. It would be better to align his regiments along the lower edges of the southern and western slopes, thus cutting down the enemy's room to maneuver. He gave his orders, and as Chamberlain's men came stumbling down the southern face of the hill, Vincent was there waiting to point out their position at the end of a spur with the ground falling away on three sides.[25] This was the extreme left of Meade's main line, and it would be up to the 20th Maine, Vincent said, to beat off enemy efforts to crush it. His last words to Chamberlain were a command to "hold that ground at all hazards." [26] "Josh" Chamberlain willingly met the challenge. Trained for the classroom and the pulpit, this man of peace had an unusual affinity for combat, and now his blood was up; there would be no retreating today.[27]

The occupation of Little Round Top at the right time and right place by Vincent's brigade was the result of a combination of circumstances and a stroke of rare good luck for which no one person in the Union high command could claim the credit, and in fact none tried to. Warren did observe the danger to the position, and knowing the Fifth Corps to be on its way to the Federal left, he took the trouble to find Sykes and urge him to protect it. Sykes did not need much urging because Meade had personally instructed him to pin down the extreme left. Once Sykes had agreed to send a brigade to occupy Little Round Top, Warren rode away and very properly left the execution of the movement to him. What Warren did and where he went immediately after this encounter is not known. According to his story, he was back on Little Round Top near the signal officers by the time Vincent's brigade arrived, yet he did not see it coming. There seems to be no doubt that in approaching the hill the brigade crossed the open ground to the west, for Chamberlain three days after the battle clearly described the route it took. If Warren stood where he said he did and was anxiously awaiting the arrival of the regiments, it is inconceivable that he did not see their approach. The solution to the enigma must be that he was away from the hill longer than he or anyone else remembered.[28]

As for Sykes's role in seizing Little Round Top, he deserved credit for having sent a stream of reinforcements to Vincent. He had perceived the military importance of the height when he examined the Union left just before the fighting started, but his first concern had been for the safety of Captain James E. Smith's 4th Battery, New York Light, at Devil's Den. He had suggested that if Birney would place more of his men in support of the battery, he himself would fill the gap with two brigades of Barnes's division. Sykes claimed no honors for the measures taken to hold Little Round Top. Instead he gave Warren a complimentary bow for its successful defense,[29] though Warren in turn belittled the part he had played. He denied having had anything to do with posting Vincent's brigade, and rightly so.[30] Through sheer chance Vincent had spied Sykes's messenger on his way to Barnes, and without wasting precious minutes looking for Barnes, he had taken the initiative and placed his men in position just before the Confederates came pouring through the gorge of Plum Run.

As General Law led his brigade across the fields toward the left end of the Federal line, he shifted his regiments about to meet unforeseen obstacles as they arose. At the beginning of the advance Colonel William C. Oates's 15th Alabama regiment had occupied the center of the battle line. Suddenly it found itself on the extreme right after Law had moved his two end regiments by left flank across the rear of the 15th to assist General Robertson in his attack on Devil's Den.[31] From then on Oates's troubles began. In addition to the increased responsibilities of guarding the flank, he regretted having to advance before a detail of twenty-two men who had gone to a spring to fill canteens for the regiment could return with the water. As years later he looked back to that hot afternoon, he was convinced that the lack of water "contributed largely" to his failure to take Little Round Top.[32] More realistically, it was the major shift in the position of his regiment in Law's battle line that led to his defeat, because it brought his 15th Alabama into what proved to be a famous encounter with the 20th Maine.

With the 47th Alabama on their left Oates's men pressed on, brushed aside a detachment of Major Homer R. Stoughton's 2nd

United States Sharpshooters posted behind a stone wall, and started the difficult climb up Big Round Top by "catching to the bushes and crawling over the immense boulders." The sharpshooters, slowly retreating, kept up a persistent fire from behind rocks and crags. Just before Oates reached the highest part of the hill, the Federals suddenly evaporated from his front "as though commanded by a magician." [33] This disappearing act fooled him into believing that a large force confronted him. When he received Law's order to make a left wheel with his regiment and join in the attack on Devil's Den, he refused to obey for fear that in executing the movement he would expose his flank and rear to the elusive foe. Another difficulty was that the 47th Alabama kept crowding his left, causing confusion and making it hard for him to maneuver in the way Law had directed.[34]

As Oates's men lay panting from their exertions, Captain L. R. Terrell of General Law's staff rode up and inquired why Oates had halted. As an excuse the colonel offered his considered opinion on the strategic importance of Big Round Top and the need for the Confederates to hold it. There is the faint suspicion that hindsight and not a careful reconnaissance at the time prompted him to make his observation. Such speculations were none of Terrell's concern, however, and he merely transmitted orders for Oates to press on, as obviously the enemy was ahead. At Oates's command the regiment got quickly into line and without skirmishers to precede it went crashing down the northern and northeastern slopes of the hill.[35] The Confederates came out in the level and thinly wooded hollow between the Round Tops [36] and immediately saw at a distance of about six hundred feet to the northeast "an extensive park of Federal ordnance wagons." [37] It looked large at the time and undoubtedly became bigger over the years, but no matter how large, the fact was that there were some wagons and they were attached to Lieutenant Charles E. Hazlett's Battery D, 5th United States Artillery, which was soon to play an important role in the fight for Little Round Top.[38] At first Oates thought nothing stood in his way to seizing them and roaming through the rear of the Union lines. Then he received an unpleasant surprise. What he called a "heavy force" of enemy posted behind some large rocks upon a slight elevation [39] poured into his ranks "a most destructive fire." [40] He thought Stoughton's sharpshooters had evaded him and were now taking a stand in a second line on the lower slopes of Little Round Top.[41]

But it was a much larger and more formidable group of men that had arrived just in time to greet him with a volley. It was Chamberlain's 20th Maine.

Oates had the advantage of numbers, 644 riflemen to 360 men from "down Maine," but Chamberlain offset this superiority with strength of position, iron determination, and better tactics. Each opponent had one of his flanks covered by a companion unit, the 47th Alabama with between 210 and 290 muskets on Oates's left, and the 83rd Pennsylvania with 375 riflemen on Chamberlain's right.[42] Though all the troops became bitterly involved, the heaviest fighting developed along Chamberlain's front because Oates concentrated the strength of his regiment on his right in a supreme effort to crush the left of the 20th Maine. Chamberlain, worried about the possibility of such a move, had sent Company B under Captain Walter G. Morrill forward to form a skirmish line and extend it across the hollow as protection for his left flank. Before the company could deploy, however, brisk firing broke out on its right, and Oates's men appeared marching rapidly to the east through the ravine. Cut off from their comrades, Morrill's men ran and hid behind a stone wall which closed the eastern end of the hollow. There they found a little over a dozen United States Sharpshooters who had previously pestered Oates as he went over Big Round Top and had fooled him into thinking they were a large force.[43] It was a happy meeting and would have important consequences, for which Chamberlain's soldierly instincts deserved considerable credit.

When Chamberlain saw how Oates's attack threatened to turn his flank and in so doing unhinge the Union defense of Little Round Top, he stretched his line to the left and then refused the end companies at right angles to the rest of the regiment. He had no fears about his right, for he had great confidence in the men of the 83rd Pennsylvania. As he later testified, they "behaved with admirable steadiness . . . [and] their heroic fortitude enabled us to accomplish our great results."[44] Through the confusion, noise, and blinding smoke of combat Chamberlain kept firm control over his men, quickly parrying the blows of his adversary who, after regrouping his forces with every repulse, struck the Union line time and again.[45] Finally the men on both sides reached the limits of their endurance, for they had been locked in combat for many hours. Oates saw the 47th Alabama on his left give way and knew that his own men had had about enough fighting for the day.[46] Chamber-lain too recognized signs of exhaustion in his men, who had run low in energy and bullets. Some of the more defiant gripped their muskets ready to swing them as clubs when the enemy seemed ready to renew the assault. Sounds of battle to the rear of the 20th Maine reached a new crescendo, and Chamberlain feared the enemy had surrounded all of Little Round Top. For him there was only one thing left to do: a swift counterattack. He ordered the bayonet. To his veterans the word was enough. "It ran like fire along the line, from man to man," he reported, "and rose into a shout, with which they sprang forward upon the enemy, now not 30 yards away." In a beautifully executed move Chamberlain used the right of his line as the shaft and swung the left as the bar of a flail.[47] Knocked off balance by this sudden move, the surprised Confederates in the front ranks dropped their guns and surrendered. The others started off hastily toward Big Round Top. They had gone but a few paces when a sheet of flame burst out on their right. Captain Morrill's skirmishers and Stoughton's wandering sharpshooters rose up from behind the stone wall and smote them with a deadly volley. The effect was devastating. Oates and his men, having visions of Union soldiers swarming out from behind the hundreds of rocks strewn along the valley and slopes, ran for their lives.[48] Chamberlain's thin line followed them, picking up the slow-footed and the weak as prisoners.[49]

The valor of the 20th Maine and the other regiments in the brigade had stopped the Confederate advance except on the right where Law's men, strengthened by two regiments of Robertson's Texans, began curling around the flank and pushing up the west slope of Little Round Top.[50] The weakest regiment of the brigade held that end of Vincent's line.[51] Its commanding officer, Lieuten-ant Colonel Norval E. Welch, who had a good war record, was having a bad day. As Confederate pressure on his regiment in-creased and became overwhelming, he and forty-five of his men left the line and sought safety in the rear of the hill. Welch afterward claimed the unfortunate move arose from a misunderstanding.[52] When Vincent saw signs of disintegration on the right of his line, he rushed forward and while cheering his men on fell mortally wounded.[53] For a moment it seemed as if the Confederate drive to seize Little Round Top would succeed after all.

Here the smoke of battle clears away and reveals again the calm and reassuring figure of General Warren, who had arrived on the scene no one knows when. A short time before Vincent fell, when Lieutenant Charles E. Hazlett appeared with his battery of rifled cannon, Warren helped some stragglers from the Third Corps haul one of the pieces over the projecting rocks on the summit. Hazlett figured that the bark of his guns would give added confidence to the Union infantry on the slope just below him, though the shot and shell would fly harmlessly over the heads of the enemy climbing the hill. An unexpected benefit was that the battery did real harm to the Confederates attacking Devil's Den.[54]

As the Union line began to crumble on Little Round Top, Warren, vested with the authority of Meade's chief representative, emerged as the right man at the right place at the right time. He stood near the top of the hill, but the thick smoke obscured the scene of fighting and he was not able to see the condition of Vincent's brigade. Then a call from Colonel James C. Rice,[55] who had succeeded the fallen Vincent, made him realize that immediate help was needed. Seeing a column of troops starting out on the road to the Peach Orchard, he and his aide, Lieutenant W. A. Roebling, quickly rode down to intercept them. To Warren's delight they were men of his old brigade in Brigadier General R. B. Ayres's Second Division of the Fifth Corps, now commanded by Brigadier General Stephen H. Weed.[56] Sykes had ordered them to reinforce Vincent on Little Round Top, but before they could get there Sickles had interfered by sending one of his aides to divert them to another part of the battlefield.[57] Weed had hurried ahead to get in touch with Sickles and select a position for his men near the Peach Orchard. He left his adjutant, Captain A. S. Marvin, in charge of the column with the understanding that in case of an emergency he would turn over the command to the next ranking officer, who was Colonel Patrick H. O'Rorke of the 140th New York regiment.[58] As Warren came plunging down the hill he called out to Colonel O'Rorke, whom he knew, that the troops were needed on Little Round Top, not somewhere else, and he ordered all of them to be brought up the hill immediately. Warren's few words of explanation were enough for O'Rorke, and in short order he had his regiment scrambling up the north side of the hill and onto the top. Before the rest of the brigade could follow, Warren's brother Edgar, who was one of Weed's aides, rode

395

up and wanted to know what was going on; Weed, he said, was waiting for his men as reinforcements for Sickles. Warren told him of the crisis on Little Round Top, but agreed to let the other regiments go if he could keep O'Rorke's,[59] which was one of the largest, numbering 526 officers and men.[60] Upon reaching the top of the hill, O'Rorke at Warren's urging did not take time to align his men but ordered them to follow him pell-mell down the southern face of it. As they met the enemy O'Rorke fell instantly killed by a fusilade of shots, but his men hurled back the advancing foe, and he died a hero.[61]

By the time the Confederates could regroup to renew the attack, the other regiments of Weed's brigade upon orders of General Sykes had rejoined their comrades of the 140th New York. Sykes had seen Weed's men going away from Little Round Top toward the Peach Orchard, and he quickly sent an aide ahead to find Weed and instruct him to disregard Sickles' orders and countermarch his men to Little Round Top. Their return and the arrival of the other brigades of Ayres's division firmly anchored the key point in the Union line and discouraged further attempts of the Southerners to take it.[62] By that time the Confederate drive had lost its punch; heavy casualties among field officers, the intermingling of the regiments of Law's and Robertson's brigades, and the rugged character of the terrain had caused confusion and a breakdown of discipline among the rank and file.[63]

The price of victory for Northern arms at Little Round Top had been high. With Vincent and Weed mortally wounded and Hazlett and O'Rorke killed outright, the loss in commanding officers was especially heavy. Warren too had been hit while talking with Hazlett on the hill, but his was only a slight wound.[64]

Assured of the safety of Little Round Top, Warren left it to rejoin General Meade near the center of the battlefield, where another crisis was now at hand. During the bitter fight for Little Round Top Warren had seen the whole Union line to the front and right of the hill yield and melt away before the enemy's assaults.[65] What happened to cause the collapse of Union resistance there neither he nor anyone since has been able to tell exactly. The peculiar features of the battleground, the continual shifting of regiments from position to position, the constant stream of reinforcements, and the lack of unified command conspire to obscure the order of events leading to the catastrophe.

In describing the Union battle line as established by Sickles it is convenient to say that it stretched from Devil's Den straight northwest to the Peach Orchard. Actually there was no continuous line connecting the two points, for it changed repeatedly with the fortunes of the battle. At its beginning near the den it faced more or less toward the southwest following the irregular contours of two rocky and partly barren ridges on both sides of the west branch of Plum Run. When within 1,000 feet of the Peach Orchard the line curved sharply to the east; then north to the Fairfield crossroad; then west along the road and through a narrow, shallow depression with open fields on both sides to the higher ground of the Peach Orchard, which occupied the southeast corner at the intersection of the Fairfield crossroad and the Emmitsburg road. Here the line formed a sharp right angle to the northeast and continued along the Emmitsburg road toward Gettysburg.[66] With all of these curves and turns several regiments occupied positions at right angles to each other, with consequent difficulties in firing their weapons and controlling their movements. As for the artillery, the best positions were along the Fairfield crossroad and at the Peach Orchard. Four batteries totalling twenty guns were massed here with their barrels pointing west and south.[67]

When, by Sickles' orders, General Birney moved his division to establish his new front, he kept his center brigade, the Third under Colonel De Trobriand, in column by regiments ready to support the other two brigades on the flanks. De Trobriand had five regiments numbering in all about 1,800 officers and men, and before long they were shifted about to fill gaps in the line on both sides of him. Two were used to strengthen Ward's Second Brigade in the area of Devil's Den and the gorge,[68] although De Trobriand could not meet all of Ward's demands for aid and at the same time pretend to defend his own part of the front. Ward was extremely vulnerable to a flanking attack, and he had need of many more than the 1,500 or so men he brought into action. Two of his regiments had been temporarily assigned to General Graham's First Brigade [69] which occupied the salient at the Peach Orchard and was exposed to assaults from two directions. Because of the peculiarities of his position Graham

397

required more assistance for his 1,800 men than the other brigades in the division could furnish him.[70] Since Humphreys with about the same number of men as Birney defended a narrower front, Sickles detached Colonel George C. Burling's brigade, the smallest of Humphreys' three, and placed it in reserve for Birney's use.[71] Burling brought six regiments with him, which altogether had between 1,500 and 1,600 officers and men.[72] With the arrival of these men on his sector to back up his three brigades, Birney had under his immediate command about 7,300 officers and infantry-men.

During the course of the fighting Birney either ordered or permitted the cannibalization of De Trobriand's and Burling's brigades. In addition to the two regiments of De Trobriand which went to help Ward, one was sent in support of Graham, so that De Trobriand had left only two regiments, one of them quite weak, with which to hold the center of the Union position. Burling soon ended up in an even worse situation; he had no troops at all to command. One of his regiments received orders to return to Humphreys, two reinforced Graham, and three fought along Ward's part of the line.[73]

Just where these reserve units went, the times when they became engaged, and what roles they played are facts impossible to determine precisely. The participants themselves had trouble remembering exactly what had happened. The comment of an officer in the 17th Maine of De Trobriand's brigade is perhaps typical. "We were marched and countermarched till I lost all direction," he said, "and it being so near noon the sun, the only guide we had, and which we had hardly time to consult, didn't aid us much." [74] The combat effectiveness of these detailed regiments was not improved by being removed from their old commands and assigned to new ones. There are indications that some of the regiments never became firmly attached to their new commands. Instead they remained relatively free of authority other than their own unless Birney or a member of his staff happened to come by. In such situations coordinated effort became difficult, if not impossible.[75] Burling, having been deprived of his troops, became a supernumerary, and his talents as a commander were lost at a moment when huge casualties among field officers seriously reduced the efficiency of many units in Birney's part of the line. With nothing to do, he and his staff reported back to

Humphreys for instructions.[76] In reviewing the battle on July 2 Humphreys snorted in disgust at Sickles' and Birney's generalship. "Had my Division been left intact," he wrote, "I should have driven the enemy back, but this ruinous *habit* (it don't deserve the name of system) of putting troops in position & then drawing off its reserves & second line to help others, who if similarly disposed would need no such help, is disgusting." [77]

General Sickles not only rearranged the Third Corps in an effort to strengthen the left section of its line. He also secured permission from army headquarters to draw on General Caldwell's division of the Second Corps to support Humphreys on the Emmitsburg road, and to borrow a brigade from the Fifth Corps. Subsequently Sykes received a message from Meade personally, after the Confederates opened with their artillery fire but before they launched their infantry attack, in which the commanding general ordered him to throw all of his corps to the Union left and to hold it at "all hazards." [78] Sykes considered that this order relieved his troops from "any call from the commander of the Third Corps." [79] Sickles and Birney remained unaware of the changed status of the Fifth Corps and persisted in considering its role to be subordinate to that of the Third and its commander. As the Fifth moved to the front Sykes resisted the importunities of various staff officers from Sickles' headquarters for assistance, on the grounds that the "key to the battlefield" was entrusted to his keeping and he "could not and would not jeopardize it by a division of . . . [his] forces." [80] Sykes had perhaps a clearer idea than did the other two officers of what Meade had in mind for him to do. Meade's order for him to send a brigade to Sickles had come while the Fifth Corps was massed as a reserve in the rear of the Twelfth Corps. Upon news of the arrival of the Sixth Corps, Meade ordered the Fifth to move to the Union left and act as a reserve there.[81] Presumably he expected it to cooperate with the Third as an autonomous military unit—at least that is the way Sykes regarded its function—rather than to be used in a piecemeal fashion to bolster the Third Corps. If so, either Meade did not make his purposes clear to Sickles and Birney, or they chose to run affairs their own way, for after Sykes's rebuffs to requests for aid they still presumed to order units of the Fifth Corps for use by the Third.[82]

When Sykes came to survey the area around Little Round Top,

Devil's Den, and the Wheatfield, just before the arrival of Barnes's First Division, he saw the impossibility of keeping his corps intact. In conversation with Birney he suggested that the First Brigade under Colonel William S. Tilton and the Second under Colonel Jacob B. Sweitzer could be used to plug the gap in the Third Corps line so Birney could shift regiments from De Trobriand to reinforce Ward. Meanwhile Vincent had gone to take position on the slopes of Little Round Top.[83] Birney admitted in his battle report that Sykes reached his left "opportunely, and protected that flank,"[84] but seven months later he changed his tune. He accused Sykes of delaying his arrival for an hour to give his men time to make coffee and rest from the fatigue of the previous night's march. This charge continued to plague Sykes in postwar reviews of the battle, despite evidence that he moved his men quickly to the left of the Union line once he received Meade's orders.[85]

The arrival of the two brigades from Barnes's division, though together they mustered only about 1,700 officers and men,[86] brought welcome strength to the center of Birney's line, but also created a serious problem in the chain of command. Sykes, who personally posted them, did not turn them over to Birney for further orders. Instead he kept them under Barnes's direction as an extension of his own front, though their positions, which were half a mile west of Sykes's main line as it finally formed around Little Round Top, in fact constituted a part of the line held by the Third Corps.[87] Stationed on a wooded knoll in the rear of De Trobriand's right, they only partially closed the gap between him and Graham at the Peach Orchard, as no infantry was located nearby to support their right flank.[88] They were equally unsure about their left, for at no time did they see or know the whereabouts of De Trobriand's brigade.[89] Their situation revealed a want of coordination between Birney and Sykes. As the battle along the left wing reached its full fury, the need for someone with authority above and beyond that of a corps commander became painfully apparent.

The result was confusion and conflict in orders. Sickles and Birney continued to regard all reinforcements from whatever corps as coming within the province of their command. Desperate for help, they seized units as they or their aides came upon them and, without permission from anyone, took them off for their own purposes. In this manner they diverted Weed's brigade from the spot where

Sykes had ordered it posted, and they placed two batteries of the Fifth Corps in their own sector of the front, much to the annoyance of everyone.[90] Then Meade ordered Hancock to send Caldwell's division to the assistance of General Sykes instead of Humphreys as previously arranged. Caldwell was specifically instructed to report to Sykes, not Sickles or Birney.[91] Hancock said later he did not know why Meade made this change, but guessed that perhaps the Fifth Corps had not as yet gotten to the battleground and that Meade wanted Sykes to place Caldwell's men on Little Round Top until it did.[92] Hancock was unaware that by the time Caldwell received his orders to move from his position on Cemetery Ridge, part of the Fifth Corps was already fighting on Little Round Top and part in the timber west of the Wheatfield. In obedience to his instructions Caldwell sent an aide to locate Sykes, but he could not find him. As his division approached the Wheatfield, a staff officer who Caldwell thought was Lieutenant Colonel Fred T. Locke, Sykes's assistant adjutant general, met it and directed it to its place in line. Caldwell later reported his position to have been between the right of the Fifth and the left of the Third Corps, but he was wrong.[93] Actually his division went into action in the part of the line held by Ward's men and De Trobriand's brigades of the Third Corps, to replace rather than to reinforce them. Both Ward and De Trobriand later reported that their men had run out of ammunition and had had enough fighting for the day.[94] The staff officer whom Caldwell mentioned meeting was very likely Major H. E. Tremain, senior aide to General Sickles, for neither Sykes nor Locke said anything in his account about assigning a position to Caldwell's division.[95] Birney and Tremain, however, told how Tremain brought up a brigade, if not a division, from the Second Corps to drive the enemy from the center of Birney's line.[96] Here was another instance where officers of the Third Corps interfered with the movement of troops from other commands.

Apparently once Caldwell knew where his men were to go, he took charge of affairs on his immediate front, since no one of superior rank seemed to be around to direct operations. Through his own efforts he coordinated the movements of his division with units adjacent to it. Otherwise, as one of his officers commented later, if there was anyone directing the fighting on the left on the second day of the battle, it was "not especially visible."[97] Finally when

Meade learned that Sickles had been wounded, he put Hancock in command of the Third Corps as well as his own. The effect of this arrangement was to place him in control of all Union troops in the combat area from Cemetery Hill to Little Round Top. By that time it was no longer possible for even as able a general as Hancock to hold the line which the Third Corps had formed at the beginning of the engagement.[98] Why did Meade not make the change sooner? Perhaps he did not realize until it was too late how much he needed someone else besides Warren to assist him in exercising tactical control on a front in which thousands of troops from six corps fought over terrain so difficult in character as to prevent easy supervision of movements. Then too his recollection of Howard's unhappiness at being superseded by someone he outranked may have stopped Meade, should he have been so inclined, from placing Hancock over Sickles, his superior in rank.[99]

The Confederates too were having their difficulties. From the beginning their assault had not gone as planned. Contrary to orders Hood had moved his division away from the Emmitsburg road for the purpose of taking Little Round Top and outflanking the Union position on the heights of Devil's Den.[100] The timely and tenacious occupation of the hill by Union forces ruined this maneuver and prevented an unhinging of the extreme left of Sickles' line. Soon after launching his attack, Hood was carried off the field badly wounded, and the delay in transferring command to the ranking officer, General Law, who was up front fighting with his brigade, deprived his division of someone with authority to direct its movements when it met unforeseen resistance.[101]

In the course of the fighting Law's and Robertson's brigades overlapped so that Robertson found himself confronting Ward's brigade with but two of his four regiments. The others were cooperating with Law's men in a vain effort to dislodge Union troops from Little Round Top. Feeling hard pressed, Robertson sent a call to Hood for help, and then learning of his wound appealed to Longstreet for reinforcements. At the same time he hastened couriers to Brigadier Generals Henry L. Benning and George T. Anderson, urging them to hurry their brigades to his support. The dispatch to Benning apparently went astray, but as luck would have it so did his brigade, which arrived only by accident where it was wanted. A belt of timber had cut off Benning's view and caused him to follow Robertson instead of Law, as Hood had directed. As for Anderson, he had orders to hold his brigade in reserve on the left of the division so that he did not keep pace with the other units. He received Robertson's plea for help just as he saw the wounded Hood being carried off the field, and he immediately rushed his men forward. So far during the emergency created by Hood's wound there seems no evidence that Law had taken over. Probably because of the precarious nature of his situation Robertson took the initiative in bringing up the rest of Hood's division, and in so doing concentrated the attack against Ward's and De Trobriand's brigades along a front about 2,000 feet wide.[102] These two Federal brigades, though reinforced by regiments from Burling's brigade, finally succumbed to Confederate pressure and gave up the high ground around Devil's Den, as well as the southern end of the Wheatfield. A counterthrust by Caldwell's division of the Second Corps and Ayres's two brigades of regulars from the Fifth Corps stopped this forward movement of Hood's men and temporarily hurled them back.[103]

With Hood's division battling fiercely amidst the boulders, defiles, and woods of the broken ground east of the Emmitsburg road, Longstreet finally sent three of McLaws' brigades to its support. Their movement toward Little Round Top, instead of Cemetery Hill as originally planned, had been deferred for an indeterminate length of time for reasons never satisfactorily explained.[104] Contemporary observers blamed McLaws for the delay [105] and told the story of how Longstreet in his impatience to hurry things along threw himself at the head of Brigadier General W. T. Wofford's brigade and led it forward under "such a fire as has rarely been witnessed." [106] This incident may have signified nothing more than the fact that Longstreet could not resist getting into the thick of the battle, for he and many other generals were given to displays of this sort.[107] Nevertheless, Longstreet must be assigned the greater share of the responsibility for the shortcomings, if any, in McLaws' operations, since he kept close to the division all during the fighting and gave orders directly to McLaws.[108]

In explaining his delay McLaws said that Longstreet wanted him to wait until Hood's men had taken the heights of Devil's Den so they could be in position to support him when he advanced. Stiff enemy resistance upset the timetable for both generals, and in the end McLaws had to come to Hood's assistance instead of the reverse.[109] In spite of their success at Devil's Den Hood's men needed reinforcements to maintain their advantage. They had run into un-foreseen difficulties almost from the beginning of the battle, and several of the brigade commanders in order to overcome the enemy on their parts of the field had appealed directly to Longstreet for help.[110] The situation had become critical. Anderson's brigade had gotten into real trouble when Union soldiers from Barnes's division of the Fifth Corps suddenly appeared on its right flank, forcing it to withdraw to the rear. Longstreet decided the propitious moment had arrived for McLaws' division to enter the fray, and he gave the word for Kershaw's brigade to move forward from its position on the right of McLaws' line just south of the Fairfield crossroad. Fol-lowed by Brigadier General P. J. Semmes's men, Kershaw quickly swung into action to join the left of Anderson's brigade [111] He took his brigade across the Emmitsburg road and past the John P. Rose house and farm buildings and gradually changed front toward the left so as to hit the Peach Orchard from the southeast and the ridge from the southwest. Semmes's brigade formed a second line a hun-dred or so feet directly in his rear.[112]

When Colonel Tilton, commanding the First Brigade of Barnes's division, saw Kershaw's brigade coming from the direction of the Rose house, he knew he had to act quickly, for his right flank was threatened. Previously with his brigade facing south he had bent the 118th Pennsylvania at right angles to guard his right flank and rear, because between him and a battery about 1,000 feet to his right rear there was nothing. As Kershaw approached, Tilton quickly got his men out of this position and had them form a new line in a grove north of the Fairfield crossroad and facing westward toward the Peach Orchard.[113] Tilton's retrograde movement in turn ex-posed the right of Sweitzer's Second Brigade of Barnes's division to a flanking attack. Barnes peremptorily ordered Sweitzer to break off action against Anderson's brigade and retire, although Sweitzer evinced reluctance to give up "an elegant position" which he felt the "Old Second could have held . . . against considerable odds 'till the cows came.'" [114] His brigade retired to the same grove as Tilton's but on ground east of him and took a line parallel to the crossroad.[115]

Kershaw's advance, though delayed by numerous fences, the buildings of Rose's farm, swampy ground near it, and the raking fire of Union batteries, reached the ridge overlooking the Wheatfield and brought relief to Anderson's brigade before he himself encountered the enemy's infantry. The respite was only temporary, however, for Kershaw could see two battle lines moving rapidly across the Wheatfield in the direction of his right flank. These troops were men of Caldwell's Second and Third Brigades, tough veterans who hit Kershaw with sledgehammer blows, overlapped his right wing, and began pressing it back. His left regiments were having better luck, and one of them charged a battery just east of the Peach Orchard to silence it. But Kershaw desperately needed help on his right. He hurried back to fetch up Semmes's brigade, over which he had temporary command by virtue of his seniority in rank and perhaps the exigencies of combat. Though Semmes fell mortally wounded just as the brigade started forward,[116] it continued to advance in support of Kershaw's right until Caldwell's men stopped it.

Shortly thereafter [117] Brigadier General William Barksdale's Mississippians of McLaws' division, who had been impatiently awaiting the command to start from a position on Warfield Ridge just north of the Fairfield crossroad, at last sprang forward and crushed all opposition in their irresistible sweep. Over 100 feet to the rear Wofford's men had lain in wait, and as soon as Barksdale got in motion they came rushing forward to back him up. Once across the Emmitsburg road immediately to the north of the Peach Orchard, all of Barksdale's brigade except the 21st Mississippi under Colonel B. G. Humphreys angled to the left in conformity to Lee's original plan to hit Cemetery Ridge obliquely.[118] The 21st Mississippi and Wofford's men pushed straight ahead and became one jaw of a pincers, while the left regiments of Kershaw's brigade became the other; together they soon squeezed the Union troops out of the salient of the Peach Orchard. Kershaw's men then wheeled to the right and in line with Humphreys' Mississippians and Wofford's brigade used the Fairfield crossroad as a guide to the northern edge of the Wheatfield and from there on toward Little Round Top. As the Confederates overran the Peach Orchard they captured over 250 prisoners including General Graham.[119] Immediately in the wake of the Confederate charge Colonel E. P. Alexander called up Major James Dearing with eight guns of the Reserve to help beat down the obstinate resistance of Federal artillery.[120] Annoyed by rows of fences which slowed down his advance, Dearing looked about for help and saw several hundred prisoners streaming in. Galloping up to them and waving his sword, he roared out, "God damn you, pull down those fences." The prisoners rushed at them, each grabbed a rail, and in no time at all the fences "flew into the air." [121] With the way now cleared for them, the batteries charged within canister distance of the enemy and poured a deadly fire into their retreating ranks. The other guns under Alexander followed Dearing after the area had been cleared of dead horses, and formed a new line upon the position evacuated by the enemy.[122]

Thus whether by luck or good generalship, or a combination of both, Longstreet had turned the delay in McLaws' advance and the repulse of Hood's men into an advantage which threatened seven Union brigades with the disaster of a double envelopment.[123] When Barksdale bore to the left after crossing the Emmitsburg road, he endangered the Union General A. A. Humphreys' left flank. Caught between him and a succession of brigades from General "Dick" Anderson's division of Hill's corps, Humphreys' men battled for their lives. They could be of no further assistance to their comrades to the south and east of them. The isolation of Birney's sector of the line from the rest of the Union army became almost complete as Wofford's brigade and the 21st Mississippi regiment kept on for Little Round Top.

The timing of this charge by Longstreet's men was almost perfect, for by chance it took place just as General Caldwell had committed the last of his four brigades to the drive against the Confederates in Devil's Den, the Wheatfield, and the adjoining woods. When Caldwell first arrived on the battlefield three of his brigades had formed quickly and charged Hood's men. The First Brigade under Colonel Edward E. Cross advanced toward Devil's Den on the left and relieved Ward's brigade; on the right the Second under Colonel Patrick Kelly moved to the woods south of the Wheatfield. Still further to the right the Third under General Samuel K. Zook pushed on to the ridge west and southwest of the Wheatfield.[124] While Caldwell's brigades advanced, Barnes's two, which previously had been threatened by Kershaw's attack, retired through their ranks.[125] Before long Caldwell decided to relieve a part of his First Brigade with Colonel John R. Brooke's Fourth because the First had lost its commander and was running out of cartridges. Seeing Sweitzer's brigade of the Fifth Corps near at hand, he induced General Barnes to let him use it as a support on the right for Brooke.[126] As Sweitzer's men prepared to dash across the Wheatfield, which was now thoroughly trampled down and soaked with the blood of many brave men, Barnes in conformity with the best Civil War tradition stood in front of his men and shouted a few "patriotic remarks," to which they "responded with a cheer" and a fierce charge.[127] The aggressive Caldwell then sought help on his left from General Ayres of the Fifth Corps, who with his two brigades of regular army troops had just moved across Plum Run Valley from the north shoulder of Little Round Top. Ayres readily agreed to wheel his men to the left and move toward Devil's Den.[128]

In the ensuing fighting the bloody successes of Caldwell's brigades and the troops cooperating with them proved their undoing, for while they were driving the enemy from the Fairfield crossroad over the Wheatfield to within a short distance of the Rose farm, no one in authority seemed to have anticipated a Confederate attack from the direction of the Peach Orchard on their right flank. The only general officers in the vicinity were Ayres and Caldwell, and they were busy with affairs on their immediate front. Birney's whereabouts at this time was uncertain; Sykes was probably somewhere between Little Round Top and the Taneytown road bringing up more troops; Zook was lying mortally wounded, if not dead; and Barnes after making his inspiring speech had disappeared from the scene, perhaps nursing his own wound.[129] With no one in overall control of Union operations, McLaws' men completely surprised the Yankees participating in Caldwell's counterattack in the Wheatfield.

What happened to Sweitzer's brigade of Barnes's division was typical of the experience of other units. His men had advanced to the stone fence separating the Wheatfield from the woods on the south. After taking position behind it to support troops in the timber in front of them, Sweitzer noticed regiments retiring from the woods on his right, while shots coming diagonally from his right rear began to hit uncomfortably close to his men. At first he thought they came from Union troops shooting over his brigade at the enemy beyond and misjudging the distance. He became suspicious and decided to investigate after the shots increased in frequency and his color bearer exclaimed: " 'Colonel I'll be——if I don't think we are faced

407

the wrong way; the rebs are up there in the woods behind us, on the right.'" An aide who went to warn Barnes of the threat could not find him, but discovered enemy forces swarming in the woods and along the road to the right and rear of the Wheatfield.[130] They were Wofford's men who had joined with regiments of Kershaw's and Anderson's brigades in their rapid advance.[131] Sweitzer's brigade just managed to escape from the trap and get across Plum Run Valley after incurring very heavy losses in hand-to-hand fighting.[132]

Units of Birney's, Caldwell's, and Ayres's divisions also found themselves in a trap and had no recourse but to flee, leaving their dead, wounded, and some prisoners behind. Soon the Union retreat on this part of the field became a rout. Remnants of the divisions found refuge in the rear of the main line where they could rest and regroup. All had suffered very heavy losses,[133] and Caldwell's division had met with disaster. Only a small fraction of its former strength was left, and for awhile it was without a "shadow of an organization." The news upset Hancock, for never before had this division "flinched" under him or any other general. Yet now General Sykes complained that it had "done badly." Subsequent investigation, however, satisfied Hancock that "no troops on the field had done better," though some officers found fault with Caldwell's handling of his men; several of the regiments had crowded each other and hampered operations.[134]

General Barnes's conduct became a subject of even sharper criticism. Unfavorable comments started with a complaint by Birney that Barnes had withdrawn the support of his brigades from De Trobriand sometime during the fight.[135] Then "Historicus" belabored him with the fantastic allegation that he would not or could not get his men to fight, so in desperation Birney had ordered them to lie down while Zook's brigade charged over their prostrate bodies.[136] Later one of his subordinates, Colonel Tilton, reluctantly concluded that Barnes, who had been in a position to know, had failed to comprehend the military situation on his part of the battlefield. Otherwise he would have suggested that Caldwell place some of his troops in line with Sweitzer's and Tilton's brigades to face the Peach Orchard. Should that have been done, Tilton thought this small force might have "held" Wofford's and Kershaw's men long enough to have saved Ayres's regular army regiments from "such a licking." [137]

As the Northerners fled to the safety of Little Round Top, the Confederates followed them to what one Georgian described as the "strongest natural position" he had ever seen.[138] Another rebel, flush with victory, said that "nothing but the exhausted condition of the men prevented them from carrying the heights." [139] But the heights were more formidable than he thought, and the troops holding them, as the Texans and Alabamians had found out, were not to be pushed aside in one headlong charge. Besides, reinforcements were at hand. General Samuel W. Crawford's division of two brigades, forming the major part of a brave remnant of the Pennsylvania Reserves which in 1861 had mustered 15,000 men, now stood not far from the lengthening shadow of Little Round Top, waiting patiently for orders.[140] At last Crawford received instructions from Sykes to send aid to Vincent's brigade. He at once dispatched Colonel Joseph W. Fisher with four regiments of the Third Brigade. The fifth one he attached to the First Brigade under Colonel William McCandless, and following Sykes's orders he advanced these troops in two lines, the second massed on the first, up the east slope of Little Round Top and to the summit of the north shoulder. The Reserves remained there about twenty minutes,[141] resting upon their arms and "calmly and silently" [142] gazing upon the fierce struggle going on below them. Soon the low ground in front of them was covered with fugitives who rushed through their lines. They could see "fragments of regiments . . . running back without arms, and behind them in solid column over the Wheatfield and through the woods came the masses of the enemy." [143] With perfect timing Crawford reached down from his horse, seized the colors, and led his men forward in solid mass. They fired two volleys upon the enemy and shouting the battle cry peculiar to the Reserves, charged at a run down the slope.[144] The fierceness and momentum of their attack overcame the stout resistance of the rebels and drove their tired and disorganized columns out of the valley and beyond a stone wall on the east side of the Wheatfield.[145]

In this moment of glory the Reserves added further luster to their reputation as fighters; yet they exaggerated the importance of their exploit when they claimed credit for having "turned the tide" of the battle in favor of the Union.[146] Although their charge did discourage all further attempts of the Confederates against this part of the line, it occurred just as advance units of the Sixth Corps arrived on the field. Sedgwick immediately put three of his brigades in line for action, and one of these under Colonel David J. Nevin joined the Reserves and charged with them down the hill.[147] Once Crawford had gained possession of the stone wall, the rebels did not attempt to retake it. The sight of Union reinforcements, which seemed endless in the deepening gloom, and the formidable character of the main Union position disheartened them. After four hours of fighting with all the strength they could muster the Confederates bitterly realized that they had succeeded in crushing only the outer lines of the enemy.[148] Longstreet knew it was too late to reorganize and renew the attack, for the sun had long since disappeared behind the slopes of South Mountain, and the men were too tired to try anything more. He withdrew the left of his corps toward the Peach Orchard and started preparations for the morrow.[149]

XVI

THE WHOLE UNION LINE ABLAZE

THE STRUGGLE for the Wheatfield, Devil's Den, and Little Round Top on the afternoon of July 2 continued for many hours, and before it was over it had also engulfed most of Cemetery Ridge, where Longstreet's and Hill's troops came perilously close to seizing about three-quarters of a mile of the crest. Much of the blame for the near disaster must go to Sickles, for when he moved his corps forward toward the Emmitsburg road he created a gap which no one adequately filled. Though brigades of the Fifth Corps opportunely covered and protected Little Round Top, there still remained a wide space between them and the left flank of Caldwell's division of the Second Corps on Cemetery Ridge. The departure of his men for Birney's front dangerously enlarged the opening, and General Gibbon of the Second Corps could only partially close it by bringing his reserve brigade into position.[1]

As long as Birney's and Humphreys' lines held firm this gap offered little danger, but when they broke under a succession of Confederate blows it became a question of whether the retreating forces could stop on the ridge and re-form, or whether fresh troops could pour in quickly enough to plug the hole. To their credit, some well-disciplined units kept their formations intact during their withdrawal despite constant pounding from the enemy, and they responded readily to orders to strike back. Yet it was the timely arrival of reinforcements from other parts of the Union battle front that played the major role in preventing disaster.

The crisis in the gap began about six o'clock when Kershaw's,

Barksdale's, and Wofford's brigades launched their attack to crush the Third Corps line near the Peach Orchard. At this time Birney held the position at the Peach Orchard salient, while General Humphreys' men adjoined him on the right along the Emmitsburg road. Humphreys had received adequate warning of the Confederate advance from Colonel William J. Sewell, whose 5th New Jersey regiment formed the picket line covering the Second Division.[2] Full of fight as always, Humphreys immediately prepared to throw the left of his infantry forward instead of waiting for the shock of an attack. Such tactics, he felt, were psychologically sound, for, as he said later, "There is always a great deal in the spirit of advancing, even though it be but a few paces." He thought by attacking he would suffer no greater losses than by retreating, and in addition he might be able to punish the enemy "very severely."[3] Realizing that his two brigades would need vigorous support, Humphreys called upon the Second Corps to furnish it. Caldwell's division, which he understood was earmarked to back him up, had already left for other parts of the battleground, so he asked for a brigade from some other division.[4]

Before Humphreys could carry out his intended attack, however, he received orders from Birney, who had just assumed command of the Third Corps, to change his front. Birney had conceived the idea of having Humphreys draw back his left and form a line at an angle to and in the rear of the one he was holding, while Birney's division would extend it obliquely to the high ground north of Little Round Top.[5] Humphreys characterized the idea as "all bosh," for there was "nobody to form the new line but myself—Birney's troops [having] cleared out."[6] Meanwhile Barksdale's brigade, followed by Cadmus Wilcox' and then Perry's, began to converge on Humphreys from the left, front, and right.[7] His immediate concern was for his left which was in the air.[8] For the time being his right was pretty well covered, since Gibbon in response to his call for reinforcements had sent the 15th Massachusetts and the 82nd New York, numbering in all 559 officers and men.[9] One of Humphreys' aides posted them to the right of the Codori house on the Emmitsburg road, about eight hundred feet north of the end of the Second Division line.[10] To their right and rear Gibbon placed Lieutenant T. Fred Brown's Battery B of the 1st Rhode Island Light Artillery, made up of six 12-pounders which were good for close work.[11]

✻ Map 9 ✻

THE BATTLE OF CEMETERY HILL AND CULP'S HILL,
7:30–11:00 P.M., JULY 2

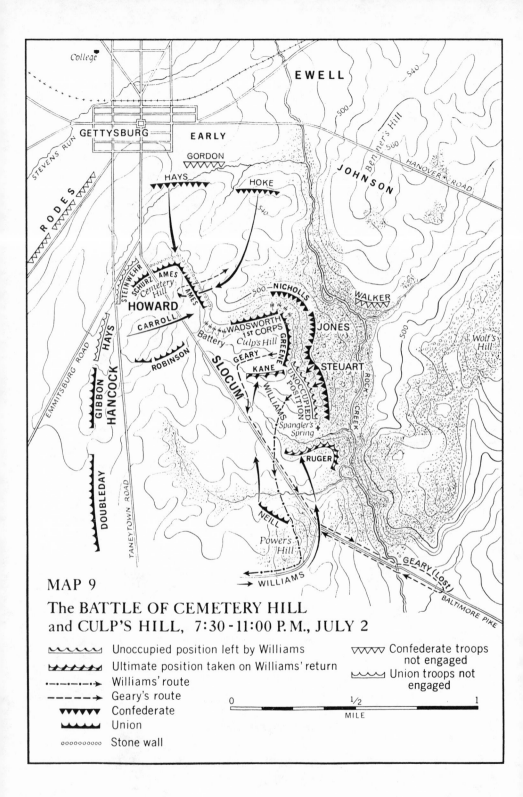

College

EWELL

540

500

GETTYSBURG   EARLY

Benner's Hill

560

HANOVER ROAD

GORDON

HAYS   HOKE

RODES

JOHNSON

540

Stevens Run

STEINWEHR
SCHURZ   AMES
Cemetery
Hill
HOWARD   AMES   500   NICHOLLS

WALKER

500

Wolf's
Hill

CARROLL   Battery   WADSWORTH
1st CORPS   JONES

Culp's Hill

ROBINSON   GEARY

GREENE

560

SLOCUM   KANE   STEUART

ROCK   CREEK

500

HANCOCK

HAYS

GIBBON

EMMITSBURG ROAD

WILLIAMS

UNOCCUPIED POSITION

Spangler's
Spring

DOUBLEDAY

TANEYTOWN ROAD

RUGER

NEILL

Power's
Hill

WILLIAMS

GEARY (Lost)

BALTIMORE PIKE

MAP 9

The BATTLE OF CEMETERY HILL
and CULP'S HILL, 7:30 - 11:00 P.M., JULY 2

〰〰〰〰   Unoccupied position left by Williams

🔺🔺🔺🔺   Ultimate position taken on Williams' return

·—·—·—·▸   Williams' route

— — —▸   Geary's route

🔻🔻🔻🔻   Confederate

🔺🔺🔺🔺   Union

ooooooooooo   Stone wall

▽▽▽▽   Confederate troops
not engaged

〰〰〰   Union troops not
engaged

0   ½   1

MILE

Following Birney's orders and despite the immense difficulties of such a move, Humphreys succeeded in forming a new line, as he modestly described it, in "pretty good order under a heavy close fire of artillery & infantry. . . ."[12] It was a credit both to his generalship and the steadiness of his troops that he could make a major shift of between 3,800 and 4,000 men[13] and two full batteries of artillery along a half-mile front without causing panic.[14] His own artillery "smashed" into the enemy "fearfully" and then retired, except for Turnbull's battery,[15] which had to leave four guns behind when all the horses in their teams were killed or wounded.[16] The division had no sooner completed this movement than Birney ordered Humphreys to retire all the way to the crest of Cemetery Ridge about half a mile farther to the rear.[17] This was an almost impossible assignment, for the enemy, sensing weakness on his part, was tearing into his division more fiercely than ever and was subjecting it to a "precise and heavy" fire from infantry and artillery.[18] As he fell back across the open ground to his rear Humphreys realized this experience was far worse than anything he had endured even in storming the sunken road below Marye's Heights at Fredericksburg the previous December.[19] For awhile he thought the day was lost,[20] but he kept on riding up and down the line and with iron discipline drew his men back very slowly, fighting all the way. To help him steady the ranks, a provost guard of seventy men stretched out behind the battle line; in spite of heavy casualties they remained faithful to his orders and turned back anyone except the wounded who might start to break away.[21] "Twenty times," Humphreys recalled, "did I bring my men to a halt & face about [to fire], myself & . . . [members] of my staff forcing the men to it."[22] Humphreys himself, according to one of his colonels, stayed "at the most exposed positions in the extreme front, giving personal attention to all the movements of the Division." His "cool and calm demeanor" inspired everyone under him with confidence and determination to hold out against the enemy.[23]

As Humphreys drew near to the section of Hancock's line previously occupied by Caldwell, Gibbon sent out two regiments, the 42nd New York and the 19th Massachusetts, to help cover his retreat. He also ordered two batteries to lob solid shot over the heads of the Union soldiers and into the ranks of the enemy. Case shot would have been more effective, but Gibbon, an old artilleryman, knew it had a tendency to explode prematurely and would do more harm than good to the defending troops. The two regiments together could muster only 290 riflemen and were but a weak barrier against the surging Confederate tide. Yet by standing firm they perhaps shamed some of their fleeing comrades in the Third Corps into slowing down to a walk.[24] More important, enough sturdy souls in Humphreys' division were inspired by his personal example to keep their formations and reach the security of the main line ready to fight again after a short pause. The price had been high. Hancock recalled riding by Humphreys' men on his way to another part of the line, and to him there seemed nothing left of the division but a mass of regimental colors still waving defiantly.[25] More than 1,500 of their comrades lay dead or wounded on the half mile of fields over which they had retreated. Very few had fallen into enemy hands, a fact which reflected their fine control under extreme adversity.[26]

While Humphreys' division was slowly retiring from its advance position to Cemetery Ridge, the sector of the Third Corps line at the Peach Orchard which General Charles K. Graham's brigade was defending finally collapsed from enemy blows coming from two directions. Soon after the Confederates began their big push against his brigade Graham became disabled from a severe wound and turned over his command to his senior colonel, Andrew H. Tippin of the 68th Pennsylvania. Before Tippin could assume his new duties, however, the situation deteriorated to a point where it was every regiment for itself. At this critical moment no general officer was on hand with the necessary authority to restore order in the ranks of the brigade and form a new line. General Birney was apparently off watching affairs near the Wheatfield, and General Sickles was lying on the ground, his right leg crushed by a cannon ball.[27]

This disintegration of the Third Corps line at its apex near the Peach Orchard uncovered the wide and dangerous gap between the Second and the Fifth Corps. Much of it was open country, which gradually sloped down from the Emmitsburg road to a depression marked by bushes and trees along the upper course of Plum Run, before rising rather quickly to Cemetery Ridge. One outstanding feature of this area was Trostle's lane; it ran parallel to the Fairfield crossroad some nine hundred feet to the north and connected the ridge and the Emmitsburg road. The Trostle house and barn, which had served as Sickles' headquarters, stood on the north side of the lane, just west of Plum Run. The regiments of Graham's brigade, broken now into small groups, retreated in the direction of the house, and as an ambulance carried Sickles away the barnyard and fields about it became scenes of wild confusion and bitter fighting. At exactly the same time Humphreys was pulling his division back to Cemetery Ridge over ground about 1,000 feet north of the farm.

The central figure in meeting the crisis which developed with the destruction of organized resistance near the Peach Orchard was Colonel Freeman McGilvery, whom General Hunt with fond respect called the "cool clear headed old sailor" from Maine.[28] All four batteries of his First Volunteer Brigade of the Artillery Reserve, the 5th and 9th Massachusetts, the 15th New York, and Battery C/F, Pennsylvania Light Artillery, with twenty-two guns in all, had formed part of a heavy concentration of cannon in the general area of the Peach Orchard. McGilvery had placed three of his batteries in line with the Fairfield crossroad facing south, and the fourth on higher ground west of the orchard in an angle formed by the crossroad and the Emmitsburg road.[29] Though hurt by enfilading fire from some of Alexander's batteries, McGilvery's guns in company with others from the Reserve and the Third Corps had exchanged blow for blow with Confederate artillerymen for about two hours and had broken up the movements of some enemy infantry columns. McGilvery had stayed close to the two Massachusetts batteries, the 5th under Captain Charles A. Phillips and the 9th under Captain John Bigelow, where in spite of clouds of smoke billowing from dozens of cannon and thousands of muskets he apparently got a good view of much of the battle line. Around 6:00 P.M. he detected signs of weakening resistance in the Union infantry. Tilton's brigade of Barnes's division had already drawn back, followed by Sweitzer's brigade, and the enemy had occupied their positions in the woods to the left of Bigelow's battery, so that McGilvery's artillery was exposed to rifle fire on its front and both flanks. One of his batteries left the field for want of ammunition, and McGilvery decided to order the other three to new positions 750 feet back toward the Trostle farm. Captain Phillips hauled one of his pieces off by hand, and Bigelow retired by prolonge, firing canister as he went. Then the batteries formed a new line and succeeded in briefly

415

checking the onrushing Confederates[30] who were spearheaded by Colonel B. G. Humphreys and the four hundred riflemen of the 21st Mississippi regiment.[31] These men were making it their business to seek out batteries, dash in, brush aside their infantry supports, and catch them on the flanks.[32] Finally the pressure of the rebels became too great, and all of McGilvery's batteries except Bigelow's retired from this part of the field.

Suddenly McGilvery realized that the crisis of the engagement had arrived.[33] He had expected Birney's division of the Third Corps to rally on Cemetery Ridge, to which he could pull back his guns and continue the fight in support of the infantry. Riding up the ridge and looking to the rear, he could see no organized body of troops for many hundreds of feet.[34] In front of him remnants of brigades and regiments still fought hopelessly in the fields and woods on the far side of Plum Run.[35] Across the lane from Trostle's barn and south of it, Bigelow's battery of six 12-pounders remained to pour canister into the ranks of the advancing rebels, but it too was getting ready to limber up before the enemy could corner it in the angle of a heavy stone wall.[36] Immediately McGilvery knew what he must do. He spurred his horse down the slope and on to the lane. Hit by a fusilade of bullets, the animal staggered but then resumed his furious pace along the lane, around the corner of the wall, and onto the field. McGilvery reared him to a stop before Bigelow. In a few words he explained why Bigelow must hold his position "at all hazards,"[37] while he himself would fill the gap by forming a new artillery line 1,200 feet to the rear. With that McGilvery was off, to round up any outfit that happened to be handy and put it in position.[38] Bigelow was left with a grim assignment, for he seemed to be completely on his own. Apparently he did not know that what was left of Tilton's small brigade was posted two hundred feet south of his position behind the stone wall. It was busy fending off Wofford's and Kershaw's men, as well as the Mississippians. By itself the brigade could not accomplish much, and it had to retreat;[39] in cooperation with Bigelow it might have been effective. Unfortunately no one appeared to bring about coordination of the two outfits.

Bigelow fought on stubbornly, keeping the Confederates at a respectful distance from his front until he had about exhausted his supply of canister and the enemy began to close in on his flanks.

Then he withdrew. He and most of his men escaped, but he lost four of his guns and practically all of his horses.[40] Nevertheless Bigelow's gallant stand gave McGilvery time to mass at least thirteen and possibly fifteen guns from four different batteries. Shortly two more batteries of four guns each came up, which McGilvery requisitioned for his new line,[41] but fire from new enemy artillery positions near the Peach Orchard and infantry operations soon reduced his force to six guns.[42] Expertly directed by McGilvery, a few stouthearted artillerymen continued to blaze away and keep the low bushes in front of them along Plum Run clear of lurking sharpshooters. Although they had no infantry supports, they somehow managed to create the illusion that the woods to their rear were filled with them, and they closed the breach in the line until the Union high command could bring up reinforcements.[43] The timing of the operation was perfect, thanks to the colonel's quick recognition of an emergency and his courageous willingness to risk his career in assuming authority beyond his rank.[44]

Just when McGilvery found he could not withstand the pressure much longer, Hancock appeared from the north end of Cemetery Ridge leading the Third Brigade, Third Division of his corps. It was about 7:15, and a quarter of an hour before sunset. Once on the scene Colonel George L. Willard commanding the brigade detached the 39th and 111th New York regiments to guard his left flank and then quickly deployed his two remaining regiments in battle formation north of Trostle's lane. Taking advantage of the downhill grade, they charged headlong into the right flank of Barksdale's brigade. Willard had made an error in his alignment, but Hancock quickly corrected it by sending the 111th New York to join the attack and prevent Willard from being outflanked on his right.[45] In the furious encounter between the two brigades Barksdale was mortally wounded. According to one account Barksdale, "almost frantic with rage," fell while he was trying to make his fleeing men hold fast.[46] After driving the rebels up the west slope of Plum Run the Union brigade returned to the run and took up position there until dark.[47]

Meantime the remaining regiment of Willard's brigade, the 39th New York, which had only four companies and was known by the more exotic name of the Garibaldi Guards, also had its work cut out for it. Shortly after Willard's arrival the ubiquitous 21st Mississippi had captured the guns of Lieutenant M. F. Watson's Battery I, 5th

United States Artillery, which McGilvery had placed on the left of his line. While Colonel Humphreys was reversing the guns to use against Union troops, the Guards struck back and retook the pieces.[48]

The magnificent work of Willard's brigade only partly relieved the situation, however, for more troops were needed on this part of the field, particularly behind McGilvery's batteries and south of them. Help arrived from a new quarter when General Alpheus Williams of the Twelfth Corps suddenly appeared in the rear of McGilvery's artillery line leading General Henry H. Lockwood and two regiments of his independent brigade. Behind them came General Thomas H. Ruger and the entire First Division of the corps. They had been sent in response to orders from Meade to go to Hancock's assistance. Earlier that day Williams, acting as commander of the Twelfth Corps while General Slocum took charge of the entire right wing, had turned over his own First Division to the exceedingly able and intelligent Ruger.[49] When Slocum in obedience to the message from Meade ordered these troops to move from Culp's Hill to the left, Williams decided to accompany them so as to avoid any complications in command. Since Lockwood outranked Ruger,[50] he would ordinarily have been in charge of the division, but not knowing his capabilities, Williams had refused to turn it over to him. As long as Williams kept the brigade as an independent unit and personally directed it and the division, he observed military protocol and gave no offense to Lockwood.

It was fortunate that these circumstances induced Williams to lead his troops because at this crucial moment army staff work broke down. No one from Meade's headquarters came to lead the way, and though Williams had no map or any other way of knowing the topography of the Cemetery Ridge area, he had the good sense and experience to find out where he was needed.[51] At first he and his men were guided by the sound of fighting and then by wounded soldiers and fugitives streaming to the rear. Their route from Culp's Hill was southeast on the Baltimore Pike to its intersection with a lane which went around the southeast and south slopes of Power's Hill and thence to the Taneytown road. After that they came to signs of battle, "broken-down fences, trodden fields, broken gun-carriages, scattered arms, knapsacks, blankets, and clothing of all kinds."[52] Soon they passed large numbers of troops "swarming in confusion" on the easterly slopes of Cemetery Ridge. When the fugitives saw the men of the Twelfth Corps they greeted them with "loud cheers and shouts to 'go in and give them Jerrie,'" but as Williams wryly observed, "Nobody seemed to know where to go in, nor did any of them offer to go in with us." [53]

The first person Williams met who seemed to understand what was going on was Colonel McGilvery. The two officers knew each other, and McGilvery expressed delight at seeing Williams and well he might, since he felt bereft without infantry support. He quickly told Williams about the loss of some of his guns and his anxiety to recover them. Without further ado Williams ordered Lockwood's leading regiment, the 1st Maryland Potomac Home Brigade under Colonel William P. Maulsby, to "pitch into" some woods ahead. In his eagerness to obey, Maulsby rashly rushed his men forward in column without waiting to form a line of battle. He met little resistance; the rebels ran and left the captured guns behind, for as it happened the main enemy forces were already beginning a general withdrawal. Maulsby's regiment, followed by the 150th New York of the same brigade, advanced almost half a mile beyond the woods on Cemetery Ridge until they were close to the Fairfield crossroad and the Peach Orchard.[54]

Meanwhile Williams deployed the rest of his division in some woods probably on Cemetery Ridge [55] and then himself rode forward to catch up with Lockwood. Seeing that his small line had gone far beyond other troops which might support it, he ordered a halt. By this time it was almost dark, and the noise of fighting was dying down to the scattered shots of wary skirmishers or the occasional boom of cannon. Any doubts about Williams' next course of action disappeared when a courier rode up with orders for him to return with his command to his original lines on Culp's Hill. On his way back Williams met Meade and many other officers in an open field near the Fairfield crossroad.[56] It was a "pleasant gathering," Williams said, in which "gratification and gratulation abounded" over the successful conclusion of the day's fighting on the left.[57]

But before this meeting took place and even as the lower end of the gap was being plugged by elements of the Twelfth Corps, the bitter struggle which had started about an hour previously between Humphreys' division and the men of Hill's corps was reaching its climax on the northern end of Cemetery Ridge. The Confederates were hurling their long lines against the tough veterans of the First, Second, and Third Corps in an effort to split the Union army at the upper end of the gap, while Hancock in his finest hour was moving heaven and earth to stop them. The commanders of four brigades in General Richard Anderson's division of Hill's corps had received orders to move forward together with Barksdale's and Wofford's brigades of McLaws' division. The signal for each brigade to begin the attack was to be the forward movement of the one on its right.[58] When at about 6:15 P.M. Barksdale's troops advanced and were followed by Wofford's men, Brigadier General Cadmus M. Wilcox wisely moved his brigade to the left so as not to crowd them. Then he faced by right flank and headed straight for the Emmitsburg road. Wilcox' brigade and those to his left, Perry's commanded by Colonel David Lang, and Brigadier General A. R. Wright's, stepped along at a lively pace for about half a mile over open, rolling fields cut up by stone and rail fences, which at first furnished the only serious obstacles to their advance. Lateral hollows between the low ridges afforded protection from enemy gunfire, which was increasing in intensity with every step, and gave the men opportunities to stop, catch their breath, and dress ranks before going on.[59] Barksdale's, Wilcox', and Perry's brigades hit Humphreys' Federals along the Emmitsburg road at about the same time. Although some of Wright's men probably participated in the assault on Humphreys' division,[60] the weight of their attack bore on the 82nd New York and the 15th Massachusetts regiments of Brigadier General William Harrow's brigade of Gibbon's division, which had formed a small breastwork of rails along the road north of the Codori house. Two batteries of six 12-pounders each, Lieutenant T. Fred Brown's Battery B, 1st Rhode Island, and Lieutenant Gulian V. Weir's Battery C, 5th United States, were located some distance to the rear, while the main Union line was another four hundred or five hundred feet farther back.[61]

As for the other two brigades of Hill's corps which were supposed to join in the attack, Brigadier General Carnot Posey's brigade never did enter the fray on Wright's left. Though Anderson had instructed him to advance once Wright had started, Posey failed to get his regiments into battle formation, probably because he misunderstood Anderson's orders. He kept his men deployed as skirmishers, and they never got much beyond the Bliss house and buildings, which were about 1,200 feet west of the Emmitsburg road.[62] The bigger mystery was the conduct of General William Mahone who did not even attempt to get his men off the ground. They were expected to move on the left of Posey's troops, but Mahone remained fixed to the idea that they were to stay as supports for some of Hill's batteries, despite Anderson's efforts to disabuse him of this notion. Even when Anderson sent an aide with blunt and unequivocal orders for the brigade to attack, Mahone refused to budge, claiming that Anderson himself had told him to remain where he was.[63]

If Anderson had been on the job, these delinquencies might have been avoided. Obviously there was a breakdown in command, and he should have exerted himself vigorously to repair the damage. When the aide came back with Mahone's reply it was Anderson's responsibility to have gone himself to secure obedience. There is the possibility, though no one has mentioned it, that Anderson referred the matter to Hill, who perhaps decided it was too late in the day to send Mahone in. Confederate writers have declared that the three brigades unassisted by the rest of the division came within a close margin of winning the battle, and with a little extra effort they might well have turned the tide in Lee's favor. However, the accomplishments of these three brigades advancing in cooperation with Barksdale's men do not warrant such contentions.[64]

When these Confederates hit Humphreys' line, his men offered but moderate resistance because they were already under orders to withdraw. From time to time as they retired Humphreys commanded them to halt and make a short stand against the enemy before resuming their retreat. Thus they unintentionally caused the Confederates to think that they had succeeded in breaking through a succession of previously prepared positions.[65] Barksdale's brigade, with the exception of the 21st Mississippi, and Hill's men fought Union troops within a triangle bounded by the Trostle land on the south, Cemetery Ridge on the east, and the Emmitsburg road on the west.[66] Nowhere did the rebels push through to the crest of the ridge. Most of them got no farther than the bottom of Plum Run Valley or the low ground north of it between the east slope of the Emmitsburg road ridge and the west slope of Cemetery Ridge.

General Wright was the only Confederate who maintained that his men after penetrating the Second Corps line finally seized the top of Cemetery Ridge. His statements, however, both in his report and in a letter to his wife written five days after the battle are literally beyond belief, and none of the Union accounts in any way supported his claim of having broken through the main line. He also pictured the features of Cemetery Ridge near the Clump of Trees, made famous the next day by Pickett's charge, as resembling the rough country around Little Round Top.[67] In reality this slope was quite gradual and free of natural obstructions except for a low outcropping of rock and a jumble of saplings and shrubs to the southwest of the clump. Wright referred to this section as a "high ledge of rocks" which he said fell away from a "rocky gorge" on the eastern slope of the "heights." The enemy's infantry fled to the gorge, he asserted, after he had overrun a heavily held line protected by a stone fence and had charged up to the "top of the crest. . . . We were now complete masters of the field," he boasted, "having gained the key, as it were, of the enemy's whole line." [68] Magnificent! If true, it meant that he had the distinction of having penetrated the main line on this part of the ridge deeper than anyone else, even farther than General L. A. Armistead the following afternoon. Wright sincerely believed that his brigade had accomplished all he claimed for it.[69] The wide discrepancies between his account and those of other participants may have been due to his total unfamiliarity with the ground which confused him, especially in the midst of a fiery encounter on a breathlessly hot and humid day.[70] Heavy clouds of low-hanging smoke could easily have obscured and distorted his vision. At one time smoke on this part of the battlefield became so thick that Gibbon, wanting to see what was going on, ordered nearby batteries to cease fire for awhile.[71] Whatever the explanation, Wright's story of the battle on July 2 should be included among the better Civil War romances.

On the right of Wright Perry's brigade, commanded by Colonel David Lang, then Wilcox' and Barksdale's, after making life miserable for Humphreys' division and pushing it back toward the ridge, had an opportunity to exploit the hole in the Union main line. They gained the Emmitsburg road and advanced over ground descending to the bottom of Plum Run Valley, where they disposed of opposition from some infantry and a battery of artillery. Before beginning the ascent of the ridge Lang stopped to rest his fagged men and to regroup them, as they had become quite scattered, while Wilcox pulled ahead. At that moment he saw a line of infantry come at him "double-quick" down the slope. These troops were the hardy men of the 1st Minnesota regiment in General William Harrow's brigade of Gibbon's division,[72] who had just moved to this part of the front as support for Lieutenant Evan Thomas' Battery C, 4th United States, of six 12-pounders. About this time Hancock had learned that the enemy had broken the Sickles' line, and he had ordered the colonel of the 1st Minnesota, William Colvill, Jr., to use his command as a dam against the stream of Third Corps fugitives. Colvill found they were too far gone from fright to halt and re-form; should he persist in the task he was fearful of demoralizing his own men, so he let them through his files. Finally the last of them passed the battery, and it was able to open with a furious cannonade on the serried ranks of the onrushing enemy. Hancock rode up and, reining his horse to a sudden stop, looked about for infantry to throw into the breach. " 'My God!' " he exclaimed, pointing to the 1st Minnesota, " 'Are these all the men we have here?' " Then he roared, " 'Advance Colonel, and take those colors.' "[73] This was very much to Colvill's taste, for he had asked to be released from arrest so he could lead his regiment into action. Hancock had deprived him of his command on June 29 because he had permitted his men to cross Monocacy Creek on a log instead of wading and had thus slowed up their march. Now his force of a little over three hundred men tore into Wilcox' right regiment and stopped it cold.[74] The price for Colvill's valor, a crippling wound; the reward, fame for his regiment. Never had Colvill seen better work done on either side, and the "destruction was awful," he said.[75] All the while Thomas' battery kept up a withering fire on the enemy below.[76] The 1st Minnesota held its position in the midst of overwhelming numbers of the enemy, who subjected it to heavy fire from all sides until Hancock could pour in reinforcements.

Hancock had previously called upon Meade for fresh troops to close the gap immediately to the left of Gibbon's division, and at just the right moment Doubleday's Third Division of the First Corps, followed by Robinson's Second, came dashing up the ridge from their positions in reserve behind Cemetery Hill.[77] Five companies of Colonel Francis V. Randall's 13th Vermont regiment led the way. These nine-month men of Stannard's Vermont Brigade, who had joined Doubleday's division the day before, had already caught the spirit of the hard-bitten veterans of the First Corps. Their first intimation of trouble came when Doubleday galloped over the hill from Hancock's line looking for his troops. Stannard was not there to greet him because he had been temporarily assigned to other duties, and Doubleday could not resist taking time to address them with a "few inspiriting remarks" before directing them to report to Hancock. Randall then rode ahead and found Hancock "encouraging and rallying" his men. Pointing to Weir's battery, the general told Randall that the rebels had captured it, and not being sure of the quality of the Vermont troops he wondered whether the colonel could retake it. With a Vermonter's gift for understatement Randall replied that he thought he could and was "willing to try." Quickly deploying his men, he ordered them to affix bayonets and to charge. The Vermonters advanced with such rapidity that many Confederates, caught by surprise, saved themselves by falling on the ground and surrendering. Pleased with this display of courage, Hancock told Randall to press on and he himself would gather up the prisoners. The Vermonters recaptured the guns and then pushed on to near the Emmitsburg road, where for good measure they seized two rebel pieces and a picket reserve of eighty-three officers and men.[78]

These rather disjointed counterattacks by separate units suddenly merged into a mighty surge of Union forces all along the left and center of Hancock's line. The remnants of Humphreys' division to the front and left of Randall's regiment called a halt to their backward movement, turned, and with much "hurrahing" lunged at the enemy. They charged back over ground they had just lost, taking many prisoners from Perry's brigade and recovering three guns of Turnbull's battery which they had abandoned.[79] To the right of Randall three regiments from three different brigades in Gibbon's division stopped Wright's drive on a line partly protected by a breastwork of fence rails and stone five hundred feet west of the top of the ridge.[80] One of the regiments, the 69th Pennsylvania, of General Alexander S. Webb's famous Philadelphia Brigade, remained steady despite heavy pressure and opened a staggering fire. Seeing the enemy ranks waver, General Webb very skillfully brought up another regiment at "double-quick" to increase his fire power. His two remaining regiments soon added their strength to his line. Within a few moments Wright's men had had enough, and they began to run with most of Webb's brigade after them. In this "very brilliant affair," for which Webb was warmly complimented, his men reached the Emmitsburg road, and on their way they recovered the guns of Brown's battery and captured about three hundred of the enemy.[81]

In their defeat Anderson's men were outgeneraled, not outfought. Both Wright and Wilcox in explaining their repulse complained of a lack of supporting columns. In his bitterness over failure Wright unfairly accused Perry's brigade of "shamefully" running to the rear, and he darkly referred to the "cowardly conduct of others." [82] He had not the "slightest doubt" of his ability to maintain his position "on the heights" if there had been a "protecting force" on his left, or if the brigade on his right had not retired.[83] Aside from the credibility of his claims of success, his evaluation of the effects of Anderson's mismanagement was questionable. Though Anderson used only about half the strength of his division for the attack,[84] employment of the remaining brigades would not have guaranteed victory. If he had continued to apply the same tactics—and there is no reason to suppose that he would not have done so—Posey's and Mahone's men would merely have broadened the front but not the depth of his attack. They would have clashed with troops of the Second Corps and possibly some of the Eleventh Corps who were well set for action in prepared positions, and they would also have faced a hail of fire from batteries in front of them on the ridge and to their left on Cemetery Hill.

It was Wilcox who put his finger on the fatal flaw in Anderson's tactical arrangements. Lack of a supporting line, he said, made it impossible for him to hold on to any advantages he might have gained. Repeatedly he called for supports, but there were none to be had, for Anderson in contrast to Longstreet had his brigades attack in one long thin line.[85] Hill, who as his immediate superior must share responsibility for this mistake, apparently had qualms about Anderson's formations, for he ordered Heth's division to move up from its position in the reserves and support him. Pettigrew, temporarily in command in place of the disabled Heth, admitted the division arrived "too late" to be of any use, but forestalled criticism by saying the order was "promptly obeyed." [86] If so, this report indicated either that Hill and Anderson had not agreed on a proper mode of attack, or that Hill belatedly decided to modify it. One thing seems clear: Neither general exercised close supervision over the operations of his attacking forces.[87] Anderson could have avoided some of his difficulties if he had stayed closer to the front, instead of setting up a command post, as he did, on the wooded western slope of Seminary Ridge. Here it was easy for couriers carrying messages to find his headquarters, but as his battle line moved forward communications between him and his brigadiers became precarious and delayed.[88] If he had been nearer to the field, he could personally have coordinated the movements of his brigades and possibly cut down their heavy losses.

Longstreet for all the criticism made of him was up near the front line with McLaws' division during the battle. When he saw the hopelessness of continuing the struggle, he withdrew most of his men to strong positions before the counterattacking Federals could take them prisoner. Anderson's brigades with fewer men assaulted as broad, if not a broader front without the immediate presence of the commanding officer and his staff to coordinate their movements. The price was a greater proportion of men captured or missing. Wilcox', Perry's, and Wright's brigades lost an estimated total of 650 men through capture, which was only slightly fewer than those taken from all the eight brigades of Longstreet's corps.[89]

These figures bear eloquent testimony to the fierceness of Union counterattacks under skillful leaders, and to the inadequacies of Southern generalship, especially in the fighting on Cemetery Ridge. Though defensive battles were admittedly easier to control then offensive,[90] Meade faced disaster when Sickles' line collapsed, for he momentarily lost his advantage of position. To regain the initiative he drew substantial reinforcements from quieter sections of his front, and placed Hancock in tactical control of all forces operating on the line between Cemetery Hill and Little Round Top. Hancock loomed magnificently above the smoke of battle as he rode up and down, quickly improvising to form a new line and close the gap at the lower end of the ridge. He seemed to be everywhere at once, and nothing escaped his notice. If he was guilty of exposing himself too recklessly, he was no more at fault than many other great Civil War captains.

His subordinates and troops responded superbly to his directions to stand and drive back the foe, and they pushed Hill's men well beyond the Emmitsburg road. As by this time it was almost dark, the Confederates continued to withdraw to their own lines on Seminary Ridge. Hancock, still on the alert, was on his way to inspect the right of his corps when suddenly he heard sounds of battle from Cemetery Hill where the Eleventh Corps was holding the line. Sensing trouble, and before receiving Howard's call for help, Hancock directed Gibbon, who was in temporary command of the Second Corps, to send Colonel S. S. Carroll with most of his brigade to the hill in a hurry.[91] Carroll needed no urging. Fearless and vigorous,[92] he was one of a small group of officers who had the reputation of attacking "wherever they got a chance, and of their own accord." [93] One soldier remembered Carroll as " 'a splendid commander to lead a forlorn hope,' " for his voice was like the blast of a trumpet, and to hear it ordering a charge was " 'worth a whole regiment in itself as a reinforcement.' " [94] Carroll was just the man to stiffen the resistance of the defenders of Cemetery Hill. Within a few minutes of sending him, Hancock heard firing which he believed came from farther to the right in the direction of Culp's Hill. Fearful that Slocum had stripped his front of soldiers to aid him, Hancock instructed Gibbon to hurry two regiments to the threatened point. Gibbon had Webb detach two regiments of his brigade. These men had hardly had time to catch their breath from pursuing rebels before they received their new assignment. Through some misunderstanding one regiment went to Cemetery instead of Culp's Hill,[95] but the other arrived at the right place.

This threat against Union lines on both hills at once had taken hours to explode into a crisis. It had started at four o'clock with a heavy and remarkably accurate cannonade by sixteen guns of General Ewell's corps against the Union batteries crowded together on East Cemetery Hill. Though but an echo of the deeper roar of Alexander's batteries off to the south, the fire of these pieces gave the appearance of extraordinary synchronization in Confederate planning. Shortly after Alexander's gunners had pulled their lanyards for the opening salvo, Hood's infantry had emerged into the open pastures and fields of grain east of the Emmitsburg road. The Union artillerymen on Cemetery Hill watched to see whether after a similar interval Ewell's brigades would wheel into battle formation and move, deliberately at first and then with quickened pace, against them. Although they could only guess at the meaning of the gunfire from this new quarter, their first duty was to accept the challenge and overwhelm the Confederate batteries promptly and efficiently.

Colonel Wainwright, in charge of artillery north of the Baltimore Pike, swung the muzzles of his 3-inch rifles around to point at Benner's Hill 4,000 feet to the northeast. The duel between his and Major J. W. Latimer's Confederate batteries continued without letup for minutes and then hours. Gradually the heavier metal hurled by Wainwright's cannon, aided by pieces in other sectors, smothered the enemy gunners and forced them to pull back from the hill out of effective range.[96] Still there were no signs of gray infantry massed to attack Cemetery or Culp's Hill. Perhaps after all Ewell's artillery was providing a "mere divertissement," [97] as Wainwright put it, rather than a covering fire for an infantry advance. Neither hypothesis was entirely correct.

During the day Ewell, according to instructions from Lee, had made preparations to divert the attention of the enemy from Longstreet's offensive; if conditions seemed favorable he was ordered to develop a "real attack." [98] As events finally unfolded, however, Ewell neither planned nor fought well. In the morning he and Early had examined the ground thoroughly along the left of the corps, but they could find no more artillery positions within range of the enemy lines to supplement the one Major Latimer had discovered on Benner's Hill soon after the break of day. It too had its drawbacks, for it furnished little shelter for the horses and caissons against enemy fire and not enough ground for a concentration of many batteries. Without an adequate number of good artillery sites Ewell and Colonel J. Thompson Brown, chief of his Artillery Reserve, could get only forty-eight of the eighty or so guns of the Second Corps placed for action. Of these only thirty-two became actively engaged on July 2.[99]

Lack of sufficient artillery support did not deter Ewell from finally ordering an infantry assault. Informed that Longstreet would start the battle at 4:00 P.M., Ewell instructed General Edward Johnson to have Latimer open fire at the same moment. Sometime during the artillery duel or shortly after it ceased around 6:30 P.M. [100] Ewell got the notion that the propitious time had arrived for a general advance of his whole corps. Unless he in some way knew of Longstreet's gains, which was not very likely at that hour, there was no reason for him to suppose he had better chances of success against the Union infantry then than earlier in the day. Certainly the violent response of Union artillery to the challenge of his own guns should have given him pause. About the time he conceived of the attack, major units of the Twelfth Corps were pulling out of their lines and forming for the march to reinforce Sickles, but there is no suggestion that Ewell knew of this movement.[101]

If Ewell had any valid reasons for an attack by his whole corps, he should have planned it earlier in consultation with Hill and Lee and arranged for Pender's troops on his right to cooperate with him. However, by his own admission it did not occur to him until just before the attack to seek Pender's help. His messenger found General James H. Lane in command, as Pender had just received a crippling wound. Lane in replying to Ewell's request said his orders from Pender permitted him to "attack if a favorable opportunity presented," [102] a statement which really promised nothing and which Ewell accepted at face value. The sun had already set and he was anxious to get started, so he at once dispatched another message to Lane saying that he was about ready to attack. In response Lane sent two brigades forward to the Confederate skirmish line, which was abreast of a sunken road running between the Bliss farm and Gettysburg.[103] This gesture toward joint operations proved meaningless, however, because General Rodes failed to synchronize the movement of his division with the rest of Ewell's corps.

There are several clues to Rodes's poor performance on July 2, among them the general inadequacy of the Confederate command system and Ewell's own lack of foresight and initiative. Nor can Rodes himself escape all blame, for he knew that he had to get into the act should a favorable situation develop along his front as a result of Longstreet's offensive. Late in the afternoon he thought he noticed a perceptible weakening of Union forces on his part of the field, in reaction to the threat by Longstreet. Now seemed to be the time to strike, so he made arrangements for joint action with Early on his left and Lane on his right. Presumably Ewell knew about these preparations but kept in the background as a silent partner. If he had been more aggressive he would have ordered Rodes to bring his men forward earlier in the day from his awkward location west of town to one closer to the enemy, from which he could have moved in concert with Early. As it was, when Rodes started to shift his position after dark, he did not give himself enough time to get his big division into formation for the attack. By the time he had completed the complicated maneuver of wheeling his brigades forty-five degrees to the left and advancing them half a mile to a good place from which to charge up Cemetery Hill, the battle was over.[104]

Ewell's decision to hurl his infantry against the enemy strongholds on Cemetery and Culp's Hills found Early fully ready for the trial and Johnson only a little less so. Early had expected the offensive on the right to start soon after daybreak on July 2, so during the night he had placed Hoke's brigade under Colonel Isaac E. Avery and General Harry T. Hays's brigade in a protected position north of the town, from which they could easily storm Cemetery Hill. Upon hearing of the delay in the attack, he brought up General J. B. Gordon's brigade within supporting distance but kept General "Extra Billy" Smith's on duty guarding the approach to the Confederate rear from the York road. During the day Johnson's division maintained a line of battle in low ground north of the Hanover road out of sight of Union observers. His skirmishers, well out in front and south of the road, kept up a desultory fire with the enemy all day. Late in the afternoon Johnson moved up Brigadier General John M. Jones's brigade in support of Major Latimer's batteries on Benner's Hill, perhaps as preliminary to a general advance of his whole division. After Latimer decided to retire as gracefully as possible from his duel with Wainwright, Ewell gave Johnson the order to attack. According to his plan, as soon as Johnson and his division had confronted the foe on Culp's Hill, two of Early's brigades would move into the fray and engage the enemy on the northeast slope of Cemetery Hill. Presumably Rodes would join the fight a little later by storming the northwest side of the hill.[105]

The advance of Johnson's division, which included the brigades of Generals Jones and Steuart, and of Colonel J. M. Williams (Nicholl's former command), did not go as smoothly as he had hoped. Contrary to plans, he had to leave General James A. Walker's Stonewall Brigade behind to settle accounts with aggressive skirmishers from General Gregg's cavalry division who had persisted in harassing his left flank and rear.[106] It took Johnson longer than he had anticipated to cross Rock Creek, which at the place of crossing was a real water hazard, and to reach the base of the hill. By the time he had driven in the persistent skirmishers, who were only expected to hit and run, and come to the main Union defenses, it was almost dark. What he found was an unpleasant surprise. The main part of Culp's Hill, with its steep rock-strewn slopes broken here and there by cliffs fifteen to twenty feet high, afforded great protection to its defenders, who had improved upon nature by digging deep entrenchments and facing them with thick abatis.[107] The troops holding this line were among the best in the Army of the Potomac, the remnants of Wadsworth's division of the First Corps and Brigadier General George S. Greene's Third Brigade of Geary's division of the Twelfth Corps. Wadsworth, battle-scarred but still defiant, had shown his mettle the day before, and the grizzled, tough Greene was an old war horse.

Wadsworth's line, running along a part of the hill near the crest, faced northwest, and Greene's descended the northeast slope from the top to the south shoulder. When other units of the Twelfth Corps had marched to the relief of Sickles, Slocum had left behind Greene's brigade of 1,424 officers and men with orders to spread itself thin and fill the vacant trenches. Greene had just started a sidling movement when the enemy made a furious assault along his entire front. He needed help and needed it fast. Wadsworth, though himself under attack, promptly sent two regiments, the 6th Wisconsin and the 84th New York. Howard in response to Greene's call had Schurz hurry over the 82nd Illinois, the 45th New York, the 157th New York, and the 61st Ohio. These six regiments, reduced to mere shadows of their strength before the first day's battle, increased Greene's force by only 755 men. As additional reinforcement the 71st Pennsylvania from Webb's brigade of the Second Corps in command of Colonel Richard Penn Smith was sent to join Greene, but probably as a result of poor staff work in Greene's brigade it was placed in an untenable position. Fearing for the safety of his men, the colonel without waiting for orders pulled them out of line almost as soon as they arrived and returned to Cemetery Ridge. Fortunately the disappearance of the 71st Pennsylvania in no way affected the outcome of the struggle, for Greene had enough men behind breastworks to stop the enemy. He maintained an incessant fire by using his reserves to relieve the troops in the trenches when they had exhausted their ammunition and fouled their rifles. Against such tactics behind fortified lines the repeated attempts of Nicholl's and Jones's brigades to break through made no headway. Theirs was a hopeless mission.[108]

Trouble began for Greene when Steuart's brigade discovered the empty entrenchments and undefended right end of his line. As the Confederates pushed ahead Greene met a threat of envelopment by refusing his right flank and using his reinforcements to extend his line as far as he could, but beyond it there was nothing. Before reaching the open fields alongside the Baltimore Pike the rebels had to cross a wooded area that was a rough and tumble mixture of rocky knolls, heavy swale, and spiney ridges. Experts at stalking game, they knew that the enemy could be lurking behind every rock, depression, or bluff, and that shadows in the moonlight could play tricks and make them see things that were not there. The lateness of the hour favored Greene; it made the Confederates hesitate in exploiting their advantage because in the dark there was great danger of a trap.[109] To reconnoiter under these conditions took time—enough time for Williams' division of the Twelfth Corps to march back from Cemetery Ridge and keep its rendezvous with Johnson's men.[110]

The lost opportunity of the Confederates, which had been fleeting at best, to envelop the right of the Union army existed less in actuality than in the minds of broken-hearted veterans seeking the reason why.[111] For one thing, they seemed to be talking about several missed chances. They pointed the accusing finger at Ewell and said he should have attacked an hour or so earlier, forgetting that if he had done so he would have met the entire Twelfth Corps head-on. It could be argued that an assault then would have materially assisted Longstreet by pinning Williams' troops down on Culp's Hill and depriving Meade of their use on the Union left flank. The soundness of this argument depends upon the debatable assumption that the arrival of the Twelfth Corps on Hancock's left was responsible for turning the tide in Meade's favor. The fact is that only Williams' division got there, and most of it never went into action. When Ewell finally did make his attack, his objective was capture of the top of Culp's Hill because the Confederates considered it the key to the Union defense on Cemetery Hill. Preoccupied with the task of accomplishing this mission, Johnson and his men persisted in storming Greene's position.[112] When they discovered the empty trenches and then the way to the pike, Williams' division was close at hand to challenge them. If Johnson's men had seized the pike, it is questionable whether they could have held it. Other than possibly Walker's Stonewall Brigade they had no supporting troops immediately in their rear to aid them in coping with Williams and later Geary's division from the south and with Robinson's division, now back from Cemetery Hill, to the northwest. The Twelfth Corps could also have been reinforced by Brigadier General Thomas H. Neill's brigade from the Sixth Corps which Meade had ordered to the area between Power's and Culp's Hills sometime after six o'clock.[113]

Johnson's unpleasant surprise at the reception given him by Wadsworth and Greene was matched by Williams' horror when greeted by the "astounding intelligence" that the rebels had taken his entrenchments during his absence.[114] As temporary commander of the Twelfth Corps he felt responsible and angry about what had happened. He did not know that Slocum had ordered Geary to follow him with most of his division as additional aid for Hancock. Before leaving, Williams had told Slocum personally that he thought the Twelfth Corps could not "safely spare" any more troops than one division. He feared that the Southerners might seize his position the moment he vacated it, and consequently he had instructed Geary to occupy the whole line. Slocum had replied that although the call for reinforcements was "urgent for all the troops he could spare," he had agreed with Williams' opinion that at least one division was necessary to hold the entrenchments. With this understanding Williams had joined the reinforcing column.[115]

Afterwards when Williams learned of Geary's orders he could not understand why he did not follow right after him, nor has anyone since then ever offered a completely satisfactory explanation. Geary complained that upon receiving his instructions no one gave him any idea of where he should go, nor why or how. He only knew that he was to "move by the right flank and to follow the First Division." [116] It seems incredible that he did not in some way learn about the critical situation on the lower end of Cemetery Ridge. An officer of his rank and responsibility might logically have asked Williams what was up, but obviously he did not do so. Once he found himself across Rock Creek on the Baltimore Pike, he should have suspected that he was lost because nothing of any importance was going on there. Yet instead of sending messengers back to headquarters for clarification of his orders, he continued south on the pike way beyond the place where he was supposed to turn right toward the battlefield. Geary's explanation was that a "crowd of stragglers" had misled him. Williams commented acidly that he had no idea where they might have come from; not, he was sure, from his units, nor had he seen any stragglers at all as he marched along the pike.[117]

What was even more exasperating, for hours nobody seemed to know where Geary had gone. Colonel Hiram C. Rodgers, assistant adjutant general of the Twelfth Corps, sent staff officers and orderlies in all directions down the pike and onto crossroads frantically looking for him. They finally found him in bivouac east of Rock Creek. As a result of his blunder 2,500 veterans had walked right off the battlefield and become lost to Meade when he needed every man who could carry a musket.[118] Both corps and army headquarters were guilty of inexcusably sloppy staff work. When the order to shift the divisions of the Twelfth Corps from the right to the left was made, Butterfield or Rodgers should have appointed smart young orderlies, if not staff officers, to guide the columns. It does not seem possible that none were available.

Before Williams himself returned to Culp's Hill he left his troops to attend a meeting of corps commanders at Meade's headquarters. Ruger and Lockwood continued with their commands, and as they appeared at the rear of the hill around ten o'clock one of Slocum's staff officers warned them of the Confederate attack against Greene. At once Ruger sent out a strong force of skirmishers and proceeded cautiously to feel out the enemy's position. He was glad to learn that the Confederates had not taken the trenches on the rocky knoll south of the swale and swampy ground around Spangler's Spring. He immediately reoccupied them with his Third Brigade and then extended his line westward into the field bordering the pike. Thus he had his men in position to outflank any Southern force attempting to gain the road.[119] Upon his return at midnight Williams, who had had experience in "trying to retake breastworks after dark," approved of Ruger's tactics and decided to await daylight for further operations.[120]

Meanwhile messengers from headquarters had gotten in touch with Geary, and he began sending his men back to their former positions. About the time Ruger was arranging his men, the first of Geary's brigades, a small one under Brigadier General Thomas L. Kane, returned from its excursion down the pike. After fumbling

434

around in the dark Kane finally located Greene's right flank, which was bent back almost at a right angle to his main position. Kane placed his men in a straight line facing south and brought Greene's flank out toward the pike. These arrangements of Kane and Ruger effectively protected the road from further danger, since no more than 1,000 feet separated the two wings of the corps, which were facing each other. It was after midnight when Geary brought back his biggest brigade under Colonel John H. Candy to a position in Greene's rear, and Slocum and Williams began preparations for a counterattack in the morning.[121]

Though General Johnson failed to gain his objective on July 2, he did obtain a foothold from which he hoped to achieve a favorable decision the next day. In contrast Early attained his goal on Cemetery Hill, but could not hold it. His men had lain hidden all day behind a low hill about half a mile from Cemetery Hill. Their line, consisting of Hays's brigade on the right and Hoke's on the left, some 3,500 men in all, stretched east from the edge of town across the fields to within a short distance of Rock Creek. As Johnson closed in on Culp's Hill around eight o'clock, Early began to whip his men into motion. When Wainwright on Cemetery Hill caught sight of them, he at once gave the signal and four of his batteries opened with a roar. They fired frantically as the attacking force came into full view at the top of the elevation immediately in front of the hill. Then the Confederates quickly descended the slope, shooting as they went. At the bottom of the depression between Cemetery and Culp's Hills they hit a line of infantry behind a stone wall, whereupon Hoke's brigade, commanded by Colonel Isaac E. Avery, made a perfect right oblique, a move which only veterans could execute while exposed to a heavy shower of canister. The enfilading fire inflicted by Captain Greenleaf T. Stevens' 5th Battery (E), Maine Light, of six 12-pounder smoothbores standing on the knoll between the hills hit the left and rear of Hoke's brigade and tore huge gaps in its ranks, while the heavy musketry of the 33rd Massachusetts from von Steinwehr's brigade in position on lower ground to the left and rear of the battery added to the woes of the attacking forces.[122]

The Confederate casualties might have been higher had it not been for some unforeseen circumstances. At one point in their advance the steepness of the northeast face of Cemetery Hill protected them from the direct fire of batteries on the top of the hill above them, and the fading daylight and the smoke of firing which lay so thick in the still air that they "could not see ten yards ahead" [123] effectively screened them from the defenders of the position. Even more fortunate for the Confederates was the feeble resistance offered by Colonel von Gilsa's and Colonel Andrew L. Harris' brigades of Ames's division of the Eleventh Corps. Von Gilsa's men, now numbering but 650 muskets and holding the right of Howard's line, had given way the previous afternoon before Gordon's frontal assaults. With their ranks seriously weakened and demoralized from this experience, the sight of Early's brigade suddenly looming over the top of the low rise east of the Union line seemed to unnerve them, though they were protected by stone walls. The same was true of Harris' brigade, which with even fewer men held a line to the left and at right angles to von Gilsa's. As the Confederates rushed at them, both brigades delivered a few scattered shots and then "ran away almost to a man." [124] One battery commander declared that the soldiers were so "panic stricken" that several ran into the canister fire of his guns. [125] Wainwright noted that the commander of another battery stretched his men along the road and with fence rails tried to stop them from running away, but he could do nothing. "Officers and men were both alike," he said. [126]

The Confederates, following after the fugitives, got to some of the guns on the hill. They first struck Captain Michael Wiedrich's Battery I, 1st New York Light, which stood on the northern end of the hill just beyond a stone wall running almost east and west. Wiedrich's German gunners refused to budge and stubbornly fought back with handspikes and fence rails, punctuating their blows with the mouth-filling oaths of the infuriated Teuton. Ames himself rushed in and stopped some of his infantrymen from running. Led by him, they turned on the enemy and aided the cannoneers in their struggle. [127] The Confederates also attacked Captain R. Bruce Ricketts' Batteries F and G, 1st Pennsylvania Light, to the south of the stone wall. Without infantry supports Ricketts' men had the nasty experience of fighting hand to hand with handspikes, rammers, and pistols against bayonets. Ricketts later recalled that Wainwright had said: " 'Captain, this is the key to our position on Cemetery Hill, and must be held and in case you are charged here, you will not limber up under any circumstances, but fight your battery as long as you can.' " [128] Whether or not these were Wainwright's words, both Ricketts and Wiedrich remained faithful to their trust and held on grimly until help arrived. It was not long in coming.

In the crisis the performance of Howard and Schurz showed up well. They were standing together in conversation when the uproar caused by the Confederate attack on the batteries attracted their attention. Upon Howard's orders Schurz quickly summoned the two regiments nearest him, ordered them to fix bayonets, and with Colonel Krzyzanowski in command, hurried them off at double-quick to the threatened point near Wiedrich's battery. Gathering up his staff, Schurz rushed forward and placed himself at the head of his men. Aided by Coster's brigade of von Steinwehr's division, these men of the Eleventh Corps came at the Confederates with a rush and after a sharp exchange of fire tumbled them down the hill away from Wiedrich's battery. [129]

When the Confederate charge began, Howard had taken the precaution of asking for supporting troops from the Second Corps. [130] As it turned out, Hancock had anticipated him by sending out Carroll with most of his brigade, but with "no precise orders" about where he was to go. More by luck than design Carroll arrived where he was needed most, near Ricketts' battery, as a result of having run into Captain J. F. Huntingdon, commander of a brigade in the Artillery Reserve, whom he knew. Carroll asked where the Confederates were, and Huntingdon, pointing in the direction of Ricketts' guns, replied that they were swarming over one of the batteries of that command. [131] This was enough for Carroll, and calling out his orders in a voice which could be heard above the roar he arranged his men with as much skill as if he were on familiar ground and in broad daylight. [132] Charging across the pike on the right of the battery, he struck Hoke's brigade and pushed it back. At the same moment some men in Hays's brigade opened a brisk fire on his left flank from behind a stone wall. Carroll quickly had the 7th West Virginia change front and drive the Louisianians away. [133] With Carroll's appearance and the stiffening of Eleventh Corps resistance Hays, who temporarily commanded both of the Confederate brigades in the assault, decided to give up his gains, and taking advantage of the darkness he led his men back down the hill.[134] Some of them did not move quickly enough to avoid capture by the hard-charging men of the Second Corps. When the enemy finally disappeared from his immediate front, Carroll gave up the chase.

The danger along Howard's front was over, though musket fire continued for awhile, finally sputtering to a stop around 10:30 P.M. Carroll, finding his brigade alone near the stone wall at the bottom of the hill and not connected with any other units, sought permission to retire. Both Ames and Howard frankly admitted they had no confidence in their troops, especially those of the First Division, and they asked Carroll to remain where he was, because he was the "mainstay" of that part of the line. Reluctantly agreeing to their wishes, he stayed on, while Ames gradually brought his men back to their old position. Several times the next day Carroll expressed a desire to get back to his division, but Howard would not hear of it.[135] The poor showing of Ames's division so shocked Howard that his fears about the security of his line on the east side of Cemetery Hill became almost an obsession. To bolster his defenses he kept the fairly strong 106th Pennsylvania regiment from Webb's brigade, as well as Carroll and his men, for the remainder of the battle.[136]

Though the struggle for Cemetery Hill was one of the more dramatic and memorable events in the three days of bloody encounter between the two armies, its military importance has perhaps been overemphasized. Early's Confederates performed brilliantly when they stormed the heights, but it is questionable whether they effected a lodgment within Union lines of sufficient strength to hold and exploit even if they had received reinforcements. Wainwright maintained that the attack failed because only a portion of Hays's command reached its objective. "Their center and left never mounted the hill at all," he said, "but their right worked its way up under cover of the houses, and pushed completely through Wiedrich's battery into Ricketts'. The cannoneers of both these batteries stood well to their guns, driving the enemy off with fence-rails and stones and capturing a few prisoners. I believe it may be claimed that this attack was almost entirely repelled by the artillery."[137] Allowing for the tendency of good artillerymen to exaggerate the effectiveness of their fire and to deprecate the role of infantrymen, Confederate reports did to some extent substantiate Wainwright's version of affairs. Though Hays made one of those typically misleading and ambiguous statements about his "whole line" having reached the summit "by a simultaneous rush," [138] Colonel Archibald C. Godwin, who reported for Hoke's brigade, admitted that in the charge up the hill "the command had become much separated, and in the darkness it was now found impossible to concentrate more than 40 or 50 men at any point for a further advance." He also mentioned that a "portion" of Hoke's 6th North Carolina regiment, aided by a "small number" of Hays's 9th Louisiana, had succeeded in "capturing a battery on the right" which was Wiedrich's. Very likely few men in either brigade advanced as far as the Union artillery positions.[139] In explaining the failure of more men to climb the hill, Wainwright said artillery fire stopped them, while Godwin blamed the darkness and such obstacles as stone walls, rocks, and rough ground for preventing "rapidity of movement and unity of action." [140] Both explanations were correct as far as they went.

Whether Hays really thought both brigades got to the top is immaterial. When he saw signs of a formidable Union counterattack instead of help from Rodes's division, he knew he had to get out, and he started to retreat. Upon hearing word that Gordon was coming to his support, he halted and evinced a willingness to renew the assault. The report proved false, however, because Early had decided that even with Gordon's help his brigades could not hold the hill unless Rodes attacked, and when he learned of Rodes's decision not to advance, he stopped Gordon from moving up.[141]

Rodes's explanation was that by the time he was ready to move, Early's attack was over. Actually Rodes had given Ramseur final say in the matter. When his brigade, which was in the lead, came within six hundred feet of the Union line, the moonlight was apparently strong enough for Ramseur to observe the great strength of the position: batteries ready to pour "direct, cross, and enfilade fires" upon his lines, and two supporting rows of infantry well protected by stone walls and breastworks. The sight gave him pause, and after consulting with the stouthearted General Doles, he concluded it would be well to warn Rodes of what he would run into should he attack. This information coming from the brave and capable Ramseur on top of everything else convinced Rodes of the wisdom of deferring the attack until daylight.[142]

After the battle the story got about that General Lee had once chided Ramseur for his failure to move up in support of General

Early "as directed." If he had done so, "what a difference there would have been," Lee was reported to have said.[143] Though probably apocryphal, for it was not like Lee to question the judgment of an able subordinate, the story reflected the tendency of the Confederates in their post mortems of the battle to attribute their defeat to a single mistake. Undoubtedly if Rodes had been able to mount an attack in conjunction with Early, which under the circumstances would have been a miracle of generalship, the defenders of Cemetery Hill would have had a hard time of it. A two-front assault on a salient always puts defenders on their mettle, but in this instance not all the advantages would have been with the Confederates. The problem of coordinating their movements would have been compounded by the dark, and once through the first and even the second lines of the defenders they would have had to contend with a number of Federal units in reserve: Robinson's Second Division of the First Corps which was back on the hill, brigades from Hancock's corps, and Neill's brigade from the Sixth Corps.[144] Of course if Rodes, Early, and Johnson had moved before dark together with all of Anderson's brigade, the story of the Confederate offensive on July 2 might have had a different ending, for Cemetery Hill was vulnerable to an attack from two directions. Coordination of such magnitude, however, was unheard of in Civil War engagements, and its possibility at Gettysburg should be relegated to the realm of pure speculation.

The thunder of battle which continued for hours after dark along the northern and eastern extremities of the Union line had a faint echo in the dark glens and rocky slopes of Big Round Top far to the south. As long as Confederates occupied that dominating height some of the commanding officers of the Fifth Corps felt they had unfinished business on their hands which they needed to complete before calling the day a success, for they feared the rebels would use the position as a base from which to renew the attack on Little Round Top during the night or early in the morning. Just who had the idea of taking the eminence in the first place has been lost in a welter of claims and counterclaims arising in part from questions about who was commanding whom. Chamberlain of the 20th Maine said that Sykes ordered Colonel Rice, who had succeeded the mortally wounded Vincent, to seize it. Rice, whose men were dead tired from battling Hood's Texans and Alabamians, suggested in turn that some regiments of Colonel Joseph W. Fisher's Third Brigade of the Pennsylvania Reserves could do the job. They had arrived in support of Rice's men after their engagement with the Confederates and were comparatively fresh.[145] For obscure reasons Fisher demurred [146] and referred the matter to his superior, General Crawford, who was then busy on another part of the field.

Crawford finally rode over to Little Round Top and saw Fisher and several other officers. Crawford thought of course Big Round Top should be taken, and as ranking officer on that part of the field he ordered Fisher to do it.[147] But Fisher took his time in getting started. Rice became impatient, for the hour was late, so he turned to Chamberlain and asked him to storm the hill. Chamberlain roused his exhausted men from sleep, quickly deployed them, and in the dark led them up the hill to the summit.[148] Fortunately the Confederates were in no mood to dispute possession, and they offered little resistance.[149] After considerable delay two of Fisher's regiments, having found a back road to the top, came up in support of the 20th Maine. Chamberlain had no sooner shown them to a position on his exposed right than much to his disgust at an outburst of fire from nervous enemy sentinels, they disappeared into the darkness. Feeling insecure with his little force of two hundred men, he asked for the 83rd Pennsylvania and the 44th New York, both of his brigade, to join him. They responded quickly to his call. As vigilant as he was brave, Chamberlain carefully posted them and pushed out a strong line of pickets with instructions for the officer in charge to report conditions to him every half hour. After making these arrangements, he allowed his men to sleep on their arms.[150] For the moment all was quiet on the battlefield.

XVII

LEE AND MEADE PONDER
AND PLAN

STILLNESS BROKEN only by the shrieks and groans of the wounded spread over the battlefield, while the warm July moon covered the carnage with soft light. The soldiers out of sheer exhaustion and futility lay down their arms for the remaining few hours of the night. Longstreet's men slept on a field "*black* with the enemy's killed and wounded," [1] and not far away Union soldiers rested behind stone walls and fences, in front of which the rebel dead were "piled in lines like winrows of hay." [2] Stepping carefully over sleeping forms, orderlies and attendants from the medical corps sought out the wounded to bring them relief from their pain or carry them off to hospitals in neighboring houses and barns. Nearby weary surgeons worked in the shelter of oak and pine trees, and by the light of overhanging lanterns operated on the wounded hour after hour with machinelike motions. [3]

The fighting on July 2 had been one of the severest contests of the war, but it had resulted in no important advantages for either side in spite of the combined casualties which totalled approximately 16,500 officers and men. Of these about 2,600 were listed as missing or captured, while the rest ended as victims of bullet or shell. A larger number of Confederate than of Federal troops were captured, a fact which attested perhaps to the effectiveness of Union counterattacks, especially along Hancock's front. In contrast, the far greater losses suffered by the Northern army in killed and wounded demonstrated the superb marksmanship of the Southerners and the

442

cost to Meade of having to repair a major break in his battle line.[4] Although both armies had received a real battering, they were not actually "shattered," as Meade described them,[5] and both were in condition to fight again. However, the cocky assurance of many Confederates on the morning of July 2 that they could easily drive the Yankees from the heights had evaporated by nightfall.[6]

In reviewing the results of the day's fighting Lee was convinced that his forces had achieved "partial successes." In actual fact he had gained not one of his major objectives, although Johnson had obtained a foothold on the lower end of Culp's Hill and Longstreet had seized the "desired ground" near the Peach Orchard.[7] This position would prove of value, however, only if Lee should decide to use it as a base from which to make a frontal assault on Cemetery Ridge; otherwise it would mean no more than so many yards of real estate for which thousands of Longstreet's men gave their lives. Its seizure by Lee did not spell disaster for Union arms, despite the importance Sickles attached to the area when he tried to justify his handling of the Third Corps on July 2. Notwithstanding his claims that it was a "key" to the Federal line [8] which, if the rebels took it, would render the Union position on the left "untenable," [9] the Yankee grip on the left was firmer than ever at the end of the day. The value of this "desired ground" was questionable even to the Confederates. Colonel Alexander found fault with it as a firing platform for his artillery because in general it sloped toward Cemetery Ridge and exposed his movements to the enemy gunners. From their vantage points they could subject his horses, limbers, and caissons to a deadly fire,[10] but he had no alternative to using the position in the Confederate attack on the 3rd.

What depressed and annoyed Lee most about Confederate operations on July 2 was the lack of what he called a "proper concert of action." [11] Contemporary critics largely agreed with him, though some of them deplored as well the late hour of the attack.[12] Longstreet admitted that the Confederates had not been as successful as they wished, but he attributed their failure chiefly to Hood's wound and Barksdale's death.[13] Other commentators blamed McLaws for not attacking soon enough and Anderson for not supporting Longstreet with his entire division.[14] McLaws himself in reviewing the "battle of the Peach Orchard," as he called it, said he considered the attack "unnecessary and the whole plan of battle a very bad one," [15] while Alexander pronounced its management "conspicuously bad." There appeared to have been "little supervision," he declared, and everywhere there was failure to conform to General Lee's original plan.[16] Alexander complained that the "whole assistance" given to Longstreet's drive by the two other corps between 4:00 P.M. and darkness was confined to a cannonade by thirty-two of Ewell's guns and fifty-five of Hill's.[17] Aside from his neglect to mention the valiant support which Anderson's three brigades in Hill's corps furnished Longstreet, Alexander's indictment was well founded. Less convincing and unduly harsh was his verdict, in referring to Longstreet's attack, that "few battle-fields can furnish examples of worse tactics" because it was based upon accounts often fragmentary, sometimes confusing, and in one or two cases misleading, if not inaccurate.[18] Many of the conditions Alexander mentioned to explain the inefficient operations of McLaws' and Hood's divisions were in fact beyond Longstreet's control. The unusually heavy loss in general officers, the physical fatigue of the men from long marches in hot weather, and the rugged nature of the battleground increased the problems of command. For these reasons the ranks became broken, and the normal volume of fire in a volley was lessened. With regiments and brigades overlapping and interfering with each other, officers had trouble keeping their men well supplied with ammunition. Though Alexander considered Longstreet responsible for the shortcomings of his assault, he felt that Lee as commanding officer should have exercised greater supervision.[19]

Supervision was hardly the word to have used in describing Lee's activities on the afternoon and evening of July 2. As soon as the firing began he joined Hill and Heth near the seminary, which was equally accessible to Longstreet and Ewell, and stayed there "nearly all the time" during the battle. Occasionally he conversed with these generals and sometimes with Colonel Long of his staff,[20] but for the most part he sat alone on a stump intently observing the movements of his infantry and artillery through a field glass. Now and then he would change his position from one stump to another, and although he was obviously much concerned about developments, yet, according to one observer, "his countenance betrayed no more anxiety than upon the occasion of a general review." [21] While the battle raged he sent only one message and received only one report by courier.[22] It was his policy to make careful plans with his corps commanders and then leave to them the duty of modifying and carrying them out to the best of their abilities.[23] Presumably he would intervene only when he saw the collapse of a major attack, such as Pickett's charge, and feared disaster. At Gettysburg this practice suffered from two serious handicaps. Lee was operating in hilly country on the exterior of a five-mile-long battlefront shaped roughly like a horseshoe, but he could not find an observation post to furnish him a view of his entire army. Furthermore, two of his three corps commanders were serving in that capacity for the first time, and they could bear close watching and the benefit of his advice. Hill stayed near him much of the time, but there is recorded only one instance in which the commanding general showed a disposition to exert direct control over his Third Corps. He apparently told Hill, when Longstreet sent word of McLaws' advance, that in accordance with previous arrangements the time had come for Anderson's division to join in the attack.[24]

Yet in spite of their freedom neither Hill nor Ewell displayed vigorous leadership on July 2; at least neither received favorable comment at the time. In contrast Longstreet, whatever his shortcomings in generalship that day, redeemed himself by keeping a close watch on affairs on McLaws' section of the line. Where necessary he and members of his staff personally participated in directing movements of the troops.[25]

Over the years as the Confederates dwelt upon their own mistakes they conveniently overlooked or underestimated the errors of their adversaries. Longstreet complained of the absence of cavalry to feel out the enemy lines and screen his preparations for an assault. Pleasonton matched this error by removing Buford's cavalry brigades and forgetting to replace them with a comparable force. As time went on Confederate critics became more and more incensed over what they charged was Longstreet's serious dereliction of duty in delaying his attack. They played the tantalizing game of "If." "If" he had attacked at sunrise, at midmorning, at noon, or at any time except when he did, there would have occurred all sorts of rosy results.[26]

It so happens that Longstreet could not have hit the Union left flank at a more inopportune moment for Meade. The timing of Sickles' move to a new position compounded the inherent defects in the line Sickles had chosen for his Third Corps. Before his men could dig in and Meade could shift the Fifth Corps from right to left, Longstreet opened his attack. From then on the Confederates held the initiative and maintained it until the last phases of the engagement. By setting the pace of the fighting, they kept Meade busy coping with one emergency after another, and only his ability to improvise and develop countermeasures quickly enough prevented the collapse of Sickles' line from turning into a catastrophe. In the process Meade had to use up an inordinate amount of manpower and materiel. Most of his brigades suffered from 30 to 40 percent casualties.[27] Nevertheless such figures do not give a true picture of the condition of many of the units immediately after the engagement, especially of those which had fought along the line from Devil's Den to the Emmitsburg road. Many brigades could not fight again until they had had time to round up their men, many of whom had been shaken from their commands during the retreat and were wandering around behind the lines unable or unwilling to rejoin their own outfits. The Third Corps, and Birney's division in particular, was not fit for further front-line duty after July 2. Caldwell's division of the Second Corps was in a similar condition,[28] and the same was true of three brigades in the Fifth Corps, the first two brigades of Ayres's division and Sweitzer's in Barnes's division. After the battle Colonel P. R. Guiney, whose 9th Massachusetts regiment had been on detached duty, described his arrival with his men at Sweitzer's headquarters. "We could scarcely be said to *join* the Brigade," he wrote; "it seemed to me that it would be more appropriate to say that we *constituted* the Brigade. There were the flags of the regiment, & a remnant of a splendid regiment around each, & there were a few officers near their respective colors. . . . The Brigade— except ourselves—had been fought nearly to extinction." Since Sweitzer's brigade could no longer fight, Sykes or Sweitzer assigned the 9th Massachusetts to Tilton's brigade, which was still in shape for further service.[29]

Contrary to Confederate opinion, Longstreet's greatest achievement lay, not in gaining ground of questionable value to the Confederates, but in temporarily knocking out thirteen of Meade's brigades. If he had mounted his offensive earlier in the day, he would have struck Sickles' corps where it should have been in the first place, and he might well have suffered the same heavy losses which he did without the compensating advantages of having pushed the enemy back and destroying the effectiveness of many of his units.

One critic of the battle commented that if Sickles had remained along the line Birney's division had originally formed near Little Round Top, the rebels would have gone through it like "an eggshell." [30] Another likened Sickles' position along the Emmitsburg road to a "breakwater upon which the fury of the attack spent itself, and by the delay enabled the Federal troops to come into line." [31] The metaphor of a breakwater is striking but not very apt, for it implies that Sickles and the Third Corps line, like any good breakwater, had something behind them to protect. But behind them was nothing—an empty harbor—and they found themselves being pounded by wave after wave of Confederates until they could hold out no longer and were overwhelmed. Many thought it an unnecessary sacrifice. If Sickles had stayed where Meade meant him to be Hood would not have been tempted to try a flanking movement at Devil's Den and Little Round Top. Instead his division, guided by the Emmitsburg road, would have moved in a northerly direction to hit the Union left where Lee thought it was on Cemetery Ridge. In that case Sickles' men, lined up on Little Round Top and north of it, would have been in position to hit Hood's right flank with raking fire and perhaps roll it up in a counterattack. But when Sickles moved his men forward, he had no intention of forming a protective barrier for the position Meade had in mind for him, and he had no prepared positions in the rear to which he could retreat should his line break. Meade felt obligated to support Sickles, who in his judgment had made a grave mistake, and he sent him reinforcements as rapidly as possible. In that connection critics more or less friendly to Sickles, and Sickles himself, implied that Meade had expected the Third Corps to hold its original position without supports from other corps. It was their thesis that in advancing to the Emmitsburg road, Sickles precipitated the Confederate attack and forced Meade to send reinforcements to battle on the left.[32] Nothing could be further from the truth. Longstreet attacked when he was ready, not because of a challenge made by Sickles. Meade also had planned to shift the Fifth Corps from right to left as soon as the Sixth Corps came in sight.[33] These troops, together with others Meade threw into the breach during the engagement, should have been able to stop Longstreet's men on the Little Round Top–Cemetery Ridge line and in all probability with far fewer casualties than they did incur. As it was, thirteen of Meade's brigades were badly battered, and some of them became unfit for further service.

In the emergency created by Longstreet's attack Meade could not afford the passive role played by Lee. Recently promoted from corps commander, he was used to leading his troops personally, and it is doubtful whether he could have restrained himself and remained quietly behind the scenes. While directing operations either from headquarters or somewhere along Cemetery Ridge he paid particular attention to the left of his front because of the critical nature of the fighting and the large number of men he sent there from six of his corps. Just where he was and just what he did at a given time may be matters of dispute, but without question he kept abreast of events and with the help of such generals as Warren and Hancock moved quickly to head off crises. He was in top form in timing his orders to his corps commanders for reinforcements; help came to hard-pressed units at precisely the right moments.[34] Though at one time "things looked a little blue" to him, so that he despaired of turning the tide in the Union favor, he encouraged his men by his presence near the battle line, so near that at one time his horse "Baldy" was badly wounded as he sat astride him.[35] At another critical moment Meade, accompanied only by a few of his aides and orderlies, stood anxiously awaiting the arrival of Doubleday's and Robinson's divisions of the First Corps to plug the still un-filled gap in Hancock's line. To some of the watchers it looked as if Meade was about to rush forward into the breach—anything to gain time—toward which the Confederates were heading. Suddenly someone called out, " 'There they come, general!' " and looking back he could see the men of the First Corps sweeping down the Taney-town road at a "sharp double quick," with their muskets on their right shoulders. Then they swung up onto Cemetery Ridge. Amid the "wildest excitement and shouting" Meade rode ahead with the skirmish line, waving his hat and urging the troops on with cries of " 'Come on gentlemen.' " When someone remarked to him that the situation had at one point seemed "pretty desperate," he replied, " 'Yes, but it is all right now, it is all right now.' "[36]

With a note of satisfaction and achievement Meade could write to his wife early next morning, "We had a great fight yesterday,"[37] but he knew as darkness closed in on that memorable Thursday that his day was not yet over. Fighting was still going on on the right side of his line, and in planning for the morrow he had to reckon the costs he had incurred in stopping Longstreet's assault. At 8:00 P.M. he dispatched a message to Halleck announcing his intention of staying in his present position. Whether his operations would be of an "offensive or defensive character" would depend, he said, upon information he received about his army. Fully aware of heavy losses from straggling and two days of fierce combat, he could not determine their extent or the general condition of his men until he could consult with his generals and obtain information and advice.[38] He was still unsure of himself in the role of commanding officer. Furthermore, he considered it conducive to efficient operations for the general of the army not to shroud his actions in secrecy, but to keep his corps commanders and other important officers informed of developments. For these reasons he decided to call a meeting at headquarters as the easiest and most satisfactory way of getting the opinions of his immediate subordinates.[39]

About 9:00 P.M. Meade, his chief of staff, General Butterfield, his chief engineer, General Warren, two wing commanders, Generals Slocum and Hancock, and seven corps commanders, Generals Gibbon, Williams, Birney, Sykes, Howard, Sedgwick, and Newton,[40] met in a hot, stuffy little bedroom not more than ten or twelve feet square in the Leister house. The room had one or two chairs, a table, and a bed, certainly not enough furniture to accommodate everyone comfortably. It began as an informal gathering with some of the officers lounging on the bed or chairs, and the rest standing or leaning against the walls. Everyone had something to say about the battle, telling of his experiences and commenting on the condition of his troops. Only Warren did not share in the conversation. Overcome by heat, fatigue, and shock from his slight wound, he slouched in a corner and quietly slept through the session which lasted until nearly midnight. As for the others, the excitement of the day and the satisfaction of having hurled back Lee's attempts to roll up their flanks and pierce the main line kept them alert and talkative. Neither the heat, the night insects, nor the sound of firing on the Union right seemed to bother them, for they were too interested in exchanging information and ideas to be distracted by physical discomfort. Meade said little but listened attentively to their talk. If he looked tired or careworn, no one seemed to notice it.[41]

They all knew that their success in holding the army's position had been dearly bought, and they wondered about the number of effective troops left to continue the battle. Butterfield added the returns from each corps, which in some instances could have been nothing more than educated guesses, and came up with a total of 58,000 able-bodied infantrymen, a sizeable reduction from previous estimates of the army's strength.[42] Assuming the accuracy of this total, which perhaps was a little too high, cold figures do not tell the whole story of the number of available soldiers. Birney considered his Third Corps "used up" and not ready for further action. Its condition affected his judgment and led him to express doubts about the ability of the army to "stay and fight it out."[43] In contrast Howard showed a positive willingness to hold on to the present position, although he had good reason to be discouraged by the sad state of the Eleventh Corps, which had not distinguished itself and had incurred heavy losses.[44]

The question of adequate supplies for the army caused concern and considerable discussion, for Meade had outrun them in his haste to concentrate his forces at Gettysburg. He had ordered the long wagon trains to stay close to the railroad between Westminster and Union Bridge over twenty miles away, because he did not want either baggage or wagons to interfere with the rapidity of his movements. But by the night of July 2 the army had rations for only one more day, and some of the corps had even less. Meade and his generals decided that if they supplemented the rations they had on hand with cattle and flour obtained from local farmers, they could "eke out a few half-fed days" and remain where they were.[45]

There was considerable talk about the merits and defects of the army's position. When Newton pronounced Gettysburg as "'no place to fight a battle in,'" many officers pricked up their ears, for they rated him highly as an engineer and a soldier. Gibbon, startled by this opinion, asked him to spell out his objections.[46] In reply Newton expressed concern that the Union left was exposed to an enveloping movement, which Lee could attempt by shifting a whole corps secretly at night while still maintaining his present lines.[47] He reasoned that Lee was not "fool enough" to attack the Union army "in front after two days' fighting which had ended in consolidating . . . [it] into a position immensely strong."[48] General Meade on the other hand objected to the irregular shape of his battle line and thought that should he need to fall back he would establish a much straighter one stretching from Wolf's Hill on the right down along the east bank of Rock Creek.[49] Some officers weighed the advantages of a general withdrawal to the Pipe Creek line in view of the shortcomings of the present position and the difficulties in keeping the army adequately supplied with food and ammunition from a base which was a long day's march away.[50]

So far the talk had been rambling and informal. Then Butterfield apparently decided that the discussion had gone far enough and it was time to bring matters to a head. On his own initiative he formulated three questions which he presented to the generals, and assuming the role of secretary of the meeting, he recorded the response of each of the wing and corps commanders, who were the only ones to vote. Meade agreed to the procedure, although it is doubtful whether he had it in mind at the beginning. He regarded such gatherings during the Gettysburg campaign—and there were several of them—not as regular councils of war but as opportunities to discuss army affairs with his generals in a more or less relaxed manner.[51] Butterfield, however, by posing set questions and recording the answers converted the meeting into a formal affair and gave it, deliberately or not, an exaggerated importance. For the sake of Meade's military reputation it was unfortunate that this change took place, for traditionally military students have considered councils of war as signs of weakness and indecision on the part of the commanding officer.

Butterfield's first question read as follows: "Under existing circumstances, is it advisable for this army to remain in its present position, or to retire to another nearer its base of supplies?" Everyone recommended that the army stay, although three of the generals advised a correction in the present line to meet the possible threat of an enveloping movement on the left. In response to the second question of whether or not the army should attack, all the generals thought it wise to remain on the defensive. Finally, in answer to the last question of how long they should wait for an enemy attack, a big majority agreed that Meade should not wait long, perhaps a day at the most, before deciding on other measures.[52] When the voting was over, Gibbon remembered Meade saying, "quietly, but decidedly, 'Such then is the decision.'"[53]

It should be noted that nowhere in the records is there the suggestion that Meade, other than contemplating a slight withdrawal to straighten his lines, wanted to retreat from Gettysburg. Yet when the Committee on the Conduct of the War reviewed the history of the campaign in the early months of 1864, Butterfield and Birney accused him of having wished to retreat and implied that he was kept from doing so only on the advice of his field commanders.[54] Thus they put the worst possible interpretation on Meade's assumed lack of self-confidence without offering any real evidence to substantiate it. In their testimony they also made factual errors about what had transpired at the meeting, but nobody could challenge their statements because the minutes of the council and the comments of the various generals which Butterfield had recorded were missing. It was not until years later that they turned up in Meade's personal files. The general, who could have used them to good effect in defending his reputation, had obviously forgotten that he had them.[55]

Meade got wind of these charges in March of 1864 when several newspaper articles purporting to be based upon a knowledge of the deliberations of the council claimed that he had wanted to retreat on July 2. Greatly disturbed by these accusations, Meade asked Gibbon, Newton, Sedgwick, Sykes, Alpheus Williams, and Slocum what they remembered of the meeting with special reference to anything he might have said about the need to withdraw from Gettysburg.[56] All except Slocum replied to his request for information.[57] None had obtained the impression that he desired to retreat.[58] Sedgwick, who was the ranking officer next to Slocum, declared positively: "At no time in my presence did the general commanding insist or advise a withdrawal of the army, for such advice would have great weight with me, and I know the matter did not engage my serious attention." [59] Alpheus Williams, who had written a long account of events in a letter to his daughters three days after the battle, declared unequivocally of Meade: "I heard no expression from him which led me to think he was in favor of withdrawing the army from before Gettysburg." [60]

Even more convincing than the records and the testimony of most of the generals who attended the council, other evidence shows that Meade's critics were wrong in saying that he had wanted to retreat. A message which he sent to Halleck prior to the meeting breathed confidence, and very positively and without any reservations declared it was his intention to hold his present position.[61] The spirit

of this dispatch bore out what Alpheus Williams said about the noticeable display of satisfaction he found in Meade and other officers
when he met them in the field at the close of the engagement with
Longstreet's troops.[62]

Since Meade had already made up his mind to stay where he was,
why did he permit the question to be raised at the meeting and put
to a vote? His purpose in calling the corps commanders to headquarters was to find out whether the condition of the army warranted offensive operations. In the course of the discussion several
officers wondered about the advisability of remaining so far away
from their base of supplies, especially in a position which struck
them as vulnerable to an envelopment or a turning movement. With
these doubts in the air Meade probably decided to include this
question among others he permitted Butterfield to formulate for a
formal vote. The answers would enable him to determine the extent
of the uncertainty of his subordinates. It must have given him satisfaction to know that they agreed with his decision to hold the army's
present position, not only because they confirmed the soundness
of his own judgment,[63] but because they demonstrated a spirit "to
do or die," as he put it in a letter to Mrs. Meade the next morning.[64]

Now that Meade and his generals had resolved to "stay and fight
it out," [65] they proceeded to get ready for a renewal of the battle in
the morning. The first commander to discover that he had his work
cut out for him was General Alpheus Williams. When he returned to
his corps from the council sometime before midnight, he learned
that the Southerners were occupying the entrenchments previously
held by his First Division. He asked Slocum's permission to drive
them out.[66] Slocum in turn secured Meade's approval of the operation.[67] For the next three hours Williams made preparations for the
attack. He was well aware of the immense strength of Johnson's position, which on the front had the double protection of log breastworks put up by men of the Twelfth Corps and a stone wall running
parallel to and about a hundred feet in advance of them. The low,
swampy, open ground between five hundred and six hundred feet
wide south of Spangler's Spring and Rock Creek secured the Confederate left flank against a major assault. Williams planned to open
his attack with a heavy cannonade by several batteries, and after fifteen minutes Geary's division on his left would advance obliquely

against the right of the Confederate entrenchments. Williams ordered his own division, the First, to keep the enemy busy by maintaining constant pressure against his left flank. His work done at 3:30 A.M., the general finally rolled up in a blanket and lay down on a "flat rock sheltered by an apple tree" for a half hour or so of sleep.[68]

Opposite Williams' line the Confederates themselves were just as busy getting ready to renew the fray in the morning. Ewell and Lee, thinking that Johnson had gained an advantage from his attack on Culp's Hill, decided to exploit it. They ordered him to advance from the breastworks he had captured on the south shoulder, outflank the Federal line, and seize the top of the hill.[69] During the night General Rodes received instructions to send Johnson all the troops he could spare in time for them to be in position before daylight. Rodes pulled out Daniel's brigade and O'Neal's, minus the 5th Alabama regiment, from his second line because they had less distance to march.[70] These reinforcements, in addition to Smith's brigade from Early's division, built up Johnson's force to seven brigades against the six under Williams.[71] Nevertheless, a complete lack of artillery support, in contrast to the four batteries available to Williams, more than offset any superiority Johnson might have had in numbers.[72] His was an impossible assignment, for he did not have nearly enough men for a successful attack over the exceedingly rough ground. It was another example of Confederate overconfidence arising from a latent contempt for the foe and the exhilarating experience of having defeated him continually despite great odds. On July 3 the toll for underestimating the valor of the ably led men of the Twelfth Corps was to prove excessively heavy.

The renewal of Ewell's offensive against Culp's Hill seemed to be an essential element in Lee's plan of operations for July 3, although ambiguities and contradictions in Confederate reports and accounts obscure what he really had in mind. Lee himself said: "The general plan was unchanged. Longstreet, re-enforced by Pickett's three brigades, . . . was ordered to attack the next morning, and General Ewell was directed to assail the enemy's right at the same time." [73] This statement at once raises questions, especially in the light of other reports. If the "general plan" remained the same as it had been on July 2, did it mean that Longstreet's two divisions facing the frowning heights of the Round Tops would begin just where they had left off when darkness fell? As for the time of the attack, the phrase "next morning" left room for considerable latitude; it could mean any hour between daylight and noon, if not the longer period from midnight to noon.

Ewell stated flatly that his orders called for an attack at daylight.[74] Lee implied that this was close to the hour he had had in mind when he said: "General Longstreet's dispositions were not completed as early as was expected, but before notice could be sent to General Ewell, General Johnson had already become engaged, and it was too late to recall him." [75] Word about the delay in Longstreet's assault came to Ewell around 5:00 A.M., half an hour after Johnson had hurled his men against the Union line.[76] Implying criticism of Longstreet's delay, Lee emphasized that it gave the Federals, who at the moment were not threatened from other quarters, a chance to build up numerical superiority by getting reinforcements from other parts of their line and thus suppress Johnson's attack.[77] Although the explanation appears convincing, poor coordination in the Confederate offensive in no way influenced the timing of the engagement or its outcome. Questions about Longstreet's delay and the hour of Ewell's attack are academic, because under any circumstances Williams would have forced the fight on Johnson. As the two lines clashed furiously for hours Williams did receive some reinforcements, but only enough to give him at best a slight edge over his opponent.[78] These forces were not needed to stop Longstreet later in the day, and if his attack had been made earlier it is doubtful that it would have changed the outcome of events on Culp's Hill in the morning or on Cemetery Ridge in the afternoon.

Longstreet got off to a slow start on July 3 because he and Lee had not previously reached a clear understanding on the nature, extent, and direction of his offensive operations. It was Longstreet's custom to ride over to Lee's headquarters after every battle to review events with him and discuss plans for the next day, but on the night of July 2 the two did not meet. Longstreet claimed that he did not feel up to the long ride to headquarters, and instead he sent a courier with a report of his activities.[79] In view of the faulty execution of his plans on the second day of the battle, Lee would have done well to have called in his three lieutenants to confer with them and spell out exactly what he wanted. That was not the way he did things, however, and he contented himself with an order to Long-

street to attack in the morning. In his report Lee did not say whether he had made clear to Longstreet his purpose to continue the
offensive according to the general plan of July 2. The only modifi-
cation in Longstreet's arrangements as Lee pictured them was the
addition of Pickett's division to the assaulting column.[80]

Either Longstreet did not consider Lee's instructions as orders,
which seems unlikely, or he concluded they were sufficiently broad
to give him a choice in the manner and direction of his attack. Because he wanted latitude, perhaps he stretched his orders out of
shape by interpreting them too liberally. There were definite orders
to attack, however, for Lee said so and so did Colonel Alexander.[81]
Alexander remembered finding his way to Longstreet's bivouac soon
after the battle ended on July 2 "to ask news from other quarters &
orders for the morning. . . . I was told," he wrote, "that we would
renew the attack early in the morning. That Pickett's Division
w[ould] arrive and would assault the enemy's line—My impression
is the *exact* point for it was not designated, but told it would be to
our left of the Peach Orchard." In accordance with his instructions
Alexander selected a place for more artillery which would come to
join him at dawn. Fortunately, he said, it was a "glorious moonlight
night, greatly facilitating all the necessary moving about." By 1:00
A.M. he had everything in shape and nothing to do but to try and get
a little sleep.[82]

In contrast Longstreet must have had almost no rest. Still hanker-
ing to try his favorite maneuver of turning Meade out of his position
or moving around his left flank and attacking his rear, he evidently
spent the night seeking ways to accomplish this purpose. Realizing
that at this stage of the battle a wide swing to strike at the Union
base at Westminster was out of the question, he thought an attack
on the immediate flank still feasible. His scouting parties had poked
around beyond Big Round Top toward the Taneytown road looking
for a route around the Union left and had come back with encouraging reports. They detected no organized forces guarding the approaches to the enemy's rear.[83] Either they were not thorough
enough, or they made the reconnaissance just before Colonel L. A.
Grant's Vermont Brigade of the Sixth Corps moved to the ground
immediately east of the hill, which it did soon after dark.[84] Their
information convinced Longstreet that he had found a solution to
his tactical problem of getting at the enemy without incurring the

bloody losses of a frontal assault. He gave orders, apparently around sunrise, to start what he himself admitted to be the "slow process" of shifting his divisions around Big Round Top for the purpose of gaining the enemy's left "by flank and reverse attack." [85]

Should he have completed the move, his men would have had the surprise of an encounter not only with Grant's brigade, but with another one as well under Brigadier General D. A. Russell of the Sixth Corps, which had come up during the night. The entire force under the command of the extremely competent Brigadier General Horatio G. Wright consisted of about 3,100 officers and men, as well as two batteries of artillery. [86] It was sufficiently large to have unmasked Longstreet's drive and contained it long enough for Union reinforcements to arrive. If Pleasonton in obedience to Meade's general instructions had maintained a strong cavalry detachment guarding this flank, Union preparations for an attack from this quarter would have been even more complete. It is not certain whether the regiment which Pleasonton had ordered General Gregg to send as a replacement for Buford's brigades finally got there. [87] Under any circumstances, the route which Longstreet felt sure "gave some promise of results" [88] was fraught with difficulties, though he failed to see or refused to admit them.

A few minutes after Longstreet issued orders for his flanking movement, General Lee rode up to his headquarters. Imagine the chagrin of the two officers when they found themselves working at cross purposes at an hour when the attack was supposed to have started. "Disappointed" was the word Longstreet used to describe his reactions, [89] but it fails to convey the feeling of depression which was to burden him all day following this meeting with the commanding general. [90] If Longstreet showed disappointment, the expression on Lee's face must have been one of amazement. Without clearing with him Longstreet had taken it upon himself to order a time-consuming maneuver which would have completely changed his plan of battle. What Lee wanted above all was to strike both extremities of the enemy line at exactly the same time, Ewell the right and Longstreet the left. Should the maneuver succeed, he was confident of victory. The formidable character of the Union position never awed him as it did Longstreet, and he felt sure his incomparable infantry if properly handled could take any height. It is not enough to say that Lee was mistaken and presumed too much for his men, because there was no guarantee of success in Longstreet's plan either, certainly not in the way he went about carrying it out. His scheme had all the characteristics of something he dreamed up at the last moment when it was too late. Newton had feared that a flanking movement of this sort in the dark might catch the Union army napping,[91] but dawn had broken before Longstreet issued his orders to attempt it, thus eliminating the element of surprise; nor did he have Pickett's division on hand to join in his operations.[92]

Lee's report was a model of restraint when he said that Longstreet's "dispositions were not completed as early as was expected." [93] He could have added that they were not completed because Longstreet had been preparing an independent course of action and had failed to bring Pickett's division up early enough to be ready for battle at daylight. Pickett's men had arrived thoroughly exhausted within three or four miles of Gettysburg on the Cashtown road late in the afternoon of July 2. Pickett reported his position to Lee and said his division would be ready for duty if given a breathing spell of two hours. Lee sent back word for the general to give his men a good rest for they were not needed that day. They went into bivouac near a stone bridge and remained there until they received instructions to move about three-thirty the next morning. Nobody bothered to explain why they were not ordered to join their corps immediately after the battle instead of many hours later. Assuming that they came to a halt near Gettysburg around 4:00 P.M.,[94] the men could have spent five or six hours in quenching their thirst, cooking their meals, and relaxing and still have reached Longstreet's part of the battlefield about the time the fighting stopped. A march by moonlight would have been no great hardship for such veteran troops, and it would have saved valuable time. In his report Lee did not go into the reasons for Longstreet's tardiness in making his dispositions. Instead he implied that his lieutenant hesitated to attack at the designated spot because he feared Union forces on the Round Tops would descend from the heights and hit his own right and rear as he advanced.[95] At best it was a lame excuse, for if Longstreet had been plagued by these doubts he should have resolved them in a conference with Lee sometime during the night.

Now that a well-coordinated attack at an early hour was no longer possible Lee had to scrap his plans for the day and start all over again. Before coming to any decision he wanted to take another look at the enemy lines. Accompanied by Longstreet and several staff officers, he rode up Seminary Ridge through the woods and out into the open. Here with his field glasses he could carefully examine much of Cemetery Ridge. Apparently it never occurred to him that the position could not be taken. The question was where would he have the best chance for complete success. One section of the ridge, and not the lowest, attracted his attention [96] for it was quite bare and furnished little cover for defending infantry and artillery. The approaches to it were open fields measuring nearly a mile square and seemingly free of any obstacles except fences. The advance of Hill's men over much of this ground the previous evening removed any fears about hidden defiles or deep depressions which could wreck formations and fatally slow down movements. Maybe Lee had heard General Wright claim that he had conquered the heights, only to be forced down again for want of supports. "The trouble is not in going there," Wright later explained to Alexander. "The trouble is to stay there after you get there. . . ." [97] Lee realized this fact too without having to be told by Wright. This time he would send over enough men to crush the defenders beyond hope of recovery. His troops would converge on one point, say that small clump of trees he could see with his naked eye; they would form something like a flying wedge of sufficient depth to sustain their momentum and sufficient breadth to protect their flanks. The objective Lee chose had another advantage. Once gained and firmly held, his men could curl around to the left and threaten Cemetery Hill from the flank and rear. Federal troops south of the captured positions would be able to do little to help their comrades for fear that their counterfire would be "as destructive to friend as foe." [98] While open country would permit a massive attack on the scale Lee visualized, it would expose his men to a raking fire from enemy muskets and artillery. He hoped to reduce this hazard by opening his assault with an extraordinarily heavy cannonade which would pulverize the Union lines and artillery before his infantry moved, and his exterior lines would give his artillery the advantage of setting up a converging fire against the defenders.

Standing out in the open field within range of Union cannon, Lee pointed to the Clump of Trees and explained his plan to his listeners who now included A. P. Hill and Henry Heth, as well as Longstreet and members of Lee's staff. [99] This gathering had become a conference in which "the mode of attack and the troops to make it were thoroughly debated." [100] Longstreet was not impressed with Lee's plan and he frankly objected to it, since he was to be responsible for its execution. How many men, he asked, did the general expect to have in the attacking force? When Lee gave a figure of 15,000, Longstreet, making a sweeping gesture with his arm toward the ridge and the broad open spaces leading to it, exclaimed vehemently: " 'I have been a soldier, I may say, from the ranks up to the position I now hold. I have been in pretty much all kinds of skirmishes, from those of two or three soldiers up to those of an army corps, and I think I can safely say there never was a body of fifteen thousand men who could make that attack successfully.' " [101] Whether these were his exact words is irrelevant. The point is that he did not like the plan and said so. Although Longstreet's manner might have made Lee impatient, he evidently did not consider his opposition an act of insubordination. Rather he chose to regard it as the professional judgment of an experienced and competent soldier with whom he happened to disagree. In the discussion that followed Lee refused to modify his plan of attack except in the matter of what troops would make the assault.[102] Here again the accounts are contradictory and far from clear.

Lee's original plan had called for Longstreet to use his entire corps in bearing again the burden of the main Confederate offensive. After Lee chose as his objective a point opposite Hill's front instead of Longstreet's, he still talked about Longstreet performing the duty with all his command. Longstreet pointed out the danger to his right and rear should Hood's and McLaws' divisions be withdrawn from their present positions on the extreme right flank to join Pickett in the attack. Lee, according to his battle report, agreed to keep these men where they were, and instead he placed at Longstreet's disposal for the assault all of Heth's division and half of Pender's, both of Hill's corps. Either then or later he also assigned to Longstreet Wilcox' and Perry's brigades from Anderson's division of Hill's corps.[103] But certain members of Lee's staff who attended the conference—Walter Taylor, Charles Venable, and A. L. Long—had a different understanding of what Lee expected of Hood's and McLaws' troops that day. With minor variations their accounts agreed that Lee intended these men to play an active role in the assault from the very beginning, as participants either in the attacking column or in the supporting one.[104] According to Taylor, the units from Hill's corps were not expected to replace these divisions in the charge but to reinforce them, "because of the apprehensions of General Longstreet that his corps was not strong enough for the movement. . . ." [105] As Lee's plans finally evolved, Taylor said, the roles were reversed and Hood and McLaws were to be used in support of Pickett's and Hill's men. Despite his knowledge of what Lee had said in his report, Taylor denied that Federal forces would have threatened the Confederate right and rear should Hood's and McLaws' divisions have joined the assault. Apparently he overlooked the fact that Lee had changed the direction of his attack when he revised his plan of operation.

Nevertheless Taylor always wondered why Longstreet kept these divisions inactive, and years later he finally asked him. Longstreet, who was smarting from increasingly intense criticism of his record, refused to explain, other than to say that Lee had given no orders for him to do otherwise.[106] In his memoirs, however, Longstreet claimed that if Pickett's and Hill's men had successfully pierced the Union lines, he had instructed Hood's and McLaws' divisions to "spring to the charge" against the enemy positions immediately confronting them.[107] In view of the various versions of what role Lee had in mind for these units, the statement in his battle report that they were needed where they were is about as satisfactory as any.[108]

With these two divisions not available Lee naturally turned to Hill's corps for troops to advance with Pickett's men. The question ultimately arose of whether he and Hill chose wisely. At the time it seemed sensible to use the four brigades of Heth's division and two from Pender's, for these troops had enjoyed over thirty-six hours of rest after the first day's encounter. Later some Confederates felt it had been a mistake to put Heth's division into action because it had suffered more heavily from the engagement on July 1 than reports made within hours of the battle had indicated. The proportionately greater loss of officers than of men had reduced its efficiency, and its temporary commander, General J. J. Pettigrew, though a soldier of ability, had had no previous experience in leading a division.[109] For reasons not clear Hill and Lee seemed not to have fully appreciated the weakened condition of the division. Inadequate staff work, the confusion of combat, and Heth's disabling wound probably deprived them of the information necessary for a correct appraisal. Nevertheless, Hill certainly should have suspected that Pender's division, in spite of the loss of its able commander on July 2, was in better shape than Heth's, since only two of its brigades, Scales's and Perrin's, had been heavily engaged in the first day's battle.[110] Furthermore, all of the brigades except one were still led by their regular commanders. To replace Pender, Lee had on hand the competent and experienced Marylander, Major General Isaac R. Trimble, who had joined the army as a supernumerary and was eager for a command. Under these circumstances Lee and Hill would have done better to have used all of Pender's division instead of half of it and kept Heth's in reserve.[111] As additional reinforcement for Pickett they could have used besides Wilcox' and Perry's brigades from Anderson's division, Mahone's and Posey's which had yet to see serious action. Their brigades were just as fresh as Pickett's division, yet they were overlooked and not assigned even a supporting role.[112]

To summarize, Lee's plan for his major offensive on July 3 as it finally evolved called for Longstreet to organize an attacking force composed of the three brigades of Pickett's division, the four of Heth's, two of Pender's, and two of Anderson's,[113] in all about 13,500 infantrymen and their officers.[114] The eight brigades of Hood's and McLaws' divisions might ultimately become involved in the attack, so altogether Lee entrusted Longstreet with authority over nineteen brigades for the day's operation.[115] As for Hill, Lee directed him "to hold his line with the rest of his command, afford General Longstreet further assistance, if required, and avail himself of any success that might be gained." [116] Lee, then, anticipated throwing another 10,000 or so infantry into the breach he expected to be made by the assaulting column.

For his offensive Lee assigned a dual role to all of his artillery except some pieces in Ewell's corps: to silence opposing batteries in a cannonade prior to the infantry advance, and to push forward with the moving columns as protection for their flanks and support for their attack. At a prearranged signal from one of Longstreet's batteries 159 guns stretching in a long line from the Peach Orchard to Oak Hill were to open simultaneously. After the artillery had effectively reduced the resistance of the enemy, the infantry would move forward. General Pickett's line would be the guide for Heth's division under Pettigrew to the left of it; it would move on the same line as Pickett's men and hit the enemy salient at the same moment. Immediately behind Pettigrew would be the two brigades of Pender's division marching abreast of one of Pickett's brigades in the second line. The two brigades of Anderson's division had instructions to move considerably in the rear of Pickett's right flank for the purpose of protecting it against a counterattack.[117] The reports do not say so, but other accounts show that the advancing battle lines were expected to converge on the Clump of Trees in order to hit the Union position on a comparatively narrow front.[118]

In planning for his grand assault Lee sought to overcome his artillery's traditional handicap through careful deployment and synchronized use of the guns. He hoped to blast Union artillery into oblivion with a cannonade unparalleled in the annals of warfare and to demoralize the Union infantry beyond the point of serious resistance. Once his artillery had gained dominance, Lee assumed that a force of 12,000 to 14,000 men stretched out in a line almost a mile wide could advance across three-quarters of a mile of open fields and by moving toward a specific landmark achieve a major breakthrough before enemy firepower could cut it down.

If Lee had employed a much larger number of troops in the attacking force, he would have risked the security of his whole army by exposing it to enemy counterthrusts in case his own assault failed. Longstreet asserted that "thirty thousand men was the minimum force necessary for the work," [119] but it is difficult to see where Lee could have gathered that many men, especially as Longstreet himself insisted upon holding back two of his own divisions. There is the suspicion that the general used the fantastic figure of 30,000 troops just to dramatize the unsoundness of Lee's tactics. For basic simplicity and audacity of concept his plan evokes admiration, though it could work only if an almost infinite number of pieces in its pattern fell into the right places at the right times.

One factor in the situation was the Union position on Cemetery Ridge which was difficult but not impossible to take; nor was it nearly as formidable as the Confederates later remembered it. Federal troops and artillery failed to cover the slopes of the ridge with field fortifications so as to give themselves maximum protection. The infantry did get some cover in hastily improvised, shallow breastworks, as well as behind low stone walls built by farmers to mark off their fields, but Union batteries south of Ziegler's Grove stood out in the open. Cemetery Ridge was far from being Marye's Heights at Fredericksburg with its wooded crest crowned by artillery and its base guarded by infantry lined up along a sunken road. Nevertheless, the ridge gave a decided advantage to determined and skillful defenders who knew enough to shoot low. Only a carefully coordinated attack with infantry and artillery acting in close cooperation could hope to succeed. In an army as loosely and informally organized as Lee's these requirements could scarcely be met. And Longstreet, entrusted with the task of carrying out the assault, had no faith in it. In later years attacks on his conduct at Gettysburg and recollections of the false position in which his own abilities and fate had placed him so embittered him that he wrote petulantly: "He [Lee] knew that I did not believe that success was possible; that care and time should be taken to give the troops the benefit of positions and the grounds; and he should have put an officer in charge who had more confidence in his plan. Two-thirds of the troops were of other commands, and there was no reason for putting the assaulting forces under my charge." [120]

Unfortunately for Longstreet and for Lee, there was no one else.[121] The facts are that Lee did help Longstreet in executing the plan, and both of them did have time to put the troops in position.[122] The question was how well they would use their opportunity.

XVIII

UNFINISHED BUSINESS: THE BATTLE FOR CULP'S HILL, JULY 3

To AN OBSERVER on Cemetery Hill the morning of July 3 offered a study in contrasts. Looking west he would notice that the two forces facing each other along the Emmitsburg road were relatively quiet, even as they maintained a wary watchfulness broken now and then by a fusillade of musketry or the roar of a solitary cannon. But upon turning around he would see signs of a violent struggle around Culp's Hill. Clouds of smoke rose from the dark woods, while the sounds of firing ranged from "intermittent" to "continuous and crashing." [1] Here brave, experienced soldiers battled desperately for possession of this key position. From sunrise to noon the struggle was a test of the endurance and determination of both the Northern and Southern infantry, yet its importance has been overlooked or underrated as a consequence of the more dramatic and spectacular demonstration of Confederate offensive power in the afternoon.

The attack of Ewell's men on the Twelfth Corps, which had started out as a major element in a two-pronged offensive, soon became a sideshow because Lee was forced to change his plans. Not knowing of his difficulties in organizing a general assault for the day, some Northern officers and observers concluded that Ewell's attack was "a feint to cover a more formidable flank movement on the left." [2] The nature of the fighting on Culp's Hill made this interpretation a plausible, if not a correct one. Neither side had much room to maneuver amid the trees, the huge boulders, the cliffs, the stone walls, and the solid breastworks built along the slopes and ridges. With the men locked in close combat and seldom moving except for a few limited charges, it was hard to realize what large numbers were engaged in the struggle, about three-quarters of the total who were to fight in the afternoon for possession of the Clump of Trees on Cemetery Ridge.[3] Whatever observers then or later might think, the crack troops of Ewell's corps were not resorting to diversionary tactics. They were fighting in earnest for a rich prize: possession of Culp's Hill and the Baltimore Pike. Slocum's men, aware of the stakes, showed equal determination to stop the invaders and hurl them off the hill.

General Meade, despite appearances, also realized the importance of this fight and kept a close check on developments from reports coming into headquarters. When it was all over General Alpheus Williams accused Meade of having had "no proper understanding or appreciation of operations of the right wing," because he had never come nearer the Twelfth Corps position than Slocum's headquarters on Power's Hill, when he was driven out of his own center of operations on the afternoon of July 3.[4] In this instance Williams was wrong. Meade did exercise control over events on Culp's Hill, as witness the fact that he sent Slocum even more reinforcements than he needed, he advised Howard to have his men stand to arms and be ready to move there, and he warned Geary that he was wasting his ammunition in excessive firing. Meade unconsciously paid Slocum and Williams a compliment in not making his appearance at their headquarters while they were busily engaged fighting the enemy. He knew they were able generals and could cope with the situation without his personal supervision.[5] He was right, for they were doing a good job in stopping the enemy, if not in driving him off.

In the few hours between the adjournment of the council of war and daybreak Williams with the help of Slocum and Geary had planned and organized well for an attack.[6] Nevertheless, he thought that Slocum's curt order, "Hell! Drive them out at daylight," was more easily said than done. The rebels were well entrenched in the Twelfth Corps lines they had seized and would be hard to dislodge. They were partly hidden by the woods, while all approaches from Williams' center and right were over "open clear ground partly marshy." He did have the advantage of excellent positions for artillery at effective range, in contrast to those of the Confederates which were too far away to be of any use.

Williams held one flank of the line as originally formed by the Twelfth Corps, that is, the section so ably defended by Greene on July 2. As he analyzed its importance: "Until they got us out of it, [the Confederates] could not safely move forward. Besides, we could work along the line on that flank. . . ." Since Geary's Second Division held the only part of the line from which Williams could advance with any hope of success, he arranged to have it operate from the Union left, while most of the First Division was held in readiness to support it directly and also push the extreme rebel left "should opportunity offer." [7] Geary's division formed a line which started on the crest of the hill, ran southward down its slope, and gradually curved to the west toward the Baltimore Pike. Greene's brigade took position on the left, Kane's in the center, and Colonel Charles Candy's on the right. Williams widened the gap between Geary's and Ruger's lines by throwing back the left of the First Division so as to give the artillery a good field of fire without endangering Union infantry. After personally putting all batteries in position, two on the west side of the pike just above his headquarters, two on Power's Hill, and one on McAllister's Hill, Williams directed their commanders to fire along the right of Geary's oblique line so as to sweep almost his entire front in the general direction of what is now known as Ario Pardee Field on the south shoulder of Culp's Hill.[8] Two brigades of Williams' First Division formed more or less the same line Ruger had established the previous night with the right flank resting near Rock Creek and the left out on the fields at right angles to the pike. The brigade on the right under Colonel Silas Colgrove had a strong position on a rocky knoll facing the Confederate left flank across the swale in the vicinity of Spangler's Spring.

On the Union left Colonel Archibald L. McDougall's First Brigade remained in reserve except for the 20th Connecticut, which Ruger under instructions from Williams advanced about 750 feet into some woods in front of a stone wall held by the enemy. He also placed the 107th New York from Colgrove's brigade within supporting distance of the 20th Connecticut.[9] The latter regiment, commanded by Lieutenant Colonel William B. Wooster, had a reputation for steadiness. On the morning of July 3 it mustered 310 riflemen, a force considered sufficiently strong for its honorable but dangerous assignment. From its advanced post it could throw up a screen of fire against the left flank of enemy columns as they tried to envelop Geary's right. Wooster also acted as a spotter for Union batteries to the rear, giving them the range of Confederate units along his front.[10] Williams completed the disposition of his forces in preparation for the battle when he placed Lockwood's brigade along the pike near the batteries of Lieutenants S. T. Rugg and David H. Kinzie. It was to act as a reserve and would be used as needed on either the right or the left.[11]

Confederate accounts do not say how Ewell and Johnson planned to gain their military objective on the morning of July 3, but the essential features of their tactics unfolded as the battle progressed. Williams was correct in his appraisal of the situation from the Southern standpoint, for Ewell and Johnson had to take the crest of Culp's Hill and the slopes immediately south and west of it before they could attempt an advance to the Baltimore Pike. Or to state the problem another way, as long as Williams' left flank remained secure the Confederate attack would fail. Very properly then Williams placed the main strength of his corps on his left side and increased it as the battle progressed, for the weight of Johnson's assaults came there. At the end of the fighting of the previous night the Confederate battle line consisted of Jones's brigade on the right, Nicholl's in the center, and Steuart's on the left. As the four reinforcing brigades, Daniel's, O'Neal's, Walker's, and Smith's, joined Johnson, he placed them toward the left of his line to protect his flank and to increase the weight of his attacking forces there. In their assaults the brigades moved somewhat obliquely to the right against Greene's and Kane's lines, pivoting so to speak on Jones's brigade which could not advance but merely held its position. However, the very rough character of the ground and the need to guard his extreme left against threats from Williams' First Division prevented Johnson from organizing his forces for one grand charge.[12]

At no time did Ewell give any indication of how he planned to follow up Johnson's attack should he achieve a breakthrough. Of course, if Longstreet had started his assault at the same moment and gained similar success, there would have been no problem. But what did Ewell expect he could do alone, after he had received word of the delay in Longstreet's advance? He perhaps figured that one of two developments would occur. If his men captured Culp's Hill, further Federal resistance on that end of the field would collapse; or if Meade should mount a counterattack, Ewell's men could dig in on Culp's Hill and hold it until help arrived. The fact that neither of these events took place is due to the superb defense made by the commander of the Twelfth Corps, his immediate subordinates, and their troops. The fundamental error in the Confederate offense was the persistence with which Ewell and Johnson continued to make frontal assaults against a determined foe situated in a naturally strong position.

The engagement started in earnest around 4:30 A.M. when three Union rifle batteries and two light 12-pounder batteries, twenty-six guns in all, opened on the Confederates and fired for fifteen minutes without intermission at a range of 1,800 to 2,400 feet. Even earlier both sides had been exchanging rifle shots on a considerable scale.[13] When the cannonade stopped, the plan was for Geary's men to advance against the enemy lines, but whether they did so, and if they did, to what extent, are questions that have never been definitely settled. According to Geary, the men of Kane's and Greene's brigades made an attack that was "most furious" and was "stubbornly met." [14] Ewell seems to bear out this claim in his report, for he wrote that before Johnson could advance, the enemy attacked him and was "repulsed with very heavy loss." [15] However, if Geary's attack did take place it made no impression on anyone else, and no other report, whether Confederate or Union, so much as intimates that such an event occurred at that time. The relatively light losses in both Kane's and Greene's brigades in spite of the long hours they were under fire seem to indicate that they did not make any charge during the engagement.[16] Furthermore, Williams' version of the beginning of the battle completely contradicts Geary, for he very categorically asserted: "On the discontinuance of the fire, the enemy, without waiting our assault, themselves attacked Geary's division with great fury. . . ." [17] It would appear then that if Geary made any attack it was a feeble attempt, or else it had barely started before Johnson launched one of his own.

Through the years the magnitude and character of Johnson's assault have remained matters of dispute, for the Confederate reports were either cryptic or vague and those made by Union officers proved almost equally unsatisfactory, although for other reasons. In contrast Geary let his pen run away with him when writing about his own accomplishments in stopping the rebels. He described how

Johnson's division, followed by Rodes's and supported by Early's, "each division massed in three lines, advanced, charging heavily upon our front and right, and yelling in their peculiar style." Then he said that "line after line of the enemy broke" under the steady fire of Greene's and Kane's brigades, but "the pressing masses from behind rushed forward to take their places." [18] Stirring as it sounds, Geary's account must be considered nothing more than romantic balderdash. Even if Johnson had had at his disposal all of Early's and Rodes's divisions, which he did not, he could not have used that many men in a single charge over the rugged terrain of Culp's Hill. How many men he did use is not clear. In referring to his attack that morning Johnson briefly mentioned ordering Walker's Stonewall Brigade to the support of the others in his division and renewing the assault "with great determination." [19] He omitted to tell what tactics he employed, other than to imply that his whole division became involved in some way. Walker's report and those of his regimental commanders suggested, however, that this famous unit alone bore the brunt of the first assault and that the Confederates maintained a heavy musket fire all along their line throughout the engagement with single regiments dashing against enemy positions and then retiring when relieved by others.[20]

After the first attack had failed the Confederates continued pressure against Geary's lines through incessant small-arms fire in mass by regiments and singly by sharpshooters. Finally at eight o'clock Johnson ordered O'Neal's brigade into line for a charge. It went up the hill in fine style, only to be pinned down, it seemed interminably, in front of the Union position by heavy cannon and rifle fire.[21] An hour or so later Walker, in obedience to a command from Johnson, moved farther to the right and made another try with his whole brigade with as "equally bad success" as in his previous efforts.[22] Finally Johnson at a little after ten o'clock decided to make an all-out drive with two of his finest brigades to crush Geary's defenses. Generals Steuart and Daniel, always challenged by danger if there was any chance of success, protested that the attempt was suicidal and a useless sacrifice of the lives of the men in their brigades. Johnson refused to listen and insisted they carry out his orders. Steuart then marched his men by the left flank out of the works they had captured the night before and formed two lines of battle in the rear of a ridge of rocks at right angles to their former position. Daniel lined up his troops to the right of Steuart's. In this order they advanced to assault the crest of Culp's Hill.[23] No sooner had they appeared from behind the rocks than the Union forces opened upon them with musketry from "every imaginable quarter" and canister from the left. One witness of what happened to Steuart's brigade wrote: "The men were mowed down with fearful rapidity. . . . It was the most fearful fire I ever encountered. . . . The greatest confusion ensued,—regiments were reduced to companies and everything mixed up. It came very near to being a rout. . . ." [24] Daniel's brigade fared better,[25] but the Union defense had broken the back of the Southern offensive and the moment had arrived for a counterattack.

Williams' well-conceived battle plans were much more efficiently executed than his opponent's. With a few exceptions Federal tactics in protecting a naturally strong position offered excellent use of manpower and increased the effectiveness of the infantry by the proper use of artillery. While keeping losses to a minimum Union commanders for almost seven hours maintained such a tremendous volume of fire as to cause comment from friend and foe alike.[26] Williams and his subordinates achieved good coordination between regiments from different brigades, and when they placed certain picked regiments beyond the main line in dangerous spots to harass the enemy with an enfilading fire, they displayed imagination as well as good understanding of the area's topographical peculiarities. In their exposed positions commanders of these regiments handled their men firmly and with good judgment as they performed balancing acts between catastrophe and success.

As the battle progressed Williams placed more and more troops at Geary's disposal mostly to back up Greene's and Kane's brigades because they had to parry the main thrusts of the enemy.[27] Three of the six regiments in Candy's brigade and all three in Lockwood's periodically manned the breastworks as relief for these units. The five regiments in Brigadier General Alexander Shaler's brigade, which had been sent over from the Sixth Corps, helped out in the same way. When regiments withdrew, they would re-form in hollows to the rear of the battle line to rest, after first cleaning their rifles and replenishing their supply of ammunition. Upon returning to their former positions they would rush over the brow of the ridge, while the men being relieved would filter quickly through

471

their ranks to the rear.[28] In this manner the main line was always occupied by relatively fresh troops with clean rifles and full cartridge boxes, who could sustain a curtain of fire without a letup "long enough for one to draw a breath." [29] Some regiments fired 150 or even 160 rounds of ammunition per man during the course of the battle, which is a lot of shooting.[30]

Of the three regiments in Candy's brigade not used to relieve the troops in Greene's and Kane's battle lines, one was the 5th Ohio, which extended Kane's front on the right. Colonel John H. Patrick advanced Company F as skirmishers to a stone wall considerably forward of his right flank and instructed them to "fret the enemy as much as possible, for the purpose of drawing him from his intrenchments." Patrick claimed that these tactics proved most satisfactory, for goaded by his skirmishers, the Confederates charged either to capture them or to drive them out, but accomplished neither objective because of the heavy fire laid down by the determined Ohioans. Patrick attributed "a large share" of the Union success to these methods,[31] but in so doing he failed to note or give credit for similar work performed by a whole regiment of Pennsylvanians who held a position comparable to that of his company of skirmishers. This was the 147th Pennsylvania Volunteer Regiment commanded by Lieutenant Colonel Ario Pardee, Jr. Early in the morning in obedience to orders directly from Geary, Pardee led his men in a charge to what was probably another section of the same stone wall that Patrick's men had seized about five hundred feet in advance of the main line. Pardee scattered the enemy skirmishers and obtained a position from which he could watch Johnson's men and harass their columns as they attacked Greene and Kane.[32] Possibly it was this Pennsylvania regiment that accomplished what Colonel Maulsby's men in Lockwood's brigade had been directed to do. Maulsby and his regiment, the 1st Maryland, Potomac Home Brigade, had driven some Confederates, who were located in the woods, back behind the stone wall and were preparing to charge them when a Union regiment crossed their right front and hit the enemy on the flank. Lockwood then withdrew the 1st Maryland because it had already suffered rather severe losses.[33] Apparent confusion in orders and poor coordination had caused a near tragedy.

One other regiment in Candy's command had an unusual assignment which most likely would have been impossible to execute if the Confederates in Jones's brigade had held lines closer to Greene's on the top of Culp's Hill. The 66th Ohio under Lieutenant Colonel Eugene Powell assumed an exposed and potentially dangerous position at right angles to Greene's entrenchments and extended it on down the hill. From there they set up an enfilading fire which seriously bothered Confederate troops on the reverse side of some former Union breastworks. The rebels used their sharpshooters to make life precarious for Powell's troops, but other than that made no serious effort to oust them.[34]

Another regiment on special assignment, the 20th Connecticut from McDougall's brigade, maneuvered skillfully and held its own for hours alone in a position thrust out close to enemy lines. Colonel Wooster had to juggle his men about constantly to keep the Confederates from overrunning them, or the Union artillery from shelling them to pieces. The harder he pushed the enemy, the more directly he was placed under the fire of Twelfth Corps guns, which severely wounded some of his men.[35] It was a situation that could not have been avoided, though Williams had tried to keep his infantry out of the path of artillery fire. Several regiments to the rear of the 20th Connecticut also went through uncomfortable moments when defective or poorly aimed shells or solid shot crashed through the tops of trees overhead and fell among them, with resultant casualties. Though regrettable, these losses were a small price to pay for the effective artillery support which contributed greatly to Union victory.[36]

On the whole the Federal command fought a well-coordinated battle. However, there was one dramatic episode involving the 2nd Massachusetts and the 27th Indiana regiments of the First Division which became an exercise in courage and futility. It resulted from a mistake in orders or in judgment or perhaps both. Between 9:00 and 10:00 A.M. Slocum, without going through Williams, sent Ruger an order which said that with the Confederates showing signs of falling back, the time had come for him to force them out of the entrenchments north of the bottom land and swale around Spangler's Spring. The order specified that the attack be made with two regiments from the Third Brigade, whose line rested on the rocky knoll south of the swale and facing the left flank of the enemy entrenchments. Ruger got Slocum to modify the order and permit him to send out a skirmish line to probe the Confederate defenses, which he suspected were too strong to be stormed.[37] Ruger then sent a staff officer with his instructions to Colonel Colgrove, the brigade commander. The officer delivered Ruger's order orally, and in the transmission completely garbled it. As Colgrove received it, the order directed him to attack with all the regiments of the brigade then with him. Nothing was said about a skirmish line. Colgrove could not carry out the instructions literally because, as he later explained, peculiarities of his position prevented him from attacking with more than two regiments in line. That being the case, he should have referred the order with this information back to division headquarters and awaited further instructions. Instead he took it upon himself to modify the order and go ahead with the attack in his own way. He had been itching to do something of this sort anyway, especially as enemy resistance seemed to him to be growing weaker and Geary's becoming stronger. There was no time to lose if he was to get into the act. He also decided against using a skirmish line to precede his main force. Again he excused himself by claiming that skirmishers without cover in the open swale would have accomplished nothing but act as good targets for Confederate marksmen lurking behind trees, rocks, and entrenchments. Anxious to attack, Colgrove had convinced himself without any real evidence or prior examination that the Confederate forces facing him had become so weak that two regiments could charge and overwhelm them. He chose the 2nd Massachusetts and the 27th Indiana, each numbering about three hundred officers and men.[38] It was a ghastly mistake, for Johnson had four fresh regiments there to greet the attackers.[39]

When Lieutenant Colonel Charles R. Mudge of the 2nd Massachusetts heard Colgrove's order, he could not believe it, and he asked the messenger if he was sure he had delivered it correctly. The messenger was sure. " 'Well,' " said Mudge, " 'it is murder, but its the order. Up, men; over the works. Forward, double quick. . . .' " [40] They lined up rapidly with the 27th Indiana on their right. The single line in double ranks charged across the swale, the 2nd Massachusetts bearing toward the left and the 27th Indiana taking an oblique right. As Mudge had said, it was murder. To his horror Colgrove saw the Confederate force, heavier than he had anticipated, set up a withering fire and cut down his regiments in swift order. A little more than halfway through the swale the 27th Indiana, after losing a third of its strength, could not take any more of it and turned back. But the 2nd Massachusetts kept on and covered itself with glory in those moments of adversity. Upon reaching its objective the full fury of the defenders' fire focused on it, and a column of Confederates advanced to envelop its right flank. Grudgingly the regiment released its hold on enemy ground, backed off slowly, then turned on its pursuers and drove them off. After being ordered to do so, it finally retreated with a little more than half of its officers and men, but its commander was dead.[41] With deepest respect Williams wrote: "There are few if any Regts. in the service that could have stood the almost instantaneous loss of half its forces & maintained as the 2d Mass. did almost perfectly the order & regularity of a battalion drill."[42] The next day as the remnants of the 2nd Massachusetts marched away from the battlefield with the rest of the brigade and passed General Slocum's headquarters, "he and a large group of general and staff officers uncovered their heads."[43]

This tragic affair might have been avoided if Slocum had followed the chain of command and cleared through Williams, since there was no emergency; if Ruger had put the order in writing; or if Colgrove had been less impulsive. Perhaps Slocum felt some responsibility, for he is alleged to have said that although the movement was the result of a blunder, the heavy losses of the 2nd Massachusetts and the 27th Indiana were not wasted, as their advance did much to "impress" the Confederates and was the beginning of the infantry fight which finally drove them from the position.[44] This statement had some of the characteristics of wishful thinking, for the drive of Union forces to recover their entrenchments had begun to succeed with the collapse of the attack by Steuart's and Daniel's brigades and the counterthrust by Geary's men. Several regiments from Ruger's division had then joined the general advance against the enemy, who began to retire down the hill toward Rock Creek.[45] The charge of the 2nd Massachusetts and the 27th Indiana was a separate operation. It accomplished nothing and proved nothing except the courage of Northern soldiers. They were the victims of bad generalship and bad timing.

Around 11:00 A.M. the battle for Culp's Hill was over.[46] The Twelfth Corps had retaken its lost entrenchments, and the Confederates had decided to give up their effort to take Culp's Hill. "The wonder is," Williams wrote, "that the rebels persisted so long in an attempt that in the first half hour must have seemed useless." [47] As Wainwright noted, "The ground was . . . a hard place for a line of battle, but capital for a cool marksman. . . ." [48] To their sorrow the Confederates found marksmen aplenty in the Union army.

The noise of the conflict on Culp's Hill reached the veterans of the Second Corps still occupying the position on Cemetery Ridge which they had held in yesterday's battle, but they gave it little notice except to stop and listen with trained ears for signs of victory or distress. The engagement was not their concern unless the commanding officer should bawl out the order, "Fall in." The command never came, so they kept themselves busy during the morning quietly preparing for anything the enemy might have in mind for them. A low stone wall badly in need of repair ran near the crest of the ridge south from Ziegler's Grove and furnished cover for anyone kneeling or lying prone behind it. The men improved and patched it with rails from nearby fences and with earth so as to make it reasonably safe against musketry and flying shell fragments. About 250 feet from the Clump of Trees the wall made a right-angled jog and extended west about two hundred feet before making another angle, a little less than ninety degrees, and continuing south along the ridge to the clump. The battle lines followed the stone wall and where it disappeared took advantage of any ground which might give the men protection and a good field of fire. In some places the contours of the ridge permitted the location of a second line from which the men could deliver volleys over the heads of their comrades holding the low breastworks in front.

Gibbon's Second Division and a major portion of General Alexander Hays's Third Division occupied the section of the Union position on Cemetery Ridge which would receive the full fury of the Confederate assault in the afternoon. Numbering about 5,500 men, the two divisions, with Hays's on the right, held a line some two thousand feet long from the edge of Ziegler's Grove on the Taneytown road south to a point about six hundred feet beyond the Clump of Trees. Hancock put all the strength of the two divisions in line without reserves, and in such a manner that "every man of them could have fired his piece at the same instant." [49] Doubleday's Third Division of the First Corps, numbering about 3,500 men, adjoined the left of Gibbon's division and continued for another six hundred feet along the ridge. Beyond Doubleday's left for almost half a mile no infantry was in position. Early in the morning Newton, who possessed a sharp eye for such matters, saw the gap and immediately reported it to army headquarters. Meade authorized him to request troops from Sedgwick's command so as to form a connection between Doubleday and the forces in positions on or near the Round Tops. On his way to see Sedgwick Newton came across Caldwell's division, sadly depleted but recovered somewhat from the shock of yesterday's encounter with the enemy. With Hancock's permission Newton put it in position on the left of Doubleday's men. Caldwell placed all his troops in one line on a slight crest and ordered them to throw up breastworks. Newton then obtained from Sedgwick Brigadier General A. T. A. Torbert's First Brigade of Wright's division, and later Sedgwick sent him the Second Brigade of the Second Division under Colonel Henry L. Eustis. Newton placed these units to the left of Caldwell. By noon, having completed his dispositions, Newton considered his line between the left of Hancock's position and the right of Sykes's on Little Round Top as "very secure." He had also made arrangements with Birney, the remnants of whose Third Corps were massed behind his line, to furnish him supports in case of need.[50]

With few exceptions the locations of troops south of Newton's line were unchanged from what they had been after darkness had ended the struggle of the day before. The Fifth Corps occupied both Little and Big Round Top, where the men strengthened their lines by building stone walls as breastworks. Most of Crawford's two brigades held a position immediately west of Plum Run behind a stone wall and astride the road running out to the Peach Orchard. To their rear and right they were supported by two brigades of the Sixth Corps, Brigadier General Joseph J. Bartlett's of the First Division and Colonel David J. Nevin's of the Third Division. Two more brigades of the Sixth Corps under General Wright extended the Union infantry line southeast from Big Round Top to the Taneytown road and slightly beyond it.[51]

Between Ziegler's Grove and the crest of Little Round Top seventy-seven pieces of artillery stood ready to throw shot and shell on the enemy. A little over half the guns came from the Artillery Reserve; Colonel McGilvery placed them in position on the lower end of the ridge where he had successfully defied Confederate infantry the day before. To his right Captain John G. Hazard, artillery chief of the Second Corps, lined up his five batteries of twenty-six cannon at intervals behind the infantry of the Second and Third Divisions. At a considerable distance to the left of McGilvery a battery of six 12-pounders attached to the Fifth Corps stood pointing down the road leading from Little Round Top to the Peach Orchard, but it was too far from enemy guns to be used effectively against them. However, the late Lieutenant Hazlett's battery of six rifled Parrotts on the crest of Little Round Top had the position and range to cause Confederate artillery and infantry considerable trouble. In the event of an enemy attack against this long shank of the Union line some of the fifty-five guns on Cemetery Hill could add the weight of their metal to those on the ridge.[52]

At 10:00 A.M. General Hunt started an inspection of the batteries on the ridge to see whether they were in good condition and well supplied with ammunition. During the night he and Brigadier General R. O. Tyler, chief of the Artillery Reserve, together with their assistants had worked to get the guns ready for service first thing in the morning. They repaired damage to equipment, refilled ammunition chests, and reorganized batteries that had lost so heavily in personnel and horses as to be unable to work a full complement of guns efficiently. Lieutenant C. Gillett, ordnance officer of the Artillery Reserve, stayed up all night issuing ammunition to batteries of several of the corps, as well as those of the Reserve. He unloaded seventy wagons of the train and sent them back in the morning to the army base at Westminster. In view of Hancock's critical comment, aimed probably at Hunt, that the artillery of his corps had been "imperfectly" supplied with ammunition, it should be noted that Gillett during the course of the battle issued 2,825 rounds to the supply train of the Second Corps.[53]

Before riding over to the ridge Hunt had spent the early part of the morning directing the fire of the batteries engaged on Culp's Hill. When the fighting seemed to ease off, he left that point and went on to Cemetery Hill to look at the batteries there. Then he continued to the ridge, from where he could see the enemy busily engaged in strengthening his artillery in front of the Union left. As chief of artillery with tactical control over all guns, Hunt set about instructing battery commanders and chiefs of artillery not to fire at small bodies or be drawn into duels without promise of good results. Should the enemy open with a cannonade, he told them not to return the fire for the first fifteen or twenty minutes at least. Then they were to concentrate on one battery at a time until it was silenced. Always they were to aim carefully, fire "deliberately," and use ammunition sparingly until the proper moment arrived.[54] In this connection Colonel Alexander wondered why Hunt's artillerymen did not send salvo after salvo at him as he was putting Longstreet's guns in position in full view of the Union lines. If they had, he maintained, they would either have driven him to cover or forced him to exhaust his limited supply of long-range shot and shell before the Confederate infantry columns were ready to advance.[55] He felt the Federals had made a "great mistake" in accepting what was tantamount to an "artillery truce" that morning, for they had, he asserted, ammunition "in abundance—literally to burn—& plenty more close at hand."[56] If asked, Hunt would have replied that due to his foresight he had plenty of ammunition on hand for a prolonged engagement, but none to waste, that is, "none for idle cannonades, the besetting sin of some of our commanders." [57] He would have pointed out too that the Union base at Westminster was twenty-five miles away, too far for him to receive fresh supplies quickly.

As Hunt went slowly from one battery to another, he could see the Confederates working to cover the Union front for two miles with what seemed like an "unbroken mass" of guns stretching from a point opposite the town south to the Peach Orchard. It was an inspiring sight to a good artilleryman, and he pronounced it "a magnificent display." He wondered what it meant. Possibly Lee was using his guns to hold that line while sending more of his infantry to Ewell, or to guard against a Union counterattack. More likely, Hunt thought, the massing of Lee's artillery indicated an assault on the Federal center to be preceded by a tremendous cannonade for the purpose of softening Meade's resistance. He suspected they wanted him to use up his ammunition in reply so that their infantry could advance without harm over the first half mile, which was beyond effective range of rifle fire and canister. Refusing to play their game, he planned to reserve most of his ammunition and subject the enemy infantry "from the first moment of their advance, to such a cross-fire of our artillery as would break their formation, check their impulse, and drive them back, or at least bring them to our lines in such condition as to make them an easy prey." He hoped through his instructions to the various artillery commanders to get this branch of the service to act as a well-integrated unit in defense of the Union line and thus greatly reduce the pressure on Federal infantry.[58]

Though not as successful in this respect as he had hoped, Hunt by virtue of his authority and foresight achieved a unity of effort in his artillery that was not even attempted in the infantry. The consensus among Union officers, Meade included, was that the enemy would make an attack during the day somewhere along the ridge. Yet no one except Meade himself had the authority to coordinate the work of the units from five separate corps [59] which would defend the position. As commander of the army it might not always be possible or desirable for him to exert personal control over the tactical dispositions of the troops during the fighting, and the need for one or two people to act in the capacity of his alter ego was perhaps greater on the third than the second day of the battle.

Because of the vicissitudes of combat on the two previous days the integrity of the corps as a separate fighting unit had been weakened, if not destroyed. With the exception of the Fifth Corps and possibly the Third, which was kept in reserve, none of the corps on July 3 went into battle as units with their organizations intact. Since the battle on July 1 the First Corps had been for all practical purposes broken up into its component parts of three divisions. On July 3 Wadsworth's division was still in position on Culp's Hill, Robinson's on Cemetery Hill as reserve for either the Eleventh or Second Corps, and Doubleday's on the center of the ridge. Newton as commander of the corps apparently established his headquarters to the rear of Doubleday's division. Hancock, in command of the Second Corps, had his headquarters near his Second and Third Divisions, which still held the same ground they had had the previous day. His First Division lay beyond the left of Doubleday's division, making it awkward for him to direct its operations.[60] As for the Sixth Corps, it had become the manpower pool of the army, from which infantry units and artillery batteries were drawn and used to plug gaps or bolster weak places in the main Union line. Its eight brigades occupied positions in various sections of the front from Wolf's Hill on the extreme right to the valley east of Big Round Top on the far left.[61] The greatest number, six of them, were posted at a point on Cemetery Ridge east of the Weikert house, and from there they covered the area south to Little Round Top. Although Sedgwick's headquarters were nearby on high ground just north of Little Round Top, he exercised no control over his brigades. As for the corps' unusually large Artillery Brigade of forty-eight pieces,[62] it was used for reserve and replacement purposes for the whole army, instead of for the Sixth Corps alone. Consequently Sedgwick felt that his position had become meaningless, for he had "not a man or gun under his command except a few orderlies." As one brigade after another slipped away from him, the general finally observed that "he might as well go home." [63]

The system of command as finally established on July 3 for the Union line from Cemetery Ridge to the Round Tops made a crazy quilt pattern. On the northern end Hancock had three divisions under him, but one of them was badly placed. Newton commanded Doubleday's division and had authority over Torbert's and Eustis' brigades of the Sixth Corps. Birney in reserve to the rear of Doubleday still temporarily commanded the two divisions of the Third Corps. Bartlett in addition to his own brigade commanded that of Colonel Nevin, also of the Sixth Corps. Sykes commanded the Fifth Corps, and Wright had under him the Sixth Corps brigades of Brigadier General David A. Russell and Colonel Lewis A. Grant.[64]

Instead of having to direct six different commanders Meade could have simplified his problems of control and increased the efficiency of the army by creating two command areas along his front. For Sedgwick to sit idle was a waste of managerial skill, because he had had more experience than most generals at Gettysburg in handling large numbers of troops.[65] Meade would have done well to have placed Sedgwick, the senior officer second only to Slocum,[66] in charge of the left wing of the army commanding all troops between the Weikert house and the Taneytown road and holding them ready for defensive or offensive operations as the occasion might demand. Meade then might have used Hancock as chief of the infantry forces on the left center of the Union line, with control over the remnants of the Third Corps, Doubleday's division, and possibly Robinson's of the First Corps, in addition to all of his own men. As Hancock remembered the battle, he thought that his authority over the left center had continued through July 3.[67] Though mistaken in his recollections, for he resumed command of his own corps around noon,[68] he acted during the course of the engagement as if he were in charge of all operations in that section of the line. He gave orders to Newton's troops and interfered, much to Hunt's annoyance, with McGilvery's direction of batteries from the Artillery Reserve.[69] It would have been much better if he had been given authority to do what he in fact did.

Although the shortcomings in Meade's command arrangements for the defense of Cemetery Ridge became obscured, if not forgotten, in light of the Union victory, there remains the possibility that with Sedgwick and Hancock in charge on the left much waste motion could have been avoided and the magnitude of Confederate defeat might have been greater. It might even have been possible for Meade to have mounted a counterattack with some hope of success. Without previous preparations and a temporary revision of the command system to concentrate the army's strength at vital points he could never have done so, however, for to reverse the defensive role of the army required more than a mere snap of the fingers. In view of the strength of the Confederate position the outcome of such an attempt even after careful planning would have been highly doubtful. Meade, confident that his troops could hold their lines on the 3rd, evidently did not see the necessity for a drastic change. Perhaps he felt that the location of his headquarters would permit him personally to supervise operations along the ridge and to bring up reinforcements "in good season." [70]

Meade rose early on July 3 and began preparations for the day by ordering Hunt to call up the Artillery Reserve, which had gone some distance to the rear during the night for repairs and fresh ammunition.[71] The outburst of heavy firing at Culp's Hill soon attracted Meade's attention, and he decided to send Shaler's brigade from the Sixth Corps to reinforce the Twelfth Corps. He requested Slocum to place it in a central position on his line so that it could be quickly returned to Cemetery Ridge as soon as it could be spared.[72] Previously he had ordered Pleasonton to have Gregg post a force of cavalry and a battery on Wolf's Hill to guard Slocum's extreme right flank and cut off the enemy's use of the Hanover road.[73]

While absorbed with these tasks Meade took time to look beyond his immediate front and plan for certain contingencies. Should the outcome of the battle prove favorable, he directed General French to reoccupy Harpers Ferry and harass the enemy on his retreat. In the same vein he asked General Couch to move in toward Gettysburg as rapidly as possible to help destroy Lee. In case the Army of the Potomac should suffer defeat, he advised Couch to return to the defenses of Harrisburg and the Susquehanna, and French to withdraw from Frederick toward Washington.[74] The tone of these messages reflected Meade's confidence in his ultimate victory rather than fear of possible disaster. His real purpose was to warn the generals that a decision by arms was soon to be made and they must be ready for action. His note to Mrs. Meade written that morning during the busy activity at his headquarters revealed even greater assurance.[75] To a visitor there Meade seemed completely self-possessed, although he moved about in a "quick and nervous" manner and his face was "lit up with the glow of the occasion." Perhaps he was growing accustomed to the heavy responsibilities of his position, for he "looked more the General, less the student." [76] Around 9:00 A.M. he sent out two circulars in anticipation of the day's engagement, which also indicated his alertness to affairs and insistence upon a taut and well-disciplined army. In one he ordered corps commanders to keep their troops under arms, fully equipped, and ready to move instantly even when not actively engaged. The other directed them to round up all stragglers and men on special assignments and bring them back to strengthen the ranks. Meade also instructed ordnance officers to pick up cast-off arms and equipment from the field and send them to the rear in empty ammunition wagons.[77]

Whenever Meade could get away from headquarters he would ride out to inspect his lines and with field glass in hand would sweep the woods and fields in the direction of the enemy, on the lookout for any unusual developments.[78] A little after nine o'clock Meade met Hancock on the ridge and discussed with him and other officers places where the Confederates might attack. There is some question of what Meade did expect to happen. According to one account, he was of the opinion that the enemy would renew his assault on the Union left, because the flank was always Lee's favorite point of attack and Union artillery did not possess such a sweeping field of fire there as it did at the center near the position of the Second Corps. Hancock held the opposite view. It was a matter of no great moment to Meade, however, because he felt prepared wherever the rebels hit. But should the attack fall on the center which was Cemetery Hill, Meade thought it would be to his advantage, for he could reinforce the line there quickly and as a countermove could advance the Fifth Corps and most of the Sixth. How thoroughly he and Hancock discussed the latter possibility is not known, but there is evidence that the commanding general did issue orders in preparation for such a development.[79]

Between 11:00 A.M. and noon in response to an invitation from Gibbon, Meade seated himself on an "empty cracker box" and enjoyed a delicious repast of stewed chickens, which were "large and in good *running* order" [80] but of uncertain age, garnished with potatoes, hot toast, bread and butter, tea and coffee. In the company of Generals Hancock, Gibbon, Newton, and Pleasonton, as well as members of the Second Corps staff, Meade spent a few moments relaxing and discussing the incidents of yesterday's battle and the probabilities for that day. He observed that some of the best men made up the provost guards of the divisions and that it would be better to have them in the line than in the rear stopping stragglers and skulkers, who were not much good even behind breastworks. After giving the order that all of the provost guards should rejoin their regiments,[81] he rode off to pay Hays's division a visit before turning around and going to Little Round Top. On the crest in company with Warren he observed the long line of enemy batteries and perhaps caught a glimpse of Confederate infantry massing for the attack. Having finished his inspection, he returned to his headquarters.[82]

The 3rd of July, 1863, was no day for a battle or for any form of physical exertion. At high noon the drowsy air and the hot sun beating down on the bare slopes of the ridge made man and beast long for a patch of shade and a snooze. The quiet which spread over the battlefield after 11:00 A.M. deepened and created the illusion that the world of struggling armies had retired to sleep off its differences. Before the lull heavy skirmishing and sniping, interspersed with the occasional roar of cannon, had persisted since dawn.[83] One of the worst outbreaks had occurred at the Bliss house and barn, which stood west of the Emmitsburg road about midway between the opposing lines. Hays's men and Hill's had quarreled bitterly for their possession since the morning of the 2nd. The barn was a large, fortresslike structure, typical of Pennsylvania farms, in which sharpshooters could hide and use the slots in the masonry as loopholes to fire at their adversaries with relative impunity.[84] Both buildings had changed hands several times, and finally around 10:00 A.M. Hays decided to burn them because they were a little too close to Confederate lines for his men to retain possession of them unchallenged. Besides, Hays anticipated a major assault by the rebels and wanted the buildings removed from the line of fire of his batteries. The 14th Connecticut did the deed with great efficiency and dispatch,[85] but in its performance set off an angry exchange between some of Hill's cannoneers and Hays's. This caused Colonel Alexander, in charge of the First Corps artillery, to comment acidly on the wanton waste of ammunition by the Confederate Third Corps. The firing died down almost as quickly as it started.[86] During the ensuing silence the Union army waited in peace, while the Confederates continued to make their preparations without interruption.

Colonel Alexander, who would have a very busy day, had gotten up before dawn to rearrange his batteries and refill their caissons and limbers with ammunition. He wondered whether his line near the Peach Orchard needed correction, because in the smoke and confusion of the battle the day before he had not been able to locate the enemy's position precisely. As it grew light he saw to his horror that he had badly placed over a dozen guns and had exposed them to the possibility of an enfilading fire from their left. Holding his breath, he quickly pulled them back before the enemy could take advantage of his mistake.[87] Around 9:00 A.M. he received word from Longstreet about his role in the forthcoming assault. Again he and not Walton had the task of preparing and directing the fire of all the guns in the First Corps in a cannonade preliminary to the advance of the infantry;[88] its purpose was not simply to "make a noise" but to try and "cripple" the enemy, to "tear him limbless, as it were. . . ." When the infantry began to move, Alexander was to advance such artillery as he could use in "aiding the attack." [89] He at once set out to make further changes in the location of his batteries. Reserving only eight guns of Henry's battalion to protect Longstreet's extreme right, he posted his other seventy-five pieces in an irregular line about 4,000 feet long so that they were virtually one battery [90] stretching between the Peach Orchard and the northeast corner of Spangler's Woods. In addition to these pieces General Pendleton placed at his disposal nine 12-pounder howitzers of Hill's corps, saying that the corps could not use guns of "such short range." Alexander put them in reserve with orders for them to be ready to accompany the assaulting columns. At 11:00 A.M. he reported to Longstreet that his preparations were completed.[91]

Alexander's counterpart in the Third Corps, Colonel R. L. Walker, also placed all his rifled guns and most of his Napoleons, a total of sixty cannon, in position for the cannonade. They stood crowded along Seminary Ridge south of the Fairfield road, except for five pieces of Major William T. Poague's battalion which Walker advanced 1,200 feet to form an extension on the left of Alexander's line. General Hill instructed Walker to place the two long-range Whitworths on Oak Hill, from where they could easily hit Union batteries on Cemetery Hill. Of the remaining twenty-one guns in the corps, Walker could not find room in the line for six Napoleons, so he kept them and fifteen short-range 12-pounder howitzers in reserve.[92] As for the Second Corps, Colonel J. Thompson Brown, acting chief of artillery, placed twenty of his guns in the long line of pieces which were to carry the main burden of the cannonade. Ten of them he ordered posted on Oak and Seminary Ridges on both sides of the railroad cut. Ten more went into position south of the Fairfield road, but Brown's order requiring them to use only solid shot for fear of dropping defective shells on Confederate infantry cut down their effectiveness considerably. Besides these pieces, Brown had twelve guns in Lieutenant Colonel William Nelson's battalion join the four under Captain A. Graham in the hills between the York and Hanover roads with orders to be ready to fire at long range at Cemetery Hill, which was about 8,000 feet away to the southwest.[93] Thus as far as can be determined, Alexander, Walker, and Brown between them arranged to have at least 170 guns and possibly 179 available for the cannonade.[94]

With Longstreet responsible for the operations of the assaulting columns, Alexander's assignment became vitally important. When he reported his artillery as "all ready," Longstreet told him the infantry needed more time for preparations. Once completed, Longstreet himself would give the signal for the batteries to open by firing two guns. He directed Alexander meanwhile to take a position from which he could get a good view of the field; he was to watch the effect of the fire and "send Pickett word *when to charge.*" [95] Accordingly Alexander with glass in hand stationed himself behind a tree near the left of Lieutenant James Woolfolk's battery, which was "just in the salient angle of the wood" between Spangler's and Pitzer's farms. He had with him two couriers, one of Pickett's and one of his own, to carry messages.[96]

About 11:45 A.M. Alexander received the following note from Longstreet: "If the Artillery fire does not have the effect to drive off the enemy or greatly demoralize him so as to make our effort pretty certain, I would prefer that you should not advise Gen. Pickett to make the charge. I shall rely a great deal upon your good judgment to determine the matter, and shall expect you to let Gen. Pickett know when the moment offers." [97] Lacking faith in the whole enterprise, Longstreet here came perilously close to evading his responsibilities and thrusting them upon an unwary subordinate. He was asking Alexander to do the impossible. Unless the cannonade should drive the enemy from the heights, which was not very likely if previous battle experience was any guide, Alexander had to decide from his observations three-quarters of a mile away and with his vision blurred by clouds of smoke, whether the fire had "greatly demoralized" the defenders of the ridge. The message amazed and disturbed Alexander, for until then he had never doubted the success of the offensive, which had been ordered by Lee despite the obvious strength of the Federal position. Now that the decision for an infantry attack was his, he began to see reasons for not making it. He also got the impression—though it is hard to see why—that Longstreet wanted him to rule on whether or not a cannonade should be made. Greatly upset, he showed the message to General Wright, who happened to be nearby. Between the two of them they composed the following reply: [98]

General: I will only be able to judge of the effect of our fire on the enemy by his return fire as his infantry is but little exposed to the view & the smoke will obscure the whole field. If as I infer from your note there is any alternative to this attack it should be carefully considered before opening our fire, for it will take all the arty. ammunition we have left to test this one thoroughly & if the result is unfavorable we will have none left for another effort & even if this is entirely successful it can only be so at a very bloody cost.[99]

Alexander's note reminded Longstreet of his duties, and he tried to erase the impression that he was trying to place on Alexander a burden which was not rightfully his to bear. Without delay he sent another message, which Alexander received about 12:15 P.M., saying: "The intention is to advance the Inf. if the Arty. has the desired effect of driving the enemy off or having other effect such as to warrant us in making the attack. When that moment arrives advise Gen. P. and of course advance such artillery as you can use in aiding the attack." [100] Though ambiguous, this note was more in keeping with the responsibilities of a commander and the traditional relationship between a superior and his subordinate. Now all Longstreet seemed to be asking was the opinion of an expert whose judgment he valued as to the most propitious moment for the infantry to advance.

Nevertheless, Alexander remained uncomfortable and felt too much was expected of him. The cannonade was to proceed as planned, but he thought that Longstreet still wanted him to decide whether Pickett should make his attack at all. He turned again to Wright and asked him about the chances of success. The general said the trouble would not be in getting to the crest of Cemetery Ridge but in holding on, for the " 'whole Yankee army is there in a bunch.' " Alexander later said that he failed to appreciate the full import of this observation. He took it to mean that penetration of the enemy's line would be easy enough but the problem was one of properly supporting the troops once they had pierced it. He now felt reassured, for from what he had seen and heard he judged that Lee had made adequate provision for supporting troops. As a final test he sought out Pickett, who was nearby, and sounded him out. Finding him "both cheerful and sanguine," Alexander decided that once the cannonade had been made Pickett should follow it with his charge.[101] To make sure that Longstreet would not expect him to be more than a neutral observer, about 12:30 P.M. Alexander sent him the following message: "When our Arty. fire is at its best I will advise Gen. Pickett to advance." [102]

It was probably after writing his second note to Alexander at noon that Longstreet dismounted, found himself a shady spot, and took a catnap. He had completed deployment of his troops into battle lines, and for the present they were lying down in the woods waiting for the batteries to open fire.[103] An appraisal of his contribution to preparations for the offensive is difficult, if not impossible, to make because Lee and Hill, as well as the division commanders, must share responsibility for them. One of the problems was to assemble the attacking column without being seen by enemy eyes.

Here topography, of which the Confederates complained so bitterly as always helping the Federals, favored them, and they very wisely took advantage of it.[104] But their greatest difficulty was to get a broken battle line, which was roughly a mile and a quarter long at its base, to focus in its advance on a salient less than half its length, and to have the various attacking columns arrive at the main objective, the Clump of Trees, at the same moment. Any alignment of the units regardless of its merits could easily disintegrate through poor handling of the troops in the advance or fail to achieve success because of enemy resistance.

In spite of his feeling of depression Longstreet escorted Pickett to a place on the ridge from which he could show him some shelter for his men, the direction of his advance, and the object of his attack. Longstreet seems to have controlled his emotions, for he did not dampen Pickett's confidence. He directed him to place two of his brigades in the front line, Brigadier General J. L. Kemper's on the right and Brigadier General R. B. Garnett's on the left, to act as guides for the brigades of Heth's division on their left. Pickett's third brigade under Brigadier General L. A. Armistead was to take a supporting position in the second line immediately to the rear of the other two. Early in the morning Wilcox' and Perry's brigades of Anderson's division had moved out to support Alexander's batteries, so that they were in good position to march on Pickett's right to protect it from an enemy flanking attack.[105] Since the men in Pickett's division were Longstreet's own troops with whom he was familiar, he had the authority and the knowledge to prepare them effectively for their trial. Whether he took equal care with the remainder of his attacking column is problematical.

Lee had given Longstreet authority to use the four brigades of Heth's division and two from Pender's, all of which were on loan from Hill's corps. Because they were not his own men Longstreet in making his preparations may have hesitated to order them about as he would have his own troops. Certainly to get best results he needed Hill's active and cordial support, but it is doubtful if he ever received it, since the relations between the two generals were not what they should have been. This situation may explain why the actual deployment of some of Hill's brigades was very different from what Longstreet said it was in his battle report. According to his report, Heth's division under Pettigrew was "arranged in two lines, and these supported by part of Major-General Pender's division, under Major-General Trimble." [106] The attacking column thus would have had four brigades abreast in the first line, three in the second, and two and possibly four in the third.[107] By sacrificing breadth the column would have gained depth and greater striking power on a narrower front. This formation was never tested, however, because the battle line as finally evolved varied greatly from Longstreet's description of it. Either the general did not know of the change or he neglected to mention it.

According to Captain Louis G. Young of Pettigrew's staff, when Pettigrew reported to Longstreet, he was directed to form in the rear of Pickett's division and support his advance. It is possible that Young's memory may have been faulty and that Pettigrew's instructions were as Longstreet described them in his report. Be that as it may, this order, Young remembered, was countermanded "almost as soon as given"—he did not say by whom—and the new instructions called for Pettigrew's division to advance in the same line with Pickett's, while Pender's two brigades were to follow as their supports.[108] In this alignment of the attacking force the brigades in the front line from right to left were thus as follows: Kemper's and Garnett's of Pickett's division; then Archer's temporarily under Colonel B. D. Fry, Pettigrew's commanded by Colonel J. K. Marshall, Davis', and Colonel J. M. Brockenbrough's under Colonel R. M. Mayo, all of Pettigrew's (formerly Heth's) division. In immediate support were Armistead's, Scales's under Colonel W. Lee J. Lowrance, and J. H. Lane's.[109] Tagging along farther to the right and rear were Perry's and Wilcox' brigades, but there was no force on the left to balance their line.

The deployment of the attacking columns was open to criticism in several respects. The most important defect was the weakness of the left flank. Longstreet had ordered Lane, who commanded Pender's division until Trimble relieved him, to form his and Lowrance's brigades behind the two right brigades of Heth's division. As a result the two left brigades had no second line to support them, and unfortunately they were the least reliable ones. Brockenbrough's had once been a splendid outfit, but as a result of heavy campaigning it had become greatly reduced in strength so that on the 1st it could muster only eight hundred men. Severe losses that day brought its strength down to five hundred, about the size of a large regiment at

Gettysburg. In addition it was without the leadership of its regular commander, who was absent recovering from a wound. In point of numbers and morale therefore it was the weakest of all four brigades, yet it held the crucial position on the extreme left flank of the line. Next to it was Davis' brigade; it had suffered heavily on July 1, and furthermore its commander and men lacked battle experience. The condition of these two brigades, however, appears to have concerned no one at the time. Their alignment on July 3 was, as it happened, a matter of chance, not choice, for on the afternoon of July 2 Pettigrew had placed them in that order when for awhile it seemed likely they would see action. He apparently saw no reason to change the order after they moved from the night's bivouac to get into position for battle on July 3.[110] If Lee wanted the two Pender brigades to advance in echelon on Pettigrew's left instead of following behind his right, either he did not make himself clear to Longstreet, or Lane misunderstood Longstreet's instructions. On the other hand Lee and Longstreet might have decided to place Pender's brigades behind Pettigrew's right so as to increase the weight of the attack near the center and ensure the penetration of the Union line near the Clump of Trees. In such an arrangement Pettigrew's two left brigades would become expendable, for their role would be to absorb enfilading fire and flanking attacks from Cemetery Hill. The question remains unanswered whether it was by accident or design that Longstreet placed Lane where he did instead of in a supporting role on the left.[111]

Whatever weaknesses the advance revealed in the deployment of the assaulting column, the Confederates did make an earnest effort to avoid mistakes and secure proper coordination between the various units. After Pettigrew had learned what Lee expected of his division in the attack and passed the information on to Colonel Fry, he told Fry to see Pickett at once and come to an understanding "as to the *dress* in the advance." Fry rode to Pickett's headquarters and found him in "excellent spirits." Pickett greeted him cordially and the two reminisced about their experiences in storming the fortress at Chapultepec in the Mexican War. In the conversation Pickett expressed "great confidence" in the ability of the Confederates to "drive" the enemy forces after they had been "demoralized" by the artillery. Garnett then joined them to discuss the work of the day. They agreed that Garnett's brigade would dress on Fry's command, which they designated as the center upon which both divisions should be aligned.[112]

During these lengthy preparations—for it took considerable time to get that many men ready—Lee rode up and down inspecting the lines and consulting with Longstreet, Hill, and other officers as he happened to meet with them.[113] Longstreet informed Lee that he and his staff had been "more particular" in giving orders than "ever before"; and that they had carefully explained the objective and difficulties of the attack to the various commanders, who in turn were expected to brief their subordinates and so on down to every private. In that way they hoped everyone would know what lay ahead and would become inspired to the task.[114] Under these circumstances it is strange that Lee with his sharp eye did not detect the hidden flaws in the deployment of his troops and the layout of its batteries.

XIX

PICKETT'S CHARGE

GENERAL LONGSTREET, satisfied that he had completed preparations for the assault, wrote a short note to Colonel J. B. Walton, his chief of artillery. It began with the fateful words: "Colonel: Let the batteries open." In a few moments two sharp reports rang out from the signal guns, and 100,000 heads turned toward the Peach Orchard.[1] Over 150 guns responded to the signal with a roar as their projectiles hurled toward the Union lines. Colonel Alexander, who was in charge of the cannonade, pulled out his watch, looked at it, and snapped it shut. It was just one o'clock. Then he got behind a tree to steady his spy glass and intently watched the effect of the fire.[2] On Cemetery Ridge members of General Gibbon's luncheon party who had tarried after the repast to lie about on the ground and doze in the heat pulled themselves up with a start. Shells suddenly came bursting all about them and momentarily caused the "wildest confusion." The servants ran about "terror-stricken" and disappeared, while the horses, which were hitched to the trees or held by orderlies, reared and neighed in fright, then "broke away and plunged riderless through the fields." General Gibbon snatched his sword and ran toward the front.[3]

Soon the surprise and excitement occasioned by the suddenness and magnitude of the cannonade subsided, and the men in the lines tried to make themselves as inconspicuous as possible while patiently waiting out the storm. Some hugged the ground; others huddled behind stone walls or curled up in convenient depressions.[4] Hancock said the cannonade was the "heaviest" artillery fire he had ever seen,[5] and he wanted to know what Gibbon, who was an old artilleryman, thought of it. Gibbon replied that it meant either a retreat or an assault.[6] Wainwright on Cemetery Hill expressed amazement at the rate and volume of fire. He had never known the enemy to be "so lavish of ammunition," and he thought that "Lee must have given special orders, and have placed much reliance on this fire." In his professional opinion, however, it was "by no means as effective as it should have been, nine-tenths of their shot passing over our men."[7] Gibbon, too, noticed that the enemy gunners did not lessen the elevation of their pieces; as a result most shells flew over the heads of men standing near the battle lines, and few suffered any harm.[8] It was safer for infantrymen on the open slopes of the ridge than in the wooded areas where shot and shell cut down small trees or broke off huge limbs from oaks and shattered them into flying splinters.[9] Most officers stayed near their men, some coolly walking about, others laughing and joking to divert attention from the ordeal. The constant roar of the cannonade was unnerving, especially for the less experienced soldiers, but most men with the pride of veterans remained steady in spite of the enemy's efforts to break their spirit.[10] They thanked the fates that at this moment they were not cannoneers, who became objects of admiration and not of envy as they worked to return the enemy fire.

The artillerymen stood right in the path of a terrific storm of shells, but they kept busy serving their guns with precision and coolness and clung to their beloved pieces to the bitter end, oblivious to the screams of wounded horses, the explosion of limbers, and the death of comrades. The Second Corps gunners on Cemetery Ridge showed just such determination when enemy fire gradually silenced or crippled several of their batteries.[11] By 2:30 P.M. it became apparent that the enemy was concentrating on General Webb's brigade, which held the angle formed by the stone wall just north of the Clump of Trees, and on the batteries on the crest behind him. Later when writing about his experiences Webb said he felt that 110 guns had been pointing right at him. "This was awful," he continued. "I lost fifty of my men lying down, and . . . excellent officers, [while I] was struck three or four times with stones, etc. I knew then that we were to have a fierce attack. . . ."[12]

On Cemetery Hill Union cannoneers fared better in spite of the apparent vulnerability of their position to a heavy cross fire. Colonel

Alexander in his critical comments on the cannonade maintained that the Confederates had missed a rare opportunity when they did not take advantage of their exterior lines to aim more of their guns toward the hill. He claimed that if they had set up a severe enfilading fire on that salient, they would have destroyed Union batteries there and demoralized the infantry. In support of his contention he cited the testimony of General Howard and Major Thomas W. Osborn, chief of artillery of the Eleventh Corps, about the destruction caused by Lieutenant Colonel William Nelson's batteries of Ewell's corps during the short time they were in action.[13] These guns and those on Seminary Ridge were able to deliver a very heavy fire from two directions upon Union artillery and infantry on Cemetery Hill. Howard reported that "shells burst in the air, in the ground to the right and left, killing horses, exploding caissons, overturning tombstones, and smashing fences. There was no place of safety. In one regiment 27 were killed and wounded by one shell. . . ."[14] Osborn also wrote about Confederate artillery raking the whole line of Union batteries, killing and wounding men and horses, and blowing up caissons.[15] Though stressing the destruction and excitement caused by this fire, nowhere did these or other accounts suggest that it had the crippling effect of knocking out many guns or spreading panic among the troops.[16] Wainwright observed that the Confederate fire was less accurate than on the previous day, owing in part, he thought, to the practice of keeping their guns "too much under cover of the hills on which they were posted."[17]

Though the cannonade hit a "great many" horses and destroyed an "unusually large number" of caissons and limbers all along the hill and the ridge, it was most effective in sweeping the slope behind the crest clear of men and beasts who could find no protection against high-flying or ricocheting shot and shell. Infantrymen in the Twelfth Corps crouching in the lee of Cemetery Hill and Ridge went through the uncomfortable experience of having "shell, shot, and missiles bursting over them, around them, and among them for hours. . . ." Nevertheless no great harm came to the men.[18] Meade's headquarters in the Leister house, because of its position at the base of Cemetery Ridge immediately to the rear of the Second Corps lines, seemed to receive more than its share of wild shots. Shells hit the house several times; a fragment of one wounded Butterfield, and another missed Seth Williams by inches. The most unfortunate victims of this hail of missiles were the horses of aides and orderlies hitched on both sides of the fence. Sixteen of them lay dead and mangled before the fire ceased.[19] Despite suggestions that he move his headquarters, Meade at first refused to budge because he felt it imperative for him to be where his subordinates would expect to find him. Toward the end of the cannonade he consented to go to Slocum's headquarters on Power's Hill, but only after he heard that a signal officer stationed there could communicate with the one located at the Leister house. No sooner had he made the change than he discovered that his man had left his post, so he started back to the old headquarters. Because of these movements he became separated for a time from his staff and found himself alone with only a few orderlies; but on returning to the Taneytown road house he came across several of them again and also his son George.[20] In temporarily disrupting Union army headquarters the Confederate artillery fire achieved a completely unforeseen result, although its consequences should not be exaggerated, for Meade managed throughout to keep in touch with developments and direct operations.

As the fury of the cannonade continued to mount, General Tyler ordered the Artillery Reserve and its train to follow the example of the ambulance drivers, wagoners, and stragglers who had long since disappeared from the fields behind the lines. They soon found a safe place to park a little over half a mile to the rear. Tyler thoughtfully posted couriers at the abandoned location, should Hunt want to get in touch with him. At the same time Major Charles Ewing, in command of the train guard, deployed his regiment, the 4th New Jersey, behind the ridge with fixed bayonets for the purpose of rounding up any fugitives from the battle line and turning them over to General Patrick.[21] The withdrawal of the reserve batteries and their ammunition to a safer place a short distance away caused Hunt but slight inconvenience, for he had on hand the huge Sixth Corps Artillery Brigade from which he could draw to replace batteries running out of ammunition or disabled by enemy fire.

During the cannonade Hunt kept constantly on the move checking the condition of his batteries and observing the poor shooting of Confederate cannoneers with mixed emotions. Though delighted that for all the metal they threw they were causing comparatively little damage, as an artillery instructor it offended him to see his former students perform so badly.[22] When the enemy opened, Hunt had finished his morning's inspection and was standing chatting with Lieutenant Benjamin F. Rittenhouse on the crest of Little Round Top. He could not have had a better observation point from which to judge the magnitude of the cannonade. The number of guns bearing on the Union west front he estimated to be from 100 to 120, but because his own line was shorter he decided he himself could use no more than 80 pieces to advantage.[23] In this reckoning he apparently did not include batteries on Cemetery Hill, which joined in returning the enemy's fire and increased the number of Union guns to approximately 118.[24]

After Hunt had determined the extent of the cannonade, he rode back to the Artillery Reserve park; there he found messengers, with whom he left orders for all batteries to be ready to move at a moment's notice. The remains of a dozen exploded caissons made very clear to him why Tyler had pulled the reserve batteries and ammunition train back out of range of enemy fire. He went to the ridge to inspect the batteries there and was pleased to notice that they seemed to be obeying his instructions about firing slowly and only after careful aim.[25] What he did not know was that General Hancock thoroughly disapproved of his tactics and felt that Union batteries should reply vigorously and rapidly in order to maintain the morale of the infantry. Hancock had ordered Hazard and McGilvery to ignore Hunt's commands. Hazard did so, but McGilvery defied him on the grounds that as a commander of one of the brigades in the Artillery Reserve he was not subject to Hancock's authority. Before the end of the cannonade Hazard's batteries had exhausted their supplies of long-range ammunition, consisting of shells and solid shot, for which Hunt when he finally learned of it blamed Hancock's interference.[26]

But for the present Hunt was unaware of Hancock's challenge to his authority as chief of artillery. He found upon looking in the chests that McGilvery's ammunition was running low in spite of efforts to conserve it, as the duel with the enemy continued without letup. It was about time, he thought, for matters to come to a head, and he was not going to be caught short of ammunition with which to blast the infantry columns that he expected would soon pour out of the woods of Seminary Ridge. If Meade should order the Union guns to slacken their pace and then lapse into silence, the enemy might be fooled into thinking the moment had come for their infantry to advance. Hunt hurried to army headquarters to see Meade about issuing the order but found he had departed for Cemetery Hill. Meade was not there either. Hunt saw Howard and Osborn, however, and discussed the situation with them.[27] Osborn felt that although his guns were being "worked with great coolness, energy, and judgment," they were getting "no satisfactory results" and it would be better for them to stop their fire.[28] Hunt then decided to take it upon himself to issue the order to cease firing, and he rode along the ridge for that purpose. On his way to the Taneytown road to meet fresh batteries which he had summoned, Hunt ran into Captain H. H. Bingham of Hancock's staff, who told him that Meade's aides were looking for him with orders from the general to cease firing.[29] Meade had just received a message from General Warren containing the same advice that Hunt had intended to offer. Standing at his favorite post on Little Round Top, Warren had studied the cannonade carefully and had signaled Meade that Union batteries were doing the enemy "very little harm." They and the Confederates were both accomplishing little more than "filling the valley with smoke," which might conceal the advance of enemy infantry. He therefore advised that the Union guns cease their fire in the hope that the Southerners would follow suit.[30]

Both Warren and Osborn felt that the Union artillery fire was ineffective because it was failing to silence Confederate batteries and stop the cannonade. In their disappointment they perhaps underestimated the performance of Federal gunners. Though they had the same tendency as the Confederates to overshoot their mark, many of their shells reached the long lines of infantry which were lying in wait behind their guns hidden from view. In Pickett's division some regiments and companies suffered heavily in killed and wounded from the shelling, one regiment sustaining eighty-eight casualties. Out in the open field no one dared to stand up and remove the wounded or the men who had suffered prostration from the intolerable heat of the sun. The men in other parts of the line went through the terrifying experience of hearing and seeing solid shot come crashing through the woods and bringing down on them the tops of trees and branches. Now and then a shell would explode directly over the ranks and the fragments hit many of the men. They were shaken at first, never having been subjected to such a hot fire before, but their officers stood up and walked up and down the line to steady them. When the artillery finally ceased firing and orders came for the charge, everyone agreed that it seemed a relief after lying inactive for about two hours under the storm of hissing and exploding shells.[31]

Confederate batteries, especially those on Alexander's part of the front, suffered heavy losses in materiel, horses, and men in the cannonade.[32] With enemy shells frequently dropping close to the First Corps ordnance train, it was decided to move it back to a safer but less convenient place. As a result battery commanders needing ammunition had to wait a longer time to refill their chests. Soon the drivers of the caissons found that the heavy fire had exhausted their supply of long-range shot and shell, and they had to go even farther to get it from the reserve train.[33] As a result some of the guns remained mute and their gunners stood helpless during the cannonade and the charge, for Alexander had no batteries in reserve to replace them.[34] At this moment the Confederates could well have used an artillery pool for the whole army comparable to the one possessed by the enemy. The few guns in reserve in Hill's corps and the many more in Ewell's corps could not be called up as replacements for Alexander's batteries without complicated negotiations, because General Pendleton though chief of artillery lacked the authority to draft them. Federal artillery on the other hand, due to Hunt's control over operations of all batteries, had greater flexibility, which increased its initial advantage of having more guns. If the Confederates had had an artillerist of like authority and ability, Alexander would probably not have had to face the dilemma which became increasingly serious with each additional minute of the cannonade.

As Alexander stood for forty minutes behind the tree, he anxiously watched the Yankee line of fire through clouds of smoke looking for signs of weakness. Though there were none, he knew his batteries with their ammunition running low could not continue their rate of fire much longer. He sent Pickett a note saying that if he was going to advance at all he must do so immediately or the batteries could not give him adequate support.[35] A few minutes later Alexander noticed "the most formidable" of the Yankee batteries limber up and pull out. He waited to see if others would replace them but none came, and there appeared to be a gap of over 1,000 feet in the artillery line near the Clump of Trees. Although not completely accurate in his observations, he did pretty well under the circumstances, for two 6-gun batteries did leave during the cannonade. Probably he saw one of them go and possibly the other. The third one, Lieutenant Alonzo H. Cushing's Battery A, 4th United States, which Alexander thought had left, still remained in its position just north of the trees, but it could fire only a fraction of its guns because of heavy losses in men and damage to equipment.[36] Alexander, confident that a break in Federal resistance had occurred, hurriedly scribbled another note to Pickett: "For God's sake come quick. The 18 guns have gone. Come quick or my ammunition will not let me support you properly." [37] He repeated this plea in two verbal messages carried by an officer and a sergeant from the nearest guns. His impatience increased when Federal fire noticeably slackened to a few scattered shots and Pickett's line, which was scarcely 1,000 feet to his rear, still did not come forward.[38] The Confederate fire was becoming slower too as the cannoneers became exhausted and the ammunition less plentiful.[39]

The courier with Alexander's first note reached Pickett as he stood talking to Longstreet. He read it and then turned it over to Longstreet. When he made no comment, Pickett asked, "General, shall I advance?" Longstreet still said nothing, for, as he recounted later, he was overcome with emotion at the thought of the terrible sacrifice Pickett and his men must make. He merely bowed his head in affirmation and then turned quickly to mount his horse. Pickett saluted and said, "I shall lead my division forward, sir." With that he galloped off. Longstreet, leaving his staff, spurred his horse ahead and joined Alexander on the left flank of the guns. Alexander immediately told Longstreet of his worries. The nine howitzers lent him by General Pendleton had disappeared just before the cannonade.[40] He had expected to move them immediately in front of Pickett's line, for as he said, in every charge there was "a critical time when both the moral & physical effect of a prompt & close Arty. support are very powerful & may decide an action." Admittedly the scheme would be an experiment, but he bitterly regretted his inability to try it.[41] Worse than the loss of these guns was the situation in his own batteries. Their supplies of long-range ammunition were so low that only a fraction of his guns could follow Pickett's men and support the charge. Longstreet spoke sharply and ordered him to stop Pickett until the limbers could be refilled. Alexander replied that it was impossible for him to do so, for if he did it would delay the charge for an hour and give the enemy a chance to recover his losses. Besides the trains had but little ammunition left.[42]

This information came as a shock to Longstreet. Earlier in the afternoon he had gone out to the fields where the guns of Major James Dearing's battalion were pouring hot metal on the Union lines. From what he could see he thought the Confederates had gained an advantage. He feared that if he continued the cannonade much longer in the hopes of achieving decisive results he would not have enough time for a successful infantry attack before nightfall. Accordingly he gave orders for the batteries to refill their ammunition chests and be ready to follow up the advance of the infantry. Until Alexander spoke to him about it, it had not occurred to him that there might be a fatal shortage of shot and shell.[43] Nor for that matter had Lee considered this possibility when he, Longstreet, and others planned a massive cannonade, the most extraordinary one of the war, as a prelude and an accompaniment to a large-scale infantry assault. The question of ammunition supplies, with the army so far from its base and after two days of heavy fighting, should have been a matter of great concern to them in the discussion, but obviously it was not. In contrast, one of Meade's first inquiries when he arrived in Gettysburg was whether he had enough ammunition for his artillery.[44] Fortunately he had a chief of artillery who knew the answer. Pendleton might not have been able to furnish the same information without considerable trouble, but if Longstreet had asked Alexander about the matter early in the morning, he would have found his best argument against Lee's plans for a grand charge.[45] Its success, Lee knew, depended greatly upon adequate artillery support for the infantry as it moved forward. After the battle he concluded that lack of fire power had contributed significantly to the collapse of Longstreet's assault on July 3.[46]

What Alexander told Longstreet about the condition of the artillery so upset him that he seemed momentarily stunned. Finally he recovered enough to say frankly and with great emotion how much he disliked making the charge. He had no confidence in its success but felt constrained to go ahead with it because General Lee had ordered it. Alexander sensed that Longstreet was looking to him for moral support and open approval of an order to stop Pickett from advancing. Conscious of his youth and inexperience, Alexander discreetly kept silent, while Longstreet "fought his battle out alone and obeyed his orders." [47] Shortly General Garnett's brigade emerged from the woods behind them.[48] Now there was no turning back.

The movement caught Longstreet's attention, and for a moment his feelings of depression left him when he saw Pickett riding forward "gracefully, with his jaunty cap raked well over on his right ear and his long auburn locks, nicely dressed, hanging almost to his shoulders." Behind him came Generals Garnett and Armistead, veterans of nearly a quarter of a century of military service, and General Kemper, who though younger, as politician-turned-soldier had served well through many bitter engagements and was now leading Longstreet's old brigade. It made "Old Pete" proud to see them advance in "well-closed ranks and with elastic step," [49] confident of their ability to sweep everything before them. The same buoyancy pervaded the rank and file of all of Pickett's division, which in this engagement had fewer stragglers than ever before. While all the men realized that they were to have "bloody work," they felt sure of "ultimate triumph." [50] Longstreet remained mounted and watched his men march straight through the batteries toward the Emmitsburg road in "quick time." They were accompanied by the music of a band which played as if the division were passing in review.[51]

Alexander left Longstreet to greet Garnett, an old friend whom he had not seen in several months, and ride with him while his brigade swept through the guns. Tarrying briefly to wish Garnett good luck, Alexander then turned to the task of furnishing artillery support for Pickett's men. He ordered all guns with fewer than fifteen rounds to remain in position and fire over the heads of the infantry. Those with over that number—only eighteen guns in all—he moved forward in close support of the charge.[52] His energetic leadership was not duplicated by Colonel Walker of the Third Corps, who apparently ran none of his guns out in time to support Hill's infantry in the assault.[53]

At 3:00 P.M. officers and men of Hancock's Second Corps looking west saw a long gray line suddenly emerge into the bright sunlight from the dark fringe of timber on Seminary Ridge three-quarters of a mile away. They had been enjoying a short respite from the roar of artillery fire and were wondering what next the Confederates had in store for them. Then it happened. From their vantage point near the Clump of Trees they noticed the first troops swing into view, obviously heading in their direction. They were Pettigrew's men. Pickett's division was still too far to the left for them to see it, nor could they hear the band playing martial airs as it stepped smartly forth. But they had no trouble seeing Pettigrew's first line of battle, which with a strong force of skirmishers preceding it advanced in such beautiful order as to cause outbursts of admiration from friend and foe.[54] In a breeze from the west, which had blown away the smoke of the cannonade, their battle flags fluttered and snapped. With burnished rifles and bayonets flashing in the sun, the men marched with a "determined, unhesitating" pace in a mood to overcome all obstacles.[55]

Pettigrew had started his men at the same time as Pickett's,[56] in itself quite a feat in coordination, as his line had waited on the ridge about a quarter of a mile to the left and rear of Garnett's brigade. Setting out from positions about 1,000 feet apart, the divisions marched at very different angles toward the Emmitsburg road, and as they marched the gap between them gradually narrowed.[57] The road made a deep diagonal gash from northeast to southwest across the whole width of the field of the assault. In many places the ground was cut up by fences, some of them stoutly built of posts and rails about five feet high. Particularly troublesome were those on both sides of the road; they virtually stopped all forward movement as the men climbed over them or crowded through the few openings.[58] Pettigrew's line centered on the Clump of Trees and in general went straight ahead, bearing only slightly toward the right. Pickett's division, though initially closer to the Union lines, had to go just as far to reach the point of attack because it had to make an oblique left, or forty-five-degree-angle turn, as it approached the road, and march some distance before turning right again and heading once more for the Clump of Trees.[59] When both divisions had covered a little more than half of the distance to the Union line and Pickett's men had already crossed the road, the attacking columns stopped in a slight depression which partially protected them from enemy fire, to rest and dress ranks.[60] Colonel Fry, commanding Archer's brigade, heard General Garnett give an order, but amid the rattle of musketry he could not distinguish the words. Garnett, seeing Fry's look or gesture of inquiry, called out, "I am dressing on you." Pettigrew's officers then passed the command down the line to "guide right" so as to keep the division aligned with Fry's brigade as the men advanced.[61] This convergence of two long battle lines within 1,400 feet of the enemy position represented a triumph of careful planning on the part of Lee, Longstreet, and other officers.

As the Confederate brigades moved inexorably forward and went through their evolutions with almost paradelike precision Longstreet, who by this time had dismounted and perched on a fence, watched them with a professional eye. Everything seemed in order; perhaps they would accomplish the impossible after all. Although Yankee gunners had opened in full fury, the Confederates kept steadily on. A screaming shell would cut a huge swath in the line; immediately a captain would shout, "Close up, men!" and without breaking step they would move into the gap, touch elbows, and press forward.[62] Longstreet, worried about the exposure of the flanks to enemy attacks, from time to time sent officers of his staff flying after the advancing lines with orders and suggestions to their commanders. When he saw a serious threat on Pettigrew's extreme left, he hurried Major Osmun Latrobe across the fields to warn General Trimble about it.[63] Latrobe's horse was killed from under him, and by the time he delivered the message it was too late for Trimble to do much about the situation.[64] At about the same moment Longstreet sent his chief of staff, Lieutenant Colonel G. Moxley Sorrell, off in search of Pickett to advise him to watch his right and if necessary move some troops to stop any attempt to flank it. In the confusion, noise, and smoke of the battle Sorrell never found Pickett, but he did come up to Garnett and Armistead well on their way toward the Federal line.[65]

Pickett's role and performance in this most famous of infantry assaults which bears his name has remained an enigma. Reliable witnesses saw him ride proudly into battle, and others told how he came back dejected and forlorn, but everyone seems to have lost sight of him somewhere in the billows of smoke which enveloped the area between the Codori farm on the Emmitsburg road and Cemetery Ridge.[66] Many participants who studied the battle after the war worried over the question of Pickett's whereabouts, although none seemed to show the same concern about Pettigrew.[67] Perhaps they reasoned that since the grand and glorious assault was named for him, he somehow failed them when he did not immolate himself while leading his troops to the point of their farthest ad-

※ *Map 10 &* 11 ※

THIRD DAY'S BATTLE, DISPOSITION OF TROOPS:
PICKETT–PETTIGREW ASSAULT,
3:30–4:00 P.M., JULY 3

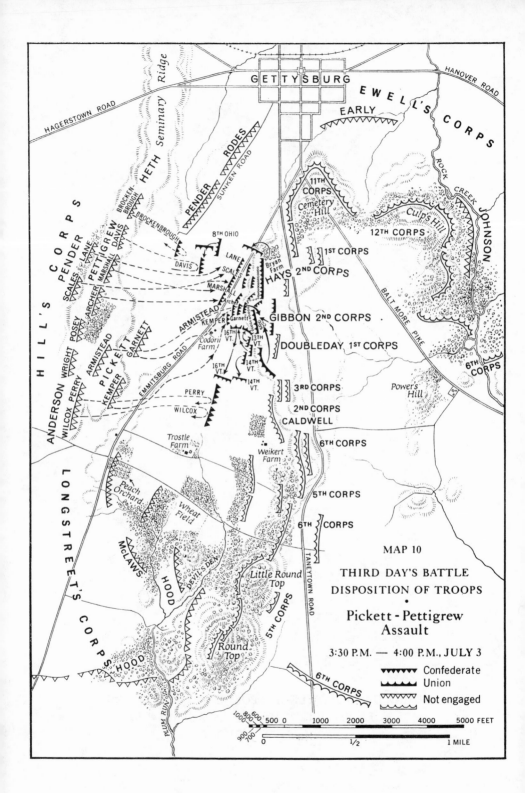

HANOVER ROAD

GETTYSBURG

EWELL'S CORPS

HAGERSTOWN ROAD

EARLY

ROCK CREEK

Broken Seminary Ridge

HETH

PENDER

RODES

SUNKEN ROAD

BROCKENBROUGH

JOHNSON

11TH CORPS

Cemetery Hill

Culp's Hill

12TH CORPS

HILL'S CORPS

PENDER

8TH OHIO

1ST CORPS

SCALES
LANE
PETTIGREW
MARSHALL
DAVIS
ARCHER
POSEY

LANE

DAVIS

SCALES

MARSHALL

Bryan Farm

HAYS 2ND CORPS

Archer

ARMISTEAD

KEMPER Garnett

GIBBON 2ND CORPS

BALTIMORE PIKE

6TH CORPS

ANDERSON

WRIGHT

ARMISTEAD

PICKETT

GARNETT

16TH VT.

Codori Farm

16TH VT.

13TH VT.

DOUBLEDAY 1ST CORPS

WILCOX

PERRY

KEMPER

EMMITSBURG ROAD

16TH VT.

14TH VT.

14TH VT.

3RD CORPS

Power's Hill

LONGSTREET'S

PERRY

WILCOX

2ND CORPS

CALDWELL

Trostle Farm

Weikert Farm

6TH CORPS

McLAWS

HOOD

Peach Orchard

Wheat Field

5TH CORPS

6TH CORPS

DEVIL'S DEN

Little Round Top

MAP 10

THIRD DAY'S BATTLE

DISPOSITION OF TROOPS

•

Pickett - Pettigrew Assault

CORPS

HOOD

5TH CORPS

Round Top

3:30 P.M. — 4:00 P.M., JULY 3

6TH CORPS

Confederate

Union

Not engaged

PLUM RUN

TANEYTOWN ROAD

1000 800 500 0   1000   2000   3000   4000   5000 FEET
900 700

0   1/2   1 MILE

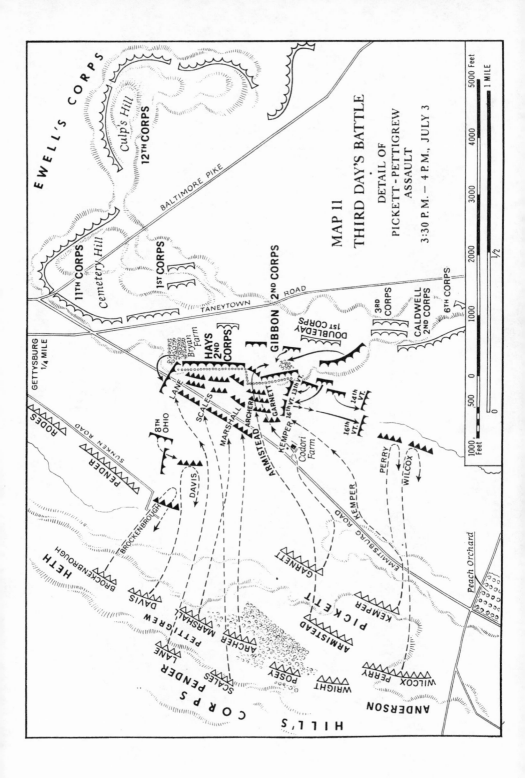

MAP II
THIRD DAY'S BATTLE
DETAIL OF
PICKETT-PETTIGREW
ASSAULT
3:30 P.M. — 4 P.M., JULY 3

vance. But unfairly he has received the onus for a defeat which must be largely attributed to the shortcomings of others, as well as to the valor of Union officers and men. Although there are indications that Longstreet used him as his assistant in coordinating the movements of all the brigades before and after the assault took place, nowhere in official or semiofficial accounts is there a suggestion that Pickett was formally entrusted with responsibility for operations on the field.[68] He neither commanded the assaulting columns nor led the larger portion of the troops engaged. As a major general of a division he naturally placed himself in a position where he could best supervise the movements of his own brigades and keep an eye on Hill's troops who were cooperating with him. It would not be surprising therefore if he stayed near the Codori farm, probably getting no farther than half the distance between it and the ridge, where he would be quite centrally located with reference to both his own and Hill's troops, as well as to Longstreet, his immediate superior. Pickett kept his staff busy carrying messages to various generals and performing other duties on the field. At different times he sent his aides back to the Confederate lines to inform Longstreet of his need for reinforcements, or to direct Wilcox when and where to advance his troops, or to ask Major James Dearing for artillery support. When he noticed men in Pettigrew's division beginning to falter, he ordered Captains E. R. Baird and W. Stuart Symington to help rally them. Then Pickett himself galloped to the left in an effort to steady the men.[69] Another aide recalled that toward the end of the advance Pickett personally gave the order to his division to "double-quick," saying, "Boys, give them a cheer;"[70] and Longstreet himself stated that it was Pickett who finally directed his men to give up their attempt to take the heights and to retreat. Although it is true that no one knows just where he was at any given moment, there is ample evidence that Pickett did play a positive role in the charge instead of skulking in the Codori barn, as one Confederate officer averred.[71]

As Pickett's division began to appear over the rise along the Emmitsburg road it received its first blast of iron and lead from McGilvery's batteries stationed on the lower end of Cemetery Ridge and Rittenhouse's Parrotts on Little Round Top.[72] Hunt had ridden to McGilvery's position in time to direct his gunners to fire on the enemy's flank. To his left Rittenhouse's battery, which had

sufficient elevation to see the Confederates easily a mile off, enfiladed almost their entire line with "fearful effect, sometimes as
many as 10 men being killed and wounded by the bursting of a single shell." [73] Though delighted at the opportunity to demonstrate
the effectiveness of his artillery against infantry, Hunt could not
help but admire the way in which the enemy advanced "magnificently, unshaken by shot and shell which tore through his ranks.
. . ." Much to his disappointment and chagrin the few Second
Corps batteries still able to function had to remain silent for want of
long-range ammunition until the advancing enemy came within
effective canister range. [74] The men in Garnett's brigade on the left
of Pickett's line remarked on a noticeable lack of artillery fire on
their front until they reached the enemy skirmish line concealed in
tall grass some three hundred feet down the slope from the Bloody
Angle. [75]

The first signs of faltering in the attacking forces due to shelling
and then musketry appeared in Colonel J. M. Brockenbrough's weak
brigade of Virginians, which was trailing behind the front line on
the extreme left. Under its temporary commander, Colonel Robert
M. Mayo of the 47th Virginia, it was the last brigade to arrive on
the field. [76] It never did get into proper alignment with the rest of
Pettigrew's brigades, and it made the whole line of the division
droop so badly on the left as to appear in echelon. [77] Not long after
it emerged from behind Seminary Ridge Major Osborn hit it with
the full force of his thirty-one guns located on Cemetery Hill. Since
the brigade had to bear right, its line became perpendicular to Osborn's artillery position and formed a perfect target for his batteries,
which threw projectiles of every description at it. Osborn made no
idle boast when he reported that "the havoc produced upon their
ranks was truly surprising." [78]

To add to its woes Brockenbrough's brigade received blows from
another source as well, the 8th Ohio, which in the afternoon of July
2 Colonel Carroll, commanding the First Brigade of Hays's division,
had posted under Lieutenant Colonel Franklin Sawyer several hundred feet west of the Emmitsburg road with instructions for it to
send out and support a skirmish line well in advance of the regiment. Carroll told Sawyer to maintain his position "at all hazards"
and the remainder of the brigade would back him up. [79] but that
evening Carroll went to Howard's rescue, leaving the 8th Ohio

behind, and he never returned because Howard wanted to keep him on the Eleventh Corps line. All through the night, the next morning, and the afternoon Sawyer held grimly to his advanced post without relief and in spite of the loss of forty-five officers and men up until noon.[80] By the time Pettigrew's division approached, Sawyer in all probability had no more than 250 officers and men in his unit.[81] Seeing the long lines bearing down on his small regiment, Sawyer coolly calculated his chances of survival and decided to make a fight for it against the Confederate flank. He advanced his regiment to the skirmish line, and as the rebels came within three hundred feet of him he ordered his men to fire. Their bullets struck down Brockenbrough's men who had just come abreast of the sunken road or perhaps a bit farther. The shelling was bad enough, but now musketry! The combined fire was too much. The brigade, sure that ten times its number confronted it, stopped in its tracks and gave up the fight. Thereupon Sawyer quickly swung his regiment around to the left and poured a devastating fire into the flank of what was probably Davis' brigade. At the same time some of Hays's troops on Sawyer's left opened up and hit Davis' men from the front. Blasted from two sides, they began to drift toward the rear. Sawyer then turned his attention to other troops as they came up.[82]

At first Pettigrew's and Archer's brigades remained hard and firm in what was the center of the assaulting forces, despite the wavering of Davis' and Brockenbrough's brigades. Just in time they received help from Lane's and Scales's brigades, which had rushed up to support them on the left.[83] Nevertheless even before reaching the Emmitsburg road their formations had lost much of their symmetry and precision, though the forward impetus continued as masses of men pushed on and on. On their part of the field the road angled much closer to the Union lines than it did where Pickett's divisions marched, and thus when the men reached it they were exposed to heavier and more accurate fire. Many, tempted by the protection provided by the low banks of the road and the strong post and rail fences, fell on their stomachs and began firing at the Union lines now within effective rifle range. Before long they had formed a line of battle along the road which never moved beyond it.[84] At this stage in the advance the number of Confederates who began to stream toward the rear, wounded in spirit as well as in body, became noticeably large.[85]

Still a vast number of Pettigrew's and Trimble's men started up the slope beyond the road. Their chances of success were quite hopeless, however, for they were contending against men of the Second Corps who were as good as they and in a much better position. All units of the Third Division of the corps were fighters and so was their leader, the fiery General Alexander Hays, a big six-foot, sandy-haired man [86] who said his division was the "fighting kind" he loved. He affectionally referred to his troops as the " 'Blue Birds' whose badge is the 'Shamrock,' " and his personal banner was borne by a "true son of the Emerald Isle, who don't fear the devil. . . ." [87] An intense and emotional man, he spoke for thousands of Union soldiers when he wrote: "I was fighting for my native state, and before I went in thought of those at home I so dearly loved. If Gettysburg was lost all was lost for them, and I only interposed a life that would be otherwise worthless." [88]

Of Hays's three brigades two were made up of old campaigners and one of garrison troops who had successfully emerged from their initiation to fierce combat the day before, though with painful losses. Trained at West Point,[89] Hays had none of the disdain of the professional for volunteers, and he seemed to know that such soldiers responded brilliantly to vigorous and fearless leadership, which he gave willingly. During the cannonade when the racket and the danger from exploding shells were making individual soldiers feel completely bereft, their commander suddenly appeared on his horse and directed them to hunt up all abandoned rifles and muskets and to clean and load them ready for use. As a result, when the charge began some of the more energetic men had four loaded weapons ready at hand, and many more had two.[90] As the Confederate columns were crossing the fields and steadily approaching the Emmitsburg road, Hays drilled some of his men in the manual of arms [91] to keep their minds off the trial ahead and probably to prevent some trigger-happy soul from firing too soon. Then he rode up and down exhorting his troops to stand fast and fight like men. Once he stopped to point at Lieutenant George A. Woodruff's Battery I, 1st United States, which was blazing away in Ziegler's Grove, and shouted, " 'Boys, don't let 'em touch those pieces.' " A minute later with a laugh he sang out, " 'Hurrah! boys, we're giving them h——l,' " whereupon he dashed up to the brow of the hill to cheer the 8th

Ohio.[92] Altogether he put on quite a show and the men loved it.

Hays's main line had in it two of his brigades, the Second and Third, consisting of seven regiments and parts of two others. Very likely they numbered no more than 2,500 officers and men, if casualties from the fighting on July 2 and detachments for special services are taken into consideration.[93] The regiments were placed in a straight line from near the angle up to and perhaps a little beyond the Bryan house and barn on the edge of Ziegler's Grove. Beginning on the left they were the 14th Connecticut, which shared the same low stone wall with several companies of the 71st Pennsylvania in Webb's brigade, the 39th New York (only four companies strong), the 1st Delaware, the 12th New Jersey, and the 111th New York. Lieutenant David Shields, an aide of Hays, brought the 111th New York up to the line as the enemy columns were advancing. The left wing of the regiment was in the rear of the 12th New Jersey and during the fighting became mixed with it. The right of the 111th New York covered the Bryan barn and the lane which ran beside it. In supporting position the 125th New York backed up part of the 14th Connecticut and all of the 39th New York. When Captain William A. Arnold's Battery A, 1st Rhode Island Light withdrew during the cannonade, it created a gap in the left end of Hays's line which Major Theodore G. Ellis of the 14th Connecticut, temporary commander of the Second Brigade, filled by shifting his men to the left. To the north of the Bryan house there was a gap between Hays's line and the left of the Eleventh Corps. Hays tried to bridge it with two regiments, the 108th New York which he placed immediately north of his line in support of Woodruff's battery of six 12-pounders, and beyond it the 126th New York which he stretched out behind a stone wall.

Just before the infantry attack on his line Hays took the 108th New York out of the grove and placed it in a kneeling position apparently to the left and rear of the 12th New Jersey. The 10th New York battalion together with a detachment from the 8th Ohio acted as a provost guard in the rear of the division.[94] In further preparation for the attack Hays ordered Lieutenant E. L. Bicknell of the 1st Massachusetts Sharpshooters to gather up all men separated from their commands who had sought shelter in Ziegler's Grove during the cannonade and form them into a line to the right of the Bryan house. Bicknell, commanding a company of twenty sharpshooters, was on loan from Gibbon's division to cope with enemy snipers who had been making life miserable for Union infantry in the grove. Now Hays saw an even better use for the services of this capable young man.[95]

Until this moment the infantry along the Second Corps line had remained quiet, but it was ready. Soldiers slid their cartridge boxes in front of them and carefully examined the capped nipples of their muskets. The men of the 12th New Jersey, armed with the Springfield smoothbore musket, caliber .69, in anticipation of close fighting converted their weapons into shotguns by breaking open their buck and ball cartridges and preparing special ones with ten to twenty-five buckshot in each. The strain of waiting became greater with each passing moment, and occasionally the click of a hammer could be heard as a soldier staring straight ahead wet his lips and absentmindedly cocked his musket.[96] The sound of artillery pouring canister into the now ragged ranks of the oncoming Confederates somewhat relieved the tension. Unfortunately few guns in the Second Corps Artillery Brigade remained in position to fire; Woodruff's six pieces and three of Cushing's were working at a furious rate, but they were about the only ones.

At just the right moment a fresh battery of six 3-inchers from the Sixth Corps, Captain Andrew Cowan's 1st New York Independent, rushed up to fill the position left vacant by Lieutenant T. Fred Brown's badly crippled Battery B, 1st Rhode Island Light.[97] Cowan had been in action on Doubleday's part of the line and had seen the Confederate infantry start its advance, when Captain C. H. Banes of Webb's staff dashed over and ordered him to support Webb's brigade. Considering himself to be under Doubleday's orders, Cowan hesitated to obey until he looked to the right and there on higher ground he saw Webb waving his hat for him to come on. Instantly he gave the command to limber to the rear and move by the left flank at a gallop. His cannoneers, mostly stripped to their undershirts, sprang upon the limber chests with loud cheers and up onto the guns; their implements which they had not time to stow away were still in their hands. As Cowan whirled his guns into firing position General Hunt and Captain Hazard rode up to commend him upon his prompt response.[98]

General Hancock, apparently unaware of Cowan's arrival, became incensed when he learned that someone had removed twelve of his guns—he did not name the batteries—thus, he thought, cutting his artillery support in almost half. He had been down at the lower end of the ridge inspecting Caldwell's First Division, when he spied enemy skirmishers moving out of the woods ahead of the assaulting columns. After warning Meade of the advance, Hancock went along his line poking here and there to see if everything was in shape. Perhaps it was he rather than Hays or Major Ellis who ordered the 39th New York to help fill the gap in Hays's line left by the withdrawal of Arnold's battery.[99]

As he rode the length of the ridge Hancock could see the final preparations being made in Gibbon's division to receive the enemy. Webb's Second Brigade held the extreme right of Gibbon's position just to the left of Hays. When the Confederate infantry approached the Emmitsburg road, Webb had Cushing push three of his guns down to the stone wall in front of the Clump of Trees and provided him with about fifty infantrymen to help work the pieces. He also ordered the 71st Pennsylvania to move forward and occupy the space between the right gun and the angle in the wall, but Colonel Richard Penn Smith found he could not put all of his men there unless he extended his line out into the open field or placed two of his companies about 250 feet to the rear behind the stone wall used by Hays's men. He wisely decided to give all his troops the advantage of protection behind a wall. As a further precaution he instructed his men to provide themselves with extra muskets which littered the ground following the previous day's engagement. To the left of Cushing's guns Webb had the 69th Pennsylvania remain behind the wall and in front of the Clump of Trees, where it had been the day before. He kept the 72nd Pennsylvania in reserve just below the crest on the east slope of the ridge. His fourth regiment, the 106th Pennsylvania, except for two companies which were on his skirmish line, had not returned from service with the Eleventh Corps.[100] South of the 71st and 69th Pennsylvania Webb's line was extended by three regiments of Colonel Norman J. Hall's brigade, from right to left the 59th New York, the 7th Michigan, and the 20th Massachusetts. These men with only a single shovel or spade for each regiment had succeeded in improving their positions either by digging shallow trenches or packing dirt around piled up fence rails.[101] About three hundred feet to their rear and to the left of the Clump of Trees and Cowan's battery Hall placed the 42nd and 19th Massachusetts. To the left of Hall General William Harrow posted all of the regiments of his First Brigade on the main line. From right to left they were the 82nd New York, the 19th Maine, the 1st Minnesota, and the 15th Massachusetts.[102]

On lower ground to the south of Gibbon, regiments of Doubleday's division of the First Corps formed a somewhat irregular line so as to take advantage of the peculiarities of the terrain. There was a gap between the left of the 15th Massachusetts and Doubleday's right regiment, Colonel Theodore B. Gates's 80th New York (20th Militia), and beyond it the 151st Pennsylvania continued the line. These regiments were of Rowley's brigade, and Gates as senior officer on that part of the field assumed command of both of them. About 250 feet in advance of his line on the left the 13th Vermont had thrown up a breastwork on a low rocky knoll which was covered with bushes and small trees. The 14th Vermont held a similar position to the left of the 13th, but on lower ground. Fortunately for the men on this hot day the right of the regiment rested near a spring and a small stream flowing through the grass behind it. Hancock, who apparently thought they were too far in advance of the main line, offered to send them supports, but the independent Yankees from Vermont wanted the honor of holding this part of the field themselves. About half of the 16th Vermont manned a cluster of picket posts in advance of the main line, and the other half stayed in their immediate rear as a reserve. The remainder of Doubleday's troops, which included two regiments from Rowley's brigade and three from Dana's, he placed, probably with Newton's advice and consent, in two parallel lines of battle as support for his first one. The comparatively level and open nature of the ground occupied by the division invited assault.[103]

The really weak point in this half mile or so of the main Union line was the salient at the angle near the Clump of Trees, but if Hancock made note of it, he said nothing. Perhaps he felt Gibbon and Webb had done everything possible to strengthen it. His real worry was about the removal of the twelve guns and the effect their absence would have on the ability of his men to repulse an attack. It also annoyed him to find that a regiment he had placed across the Taneytown road to connect his right with Howard's left had been removed. He feared an attack there, and since all of his staff had been sent on other errands, he went himself to speak to Meade about getting troops from another command to occupy this position. He probably did not know that Robinson's division was in reserve nearby and could have filled the gap then instead of later. Finding Meade's headquarters deserted, Hancock wasted no time there but rode at once to Webb's part of the line. He arrived just before the Confederate infantry struck.[104]

The battle-hardened soldiers along the front of the Second Corps, though tense with anticipation, had learned the importance of waiting until the enemy came within short range before opening fire. Here and there a few units fired volleys at distances of 600 to 750 feet to break up enemy formations,[105] but most regiments held off while the men watched the Confederates cross the Emmitsburg road, then gather together in what seemed like a huge mass, quicken their pace, and finally with a rebel yell break into a charge.[106] When they were within 300 or 400 feet of the Union line, it suddenly became ablaze with the fire of thousands of muskets.[107] Still the Confederates continued up the slope with irresistible fury. It was soon apparent that their thrust was aimed at the narrow front between the Clump of Trees and the lane running down from the Bryan house to the Emmitsburg road. Some generals, Hunt and Stannard in particular, thought the enfilading artillery and musket fire was forcing the enemy lines to sidle from their front and move toward the Clump of Trees.[108] Here the greatest danger to Union forces became focused because the advanced location of Webb's line exposed it to a cross fire, especially on the right, and to an attack before the enemy columns could lose their momentum. Here Gibbon's men displayed a truly remarkable feat of arms and valor in repulsing the desperate Confederate attempt to penetrate their line. Nevertheless their action should in no way belittle the contributions of troops on both sides of them to the victory. These men and their officers, once they perceived the direction of the Confederate assault, broke their lines on both ends of the threatened area and swinging them as doors slammed them against the enemy flanks so as to crush and pulverize them.

The right flank of this threatened area was along Hays's front. As the Confederates advanced, Trimble's two brigades came directly toward it, with Lane's on the extreme left.[109] Suddenly "four lines" rose from behind the stone wall and delivered a mighty volley. Hays, who had an especial fondness for hyperbole, described the scene as one which "the angel of death alone" could have produced.[110] No doubt the fire blew great holes in the enemy ranks, for it included shotgunlike blasts from the 12th New Jersey smoothbores and a torrent of bullets from two companies of the 14th Connecticut armed with Sharps breech-loading rifles.[111] Many of Lane's North Carolinians succeeded in coming within a few feet of the stone wall in spite of the heavy musket and cannon fire on their front, when heavy volleys from their left stopped them in their tracks.[112] The ferocity and unexpectedness of these blasts completely demoralized them. Cut off from their supports, some of the rebels found refuge in Bryan's barn nearby and continued to fight, only to be killed or captured by men from the 111th New York who finally surrounded them.[113]

Apparently two separate commands participated in this assault on the Confederate left. Hays himself led the small force Lieutenant Bicknell had previously collected down the Bryan lane and then swung by left wheel up to the fence along the edge of the byway.[114] Another group consisting of detachments from the Third Brigade under Captains Morris Brown of the 126th New York and Samuel C. Armstrong of the 125th New York also struck the enemy left flank about the same time or shortly after Hays had hit it. These men had been stationed near a house along the Emmitsburg road in front and to the right of the brigade as a reserve for the skirmish line. Seeing the North Carolinians move past their left to attack Hays's main line, Brown and Armstrong without orders from any superior officer gathered their men and quickly posted them along a rail fence at right angles to the enemy line. Leveling their guns on the top rail, they made every shot count, for the extreme left of the Confederates was within short range.[115] The combined fire from flank and front was too much. Armstrong saw many of the rebels fall "in heaps," while others "threw themselves flat on the Emmitsburg road to escape bullets, and waved hats, handkerchiefs, newspapers or whatever they had to signal surrender. . . ."[116] Sawyer's regiment was on hand to the right of Armstrong to prevent enemy attempts to outflank him by moving north on the road.[117] With the collapse of their attack as many North Carolinians as possible tried to get out of the trap, but in so doing they left behind their dead and wounded and droves of prisoners.[118]

Even as the left of the assaulting forces was being shattered, the idea of making a heavy attack on the exposed right flank of Pickett's division occurred almost simultaneously to several officers, including Hall, Gibbon, Hancock, and Stannard.[119] They all noticed that the three Vermont regiments happened to be well located for such a move. Before and during the engagement Hancock had taken an unusual interest in these regiments. They were well above the average in size of Union regiments at Gettysburg, any one of them having about three-quarters the strength of all three with Webb at the angle.[120] He had reservations about their quality, however, since their ranks were composed of short-term men with no previous experience in combat. Yet Hancock had no cause to complain about the 13th Vermont, which had performed with veteranlike precision the day before, and as a result he thought it and the other Vermont regiments were capable of performing more important tasks than the ones they had been assigned. Perhaps this appreciation of their worth explains his repeated visits to the units to give them the benefit of his "advice and encouragement." [121]

During the critical moments on Webb's front Hancock quickly rode over to Stannard to get him to make a flanking attack. Under the pressure of Pickett's advance Stannard had pulled the 16th Vermont regiment back from the skirmish line and massed it in the rear of the 14th Vermont.[122] The 13th Vermont on the right of the 14th would have to go forward but a short distance and swing its line clockwise to hit the enemy flank. In recalling the incident Stannard insisted that he had ordered the movement and it was already under way when Hancock arrived. Hancock and one of his aides said that, on the contrary, it was his idea all along, and that just as the general was leaving Stannard to go back to Webb's line the regiments stood poised for the attack. Regardless of who deserved all or part of the credit, the important thing is that the 13th Vermont, followed by the 16th Vermont on its left, pivoted ninety degrees to the right and fired a succession of volleys at pistol range on Pickett's right flank.[123] Despite the efforts of five Confederate guns advanced beyond Alexander's line by Major J. C. Haskell to break up this movement, the Vermonters persisted in their attack.[124] The effect of their assault cannot be precisely gauged, but without doubt it was largely instrumental in destroying the ability of the Confederates to exploit their gains along Webb's line. The Vermonters exacted a heavy toll from the Virginians in lives and prisoners and threatened to cut them off completely.[125]

Still nothing seemed to stop the rebels. With both ends of their line crumbled, on their right by the Vermonters and on their left by Hays's men, they drove relentlessly on toward the Clump of Trees and the Bloody Angle. Though greeted by a fierce fire of canister from Cowan's battery and Cushing's three guns, as well as repeated volleys from thousands of muskets, they took their losses and came on up the slope to the stone wall along Webb's line. Opposite that point they had succeeded in concentrating great strength in depth, and their impetus carried them on.[126] The heavy pall of smoke obscured their movements and permitted them to get almost on top of Gibbon's men, some of whom suddenly found hostile muskets pressing against their chests.[127] One company of the 71st Pennsylvania fled without orders, while several others upon command of Lieutenant Colonel C. Kochersperger beat a quick retreat toward the crest. Sergeant John Stockton with six other members of the regiment stubbornly held their ground at the angle and miraculously escaped death or capture. Colonel Smith of the 71st, standing on the crest with his right wing in line with Hays's men, steadied his fleeing companies and faced them about toward the enemy.[128] Cushing fell dead after firing his last load of canister. Captain Cowan continued to pour canister and then double canister into the oncoming Confederates only a few paces away. Hunt, still on his horse, shouted to Cowan that he might be firing into Union soldiers, but the captain yelled for him not to worry because on foot he could peer under the smoke and see what he was doing. Much to Cowan's disgust some infantry began to give way. One of his men, Corporal Plunkett, irate at seeing one man run to the rear, hit him over the head with a coffee pot; the bottom gave way, and down it went wrapped around his neck.[129]

The time had come for the artillery to clear out. The issue had been reduced to the lowest common denominator: a bitter contest between equally brave and determined infantrymen. The Confederates had gained a toehold and thrown their foe into confusion, but just at the point of success their drive lost its momentum. When they reached the wall they hesitated, and the moment of hesitation, as Webb said, is "the moment of defeat." [130] The ground, which was strewn with rocks and timber slashings, and the wall itself gave them some protection as they stopped to return the Union fire.[131] However, if they stayed there long Union troops would close in on them. Armistead, the only general officer remaining, quickly saw that they must press on.[132] Precariously balancing his hat on the top of his sword and crying, "Boys, give them cold steel," he led some 150 of his men over the wall.[133] But instead of chasing the fleeing enemy with the end of the long cold bayonet, they themselves received hot lead as Union officers quickly and skillfully maneuvered their men in an effort to hurl the rebels back to the far side of the wall.[134] This was the moment of truth for the Southerners, the moment that would be known in history as the High Water Mark of the Confederacy.

As Webb struggled to rally his troops, for a time he despaired of preventing a major breakthrough and feared personal disgrace for himself and disaster for the Army of the Potomac. Refusing to give up, he set an example of bravery and undaunted leadership for his men to follow, although many of them barely recognized him since he had been appointed their commander but a few days before. To organize a counterattack he rushed back to his reserve regiment, the 72nd Pennsylvania, which was several hundred feet behind his line. In the confusion Webb neglected to go through channels and give Lieutenant Colonel Theodore Heiser the order to charge. Instead he himself shouted out the order; when the soldiers did not budge, Webb in desperation seized the regimental standard and tried to drag the color bearer ahead in hopes of getting the regiment to follow. The bearer, apparently not knowing him, pulled back and then, riddled by bullets, fell over dead. Finally the men advanced a few paces and fired at the Confederates. They refused to go any farther, however, and steadfastly remained in a position about 250 feet back from the wall, where though without protection they kept up their fire.

Webb, almost frantic, then left the line of the stubborn 72nd and, fully exposed to enemy bullets, rushed over to the 69th Pennsylvania, the left regiment of his brigade. It had stoutly held its ground, although the right half of the regiment had pulled away from the wall at almost a forty-degree angle to give the men elbow room and to keep them from being outflanked. When Webb cried out for them to fire across the front of the 72nd regiment, they raked the Confederates with a crippling cross fire. To their rear two companies of Webb's fourth regiment, the 106th Pennsylvania, remained steady and resolutely blazed away at the charging enemy. On his way to the 69th regiment Webb passed within a few feet of Armistead as he was leading his men up the slope beyond the wall. The two generals narrowly missed a personal encounter just as the fierce contest between their forces reached its climax. Within minutes Armistead fell mortally wounded, while Webb survived to relive the scene of his triumph for years to come.[135]

But before Webb could turn back this surge of Confederate power, he needed help. Fortunately Colonel Hall, a young West Pointer commanding the brigade to his left, was very perceptive and cooperative.[136] Without being told he immediately saw what he should do. His front-line regiments, the 59th New York, the 7th Michigan, and the 20th Massachusetts, had previously turned back a Confederate thrust. Now to meet the new threat Hall pushed the three regiments out of their line and ordered them to make a quarter turn to the right and charge for the Clump of Trees. In the din of battle the men mistook the command to mean withdrawal, which resulted in confusion until some of the officers rushed ahead to show them what was really intended. About then Hancock came up the eastern slope of the ridge not far from the critical area. Colonel Arthur F. Devereux of the 19th Massachusetts in Hall's brigade, seeing him, ran over and asked permission to move his men and those of the 42nd New York to the threatened point. Hancock readily gave consent, and with the 42nd New York in the lead the two regiments at "double-quick" took a right oblique, which brought them to the Clump of Trees between the 69th and 72nd Pennsylvania. Soon afterwards Harrow rushed over the four regiments of his brigade, the 82nd New York, the 19th Maine, the 1st Minnesota, and the 15th Massachusetts.[137] In their eagerness to get at the enemy the various commands became so intermingled and packed in as to be practically immobile. To the left of this mass of struggling men Colonel Gates of the First Corps, directing operations of his own regiment, the 80th New York, and of the 151st Pennsylvania, ordered his force of six hundred infantrymen to move by right flank and take a position a little obliquely to the general line. From there they poured a heavy fire into rebels who were still trying to push ahead in the center.[138] At this critical moment both Gibbon and Hancock fell wounded, leaving no one to assert general authority over this part of the field.[139] Finally, after several minutes of heaving and hauling, the efforts of many officers, and the raising of regimental colors as rallying points, there emerged a semblance of a battle line which could be directed to close in on the enemy. Desperate, often hand-to-hand fighting took place before the Confederates on both sides of the wall threw down their arms and were taken prisoners of war. All those who could do so streamed back to their own lines, some of them still defiant and embittered,[140] wondering what had happened to their supports, particularly Wilcox' and Perry's brigades.

These two brigades had been put in position to follow after Pickett's division and protect its right flank. For some reason Wilcox, who had Perry's small brigade also in his charge, did not receive the command to advance until about twenty minutes after the Virginians' departure. He set out at once, but after crossing the Emmitsburg road, instead of bearing to the left he kept more or less straight ahead and went down the slope toward the upper course of Plum Run.[141] From the beginning of his advance "a terrible fire of artillery" [142] from McGilvery's batteries cut down his ranks at an alarming rate, and near the creek heavy musketry from the 14th Vermont greeted him on his front. The situation became unbearable when the 16th Vermont, having just completed its work of destruction on Pickett's lines, turned about, re-formed, and charged the left flank of Perry's brigade, taking most of the 2nd Florida as prisoners.[143] Wilcox rode back to ask for artillery support, but the battery commanders said they could give none, as they had no ammunition. They also asked why he was so far out in front. Wilcox replied that since Pickett had "gone over the enemy works," his job was to do the same farther down the line. When they told him he was mistaken and that Pickett rather than taking the works had been repulsed, Wilcox pulled his men out quickly and returned to his own lines.[144] The foray accomplished nothing and caused futile bloodletting, because it was poorly directed and started too late. If Wilcox had been ordered to follow more closely on Pickett's heels, he might have turned the flanking attack of the Vermonters into a bloody shambles. The mystery is why Longstreet let the brigades start out at all. During the charge his eyes never left the scene of

combat, and it was probably he who first perceived the gradual disintegration and final collapse of the attack. General R. H. Anderson
had been about to order Wright's and Posey's brigades to move forward when Longstreet directed him to halt them, saying that such a
maneuver would be "useless" and would only involve "unnecessary
loss," because the assault had failed.[145] It is barely possible that
Longstreet in his anxiety to rally the broken brigades and prepare
for a possible enemy counterattack had forgotten his approval of
Pickett's earlier request for Wilcox' help, and before he remembered
it, Wilcox had already started.

Even as Longstreet's infantry assault was threating the Union
center, cavalry forces were clashing several miles northeast of the
battlefield. General Stuart, who had finally ridden into Gettysburg
about noon on July 2, had consulted with General Lee about operations for July 3. Though a late arrival for the battle, Stuart's unerr-
ing eye and quick appreciation of the controlling topographical features in a strange land quickly showed him where he could best use
his cavalry for an offensive movement. He and Lee worked out a
scheme to put Stuart's entire cavalry force in a position from which
he could separate the Union cavalry from the main body of the
army and at the proper moment swoop down onto its rear. Taking
the three brigades of his command and Jenkins' troopers, he rode
out in the morning on the York road for about two and a half miles
beyond Gettysburg before turning off on a crossroad to the right,
which led him to Cress Ridge a mile away. The position controlled a
wide area of cultivated fields stretching east toward Hanover and
south to the frowning hills of the Union lines. With Stuart occupying it Ewell's left and rear would be secure against attack, but more
important, Stuart would obtain a view of the routes leading to the
enemy's rear.[146] If Lee should achieve his purpose in the Pickett-
Pettigrew assault, Stuart knew he would be "in precisely the right
position to discover it and improve the opportunity," by spreading confusion in the Union rear and rounding up fleeing soldiers.[147]
He had hoped to get to the top of the ridge undetected and to remain hidden behind a thick woods which crowned it, but unfortunately, as he later charged, Hampton's and Fitz Lee's brigades
bringing up the rear of the column debouched onto the open ground
and disclosed his presence.[148] Stuart blamed them unjustly, however, for their untimely arrival only confirmed an earlier discovery

by watchful United States signal officers of large columns of cavalry moving toward the right of the Union line. Their message wig-wagged to General Howard finally reached General Gregg by way of cavalry corps headquarters at noon.[149]

Stuart himself was also guilty of clumsiness in his attempts at deception, for reasons that his faithful assistant adjutant general, Major McClellan, could never fathom to his complete satisfaction. While carefully concealing Jenkins' and Chambliss' brigades from view and before Hampton and Fitz Lee came up, Stuart pushed one gun of Captain W. H. Griffin's 2nd Maryland Battery to the edge of the woods and personally ordered it to fire a number of "random shots in different directions."[150] McClellan supposed that these shots might have been a prearranged signal to notify Lee of Stuart's arrival at the designated spot, or perhaps Stuart, not finding any Federal cavalrymen about, wanted to flush them out before making any further moves. Not receiving an immediate reply to this fire, he then sent for Hampton and Fitz Lee to plan with them for an advance and an attack upon the enemy's rear. In the meantime he ordered a battalion of Jenkins' brigade to dismount, occupy a barn on the Rummel farm about 1,000 feet south of him, and form a line behind a fence on the right.[151]

When Gregg received the warning about Stuart's movements, he was somewhere on the long skirmish line formed by two brigades of his division running from Wolf's Hill to the Hanover road. Gregg had previously placed General Custer's strong Michigan brigade of Kilpatrick's division, which was temporarily under his command, at the crossing of the Low Dutch and Hanover roads three miles east of Gettysburg. General Pleasonton in transmitting the message from Howard evidently did not appreciate its importance, because at the same time he ordered Gregg to relieve Custer and send him back to his division on the extreme left of the Federal line. Gregg chose Colonel John B. McIntosh's brigade to replace Custer and decided to accompany it to its new position. Arriving there, he discovered the enemy to be in great strength and so situated as to pose a serious threat to the Union rear. When Custer voiced the opinion that Gregg would soon have a fight on his hands, Gregg replied that in that case he would like to have the assistance of his Michigan brigade. Custer answered that if Gregg gave him an order, he would be "only too happy" to stay. Without taking precious time to clear with Pleasonton, Gregg assumed the responsibility of ordering Custer to remain with him and willingly risked endangering his military career and reputation in his anxiety to protect the rear of the Union army.[152]

General Gregg now felt he could maintain the line from Wolf's Hill to the Hanover road with Colonel J. Irvin Gregg's brigade and at the same time confront Stuart's larger force with Custer's and McIntosh's brigades.[153] Stuart's advantage in numbers was lessened when Jenkins' brigade, commanded by Colonel M. J. Ferguson in place of the wounded Jenkins, soon had to retire for want of ammunition. Much to Stuart's disgust, through someone's senseless inefficiency the men in the unit who were equipped with Enfield rifles of the latest design came into action with only ten rounds of ammunition.[154] Gregg also balanced out the initial disparity of numbers against him with the greater efficiency of his two full batteries of horse artillery which carried much better ammunition in their chests than their Confederate antagonists. Gregg described the fire of his guns as "the most accurate" he had ever seen,[155] and even the Confederates commented upon the devastating effectiveness of the shells thrown by Battery M, 2nd United States, under Lieutenant A. C. M. Pennington, Jr.[156] Fortunately for Gregg, he had in Custer and McIntosh two brigade commanders who eagerly sought combat, and he skillfully used them to strike back at Stuart.

The main action between the opposing cavalry forces took place about 3:00 P.M., near the end of the cannonade, which some of the Union cavalry officers had observed as their dismounted troopers skirmished with Jenkins' men and some of Stuart's sharpshooters. The cavalry fought in the open fields north of the Hanover road between the Rummel and Lott farms, which were about a mile apart. Many of the fences intersecting the fields hindered freedom of movement[157] but did not prevent charges and countercharges, ending in a final effort by almost all of Stuart's force. After a furious hand-to-hand melee the Federal troopers, according to Union accounts, drove Stuart back to his original position, while Confederate partisans insisted on the contrary that the rebels had forced Gregg back to his line.[158] Whatever the truth, it seemed all at once that everyone had had enough of fierce combat on a hot day, and they all withdrew to their respective positions, where they continued nevertheless to send out skirmishers and keep up a sharp exchange of shots.[159] The losses on both sides were relatively light, and as for skill and bravery the honors were even.[160] Probably the true verdict was given by a sergeant of the 1st Virginia Cavalry who pronounced the fight a "draw." [161] Gregg might not have whipped Stuart, but he had forced him to enter a battle in which the Confederates gained nothing except the "glory of the fighting." [162] Gregg's aggressiveness had stopped Stuart from going forward and had given the Union right the best of protection.[163]

It could be argued that Lee might have done better to have assigned Stuart's cavalry the task of guarding his right flank instead of using it in his offensive thrust against Meade. Lee had Jenkins' brigade to protect Ewell's left and rear, but no cavalry worth mentioning on Longstreet's right. Robertson's and Jones's brigades had come up from the Shenandoah Valley through Williamsport and Chambersburg and finally reached Cashtown on the morning of the 3rd. After a short rest Jones's brigade pushed on to Fairfield and arrived in time to batter the 6th United States Regular Cavalry of Merritt's brigade. It was about to capture Stuart's supply train which had been parked near the town, apparently in search of forage.[164] From Fairfield to Big Round Top, however, Lee's right and rear, especially west of the Emmitsburg road, was exposed to slashing attacks from fast-moving columns of enemy horsemen. What happened on that part of the battlefield confirmed Longstreet's judgment in keeping Hood's and McLaws' divisions on ground they had won the day before. Without cavalry to furnish them mobility these infantrymen were vulnerable to any serious threat to their flank, and should the Federal command have worked out a closely coordinated attack by both infantry and cavalry against them, the result might have been a catastrophe for Lee. As it was, the poorly conceived and badly conducted assault of Kilpatrick and Merritt in the afternoon of July 3 was enough of a threat to make Longstreet's infantrymen hustle from one part of the field to another in their efforts to stop it.

At eight o'clock that morning Kilpatrick had received orders from Pleasonton to move his division from Two Taverns to the left of the Union line, and to attack the enemy's right and rear in conjunction with the regular cavalry brigade of Buford's division under General Merritt. Kilpatrick started out with his First Brigade under Brigadier General Elon J. Farnsworth, expecting his Second Brigade under

Custer to follow. Kilpatrick complained that through an error it never caught up with him, but there had been no mistake unless Gregg's intervention to keep Custer with him could be called a mistake. Merritt's brigade, which had been in Emmitsburg the day before, started out from its bivouac at noon. The two forces apparently reached their rendezvous about the same time, and the Confederates became aware of their presence sometime during the cannonade.[165] General Law, who had charge of operations on that part of Lee's line in place of the wounded Hood, ordered two batteries of Henry's battalion to change front. He also pulled three regiments of General George T. Anderson's brigade out from their lines and arranged them so as to cover the ground from Big Round Top to the Emmitsburg road as effectively as possible. Law received slim reinforcements from Colonel John L. Black of the 1st South Carolina Cavalry, who reported to him with three guns of Captain J. F. Hart's battery of horse artillery and a scratch force of between two hundred and three hundred mounted men, the "ragtag & bobtail" of the hospital and wagon trains, which he considered proved "a nuisance" rather than a "benefit."[166] As the Federals increased their pressure Law stretched his defenses even more by moving the remaining two regiments of Anderson's brigade toward the right, making a total of five in all with which to extend his flank.

Kilpatrick and Merritt made Law's task easier by using faulty tactics. For one thing Merritt, who kept pushing north up the Emmitsburg road against Law's extreme right, discarded his advantage of mobility by dismounting his troopers and fighting them as infantry.[167] With their different training and equipment they fared poorly against Law's experienced foot soldiers. Their more rapid firing, breech-loading carbines had neither the range nor the accuracy of the infantryman's muzzle-loading rifle. As for Kilpatrick, who was east of the Emmitsburg road and to the right of Merritt, his men fought over ground too broken and rocky for operations by large bodies of cavalry, so quite properly he dismounted them to skirmish with the enemy's infantry. When about 5:30 P.M. Kilpatrick received word of the Union success in the center, he ordered an all-out effort by both brigades. However, instead of having Merritt mount his men and make a sweeping movement around Law's right, where there were fewer natural obstacles, while he would maintain pressure with his own dismounted troopers, he did just the opposite.

Although Farnsworth protested that it was suicide, Kilpatrick insisted that he should charge with half of his brigade against the center of Law's slender line. Law by juggling his men about had neutralized Merritt's threat and had shifted what little weight he could spare against Farnsworth, who soon found himself running through a gauntlet of Confederate infantry no matter which way he turned.[168] He put on a brilliant display of courage and horsemanship, but the attack ended in a fiasco, including the death of Farnsworth.[169] If Kilpatrick had assumed that Law's men were demoralized by the repulse of Pickett and Pettigrew, he was sadly mistaken.

Both Kilpatrick and Pleasonton in their reports exaggerated the impact of this attack on the enemy, but when Pleasonton claimed that it had caused the enemy "to detach largely from his main attack" on the left of the Union line, he was completely fatuous.[170] Kilpatrick had a point, however, when he observed that some Union infantry should have advanced on his right at the time he made his charge.[171] The fault in this instance lay in part with Meade for not putting Sedgwick in overall command of the forces on the extreme left and giving him instructions to take advantage of any weakness in enemy resistance without awaiting orders from headquarters. But neither can Pleasonton escape responsibility, for he should have alerted Federal commanders to Kilpatrick's operations and asked them to cooperate. Nevertheless Kilpatrick's complaint about the inactivity of Union infantry does not excuse him from the charge of bad generalship.

The defeat of Kilpatrick was small comfort to the proud Confederates for a day of disappointment and disaster. To them their repulse by the despised Yankees in spite of careful preparations and a massive concentration of power was gall and wormwood; yet more devastating to their morale was the excessively high casualty rate, especially among line, field, and general officers. A few statistics about Pickett's division graphically tell the story. Of its generals the division lost Garnett killed outright, Armistead fatally wounded, and Kemper desperately so. Of the whole complement of field officers in the fifteen regiments, only one escaped unhurt. Many of the rank and file who were shaken loose from the division as a result of its shocking experience eventually returned, but the morning after the battle not even a thousand riflemen reported for duty, although all cooks and ambulance men had been put back into line. The loss in some units was so great that they virtually passed out of existence. One captain reported that in the 18th Virginia twenty-nine out of thirty-one regimental officers were struck down, and everyone in his company except himself and one other man had fallen or disappeared. The casualties in the North Carolina regiments were proportionately as great, and perhaps greater. The 47th Carolina of Pettigrew's brigade went into the fight with 600 men and came out with 100. In Scales's brigade the 13th North Carolina lost 155 out of 180 in killed, wounded, or captured.[172]

For the first hour after the repulse a large segment of the Confederate army might well have been seized by unreasoning fear, started running, and swept the rest along, had it not been for the grim determination of "Pete" Longstreet and the reassuring presence of Robert E. Lee.[173] Longstreet rode out to Alexander's batteries to get Confederate defenses in shape in case the enemy should counterattack. He tightened and shortened his lines by pulling McLaws' and Hood's divisions back to the west side of the Emmitsburg road from their advanced positions near the Round Tops. Previously he had ordered General Wright and all of his officers to help him and members of his staff rally and collect the scattered troops behind R. H. Anderson's division. Lee then ordered Wright to move his brigade to the right to strengthen the remnants of Wilcox' brigade, which was back in support of Alexander's batteries.[174]

For General Lee the emergency was one of the few occasions when he felt impelled to intervene personally in the affairs of the army below the command level. He had watched the advance intently in the fields north of Spangler's Woods and then had ridden alone to join Alexander as Wilcox made his charge. He stayed with Alexander perhaps an hour, obviously for the purpose of greeting every man who came back to lessen his grief over the defeat and urge him to stand firm.[175] Partly to head off an outbreak of recriminations between officers and soldiers which might have racked the army with dissension, and partly as a result of sincere conviction, Lee told the men that he alone was to blame for what had happened. Few, if any, believed him, but he did restore their confidence in themselves. In this display of leadership Lee was, as one writer expressed it, "perfectly sublime." [176] Nevertheless his efforts and those of other Confederate officers to rally the fugitives were not completely successful. One account described how a large number of demoralized officers and men, frightened by Federal artillery fire which persisted as they retreated, became panic-stricken and, ignoring the appeals of their superiors, started a stampede for the rear, throwing away guns, blankets, and haversacks as they rushed on in confusion. It is impossible to say how many men lost control of themselves, but it could not have been as many as the account implied for Confederate commanders soon established a picket line across the road as a barrier to further retreat and gradually restored order.[177] Most of the survivors, it seemed, responded in good spirit to the appeals for them to find their commands and get ready to meet an attack from the enemy. Within an hour or so after the repulse the Army of Northern Virginia had pulled itself together and was prepared to give a good account of itself should an assault occur.[178]

It was a day of glory and well-earned praise for all the officers and men of the Union Second Corps and for many in the First Corps, especially the Vermonters. A few officers deserved even greater acclaim because of their superb indifference to danger and their qualities of leadership. Among the most outstanding was General Hays, who by virtue of his foresight in preparing for the attack and his reckless bravery, inspired his men to victory. Gibbon, the tough, hardheaded realist, exerted a steadying influence over his men until he was struck down as he was bringing up reinforcements near the Clump of Trees. Hancock reached the climax of a three-day demonstration of brilliant generalship in his new role as a corps commander. In preparation for the struggle on the afternoon of the 3rd he constantly inspected his lines, and during the assault he remained close at hand to intervene personally if need be and to devise countermeasures. Very likely he approved and encouraged Hays's formation of a flanking force on Pettigrew's and Trimble's left. At the right moment he gave Devereux the order to strike back at the Confederates. Whether he ordered the Vermonters to attack is uncertain, but he went to see Stannard about it and was with him when they struck the enemy columns. Turning his horse to gallop back to Gibbon's front, he fell seriously wounded in the thigh near the scene of his greatest endeavors. As he lay in the ambulance pale and weak from loss of blood he forced himself to dictate a report to Meade with a suggestion for a counterattack.[179] Arrived at the hospital, when the stretcher-bearers brought Hancock in, wounded soldiers hobbled over and crowded about him in wildest enthusiasm. Moved by this display of respect and affection, he tried to address them but fell back into the arms of his attendants faint and exhausted.[180]

Of all the young officers cited for gallantry none received more acclaim than Lieutenant Frank Haskell, Gibbon's favorite aide. His superiors were universal in their praise of his conduct. When it seemed that the enemy would overwhelm Webb's men, as the only mounted officer on that part of the field he rode out in front of them, encouraged them to stand firm, and finally helped to lead them forward.[181] Haskell had to share his honors with Webb, who in his first assignment as a field officer performed brilliantly and gained for himself an undying reputation. Faced with defeat, he accepted the challenge and held his men together through great personal exertion and a willingness to risk his life. Sometime later, in response to a toast at a dinner given by General Butterfield, Hancock said of Webb: " 'In every battle and on every important field there is one spot to which every army [officer] would wish to be assigned—the spot upon which centers the fortunes of the field. There was but one such spot at Gettysburg and it fell to the lot of Gen'l Webb to have it and to hold it and for holding it he must receive the credit due him.' " [182] Belatedly his country recognized his services and pinned on him the Medal of Honor.[183] Webb felt, however, that he must share his triumph with Colonel Hall who had helped him at the right time, and who for his initiative and skill deserved more credit than he got.[184]

Webb's opponent on the far side of the wall, George Edward Pickett, with head down rode away from the scene of his defeat into a fading military career. He had given his name to a magnificent effort by a "damned brave set of fellows," as one Yankee put it,[185] but it would have been better for his reputation if he had been called upon to give his life or if the attack had been known for what it was, Longstreet's Second Assault. In explaining the utter collapse of one of the most spectacular charges in history the Confederates used the stock excuses that Cemetery Ridge was unassailable even if held by the lowliest troops, and that the Yankees overwhelmed them as usual by sheer weight of numbers. These explanations were just a little too pat, for the slopes of Cemetery Ridge were no more forbidding than those of Seminary Ridge, and the Yankee lines were unbelievably thin. The expletive "pshaw!" uttered by one rebel colonel summed up the amazement of Confederate prisoners when they saw how few Yankees there were along the battle lines.[186] Two years of war had not completely dispelled the preposterous notion that one Southerner could lick ten Northerners. They overlooked the fact that a handful of Yankee veterans behind a stone wall could stop an attacking force many times their size—something the rebels had done themselves on many occasions. Of course Northern soldiers in reliving the great moments of the charge were apt to exaggerate the thinness of their lines to make the victory more impressive.[187]

In trying to understand the debacle Confederates from the highest officer to the lowliest private played an ever recurring theme: the lack of support given the attacking forces. It had variations, and one of them led to the undignified and bitter quarrel between the North Carolinians and Virginians over who failed to support whom. The universal complaint, whether the soldier was a Pettigrew or a Pickett man, was the lack of help from troops in the rear who remained idle while the assaulting columns tried to hold on to their gains.[188] In developing this theme in their battle reports and continuing with it in their recollections, the Confederates stressed the achievements of the assaulting forces in such a way as to imply that they had gained a major break through the enemy lines and only needed reinforcements to exploit it. The reports contained such statements as, "The intrenchments were carried, the enemy was driven from his guns";[189] or, "We pressed forward until our flag was planted upon the breastworks of the enemy";[190] or, "His strongest and last line was instantly gained; the Confederate battle-flag waved over his defenses. . . ."[191] All were true up to a point, although exaggerated and misleading, and Longstreet knew his forces had not accomplished what Lee had hoped. He had witnessed the first signs of disintegration in the assaulting lines, their lack of success except at the Clump of Trees, and the growth of Federal power on their flanks. Considering the attack a failure, he had refused to allow supporting columns to be sacrificed needlessly.[192]

Confederate critics seem to have ignored the ability of the Union command to reinforce its lines with greater facility than they and with less exposure of the supporting columns to hostile fire. Before Pickett's charge Meade, not knowing where Lee would strike, distributed his infantry supports where he could move them quickly to any threatened point from Cemetery Hill to Big Round Top; most of them he placed south of Gibbon's division. Although his infantry reserves were not much greater than Lee's, those of his artillery certainly were. Meade had seventy-nine more guns than the Confederates immediately available, fully-equipped, and ready for action. Hunt also brought up almost twice as many rounds of ammunition per gun as did Pendleton, 270 as compared to 150. In three days of fighting Hunt used an average of 100 rounds a gun, leaving plenty of ammunition on hand in spite of heavy losses from exploding caissons and limbers. When he received word about the heavy attrition in batteries along Hancock's front and also saw the situation for himself, he quickly advanced three full batteries in addition to Cowan's as replacements. Though the time of their arrival is uncertain, their commanders reported having taken position and gone into action near Webb's brigade just before the enemy infantry hit it. Additional help for the Second Corps came from Osborn who sent, probably at Hancock's request, Lieutenant William Wheeler's small battery of three guns. Since Hancock himself directed Wheeler where to place the guns, his battery must have arrived before or during the assault.[193]

During the furious action on the afternoon of July 3 Meade gave the illusion of having been swallowed up by the smoke of battle, for he did not make his presence felt to the same extent as he had the day before. He knew Hancock would have a firm grip on affairs on his part of the front, and apparently he placed a great deal of reliance on Newton's judgment. As an indication of his confidence in Newton, after Hancock was wounded Meade placed him in command of all the battle line between Sykes and Howard.[194] Though generally staying away from the field, Meade kept abreast of developments and when necessary exerted influence. His concern for the security of Cemetery Hill, for instance, induced him to visit it personally during the cannonade to see how well the men were taking the shelling. Osborn was impressed by his "cool and collected" judgment, as well as his alert and nervous manner which showed a quick comprehension of the situation.[195] When Confederate infantry started to advance, Gibbon sent Lieutenant Haskell to warn Meade of it, and as the point of attack became apparent Newton must have informed him about reinforcements he was sending Hancock, for Meade made one important change in their disposition. In addition to these troops Meade himself ordered three more brigades to back up the threatened sector before the culmination of the Confederate assault.[196] By means of prior arrangements and good management he thus quickly concentrated almost 13,000 infantrymen from four different corps and every part of his battle line, ready to relieve Hancock's men should the pressure become too great for them, or to pounce on enemy columns should they break through.[197]

During the cannonade and more particularly the infantry assault Meade kept his staff busy carrying messages and orders and leading supporting columns to their positions.[198] Toward the end of the struggle along Hancock's line Captain Meade found his father alone in an open field not far from the Leister house. He had just been talking to an officer who had come up, reported something, and dashed off again. The general turned smiling toward his son as he rode up and said, " 'Hello, George, is that you? I am glad you are here. You must stick by me now; you are the only officer left.' " He then added something about its being " 'a pretty lively place,' " and suggested that they go forward and find out what was going on. As they got near the front line they were unable to see anything and so turned to the right toward Hays's position to get out of the smoke. Soon they met Lieutenant John Egan,[199] whose section of Wood-ruff's battery was firing canister down the Bryan farm lane. General Hays had just ridden up from the right and had jumped his horse over the wall, followed by some of his troops. Meade inquired about Hays, and Egan pointed to him riding on the far side of the wall and trailing a Confederate flag behind him. When Meade asked if the rebels had " 'turned,' " Egan said, " 'Yes. See Hays has one of their flags.' " Egan recalled that Meade, "mighty cross," replied, " 'I don't care for their flag. Have they turned?' " The answer was, " 'Yes, sir. They are just turning.' " [200]

Satisfied with this answer, Meade and George rode down Hays's line toward Webb's front; there they met Lieutenant Haskell, who confirmed Egan's information. By then Confederate prisoners were streaming back through the lines. Seeing Meade, they recognized him as someone in authority and gathered about him to ask where they should go. In fine spirits he pointed to the rear and said, " 'Go

along that way [and] you will be well taken care of.' " Almost immediately enemy batteries resumed their fire, and shells began falling all about. The prisoners scampered off cheering and shouting
such expressions as, " 'Why it's hotter here than it was in front.' " [201]
After going a little farther toward the left Meade remarked that
since everything seemed all right on this part of the line, he would
go and see how affairs were with Howard. George had to stay behind because his horse had been struck by a shell fragment, and he
did not see the general again until he returned from Howard's headquarters with his whole staff and a crowd of other mounted officers.
As Meade was returning from the hill to Cemetery Ridge, Major
W. G. Mitchell brought official word from the wounded Hancock
announcing a "great victory." Meade expressed regrets about the
wound and asked Mitchell to thank Hancock " 'for the country and
for myself for the service he has rendered today.' " [202]. As Meade
and his entourage approached the ridge, troops on the front commenced to cheer, and some called out congratulations to the general. He then made a triumphal ride from Ziegler's Grove all the
way to Little Round Top, and strangely enough the enemy fired not
a shot at him, although the cavalcade was often within easy
range.[203]

At Little Round Top, as Meade remembered it, he gave the necessary orders for pickets and skirmishers to be thrown forward to
feel the enemy, as part of his preparations for a possible counterattack. He was forced to abandon the idea, he said, because by the
time he could get a reconnaissance organized and receive a report of
its findings, it was too late in the evening for him to start an offensive.[204] It would also take longer than usual to organize an attack,
he felt, because "fatigue and other results of the three days' fighting" had greatly slowed up the movements of the troops.[205] Critics
of Meade's generalship have tended to overlook this explanation as
given by Meade himself. Certainly the men were tired—that was
quite plain to see—but nobody then or later bothered to ask the
general about the "other results" of the fighting which he thought
would lessen the army's efficiency. He might have explained that
during the battle he had shuffled major units about so frequently
that systems of command had become seriously impaired, if not
broken up; and he had lost a number of his most valuable officers,
on whom he had placed great reliance. Furthermore, with his troops

arranged for defensive operations he would need more time to reorganize them for a counterattack than if they had been engaged in an offensive battle. Time, he knew, was the crux of the situation, and unless he could mount a well-planned counterattack within an hour of the repulse his chances of success would virtually disappear. Under the circumstances such speedy preparations were impossible.

Nevertheless many students of the battle, including some of Meade's friends and all of his enemies,[206] have felt that he should have obeyed the maxim, "When you repulse or defeat an enemy you should pursue him." [207] When he failed to do so, he became in their eyes guilty of timid or at best sluggish generalship. No one explained just how Meade should have made the attack, nor did his critics examine carefully some of the assumptions which formed the basis for their judgment of his conduct. Presumably the counterattacking force would have been composed of the Fifth and Sixth Corps, with help from troops stationed on or near the lines that had been under attack. Hancock said he had told Caldwell to start a counterattack should the Confederates be repulsed. Rather optimistically he assured Caldwell that the Fifth and Sixth Corps on his left would help him, but he did not say who would advance with him on the right or who would have overall command of the whole movement.[208] It is questionable whether the other divisions of Hancock's corps, especially the Second, were in shape for an advance. Their losses had been heavy, particularly in Webb's brigade, and the commands had become completely disorganized.[209] The Vermonters would not have been of much help either, for they had been without food for two days and were worn out from their exertions.[210] It was all very well for armchair strategists to talk about using the Sixth Corps to bear the brunt of the attack, but they forgot that after two days of assault by Longstreet's men its units were widely scattered, with five of its eight brigades having positions on parts of the line other than the area of the Round Tops.[211]

Nor did Meade's critics indicate just where he should have attacked. If the Fifth and Sixth Corps had moved from Little Round Top immediately after the Pickett-Pettigrew assault, they would have had to push Hood's and McLaws' divisions out of the way, which operation might have taken some doing. They would have run into more serious problems if they had sidestepped these divisions and aimed for the gap in the Confederate lines left vacant by the defeated columns; Hancock by a process of questionable logic claimed it was a mile wide.[212] To reach it they would have had to cross the same open and ill-fated fields as their opponents had done, face enfilading fire from Confederate batteries still well supplied with canister, and encounter flanking attacks from Longstreet's men on their left and some of Hill's and Ewell's on their right.[213] Success under these circumstances was highly dubious.

Meade obviously thought if he were going to attack at all, it would be sounder for him to move against Lee's right flank with units of the Fifth and Sixth Corps than to try to strike at other parts of the Confederate line. His moves were only tentative in character, however, for both Sedgwick and Sykes denied having received instructions to prepare for a general advance.[214] Sykes did get orders, very likely before Meade arrived at the left of the line, to make a reconnaissance in force to see whether the enemy was retreating, and if not to induce him to do so.[215] Sykes sent Crawford word to advance Colonel William McCandless' brigade and one regiment of Fisher's brigade of the Pennsylvania Reserves across the Wheatfield and into the woods southwest of it. At Crawford's request Colonel Nevin's brigade of the Sixth Corps formed a second line behind the Reserves. They charged across the field and struck not George T. Anderson's brigade, as Crawford reported, but one regiment of Benning's, which through an ambiguity in orders had advanced to a new position instead of withdrawing with Hood's and McLaws' divisions. Crawford claimed that he had forced Hood's division to retreat. Actually it and McLaws' division were well on their way back to a new line along the Emmitsburg road when Crawford attacked. Subsequently skirmishers thrown out by McCandless and Nevin located it.[216] From them Meade learned that Longstreet's men held the line "in force" and were still full of fight.[217]

By the time these operations had ceased, it was dark, and any chance for a counterattack was gone—assuming that there had ever been one. Meade in failing to comply with one rule of war had been faithful to an even more important adage: "Avoid doing what your antagonist desires." [218]

XX

RETREAT AND PURSUIT

As DARKNESS closed in on July 3, except for the occasional spiteful crack of a sniper's rifle the noise of combat had subsided to the moans of thousands of wounded who lay among the dead "thick as fallen leaves of autumn." [1] The Union soldiers, after long forced marches and three days of fierce battle, sagged from fatigue and desperately needed rest and food. They perhaps suspected that the enemy might now give them a respite, but they were not sure, nor for that matter was their commander. Meade waited until he felt that all fighting had ceased for the day; then he sent Halleck a concise and modest report of the events of the afternoon and evening. He made no claim to victory but merely said that the enemy after a prolonged cannonade had assaulted his left center twice, "being upon both occasions handsomely repulsed, with severe losses to him." [2] The tone of the dispatch revealed Meade's uncertainty about what the morrow might bring and what his next move should be.

Lee on the other hand had little doubt about his next step when all expectations of a Yankee counterattack faded with the setting sun. [3] He realized that his army had lost its offensive punch after its three days of persistent and futile pounding of Union positions, and he could hope to retrieve his fortunes only if Meade should decide to attack his strong lines on Seminary Ridge on July 4. As that day came and went and no attack developed, Lee knew that with a favorable decision no longer possible at Gettysburg he had no recourse but to withdraw from his exposed position. If enemy forces should close in on him from all sides—and they were bound to do so

535

before long—he could no longer hope to live off the country; even if he managed to fend off efforts to destroy him, he realized that in the process he would exhaust his already depleted supplies of ammunition and wear out his horses.[4] Furthermore, he had no chance of getting substantial reinforcements to replace his heavy casualties. Whatever his reasons, it was not the condition of his men which forced Lee to retreat, for they were far from being a "demoralized horde of fugitives," [5] as was claimed in the optimistic reports of Northern newsmen at the time and in testimony later offered to the Committee on the Conduct of the War by officers unfriendly to Meade.[6] Though weary and badly cut up, his army retained confidence in itself and its commander. The blasted hopes of victory and the retreat did not dim the respect of the men for Lee. They greeted him with "enthusiastic cheers" whenever he rode by and remarked to themselves that as long as he continued to lead them, all was well.[7]

The loss of 20,451 officers and men, and very likely more, in the three-day battle had greatly thinned out the ranks of Lee's infantry, in some units to a small fraction of what they had been, and in the army as a whole to about two-thirds of their former strength.[8] Nevertheless the corps were still led by their permanent commanders and therefore they remained formidable military forces, although Pickett's division and two or three brigades of Heth's division had suffered excessive losses in field and general officers.[9] Most of Lee's batteries too were ready for further service, despite the disabled condition of some of the guns and equipment and the very heavy casualties in men and horses in a few of the outfits.[10] An "anxious" inventory of artillery ammunition showed there was enough on hand for one more day's heavy fighting.[11] As for the cavalry, for the first time on July 3 Lee had had all of the units available to screen his operations, pry into enemy activities, and guard his flanks, and by the end of the day these forces continued strong enough to cope with the slightly larger Federal cavalry.[12] All in all, on July 4 Lee's army, instead of being ripe for the plucking, still had the determination and capacity to punish severely, if not wreck any incautious or unskillful foe who might pursue it.

Lee began preparations for his retreat during the night of July 3 after holding a council of war with some of his officers. They decided to fall back in the hope of inducing the enemy to follow them to a place where they could fight to better advantage than among the hills of Gettysburg. At the same time the Confederates felt it wise to send to Virginia the long train of wagons, horses, equipment, and supplies which they had captured in great quantity.[13] As the first step in getting ready for the retreat Lee shortened and straightened his main battle line by pulling Ewell's corps back through town and placing it in position along Oak and Seminary Ridges. The men dug in and soon had long lines of breastworks and rifle pits, in some cases two parallel lines, extending two and a half miles from the Mummasburg to the Emmitsburg road. The trees on top of the ridges hid the entrenchments because the Southerners placed them on the western side of the slopes. Should Meade have attacked on July 4, his men would have been exposed to heavy fire as they crossed the fields separating the two forces, and once into the woods they would have been surprised by volleys from the concealed pits.[14] Meade had no intention, however, of giving the rebels a chance, as he said, to "play their old game of shooting us from behind breastworks . . .";[15] and he stayed within his own lines. Lee's soldiers meanwhile manned their defenses all day for the purpose of "inviting" attack, as well as to furnish Lee cover as he completed arrangements for the withdrawal.[16]

His immediate concern was to get his wagons and ambulances well on their way before the infantry and artillery started to move. The wagons carried much of the booty of the campaign,[17] and the ambulances as many of the wounded as were fit to travel. They also carried a few like Generals Hood, Hampton, Pender, and Scales who were *not* fit to travel but were too important to be left behind. As the army departed from the battlefield, 6,802 Confederates still lay in scores of houses, barns, churches, schools, and other public buildings in Gettysburg and the surrounding countryside. A few of their own surgeons and orderlies remained with them, but for the most part they had to depend upon their enemies for care.[18]

Lee's control of the two important mountain passes west of Fairfield and Cashtown gave him a choice of routes to the Cumberland Valley.[19] The defeat of the 6th United States Cavalry of General Merritt's Reserve Brigade by General "Grumble" Jones's brigade in its attempt to seize Fairfield on the afternoon of July 3 had far greater consequences than indicated by the number of troops engaged,[20] for it was through Fairfield, the shortest way to Hagerstown and then Williamsport, that Lee would march all of his infantry and most of his artillery. The greater part of the wagons and ambulances he sent over the Cashtown road in charge of General Imboden, whose command of 2,100 mounted men and a battery of guns, indifferently disciplined and inefficiently directed,[21] was of little use for any assignment other than guard duty or fighting militia.[22] Lee reinforced Imboden with five batteries selected from his three corps, and he had Stuart assign General Fitz Lee with his own and Hampton's brigades to protect the flanks and rear of Imboden's seventeen-mile-long column. He gave Imboden very specific instructions on how to proceed. The head of the column of wagons and ambulances was to leave Cashtown no later than five-thirty in the afternoon of July 4, avoid Chambersburg by turning south at Greenwood, and push on all night so as to arrive in the comparative safety of Greencastle by morning. From there the train was to take the direct road to Williamsport, where it could use the ford across the Potomac River. Imboden would escort the train to a point beyond Martinsburg; then according to Lee's directions, he was to return with his command to a position near Hagerstown and guard the army's route to Williamsport and to Falling Waters, where a pontoon bridge had been laid across the river. Through Imboden Lee instructed the commanding officer at Winchester to send troops to Falling Waters as further protection for the bridge.[23] The wagons and ambulances which did not go with Imboden Lee sent to Williamsport by way of Fairfield. They were to have been escorted by General Iverson and his small brigade, but for undisclosed reasons Iverson's command got off to a late start and did not catch up with the train until it was beyond Jack Mountain, several miles west of Fairfield. From that point on even without guards it was safe because Generals Robertson and Jones with their cavalry held both Monterey and Fairfield Passes through Jack Mountain.[24]

On July 4 even as Confederate positions along the ridges bristled defiantly with thousands of muskets and hundreds of guns, the two wagon trains began to roll slowly up and over the mountains in a pouring rain. When darkness fell and Meade still was not heard from, Lee had Hill's Third Corps head out onto the Fairfield road, to be followed by Longstreet's First Corps and finally Ewell's Second over the same route. To cover his left rear as he moved toward Hagerstown he ordered Stuart with Chambliss' and Jenkins' brigades to proceed by way of Emmitsburg. Meanwhile Fitz Lee with two brigades was protecting Imboden's train and at the same time covering Lee's right rear along the Cashtown road. Lee, planning his retreat carefully and without hurry, specified the order of march and the departure time of every major unit.[25] Because of his position on the west side of the battlefield he had access to a route from Gettysburg to Williamsport which was about half the length of the one available to the Army of the Potomac when it undertook to pursue him. Lee had the added advantage, one which is always possessed by an army withdrawing under the cover of night, of being able to gain several hours headstart over his adversary.[26] But for the torrential rain which turned an unimproved dirt road into a quagmire, he would have gained even more time in his effort to get beyond the mountains and close to the crossings of the Potomac.[27]

Though both Lee and Meade faced similar problems at this time, there was an important difference in their situations. After the repulse on July 3 and the refusal of Meade to counterattack, Lee knew what he had to do, but Meade was uncertain about his next step because it depended upon what his opponent did. Meade did not think Lee would resume the offensive, but he was not sure.[28] Under any circumstances he had to remain at Gettysburg with most of his army as long as Lee stayed there. If he moved prematurely he might uncover Baltimore and Washington. Worse still, he might unintentionally create the impression that he had conceded the victory to Lee, for according to an odd medieval notion of warfare, which was still cherished during the Civil War, leaving the field before one's adversary was considered an admission of defeat.[29] In case Lee should withdraw down the Cumberland Valley, Meade planned to follow him along the east side of the mountains, because he understood that the Confederates had so well fortified the passes west of Gettysburg [30] that "a small force could hold a large body in check for a considerable time." [31] He would make up for the time lost in taking the longer route by means of forced marches; then he would seize the passes west of Frederick and threaten Lee's left flank as he retreated down the valley.[32] Apparently it never occurred to Meade to send an expeditionary force of infantry and cavalry to Fairfield on July 4 to seize the gaps in the nearby mountains, perhaps because he thought Lee had anticipated him and already had a firm grip on them. Other circumstances also kept

Meade from attempting a major move on Fairfield. The rain on July 4, which became a downpour late in the day, made large-scale operations difficult, if not impossible. Meade felt it imperative that he have time to bring up urgently needed supplies and ammunition while his army rested from its long marches and three days of hard fighting.[33]

However, if Meade had wanted to catch Lee at a serious disadvantage, Fairfield was the key to the strategical problem, for the Confederates held it with only two small cavalry brigades, and Lee had not fortified the passes as Meade thought. Seizure of Fairfield by strong elements of the Union army would have forced Lee to fight his way through, with his rear exposed to attack from the rest of Meade's men near Gettysburg. If he had wanted to avoid a battle under such circumstances, he would have had the unpleasant prospect of trying to march his entire army through Cashtown Pass, which was a much longer and harder way to Hagerstown and Williamsport than the one he took. Restricted to one main route through the mountains, the movements of his army would have been seriously retarded. Federal occupation of Fairfield then, before Lee had really gotten his retreat under way, might have given Meade a real opportunity to cripple, if not destroy the rebel army, but he had only a few hours—until midnight of July 4—to make a move which would have involved major changes in the disposition of his forces. It was virtually an impossible task. In view of the heavy criticism of his pursuit of Lee this lost opportunity, if it existed at all, should at least be mentioned, for never again in this campaign would Meade be able to maneuver his opponent into such a tight corner.

Although by the morning of July 4 Meade was unsure about the nature and extent of Lee's movements from information he had already received,[34] he realized he had a busy day ahead. The army needed to be fed and reequipped. It had adequate supplies at Westminster, largely because of the exertions of Brigadier General Herman Haupt, one of the engineering geniuses of the nineteenth century and an efficient administrator who refused to let the woefully inadequate facilities of the Western Maryland Railroad thwart him. His achievements in railroad transportation, though vitally important, only partly solved Meade's logistical problems, for it was one thing to get supplies to Westminster, where they were of no use to anyone, and another to cart them twenty-five miles in thousands of creaking wagons over the Baltimore Pike to Gettysburg. This task was the responsibility of Brigadier General Rufus Ingalls, chief quartermaster of the army, but in spite of his best efforts he did not get the wagons rolling until early on July 4. Railroad trains moved slowly in those days, but wagons even more so,[35] and they were many hours on the way.

While waiting for them to come up, Meade ordered his corps commanders to regroup their forces and get them ready for further action. This was a large assignment, for the casualties of 23,049 troops suffered by the army had reduced scores of regiments to small companies, and companies to a few pitiful survivors, many without an officer to lead them. Furthermore, many of their men had fled or wandered away in the heat of the fighting, and General Patrick, Meade's provost marshal general, had the job of ferreting them out of their hiding places and sending them back to their units. Many of their more stouthearted comrades on orders from their officers went out beyond the battle lines, gathered up the countless dead, and buried them. Others served on the skirmish lines, probing the enemy's defenses, while signal officers at high points along the line kept a sharp lookout for any unusual movements on the enemy's front.[36]

Early in the morning a Confederate officer carrying a flag of truce appeared at a Union outpost and asked permission to bring a message from Lee to Meade through the lines. Lee proposed an exchange of prisoners on the grounds that it would promote their comfort and convenience. More likely his real reason was that he wanted to avoid the drain upon his manpower and supplies of having to guard and feed thousands of Union prisoners during his retreat. He had already paroled around 1,500 men of the First Corps and sent them under escort toward Carlisle, but he decided that since Union authorities might not honor this arrangement, he ought to effect another one. The task of herding prisoners in enemy country required a much heavier detail of valuable soldiers than in the comparative safety of Virginia. In contrast General Patrick simply rounded up some otherwise useless stragglers and gave them the job of watching over nearly 2,000 Confederates. Very properly Meade refused to accommodate Lee, saying that he had no authority to make the exchange.[37] He did not mention that there were practical difficulties in the plan, since his own captives already were on the way to distant prison pens. Meade liked to keep his immediate rear free of all unnecessary encumbrances.

Meade's dispatches during the day to Generals French, Couch, and W. F. Smith of Couch's command reflected his uncertainty about Lee's moves. Early in the morning of the 4th, thinking Lee had started to retreat, Meade ordered French to leave Frederick and occupy the South Mountain passes and Maryland Heights. A few hours later, in view of Lee's evident determination to remain where he was, Meade rescinded his order and told French to stand by. French had already shown commendable initiative; without waiting word from Meade he had sent a cavalry detachment up the river, which on the 4th succeeded in destroying at Falling Waters Lee's one and only pontoon bridge over the Potomac. It also captured an ammunition train and dumped it into the river. With the water beginning to rise rapidly from the heavy rains, and no bridge,[38] Lee's difficulties in getting his booty, prisoners, and wounded back to Virginia were greatly increased.

While Meade considered his next moves against Lee, he wondered how best to use Couch's troops. These included some 9,000 inexperienced militia, who since July 1 had been kept at Carlisle under General Smith. He also had over 2,000 infantrymen and cavalry troopers concentrated under Colonel Lewis B. Pierce at Bloody Run (Everett).[39] Looking at their positions pinpointed on a map, it would seem that they were well located to cause trouble for the retreating army, but distances were deceiving and the quality of the troops uncertain. Couch wrote Meade about starting Smith's men from Carlisle at midnight July 3, for the purpose of striking the Confederates near Cashtown.[40] Smith blasted these hopes by reporting that he could not possibly get off at that hour. A night march with "these troops" he thought would be a waste of time, for they would not get far. To add to his woes, his supply of ammunition had not yet arrived, and he was not sure whether his ordnance officer knew enough to bring it up.[41] A very efficient commander, Smith apparently straightened out affairs in time to get his columns off at six o'clock on the morning of the 4th. In spite of their inexperience and the heavy rain, his advance units marched the seventeen miles from Carlisle to Pine Grove Furnace in the mountains by six that night, a very creditable performance; still they were another twenty miles from Cashtown. Meanwhile Halleck sent messages urging Couch to hasten his troops forward to the aid of Meade, and Stanton, not appreciating what Couch had to work with, on the 4th accused him of tardiness in cooperating with the Army of the Potomac. Meade, though showing no great eagerness for the help of raw militia, still did not know whether to have Smith join him at Gettysburg or pursue Lee down the valley. He was afraid that if Smith attacked Lee near Cashtown prematurely, that is, before the Army of the Potomac came within supporting distance, the Confederates would rip the emergency troops to shreds.[42]

As for Colonel Pierce's little command, located as it was almost fifty long miles over the mountains west of Chambersburg, it was too far away for Meade to show any concern about it. Couch, thinking if Pierce moved quickly enough he could be useful in harassing Lee's rear, ordered him on the 3rd to get as close as possible to Chambersburg and Mercersburg.[43] Pierce reported that he could depend upon his cavalrymen, who were three-year volunteers and had previously served under Milroy at Winchester; his infantrymen, however, which made up about half his force, had been recruited for the emergency, and he considered them of "no account."[44] Though worried about a shortage of ammunition for his command, Pierce in response to Couch's orders promptly started advancing his cavalry toward the Cumberland Valley on the night of July 3.[45]

Whatever worries Meade may have had about timing the movements of his own infantry and artillery, they did not include his cavalry. As long as Lee maintained his defiant posture before Gettysburg, Meade confronted him with the bulk of his forces, but early on July 4 he sent his cavalry [46] to strike at the enemy's rear and his lines of communication so as to "harass and annoy him as much as possible in his retreat."[47] Under General Pleasonton's direction each of the eight brigades, except Colonel McIntosh's of Gregg's division, took to the roads and fields in search of Confederate columns and trains. The Third Brigade of General Gregg's division under Colonel J. Irvin Gregg moved northeast to Hunterstown and then west on the Mummasburg road toward Cashtown. All the others kept south of Gettysburg with the intention of cutting off the Confederates, if possible, at Fairfield, Hagerstown, or Williamsport. Buford with Gamble's and Devin's brigades went directly from Westminster to Frederick, where Merritt's troopers joined them on the night of the 5th. On the morning of the 4th Pleasonton had ordered Kilpatrick to Emmitsburg, where he would find Colonel Pennock Huey's brigade of Gregg's division; it had come from Westminster to bolster his command for a move against any trains Lee might be sending from Gettysburg to Hagerstown by way of Fairfield. In making these dispositions Pleasonton, for reasons not known, stripped General Gregg, an able and experienced brigadier, of his entire command and apparently left him with nothing to do until July 9, when one of his brigades finally reported back to him for orders.[48] Whatever his shortcomings in the handling of one of his chief subordinates, Pleasonton did succeed in quickly spreading his cavalry over the countryside in pursuit of Lee's train long before the Union infantry could get under way. His one mistake in the disposition of his command may have been that he scattered it too much.

Very late on the afternoon of the 4th Meade received reports from his signal officers which led him to believe that the Confederates had started a retreat over the Cashtown and Fairfield roads,[49] but he was not sure of it when he met with his corps commanders that night. Once more Meade was seeking advice when perhaps it was not necessary, and he was again exposing himself to the charge that he lacked moral courage. He asked the generals about the condition and strength of their various corps, and from their field returns he learned that he would have at the most 56,000 officers and men available for front-line duty.[50] Then Meade and Butterfield posed four questions about strategy. In a vote which was carefully tabulated by Butterfield a majority of the officers concurred with Meade's judgment of what to do. Most of them agreed that the army should remain at Gettysburg until Lee moved or tipped his hand; no one wanted to assume the offensive under any circumstances. Should Lee retreat, a majority voted to have only cavalry pursue him directly.[51] Presumably they accepted Meade's plan of marching Union infantrymen along roads roughly parallel to the Confederate route until they were in a position to turn west and move against Lee's left flank.[52] Before making any major move, however, Meade decided to have Warren take a division and probe the enemy lines in the hope of learning Lee's intentions.[53] He instructed Sedgwick to furnish the troops, which would include his whole corps if Warren thought it necessary, and have them ready to start out by daylight.[54]

On the morning of the 5th Meade directed Butterfield to prepare orders for a general movement of the army; their execution would depend upon the results of Warren's reconnaissance. For the march to Middletown, Maryland, Meade grouped the various corps into three wings. One included the First, Sixth, and Third under Sedgwick; another the Second and Twelfth under Slocum; and the last the Fifth and Eleventh under Howard. By arranging for them to take three different routes, he was confident they would be able to assemble at Middletown by the night of July 7. At 8:30 A.M. on the 5th Meade sent Halleck a message saying that he and his staff would be at Creagerstown that night, which would place him about ten miles north of Frederick after a ride of thirteen or fourteen miles.[55] Before his headquarters issued the orders and apparently before Meade heard from either Warren or Sedgwick, General Herman Haupt pulled up in a buggy to pay him a visit.

Haupt had been busy all day on the 4th at Hanover and Hanover Junction, directing the men of his construction corps as they repaired the railroad between Hanover Junction and Gettysburg. That night he had walked to New Oxford and from there driven on to see Meade. Gettysburg and the immediate countryside he knew intimately, for he had married a Gettysburg girl, laid out the route for a railroad across South Mountain, played a prominent role in the construction of the York and Wrightsville Railroad, and served for a time as Professor of Mathematics and Engineering at Pennsylvania (now Gettysburg) College. During his feverish activities to repair damaged railroads and to improve the efficiency of those left intact, he had kept close watch on Lee's invasion and the battle. Now Haupt concluded from fragmentary and somewhat misleading reports that Meade had won a decisive victory and had a rare opportunity to crush the Confederate army, if only he would follow up his advantage. Believing that Lee had already started his retreat before dawn on July 4, Haupt in a message to Halleck that night had revealed his fear that while Meade rested his men and collected supplies, Lee would slip unmolested across the Potomac. In this disapproving and self-righteous mood Haupt arrived in Gettysburg for the purpose of prodding his sluggish West Point classmate, George G. Meade, on to ever greater glory.

For Haupt the interview proved far from satisfactory, though Meade was polite and cordial enough. Both he and Pleasonton, who was there at the time, gave Haupt an account of the battle and presented him with some mementos of the engagement. After an hour or so of rambling conversation Haupt at last got down to business and asked Meade about his plans so that arrangements could be made for supplying the army. He made the pointed observation that he presumed Meade would march at once to the Potomac and cut off Lee's retreat. Meade replied that it could not be done, because the men needed a rest. Obviously annoyed, Haupt brashly ventured his opinions about the relative condition of the two armies, although he was surely not in as good a position to know about this subject as was Meade. Judging from Haupt's own account, Meade remained uncommunicative, and other than saying that his men needed a rest and Lee could not cross the Potomac because of rising waters, he offered no reasons for the delay in his movements. Very likely he resented Haupt's rather officious interference, and for that reason he chose not to explore with him all aspects of his strategical problem nor fully reveal the current operations of the army. Meade did say that he proposed to move his headquarters to Creagerstown later in the day, but Haupt attached no importance to the remark. He came away with the impression that while the victorious general was sitting around in a relaxed and genial mood waiting for his men to recover from their exertions in a battle which could not possibly have tired them much anyway, Lee's defeated and demoralized army was fleeing to escape greater disaster. These views Haupt unhesitatingly and bluntly passed on to Halleck, Stanton, and Lincoln in separate private interviews the next day in Washington.[56]

His unfavorable report thoroughly depressed President Lincoln and increased his fear that Meade would let Lee slip away and thus lose a superb chance to end the war right then and there on the slopes of Seminary Ridge.[57] Lincoln for some time had been of the opinion, without real justification, that should the rebel army go north of the Potomac, it could "never return, if well attended to."[58] News of the Confederate repulse at Gettysburg confirmed his belief, although he could have known very little about the actual condition of either army immediately following the battle.[59] His hopes for the swift destruction of Lee's forces began to fade as he received various Union dispatches which seemed to indicate that his military leaders were more anxious to shoo Lee out of Pennsylvania and Maryland than to crush him.[60] Lincoln became particularly upset upon reading a copy of Meade's order of July 4, in which he thanked the army in behalf of the country "for the glorious result of the recent operations." [61] On issuing it Meade was merely employing a method commonly used by Civil War generals to maintain the morale of their soldiers. Sometimes they got carried away by their own enthusiasm and made statements which later proved embarrassing. Meade in this instance reminded his men that their task remained unfinished and urged them on to "greater efforts to drive from our soil every vestige of the presence of the invader." [62] This windy version of the old ringing cry of "drive the invader from our soil" may have been a good rhetorical device, but it impressed Lincoln not one whit. Though open to several interpretations, Lincoln took Meade's words at face value and accused him of wanting "to get the enemy across the river again without a further collision. . . ." [63] From then on nothing Meade said or did could wipe out the unfavorable impression Lincoln obtained of his generalship during this crucial phase of the Gettysburg campaign. The tenor of Meade's dispatches to Halleck increased Lincoln's impatience, and it seemed to him that Meade vacillated and moved too cautiously once Lee started his retreat.

In Lincoln's appraisal of Meade his instincts served him well, up to a point. Perhaps the general did show undue concern about the condition of his army, the reduced size of his regiments, and the need to keep his forces always between Lee and Washington, as Halleck had instructed him to do.[64] Before deciding on a course of action he felt he must be certain of his facts; hence his frequent complaints about the lack of accurate information of enemy movements.[65] Should he clash with Lee's army again, he wanted to make sure that circumstances favored him. Nevertheless for Lincoln to charge Meade with a desire to maneuver Lee out of the Northern states without renewing the engagement was quite unfair. Contrary to the President's belief, Meade set out after Lee for the express purpose of battling him again, the sooner the better, for as he revealed to his wife, he would rather fight again "at once . . . in Maryland than to follow in Virginia." [66] Lincoln might have felt better if he had know of that letter, but unfortunately he saw only some of the general's dispatches which were not always as carefully worded as they should have been.

As Lincoln wishfully waited on July 5 to hear that Meade had finally pounced upon his crippled adversary and crushed him, the general stood poised to pursue Lee swiftly with his whole army. By eight-thirty that morning he knew of Lee's departure the night before for Fairfield and Cashtown,[67] but until he learned positively that the Confederate columns were well on their way through the mountain passes he hesitated to give the signal for his men to march. Although it would be some hours before he could hear the results of the reconnaissance from Warren or Sedgwick, Meade concluded from reports arriving from other sources that the enemy was in "full retreat," and he authorized Butterfield late in the morning to start a general movement of the army toward Maryland.[68] Early in the afternoon he learned from Pleasonton that Kilpatrick's cavalry on its way from Emmitsburg had reached South Mountain and in a night action had succeeded in slicing through Ewell's trains in one of the passes near Fairfield. Kilpatrick claimed great deeds for his forces: the destruction or seizure of all of Ewell's wagons, and the capture of 1,500 prisoners, as well as a large number of horses, mules, and Negroes.[69]

The news must have pleased Meade as an auspicious start for his pursuit, but the exploit in reality was less impressive than it sounded. Kilpatrick's column had arrived near Fairfield on the 4th just before dark, and after easily brushing aside General Robertson's pickets it struck a company of the 1st Maryland Cavalry which was guarding the road to Monterey Pass. This determined little force, aided by a detachment of the 4th North Carolina Cavalry and a single cannon, took advantage of the dark, rainy night and delayed the advance of several thousand Union troopers until long after midnight. Kilpatrick, not being able to see anything, considered his command to be in "a perilous situation." Finally in desperation he ordered Custer to charge, and the ensuing headlong rush brought his men to the wagon train and success. The Southern cavalry detachments which had been opposing him quickly slipped away in the dark before he could do them any harm.[70] Confederate accounts either belittled the consequences of this affair or ignored it entirely. Even Kilpatrick subsequently scaled down his figures a bit,

ROUTES TO THE POTOMAC, JULY 5
TO JULY 12, 1863

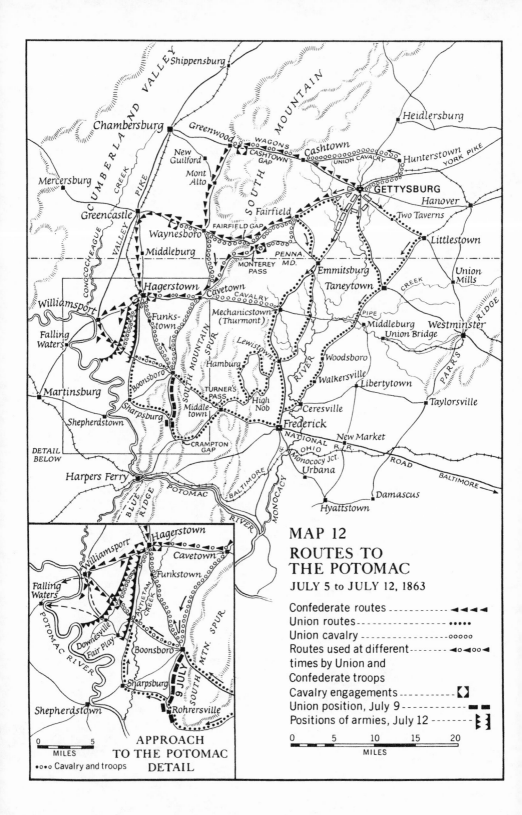

MAP 12
ROUTES TO
THE POTOMAC
JULY 5 to JULY 12, 1863

Confederate routes --------- ◄◄◄◄
Union routes -------------- ••••
Union cavalry ------------- ooooo
Routes used at different ------ ◄o◄oo◄
times by Union and
Confederate troops
Cavalry engagements --------- 〔〕
Union position, July 9 --------- ▰ ▰
Positions of armies, July 12 ------ ⟩⟩

0   5   10   15   20
MILES

APPROACH
TO THE POTOMAC
DETAIL

•o•o Cavalry and troops

0   5
MILES

though he still insisted that he had destroyed or captured all of Ewell's train. How he thought he knew its size is one of the mysteries of Civil War battle reporting.[71] As for the prisoners, many, if not most of them were wounded officers and men who were caught helpless in their ambulances.[72] In no respect did this attack cripple Lee's army or perceptibly reduce its power to fend off any major assault Meade might be able to mount.

In the meantime, before dawn on the morning of the 5th Sedgwick had aroused the men of the Sixth Corps to prepare them for the reconnaissance which he and Warren had been instructed to undertake. With Meade's approval they took the whole corps instead of a division, turning the movement into a pursuit as well as a reconnaissance. The columns did not get under way until almost noon, and then they employed a formation which was not conducive to a rapid advance. Covered by a heavy line of skirmishers, General Torbert's First Brigade of the First Division led the corps and marched in line of battle for about six miles until it finally struck the rear guard of Ewell's corps late in the afternoon near Fairfield. After a sharp exchange of fire Sedgwick's men cautiously pressed Gordon's brigade, which discreetly retired for two miles into Fairfield. In contrast to the thunderous fury of the battle at Gettysburg the skirmish was a pretty tame affair, and it ended with the Confederates setting up their main camp a mile and a half west of town and holding it with their pickets.[73]

After this brief encounter Warren returned to Gettysburg some time after dark and discussed the situation at Fairfield with Meade. He told the commander that he and Sedgwick believed Lee had concentrated the main body of his army around Fairfield for the purpose of giving battle to the Union forces. Upon receiving this report Meade at once halted the movement of his army toward Middletown. Some of the troops had already started out; the Twelfth Corps had reached Littlestown, the Second Two Taverns, the Eleventh Rock Creek on the Taneytown road, and the Fifth Marsh Creek on the Emmitsburg road. The First and Third Corps, which he had previously placed under Sedgwick's marching orders, he now alerted to support the Sixth Corps should it become engaged.[74]

Early on the morning of the 6th Meade sent instructions to Sedgwick to push his reconnaissance for the purpose of determining the exact nature of Lee's movements. Sedgwick was also to examine the character of the gaps and decide whether Meade could seize them without heavy losses should he choose to follow directly after Lee. Sedgwick in reply said that he considered it dangerous and a waste of time to move his whole corps forward in view of the rugged nature of the country and the dense fog which lay over the valley. From the large number of campfires he had seen glowing through the dark of the previous night he judged that the Confederates held the passes with a strong rear guard, but to make sure in the morning he had sent General Neill's brigade to probe their defenses. Should they turn out to be as sturdy as he anticipated, he recommended that Meade permit him to pull his forces back to Emmitsburg. Meade disagreed and ordered Sedgwick to make a vigorous thrust forward with his whole corps. He had already directed the Eleventh and Fifth Corps to occupy Emmitsburg, and from there they could easily assist the Sixth Corps in conjunction with the First and Third if they were needed. Sedgwick, Meade said, had no need to worry about a Confederate flanking movement from Cashtown, for Union cavalry now controlled the Chambersburg Pike beyond Greenwood. As soon as Sedgwick knew the results of Neill's operations— whether the Confederates withdrew or bristled and turned on him —Meade wanted a report. Only when he became satisfied that the main body of Lee's army was retiring from the mountains would he continue his flanking movement by way of Frederick and Middletown.[75]

Soon after noon on the 6th Meade abandoned any thoughts he might have entertained of pursuing Lee by way of Fairfield. He decided it would be fruitless for the Northern army to follow in Lee's tracks, because, judging by what Sedgwick had told him about the formidable character of the passes, a small Confederate force occupying them could keep his columns in check for a long time.[76] Furthermore, information from other sources led him to believe that Lee had already reached Hagerstown.[77] Accordingly he reversed his orders of that morning to Sedgwick and instructed him to withdraw most of the Sixth Corps from Fairfield to Emmitsburg. Neill's brigade and rifled battery were to be detached from the corps and, reinforced by a brigade of cavalry under Colonel McIntosh, were to keep in direct touch with the retreating Confederates and send a constant stream of information about their movements back to headquarters. Meade then ordered the rest of the army to resume its progress for a rendezvous at Middletown early the next morning.[78]

The suspension of the army's movement for over a day and a half put the commanding general in a bad light; he was considered overly cautious, if not timid, because he seemed to have no other purpose in mind than to verify the fact of Lee's retreat into the Cumberland Valley. In addition, his use of an entire infantry corps for a mere reconnaissance appeared absurd, especially as McIntosh's cavalry brigade could have done the errand just as well alone. When Sedgwick asked to have his ordnance train accompany him, he inadvertently raised the question of whether he was to do more than ascertain the position and movements of the enemy. Butterfield in reply said that Meade in ordering a reconnaissance wanted him to obtain information, but not to fight.[79] It seems, however, that Butterfield misread Meade's intentions; in reality Meade wanted Sedgwick to advance aggressively and come to grips with the enemy in the hope of causing his rear guard to turn and fight back. If he could provoke the Confederates into a general engagement and they became too much for him to handle, Meade would have supports available for him. Above all, Meade as early as noon on July 5 urged Sedgwick to move rapidly while getting "explicit information," for time was "of great importance." [80]

Sedgwick and Warren, who very likely rode together, chose to interpret Meade's instructions conservatively. Before starting their reconnaissance they waited until Ewell's corps, which had been delayed by the overcrowded condition of the Fairfield road, had pulled out of its lines and gotten under way. As they followed it they continued to stay at a safe distance until the Confederate rear guard took position about two miles east of Fairfield. Sedgwick had no intention of precipitating a battle, and he issued no orders to the commanders of the supporting units to come up, as Meade had authorized him to do. Even after receiving Meade's instructions early on the 6th to probe the Confederate defenses more vigorously, Sedgwick permitted a stiffening of rebel resistance to stop the forward movement of his corps. At any time between noon of the 5th and noon of the 6th, while the Southern army was in motion and its defenses were not yet set, Sedgwick might have caused a renewal of a general engagement if he had dashed ahead and led a slashing attack upon Lee's rear guard.[81] And Lee, undaunted by his reverses, would have struck back. He sent word to Ewell on the 6th that "if these people keep coming on, turn back and thresh them." Ewell swore, "By the blessing of Providence I will do it" and snapped out orders for Rodes's division to form battle lines, but the Yankees continued only to the top of Monterey Pass and allowed the enemy to retreat down the other side unmolested.[82] In view of Sedgwick's lack of aggressiveness in the advance to Fairfield his remark after the campaign that Meade in his pursuit "might have pushed Lee harder" [83] seems singularly inappropriate.

Before Meade's infantry started to march in earnest toward Maryland on the morning of July 7,[84] elements of his cavalry had struck at Lee's wagon trains as they rolled slowly over the various roads to Williamsport. General Kilpatrick's foray against Ewell's train in the early hours of July 5 was matched by a raid made by a small force of Colonel Pierce's cavalry which attacked some wagons of Stuart's division travelling on the road to Greencastle in charge of General Imboden. General Stuart became so incensed over the loss of ninety wagons, one gun, and 645 soldiers, almost half of whom had been wounded at Gettysburg, that he demanded a court of inquiry to investigate the affair.[85]

Late the next day Generals Buford and Kilpatrick carried on operations of larger proportions against Generals Stuart and Imboden at Hagerstown and along the road to Williamsport seven miles to the southwest. The three brigades of Buford's division, which were together for the first time in a week and numbered at the most a little over 4,000 effectives,[86] left Frederick at 4:00 A.M. for Williamsport twenty-five miles to the northwest. Buford had learned of the arrival there of the train entrusted to Imboden and set out to destroy it before it could cross the Potomac. General French, whose headquarters were at Frederick, had undoubtedly told Buford that the flood waters of the Potomac had reached such a depth that the fords could not be used. Around five o'clock that afternoon Buford drove in the enemy pickets stationed outside the town and followed them within half a mile of the parked trains. There the stiffening resistance of Imboden's command stopped his further advance. The rebels counterattacked but were just as unsuccessful in their efforts to force Buford back as he was in capturing the town with all its loot. At the height of the contest Buford heard Kilpatrick's guns in the direction of Hagerstown, and as the sound grew louder he sent word for Kilpatrick to connect with his right for mutual support.[87]

Until then Kilpatrick had been busily engaged in fighting the Confederates in and around Hagerstown. After his attack on Ewell's train near Monterey early on July 5 he had gone to Boonsborough for the rest of the night, where he regrouped his forces and turned his prisoners and captured property over to General French. The next day Kilpatrick moved toward Hagerstown to attack Stuart's cavalry, which he heard had occupied the town. Actually the occupying force consisted only of the two small brigades under Chambliss and Robertson. Kilpatrick quickly pushed them out, but then he ran into Iverson's infantry; by a forced march it had arrived at the opportune moment on the north side of town. Iverson, who had recovered from the mental shock of the bloody fight of July 1, rapidly and skillfully arranged his men in line of battle and drove the Union cavalry down the streets of the town. At this moment Stuart, with all of his cavalry with him except for two brigades under Fitz Lee, came pounding onto the scene. Parts of two brigades of Hood's division also appeared and helped to recapture Hagerstown.[88]

Meanwhile Kilpatrick in response to Buford's instructions gave up trying to hold the town, and leaving Farnsworth's brigade, now under Colonel Nathaniel P. Richmond, to guard his rear, he turned his command around to cooperate in Buford's attack on Imboden at Williamsport. The joint efforts of the two Union leaders did little good because Stuart, aided by Confederate infantry and the arrival of Fitz Lee's brigades, put increasing pressure on Kilpatrick's rear and right flank. Kilpatrick's troopers gave way and exposed Buford's rear to attack. Buford gave up and under cover of night gradually withdrew his men to camp with Kilpatrick's division near Jones's Crossroads (Lappans) on the way to Boonsborough, thus ending an expedition which he honestly admitted failed to accomplish its objective.[89]

In their accounts of this engagement the participants seem to have put more than their usual emphasis on claims that the other side possessed great superiority in numbers. In truth both forces were quite evenly matched, with the odds in favor of the Confederates as the day wore on. Buford's and Kilpatrick's two divisions, plus Huey's brigade of Gregg's division, had on paper no more than 9,000 troopers available for front-line duty, but in this encounter it is doubtful whether they had anywhere near that number of men in view of the long marches they had had to make to catch up with the enemy. They were supported by eighteen guns of the horse artillery.[90] Imboden's forces consisted of 2,100 of his own men, twenty-three pieces of artillery, and 700 wagoners whom he armed and placed in command of experienced officers. One of these was Colonel William R. Aylett of Pickett's division who though wounded was able to move about.[91] Before the engagement began two infantry regiments of General Early's division, which were guarding an ordnance train carrying a supply of ammunition from Winchester, joined Imboden and strengthened his battle lines with between 600 and 700 muskets.[92] He therefore had a combined force of about 3,500 effectives, which were enough to cope with Buford's division of some 4,000 men. In his attack Buford used only two of his three brigades, keeping one in reserve to follow up any advantage he might gain or cover a retreat should he run into trouble. When Kilpatrick turned to help Buford, both Stuart and Fitz Lee were available to come to Imboden's rescue with an estimated total of about 5,000 cavalry. In addition they had the help of the 650 survivors of Iverson's brigade, who formed the vanguard of Lee's infantry columns as they rapidly approached Hagerstown.[93] Under these circumstances it is not surprising that the Confederates thwarted the efforts of Union cavalry to seize Lee's supply train at Williamsport. Though Imboden handled his forces well, for which achievement Stuart gave him no credit, he was not battling against the great odds he pictured so dramatically in his account.[94]

For the next several days, despite pressure from Stuart's cavalry, Buford and Kilpatrick continued to hold their advanced position around Boonsborough until Meade could bring up the Army of the Potomac. They performed the important service of guarding the South Mountain passes against enemy forces moving out from Hagerstown on the northwest, while a brigade in French's command covered the lower gaps which were near the Potomac. General French, after destroying the railroad bridge at Harpers Ferry, had sent a brigade on July 7 to reoccupy Maryland Heights.[95] Both of these moves were designed to prevent any Confederate force from outflanking the lower end of South Mountain and threatening Frederick from the southwest. French's troops were sufficiently strong to give Meade time to counteract any drive Lee might make toward Washington by way of Frederick. They would not have had to hold on for long, for by the end of the day on July 7 the scene of operations of both armies had shifted from Pennsylvania to Maryland.

Early on the morning of the 7th Meade's Army of the Potomac struck out in full pursuit after Lee's retreating Confederates. With all of his doubts resolved Meade gave the sign for his corps to move rapidly over different roads and converge on Middletown, seven miles west of Frederick in the valley between the Catoctins and South Mountain. Soon his infantrymen were swinging along hour after hour as they began to execute a wide wheeling movement to the right, which in the next few days would bring them in position beyond the western slopes of South Mountain. There they would confront once more all of the Southern army already arrived in the Cumberland Valley.

July 7, the first day on the road, was a long one for Meade's soldiers. Most of them made marches of between fifteen and twenty miles over roads soggy from rain, which began to pour down again toward nightfall. The Eleventh and Twelfth Corps made the records for distance that day. Slocum reported that his men trudged steadily, some of them without shoes, for the twenty-nine miles from Littlestown, Pennsylvania, to Walkersville, Maryland. Parts of the Eleventh Corps did even better by covering distances variously estimated at thirty, thirty-two, and thirty-four miles from Emmitsburg to Middletown. The road over High Knob Pass in the Catoctins was so steep, narrow, and rocky that the artillery and trains could be brought over only with the greatest exertion. When the men stumbled into their bivouac at 10:00 P.M., they sank footsore, drenched, and exhausted onto the sodden ground. By 11:00 P.M. all the corps except the Second and Twelfth had reached positions on both sides of the Catoctins from Middletown to Mechanicstown. The Second Corps, bringing up the rear behind the Artillery Reserve, had had the shortest distance to go, and it practically loafed as it marched the nine miles or so from Two Taverns to Taneytown. Meade, greatly refreshed after his first good night's sleep in days, probably travelled farther than anyone when he moved his headquarters thirty-three miles from Gettysburg to Frederick, rather than to Creagerstown as he had planned to do.[96] Thus by making forced marches the Union army came near to accomplishing in one day what Meade had thought would take two or three days.

The pursuit of the rebels was now well under way. Meade needed another day before he could get his army over South Mountain into the Cumberland Valley, but by the 9th most of it was concentrated in a line from Rohrersville on the south to Boonsborough five miles away. To protect his outer flanks and anchor his hold on the Potomac he had a force on Maryland Heights that was being constantly increased and another at Waynesboro consisting of Neill's and McIntosh's brigades and about 4,000 emergency troops under General Smith.[97] From then on his problem became mainly one of maneuvering his forces so as to get in position to attack Lee, but before he could reach that stage in his pursuit of the enemy he had much work to do.

The torrential rains of the 7th had made all roads except the pikes almost impassable. Countless wagons and pieces of artillery became stalled in the mud, and it took time and great effort to pull them out. The Sixth Corps spent all of the 8th and until noon of the next day getting its batteries over South Mountain, and when the task was finished the horses were unfit for further use. For this reason the infantry in the Sixth and the First Corps marched ahead without their artillery until the horses could rest up or be replaced. Because of the frightful condition of the roads the Third and Fifth Corps had to take long detours to get to their appointed destinations. Thousands of the men wore out their shoes and had to wait for new footwear before they could go on.[98]

The disadvantages of taking a longer route, though accentuated by bad weather, were more than offset by placing the army within a short distance of Frederick, a town connected by the Baltimore and Ohio Railroad, as well as hard-surfaced turnpikes, to such important military centers as Washington and Baltimore. No other place in this part of Maryland possessed its facilities as a supply base, and it was partly for this reason that Meade decided to move along Lee's flank rather than pursue him directly over the mountains. Before Meade halted the movement of his army late on the 5th General Rufus Ingalls notified the quartermaster general in Washington, General Montgomery C. Meigs, that the army would establish a new base of operations at Frederick. The efficient Meigs immediately started vast shipments of horses, forage, rations, clothing, and shoes to Frederick, but because of the delay in the army's departure from the vicinity of Gettysburg Ingalls did not arrive in Frederick to take charge of affairs until around noon of July 7. When he got there he found that General French had snarled traffic at Monocacy Junction, on the main line of the Baltimore and Ohio just south of Frederick, by holding up ten troop trains going west toward Harpers Ferry. The soldiers had come from Baltimore as reinforcements for French improperly provisioned and ill-equipped. Instead of unloading the trains and sending them back empty to Baltimore and then finding other trains for his troops after they had been issued rations and ammunition, French kept them all sitting idle for many hours.

If Ingalls had been on hand, the delay of these trains and a great many others might well have been avoided. Ingalls placed most of the blame on the railroad for not keeping a dispatcher in Frederick with power to control the movement of traffic. He also admitted that officers in charge of posts along the line could not resist displaying their authority and interfering with the working of the railroad. Although the ubiquitous General Haupt had rushed to Frederick upon hearing of the snarl and had reported early in the afternoon of the 8th that he had straightened matters out, Ingalls was not quite so sure. As a precaution, on the same day Ingalls wired Meigs's office not to send any more horses by rail until the army could begin to get provisions, clothing, and forage and could regulate the movement of trains, which he hoped would be accomplished the next day. He desperately needed boots, but they had not as yet arrived.[99] Although Meigs's department performed admirably as usual, Meade's army did not receive supplies in adequate amounts for several days after establishing its base at Frederick.[100] Time was lost too in apportioning the fresh horses among the artillery and cavalry. Meigs had scoured the country for them and had sent them to Frederick in large numbers.[101] How much all of these factors hampered the forward movement of the army is hard to say, but undoubtedly they had considerable effect.

During the several days Meade took to move his army and get it ready for an offensive, he effected certain changes in organization and began receiving reinforcements to replace his losses and to increase his numerical edge over Lee. Heavy casualties in his top echelon forced him to look for new talent. Although he did his best, he was not too successful in finding suitable replacements. The loss of Reynolds and Hancock Meade considered insurmountable, and he felt he could get no one of comparable structure to take their places as corps commanders.[102] When Butterfield, after receiving a painful wound on July 3, went home, "fortunately for him & to the joy of all," as General Patrick observed,[103] Meade succeeded in securing just the right person to fill the vacancy. As his new chief of staff on July 8 he appointed General A. A. Humphreys, to the immediate surprise but ultimate satisfaction of everyone. In the interval between Butterfield's departure on the 5th and Humphreys' assumption of his duties on the 9th Generals Pleasonton and Warren performed the work of the office.[104] Another major change in top command occurred on the same day, partly in connection with the transfer of Humphreys from the field to headquarters. General French, previously in charge of the Harpers Ferry garrison, received orders to take the place of the wounded Sickles as commander of the Third Corps. Although Meade at first had great confidence in French, it is questionable whether he was any real improvement over Sickles. On the 10th Brigadier General Henry Prince, who had been on duty in North Carolina, joined the Army of the Potomac, and Meade put him in charge of Humphreys' old division.[105]

Other changes in corps command had taken place earlier when General John Newton succeeded Reynolds on July 2, and Brigadier General William Hays replaced Hancock on July 3 at the conclusion of the battle.[106] With his appointment there were two General Hays in the Second Corps, but the new commander should not be confused with General Alexander Hays who at the head of the Third Division had greatly distinguished himself on July 3. Of these two new corps commanders Newton had by far the more outstanding career before and during the war. Though his chief of artillery, Colonel Wainwright, thought highly of his intelligence and competence as an engineer, as did everyone else, he considered him "intensely lazy" and a lover of creature comforts in contrast to the beloved Reynolds.[107] Hays apparently made little impression as head of the Second Corps, and he remained with the Army of the Potomac for only a short time.[108] The three new corps commanders, especially Newton, were by ordinary standards very adequate replacements, but they could not compare to Reynolds and Hancock, without whom Meade felt his effectiveness as a leader had become seriously, if not fatally, impaired.

Meade also felt keenly the loss of thousands of veteran troops, for he knew there were few soldiers of their caliber available to serve as replacements. To compound his woes as he approached another showdown with Lee, hundreds of his short-term volunteers, who had been tempered by the fires of Gettysburg, began leaving the ranks upon the expiration of their periods of enlistment. Unfortunately most of them were the nine-month regiments of Stannard's brigade of the First Corps, which had won glory for themselves on the slopes of Cemetery Ridge.[109] In high dudgeon General Schenck wired Secretary Stanton from Baltimore on July 11 that he was "astounded" to see that a "fine regiment," the 13th Vermont numbering 663 men, had just arrived from Middletown and was headed for home. "Can nothing be done to stop this?" he protested. Then rather in despair he added: "I suppose I must give them transportation, but I cannot help denouncing them." [110] What he should have denounced instead of the Vermonters was the haphazard system of recruiting which by a strange irony was depriving a general of the tools of his profession when he needed them most. In July, 1861, when troops marched away from the battlefield at the expiration of their terms of enlistment, the situation could be explained as one of the expected consequences of unpreparedness. Two years later it could only be labelled a cruel jest.

The immediate source of reinforcements and replacements for Meade was a force of some 10,000, most of them infantrymen, which had been with French at Maryland Heights. Upon evacuation of that stronghold about two-thirds of the men had remained under French at Frederick. The rest had retired to Washington, but after the battle they rejoined their commander to participate in the pursuit of Lee. When French was assigned to the Third Corps, between 8,000 and 9,000 of his men became incorporated into the Army of the Potomac, the bulk in the Third Corps and the rest in the First. Allowing for the departure of some regiments at about the same time, the attachment of these troops to the army represented a net gain in numerical strength of around 6,000 men. Their quality, however, was uncertain. In contrast to the lean and sinewy regiments of the Army of the Potomac, some of which were now reduced to fewer than 150 veterans, their ranks were fat and oversized in numbers, reflecting the ease of garrison life.[111]

Though not yet hardened to the rigors of campaigning, French's men had rendered essential service by guarding the rear of Meade's army around Frederick, occupying some of the passes in South Mountain, and maintaining control of Maryland Heights. To take their places Halleck arranged to have General Schenck transfer about 3,900 troops from Baltimore, including two new Maryland six-month regiments and one New York thirty-day militia regiment. Most of the replacements, however, came from General John G. Foster's Eighteenth Corps in North Carolina, who were on their way home to be mustered out. All of these units went to Maryland Heights, where they were joined by others transferred from North Carolina and Virginia. On July 8 Meade assigned Brigadier General H. M. Naglee, who had held a command at Beaufort, North Carolina, to take charge of the posts at Harpers Ferry and Maryland Heights. He reported on July 9 that he had almost 6,500 men there; most of them were infantry, and 70 percent were soon to be mustered out of service. The rest of his men, three-year volunteers, apparently never became attached to the Army of the Potomac. In fact, the only three-year men who did reinforce Meade before Lee crossed the Potomac were units from French's command and also the 39th Massachusetts, a large regiment mustering 671 men which had been on garrison duty at Washington and joined Meade on July 10. Four days later strong reinforcements began to arrive from the Department of Virginia, but by this time most of the Confederates were already across the river.[112]

Meade had grave doubts about the reliability of men whose terms of enlistment were about to expire. Unless they had at least ten more days to serve or pledged themselves to remain in the ranks for the duration of the emergency, he kept them out of harm's way at Maryland Heights, the South Mountain passes, or other points in the rear.[113] Apparently five regiments of nine-month men met the requirements for service in his command, and on the 13th two of them joined the First Corps and three the Eleventh, bringing in a total of 2,411 men. Altogether it seems that Meade thus acquired before the 14th between 11,000 and 12,000 men. Of course from this figure there must be deducted the 3,500 or so who left his army after the battle, in order to get a fair estimate of the actual increase in the size of his force. Meade also obtained six fresh batteries, which he distributed evenly between the Second and Third Corps.[114]

On July 10 in addition to the Army of the Potomac numerous other Union forces of various sizes and descriptions were slowly closing in on the Army of Northern Virginia from practically all directions. General Naglee was holding Maryland Heights with a mixed force of uncertain quality. To the north of him General Couch had sizeable bodies of troops concentrated in three locations: General Smith at Waynesboro with 7,600 men, General N. P. Dana at Chambersburg with 11,000, and Colonel Pierce near Mercersburg with 6,700. Both Naglee's and Couch's commands consisted mostly of emergency troops and were subject to Meade's orders.

By the 10th another force numbering about 4,500 men in two infantry brigades and a regiment of cavalry appeared in western Maryland within thirty miles of the scene of operations. They were from Brigadier General B. F. Kelley's Department of West Virginia. Meade had no authority over them, but General Kelley had moved them to Hancock, Maryland, in response to an order from Halleck on July 4; he wanted as many as possible of a total of 17,000 men in the department brought into position to attack Lee from the west. After constant prodding from both Halleck and Stanton, Kelley finally succeeded in bringing up about half of his scattered forces just as Lee crossed the Potomac.[115]

Although all of these commands looked impressive on paper and appeared as a great threat to the enemy, none of them, especially those in Couch's department, dared to confront any significant portion of Lee's army for fear of annihilation. Nevertheless, collectively they rendered one important service. As they crept slowly forward without serious opposition from rebel outposts, they further constricted the area over which Confederate foraging parties could roam, thus making Lee's position uncomfortable, if not untenable.

If Meade showed reluctance in accepting nine-month regiments because of their limited usefulness and unreliability in combat, he had a real aversion to Couch's emergency troops, although Simon Cameron, Lincoln's erstwhile Secretary of War, blithely referred to them as a "fine army." [116] This opinion, which many leaders in Washington seemed to accept without question, was the sort of thinking that plagued Meade in the post mortems of the campaign. His critics could not understand why, with such a splendid body of men available, he did not use them to smash the crippled Lee. Considering their hasty recruitment and almost complete lack of training it was amazing they were worth anything at all. Professional army men naturally viewed them with dismay. On July 8 Smith referred to his command as "quite helpless" and an "incoherent mass" which could not be maneuvered. He suggested that if they joined the army they should be attached to old divisions so as to "disperse the greenness." [117] Although Couch thought that a good many of the Pennsylvania troops would do well, he worried about the effect on the Army of the Potomac if any of his men should refuse to cross the Mason and Dixon line or should "break on the field." [118] The regiments suffered from inefficient or nonexistent supply systems, and some from very inadequate equipment. General Ingalls was appalled to learn that General Smith with nearly 7,000 troops had arrived near Hagerstown on the night of July 12 without supplies or the means of procuring them. In his report Smith admitted that he had entered the campaign with no wagons or quartermasters. And this was the "fine army" about which Simon Cameron wired Lincoln on July 14! [119]

Meade thoroughly disliked the responsibility of exercising control over these troops, for he felt he could not rely upon them in combat, and Halleck's wire of July 5 categorically placing them directly under his authority pained him greatly. In spite of his feelings he dutifully asked Couch the next day about the disposition of his forces and what plans he had for their movements. Then on second thought he wired Couch again and himself made several suggestions about their use. Couch, he said, could do one of several things: reinforce the Army of the Potomac, move down the Cumberland Valley and keep in touch with army headquarters, or confine himself to threatening gestures in the hope of distracting Lee from his real source of danger. The last possibility was the one Meade preferred. However, since Smith's force had arrived near Cashtown and was close at hand, Meade decided it could do the most good by coming to Gettysburg to cover the withdrawal of the Army of the Potomac and at the same time protect hospitals and public property.[120] On the 7th Meade once more changed his mind and directed Smith to keep on his course through the mountains in pursuit of Lee; and he added something vague about Smith joining the army in Middletown "after pushing the enemy to the best advantage." [121]

Smith went ahead and reached Waynesboro on the 8th, where he found Neill's flying column of infantry and cavalry. While there he sent out an expedition made up of three regiments of emergency men; it succeeded in destroying all of twenty-four barrels of flour and one hundred bushels of grain which the Confederates had requisitioned at a place called Marsh Mill. Because Meade's orders had left him so uncertain about what to do next, Smith finally went to see the general in person and recommended that his command be divided among the old divisions of the Army of the Potomac. Meade rejected the idea but agreed to have Smith's command become associated with the Army of the Potomac, though not be formally a part of it. In this anomalous capacity one of Smith's regiments known as the Blue Reserves took part with General Kilpatrick's cavalry in a skirmish near Hagerstown on the 13th and suffered the loss of one killed and nine wounded. This minor affair represented the extent of any fighting done by the emergency troops in cooperation with the main body of the Army of the Potomac.[122] The next day, perhaps because Lee had already crossed the river and Meade had no further need of these soldiers, he declined to take the responsibility of ordering the rest of Couch's men to join him.[123] On the 15th he released General Smith from his command with appropriate words of gratitude for the "zeal and promptitude" with which he and his troops "amid no little privations" had given the army "all the assistance of their power," [124] sentiments that were just so much window-dressing.

The truth of the matter is that authorities in Washington expected too much of these scattered commands, even as they did of the Army of the Potomac. They exhorted Kelley and Couch not to rest night or day in their efforts "to inflict a heavy blow upon the enemy," [125] and Lincoln, becoming impatient with their clumsy and poorly coordinated movements, commented acidly that they were "as likely to capture the 'man in the moon' as any part of Lee's army." [126] The officials' optimistic but distorted picture of the situation resulted partly from dispatches sent by officers in the Army of the Potomac right after the battle, in which they used such words, when referring to the condition of the enemy, as "very much crippled," "hampered with his trains," [127] or "in retreat, demoralized, and embarrassed with muddy roads." [128] Actually except for Ewell's train Lee through careful planning got most of his wagons away from Gettysburg, and the sodden roads in the mountains hindered him no more than they did his pursuers.

From the very moment leaders in Washington heard of Lee's defeat at Gettysburg until his retreat across the Potomac they intently watched every move Meade made to finish what Lincoln considered to be an incomplete victory. For the first few days after the battle they showed forbearance and waited for him to resolve his uncertainties and evolve his plans. Halleck on the 5th expressed satisfaction with his movements, but two days later his mood changed and he began to reflect the growing impatience of official Washington.[129] Now the prodding of Meade began in earnest. Lincoln sent Halleck a message to pass on to Meade confirming the surrender of Vicksburg. "Now," the President added, "if General Meade can complete his work, so gloriously prosecuted thus far, by the literal or substantial destruction of Lee's army, the rebellion will be over."[130] Again using Halleck as an intermediary, Lincoln followed up this jab with another message informing Meade that the enemy was crossing at Williamsport and he was most anxious that the Union army should move against him by forced marches. The opportunity to attack Lee's forces while they were straddled over the Potomac should not be lost, Halleck warned. Meade bristled and wired back a tart reply, saying that according to his information the enemy was *not* crossing the Potomac and the Union army was already making forced marches. Thereupon Halleck backed down. He decided that if Lee was massing his forces west of Antietam Creek between Williamsport and Hagerstown, Meade should take time to concentrate his troops and wait until he could hurl all of his men, good, bad, and indifferent, into the fray at one time so as to gain a decisive victory. And Meade fully agreed with this advice.[131]

On July 9 as the two Union generals began to see eye to eye about strategy, the advance elements of Meade's army established a line just west of South Mountain, from Boonsborough five miles south to Rohrersville. Meade correctly assumed that the whole of Lee's army lay somewhere between Hagerstown and Williamsport and that in view of the flooded condition of the river it had stopped its retreat and was getting ready to receive an attack. For the next three days Meade maneuvered his troops carefully for a distance of about eight miles west of South Mountain. The enemy abandoned Hagerstown on the morning of the 12th, and by that afternoon the Union line, running roughly parallel to the Hagerstown-Sharpsburg Pike, extended from Hagerstown to the little town of Fair Play. Meade advanced cautiously, perhaps too much so, for fear of being surprised into a premature engagement which could have unfortunate results for him, since the enemy was holding very strong positions.[132] During this three-day period he reorganized his army with the arrival of reinforcements, and made changes in commanders. With his base still at Frederick the problem of bringing supplies to the front lines became greater as he moved west. The occupation of Hagerstown would bring him no relief, for the railroad from Harrisburg to that town had not been repaired even as far as Chambersburg and would not be for the next five days. Neill's detachment of infantry and cavalry together with Smith's forces near Waynesboro had to get their supplies from as far off as Gettysburg, where there was a vast accumulation after Haupt got the trains running again from Hanover Junction.[133] The problem of supplies for Meade was minor, however, compared to the one of getting his troops into good positions from which to attack. His operations were slowed down by the exhausted condition of his men and draft animals, who had to advance over rough country soaked from rain or through lowlands covered with water from overflowing streams.[134]

Meade's suspicions that Lee had made careful preparations to meet an assault were well founded. Soon after the rear guard of the Confederate army arrived in Hagerstown on the morning of July 7, Lee began to inspect the approaches to the river by way of the Williamsport-Hagerstown Pike. Stuart with his customary skill and agility had previously forced the Yankee cavalry back considerably east of this road, thus clearing the ground for Lee.[135] The country around Williamsport, Falling Waters, Downsville, and Jones's Crossroads had many good defensive positions,[136] and Lee spent several days in riding about, consulting with his chief subordinates, and instructing "Jed" Hotchkiss and others of his engineers to draw maps of the area. By July 11 the engineers and generals had selected a line along high ground with the right resting on the river near Downsville and the left about a mile and a half southwest of Hagerstown, so that the road from there to Williamsport was covered. The Conococheague Creek, a sizeable stream emptying into the Potomac from the north at Williamsport, and the open country through which it flowed protected the Confederate position from a surprise attack from the west.[137] The Southerners proceeded to fortify their line by throwing up earthworks which Colonel Wainwright later pronounced by far the strongest he had yet seen, "built as if they [were] meant to stand a month's siege." The parapet, a good six feet wide on top and with frequent gun emplacements, was designed so the men could get a perfect cross-fire while sweeping the front.[138] They also put up inner defenses at Falling Waters and Williamsport to cover the passage of the river. A possible weakness in the fortified line was its length of six to eight miles, making it difficult to defend. By the morning of July 12 the Confederates had almost finished preparing their fortifications, and at this exact time Meade finally brought up his forces to confront them.[139]

Until then Lee had had his troops occupy as much area as possible without running into serious clashes with the enemy, in order to have room to maneuver and give his foraging parties access to adequate supplies. His men continually challenged the Yankees to keep them off balance and then withdrew as the pressure became too great. Lee's purpose was not to take the offensive but to fight a defensive battle if fight he must. He became restive when Meade did not show up as soon as anticipated, because he figured that the longer he remained in his present position, the stronger the enemy was becoming and the slimmer his own supplies. The flooding of the Potomac upset Lee, not so much because it endangered his army as because it prevented him from coming and going as he pleased. In planning his campaign he had assumed that the river would remain fordable all during the summer. All communication with Virginia was not cut off, however, for he had at least one flatboat attached to a wire rope, which could cross the river in about seven minutes. Lee used it to send off his sick and wounded to Virginia and bring back ammunition and other essentials. Besides, work on repairing the pontoon bridge was progressing very satisfactorily in spite of a lack of tools and the inclement weather. Whatever his worries, Lee seemed in good spirits and confident that his army if attacked would do well and perhaps might even retrieve its fortunes.[140] On the 12th and 13th all his infantry and artillery were in their works with Longstreet's corps holding the right of the line toward the Potomac, Hill's the center, and Ewell's the left. Most of Stuart's cavalry was massed guarding the left flank and in position to bear down on the enemy's right should he mount an offensive.[141] Fully prepared for an engagement, Lee's army lay waiting for the Federals to attack; everyone was convinced, as one Confederate officer expressed it, that "Mr. Yank would have smelt powder & ball before getting us out of the breastworks. . . ." [142]

On July 12 Meade wired Halleck his intention to attack the next day because a further delay would strengthen the enemy while not increasing the power of his own force. So far so good, but then he weakened his decision with an unfortunate qualifying phrase: "unless something intervenes to prevent it." [143] Meade, because he still lacked confidence in himself and because it was a good way of obtaining information, once more called a meeting of his corps commanders for eight o'clock on the night of July 12, in which he included Pleasonton, Warren, and of course Humphreys, his new chief of staff. Wadsworth attended in place of Newton, who was sick. Before the meeting Meade asked Humphreys, in whose judgment he had great confidence, what he thought of advancing the army and making a reconnaissance in force which could be converted into an attack if an opportunity developed. Although they had only a very superficial knowledge of the enemy's position, Humphreys was in favor of the idea. Meade then outlined this plan to the corps commanders and asked them for information about the positions of their corps, what they knew about the enemy, and their reactions to his proposal. Of the seven, five including the two senior officers, Sedgwick and Slocum, were unalterably opposed to an attack. Only Wadsworth and Howard were for it. Wadsworth, that stouthearted gentleman from New York State, was always spoiling for a fight whether it was militarily sound or not, but he lacked the rank to carry much weight. As for Howard, the questionable record of his corps in two battles greatly discounted the importance of his opinions in the minds of his hearers. Pleasonton thought well of Meade's proposal, and Warren argued eloquently for it,[144] but these generals could not properly be considered participants in the council of war, since they did not command infantry units.

The adverse opinion of the majority of the infantry generals was the "something" that intervened to prevent the attack, at least for the moment, for Meade, though not agreeing with the decision, deferred an assault until he could personally reconnoiter the positions of the opposing forces. The next morning he and Humphreys rode out from headquarters together and in spite of rain and mist saw the character of the ground held by Federal troops and some of that occupied by the enemy. Upon returning, Humphreys, by direction of General Meade, prepared instructions for the corps commanders to move on the morning of the 14th and make reconnaissances in force, with the whole army ready to spring into action. It was to be a movement, according to Humphreys, "similar in most respects" to the one Meade had wanted to make the day before.[145]

When Meade reported to Halleck about the postponement of his attack and the reasons for it, the general in chief sharply advised him to follow his own judgment and make his generals carry out orders. He added sententiously that it was "proverbial that councils of war never fight." [146] Criticis of Meade have never forgiven him for his evasion of responsibility when he allowed the decision of his generals to control his actions. Some of them went so far as to claim that by this show of weakness he nullified his accomplishments at Gettysburg. But many of these same people would have been the first to accuse him of rashness if he had attacked, as he suggested doing, before making a careful examination of the ground and had thereby suffered a serious reverse. Lack of precise information of the enemy's position bothered Meade's engineering mind very much. Although he was "rather inspired" to try an attack on the 13th, he admitted that his own conviction was not strong enough to warrant his overruling the opinions of most of his corps commanders.[147] After the Confederate departure when Meade and some of his more capable officers—Sedgwick, Hunt, and Wainwright, to name a few—inspected the Confederate fortifications, they concluded that the Yankees had escaped disaster by putting off the attack,[148] but Meade's critics would never agree to this point of view.

In this controversy Humphreys took a position midway between the censors and defenders of Meade. Although in his estimation the strength of enemy positions would have made an attack on them very costly, he still thought Meade should have risked a reconnaissance in force on the 13th.[149] Should the attacking columns have been severely repulsed, they could have fallen back to the entrenchments which veteran units had dug without waiting for orders as soon as they came close to enemy lines,[150] and from there they could have fought off Confederate counterattacks. On the other hand, if Meade's operations had succeeded in breaking Lee's lines, Humphreys doubted—contrary to the Lincoln thesis—that the Federals could have annihilated the enemy and ended the war right there. An army as large as Lee's, he observed, could not have been "knocked in pieces" and prevented from rallying and taking new and formidable positions, especially in the broken country of western Maryland. In other words, a defeat might have badly battered Lee's army but not utterly ruined it.[151]

Humphreys' analysis of Meade's opportunities on the 13th was most convincing. He did not intend criticism of Meade's postponement, for he emphasized that the order to advance was issued before the Confederates had crossed the river and before headquarters had any intimation of their imminent departure.[152] Nonetheless one cannot help wondering why if the reconnaissance in force was feasible on the 14th, it was not just as much so on the 13th. The stakes were high enough for Meade to have taken the chance. He should have heeded his own counsel which was so ably seconded by his two valued advisers, Warren and Humphreys. In Humphreys he had a general with aggressiveness and military sense on a par with Reynolds and Hancock, whose absence he so keenly felt.[153] Meade's unfortunate moment of hesitation gave his reputation a blow from which it never fully recovered. His detractors attached to it a significance out of proportion to its true meaning, and Lincoln never forgave him for not venturing an attack of some sort when he seemed to have the opportunity. Whether the opportunity was as great as Lincoln thought is questionable, for he apparently assumed the Union army to be stronger and the Confederate army weaker than they really were. On July 10 the Army of the Potomac had no more than 80,000 officers and men available for combat, while Lee had at least 50,000 troops with which to confront them.[154] This ratio of eight to five, which is based on a conservative estimate of Confederate strength, seemed to show Union arms as having an overwhelming advantage. In reality the Army of the Potomac, though inspired by victory, had lost much of its hitting power from excessively high casualties in veteran soldiers and officers. The outcome of the battle had reversed the roles of the two commanding generals and forced Meade to assume the offensive with a weakened and inadequately reinforced army, against a force noted for its unusual aptitude and skill in defensive fighting.

As Meade and Humphreys inspected the front lines on the morning of July 13, Lee anxiously and hopefully looked for signs of a massive assault against his position. The outbreak of skirmishing at dawn had given him reason to expect it at any moment, but as the firing died down [155] and information filtered back about the Yankees busily digging entrenchments, he became impatient and said, "'That is too long for me; I can not wait for that.'" Then he added: "'They have but little courage!'" [156] Within a short while Lee ordered a retreat, for the engineers and sappers had finished the pontoon bridge and the Potomac had subsided enough to be forded. The troops started out at dark, with orders for Longstreet's and Hill's corps together with the artillery to march across on the pontoon bridge at Falling Waters and for Ewell's men to ford the river at Williamsport. It was a beautifully executed move. Despite the pitch-dark night, a heavy rain, the flooded roads, and several accidents, all units of the army except Heth's and Pender's divisions reached the south bank by 11:00 A.M. on the 14th.[157]

During the night even as the Confederates were evacuating their works Meade's headquarters issued orders that the reconnaissance in force by four of his corps be started punctually at 7:00 A.M. Though no reason was given for the time of the move, Meade probably set it at what was considered rather late in the morning so as to make sure the various commanders would act in concert and begin operations simultaneously.[158] Before seven o'clock, however, General H. G. Wright of the Sixth Corps and then General Howard got wind of an enemy withdrawal. Upon ordering his skirmishers forward, Wright found the Confederates had left their entrenchments and were nowhere in sight. He pressed on with his division toward Williamsport, followed by the rest of the corps. When Meade learned of Lee's departure he ordered a general pursuit at 8:30 A.M., but it was too late.[159]

As consolation for his bitter disappointment Meade in good conscience claimed signal success against Lee's rear guard under General Henry Heth at Falling Waters. From the reports of his cavalry generals, Buford and Kilpatrick, he concluded that the Confederates had suffered the capture of an infantry brigade, 1,500 strong, as well as five hundred other prisoners, two guns, two caissons, two battle flags, and a large number of small arms.[160] But when Northern and Southern newspapers published Meade's report of the affair, Lee took the unusual step of officially challenging its facts and figures. He went so far as to state positively that "no arms, cannon, or prisoners were taken by the enemy in battle"; the guns had been abandoned, he said, and the prisoners were only stragglers "worn down by fatigue" who were caught asleep in barns and along the road.[161] Both Meade and Lee, it seems, were victims of inaccurate reporting. If Kilpatrick did not tell a downright falsehood, he at least grossly exaggerated his accomplishments, while Henry Heth recounted only part of the story of what took place. Buford's more modest report was closer to the truth than the other two versions.

What seems to have happened was that in the morning of the 14th, while in pursuit of Lee's army, Buford's division coming from the east and Kilpatrick's from the north approached the position occupied by Heth's division on a ridge about a mile and a half from Falling Waters. Pender's division lay back of Heth's waiting its turn to march over the pontoon bridge. Kilpatrick arrived a little ahead of Buford. His attack was a complete surprise, and he caught the Confederates, who were tired out from the night's hard march, napping amidst their stacked and unloaded arms. Fortunately for the Southerners Kilpatrick's generalship was faulty. He permitted two small squadrons without any supports to rush ahead and make the initial charge, but they only served to alert the enemy without causing him much harm, except for the loss of General Pettigrew who in the melee received a mortal wound. The Confederates, wielding their rifles as clubs and in some instances using fence rails or axes, knocked most of the troopers from their horses and killed or wounded them. Kilpatrick, however, renewed his attack, while Buford struck the Confederates on their right and rear. Before Heth could get his own and Pender's division across the river, they had lost 719 officers and men as prisoners; of these about 230 came from Brockenbrough's brigade, which had borne much of the fighting, and nearly 200 from Colonel Lowrance's (Scales's).[162] Buford reported he had captured over 500 prisoners, Kilpatrick claimed upwards of 1,500, Meade combined the two and set the figure at 2,000, but Lee admitted the loss of only an indeterminate number of stragglers. However, General Patrick, whose responsibility it was to herd all prisoners, confirmed that Buford's figures were quite accurate. The Yankees might have made an even greater haul of rebels if Kilpatrick had exercised greater control over his men and coordinated his movements with Buford's.[163] Ironically Henry Heth, who had opened hostilities at Gettysburg, also fired the closing volleys fourteen days later at Falling Waters—and in both instances he was caught unprepared.[164]

Meade's announcement of success against Lee's rear guard did little to assuage Lincoln's distress and grief over the earlier news of what Washington called Lee's "escape." The word "escape" reflected a highly questionable analysis of the military situation. Lincoln had become obsessed with the notion that Meade's dispatches before the 14th were breathing the spirit of McClellanism and that he was using his difficulties as excuses for doing nothing.[165] In his impatience with what he considered the prevailing attitude in the Meade camp the President overlooked certain hard realities as in the beautiful cadences of the King James Bible he made Meade's task seem so simple. " 'We had them within our grasp,' he said, 'We had only to stretch forth our hands and they were ours. And nothing I could say or do could make the Army move.' " [166] Again he said, " 'Our Army held the war in the hollow of their hand and they would not close it.' " [167] In these utterances Lincoln assumed that Lee was surrounded. On the face of it Lee did seem trapped with Federal forces on three sides of him and a flooded river on the fourth, but of all these elements in the situation only the Army of the Potomac to the east gave Lee any real concern. Although the appearance of Kelley's three-year brigades from the west created the illusion of a serious threat, Kelley approached Lee's army with as much courage as a beagle hound coming up to sniff a pit bull.[168] At the first quick move he would be off and away. Neither Kelley nor the thousands of emergency troops to the north could have prevented Lee from escaping up the river if the Army of the Potomac had succeeded in defeating him. Yet Lincoln tended to equate these troops with the veterans of Meade's army, when they were nothing but straw soldiers compared to the battle-hardened three-year volunteers.[169] It might have been more fitting if Lincoln and members of his administration, instead of castigating Meade, had acknowledged that the Army of the Potomac in 1863 had reached the nadir of its strength and effectiveness largely as a result of their own timid and unrealistic recruitment policies and their practice of filling the legal quotas of generals with political appointees.[170]

In their extreme dissatisfaction with Meade some of the leaders in Washington went so far as to take the view that Lee had not only won the "laurels of the campaign," [171] but had "really won . . . [the] battle!" [172] In a limited sense they were right, for Lee had in fact achieved many of his objectives. He had disrupted Union plans for a summer campaign by carrying the war into the North, and he had relieved his own people of the presence of the invader. For days his men had lived well while carrying off vast supplies of stores and food which would permit them to prolong the struggle. These accomplishments were truly substantial, but in return Lee paid an excessively high price in lives lost and the destruction of the myth of his invincibility. Nor did he succeed in forcing the withdrawal of a single Federal soldier from the siege of Vicksburg, which had been one of the main reasons for the campaign.

Although the real meaning of Meade's victory at Gettysburg emerged only with the passage of time, its immediate effect was to give the Army of the Potomac a sense of triumph which grew into an imperishable faith in itself. The men knew what they could do under an extremely competent general; one of lesser ability and courage could well have lost the battle. The Confederates had put forth their best efforts and their best army but they were not strong enough, for the Army of the Potomac, weak as it was, finally lived up to its promise. The mistakes of the Confederates which in another battle would have been mere slips of the tongue, so to speak, became fatal at Gettysburg. Unfortunately the people of the country, frustrated at seeing Lee retreat across the Potomac without another challenge from Meade, seemed to ignore the magnitude of the Union victory and its enormous cost. They failed to realize that after the battle Meade no longer possessed a truly effective instrument for the accomplishment of his tasks. The army needed a thorough reorganization with new commanders and fresh troops, but these changes were not made until Grant appeared on the scene in March of 1864.

Unfortunately Meade had never inspired in his men the adulation of a Lee or a McClellan, and his caution at Williamsport and Hagerstown dimmed in the eyes of many of his soldiers the luster of his achievement at Gettysburg. Some were as bitter in their disappointment as the fiery General Alexander Hays who wrote: "We are tired of scientific leaders and regard strategy as it is called—a humbug. Next thing to cowardice. What we want is a leader who will go ahead." [173] Others, though regretting it, accepted the result more philosophically and undoubtedly agreed with General Slocum's warning to a friend: "Please don't believe the newspapers when they tell you that we could have captured (bagged) the rebel army—our best officers think everything was done for the best—the reporters often differ in opinion with [the] Army." [174] But the majority, out of confidence born on the slopes of Cemetery Ridge or repugnance at the thought of another campaign in that "God-forsaken, desolated country of Virginia," [175] wanted to make one more tremendous effort in the hope of ending the war on the north bank of the Potomac. [176] Instead their columns once more headed south across the river and into Virginia.

At three o'clock in the afternoon of the 14th of July, 1863, General G. K. Warren sent the following message to the War Department: "The Maryland campaign is ended. Have sent to me . . . all the maps you can spare of the Shenandoah Valley and the routes east of the mountains to Gordonsville." [177] And so the war went on.

Official Rosters

(Corps and division commanders are listed in the order that they assumed command.)

UNITS OF THE ARMY OF THE POTOMAC, U.S.A., AT THE BATTLE OF GETTYSBURG, JULY 1–3, 1863

Maj. Gen. GEORGE G. MEADE, commanding

ARMY HEADQUARTERS

Maj. Gen. DANIEL BUTTERFIELD, chief of staff
Brig. Gen. G. K. WARREN, chief of engineers
Brig. Gen. HENRY J. HUNT, chief of artillery
Brig. Gen. MARSENA R. PATRICK, provost marshall general
Brig. Gen. SETH WILLIAMS, assistant adjutant general
Brig. Gen. RUFUS INGALLS, chief quartermaster
Dr. JONATHAN LETTERMAN, medical director
Capt. LEMUEL B. NORTON, chief signal officer
Lt. JOHN R. EDIE, acting chief ordnance officer

Command of the Provost Marshal General

2d Pennsylvania Cavalry
6th Pennsylvania Cavalry, Companies E and I
Regular cavalry (detachments from 1st, 2d, 5th, and 6th Regiments)

FIRST ARMY CORPS

Maj. Gen. JOHN F. REYNOLDS
Maj. Gen. ABNER DOUBLEDAY
Maj. Gen. JOHN NEWTON

GENERAL HEADQUARTERS

1st Maine Cavalry, Company L

FIRST DIVISION

Brig. Gen. JAMES S. WADSWORTH

First Brigade	Second Brigade
Brig. Gen. SOLOMON MEREDITH	Brig. Gen. LYSANDER CUTLER
Col. WILLIAM W. ROBINSON	

19th Indiana	7th Indiana
24th Michigan	76th New York
2d Wisconsin	84th New York (14th Militia)
6th Wisconsin	95th New York
7th Wisconsin	147th New York
	56th Pennsylvania (nine companies)

SECOND DIVISION

Brig. Gen. JOHN C. ROBINSON

First Brigade	*Second Brigade*
Brig. Gen. GABRIEL R. PAUL	Brig. Gen. HENRY BAXTER
Col. SAMUEL H. LEONARD	
Col. ADRIAN R. ROOT	
Col. RICHARD COULTER	
Col. PETER LYLE	
Col. RICHARD COULTER	
16th Maine	12th Massachusetts
13th Massachusetts	83rd New York (9th Militia)
94th New York	97th New York
104th New York	11th Pennsylvania
107th Pennsylvania	88th Pennsylvania
	90th Pennsylvania

THIRD DIVISION

Brig. Gen. THOMAS A. ROWLEY
Maj. Gen. ABNER DOUBLEDAY

First Brigade	*Second Brigade*
Col. CHAPMAN BIDDLE	Col. ROY STONE
Brig. Gen. THOMAS A. ROWLEY	Col. LANGHORNE WISTER
Col. CHAPMAN BIDDLE	Col. EDMUND L. DANA
80th New York (20th Militia)	143d Pennsylvania
121st Pennsylvania	149th Pennsylvania
142d Pennsylvania	150th Pennsylvania
151st Pennsylvania	

Third Brigade

Brig. Gen. GEORGE J. STANNARD
Col. FRANCIS V. RANDALL

13th Vermont
14th Vermont
16th Vermont

ARTILLERY BRIGADE

Col. CHARLES S. WAINWRIGHT
Maine Light, 2d Battery (B)

Maine Light, 5th Battery (E)
1st New York Light, Battery L and E
1st Pennsylvania Light, Battery B
4th United States, Battery B

SECOND ARMY CORPS

Maj. Gen. WINFIELD S. HANCOCK
Brig. Gen. JOHN GIBBON
Maj. Gen. WINFIELD S. HANCOCK

GENERAL HEADQUARTERS

6th New York Cavalry, Companies D and K

FIRST DIVISION

Brig. Gen. JOHN C. CALDWELL

First Brigade	*Third Brigade*
Col. EDWARD E. CROSS	Brig. Gen. SAMUEL K. ZOOK
Col. H. BOYD McKEEN	Lieut. Col. JOHN FRASER
5th New Hampshire	52d New York
61st New York	57th New York
81st Pennsylvania	66th New York
148th Pennsylvania	140th Pennsylvania
Second Brigade	*Fourth Brigade*
Col. PATRICK KELLY	Col. JOHN R. BROOKE
28th Massachusetts	27th Connecticut (two companies)
63d New York (two companies)	2d Delaware
69th New York (two companies)	64th New York
88th New York (two companies)	53d Pennsylvania
116th Pennsylvania (four companies)	145th Pennsylvania (seven companies)

SECOND DIVISION

Brig. Gen. JOHN GIBBON
Brig. Gen. WILLIAM HARROW
Brig. Gen. JOHN GIBBON

First Brigade	*Second Brigade*
Brig. Gen. WILLIAM HARROW	Brig. Gen. ALEXANDER S. WEBB
Col. FRANCIS E. HEATH	
19th Maine	69th Pennsylvania
15th Massachusetts	71st Pennsylvania
1st Minnesota and 2d Company	72d Pennsylvania
Minnesota Sharpshooters	106th Pennsylvania
82d New York (2d Militia)	

Third Brigade	*Unattached*
Col. Norman J. Hall	
19th Massachusetts	Massachusetts Sharpshooters, 1st
20th Massachusetts	Company
7th Michigan	
42d New York	
59th New York (four companies)	

THIRD DIVISION

Brig. Gen. Alexander Hays

First Brigade	*Second Brigade*
Col. Samuel S. Carroll	Col. Thomas A. Smyth
	Lieut. Col. Francis E. Pierce
14th Indiana	14th Connecticut
4th Ohio	1st Delaware
8th Ohio	12th New Jersey
7th West Virginia	10th New York (battalion)
	108th New York

Third Brigade

Col. George L. Willard
Col. Eliakim Sherrill
Lieut. Col. James M. Bull

39th New York (four companies)
111th New York
125th New York
126th New York

ARTILLERY BRIGADE

Capt. John G. Hazard

1st New York Light, Battery B and 14th New York Battery
1st Rhode Island Light, Battery A
1st Rhode Island Light, Battery B
1st United States, Battery I
4th United States, Battery A

THIRD ARMY CORPS

Maj. Gen. Daniel E. Sickles
Maj. Gen. David B. Birney

FIRST DIVISION

Maj. Gen. David B. Birney
Brig. Gen. J. H. Hobart Ward

578

First Brigade

Brig. Gen. CHARLES K. GRAHAM
Col. ANDREW H. TIPPIN

57th Pennsylvania (eight companies)
63d Pennsylvania
68th Pennsylvania
105th Pennsylvania
114th Pennsylvania
141st Pennsylvania

Second Brigade

Brig. Gen. J. H. HOBART WARD
Col. HIRAM BERDAN

20th Indiana
3d Maine
4th Maine
86th New York
124th New York
99th Pennsylvania
1st United States Sharpshooters
2d United States Sharpshooters
(eight companies)

Third Brigade

Col. P. REGIS DE TROBRIAND

17th Maine
3d Michigan
5th Michigan
40th New York
110th Pennsylvania (six companies)

SECOND DIVISION

Brig. Gen. ANDREW A. HUMPHREYS

First Brigade

Brig. Gen. JOSEPH B. CARR

1st Massachusetts
11th Massachusetts
16th Massachusetts
12th New Hampshire
11th New Jersey
26th Pennsylvania

Second Brigade

Col. WILLIAM R. BREWSTER

70th New York
71st New York
72d New York
73d New York
74th New York
120th New York

Third Brigade

Col. GEORGE C. BURLING

2d New Hampshire
5th New Jersey
6th New Jersey
7th New Jersey
8th New Jersey
115th Pennsylvania

ARTILLERY BRIGADE

Capt. GEORGE E. RANDOLPH
Capt. A. JUDSON CLARK

New Jersey Light, 2d Battery
1st New York Light, Battery D

New York Light, 4th Battery
1st Rhode Island Light, Battery E
4th United States, Battery K

FIFTH ARMY CORPS

Maj. Gen. GEORGE SYKES

GENERAL HEADQUARTERS

12th New York Infantry, Companies D and E
17th Pennsylvania Cavalry, Companies D and H

FIRST DIVISION

Brig. Gen. JAMES BARNES

First Brigade	*Second Brigade*
Col. WILLIAM S. TILTON	Col. JACOB B. SWEITZER
18th Massachusetts	9th Massachusetts
22d Massachusetts	32d Massachusetts
1st Michigan	4th Michigan
118th Pennsylvania	62d Pennsylvania

Third Brigade

Col. STRONG VINCENT
Col. JAMES C. RICE

20th Maine
16th Michigan
44th New York
83d Pennsylvania

SECOND DIVISION

Brig. Gen. ROMEYN B. AYRES

First Brigade	*Second Brigade*
Col. HANNIBAL DAY	Col. SIDNEY BURBANK
3d United States (six companies)	2d United States (six companies)
4th United States (four companies)	7th United States (four companies)
6th United States (five companies)	10th United States (three companies)
12th United States (eight companies)	11th United States (six companies)
14th United States (eight companies)	17th United States (seven companies)

Third Brigade

Brig. Gen. STEPHEN H. WEED
Col. KENNER GARRARD

140th New York
146th New York

91st Pennsylvania
155th Pennsylvania

THIRD DIVISION

Brig. Gen. SAMUEL W. CRAWFORD

First Brigade	*Third Brigade*
Col. WILLIAM McCANDLESS	Col. JOSEPH W. FISHER
1st Pennsylvania Reserves (nine companies)	5th Pennsylvania Reserves
2d Pennsylvania Reserves	9th Pennsylvania Reserves
6th Pennsylvania Reserves	10th Pennsylvania Reserves
13th Pennsylvania Reserves	11th Pennsylvania Reserves
	12th Pennsylvania Reserves (nine companies)

ARTILLERY BRIGADE

Capt. AUGUSTUS P. MARTIN

Massachusetts Light, 3d Battery (C)
1st New York Light, Battery C
1st Ohio Light, Battery L
5th United States, Battery D
5th United States, Battery I

SIXTH ARMY CORPS

Maj. Gen. JOHN SEDGWICK

GENERAL HEADQUARTERS

1st New Jersey Cavalry, Company L
1st Pennsylvania Cavalry, Company H

FIRST DIVISION

Brig. Gen. HORATIO G. WRIGHT

PROVOST GUARD

4th New Jersey (three companies)

First Brigade	*Second Brigade*
Brig. Gen. A. T. A. TORBERT	Brig. Gen. JOSEPH J. BARTLETT
1st New Jersey	5th Maine
2d New Jersey	121st New York
3d New Jersey	95th Pennsylvania
15th New Jersey	96th Pennsylvania

Third Brigade

Brig. Gen. DAVID A. RUSSELL

6th Maine
49th Pennsylvania (four companies)
119th Pennsylvania
5th Wisconsin

SECOND DIVISION

Brig. Gen. ALBION P. HOWE

Second Brigade	*Third Brigade*
Col. LEWIS A. GRANT	Brig. Gen. THOMAS H. NEILL
2d Vermont	7th Maine (six companies)
3d Vermont	33d New York (detachment)
4th Vermont	43d New York
5th Vermont	49th New York
6th Vermont	77th New York
	61st Pennsylvania

THIRD DIVISION

Maj. Gen. JOHN NEWTON
Brig. Gen. FRANK WHEATON

First Brigade	*Second Brigade*
Brig. Gen. ALEXANDER SHALER	Col. HENRY L. EUSTIS
65th New York	7th Massachusetts
67th New York	10th Massachusetts
122d New York	37th Massachusetts
23d Pennsylvania	2d Rhode Island
82d Pennsylvania	

Third Brigade

Brig. Gen. FRANK WHEATON
Col. DAVID J. NEVIN

62d New York
93d Pennsylvania
98th Pennsylvania
139th Pennsylvania

ARTILLERY BRIGADE

Col. CHARLES H. TOMPKINS

Massachusetts Light, 1st Battery (A)
New York Light, 1st Battery
New York Light, 3d Battery

1st Rhode Island Light, Battery C
1st Rhode Island Light, Battery G
2d United States, Battery D
2d United States, Battery G
5th United States, Battery F

ELEVENTH ARMY CORPS

Maj. Gen. OLIVER O. HOWARD
Maj. Gen. CARL SCHURZ
Maj. Gen. OLIVER O. HOWARD

GENERAL HEADQUARTERS

1st Indiana Cavalry, Companies I and K
8th New York Infantry (one company)

FIRST DIVISION

Brig. Gen. FRANCIS C. BARLOW
Brig. Gen. ADELBERT AMES

First Brigade	*Second Brigade*
Col. LEOPOLD VON GILSA	Brig. Gen. ADELBERT AMES Col. ANDREW L. HARRIS
41st New York (nine companies) 54th New York 68th New York 153d Pennsylvania	17th Connecticut 25th Ohio 75th Ohio 107th Ohio

SECOND DIVISION

Brig. Gen. ADOLPH VON STEINWEHR

First Brigade	*Second Brigade*
Col. CHARLES R. COSTER	Col. ORLAND SMITH
134th New York 154th New York 27th Pennsylvania 73d Pennsylvania	33d Massachusetts 136th New York 55th Ohio 73d Ohio

THIRD DIVISION

Maj. Gen. CARL SCHURZ
Brig. Gen. ALEX. SCHIMMELFENNIG
Maj. Gen. CARL SCHURZ

First Brigade	*Second Brigade*
Brig. Gen. ALEX. SCHIMMELFENNIG Col. GEORGE VON AMSBERG	Col. W. KRZYZANOWSKI

82d Illinois	58th New York
45th New York	119th New York
157th New York	82d Ohio
61st Ohio	75th Pennsylvania
74th Pennsylvania	26th Wisconsin

ARTILLERY BRIGADE

Maj. THOMAS W. OSBORN

1st New York Light, Battery I
New York Light, 13th Battery
1st Ohio Light, Battery I
1st Ohio Light, Battery K
4th United States, Battery G

TWELFTH ARMY CORPS

Maj. Gen. HENRY W. SLOCUM
Brig. Gen. ALPHEUS S. WILLIAMS

PROVOST GUARD

10th Maine (four companies)

FIRST DIVISION

Brig. Gen. ALPHEUS S. WILLIAMS
Brig. Gen. THOMAS H. RUGER

First Brigade	*Second Brigade*
Col. ARCHIBALD L. McDOUGALL	Brig. Gen. HENRY H. LOCKWOOD
5th Connecticut	1st Maryland, Potomac Home Brigade
20th Connecticut	1st Maryland, Eastern Shore
3d Maryland	150th New York
123d New York	
145th New York	
46th Pennsylvania	

Third Brigade

Brig. Gen. THOMAS H. RUGER
Col. SILAS COLGROVE

27th Indiana
2d Massachusetts
13th New Jersey
107th New York
3d Wisconsin

SECOND DIVISION

Brig. Gen. JOHN W. GEARY

584

First Brigade

Col. CHARLES CANDY

5th Ohio
7th Ohio
29th Ohio
66th Ohio
28th Pennsylvania
147th Pennsylvania (eight companies)

Second Brigade

Col. GEORGE A. COBHAM, JR.
Brig. Gen. THOMAS L. KANE
Col. GEORGE A. COBHAM, JR.

29th Pennsylvania
109th Pennsylvania
111th Pennsylvania

Third Brigade

Brig. Gen. GEORGE S. GREENE

60th New York
78th New York
102d New York
137th New York
149th New York

ARTILLERY BRIGADE

Lieut. EDWARD D. MUHLENBERG

1st New York Light, Battery M
Pennsylvania Light, Battery E
4th United States, Battery F
5th United States, Battery K

CAVALRY CORPS

Maj. Gen. ALFRED PLEASONTON

FIRST DIVISION

Brig. Gen. JOHN BUFORD

First Brigade

Col. WILLIAM GAMBLE

8th Illinois
12th Illinois (four companies)
3d Indiana (six companies)
8th New York

Second Brigade

Col. THOMAS C. DEVIN

6th New York
9th New York
17th Pennsylvania
3d West Virginia (two companies)

Reserve Brigade

Brig. Gen. WESLEY MERRITT

6th Pennsylvania
1st United States
2d United States
5th United States
6th United States

OFFICIAL ROSTERS

SECOND DIVISION

Brig. Gen. DAVID MCM. GREGG

Headquarters Guard
1st Ohio, Company A

First Brigade

Col. JOHN B. McINTOSH

1st Maryland (eleven companies)
Purnell (Maryland) Legion, Company A
1st Massachusetts
1st New Jersey
1st Pennsylvania
3d Pennsylvania
3d Pennsylvania Artillery, Section
  Battery H

Third Brigade

Col. J. IRVIN GREGG

1st Maine (ten companies)
10th New York
4th Pennsylvania
16th Pennsylvania

THIRD DIVISION

Brig. Gen. JUDSON KILPATRICK

Headquarters Guard
1st Ohio, Company C

First Brigade

Brig. Gen. ELON J. FARNSWORTH
Col. NATHANIEL P. RICHMOND

5th New York
18th Pennsylvania
1st Vermont
1st West Virginia (ten companies)

Second Brigade

Brig. Gen. GEORGE A. CUSTER

1st Michigan
5th Michigan
6th Michigan
7th Michigan (ten companies)

HORSE ARTILLERY

First Brigade

Capt. JAMES M. ROBERTSON

9th Michigan Battery
6th New York Battery
2d United States, Batteries B and L
2d United States, Battery M
4th United States, Battery E

Second Brigade

Capt. JOHN C. TIDBALL

1st United States, Batteries E and G
1st United States, Battery K
2d United States, Battery A

ARTILLERY RESERVE

Brig. Gen. ROBERT O. TYLER
Capt. JAMES M. ROBERTSON

Headquarters Guard
32d Massachusetts Infantry, Company C

586

First Regular Brigade

Capt. DUNBAR R. RANSOM

1st United States, Battery H
3d United States, Batteries F and K
4th United States, Battery C
5th United States, Battery C

Second Volunteer Brigade

Capt. ELIJAH D. TAFT

Connecticut Light, 2d Battery
New York Light, 5th Battery

First Volunteer Brigade

Lieut. Col. FREEMAN McGILVERY

Massachusetts Light, 5th Battery (E) and
  10th New York Battery
Massachusetts Light, 9th Battery
New York Light, 15th Battery
Pennsylvania Light, Batteries C and F

Third Volunteer Brigade

Capt. JAMES F. HUNTINGTON

New Hampshire Light, 1st Battery
1st Ohio Light, Battery H
1st Pennsylvania Light, Batteries F and G
West Virginia Light, Battery C

Fourth Volunteer Brigade

Capt. ROBERT H. FITZHUGH

Maine Light, 6th Battery (F)
Maryland Light, Battery A
New Jersey Light, 1st Battery
1st New York Light, Battery G
1st New York Light, Battery K and 11th New York Battery

Train Guard

4th New Jersey Infantry (seven companies)

UNITS OF THE ARMY OF NORTHERN VIRGINIA, C. S. A., AT THE BATTLE OF GETTYSBURG, JULY 1–3, 1863

Gen. ROBERT E. LEE, commanding

ARMY HEADQUARTERS

Col. R. H. CHILTON, chief of staff and inspector general
Brig. Gen. W. N. PENDLETON, chief of artillery
Dr. LAFAYETTE GUILD, medical director
Lt. Col. BRISCOE G. BALDWIN, chief of ordnance
Lt. Col. ROBERT G. COLE, chief of commissary
Lt. Col. JAMES L. CORLEY, chief quartermaster
Maj. H. E. YOUNG, judge advocate general
Col. A. L. LONG, military secretary and acting assistant chief of artillery
Lt. Col. WALTER H. TAYLOR, aide de camp and assistant adjutant general
Maj. CHARLES MARSHALL, aide de camp and assistant military secretary
Maj. CHARLES S. VENABLE, aide de camp and assistant inspector general
Capt. S. R. JOHNSTON, engineer

FIRST ARMY CORPS

Lieut. Gen. JAMES LONGSTREET

MCLAWS' DIVISION

Maj. Gen. LAFAYETTE MCLAWS

Kershaw's Brigade	*Semmes' Brigade*
Brig. Gen. J. B. KERSHAW	Brig. Gen. P. J. SEMMES
	Col. GOODE BRYAN
2d South Carolina	10th Georgia
3d South Carolina	50th Georgia
7th South Carolina	51st Georgia
8th South Carolina	53d Georgia
15th South Carolina	
3d South Carolina Battalion	

Barksdale's Brigade	*Wofford's Brigade*
Brig. Gen. WILLIAM BARKSDALE	Brig. Gen. W. T. WOFFORD
Col. B. G. HUMPHREYS	
	16th Georgia
13th Mississippi	18th Georgia
17th Mississippi	24th Georgia
18th Mississippi	Cobb's (Georgia) Legion
21st Mississippi	Phillips (Georgia) Legion

Artillery

Col. H. C. CABELL

1st North Carolina Artillery, Battery A
Pulaski (Georgia) Artillery
1st Richmond Howitzers
Troup (Georgia) Artillery

PICKETT'S DIVISION

Maj. Gen. GEORGE E. PICKETT

Garnett's Brigade	*Kemper's Brigade*
Brig. Gen. R. B. GARNETT	Brig. Gen. J. L. KEMPER
Maj. C. S. PEYTON	Col. JOSEPH MAYO, Jr.
8th Virginia	1st Virginia
18th Virginia	3d Virginia
19th Virginia	7th Virginia
28th Virginia	11th Virginia
56th Virginia	24th Virginia

Armistead's Brigade

Brig. Gen. L. A. ARMISTEAD
Col. W. R. AYLETT

9th Virginia
14th Virginia
38th Virginia
53d Virginia
57th Virginia

Artillery

Maj. JAMES DEARING

Fauquier (Virginia) Artillery
Hampden (Virginia) Artillery
Richmond Fayette Artillery
Virginia Battery

HOOD'S DIVISION

Maj. Gen. JOHN B. HOOD
Brig. Gen. E. M. LAW

Law's Brigade	*Robertson's Brigade*
Brig. Gen. E. M. LAW	Brig. Gen. J. B. ROBERTSON
Col. JAMES L. SHEFFIELD	
4th Alabama	3d Arkansas
15th Alabama	1st Texas
44th Alabama	4th Texas
47th Alabama	5th Texas
48th Alabama	

Anderson's Brigade	*Benning's Brigade*
Brig. Gen. GEORGE T. ANDERSON	Brig. Gen. HENRY L. BENNING
Lieut. Col. WILLIAM LUFFMAN	
7th Georgia	2d Georgia
8th Georgia	15th Georgia
9th Georgia	17th Georgia
11th Georgia	20th Georgia
59th Georgia	

Artillery

Maj. M. W. HENRY

Branch (North Carolina) Artillery
German (South Carolina) Artillery
Palmetto (South Carolina) Light Artillery
Rowan (North Carolina) Artillery

ARTILLERY RESERVE

Col. J. B. WALTON

Alexander's Battalion	*Washington (Louisiana) Artillery*
Col. E. P. ALEXANDER	Maj. B. F. ESHLEMAN

Ashland (Virginia) Artillery	First Company
Bedford (Virginia) Artillery	Second Company
Brooks (South Carolina) Artillery	Third Company
Madison (Louisiana) Light Artillery	Fourth Company
Virginia Battery	
Virginia Battery	

SECOND ARMY CORPS

Lieut. Gen. RICHARD S. EWELL

Escort

Randolph's Company Virginia Cavalry

EARLY'S DIVISION

Maj. Gen. JUBAL A. EARLY

Hays's Brigade	*Smith's Brigade*
Brig. Gen. HARRY T. HAYS	Brig. Gen. WILLIAM SMITH
5th Louisiana	31st Virginia
6th Louisiana	49th Virginia
7th Louisiana	52d Virginia
8th Louisiana	
9th Louisiana	

Hoke's Brigade	*Gordon's Brigade*
Col. ISAAC E. AVERY	Brig. Gen. J. B. GORDON
Col. A. C. GODWIN	
6th North Carolina	13th Georgia
21st North Carolina	26th Georgia
57th North Carolina	31st Georgia
	38th Georgia
	60th Georgia
	61st Georgia

Artillery

Lieut. Col. H. P. JONES

Charlottesville (Virginia) Artillery
Courtney (Virginia) Artillery
Louisiana Guard Artillery
Staunton (Virginia) Artillery

JOHNSON'S DIVISION

Maj. Gen. EDWARD JOHNSON

Steuart's Brigade	*Nicholls' Brigade*
Brig. Gen. GEORGE H. STEUART	Col. J. M. WILLIAMS
1st Maryland Battalion Infantry	1st Louisiana
1st North Carolina	2d Louisiana

3d North Carolina
10th Virginia
23d Virginia
37th Virginia

10th Louisiana
14th Louisiana
15th Louisiana

Stonewall's Brigade

Jones's Brigade

Brig. Gen. JAMES A. WALKER

Brig. Gen. JOHN M. JONES
Lieut. Col. R. H. DUNGAN

2d Virginia
4th Virginia
5th Virginia
27th Virginia
33d Virginia

21st Virginia
25th Virginia
42d Virginia
44th Virginia
48th Virginia
50th Virginia

Artillery

Maj. J. W. LATIMER
Capt. C. I. RAINE

1st Maryland Battery
Alleghany (Virginia) Artillery
Chesapeake (Maryland) Artillery
Lee (Virginia) Battery

RODES'S DIVISION

Maj. Gen. R. E. RODES

Daniel's Brigade

Iverson's Brigade

Brig. Gen. JUNIUS DANIEL

Brig. Gen. ALFRED IVERSON

32d North Carolina
43d North Carolina
45th North Carolina
53d North Carolina
2d North Carolina Battalion

5th North Carolina
12th North Carolina
20th North Carolina
23d North Carolina

Doles's Brigade

Ramseur's Brigade

Brig. Gen. GEORGE DOLES

Brig. Gen. S. D. RAMSEUR

4th Georgia
12th Georgia
21st Georgia
44th Georgia

2d North Carolina
4th North Carolina
14th North Carolina
30th North Carolina

O'Neal's Brigade

Col. E. A. O'NEAL

3d Alabama
5th Alabama
6th Alabama

12th Alabama
26th Alabama

Artillery

Lieut. Col. THOMAS H. CARTER

Jeff. Davis (Alabama) Artillery
King William (Virginia) Artillery
Morris (Virginia) Artillery
Orange (Virginia) Artillery

ARTILLERY RESERVE

Col. J. THOMPSON BROWN

First Virginia Artillery	*Nelson's Battalion*
Capt. WILLIS J. DANCE	Lieut. Col. WILLIAM NELSON
2d Richmond (Virginia) Howitzers 3d Richmond (Virginia) Howitzers Powhatan (Virginia) Artillery Rockbridge (Virginia) Artillery Salem (Virginia) Artillery	Amherst (Virginia) Artillery Fluvanna (Virginia) Artillery Georgia Battery

THIRD ARMY CORPS

Lieut. Gen. AMBROSE P. HILL

ANDERSON'S DIVISION

Maj. Gen. R. H. ANDERSON

Wilcox's Brigade	*Wright's Brigade*
Brig. Gen. CADMUS M. WILCOX	Brig. Gen. A. R. WRIGHT Col. WILLIAM GIBSON Brig. Gen. A. R. WRIGHT
8th Alabama 9th Alabama 10th Alabama 11th Alabama 14th Alabama	3d Georgia 22d Georgia 48th Georgia 2d Georgia Battalion
Mahone's Brigade	*Perry's Brigade*
Brig. Gen. WILLIAM MAHONE	Col. DAVID LANG
6th Virginia 12th Virginia 16th Virginia 41st Virginia 61st Virginia	2d Florida 5th Florida 8th Florida

OFFICIAL ROSTERS

Posey's Brigade

Brig. Gen. CARNOT POSEY

12th Mississippi
16th Mississippi
19th Mississippi
48th Mississippi

Artillery (Sumter Battalion)

Maj. JOHN LANE

Company A
Company B
Company C

HETH'S DIVISION

Maj. Gen. HENRY HETH
Brig. Gen. J. J. PETTIGREW

First Brigade	*Third Brigade*
Brig. Gen. J. J. PETTIGREW	Brig. Gen. JAMES J. ARCHER
Col. J. K. MARSHALL	Col. B. D. FRY
	Lieut. Col. S. G. SHEPARD
11th North Carolina	13th Alabama
26th North Carolina	5th Alabama Battalion
47th North Carolina	1st Tennessee (Provisional Army)
52d North Carolina	7th Tennessee
	14th Tennessee
Second Brigade	*Fourth Brigade*
Col. J. M. BROCKENBROUGH	Brig. Gen. JOSEPH R. DAVIS
40th Virginia	2d Mississippi
47th Virginia	11th Mississippi
55th Virginia	42d Mississippi
22d Virginia Battalion	55th North Carolina

Artillery

Lieut. Col. JOHN J. GARNETT

Donaldsonville (Louisiana) Artillery
Huger (Virginia) Artillery
Lewis (Virginia) Artillery
Norfolk Light Artillery Blues

PENDER'S DIVISION

Maj. Gen. WILLIAM D. PENDER
Brig. Gen. JAMES H. LANE

Maj. Gen. I. R. TRIMBLE
Brig. Gen. JAMES H. LANE

First Brigade

Col. ABNER PERRIN

Third Brigade

Brig. Gen. EDWARD L. THOMAS

1st South Carolina (Provisional Army)	14th Georgia
1st South Carolina Rifles	35th Georgia
12th South Carolina	45th Georgia
13th South Carolina	49th Georgia
14th South Carolina	

Second Brigade

Brig. Gen. JAMES H. LANE
Col. C. M. AVERY
Brig. Gen. JAMES H. LANE
Col. C. M. AVERY

Fourth Brigade

Brig. Gen. A. M. SCALES
Lieut. Col. G. T. GORDON
Col. W. LEE J. LOWRANCE

7th North Carolina	13th North Carolina
18th North Carolina	16th North Carolina
28th North Carolina	22d North Carolina
33d North Carolina	34th North Carolina
37th North Carolina	38th North Carolina

Artillery

Maj. WILLIAM T. POAGUE

Albemarle (Virginia) Artillery
Charlotte (North Carolina) Artillery
Madison (Mississippi) Light Artillery
Virginia Battery

ARTILLERY RESERVE

Col. R. LINDSAY WALKER

McIntosh's Battalion

Maj. D. G. McINTOSH

Pegram's Battalion

Maj. W. J. PEGRAM
Capt. E. B. BRUNSON

Danville (Virginia) Artillery	Crenshaw (Virginia) Battery
Hardaway (Alabama) Artillery	Fredericksburg (Virginia) Artillery
2d Rockbridge (Virginia) Artillery	Letcher (Virginia) Artillery
Virginia Battery	Pee Dee (South Carolina) Artillery
	Purcell (Virginia) Artillery

CAVALRY

STUART'S DIVISION

Maj. Gen. J. E B. STUART

Hampton's Brigade

Brig. Gen. WADE HAMPTON
Col. L. S. BAKER

1st North Carolina
1st South Carolina
2d South Carolina
Cobb's (Georgia) Legion
Jeff. Davis Legion
Phillips (Georgia) Legion

Robertson's Brigade

Brig. Gen. BEVERLY H. ROBERTSON

4th North Carolina
5th North Carolina

Jones's Brigade

Brig. Gen. WILLIAM E. JONES

6th Virginia
7th Virginia
11th Virginia

Fitz. Lee's Brigade

Brig. Gen. FITZ. LEE

1st Maryland Battalion
1st Virginia
2d Virginia
3d Virginia
4th Virginia
5th Virginia

Jenkins' Brigade

Brig. Gen. A. G. JENKINS
Col. M. J. FERGUSON

14th Virginia
16th Virginia
17th Virginia
34th Virginia Battalion
36th Virginia Battalion
Jackson's (Virginia) Battery

W. H. F. Lee's Brigade

Col. J. R. CHAMBLISS, Jr.

2d North Carolina
9th Virginia
10th Virginia
13th Virginia

Stuart Horse Artillery

Maj. R. F. BECKHAM

Breathed's (Virginia) Battery
Chew's (Virginia) Battery
Griffin's (Maryland) Battery
Hart's (South Carolina) Battery
McGregor's (Virginia) Battery
Moorman's (Virginia) Battery

IMBODEN'S COMMAND

Brig. Gen. J. D. IMBODEN

18th Virginia Cavalry
62d Virginia Infantry, Mounted
Virginia Partisan Rangers
Virginia Battery

595

List of Abbreviations

Alpheus Williams Letters   Milo M. Quaife, ed., *From the Cannon's Mouth, The Civil War Letters of General Alpheus S. Williams*, Detroit, 1959.

Annals   *The Annals of the War, Written by Leading Participants, North and South*, Philadelphia, 1879.

B&L   *Battles and Leaders of the Civil War*, Robert U. Johnson and Clarence C. Buel, eds., 4 vols., New York, 1884–1888.

Bachelder Papers   John B. Bachelder Papers, New Hampshire Historical Society.

Bates Collection   Samuel P. Bates Collection, Pennsylvania Division of Public Records, Harrisburg.

CCW, *Report*   U.S. Congress, *Report of the Joint Committee on the Conduct of the War at the Second Session, Thirty-Eighth Congress*. Vol. I, Washington, 1865. *Supplemental Report*, Part 2, Washington, 1866.

CWH   *Civil War History*.

DU   Duke University Library.

HSP   Historical Society of Pennsylvania.

Howard Papers   O. O. Howard Papers, Bowdoin College Library.

LC   Library of Congress.

Longstreet, *Memoirs*   Longstreet, James, *From Manassas to Appomattox, Memoirs of the Civil War in America*, Philadelphia, 1896.

MHS   Massachusetts Historical Society.

MOLLUS   Military Order of the Loyal Legion of the United States.

NA   National Archives.

NYHS   New York Historical Society.

OR   *The War of the Rebellion: A Compilation of the Official Records of the Union and Confederate Armies* (unless otherwise noted, assumed to be Series I), Washington, 1880–1901.

PDMA, PDPR	Pennsylvania Department of Military Affairs, Pennsylvania Division of Public Records.
PMHB	*Pennsylvania Magazine of History and Biography.*
PU	Princeton University Library.
SHSP	*Southern Historical Society Papers,* 50 vols., Richmond.
UNC	*Southern Historical Collection,* University of North Carolina Library.
UV	University of Virginia Library.
VHS	Virginia Historical Society.
Wainwright Journals	Allan Nevins, ed., *A Diary of Battle, The Personal Journal of Colonel Charles S. Wainwright, 1861–1865,* New York, 1962.
Webb Collection	Alexander S. Webb Collection, Yale University Library.
YU	Yale University Library.

Notes

1. Entry for May 26, 1863, quoted in Edward Younger, ed., *Inside the Confederate Government, The Diary of Robert Garlick Hill Kean* (New York, 1957), 66.

2. See Archer Jones, *Confederate Strategy from Shiloh to Vicksburg* (Baton Rouge, La., 1961) for a detailed analysis of the military problems confronting Confederate leaders and their efforts to solve them. For a discussion of the grand strategy leading to the Gettysburg campaign Chap. XI is particularly important.

3. *The War of the Rebellion: A Compilation of the Official Records of the Union and Confederate Armies* (Washington, D. C., 1880–1901), Ser. I, Vol. XXV, pt. 2, pp. 700, 713, 725–726 (cited hereafter as *OR* and unless otherwise noted assumed to be Series I).

4. Pender wrote to his wife on June 28, 1863, that "Gen. Lee intimates to no one what he is up to, & we can only surmise." William D. Pender Papers, Southern Historical Collection, University of North Carolina Library (cited hereafter as UNC). See also Younger, ed., *Inside the Confederate Government*, 75. Lee wrote to Seddon on June 13, 1863, that he thought the enemy had been "mystified" as to his movements until the "publication" of his dispatch to the War Dept. about the cavalry fight on the 9th and the "comments and assertions" of some of the Richmond papers. *OR*, XXVII, pt. 3, p. 886. After the war Gen. Longstreet said in his memoirs that Lee's early experience with Richmond authorities had made him overly cautious in disclosing his views. Less than frank presumably even with the President, Lee failed to convey to them a clear idea of his intentions. As a result, Longstreet claimed, they allowed the importunities of commanders in other areas to hold back forces which Lee needed for his grand design in the summer of 1863. James Longstreet, *From Manassas to Appomattox, Memoirs of the Civil War in America* (Philadelphia, 1896), 336–337 (cited hereafter as Longstreet, *Memoirs*). This criticism of Lee was Longstreet's way of explaining why the strength of the Army of Northern Virginia was not as great as it should have been for the invasion of Pa. It contains an element of truth, but reduces a complex military situation to the simpler one of personal relations between Lee and Davis. Though Davis did not always understand at first what Lee wanted, these two

599

leaders had frank exchanges of view. Lee might not have volunteered information as readily as he should, but there is no doubt that he would make an honest answer to a point-blank question if Davis asked him one.

5. John H. Reagan, *Memoirs with Special Reference to Secession and the Civil War* (New York, 1906), 150–153; Rembert W. Patrick, *Jefferson Davis and His Cabinet* (Baton Rouge, La., 1944), 137–138; Douglas S. Freeman, *R. E. Lee, A Biography* (New York, 1935), III, 19; *OR*, XXV, pt. 2, p. 783. Longstreet charged that the authorities did not comprehend the strategic opportunities of utilizing the Confederacy's interior lines. This is not true. Seddon was quite aware of them, but Lee felt the advantage of using them was not as great as it seemed, owing probably to the poor condition of Southern railroads. See *Ibid.*, pp. 708, 713–714.

6. *Ibid.*, p. 842.

7. *Ibid.*, pp. 831–833; XVIII, pp. 1071, 1074–1077.

8. *Ibid.*, XXV, pt. 2, p. 842.

9. *Ibid.*, XXVII, pt. 2, p. 305. Lee wrote a preliminary report on July 31, 1863. His final and official report, which was completed in Jan., 1864, was even more concise than the first one, but in one respect it was more definite. Instead of making vague references to possible "military success," presumably north of the Potomac River, Lee mentioned the "valuable results which might be expected to follow a decided advantage gained over the enemy in Maryland or Pennsylvania." The final report on the other hand omitted two rather important points which had been included in the preliminary one. Taking advantage of hindsight, Lee made no reference to relieving enemy pressure along the coast, a result he had predicted would occur should he undertake a northern invasion, as he had found that his prediction was a poor one. Some of the Federal forces were withdrawn from the coast to reinforce the Army of the Potomac but not until after the battle. Federal attacks against Charleston actually stepped up in August, rather than becoming less. The second statement Lee deleted from his final report concerned "other important considerations" that had impelled him to assume the offensive in the first place. He did not mention them. In neither report did he say anything about loosening Grant's grip on Vicksburg or preventing any move by Rosecrans against Bragg. *Ibid.*, p. 313.

10. Armistead L. Long, *Memoirs of Robert E. Lee* (New York, 1886), 268; Sir Frederick Maurice, ed., *An Aide-de-Camp of Lee, Being the Papers of Colonel Charles Marshall, Sometime Aide-de-Camp, Military Secretary, and Assistant Adjutant General on the Staff of Robert E. Lee, 1862–1865* (Boston, 1927), 185–186.

11. Memorandum Book, Entry for Feb. 23, 1863, Jedediah Hotchkiss Papers, Library of Congress (cited hereafter as LC). Hotchkiss finished the project Mar. 10. E. P. Alexander in his *Military Memoirs of a Confederate Artillery Officer* (New York, 1907), 322 note, refers to Hotchkiss' work as a "remarkable map" of the country from Winchester to the Susquehanna, compiled from country maps of Md., Va., and Pa. It was on a large scale and noted the location of farmhouses and the names of their occupants. Lee used it during the

Gettysburg campaign, and it is reproduced on a smaller scale in *OR Atlas*, Plate CVVI. At the time of the Gettysburg campaign Hotchkiss was still a civilian. Later he became a captain in the Confederate army. Wilbur S. Nye, *Here Come the Rebels!* (Baton Rouge, La., 1965), 368, 12 note.

12. Long, *Memoirs of Lee*, 267–269; Maurice, ed., *Aide-de-Camp of Lee*, 182–188, 250–252; I. R. Trimble to Bachelder, Feb. 8, 1883, Typescript, John B. Bachelder Papers, New Hampshire Historical Society (cited hereafter as Bachelder Papers); Justus Scheibert, *Seven Months in the Rebel States during the North American War, 1863*, Joseph C. Hayes, trans., William Stanley Hoole, ed. (Tuscaloosa, Ala., 1958), 98–99, 117–118; William Allan, "The Strategy of the Gettysburg Campaign. Objects, Progress, Results," *Campaigns in Virginia, Maryland and Pennsylvania, 1862–1863* (Papers of the Military Historical Society of Massachusetts, Boston, 1903), III, 415–448; Walter H. Taylor, "The Campaign in Pennsylvania," *The Annals of the War, Written by Leading Participants, North and South* (Philadelphia, 1879), 305 (cited hereafter as *Annals*). There seems to be a basic contradiction in the testimony of these writers; some talked about Lee's wish to avoid battle in Pa., and others stressed the importance of a Confederate victory in the area north of the Potomac. It can be resolved only by assuming that they meant that Lee would try to gain his objectives without a major battle and fight one only as a last resort. The phrase "military success" which Lee used has many different shades of meaning, but it does not necessarily include a major victory. As for Gettysburg as a possible battleground should an engagement occur, both Gens. Long and Trimble noted that Lee talked to them about it.

13. Quoted in Maurice, ed., *Aide-de-Camp of Lee*, 186.

14. James Longstreet, "Lee in Pennsylvania," *Annals*, 417. For substantially the same account see also Longstreet, "Lee's Invasion of Pennsylvania," *Battles and Leaders of the Civil War*, Robert U. Johnson and Clarence C. Buel, eds. (New York, 1888), III, 245–247 (cited hereafter as *B&L*); Longstreet, *Memoirs*, 330–331. In none of these accounts did Longstreet say that Lee "promised" to employ "defensive tactics." William Swinton used the word in his *Campaigns of the Army of the Potomac* (New York, 1866), 340. In a footnote on the same page he made the following statement: "This, and subsequent revelations of the purposes and sentiments of Lee, I derive from General Longstreet, who, in a full and free conversation with the writer, after the close of the war, threw much light on the motives and conduct of Lee during this campaign." Longstreet never repudiated Swinton's words, although he did not use them himself in his own accounts. In this way he escaped responsibility for the impression Swinton had created that Lee had made a "promise." There is a species of dishonesty here. Freeman makes somewhat the same point in his discussion of Longstreet's and Swinton's versions of Lee's plans. See *R. E. Lee*, 21 note.

15. Longstreet to Wigfall, May 13, 1863, Correspondence of Louis T. Wigfall, Wigfall Family Papers, LC. In mentioning a letter from Seddon to Lee, Longstreet was probably referring to a dispatch from Seddon on May 9 asking

Lee to consider the desirability of sending troops from his army to reinforce Pemberton. See *OR*, XXV, pt. 2, p. 790. The date of Longstreet's return to Lee's army is uncertain.

Col. William Allan, who had been chief of ordnance in the Second Corps, on Apr. 15, 1868, made a memorandum of a conversation he had just had with Gen. Lee. The general referred to a remark attributed to Longstreet to the effect that Lee had promised him "not to fight a general battle" in Pa. Lee stated he did not think Longstreet ever said this; furthermore, the idea was absurd, and he never made such a promise or thought of so doing. A printed version of the memorandum is in Maurice, ed., *Aide-de-Camp of Lee*, 248–252.

16. *OR*, XXV, pt. 2, pp. 774, 782, 813, 830; Douglas S. Freeman, *Lee's Lieutenants: A Study in Command* (New York, 1943), II, 648–650, 659–665.

17. *OR*, XXV, pt. 2, p. 810.

18. Quoted in J. B. Hood, *Advance and Retreat: Personal Experiences in the United States and Confederate Armies* (New Orleans, 1880), 53.

19. Freeman, *Lee's Lieutenants*, II, 659–666, 689–706; *OR*,. XXV, pt. 2, pp. 787, 810–811, 816, 824–825, 827, 830, 840; Douglas S. Freeman and Grady McWhiney, eds., *Lee's Dispatches, Unpublished Letters of General Robert E. Lee, C. S. A., to Jefferson Davis and the War Department of the Confederate States of America, 1862–65* (New York, 1957), 91–97.

20. Freeman, *Lee's Lieutenants*, II, 712.

21. See *OR*, XXV, pt. 2, p. 830. Lee wrote Adj. Gen. Samuel Cooper, May 28, 1863, that colonels of a N. C. brigade objected to having a Virginian as commander. He suggested that Gen. George H. Steuart, a Marylander and an officer of the old army, be given the brigade, because in a similar instance he had assigned Gen. James Archer, who had also come from Md. with the same military background, to a brigade composed of Ala. and Tenn. regiments. "All difficulties were thus obviated. . . ."

22. *OR*, XXV, pt. 2, pp. 614–619, 625–626, 651. For the table of organization and names of the commanders of the various battalions and batteries see Jennings C. Wise, *The Long Arm of Lee, The History of the Artillery of the Army of Northern Virginia* (New York, 1959), 419–422.

23. Freeman, *Lee's Lieutenants*, II, 589, 592; *OR*, XXV, pt. 1, pp. 822–824, 998–1000; Wise, *Long Arm of Lee*, 548–551.

24. *OR*, XXV, pt. 2, pp. 850–851.

25. G. Moxley Sorrell, *Recollections of a Confederate Staff Officer* (New York, 1917), 121.

26. *OR*, XXV, pt. 2, pp. 837–838, 840, 850–851; Wise, *Long Arm of Lee*, 565–572. Col. (later Gen.) E. P. Alexander, one of the more discerning and objective of the Confederate writers after the war and Longstreet's acting chief of artillery at Gettysburg, wrote that the discontinuance of the Artillery Reserve under Pendleton was due to Confederate poverty of guns, not to dissatisfaction with the system. He added that the "fine service" at Gettysburg by the Federal Reserve of 110 guns under Hunt seemed to "demonstrate the advantage of such

an organization in every large army." Alexander, *Military Memoirs*, 370.

In a letter to A. L. Long many years later the Union Gen. Henry J. Hunt expressed his appreciation of what the Confederates had accomplished in the reorganization of their artillery, "all of which I liked except the name 'battalion,' which is not applicable to artillery, it being an infantry term. . . . You were infinitely better off than we were, as you were allowed '*field officers*'. . . . I see that Gen Pendleton complained *formally* of the injustice of not giving you (sufficient rank) general officers. He was right, not only the artillery of the army, but that of each corps should be commanded by a general officer." Hunt to Long, Oct. 5, 1884, A. L. Long Papers, UNC.

27. Pendleton to his wife, May 14, 1863, William N. Pendleton Papers, UNC; *OR*, XXV, pt. 2, pp. 793, 808–809, 812–813, 828, 837–839; Col. William Allan, "Reminiscences of Field Ordnance Service," *Southern Historical Society Papers*, XIV, 141 (cited hereafter as *SHSP*); Wise, *Long Arm of Lee*, 340–341, 570.

28. *Ibid.*, 571–573; *OR*, XXV, pt. 2, p. 838.

29. Jac Weller, "The Confederate Use of British Cannon," *Civil War History*, III (June, 1957), 150–151 (cited hereafter as *CWH*). Aside from defects in workmanship, Civil War shells proved less lethal than more modern types because, as Weller points out, they were designed to break into only a few pieces, seldom more than six, and the black powder bursting charge did not have sufficient power to cause real destruction.

30. *OR*, XVIII, pp. 1075, 1084, 1088; XXV, pt. 2, pp. 788–790, 804–805, 820–821, 825–828, 836–837; XXVII, pt. 3, pp. 1006–1007. On May 9 Lee explained to Gen. Samuel Jones, commanding the Dept. of Southwestern Va., that he needed more cavalry to stop raiding forces, such as those under the Union Gen. George Stoneman who had been "running wild over the State, cutting our railroads, etc., and even going to within sight of Richmond." *Ibid.*, XXV, pt. 2, p. 789. He did not even hint that he might want to use them for other purposes, such as an offensive move against the North.

In answer to Lee's query about Jenkins, Jones referred to him as a "bold and gallant soldier," but not a "good administrative officer." He believed him capable of great improvement in this respect, but "unfortunately many of his men are his constituents, and he has been a politician . . . and still has aspirations that way." *Ibid.*, p. 804. For a good summary of Lee's efforts to strengthen his cavalry see Freeman, *Lee's Lieutenants*, II, 710–712.

31. *OR*, XXV, pt. 2, p. 820. See also *ibid.*, pp. 681–682, 693, 697, 709, 740–741, 747–749; XXVII, pt. 3, pp. 867–868; Angus J. Johnston, II, *Virginia Railroads in the Civil War* (Chapel Hill, N. C., 1961), 120–156.

Capt. Justus Scheibert, a Prussian observer in Lee's army, in commenting on the condition of Confederate cavalry during the Chancellorsville campaign, said that "the lack of fodder, the rough season, and a disease that the cavalry had brought back from the North on the last expedition threatened to deal the mounted troops a mortal blow, so that after most of the brigades had been dispersed far into the country, General Stuart had with him only two very weak brigades, (Fitz Lee and W. Lee), whose horses, moreover were in a very real sad condition at this time." Scheibert, *Seven Months in the Rebel States,* Hoole, ed., 50.

32. H. B. McClellan, *The Life and Campaigns of Major-General J. E. B. Stuart, Commander of the Cavalry of the Army of Northern Virginia* (Boston and New York, 1885), 257–260; *OR,* XXV, pt. 2, p. 825.

33. Freeman, *Lee's Lieutenants,* II, 709–710; III, 1–5; McClellan, *Campaigns of Stuart,* 261–262; *OR,* XXV, pt. 2, pp. 711–712, 819, 831, 837, 844, 847, 852; XXVII, pt. 2, p. 291. Jenkins' cavalry was not at the review.

Gen. Samuel Jones raised the question of Imboden's status, and Lee quickly told him that Imboden was attached to the Army of Northern Virginia. An idea of the quality of his command can be obtained from its roster, which listed the 18th Va. Cavalry, the 62nd Va. Infantry (mounted), the Va. Partisan Rangers, and the Va. Battery.

Jones was not the only one who was puzzled about the nature and status of Imboden's command. On Oct. 5, 1884, while preparing his articles on Gettysburg for *B&L,* Gen. Hunt wrote to Long that he was "glad to get some idea of what sort of a body Imboden's command was. I never could make out—nor could Col. *Scott* (the 'Rebellion Record' man) who has been trying to place him, and find out what sort of a command he had." A. L. Long Papers, UNC.

34. He made this suggestion as early as May 7 in a letter to Davis on the grounds that "no more [troops] can be needed then this summer than enough to maintain the water batteries. Nor do I think that more will be required at Wilmington than are sufficient for this purpose. If they are kept in their present positions in these departments, they will perish of disease. . . . It will be better to order General Beauregard in with all the forces which can be spared, and to put him in command here, than to keep them there inactive and this army inefficient from paucity of numbers." Lee's exact meaning is not clear in this last sentence, but in view of a later suggestion that he be allowed to use Beauregard and some forces under him as a feint against Washington, this may be the first intimation of the idea. *OR,* XXV, pt. 2, pp. 782–783.

35. *OR,* XVIII, p. 1063; LI, pt. 2, p. 720.

36. *Ibid.,* XVIII, p. 1063.

37. *Ibid.,* p. 1066. On May 11 Lee had written Davis that certain Northern papers, the *Washington Chronicle,* the *New York Herald,* and the *New York World,* had said "positively" that the administration was going to reinforce Hooker's army. The *World* "represents that General Heintzelman is ordered to re-enforce it with 30,000 men, and that 18,000 are ordered to it from other quarters." *Ibid.,* XXV, pt. 2, p. 791.

38. *Ibid.,* XVIII, pp. 1078–1079. Longstreet had been the departmental commander before his return to Lee's army.

39. Lee assumed that Union troops along the coast south of Va. would be withdrawn to concentrate against him, thus reducing the threat to D. H. Hill. A study of Union dispatches and letters shows that there were other reasons for a possible reduction in the threat to Hill. On May 5 Foster warned Halleck that by July 1 his department would have no more than 5,000 effectives. In May

500 artillerymen, their terms of two years' service having expired, were being mustered out, and in June twelve of his fullest regiments, composed of men who had enlisted for nine months, would also leave. Feeling threatened "at all points," he too asked that those of his troops which had apparently been assigned to the Dept. of the South be returned. *Ibid.*, p. 700. For information on the size and dispositions of Federal forces along the coast during April, May, and June see *ibid.*, pp. 675–679, 711–712, 731–739; XXVII, pt. 3, pp. 450–457.

40. *Ibid.*, XVIII, pp. 1078–1079.

41. *Ibid.*, pp. 1083–1084. To replace Cooke's brigade Davis said he would authorize Hill to organize a scratch force of odds and ends of military units at Salisbury, N. C. See *ibid.*, p. 1083. Lee lost Ransom and his brigade through a misunderstanding that arose between him and Davis over the promotion of Brig. Gens. Henry Heth, William D. Pender, and Robert Ransom, Jr. He needed two major generals to command two newly created divisions. Though Lee on May 20 explicitly recommended Heth and Pender, the President inferred that he had Ransom in mind also. When Lee realized the error, he offered on May 25 to withdraw his nomination of Heth, but the President felt it was too late to do so, as the news of his promotion had probably leaked out to Heth. If Heth had not been promoted, he and his weak brigade (Brockenbrough's) might have been left behind in place of Ransom and his very large one. *Ibid.*, XVIII, pp. 1077–1079, 1083–1085; XXV, pt. 2, pp. 810–811, 827; LI, pt. 2, pp. 716–717; Freeman and McWhiney, eds., *Lee's Dispatches*, 91–93, 96–99.

42. Freeman, *Lee's Lieutenants*, II, 711. Daniel's large brigade replaced Colquitt's, which was considerably reduced in size. *OR*, XXV, pt. 2, pp. 798, 833.

43. *Ibid.*, XVIII, pp. 943. According to official returns for May the strength of the brigades involved in the transactions was as follows:

Effectives:	*Officers and Men*
Jenkins	2,644
Ransom	3,067 including a battery
Colquitt	1,854
Evans	1,500 as of March 25
Davis	2,577
Cooke	2,332 including a battery
Daniel	2,500
Pettigrew	3,683

Ibid., pp. 943, 1086; XXV, pt. 2, p. 798. The voluminous correspondence arising from Lee's negotiations to strengthen his army and speculations about enemy movements is found in *ibid.*, XVIII, pp. 943, 1034, 1045–1047, 1049, 1053–1063, 1066–1067, 1069–1071, 1073–1086, 1088–1090, 1092; XXV, pt. 2, pp. 782–783, 790–792, 797–798, 813, 816, 826–827, 849, 851–852 (some of the same letters and dispatches are published in both volumes); LI, pt. 2, pp. 698, 716–717, 720; Freeman and McWhiney, eds., *Lee's Dispatches*, 99–100. From the standpoint of sound analysis and thorough research the best account of the difficulties between Lee and Hill over the question of reinforcements for the Army of Northern Virginia is in Hal Bridges, *Lee's Maverick General, Daniel Harvey Hill* (New York, 1961), 183–193.

44. *OR*, XXV, pt. 2, p. 848; XXVII, pt. 3, pp. 860, 909, 946–947.

45. Scheibert, *Seven Months in the Rebel States*, Hoole, ed., 74; Jubal A. Early, *Autobiographical Sketch and Narrative of the War between the States* (Philadelphia, 1912), 238; Frank Moore, ed., *Rebellion Record: A Diary of American Events with Documents, Narratives, Illustrative Incidents, Poetry, etc.* (11 vols. and supplement, New York, 1861–68), *Documents*, VII, 122–123.

46. Special Correspondent, Hagerstown, Md., July 8, 1863, in the *Times* [London], Aug. 18, 1863; Charles Minor Blackford, III, ed., *Letters from Lee's Army or Memoirs of Life in and out of the Army in Virginia during the War between the States* (New York, 1947), 194–195.

47. J. B. Jones, *A Rebel War Clerk's Diary at the Confederate States Capitol*, Howard Swiggett, ed. (New York, 1935), I, 343; Johnston, *Virginia Railroads*, 158, 162.

48. Blackford, ed., *Letters from Lee's Army*, 194–195.

49. Pender to his wife, June 28, 1863, William D. Pender Papers, UNC; Blackford to [his wife], June 25, 1863, Blackford, ed., *Letters from Lee's Army*, 181. See also Spencer G. Welch, *A Confederate Surgeon's Letters to His Wife* (Washington, 1911), 56.

50. Long, *Memoirs of Lee*, 265.

51. J. G. de Roulhac Hamilton, ed., *The Papers of Randolph Abbott Shotwell* (Raleigh, N. C., 1929), I, 475–476.

52. Pender to his wife, June 28, 1863, William D. Pender Papers, UNC. Other writers ventured similar opinions of Lee's army. See Hampton to his sister, May 13, 1863, Wade Hampton Papers, UNC; Welch, *Letters to His Wife*, 56, 58; Walter H. Taylor, "Causes of Lee's Defeat at Gettysburg," *SHSP*, IV, 82; William C. Oates, "Gettysburg—The Battle on the Right," *SHSP*, VI, 172; Sorrel, *Recollections*, 159.

53. Charles W. Ford, ed., *A Cycle of Adams Letters, 1861–1865* (Boston, 1920), II, 55–56.

54. Barlow to his mother, July 7, 1863, Francis C. Barlow Papers, Massachusetts Historical Society (cited hereafter as MHS).

55. Henry N. Comey to his father, May 27, 1864, Civil War Letters of Captain Henry N. Comey of 2nd Mass. Infantry, MSS in possession of Morton C. Jaquith, Worcester, Mass.; George R. Agassiz, ed., *Meade's Headquarters, 1863–65, Letters of Colonel Theodore Lyman from the Wilderness to Appomattox* (Boston, 1922), 125–126; John W. De Forest, *A Volunteer's Adventures*, James H. Croushore, ed. (New Haven, 1946), 190.

56. Agassiz, ed., *Meade's Headquarters*, 100.

57. Hooker to Bates, July 2, 1878, Samuel P. Bates Collection, Pennsylvania Division of Public Records, Harrisburg (cited hereafter as Bates Collection).

58. For remarks on the overconfidence of the army see Hood, *Advance and Retreat*, 54; James A. L. Fremantle, *Three Months in the Southern States: April–June, 1863* (New York, 1864), 274; Barlow to his mother, July 7, 1863, Francis C. Barlow Papers, MHS.

NOTES TO CHAPTER II

1. Darius N. Couch, "The Chancellorsville Campaign," *B&L*, III, 154. See comment by Col. Lucius Fairchild of the 2nd Wis. regiment: "The administration part of this army is being run splendidly; all departments work like a clock compared with when we first began soldiering." Fairchild to his sister, Apr. 13, 1863, Fairchild Letters, Typescript in possession of Miss Lee Bacon, Milwaukee, Wis. (MS in the State Historical Society of Wisconsin).

2. Hooker to Bates, Feb. 18, 1879, Bates Collection. Bates was state historian of Pa. and a good friend of the general. Hooker also rated Gen. Rufus Ingalls, his chief quartermaster, very highly. He conceded that Hunt was able, though opinionated.

3. George W. Adams, *Doctors in Blue: The Medical History of the Union Army in the Civil War* (New York, 1952), 196–199.

4. *Ibid.*, 206–210, 212. Soldiers' letters and diaries make constant reference to boxes of clothing and food received from home.

The sutler was one of the most frequently damned and bedevilled civilians in Civil War history. In case of an enemy raid his goods were the first to be seized, destroyed, or carried off. Should the discipline of the army break down momentarily because of a retreat, a raid, or some other unexpected development, the sutler's property would be among the first to suffer damage. Sometimes he deserved such treatment, especially when he illegally sold liquor or charged unusually high prices. Often he was the victim of unwarranted contempt on the part of government and army officials who with their absurd rules and regulations greatly impaired his efficiency. In spite of his shortcomings—and he had many—he performed a function similar to the army PX's of World War II, but he did not enjoy their status and advantages. The uncertainties of his business and costs of transportation largely justified the prices he charged for his goods. See *ibid.*, 217; John C. Gray and John C. Ropes, *War Letters, 1862–1865* (Boston, 1927), 86–87.

5. James A. Huston, "Logistical Support of Federal Armies in the Field," *CWH*, III, 40.

6. *OR*, XXV, pt. 2, pp. 239–240.

7. Hooker also explained what led him to order corps insignia. During Gen. George B. McClellan's Peninsular campaign of 1862 he had observed that every march was "equivalent to a defeat, from the men straggling and when you enquired of the men the Corps to which they belonged they would tell you any one but the true one. Hence it was impossible to fasten the responsibility and neglect on any one officer." Hooker to Bates, Dec. 8, 1876, Bates Collec-

tion; *OR*, XXV, pt. 2, p. 152. See also Couch, "The Chancellorsville Campaign," *B&L*, III, 154. Gen. Couch agreed with Hooker's appraisal of the badges and said they were very popular with the officers and the men.

Although Gen. Butterfield designed the badges and administered the whole system, the idea of identification marks originated with Gen. Philip Kearny. According to Swinton in his *Campaigns of the Army of the Potomac*, 268 note, Kearny ordered the soldiers of his division at Fair Oaks to sew a piece of red flannel to their caps so he could recognize them in the confusion of battle.

8. *OR*, XXV, pt. 2, pp. 10–12, 44, 57–59, 73, 86, 109, 119–123; Ser. III, Vol. III, pp. 60–61; Regis De Trobriand, *Four Years with the Army of the Potomac* (Boston, 1889), 416, 422–423.

9. The order was dated Feb. 5, 1863. *OR*, XXV, pt. 2, pp. 51, 61; George Meade [son], *The Life and Letters of George Gordon Meade*, George Gordon Meade [grandson], ed. (New York, 1913), I, 350–351; Swinton, *Campaigns of the Army of the Potomac*, 268.

10. Henry J. Hunt, "The First Day at Gettysburg," *B&L*, III, 261. In commenting in his diary in Jan., 1864, on a rumor that the First and Third Corps were to be broken up and consolidated with the Second, Fifth, and Sixth, Col. Charles S. Wainwright wrote: "It would be a good move in my opinion, as a corps d'armée of 15,000 men is simply absurd, causing a vast increase in the amount of writing to be done, and the time necessary to get orders to their destination. Were all the companies reasonably full, and the army not stronger numerically than at present, two-thirds of the writing could be dispensed with, two-thirds of the clerks returned to the ranks, and one-half the officers dispensed with." Allan Nevins, ed., *A Diary of Battle, The Personal Journals of Colonel Charles S. Wainwright, 1861–1865* (New York, 1962), 314 (cited hereafter as *Wainwright Journals*).

11. *OR*, XXV, pt. 2, pp. 51, 61; Swinton, *Campaigns of the Army of the Potomac*, 268.

12. Wise, *Long Arm of Lee*, 546; John Bigelow, Jr., *The Campaign of Chancellorsville* (New Haven, 1912), 26; *OR*, XXV, pt. 1, p. 252.

13. Hooker to Bates, Aug. 28, 1876, Bates Collection.

14. Wise, *Long Arm of Lee*, 547.

15. *OR*, XXV, pt. 1, pp. 252–253. Wise fully subscribed to Hunt's views and had some strong comments of his own to make on Hooker's generalship.

16. Dunn Browne [S. W. Fiske], *Mr. Dunn Browne's Experiences in the Army* (Boston, 1866), 150–151.

17. *OR*, XXV, pt. 1, pp. 658–659; Carl Schurz, *Reminiscences* (New York, 1907), I, 438–443. Immediately after the war Schurz claimed that the stories about the Eleventh Corps at Chancellorsville were "mostly untrue." He admitted that the enemy drove the corps out of its position, but statements about the men throwing away their arms, equipment, and the like were "all false"; two hours after its defeat the corps was completely reorganized and "in good fighting condition." No corps in the battle, he boasted, had "fewer stragglers." Schurz to Frank Moore, June 6, 1865, Andre de Coppet Collection, Princeton University Library (cited hereafter as PU). These assertions sound convinc-

ing, but it should be noted that for the remainder of the battle the Eleventh Corps was tucked away in some quiet spot on the battle line.

Admitting a prejudice against the "Dutch," Barlow said it was not fair to charge the poor record of the corps against them. "Some of the Yankee Regts. behaved just as badly. . . ." Barlow to his mother and brothers, May 8, 1863, Francis C. Barlow Papers, MHS. For the fairest appraisal of the role of the Eleventh Corps at Chancellorsville see Bigelow, *Campaign of Chancellorsville*, 478–480.

18. Barlow to his mother, May 19, 1863, Francis C. Barlow Papers, MHS.

19. Howard to [his wife], May 26, 1863, O. O. Howard Papers, Bowdoin College Library (cited hereafter as Howard Papers).

20. Williams to his daughter, May 7, 1863, found in Milo M. Quaife, ed., *From the Cannon's Mouth, The Civil War Letters of General Alpheus S. Williams* (Detroit, 1959), 178 (cited hereafter as *Alpheus Williams Letters*). Later Williams wrote: "I cannot conceive of greater imbecility and weakness than characterized that campaign from the moment Hooker reached Chancellorsville and took command." Williams to his daughter, June 29, 1863, *ibid.*, 220–221. See also W. F. Parmelee, Jr., to Bates, Dec. 9, 1882, Bates Collection. Parmelee, formerly a private in the 1st Ohio Light Artillery, Battery H, observed that in none of the battles he had experienced were the commanding officers more confused than at Chancellorsville.

21. Capt. R. F. Halsted to Miss [Emily] Sedgwick, May 13, 1863, Sedgwick Commissions, etc., Cornwall Historical Collection, No. 400, Cornwall, Conn., Public Library.

22. Webb to his father, May 12, 1863, Alexander S. Webb Collection, Yale University Library (cited hereafter as Webb Collection, and Yale as YU).

23. Adams to his father, May 24, 1863, found in Ford, ed., *Adams Letters*, II, 14.

24. For one of the neatest appraisals of Hooker's generalship see Wise, *Long Arm of Lee*, 547.

25. Couch, "The Chancellorsville Campaign," *B&L*, III, 161.

26. *OR*, XXV, pt. 2, p. 438.

27. Hooker to Col. Samuel Ross, Feb. 28, 1864, quoted in *B&L*, III, 223. Even more astonishing was the statement he made to his friend Bates: "You may like to know my opinion of the battle of Chancellorsville, so far as my individual efforts were concerned, and I feel no hesitation in giving it to you. I won greater success on many Fields, in the War, but no where did I deserve it half so much, and when all of the Records (North & South) are correctly published, I believe it will be conceded by all of my Countrymen." Hooker to Bates, Apr. 2, 1877, Bates Collection.

28. Even Hooker's friends on the Joint Committee on the Conduct of the War admitted there was a defeat, but they found him blameless. Of the four causes named by the committee, the "stampede" of the Eleventh Corps was put first. *Report of the Joint Committee on the Conduct of the War*, 38 Cong., 2 Sess. (Washington, 1865), I, p. XLIX (cited hereafter as CCW, *Report*).

29. In Hooker's message of May 13 to the President he talked about the

necessity of delay in order to get his army in shape before resuming the offensive, and at the same time he expressed the hope of making the move "tomorrow." The tenor of the letter suggests weakness and confusion on Hooker's part, which he tried to cover up by talking bravely and too much. *OR*, XXV, pt. 2, pp. 438, 473, 479.

30. Fairchild to Sarah [his sister], June 1, 1863, Fairchild Letters, Typescript of Miss Lee Bacon.

31. Weld to his mother, June 10, 1863, in Stephen Minot Weld, *War Diary and Letters* (Boston, 1912), 213.

32. John Gibbon, *Personal Recollections of the Civil War* (New York, 1928), 424–425.

33. Webb to his father, Oct. 16, 1863, Webb Collection.

34. Gouverneur K. Warren to W. I. Warren [his brother], May 8, 1863, Copy, Letters and Miscellaneous Manuscripts of Gouverneur Kemble Warren, Sylvanus Warren, William Warren, Gouverneur Kemble, and Others, 1849–1865, New York State Library. Immediately after Chancellorsville Col. (later Gen.) Alexander S. Webb, a West Point graduate, complained of the quality of generalship in various units of the army and referred to many officers as "contemptible blocks with 'stars' on their shoulders [who] in moments of trial have asked me what to do! how to do it! & look like sheep when they ought to show character. This is known to all and yet you see no improvement in the appointments." Webb to his father, May 12, 1863, Webb Collection. See also Col. Lucius Fairchild to Sarah [his sister], June 1, 1863, Fairchild Letters, Lee Bacon Typescript. Fairchild said he sometimes got "so disgusted" with the service that he was almost ready to resign, and when he thought of the "many Generals under whom I may chance to be thrown—political generals who are perfect failures—Generals who are drunkards—Generals who are not fit for the places they hold, I get a big disgust on—When I see the reputation of a good regiment resting on the reports of popinjay staff officers who would not make first class corporals—then I get mad as the d——l and swear *some*."

35. De Trobriand, *Four Years with the Army of the Potomac*, 471–472; Weld to his father, May 7, 13, 1863, in *War Diary and Letters*, 194, 198; Gibbon, *Recollections*, 122; Ford, ed., *Adams Letters*, II, 6, 14–15, 38; Williams to his daughter, May 29, 1863, *Alpheus Williams Letters*, 204; Meade, *Life and Letters*, I, 373, 379; Webb to Annie [his wife], May 20, 1863, Carswell McClellan to Webb, Oct. 25, 1890, Darius Couch to Webb, Oct. 20, 1890, Webb Collection. In this letter to Webb, Couch recalled the circumstances of his nomination of Meade to succeed Hooker: "The day our Army recrossed U.S. Ford, Sedgwick and myself rode in company after leaving Hooker near the Ford. During the conversation referring to a probable new commander I remarked 'Meade is the man, he is my choice.' . . . A few days after I went home on a sick leave, stopping in Washington on my way I called upon Mr. Lincoln and had an earnest conversation with him upon the same subject, in which I advised that Gen Meade should have the position." There is good evidence that Couch also spoke to Lincoln when the President made his visit to the army May 6–7. See Meade, *Life and Letters*, I, 373. For further information on moves against

Hooker see John H. Alley to Bates, Sept. 26, 1877, Bates Collection. Alley, who had been a captain during the war, claimed that Gens. George Stoneman and David B. Birney had plotted to get Hooker removed from command after Chancellorsville. Alley discovered the plan and told Hooker, who then had Stoneman removed from command of the cavalry corps.

36. See Freeman Cleaves, *Meade of Gettysburg* (Norman, Okla., 1960), 115–126, for a careful treatment of the relations between Meade and Hooker after the Chancellorsville campaign.

37. *OR*, XXV, pt. 2, p. 479; LI, pt. 2, p. 1043; Webb to Annie [his wife], May 18, 1863, Webb Collection; Noah Brooks, *Washington in Lincoln's Time* (New York, 1958), 26.

38. Howard to his brother, May 16, 1863, Howard Papers.

39. Bigelow, *Campaign of Chancellorsville*, 487; F. A. Walker, *History of the Second Corps in the Army of the Potomac* (New York, 1886), 253–254; Nelson A. Miles to Hon. E. J. Hill, May 17, 1900, Cornwall Men, Sedgwick Monument Dedication, Cornwall Historical Collection, No. 400, Cornwall, Conn., Public Library; Hancock to his wife [no date, but obviously just after Chancellorsville] in [Mrs. W. S. Hancock, ed.], *Reminiscences of Winfield Scott Hancock* (New York, 1887), 95. Hancock wrote: "I have been approached again in connection with the command of the Army of the Potomac. Give yourself no uneasiness— under no conditions would I accept the command. I do not belong to that class of generals whom the Republicans care to bolster up. I should be sacrificed." Hancock was a good Democrat and therefore politically undesirable. In view of this fact it is doubtful whether he received a definite offer directly from the War Dept., although somebody might have sounded him out informally.

40. Edward J. Nichols, *Toward Gettysburg, A Biography of General John F. Reynolds* (University Park, Pa., 1958), 140–148, 182–184. Reynolds outranked Meade by one week. Everything else being equal, Reynolds would for this reason have received first consideration.

For a thorough and able analysis of the question of whether Reynolds was offered the command, see *ibid.*, Appendix, 220–223. Nichols questions the reliability of the account by Charles F. Benjamin, "Hooker's Appointment and Removal," *B&L*, III, 239–243, which Civil War specialists generally have accepted as authentic. Benjamin says that Reynolds was offered the command at the time of Gen. Ambrose Burnside's dismissal in Jan. of 1863 but offers no evidence to support his statement. Nichols has based his version on three documents which dovetail pretty well in their essentials. First there is the circular of Gen. Abner Doubleday dated May 31, 1863, announcing his assumption of temporary command of the First Corps because Reynolds had gone to Washington for a few days. *OR*, LI, pt. 1, p. 1043. Then Meade's letter to his wife, June 13, 1863, tells of Reynolds' conversation with Lincoln about the command. Meade did not say that Reynolds had received a positive offer or why he might have turned it down. Meade, *Life and Letters*, I, 385. Finally, a maiden sister of Reynolds, Eleanor, in a letter to her nephew, Lt. Col. J. F. Landis, Aug. 20, 1913, put in writing a family legend of how Reynolds had received an offer of the command on June 2 and turned it down because the

President refused to promise him freedom from interference by Washington. Although written fifty years after the event, the account has a strong ring of truth about it, as Nichols proceeds to show. For the copy of the letter and analysis see Nichols, *Toward Gettysburg*, Appendix, 220–221.

Recent evidence confirms Nichols' version. Col. Charles S. Wainwright, commander of the Artillery Brigade of the First Corps, wrote in his diary on June 28, 1863: "General Reynolds told me today that the command of this army was offered to him when he was summoned up to Washington a month ago; but he refused it, because, to use his own expression, 'he was unwilling to take Burnside and Hooker's leavings.'" *Wainwright Journals*, 229. After Reynolds turned down the offer Lincoln apparently gave up his search for Hooker's replacement. One Washington observer, who was in close touch with the President, wrote on June 2 that Lincoln had "resolved" to try Hooker once more; at least he had said so a night or so previously, although many "leading" Republicans were "bitterly" opposed to it. Four days later he reported Lincoln as disposed, "if not determined," to "re-try" Hooker. T. B[arnett] to Barlow, June 26, 1863, S. L. M. Barlow Collection, Huntington Library.

41. *OR*, XXV, pt. 2, pp. 243, 532; Ser. 3, Vol. III, pp. 88–93; Fred A. Shannon, *The Organization and Administration of the Union Army, 1861–1865* (Cleveland, 1928), I, 306; II, 16, 26, 55–64, 72–73, 107, 115. About May 25 the enrollment began, and the first drawing of names occurred in R. I. on July 7, 1863.

42. Webb to his wife, May 20, 1863, Webb Collection.

43. Webb to his father, June 21, 1863, Webb Collection; De Trobriand, *Four Years with the Army of the Potomac*, 333.

44. *OR*, XXV, pt. 2, pp. 233, 466.

45. Meade to his wife, May 19, 1863, in Meade, *Life and Letters*, I, 378; Webb to his wife, May 18, 1863, Webb Collection.

46. Williams to his daughters, July 21, 1863, in *Alpheus Williams Letters*, 239.

47. Office Memoranda of War Statistics, 1861–65, pp. 16–17, Record Group 94, National Archives (cited hereafter as NA). The number of men listed by Union officials as captured or missing was 5,919. Lee reported that he had captured about 5,000 Union soldiers. Some of the difference in these figures could have been made up of stragglers, especially from the First, Eleventh, and Twelfth Corps, who were reputed on May 13 to have been swarming over the country north of the Rappahannock to Aquia Creek. *OR*, XXV, pt. 1, p. 804; pt. 2, pp. 476–477.

48. *Ibid.*, pp. 320, 473.

49. *Ibid.*, pp. 320, 533.

50. *Ibid.*, p. 473; L. Van Loan Naisawald, *Grape and Canister, The Story of the Field Artillery in the Army of the Potomac, 1861–1865* (New York, 1960), 332–333.

51. *OR*, XXV, pt. 2, pp. 471–472; Naisawald, *Grape and Canister*, 329–332; Wise, *Long Arm of Lee*, 567–570.

52. *OR*, XXV, pt. 2, pp. 509–510, 514, 525–529, 531, 538, 540–542, 566–567, 570–571, 595; XVIII, 738–739, 1080; XXVII, pt. 3, p. 3.

53. *Ibid.*, XXV, pt. 1, p. 156; pt. 2, pp. 505–506; XXVII, pt. 1, p. 47; Benjamin P. Thomas and Harold M. Hyman, *Stanton, The Life and Times of Lincoln's Secretary of War* (New York, 1962), 271. Hooker ignored not only Halleck but Stanton as well.

54. *OR*, XXV, pt. 2, p. 473.

55. *Ibid.*, pp. 503–506, 527–528. Hooker heard about Halleck's report and asked Stanton to send him a copy. Stanton sent one as soon as his clerks had made one. For another example of the embarrassing lack of coordination between Hooker and the War Dept. see *ibid.*, pp. 514–516.

56. *Ibid.*, pp. 513, 533; Hooker to Bates, Apr. 2, 1877, Bates Collection.

57. Mark M. Boatner, III, *The Civil War Dictionary* (New York, 1959), 97, 655–656.

58. *Ibid.*, 372, 760, 765.

59. Anyone familiar with Southern newspapers during the war knows how free they were with opprobrious terms in referring to Northern armies. For similar feelings shared by Confederate officers see Blackford, *Letters from Lee's Army*, 179–180; Sale to his aunt, July 27, 1863, John F. Sale Letters, Virginia State Library. For opposite views see Gray to Ropes, Nov. 3, 1863, in Gray and Ropes, *War Letters*, 256–257.

60. Hunt to Long, Oct. 5, 1884, A. L. Long Papers, UNC.

NOTES TO CHAPTER III

1. "Richmond papers are not easily obtainable at present, stringent orders restraining all communications between the pickets." T. Grey to Gay, June 2, 1863, S. H. Gay Collection, Columbia University Library.

2. *OR*, XXV, pt. 2, pp. 265, 572–573.

3. Benson J. Lossing, *Pictorial History of the Civil War* (Hartford, 1874), III, 49–50; *OR*, XXV, pt. 2, pp. 509–510, 514, 525–527, 528–531, 540–542.

4. *Ibid.*, 528. On the same day as Sharpe's report Gen. Milroy at Winchester sent word to Gen. R. C. Schenck in Baltimore that Longstreet had joined Lee on May 21 for an offensive move which would involve crossing the river above Hooker's right flank. See *ibid.*, 531.

5. *Ibid.*, 542.

6. *Ibid.*, 534–538.

7. *Ibid.*, 529.

8. Williams to his daughter, May 29, 1863, in *Alpheus Williams Letters*, 204.

9. Freeman, *R. E. Lee*, III, 24.

10. *OR*, XXV, pt. 2, pp. 820, 827–828, 832–833, 844.

11. *Ibid.*, p. 792. For orders to other units alerting them to possible enemy moves see *ibid.*, pp. 809, 839, 844–845; LI, pt. 2, pp. 711, 717–719, 721.

12. *Ibid.*, XVIII, 733. As is true of many army and departmental reports

during the Civil War, the figures giving the strength of various commands in the Dept. of Va. for the three months' period ending May 31 are at best approximations. In this instance there is no way of knowing whether deductions were made for regiments that had just been mustered out or were in the process of leaving the army. Dix said on May 30 that he had lost three regiments and would lose fourteen more by expiration of service. See Dix to Gen. H. W. Halleck, May 30, 1863, *ibid.*, 732.

13. *Ibid.*, XXV, pt. 2, p. 463. Halleck suggested its occupation as a base for a movement in support of Hooker in his coming Chancellorsville campaign. The troops did not arrive there until after Hooker had retreated following his defeat. See *ibid.*, XVIII, pp. 649, 706.

14. *Ibid.*, XXV, pt. 2, pp. 847, 851. Among the several reasons Dix gave for withdrawing his troops from West Point the most important one was the retreat of Gen. Hooker. He planned to use the withdrawn troops in cooperation with those under Gen. E. D. Keyes at Gloucester Point, Yorktown, and Williamsburg for an attack on Diascund Bridge, which was as close to Richmond as West Point. Consequently, if Lee thought the withdrawal of Federal forces from West Point lessened the danger to Richmond, he was mistaken. See *ibid.*, XVIII, pp. 727–728, 732.

15. *Ibid.*, XXV, pt. 2, pp. 849–850.

16. Freeman implies that Lee had completed his preparations for the offensive and was only waiting to hear the news of a lifting of an enemy threat to Richmond before giving the word to his commanders. Actually he did not put the final touches to his reorganization of the army until May 30 and June 2. Lee and Davis finally came to an agreement on May 31 about the recall of brigades which had been detached from the army. At that time there was no intimation from Davis that he would prevent Lee's departure for fear of threats to Richmond. In his letter to Davis on June 2 Lee, who showed just as much concern about the safety of Richmond as anyone, said that for the present he would leave Pickett and Pettigrew at the Junction. See Freeman, *R. E. Lee*, III, 25–26; *OR*, XXV, pt. 2, pp. 840–843, 848, 850.

17. *Ibid.*, p. 848; XXVII, pt. 2, p. 293; pt. 3, p. 859.

18. *Ibid.*, pt. 1, p. 30; pt. 3, pp. 8, 10–13.

19. *Ibid.*, pt. 1, p. 30.

20. *Ibid.*, p. 31.

21. *Ibid.*

22. *Ibid.*, pt. 3, pp. 859–860, 862. A biographer of Hooker asserts that most military authorities now agree that Hooker was right in proposing to storm Confederate defenses at Fredericksburg because Lee was most sensitive of his rear, and an attack there would have stopped the invasion. See Walter H. Hebert, *Fighting Joe Hooker* (Indianapolis, 1944), 233–234. When discussing an "if" in history experts can always marshal convincing arguments. An examination of the ill-fated nature of Federal military operations around Fredericksburg clearly reveals why Lincoln and Halleck were both apprehensive about another venture at that place.

23. *OR*, XXVII, pt. 1, p. 32. Buford was misinformed, for Jenkins' brigade was not with Stuart at that time. See *ibid.*, pt. 2, p. 305.

24. *Ibid.*, pt. 3, pp. 15–16, 26–30. By midafternoon of June 6 Hooker had decided to break up "in its incipiency" the accumulation of the heavy rebel force of cavalry about Culpeper, and he wired Halleck to that effect. *Ibid.*, pt. 1, p. 33.

25. Maj. C. H. Howard wrote that Gen. Adelbert Ames had been sent up the river with a brigade of infantry and some artillery. He had taken with him "the best troops of the Army. *One* Regt. from this Corps [Eleventh] 33d *Mass.* . . ." Howard to his sister [-in-law], Lizzie, June 9, 1863, Howard Papers.

26. *OR*, XXVII, pt. 3, p. 27.

27. *Ibid.*, pp. 27–28.

28. *Ibid.*, XXV, pt. 2, pp. 542–543. Hooker blamed Stoneman for the poor condition of his cavalry. *Ibid.*, XXVII, pt. 1, p. 33. Pleasonton made three reports to Hooker late in May about the unsatisfactory condition of the cavalry. Pleasonton felt that many of the horses reported as serviceable were not really so. He estimated the effective strength of the corps to be one-third of the 12,000 men and horses reported in the March returns. Memo from Pleasonton, May 21, 1863; *id.* to Seth Williams, May 24, 1863, MSS, Joseph Hooker Papers, Huntington Library. Pleasonton made the third report on May 27. See *OR*, XXV, pt. 2, pp. 533–534.

29. *Ibid.*, pt. 3, p. 28. See Boatner, *Civil War Dictionary*, 657, for a definition of this term. According to him, it was a tactical or strategic base which performed somewhat the same function as castles or fortified towns.

30. Pleasonton reported that of his 10,981 effectives, 7,981 were cavalry and 3,000 infantry. *OR*, XXVII, pt. 1, p. 906. Meade reported he had ordered Gen. Barnes to have 1,000 men ready to push forward from Kelly's Ford, if needed, and to supply their places with his reserves. *Ibid.*, pt. 3, p. 40. Barnes sent about 500 men of this force under Col. Jacob B. Sweitzer to accompany Gen. D. McM. Gregg's column far enough to guard its left flank while driving for Stevensburg. *Ibid.*, pp. 608–610; LI, pt. 1, p. 1047.

31. *Ibid.*, XXVII, pt. 1, p. 32. Hooker also received other reports which exaggerated the size of Stuart's cavalry. See *ibid.*, p. 31; Pleasonton to Seth Williams, May 28, 1863, enclosing an intercepted Confederate letter dated May 13, 1863, MSS, Joseph Hooker Papers, Huntington Library.

32. Stuart's five brigades and horse artillery had an effective strength of 9,536. McClellan, *Campaigns of Stuart*, 293. Hooker's more correct estimate is inferred from the number of infantry he sent to cooperate with the approximately 8,000 Union cavalry.

33. *OR*, XXVII, pt. 3, p. 14. This report came from Buford, who said he could not learn whether there was any infantry north of the Rapidan but was very certain that a heavy cavalry force was on the grazing grounds of Culpeper County.

34. If Hooker had decided to attack Lee at Culpeper with a major portion of his army, he would then have had to depend upon the Orange and Alexan-

dria Railroad for supplies, as Meade did in the fall of 1863. The capacity of that road is indicated by a statement of J. H. Devereux, military superintendent. He reported that in one trip the road could carry 7,500 troops from Alexandria to Bealeton, Va., provided he had six hours notice to collect the necessary cars. See *ibid.*, p. 42.

35. *Ibid.*, LI, pt. 1, p. 1047; XXVII, pt. 1, p. 906; pt. 2, p. 686; F. C. Newhall, "The Battle of Beverly Ford," *Annals*, 137–138; McClellan, *Campaigns of Stuart*, 263–264.

36. For an excellent account of the two reviews, June 5 and 8, see Freeman, *Lee's Lieutenants*, III, 1–5.

37. McClellan, *Campaigns of Stuart*, 262–263.

38. *Ibid.*, 264–269; *OR*, XXVII, pt. 1, pp. 902–904, 1043–1048; pt. 2, pp. 679–685, 721–723, 727–728, 748–750, 754–755, 757–758, 762–763, 768–770, 771–773; Newhall, "The Battle of Beverly Ford," *Annals*, 137–143; Battle Reports of Gen. John Buford, Col. T. C. Devin, Capt. G. C. Cram, Lt. S. G. Elder, Maj. H. C. Wheelan, Capt. J. E. Harrison, Capt. R. S. C. Lord, Maj. Chas. J. Whiting, MSS, Joseph Hooker Papers, Huntington Library.

E. P. Alexander in a few lines summed up the nature of the fighting during the morning when he said that "Pleasonton did it in fine style, & but for bad luck in the killing of Col. Davis, leading his advance, would probably have surprised & captured the most of Stuart's artillery. But as soon as Stuart's people could get together they were able to hold their own & after hard fighting all the morning, in the afternoon Pleasonton, as we put it, was forced to withdraw." Alexander, "Battle of Gettysburg," MS, E. P. Alexander Papers, UNC.

39. Scheibert, *Seven Months in the Rebel States*, Hoole, ed., 90; McClellan, *Campaigns of Stuart*, 268–292; *OR*, XXVII, pt. 1, pp. 608–610, 903, 949–952, 961–962, 965–966, 985–986, 996–997, 1023–1028, 1034; pt. 2, pp. 679–685, 733–739, 743–744, 762–766.

40. In three communications Pleasonton gave different but not necessarily contradictory reasons for withdrawing. They showed confusion in reporting on his part, which must have annoyed Hooker. At 8:00 P.M. on June 9 he sent a message giving two reasons for retreating: reports of large forces of Confederate infantry nearby, and the crippled condition of the enemy cavalry which prevented it from following Union forces. Early the next day Pleasonton said that since he had used up all his reserves he decided to recross the river. In his full battle report of June 15 he again said that the menace of enemy infantry caused him to retire from the field. *Ibid.*, pt. 1, pp. 903–904, 1045.

There is no doubt that Stuart had plenty of infantry support near at hand during most of the battle. Gen. Robert E. Rodes, in command of a division with over 8,000 officers and men in Ewell's Corps, said that during the fight he gradually moved toward Brandy Station. *Ibid.*, pt. 2, p. 546. A member of the 23rd N.C. regiment in Rodes's division recorded in his diary that they moved at eleven o'clock and formed a line of battle near Brandy Station. Leonidas Torrence Diary, June 9, 1863, found in Haskell Monroe, ed., " 'The Road to Gettysburg'—The Diary and Letters of Leonidas Torrence of the Gaston

Guards," *North Carolina Historical Review*, XXXVI, 510. Lee was ready to send reinforcements from other units of his army. E. P. Alexander wrote his father on June 14, 1863, to say that "on the day of the Cavalry Battle . . . we were hitched up all day long, with wagons packed & everything ready for a fight. . . ." Alexander-Hillhouse Papers, UNC. Whether Alexander's artillery battalion was alerted to support Stuart in addition to a Longstreet division sent toward Stevensburg is not clear. See Lee's dispatch to Stuart, June 9, 1863, in *OR*, XXVII, pt. 3, p. 876.

41. *Ibid.*, pt. 2, pp. 679–685, 719–720. Stuart would not admit he had been surprised, not even to his wife. Of course she might be the last person to whom the general would confess a mistake. See John W. Thomason, Jr., *Jeb Stuart* (New York, 1930), 410. The two regiments which behaved badly were the 4th and 12th Va. Cavalry. A portion also of the 2nd S.C. Cavalry at one time during the fight did not do well.

In his reminiscences Lt. Col. W. W. Blackford, who at the time was Capt., Corps of Engineers, and a member of Stuart's staff, used the following criteria to adjudge Brandy Station a Confederate victory: "By all the tests recognized in war the victory was fairly ours. We captured three cannon and five hundred prisoners, and held the field. . . ." W. W. Blackford, *War Years with Jeb Stuart* (New York, 1945), 217. Such self-deception does not win wars.

42. McLaws to Emily, June 10, 1863, Lafayette McLaws Papers, UNC. For Lee's dispatch of June 9 to Gen. S. Cooper in Richmond saying that "General Stuart drove them [the Yankees] across the river," see *OR*, XXVII, pt. 3, p. 880. For a Northerner's version of the Federal retreat from the battlefield see the statement of [Lt. Col.] William Brooke Rawle to Col. Denison, Dec. 29, 1878. Rawle asserted that after driving the Confederate cavalry back on their infantry supports, "we leisurely withdrew across the river unmolested." Rawle was with the extreme Union rear guard so was able to state "positively" that Confederate claims that "they pursued us across the river are incorrect." William Brooke Rawle Papers, Historical Society of Pennsylvania (cited hereafter as HSP).

43. Charles M. Blackford to his wife, June 12, 1863, in Blackford, *Letters from Lee's Army*, 175. Further corroborating evidence of Stuart's surprise is found in other Confederate sources. Capt. Jasper Hawse of the 11th Va. Cavalry made the following entry in his diary on June 9: "The Bugle had scarcely sounded 'Roll Call,' when busy preparing breakfast, the sound of artillery near our camp burst upon our ears. The men, without their breakfasts, were ordered to 'Fall in' & the camp to move immediately. . . . The fight was probably the most desperate of any cavalry fight of the war." Jasper [Hawse] Diary, 1861–1864, Microfilm, University of Virginia Library (cited hereafter as UV). A lieutenant in Stuart's horse artillery wrote two days after the battle that "about daylight the Yanks drove in our Picket stationed at Beverly Ford on the Rappahannock, and came near surprising us in bed. . . . They charged up to our camp and killed & wounded several Horses, before we could get out." Phelps to his aunt, June 11, 1863, Charles R. Phelps Letters, UV. See also Robert A. Moore, *A Life for the Confederacy*, James W. Silver, ed. (Jackson, Tenn., 1959), 150.

44. Wade Hampton to McClellan, Jan. 14, 1878, Henry B. McClellan Papers, Virginia Historical Society (cited hereafter as VHS).

45. For a careful study of the meaning of Brandy Station to Stuart see Freeman, *Lee's Lieutenants*, III, 18–19, 51–53. Freeman suggests that Brandy Station rankled so in Stuart's mind that it warped his judgment and caused him to make mistakes. Thomason accepts at face value Stuart's declared indifference to the attacks of his critics. He does not even imply that Brandy Station affected Stuart's conduct in the campaign. See Thomason, *Jeb Stuart*, 409–410, 412.

46. *OR*, XXVII, pt. 1, p. 1045.

47. Pleasonton to Hooker, 9:30 P.M., June 9, 1863, MS, Joseph Hooker Papers, Huntington Library.

48. *OR*, XXVII, pt. 1, pp. 903–904, 1045.

49. CCW, *Report*, I, 32; *Supplement*, II, Report of Major General A. Pleasonton, p. 9; Pleasonton, "The Campaign of Gettysburg," *Annals*, 449.

50. *Ibid.*, 448.

51. The following accounts agree that Pleasonton's assignment was a reconnaissance in force: McClellan, *Campaigns of Stuart*, 263–264; Freeman, *Lee's Lieutenants*, III, 6–7; Newhall, "The Battle of Beverly Ford," *Annals*, 137; George B. Davis, "The Operations of the Cavalry in the Gettysburg Campaign," *Cavalry Studies from Two Great Wars*, Arthur L. Wagner, ed. (Kansas City, Mo., 1896), 232; Fairfax Downey, *Clash of Cavalry. The Battle of Brandy Station, June 9, 1863* (New York, 1959), 77, 146. Col. John S. Mosby refused to accept this version and said bluntly: "He [Pleasonton] went after a fight." See Mosby, *Stuart's Cavalry in the Gettysburg Campaign* (New York, 1908), 13. Thomason in one of the best accounts of the battle also stressed that the purpose of Pleasonton's expedition was to destroy Stuart. See Thomason, *Jeb Stuart*, 400. At the time Lee adjudged Pleasonton's attack to be only a reconnaissance in force, not to be taken too seriously. Consequently he advised Stuart to fight cautiously and save his men. He assured him that in case of necessity he would support him with infantry. *OR*, XXVII, pt. 3, p. 876.

52. MSS, Joseph Hooker Papers, Huntington Library. E. B. Long, who surveyed and processed the Hooker Papers for the library, wrote the following note in Mar., 1964, about these papers: "There were only two documents in this envelope: the letter of a Confederate soldier and an order of march for Jones's brigade for review June 8. . . . E. C. Fishel in his memo of Dec. 8, 1863 [sic], mentions three papers in the envelope; we found only two and one was misplaced."

53. Pleasonton reported that Stuart had "upward" of 12,000 cavalry. *OR*, XXVII, pt. 1, p. 903.

54. *Ibid.*, pt. 2, pp. 680, 736; McClellan, *Campaigns of Stuart*, 266, 294–295.

55. *OR*, XXVII, pt. 1, pp. 35–36, 903, 1045; pt. 2, pp. 439–440; pt. 3, pp. 47–48, 62.

56. *Ibid.*, p. 38.

57. *Ibid.*, p. 39.

58. *Ibid.*, pt. 1, p. 950.

59. The phrase was used by Thomason, *Jeb Stuart*, 415.

60. *OR*, XXVII, pt. 1, p. 904.

61. *Ibid.*, p. 1045.

62. Scheibert, *Seven Months in the Rebel States*, Hoole, ed., 90.

63. McClellan, *Campaigns of Stuart*, 294.

64. *OR*, XXVII, pt. 2, p. 687; McClellan, *Campaigns of Stuart*, 296. Hooker on June 10 expressed scepticism of Pleasonton's claims of having crippled Stuart. He thought Pleasonton's attack might have delayed Stuart's raid a few days but not caused its abandonment. See *OR*, XXVII, pt. 1, p. 34.

65. General John Buford's Report, June 13, 1863, and Colonel Thos. C. Devin's Report, June [no date], 1863, MSS, Joseph Hooker Papers, Huntington Library; *OR*, XXVII, pt. 1, p. 906.

66. In his congratulatory order to his command Stuart made much of the fact that Confederate cavalry and horse artillery alone confronted the Union cavalry and artillery "escorted by a strong force of infantry." *OR*, XXVII, pt. 2, p. 719. He conveniently overlooked his continual use of dismounted troopers as infantry in the battle and the presence in the afternoon of Rodes's division ready to reinforce him. The Confederate battle reports made constant reference to the employment of squadrons of sharpshooters who would fight dismounted. *Ibid.*, pp. 680, 682–683, 721, 723, 727–732, 734, 737–738, 744, 757, 763, 765, 771.

67. Buford Report, Joseph Hooker Papers, Huntington Library.

68. *OR*, XXVII, pt. 1, pp. 168–169, 904; pt. 2, pp. 719, 768. McClellan in his careful study of the battle estimated casualties for both sides to be greater than the official figures. He said that Confederate losses were 523 officers and men; Union 936 including 486 taken prisoner. He did not state how many Confederates were captured. McClellan, *Campaigns of Stuart*, 292–293. It is interesting to note that even in the downward revision of losses for both sides in the *OR*, the ratio of Confederate to Union casualties remains approximately 1:2.

69. John O. Casler wrote in his memoirs: "I saw more men cut with the sabre that day [Brandy Station, June 9] than I ever saw before or have seen since." Casler, *Four Years in the Stonewall Brigade* (Guthrie, Okla., 1893), 165. Even more precise was the testimony of Capt. W. W. Blackford who said: "The next morning we rode over the field and most of the dead bore wounds from the sabre, either by cut or thrust. I mean the field around Fleetwood; in other places this was not the case to so great an extent." Blackford, *War Years with Jeb Stuart*, 217. Gen. Buford, however, clearly indicated in his report that Union cavalrymen used sabers only as a last resort; the same was true even of U. S. Regulars. In describing their fight on Fleetwood Hill he wrote: "After exhausting the little ammunition . . . [they] had left, out flew the Sabres and most handsomely were they used." MS, Joseph Hooker Papers, Huntington Library.

70. E. P. Alexander to his father, June 14, 1863, Alexander-Hillhouse Papers, UNC.

71. *OR*, XXVII, pt. 1, pp. 34–35.

72. *Ibid.*, p. 35.

73. *Ibid.*, pt. 2, pp. 294–295; pt. 3, pp. 868–869, 874–876, 882, 885; Freeman, *R. E. Lee*, III, 24.

74. *OR*, XXVII, pt. 3, pp. 868–869.

75. *Ibid.*, pp. 874, 879–880.

76. *Ibid.*, p. 886.

77. *Ibid.*, p. 885.

78. *Ibid.*, p. 882.

79. *Ibid.*, pt. 2, p. 295.

80. *Ibid.*, pp. 295, 306, 315; pt. 3, pp. 890–891, 896.

81. *Ibid.*, pp. 3–4, 9, 17–18, 24, 26, 28, 39–41, 47, 49, 56–62, 67–68; LI, pt. 1, p. 1050. Berea Church was not far from Bealeton on the Orange and Alexandria Railroad.

82. *Ibid.*, XXVII, pt. 3, pp. 69–73. Pleasonton was bubbling over with confidence at this time. Failing to obtain any news of enemy movements after Brandy Station, he rashly concluded that Lee had been stopped in his tracks. He summarized the situation by saying that "the rebels are like that boy the President tells about, who stumped his toe, and was too big to cry." As a further indication of his overconfidence, in the same letter he clearly intimated that with enough money he could bribe Col. Mosby. One wonders who was fooling whom in this instance. See Pleasonton to Gen. R. Ingalls, chief quartermaster, June 12, 1863, in *ibid.*, p. 72.

83. *Ibid.*, p. 87.

84. *Ibid.*, pp. 80–82, 84, 86–88; pt. 1, p. 38. The exact time of the sending and receiving of dispatches was often recorded, but the same unfortunately was not true of letters. Hooker wrote his letters to Reynolds and Meade sometime on the 13th, and internal evidence suggests that he composed and sent them early in the day. He expressed uncertainty about Lee's intentions; but before seven o'clock that night he sent a message to Halleck stating positively that Ewell and Longstreet were going to the valley. During the morning and early afternoon he had received a series of messages from Pleasonton which suggested more and more definitely that Ewell's and Longstreet's corps had passed through Culpeper headed for the mountains. See also Butterfield's dispatch to Reynolds at 9:10 A.M. in which he said that Hooker did not want to abandon the "Fredericksburg line" until he had received information of "such a settled character" as to "warrant" the move. *Ibid.*, pt. 3, p. 81.

85. *Ibid.*, pt. 1, p. 38; pt. 3, pp. 88–95.

86. *Ibid.*, pt. 1, p. 38. He gave his real reason in a dispatch to Lincoln on June 15. See *ibid.*, pp. 43–44.

NOTES TO CHAPTER IV

1. *OR*, XXVII, pt. 2, pp. 440, 546–547.

2. *Ibid.*, pp. 295, 357, 613, 687; pt. 3, pp. 859, 887–888, 890, 896; McClellan, *Campaigns of Stuart*, 296.

3. *OR*, XXVII, pt. 2, pp. 295–296, 357, 440–442, 550; pt. 3, pp. 890, 896.

4. Selden Connor Correspondence, Brown University Library. The 7th Maine was in Gen. Thomas H. Neill's brigade, Second Division, Sixth Corps.

5. *OR*, XXVII, pt. 3, pp. 118, 147. Though a strict disciplinarian, Hancock fully appreciated that a combination of circumstances had caused real suffering among his men, and he denied the commander of the provost guard "permission to fire a few shots of artillery towards the mass of stragglers to give them the impression that the enemy were following. . . ." Apparently this was an old army trick to get the stragglers to step along. Extract from Account of Movements of Second Army Corps by Lieut. Col. C. H. Morgan, Inspector-General and Chief of Staff, Typescript, Bachelder Papers. For other accounts of the hardships endured by Federal soldiers in their rapid maneuvers between the Rappahannock and the railroad, see the following: Horatio Dana Chapman Diary, MS, Connecticut State Library; Harlan P. Rugg Diary and Memorandum, 1861–1865, MS, copy, Connecticut State Library; De Trobriand, *Four Years with the Army of the Potomac*, 474–477; Williams to his daughter, June 16, 1863, in *Alpheus Williams Letters*, 212; O. O. Howard, *Autobiography* (New York, 1908), 386; Jesse Bowman Young, *What a Boy Saw in the Army* (New York, 1894), 267–268. A newspaper correspondent, T. Grey, said that the thermometer on June 15 stood at 102 in the shade. Grey to Gay, June 17, 1863, S. H. Gay Collection, Columbia University Library. Gen. Webb wrote: "We remain here [Gum Springs] today to rest. Our men terribly exhausted yesterday. Lt. Col. Gleason of the 25th New York died last night from sun stroke." Webb to his wife, June 18, 1863, Webb Collection.

6. Hamilton, ed., *Shotwell Papers*, I, 477.

7. *Ibid.*, 483–484, 486. See also Moore, *A Life for the Confederacy*, Silver, ed., 150–151. For the marching prowess of Confederate columns see Scheibert, *Seven Months in the Rebel States*, Hoole, ed., 99–100; E. P. Alexander to his father, June 14, 1863, Alexander-Hillhouse Papers, UNC.

8. Hamilton, ed., *Shotwell Papers*, I, 479–480.

9. *OR*, XXVII, pt. 1, pp. 50, 142, 906–907, 952–953, 962–963, 979–980, 1051–1052; pt. 2, pp. 688, 739–743, 745–748; pt. 3, pp. 171–173, 178, 193; LI, pt. 1, p. 1061; McClellan, *Campaigns of Stuart*, 296–303. McClellan said that Munford's flanks were secured by the Little River and its tributaries, which forced the enemy to attack his front. The sunken road the enemy had to use compelled an attack in column of fours and prevented a spread formation. Munford's sharpshooters commanded the road and were protected in front by a stone wall and on the flanks by post and rail fences. *Ibid.*, 299.

10. Pleasonton's reports of the engagement, consisting of a series of dispatches to Hooker and to army headquarters, were either contradictory or incomplete. As to the time of his arrival at Aldie it is hard to determine whether he was confused about the hour or made a mistake in putting down the time of one of his dispatches. Gregg's report of the engagement is very sketchy and for that reason is unsatisfactory. Col. Horace B. Sargent of the 1st Mass. Cavalry gave the most detailed account of all Union participants. *OR*, XXVII, pt. 1, pp. 906–907, 952–953, 1051–1052; pt. 3, p. 173. For a statement that the

Union cavalry arrived about four o'clock see the Diary of Charles Francis Adams, [Jr.], 1863, Entry for June 17, MHS.

11. *Ibid.*, Entries for June 17 and 18.

12. *OR*, XXVII, pt. 2, pp. 688, 741; [Rosser] to his wife, June 18, 1863, Thomas L. Rosser Papers, UV.

13. *OR*, XXVII, pt. 1, pp. 962–963.

14. *Ibid.*, pp. 964–965.

15. *Ibid.*, pp. 962–964; McClellan, *Campaigns of Stuart*, 303–305. If Pleasonton left Aldie during the night, he must have returned the next day because at 1:10 P.M. he sent a message from there to army headquarters, saying that he had received at second hand word about Duffié's disaster at Middleburg. Duffié, he said, had "permitted himself to be surrounded. . . ." The damning word was "permitted." In view of Pleasonton's orders to Duffié through Gregg, and the likelihood of his presence at Aldie when Capt. Allen arrived to request reinforcements, this message appears suspiciously like the clever dodge of a superior to escape responsibility for his own shortcomings at the expense of his subordinate. See *OR*, XXVII, pt. 3, p. 193. The next day in writing to Butterfield he said he could not understand Duffié's conduct. See *ibid.*, pt. 1, pp. 909–910. Pleasonton was furious with Duffié and accused him of having "failed to obey his instructions, & permitted the enemy to obtain such a position as to be able to kill, wound, & capture a large number of his men & officers." He then pronounced him "totally unfitted to command a Regiment." Report of Operations of Cavalry Corps of Battles of Aldie, Middleburg & Upperville on the 17th, 19th & 21st June under Command of Brigadier General Pleasonton, MS, Huntington Library. Though perhaps guilty of reckless bravery and questionable judgment, under the circumstances it is hard to see what else Duffié could have done, because he did obey orders. That was the trouble. See *OR*, XXVII, pt. 1, pp. 949–950.

16. In reporting his losses Pleasonton conveniently forgot to mention the large number of his men who were captured. *Ibid.*, p. 907. The total Union casualties at Aldie were 305 officers and men, of which 124 were captured. If the 200 losses of the 1st R. I. Cavalry are added in, there was a sizeable total of 505 casualties. The Confederate casualties were 119, of which 63 were captured. *Ibid.*, pp. 171, 964; pt. 2, p. 741; McClellan, *Campaigns of Stuart*, 305.

17. *OR*, XXVII, pt. 1, p. 50.

18. *Ibid.*, pp. 908–910, 953–954.

19. *Ibid.*, pt. 2, p. 689.

20. *Ibid.*, pt. 1, p. 911.

21. *Ibid.*, pp. 911–913, 954–955; pt. 2, pp. 689–691; pt. 3, pp. 227–230. Stuart said he did not attack on June 21 because it was Sunday. Then he added it was fortunate he had observed the Sabbath because he would have encountered a heavy force of infantry and artillery, as well as cavalry, and "the result would have been disastrous, no doubt." *Ibid.*, pt. 2, p. 690.

22. *Ibid.*, pt. 1, pp. 912–913.

23. *Ibid.*, pp. 912, 955; pt. 2, p. 690; pt. 3, p. 914. Gregg claimed that his two brigades had captured 250 officers and men. These figures cannot be rec-

onciled with those given in the return of casualties in Stuart's cavalry near Middleburg and Upperville for the period from June 10 to 24 inclusive. These amounted to a loss of 510 officers and men who were listed as killed, wounded, or missing. The number of those missing, presumably most of them captured, was 166 officers and men. See *ibid.*, pt. 1, p. 955; pt. 2, pp. 712–713.

24. *Ibid.*, pt. 1, pp. 53–55, 912; pt. 3, p. 211. Highly gratified with the generalship of Buford and Gregg, Pleasonton reported that the "manner in which . . . [they] handled their respective Divisions is worthy of special mention." He also had kind words for Kilpatrick's gallantry. He was pleased with the help given him by Gen. Barnes's infantry division and particularly Vincent's brigade, which "were most efficient as sharpshooters and skirmishers in the advance." Pleasonton's Report of Battles of Aldie, Middleburg & Upperville, MS, Huntington Library.

25. *OR*, XXVII, pt. 3, pp. 247–249, 266, 268, 272, 275–276, 281. Gen. Slocum at Leesburg obtained some very accurate information.

26. *Ibid.*, pt. 2, p. 167; pt. 3, pp. 80–81, 84, 101; LI, pt. 1, p. 1055.

27. *Ibid.*, XXVII, pt. 1, pp. 38–39.

28. *Ibid.*, pt. 3, p. 101. Pleasonton addressed the dispatch to both Hooker and Stanton.

29. *Ibid.*, pt. 1, p. 39.

30. *Ibid.*, pt. 2, p. 313.

31. *Ibid.*, pt. 1, p. 39.

32. *Ibid.*, pp. 39–40.

33. *Ibid.*, p. 38.

34. *Ibid.*, p. 40.

35. *Ibid.*

36. *Ibid.*, pp. 40–42; pt. 3, pp. 114–115. Hooker made very improbable guesses about Lee's intentions. From the beginning of the campaign he had had the idea that Stuart was going to make a gigantic cavalry raid. This presupposition, fed by Pleasonton's false interpretation of information, persisted for some time and blinded him to a more realistic appraisal of enemy moves. On June 17 he thought of the raid as a feint for something bigger, perhaps "Lee's re-enforcing Bragg or moving troops to the West." *Ibid.*, pt. 1, p. 50. In a conversation with Gen. Samuel W. Crawford in the afternoon of June 21 Hooker said that although he could not locate Lee, he thought that he had yielded to pressure from Richmond and was heading for Pittsburgh. S[amuel] W. C[rawford] to Gen'l. [?], 5:00 P.M., June 21, 1863, de Coppet Collection, PU. Hooker knew better than to depend upon Pleasonton's intelligence reports, for he admitted after the war that he "never dared rely upon his statements too fully." Hooker to Bates, July 12, 1878, Bates Collection.

37. *OR*, XXVII, pt. 1, pp. 41–42.

38. *Ibid.*, pp. 43–44.

39. *Ibid.*, XXV, pt. 2, pp. 12–13.

40. *Ibid.*, XXVII, pt. 3, p. 175. These were Butterfield's words in a message to Gen. R. Ingalls on June 17.

41. *Ibid.*, pt. 1, pp. 30–32, 34–35, 39, 45, 49; CCW, *Report*, I, 160–161.

42. Marsena R. Patrick Journal, Entries for June 17, 19, 1863, LC. As a member of the general staff Patrick had a ringside seat to watch what was going on.

43. *OR*, XXV, pt. 2, pp. 505–506; XXVII, pt. 1, p. 45.

44. *Ibid.*, p. 47. Lincoln tried to soften the harshness of the official dispatch by sending Hooker a personal note. He said that Halleck had faith in Hooker's competence as a military commander and disagreed with him only on matters of no real importance. Lincoln then appealed for effective cooperation between the two generals because he had need of their "professional skill." See Roy P. Basler, ed., *The Collected Works of Abraham Lincoln* (New Brunswick, N.J., 1953), VI, 281–282.

45. For a good summary of Halleck's training, temperament, and record before the Gettysburg campaign see Thomas and Hyman, *Stanton*, 214–225, 255–256, 258, 265–266, 270–271, 284–285; Stephen E. Ambrose, *Halleck: Lincoln's Chief of Staff* (Baton Rouge, 1962), Chs. I–X.

46. Howard K. Beale and Alan W. Brownsword, eds., *Diary of Gideon Welles* (New York, 1960), I, 83, 121, 179–180. After a conversation with Lincoln on July 16, 1863, John Hay made this comment: "Tycoon [Lincoln] says, however you may doubt or disagree with Halleck he is very apt to be right in the end." John Hay Diary, Typescript, Brown University Library.

47. *OR*, XXVII, pt. 2, pp. 186–197.

48. *Ibid.*, XXV, pt. 2, pp. 589–590; XXVII, pt. 2, p. 186; Thomas Weber, *The Northern Railroads in the Civil War, 1861–1865* (New York, 1952), 77, 79–80.

49. *OR*, XXVII, pt. 2, pp. 158–159.

50. *Ibid.*, p. 186.

51. *Ibid.*, pp. 186–187.

52. *Ibid.*, pp. 189–192. Just as Ewell's men poured into the valley and when a few hours warning would have made considerable difference, for some unaccountable reason there was loose play in the transmission of intelligence about enemy movements. See *ibid.*, pp. 167, 184–185; pt. 3, pp. 80–81.

53. *Ibid.*, pt. 2, p. 190.

54. *Ibid.*, pt. 2, pp. 49, 53, 189–190, 193–195, 456, 464; Freeman, *Lee's Lieutenants*, III, 23–24, 26–27. The Confederates improved the quality of their artillery by their captures at Winchester. They took the Parrotts and the 3-inch rifles with them, leaving behind inferior guns. In addition to the artillery, they acquired three hundred loaded wagons, more than three hundred horses, and quite a large amount of commissary and quartermaster's stores. *OR*, XXVII, pt. 2, pp. 442, 456.

55. *Ibid.*, pt. 3, p. 124.

56. *Ibid.*, pt. 2, pp. 45, 440, 546–549.

57. *Ibid.*, pp. 440–441, 460–463. Col. Nye after a careful study of the battle concluded that Early did not launch his attack from Round Hill and Little North Mountain as a number of writers have suggested, but from a ridge closer to the Union position and running north from Dr. John S. Lupton's house to the Pughtown road. See Nye, *Here Come the Rebels!*, 97–98.

58. Milroy sent a message to Schenck at 8:00 P.M., June 13, which contained the following sentence: "They [the enemy] will surround, but can't take, my fortification." *OR*, XXVII, pt. 2, 182. He forgot one important qualification in this amazing statement. A fortified area is no better than the troops who hold it.

59. *Ibid*, pp. 441–442, 501–502.

60. Freeman, *Lee's Lieutenants*, I, 25. Col. Nye has written the most recent and best balanced account of the engagement in his *Here Come the Rebels!*, 66–123.

61. The figure of around 7,000 men is estimated in the following manner: Milroy lost 4,443 officers and men in action and during the retreat. The 2,700 survivors, more or less, who finally gathered at Bloody Run, Pa., were demoralized, disorganized, and partly disarmed. The other troops who escaped Ewell reached Harpers Ferry, where they could be put into service. *OR*, XXVII, pt. 3, pp. 295–296, 325, 357, 389. The figures given for those troops who reached Bloody Run vary from 2,000 to 2,700. Schenck said that 1,559 of Milroy's men finally got to Harpers Ferry. See *ibid.*, p. 220.

62. *Ibid.*, pt. 2, pp. 19–21, 198–201; pt. 3, pp. 96–97, 124, 237. Tyler charged that his predecessor at Harpers Ferry, Gen. Kelley, had allowed the defenses to suffer woefully from neglect, and that in spite of warnings of a possible enemy attack Kelley had not taken the precaution of removing subsistence, forage, ammunition, hospitals and hospital stores, and other supplies from the town, where they were exposed to capture. He also accused Kelley of unmilitary conduct in turning the post over to Tyler. When Kelley received orders relieving him of command, he merely reported the order to Tyler and left with his whole staff without briefing his successor or leaving records indicating the location, quantity, and quality of supplies and equipment. See *ibid.*, pt. 2, pp. 36–37.

63. Tyler's entire force including the refugees from Winchester numbered 4,680 men on June 16. *Ibid.*, pp. 22–24; pt. 3, p. 218. Col. Edward C. James of the 106th N. Y. shared this confidence in the defenses on Maryland Heights. On June 19 he wrote that he regarded Harpers Ferry as "impregnable if the defence is properly conducted." They had on hand plenty of provisions and forage, and "enough ammunition to lay out all the rebels that will come and see us." Three days later he claimed that they were now prepared for the enemy, for the "position is a Gibratter [sic], and although if attacked at all, it will be with greatly superior numbers, yet with any kind of generalship we need not fear the result." James to his mother, June 19, 22, 1863, E. C. James Collection, YU.

64. *OR*, XXVII, pt. 2, p. 24.

65. James to his father, June 24, 1863, E. C. James Collection, YU.

66. *OR*, XXVII, pt. 2, pp. 22–33; pt. 3, p. 245. According to Schenck, Tyler on June 21 had not more than four companies of cavalry. On June 26 he received a part of a cavalry regiment as reinforcement. James to his mother, June 26, 1863, E. C. James Collection, YU.

67. *OR*, XXVII, pt. 1, pp. 41–42, 45.

68. *Ibid.*, pt. 3, pp. 148–149.
69. *Ibid.*, pt. 1, pp. 45–46.
70. *Ibid.*, pp. 44–45, 47–48.
71. *Ibid.*, p. 48.
72. *Ibid.*
73. *Ibid.*, p. 47.
74. *Ibid.*, pp. 48, 142.
75. *Ibid.*, pp. 48–51.
76. *Ibid.*, p. 30.
77. *Ibid.*, pp. 51–52, 54–55.
78. *Ibid.*, p. 56; pt. 3, pp. 358–359.
79. *Ibid.*, pt. 1, p. 56.
80. *Ibid.*, pp. 56–57; pt. 3, pp. 355–358.
81. CCW, *Report*, I, 111, 166, 170, 173, 175.
82. *Ibid.*, 166.
83. OR, XXV, pt. 2, pp. 586–587; XXVII, pt. 1, pp. 59, 156, 258, 348–351, 371. The First Brigade consisting of two regiments was apparently mustered out before the battle. The morning report for June 20, 1863, had the following statistics for the Vermont brigade: Present for duty: 144 officers; 3,360 men. Sick: 14 officers; 143 men. Extract from General Stannard's Diary, Typescript, Bachelder Papers.
84. OR, XXV, pt. 2, p. 587; XXVII, pt. 1, pp. 158–159.
85. *Ibid.*, p. 453; William F. Fox, ed., *New York at Gettysburg* (Albany, 1900,) I, 284.
86. OR, XXVII, pt. 1, pp. 167–168, 872, 882–883.
87. *Ibid.*, XXV, pt. 2, pp. 587–588; XXVII, pt. 1, pp. 162, 167, 593, 653–654, 657–658, 914–916, 956–957, 992–993; pt. 3, p. 242.
88. *Ibid.*, pt. 3, p. 331.
89. *Ibid.*, pp. 331–332, 345–346, 356–357, 440–442. The nucleus of the camp convalescents and paroled prisoners consisted of two regiments from the Second Brigade, Pa. Reserves. Heintzelman said on June 26 that Hooker received from him a total of 15,249 men. This figure is swollen, for he included men whose terms of enlistment had expired, troops for various reasons not available for front-line duty, and the corps of observation which was apparently a scratch force under Col. Albert B. Jewett. Jewett's men never saw service at Gettysburg either at the rear or on the battle line. See *ibid.*, XXV, pt. 2, pp. 586–589; XXVII, pt. 3, p. 345. The corps commanders met at Fairfax Court House in Gen. McClellan's headquarters and decided that in addition to the large garrison of artillerymen the Washington defenses should always have 25,000 infantry and 3,000 cavalry. They also added the stipulation that whenever the enemy was within striking distance of the capital, "a covering army of not less than 25,000 should be held in position ready to march to meet the attacking column." See *ibid.*, pp. 331, 345.
90. Allowing for termination of terms of enlistment of some of his men, Abercrombie's division furnished about 6,000 troops. In round figures Crawford had 3,800 and Stahel 3,600. Lockwood's brigade became the second in Gen.

Alpheus S. Williams' First Division of the Twelfth Corps. *Ibid.*, pt. 1, p. 165; pt. 3, pp. 356–358. The figures for Lockwood's brigade were based upon the returns for June 20, 1863. By the time his brigade arrived at Gettysburg, according to careful estimates it probably mustered no more than 1,700 officers and men. See Selected Pages from Historical and Statistical Records of the Principal Military Commands in the Union and Confederate Armies, IV, 42, Entry 161, Record Group 94, NA.

91. *OR*, XXVII, pt. 1, p. 59. When on June 24 Hooker sent Butterfield to Washington and Baltimore to beat the bushes for more troops, he instructed his chief of staff to organize a column of 15,000 troops to move without delay to Frederick. Presumably this force would be made up of troops other than those already sent to the Army of the Potomac as reinforcement. There was something weirdly unrealistic about this scheme. How Hooker expected Butterfield to find this number of men, gather them together, and send them off as an organized body to Frederick, all with the snap of a finger, is a mystery. See *ibid.*, pt. 3, pp. 355–356.

92. *Ibid.*, pt. 1, pp. 156, 158–159, 167–168; pt. 3, pp. 274, 291–292, 373.

93. *Ibid.*, XVIII, pp. 711–712, 716–718, 727–728, 732; XXV, pt. 2, pp. 847, 851; XXVII, pt. 3, p. 875.

94. *Ibid.*, XVIII, p. 732; XXVII, pt. 3, pp. 6–7, 20, 44.

95. According to the abstract of the tri-monthly return for May 31, 1863, Dix had 32,668 officers and men present for duty and equipped. Of this number 27,369 were infantry, 2,640 cavalry, and 2,659 artillery. He also had 136 pieces of artillery. *Ibid.*, XVIII, p. 733.

96. Gen. E. R. Keyes, a West Pointer and commander of the Fourth Corps in Dix's department, perhaps had influenced his superior's thinking on the value of raids. On June 16 he protested against Dix's order forbidding any more raids, arguing that they had a "wonderful effect by producing discontent among the people against the Confederate Government. They demand protection, and, if the raids are repeated, the old and sick will call home their sons and brothers to protect their homesteads, and in that way the rebel army will be melted away." *Ibid.*, XXVII, pt. 3, pp. 168–169. The effect of such methods of warfare in bringing the enemy to his knees during the Civil War needs further study. Jefferson Davis was well aware of the ulterior purpose of the raid on Walkerton and similar ones within the area of Middlesex, King and Queen, and King William Counties. In referring to them he bitterly called them "atrocious." When he said, however, that such a system of warfare "has never been practiced by any people professing civilization and Christianity," he revealed a profound ignorance of the history of Western civilization. It should be noted that though he was highly outraged and rightly so, he showed no signs of succumbing to this kind of pressure. He and Seddon refused to dissipate the strength of Lee's army by sending troops to areas threatened by enemy raids. According to Keyes's reasoning, the incidence of desertion should have been higher among Va. troops, especially from those counties, than other groups. It so happened that during this period it was highest among troops from N. C. *Ibid.*, pp. 875, 883. See also *ibid.*, XXV, pt. 2, pp. 814–815.

97. *Ibid.*, XXVII, pt. 3, p. 111.

98. *Ibid.*, pt. 1, pp. 17–20.

99. Gen. Keyes on June 16 remarked that with Lee's army moving up the Shenandoah, if he had 25,000 men and some gunboats he would take the rebel capital or destroy the railroads in its vicinity. *Ibid.*, pt. 3, pp. 168, 412–413. See also *ibid.*, pt. 1, pp. 17–18.

100. Quoted in Bridges, *Lee's Maverick General*, 193.

101. *Ibid.*, XXVII, pt. 1, pp. 19, 75–77.

102. Secy. Welles mentioned on June 28 that the President thought it a good time to strike a blow at Richmond but had little faith in Dix's ability to accomplish it. Though Dix was not much of a general, Lincoln had reasons for not wanting to replace him. Two days later Welles said Lincoln and Stanton were anxious for Dix to make a "demonstration" on Richmond but Halleck did not respond "favorably." In this instance Welles allowed his intense dislike for Halleck to warp his judgment. Beale and Brownsword, eds., *Diary of Gideon Welles*, I, 350–351.

NOTES TO CHAPTER V

1. *OR*, XXVII, pt. 3, p. 940. Seddon on June 27 sent a message to Gen. D. H. Hill at Petersburg, saying that Dix with some 25,000 or 30,000 men had concentrated at Yorktown, and he ordered Hill to bring his whole force to Richmond. Reports of an enemy concentration at Yorktown had been filtering in to Seddon for six days previous to his order to Hill. See *ibid.*, p. 912.

2. *Ibid.*, pt. 2, pp. 316, 751–752.

3. *Ibid.*, pp. 549–550; pt. 3, pp. 131, 161; "Extracts from the Diary of Lieut. Hermann Schuricht," *SHSP*, XXIV, 340; Dr. Philip Schaff, "The Gettysburg Week," *Scribner's Magazine*, XVI, 22–23.

4. *OR*, XXVII, pt. 1, pp. 49–51; pt. 3, pp. 186, 201.

5. *Ibid.*, pt. 2, pp. 464, 503.

6. *Ibid.*, pt. 3, p. 896.

7. *Ibid.*, pt. 1, pp. 38–39, 44; pt. 2, p. 295.

8. *Ibid.*, pt. 3, pp. 900–901.

9. *Ibid.*, p. 905.

10. Pender to his wife, June 23, 1863, William D. Pender Papers, UNC. Gen. Hood, whose headquarters were close to Lee's, testified that his commander had the "same buoyant spirits which pervaded his magnificent army." Hood, *Advance and Retreat*, 55. There is indirect evidence that Lee had recovered fully from the attack of pericarditis from which he suffered in April. Within a twenty-four-hour period on June 16 and 17 he rode over thirty miles from Culpeper to Markham. For a man who, according to one writer, was "at a point of complete physical and spiritual exhaustion and needed a rest badly," this trip over mountain roads showed he was quite a healthy invalid. See Donald B. Sanger and Thomas Robson Hay, *James Longstreet* (Baton Rouge,

1952), 160; Clifford Dowdey and Louis H. Manarin, eds., *The Wartime Papers of Lee* (Boston, 1961), 421; *OR*, XXVII, pt. 3, pp. 896, 900.

11. *Ibid.*, pp. 905–906.

12. *Ibid.*, pt. 2, pp. 297–298.

13. *Ibid.*, p. 298.

14. *Ibid.*, p. 296.

15. *Ibid.*, pp. 613, 673.

16. *Ibid.*, pt. 3, p. 914.

17. *Ibid.*

18. *Ibid.*, pp. 914–915.

19. *Ibid.*, p. 913.

20. *Ibid.*, p. 923. At 7:30 P.M. on June 22 Longstreet acknowledged receipt of a message from Lee enclosing a letter to Stuart, which he then forwarded with a covering note. Judging from Longstreet's comments to both Lee and Stuart, the letter was not one of those reproduced in the *OR*. See *ibid.*, p. 915.

21. *Ibid.*, p. 923.

22. In his report Stuart made no mention of having discussed with Mosby the possibilities of taking a route through or around Hooker's army. Both Mosby and McClellan, who spent years studying Stuart's campaigns, agreed that Mosby suggested the route by way of Seneca Ford. *Ibid.*, pp. 691–692; McClellan, *Campaigns of Stuart*, 315; Mosby, *Stuart's Cavalry*, 72, 76–78, 174.

23. Thomason, *Jeb Stuart*, 420–421.

24. *OR*, XXVII, pt. 3, p. 923. McClellan wrote that Stuart received a dispatch from Lee late on the night of June 23. If McClellan's recollection of the contents of that message, which he read, was correct, then it was not the one dated 5:00 P.M., June 23, 1863, which is in the *OR*. The letter McClellan referred to informed Stuart that Gen. Early would move to York and Stuart should join him there as soon as possible. McClellan, *Campaigns of Stuart*, 316–318. It was also Stuart's understanding that the rendezvous would be at York. See *OR*, XXVII, pt. 1, p. 708.

25. *Ibid.*, pt. 3, p. 923.

26. *Ibid.*, p. 915.

27. *Ibid.*, pt. 2, pp. 27–30; pt. 3, pp. 275–276, 284, 292, 294.

28. The estimate of the comparative distances from Rector's Crossroads to York via Rowser's Ford at Seneca and the ford at Shepherdstown is based on the detailed map showing the routes of Stuart's cavalry division from Oct. 9 to 12, 1862, and June 25 to July 2, 1863, in back pocket of McClellan, *Campaigns of Stuart*. For the rate of travel of a cavalry column with artillery see Thomason, *Jeb Stuart*, 428.

29. Mosby, *Stuart's Cavalry*, 78, 81, 169; McClellan, *Campaigns of Stuart*, 318–320.

30. *OR*, XXVII, pt. 3, p. 915.

31. Mosby, *Stuart's Cavalry*, 215–216.

32. *OR*, XXVII, pt. 3, pp. 927–928.

33. *Ibid.*, pt. 2, pp. 691–692. When Mosby on his way to the rendezvous with Stuart found Hooker's army in motion and heard artillery fire near Hay Market, he assumed Stuart had not been able to get through and had turned back. Mosby, *Stuart's Cavalry*, 175.

34. *OR*, XXVII, pt. 2, p. 693. McClellan, convinced that the messenger did not reach Gen. Lee's headquarters, exaggerated what would have been the importance to Lee if he had known of Hancock's movement. Stuart did not say how he knew Hancock was on his way to Gum Springs, a good fifteen miles from Hay Market, and he made no mention of having captured any prisoners. Perhaps Fitz Lee had discovered Hancock's destination as a result of his reconnoitering around Gainesville. The movement of one corps to Gum Springs, however, did not indicate a general movement of the Union army. In this instance McClellan is guilty of reading into history. See McClellan, *Campaigns of Stuart*, 321–322.

35. *OR*, XXVII, pt. 2, p. 693.

36. *Ibid.;* McClellan, *Campaigns of Stuart*, 323.

37. *OR*, XXVII, pt. 2, p. 694; McClellan, *Campaigns of Stuart*, 324.

38. *OR*, XXVII, pt. 2, pp. 297, 306, 316, 358, 613.

39. Westwood H. Todd, "Reminiscences of the War between the States," Typescript, I, 119, UNC.

40. Hamilton, ed., *Shotwell Papers*, I, 486–487.

41. Lafayette McLaws, "Gettysburg," *SHSP*, VII, 65.

42. William A. Fletcher, *Rebel Private, Front and Rear* . . . (Beaumont, Texas, 1908), 54–55.

43. *OR*, XXVII, pt. 2, pp. 306–307.

44. *Ibid.*, pt. 3, p. 913.

45. *Ibid.*, pt. 2, p. 297. On June 25 Lee wrote Davis that he thought he could "throw General Hooker's army across the Potomac. . . ." *Ibid.*, pt. 3, p. 931.

46. *Ibid.*, pp. 925–926.

47. *Ibid.*, pp. 924–925.

48. *Ibid.*, p. 925.

49. *Ibid.*, p. 931.

50. *Ibid.*, pt. 1, pp. 75–76. The date of this letter was June 29.

51. *Ibid.*, pp. 76–77. Davis' letter was dated June 28.

52. *Ibid.*, XXV, pt. 2, p. 842.

53. *Ibid.*, XXVII, pt. 1, p. 77.

54. *Ibid.*, pt. 3, p. 944. Apparently the order was rescinded, for Corse remained in Gordonsville. *Ibid.*, pp. 954, 956, 971.

55. Lee never received these letters, as Union scouts under Capt. Ulric Dahlgren on July 2 intercepted them. *Ibid.*, pt. 1, p. 75.

56. *Ibid.*, pt. 3, p. 931.

57. E. P. Alexander to his father, June 14, 1863, Alexander-Hillhouse Papers, UNC.

58. *OR*, XXVII, pt. 3, p. 191.

59. *Ibid.*, pp. 209, 224.

60. *Ibid.*, p. 208; Williams to his daughters, June 20 and 23, 1863, in *Alpheus Williams Letters*, 214–215.

61. *Ibid.*, 218–219.

62. *OR*, XXVII, pt. 3, pp. 208–209. With Slocum situated at Leesburg Hooker was in a position to control the use of other fords. The best ford in the vicinity was White's, three miles above Edwards Ferry, and a mile above that was White's Ferry. Below Point of Rocks was Noland's Ford, which Lee used in 1862. Since the river was high in June of 1863, Noland's was not useful even for infantry. Seneca Ford two miles below Goose Creek was reported to be practicable for all branches of the service. See *ibid.*, pp. 149, 209, 266–267, 272–273.

63. *OR*, XXVII, pt. 3, pp. 211, 228–229, 272, 279, 282–283, 310–311, 316; Williams to his daughters, June 20 and 23, 1863, in *Alpheus Williams Letters*, 217–218. The first bridge was laid either June 21 or 22.

64. *OR*, XXVII, pt. 3, p. 273.

65. *Ibid.*, p. 194. For uncertainty about the enemy in Pa., see *ibid.*, pp. 157, 160–161, 163, 171–172, 174–175, 180, 199–202, 248.

66. Patrick Journal, Entry for June 23, 1863, LC. On June 22 Meade sent Howard a long dispatch about Pleasonton's engagements and added this postscript: "I don't know what we are going to do. I have had no communication from headquarters for three days." *OR*, XXVII, pt. 3, p. 255. These messages indicate that Hooker still could not make up his mind about what to do, or else he was being unduly secretive as usual about his plans. An alert to his corps commanders to be ready for a major shift in the army's position was the least he could have done. Gen. Webb wrote to his wife on June 24 that they had had no orders from Hooker for some days and supposed he was "awaiting the developement [sic] of the enemy's plans." Webb Collection.

67. *OR*, XXVII, pt. 3, pp. 249, 281.

68. *Ibid.*, pt. 1, pp. 142–143.

69. Slocum had no cavalry at his disposal, and Tyler had no more than four companies. *Ibid.*, pt. 3, pp. 245, 281. For Slocum's work in obtaining information about the enemy see *ibid.*, pp. 247, 249, 268, 272, 281, 284, 307.

70. *Ibid.*, pt. 1, pp. 912–913; pt. 3, p. 211.

71. *Ibid.*, pp. 247–249, 251, 253, 266, 272, 275–277.

72. *Ibid.*, pt. 1, p. 55; pt. 3, p. 291.

73. *Ibid.*, p. 271.

74. *Ibid.*, pp. 285, 288–291, 305–306.

75. *Ibid.*, pp. 284–285, 305–307.

76. *Ibid.*, pp. 305–307. At first Hooker gave Reynolds only a brigade with four pieces of artillery from Stahel's cavalry. About noon on the 25th he left word for all of Stahel's division to report to Reynolds. *Ibid.*, p. 312.

77. *Ibid.*, pp. 308, 313, 317.

78. *Ibid.*, pp. 312, 316; Rowland Howard to his sister[-in-law], Lizzie, June 26, 1863, Howard Papers. The Eleventh Corps while marching stretched out for over twelve miles, which shows much straggling or poor control. At 11:15 A.M., June 25, Gen. Howard sent a message to army headquarters that his lead-

ing division was between the Monocacy and Point of Rocks. Reynolds fifteen minutes later sent a message from Edwards Ferry that the rear column of the Eleventh Corps had just about crossed the bridge. He implied that its march had been slowed down by an "immense number of led horses and colts, evidently stolen, blocking up the roads and bridges." *OR*, XXVII, pt. 3, pp. 312–313.

79. *Ibid.*, pp. 306, 312, 337–338.

80. *Ibid.*, pp. 315, 317.

81. Report of Maj. Charles Hamlin, Asst. Adj. Gen., Aug. 11, 1863, A. A. Humphreys Papers, HSP; Col. C. B. Baldwin, 1st Mass. Regt., to Bachelder, May 20, 1865, Bachelder Papers. For distance from Gum Springs to Edwards Ferry via Farmwell, Farmwell Station, and Frankville see G. K. Warren's Memo on Distances, Joseph Hooker Papers, Huntington Library.

82. *OR*, XXVII, pt. 3, pp. 313, 322.

83. *Ibid.*, pp. 307, 335.

84. Diary of Newton Heston Mack, Co. K, 153rd Pa. Regt., Entry for June 27, 1863, Typescript in possession of author; *OR*, XXVII, pt. 3, p. 337.

85. *Ibid.*, pp. 350–352; pt. 1, p. 58.

86. *Ibid.*, pt. 3, p. 373.

87. *Ibid.*, p. 314.

88. To prevent confusion and hardship Hooker wanted the trains of each corps to follow behind their own men. He ordered the corps commanders to halt the heads of their columns until the wagons of the corps in advance had crossed the bridges. *Ibid.*, p. 334. The train of the Army of the Potomac, including the artillery, when it left Fredericksburg would have extended over seventy miles if placed in a single line with the teams at the proper distance for marching. Wherever possible the wagons went along four or five abreast so as to increase their rapidity of movement. At Fairfax Court House and again at Fairfax Station the trains were reduced in size. Meade also cut them down. After these reductions their trains were between thirty and forty miles long. George T. Stevens, *Three Years in the Sixth Corps* (New York, 1870), 223. See also a lithograph by John B. Bachelder entitled "The Wagon Trains of the Army of the Potomac en Route from Chickahominy to James River, Va., during the Seven Days Fight, June 29th, 1862," in possession of author.

89. Patrick Journal, Entry for June 26, 1863, LC. There is more evidence of confusion during the crossing. Gen. Crawford sent a dispatch at 9:25 A.M., June 27, from Edwards Ferry, saying that the road was "encumbered by trains of Third Corps." Birney's men had crossed in the late afternoon and early evening of June 25 and by the morning of the 27th were not far from Middletown. Their trains were miles behind them. *OR*, XXVII, pt. 3, pp. 350, 353. A member of the Second Corps complained that confusion arising from poor traffic control exhausted the troops and delayed their arrival in Frederick by a whole day. Browne, *Dunn Browne in the Army*, 175–176.

90. General Stannard's Diary, June 26 and 27, 1863, Typescript, Bachelder Papers; Frank Rauscher, *Music on the March* . . . (Philadelphia, 1892), 80–81, 84–85; St. Clair A. Mulholland, *The Story of the 116th Regiment Penn-*

sylvania Volunteers . . . (Philadelphia, 1903), 117; Thomas Chamberlain, *History of the One Hundred and Fiftieth Regiment Pennsylvania Volunteers* . . . (Philadelphia, 1905), 114–115.

91. *OR*, XXVII, pt. 1, p. 143; pt. 3, pp. 353–354.

92. Connor to his father, June 25, 1863, Selden Connor Correspondence, Brown University Library. For the mental and physical conditions of the army see also Gen. and Chief Quartermaster Rufus Ingalls' message to Gen. M. C. Meigs, June 27, 1863, in *OR*, XXVII, pt. 3, p. 355.

93. Column by Agate [Whitelaw Reid], Washington, June 28, in *Cincinnati Daily Gazette*, July 1, 1863; Dispatch from C. C. Coffin, Frederick, Md., June 28, in *Boston Morning Journal*, July 3, 1863.

94. *OR*, XXVII, pt. 3, p. 349.

95. *Ibid.*, pp. 353, 370.

96. Hooker to [E. D.] Townsend, Sept. 28, 1876, MS copy; Alfred Pleasonton to Hooker, Aug. 17, 1876, MS copy; Hooker to Bates, Aug. 29, 1876, Bates Collection. If Pleasonton had gained knowledge of the country about Gettysburg, he did not get it first-hand during the Antietam campaign or afterwards. On Sept. 13, 1862, he sent one of his cavalry brigades with a section of artillery in the direction of Gettysburg, but he himself did not go. A month later during Stuart's raid on Chambersburg, Pleasonton was ordered to send scouts on the road from Hagerstown to Gettysburg, Emmitsburg, and beyond to ascertain the movements of Stuart's cavalry. Again there is no indication that he accompanied them. *OR*, XIX, pt. 1, pp. 208–213; pt. 2, pp. 68–69.

97. *Ibid.*, XXVII, pt. 3, pp. 375, 400.

98. CCW, *Report*, I, 177, 418–419.

99. *Ibid.*, 329.

100. *Ibid.*, 418.

101. *Ibid.*, 174, 418.

102. *OR*, XXVII, pt. 3, pp. 314, 317, 354. Apparently Slocum had some idea beforehand of what he was to do. Gen. Williams said that after dark on June 27 he rode to headquarters in Knoxville for consultation on the order to advance to Williamsport to burn the pontoon bridges. Williams to his daughters, July 6, 1863, in *Alpheus Williams Letters*, 223.

103. *OR*, XXVII, pt. 1, p. 151; pt. 3, p. 440. According to the returns for June 30, Slocum had 8,597 officers and men, and Lowell 242. French in a dispatch on June 30 said that he had 5,000 untried men and 3,000 who came from Winchester, "ready to take the rear at the first alarm." *Ibid.*, pt. 1, p. 70.

104. Hooker had the foresight to have Gen. Warren investigate the possibilities of moving the army to Harpers Ferry and using it as a base of operations against Lee. Warren in a report dated June 24, 1863, recommended that the move be made at once. *Ibid.*, pt. 3, p. 292. His reasons were sound providing the Confederates remained for several days where they were. But Lee was going too fast, and by the time Hooker could have moved his forces, it was too late.

105. *Ibid.*, pt. 1, p. 60; pt. 3, p. 354.

106. *Ibid.*, pt. 1, p. 58.

107. *Ibid.*, pp. 58–60.

108. It is difficult to see how Cullum could have forced Hooker out of his command, except by advising Halleck to take Hooker's resignation seriously and refer it to the President. His claim to fame in this affair is the following sentence in a letter to Henry Lane Kendrick: "I did my share in getting rid of Hooker, in whom I never had confidence, and getting Meade appointed, who I thought was the best man under the circumstances, to say nothing of his ability to eat the *pork* ration." G. W. C[ullum] to Kendrick, July 4, 1863, Henry Lane Kendrick Papers, New York Historical Society (cited hereafter as NYHS). There is the tantalizing suggestion in this cryptic passage of important and unrecorded manipulation behind the scene. Then again it may be nothing but an idle boast.

109. Hooker sent the notice of his resignation from Sandy Hook at 1:00 P.M. on June 27. Halleck received it at 3:00 P.M. *OR*, XXVII, pt. 1, p. 60. Hooker's dispatch ordering Slocum into the valley went out at 8:00 P.M.; Halleck's response to Hooker's resignation was sent at exactly the same time. By then Hooker was at his headquarters in Frederick. It is not known when Hooker received Halleck's message, but it conceivably could have arrived within half an hour after being sent. Messages from army headquarters to Washington and vice versa did occasionally get through in that short a time, although they usually took longer. The fact that Hooker sent a wire at 8:30 to Slocum countermanding his march to Harpers Ferry suggests something important had occurred to change his mind, such as the arrival of Halleck's dispatch announcing that he had referred the resignation to Lincoln. Hooker then knew that Halleck was not accepting his views about Harpers Ferry, and that there was also a good chance that he would shortly be relieved of his command. *Ibid.*, p. 60; pt. 3, p. 354.

110. In his dispatches of June 5, 10, and 24 Hooker suggested countermoves in the direction of Richmond, while avoiding an attack on the main body of Lee's army. *Ibid.*, pt. 1, pp. 30, 34, 55. His plan of operations for June 28 was conceived in the same spirit.

111. *Ibid.*, pp. 59, 62–63.

112. *Ibid.*, p. 63.

113. *Ibid.*, pp. 66–67.

114. *Ibid.*, pp. 20–21.

115. Not unexpected was the unfavorable reaction to Hooker's replacement on the part of the men who had served directly under him, particularly the soldiers of the Third Corps. A typical comment was: "The army received the news of the removal of Gen. Hooker . . . with amazement, and refused to believe the fact until the orders were read; and the opinion was expressed that he had fallen a victim to the implacable hatred of Gen. Halleck and the machinations of Pennsylvania politicians." Henry N. Blake, *Three Years in the Army of the Potomac* (Boston, 1865), 201–202. More important were the comments of people who had no personal feelings in the matter. There was a tendency for many of them to blame the administration for what had happened. Thomas A. Scott, former Asst. Secy. of War, worried for fear the change in commanders would delay the army's movements and prove fatal to Pa. Thomas A. Scott to

S. L[ewis], [June 28, 1863], Dispatches, Pennsylvania Department of Military Affairs, Pennsylvania Division of Public Records (cited hereafter as PDMA, PDPR). Capt. Charles Francis Adams, Jr., who was no admirer of Hooker, wrote: "Again a change in face of the enemy & yet the government ask us to believe that they know what they are about!" Diary of Charles Francis Adams, Jr., Entry for June 28, 1863, MHS. An aide on Gen. Reynolds' staff blamed the administration; he said they would not let Hooker withdraw "our forces from Harper's Ferry, nor would they give him any reinforcements from Washington or Baltimore, and so he properly resigned. This suicidal policy of the government is strange." Stephen M. Weld to his father, June 28, 1863, in *War Diary and Letters*, 227. T. C. Grey, attached to headquarters of the Second Brigade, Third Division, Second Corps, wrote on June 29, 1863, to Gay: "The relieving of Hooker is received with a kind of apathetic indifference by the army although many are loud in denouncing the act *at this particular moment*." S. H. Gay Collection, Columbia University Library. A newspaper correspondent wrote that when Washington heard about Hooker's removal "apparently without good cause largely through Halleck's efforts, it forgot its blasé air and for a few hours there was genuine, old-fashioned excitement." Writing after the battle, he admitted that Hooker's successor was "perhaps better," but the "timing most unfortunate. . . ." Column by Agate [Whitelaw Reid], Washington, July 6, in *Cincinnati Daily Gazette*, July 8, 1863.

116. Charles F. Benjamin wrote a full but untrustworthy account of Hardie's mission to Frederick. He made an inexcusable factual error by referring to Hardie as a general and chief of staff of the Secretary of War, and he overdramatized the whole affair. It was he also who firmly established the thesis that the War Dept., Stanton, and particularly Halleck were determined to get rid of Hooker and had made life so miserable for him that he had no alternative but to resign. Benjamin, "Hooker's Appointment and Removal," *B&L*, III, pt. 1, pp. 239–243. The most reliable account, giving the time of Hardie's arrival and his interview with Meade, is found in Meade, *Life and Letters*, II, 2–3, 11–12.

117. Beale and Brownsword, eds., *Diary of Gideon Welles*, I, 348–349.

118. The traditional appraisal of Hooker's generalship during the Gettysburg campaign until his removal has been favorable to him. A close examination of the *OR*, however, reveals the opposite: that if left to himself he might have made some egregious errors and that he also lacked the aggressiveness and confidence required of a successful general. Furthermore, what aggressiveness he had seemed to be directed against the wrong person—against Halleck instead of Lee. Yet the version that he was doing well until inopportunely relieved by the administration has become accepted as valid. It started with such newspapermen as Whitelaw Reid, who wrote that Hooker had by "brilliant" forced marches brought his army "face to face" with the enemy; yet he was removed when he had made no "mistakes." Column by Agate, Washington, July 6, in *Cincinnati Daily Gazette*, July 8, 1863. These statements are gross exaggerations. Hooker had made mistakes, and he had not brought his army face to face with the enemy. Separated by a distance of thirty-five miles, the two

forces could hardly be said to have been within shooting distance of one another. Benjamin in his article, "Hooker's Appointment and Removal," B&L, III, pt. 1, p. 241, continues the same interpretation. Most surprising, this favorable view of Hooker's generalship was accepted without question by John G. Nicolay and John Hay in their *Abraham Lincoln, A History* (New York, 1890), VII, 215, 227–228. There is good reason to believe that Hay was carried away by his fondness for Hooker, who without any doubt was a very charming person and a delightful companion. In his diary Hay mentioned having had dinner with Butterfield and Hooker several times in late summer of 1863. The entry for Sept. 9, 1863, illustrates the relationship between him and Hooker: "Dined with Wise, Met Hooker, Butterfield and Fox. Hooker was in a fine flow. Before dinner we talked about Halleck and his connection with Hooker's resignation. He says he was forced to ask to be relieved by repeated acts which proved that he was not to be allowed to manage his army as he thought best but that it was to be maneuvered from Washington." John Hay Diary, Typescript, Brown University Library. For a more critical appraisal of Hooker's generalship see Kenneth P. Williams, *Lincoln Finds a General* (New York, 1950), II, 624–654.

NOTES TO CHAPTER VI

1. *OR*, XXVII, pt. 3, pp. 79–80.
2. *Ibid.*, XXV, pt. 2, pp. 514, 542. The meeting took place the evening of May 28 or morning of May 29.
3. *Ibid.*, XXVII, pt. 3, pp. 44–45, 54–55, 68–69. Each corps was to include infantry, artillery, and cavalry, but nothing was mentioned about the total number of soldiers needed in each department.
4. *Ibid.*, pp. 77, 111.
5. *Ibid.*, p. 68.
6. *Ibid.*, p. 111.
7. *Ibid.*, p. 77.
8. *Ibid.*, pp. 112–113.
9. *Ibid.*, pp. 135–137. In addition to the 50,000 men from Pa., the quotas were as follows: Md., 10,000; Ohio, 30,000; West Va., 10,000.
10. *Ibid.*, p. 135. The President apparently was not at the conference and certainly did not force this arrangement on Stanton. *Ibid.*, pp. 113, 134. As the Secretary explained to Gen. Brooks, "in view of the urgency of the case," the President's call for 100,000 militia would provide "more speedily than anything else for the present exigency, and the more permanent organization can follow, if needed." *Ibid.*, p. 133. Brooks did not understand the President's proclamation as having superseded the orders establishing a departmental corps. See *ibid.*, p. 161.
11. *Ibid.*, pp. 136, 145.
12. *Ibid.*, p. 144; [Anonymous], *Life of David B. Birney, Major-General United States Volunteers* (Philadelphia, 1867), 163.

13. *OR*, XXVII, pt. 3, p. 164.

14. *Ibid.*, p. 169.

15. *Ibid.*, p. 185. See also *ibid.*, p. 203.

16. *Ibid.*, pp. 137–144, 163–167, 206.

17. *Ibid.*, pp. 138–139.

18. *Ibid.*, pp. 264, 329–330, 343.

19. A. G. Curtin to Kate Curtin, [No date, but filed in folder of June 25, 1863], Dispatches, PDMA, PDPR. Internal evidence suggests that Curtin wrote the letter on June 25, for he mentioned the enemy advance on Carlisle. Couch reported to Halleck late on June 25 that enemy cavalry were within five miles of the town. *OR*, XXVII, pt. 3, p. 328.

20. *Ibid.*, pp. 347–348. Curtin had carefully discussed the matter of another proclamation and its contents with his advisers and Gen. Couch, who accepted the proposal as a wise one. *Ibid.*, pp. 342–343. Not having a good opinion of Stanton, Curtin had worried about the reaction of the War Dept. and the President to his proposal to call for state militia. Apparently Scott had no trouble in getting approval in Washington. See *ibid.*, pt. 2, p. 213; Thomas A. Scott to Gov. Curtin, June 25, 1863, Dispatches, PDMA, PDPR.

21. Winnifred K. MacKay, "Philadelphia during the Civil War," *Pennsylvania Magazine of History and Biography*, LXX, 31–32 (cited hereafter as *PMHB*).

22. Basler, ed., *Collected Works of Lincoln*, VI, 298. The N.Y. State Militia entered the Federal service for thirty days. *OR*, XXVII, pt. 2, p. 212. At the beginning of the war militia from all the Northern states was mustered in similar fashion but for ninety days instead of thirty. The states recruited, organized, and maintained the men until they joined the Federal forces, and also furnished all their officers, even brigadier and major generals. In contrast, in the 1863 emergency most general officers were already in Federal service. Only N.Y. State had a militia organization comparable to what it had been two years earlier. See Shannon, *Organization and Administration of the Union Army*, I, 34, 53.

23. *OR*, XXVII, pt. 3, pp. 343–344, 363–365.

24. All troops in the Dept. of the Susquehanna, whether mustered into the Federal or state service, for the emergency remained under Couch's command. Couch continued to take orders from Stanton and Halleck. *Ibid.*, pp. 329–330, 342–343, 363, 391–393, 433.

25. *Ibid.*, pp. 168, 391, 409–410, 435–437. For an account of Stanton's suspicions that Curtin, Scott, and others were maneuvering to force Lincoln to appoint McClellan commander of the emergency troops, see Samuel R. Kamm, *The Civil War Career of Thomas A. Scott* (University of Pennsylvania Press, 1940), 159–161. Whatever suspicions Stanton might have entertained they apparently had no effect upon his official relations with Curtin.

26. *OR*, XXVII, pt. 3, pp. 409, 436–437; Basler, ed., *Collected Works of Lincoln*, VI, 311–312.

27. On June 22 in a dispatch to Stanton, Couch referred to his forces in the following manner: "I speak of the quality and condition of my troops, in order

that you may not wonder why I do not boldly face them against the rebels in the Cumberland Valley. . . . Of course, I would like some old regiments, batteries, etc., but you know if they can be spared from other points." *OR*, XXVII, pt. 3, p. 264.

28. For a description of Couch's powers see *ibid.*, pp. 130–132, 162, 185, 203, 239–240. Stanton wired Couch on June 20 to ask whether the powers granted him were as large and discretionary in the present emergency as he wished. Couch's reply was a model of its kind, for he said: "My powers are ample. I require nothing more." *Ibid.*, p. 240.

29. For Couch's reports to Curtin and Stanton indicating his relationship with them see *ibid.*, pp. 391–392, 407–408.

30. Kamm, *Civil War Career of Scott*, 155–156. For work done in Chambersburg to keep in touch with enemy movements and make reports to Harrisburg, see A. K. McClure, *Lincoln and Men of War Times* (Philadelphia, 1892), 378–381. For information which Couch furnished authorities in Washington or the commander of the Army of the Potomac, see *OR*, XXVII, pt. 3, pp. 130–131, 159–163, 186, 201, 253, 263, 295, 328–329.

31. C. C. Coffin, *The Boys of '61, or Four Years of Fighting* . . . (Boston, 1883), 258–259.

32. Kamm, *Civil War Career of Scott*, 151–152.

33. S. W. Pennypacker, "Six Weeks in Uniform in the Gettysburg Campaign, 1863," *Historical and Biographical Sketches* (Philadelphia, 1883), 308; M. Jacobs, *Notes on the Rebel Invasion of Maryland and Pennsylvania and the Battle of Gettysburg, July 1st, 2nd, and 3d, 1863* (Philadelphia, 1864), 10.

34. Both Northern and Southern observers referred to the "great many Copperhead Democrats" in the invaded portions of Pa. See A. A. Anderson, 1st Battalion, Hoke's Brigade to his brother, July 5, 1863, Patrick H. Cain Letters, UNC; McLaws to Emily [his wife], June 28, 1863, Lafayette McLaws Papers, UNC; Chambersburg *Repository* in Moore, ed., *Rebellion Record, Documents*, VII, 197; "Extracts from the Diary of Lieut. Hermann Schuricht," *SHSP, XXIV*, 340; Dispatch from Thomas Maguire, Harrisburg, July 1, in *Boston Morning Journal*, July 4, 1863; Dispatch from Agate [Whitelaw Reid], Washington, June 27, in *Cincinnati Daily Gazette*, July 1, 1863. One Southerner described their reception in a small town just over the Pa. border as warmer than anything experienced in Md. There was a great display of miniature Confederate flags, while the women waved handkerchiefs and scarves from porches and upper windows. He suspected that these demonstrations were not sincere and wondered whether they were merely a part of "Dutch cunning to placate the oft-pictured, wild, rantankerous, ravenous Rebs." Hamilton, ed., *Shotwell Papers*, I, 490–491.

35. John B. Gordon, *Reminiscences of the Civil War* (New York, 1903), 143.

36. Patrick Journal, Entry for July 5, 1863, LC; L. F. Lyttle, Capt. & Provost Marshal, to Capt. E. W. Andrews, July 16, 1863, U. S. Army Command, Army of the Potomac, LXVII, 100, Record Group 98, NA.

37. Fitzgerald Ross, *Cities and Camps of the Confederate States*, Richard B. Harwell, ed. (Urbana, Ill., 1958), 39. Very possibly many of these young men came from Scotch-Irish families who, contrary to the impressions of most Confederates, actually outnumbered the "Dutch" in the Cumberland Valley. For more evidence of the Pennsylvanians' indifference to the war and excessive concern for their property, see Hamilton, ed., *Shotwell Papers*, I, 492–493; Browne, *Dunn Browne in the Army*, 207–208; Blake, *Three Years in the Army of the Potomac*, 220; [J. T. Trowbridge], "The Field of Gettysburg," *Atlantic Monthly*, XVI, 616; *OR*, XXVII, pt. 1, p. 926.

38. Samuel P. Bates, *Martial Deeds of Pennsylvania* (Philadelphia, 1875), 168; Jacobs, *Rebel Invasion*, 9–10.

39. A. Kopelin to Curtin, June 27, 1863; A. L. Russell to Geo. W. McConnell, June 30, 1863; Thos. M. Howe to Curtin, June 2, 1863, Dispatches, PDMA, PDPR.

40. H. M. Johnson to Col. Jno. A. Wright, June 25, 1863, *ibid.*

41. A. Sutton to State Adjutant General [Russell], July 1, 1863; F. Johnston to Curtin, June 4, 1863, General Correspondence, January–August, 1863, *ibid.*

42. "Extracts from Diary of Lieut. Hermann Schuricht," [Entry for June 23], *SHSP*, XXIV, 342; Berry G. Benson Reminiscences, Typescript, I, 164–165, Berry G. Benson Papers, UNC; *OR*, XXVII, pt. 2, p. 213; LI, pt. 2, pp. 727–728.

43. *Ibid.*, XXVII, pt. 2, pp. 215, 219. The total number of N.Y. troops is based upon the strength given for each regiment in the Annual Report of the Adjutant General of the State of New York. His figures were usually much higher than those given in the regimental reports. On June 27 Couch reported that he had 2,075 N.Y. troops mustered into the U.S. service, and 5,131 not mustered, making a total of 7,206. See *ibid.*, pt. 3, p. 363.

44. *Ibid.*, p. 264.

45. *Ibid.*, pp. 328, 389; Col. Jacob Higgins [commanding militia] to Col. J. A. Wright, [June] 25, 26, 1863, Dispatches, PDMA, PDPR.

46. *OR*, XXVII, pt. 3, p. 407. For other Northern comments see Williams to his daughters, Aug. 6, 1863, in *Alpheus Williams Letters*, 252.

47. Jubal A. Early, *Autobiographical Sketch and Narrative of the War between the States; with Notes by R. H. Early* . . . (Philadelphia, 1912), 264. See also Pettit to his wife, June 28, 1863, in William B. Pettit Papers, UNC. As a good lawyer Early could argue convincingly in favor of the other side of the coin. After the war in an argument with the Count of Paris about the size of the opposing forces in the Gettysburg campaign, he cited the number of emergency troops furnished by Pa. and N.Y. to help the Army of the Potomac, in an effort to prove his thesis that the Confederates had fought against overwhelming odds. "General Early's Reply to the Count of Paris," *SHSP*, IV, 24–25.

48. *OR*, XXVII, pt. 3, p. 347.

49. MacKay, "Philadelphia during the Civil War," *PMHB*, LXX, 32–33; Jacobs, *Rebel Invasion*, 11.

50. Moore, ed., *Rebellion Record, Documents*, VII, 327.

51. J. Sillman to Curtin, June 29, 1863, Dispatches, PDMA, PDPR. Many people wired they had groups all ready and waiting for instructions and transportation.

52. John P. Ilsley to Maj. O. W. Lees, June 26, 1863; [Maj.] O. W. Lees to Col. R. B. Roberts, July 2, 1863; A. L. Russell to H. W. Finley, July 4, 1863, Dispatches, *ibid.*

53. Maj. J. S. Hoyer to Adj. Gen. A. L. Russell, July 1, 2, 1863; Col. Chas. Albright to *id.*, July 2, 1863, *ibid.*

54. John Scott to Col. Jno. A. Wright, [July 2, 1863], *ibid.*

55. Wm. H. Ely to Curtin, July 26, 1863, General Correspondence, *ibid.* For the difficulties emergency troops had in getting supplies, see also *OR*, XXVII, pt. 2, pp. 238, 242, 246–247, 256, 262–264.

56. A. G. Curtin to Horatio Seymour, July 2, 1863; *id.* to Joe[l] Parke[r], July 2, 1863; *id.* to John A. Andrew, July 2, 1863; Joe[l] Parker to Curtin, July 2, 1863; Horatio Seymour to *id.*, July 2, 3, 1863, Dispatches, PDMA, PDPR. Curtin apologized to Andrew for not going through channels in Washington when asking for aid. He had requested the Secy. of War to call for troops from Mass. and other New England states for temporary service in Pa., but as yet he had received no answer from Stanton. He could not wait for it because the "necessity for the immediate presence of assistance becomes more imminent every hour." He asked Andrew to get in touch with the other New England governors about Curtin's need for troops. Curtin seemed excited, but under the circumstances it was perfectly understandable. What he apparently did not know was that Stanton had wired all governors for emergency troops on June 15. For their response see *OR*, XXVII, pt. 3, pp. 138–144, 163–167, 187–188, 205–206. For an example of how Curtin kept up to date on news from Gettysburg see his message to J. R. Fry, Chairman of the Military Committee of Philadelphia. Curtin wired on July 2: "Our affairs look worse today than yesterday. Neither of the battles were decisive." Therefore he urged Fry to devote his time and energy to raising and arming troops to defend the state. Dispatches, PDMA, PDPR.

57. *OR*, XXVII, pt. 3, pp. 95, 113, 129.

58. Either Couch was whistling to keep up his courage or was unduly optimistic about the river as a barrier against the Confederate invasion. The water level of the river was so low at this time that Union military authorities estimated that a force of 3,000 men could have forced passage "at any moment." Cyphered Dispatch signed Optic for Pardon Cola, July 4, 1863, Dispatches, PDMA, PDPR. Gen. Lorenzo Thomas, Adj. Gen. in the War Dept., pronounced the city a "difficult place to defend." *OR*, XXVII, pt. 3, p. 478.

59. *Ibid.*, pp. 80, 129, 163, 223, 264, 330, 385, 401, 403, 478; Pennypacker, "Six Weeks in Uniform," *Historical and Biographical Sketches*, 354, 357, 362; [Trowbridge], "Field of Gettysburg," *Atlantic Monthly*, XVI, 616; Kamm, *Civil War Career of Scott*, 157. In addition to the bridges at Harrisburg there were two railroad bridges nine miles north of the city at Dauphin. Information about the bridges at or near Harrisburg in 1863 was furnished by William Work of the Pa. Historical and Museum Commission.

60. *OR*, XXVII, pt. 3, pp. 297–298.

61. Frederic S. Klein, *Lancaster County, 1841–1941* (Lancaster, Pa., 1941), 46; *OR*, XXVII, pt. 2, pp. 278–279.

62. *Ibid.*, pp. 278–279; pt. 3, pp. 160, 410–411. A message from Thomas A. Scott to J. Edgar Thomson, 9:00 P.M., July 5, 1863, read as follows: "Couch has consented today to have water put in canal. Men have started to fill up canal from Clark's Ferry East." Dispatches, July 1–8, 1863, PDMA, PDPR. Clark's Ferry is fifteen miles northwest of Harrisburg on the east bank of the Susquehanna River. There is no indication of how far east Couch had the canals drained; probably far enough to deprive the Confederates of their use for transportation purposes for a good distance east of Harrisburg. The route of the central division of the Pa. Canal was from Columbia past Harrisburg to Hollidaysburg. The Union Canal came from Reading and intersected the Pa. Canal at what is now the city of Middletown, about nine miles south of Harrisburg. Seymour Dunbar, *A History of Travel in America* (New York, 1937), 793–794, 801–802.

63. *OR*, XXVII, pt. 2, pp. 278–279, 995–999; pt. 3, pp. 410–411.

64. Benson J. Lossing, *Field Book of the Civil War* (New Haven, Conn., 1878), III, 55; Samuel Hunt to Knight, July 2, 1863, John Knight Papers, Duke University Library (cited hereafter as DU); Harold R. Manakee, *Maryland in the Civil War* (Baltimore, 1961), 74.

65. *OR*, XXVII, pt. 3, p. 204; Bates, *Martial Deeds of Pennsylvania*, 171; MacKay, "Philadelphia during the Civil War," *PMHB*, LXX, 32–33; Lossing, *Field Book of the Civil War*, III, 55. While the people in Pittsburgh were perfectly willing to build fortifications, they responded poorly to calls to enlist, even the Governor's call made on June 26. See Thomas M. Howe, Pittsburgh, to Curtin, June 28, 1863, [Part of letter sent in code], Dispatches, PDMA, PDPR. Believing in the efficacy of fortifications against enemy raids, the War Dept. aided and abetted these preparations of civilians by sending military experts to advise and direct them. *OR*, XXVII, pt. 3, pp. 32, 36, 53.

66. *Ibid.*, pp. 188, 204, 366; William Dashington, West Chester, to Curtin, June 28, 1863; Isaac P. Walter, C. Burguess [sic], Tyrone, to Curtin, June 29, 1863, Dispatches, PDMA, PDPR. The petitioner in the dispatch of June 29 did not ask for martial law per se but wanted powers that were tantamount to it. He requested authority of the Governor to close stores and stop all kinds of business in his borough. In this way he hoped to counteract the influence of "many rebel sympathizers who reside here and will not go themselves or encourage others to go."

67. *OR*, XXVII, pt. 3, pp. 437, 504. As a result of martial law, travel without passes was forbidden, the homes of suspected Southern sympathizers were searched for arms, and business was brought to a standstill. Manakee, *Maryland in the Civil War*, 74. In contrast a contemporary in commenting on affairs in Baltimore during martial law said the city was now quiet and business was going on as usual but was dull owing to the invasion. Samuel Hunt to Knight, July 2, 1863, John Knight Papers, DU.

68. Kamm, *Civil War Career of Scott*, 156; Thomas A. Scott to E. L[ewis],

Altoona, [No date, in folder of June 27, 1863]; *id.* to Jos. N. Black, Columbia, [No date, in folder of June 27, 1863], Dispatches, PDMA, PDPR. For mention of stockades and blockhouses along the line of the Northern Central Railroad see Lossing, *Field Book of the Civil War*, III, 55, 76. The Baltimore and Ohio Railroad sent many locomotives and cars to the city of Baltimore as a precaution against their destruction. Manakee, *Maryland in the Civil War*, 74.

69. *OR*, XXVII, pt. 3, pp. 95, 113, 129–130.

70. Schaff, "Gettysburg Week," *Scribner's Magazine*, XVI, 22, 25–26; Ross, *Cities and Camps of the Confederate States*, 40–41; Fremantle, *Three Months in the Southern States*, 241, 245; "Extracts from Diary of Lieut. Hermann Schuricht," *SHSP*, XXIV, 341; Francis Milton Kennedy Diary, Microfilm of Typescript, UNC; Chambersburg *Repository*, in Moore, ed., *Rebellion Record, Documents*, VII, 197; Westwood A. Todd Reminiscences, I, 125, Typescript, UNC.

71. Bates, *Martial Deeds of Pennsylvania*, 169–170; Pennypacker, "Six Weeks in Uniform," *Historical and Biographical Sketches*, 354.

72. Bates, "William H. Boyd," MS, Bates Collection; Chambersburg *Repository*, in Moore, ed., *Rebellion Record, Documents*, VII, 194–195. For a description of the panic in Mercersburg, which fugitive soldiers, "most of them drunk," from Milroy's command helped to accentuate, see Schaff, "Gettysburg Week," *Scribner's Magazine*, XVI, 22–23.

73. Coffin, *Boys of '61*, 259. Coffin was a reporter for the *Boston Morning Journal* and entered Harrisburg on June 15. For further information on the flight see *New York Tribune*, July 14, 1863. On July 8 refugees in great numbers passed through Harrisburg on their return home.

74. *OR*, XXVII, pt. 2, pp. 443, 466.

75. *Ibid.*, p. 995.

76. Ramseur to [Nellie], June 28, 1863, Stephen D. Ramseur Papers, UNC.

77. Dispatch from Thomas Maguire, Harrisburg, July 1, in *Boston Morning Journal*, July 4, 1863; Thomas A. Scott to W. F. L., Columbia, [No date, in folder of June 27, 1863], Dispatches, PDMA, PDPR. To set the number of fleeing Negroes in the "thousands" seems like an exaggeration, but the Census of 1860 bears out the reliability of this estimate by giving the number of Negroes living in the invaded counties as 5,622. If the Negroes living in two of the immediately threatened counties, Dauphin and Lancaster, are included, the total becomes 10,790. *Eighth Census of the United States, 1860, Population* (Washington, D.C., 1864), 412.

78. W. H. Armstrong, Harrisburg, to Adams Express Co., Philadelphia, June 27, 1863, Dispatches, PDMA, PDPR; Bates, *Martial Deeds of Pennsylvania*, 171; James Ford Rhodes, "The Battle of Gettysburg," *American Historical Review*, IV, 669; Lossing, *Field Book of the Civil War*, III, 55 note; Pennypacker, "Six Weeks in Uniform," *Historical and Biographical Sketches*, 357; Dispatch from Thomas Maguire, Harrisburg, July 1, in *Boston Morning Journal*, July 4, 1863; Coffin, *Boys of '61*, 259.

79. Rhodes, "Battle of Gettysburg," *American Historical Review*, IV, 669.

80. *OR*, XXVII, pt. 3, p. 409.

81. *Ibid.*, pt. 2, pp. 212–216, 219; pt. 3, pp. 1081–1082.

82. For condemnation of Pennsylvanians see *Wainwright Journals*, 229–230, 254, 256; Julian W. Hinkley, *A Narrative of Service with the Third Wisconsin Infantry* (Wisconsin Historical Commission, 1912), 91; Browne, *Dunn Browne in the Army*, 207–208; [Trowbridge], "Field of Gettysburg, *Atlantic Monthly*, XVI, 616; Sedgwick to his sister [Emily], July 26, 1863, *Correspondence of Major-General John Sedgwick* (Boston, 1902–1903), II, 137; Paul Fatout, ed., *Letters of a Civil War Surgeon* [Maj. William Watson] (Lafayette, Ind., 1961), 69; Ford, ed., *Adams Letters*, II, 45; Blake, *Three Years in the Army of the Potomac*, 220; Allan Nevins and Milton Halsey Thomas, eds., *Diary of George Templeton Strong* (New York, 1952), III, 325; Gray and Ropes, *War Letters*, 133–134; *New York Times*, July 9, 1863. For commendations of the generosity of Pennsylvanians toward Union troops see Pennypacker, "Six Weeks in Uniform," *Historical and Biographical Sketches*, 372; Coffin, *Boys of '61*, 265–266; Elizabeth Eaton Hincks, *Undismayed, The Story of a Yankee Chaplain's Family in the Civil War* (Privately Printed, 1952), 50; David Stevenson, *Indiana's Roll of Honor* (Indianapolis, 1864), 374–375. For the fine reception Union troops received in Md. see Brooks, *Washington in Lincoln's Time*, 84–85; Blake, *Three Years in the Army of the Potomac*, 199–200; The Survivors' Association, *History of the 118th Pennsylvania Volunteers* (Philadelphia, 1905), 233; *Wainwright Journals*, 259; *New York Times*, July 13, 1863.

83. For the interpretation that the breakdown of the Federal recruitment policies during the invasion was due to a resurgence of states rights feeling and that controversies between states rightists and nationalists hampered mobilization of emergency troops, see William B. Hesseltine, *Lincoln and the War Governors* (New York, 1948), 295–297.

84. Gen. P. G. T. Beauregard to Wigfall, May 16, 1863, Correspondence of Louis T. Wigfall, Wigfall Family Papers, LC; McLaws to his wife, June 10, 1863, Lafayette McLaws Papers, UNC; Jones, *Rebel War Clerk's Diary*, I, 357.

NOTES TO CHAPTER VII

1. Gordon, *Reminiscences*, 144–145. Gen. Early made the astounding statement in his memoirs that "not even a rail had been taken from the fences for firewood." See Early, *Narrative of the War*, 264.

2. *Report of the Auditor General on the Finances of the Commonwealth of Pennsylvania for the Year Ending November 30, 1880* (Harrisburg, 1881), 14. This figure at best is a rough approximation of the financial loss the Confederates caused the people of Pa. in 1863. A state board of commissioners adjudicated all claims for actual physical damage during the war and allowed only those which could be established by judicial rules of evidence. Many bona fide claims which could not pass the test were not considered valid. There was also no attempt by anyone to estimate indirect losses, such as those suffered by

farmers when they could not harvest their crops on time for want of draft animals.

3. *OR*, XXVII, pt. 3, pp. 912–913. General Orders No. 72 were issued June 21.

4. In referring to the invasion of the enemy's soil Gen. Longstreet remarked that "although it might be fair, in just retaliation, to *apply the torch*, yet doing so would demoralize the army and ruin its now excellent discipline. Private property is to be therefore rigidly protected." Fremantle, *Three Months in the Southern States*, 237–238. See also Longstreet's instructions to his division commanders, June 26, 1863, in *OR*, LI, pt. 2, pp. 727–728. Col. John S. Mosby, who was pretty much the hard-headed realist, maintained that Lee's order was issued not from any feeling of tenderness toward the Pennsylvanians, but to preserve the morale and discipline of his army. He did not want it to "degenerate into a band of marauders and stragglers." Mosby to H. C. Jordan, Aug. 23, 1909, John S. Mosby Papers, DU.

5. Freeman takes the position that Lee had the peace movement in mind when he drafted the regulations, but offers no supporting evidence for his view. *R. E. Lee*, III, 57.

6. "Advance into Pennsylvania," Moore, ed., *Rebellion Record, Documents*, VII, 324.

7. Alexander, "Battle of Gettysburg," MS, E. P. Alexander Papers, UNC. See also Thomas L. Ware Diary, Entry for June 27, 1863, Typescript, UNC, for a short description of the march from Greencastle to Chambersburg. For marching of infantry through fields of wheat because heavy rains and artillery trains had made the roads impassable, see Dr. J. E. Green Diary, Entry for July 5, 1863, North Carolina State Department of Archives and History.

8. "Advance into Pennsylvania," Moore, ed., *Rebellion Record, Documents*, VII, 324; *OR*, XXVII, pt. 2, p. 550.

9. Pender to his wife, June 28, 1863, William D. Pender Papers, UNC.

10. Chandler to his sister, July 17, 1863, John J. Chandler Papers, Virginia State Library. Better expressed is the comment of William Calder: "They live in real Yankee style wife & daughters & a help doing all the work. It makes me more than ever devoted to our own Southern institutions & customs." Calder to his mother, June 26, 1863, William Calder Papers, UNC.

11. J. B. Clifton Diary, North Carolina State Department of Archives and History; Pettit to his wife, June 28, 1863, W. B. Pettit Papers, UNC; Thomas L. Ware Diary, Typescript, UNC; Hotchkiss to his wife, June 28, 1863, Jedediah Hotchkiss Papers, LC; Ross, *Cities and Camps*, 36, 38–39; Fremantle, *Three Months in the Southern States*, 238–239.

12. *Ibid.*, 239–240.

13. Dispatch of Special Correspondent, Headquarters of General Lee near Chambersburg, June 29, in the *Times* [London], July 29, 1863.

14. Hotchkiss, near Chambersburg, to his wife, June 25, 1863, Jedediah Hotchkiss Papers, LC. See also letter to his wife, June 28, 1863, and entry of June 30, 1863, in his Memorandum Book, *ibid.*

15. Halsey [Wigfall] to Louly, July 18, 1863, Wigfall Family Papers, LC.

Another Confederate correspondent said: "The people [around York] all treated us very kindly . . . though I think that their kindness was more through fear than anything else." A. G. Cleek to his father, July 19, 1863, John Cleek Papers, DU. See also Ross, *Cities and Camps*, 38–39; Welch, *Letters to His Wife*, 62–63.

16. Early, *Narrative of the War*, 265.

17. *OR*, XXVII, pt. 1, p. 926.

18. Gordon, *Reminiscences*, 147–148. About the lack of open resistance see also Calder to his mother, June 26, 1863, William Calder Papers, UNC.

19. Pender to his wife, June 28, 1863, William D. Pender Papers, UNC; Walter Harrison, *Pickett's Men, A Fragment of War History* (New York, 1870), 86–87; Ross, *Cities and Camps*, 35; Francis Milton Kennedy Diary, Entry for July 6, 1863, Microfilm of Typescript, UNC.

20. Calder to his mother, June 20, 26, 1863, William Calder Papers, UNC; Hotchkiss to his wife, June 25, 1863, Jedediah Hotchkiss Papers, LC.

21. G. Campbell Brown, "Reminiscences of the Civil War," I, MS, Campbell Brown Books, UNC.

22. *Ibid.*; Hotchkiss to his wife, June 25, 1863, Jedediah Hotchkiss Papers, LC.

23. *Id.* to *id.*, June 25, 1863, *ibid.*

24. Mercersburg received six visitations; the last occurred July 1 and was the worst. Schaff, "Gettysburg Week," *Scribner's Magazine*, XVI, 26.

25. Jacob Hoke, *The Great Invasion of 1863; or General Lee in Pennsylvania* (New York, 1959), 97–107, 109–111; Chambersburg *Repository* in Moore, ed., *Rebellion Record, Documents*, VII, 196; "Extracts from Diary of Lieut. Hermann Schuricht," *SHSP*, XXIV, 340.

26. Hoke, *Great Invasion*, 111. Someone broke into two vacant houses just outside of Chambersburg and plundered them of clothing, kettles, and other articles. Presumably some of Jenkins' men were guilty of this act, but no one really knew. Chambersburg *Repository* in Moore, ed., *Rebellion Record, Documents*, VII, 197. In Chambersburg panic-stricken inhabitants fleeing the town left clothes and household utensils scattered in the streets. Jenkins detailed a company of men to gather up the goods and put them in the houses of their probable owners. "Extracts from Diary of Lieut. Hermann Schuricht," *SHSP*, XXIV, 340.

27. Chambersburg *Repository* in Moore, ed., *Rebellion Record, Documents*, VII, 197; Schaff, "Gettysburg Week," *Scribner's Magazine*, XVI, 22–25; *OR*, II, pt. 2, pp. 732–733.

28. Schaff, "Gettysburg Week," *Scribner's Magazine*, XVI, 22–23; Chambersburg *Repository* in Moore, ed., *Rebellion Record, Documents*, VII, 196–198; Jacobs, *Rebel Invasion*, 8–9, 11; Bates, *Martial Deeds of Pennsylvania*, 173–174; Hoke, *Great Invasion*, 111–113. According to the Chambersburg *Repository*, horses seemed to be considered by Jenkins as "contraband of war, and were taken without the pretence of compensation; but other articles were deemed legitimate subjects of commerce even between enemies, and they were generally paid for after a fashion." Jacobs, who at the time of the battle was

645

a professor at what is now Gettysburg College, agreed with this statement about Jenkins' seizure of horses; so did the Confederate Gen. R. E. Rodes. See *OR*, XXVII, pt. 2, p. 550.

29. On p. 113 of his *Great Invasion* Hoke makes the following statement: "The effect of this raid, however, was to arouse the people of Pennsylvania and the whole North, and volunteers for the defense of the border hurried to Harrisburg." If so, their reaction to the news was greatly overdue. It was not until all of Lee's army had crossed the Potomac and the Governor had issued his last proclamation that volunteers came pouring in. By then it was much too late.

30. *OR*, XXVII, pt. 2, pp. 550–551.

31. Hoke, *Great Invasion*, 123–130.

32. *Ibid.*, 131; Copy of Order of Gen. Ewell, R. S. Ewell Papers, LC; *OR*, XXVII, pt. 2, p. 551. Ewell prohibited marauding and plundering and stipulated that anything taken for army use would be in obedience to "regulations to be established by the commanding-general, according to the rules of civilized warfare." Ewell evidently knew Lee intended to formulate and publish such regulations, but he had not as yet received them.

33. Hoke, *Great Invasion*, 132–135, 137–144; *OR*, XXVII, pt. 2, pp. 442–443, 464, 503, 551.

34. Schaff, "Gettysburg Week," *Scribner's Magazine*, XVI, 23–25.

35. *OR*, XXVII, pt. 2, pp. 443, 503; Randolph H. McKim, *A Soldier's Recollections. Leaves from the Diary of a Young Confederate* (London, 1910), 166. McKim recalled that Steuart's expedition had not gathered nearly as many cattle as had been expected.

36. In 1863 the center of Greenwood was about three miles east of Fayetteville.

37. *OR*, XXVII, pt. 2, pp. 443, 464–465; Richard N. Current, *Old Thad Stevens. A Story of Ambition* (Madison, Wis., 1942), 179. Ewell and Early gave no reasons for the order to destroy the Wrightsville-Columbia bridge.

38. *OR*, XXVII, pt. 2, pp. 464–465, 768–770.

39. Early to J. Fraise Richard, May 7, 1886, Jubal A. Early Correspondence, LC; Hoke, *Great Invasion*, 170–171. The works were at the base of South Mountain about two miles east of Greenwood.

40. Current, *Old Thad Stevens*, 38, 177, 180–183. Lee was distressed to see the ruins of the buildings three days later. Both he and Stevens worried about the plight of the families of men who had lost their jobs. Lee's quartermaster told John Sweeney, the works manager, that needy families could draw upon him for supplies. See *ibid.*, 179, 183.

41. *OR*, XXVII, pt. 2, p. 465; Pennypacker, "Six Weeks in Uniform," *Historical and Biographical Sketches*, 319, 323–324, 340.

42. Early, *Narrative of the War*, 257–258.

43. Pennypacker, "Six Weeks in Uniform," *Historical and Biographical Sketches*, 342–343.

44. *OR*, XXVII, pt. 2, p. 465.

45. *Ibid.*, pt. 3, p. 923; Jacobs, *Rebel Invasion*, 16–18. According to Jacobs, Early's demand for provisions included the following items: 1,200 lbs. of sugar,

600 lbs. of coffee, 60 bbls. of flour, 1,000 lbs. of salt, 7,000 lbs. of bacon, 10 bbls. of onions, and 10 bbls. of whiskey.

46. *Ibid.*, 17.

47. J. Warren [Jackson] to Lt. R. Stark Jackson, July 22, 1863, Typescript in possession of Prof. Merl E. Reed, Dept. of Social Studies, Ball State Teachers College (Original in David F. Boyd Civil War Papers, 1863, Department of Archives, Louisiana State University).

48. *OR*, XXVII, pt. 2, p. 465.

49. The columns with Early were slowed down by mud nearly knee-deep, which caused hundreds of men to straggle. See J. W. [Jackson] to R. S. Jackson, July 22, 1863, Reed Typescript.

50. Hanover Junction was about three and a half miles due west of the present town of Logansville.

51. Hoke, *Great Invasion*, 183–185; *OR*, XXVII, pt. 2, pp. 465–466; Early, *Narrative of the War*, 262; "The Occupation of York, Pa.," Moore, ed., *Rebellion Record, Documents*, VII, 321, from the *York Gazette*, June 29, 1863; "Report of Dr. Douglas [United States Sanitary Commission]," *ibid.*, 122. Town authorities collected the articles and money, for which they gave certificates or receipts to citizens making the contributions. Presumably these certificates could be used in the future as claims against the Confederate government. The requisitions for food were as follows: 165 bbls. of flour or 28,000 lbs. of baked bread; 3,500 lbs. of sugar; 1,650 lbs. of coffee; 300 gals. of molasses; 1,200 lbs. of salt; 32,000 lbs. of fresh beef or 21,000 lbs. of bacon or pork. Sugar, molasses, coffee, and salt were very scarce items in the Confederacy. In some areas they were not to be had at all.

52. "Report of Dr. Douglas," *ibid.*, 122–123; "The Occupation of York, Pa.," *ibid.*, 321–322.

53. *OR*, XXVII, pt. 2, pp. 466–467; J. A. Early to McClellan, Feb. 2, 1878, Henry B. McClellan Papers, VHS.

54. *OR*, XXVII, pt. 2, pp. 277–279, 466, 491–492, 995–999. Gordon claimed the Yankees had 1,200 men, a number "nearly equal" in strength to his brigade. This figure was given him, he said, by the commanding officer who had been captured. The commanding officer, Col. Jacob G. Frick, who was not captured, gave no precise figures for the size of his force. From a careful reading of his report it is doubtful whether he had altogether as many as 1,000 men. They were a hodgepodge of separate companies and detachments from various regiments.

55. *Ibid.*, p. 466.

56. *Ibid.*, pp. 466–467, 492, 998; "The Occupation of York, Pa.," Moore, ed., *Rebellion Record, Documents*, VII, 321, from the *York Gazette*, June 29, 1863. Early and Gordon denounced the ingratitude of the Yankee press in accusing the Confederates of arson in Wrightsville. Maj. Haller of the staff of Gen. Darius N. Couch paid generous tribute to the Confederates for saving the town.

57. *Ibid*; *OR*, XXVII, pt. 2, pp. 467, 492; J. A. Early to McClellan, Feb. 26, 1878, Henry B. McClellan Papers, VHS. In his battle report Early said he decided against burning the railroad car shops and other buildings for fear of

destroying a large part of York. Later he told McClellan that the head of a mercantile firm had offered him $50,000 if he would not burn them. Early hesitated to give his word because Stuart might go through York after he was gone. Should Stuart burn the buildings, the Confederates would then be charged with having committed a "breach of faith."

58. "Report of Dr. Douglas," Moore, ed., *Rebellion Record, Documents*, VII, 122–123.

59. *OR*, XXVII, pt. 2, pp. 565–566, 599–600.

60. *Ibid.*, pp. 443, 503.

61. *Ibid.*, p. 443; *New York Times*, July 1, 1863; Hotchkiss to his wife, June 28, 1863, Jedediah Hotchkiss Papers, LC; R. M. Evans to T. A. Scott, June [27], 1863, Dispatches, PDMA, PDPR.

62. *Ibid.*

63. *New York Times*, July 3, 1863.

64. *OR*, XXVII, pt. 2, p. 443; Brown, "Reminiscences," MS, Campbell Brown Books, UNC.

65. Diary of John I. Murray–1863 [Co. A, 22nd N.Y. regiment], Entries of July 1, 3, 1863, NYHS.

66. Ewell to Lizzie [Ewell], June 24, 1863, R. S. Ewell Papers, LC.

67. I. A. Wilson to William Wilson, July 1, 1863; Thomas A. Scott to E. Lewis, [July 1, 1863]; Thomas A. Scott to J. Edgar Thomson, July 5, 1863; Cypher signed Optic [Couch] to Austria Lucy [Halleck], July 7, 1863; Halleck to Couch, [July 8, 1863], Dispatches, PDMA, PDPR.

68. Pennypacker, "Six Weeks in Uniform," *Historical and Biographical Sketches*, 375–377.

69. Hoke, *Great Invasion*, 160–161, 169, 173; *OR*, XXVII, pt. 2, pp. 358, 366, 388, 428.

70. Fremantle, *Three Months in the Southern States*, 240, 242, 249–250; Sorrel, *Recollections*, 177–179; Scheibert, *Seven Months in the Rebel States*, Hoole, ed., 110.

71. *Ibid.*

72. *OR*, XXVII, pt. 3, pp. 942–943.

73. Fremantle, *Three Months in the Southern States*, 241, 244–245; Hoke, *Great Invasion*, 191–199.

74. A. K. McClure to William [?] McLellan, July 4, 1863, Dispatches, PDMA, PDPR. Part of the message read: "[Judge] Kimmell here [Harrisburg], all safe at home [Chambersburg]. . . . Mrs. McLellan entertained General Battle and had interview as to supplies. . . . Mrs. McClure saved everything but the sheep—had a fight over the corn and farm-wagon but saved both." Cullen A. Battle was a colonel at the time and did not become brigadier general until Aug. 20, 1863. Boatner, *Civil War Dictionary*, 50–51.

75. Schaff, "Gettysburg Week," *Scribner's Magazine*, XVI, 25–26.

76. Daniel to his grandfather, Aug. 3, 1863, John W. Daniel Papers, UV.

77. *OR*, XVII, pt. 2, pp. 443, 550.

78. Ross, *Cities and Camps*, 34.

79. Fremantle, *Three Months in the Southern States*, 242, 275.

80. G. W. Nichols, *A Soldier's Story of His Regiment* (Kennesaw, Ga., 1961), 123.

81. Welch, *Letters to His Wife*, 60. This letter was written from near Bunker Hill, Va., on July 17, 1863. See also Ross, *Cities and Camps*, 67–68. Ross said enough supplies had been obtained to sustain the army for several months. The Confederates also got wagons and horses in "incalculable numbers." He also said that the army in order to give the men a daily ration of a pound and a half of beef butchered 300 head of cattle a day. As corroboration see the letter of the Union Gen. John Sedgwick, July 26, 1863: "We captured twelve thousand head of cattle and eight thousand head of sheep that the enemy had driven from Pennsylvania." Sedgwick to his sister [Emily], in *Correspondence of Sedgwick*, II, 136–138.

82. Papers of the Board of Claims under Act of April 16, 1862, Auditor General of State of Pennsylvania, Border Claims, Adjudicated under Act of May 22, 1871, PDPR. These claims are illustrative of thousands of others. It is not clear whether the monetary value of these claims was based upon the price level of commodities in 1863 or 1871 or later. For the sake of convenience probably market prices in 1871 or later, depending upon the time of the adjudication, were used as the standard to determine values. If so, claimants were allowed less in monetary compensation, since the dollar had greatly appreciated since the war. Therefore the following figures do not accurately reflect the losses of the claimants:

Barr	Value of claim which was allowed—			$ 5,190.25
Hargbroad	"	"	"	10,802.79
Eyster & Brothers	"	"	"	7,553.22
Bitner	"	"	"	4,167.40

83. *OR*, XXVII, pt. 3, p. 943.

84. Casler, *Four Years in the Stonewall Brigade*, 168.

85. George W. Beale to his mother, July 13, 1863, in *SHSP*, XI, 327; *OR*, XXVII, pt. 2, p. 550; Schaff, "Gettysburg Week," *Scribner's Magazine*, XVI, 23.

86. *Ibid.*, 24–26; Samuel C. Means [Capt. Va. Rangers] to Halleck, July 3, 1863, General Halleck Telegrams Received, Generals' Papers and Books, Record Group 107, NA.

87. For Confederate stragglers or skulkers see Fremantle, *Three Months in the Southern States*, 246; John L. Hubbard [1st Md. Battalion] to Ignatius Brown, July 19, 1863, Intercepted Letters, Confederate Records, U. S. Army Command, Record Group 109, NA. For Union stragglers or skulkers see *Cincinnati Daily Gazette*, July 8, 1863; *New York Times*, July 9, 1863; *OR*, XXVII, pt. 3, p. 398.

88. Hoke, *Great Invasion*, 176; John C. Haskell, *The Haskell Memoirs*, Gilbert E. Govan and James W. Livingood, eds., (New York, 1960), 48. It is not clear whether Hoke and Haskell are citing the same murder or two different acts.

89. Casler, *Four Years in the Stonewall Brigade*, 170; Brown, "Reminiscences," MS, Campbell Brown Books, UNC; *Cincinnati Daily Gazette*, July 8, 1863.

90. Fremantle, *Three Months in the Southern States*, 246.

91. *Ibid.*, 235; Holley to his wife, July 10, 31, 1863, Turner W. Holley Letters, DU; Joseph A. Trundle to his sister, July 7, 1863, in "Gettysburg as Described in Two Letters from a Maryland Confederate," *Maryland Historical Magazine*, June, 1959, 212.

92. Fletcher, *Rebel Private*, 54–57; Sale to his aunt, July 27, 1863, John F. Sale Letters, Virginia State Library; Paul Turner Vaughan Diary, Mar. 4, 1863, to Feb. 12, 1864, DU; Moore, *A Life for the Confederacy*, 152; Boatwright to his wife, June 25 [?], July 9, 1863, Thomas F. Boatwright Papers, UNC; Entry in Diary for June 29, 1863, found in Berry G. Benson Reminiscences, I, Typescript, UNC; J. B. Polley, *A Soldier's Letters to Charming Nellie* (New York, 1908), 125–127.

93. Thomas L. Ware Diary, Entries for June 27, 28, 1863, Typescript, UNC.

94. Pender to his wife, June 28, 1863, William B. Pender Papers, UNC.

95. Claims of Benjamin Albert, Reading Twp., Adams Cty.; George Biesecker and Henry Biesecker, Franklin Twp., Adams Cty.; Berkley Buhrman, Hamilton Twp., Adams Cty.; Joseph Culbertson, Hamilton Twp., Adams Cty.; John S. Deardorf, Guilford Twp., Adams Cty.; James Brumback, Washington Twp., Franklin Cty.; William Boadenhamer, Hanover Borough, York Cty.; David Bricker, Butler Twp., Adams Cty.; Margaret Anderson, Hamiltonban Twp., Adams Cty.; William M. Bigham, Freedom Twp., Adams Cty.; Mary J. Baumgardner, Cumberland Twp., Adams Cty., Papers of the Board of Claims under Act of April 16, 1862, Auditor General of State of Pennsylvania, Border Claims, Adjudicated under Act of May 22, 1871, PDPR.

96. Francis Milton Kennedy Diary, Entry for June 28, 1863, Microfilm of Typescript, UNC.

97. Reed to his mother and sister, July 11, 1863, Charles W. Reed Letters, Typescript, PU.

98. Claims of William Comfort, Cumberland Twp., Adams Cty.; Daniel Stallsmith, Executor of Peter Trostel Estate, Straban Twp., Adams Cty.; John H. Eckert, Straban Twp., Adams Cty.; David Finefrock, Cumberland Twp., Adams Cty., Papers of the Board of Claims under Act of April 16, 1862, Auditor General of State of Pennsylvania, Border Claims, Adjudicated under Act of May 22, 1871, PDPR.

99. Claims of William Comfort, Cumberland Twp., Adams Cty.; Adam Doersom, Gettysburg, Adams Cty.; John Q. Allewelt, Cumberland Twp., Adams Cty.; David K. Beams, Cumberland Twp., Adams Cty.; Adam Beisecker, Franklin Twp., Adams Cty.; May J. Baumgardner, Cumberland Twp., Adams Cty.; Daniel Heintzelman, Franklin Twp., Adams Cty.; Samuel Martin, Liberty Twp., Adams Cty.; Paxton & McCreary, Hamiltonban Twp., Adams Cty., *ibid.*; Diary of Sarah M. Broadhead, Typescript, Library of Gettysburg National Military Park; Pennypacker, "Six Weeks in Uniform," *Historical and Biographical Sketches*, 354; "South Carolinians at Gettysburg," by Col. Joseph

N. Brown, in Varina D. Brown, *A Colonel at Gettysburg and Spotsylvania* (Columbia, S. C., 1931), 85–86; Casler, *Four Years in the Stonewall Brigade*, 178.

100. Noah Brooks, *Washington in Lincoln's Time*, 85; [J. Y. Foster], "Four Days at Gettysburg," *Harper's Monthly*, XXVIII, 281.,

101. Howard to [his wife], July 22, 1863, Howard Papers.

102. McIntosh to his wife, July 22, 1863, John B. McIntosh Correspondence, Brown University Library.

NOTES TO CHAPTER VIII

1. *OR*, XXVII, pt. 1, pp. 64, 67, 143; pt. 2, pp. 307, 316, 358, 694.

2. Freeman, *Lee's Lieutenants*, III, 48–49. Harrison was born in the early 1830's and made his stage debut at the Old Museum, Baltimore, Sept. 8, 1852, with Joseph Jefferson as stage manager. He became an associate of Edwin Booth and though never a star, attained distinction as one of the better known actors in the country. Information furnished through the kindness of John Bakeless of Seymour, Conn.

3. *OR*, XXVII, pt. 2, p. 316. See also *ibid.*, pp. 307, 321.

4. *Ibid.*, pt. 1, p. 143; pt. 3, p. 923.

5. *Ibid.*, pt. 2, p. 297.

6. *Ibid.*, pt. 3, p. 913.

7. *Ibid.*, pt. 2, p. 297.

8. *Ibid.*, pt. 3, pp. 923, 931.

9. *Ibid.*, pt. 2, p. 306.

10. *Ibid.*, pp. 307, 316. The first quotation comes from Lee's first report of the campaign, the other from the final one.

11. *Ibid.*, p. 316.

12. McClellan, *Campaigns of Stuart*, 318; Longstreet, *Memoirs*, 341–343; *OR*, XXVII, pt. 3, p. 915.

13. *Ibid.*, p. 927.

14. Butterfield at 9:20 P.M. on June 20 ordered Capt. Turnbull, who was in command of the engineers at Edwards Ferry, to delay building the bridge. On June 22 Gen. Alpheus Williams mentioned riding out on the bridge. It is reasonable to assume therefore that it was laid sometime on June 21 or 22. Gen. Lee referred to it in his letter to Davis on June 23. *Ibid.*, pt. 2, p. 297; pt. 3, p. 229; Williams to his daughters, June 20 and 23, 1863, in *Alpheus Williams Letters*, 217–218.

15. There is another question which has not been satisfactorily answered: What happened to Maj. Mosby when he and Stuart did not meet as planned near Dranesville because Stuart had to make a detour around the Federal army? Mosby said that when Stuart's artillery ceased firing, he concluded that Stuart had gone back and therefore he did the same. He did not say where he went, nor why he did not try to get in touch with Stuart or someone else in the

Confederate cavalry. Since he had developed the art of going back and forth through the opposing lines with impunity, it is strange he did not report Hooker's moves toward the Potomac. See Mosby, *Stuart's Cavalry*, 177.

16. Gen. Slocum, who at this time held Leesburg with the Twelfth Corps and formed the vanguard of Hooker's army, kept a sharp eye out for signs of enemy activity between Leesburg and Snickersville. With only a regiment of cavalry at his disposal he knew what was going on in an extensive area to the west and south of him. *OR*, XXVII, pt. 3, pp. 281, 307.

17. *Ibid.*, pt. 1, p. 143.

18. *Ibid.*, pt. 2, pp. 751–752, 760, 763–764, 766; B. H. Robertson to [Henry] Heth, Dec. 27, 1877, in Mosby, *Stuart's Cavalry*, 200–201. Robertson's report of the Gettysburg campaign covered only his operations at Brandy Station.

19. *OR*, XXVII, pt. 3, p. 336. Gen. Stahel also reported a small force of rebel cavalry as having been in Boonsborough on the morning of June 26. See *ibid.*, p. 334.

20. B. H. Robertson to [Henry] Heth, Dec. 27, 1877; [T. B.] Massie to [John Mosby], [No date], in Mosby, *Stuart's Cavalry*, 200–203. Maj. McClellan, while writing his fair-minded history of Stuart's cavalry campaigns, made the following observation: "I have never been able to understand how General Lee could have allowed Robertson & Jones to remain inactive during all those days—especially since Walter Martin [Jones's asst. adj. gen.] tells me that he was in constant communication with him.—They had as many men as Stuart had with him, and it seems to me that they ought to have found out all that General Lee wanted to know." McClellan to Early, Aug. 2, 1863, Jubal A. Early Papers, LC. See also McClellan, *Campaigns of Stuart*, 335–336, for similar views. Mosby thought it "highly probable" that Jones and Robertson got instructions from Lee or Longstreet to wait at the gaps for further orders. Mosby, *Stuart's Cavalry*, 198.

21. *Cf. ante*, V, 122; *OR*, XXVII, pt. 3, pp. 334, 336.

22. Although Lee kept in touch with Robertson, who had his headquarters near Berryville, he sent him no new instructions until June 29, when the brigades were ordered to join the main body of the army. According to Martin, Lee showed great anxiety to hear from Stuart; he repeatedly sent couriers with inquiries as to his whereabouts. W. K. Martin to McClellan, Oct. 28[?], 1877, Henry B. McClellan Papers, VHS. One question which has not been satisfactorily answered is why it seemed to take Robertson so long to rejoin the army. In one of his accounts Robertson admitted that he received the order on June 29 and that he left Ashby's Gap in the evening of the same day, went through Chambersburg July 2, and reached Cashtown on the morning of July 3. In another account he said that he was in Martinsburg when he received the order, but he did not give the day. He also claimed that he had to go by way of Martinsburg and cross the river at Williamsport because he had had orders to avoid the hard-surfaced turnpikes, which were rough on the hoofs of shoeless mounts. His excuse for taking the longer route to Chambersburg seems like a bit of rationalization. In both accounts Robertson claimed that he made good

time as a result of rapid marching. Actually he did no better with his cavalry than Lee did with his infantry. See B. H. Robertson to [Henry] Heth, Dec. 27, 1877, in Mosby, *Stuart's Cavalry*, 200–201; B. H. Robertson, "The Confederate Cavalry in the Gettysburg Campaign," *B&L*, III, pt. 1, p. 253. Stuart was dissatisfied with Robertson's conduct but for some reason "refrained from making any strictures" on him. H. B. McClellan to Longstreet, Feb. 28, 1887, James Longstreet Letters, DU.

23. *OR*, XXVII, pt. 2, p. 316.

24. *Ibid.*, p. 302.

25. *Ibid.*, pt. 3, pp. 858–859, 891; LI, pt. 2, p. 730.

26. According to Charles Marshall, Lee said that while he did not consider that he had "complete communication with Virginia, he had all the communication he needed, as long as the enemy had no considerable force in the Cumberland Valley. His principal need for communicating with Virginia was to procure ammunition, and he thought that he could always do that with an escort, if the valley were free from a Federal force, but should the enemy have a considerable force in the valley this would be impossible." Charles Marshall, "Events Leading up to the Battle of Gettysburg," *SHSP*, XXIII, 226.

27. *OR*, XXVII, pt. 2, pp. 307, 316. The report of July 31 stressed that the purpose of Early's occupation of York was to keep Hooker east of the mountains, whereas the one of Jan., 1864, made no mention of it. Instead it referred to Early's role in preparing for the advance on Harrisburg. Charles Marshall claimed that Lee, thinking Hooker had not yet crossed the Potomac, on June 28 planned the move on Harrisburg so as to "compel the enemy to leave Virginia, and deter him from any attempt upon Richmond. . . ." Apparently before Harrison appeared that night Lee gave Marshall the assignment of drawing up orders for a general advance on Harrisburg. The orders were as follows: Ewell to move directly upon the city; Longstreet to follow him by way of Carlisle, June 29; Hill to go eastward over the mountain, cross the river below Harrisburg, and seize the railroad between Harrisburg and Philadelphia to cut off Union reinforcements presumably coming from the east. Marshall, "Events Leading up to the Battle of Gettysburg," *SHSP*, XXIII, 225–226.

28. *OR*, XXVII, pt. 2, pp. 464–465. According to a memorandum Early made of his conference with Ewell in Chambersburg June 25, his objectives for the next four days were as follows: June 26, Mummasburg and Hunterstown; June 27, come within five miles of Dover; June 28, "gut" York and destroy the Columbia-Wrightsville bridge; June 29, pass through Dillstown [Dillsburg] and approach Carlisle. Early's Memorandum, Henry B. McClellan Papers, VHS. In a letter to McClellan, Feb. 11, 1878, Early said that Ewell was to have sent him Jenkins' cavalry by the 28th to burn the bridge at Wrightsville. *Ibid.*

29. "Extracts from the Diary of Lieut. Hermann Schuricht," *SHSP*, XXIV, 242–244; *OR*, XXVII, pt. 2, p. 443; Hoke, *Great Invasion*, 182–183; Robert G. Crist, "Highwater, 1863: The Confederate Approach to Harrisburg," *Pennsylvania History*, XXX, 171–180.

30. Bates, *Martial Deeds of Pennsylvania*, 182.

31. Harrisburg Correspondent, June 29, in *New York Times*, July 1, 1863.

32. Ewell sent Early a message from Carlisle, dated 2:00 P.M., June 28, in which he said among other things: "Gen'l Lee seems inclined to concentrate about Chambersburg, so that I don't know yet whether I move towards Harrisburg or not. . . ." Early's copy of Ewell's note to him, Henry B. McClellan Papers, VHS.

33. Brown, "Reminiscences," MS, Campbell Brown Books, UNC. Ewell said he was starting for Harrisburg when he received word from Lee on the 29th. See OR, XXVII, pt. 2, p. 443.

34. Ibid., pp. 307, 316, 358.

35. Ibid., pt. 3, pp. 943–944. It could have been copied in the letter book as late as July 1 when a copy of the next message was put into the book. See ibid., p. 947. Col. Mosby, in a long and involved effort to close all loopholes in his lawyer-like defense of Stuart's record in the Gettysburg campaign, refused to admit any possibility of error in the date of Lee's second dispatch to Ewell. He was positive that since the second note was written early on June 28, the first one must have been composed late on June 27. Mosby rejected the reliability of official reports and postwar accounts of some officers on Lee's and Longstreet's staffs which stated that Harrison reported on the night of June 28, and he insisted that Lee knew about Hooker's advance at least twenty-four hours before the appearance of Harrison. Thus the spy's report came too late to change Lee's plan of campaign, he said. All stories and reports attaching great importance to Harrison's work he thought were designed to throw the onus for Confederate defeat at Gettysburg on Stuart's shoulders. See Mosby, Stuart's Cavalry, 117–130, 207–215.

36. OR, XXVII, pt. 3, p. 943. Johnson in his report said that he received his orders on June 29, not giving the hour. See ibid., pt. 2, p. 503. Lt. McKim, one of Johnson's staff officers, kept a diary of the campaign, in which he put down the hour of the arrival of the order as nine o'clock in the morning. R. H. McKim, "A Reply to Col. J. S. Mosby," SHSP, XXXVII, 212–213.

37. OR, XXVII, pt. 3, p. 943.

38. Ibid., pt. 2, p. 456; Pettit to his wife, July 8, 1863, W. B. Pettit Papers, UNC. Pettit served with Capt. J. L. Massie's battery of Lt. Col. William Nelson's battalion, which must have been stationed about eight miles south of Carlisle. Pettit said they marched twelve miles that day. Johnson's division was also on the Chambersburg side of Carlisle, which probably explains why it was the first in Ewell's corps to be ordered back. For the departure time of Johnson's columns see also S. A. Firebaugh War Diary, Entry for June 29, 1863, Typescript, UNC.

39. Pettit to his wife, July 8, 1863, W. B. Pettit Papers, UNC; S. A. Firebaugh War Diary, Entry for June 30, 1863, Typescript, UNC; Casler, Four Years in the Stonewall Brigade, 180–181; H. J. Hunt to Long, Aug. 14, 1885, A. L. Long Papers, UNC; Hoke, Great Invasion, 227–228; OR, XXVII, pt. 2, pp. 358, 504; LI, pt. 2, p. 732.

40. Calder to his mother, July 8, 1863, William Calder Papers, UNC.

41. OR, XXVII, pt. 2, p. 552.

42. *Ibid.*, pp. 467–468; Early to McClellan, Feb. 11, 26, 1878, Henry B. McClellan Papers, VHS.

43. Besides the Hotchkiss map Lee undoubtedly had the readily available county maps. Of these Early said that they were "so thorough and accurate that I have no necessity for a guide in any direction." Early, *Narrative of the War*, 264.

44. *OR*, XXVII, pt. 3, p. 943.

45. H. J. Hunt to Long, Aug. 14, 1885, A. L. Long Papers, UNC. The Union General Hunt, who made a study of the campaign, after the war characterized Ewell's handling of his corps on June 29 and 30 as "quick work and good work. . . ."

46. The strength of Rodes's command at Carlisle was 8,052 officers and men. *OR*, XXVII, pt. 2, p. 562. Early's division at Shepherdstown on June 20 numbered 5,611 officers and men present for duty on the battle line. Early, *Narrative of the War*, 253. Actually Early had 6,476 in his command at that time, but 343 officers and men were sick, 468 on extra duty, and 32 under arrest. Field Return of Early's Division, Camp near Shepherdstown, Va., June 20, 1863, War Department Collection of Confederate Records, Record Group 109, NA.

47. This figure is the result of an educated guess. The cavalry were Jenkins' men, except about 200 troopers in Lt. Col. E. W. White's 35th Va. Battalion from Gen. "Grumble" Jones's brigade. Early to McClellan, Feb. 2, 1878, Henry B. McClellan Papers, VHS; *OR*, XXVII, pt. 2, pp. 770–771. It is virtually impossible to get even reasonably accurate figures for the size of Jenkins' brigade. Of the two reliable contemporary sources of information, Gen. Rodes gave about 1,600 men as the strength of the command, while Lt. Hermann Schuricht, who was in the brigade, set the figure at 3,200. *Ibid.*, p. 547; "Diary of Lieut. Hermann Schuricht," *SHSP*, XXIV, 340.

48. Ewell ordered Jenkins to "retreat from before Harrisburg" on June 29. Memorandum Book, Entry for June 29, 1863, Jedediah Hotchkiss Papers, LC.

49. "Diary of Lieut. Hermann Schuricht," *SHSP*, XXIV, 343–344. Early had little respect for the efficiency of Jenkins' cavalry and said they had had "little real training as soldiers." He also referred disparagingly to the 17th Va. Cavalry from the brigade as partaking of "the character of all the 'Wildcat Cavalry.'" Early to McClellan, Feb. 2, 1878, Henry B. McClellan Papers, VHS.

50. *OR*, XXVII, pt. 2, p. 468. White never received this order from Early to picket Mummasburg and Hunterstown and to scout around Gettysburg because Buford's men captured the courier. However, Buford reported that roving detachments of enemy cavalry infested the area north of Gettysburg on the night of June 30. *Ibid.*, pt. 1, pp. 923–924; pt. 3, p. 414. Of Early's cavalry force of 500 men, 300 were from the 17th Va. Cavalry and the rest from White's battalion. Early to McClellan, Feb. 2, 1878, Henry B. McClellan Papers, VHS.

51. Memorandum Book, Entry for June 29, 1863, Jedediah Hotchkiss Papers, LC.

52. *OR*, XXVII, pt. 3, p. 943.

53. *Ibid.*, pt. 2, p. 444.

54. Memorandum Book, Entry for June 26, 1863, Jedediah Hotchkiss Papers, LC.

55. The story about Ewell's annoyance and perplexity over the ambiguous clause, "as circumstances might dictate," in Lee's message came from an account written by Maj. Gen. Isaac R. Trimble after the war. It first appeared in a letter from Trimble to John B. Bachelder almost twenty years after the battle, again fifteen years later in the *Southern Historical Society Papers,* and subsequently in the *Confederate Veteran.* Trimble, who had just recovered from a severe illness, was without a command, and Lee sent him to Carlisle to work in some capacity agreeable to Ewell. He was at Heidlersburg the night of June 30 and told how Ewell, troubled over the "indefinite phraseology" of Lee's order, consulted with Rodes, Early, and himself. The first two generals were not of much help, but Trimble, who claimed to have talked to Lee a few days previously, had many bright suggestions. In his opinion there was only one thing for Ewell to do and that was to get to Gettysburg as fast as possible, by pushing on that night or by starting early next morning so as to arrive by sunrise. Trimble was sure that Hill had similar orders and Ewell would find him at Gettysburg when he got there. Ewell remained undecided. Implicitly critical, Trimble gave the impression that Ewell's indecision was bad enough to have impaired the efficiency of his command.

There are several things wrong with this story. Written many years after the event when Confederate officers finally appreciated the importance of their defeat at Gettysburg and understood more of their mistakes, Trimble exaggerated Ewell's want of decisiveness. He claimed to have perceived the importance of getting to Gettysburg in a hurry, which no one else saw until after the battle. He overlooked Hill's message to Ewell, telling him that the Third Corps was at Cashtown. He ignored the fact that Ewell's marching route was admirably chosen to get his men as quickly as possible to either Cashtown or Gettysburg. Trimble to Bachelder, Feb. 8, 1883, Typescript, Bachelder Papers; Trimble, "The Battle and Campaign of Gettysburg" *SHSP,* XXVI, 122; Trimble, "The Battle and Campaign of Gettysburg," *Confederate Veteran,* XXV, 211.

56. One member of the 23rd N. C. regiment of Iverson's brigade, Rodes's division, set the departure time at 6:00 A.M. Calder to his mother, July 8, 1863, William Calder Papers, UNC. Col. Bryan Grimes of the 4th N. C. regiment, Ramseur's brigade, Rodes's division, said they left Heidlersburg at sunrise. Ramseur's brigade guarded the rear of the division train. *OR,* XXVII, pt. 2, pp. 587, 589. Maj. G. Campbell Brown, a member of Ewell's staff, said they began the march "not long after sunrise." See his "Reminiscences," MS, Campbell Brown Books, UNC.

57. *OR,* XXVII, pt. 2, pp. 444, 468, 552. Ewell, Early, and Rodes all agreed in their reports that Hill's message announcing his advance on Gettysburg came to Ewell in the morning of July 1 while his columns were on the march. Hill said that he had notified Ewell of his intention to move toward Gettysburg the next morning, thus clearly implying that he had sent the message the night of

June 30. Also according to his report he sent only one message to Ewell instead of the two that Ewell mentioned, one which arrived on June 30 and the other on July 1. See *ibid.*, p. 607. Hill's version is unacceptable for several reasons. If Ewell had known the night of June 30 or very early the next morning of Hill's plans about Gettysburg, he would have headed both of his divisions in that direction when they started out. Hill's battle report for July 1 and events leading up to it was misleading and inaccurate because of important omissions and ambiguous phraseology, whereas Ewell, Early, and Rodes wrote very complete and generally clear reports which agree on the essentials. See also Brown, "Reminiscences," MS, Campbell Brown Books, UNC. Brown said that the message from Hill came between 8:00 A.M. and 9:00 A.M., July 1.

58. Hamilton, ed., *Shotwell Papers*, I, 493.

59. *Ibid.*, 494.

60. Lee mentioned "inclement" weather in his second report. *OR*, XXVII, pt. 2, p. 317. The weather was bad from the time Lee arrived in Chambersburg until he left it. Charles Marshall to Early, Apr. 10, 1876, Jubal A. Early Papers, LC. One Confederate writing from Hagerstown after the battle said: "It has [been] raining or cloudy & threatening ever since we crossed the Potomac. . . . It is now clearing off. . . ." Pettit to his wife, July 8, 1863, W. B. Pettit Papers, UNC.,

61. *OR*, XXVII, pt. 2, pp. 317, 358, 366, 371, 606–607, 613, 637, 656; LI, pt. 2, pp. 729–731. Gen. Buford mentioned in his battle report an enemy force consisting of two Miss. regiments and a section of artillery which he discovered early in the morning of June 30 near Fairfield. They had been there the night before, but out of fear for their property the people in the area did not tell Buford of their presence when his two brigades reached Fairfield and camped there for the night. Buford did not identify the brigade to which the regiments belonged. See *ibid.*, XXVII, pt. 1, p. 926.

62. See report of Capt. E. B. Brunson, commanding Reserve Artillery Battalion, Third Corps, in which he complains of the crippling effect of limestone pikes on the hoofs of horses without shoes. *Ibid.*, pt. 2, p. 677. For a reference to the steep roads up South Mountain, see Ross, *Cities and Camps*, 46.

63. Charles Marshall, a member of Lee's staff in the campaign, explained later why the divisions in the valley were not pushed over the mountain at a faster clip on June 29 and 30. He said that Lee and his staff assumed that the enemy was moving west from Frederick and would reverse himself once he heard of a rebel movement toward the east. This change in the direction of the Northerners' movement would take time. Until then it would be well to keep a large part of the Confederate army on the west side of the mountain. In making this statement Marshall ignored the enervating effect of the weather on military operations, as suggested in Lee's report, and implied that Lee had no inkling of enemy moves since the spy, Harrison, made his report late on June 28. Marshall to Early, Apr. 10, 1876, Jubal A. Early Papers, LC.

64. *Address of Edward Everett at the National Cemetery, Gettysburg, November 19, 1863* (Boston, 1864), 44, Edward Everett Papers, No. 278, MHS. Everett's famous two-hour address was in large measure a history of the cam-

paign and battle. He worked hard and carefully in getting information, much of which he obtained from correspondence with Gen. Halleck, Col. Theodore Lyman of Meade's staff, and Prof. Jacobs at the college in Gettysburg. For further information on the foraging activities of Hill's men, see Jacobs, *Rebel Invasion*, 21.

65. Freeman, *Lee's Lieutenants*, III, 78; Fremantle, *Three Months in the Southern States*, 250. Campbell Brown recalled a conversation he had with Lee in Cashtown the afternoon of July 1, in which the general indicated that what little he knew of Meade's army was through a scout's report. Brown, "Reminiscences," MS, Campbell Brown Books, UNC.

66. Freeman, *Lee's Lieutenants*, III, 78; Henry Heth, "Causes of Lee's Defeat at Gettysburg," *SHSP*, IV, 157. There is evidence to suggest that Lee knew by June 30 that units of the Army of the Potomac had reached Emmitsburg. After the war the then Gen. A. L. Long, who was Lee's military secretary during the campaign, made the following statement: "While waiting for information at Chambersburg, the first intelligence received of the movements of the enemy was his arrival at Emmettsburg [sic]." Long, "Causes of Lee's Defeat at Gettysburg," *ibid.*, 122. The First Corps of the Army of the Potomac marched from Frederick to Emmitsburg on June 29. See *OR*, XXVII, pt. 1, p. 243. Probably Lee heard of its presence there no sooner than early in the morning of June 30. Maj. Brown recollected that Lee said on July 1 that Meade was "marching this way," but that was about all he knew about the enemy's position. "Reminiscences," MS, Campbell Brown Books, UNC.

67. *OR*, XXVII, pt. 2, pp. 317, 607, 637.

68. Longstreet told Fremantle in the evening of June 30 that he had "just" received intelligence that Hooker had been "disrated" and that Meade had been appointed in his place. Fremantle, *Three Months in the Southern States*, 250. The story that Lee heard from the spy, Harrison, on the night of June 28 of the change in commanders apparently started with A. L. Long, for none of the official reports mentioned it, nor any other Confederate authority before Long. Gen. Henry J. Hunt in writing his articles on Gettysburg for *B&L* accepted Long's version as a reasonable one. Since Meade, he said, relieved Hooker very early in the morning of June 28, Harrison could have carried news of the change to Chambersburg by 10:00 P.M. that night. Hunt to Long, Aug. 14, 1885, A. L. Long Papers, UNC; H. J. Hunt, "The First Day at Gettysburg," *B&L*, III, pt. 1, p. 271. No contemporary account of the spy incident said that Harrison reported a change of commanders.

69. George Cary Eggleston, *A Rebel's Recollection*, David Donald, ed. (Bloomington, Ind., 1959), 130.

70. Long, *Memoirs of Lee*, 274.

71. Fremantle, *Three Months in the Southern States*, 250.

72. *Ibid.*, 248; Scheibert, *Seven Months in the Rebel States*, Hoole, ed., 38–39.

73. Fremantle, *Three Months in the Southern States*, 248.

74. *Ibid.*, 249.

75. Hood, *Advance and Retreat*, 55.

76. *OR*, XXVII, pt. 2, pp. 317, 358; pt. 3, pp. 947–948; Longstreet, *Memoirs*, 351.

77. James P. Smith, "General Lee at Gettsyburg," *Petersburg, Chancellorsville, Gettysburg* [Papers of the Military Historical Society of Massachusetts, V] (Boston, 1906), 384. Smith, who had been an aide on Gen. Ewell's staff, did not accompany the army on its march to Pa. but followed it later. When he reached Chambersburg before dawn on June 29, he reported to Lee who was up and preparing to mount Traveller. Lee asked about Stuart and was "surprised and disturbed" to learn that on June 27 he was still in Prince William County, Va. For further evidence of Lee's growing concern over Stuart's absence see the following: Gen. R. H. Anderson's account of his interview with Lee on July 1 in Longstreet, *Memoirs*, 357; Scheibert, *Seven Months in the Rebel States*, Hoole, ed., 113; Brown, "Reminiscences," MS, Campbell Brown Books, UNC; Long, *Memoirs of Lee*, 275.

78. *OR*, XXVII, pt. 2, p. 694.

79. *Ibid.*, pt. 3, p. 923.

80. Russell F. Weigley, *Quartermaster General of the Union Army, A Biography of M. C. Meigs* (New York, 1959), 276–277; *OR*, XXVII, pt. 2, p. 694.

81. *Cf. ante*, Chap. VII.

82. *OR*, XXVII, pt. 2, p. 694.

83. McClellan, *Campaigns of Stuart*, 324–326; *OR*, XXVII, pt. 2, p. 694.

84. McClellan, *Campaigns of Stuart*, 326; *OR*, XXVII, pt. 2, p. 695.

85. *Ibid.*

86. *Ibid.*

87. For accounts of Stuart's overnight stay in Union Mills at the home of a Confederate sympathizer, William Shriver, see Frederic S. Klein, ed., *Just South of Gettysburg* (Westminster, Md., 1963), 178–205.

88. *OR*, XXVII, pt. 2, p. 695.

89. *Ibid.*, p. 696.

90. Maj. McClellan, Stuart's friendly critic, said that his former commander made a great mistake in not destroying the captured wagons the night of June 29 when he heard of Kilpatrick's presence in Littlestown. Realizing the probability of an encounter the next day, Stuart he felt he should have stripped himself for action. He then made the following observation: "It was not in Stuart's nature to abandon an attempt until it had been proven to be beyond his powers; and he determined to hold on to his prize until the last moment. This was unfortunate." McClellan, *Campaigns of Stuart*, 327. Stuart had the sixteen-year-old Herbert Shriver guide him over the back road from Union Mills to Hanover. Klein, ed., *Just South of Gettysburg*, 178.

91. McClellan, *Campaigns of Stuart*, 327–328; *OR*, XXVII, pt. 1, pp. 986–988, 991–992, 997–1000, 1005, 1008–1009, 1011–1012, 1018; pt. 2, pp. 695–696. Both Stuart and Kilpatrick agreed in their reports that the engagement began at 10:00 A.M.

92. McClellan, *Campaigns of Stuart*, 328–330; *OR*, XXVII, pt. 2, p. 696.

93. *Ibid.*

94. *Ibid.*, pp. 308, 696–697; McClellan, *Campaigns of Stuart*, 330. Ven-

able, who was inspector general of Stuart's cavalry division, and a courier rode to Gen. Ewell's headquarters near Oak Hill on the afternoon of July 1. Ewell sent them to Lee, who was riding toward Gettysburg from Cashtown. Brown, "Reminiscences," MS, Campbell Brown Books, UNC; W. Gordon McCabe, "Major Andrew Reid Venable, Jr.," SHSP, XXXVII, 65.

95. OR, XXVII, pt. 2, pp. 220–221, 224, 236–237, 696–697.

96. Years later Gen. Wade Hampton aptly summed up the character of Stuart's report when he wrote: "Lately I saw for the first time Stuart's report of the Gettysburg campaign & I never read a more erroneous—to call it no harsher name—one than it was." Hampton to Thomas T. Munford, Dec. 18, 1887, Munford-Ellis Family Papers, DU.

97. OR, XXVII, pt. 2, p. 694.

98. Ibid., p. 708.

99. Ibid., pt. 3, pp. 378–379.

100. Ibid., pt. 1, pp. 67–68, 70–71.

101. Ibid., pt. 2, p. 708. Stuart did not give an exact accounting of where he captured so many prisoners.

102. Ibid., pt. 1, pp. 64–67, 68–69, 666; pt. 3, p. 375.

103. Ibid., pt. 1, pp. 663, 665.

104. Ibid., p. 67.

105. Ibid., pp. 62, 67; pt. 3, pp. 376–377, 396–397, 417.

106. Ibid., pt. 1, pp. 69–70, 991–992; pt. 3, p. 400; H. J. Hunt to Long, Aug. 14, 1885, A. L. Long Papers, UNC.

107. OR, XXVII, pt. 1, pp. 62–64, 66–68, 70–71; pt. 3, pp. 380, 401–402. Stuart reported that Meade used 4,000 men to escort the government property, whereas Meade ordered Gen. French to assign not more than 3,000 soldiers for this duty. On July 1 Halleck ordered the 2nd Mass. Cavalry under Col. Charles R. Lowell, Jr., which numbered 462 officers and troopers, to escort the stores from Maryland Heights in place of the 3,000 or so men from Gen. French's command, thus releasing them for Meade's use. See ibid., pt. 1, pp. 67, 71; pt. 2, p. 708; pt. 3, p. 440.

108. Meade reported to Halleck on June 30 that the "Pennsylvania Reserves can't keep up—still in rear. General Lockwood with the troops from Schenck, still behind; these troops cannot keep up with the marches made by the army." Ibid., pt. 1, pp. 68–69.

109. H. J. Hunt to Long, Aug. 14, 1885, A. L. Long Papers, UNC.

110. OR, XXVII, pt. 2, p. 707.

111. Ibid., pp. 708–709.

112. While preparing his book on Stuart's campaigns McClellan asked Early whether he had received instructions to send out scouts to get in touch with Stuart. H. B. McClellan to Early, Nov. 29, 1877, Jubal A. Early Papers, LC. In his answer to McClellan Early said it had been impossible for Ewell to order his cooperation with Stuart, for none of the Confederate general officers in Pa. knew of Stuart's intention to cross the Potomac between Hooker's army and Washington. Even if Early had known of Stuart's intentions, where would he have sent scouts to meet the constantly moving cavalry? Early could not

understand why Stuart did not discover his route on July 1, if not from the local inhabitants, then "certainly from the tracks of my wagons and artillery, and by sending couriers along them he could have ascertained my exact route and destination." Early to McClellan, Feb. 2, 1878, Henry B. McClellan Papers, VHS. McClellan accepted Early's denial without question but defended Stuart's intelligence by saying that he "crossed your *trail* during the night of the 30th, and under circumstances which rendered it almost impossible that he could have received from it any information concerning the direction of your march." H. B. McClellan to Early, Feb. 6, 1878, Jubal A. Early Papers, LC.

113. Early to McClellan, Feb. 26, 1878, Henry B. McClellan Papers, VHS.

114. Lee told Ewell on June 22 to move toward the Susquehanna. *OR*, XXVII, pt. 3, p. 914. There are indications, however, that Lee let Ewell work out for himself the precise nature of the move. Ewell sent Early a message on June 28 and among other things said, "I notified Genl Lee that you had gone there [York]." Early's copy of Ewell's note to him, Henry B. McClellan Papers, VHS. If Lee did not know on June 22 and 23, when he conferred with Stuart, how Ewell was going to use his troops in Pa., then it was impossible for him to tell Ewell to order Early to look out for Stuart's arrival in York. See also Maurice, ed., *Aide-de-Camp of Lee*, 210–211.

115. *OR*, XXVII, pt. 2, p. 708.

116. *Ibid.*, XXV, pt. 2, p. 789; XXVII, pt. 3, p. 913.

117. *Ibid.*, pt. 2, pp. 467–468.

118. Hampton's brigade reached Hunterstown on the morning of July 2 and soon took a position on the left of Lee's line. Stuart himself, with Fitz Lee's and Chambliss' commands, reached Gettysburg on the afternoon of the 2nd and joined Hampton. McClellan, *Campaigns of Stuart*, 331–332.

119. Indicative of the feeling against Stuart was a rumor of his dismissal from command of the cavalry of the Army of Northern Virginia, because of his absence "before and at [the] battle of Gettysburg against orders. . . ." Kean Diary, Entry of Aug. 9, 1863, found in Younger, ed., *Inside the Confederate Government*, 90.

Appraisals by Confederate officers of the consequences of Stuart's delinquencies ranged from a statement in Lee's second report that movements of the army preceding the battle had been "much embarrassed" by the absence of the cavalry, to Gen. G. Moxley Sorrel's unvarnished accusation that they lost the campaign for Lee. *OR*, XXVII, pt. 2, p. 321; Sorrel, *Recollections*, 162. For opinions of other officers who felt that Stuart's delay in reaching Gettysburg was an important reason, but by no means the only one, for the Confederate defeat, see C. M. Wilcox, "Causes of Lee's Defeat at Gettysburg," *SHSP*, IV, 117; Fitzhugh Lee, "Causes of Lee's Defeat at Gettysburg," *ibid.*, 74; Henry Heth, "Causes of Lee's Defeat at Gettysburg," *ibid.*, 159–160; Alexander, *Military Memoirs*, 377; Longstreet, *Memoirs*, 341–343; Long, *Memoirs of Lee*, 272, 277; Henry Heth, "Gen. Lee's Orders to His Cavalry," *Philadelphia Weekly Times*, Mar. 23, 1878; R. H. McKim, "A Reply to Col. J. S. Mosby," *SHSP*, XXXVII, 226. Gen. Early disagreed with these appraisals by saying that though Stuart's absence was a source of embarrassment to Lee, it caused "no real harm." Early to McClellan, Feb. 2, 1878, Henry B. McClellan Papers, VHS.

The bitterest critic of Stuart was Maj. Charles Marshall of Lee's staff, the author of the letters of June 22 and 23 to Stuart, which were anything but models of clear, crisp, and definite English. He wanted Stuart court-martialled and sought to put in Lee's report of Jan., 1864, which he also wrote, the charge that Stuart had deliberately disobeyed orders. Lee made him cross it out. Maurice, ed., *Aide-de-Camp of Lee*, 209–211, 214–216, 224 note; David G. McIntosh, "Review of the Gettysburg Campaign," *SHSP*, XXXVII, 94–95.

120. Gen. Trimble remembered Lee as saying on June 25 that his plan was to "throw an overwhelming force against the enemy's advance, as soon as I learn the road they take, crush them, and following up the sweep beat them in detail. . . ." I. R. Trimble to Bachelder, Feb. 8, 1883, Typescript, Bachelder Papers.

121. An example of their thinking was the following statement made by Gen. Heth: "Not one of the alleged mistakes or shortcomings which occurred on July 1 and 2 would or could have happened had General Lee been promptly notified of the enemy's movements, which surely would have been done had his cavalry been in place." Henry Heth, "Gen. Lee's Orders to His Cavalry," *Philadelphia Weekly Times*, Mar. 23, 1878.

122. Fitzhugh Lee to McClellan, July 31, 1878, Henry B. McClellan Papers, VHS.

NOTES TO CHAPTER IX

1. Meade, *Life and Letters*, II, 1. The Fifth Corps camped at Ballinger's Creek three miles directly south of Frederick.

2. Meade to his wife, June 29, 1863, in *ibid.*, 11.

3. Meade to his wife, June 29, 1863, in *ibid.*, OR, XXVII, pt. 3, p. 369.

4. *Ibid.*, pt. 1, p. 61.

5. For soldier reaction to his appointment, *cf. ante*, V, 115 note.

6. Theodore Lyman to [Col.] George Meade, Dec. [No date], 1872, Official Letters to and from Gen. Meade Relating to the Civil War Conduct, 1863–1881, George Gordon Meade Papers, HSP; J. C. Biddle, "General Meade at Gettysburg," *Annals*, 217–218; Brooks, *Washington in Lincoln's Time*, 85; Charles Leonard Moore, "The Hero of Gettysburg," *The Dial*, LV, 13–15.

7. Dispatch from C. C. Coffin, Frederick, June 28, in *Boston Morning Journal*, July 3, 1863.

8. Webb to William H. Seward, Aug. 22, 1863, James Watson Webb Papers, YU. Even Dan Butterfield had kind words to say about Meade. See Daniel E. Sickles, D. McM. Gregg, John Newton, and Daniel Butterfield, "Further Recollections of Gettysburg," *North American Review*, CLII, 280–281.

9. Williams to his daughters, June 29, 1863, in *Alpheus Williams Letters*,

221. For other contemporary expressions of pleasure at Meade's appointment see: Weld, *War Diaries and Letters*, 227; Gibbon, *Recollections*, 128–131; *Wainwright Journals*, 227. After Chancellorsville Gens. Couch, Sedgwick, Reynolds, and many lesser officials felt Meade should replace Hooker. See *ibid.*, 202, 229; Couch to Webb, Oct. 20, 1890, Webb Collection.

10. Olmsted to [E. L.] Godkin, July 15, 1863, in Evelyn Page, ed., "After Gettysburg, Frederick Law Olmsted on the Escape of Lee," *PMHB*, LXXV, 437.

11. [Lyman to his wife], Sept. 29, 1863, in Agassiz, ed., *Meade's Headquarters*, 25.

12. [*Id.* to *id.*], July 10, 1864, in *ibid.*, 188. See also an appraisal of Meade's character in a book review of *Battle of Gettysburg* by Comte de Paris, *Atlantic Monthly*, LVIII, 852. The name of the reviewer was not published, but very likely it was Gen. Francis A. Walker, who wrote *A History of the Second Corps* and a biography of Gen. Winfield S. Hancock. The review appeared in the Dec., 1886, issue of the *Atlantic*, and Walker wrote Webb a year earlier, on Dec. 9, 1885, that he had found Comte de Paris "faulty in many respects." Webb Collection.

13. For a comment on Meade's moral courage and his refusal to act against his better judgment in the Mine Run campaign, see [Lyman to his wife], Dec. 12, 1863, in Agassiz, ed., *Meade's Headquarters*, 61. For a careful appraisal of Meade's temper see Leslie Perry, Jr., "General Meade's Temper," *SHSP*, XI, 248.

14. Charles A. Dana, *Recollections of the Civil War, with the Leaders at Washington and in the Field in the Sixties* (New York, 1913), 190, 226–227.

15. [Lyman to his wife], June 1, 24, 1864, in Agassiz, ed., *Meade's Headquarters*, 138, 176.

16. Webb to his wife, Jan. 27, 1864, Webb Collection.

17. [Lyman to his wife], Apr. 5, 1865, in Agassiz, ed., *Meade's Headquarters*, 345.

18. Richard M. Bache, *Life of General George Gordon Meade* (Philadelphia, 1897), 572.

19. [Lyman to his wife], Oct. 26, 1863, in Agassiz, ed., *Meade's Headquarters*, 39.

20. [*Id.* to *id.*], Feb. 22, 1864, in *ibid.*, 73.

21. Webb to his wife, Apr. 18, 1865, Webb Collection.

22. [Lyman to his wife], Oct. 14, 1864, in Agassiz, ed., *Meade's Headquarters*, 247.

23. [*Id.* to *id.*], May 27, June 24, 1864, in *ibid.*, 129, 177.

24. George G. Meade to Webb, Nov. 1, 1866, Webb Collection. Webb was Meade's loyal supporter and friend. He served as asst. inspector general of the Fifth Corps at the time Meade commanded it. When Gen. Humphreys replaced Hancock as commander of the Second Corps in the fall of 1864, Webb succeeded him as chief of staff of the Army of the Potomac. Webb to Maj. Samuel Breck, Feb. 8, 1864, Webb Collection; [Lyman to his wife], Nov. 27, 1864, Mar. 3, 1865, in Agassiz, ed., *Meade's Headquarters*, 279, 307.

25. [*Id.* to *id.*], Apr. 17, 1865, in *ibid.*, 359; Moore, "The Hero of Gettysburg," *The Dial*, LV, 13. Meade explained to Lyman his attitude toward the newspapers by saying: "You are mistaken in supposing I am indifferent to public opinion, tho it is true I have great contempt for the way it is manufactured and directed in this country." Meade to Lyman, May 5, 1865, Theodore Lyman Papers, MHS.

26. Warren became increasingly provoked with Meade. G. K. Warren to his brother, W. I. Warren, Dec. 8, 1863, May 27, 1865, MS copy, G. K. Warren Letters, New York State Library. Meade said in the winter of 1865 that he feared he would have to number Warren and Patrick among those unfriendly to him. Meade to Lyman, Jan. 14, 1865, Theodore Lyman Papers, MHS.

27. G. K. Warren to Bates, Oct. 15, 1875, Bates Collection.

28. Cleaves, *Meade of Gettysburg*, 11, 18, 53–55, 64–68, 75–80, 90–93, 96, 103–115; Boatner, *Civil War Dictionary*, 539.

29. Cleaves, *Meade of Gettysburg*, 74, 117–118; Meade, *Life and Letters*, I, 308, 373–374, 379, 388–389.

30. Nicolay and Hay, *Abraham Lincoln*, VII, 226. The account of Col. Hardie's mission to Frederick which historians have most frequently cited was found in Benjamin's article, "Hooker's Appointment and Removal," *B&L*, III, pt. 1, pp. 239–243. Close examination of it reveals that his story was quite untrustworthy and contained many errors. Benjamin tended to be melodramatic and created the impression that Hardie carried out his assignment without help from others and at great danger to himself. He even spoke of the possibility of Hardie's capture by Stuart's raiders and his trouble with drunken Union soldiers in Frederick. At the time Hardie left Washington Stuart was nowhere near the Baltimore and Ohio Railroad. As for drunken soldiers in Frederick, it is doubtful whether many were there, since a very small fraction of the army was near that town on the night of June 27. The trouble with drunken stragglers developed later on.

A more convincing account appeared in George C. Gorham, *Life and Public Service of Edwin M. Stanton* (Boston, 1899), II, 98–100. This story told how Hardie was carried to Frederick quite safely in a special train, a feature borne out by a contemporary account. See dispatch from C. C. Coffin, Frederick, June 28, in *Boston Morning Journal*, July 3, 1863. Gen. Sickles recalled that in returning to his command from convalescence in New York City, he rode on the train with Hardie from Washington to Frederick. They chatted pleasantly without Hardie revealing a word of his mission. Daniel E. Sickles et al., "Further Recollections of Gettysburg," *North American Review*, CLII, 259.

31. Thomas A. Scott expressed deep concern over the timing of the change of commanders because it would "cause delay in its [the army's] movements and may prove fatal to Pennsylvania as it gives enemy time to over run us and concentrate if need be in the Heart of our State—or possibly it may enable Lee to crush Army of Potomac before new commander finds where his forces are." Scott to E. L[ewis], [June 28, 1863], Dispatches, PDMA, PDPR.

32. *OR*, XXVII, pt. 1, p. 61.

33. W. A. Croffut, ed., *Fifty Years in Camp and Field, Diary of Major-General Ethan Allen Hitchcock, U. S. A.* (New York, 1909), 445–446.

34. *OR*, XXVII, pt. 1, p. 61.

35. *Ibid.*, pp. 51, 61, 63.

36. *Ibid.*, pt. 3, p. 385.

37. *Ibid.*, pt. 1, p. 61.

38. Meade, *Life and Letters*, II, 2–3; Benajmin, "Hooker's Appointment and Removal," *B&L*, III, pt. 1, p. 243. In Benjamin's account Hooker showed the bitterness of his disappointment. Benjamin also included Hardie in the conference of the three generals. Though Hardie was a man of great ability and undoubtedly well known to Hooker, it is questionable whether he, then asst. adj. gen. in the War Dept., would have been asked to stay or would have wanted to do so. From available evidence it seems that Hardie, after personally delivering to the two generals the order effecting the change in command, spent the remainder of his stay in Frederick visiting with many officers to determine the morale of the army. *OR*, XXVII, pt. 3, pp. 373–374.

39. Meade, *Life and Letters*, II, 2.

40. *OR*, XXVII, pt. 1, pp. 20–21.

41. *Ibid.*, p. 61.

42. CCW, *Report*, I, 329.

43. See the famous Pipe Creek Circular of July 1, 1863, in *OR*, XXVII, pt. 3, pp. 458–459. In testimony before the Committee on the Conduct of the War on Mar. 25, 1864, Butterfield put Meade in a very bad light. According to his story, after he consented to continue as chief of staff in the afternoon of June 28, with advice from Hooker he proceeded to straighten out the thinking of the bewildered Meade and finally got the army under way in pursuit of Lee. It was a nice little yarn designed to blow up the importance of Butterfield and Hooker and to belittle Meade. There are several things wrong with it. In the first place, it draws a picture of Meade which is completely out of character. Secondly, as early as 7:00 A.M. Meade knew in general what he was going to do. Thirdly, Butterfield mentioned a dispatch from Stanton, of which there is no record, about enemy forces near Winchester; he said it made Meade hesitate about going forward toward Pa. Halleck did mention a report of an enemy cavalry brigade south of the Potomac, but Meade did not believe it to be true. CCW, *Report*, I, 418–420; *OR*, XXVII, pt. 1, pp. 61–63. Years after the war Butterfield told how Meade upon assuming command wanted to have a review at Frederick in order to get to know the troops, but Butterfield talked him out of it. Daniel Butterfield et al., "Further Recollections of Gettysburg," *North American Review*, CLII, 281. This story appears to be another attempt to disparage Meade, for it is inconceivable that at this critical juncture a man of his ability would waste the time and energy of the army by holding a review.

44. *OR*, XXVII, pt. 1, p. 61; pt. 3, p. 374; Patrick Journal, Entry for Sunday Night, June 28, 1863, LC.

45. George G. Meade to [Col.] G. G. Benedict, Mar. 16, 1870, Copy, in *B&L*, III, pt. 2, p. 413. In this letter Meade asserted that he did not see Hum-

665

phreys until after the battle, but he forgot that he had called him to headquarters on June 28 for the purpose of asking him to be chief of staff. *OR*, LI, pt. 1, p. 1064. Although Warren would not vouch for the hour, he said Meade woke him up at 2:30 A.M. to offer him the position of chief of staff. Warren refused to accept it, because he said Meade would lose a good chief engineer without gaining a better chief of staff. He then advised Meade to keep Butterfield because of his knowledge of actual affairs, recent orders, and other important data. Copy of a Warren letter, no date, in Emerson G. Taylor, *Gouverneur Kemble Warren* (Boston, 1932), 119–120. More is the pity, Taylor did not indicate the location of the original letter or its copy.

46. CCW, *Report*, I, 419.

47. W. A. Swanberg, *Sickles the Incredible* (New York, 1956), 128–129, 143, 191–192, 221–222, 238–240; Thomas Newbould to Gay, June 24, 1863, S. H. Gay Collection, Columbia University Library; Julia L. S. Butterfield, ed., *A Biographical Memorial of General Daniel Butterfield* (New York, 1904), 111–112.

48. *Ibid.*

49. Patrick Journal, Entry for June 2, 1863, LC.

50. Humphreys to his wife, Sept. 1, 1864, A. A. Humphreys Papers, HSP. Col. Charles Wainwright said that Butterfield often lacked practical common sense and had not made as good a chief of staff as expected. He referred to him as the "little Napoleon" who was thoroughly hated by all officers at headquarters as a "meddling, over-conceited fellow." *Wainwright Journals*, 215. When Gen. Sedgwick heard that Meade had retained Butterfield, he said he "regretted it, that he knew Butterfield well, that he was a bold bad man & that Meade would live to regret it." [Jas. C. Biddle] to Webb, Dec. 10, 1885, Webb Collection.

51. Meade, *Life and Letters*, I, 351; [Col.] George Meade to his mother, July 1, 1863, George Gordon Meade Papers, HSP; CCW, *Report*, I, 429. After Butterfield in his testimony before the Committee on the Conduct of the War joined the attack on Meade's record at Gettysburg, Meade, thoroughly disillusioned, wrote to his wife on Mar. 20, 1864, that he believed that from the time he assumed command Butterfield had deliberately begun to "treasure up incidents, remarks and papers to pervert and distort in the future to my injury." Meade, *Life and Letters*, II, 181.

52. Patrick Journal, Entry for Sunday Night, June 28, 1863, LC.

53. *Ibid.;* [Col.] George Meade to his mother, July 1, 1863, George Gordon Meade Papers, HSP.

54. *OR*, XXVII, pt. 3, pp. 61–62.

55. Williams to his daughters, July 6, 1863, in *Alpheus Williams Letters*, 223.

56. *OR*, XXVII, pt. 1, pp. 143–144; pt. 3, p. 371.

57. *Ibid.*, pt. 1, pp. 143–144; pt. 3, p. 372.

58. *Ibid.*, pt. 1, p. 144; pt. 3, p. 395.

59. *Ibid.*, pt. 1, p. 144. Apparently the Sixth Corps was strung out along the road from Edwards Ferry to Poolesville. To get to Hyattstown from its camp

near Edwards Ferry the First Division under Gen. H. G. Wright had to march eighteen miles, which was a good day's work at any time. *Ibid.*, pp. 666, 669, 689, 692–694. Meade for some reason expected the Sixth Corps to push on and reach New Market the night of June 28. *Ibid.*, p. 64.

60. Seth Williams to [Pleasonton], June 28, 1863; [Meade] to Halleck, June 28, 1863, Telegrams Sent, XCII, 3, 7, U. S. Army Command, Army of the Potomac, Record Group 98, NA; *OR*, XXVII, pt. 1, pp. 166–167; pt. 3, pp. 373, 376; Theodore Lyman Diary, Entries for Sept. 13, 1863, Feb. 23, 1864, MHS; Ford, ed., *Adams Letters*, II, 44–45. At the time of their appointments the ages of the three generals were: Custer 23, Farnsworth 26, and Merritt 29. Boatner, *Civil War Dictionary*, 216, 275, 544.

61. *OR*, XXVII, pt. 1, pp. 62, 67; pt. 3, pp. 275–276, 376–377.

62. *Ibid.*, pt. 1, p. 63; pt. 3, pp. 377, 381.

63. *Ibid.*, pt.1, pp. 20–21, 62–65; CCW, *Report*, I, 335.

64. *OR*, XXVII, pt. 3, pp. 378, 382. In another dispatch French referred to the men with whom he started out to join Meade as "untried," and the 3,300 or so he left behind to guard the stores and transport them to Washington as ready "to take the rear at the first alarm." *Ibid.*, pt. 1, pp. 69–70. Halleck said in his report of the campaign that there were supposed to be 11,000 men at Harpers Ferry, while French set the figure in his dispatch of July 1, 1863, at 10,000. *Ibid.*, pt. 1, p. 15; pt. 3, p. 473.

65. *Ibid.*, pt. 1, p. 21; CCW, *Report*, I, 335.

66. *OR*, XXVII, pt. 1, pp. 67–71; pt. 3, pp. 401–402, 428, 462–463, 473. Stanton sent a dispatch to Meade saying that French had blown up his magazine, spiked the large cannon, and destroyed the surplus stores. *Ibid.*, pt. 1, p. 69.

67. *Ibid.*, pp. 490–491, 501–502, 517–518.

68. These estimates are based on various sources. The number of wagons needed to carry seven days' subsistence, forage, ammunition, baggage, hospital stores, and miscellaneous items was derived from a ratio of one wagon to fifty officers and men, which army authorities considered desirable. Actually in the Army of the Potomac the ratio of wagons to officers and men was larger. See *ibid.*, pp. 212–213; [Lyman to his wife], Nov. 28, 1863, in Agassiz, ed., *Meade's Headquarters*, 55; Cecil Battine, *The Crisis of the Confederacy, A History of Gettysburg and the Wilderness* (London, 1905), 399.

69. Ford, ed., *Adams Letters*, II, 3.

70. Most corps received orders to start at 4:00 A.M. *OR*, XXVII, pt. 3, p. 375.

71. *Ibid.*, pt. 1, pp. 64–67; pt. 3, p. 370.

72. John C. Ropes to John C. Gray, Jr., Apr. 16, 1864, in Gray and Ropes, *War Letters*, 316.

73. *OR*, XXVII, pt. 1, p. 67. Indulging in a bit of wishful thinking, Meade hoped Couch would be able to check Lee "for a few days." Meade, from Frederick, Md., to his wife, June 29, 1863, George Gordon Meade Papers, HSP.

74. The objectives for the first day's march were as follows: Emmitsburg, First and Eleventh Corps; Taneytown, Twelfth and Third Corps; Union or

Uniontown, Fifth Corps; Frizzelburg, Second Corps; New Windsor, Sixth Corps; between Middleburg and Taneytown, Reserve Artillery; Middleburg, army headquarters. *OR,* XXVII, pt. 3, p. 375.

75. Humphreys to his wife, May 2, 1864, A. A. Humphreys Papers, HSP. John Gray, a confirmed McClellan man who considered Meade a mediocre general, admitted that off the field of battle he "certainly manoeuvres his army beautifully." Gray to Ropes, Nov. 3, 1864, in Gray and Ropes, *War Letters,* 407. Theodore Lyman wrote his wife on Nov. 16, 1864, that Meade's handling of his troops "when a mistake would be the destruction of the entire plan, has been a wonder; without exaggeration, a wonder. His movements and those of Lee are only to be compared to two exquisite swordsmen, each perfectly instructed, and never erring a hair in attack or defense." Agassiz, ed., *Meade's Headquarters,* 271.

76. Williams to his daughters, June 29, 1863, in *Alpheus Williams Letters,* 220.

77. The Survivors' Association, *History of the 118th Pennsylvania Volunteers,* 232.

78. Coffin, *Boys of '61,* 263–264.

79. Patrick Journal, Entry for Sunday Night, June 28, 1863, LC.

80. Dispatch from C. C. Coffin, Frederick, June 29, in *Boston Morning Journal,* July 4, 1863.

81. Column by Agate [Whitelaw Reid], Frederick, June 30, in *Cincinnati Daily Gazette,* July 8, 1863.

82. Dispatch from C. C. Coffin, Frederick, June 29, in *Boston Morning Journal,* July 4, 1863.

83. Gen. Slocum sent Meade a dispatch saying that when he left Frederick there were a "great number of men from every corps lying about the streets beastly drunk." *OR,* XXVII, pt. 3, p. 398.

84. Column by Agate [Whitelaw Reid], Two Taverns, Pa., July 1, in *Cincinnati Daily Gazette,* July 8, 1863.

85. Extract from Gen. Stannard's Diary, Entry for June 29, 1863, Typescript, Bachelder Papers.

86. *OR,* XXVII, pt. 3, pp. 398, 1083; Patrick Journal, Entry for June 30, 1863, LC. Meade personally ordered the commanding officers of the 2nd Pa. Cavalry to help Patrick.

87. *Wainwright Journals,* 229. See also dispatch from C. C. Coffin, Uniontown, Md., June 30, in *Boston Morning Journal,* July 4, 1863.

88. Meade, *Life and Letters,* II, 12; Gen. Stannard's Diary, Entries for June 29 and 30, 1863, Typescript, Bachelder Papers; Patrick Journal, Entry for June 30, 1863, LC.

89. *Ibid.; OR,* XXVII, pt. 1, p. 144; pt. 3, pp. 398–399.

90. *Ibid.,* pt. 1, p. 144; pt. 3, pp. 375, 395–396; St. Clair A. Mulholland, "The Gettysburg Campaign," *Philadelphia Weekly Times,* Feb. 14, 1880; Dispatch from C. C. Coffin, Uniontown, Md., June 30, in *Boston Morning Journal,* July 4, 1863; Extract from the Account of Movements of Second Army Corps by Lt. Col. C. H. Morgan, Inspector-General and Chief of Staff, Typescript,

Bachelder Papers; [Second] Battle Report of Col. A. F. Devereux, May 1, 1878, Selected Documents from Union Battle Reports, 1861–1865, Entry 729, Record Group 94, NA. Night marches were regarded as much more tiring. One observer wrote: "I consider fifteen miles by night equal to twenty-five by day. . . ." [Lyman to his wife], June 2, 1864, in Agassiz, ed., *Meade's Headquarters*, 139.

91. Hancock sent his message at 9:30 P.M., and headquarters dispatched its reply at 12:15 A.M. Assuming he received the answer within two and a half hours, he had plenty of time to send all or part of his corps to Westminster and Union Mills before Stuart left in the morning. Stuart apparently was unaware of Hancock's arrival at Uniontown. *OR*, XXVII, p. 1084; Lt. Col. C. H. Morgan's Account, Typescript, Bachelder Papers.

92. *Wainwright Journals*, 228.

93. *OR*, XXVII, pt. 1, pp. 144, 926, 943; pt. 3, p. 400; Theo. W. Bean, "Who Fired the Opening Shots?", *Philadelphia Weekly Times*, Feb. 2, 1878.

94. *Wainwright Journals*, 228.

95. Meade, *Life and Letters*, II, 12; Lt. Col. C. H. Morgan's Account, Typescript, Bachelder Papers. They were delayed by units which preceded them from Frederick. *OR*, XXVII, pt. 3, pp. 395–397.

96. *Ibid.*, p. 398.

97. *Ibid.*, pt. 1, pp. 144, 666.

98. *Ibid.*, pt. 3, p. 399. The editor of the *OR* corrected what he thought was an error when Gen. Seth Williams addressed the dispatch of 6:45 P.M. on June 29 to the commander of the Fifth Corps instead of the First. An examination of other communications on the same date clearly indicates that Williams made no mistake. See *ibid.*, pp. 375, 395–396.

99. *Ibid.*, pp. 399, 420. On June 28 the Third Corps marched to Walkersville, a town seven miles northeast of Frederick on the main road to Taneytown. Headquarters instructed Sickles to start on June 29 for Taneytown at the same hour, 4:00 A.M., as the other corps which were nearer Frederick. Since Sickles had a good head start on the same road over which the Twelfth Corps, the Artillery Reserve, and the headquarters train would travel, Meade naturally expected him to be well out of the way long before the others arrived. Under the circumstances Meade's anger was thoroughly justified.

100. *Ibid.*, pt. 1, p. 144; pt. 3, p. 375.

101. CCW, *Report*, I, 329–330.

102. Meade, from Middleburg, Md., to Mrs. Meade, June 29, 1863, in Meade, *Life and Letters*, II, 13.

103. *OR*, XXVII, pt. 3, p. 375.

104. *Ibid.*, pt. 1, pp. 66–67. Meade sent this message at 11:00 A.M. by courier, since the Confederates had cut telegraphic communications of the Army of the Potomac with Washington, Baltimore, and Harrisburg.

105. *Ibid.*, pt. 3, p. 402.

106. *Ibid.*, pp. 414–415, 419, 422–425. Bridgeport was five miles west of Taneytown, halfway to Emmitsburg.

107. There is no record of the time when the order appointing Reynolds as

left-wing commander was issued. Without doubt it was sent before 12:45 P.M. and perhaps even before 9:45 A.M. *Ibid.*, pp. 418–419, 422.

108. Memo from J. G. Rosengarten to Bates regarding the death of his late chief, Gen. Reynolds [sent sometime late in 1875 or early in 1876]; Hooker to Bates, July 12, 1878, Bates Collection; John Hay Diary, Entry for Sept. 10, 1863, Typescript, Brown University Library; [Theodore Lyman to his wife], Sept. 22, 1863, in Agassiz, ed., *Meade's Headquarters*, 21; Humphreys to Gov. [Horatio] Seymour, July 15, 1864, A. A. Humphreys Papers, HSP; [Obituary of Gen. John Buford], *Harper's Weekly*, Jan. 2, 1864.

109. *OR*, XXVII, pt. 1, p. 144; pt. 3, p. 400.

110. *Ibid.*, pt. 1, p. 926.

111. *Ibid.*, p. 923. Buford gave the time of his arrival in a dispatch to Pleasonton from Gettysburg on June 30. In his report he said his force arrived in town in the afternoon.

112. *Ibid.*, pp. 922–924.

113. *Ibid.*, pt. 3, pp. 417–418.

114. *Ibid.*, pp. 419–420.

115. *Ibid.*, p. 420.

116. *Ibid.*, pp. 417–419.

117. Nichols, *Toward Gettysburg*, 195; Boatner, *Civil War Dictionary*, 413, 694.

118. Howard to Prof. M. Jacobs, Mar. 23, 1864, Howard Papers.

119. Meade to his wife, June 30, 1863, in Meade, *Life and Letters*, II, 18.

120. *OR*, XXVII, pt. 1, pp. 69, 71.

121. *Ibid.*, pt. 3, p. 415.

122. *Ibid.*

123. *Ibid.*, pp. 416–417, 420–423. He ordered the empty wagons, surplus baggage, and other impedimenta to be sent to Union Bridge, three miles from Middleburg. Union Bridge was the railhead of the Western Maryland Railroad, which ran from there to Baltimore by way of Westminster.

124. Meade to his wife, Apr. 18, 1863, in Meade, *Life and Letters*, I, 367. Meade could see the advantage of secrecy to prevent the enemy from becoming aware of plans but felt Hooker carried it too far. See also his postscript to Howard in message of June 22, 1863, in which he said: "I don't know what we are going to do. I have had no communication from headquarters for three days." *OR*, XXVII, pt. 3, p. 255.

125. *Ibid.*, pp. 416, 420–421.

126. *Ibid.*, p. 421.

127. *Ibid.*

128. *Ibid.*, pt. 1, pp. 924, 987–988.

129. On the night of the 30th Buford sent two long messages from Gettysburg, one at 10:30 P.M. to Reynolds, and the other ten minutes later to Pleasonton, who sent it on to army headquarters but did not indicate when. The first one gave a more complete picture of the situation, and when it finally reached Meade he became convinced that the danger point was Gettysburg, as he had suspected. He testified to the Committee on the Conduct of the War in Mar. of

1864 that he did not get the message until late in the morning of July 1. CCW, *Report*, I, 347; *OR*, XXVII, pt. 1, pp. 923–924. Couch and Brig. Gen. Herman Haupt, who was in charge of railroads for military use, wired Halleck on June 30 that they had definite information that Lee had withdrawn from the Susquehanna. In his message Haupt said that indications pointed to a "sudden movement against Meade," while Couch mentioned Gettysburg or Hanover as the rendezvous for the Confederates. Meade said he did not get the dispatches until after he had ordered army movements for July 1. *Ibid.*, pp. 69–70; pt. 3, pp. 434, 460. At 7:00 A.M., July 1, he acknowledged receipt of the dispatches, which the War Dept. had forwarded.

130. Howard said he did not receive the order to advance to Gettysburg until near daylight, July 1. Howard to Prof. M. Jacobs, Mar. 23, 1864, Howard Papers. In his report he gave the time as 3:30 A.M. *OR*, XXVII, pt. 1, p. 701. The orders for the movements of the various corps for July 1 were drawn up sometime on June 30. *Ibid.*, pt. 3, p. 416. Meade said he wrote the Pipe Creek Circular and sent it out to his commanders on the morning of July 1 before he received the dispatch Buford sent to Reynolds at 10:30 P.M., June 30. Buford reported that enemy columns were moving on the Chambersburg Pike to Gettysburg. CCW, *Report*, I, 347–348.

131. This phrase was used by Kenneth Williams in *Lincoln Finds a General*, II, 675. Williams thought Meade did not possess sufficient moral fortitude to move aggressively and he missed fleeting opportunities to gain advantages over Lee. To Williams Gettysburg was the obvious place for a battle; if Meade had acted on that assumption with confidence he could have defeated Lee in detail. *Ibid.*, II, 672–694. Butterfield claimed that when Meade presented him with a draft of the Pipe Creek Circular as early as the morning of June 30, Butterfield expressed a fear that a retreat, even though prearranged, would have an adverse effect on army morale. He talked about it, he said, with Hancock and others who were at headquarters at the time for the purpose of getting them to induce Meade to change his mind. CCW, *Report*, I, 403, 421–422. He may have discussed it with several generals on June 30, but Hancock was nowhere near headquarters then. It is also highly doubtful that Meade had even considered establishing a line along Pipe Creek before the night of June 30. At 4:30 P.M., June 30, he wired Halleck that because of the intelligence reports he had received of enemy movements, he would push on in the direction of Hanover and Hanover Junction on July 1, where he could establish direct rail and telegraphic connections with Baltimore. He sent the same message to Couch at 5:30 P.M. *OR*, pt. 1, pp. 68–69.

132. *Ibid.*, pt. 3, pp. 416, 422–423.

133. According to returns of the Army of the Potomac, June 30, 1863, the First Corps had a strength of 10,355 officers and men; the Eleventh had 10,576. Gen. Abner Doubleday, who assumed command of the First Corps upon the death of Gen. Reynolds, asserted in his report that his command went into battle with about 8,200 men, a difference of 2,155 from the first figure. Buford had only two of his brigades with him, numbering 2,900 in round figures on July 1. *Ibid.*, pt. 1, pp. 151, 154, 251, 934; Selected Pages from His-

torical and Statistical Record of the Principal Military Commands in the Union and Confederate Armies, IV, 53, 60, 75, Entry 161, Record Group 94, NA. The smaller total is probably the more correct one.

134. Manchester to Gettysburg via Westminster is thirty-three miles, via Hanover twenty-seven.

135. OR, XXVII, pt. 3, pp. 458–459; CCW, Report, I, 380. Among those who laid out the line were Gens. Warren and Hunt. Copy of Warren letter, no date, in Taylor, G. K. Warren, 122; H. J. Hunt to Webb, Jan. 19, 1888, Webb Collection.

136. CCW, Report, I, 330.

137. OR, XXVII, pt. 3, p. 459.

138. Ibid., p. 458.

139. For some of the virtues of the Pipe Creek line see Andrew Brown, Geology of the Gettysburg Campaign (Educational Series No. 5, Bureau of Topographic and Geologic Survey, Pa. Dept. of Internal Affairs, [no date]), 9; H. J. Hunt to Webb, Jan. 19, 1888, Webb Collection. Hunt wrote: "He [Meade] did ask or direct me to look for a battle-field behind Pipe Creek, and of course I inquired of my own mind his reasons, as he did not give them to me himself. I did not have to look far, for the only reasonable solution presented itself. . . . I believe . . . that Pipe Creek was our true place, and it was Meade's order to me to look for a field there that suggested that fact to me."

140. Lincoln wrote Gov. Joel Parker of N.J.: "I really think the attitude of the enemy's army in Pennsylvania presents us the best opportunity we have had since the war began." OR, XXVII, pt. 3, pp. 436–437. With this view of the situation, his feelings could well be imagined should the Army of Northern Virginia have escaped without a scratch.

141. CCW, Report, I, 330, 347; Ropes to Gray, Apr. 16, 1864, in Gray and Ropes, War Letters, 317. Gen. Warren in a letter telling of his experiences in the Gettysburg campaign referred to the line at Pipe Creek as "provisional." Copy of letter, no date, in Taylor, G. K. Warren, 122. For a map and a sound study of the Pipe Creek line, see a reprint of an article about it by Frederic S. Klein in Klein, ed., Just South of Gettysburg, 158–174.

142. Although it really had no effect on events, it is almost certain that Reynolds received neither the Pipe Creek Circular nor the special message. A copy of the latter was sent to Howard. Meade thought that perhaps Reynolds did not get the Pipe Creek Circular. See OR, XXVII, pt. 3, p. 461. For a list of those people who were sure Reynolds did not get it, see Nichols, Toward Gettysburg, 251, 2 note.

143. OR, XXVII, pt. 3, pp. 460–461. The astute Confederate Col. E. P. Alexander resorted to an ingenious interpretation to reconcile the orders for a general advance on July 1 with the Pipe Creek Circular. He claimed that Meade's order to advance was not for the purpose of bringing on a battle, but "to cover the position selected, allowing space in front to delay the enemy's approach and give time for preparation. The instructions to Reynolds, who was in command on the left, were not to bring on a general engagement." Alexander,

Military Memoirs, 282. There are two things wrong with this explanation. It is doubtful whether Meade would have used almost half his army for a mere covering movement, and he did not direct Reynolds to avoid a general engagement. On the contrary, he told him to decide whether Gettysburg was a suitable place for one.

144. *OR*, XXVII, pt. 1, pp. 67–71.

145. Ropes to Gray, Apr. 16, 1864, in Gray and Ropes, *War Letters*, 317.

NOTES TO CHAPTER X

1. Longstreet, *Memoirs*, 335.

2. *OR*, XXV, pt. 2, pp. 239–241, 790–791, 846. Col. Long of Lee's staff said that since the battle of Chancellorsville the Federal army had been increased to its "former dimensions," which was not true. Long, *Memoirs of Lee*, 269. Taylor, also of Lee's staff, was aware that certain Northern regiments were not used at Chancellorsville because they were being discharged, he thought, from service. Other than this vague reference to discharged troops he made no mention of the substantial reduction in the size of Hooker's army. Walter H. Taylor, *Four Years with General Lee* (New York, 1877), 89, 112–113. Lee must have known that a large number of Union regiments had gone home, but apparently he accepted the notion that they would be replaced shortly. In the existing records he himself said nothing about this loss of Hooker's manpower, but the armchair strategists in Richmond talked openly about it. *OR*, XXV, pt. 2, pp. 566–567.

3. *Ibid.*, p. 832.

4. CCW, *Report*, I, 173, 337–338. In a message to Reynolds on July 1, Meade said the two armies were equal in size. *OR*, XXVII, pt. 3, p. 460.

5. As a further example of conflicting evidence, Meade said he had about 105,000 men including the 11,000 of French's command which he did not bring up to Gettysburg, whereas Hooker wired Halleck on June 27 that his "whole force of enlisted men for duty" would not exceed 105,000. If by this statement he meant only the rank and file, his total force of officers and men would have been in the neighborhood of 115,000. It does not seem likely that at a time when he was asking for reinforcements he would have exaggerated the size of his army. The returns on June 30 gave the number of those troops and officers present for duty as 104,256. See CCW, *Report*, I, 337–338; *OR*, XXVII, pt. 1, pp. 59, 151.

6. *Ibid.*, XXV, pt. 1, pp. 156–170, 789–794; XXVII, pt. 1, pp. 155–168; pt. 2, pp. 283–291.

7. The returns of June 30, 1863, for the Army of the Potomac placed the number of pieces in the light field artillery at 312 and in the horse artillery at 50, for a total of 362. Hunt's figures were 320 light field artillery, 44 horse artillery, total 364. Naisawald counted 324 light field pieces and 50 in the horse

artillery, total 374. In his tabulation he included eight 4.5-inch rifles which were not brought to Gettysburg. According to his estimate, therefore, Meade had 366 guns on the field. See *ibid.*, pt. 1, pp. 151, 241–242; Naisawald, *Grape and Canister*, Appendix II, 553–556, 2 Note, p. 573; Wise, *Long Arm of Lee*, 576. After the battle Pendleton inspected the condition of the batteries of the Army of Northern Virginia. According to his tabulations, Lee had 251 pieces at the battle. In addition he had 24 pieces of horse artillery in Stuart's division and a battery of 6 guns in Imboden's command, in all 281 guns. Wise and Alexander gave a total of 272 guns. See *OR*, XXVII, pt. 2, pp. 355–356; Wise, *Long Arm of Lee*, 578–579, 692; Alexander, *Military Memoirs*, 368; John D. Imboden, "The Confederate Retreat from Gettysburg," *B&L*, III, pt. 2, p. 423.

8. Albert B. Moore, *Conscription and Conflict in the Confederacy* (New York, 1924), 228–296.

9. *OR*, Ser. III, Vol. III, pp. 58, 109, 112–113, 219, 224, 329, 373–374, 378, 386–390, 424–425, 487. On Dec. 3, 1861, Gen. McClellan established a system of getting recruits to keep the regiments up to full strength. Just when the new machinery was working smoothly Stanton decided to scrap it in an order issued on Apr. 3, 1862. Why he committed what has been called one of the "colossal blunders of the war" has never been satisfactorily explained. Shannon, *Organization and Administration*, I, 265–268. The explanation offered in a recent biography of Stanton is inadequate. See Thomas and Hyman, *Stanton, Life and Times*, 201–202.

10. Thomas L. Livermore, *Numbers and Losses in the Civil War in America, 1861–65* (Boston, 1900), 68.

11. The 61st N.Y., which was Gen. Barlow's old regiment, brought only ninety muskets into action at Gettysburg. Barlow to his mother, June 2, 1863, Francis C. Barlow Papers, MHS; *OR*, XXVII, pt. 1, p. 384. By the time of Gettysburg the 14th Conn., which had been in the field less than a year, could muster only 200 effective men out of 1,000 as a result of losses from marching, sickness, and casualties at Antietam, Fredericksburg, and Chancellorsville. Browne, *Dunn Browne in the Army*, 189.

12. Out of fifty-one Union brigades at Gettysburg, there are records which give the strength of forty-two of them on June 30, July 1, or July 2. Twenty-seven mustered between 1,000 and 2,000 officers and men; ten between 2,000 and 2,500; and five below 1,000. Most brigades reporting over 2,000 officers and men as present on June 30 brought into action far fewer than that number. Selected Pages from the Historical and Statistical Record of the Principal Military Commands in the Union and Confederate Armies, IV, 42, 53, 75, 80, 143–144, Entry 161, Record Group 94, NA; *OR*, XXVII, pt. 1, pp. 291, 313, 338, 381, 386, 418, 421, 494, 560, 601, 604, 645, 668, 833, 858; Richard Robbins, "The Regular Troops at Gettysburg," *Philadelphia Weekly Times*, Jan. 4, 1879.

Information available about twenty-four out of thirty-seven Confederate brigades at Gettysburg shows that eighteen mustered between 1,000 and 2,000 officers and men for the battle; three had more than 2,000; and three had less than 1,000. *OR*, XXVII, pt. 2, pp. 387, 493, 562, 619–620, 633, 647, 667; Harrison, *Pickett's Men*, 90–91; B. G. Humphreys to Bachelder, May 1, 1876, Bachelder Papers; Notes for Gen. E. P. Alexander by Henry L. Benning, 1866 [?], MS, Henry L. Benning Papers, UNC; Field Return of Early's Division, June 20, 1863, War Department Collection of Confederate Records, Record Group 109, NA; Alexander, *Military Memoirs*, 402; Abner Perrin to Governor [Bonham], July 29, 1863, in *Mississippi Historical Review*, XXIV, 522; Battle report of R. M. Mayo, Aug. 13, 1863, Henry Heth Collection, Confederate Museum; Louis G. Young to Early, Mar. 14, 1878, Jubal A. Early Papers, LC.

13. H. J. Hunt to Long, Oct. 5, 1884, A. L. Long Papers, UNC.

14. Hunt's marginal comments on "General Early's Reply to the Count of Paris," *SHSP*, VI, 22, 28, 30. Hunt wondered why Confederates did not make out reports during periods of active campaigning before a major engagement and decided that perhaps they had felt it was a hopeless task.

15. Gray to Ropes, Aug. 30, 1863, in Gray and Ropes, *War Letters*, 190.

16. James Beall [Beale], "Strength of the Armies," *Philadelphia Weekly Times*, Nov. 9, 1878. The newspaper editor spelled Beale's name wrong and placed him in the 1st instead of the 12th Mass. See James Beale to Nicholson, Apr. 25, 1880, John Page Nicholson Collection, Huntington Library.

17. Greely S. Curtis, "Gettysburg (Report of Committee)," *Campaigns in Virginia, Maryland and Pennsylvania*, 357–358.

18. Comte de Paris to Early, Apr. 20, 1878, Jubal A. Early Papers, LC.

19. Curtis, "Gettysburg," *Campaigns in Virginia, Maryland and Pennsylvania*, 358.

20. Bates, *Martial Deeds of Pennsylvania*, 341–342; Sickles *et al.*, "Further Recollections of Gettysburg," *North American Review*, CLII, 274.

21. Selected Pages from Retained Copies of Reports, 1861–1865, Vol. 3, War Records Office, Entry 87, Record Group 94, NA. Col. Thomas L. Livermore made an equally careful study of the strength of the two armies. He estimated the total Confederates engaged at Gettysburg to be 75,054. In judging the strength of Meade's forces at Gettysburg he came up with a figure of 83,289, not counting the brigades of Brig. Gen. A. T. A. Torbert, Brig. Gen. David A. Russell, and Col. Lewis A. Grant of the Sixth Corps because, though present at the battlefield, they were not engaged. A questionable formula at best, he should have applied it to Brig. Gen. William Mahone's and Brig. Gen. Carnot Posey's brigades of A. P. Hill's corps, neither of which went into action. See Livermore, *Numbers and Losses*, 102–103.

22. Selected Pages from Retained Copies of Reports, 1861–1865, Vol. 3, War Records Office, Entry 87, Record Group 94, NA. The study underestimated the size of Pettigrew's brigade by at least 800 troops and did not include Davis' brigade and the 1st Md. Infantry Battalion among the reinforcements, over 4,000 men in all. Davis' brigade joined the army as a replacement for Jenkins' brigade which, however, had been on detached service for some time and was not included in the returns for May 31. See *OR*, XXV, pt. 1, pp. 789–794; pt. 2, pp. 841–842, 845–846; XXVII, pt. 2, pp. 286, 289, 645;

Louis G. Young to Early, Mar. 14, 1878, Jubal A. Early Papers, LC. The size of the 1st Md. Infantry Battalion was estimated to be about 700. See *OR*, XXVII, pt. 1, p. 65.

23. *Cf. ante*, I, 23–24.

24. *OR*, XXVII, pt. 2, pp. 336–337, 712–714, 719. Very likely Lee started from Fredericksburg with almost 78,000 of all arms, but not including Corse's brigade, and picked up along the way at least 3,600 troops in Jenkins' and Imboden's commands. The 1st Md. Infantry Battalion and the Baltimore Light Artillery battery joined Ewell's corps in the Shenandoah Valley. *Ibid.*, p. 440. Two officials in the Confederate War Dept. reported in their diaries, apparently independently of each other, that Lee took with him 70,000 effectives or fighting men. As it was a common practice among Confederates not to include officers in their estimates, these figures probably do not do so, although they made up on the average 8 percent of the total. See Kean, *Inside the Confederate Government*, 76; Jones, *Rebel War Clerk's Diary*, 343. The estimate of 75,000 for Lee's strength at Gettysburg is therefore a conservative one.

25. Selected Pages from Retained Copies of Reports, 1861–1865, Vol. 3, War Records Office, Entry 87, Record Group 94, NA.

26. The First, Second, Fifth, and Eleventh Corps reported all those "present for duty," the Twelfth "present for duty equipped," and the Third its "effective strength." *OR*, XXVII, pt. 1, p. 153.

27. Col. Walter Taylor of Lee's staff set the figure for Lee's army at Gettysburg at 67,000; Gen. Early cut it to 59,900 and then to 50,742; Col. William Allan placed it at about 60,000; Gen. Heth at 62,000; and Gen. Longstreet said there were 67,000 bayonets or above 70,000 men of all arms. John Esten Cooke was the exception to the rule when he estimated the entire force to have been about 80,000. For their estimates of the Union army these Confederates used the highest figures available, usually the 104,256 reported as present for duty in the June 30 returns. Before publication of the *OR* the Confederates would cite Butterfield's testimony before the Committee on the Conduct of the War, in which he said the Union army had 78,245 officers and men in the infantry on June 10; or Meade's, in which he set the figure of about 95,000 men for all arms. Curtis, "Gettysburg," *Campaigns in Virginia, Maryland and Pennsylvania*, 362–365; William Allan, "Gen. Lee's Strength and Losses at Gettysburg," *SHSP*, IV, 40–41; "General Early's Reply to Count of Paris," *ibid.*, VI, 18–21; "General Heth's Letter," *ibid.*, IV, 151; W. H. Taylor to Early, Feb. 26, 1878, Jubal A. Early Papers, LC; CCW, *Report*, I, 337, 428; *OR*, XXVII, pt. 1, p. 151. In referring to the tendency of Confederate officers to exaggerate the odds against them Gen. Warren wrote: "Be careful in statements of facts, for I see Longstreet, like everyone in the South, always gets whipped with overwhelming numbers . . . according to his own statement, which I know were quite as often just the reverse." Warren to Porter Farley, Nov. 24, 1877, in Oliver W. Norton, *The Attack and Defense of Little Round Top, Gettysburg* (New York, 1913), 323.

28. Notes on "Gettysburg to the Rapidan," MS, A. A. Humphreys Papers,

HSP. A breakdown of the Field Return on July 5, 1863, as recorded by Humphreys, is as follows:

Corps	Officers	Enlisted Men	
1	472	4,500	300? guns
2	500	5,600	
3	438	5,100	Cavalry—
5	635	7,850	7,000 officers
6	783	11,042	& enlisted men
11	301	4,818	
12	442	7,375	
	3,571	46,285	

29. Olmsted to [E. L.] Godkin, July 19, 1863, in Page, ed., "After Gettysburg," *PMHB*, LXXV, 441. Gen. Alpheus Williams complained of the great exaggeration in the press of the real strength of the Union army at Gettysburg. It was a fact, he said, that Meade had fewer than 60,000 "fighting men" there. Williams to his daughters, July 21, 1863, in *Alpheus Williams Letters*, 238–239. Gen. Joseph J. Bartlett of the Sixth Corps set an even lower figure when he wrote: "We fought this last battle at Gettysburg with *48,000 men all told!* Isn't it sad to think that the old army is so reduced?" Bartlett to Howland, July 16, 1863, Miscellaneous Manuscripts of [Col.] Joseph Howland, NYHS. Col. Theodore Lyman of Meade's staff stated that the number of Union troops present at the battle was about 85,000 of all arms. Lyman to Everett, Oct. 5, 1863, Edward Everett Papers, MHS. During this correspondence with Everett, Lyman made a puzzling request: "Gen. Meade desires me to ask you not to mention the *number of troops* engaged on *our* side, at Gettysburg, as it is the intention of the Secretary of War to suppress these figures in the published report. You could say our numbers were inferior, or words to that effect." *Id.* to *id.*, Oct. 26, 1863, *ibid*. This desire for secrecy helps to explain the insuperable difficulties of the historian in ascertaining the number of troops engaged in the battle.

30. *Cf. ante*, I, 14; Wise, *Long Arm of Lee*, 511–513; *OR*, XXV, pt. 2, p. 838; Weller, "Confederate Use of British Cannon," *CWH*, III, 150–151. Weller said both sides suffered from defective ammunition, but the South especially so. The proportion of "duds" among shells of Confederate manufacture ran as high as 50 percent, "a high figure even by contemporary performance."

31. *OR*, XXVII, pt. 1, p. 241; pt. 2, pp. 355–356. For total number of guns *cf. ante*, X, 244.

32. Harold L. Peterson, *Notes on Ordnance of the American Civil War, 1861–1865* (The American Ordnance Association, Washington, 1959); Bell I. Wiley and Hirst D. Milhollen, *They Who Fought Here* (New York, 1959), 126; Naisawald, *Grape and Canister*, 37. On pp. 38–39 Naisawald described

the howitzer and referred to it as a "weird" breed of cannon, made especially to fire the "hollow explosive type of projectile—shell and spherical case." In contrast to the Napoleon it lacked the bulge at the muzzle and weighed less. Unlike the modern howitzer it was not designed for high-angle fire.

33. Wiley and Milhollen, *They Who Fought Here*, 133–135. Canister, unlike shrapnel, contained no powder charge. The velocity with which the can flew out of the cannon hurled the pellets off in all directions. Canister and grape should not be confused, although their purposes and operations were similar. The word grape has literary and historical connotations lacking in the more deadly but prosaic canister. It was the latter that students of Civil War artillery feel was used exclusively by Union gunners and only a little less so by Confederates because of a scarcity of ammunition. Grape shots, though arranged in much the same way as canister balls, were much larger in size and fewer in number in each charge. See also Naisawald, *Grape and Canister*, Appendix I, 540–541.

34. *OR*, XXV, pt. 2, pp. 837–839; XXVII, pt. 1, p. 241; pt. 2, pp. 355–356; Weller, "Confederate Use of British Cannon," *CWH*, III, 143–145. At first glance it would appear that the British-made breech-loading rifled cannon, the Armstrong, Blakeley, and Whitworth, especially the last, had immediately outmoded all other types of guns. In his excellent article Weller pointed out that the shortcomings of the Whitworth outweighed its virtues. The heavy breech and long barrel made it an unwieldy weapon for the march. The most important disadvantages were in the inefficiency of its shell and the uselessness of the gun for close work. It could fire canister only with danger of causing serious damage to itself. Also there was little advantage to any breech-loader unless it possessed an improved recoil system. Every field gun in the Civil War when fired, recoiled from five or six feet to a dozen or so yards. "In fast action part of the crew rolled the piece forward and realigned it while the rest sponged and loaded." By the time it was brought back into its original position the gun was loaded, whether a muzzle- or breech-loader. Therefore rapidity of loading did not give a gun any advantage.

35. *Cf. ante*, X, 242.

36. The name "rifled musket" seems another of those contradictions in terms so frequent in Civil War literature, but it reflects a transition from the old 18th-century smoothbore musket to the modern rifle. The rifled muskets had the "long, relatively thin barrels of the old muskets instead of the shorter, thicker barrels of the rifles proper which later supplanted them." Wiley and Milhollen, *They Who Fought Here*, 104.

37. *Ibid.*, 114–115; Peterson, *Notes on Ordnance*.

38. Alexander said nine-tenths of the Confederate infantry were armed with muzzle-loading rifled muskets, mostly .58 caliber, but some .54 caliber. Alexander, *Military Memoirs*, 370. Fremantle exaggerated in saying the troops were "entirely" armed with rifles, for Scheibert noticed one brigade had smoothbores "by request because the trajectory was flatter." See Fremantle, *Three Months in the Southern States*, 225; Scheibert, *Seven Months in the Rebel States*, Hoole, ed., 37. For evidence that Lee's Confederates perhaps carried a greater

variety of small arms to Gettysburg than these accounts indicated, see the inventory of weapons picked up by Gen. Crawford's Pa. Reserves on July 2 and 3. Of course many of these arms could well have been dropped by Yankee soldiers in the fighting of July 2. *OR*, XXVII, pt. 1, p. 656. Over 80 percent of the 2,958 Confederate arms picked up by the Union First Corps were Enfield rifled muskets. *Ibid.*, p. 264.

39. Allan, "Reminiscences of Field Ordnance Service," *SHSP*, XIV, 139–140. As for the rifles taken at Winchester, an agent of the U. S. Sanitary Commission at York, Pa., talked to an officer from La. who said that his own and a N. C. brigade had equipped themselves there with these arms. Moore, ed., *Rebellion Record, Documents*, VII, 123. Obviously these were Gen. Harry T. Hays's and Gen. Robert F. Hoke's brigades of Early's division.

40. Allan Nevins, *The War for the Union: The Improvised War, 1861–1862* (New York, 1959), I, 344–345, 361–364.

41. For appraisals of Ripley and his work see *ibid.*, 351–352, 358, 361, 365–366; Shannon, *Organization and Administration*, I, 107–148; Robert V. Bruce, *Lincoln and the Tools of War* (New York, 1956), 22–58, 69–71, 99–117.

42. Lt. Mark Poore to Lt. Chas. S. Isaacs, Apr. 23, 1863, Selected Documents from Letters Received, 1863, Record Group 156, NA.

43. Summary Statement of Ordnance and Ordnance Stores on Hand in Infantry Regiments in the Service of the United States, 2d Quarter, June 30, 1863, Inventory No. 232, Record Group 156, NA.

44. Nevins, *War for the Union*, I, 355.

45. Kenneth W. Munden and Henry P. Beers, *Guide to Federal Archives Relating to the Civil War* (Washington, 1962), 277–278.

46. Record of Purchases of Ordnance, 1861–1867, Inventory No. 147, Record Group 156, NA.

47. Summary Statement of Ordnance and Ordnance Stores on Hand in Infantry Regiments, 2d Quarter, June 30; 4th Quarter, December 31, 1863, Inventory No. 232, Record Group 156, NA.

48. Summary Statement of Ordnance, 2d Quarter, June 30, 1863, Inventory No. 232, Record Group 156, NA. Because the inventories were incomplete the fraction or percentage of regiments uniformly equipped with Springfields or Enfields is only an estimate. Also regiments which appeared to have had only one kind of shoulder arm might have had other makes as well. Purportedly inventories were taken every quarter, but the returns generally reached the department about six to eight weeks after the end of the quarter. A few came in months later. In most regiments more companies took inventory of their arms and accoutrements than not and in a few all of them did. Out of 238 infantry regiments at Gettysburg only four failed to make any report. For the preference of some of the soldiers for Springfields see John J. Pullen, *The Twentieth Maine, A Volunteer Regiment in the Civil War* (New York, 1959), 134.

49. Lt. Col. J. Ford Kent to Lt. Col. Robert A. Hutchins, Jan. 28, 1863, Selected Documents from Letters Received, Summary Statement of Ordnance, 2d Quarter, June 30, 1863, Inventory No. 232, Record Group 156, NA; Shannon,

Organization and Administration, I, 124–125. See also George F. Davis, Vermont Quartermaster General, to Gen. Ripley, July 31, 1863, Selected Documents from Letters Received, Record Group 156, NA. Davis reported that the 12th, 13th, 14th, 15th, and 16th regiments of Vermont when mustered out had turned over their arms and accoutrements to him. Most of the arms returned by the 14th regiment, he said, were Austrian rifled muskets "unfit for use in the field." He then added: "I understand that they were condemned before the Regiment was engaged in the battle of Gettysburg."

50. For accounts of entire regiments reequipping themselves on the battlefield, see Pullen, *Twentieth Maine*, 134; Blake, *Three Years in the Army of the Potomac*, 219; Stevenson, *Indiana's Roll of Honor*, I, 234; Alanson A. Haines, *History of the Fifteenth Regiment New Jersey Volunteers* (New York, 1883), 94; John T. Porter, ed., *Under the Maltese Cross . . . Campaigns 155th Pennsylvania Regiment . . .* (Pittsburgh, 1910), 189–190.

51. Two companies in the 7th U.S. regiment and one in the 8th U.S. regiment had Colt rifles. Whether they were repeaters is not indicated. Summary Statement of Ordnance, 2d Quarter, June 30, 1863, Record Group 156, NA; Edwin A. Glover, *Bucktailed Wildcats, A Regiment of Civil War Volunteers* (New York, 1960), 209–210. There is evidence that in some regiments the companies entrusted with guarding their flanks were armed with Sharps rifles. See John F. Dearborn [of 2nd N. H.] to Bachelder, Apr. 22, 1889, Bachelder Papers.

52. Record of Purchases of Ordnance, 1861–67, Inventory No. 147, pp. 187–189, Record Group 156, NA.

53. *Ibid.*, pp. 201–202; Register of Letters Received, No. 449, Received in Washington, June 8, 1863, Vol. 34, 1863, Inventory No. 31, Record Group 156, NA. The first order made on July 13, 1863, for 7,000 Spencer carbines at $25.00 apiece was a large one for the cautious department. The first 1,000 of them were delivered Oct. 3, 1863. Record of Purchases, Inventory No. 147, pp. 201–202, Record Group 156, NA.

54. The Ordnance Dept. listed the following makes of breech-loading carbines in its inventory book for cavalry regiments during the second quarter of 1863: the Ballard, Burnside, Cosmopolitan, Joslyn, Gallagher, Gibb, Greene, Hall, Lindner, Merrill, Maynard, Sharps, Smith, and Starr. It also had the following rifles in the inventory rated as first-class: Austrian, U.S., Ballard breechloading, Colt's revolving, Merrill breech-loading, Spencer breech-loading, Sharps breech-loading, Enfield, and Light French. Summary Statement of Ordnance and Ordnance Stores on Hand in the Cavalry Regiments in Service of the United States, 2d Quarter, June 30, 1863, Inventory No. 231, Record Group 156, NA. For preferences troopers had in carbines see Gen. [Julius] Stahel to Gen. James S. Ripley, June 19, 1863; Capt. D. W. Flagler to Ripley [telegram], Aug. 3, 1863, Selected Documents from Letters Received, 1863, Record Group 156, NA.

The Sharps Rifle Mfg. Co. made constant improvements in its ammunition. At first it produced a paper cartridge, to which soldiers objected because the paper tore easily and broke open from jolting in the cartridge box, thus ruining the ammunition. The company then came out with a linen cartridge which was satisfactory, and finally in the summer of 1863, "metallic, pointed cartridges." They could only be used in a newly designed carbine. They were rapidly issued to troops in the field. Flagler to Ripley, Aug. 6, 1863; Maj. T. T. S.[?] Laidley to id., Aug. 29, 1863, ibid.

55. McClellan, Campaigns of Stuart, 260–261; OR, XXV, pt. 2, p. 820. Scheibert reported that one squadron in each cavalry regiment was armed with carbines in order to be able to fight dismounted as sharpshooters. He criticized the cavalry saber as being too light to be an effective weapon. Scheibert, Seven Months in the Rebel States, Hoole, ed., 37. McClellan made the unbelievable statement that in some regiments the men were not even armed with pistols or revolvers. McClellan, Campaigns of Stuart, 260.

NOTES TO CHAPTER XI

1. Cf. ante, V, 127–128.

2. For Meade's appraisal of the situation and moves to cope with it, cf. ante, VIII, 196; IX, 231. A general expectation of battle is not the same, however, as planning it at a certain place and time. Indicative of a prevailing attitude among Confederate officers was the following comment from Gen. Ramseur: "We are surprised that we have met with feeble resistance thus far. We feel sure however that we will have some stern and bloody work to do before this campaign is ended." Ramseur, at Carlisle, to [Nellie, his fiancée], June 28, 1863, Stephen D. Ramseur Papers, UNC. As the campaign progressed the Confederates began to narrow the possible locations of an engagement. Col. Fremantle noted in his diary on June 30 that he had had long talks with many officers about the "approaching battle," which they predicted could not be "delayed long, and will take place on this road [Chambersburg-Gettysburg Pike] instead of in the direction of Harrisburg, as we had supposed." Three Months in the Southern States, 250.

3. Nichols, Toward Gettysburg, 195–197.

4. Wainwright Journals, 232. According to Reynolds' staff officers, the general was not expecting a battle but intended "camping" at Gettysburg with his corps. Jennie [Reynolds] to her brother, July 5, 1863, Reynolds Family Papers, Franklin and Marshall College Library.

5. William Riddle to Le Bouvier, Aug. 4, 1863, copy, ibid.; Nichols, Toward Gettysburg, 196, 198; Weld, War Diaries and Letters, 229.

6. Wainwright Journals, 232.

7. Ibid.; OR, XXVII, pt. 1, p. 244; pt. 3, p. 457; LI, pt. 1, pp. 1065–1066. According to Doubleday, Reynolds told him before they started that he was going to modify the order of the march by placing the First Division to the front instead of the rear of the column. The First Division had led the corps on June 30, and ordinarily it would have brought up the rear on the following day's march. Ibid., XXVII, pt. 1, p. 244. Very likely before he talked to

Doubleday Reynolds rode to Wadsworth's headquarters and asked him about Doubleday's marching orders. When he learned that Wadsworth was waiting for the other divisions to pass, Reynolds said it was a mistake and for Wadsworth to move on directly. CCW, *Report*, I, 413.

8. *Ibid.; OR*, XXVII, pt. 1, pp. 244, 265.

9. Alan T. Nolan, *The Iron Brigade, A Military History* (New York, 1961), 130.

10. Boatner, *Civil War Dictionary*, 340–341.

11. For weather see Weld, *War Diaries and Letters*, 229; *Wainwright Journals*, 232; Louis R. Fortescue Diary, 1863–1864 [Lt. and signal officer, U. S. Army], UNC; *OR*, XXVII, pt. 1, p. 202. Col. William W. Robinson of the 7th Wis. said their camp was about five miles from Gettysburg. *Ibid.*, p. 278.

12. The order of march of the Iron Brigade was as follows: 2nd Wis., 7th Wis., 19th Ind., 24th Mich., and 6th Wis. Report on Iron Brigade by Brvt. Brig. Gen. William W. Dudley [19th Ind.], 1878, Selected Documents from Union Battle Reports, 1861–1865, Entry 729, Record Group 94, NA; R. R. Dawes to Bachelder, Mar. 18, 1868, Bachelder Papers.

13. *Id.* to *id.*, Mar. 18, 1868, *ibid.*

14. Charles H. Veil to D. McConaughy, Apr. 7, 1864, Peter F. Rothermel Collection, PDPR; Weld, *War Diaries and Letters*, 229–230; *OR*, XXVII, pt. 1, p. 265. Veil was Reynolds' orderly and kept close to his side. There is some question about where Reynolds found Buford. Veil specifically mentioned McPherson's Ridge, while Weld by implication agreed with him. The traditional account, dear to the heart of the romanticists, placed the meeting at the Theological Seminary. According to Buford's signal officer, Lt. A. B. Jerome, who is the source for the account, he and the general were up in the steeple of the building observing the fight and the approach of the First Corps when Reynolds and some of his staff rode up at a gallop. "In a familiar manner Gen. Reynolds asked Buford 'how things were going on,' and received the characteristic answer 'let's go and see.'" Jerome to Gen. Hancock, Oct. 18, 1865, Typescript, Bachelder Papers. Certain things should be noted. Both Veil and Weld were members of Reynolds' staff, and their accounts are more contemporary than Jerome's. Also it seems more logical, when the situation was getting tight, for Buford to have been at the front than a half mile to the rear. Jerome's account also is not too convincing in other respects.

Reynolds reached Gettysburg and conferred with Buford a little after 10:00 A.M., ahead of his troops probably by as much as half an hour. The time of his arrival can only be estimated by inference and from reminiscences based upon the diary of one of his staff officers, Stephen M. Weld. Starting with the positive fact of the entry in his diary that they had started at 8:00 A.M., Weld estimated that they could not have taken more than two hours to get to Gettysburg. "They" referred most likely to Reynolds and his staff. At 10:10 A.M. Buford sent Meade a message about the advance of the enemy and said Reynolds was advancing and was within three miles of "this point" with his leading division. Although ambiguous, this statement might have referred only to Reynolds' force and not to the general himself, who had either just arrived or was just moments away. Weld recorded that Reynolds had him carry a message to Meade around 10:00 A.M., and the tenor of the dispatch was the same as Buford's. Nothing was said about any of Reynolds' troops fighting. *OR*, XXVII, pt. 1, p. 924; Weld, *War Diaries and Letters*, 229–231.

15. *OR*, XXVII, pt. 1, pp. 923, 927.

16. *Ibid.*, pt. 2, p. 637.

17. There was general agreement among Confederate writers that Pettigrew's brigade numbered about 3,000 men. He took but three of his four regiments to Gettysburg on June 30. The largest regiment with between 800 and 1,000 men apparently was the 26th N. C., which went to Gettysburg with him. The other regiments numbered between 550 and 750 men. If one of these is deducted, he had a force of between 2,300 and 2,500 men for the march to Gettysburg. See Louis G. Young, "Pettigrew's Brigade at Gettysburg," Walter Clark, ed., *Histories of the Several Regiments and Battalions from North Carolina in the Great War, 1861–65* (Raleigh, 1901), V, 115–116, 120. The brigade marched from near Cashtown to very close to Gettysburg, a distance of eight miles. There is evidence to suggest that it returned to its old camp, another eight miles, and then went on picket duty four miles or so from Cashtown. The likelihood is that these men covered around twenty miles that day. See Henry C. Albright War Diary, North Carolina State Department of Archives and History. See also *OR*, XXVII, pt. 2, p. 642. Heth recalled that Pettigrew went all the way back to Cashtown. See James L. Morrison, Jr., ed., "Memoirs of Henry Heth," *CWH*, VIII, 303.

18. Gen. Lee reported that Pettigrew, being ignorant of the size of Buford's forces, did not "hazard" an attack. *OR*, XXVII, pt. 2, p. 317. Capt. Louis G. Young, who was on Pettigrew's staff, said the general was under strict orders not to precipitate a fight with any portion of the Army of the Potomac. He also said that Longstreet's spy, Harrison, and a member of the Knights of the Golden Circle, a Copperhead group, gave warning about Buford's arrival. Young, "Pettigrew's Brigade at Gettysburg," Clark, ed., *North Carolina Regiments*, V, 115–116.

19. *Ibid.*, 116–117.

20. "Gen. Henry Heth's Letter," *SHSP*, IV, 157. The wording of the conversation as Heth remembered it in his memoirs was different, but the gist of it was the same. Morrison, ed., "Heth Memoirs," *CWH*, VIII, 304.

21. *OR*, XXVII, pt. 2, p. 607.

22. Young, "Pettigrew's Brigade at Gettysburg," Clark, ed., *North Carolina Regiments*, V, 117.

23. *OR*, XXVII, pt. 2, p. 607. Heth maintained that he went to Gettysburg to get those shoes which Pettigrew failed to obtain. Henry Heth, "Gen. Lee's Orders to His Cavalry," *Philadelphia Weekly Times*, Mar. 23, 1878; Morrison, ed., "Heth Memoirs," *CWH*, VIII, 304. Other reports agree with Hill's that Heth and Pender were sent to reconnoiter. *OR*, XXVII, pt. 2, p. 317; Louis G. Young to William J. Baker, Feb. 10, 1864, Francis D. Winston Papers, North Carolina Department of Archives and History.

24. *OR*, XXVII, pt. 3, pp. 947–948.

25. Alexander, "Battle of Gettysburg," MS, E. P. Alexander Papers, UNC.
26. Ropes to Gray, Oct. 19, 1863, in Gray and Ropes, *War Letters*, 240.
27. *Eighth Census of U. S., 1860*, Vol. I.
28. [Trowbridge], "The Field of Gettysburg," *Atlantic Monthly*, XVI, 617; Comte de Paris, *The Battle of Gettysburg* (Philadelphia, 1907), 94. Trowbridge and the Count said the surface of the Chambersburg Pike was macadamized, but Professor Robert L. Bloom of Gettysburg College questions their statements. He said photographs taken soon after the battle show the pike to have been a dirt and gravel road.
29. *Wainwright Journals*, 233. Oak Ridge attains a height of 640 feet above sea level or 140 feet above the ground north of Gettysburg.
30. These descriptions are based upon personal observations and a perusal of the maps of the U. S. Geological Survey and of a relief map prepared by U. S. Army Engineers, 1952. Wainwright's comments in his *Journal*, 233–234, have also been used.
31. *OR*, XXVII, pt. 2, pp. 607, 637.
32. *Ibid.*, pt. 1, p. 927. Buford's remark that he would hold on until Reynolds arrived suggests that he knew the First Corps was on its way to Gettysburg. Although Meade's order to advance did not reach Reynolds until a little after daylight, a courier on a good horse could have gotten a copy of it to Buford long before the Confederate advance developed into a real threat. By that time Reynolds was on his way.
33. Gen. Buford, Col. Gamble, Col. George H. Chapman of the 3rd Ind. Cavalry regiment, and Lt. Calef all agreed that the main action between Gamble's brigade and Heth began between eight and nine o'clock in the morning. *OR*, XXVII, pt. 1, pp. 927, 934, 1030; George H. Chapman to Bachelder, Mar. 30, 1864, Typescript, Bachelder Papers.
34. In his report Lt. Calef offered an interesting and puzzling bit of information. He said that Lt. Roder, who commanded the section to the right of the Cashtown road, fired the first gun to open the battle on the "head of a column of rebel cavalry advancing on the right of the road." *OR*, XXVII, pt. 1, p. 1031. None of the Confederate reports mentioned any cavalry with Heth. It is possible, however, that a detachment from Jenkins' cavalry had ridden west from near Heidlersburg to meet up with Heth's advancing columns. See a letter of Capt. E. E. Bouldin to Bachelder, July 29, 1886, in which he said that "some of his [Jenkins'] command were the first to get to Gettysburg 1 July 1863." Bachelder Papers.
35. *OR*, XXVII, pt. 1, pp. 927, 934, 1030–1031. Although Calef had only six guns to the eight used by the enemy when the fighting began, they were 6-inch rifled pieces against no more than four guns of the same caliber. See *ibid.*, pt. 2, pp. 290, 356.
36. Charles H. Veil to D. McConaughy, Apr. 7, 1864, Peter F. Rothermel Collection, PDPR. For discussion of Reynolds' arrival, *cf. ante*, XI, 14 note.
37. The effective strength of the First Brigade on July 1 was 1,883 officers and men, and of the Second Brigade 1,626; the total for the division was 3,509. *OR*, XXVII, pt. 1, p. 282; Fox, ed., *New York at Gettysburg*, II, 681, 735;

Corrected Statement of Strength and Losses, Iron Brigade, Gettysburg, July 1, 1863, Copied War Records, 1861–1865, Selected Documents from Union Battle Reports, 1861–1865, Entry 729, Record Group 94, NA. The 7th Ind. arrived after the action of the first day so was not included in the total for the Second Brigade. Its strength of 530 represented the difference between the reported strength of the brigade on June 30 and the number of officers and men said to have been in action on July 1. OR, XXVII, pt. 1, pp. 284–285.

38. Though it is impossible to know definitely the hour of the First Division's arrival, largely because the watches of many commanding officers did not agree, the best evidence suggests the time as no sooner than 10:30 A.M. Ibid., pp. 265, 273, 278, 285, 288, 359, 924; Jacobs, Rebel Invasion, 23. James Beale of the 12th Mass. regiment of Robinson's division made a study of the first day's battle. He was convinced that the First Corps, not just the First Division, arrived long before 10:00 A.M. If he had had the opportunity to see the OR, he would have found that only one report sustained his contention. See [James Beale], "Gettysburg on July 1, 1863," MS, Bates Collection; Beale to Nicholson, Apr. 25, Aug. 24, 1880, John Page Nicholson Collection, Huntington Library.

39. Veil said that Reynolds also sent Sickles a message to start for Gettysburg. If so, there is no record that Sickles ever received it. Charles H. Veil to D. McConaughy, Apr. 7, 1864, Peter F. Rothermel Collection, PDPR. Joseph G. Rosengarten, who had been ordnance officer of the First Corps, also maintained that Reynolds ordered Sickles to come to Gettysburg. His evidence is more in the form of conjecture than anything else. Rosengarten to Nicholson, June 19, 1886, John Page Nicholson Collection, Huntington Library. In view of Reynolds' fears about the possibility of a Confederate turning movement starting from Fairfield, it is doubtful whether he would have stripped Emmitsburg of defenders without notifying Meade. For an account of the nature of Reynolds' message to Meade, see Weld, War Diaries and Letters, 229–230; Meade, Life and Letters, II, 35–36.

40. Wainwright did not like the "advanced position" on McPherson's Ridge for these reasons. Wainwright Journals, 234. References to tall wheat are found in OR, XXVII, pt. 1, p. 285; Statement of H. H. Lyman of 147th N.Y. regiment in John B. Bachelder, "Gettysburg Campaign," II, 24–25, Typescript, Bachelder Papers.

41. Jacobs, Rebel Invasion, 23; OR, XXVII, pt. 1, pp. 265–266; Dudley Report, Selected Documents from Union Battle Reports, 1861–1865, Entry 729, Record Group 94, NA.

42. OR, XXVII, pt. 1, p. 1031.

43. James A. Hall to Bachelder, Feb. 27, 1868, Bachelder Papers. In his report written July 16, 1863, Hall said that Gen. Reynolds ordered him into position on the right of the Cashtown road. OR, XXVII, pt. 1, p. 359.

44. Daniel Hall to Col. L. Livermore, Feb. 17, 1877, Howard Papers.

45. Howard to Prof. Henry Coppie [Coppee?], Mar. 4, 1864; id. to Maj. [William] Riddle, Mar. 22, 1864, Howard Papers. Howard believed that Reynolds had sent Riddle with the order before the battle began. It is hardly pos-

sible that Reynolds would have picked out an exact spot for Howard to camp before he got to Gettysburg. Upon his arrival the battle had already started.

46. Gen. L[ysander] Cutler to Gov. of Pa. [Curtin], Nov. 5, 1863, Peter F. Rothermel Collection, PDPR. Questions about who fired the first shot or what unit arrived first were taken very seriously by Civil War veterans and became the occasion for debates, some of them quite acrimonious. Members of the Iron Brigade said it started the battle between infantry on July 1 and the 2nd Wis. was the first regiment to open fire. For these claims see H. B. Harshaw to Col. [Lucius] Fairchild, May 16, 1884; Fairchild to Gen. Chauncy M. Reeve, June 15, 1884; John Mansfield to Fairchild, Apr. 29, 1884, Selected Documents from Union Battle Reports, 1861–1865, Entry 729, Record Group 94, NA; Cornelius Wheeler, "Reminiscences of the Battle of Gettysburg," War Papers, Commandery of the State of Wisconsin, Military Order of the Loyal Legion of the United States [MOLLUS] (Milwaukee, 1896), II, 214–220. For acceptance of Cutler's claim see E. B. Quiner, The Military History of Wisconsin: A Record of the Civil and Military Patriotism of the State, in the War for the Union . . . (Chicago, 1866), 461; J. A. Kellogg [late Col. of 6th Wis. regiment] to Bachelder, Nov. 1, 1865, Bachelder Papers.

47. Dudley Report, Selected Documents from Union Battle Reports, 1861–1865, Entry 729, Record Group 94, NA; OR, XXVII, pt. 1, pp. 267, 273.

48. B. D. Fry [late Col. of 13th Ala. regiment] to Bachelder, Dec. 27, 1877, Bachelder Papers.

49. OR, XXVII, pt. 1, p. 256.

50. Charles H. Veil to D. McConaughy, Apr. 7, 1864, Peter F. Rothermel Collection, PDPR. The general's sister, Jennie, used almost exactly the same words. Jennie to her brother, July 5, 1863. Reynolds Family Papers, Franklin and Marshall College Library.

51. Wheeler, "Reminiscences of the Battle of Gettysburg," War Papers, Wisconsin Commandery, MOLLUS, II, 211; OR, XXVII, pt. 1, p. 273.

52. Jennie [Reynolds] to her brother, July 5, 1863, Reynolds Family Papers, Franklin and Marshall College Library; James L. Reynolds to Bates, Dec. 9, 1870; Memorandum from J[oseph] G. Rosengarten to S. P. Bates regarding the death of his late chief, General Reynolds [sent sometime late in 1875 or early in 1876], Bates Collection; Weld, War Diaries and Letters, Entry for July 1, 230. Jennie's account said that after the bullet hit him behind the right ear it passed down and around the skull and lodged in his chest. Other versions had the bullet striking him at the base of the brain and travelling upward. All accounts agreed that he never spoke after he was struck, but there is disagreement about how long he lived. The general's sister, Jennie, who got the story from his staff officers, said he was alive as they carried him from the field. While on the way Capt. Mitchell asked him if he suffered, but Reynolds, turning his glazed eyes toward him, smiled slightly, gasped for breath, and died.

Reynolds' biographer, Edward J. Nichols, who is a thorough and honest scholar, has carefully examined the circumstances of the general's death and particularly the story of the bullet having been fired by a sharpshooter. Nichols, Toward Gettysburg, 253, 48 note. There is some additional information, however, that Nichols apparently overlooked. In his memo to Bates, Rosengarten said Reynolds was hit by sharp fire from rebel skirmishers. Yet in writing an article for the *Philadelphia Weekly Times* a few years later, which was reprinted in the *Annals of the War* in 1879, he changed his story and said (p. 63) that Reynolds was killed by a sharpshooter hidden in the branches of a tree almost overhead. The sharpshooter legend became current even before the end of the battle. Lorenzo L. Crounse, a newspaper reporter, sent a dispatch at noon on July 2 reporting the first day's fight, and he said Reynolds was killed by a sharpshooter. *New York Times*, July 4, 1863. If his sister's version is correct, the downward path of the bullet which killed him suggests the possibility that Reynolds was the victim of a sniper hidden in a nearby tree.

53. Bachelder, "Gettysburg Campaign," II, 46, Typescript, Bachelder Papers.

54. *OR*, XXVII, pt. 1, pp. 281–282, 285; Bachelder, "Gettysburg Campaign," II, 24–25, Typescript, Bachelder Papers; [Maj.] George Harney to Gen. J. W. Hofmann, Aug. 16, 1865; [Col.] J. A. Kellogg to Bachelder, Nov. 1, 1865, *ibid.*

55. James A. Hall to Bachelder, Feb. 27, 1868, *ibid.; OR*, XXVII, pt. 1, p. 359.

56. *Ibid.*, pp. 359–360. Hall recovered the gun later on.

57. James A. Hall to Bachelder, Feb. 27, 1868, Bachelder Papers.

58. *OR*, XXVII, pt. 1, pp. 355–356, 360, 1031–1032; *Wainwright Journals*, 234. When Wadsworth could not induce Wainwright to permit the return of Hall's battery and finding Lt. Calef's horse battery nearby, he ordered it to the position. Calef refused to go because he felt it was not a proper place for a battery. Wadsworth ordered him to the rear in arrest and had the second in command post the battery. Buford then wanted Calef's battery relieved, and Wainwright agreed to send out Captain Gilbert H. Reynolds' Battery L, 1st New York Light, in its place providing it did not have to report to Wadsworth. His request was granted on condition that he remain with it himself. Just as Reynolds was getting into position to permit the horse battery to withdraw, the enemy opened fire and drove off both of them. *Wainwright Journals*, Entry for July 1, 1863, MS, 213–214, Huntington Library. This part of the journal has not been included in the printed edition. Much to his disgust Wainwright had had trouble previously with Wadsworth about the proper use of artillery. See *Journals*, Entry for June 30, 1863, MS, 206–207.

59. Dudley Report, Selected Documents from Union Battle Reports, 1861–1865, Entry 729, Record Group 94, NA; *OR*, XXVII, pt. 1, pp. 266–267, 273–274, 279. The regiments entered the charge in the following order: 7th Wis., 19th Ind., and 24th Mich.

60. Freeman, *Lee's Lieutenants*, III, 80.

61. The figures for the number of prisoners taken varies from the sixty or seventy men Heth admitted having lost to Dudley's claim of the "larger portion" of the brigade. Doubleday said practically the same thing when he placed the number at 1,000. Wadsworth set the figure at "several hundred," Col. Morrow of the 24th Mich. settled for a "large number," Maj. John Mansfield of the

2nd Wis. said the same, and Col. W. W. Robinson of the 7th Wis. mentioned taking one regiment. Two other Southern accounts besides that of Heth deserve comment. Lt. Col. S. G. Shepard of the 7th Tenn. admitted the capture of seventy-five men. He also said that the brigade went into action on July 1 with 1,048 men, with no figure given for officers, and the total loss for three days of fighting was 677. The return of casualties for the Army of Northern Virginia for the entire battle sets a figure of 517 men and officers captured or missing for this brigade. Many men in Archer's brigade were captured in Pickett's charge. Perhaps Col. B. D. Fry of the 13th Ala., who succeeded Archer in command after his capture, was as close to the truth as anyone when he said that Archer lost a "considerable part" of the brigade on July 1. *OR*, XXVII, pt. 1, pp. 245, 266–267, 274, 280; pt. 2, pp. 344, 637, 646–647; B. D. Fry to Bachelder, Dec. 27, 1877, Bachelder Papers.

62. *Ibid.*; *OR*, XXVII, pt. 1, pp. 245, 267–268, 274, 279.

63. R. R. Dawes to Bachelder, Mar. 18, 1868, Bachelder Papers; *OR*, XXVII, pt. 1, p. 275.

64. Corrected Statement of Strength and Losses, Iron Brigade, Gettysburg, July 1, 1863, Copied War Records, Selected Documents from Union Battle Reports, 1861–1865, Entry 729, Record Group 94, NA.

65. R. R. Dawes to Bachelder, Mar. 18, 1868, Bachelder Papers. The two officers who brought the orders were Lt. Benjamin T. Martin of Doubleday's staff and Capt. Wood of Meredith's.

66. Rufus R. Dawes, "With the Sixth Wisconsin at Gettysburg," *Sketches of War History, 1861–1865*, Papers Prepared for the Ohio Commandery, MOLLUS, 1888–1890, Robert Hunter, ed. (Cincinnati, 1890), III, 368–369. On p. 374 Dawes said that Doubleday in his report fell into the "time-honored line of battle fiction" when he said that the cut was carried at the point of the bayonet. Not a single bayonet, Dawes added, was fixed for use in the regiment.

67. R. R. Dawes to Bachelder, Mar. 18, 1868, Bachelder Papers. For further information on the counterattack of the 6th Wis. and other regiments see J. A. Kellogg to Bachelder, Nov. 1, 1865, *ibid.*; *OR*, XXVII, pt. 1, pp. 275–276, 282, 286–287; pt. 2, pp. 637–638, 649; Dudley Report, Selected Documents from Union Battle Reports, 1861–1865, Entry 729, Record Group 94, NA.

68. This is another instance where the exact number of prisoners is not known, although the spread between the top and low figures is not as great as in the case of Archer's brigade. Doubleday and Wadsworth said two regiments were taken. Cutler vaguely mentioned a "large body" of the enemy. Dawes, who wrote a complete account of the action, was more exact and perhaps more modest when he set the figure at seven officers and about 225 men of the 2nd Miss. *OR*, XXVII, pt. 1, pp. 246, 266, 276, 282. In a later account Dawes said that only the 2nd Miss. regiment was captured as an organization and only a part of that. He also gave the 95th and 84th N. Y. regiments credit for capturing some prisoners. All the troops in the cut threw down their muskets, and the men either surrendered or escaped by running out of the other end of the cut. Dawes asserted that later in the day men in his regiment while marching

through the cut counted at least 1,000 muskets lying there. Dawes, "With the Sixth Wisconsin at Gettysburg," *Sketches of War History*, Ohio Commandery, MOLLUS, III, 374–375. H. H. Lyman, adjutant of the 147th N. Y., in a letter to Bachelder, Apr. 15, 1889, identified the 42nd Miss. and the 55th N. C. as the other regiments in the cut and said some of their men were captured too. Before writing Bachelder he had been in touch with J. M. Stone, formerly colonel of the 2nd Miss. (Bachelder Papers). Stone had been wounded before the fight in the cut took place. *OR*, XXVII, pt. 2, p. 649. Years after the war Davis admitted that he had lost at the cut a major and eighty or ninety men. Joseph R. Davis to Early, Mar. 12, 1878, Jubal A. Early Papers, LC.

69. *OR*, XXVII, pt. 1, pp. 274, 276, 279, 282; pt. 2, pp. 317, 637–638, 646, 649; George Harney to Gen. J. W. Hofmann, Aug. 16, 1865; R. R. Dawes to Gen. W. W. Dudley, Dec. 2, 1878; J. A. Kellogg to Bachelder, Nov. 1, 1865, Bachelder Papers; Dudley Report, Selected Documents from Union Battle Reports, 1861–1865, Entry 729, Record Group 94, NA. The 6th Wis. cooperated with the Second Brigade during the rest of the day.

70. Heth, "Gen. Lee's Orders to His Cavalry," *Philadelphia Weekly Times*, Mar. 23, 1878.

71. *OR*, XXVII, pt. 2, p. 637.

72. *Ibid.*, p. 638. The object of a reconnaissance is to get information that will enable a general to determine whether he should attack or withdraw. Heth did just the opposite. He attacked first and then got his information. See Mosby, *Stuart's Cavalry*, 155.

73. *OR*, XXVII, pt. 2, p. 637.

74. Heth, "Gen. Lee's Orders to His Cavalry," *Philadelphia Weekly Times*, Mar. 23, 1878. In a later account he had second thoughts about what happened, for he wrote that Davis' and Archer's brigades became engaged with Buford's "dismounted cavalry" before Reynolds attacked them. See Morrison, ed., "Heth Memoirs," *CWH*, VIII, 304.

75. *OR*, XXVII, pt. 1, pp. 934, 938–939.

76. The John S. Mosby Letter, [no date], Typescript signed by Mosby, Coles Collection, UV. Col. B. D. Fry recalled that the resistance made by the Union cavalry was "inconsiderable" and did them "no damage." The skirmish line for the brigade, consisting of the 5th Ala. Battalion under Maj. A. S. Van de Graaff, kept one hundred paces ahead of the main body, but near enough for Fry to see them all the time. Fry to Bachelder, Feb. 10, 1878, Bachelder Papers in possession of Francis C. Carleton, Belmont, Mass., Microfilm, MHS.

77. Heth, "Gen. Lee's Orders to His Cavalry," *Philadelphia Weekly Times*, Mar. 23, 1878; Morrison, ed., "Heth Memoirs," *CWH*, VIII, 304–305.

78. *OR*, XXVII, pt. 2, pp. 317, 638, 649.

79. The total effective strength of the Iron Brigade was 1,883 officers and men. The 6th Wis. had a total of 344 and the brigade guard of 102. Copied War Records, 1861–1865, Corrected Statement of Strength and Losses, Iron Brigade, Gettysburg, July 1, 1863, Selected Documents from Union Battle Reports, 1861–1865, Entry 729, Record Group 94, NA. Lt. Col. S. G. Shepard, who finally assumed command of Archer's brigade, said in his report that the

brigade went into action on July 1 with 1,048 men. Adding 8 percent for officers, which was the average ratio in those days, the total strength of the brigade was 1,132. *OR*, XXVII, pt. 2, p. 647. Buford said a portion of the 3rd Ind. Cavalry regiment found "horse-holders"; then they borrowed muskets and fought with the Wis. regiment that came to relieve them. *Ibid.*, pt. 1, p. 927.

80. Heth said his division numbered on July 1 "some seven thousand muskets." Adding the usual 8 percent for officers would put the strength of his division at about 7,500 officers and men. Pettigrew's brigade numbered about 3,000 officers and men, Archer's 1,132, and Brockenbrough's approximately 880. Henry Heth to the Rev. Dr. J. William Jones, June, 1877, in *SHSP*, IV, 158; Young, "Pettigrew's Brigade at Gettysburg," Clark, ed., *North Carolina Regiments*, V, 128; *OR*, XXVII, pt. 2, p. 647; Battle Report of R. M. Mayo of Brockenbrough's Brigade, Aug. 13, 1863, Henry Heth Collection, Confederate Museum. The size of Davis' brigade was the difference between the estimated total of the three other brigades and the entire division, or about 2,400. Its size on May 31 was placed at 2,577. *OR*, XVIII, 943, 1086. On July 1, however, the 11th Miss., which according to various estimates had between three and four hundred men, was not at Gettysburg. W. A. Love, "Mississippi at Gettysburg," *Publications of Mississippi Historical Society*, IX, 44. For size of Cutler's brigade *cf. ante*, XI, 37 note.

81. Bachelder, "Gettysburg Campaign," II, 51, Typescript, Bachelder Papers. Bachelder pointed out that Col. Fowler of the 84th N.Y. was the ranking officer on that part of the field and undoubtedly directed movements of the two regiments of his brigade; but Lt. Col. Dawes was commander of the division's reserve regiment and moved under direct orders from the corps commander. In this situation Dawes could assume theoretical control and in practice he did so because his regiment was in the lead.

82. For some reason Doubleday did not inspire confidence as a commanding officer. Capt. William Brooke Rawle, a friend of the Meade family, said flatly that Meade had no confidence in Doubleday. Rawle to Capt. G. S. L. Ward, Apr. 2, 1883, William Brooke Rawle Papers, HSP. Charles F. Benjamin, who had been a clerk in Gen. Seth Williams' office, recalled writing the order which sent Newton to command the First Corps. Meade, he said, told Williams in his "blunt way" that he had " 'no confidence in Doubleday.' " Benjamin to J. G. Rosengarten, Aug. 13, 1883, Reynolds Family Papers, Franklin and Marshall College Library. Wainwright commented in his diary that upon hearing of Reynolds' death he felt Doubleday was a "weak reed to lean upon," and therefore he himself went ahead to do what he thought best without waiting for orders. *Wainwright Journals*, 233. The brother of Lucius Fairchild, colonel of the 2nd Wis., visited him in May and met both Reynolds and Doubleday. "Reynolds," he said, "looks like a splendid officer and Doubleday does not." Charlie to Sarah [sister], May 20, 1863, Charles Fairchild Letters, Typescript of Lee Bacon.

Doubleday's commission as major general happened to antedate Newton's by several months. Boatner, *Civil War Dictionary*, 244, 593. Doubleday requested permission to leave the Army of the Potomac if Meade would not allow him to command the First Corps. Meade obviously did not change his mind, for

Doubleday left for Washington at daylight on July 7, 1863. Nathaniel G. Shepherd to Gay, July 6, 1863, S. H. Gay Collection, Columbia University Library. Shepherd expressed indignation at Doubleday's removal and accused Meade of disregarding all claims of rank in order to appoint "democratic general[s] to take the places of those removed by wounds or death." *Id.* to *id.*, *ibid.* This baseless charge became one source for the indictment of Meade's generalship by his enemies.

83. Perhaps there is a correlation between the length of an officer's battle report and his career as a historian. Henry Hunt's report was second only to Doubleday's in length. Both of these generals wrote well-known accounts of the battle.

84. *OR*, XXVII, pt. 1, pp. 244–245.

85. *Ibid.*, pp. 267, 273.

86. *Wainwright Journals*, 232–233. See also Wainwright's report, *OR*, XXVII, pt. 1, p. 354. In his report, which was written on July 4, 1863, Gen. Wadsworth said that Doubleday "arrived on the ground about the time, or very soon after, General Reynolds fell, with the Second and Third Divisions." *Ibid.*, p. 266. The Second Division followed immediately behind the Artillery Reserve, while the Third Division marched on a road roughly parallel to and about a mile and a half west of the Emmitsburg road. *Wainwright Journals*, 233; *OR*, XXVII, pt. 1, p. 354.

87. *Ibid.*, p. 275; R. R. Dawes to Bachelder, Mar. 18, 1868, Bachelder Papers. Dawes's report was written on July 17, 1863. The letter to Bachelder and the report do not fully agree in certain particulars.

88. In his testimony before the Committee on the Conduct of the War Gen. Wadsworth said that upon receiving a report of the enemy attack on Buford's cavalry Reynolds and he decided to take a position in front of Gettysburg instead of going into town, for fear the enemy would shell and destroy it. This statement was rather misleading, for it suggested that Reynolds chose a position before he got to the front and consulted with Buford. It was not like him to make a decision before he got the facts. CCW, *Report*, I, 413.

89. [Maj.?] H. T. Lee to Bates, Feb. 6, 1871, Bates Collection.

90. For a discussion of Reynolds' propensity for staying near the front line and his methods of handling volunteers, see Nichols, *Toward Gettysburg*, 27–28, 79–80, 115–116, 144–145, 210, 254, 62 note. Officers on Reynolds' staff told Weld that the general was not three hundred feet from the Confederates when he was shot. Weld, *War Diaries and Letters*, 233. Jennie Reynolds placed the general not half that distance from the rebel line when he was hit. Jennie to her brother, July 5, 1863, Reynolds Family Papers, Franklin and Marshall College Library.

91. Howard to Prof. M. Jacobs, Mar. 23, 1864, Howard Papers.

92. In reviewing the battle of the first day Wainwright felt the fight would have gone better for the North if only a "brigade of observation" had been sent to McPherson's Ridge and the rest of the corps had been properly posted on Seminary Ridge with its flanks extended by the cavalry and all covered by such breastworks as could have been thrown up. *Wainwright Journals*, 239.

93. *OR*, XXVII, pt. 1, pp. 696, 701–702; Howard, *Autobiography*, 408–410,

412; Howard to [S. P. Bates], Sept. 14, 1875, Pressed Copy, Howard Papers. In his *Autobiography* Howard said his columns did not start until 8:30 A.M. because he had to wait for Reynolds' marching orders.

94. Howard in a dispatch to Meade late in the afternoon said Reynolds was killed at 11:15 A.M. In his report Howard said Riddle brought him word about 11:30 A.M., apparently while he was up in Fahnestock's Observatory. *OR,* XXVII, pt. 1, pp. 696, 701–702. According to Jennie Reynolds, the general fell between 10:30 and 11:00 A.M. Jennie to her brother, July 5, 1863, Reynolds Family Papers, Franklin and Marshall College Library.

95. *OR,* XXVII, pt. 1, pp. 702, 727; Howard, *Autobiography,* 413–415; Howard, "Campaign and Battle of Gettysburg, June and July, 1863," *Atlantic Monthly,* XXXVIII, 55–56.

96. The hours given for the arrival of the Second Division ranged from 10:00 A.M. to 1:00 P.M. Robinson did not say when his men got there but reported that they heard firing when they were about three miles from Gettysburg, or about an hour's march away. Upon his arrival the fighting had subsided, and his division was not put into battle line until later. An officer in the 12th Mass. said that the First and Third Divisions were already engaged when Robinson's men got there. Most likely therefore the division arrived around noon. As for the Third Division, the discrepancies in time are not so great. Most reports place the hour between 11:00 A.M. and noon. None is earlier than 10:30 A.M. *OR,* XXVII, pt. 1, pp. 289, 292, 300, 304, 307, 309, 311–312, 315, 319–20, 327, 329, 331, 341, 344, 346; [Maj.] Benjamin F. Look [or Cook?] to Bachelder, Dec., 1863, Typescript, Bachelder Papers.

97. *OR,* XXVII, pt. 1, pp. 715–716, 720–721, 727, 734, 738, 742, 745–748; Howard, "Campaign and Battle of Gettysburg," *Atlantic Monthly,* XXXVIII, 55–56; Howard to [S. P. Bates], Sept. 14, 1875, Pressed Copy, Howard Papers; Schurz, *Reminiscences,* III, 7. Most accounts agree that the First and Third Divisions of the Eleventh Corps arrived between 1:00 and 2:00 P.M. Howard said the First Division arrived before the Third, whereas Schurz reported that the Third got there slightly ahead of the First. The only report which disagreed widely with the others was that of Maj. Thomas W. Osborn. His watch must have been hours slow, for the times he gave for the arrival and movements of his various batteries made no sense at all. *OR,* XXVII, pt. 1, pp. 747–748. Howard said Barlow pushed his men vigorously, but because of the heat, the poor condition of the road, and the congestion created by supply wagons of the preceding corps they made an average of but two and a half miles per hour. *Autobiography,* 403–409.

98. *OR,* XXVII, pt. 2, pp. 638, 643, 674.

99. *Ibid.,* p. 638.

100. Fremantle mentioned that Hill had been unwell all day and "in fact he looks very delicate," *Three Months in the Southern States,* 254. Taylor said when Lee arrived in Cashtown, Hill told him of Heth's advance and his encounter with Union cavalry. Lee then sent instructions to Heth for him to ascertain more precisely the nature of the enemy's force without precipitating an engagement and to report the fact to him immediately. Later Lee heard the

sound of artillery. Taylor, *Four Years with General Lee*, 92–93. Long asserted that Lee while ascending South Mountain with his staff heard firing from the direction of Gettysburg. When he got to Cashtown he received a message from Hill reporting the engagement and asking for reinforcements. Anderson's division then was rushed forward by Lee. Long, *Memoirs of Lee*, 275–276. Gen. Pendleton, who apparently was with Lee at the time, said in his battle report that Lee heard firing before he reached Cashtown. He made no mention of a message from Hill or conversations between Hill and Lee at Cashtown. *OR*, XXVII, pt. 2, p. 348.

101. Freeman, *R. E. Lee*, III, 66; Long, *Memoirs of Lee*, 275; Taylor, *Four Years with General Lee*, 92–93; Longstreet, *Memoirs*, 359; Campbell Brown to Abner Doubleday, Dec. 6, 1881, Polk-Brown-Ewell Collection, UNC.

102. Quoted in Longstreet, "Lee in Pennsylvania," *Annals*, 420. Longstreet said Lee made this statement to Anderson in Cashtown about 10:00 A.M. Apparently Longstreet learned that Anderson could not have been there at that early hour and asked Anderson about it, for in his *Memoirs*, 357, he quoted a letter from Anderson saying that the conversation took place about noon. Longstreet might not have been much of an historian, but he did make it a practice to write to his old colleagues for information.

103. *OR*, XXVII, pt. 2, pp. 444, 468, 552; Brown, "Reminiscences," Campbell Brown Books, UNC.

104. *OR*, XXVII, pt. 2, p. 444.

105. *Ibid.*, p. 552.

106. *Ibid.*, pt. 1, pp. 702, 727–728.

107. Both Howard and Wadsworth mentioned Howard's visit to the First Corps and agreed as to the time it was made. Howard first told of it in his battle report of Aug. 31, 1863, and repeated it in his letters, articles, and autobiography written after the war. Wadsworth in his testimony on Mar. 23, 1864, before the Committee on the Conduct of the War said Howard had come to his line. Doubleday for reasons best known to himself breathed not a word of the visit in anything he wrote during and after the war. In this connection it should be noted that Doubleday disliked Howard and accused him of trying to blacken the reputation of the First Corps and its temporary commander by reporting to Meade on the flight of the corps before the enemy's attack in the morning. Doubleday, however, never denied that Howard made a visit to the First Corps. *Ibid.*, pp. 244, 246–247, 266, 702–703; CCW, *Report*, I, 413; Howard, "Campaign and Battle of Gettysburg," *Atlantic Monthly*, XXXVIII, 56; Howard to [S. P. Bates], Sept. 14, 1875; Howard to [Messrs. T. H. Davis], Sept. 14, 1875; Doubleday to [S. P. Bates], Oct. 18, 1875, Bates Collection; Howard, *Autobiography*, 416; Abner Doubleday, *Chancellorsville and Gettysburg* (New York, 1882), 134–137. As for the idea of retiring presumably to Cemetery Hill, it probably had not occurred to Doubleday until he reviewed events in his mind when writing his report. He said in view of the fact that they had been finally forced to retreat, it might have been well if they had retired after the successful counterattack against Davis' brigade. There were two arguments against the idea, Doubleday thought. To retreat without orders from

the commanding general would have brought "lasting disgrace" upon the corps. Also since Reynolds had formed his lines to resist the entrance of the enemy into Gettysburg, Doubleday "naturally supposed" that it was his intention to defend the place. *OR*, XXVII, pt. 1, p. 246.

108. *OR*, XXVII, pt. 1, p. 702; pt. 3, pp. 457–458, 463–464.

109. Column by Agate [Whitelaw Reid], July 1, in *Cincinnati Daily Gazette*, July 8, 1863.

110. *OR*, XXVII, pt. 1, p. 924; Meade, *Life and Letters*, II, 35–36; Weld, *War Diaries and Letters*, 229–232.

111. *Ibid.*, 231–232.

112. *OR*, XXVII, pt. 3, p. 461.

113. *Ibid.*, p. 458.

114. Meade received the news about 1:00 P.M. CCW, *Report*, I, 348.

115. James C. Biddle, an officer on Meade's staff, wrote to Gen. Alexander S. Webb, Nov. 31, 1886, the following recollection: "I joined Genl Meade as you remember a short time before the Chancellorsville campaign began. . . . I was there impressed with the mutual feeling of confidence between Genl Meade & Reynolds. I do not think a day passed without their [sic] being a visit paid by one or the other to their respective Head Quarters, & during the campaign whenever possible they visited each other." Webb Collection.

116. For the personal relations between Meade and Hancock see [Lyman to his wife], July 12, 1864, in which he said: "When he [Meade] gets down with Hancock they talk, and talk, and talk, being great friends." Quoted in Agassiz, ed., *Meade's Headquarters*, 189.

117. *OR*, XXVII, pt. 1, pp. 367–368; pt. 3, p. 461; CCW, *Report*, I, 377, 404–405; Winfield Scott Hancock, "Gettysburg, Reply to General Howard," *The Galaxy*, XXII, 821–822. The official and written order assigning Hancock to command of the troops at Gettysburg went to him at 1:10 P.M. According to Hancock's chief of staff, Lt. Col. C. H. Morgan, Meade told Hancock he knew him much better than Howard and that "at this crisis he must have a man he knew and could trust." Lt. Col. Morgan's Account, Typescript, Bachelder Papers.

NOTES TO CHAPTER XII

1. Gen. Lee was the only person to set the hour of the attack around 2:30 P.M., but Howard pretty well agreed with him by saying that the enemy appeared in force in front of the Eleventh Corps about 2:45 P.M. Schurz reported that the two divisions under him had completed their deployment around 2:00 P.M. and before the enemy attacked. Rodes made no mention of the hour of his attack, but he did say that by the time he was ready the enemy had deployed north of the town. So 2:30 P.M. seems about right. Confederate brigade and regimental reports varied so widely as to be practically worthless. *OR*, XXVII, pt. 1, pp. 115, 249, 292, 329, 703, 728, 734, 738, 745; pt. 2, pp. 317, 552, 571, 573, 576, 577, 581, 584, 590, 601–602.

2. *Ibid.*, pt. 1, pp. 248–249, 266, 702, 727–728, 927, 939; pt. 2, pp. 552, 602. Although he did not say so explicitly, the wording of Rodes's report strongly suggested that he had gone ahead to survey the battlefield. Since Buford's troopers infested the whole area, he risked capture or worse unless a strong escort accompanied him. Nevertheless the risks were worth the advantages he gained in making the reconnaissance.

Doubleday knew of Ewell's approach as did Howard and Reynolds and expected Howard to cope with him. Although he was not clear about where he expected Howard's forces to be deployed, Doubleday found that the Eleventh Corps had apparently gone too far north of the town and thus had created a serious gap between his right flank on Seminary Ridge and Howard's left in the valley. With Ewell coming on, this situation was dangerous so Doubleday moved Baxter's brigade out onto Oak Ridge, to be followed later by Paul's.

3. *Ibid.*, pt. 1, pp. 247–248, 274, 276–277, 279, 282, 312–313, 315, 327, 329–330, 334–338; *cf. ante*, XI, 271–272. The 151st Pa. of the First Brigade, Third Division, was kept in reserve for awhile at the seminary. Before the final onslaught took place it was put in line between the right flank of the First Brigade, Third Division, and the Iron Brigade. The brigade guard of twenty men from each regiment was broken up, and the men went back to their respective commands in the Iron Brigade.

4. *OR*, XXVII, pt. 1, pp. 248–249, 266, 276, 282, 289–291, 297–298; *cf. ante*, XI, 37, 79 notes. Robinson reported his strength to be about 2,500; Cutler's was 1,626 and the 6th Wis. 364, for a total of 4,490. Deduct from this figure the 615 officers and men reported to have been lost in Cutler's brigade and the 6th Wis. in the morning's action for a correct total. See *OR*, XXVII, pt. 1, pp. 276, 282.

5. The battle reports of the Eleventh Corps were few in number and usually meager in content. Only Howard and Schurz wrote reports in any way satisfactory, but with respect to information about the positions of the First and Third Divisions on July 1 they were both vague and confusing. Howard gave the impression that the lines of the First and Eleventh Corps were at right angles to each other and came together at the Mummasburg road. Schurz's account was even more misleading because it appeared at first glance to be clear and exact. See *ibid.*, pp. 702–703, 727–728. Col. John B. Bachelder, who made a careful study of troop positions right after the battle and whose work was largely responsible for the location of regimental markers and monuments on the battlefield, had trouble determining the position of the Eleventh Corps on July 1. For his efforts to secure information see the following correspondence in his papers: J. M. Brown to Bachelder, Apr. 8, 1864; P[hilip] P. Brown to *id.*, Apr. 4, 1864; Andrew L. Harris to *id.*, Mar. 14, 1881, Sept. 18, 1882. Also as a result of Bachelder's inquiries Howard wrote to his chief of staff, Lt. Col. T. A. Meysenberg, who replied to Howard Apr. 13, 1864. Howard Papers.

6. The round figure given by Schurz was pretty close to the number of 6,167 officers and men who were probably in the engagement. Sizes of the four brigades present for duty according to the monthly return for June were as fol-

lows: First Brig., First Div., 1,491; Second Brig., First Div., 1,465; First Brig., Third Div., 1,933; Second Brig., Third Div., 1,672; total, 6,571. However, one regiment on detail to the rear did not reach Gettysburg that night, and two other regiments were considerably reduced in strength because many of their men had other assignments. Total of officers and men absent was 404. See *OR*, XXVII, pt. 1, pp. 713, 715, 739; Selected Pages from the Historical and Statistical Record of the Principal Military Commands in the Union and Confederate Armies, IV, 53, Record Group 94, NA.

7. *OR*, XXVII, pt. 1, pp. 248, 297, 315, 317, 320, 329–348.

8. *Ibid.*, pp. 154, 229–230. The Artillery Brigade of the First Corps had twelve 12-pounder smoothbores and sixteen 3-inch rifles; the Eleventh Corps Artillery Brigade had sixteen 12-pounders and ten 3-inch rifles.

9. *Ibid.*, pt. 2, pp. 287, 552–553, 564.

10. Ezra J. Warner, *Generals in Gray, Lives of the Confederate Commanders* (Baton Rouge, La., 1959), 66–67, 74, 147–148, 226, 251–252.

11. *OR*, XXVII, pt. 2, p. 553.

12. *Ibid.*; V. E. Turner and H. C. Wall, "Twenty-third Regiment," Clark, ed., *North Carolina Regiments*, II, 235.

13. Freeman, *Lee's Lieutenants*, III, 83.

14. *OR*, XXVII, pt. 2, p. 553; Turner and Wall, "Twenty-third Regiment," Clark, ed., *North Carolina Regiments*, II, 235.

15. *OR*, XXVII, pt. 1, pp. 289, 292, 295, 297–299, 301, 307, 309–311; pt. 2, pp. 553–554, 592–593.

16. Turner and Wall, "Twenty-third Regiment," Clark, ed., *North Carolina Regiments*, II, 235.

17. *OR*, XXVII, pt. 2, p. 579. See also Henry Robinson Berkeley Diary, Entry for July 2, 1863, MS, VHS.

18. *Ibid.*, pt. 1, pp. 282, 289, 307, 329–330; pt. 2, pp. 554, 579; [Maj.] Benjamin F. Look to Bachelder, Dec., 1863, Typescript, Bachelder Papers.

19. Both Ramseur and Iverson commanded brigades made up entirely of N. C. troops, so the attachment of Iverson's men to Ramseur's command was not offensive to state pride. On the contrary, since Ramseur was a good North Carolinian, while Iverson was a rank outsider from Ga., Iverson's men were undoubtedly happier under Ramseur. Furthermore, Ramseur was an unusually fine general. The collapse of Iverson's morale was only implied in Ewell's and Rodes's reports, but in his own report he frankly said that he waived his rank and submitted himself to Ramseur's command. *Ibid.*, pp. 445, 554, 580. In the day of modern psychiatry his trouble would probably have been diagnosed as a case of battle fatigue. To the less sophisticated Civil War mind there was but one answer to his difficulty; he was guilty of nothing less than "cowardly behavior." See Brown, "Reminiscences," MS, Campbell Brown Books, UNC. Not so blunt was the somewhat ambiguous expression used by Ramseur, who said that Iverson had been relieved from the command of his brigade for "misconduct at Gettysburg." Ramseur to [Nellie], July 29, 1863, Stephen D. Ramseur Papers, UNC. Iverson was not court-martialed, and he served with credit during the retreat. After the campaign he was transferred to command of

the state forces at Rome, Ga. Later in 1864 he redeemed himself as a brigadier in Martin's division of Wheeler's cavalry corps by capturing the Federal Gen. Stoneman and five hundred of his troopers at Sunshine Church. Brown, "Reminiscences," MS, Campbell Brown Books, UNC; Warner, *Generals in Gray*, 148.

20. Very properly Freeman emphasized mistakes made by Rodes and his subordinates, but he failed to show the contributions of skillful Yankee generalship to Rodes's humiliation. See Freeman, *Lee's Lieutenants*, III, 87. For a comment on Robinson's good generalship see Abner Small, *Road to Richmond* (Berkeley, Calif., 1939), 100.

21. *OR*, XXVII, pt. 2, pp. 445, 554, 564, 595. Although it was not mentioned in the reports, Ramseur in the final drive assumed temporary command of three brigades: Iverson's, O'Neal's, and his own. Calder to his mother, July 8, 1863, William Calder Papers, UNC.

22. *OR*, XXVII, pt. 2, pp. 445, 564, 581–582, 596–597; "Report of Col. Edward Willis, Twelfth Georgia Infantry, Doles' Brigade," *SHSP*, XVII, 184–185.

23. *OR*, XXVII, pt. 2, pp. 445, 468, 495.

24. Brown, "Reminiscences," MS, Campbell Brown Books, UNC.

25. *Ibid.*; *OR*, XXVII, pt. 2, pp. 468, 493.

26. According to the monthly return for June von Gilsa's First Brigade had 1,491 officers and men present for duty. However, on July 1 the brigade numbered only 1,290 because the 41st N.Y. regiment with 201 officers and men was still at Emmitsburg. Selected Pages from Historical and Statistical Record of the Principal Military Commands in the Union and Confederate Armies, IV, 53, Record Group 94, NA; *OR*, XXVII, pt. 1, p. 713; pt. 2, p. 493.

27. *Ibid.*, p. 492. Since the battle this spot has been called Barlow's Knoll. No longer wooded, it is easily seen from the Heidlersburg (Harrisburg) road about a mile north of the center of town.

28. The positions of the First and Second Brigades were indicated in the following source: Lt. Col. T. A. Meysenberg to Howard, Apr. 13, 1864, Howard Papers.

29. Brown, "Reminiscences," MS, Campbell Brown Books, UNC.

30. *OR*, XXVII, pt. 2, p. 492.

31. There has been some question of just how the Confederates took the knoll. Schurz's report was misleading because he confused the First Brigade with the Second. Then he implied that the men in Barlow's division gave up the position because of an attack on their right flank. *Ibid.*, pt. 1, pp. 728–729. In his *Reminiscences*, III, 8–10, Schurz was more explicit; he said that von Gilsa's brigade was crushed by the enemy rushing in from the front and both flanks. On the other hand Barlow stoutly maintained that Gordon hit him "fair & square *in front*," and that the enemy troops which came up on the flank, came "*later in the day*, & perhaps attacked my command after they had rallied." Gen. F. C. Barlow to Bachelder, Mar. 31, 1883, Bachelder Papers. J. Clyde Millar of the 153rd Pa. regiment disputed this statement and recalled that the attack came from the right and rear. Since he also talked about falling back and coming in line with skirmishers of the 41st N.Y. regiment, which was no-

where near Gettysburg then, his memory does not seem too reliable. Millar to Bachelder, Mar. 2, 1886, Bachelder Papers. For corroboration of Barlow's recollection see Ewell's and Early's reports, in which they said Hays and Avery attacked *after* Gordon's attack had succeeded. *OR*, XXVII, pt. 2, pp. 445, 468–469. For the cooperation of Doles and O'Neal's sharpshooters with Gordon, as well as further corroboration of Barlow, see Col. Andrew L. Harris to Bachelder, Mar. 14, 1881, Bachelder Papers.

32. *OR*, XXVII, pt. 1, p. 729.

33. *Ibid.*, pp. 712, 729; pt. 2, pp. 445, 469.

34. *Ibid.*, pp. 445, 449, 479, 554, 582. Once the Confederate attack gained momentum, the few Eleventh Corps regiments which tried to stop it became badly chewed up. See *ibid.*, pt. 1, p. 745; John S. Applegate, *Reminiscences and Letters of George Arrowsmith of New Jersey* (Red Bank, N.J., 1893), 216–222.

35. *OR*, XXVII, pt. 2, pp. 554–555, 566–567, 587.

36. Actually only seven of the eight brigades became seriously engaged. Gen. Hill kept Gen. Edward L. Thomas' brigade of Pender's division out of the advance to meet a threat from the left. It is not clear what was the nature of the threat, especially on Hill's left. *Ibid.*, pp. 656, 668.

37. *Ibid.*, pp. 646–647.

38. The reports do not indicate just what the men of Davis' brigade did in the final assault of Heth's division. Heth said vaguely that they participated, and Davis did not elaborate. Daniel claimed they refused to cooperate with him when he asked for their help on his right just before all of Heth's division advanced again. *Ibid.*, pp. 567, 638, 649.

39. *Ibid.*, pt. 1, pp. 329–336; pt. 2, pp. 554, 567.

40. [Capt.] Louis G. Young to Maj. William J. Baker, Feb. 10, 1864, Francis D. Winston Papers, North Carolina State Department of Archives and History. For further information on Pettigrew's attack see *OR*, XXVII, pt. 1, pp. 268, 274, 279–280, 313, 315, 320–321, 323, 327–328; pt. 2, pp. 638, 645.

41. *Ibid.*, pt. 1, pp. 329–336; pt. 2, pp. 567, 638.

42. Confederate and Union reports seem to indicate without saying so that Stone's Second Brigade was the last to leave the ridge. The left of the First Corps line gave way first. *Ibid.*, pt. 1, pp. 268, 274, 279–280, 313, 315, 320–321, 323, 330; pt. 2, p. 638.

43. *Ibid.*, p. 657; Welch, *Letters to His Wife*, 64–65.

44. Perrin to Governor [Bonham], July 29, 1863, in the *Mississippi Valley Historical Review*, XXIV, 522.

45. *OR*, XXVII, pt. 2, p. 661.

46. Perrin to Governor [Bonham], July 29, 1863, in the *Mississippi Valley Historical Review*, XXIV, 522. See also *OR*, XXVII, pt. 2, p. 670.

47. *Ibid.*, pt. 1, pp. 250–251, 274, 280, 282–283, 313–314, 321, 323, 328, 330, 336, 343, 927, 934–935; pt. 2, pp. 656–657, 661–62; *Wainwright Journals*, 235; Varina D. Brown, *A Colonel at Gettysburg and Spotsylvania* (Columbia, S. C., 1931), 230; William R. Ramsey [Sgt. F Co., 150th Pa. Vols.] to

Bachelder, Apr. 16, 1883; Lt. Col. George F. McFarland to *id.*, Feb. 7, 1867, Bachelder Papers; Dawes, "With the Sixth Wisconsin at Gettysburg," *Sketches of War History*, Ohio Commandery, MOLLUS, III, 378.

48. Perrin to Governor [Bonham], July 29, 1863, in the *Mississippi Valley Historical Review*, XXIV, 522.

49. *OR*, XXVII, pt. 1, pp. 290, 292, 295, 307, 310; pt. 2, pp. 567, 575–576, 578, 587. Gen. Robinson ordered the 16th Maine regiment to counterattack along the extreme right flank of the Union position on Oak Ridge so as to slow up Ramseur's advance and cover the retreat of the rest of the Second Division. Small, *Road to Richmond*, 101–102.

50. Gen. J. B. Hardenburgh to Gen. [Theodore B. Gates], Oct. 9, 1878, Miscellaneous [Papers] Theodore Burr Gates, NYHS; Brown, *A Colonel at Gettysburg*, 217; [Craig Wadsworth?], "First Day of Battle of Gettysburg," MS, James W. Wadsworth, Jr., Family Papers, LC; *Wainwright Journals*, 236–237.

51. *OR*, XXVII, pt. 1, p. 704; pt. 2, pp. 317, 607.

52. Schurz in his *Reminiscences*, III, 12, used this phrase in his complaint against Confederate accounts of the Federal defeat in the afternoon of July 1.

53. *OR*, XXVII, pt. 1, p. 704.

54. *Wainwright Journals*, 237.

55. *OR*, XXVII, pt. 1, p. 277.

56. Dawes, "With the Sixth Wisconsin at Gettysburg," *Sketches of War Hisory*, Ohio Commandery, MOLLUS, III, 381–382; Welch, *Letters to His Wife*, 64–65; Calder to his mother, July 8, 1863, William Calder Papers, UNC; *OR*, XXVII, pt. 1, pp. 286, 718.

57. *Wainwright Journals*, 237.

58. Diary of William H. Warren [17th Conn.], Entry for July 1, 1863, YU; Schurz, *Reminiscences*, III, 12; Howard, *Autobiography*, 418; C. P. Horton to Bachelder, Jan. 23, 1867; Lt. Col. C. H. Morgan's Account, Typescript, Bachelder Papers. Morgan recalled that Slocum said his provost guard had stopped "many hundreds" of the Eleventh Corps. In a version apparently reproduced later in the *Reminiscences of Winfield Scott Hancock* Morgan on page 189 set the number of Eleventh Corps fugitives which the provost guard caught at 1,500.

59. *OR*, XXVII, pt. 1, pp. 173, 298–299, 310, 704, 735; "Army Experience of Major Morton Tower from 1861 to 1864," Typescript, C. S. A. Army Prisons, VHS; Schurz, *Reminiscences*, III, 12. The famous correspondent, Whitelaw Reid, reported that in trying to avoid the fire of the advancing Confederates and to hasten the movements of their men through the crowded streets, officers of the Eleventh Corps resorted to rather complicated maneuvers which seemed to confuse the troops. Perhaps it was that, or, in the words of Reid, "perhaps the old panic at the battle-cry of Jackson's flying corps comes over them; at any rate they break in wild confusion, some pouring through the town . . . , and are with difficulty formed again on the hights [sic] to the southward. They lost over twelve hundred prisoners in twenty minutes." Column by Agate, Near Get-

tysburg, July 2, in *Cincinnati Daily Gazette*, July 8, 1863. The total number of officers and men in the Eleventh Corps captured or missing in the three days of the battle was 1,510. All but a few of these losses occurred the first day. *OR*, XXVII, pt. 1, p. 183.

60. Lt. Col. George F. McFarland to Bachelder, Feb. 7, 1867, Bachelder Papers; Brown, *A Colonel at Gettysburg*, 77–83.

61. Perrin said he went into action with 1,100 men and came out with five hundred. Perrin to Governor [Bonham], July 29, 1863, in *Mississippi Valley Historical Review*, XXIV, 522–523; *OR*, XXVII, pt. 1, pp. 927, 934–935; pt. 2, p. 657; Doubleday, *Chancellorsville and Gettysburg*, 147–148.

62. *OR*, XXVII, pt. 1, pp. 230, 703–704, 927, 939; CCW, *Report*, I, 377; Michael Wiedrich to Bachelder, Jan. 20, 1886, Bachelder Papers. For size of Smith's brigade *cf. post*, XII, 98 note.

63. Edward N. Whittier, "The Left Attack (Ewell's), Gettysburg," *Campaigns in Virginia, Maryland and Pennsylvania*, 316. Other people noticed this habit of Hancock. Theodore Lyman referred to the "stout General Hancock, who always wears a clean *white* shirt (where he gets them nobody knows). . . ." Agassiz, ed., *Meade's Headquarters*, 107.

64. Both Hancock and Howard were inconsistent in their accounts of the hour of Hancock's arrival at Gettysburg. Hancock in his battle report set the time at 3:00 P.M.; in his dispatch of July 1, at 4:25 P.M.; in his testimony before the Committee on the Conduct of the War, "not later" than 3:30 P.M.; and in an article written after the war, "about" 3:30 P.M. Howard in his report said Hancock came to him with Meade's instructions about 4:30 P.M., but in a dispatch sent to Meade at 5:00 P.M. he placed the time of Hancock's arrival half an hour earlier. Because of the close agreement between Hancock's and Howard's dispatches of July 1 it is safe to say that Hancock arrived between 4:00 and 4:30 P.M. *OR*, XXVII, pt. 1, pp. 366, 368, 696, 704; CCW, *Report*, I, 405; Hancock, "Gettysburg," *Galaxy*, XXII, 822–823.

65. Lt. Col. C. H. Morgan's Account, Typescript, Bachelder Papers. Morgan said as they came near Gettysburg the road was blocked by the wagon trains of the Eleventh Corps. Hancock immediately ordered them to the rear. He and the general arrived as the "remnants" of the First Corps were regrouping on Cemetery Hill.

66. *OR*, XXVII, pt. 1, pp. 368, 696–697; Hancock, "Gettysburg," *Galaxy*, XXII, 822–825.

67. Howard to Prof. M. Jacobs, Mar. 23, 1864, Howard Papers.

68. Lt. Col. C. H. Morgan's Account, Typescript, Bachelder Papers.

69. *OR*, XXVII, pt. 1, p. 927.

70. *Ibid.*, p. 704.

71. Hancock, "Gettysburg," *Galaxy*, XXII, 822–825. Without a doubt Meade put Hancock in command of all the troops at Gettysburg. See Meade's dispatch to Hancock at 6:00 P.M., July 1, 1863, in *OR*, XXVII, pt. 1, pp. 71–72. Whether Hancock exercised his plenary powers in the manner his account suggested is less certain.

72. *Wainwright Journals*, 237–238. Wainwright said he heard later about

Hancock's claims to have been in command, but he neither saw nor heard anything of him at the time.

73. Hunt and Osborn in their reports merely said Wainwright was given command of Wiedrich's battery, normally attached to the Eleventh Corps, because it was on the right of the Baltimore Pike facing the town. According to Osborn, Wainwright commanded the batteries on the right side of the pike and Osborn those on the left. *OR*, XXVII, pt. 1, p. 748; Col. Thomas W. Osborn, "The Artillery at Gettysburg," *Philadelphia Weekly Times*, May 31, 1879.

74. *OR*, XXVII, pt. 1, p. 366.

75. *Ibid.*, pp. 368, 758–759. Slocum said Howard had suggested the location of Williams' division, thus lending credence to Howard's claim about the division of authority between him and Hancock. If it did not exist, Slocum at least thought so and acted accordingly. He never took back what he had written in his official report. See Howard, *Autobiography*, 418.

76. Howard asserted that before Hancock's arrival he had given "the order generally to arrange the 11th Corps on the ridge, or north of the Baltimore Pike, and the 1st Corps south of the same." Howard to Prof. M. Jacobs, Mar. 23, 1864, Howard Papers. It is reasonable to suppose that when Howard ordered the retreat he gave the commanders some idea of where to go. See also Howard to [Messrs. T. H. Davis], Sept. 14, 1875, Bates Collection.

77. Hancock never wrote a critique of the battle and Howard's generalship, but he did think that Howard claimed "too much" for his services at Gettysburg and received "greater honor for the same then he . . . [was] legitimately entitled to." Hancock to Hooker, July 27, 1876, [Copy], Bates Collection. He also questioned Howard's version of events after Hancock appeared on the field and of the settlement of the dispute over Hancock's authority. See Hancock, "Gettysburg," *Galaxy*, XXII, 821–831.

78. Two articles appearing in the spring of 1864 in a newspaper and in the *Army and Navy Journal* deprecated Howard's accomplishments at Gettysburg, causing him to enter into correspondence in his own defense. See Howard to Henry Coppie, Mar. 4, 1864; *id.* to Prof. M. Jacobs, Mar. 23, 1864, Howard Papers. Then in 1875 Samuel P. Bates published his *Battle of Gettysburg* in which he was very critical of Howard. After protesting to Bates and his publishers, Howard wrote a letter to the *New York Herald*, Oct. 2, 1875, and then an article for the July, 1876, issue of *Harper's Magazine*, defending himself. See Howard to [Bates], Sept. 14, 1875, Howard Papers; Howard to [Messrs. T. H. Davis], Sept. 14, 1875; Doubleday to [Bates], Oct. 18, 1875, Bates Collection. Of course in his *Autobiography*, which came out in 1908, he again tried to vindicate his record at Gettysburg.

79. *OR*, XXVII, pt. 1, p. 696.

80. Howard to [S. P. Bates], Sept. 14, 1875, Howard Papers.

81. *OR*, XXVII, pt. 1, p. 248.

82. Reference to entrenchments on Seminary Ridge was made by Doubleday, Robinson, and others in their reports. Others mentioned breastworks made of rails and the like. Rowley said the fortification consisted of hastily

thrown up rails. See *ibid.*, pp. 247, 289, 299, 301, 313, 321, 326. Lt. Col. George F. McFarland of the 151st Pa. regiment spoke of how breastworks and woods on Seminary Ridge helped in stopping an enemy attack. *Ibid.*, p. 328.

83. One writer, J. W. De Peyster, using the authority of a general in the Army of the Potomac, probably Gen. John Newton, said that Howard should not have tried to hold the low ground north of Gettysburg with long weak lines. He should have kept closer to Gettysburg and Cemetery Hill and swept the ground with the fire of his artillery. See De Peyster, *The Decisive Conflicts of the Late Civil War* (New York, 1867), 40. In 1891 Newton said that the position of the Eleventh Corps in a military sense was a "nearly smooth plain" which afforded an opportunity for a "magnificent display of artillery." A competent force of guns here, he went on, would have checked or seriously delayed Ewell and thus have prevented turning the flank and rear of the First Corps. See John Newton et al., "Further Recollections of Gettysburg," *North American Review,* CLII, 273.

84. In his report Schurz was less outspoken than in his *Reminiscences.* In the latter he said that Barlow either misunderstood his orders or was carried away by the "ardor of the conflict" when he advanced his whole line and lost connection with the Third Division. *OR,* XXVII, pt. 1, p. 728; Schurz, *Reminiscences,* III, 8–10.

85. Barlow stoutly maintained that he had an "admirable" position. He also said that Schurz ordered him through town, and that he "went through and formed as directed." Barlow to his mother, July 7, 1863, Francis C. Barlow Papers, MHS. There is a strong possibility that Howard had a hand in the formation of Barlow's line, for he said: "I rode with Barlow through the city, and out to what is now Barlow Hill." Howard, *Autobiography,* 414.

86. Alfred E. Lee to Bachelder, Feb. 16, 1888, Bachelder Papers.

87. C. H. Howard to [Maj. E. Whittlesey], July 9, 1863, Howard Papers. Charles Howard was O. O. Howard's brother and an aide on his staff.

88. *OR,* XXVII, pt. 1, p. 246.

89. *Ibid.*, p. 140. Many people felt that Hancock deserved this honor more than Howard.

90. Howard's claim that it was he who chose Cemetery Hill was made in his battle report. *Ibid.*, p. 702. This question of who thought of the strategic importance of the hill was brought up as early as 1864. It upset Howard very much, and he sent out inquiries to various people asking for supporting evidence for his claim. Maj. William Riddle, who had been on Reynolds' staff, wrote: "I did not carry to you any order to place any troops on Cemetery Hill, nor do I know that General Reynolds sent you such [an] order by any of his staff at Gettysburg." Riddle to Howard, Apr. 3, 1864, Howard Papers. Prof. M. Jacobs, who wrote one of the first accounts of the battle, after careful examination came to the conclusion that Howard had received no order from Reynolds about Cemetery Hill. See Jacobs to Howard, Mar. 15, 1864, *ibid.* The controversy flared up again in 1875 when Bates in his *Battle of Gettysburg* accepted the Doubleday and Maj. Joseph G. Rosengarten version about who chose Cemetery Hill as a defensive position. See Howard to [Col.] T. A. Meysenberg,

Sept. 13, 1875; Daniel Hall to Howard, Feb. 19, 1877, Howard Papers; Doubleday to [S. P. Bates], Oct. 4, 18, 1875, Bates Collection; Rosengarten, "General Reynolds' Last Battle," *Annals*, 62.

91. Howard said Cemetery Hill was "partially fortified" under his personal supervision. Howard to [S. P. Bates], Sept. 14, 1875, Howard Papers.

92. *OR*, XXVII, pt. 1, pp. 924–925. Buford sent this dispatch to Pleasonton at 3:20 P.M.

93. Howard to [S. P. Bates], Sept. 14, 1875, Howard Papers.

94. In his report and his diary Wainwright told how upon overhearing an order from one of Howard's aides he mistook Seminary Ridge for Cemetery Hill. In the latter account he elaborated and became more explicit. The aide, according to Wainwright, said that Howard wanted Cemetery Hill to be held at all costs, but "with the aide's broken English and our being on this hill and not knowing that there was a *cemetery*, I thought it was the *Seminary* Hill we were to hold." *Wainwright Journals*, 235. As a result of this mistake Wainwright came near losing several of his batteries by holding on too long. See *ibid.*, 236–237; *OR*, XXVII, pt. 1, p. 356.

95. Doubleday finally admitted that Howard had told him to go to Cemetery Hill in case of retreat. Doubleday, *Chancellorsville and Gettysburg*, 141.

96. *OR*, XXVII, pt. 1, p. 702. Wainwright, who knew both Reynolds and Howard, was confident that Reynolds would have conducted the retreat much more expertly and with "half the loss to ourselves." *Wainwright Journals*, 239. Howard admitted that clogging of the streets was due to the "small neck for egress at the Baltimore pike." Howard to [Messrs. T. H. Davis], Sept. 14, 1875, Bates Collection.

97. Doubleday admitted he never received an order to retreat, but Schurz reported that he had. Doubleday to [Bates], Sept. 14, 1875, Bates Collection; Doubleday, *Chancellorsville and Gettysburg*, 149; *OR*, XXVII, pt. 1, p. 729.

98. *Ibid.*, pp. 703–704, 729, 755; Dan B. Allen [Lt. Col., 154th N.Y. Vols.] to Bachelder, Apr. 5, 1864, Bachelder Papers. Howard said that Coster's brigade made demonstrations and used artillery, probably Heckman's battery. Its work, he claimed, was efficient. The figures for the two brigades in von Steinwehr's division are in Selected Pages from the Historical and Statistical Record of the Principal Military Commands in the Union and Confederate Armies, IV, 53, Record Group 94, NA. Orland Smith's brigade had 1,940 officers and men present for duty.

99. *OR*, XXVII, pt. 1, p. 366.

100. Barlow to his mother, July 7, 1863, Francis C. Barlow Papers, MHS.

101. Howard to H. W. Halleck, July 29, 1863, Howard Papers.

102. C. H. Howard to [Maj. E. Whittlesey], July 9, 1863, Howard Papers.

103. *OR*, XXVII, pt. 2, p. 492.

104. From the Special Correspondent, Hagerstown, July 8, in the *Times* [London], Aug. 18, 1863. The correspondent, Francis Lawley, reflected the sneering attitude of many Confederates toward Union soldiers, whom they considered to be mostly foreign hirelings and the scum of the earth. Information furnished by Prof. Robert L. Bloom of Gettysburg College.

105. *OR*, XXVII, pt. 1, p. 728.

106. *Ibid.*, p. 728; pt. 2, p. 562; Field Return of Early's Division, June 20, 1863, War Department Collection of Confederate Records, Record Group 109, NA. The figure of 5,800 includes one of Rodes's brigades plus his 5th Ala. regiment and sharpshooters with an estimated total of 400 officers and men, and three of Early's brigades. Gen. William Smith's small brigade in Early's division was kept in reserve.

107. *OR*, XXVII, pt. 1, pp. 728–729.

108. *Cf. ante*, XII, 304; *OR*, XXVII, pt. 1, pp. 182–183, 697; pt. 2, pp. 474–475, 480, 562, 596–597. Losses of Early's brigades on July 1 were as follows: Gordon's 378; Hays's 63; Hoke's 145. The casualty figures in Rodes's division, however, represented totals of fighting for the three days of the battle. Doles reported a loss of 241 officers and men; Col. J. M. Hall of the 5th Ala. put his casualties at 209.

109. One Yankee officer who saw a review of troops said that the regiment which marched best was the 41st N.Y., composed entirely of Germans "who have run away several times." Then he observed: "The Germans certainly have a natural gift which makes them march well and hold themselves in a soldierly manner." Gray to his mother, Sept. 23, 1863, in Gray and Ropes, *War Letters*, 213. Barlow made the following comment to his Harvard classmate, Robert Treat Paine, on Aug. 12, 1863: "But these Dutch won't fight. Their officers say so & they say so themselves & they ruin all with whom they come in contact." Francis C. Barlow Papers, MHS.

110. *OR*, XXV, pt. 1, pp. 658–663; pt. 2, p. 464; CCW, *Report*, I, p. XLIX: Boatner, *Civil War Dictionary*, 761; Ella Lonn, *Foreigners in the Union Army and Navy* (Baton Rouge, La., 1951), 179–180, 594–596.

111. *Ibid.*, 180–182; Williams to his daughter, Feb. 22, June 7, 1863, in *Alpheus Williams Letters*, 166, 206; Gray to his mother, Sept. 23, 1863, in Gray and Ropes, *War Letters*, 213. In speaking of the conduct of his division July 1 Barlow said: "Some of the German officers behaved well. Col. Von Gilsa I did not notice after the fight began. Probably he behaved well as he is personally brave." Barlow to ? [first part missing], July 11 [?], 1863, Francis C. Barlow Papers, MHS. For opinions of Howard, most of which were favorable, see Webb to his wife, Aug. 1, 1863, Webb Collection; W. S. Hancock to Howard, Mar. 14, 1864; William Riddle to Howard, Apr. 3, 1864; W. T. Sherman to Howard, Dec. 18, 1863, Howard Papers.

112. Ford, ed., *Adams Letters*, II, 167. For Schurz's opinion of Barlow, which on the whole was favorable, see Schurz, *Reminiscences*, III, 8. For favorable opinions of Ames see B. F. Young to Bachelder, Aug. 12, 1867, Bachelder Papers; Barlow to ? [first part missing], July 11 [?], 1863, Francis C. Barlow Papers, MHS.

113. The irrelevance of national origins as a standard for determining the quality of troops is made obvious by the fact that in the Union army there was "hardly a regiment or a company to be found in which there were no foreign-born." Lonn, *Foreigners in the Union Army*, 154.

114. Many of the men and most of the officers did not wear the corps badge,

although in all the other corps it was universally worn. Gray to Elizabeth Gray, July 17, 1863, in Gray and Ropes, *War Letters,* 146.

115. From Special Correspondent, Hagerstown, July 8, in the *Times* [London], Aug. 18, 1863; Fremantle, *Three Months in the Southern States,* 254; *OR,* XXVII, pt. 1, p. 272.

116. Boatner, *Civil War Dictionary,* 187–188; Nichols, *Toward Gettysburg,* 148, 150–153, 166–167, 173–177.

117. The number and loss figures are for infantry units only. For the number of men in the First Corps see IX, 133 note. Heth and Pender had four brigades each in their divisions. All four of Heth's brigades numbering over 7,000 men fought against the First Corps, but only two of Pender's brigades, Perrin's and Scales's with a total of about 2,300 officers and men, attacked it. Of Pender's other two brigades, Thomas' was kept in reserve and Lane's fought Gamble's cavalry south of the Fairfield road. Rodes had five brigades, but one of them, Doles's, and a regiment of O'Neal's were used against the Eleventh Corps. Deducting an estimated 400 men in the 5th Ala. regiment and sharpshooters, the number of troops in O'Neal's brigade to fight the First Corps came to about 1,400. Adding this number to the total of the other three brigades, Rodes hurled about 6,350 men against part of the First Corps. *OR,* XXVII, pt. 2, pp. 562, 564, 670–671; Perrin to Governor [Bonham], July 29, 1863, in *Mississippi Valley Historical Review,* XXIV, 522; Heth to Jones, June, 1877, *SHSP,* IV, 158.

118. The regimental losses as tabulated in the *OR* are totals for the three days of the battle. Losses incurred on the first day can be reasonably inferred, estimated, or obtained from explicit statements in the *OR* or elsewhere. *OR,* XXVII, pt. 2, pp. 342, 344–345, 670–671; Perrin to Governor [Bonham], July 29, 1863, in *Mississippi Valley Historical Review,* XXIV, 522; Heth to Jones, June, 1877, *SHSP,* IV, 158; *New York Times,* July 4, 1863; Love, "Mississippi at Gettysburg," *Mississippi Historical Society Publications,* IX, 31; Capt. George Wilcox to Messrs. Editors [Raleigh *Observer*], Oct., 1877, Bryan Grimes Papers, North Carolina State Department of Archives and History; Louis G. Young to Early, Mar. 14, 1878, Jubal A. Early Papers, LC. There is a strong suspicion that the figures in the *OR* for losses during the three days' fighting in Pettigrew's brigade are too low. All other accounts agree that on the first day his brigade lost 1,000 to 1,100 men. The total given in *OR,* XXVII, pt. 2, p. 344, is only 1,105, and Pettigrew's brigade participated in the famous charge of July 3.

119. *OR,* XXVII, pt. 1, pp. 173–174, 290, 295, 307, 310. Except for Stannard's brigade which arrived at night on July 1, practically all the losses of the First Corps occurred during the fight and retreat of the first day.

120. It was unusual for a subordinate officer to make special mention of the conduct of his superiors. In his report Col. Charles Wheelock of the 97th N.Y. regiment wrote: "I wish to say one word outside of my regiment in regard to Generals Baxter and Robinson. They were on every part of the field, encouraging and stimulating the men by their presence and bravery." *Ibid.,* p. 310.

Col. Morgan said that during the retreat Gen. Wadsworth was "still full of fight." Lt. Col. C. H. Morgan's Account, Typescript, Bachelder Papers.

121. The court-martial convened at Culpeper, Va., Apr. 23, 1864, and included as judges such outstanding officers as Gens. John C. Robinson, President, Alexander Hays, Thomas H. Neill, and Alexander S. Webb. Rowley, it seems, had made himself thoroughly obnoxious to commanding officers of other brigades by suddenly getting the idea that he was in command of the corps. Judge Advocate General Holt said that although the weight of evidence supported the court's decision of dismissal from the service, there was such a conflict of testimony that he recommended to Lincoln that the sentence not be upheld. What happened was that some of Rowley's friends and aides staunchly swore to his sobriety. His surgeon said Rowley was suffering from boils on his legs and hence he could not sit well on his horse, while Doubleday gave equivocal testimony which proved damaging to the prosecution. Wainwright, who was not asked to testify, recorded in his diary that during the retreat he had found Rowley drunk. General Court Martial, Orders No. 120, Judge Advocate General J. Holt to [Lincoln], May 6, 17, 1864, M. M. 1416, Record Group 153, NA; *Wainwright Journals*, 237.

122. *Ibid.*, 235, 237.

123. *OR*, XXVII, pt. 1, pp. 312–315, 317–318, 320–321, 327, 329–338. Rowley's report is confusing, to say the least. See also Theodore B. Gates, *The "Ulster Guard" [20th N. Y. State Militia] and the War of the Rebellion* (New York, 1879), 429–430, 440–446. Gates said the promotion of Rowley to temporary command was "detrimental" to the efficiency of the division, and left the brigades to act very much upon their own discretion. At another place he hints something was wrong with Rowley by saying that he was hardly competent to judge correctly the condition of things, or to know what transpired on the field on July 1. See *ibid.*

124. See testimonies of Doubleday and of Maj. H. N. Warren, as well as the deposition of Lt. Col. A. B. McCalmont. Both Warren and McCalmont were of the 142nd Pa. regiment. General Court Martial, Orders No. 120, Judge Advocate General's Office, M. M. 1416, Record Group 153, NA; *OR*, XXVII, pt. 1, p. 256; *New York Tribune*, July 9, 1863.

125. In a critical manner Doubleday said he received only two orders from Howard but never a specific order to retreat. CCW, *Report*, I, 307; Doubleday to [S. P. Bates], Oct. 4, 18, 1875, Bates Collection. In his first account Doubleday said that Howard's second order directed him to hold the seminary if forced back, but he then changed his story in the second account to say that Howard told him to retreat to Cemetery Hill if necessary. Finally in his *Chancellorsville and Gettysburg*, pp. 141, 145–146 he wrote that Howard gave him but one order and that was to fall back to Cemetery Hill should he be forced to retreat. He also charged that when he asked that he be given reinforcements or be allowed to retreat, Howard refused both the reinforcements and the order.

126. *Cf. ante*, IX, 238, XII, 106, 117 notes; Selected Pages from the Historical and Statistical Record of the Principal Military Commands in the Union and Confederate Armies, IV, 53 ,60, 75, Entry 161, Record Group 94, NA; *OR*

XXVII, pt. 1, pp. 284, 291; pt. 2, p. 667. These figures do not include the following brigades because they were kept in reserve: Orland Smith's of von Steinwehr's division, Thomas' of Pender's division, William Smith's of Early's division, and Jenkins' cavalry. Lane's brigade had an effective total of 1,355 officers and men.

127. OR, XXVII, pt. 1, pp. 173–174, 183; pt. 2, p. 317. Gen. Lee said they captured more than 5,000 prisoners, exclusive of a large number of Union wounded presumably left on the battlefield and in town.

128. Ibid., pt. 1, pp. 229–230, 1031; pt. 2, pp. 348–349, 355–356, 495, 602–603, 652, 673–675, 677–678. The Confederates had 95 guns available, while the Yankees had 60. Twenty-three guns were not used by the Confederates; one of them became damaged and unfit for use as it was being drawn into position.

129. Ibid., p. 444.

130. "Gen. Heth's Letter," SHSP, IV, 158; Morrison, ed., "Heth Memoirs," CWH, VIII, 305. Fremantle in a footnote said he had "best reason" for supposing that the first day's fight came off "prematurely," and neither Lee nor Longstreet intended that it should have begun that day. He also thought that "their plans were deranged by the events of the first." Fremantle, Three Months in the Southern States, 256. See also Scheibert, Seven Months in the Rebel States, Hoole, ed., 112. Scheibert offered similar reasons for Lee's hesitation in bringing on a general engagement on July 1. He said Lee had "a long extended column on the march," while assuming that he was confronted with the entire force of the enemy.

131. OR, XXVII, pt. 2, p. 317.

132. For relations between Lee and Heth see Freeman, R. E. Lee, III, 160. It is also possible that Hill's indisposition during the day caused Heth to turn to Lee for guidance. Fremantle, Three Months in the Southern States, 254. According to Heth, he found Hill with Lee when he sought permission to attack. Morrison, ed., "Heth's Memoirs," CWH, VIII, 305.

133. OR, XXVII, pt. 2, pp. 348, 444.

134. Ibid., p. 559.

135. Fremantle, Three Months in the Southern States, 254.

136. OR, XXVII, pt. 2, p. 607.

137. Frederick Phisterer, The Army in the Civil War, Statistical Record of the Armies of the United States (New York, 1882, 1885), 252, 269.

138. Gen. John W. Geary in command of the Second Division reported his arrival at 11:00 A.M. OR, XXVII, pt. 1, p. 825. Williams did not give the time of his arrival, but since he said his division was in the lead he must have marched into Two Taverns no later than midmorning. Williams to his daughters, July 6, 1863, in Alpheus Williams Letters, 224. The asst. adj. gen. of the Third Brigade of the Second Division said they arrived early in the forenoon. C. P. Horton to Bachelder, Jan. 23, 1867, Bachelder Papers. Slocum said they got in about noon. H. W. Slocum to Messrs. Davis & Co., Sept. 8, 1875, Bates Collection.

139. Id. to id., Sept. 8, 1875, ibid.

140. C. P. Horton to Bachelder, Jan. 23, 1867, Bachelder Papers; Buckingham to his wife, July 18, 1863, Civil War Letters of Lt. Col. Philo B. Buckingham, American Antiquarian Society. These two accounts agree pretty well in their timing of important developments on that day.

141. *OR*, XXVII, pt. 3, pp. 416, 463.

142. *Ibid.*, pt. 1, pp. 704, 825. Other accounts set the departure time about an hour later. If Williams' division, which took the lead in the morning march, headed the column in the afternoon, the hours given by two staff officers, one in the First and the other in the Second Division, appear reasonable. Maj. [later Lt. Col.] Buckingham, who was asst. inspector general on Williams' staff, said they left "at about 3 o'clock," while C. P. Horton set their time at 3:30 or 4:00 P.M. Buckingham to his wife, July 18, 1863, Civil War Letters of Lt. Col. Philo B. Buckingham, American Antiquarian Society; C. P. Horton to Bachelder, Jan. 23, 1867, Bachelder Papers.

143. This interpretation is based upon the rather lame excuse Slocum later offered Howard for his strange conduct on the afternoon of July 1. He expressed the "opinion," according to Howard, that Meade did not want to "bring on a general engagement at that point [Gettysburg]." *OR*, XXVII, pt. 1, p. 704.

144. *Ibid.*, pt. 3, pp. 416, 458–459, 462.

145. *Ibid.*, pt. 1, p. 126; pt. 3, p. 466.

146. *Ibid.*, pt. 1, pp. 703–704.

147. C. H. Howard to [Maj. E. Whittlesey], July 9, 1863, Howard Papers. Italics are Howard's.

148. Lt. Col. C. H. Morgan's Account, Typescript, Bachelder Papers. Both Morgan and Hancock agreed that Slocum relieved Hancock between 5:00 and 6:00 P.M. In his dispatch to Meade, which was sent at 5:25 P.M., Hancock said he would communicate in a few moments with Slocum and transfer the command to him. *OR*, XXVII, pt. 1, p. 366. It is safe to say, therefore, that Slocum did not assume command *before* 5:25 P.M. Hancock knew that he was to turn the command over to Slocum as soon as he came to the battlefield. Before Hancock left Taneytown Butterfield told him to do so, and at 6:00 P.M. Meade sent a special dispatch to that effect. *Ibid.*, pt. 3, p. 466; CCW, *Report*, I, 405. Howard, however, who questioned Hancock's right to supersede him, assumed he was still in command until he got written orders to the contrary from Meade, or Slocum came on the field and personally took over from Howard. Both events occurred almost exactly at 7:00 P.M. *OR*, XXVII, pt. 1, p. 696.

149. It just so happened that Slocum practiced law before the war. A graduate of West Point, he resigned his commission in 1856. Boatner, *Civil War Dictionary*, 765. Other than the Howard brothers no one seems to have been upset by Slocum's stuffy attitude. Meade learned of Slocum's "hesitation about reinforcing Howard" but apparently made nothing of it. See his letter to Mrs. Meade, Dec. 3, 1864, in Meade, *Life and Letters*, II, 249. Gen. Howard in his battle report showed due Christian forebearance, but Charlie in a private letter made acid comments. He wrote: "He [O. O. Howard] hoped that Slocum would come up to assist in the retreat as he was but 2 miles away but he was

too willing to demonstrate the fitness of his name *Slow Come.*" C. H. Howard to [Maj. E. Whittlesey], July 9, 1863, Howard Papers.

150. *OR,* XXVII, pt. 3, p. 465. In sending a dispatch at 3:35 P.M. addressed to either Hancock or Howard, Slocum unwittingly complicated the problem of determining the time of Hancock's arrival on Cemetery Hill. The presumption is that the courier carrying the message for Slocum from Meade's headquarters in Taneytown telling about the situation at Gettysburg reached him before 3:35 P.M. Otherwise why would Slocum at that hour address a message for either Hancock or Howard? For Meade's message see *ibid.,* pt. 1, p. 126.

151. Alpheus Williams to Bachelder, Nov. 10, 1865, Bachelder Papers; Williams to his daughters, July 6, 1863, in *Alpheus Williams Letters,* 224–225. Traditional accounts all state that Williams got only as far as Wolf's Hill, which is northeast of Culp's Hill with Rock Creek running in between. See Fox, ed., *New York at Gettysburg,* I, 30; Charles E. Slocum, *The Life and Services of Major General Henry Warner Slocum* (Toledo, Ohio, 1913), 102. For Slocum to have sent Williams to Wolf's Hill would have been a meaningless gesture. His purpose was to threaten the flank of Ewell's men near Gettysburg, and Wolf's Hill was too far away from town. Also Williams in his letters makes it very clear that he reached the bottom of Benner's Hill. On Nov. 1, 1961, Dr. Frederick Tilberg, who at the time was Gettysburg National Military Park Historian, and the author drove carefully through the country between the Baltimore and Hanover roads in an effort to determine the road Williams might have taken. From Tilberg's expert knowledge of the area and a careful perusal of the records it seems evident that Williams followed a road which started off on the first ridge southeast of Rock Creek and came out on the Hanover road almost a mile from the crest of Benner's Hill. Before Williams reached the Hanover road his men must have cut through the woods over the north shoulder of Wolf's Hill and down to the stream which runs along the southeast face of Benner's Hill.

152. *OR,* XXVII, pt. 2, p. 318.

153. *Ibid.,* p. 607.

154. *Ibid.,* p. 318.

155. Dispatch from Special Correspondent, Hagerstown, July 8, in the *Times* [London], Aug. 18, 1863.

156. Perrin to Governor [Bonham], July 29, 1863, in *Mississippi Valley Historical Review,* XXIV, 523.

157. *OR,* XXVII, pt. 2, pp. 318, 607, 613.

158. *Ibid.,* p. 607.

159. *Ibid.,* p. 622.

160. Anderson said he started soon after daylight and arrived in Cashtown early in the afternoon. It took Anderson therefore probably eight hours to march eleven miles. This was not good time for veteran troops unless they were held up by a traffic jam, which was very likely. Assuming again that he left Cashtown at 2:00 P.M. and arrived in his position at 5:00 P.M., his division made the next six miles in three hours, which was more like it. See *ibid.,* p. 613.

161. Louis G. Young, "Pettigrew's Brigade at Gettysburg," Clark, ed., *North Carolina Regiments*, V, 121 note. In relating this story at second-hand Young had Anderson in command of only a brigade.

162. Calder to his mother, July 8, 1863, William Calder Papers, UNC.

163. The case against Ewell is exceedingly well discussed by Freeman in *Lee's Lieutenants*, III, 90–100. He accepts the judgment of Ewell's critics without much question. Accounts of the Second Corps and analyses of Ewell's generalship are to be found largely in the *Southern Historical Society Papers*.

164. Gordon, *Reminiscences*, 153–157; I. R. Trimble to Bachelder, Feb. 8, 1883, Bachelder Papers.

165. This is the point made by Maj. Campbell Brown, Ewell's stepson. See Brown, "Reminiscences," MS, Campbell Brown Books, UNC.

166. Trimble referred to the enemy retreat as a "rout." It should be noted also that he was one of the very few Confederate witnesses who claimed the fight ended as early as 3:30 P.M. The longer the interval between the close of the engagement and darkness, the greater the damnation of Ewell for not accomplishing what Trimble insisted was possible. Trimble to Bachelder, Feb. 8, 1883, Bachelder Papers.

167. Gen. W. S. Hancock to Gen. Fitz Lee, Jan. 17, 1878, quoted in Fitz Lee, "A Reply to General Longstreet," *SHSP*, V, 168.

168. Gordon, *Reminiscences*, 157; Brown, "Reminiscences," MS, Campbell Brown Books, UNC; Early, *War Memoirs*, 269.

169. For the need of the men to reorganize and obtain ammunition, as well as to recover from general fatigue, see *OR*, XXVII, pt. 2, pp. 469, 484, 555, 582, 586, 589–590, 601; Col. R. T. Bennett, "Fourteenth Regiment," Clark, ed., *North Carolina Regiments*, I, 719; Early, "Causes of Lee's Defeat at Gettysburg," *SHSP*, IV, 257; James Power Smith, "With Stonewall Jackson in the Army of Northern Virginia," *SHSP*, XLIII, 56–57.

170. *Ibid.*

171. Trimble to Bachelder, Feb. 8, 1883, Bachelder Papers. See also Freeman, *Lee's Lieutenants*, III, 95–96, for a different reaction to Trimble's story of his conversation with Ewell on the afternoon of July 1.

172. Fremantle said the "tops of the ridges being covered with pine woods," the enemy troops were concealed very well. *Three Months in the Southern States*, 255. Early asserted that Ewell was on low ground at the foot of the hill and could neither see the enemy nor form an estimate of his strength. He also emphasized the difficulties of an advance against Cemetery Hill from the north through the town and also from the east. "General Early's Reply to the Count of Paris," *SHSP*, V, 32; Early, *War Memoirs*, 269–270. In his report Ewell also said that the hill was not assailable from the town and added that he could not bring artillery to "bear on it." *OR*, XXVII, pt. 2, p. 445.

173. Gordon implied censure of both Early and Ewell because his brigade was halted for awhile after it broke through Barlow's first position. See *Reminiscences*, 154–155. As Early clearly indicates in his report, he halted Gordon's brigade after it had driven the enemy for a distance so it would not be in the way of Hays's and Avery's brigades when they cut across Gordon's front in

charging into the enemy's right flank. See *OR*, XXVII, pt. 2, p. 469. For Early's ranking position among the major generals in Ewell's corps see Warner, *Generals in Gray*, 79, 159, 263.

174. For an estimate of the number of troops possibly available for the attacking column *cf. ante*, XII, 106 note. In retrospect Early became convinced that an attack by his whole division, even with Rodes's support, would have met with repulse because of "subsequent developments." Early, "Causes of Lee's Defeat at Gettysburg," *SHSP*, IV, 257–258.

175. The accounts of this exchange of messages are, as so often happens, vague about time. Ewell said he received the message from Lee as he was entering town, which would probably be around 4:30 P.M.; whereas Fremantle, who was with Hill, said the dispatch from Ewell suggesting a joint attack reached Hill sometime after 4:30 P.M. Early asserted that before meeting Ewell in town he made the same suggestion to Hill through a staff officer of Gen. Pender. Whether Hill received the message is not known, although other witnesses agreed Early sent one. *OR*, XXVII, pt. 2, pp. 318, 445, 469–470; Taylor, *Four Years with General Lee*, 95; Smith, "With Stonewall Jackson in the Army of Northern Virginia," *SHSP*, XLIII, 56–58; James McDowell Carrington, "First Day on the Left at Gettysburg," *SHSP*, XXXVII, 326; Campbell Brown to Early, July 4, 1885, Jubal A. Early Papers, LC.

176. *OR*, XXVII, pt. 2, 469–470. Campbell Brown maintained that Ewell, having decided to attack if Hill concurred, had ordered Early and Rodes to get ready when Freddy Smith, aide and son of General "Extra Billy" Smith, arrived to say that a heavy force was reported to be moving up in the rear of Smith's position. Brown also claimed that because of Hill's inactivity and the alarm sounded by Smith, Early and Rodes expressly concurred in Ewell's decision to await the arrival of Johnson before making any further moves. Brown, "Reminiscences," MS, Campbell Brown Books, UNC. At another time Brown said that an entry in his diary recorded the fact that Ewell had actually begun to arrange for an attack on Cemetery Hill when Smith's report came in. Campbell Brown to Abner Doubleday, Dec. 6, 1881, Draft of a letter, Polk-Brown-Ewell Collection, UNC.

177. *OR*, XXVII, pt. 2, pp. 445, 469; Early, "Causes of Lee's Defeat at Gettysburg," *SHSP*, IV, 256. Lt. B. B. Coiner of the 52nd Va. regiment was convinced that Gen. Smith "mistook a fence with a growth of small trees along it for a line of troops." Becoming thoroughly alarmed, he at once sent his son to Early for reinforcements, since he was sure the enemy was advancing. B. B. Coiner Report, Microfilm, UV.

178. For the location of Ewell's headquarters and the time he returned to them, see Freeman, *Lee's Lieutenants*, III, 99–100. For the time of arrival of Johnson's division and the hour it bivouacked, see *OR*, XXVII, pt. 2, pp. 504, 513, 518, 526, 530–531; R. W. Hunter to Early, Oct. 10, 1877; J. A. Walker to *id.*, Oct. 13, 1877, Jubal A. Early Papers, LC; S. Thomas McCullough Diary, Entry for July 1, 1863, UV.

179. A. L. Long, who was Lee's military secretary, said the general decided against further advance on July 1 because of the tired and disorganized condi-

tion of the troops after rapid marching and hard fighting, and Long's report of his reconnaissance of the Federal position on Cemetery Ridge, which he found strong and occupied in considerable force. Long, *Memoirs of Lee*, 276–277. He placed none of the onus for the failure to advance on Ewell.

180. With few exceptions Confederate and Federal accounts show amazing agreement in setting the time of the retreat as no earlier than 4:00 P.M. It took Union forces at least another half hour to get up the hill. For Confederate sources see Trimble, "The Battle and Campaign of Gettysburg," *SHSP*, XXVI, 123–124; Memorandum Book, Entry for July 1, 1863, Jedediah Hotchkiss Papers, LC; Fremantle, *Three Months in the Southern States*, 254; Welch, *Letters to His Wife*, 66; Campbell Brown to Abner Doubleday, Dec. 6, 1881, Draft of a letter, Polk-Brown-Ewell Collection, UNC; Dr. J. E. Green Diary, North Carolina Department of Archives and History; *OR*, XXVII, pt. 2, pp. 656–657, 661. For Northern accounts see *ibid.*, pt. 1, pp. 250, 266, 283, 290, 293, 315, 328, 333, 335–336, 704, 730, 735, 739, 751.

181. *Ibid.*, p. 366.

182. The 7th Ind. regiment of Wadsworth's division arrived before 6:00 P.M., probably around 5:00 P.M. It was immediately ordered to the crest of Culp's Hill, where it constructed temporary breastworks. *Ibid.*, pp. 283–284. For the arrival of Eleventh Corps units see *ibid.*, pp. 715, 739–740.

183. *Ibid.*, pp. 349, 351; General Stannard's Diary, Typescript, Bachelder Papers; C. C. Benedict, *Vermont at Gettysburgh* [sic] (Burlington, 1870), 5; John B. Bachelder, Notes Relating to the Services of Troops at Gettysburg, 1863, MS, Huntington Library. Col. Francis V. Randall of the 13th Vt. said they arrived "at about 5 P.M." Gen. Stannard said they were in position at 7:30 P.M. There is often a considerable lapse of time between arrival and getting into position.

184. Geary said he was in position at 5:00 P.M. He must have been mistaken about the time because when Hancock sent his message to Meade at 5:25 P.M. he said there were no troops on the left. *OR*, XXVII, pt. 1, pp. 366, 825, 867. The strength of the Second Division was 4,338 on June 30. Selected Pages from Historical and Statistical Record of the Principal Military Commands in the Union and Confederate Armies, IV, 42, Entry 161, Record Group 94, NA. However, Geary said he took only 3,922 officers and men into the battle. *OR*, XXVII, pt. 1, p. 833. The smallest of Geary's three brigades was held in reserve to the left of the Baltimore Pike, probably near Power's Hill. *Ibid.*, pp. 825, 848.

185. Birney claimed he received an order to proceed to Gettysburg from Emmitsburg at 2:00 P.M. and made the ten miles or so over roads made "almost impassable by mud and the passage over it of the First and Eleventh Corps through the rain" in three and a half hours. This is truly a tall story. For one thing, it seems incredible that his men marched at a rate of about three miles an hour over bad roads. Secondly, he could not have started at 2:00 P.M. for Sickles did not give the order to advance before 3:15 P.M. The report of Gen. J. H. Hobart Ward is far more convincing. He said that upon receiving the order to move at 3:00 P.M., he and his men made a forced march, and they

arrived about dark. His statement checks more closely with other reports in his division and with that of C. P. Horton of the Twelfth Corps. *Ibid.*, pp. 482, 493, 502, 513; pt. 3, p. 463; Horton to Bachelder, Jan. 23, 1867, Bachelder Papers. The combined strength of these brigades was 4,393 on June 30. Selected Pages from Historical and Statistical Record of the Principal Military Commands in the Union and Confederate Armies, IV, 80, Entry 161, Record Group 94, NA.

186. According to returns of June 30 Williams' First Division of the Twelfth Corps had 3,770, but Gen. Thomas H. Ruger reported he had only 3,401 on July 1. *Ibid.*, IV, 42; *OR*, XXVII, pt. 1, p. 782.

187. During the course of the fighting Wainwright's Artillery Brigade lost seven of its twenty-eight guns, one being captured and the others disabled. Osborn lost four of twenty-six guns, two disabled and two captured. Heckman's battery with only two guns remaining was so used up that it was retired from the front line. Osborn had enough ammunition on hand to enable Wainwright to fill his depleted chests. Calef's Horse Battery remained with Buford's cavalry and so was not placed on Cemetery Hill. The Artillery Brigade of the Twelfth Corps had twenty guns. Birney brought eighteen guns with him in his march from Emmitsburg on July 1. *Ibid.*, pp. 154, 157, 161, 165, 229–235, 357–358, 360, 363, 365, 581, 748–749, 751, 753–758.

188. Col. John B. Bachelder, who spent years studying the battle, wrote the following estimate of the situation after the retreat: "There is no question but what a combined attack on Cemetery Hill made within one hour would have been successful. At the end of an hour the troops had been rallied, occupied strong positions . . . , and under the command . . . of General Hancock who . . . had reached the field would, in my opinion, have held the position against any attack from the troops then up." Bachelder to Gen. Fitzhugh Lee, Jan. 18, 1875, Bachelder Papers. It should be noted that Bachelder emphasized that to be successful the attack would have had to include the troops of both Ewell's and Hill's corps and have occurred within the hour.

NOTES TO CHAPTER XIII

1. After the battle Howard, Slocum, and Sickles set up headquarters near the caretaker's cottage. Howard, *Autobiography*, 419.

2. The hours of Meade's departure from Taneytown and arrival in Gettysburg are another matter of dispute. Meade said he broke up his headquarters at 10:00 P.M. and arrived on the field at 1:00 A.M. Other evidence suggests pretty conclusively that the hours he mentioned were too early and that he waited until midnight to see Sedgwick. Meade, *Life and Letters*, II, 41, 62; *OR*, XXVII, pt. 1, p. 115; Butterfield to Sedgwick, July 2, 1863, in *ibid.*, pt. 3, p. 484. Gen. Patrick said Meade left at 12:30 A.M. See Patrick Journal, Entry for July 6, 1863, LC. Howard was confident that the time of Meade's arrival was about 3:00 A.M., because there seemed so short an interval between it and day-

light. Howard, *Autobiography*, 422–423. There is also contradictory evidence about the weather on the night of July 1. Some contemporary accounts suggest that all day and throughout the night it was warm and cloudy with intermittent rain, whereas later ones stressed the brightness of the moon in a clear sky. See S. Thomas McCullough Diary, UV; William Byrnes Diary, 1863, DU; Hinkley, *With the Third Wisconsin*, 84; Comte de Paris, *Battle of Gettysburg*, 131; De Peyster, *The Decisive Conflicts of the Late Civil War*, 28, 74; Edward N. Whittier, "The Left Attack (Ewell's), Gettysburg," *Campaigns in Virginia, Maryland and Pennsylvania*, 340.

3. Meade, *Life and Letters*, II, 62. The description of Meade's manner came from Carl Schurz's recollections of him at 8:00 A.M. on July 2. Schurz, *Reminiscences*, III, 20.

4. Howard in his report said that this comment was directed to him at 3:00 A.M. *OR*, XXVII, pt. 1, p. 705. In his *Autobiography*, 422–423, he gave the impression that he was the first general Meade saw upon his arrival.

5. The Comte de Paris was very critical of Meade for not going immediately to Gettysburg. If Meade had done so, according to the count, he would have effected concentration of his army more rapidly. It is difficult to see how Meade could have brought his forces together much sooner than he did. Certain developments were beyond his control. He might, however, have gotten Slocum to move a little faster and prevented any misunderstanding between Hancock and Howard. Comte de Paris, *Battle of Gettysburg*, 238–239.

6. *OR*, XXVII, pt. 1, p. 368; CCW, *Report*, I, 405.

7. *Ibid.*; *OR*, XXVII, pt. 1, pp. 366, 369; pt. 3, pp. 466–468. Why Meade's dispatch was addressed to Hancock and Doubleday instead of Hancock and Howard is difficult to understand. Slocum acknowledged receipt of the message at 9:20 P.M.

8. *Ibid.*, pt. 1, p. 115; pt. 3, p. 465; CCW, *Report*, I, 405; Meade, *Life and Letters*, II, 39.

9. Memo prepared by George Meade and sent to Gen'l [Webb?], Dec. 9 or 11, 1885, Webb Collection. Though according to Hancock Mitchell left for Taneytown about 4:00 P.M., the salutation and contents of Meade's six o'clock dispatch clearly indicate that Mitchell arrived after it was sent. George Meade, for reasons he never gave, also concluded that Mitchell reached headquarters after 6:00 P.M. See Meade, *Life and Letters*, II, 39.

10. Taylor, *G. K. Warren*, 121–122; *OR*, pt. 1, p. 115; pt. 3, p. 466. Meade obtained the services of four natives from Taneytown to guide the Second and Third Corps to Gettysburg. Klein, ed., *Just South of Gettysburg*, 227–228.

11. *OR*, XXVII, pt. 3, pp. 462, 465. Meade said he sent the dispatch to Sedgwick after receiving Buford's message to Reynolds the night before warning him of a "strong concentration of the enemy at Gettysburg." CCW, *Report*, I, 348.

12. *OR*, XXVII, pt. 3, pp. 416, 457–458, 463–464, 468; LI, pt. 1, p. 1066; CCW, *Report*, I, 296–297.

13. *Ibid.*, 405.

14. *OR*, XXVII, pt. 1, p. 872. Meade sent an earlier message to Slocum

ordering him to advance Sykes's Fifth Corps. It was this dispatch which Sykes received. Meade's second message ordering the night march of the Fifth Corps which he sent directly to Sykes left headquarters at 7:00 P.M., the time the corps left Hanover. See *ibid.*, p. 126; pt. 3, pp. 467, 483.

15. *Ibid.*, pp. 465, 467–468.

16. On the present road from Taneytown to Westminster (Md. Route 97), which goes through Frizzelburg, the distance is eleven miles. The shortest way to Manchester from Westminster is over Md. Route 31, a distance of nine miles. In Civil War days the route was known as the Old Manchester Road.

17. Sedgwick did not say in his battle report when he received the message or when the corps got on the road. In testifying, probably from memory, he said the message reached him about seven o'clock the night of July 1. In the next breath he said the corps marched from 7:00 P.M., July 1, until 2:00 P.M. the next day. Sedgwick was off by at least an hour, for most of the battle reports mentioned 9:00 P.M. as the starting time. Two of them set 8:00 P.M. as the hour, and the rest with one exception gave 10:00 P.M. as the time. Since the big Sixth Corps formed a very long column, the spread of two hours in times of departure is understandable. However, 7:00 P.M. is way too early, and 1:00 A.M., July 2, much too late. See CCW, *Report,* I, 460; *OR,* XXVII, pt. 1, pp. 665, 667–668, 673, 675, 684, 686, 690, 692–693, 695.

18. The last message left headquarters at 11:00 P.M. *Ibid.,* pt. 3, pp. 469, 1086. About two miles from the center of Westminster the Sixth Corps took the Meadow Branch road to get to the Baltimore Pike. See map of the Civil War in Carroll County, Maryland: The Gettysburg Campaign, prepared by the Historical Society of Carroll County, Maryland, and Carroll County Planning and Zoning Commission, 1963.

19. The distance by modern road from Westminster to Gettysburg is the same by way of Littlestown or Taneytown. For a comparison of the routes and the distance the corps detoured, see *OR,* XXVII, pt. 1, pp. 665, 684.

20. *Ibid.*, pt. 3, p. 483.

21. *Ibid.*, pp. 484–485. For the suggestion that Meade wanted the presence of Sedgwick to boost his sagging morale see Williams, *Lincoln Finds a General,* II, 692.

22. Meade, *Life and Letters,* II, 41; Gibbon, *Recollections,* 133–134.

23. Sickles to Humphreys, Emmitsburg, July 1, 1863, 3:15 P.M., with Humphreys' note at bottom, A. A. Humphreys Papers, HSP. A copy of the dispatch but not of Humphreys' note is in *OR,* LI, pt. 1, p. 1066.

24. *Ibid.*, XXVII, pt. 1, p. 531.

25. C. B. Baldwin, Col. of 1st Mass. regt., to Bachelder, May 20, 1865, Bachelder Papers.

26. Humphreys to Archibald Campbell, Aug. 6, 1863, A. A. Humphreys Papers, HSP.

27. CCW, *Report,* I, 376.

28. *Ibid.*, 421. Butterfield, who was an expert on such matters, also said that this railroad was not shown on any of the railroad maps.

29. *OR,* XXVII, pt. 3, p. 419.

30. Hunt, "The Second Day at Gettysburg," *B&L*, III, pt. 1, p. 291; CCW, *Report*, I, 376–377, 448; Taylor, *G. K. Warren*, 121–122.

31. *OR*, XXVII, pt. 3, p. 417.

32. *Ibid.*, pt. 1, p. 531; Humphreys to Archibald Campbell, Aug. 6, 1863; Report of Maj. Charles Hamlin, asst. adj. gen., Second Division, Third Corps, Aug. 11, 1863, A. A. Humphreys Papers, HSP; Meade, *Life and Letters*, II, 41.

33. Reynolds, Howard, and Sickles used different roads to hasten the movements of their corps to Gettysburg. Stannard's brigade followed for at least part of the way the route taken by Rowley's Third Division of the First Corps in the morning. There is no doubt that Stannard had a guide who knew the location of the Confederate right flank near the Fairfield road upon the conclusion of the first day's battle. Otherwise the brigade might have gone through the same experience as Humphreys' division. See General Stannard's Diary, Entry for July 1, 1863, Typescript, Bachelder Papers.

34. Meade, *Life and Letters*, II, 62–63. As young George Meade described it, the general continued beyond Cemetery Ridge "to where the land dips before it rises abruptly at the base of Little Round Top. . . ." *Ibid.*, 63. George recalled that he had among his papers somewhere a copy of a statement made by Gen. Hunt, saying that he and Meade rode "as far as the Round Tops" after daylight on July 2. George Meade to Webb, Dec. 2, 1885, Webb Collection.

35. What happened to the Leister house was typical of the fate of private property within the area of the battlefield. It was "sadly shattered," and the poor widow who owned it complained "bitterly" of her losses. George J. Gross, *The Battlefield of Gettysburg* (Philadelphia, 1866), 20.

36. This information is the result of many personal visits to the battlefield, and an examination of John B. Bachelder's Isometric Drawing made of the Battlefield drawn in 1863, and maps of the United States Geological Survey. Walter Harrison, who wrote an account of Pickett's charge, told how he revised his impressions of the battlefield. "The ascent," he said, "from the point of starting under fire to the front line of the enemy, I find, upon subsequent examination, is not so precipitous as it appeared to me on the day of the battle, but it is gradual, and endures for fully *three quarters of a mile*, to the Emmettsburg road. . . ." [Walter Harrison] to Kemper, Oct. 2, 1869, James L. Kemper Correspondence, UV. Maj. Campbell Brown also visited Gettysburg after the battle and made the following observations about Cemetery Hill: "1. It is quite as high as I thought it, but the rise is more gradual and it is hardly so steep as I imagined. 2. The main street of the town (the Balto Pike) makes a slight angle at a point 250 or 300 yards below the summit of the hill, so that the guns of the battery there could not rake the streets so completely as I supposed." Maj. Campbell Brown's Notes on Gettysburg, July 2 and 3, 1878, R. S. Ewell Papers, UNC.

37. Patrick said he arrived a little before 6:00 A.M. Patrick Journal, Entry for July 6, 1863, LC. Meade testified that Butterfield reached headquarters between nine and ten in the morning. CCW, *Report*, I, 436.

38. *Ibid.*, 377, 436–437; Patrick Journal, Entry for July 6, 1863, LC; Gib-

bon, *Recollections*, 133–134; Column by Agate [Whitelaw Reid], July 4, in *Cincinnati Daily Gazette*, July 8, 1863.

39. *Ibid.*

40. CCW, *Report*, I, 349.

41. George Meade said he saw his father between 8:00 and 9:00 A.M. when there was a momentary lull in activity at headquarters. The general seemed relaxed and in a very good mood, evidently pleased with the way affairs were going. Meade, *Life and Letters*, II, 66.

42. *Ibid.*, 63; Gibbon, *Recollections*, 133–134; *OR*, XXVII, pt. 1, pp. 369, 400, 403, 407, 409, 415, 427, 456, 463–464; pt. 3, p. 1086; CCW, *Report*, I, 406. Lt. Col. Nelson H. Davis, asst. inspector general, U. S. Army, in response to an order from Meade at 11:00 A.M. described and drew a sketch of the position of the Second Corps. He said that the line extended from the Taneytown road, east of and roughly parallel to the Emmitsburg road for one-half mile. His sketch, however, showed the brigades in mass formation. *OR*, XXVII, pt. 3, pp. 487, 1087. When the brigades formed a line, the Second Corps was pushed farther south along the ridge, for Hancock said his line extended from the Taneytown road about halfway to Round Top. It is not clear whether he meant Little Round Top or Big Round Top. If the former, his corps covered a front about three-quarters of a mile in length, and if the latter, a good full mile. CCW, *Report*, I, 405–406.

43. Statement of Capt. Joseph M. Leeper, [no date], Typescript, Bachelder Papers. See also Col. Joshua L. Chamberlain's report of July 6, 1863, which substantiated Leeper's recollections, in *OR*, XXVII, pt. 1, p. 622. Sykes recorded the distances the corps had marched each day since Frederick. See *ibid.*, p. 595.

44. Chamberlain reported: "My men moved out with a promptitude and spirit extraordinary, the cheers and welcome they received on the road adding to their enthusiasm." *Ibid.*, p. 622. One diarist of the 118th Pa. regt. probably reflected the feeling of many Pennsylvanians when he wrote: "We may in all probability get into Penna. and I hope we shall, for if I am to die, I want to die on my native soil." Diary of William H. Read, Entry for June 29, 1863, private collection.

45. In identical dispatches to Butterfield and Slocum dated Bonaughtown, July 2, 1863, 12:30 A.M., Sykes said his corps had left Hanover at 7:00 P.M. and marched nine miles. He expected to resume his march at 4:00 A.M. *OR*, XXVII, pt. 3, p. 483. Apparently he got his men a little beyond Bonaughtown. Ewell's men captured the courier carrying the dispatch to Slocum. See *ibid.*, pt. 2, p. 446. As for the march, Read recalled that the moon shone brightly and the roads were "pretty good, so we got on very well, although exceedingly tired." Diary of William H. Read, Entry for July 6, 1863. For information on the first position of the Fifth Corps near Gettysburg see Statement of Capt. Joseph M. Leeper, [no date], Typescript, Bachelder Papers.

46. *Ibid.*; *OR*, XXVII, pt. 1, pp. 592, 595, 621, 633, 759; Survivors' Association, *History of the Corn Exchange Regiment, 118th Pennsylvania Volunteers* (Philadelphia, 1888), 238–241.

47. Asst. Adj. Genl. F. F. Kocke to Crawford, 10:00 A.M., June 30; 9:20 A.M., July 1; [7:00 P.M., July 1?], 1863, Samuel W. Crawford Papers, LC; *OR*, XXVII, pt. 1, p. 68; pt. 3, pp. 424–425.

48. A. P. Morrison to his brother Will, July 21, 1863, Torrance Collection, PDPR; *OR*, XXVII, pt. 1, pp. 652–653, 657.

49. The brigades were the following: Third Brigade from the First Division under Col. P. Regis De Trobriand, and Third Brigade from the Second Division under Col. George C. Burling. The batteries were the 1st N.Y. Light, Battery D, Capt. George B. Winslow, and N.Y. Light, 4th Battery, Capt. James E. Smith. Most accounts agree that these units reached the battlefield between 9:00 and 10:00 A.M. *Ibid.*, pp. 159–161, 482, 519, 522–523, 531, 570, 575, 577; pt. 3, p. 467.

50. *Ibid.*, pt. 1, pp. 519, 570; pt. 3, p. 467.

51. *Ibid.*, pt. 1, p. 484.

52. *Ibid.*, p. 570.

53. *Ibid.*, pp. 531, 570, 575; pt. 3, p. 467. De Trobriand explained that it had rained and the road was bad. His brigade followed Burling's. As they took the crossroad from the Peach Orchard to Cemetery Ridge, enemy sharpshooters fired a few shots at them. De Trobriand, *Four Years in the Army of the Potomac*, 493–494.

54. Fremantle, *Three Months in the Southern States*, 258.

55. Boatner, *Civil War Dictionary*, 64, 84, 106, 128, 237–238, 350, 417, 760, 889.

56. *OR*, XXVII, pt. 1, p. 872.

57. *Ibid.*, p. 241. The canny Hunt was well aware of the frailties of commanders of infantrymen, and unbeknownst to Hooker in the Chancellorsville campaign he had formed a special ammunition column attached to the Artillery Reserve which carried twenty rounds per gun over and above the authorized amount. He assured Meade he had enough ammunition for the battle, but "none for idle cannonades, the besetting sin of some of our commanders." Henry J. Hunt, "The Second Day at Gettysburg," *B&L*, III, pt. 1, pp. 299–300.

58. *OR*, XXVII, pt. 3, p. 468.

59. *Ibid.*, pp. 486–487; CCW, *Report*, I, 377.

60. Hancock to Humphreys, Oct. 10, 1863, A. A. Humphreys Papers, HSP; *OR*, XXVII, pt. 1, p. 72. Meade freely admitted to the Committee on the Conduct of the War, a group which favored action rather than thought, that it had been his "desire . . . to receive the attack of the enemy, and fight a defensive rather than an offensive battle, for the reason that . . . [he] was satisfied . . . [his] chances of success were greater in a defensive battle than an offensive one. . . ." CCW, *Report*, I, 439.

61. Circular to Corps Commanders, July 2, 1863, 11:00 A.M., George Gordon Meade Papers, HSP.

62. *OR*, XXVII, pt. 3, p. 487.

63. CCW, *Report*, I, 436.

64. *Ibid.*, 442.

65. Meade, *Life and Letters,* II, 169–170; CCW, *Report,* I, 298.

66. *Ibid.,* 349.

67. *Ibid.,* 466.

68. This passage was omitted from the first sentence on p. 182 in Meade, *Life and Letters,* II. For some reason the general's grandson left it out when he edited the original letters for publication. See Meade to Mrs. Meade, Mar. 20, 1864, George Gordon Meade Papers, HSP.

69. CCW, *Report,* I, 436, 452. Gen. Hunt recalled a conversation with Meade about supplies of artillery ammunition which may have contributed to the idea that Meade intended to withdraw from Gettysburg. Meade had heard that someone had neglected to bring up the entire artillery ammunition train of one corps. He feared that this oversight, plus the heavy expenditure of shells the previous day, had reduced supplies to a dangerous level and there would not be enough for a major battle. Assured by Hunt of sufficient supplies, Meade was "much relieved and expressed his satisfaction." Hunt commented that if Meade was considering retreat, then was the time for him to have said something about it to his chief of artillery. Hunt, "Second Day at Gettysburg," *B&L,* III, pt. 1, pp. 299–300.

70. CCW, *Report,* I, 425.

71. *Ibid.,* 436.

72. Webb to William F. Fox, Nov. 1, 1898, Webb Collection. Fox's account gave Butterfield credit for the rapid concentration of the army, and tended to deprecate Meade's generalship in other respects as well. See Fox, ed., *New York at Gettysburg,* I, 34–37.

73. Commenting on Butterfield in a letter to Gibbon on Mar. 15, 1864, Meade said: "To be sure when the question is asked, why was not the order *issued* and why did not the army retreat? the gentlemen will be puzzled for an answer because you know from the time I arrived on the ground, up to 4 P.M., when Lee attacked, and after the attack *all day* and *night* there was no difficulty at any moment in withdrawing by the Taneytown road, Baltimore Pike, and Bonnaughtown road." Gibbon, *Recollections,* 186–188.

74. Years later when repeating his story Butterfield offered a questionable explanation as to why the order was not issued, in the following words: "The withdrawal in *echelon* ordered, but not begun,—stopped by Longstreet's attack on Sickles. . . ." Butterfield et al., "Further Recollections of Gettysburg," *North American Review,* CLII, 282.

75. OR, XXVII, pt. 1, p. 261; pt. 3, p. 1086. Newton arrived before 6:15 A.M.

76. The consolidated field return for the Army of the Potomac on July 4, 1863, gave the strength of Lockwood's brigade as 1,462 officers and men. His losses during the battle were 174, so it is safe to say that his command numbered a little over 1,600. Since there is a record of the size of only one of the regiments, the figure of 1,100 is based upon a reasonable guess. The 150th N.Y. reported having 579 enlisted men but mentioned nothing about the number of officers. This group and the First Potomac Home Brigade, Md. Infantry, arrived July 2. The First Regiment, Eastern Shore Md. Volunteers, came July 3.

The two Md. regiments are assumed to be of the same size. *Ibid.*, pt. 1, pp. 153, 184, 810.

77. Williams to his daughters, July 6, 1863, in *Alpheus Williams Letters*, 227.

78. Williams to Bachelder, Apr. 21, 1864, Bachelder Papers.

79. *OR*, XXVII, pt. 1, pp. 261, 369, 759, 773, 778, 825–826; Gibbon, *Recollections*, 133–134; CCW, *Report*, I, 405. Lt. Col. Rufus Dawes recalled that as his regiment went to rejoin the Iron Brigade on Culp's Hill late in the afternoon of July 1, the regimental wagon came up bringing a dozen spades and shovels. When the 6th Wis. took a place on the right of the brigade, he ordered the men to entrench without being told by division headquarters. They worked with a will. As soon as one man became tired, another would seize a spade and begin to dig furiously. Dawes, "With the Sixth Wisconsin at Gettysburg," *Sketches of War History*, Ohio Commandery, MOLLUS, III, 383.

80. Meade, *Life and Letters*, II, 66.

81. *Ibid.*, 67. Up to this point father and son agreed in their stories. For the general's version see CCW, *Report*, I, 331. Meade said his original instructions to Sickles were for him to connect with Hancock's left and to extend his left to the "Round Top mountain, plainly visible, if it was practicable to occupy it." *Ibid.* In the context of his testimony, when he referred to "Round Top mountain" he meant Little, not Big, Round Top.

82. *Ibid.*

83. *Ibid.* Capt. Meade's version adds something omitted from his father's account. He said that after delivering his second message, he was told by Sickles that his troops were then moving and would be in position shortly. Before he mounted his horse to go to the front, Sickles murmured something about Geary's troops not having had any position, because they had been only massed in the vicinity. Then Randolph asked Capt. Meade to get Hunt to come out there to look at some positions he had selected for artillery. Meade, *Life and Letters*, II, 67. Apparently nothing came of the request for Hunt's help at this time, because he was busy inspecting the battlefield. When Hunt returned to headquarters about 11:00 A.M. Meade called him over and said Sickles, who was there, wanted him to examine his line or the line he wished to occupy. Meade told him to do it. CCW, *Report*, I, 449.

84. *Ibid.*, 449–451.

85. *Ibid.*, 332. In his battle report Sedgwick did not give the time of his arrival, but in testifying before the Committee on the Conduct of the War he gave the hour as about 2:00 P.M. See CCW, *Report*, I, 460. None of the reports gave an hour earlier than 2:00 P.M., and most of them set the arrival time as between 3:30 and 5:00 P.M. Meade in his message of 3:00 P.M. said the Sixth Corps "is just coming in." See *OR*, XXVII, pt. 1, pp. 72, 665, 668, 671, 673, 675, 678, 680, 684, 686, 688, 690, 693, 695.

86. *Ibid.*, 72.

87. *Ibid.*, pt. 3, p. 1086. The enemies of Meade, referring to this gathering as a council of war probably because it sounded more portentous, implied, if they did not say so, that it was held for the purpose of considering Meade's

proposal to retreat. See Sickles' and Butterfield's testimonies in CCW, *Report*, I, 298–299, 424–425. In contrast Warren said the conference was nothing more than one of many informal meetings where the officers explained to each other how things stood. *Ibid.*, 378. In his battle report Gen. Sykes said Meade sent for him at 3:00 P.M., and while he and other corps commanders were conversing with him the battle started. *OR*, XXVII, pt. 1, p. 592. Hancock recalled that he had just left Meade a few minutes before. He said Sickles' advance surprised him, for he understood from Meade that he would keep on the defensive. Hancock to Humphreys, Oct. 10, 1863, A. A. Humphreys Papers, HSP. See also Meade, *Life and Letters*, II, 71–72.

88. CCW, *Report*, I, 332.

89. Letter of G. K. Warren, [no date], in Taylor, *G. K. Warren*, 122–123. See also Warren's testimony in CCW, *Report*, I, 377.

90. *Ibid.*, 332.

91. Quoted in Isaac R. Pennypacker, "Military Historians and History," *PMHB*, LIII, 40. Whether Meade actually said this is another matter, but the quotation reflects very well the temperament of the man and the extent to which he was provoked.

92. CCW, *Report*, I, 297–298.

93. *Ibid.* The respective accounts of Meade and Sickles about their meeting before the battle are so far apart that it is virtually impossible to reconcile the discrepancies. Sickles placed Meade near headquarters, thus heightening the suggestion of a petty, querulous, spineless general who exerted no leadership, but nevertheless wasted the time of his more able and active subordinates by demanding their attendance at useless conferences. Meade on the other hand naturally wanted to convey the idea of an alert, vigorous, and very busy commander who, though giving his generals considerable latitude to work out problems for themselves, kept a sharp eye on their conduct. It is not surprising then that he pictured himself going out to inspect Sickles' line and having his encounter with the general there. Meade's self-portrayal, though not without blemishes, is more in keeping with his character and his career than Sickles' unlovely caricature. It is quite reasonable to suppose that Sickles had started out in response to the second summons to headquarters when Meade met him well on his way to the Third Corps line.

94. *OR*, XXVII, pt. 1, pp. 16, 116.

95. CCW, *Report*, I, 298.

96. His personal characteristics and his political activities are brought out clearly in Swanberg's excellent biography, *Sickles the Incredible*, 77–125, 236–240.

97. Edwin B. Coddington, "The Strange Reputation of General George G. Meade: A Lesson in Historiography," *The Historian*, XXIII, 154–155, 157–159.

98. A copy of the letter of Mar. 12 is in *OR*, XXVII, pt. 1, pp. 128–136, and also in Meade, *Life and Letters*, II, 323–331. Copies of the replies to "Historicus," which also appeared in the *Herald*, and his rebuttal are included in *ibid.*, 331–340. Meade believed that Sickles either wrote or dictated the let-

ters. Halleck, Humphreys, and Webb agreed with him; so does Sickles' twenti-eth-century biographer, A. W. Swanberg. *OR*, XXVII, pt. 1, pp. 128, 137; Humphreys to his wife, Mar. 22, 1864, A. A. Humphreys Papers, HSP; Webb to his father, Mar. 15, 23, 1864, Webb Collection; Swanberg, *Sickles the Incredible*, 252, 257. In contrast Freeman Cleaves, Meade's latest biographer, disagrees with these conclusions and accuses Col. John B. Bachelder of having been the author of the letters. He bases his charge upon a statement written Apr. 23, 1925—more than sixty years after the event—by one R. G. Carter, a retired captain of the regular army and veteran of the Fifth Corps. Carter claimed that Bachelder had been a "henchman" of Sickles and as such had convinced historians by "an avalanche of propaganda that Sickles held back Longstreet"; but he did not directly identify Bachelder as the writer of the "Historicus" letters. Quoted in W. A. Graham, *The Custer Myth* (Harrisburg, Pa., 1953), 318. Nowhere in the Bachelder Papers, which include extensive correspondence with former Northern and Southern soldiers and the manu-script of his own history of the battle, can there be found evidence to bear out Carter's statement and Cleaves's accusation. The timing and character of the "Historicus" letters, Sickles' attack on Meade's generalship before the Commit-tee on the Conduct of the War, and his other activities against his former com-mander force the conclusion that Carter and Cleaves were in error and that Meade correctly guessed the identity of "Historicus."

99. See also Coddington, "Strange Reputation of General Meade," *Historian*, XXIII, 154–160, 164. A good summary of the Sickles thesis is found in a letter of G. G. Benedict to the editors of the *Philadelphia Weekly Press*, Aug. 7, 1886, quoted in Meade, *Life and Letters*, II, 350–351. Sickles consistently main-tained throughout his life that he made the advance on his own responsibility and that he would have welcomed a court-martial or a court of inquiry for his conduct at Gettysburg. Yet he protested too much, for he wanted everyone far and wide, from President Theodore Roosevelt to a son of one of his old com-rades at arms, to know how right he had been. Eagerly and almost pathetically he continued to cite the testimony of two famous generals as vindication for his conduct. Gen. Phil Sheridan, no admirer of Meade, who really knew nothing about the battle, pronounced Sickles' move as "well advised and proper." A. G. Curtin to Maj. Gen. Daniel E. Sickles, Oct. 18, 1889, Copy, Bachelder Papers. What pleased Sickles most was to have his old enemy "Pete" Longstreet say that the Third Corps won the battle of Gettysburg. In writing to an old friend about Longstreet's opinion Sickles said: "Put that feather in your caps. Dia-monds were trumps that day." A figure of a diamond was the insignia of the Third Corps. Sickles to F. M. Thayer, Oct. 9, 1903, D. E. Sickles Press Letter Book, 1899–1912, DU. See also Sickles to Pres. Theodore Roosevelt, June 6, 1904; *id.* to Capt. Richard B. Bartlett, Feb. 19, 1904; *id.* to Col. William Jay, Feb. 27, 1912, *ibid.* The immediate adversaries of July 2, Longstreet and Sick-les, both of whom were greatly criticized by their respective comrades, turned to each other for comfort and ultimately became intimate friends and admirers. Sickles told a story of a reunion the two crippled old veterans enjoyed at a St. Patrick's day banquet in 1892 in Atlanta, Ga. After indulging perhaps too

freely in hot Irish whiskey punch, they were unable to find a carriage so Longstreet courteously guided Sickles to his hotel on foot. Not to be outdone, Sickles insisted on escorting Longstreet to his quarters, and so they kept up their peregrinations between the hotels until the wee hours of the morning. *Id.* to Mrs. James Longstreet, June 14, 1904, *ibid.*

100. Hancock to Humphreys, Oct. 10, 1863, A. A. Humphreys Papers, HSP; Gibbon, *Recollections,* 136.

101. *OR,* XXVII, pt. 1, p. 759.

102. *Ibid.,* pp. 778–779.

103. George G. Meade to G. G. Benedict, Mar. 16, 1870, in Meade, *Life and Letters,* II, 353. Geary said he formed a line about half a mile west of the Baltimore Pike which stretched from the left of the First Corps on Cemetery Ridge to a range of hills south of the town. He placed two regiments of the First Brigade on the hills. *OR,* XXVII, pt. 1, p. 825. These regiments were the 5th Ohio and the 147th Pa. *Ibid.,* pp. 836, 839, 846; C. P. Horton to Bachelder, Jan. 23, 1867, Bachelder Papers.

104. *OR,* XXVII, pt. 1, p. 482.

105. *Ibid.,* p. 531. Humphreys mentioned that Caldwell's division of the Second Corps to the right of him was also massed on the crest. At a preparatory stage before a battle, this formation was not unusual.

106. CCW, *Report,* I, 449.

107. Letter of Tremain to his family, July 10, 1863, quoted in H. E. Tremain, *Two Days of War, A Gettysburg Narrative and Other Excursions* (New York, 1905), 104–105. The italics were Tremain's.

108. None of the reports gave the time of departure, but judging by references to certain other developments they probably left between 10:00 A.M. and noon. *OR,* XXVII, pt. 1, pp. 515, 914, 927–928, 939, 1032.

109. CCW, *Report,* I, 359.

110. *OR,* XXVII, pt. 3, p. 490.

111. Gen. Gibbon recalled an incident at headquarters during the battle which threw light both on Meade's temperament and his system of command: "Pleasonton came to ask him [Meade] some question about the disposition of his cavalry. It struck me that Meade answered him very curtly by saying, 'I can give you no detailed instructions but simply want you to protect well the front and flanks of this army with your Cavalry.'" Gibbon, *Recollections,* 129.

112. Meade, *Life and Letters,* II, 71; *OR,* XXVII, pt. 1, p. 956; pt. 3, pp. 489–490; CCW, *Report,* I, 298.

113. *Ibid.,* 359. See also Meade, *Life and Letters,* II, 71.

114. Selected Pages from Historical and Statistical Record of the Principal Military Commands in the Union and Confederate Armies, IV, 60, Entry 161, Record Group 94, NA; *OR,* XXVII, pt. 1, p. 185.

115. *Ibid.,* p. 202; pt. 3, pp. 486–489. The signal officers kept referring to a station on Round Top Mountain. Whether they meant Big or Little Round Top or both is not clear. At the time of the battle Union officers used the names loosely or called the hills by other names. As a result their reports were confusing. It is known that the signal corps used Little Round Top as a signal station,

and they might have used Big Round Top as well, though it was heavily wooded.

116. *Ibid.*, pt. 2, p. 697.

117. *Ibid.*, pt. 1, pp. 943, 956, 970, 991–992; Selected Pages from Historical and Statistical Record of the Principal Military Commands in the Union and Confederate Armies, IV, 60, Entry 161, Record Group 94, NA.

118. *OR*, XXVII, pt. 1, pp. 482, 514–518; Francis A. Lord, *They Fought for the Union* (Harrisburg, Pa., 1960), 144–145.

119. *OR*, XXVII, pt. 1, pp. 515, 927–928, 939, 1032.

120. CCW, *Report*, I, 449.

121. There is conflicting evidence about who deserved credit for the idea of reconnoitering the woods. Hunt said that after he had pointed it out to Sickles, Sickles decided to send a couple of companies of Berdan's sharpshooters to investigate. Berdan said he perceived danger there and asked permission to send a group to scout, while Birney claimed he worried about the woods and got permission to send Berdan's men and the 3rd Maine to feel the enemy's right. *Ibid.*; *OR*, XXVII, pt. 1, pp. 482, 515–517.

122. *Ibid.*, pp. 482, 507, 515–517; pt. 3, p. 488; CCW, *Report*, I, 366, 449. None of the Union officers who referred to Berdan's reconnaissance and his clash with Wilcox' men mentioned the time of the affair. Judging by the hours they gave for other events and developments connected with it, this skirmish occurred around noon. Wilcox, however, said it was over as early as 9:00 A.M. The agreement among Union reports leads to the conclusion that he may have confused this brush with an earlier but less important one. Skirmishers on both sides periodically fired away at each other during the morning. At 11:55 A.M. the signal station on Little Round Top reported that the rebels were in force and Union skirmishers had given way; and that one mile west of the station the woods were full of Confederates. Although Berdan's skirmish took place one and a half miles northwest of the station, the message might have been referring to this affair.

123. Berdan may have seen Longstreet's columns off at a distance. According to Wilcox, they did not move south past his right flank until about 2:00 P.M., the time Berdan reported to Birney. Birney claimed he plainly saw enemy columns from the left of his position about 2:30 P.M. Capt. L. B. Norton, chief signal officer of the army, reported that the signal officer on "Round Top Mountain" discovered the enemy "massing upon General Sickles' left" at 3:30 P.M. Allowing for the time it took Berdan to withdraw from his advanced position and report to Birney around 2:00 P.M., he most likely did not observe Longstreet's men later than 1:30 P.M. See *ibid.*, 366; *OR*, XXVII, pt. 1, p. 202; pt. 2, p. 617.

124. CCW, *Report*, I, 298.

125. These comments are the result of visits to the battlefield and study of the maps of the U.S. Geological Survey.

126. Swanberg, *Sickles the Incredible*, 208; Sickles to H. P. Smith, Aug. 11, 1911, D. E. Sickles Press Letter Book, 1899–1912, DU. Doubleday, who certainly was no defender of Meade, said there was some low ground in every

position. This fact alone, he said, "hardly justified" Sickles' advance so far to the front. Doubleday to Bates, Apr. 4, 1874, Bates Collection.

127. CCW, *Report*, I, 453–454; Hunt, "Second Day at Gettysburg," *B&L*, III, pt. 1, pp. 295–296, 302.

128. *Ibid.*, 301–303; CCW, *Report*, I, 332, 377, 391, 449; *OR*, XXVII, pt. 1, pp. 482–483, 532.

129. CCW, *Report*, I, 391.

130. Hunt, "Second Day at Gettysburg," *B&L*, III, pt. 1, p. 301. Gibbon observed that the position of the Third Corps all the way to the Peach Orchard was well commanded by batteries of the Second Corps, which, however, could not be used without hurting Humphreys' men should an enemy attack force them back to Cemetery Ridge. Gibbon, "Another View of Gettysburg," *North American Review*, CLII, 712. See also Gibbon, *Recollections*, 135. One Confederate critic stressed the faulty character of the line because of the salient at the Peach Orchard. Long, *Memoirs of Lee*, 283. Alexander found nothing good about the position and called it "bad tactics," for it exchanged strong ground for weak and gave the Confederates an opportunity not otherwise possible. Alexander, *Military Memoirs*, 393. Generally agreeing with Alexander, Wilcox said that "Sickles' position was certainly such as to invite attack, not so much from any salient that may have been formed by refusing his left, but from the fact that his right flank was exposed. His position was faulty in the extreme, as the result of the collision must have shown him." [Review of John Esten Cooke's *Life of Lee* for the Southern Historical Society, no date], Cadmus M. Wilcox Papers, LC.

131. Sickles said that Little Round Top, "the key of our position on the left flank," was unoccupied, as he was unable to extend his line "further than the base of the hill, and, of course was wholly unable to defend it." Sickles to H. P. Smith, Aug. 11, 1911, D. E. Sickles Press Letter Book, DU. In this letter he was claiming that his corps could not cover a section of Meade's main line of a little less than a mile in length. In earlier accounts he asserted or implied that by advancing his men on the other line which everyone recognized was longer, he could and did find by some sleight of hand enough men to occupy Little Round Top. In other words, Sickles changed his story to justify his conduct and also revealed faulty logic. CCW, *Report*, I, 298; *OR*, XXVII, pt. 1, pp. 130–131 ["The Battle of Gettysburg" by "Historicus" in the *New York Herald*, Mar. 12, 1864].

132. Though the Second Corps was usually judged to be larger than the Third by as few as 145, or by as many as 1,071 officers and men, there is rather impressive evidence that on July 2 the opposite was true: that the Third Corps was stronger than the Second. Hancock reported that he went into battle with 10,000 officers and men, while on July 1 the Third Corps headquarters reported the corps as having 12,169 officers and men. *OR*, XXVII, pt. 1, p. 375; Memoranda Field Return, Hdqu. 3d Army Corps, July 1, '63, signed by Sickles [?], Field Reports, George Gordon Meade Papers, HSP. See also *OR*, XXVII, pt. 1, pp. 151, 375, 534; Selected Pages from Historical and Statistical Record of the Principal Military Commands in the Union and Confederate Armies, IV, 80,

143–144, Entry 161, Record Group 94, NA; *Philadelphia Weekly Times*, Feb. 2, 1878; Tremain, *Two Days of War*, 104; Gross, *Battlefield of Gettysburg*, 8.

133. In commenting on Sickles' move one student of the battle emphasized the ruggedness of the terrain, rather than the distance of the new position from the main line, as making it "difficult if not impossible to reinforce" the Third Corps. See Battine, *Crisis of the Confederacy*, 216. He got the cart before the horse, for the reverse was true.

134. Sickles advanced his corps in two stages. The final advance was made just before the Confederate attack, which started around 4:00 P.M. CCW, *Report*, I, 298; *OR*, XXVII, pt. 1, pp. 531–532. See also *ibid.*, pp. 500, 511, 525, 543, 558, 573, 578. Capt. George Meade said the advance began about two o'clock. He was probably referring to the first stage during which Sickles moved the line a few hundred yards in advance of the original one. Meade, *Life and Letters*, II, 77.

135. A. A. Humphreys, "The Fight for Round Top," *Philadelphia Weekly Times*, Feb. 2, 1878.

136. Meade to G. G. Benedict, Mar. 16, 1870, in Meade, *Life and Letters*, II, 353.

137. *Cf. post*, XVII, 442–443.

138. On June 30 the Sixth Corps had present for duty equipped 14,516 officers and men in the infantry, 124 in the cavalry, and 1,039 in the artillery. Its 48 guns made a sizeable contribution to the strength of the Union artillery. *OR*, XXVII, pt. 1, p. 151.

139. On June 30 all of Gregg's division reached Westminster and from there went on to Hanover Junction. At 1:30 P.M., July 1, army headquarters ordered Gregg to Hanover to join the Third Cavalry Division and assume command of both divisions. Before doing so he was to place one brigade and a battery at Manchester to cover the right flank and protect the depot at Westminster. *Ibid.*, pt. 1, p. 970; pt. 3, pp. 469–472.

140. Charles A. Harrison, Diary of Three Years Service in the United States Army . . . , PU; Diary of Charles Francis Adams, Entry for July 2, 1863, MHS; Sanford N. Truesdale to [his brother, Ozias E. Truesdale], July 9, 1863, Connecticut State Library; Stevens, *Three Years in the Sixth Corps*, 240–241, 252–253; Mason W. Tyler, *Recollections of the Civil War* (New York, 1912), 102–103; Report of Col. Oliver Edwards, 37th Mass. regt., May 11, 1878, MS, Union Battle Reports, 1861–1865, Record Group 94, NA.

141. James S. Anderson, "The March of the Sixth Corps to Gettysburg," *War Papers*, Wisconsin Commandery, MOLLUS, IV, 80–81.

142. Tyler, *Recollections*, 102–103.

143. Connor to his father, July 10, 1863, Selden Connor Correspondence, Brown University Library.

144. An aide on Sedgwick's staff summed up well the significance of the army's marching in the Gettysburg campaign: "Now and then well ordered marches as effectively beat an enemy as the most decisive battle could do. . . ." Capt. R. F. Halsted to Miss [Emily] Sedgwick, July 17, 1863, Sedg-

wick Commissions, etc., Cornwall Historical Collection, No. 400, Cornwall, Conn., Library.

NOTES TO CHAPTER XIV

1. Fremantle, *Three Months in the Southern States*, 256.
2. Ross, *Cities and Camps*, 47.
3. Jacobs, *Rebel Invasion*, 28.
4. Fremantle, *Three Months in the Southern States*, 256; Jacobs, *Rebel Invasion*, 28.
5. Fremantle, *Three Months in the Southern States*, 256. See also Pettit to his wife, July 8, 1863, William B. Pettit Papers, UNC.
6. Longstreet, "Lee in Pennsylvania," *Annals*, 416–417, 420–422; Longstreet, "The Mistakes of Gettysburg," *Annals*, 626–627; Longstreet, "Lee's Right Wing at Gettysburg," *B&L*, III, pt. 1, pp. 329–330. In his various accounts Longstreet changed the wording of the dialogue between him and Lee. Also he failed to make clear the precise nature of his proposal.
7. Col G. F. R. Henderson, author of the classic biography of "Stonewall" Jackson, was sharply critical of Longstreet's statement in his memoirs that when the invasion of Pa. was first broached, he assented to Lee's plan on condition that Confederate tactics be purely defensive. Henderson said Longstreet did not explain "on what grounds he considered himself entitled to dictate conditions to his superior officer." He had no mandate from the government to act as Lee's adviser, for he was a subordinate officer; yet he entered on the campaign with the idea that Lee must obey his suggestions. Henderson, "Review of General Longstreet's Book 'From Manassas to Appomattox,'" *SHSP*, XXXIX, 110. Gen. Hooker, who for reasons not clear considered Longstreet a greater general than Lee, in this instance disagreed with Longstreet's idea that it would be possible to conduct a campaign defensive in tactics and offensive in strategy. Hooker to Bates, Nov. 13, 1877; July 26, 30, 1879, Bates Collection. For further discussion of whether Lee agreed to Longstreet's views on the way to operate during the campaign, *cf. ante*, I, 10–11.
8. Longstreet, "Lee in Pennsylvania," *Annals*, 421.
9. Longstreet, *Memoirs*, 384.
10. E. P. Alexander, who was a great admirer of Longstreet, wrote of this statement: "Many an old soldier will *never forgive* Longstreet such a sentiment & yet I do not believe he ever knew how it reads to a lover of Lee." Alexander to Mr. Bancroft, Oct. 30, 1904, James Longstreet Letters, DU.
11. "Letter from Major Scheibert, of the Prussian Royal Engineers," *SHSP*, V, 91–92. Longstreet said that Lee suffered from his old trouble, sciatica, during the campaign. Longstreet, *Memoirs*, 432. W. W. Blackford of Stuart's staff told how on a visit to army headquarters he observed that Lee walked as if "he was weak and in pain." A staff officer told him upon inquiry that the general was suffering "a good deal from an attack of diarrhea." Blackford, *War Years with*

Jeb Stuart, 230. There is no evidence, however, that these ailments, if they plagued Lee, in any way incapacitated him for command.

12. "Letter from Major Scheibert," *SHSP,* V, 90–93.

13. The suggestion that Longstreet's attitude might have had a great deal to do with Lee's unhappy frame of mind came from Longstreet himself. In his memoirs he said that on the morning of the 1st Lee was in his "usual cheerful spirits." Longstreet, *Memoirs,* 351–352. What occurred to cause Lee's agitation? Certainly not the defeat of two corps of the Army of the Potomac. Maj. G. M. Sorrel, Longstreet's chief of staff, summed up the difficulty between the two generals when he said: "He [Longstreet] did not want to fight on the ground or on the plan adopted by the general-in-chief. As Longstreet was not to be made willing and Lee refused to change or could not change, the former failed to conceal some anger." Sorrel, *Recollections of a Confederate Staff Officer,* 167.

14. Fremantle said that Longstreet was never far from Lee, "who relies very much upon his judgment." Then he added that the soldiers "invariably" spoke of Longstreet as "the best fighter in the whole army." Fremantle, *Three Months in the Southern States,* 190, 198. For further information on the close collaboration between Lee and Longstreet, see Thos J. Goree to Longstreet, May 17, 1875, Microfilm, James Longstreet Papers, DU; Sorrel, *Recollections,* 166. The exact nature of the relationship between Lee and Longstreet has been lost to posterity because, as Sorrel said, communications between the two men were "in the main . . . verbally or occasionally by note direct."

15. "Letter from Major Scheibert," *SHSP,* V, 90–91. In fine print, so to speak, Longstreet admitted that Lee had considered all worthwhile ideas proposed to him in the campaign. Longstreet to Dr. A. B. Longstreet, July 24, 1863, in Longstreet, "Lee in Pennsylvania," *Annals,* 415.

16. Maurice, ed., *Aide-de-Camp of Lee,* 232.

17. *OR,* XXVII, pt. 2, pp. 308, 318. See Long, *Memoirs of Lee,* 276–279, for a full discussion of various courses of action Lee considered. At the same time Meade was shrewdly appraising the situation in much the same way as Lee. Though not appreciating Lee's worries about his long trains in case of retreat, Meade decided that Lee could not wait around to maneuver, but would have to attack or retire. CCW, *Report,* I, 349

18. *OR,* XXVII, pt. 2, pp. 308, 318. In contrast to the prevailing jubilation in the Confederate camp over the first day's victory, Longstreet felt depressed because to him it would have been better had they not fought than to have left undone what they did. He went on to say that when action broke off on July 1, Union forces were left occupying a position from which it would take the "whole army to drive them . . . at . . . great sacrifice." [Dr.] J. S. D. Cullen [medical director of First Corps] to Longstreet, May 18, 1875, in Longstreet, *Memoirs,* 383–384. Col. Henderson thought Longstreet's idea of a turning movement had merit, but it would take time to execute it and this would allow the enemy to concentrate his army, which he estimated was stronger than the Confederates' by 25,000 men. Henderson, "Review of General Longstreet's

Book," *SHSP*, XXXIX, 111. Maj. Scheibert believed it would not have been difficult to maneuver Meade out of his formidable position by marching vigorously either to the north or east. Scheibert, *Seven Months in the Rebel States*, Hoole, ed., 118. In rebuttal Gen. Howard told Longstreet thirty years after the event that a Confederate movement toward the right would have "exposed Lee's communications. . . ." H. W[hite], "Gettysburg Thirty Years After," *The Nation*, LVI, 327. Gen. Bradley T. Johnson, C. S. A., summed up as well as anyone the difficulties of a turning movement: "I have . . . [wondered] why Lee attacked instead of maneuvering & making Meade attack him—but have long since come to the conclusion—that owing to the absence of Stuart—he found himself in the presence of the enemy before he knew it, & then it was too late to move around Meade's left toward Emmittsburgh or Middletown & fight Meade. . . . Such a move w[oul]d have exposed his whole flank—yet he did it at Chancellorsville. He could not repeat it in the open country . . . where all his movements were at once known. . . ." Johnson to Early, Mar. 19, 1876, Jubal A. Early Papers, LC.

19. Dispatch from Special Correspondent, Hagerstown, July 8, in the *Times* [London], Aug. 18, 1863. This correspondent had been with Lee for a year and possessed the perspective with which to judge affairs at Gettysburg. He prefaced this quotation by saying that it struck him that both Gens. Lee and Longstreet yielded "reluctantly, and *contre-coeur* to the policy of pressing forward at once. . . ." Undoubtedly, he said, Longstreet wanted to wait for Pickett's division. Lee was "more anxious and ruffled than I had ever seen him before, though it required close observation to detect it." However, he went on to say, the success of the first day's battle, memories of previous victories, the impracticality of turning either Federal flank, and the impatience of Gen. Hood and his fine division (lightly engaged at Fredericksburg and absent at Chancellorsville) "combined to inspire the leading Confederate Generals with an undue contempt for the enemy," in spite of the strength of the Federal position which for "strength and eligibility for defence has not been surpassed during 27 months of warfare." Therefore it was deemed desirable not to wait for Pickett.

20. Longstreet to Wigfall, Aug. 2, 1863, Correspondence of Louis T. Wigfall, Wigfall Family Papers, LC. In this letter Longstreet said that "many other causes combined to prevent our success but I think the first the principal." This statement contradicted his claim in the letter to his uncle written a little over a week before, that if his idea had been followed of placing the Confederate army in a strong position between Washington and the enemy and forcing the enemy to attack, the Federal army would have been destroyed, Washington captured, and peace established on terms dictated by the South. See Longstreet to [Dr.] A. B. Longstreet, July 24, 1863, in Longstreet, "Lee in Pennsylvania," *Annals*, 414–415. Gen. Early and Col. Henderson felt that if Lee were going to attack he should have done so as early as possible on July 2, thus giving Meade less time to bring up all his forces. The English correspondent on the other hand thought it would have been better for Lee to have waited until July 3, when Pickett could have joined with McLaws and Hood. Early, "Reply to

General Longstreet's Second Paper," *SHSP*, V, 287; Henderson, "Review of General Longstreet's Book," *SHSP*, XXXIX, 111; Dispatch from Special Correspondent, July 8, in the *Times* [London], Aug. 18, 1863.

21. Lee apparently had his headquarters in two places: a small house east of Seminary Ridge and just north of the Chambersburg Pike, and a cluster of tents in an orchard nearby. Maurice, ed., *Aide-de-Camp of Lee*, 232–234.

22. Longstreet said that he made his proposal to Lee for a turning movement about 5:00 P.M. When he rode back to his headquarters two hours later he knew Lee had formed no plans "beyond that of seizing Culp's Hill as his point from which to engage, nor given any orders for the next day. . . ." Longstreet, *Memoirs*, 361. The accuracy of Longstreet's recollection that Lee discussed matters with him before going to see Ewell is borne out by the testimony of Dr. J. S. D. Cullen, Gen. Early, and Col. Fremantle. See *ibid.*, 383–384; Fremantle, *Three Months in the Southern States*, 255–256; Early, "Causes of Lee's Defeat at Gettysburg," *SHSP*, IV, 271. Charles Marshall reversed the order of the consultation. He said that after talking to Gens. Hill and Ewell, Lee contemplated a turning movement around Meade's left flank. For various reasons he decided against it and in favor of an attack on the Union left flank. Following his meeting with Hill and Ewell, Lee returned to Seminary Ridge where he saw Longstreet, who proposed the move that Lee had rejected as impracticable. Lee then informed him of his decision to attack the enemy the next day as early as feasible, and directed him to place McLaws and Hood's divisions on the right of Hill, partially enveloping the enemy's left which he was to drive in. Hill's right division would cooperate in the attack, while the rest of his corps threatened the enemy's center to prevent Meade from shifting his troops. Ewell would make a simultaneous demonstration upon the enemy's right, to be converted into a real attack should he have the opportunity. Maurice, ed., *Aide-de-Camp of Lee*, 232–234.

23. Early, "Causes of Lee's Defeat," *SHSP*, IV, 271–274.

24. *OR*, XXVII, pt. 2, pp. 318–319, 446. Early asserted that all during the talk they assumed Longstreet would be up in time to begin the battle at dawn next morning. In connection with their recommendation for an attack from the Confederate right, Lee made a remark that became "indelibly impressed" on Early's memory: " 'Well, if I attack from my right,' he said, 'Longstreet will have to make the attack,' and after a moment's pause, during which he held his head down in deep thought, he raised it and added: 'Longstreet is a very good fighter when he gets in position and gets everything ready, but he is *so slow*.' " The words, as Early recalled them, seemed to come from Lee in great pain. Until 1877 Early said he had not repeated them, but Longstreet's article in the *Philadelphia Weekly Times*, in which he deprecated Lee's generalship, removed the "last scruple." Early, "Causes of Lee's Defeat," *SHSP*, IV, 273–274. This comment, if Lee made it, seems out of keeping with his character, for it certainly was most indiscreet. It suggests furthermore that Longstreet's truculence may have unduly provoked him.

25. Judging from Ewell's report, Lee did not give him his final instructions until early in the morning of July 2. See *OR*, XXVII, pt. 2, p. 446.

26. *Ibid.;* Charles Marshall to Early, Mar. 23, 1870, Jubal A. Early Papers, LC.

27. *OR*, XXVII, pt. 2, pp. 445–446; "Gettysburg," Typed Statement by Capt. [T. T.] Turner, [no date], Jubal A. Early Papers, LC. Turner, who was then a lieutenant, and Lt. Robert D. Early were the two officers sent by Ewell to ride up Culp's Hill.

28. Freeman said that "Lee's one reason for deciding to shift Ewell to the right had been doubt of the ability of Ewell to make up his mind to do anything." Consequently he was glad to learn of Ewell's determination to attack Culp's Hill. See Freeman, *Lee's Lieutenants,* III, 103.

29. Charles Marshall recalled that when Ewell received Lee's order to withdraw the Second Corps from its position, he referred the message to Rodes and Early for discussion. Early urged that the Confederates should not abandon the idea of an "attack on that side." Marshall to Early, Mar. 23, 1870, Jubal A. Early Papers, LC. Capt. Turner said that upon his return from the ride up Culp's Hill Ewell asked Rodes and Early whether he should send Johnson's division to occupy the eminence. Early strongly advised him to do so, whereas Rodes thought Johnson's men were too tired from the long day's march to make the move. "Gettysburg," Typed Statement by Capt. [T. T.] Turner, [no date], in *ibid.*

30. Lee always expressed the "strongest conviction" that if the Confederate corps had attacked together on either day, he would have won. He also said that he used every effort to obtain the necessary "concert of action and failed." Col. William Allan, "Causes of Lee's Defeat at Gettysburg," *SHSP*, IV, 79.

31. Alexander, "Battle of Gettysburg," MS, E. P. Alexander Papers, UNC.

32. Alexander, "Causes of Lee's Defeat at Gettysburg," *SHSP*, IV, 110.

33. *OR*, XXVII, pt. 2, p. 446. Capt. Turner said Ewell rode over to Lee's headquarters at 10:00 P.M., and Charles Marshall thought the two generals conferred at least an hour. "Gettysburg," Typed Statement by Capt. Turner, [no date]; Charles Marshall to Early, Mar. 23, 1870, Jubal A. Early Papers, LC.

34. *OR*, XXVII, pt. 2, p. 446; pt. 3, p. 483. Sykes reported that his march to Gettysburg on July 2 did start at 4:00 A.M. *Ibid.*, pt. 1, p. 595.

35. *Ibid.*, pt. 2, p. 446.

36. *Ibid.*, pp. 318–319, 446.

37. Maurice, ed., *Aide-de-Camp of Lee*, 232–234; Early, "Causes of Lee's Defeat," *SHSP*, IV, 289.

38. Longstreet, *Memoirs*, 361.

39. Smith, "With Stonewall Jackson in the Army of Northern Virginia," *SHSP*, XLIII, 57–58.

40. *OR*, XXVII, pt. 3, pp. 947–948; LI, pt. 2, pp. 732–733.

41. *Ibid.*, p. 733. The order was sent from near Gettysburg at 5:30 P.M. As reproduced in the *OR*, Longstreet addressed the message only to Col. J. B. Walton, chief of artillery. In Longstreet's *Memoirs*, 359, this same message was designated "circular orders" sent to "commanders of columns, First Corps." It also omitted the last six sentences which gave a short account of

the outcome of the day's fighting. Neither Hood nor McLaws mentioned receiving the second order from Longstreet telling them to push on as far as possible. McLaws said about 10:00 P.M. he met Longstreet, probably near Cashtown; Longstreet directed McLaws to go into camp at Marsh Creek, which he reached a little after midnight. Gen. Lafayette McLaws, "Gettysburg," *SHSP*, VII, 67–68; Hood, *Advance and Retreat*, 56. In his battle report Longstreet said McLaws arrived at Marsh Creek a little after dark July 1 and Hood at midnight. Gen. J. B. Kershaw in his report gave the hour of McLaws' arrival as midnight. If Johnson's division which arrived about dark had a train fourteen miles long, as was claimed, the time Kershaw gave seems more likely. *OR*, XXVII, pt. 2, pp. 358, 366.

42. McLaws said he had in his division at Gettysburg "about 6,000 aggregate." He did not say whether this number included his artillery as well. This figure seems a little low. The Field Return for July 20 reported that he had 4,604 officers and infantrymen present for duty. Judging from the return for July 31, not many stragglers or slightly wounded had as yet returned to the division. The total in killed, wounded, and missing in the division's infantry at Gettysburg was 2,141. Add this figure to the number in the July 20 return and the result is 6,745 infantry. It would be safe then to say that McLaws had about 6,500 infantrymen when he went into battle. McLaws, "Gettysburg," *SHSP*, VII, 70; *OR*, XXVII, pt. 2, pp. 283, 291–292, 338; pt. 3, p. 1058.

43. The time of Hood's arrival is based upon inferences from his statement that his troops were allowed to rest only two hours during the night, and statements in two separate battle reports which gave the hour for the division's departure for Gettysburg after the halt as 3:00 A.M. Hood, *Advance and Retreat*, 56; *OR*, XXVII, pt. 2, pp. 420, 424.

44. Walton said he got the 5:30 P.M. order from Longstreet about 10:00 P.M. The order reached Col. Alexander between 10:30 and 11:00 P.M. The two battalions started at midnight. In spite of a delay caused by a wagon train and their easy pace, they reached the vicinity of Gettysburg about sunup. "Letter from Colonel J. B. Walton," *SHSP*, V, 49–50. Alexander said they left at 1:00 A.M. and according to his notes arrived a mile or so west of Seminary Ridge at 9:00 A.M., but his impression was they got there about two hours sooner. Alexander, "Battle of Gettysburg," MS, E. P. Alexander Papers, UNC. His battle report, dated Aug. 3, 1863, said they arrived at 9:00 A M. *OR*, XXVII, pt. 2, p. 429. See also Alexander, *Military Memoirs*, 388.

45. Alexander, "Battle of Gettysburg," MS, E. P. Alexander Papers, UNC.

46. *OR*, XXVII, pt. 3, p. 948.

47. If this information is vague it is because as usual there was conflicting testimony about the marching schedules of these two units of Longstreet's corps. Also the accounts disagreed about the distances they marched. *Ibid.*, pt. 2, pp. 358, 391, 395; Longstreet, *Memoirs*, 364–365; Col. William C. Oates, "Gettysburg—The Battle on the Right," *SHSP*, VI, 173; Paul Turner Vaughan Diary, Entry for July 2, 1863, Paul Turner Vaughan Papers, DU; E. M. Law, "The Struggle for 'Round Top,'" *B&L*, III, pt. 1, p. 319; Gen. [E. M.] Law to Bachelder, Feb. 2, 1891, Bachelder Papers; Harrison, *Pickett's Men*, 87–88;

Col. W. W. Wood, "Pickett's Charge at Gettysburg," *Philadelphia Weekly Times,* Aug. 11, 1877.

48. Hamilton, ed., *Shotwell Papers,* Entry for July 2, 1863, I, 499–500. For further information about the exhausted condition of Pickett's men see T. Joseph Durkin, ed., *John Dooley, Confederate Soldier, His War Journal* (Washington, 1945), 101; Harrison, *Pickett's Men,* 87.

49. Ross, *Cities and Camps,* 50. For further information on shortage of water see Henry Robinson Berkeley Diary, Entry for July 4, 1863, MS, VHS.

50. See Longstreet, *Memoirs,* 359, 364–365; Law, "The Struggle for 'Round Top,' " *B&L,* III, pt. 1, p. 319; Oates, "Gettysburg—The Battle on the Right," *SHSP,* VI, 173; *OR,* XXVII, pt. 2, pp. 391, 395.

51. *Ibid.,* pt. 3, pp. 947–948; LI, pt. 2, pp. 732–733. In a letter to Stuart on July 9 Lee referred to Imboden's cavalry as "unsteady, and . . . inefficient." *Ibid.,* XXVII, pt. 3, p. 985.

52. The words and italics are Long's. Long to Longstreet, May 31, 1875, A. L. Long Papers, UNC. Pendleton claimed that as a result of a reconnaissance he personally made late on July 1, he discovered the low section of Cemetery Ridge just before the ground begins to rise toward Little Round Top. He passed the information on to Lee, who said he had ordered Longstreet to attack there "at sunrise next morning." "Personal Recollections of Genl. Lee. An Address delivered by request. In Lexington, Virginia, Jany 19th, 1873," MS copy, William N. Pendleton Papers, UNC. The story is so improbable that it is amazing anyone gave it any credence. Gen. Early said he knew nothing about a sunrise order, but he would assert that Lee announced to him, Ewell, and Rodes his purpose to attack at dawn on July 2, and that Lee left them for the purpose of ordering up Longstreet's troops to begin the attack then. Early, "Causes of Lee's Defeat," *SHSP,* IV, 286. This statement also strains belief unless Lee expected the men of Longstreet's corps to march all night and then move to their positions without rest. But as Alexander pointed out, if the latter was true Lee would then have had to furnish guides to put the men in position. He also said that the Confederates could not determine the enemy's position until morning. Alexander, "Battle of Gettysburg," MS, E. P. Alexander Papers, UNC. Charles Marshall, Charles Venable, W H. Taylor, and A. L. Long all said, when the question was first raised, that they had never heard of the sunrise order. Long to Early, May 3, 1875, Jubal A. Early Papers, LC; Taylor to Longstreet Apr. 28, 1875; Marshall to *id.,* May 7, 1875; Venable to *id.,* [no date], James Longstreet Papers, 1875–1904, Microfilm, DU. Years after his letter to Longstreet and the publication of his *Four Years with General Lee* Taylor for some reason changed his mind and decided that Lee had proposed to order an attack at sunrise or soon afterwards, provided Longstreet had his men up. Taylor, "Lee and Longstreet," *SHSP,* XXIV, 78.

53. [Dr.] J. S. D. Cullen to Longstreet, May 18, 1875, in Longstreet, *Memoirs,* 383–384. Fremantle reported that at supper Longstreet spoke of the enemy's position as being "very formidable" and that he expected the Yankees to entrench during the night. *Three Months in the Southern States,* 256.

54. McLaws, "Gettysburg," *SHSP,* VII, 68.

55. Fremantle, *Three Months in the Southern States*, 256–257. Longstreet's memory was completely at fault when he said the stars were shining when he reported to Lee's headquarters on July 2. Longstreet, *Memoirs*, 362. His medical director, Dr. Cullen, agrees with Fremantle as to the time of his arrival at army headquarters. See [Dr.] J. S. D. Cullen to Longstreet, May 18, 1875, in *ibid.*, 384.

56. Longstreet, "Lee in Pennsylvania," *Annals*, 422. In another account he merely said that he "again proposed the move to Meade's left and rear." Longstreet, "Lee's Right Wing at Gettysburg," *B&L*, III, pt. 1, p. 340. Marshall said Longstreet came to see Lee early on the 2nd to renew his proposal for a turning movement, but Lee affirmed his decision to fight where he was. Maurice, ed., *Aide-de-Camp of Lee*, 232–233.

57. Morrison, ed., "Heth Memoirs," *CWH*, VIII, 306. Judging from Longstreet's statement in his memoirs that he reported to headquarters in the morning for orders, it would seem that he did not know then where Lee intended to make the main attack on July 2. *Memoirs*, 362.

58. Longstreet, "Lee in Pennsylvania," *Annals*, 422.

59. Hood, *Advance and Retreat*, 57.

60. The hour of 8:30 A.M. was the very outside figure. Probably both divisions came in earlier. Hood's possibly could have started to file into the open field west of Seminary Ridge between 5:30 and 6:00 A.M. *Ibid.*, 56. Fremantle said that at 7:00 A.M. he rode with Longstreet and saw him arranging McLaws' division for the day's fight. *Three Months in the Southern States*, 257. For information on disposing of the troops for rest see *OR*, XXVII, pt. 2, pp. 366, 372; Hood, *Advance and Retreat*, 56; McLaws, "Gettysburg," *SHSP*, VII, 76; Alexander, "Battle of Gettysburg," MS, E. P. Alexander Papers, UNC; Alexander, *Military Memoirs*, 388.

61. Long, *Memoirs of Lee*, 280; A. L. Long to Early, Mar. 30, 1876, Jubal A. Early Papers, LC.

62. For an analysis of how the ridge on which the Emmitsburg road is located hid the southern end of Cemetery Ridge from Confederate observers, see a report by Frederick Tilberg, Park Historian, and J. Walter Coleman, Supt. Gettysburg National Military Park, in Freeman, *Lee's Lieutenants*, III, Appendix, I.

63. Gen. Humphreys testified that it was a moonlight night but hazy on July 1, suggesting a ground fog in the lower places which could linger until the sun burned it away. CCW, *Report*, I, 390. Col. R. McAllister of the 11th N. J. regt. reported "considerable fog" in the morning of July 2. *OR*, XXVII, pt. 1, p. 552.

64. *Ibid.*, pt. 2, p. 350. Johnston positively denied having gone with Pendleton. See Freeman, *Lee's Lieutenants*, III, 174.

65. *OR*, XXVII, pt. 1, p. 927. See also John B. Bachelder, Map of the Battlefield of Gettysburg, Second Day, 1876.

66. *OR*, XXVII, pt. 2, 350. In his address honoring Lee's birthday on Jan. 19, 1873, Pendleton used language which gave the impression that he had reconnoitered the Federal lines on Cemetery Ridge. Actually he had only exam-

ined them at a distance from different vantage points. He did go over quite thoroughly the ground later occupied by Confederate forces on Seminary and Warfield Ridges. See Pendleton, "Personal Recollections of Genl. Lee," MS, Copy, William N. Pendleton Papers, UNC.

67. Notes on Gettysburg [by Maj. Johnston, 1886 (?)], Lafayette McLaws Papers, DU.

68. This part of the story of Johnston's reconnaissance is based upon Freeman, *Lee's Lieutenants*, III, 111, 113, 174. Freeman had access to the S. R. Johnston MSS which contain a much more detailed account of the mission.

69. Freeman said that Johnston arrived at Little Round Top about 5:30 A.M. Since he started at 4:00 A.M. and travelled slowly and cautiously to avoid enemy pickets, this is as good a guess as any. *Ibid.*, 113.

70. *OR*, XXVII, pt. 1, pp. 368, 825, 836, 839, 855. Col. John H. Patrick of the 5th Ohio Infantry, who temporarily commanded both his own regiment and Col. Ario Pardee's 147th Pa. while they occupied the Round Tops, reported that he received orders at 5:00 A.M. from Col. Charles Candy, commanding the First Brigade, to rejoin the brigade. This information indicates that the order to Geary to take a position on Culp's Hill came a good deal earlier than 5:00 A.M.

71. *Ibid.*, pt. 1, p. 368.

72. Johnston's explanation for not reconnoitering along Cemetery Ridge is not convincing. See Freeman, *Lee's Lieutenants*, III, 113, 175.

73. Notes on Gettysburg [by Maj. Johnston, 1886(?)], Lafayette McLaws Papers, DU.

74. *OR*, XXVII, pt. 2, p. 350.

75. Freeman, *Lee's Lieutenants*, III, 113–114, 118; Freeman, *R. E. Lee*, III, 86, 88.

76. Freeman, *Lee's Lieutenants*, III, 113.

77. McLaws, "Gettysburg," *SHSP*, VII, 68–69.

78. Notes on Gettysburg [by Maj. Johnston, 1886(?)], Lafayette McLaws Papers, DU.

79. "Colonel E. P. Alexander's Report on the Battle of Gettysburg," *SHSP*, IV, 235. After the war Longstreet, who was in enough trouble with his erstwhile companions in arms, tried to make public amends for "overslaughing" Walton. His explanations consisted of an amusing melange of factual mistakes and double-talk. See "Letter from Colonel J. B. Walton," *SHSP*, V, 47–52; "Letter from Genl. E. P. Alexander," *SHSP*, V, 201–203; "Letter from General Longstreet," *SHSP*, V, 52–53; Longstreet, "The Mistakes of Gettysburg," *Annals*, 631–632.

80. Alexander, "Battle of Gettysburg," MS, E. P. Alexander Papers, UNC. Alexander made a mistake when he said he went to the left. To avoid being seen he had to go to the right where the ground, sloping off toward Marsh Creek, was much lower.

81. Col. Long said he met Lee at Ewell's headquarters about 9:00 A.M. Long, *Memoirs of Lee*, 281. Longstreet recalled that Lee returned to Seminary Ridge from a conference with Ewell at nine o'clock. Longstreet, "Lee in Penn-

sylvania," *Annals*, 422. However, Johnston's testimony that he reported to Lee at 9:00 A.M. with Longstreet in attendance, and Alexander's report that he saw both Lee and Longstreet about 10:00 A.M. indicate 10:00 or a little after as the hour for Lee's departure to see Ewell.

82. Charles S. Venable to Longstreet, May 11, 1875, in Longstreet, "Lee in Pennsylvania," *Annals*, 438. Gen. Early doubted Venable's account that Lee sent him to inquire about the possibilities of an attack by Ewell. Early, "Causes of Lee's Defeat," *SHSP*, IV, 289. Charles Marshall on the other hand claimed that Lee became so impatient with the dilatory Longstreet that he went to Ewell to see whether after an inspection of Cemetery Hill in daylight an attack there showed greater promise. Maurice, ed., *Aide-de-Camp of Lee*, 232–234.

83. Long, *Memoirs of Lee*, 281–282.

84. *Ibid.;* Taylor, *Four Years with Lee*, 99; Gen. R. Lindsay Walker to [Gen. Fitz] Lee, Jan. 17, 1878, in Gen. Fitz Lee, "Reply to General Longstreet," *SHSP*, V, 181; William T. Poague, *Gunner with Stonewall, Reminiscences*, Monroe F. Cockrell, ed. (Jackson, Tenn, 1957), 71.

85. Hood, *Advance and Retreat*, 57.

86. *OR*, XXVII, pt. 2, p. 358.

87. *Ibid.*

88. *Ibid.*, pt. 1, p. 532; pt. 2, p. 358; Longstreet, "Lee in Pennsylvania," *Annals*, 422.

89. *Cf. ante*, XIII.

90. The idea that Lee thought of making the offensive in two stages, one following the other as soon as the troops could be re-formed, came from statements in Lee's reports as well as Longstreet's. In the first report Lee said the enemy held a position in front of Longstreet; if he could be driven from it "it was thought our artillery could be used to advantage in assailing the more elevated ground beyond; and thus enable us to reach the crest of the ridge." *OR*, XXVII, pt. 2, p. 308. The second report is less precise and gives the impression that seizure of artillery positions on the Emmitsburg road was Lee's real objective, instead of a means to an end. *Ibid.*, p. 318. Col. Long undoubtedly told Lee about these positions which he saw early in the morning long before the Federals occupied them. If Longstreet had acted quickly, he could have had them without a fight.

91. Freeman believed that Lee got back to Seminary Ridge after 11:00 A.M. *Lee's Lieutenants*, III, 114, 36 note.

92. *Ibid.*, 115.

93. *OR*, XXVII, pt. 2, p. 318.

94. In his battle report he said nothing about getting Lee's permission to wait for Law. In subsequent accounts he remembered asking for Lee's approval. *Ibid.*, p. 358; Longstreet, "Lee in Pennsylvania," *Annals*, 422.

95. McLaws, "Gettysburg," *SHSP*, VII, 70; Notes on Gettysburg [by Maj. Johnston, 1886 (?)], Lafayette McLaws Papers, DU, McLaws wrote the following comment on the margin of this document: "He [Johnston] seems not to realise that he was conducting my column, for he was the only one who was supposed to know or could know, the route to take. He denies that Gen. Lee or

any one else said anything to him about finding a route to go on . . . which would be invisible to the enemy & yet when I was following the route *he must* have designated as the proper one *he* tells Gen. Longstreet 'without being asked' that by this route my movements would be disclosed to the enemy."

96. Before McLaws' and Hood's divisions marched to the Emmitsburg road they probably rested along the Chambersburg Pike and from there south on the west side of Herr's Ridge. E. M. Law, "The Struggle for 'Round Top,'" *B&L*, III, pt. 1, p. 319; *OR*, XXVII, pt. 2, pp. 366, 372; John B. Bachelder's Isometric Drawing of the Gettysburg Battlefield, 1863, in possession of author.

97. Longstreet, "Lee in Pennsylvania," *Annals*, 422–423.

98. Notes on Gettysburg [by Maj. Johnston, 1886 (?)], Lafayette McLaws Papers, DU; McLaws, "Gettysburg," *SHSP*, VII, 69–70; *OR*, XXVII, pt. 2, pp. 366–367, 372. The Black Horse Tavern is in the hollow of Marsh Run on the north side of the Fairfield road.

99. Longstreet, "Lee in Pennsylvania," *Annals*, 423; Law, "The Struggle for 'Round Top,'" *B&L*, III, pt. 1, p. 320. Hood reported nothing about a long halt in the march and a retracing of steps. According to his account his division started out by following McLaws. Without giving any reason he said Longstreet ordered him to "quicken the march of my troops, and to pass to the front of McLaws. This movement was accomplished by throwing out an advanced force to tear down fences and clear the way." Hood, *Advance and Retreat*, 57.

100. *OR*, XXVII, pt. 3, p. 488. At 2:10 P.M. the signal officers reported the column was still moving north in the direction of the Chambersburg Pike.

101. Alexander, "Battle of Gettysburg," MS, E. P. Alexander Papers, UNC.

102. McLaws, "Gettysburg," *SHSP*, VII, 69.

103. *OR*, XXVII, pt. 2, p. 367.

104. McLaws to his wife, July 7, 1863, Lafayette McLaws Papers, UNC.

105. *OR*, XXVII, pt. 2, p. 367.

106. McLaws to his wife, July 7, 1863, Lafayette McLaws Papers, UNC.

107. McLaws, "Gettysburg," *SHSP*, VII, 70–72, 75; McLaws' comments on Notes on Gettysburg [by Maj. Johnston, 1886 (?)], Lafayette McLaws Papers, UNC. In his letter to his wife on July 7 McLaws did not give the reasons for the postponement but said, "The assault was delayed, but again delayed, and finally I was directed not to assault until Hood was in position." *Ibid.*

108. McLaws to his wife, July 7, 1863, *ibid.*

109. Hood, *Advance and Retreat*, 57; Law, "The Struggle for 'Round Top,'" *B&L*, III, pt. 1, p. 321. Hood said he sent the scouts out to the Emmitsburg road during the march. Soon after he got there they reported their findings.

110. Hood, *Advance and Retreat*, 58–59. Col. John W. Fairfax partly corroborates Hood's account. See Fairfax to Longstreet, Nov. 12, 1877, in Longstreet, *Memoirs*, 380–381. Gen. Law said they also received information about the defenseless condition of the area east and northeast of Round Top from some Yankee soldiers who were captured on their way to Emmitsburg with medical discharges. He also gave the impression in his account that the turning movement was his idea, which he suggested to Hood. Law wanted to put off

the attack for the day, occupy Round Top during the night, and then move the next day against the enemy's left and rear. Law, "The Struggle for 'Round Top,' " *B&L*, III, pt. 1, pp. 321–322. There is no evidence that Hood wanted to postpone the attack. If so, it can be readily seen why Longstreet refused to consider the request. It was too late to delay the attack any more.

111. E. P. Alexander, "The Great Charge and Artillery Fighting at Gettysburg," *B&L*, III, pt. 1, p. 359; Alexander, "Battle of Gettysburg," MS, E. P. Alexander Papers, UNC.

112. Bachelder, Isometric Drawing of the Gettysburg Battlefield.

113. Alexander to his father, July 17, 1863, Alexander-Hillhouse Papers, UNC.

114. Alexander, "Battle of Gettysburg," MS, E. P. Alexander Papers, UNC.

115. *OR*, XXVII, pt. 2, pp. 318, 358, 446–447, 607–608.

116. *Ibid.*, pt. 1, pp. 155–166; pt. 2, 283–290.

117. *Ibid.*, pp. 318–319, 446, 608, 614.

118. Alexander, "Battle of Gettysburg," MS, E. P. Alexander Papers, UNC.

119. *OR*, XXVII, pt. 2, pp. 608, 614. Hill said Anderson's brigades would move forward "en echelon."

120. Another name for this kind of attack is movement in oblique order. Boatner, *Civil War Dictionary*, 604.

121. *OR*, XXVII, pt. 2, p. 614.

122. Longstreet in saying Anderson's brigades would move "en echelon" made no mention of the order he employed for his own. Longstreet, "Lee in Pennsylvania," *Annals*, 424. Hill's and Anderson's battle reports were probably the basis for Longstreet's statement. Gen. Cadmus Wilcox, who commanded the right brigade in Anderson's division, however, denied ever having received an order to move in echelon. By implication Gen. A. R. Wright in his report substantiated Wilcox. See "General C. M. Wilcox on the Battle of Gettysburg," *SHSP*, VI, 98; *OR*, XXVII, pt. 2, pp. 608, 614, 622–623.

NOTES TO CHAPTER XV

1. Column by Agate [Whitelaw Reid], near Gettysburg, July 2, in *Cincinnati Daily Gazette*, July 8, 1863.

2. *OR*, XXVII, pt. 1, p. 483; CCW, *Report*, I, 391; Hunt, "The Second Day at Gettysburg," *B&L*, III, pt. 1, p. 304.

3. *OR*, XXVII, pt. 1, pp. 202, 483.

4. Alexander to his father, July 17, 1863, Alexander-Hillhouse Papers, UNC; Alexander, "Battle of Gettysburg," MS, E. P. Alexander Papers, UNC; *New York Times*, July 4, 1863. Most accounts agreed, which was unusual, that Longstreet's assault started about 4:00 P.M. *OR*, XXVII, pt. 1, pp. 72, 483, 506, 522; pt. 2, pp. 319, 351, 379, 407–408; Henry Robinson Berkeley Diary, Entry for July 2, 1863, VHS; Sorrel, *Recollections*, 168; *The Times* [London], Aug. 18, 1863. Of the reliable witnesses, Fremantle and L. L. Crounse disagreed with the majority by putting the time of the opening salvo from one-half

to three-quarters of an hour later. Fremantle, *Three Months in the Southern States*, 266; *New York Times*, July 4, 1863.

5. W. B. Sturtevant to Jimmie, July 27, 1863, Confederate Museum.

6. *OR*, XXVII, pt. 1, p. 483. A captain in the Texas brigade described their attack as "not at an orderly double-quick, but in a wild, frantic and desperate run, yelling, screaming and shouting; over ditches, up and down hill, bursting through garden fences and shrubbery. . . ." Decimus et Ultimus Barziza, *The Adventures of a Prisoner of War, 1863–1864,* R. Henderson Shuffler, ed. (Austin, Texas, 1964), 45.

7. *OR*, XXVII, pt. 2, pp. 404, 407, 411; Bachelder, Map of the Battlefield of Gettysburg, Second Day.

8. *Ibid.*; *OR*, XXVII, pt. 1, p. 493; pt. 2, pp. 392, 404; William C. Oates, *The War between the Union and the Confederacy and Its Lost Opportunities . . .* (New York, 1905), 207.

9. Longstreet, "Lee in Pennsylvania," *Annals,* 424.

10. In Longstreet's corps Gens. Hood and G. T. Anderson were severely wounded; Semmes and Barksdale mortally wounded. *OR*, XXVII, pt. 2, p. 359.

11. *Ibid.,* pt. 1, p. 493.

12. *Ibid.,* pt. 2, p. 404. See also other Confederate battle reports in *ibid.,* pp. 393, 396, 407–408, 411, 415, as well as Longstreet, *Memoirs,* 369–370.

13. Alexander, "Battle of Gettysburg," MS, E. P. Alexander Papers, UNC. Hunt drew heavily upon the Artillery Reserve to reinforce Randolph's brigade and lined up fifty guns from Devil's Den to the Peach Orchard with which to match Alexander's fifty-four cannon. Because of the salient at the Peach Orchard some of Hunt's guns were subjected to a cross-fire. Alexander had in addition to the usual Napoleons and 3-inch rifles two 20-pounder Parrotts and five 24-pounder howitzers, while Hunt had nothing heavier than 12-pounders. Since Alexander did not use all the guns he brought with him, it is not known whether he used all of his larger cannon in this cannonade. *Ibid.*; *OR*, XXVII, pt. 1, pp. 234–235, 483, 582; pt. 2, p. 355.

14. Alexander to his father, July 17, 1863, Alexander-Hillhouse Papers, UNC. Gen. S. D. Lee, who commanded Alexander's battalion at Sharpsburg or Antietam in 1862, told Alexander to pray "never to see another Sharpsburg, that 'Sharpsburg was Artillery Hell.'" Alexander, "Battle of Gettysburg," MS, E. P. Alexander Papers, UNC.

15. Dispatch of July 3 from L. L. Crounse in the *New York Times,* July 4, 1863.

16. *New York Tribune,* July 6, 1863.

17. As an indication of the close relationship between the two officers the reporter of the *New York Tribune* mistakenly referred to Warren as Meade's chief of staff. Issue of July 6, 1863.

18. Warren's Testimony in CCW, *Report,* I, 377. In a letter written apparently soon after the battle Warren said he worried so much about the unprotected position of Little Round Top that he asked Meade to send him there. In a later letter he told the story in such a way as to give the impression that

Meade directed him to examine conditions on the left and in the process of doing so he reached the crest of Little Round Top. Taylor, *G. K. Warren*, 22–23; Warren to Capt. Porter Farley, July 13, 1872, quoted in Norton, *Little Round Top*, 308, and also in Hunt, "Second Day at Gettysburg," *B&L*, III, pt. 1, p. 307, note.

19. Oliver W. Norton, *Strong Vincent and His Brigade at Gettysburg, July 2, 1863* (Chicago, 1909), 10.

20. Meade, *Life and Letters*, II, 82; CCW, *Report*, I, 377. Warren in two letters, one quoted in Taylor and the other in Norton, told the story which has been often repeated of what he did when he reached Little Round Top. Suspecting that the Confederates were forming for an attack behind a screen of trees, he sent word to Smith at Devil's Den to fire a shot from one of his cannon. Upon hearing the report, the enemy troops waiting in line all turned in its direction and through the glistening of their gun barrels and bayonets gave Warren an idea of their position and the length of their line. This romantic story puts a strain upon belief. Warren did not say when he got to Little Round Top, but very likely it was no sooner than 3:30 P.M. At that time the signal officer there reported seeing the Confederates massing upon Sickles' left. Birney said two of his batteries opened at 3:30 P.M. Warren also said that at the time he caught the glimpse of the Confederates the battle was already beginning to rage at the Peach Orchard. If by this ambiguous statement he meant infantry action as well as an artillery barrage, he was in error. The battle, or at least the infantry attack, started on Sickles' left and not at the Peach Orchard. See Warren letter [no date] in Taylor, *G. K. Warren*, 22–23, and Warren to Capt. Porter Farley, July 13, 1872, in Norton, *Little Round Top*, 308.

21. *OR*, XXVII, pt. 1, p. 138. Warren apparently forgot he had sent Lt. R. S. Mackenzie, one of his engineers, to Sickles with this message.

22. *Ibid.*, pp. 116, 592; CCW, *Report*, I, 332; Humphreys to Archibald Campbell, Aug. 6, 1863, A. A. Humphreys Papers, HSP; Warren to Capt. Porter Farley, July 13, 1872, in Norton, *Little Round Top*, 309–310.

23. Meade, *Life and Letters*, II, 82–83.

24. Norton, *Strong Vincent*, 6–7, 10–11; Norton, *Little Round Top*, 238. Barnes in his battle report claimed Warren came up while he and Sykes were riding together at the head of the column of the First Division. He said Warren asked for help to secure Little Round Top, Sykes agreed to send troops, and Barnes immediately ordered Vincent's brigade to the threatened point. *OR*, XXVII, pt. 1, p. 600. Sykes made no mention in his report of meeting Warren. When he said that he himself posted two of Barnes's brigades in the Third Corps battle line, he implied he became separated from Barnes. As for Vincent's brigade, Sykes asserted Warren put it in position on Little Round Top. *Ibid.*, pp. 592–593. Later he disclaimed any knowledge of how Vincent got to Little Round Top. To add to the confusion in the testimony, Warren himself did not remember having "detached" Vincent's brigade from Barnes's division and having led it to the hill; for that matter, apparently neither did Lt. W. A. Roebling, one of Warren's aides and later his brother-in-law. Sykes to Capt. Porter Farley, Aug. 5, 1872; Warren to *id.*, July 13, 24, 1872; W. A. Roebling

to *id.*, Dec. 13, 1877, in Norton, *Little Round Top*, 294, 310, 312. Oliver W. Norton, who made a careful study of the fight for Little Round Top, questioned the reliability of Barnes's report in general and categorically denied that Barnes sent an order directly to Vincent at the moment when Warren applied for troops. According to him, Sykes's aide finally found Barnes, who then issued the order after Vincent had already left for Little Round Top. At the time of the battle Norton was in the best position possible to witness Vincent's activities. As bugler and bearer of the brigade headquarters flag it was his duty when the brigade was in the field always to be near the commander so everyone could locate him by the flag. Norton also sounded orders for the brigade with his bugle. Norton, *Strong Vincent*, 10, 50–51; Norton, *Army Letters, 1861–1865* (Chicago, 1903), 167.

25. *OR*, XXVII, pt. 1, pp. 593, 600–601, 616–617, 622–623; Norton, *Strong Vincent*, 5–8; Norton, *Little Round Top*, 266–267; Boatner, *Civil War Dictionary*, 878. Col. James C. Rice of the 44th N.Y., who took over command of the brigade when Vincent fell mortally wounded, reported about 1,000 muskets taken into action on July 2. *OR*, XXVII, pt. 1, p. 616. Gen. Barnes evidently thought this figure was too low, for sometime after the battle he asked Col. Chamberlain, then in Washington, D. C., to check the estimate. Chamberlain placed the number at 1,350 muskets and 150 officers, which brought the total to 1,500. The number of riflemen in each regiment was as follows: 83rd Pa. 375; 44th N.Y. 365; 20th Maine 360; and 16th Mich. 250. Col. J. S. Chamberlain to Barnes, Apr. 6, 1864, Manuscripts of General James Barnes, NYHS.

26. *OR*, XXVII, pt. 1, p. 623.

27. Boatner, *Civil War Dictionary*, 135.

28. *OR*, XXVII, pt. 1, pp. 592, 600, 622–623; Norton, *Strong Vincent*, 10–11; *cf. ante*, XV, 24 note. Norton at first accepted the story that Warren returned immediately to Little Round Top and found the signal officer folding the flags in preparation for leaving, whereupon to fool the enemy Warren directed him to remain and continue waving the flags. In his later study, *Attack and Defense of Little Round Top*, pp. 331–332, Norton said he believed Warren sent aides to Sykes instead of going himself. Still he did not explain why Warren did not see the arrival of the brigade. Both Warren and Roebling of his staff asserted that the brigade must have come through the woods east of Little Round Top and reached its position by marching along the base of the hill, where it could not be readily seen. Even if true, the explanation is unconvincing for it does not seem possible for over a thousand men to come into battle unnoticed by anyone who might be standing on the crest of the hill. See W. A. Roebling to Porter Farley, Dec. 13, 1877; Warren to [*id.*], July 13, 24, 1872, Oct. 23, Dec. 16, 1877, in *ibid.*, 308–312. More valid evidence shows that the brigade, instead of coming from the Taneytown road east of Little Round Top, approached it from a location near the Wheatfield, which was west of the hill, by taking the road across Plum Run. See Col. Chamberlain's report in *OR*, XXVII, pt. 1, pp. 622–623.

29. *Ibid.*, pp. 592–593.

30. Norton said no general or staff officer directed or accompanied Vincent.

None of the battle reports except Sykes's mentioned anyone being sent to guide the column. In referring to Vincent's and Weed's brigades Sykes rather ambiguously said that these troops were posted on the height under the direction of General Warren. Since he was on another part of the field at the time, Sykes did not see Warren or anyone else do it. See Norton, *Little Round Top*, 266–267; Warren to Porter Farley, July 24, 1872, in *ibid.*, 312; also *OR*, XXVII, pt. 1, pp. 593, 600–601, 616–617, 623, 628.

The confusion about who deserves credit for saving Little Round Top is compounded by statements in a diary of Lt. Ziba B. Graham of the 16th Mich., which was published in 1893. Graham noted that Warren found Vincent's brigade near the Trostle house, which was Sickles' headquarters, and assumed the responsibility of detaching it from the division and leading it to Little Round Top. According to Graham, when they reached the position, Warren pointed out to Vincent the movements of Hood's division and then gave him strict orders to hold the hill to the last man, while he went and searched about for reinforcements. Graham, *On to Gettysburg. Ten Days from My Diary of 1863* (Detroit, 1893), 9. This diary seems to have been dressed up for a speech which was later published. Graham's statements about Warren's role on July 2 cannot possibly be reconciled with Warren's own account.

31. *OR*, XXVII, pt. 2, pp. 392–393; W. C. Oates to Bachelder, Mar. 29, 1876, Bachelder Papers. According to Oates, the order of the regiments in the brigade from left to right at the start of the advance was as follows: 4th, 47th, 15th, 44th, 48th Ala.

32. Oates, *War Between the Union and the Confederacy*, 212. To add to Oates's woes, the water detail which was following the brigade with well-filled canteens got lost in the woods of Big Round Top and walked right into the Yankee lines and was captured, canteens and all. See Maj. Homer R. Stoughton's battle report in which he told how Adj. Norton of the Second U.S. Sharpshooters with about a dozen men captured twenty-two prisoners. *OR*, XXVII, pt. 1, p. 519. By stressing the lack of water as a reason for his defeat Oates made the unwarranted assumption that his men were more thirsty than their foe. Actually men on both sides suffered from thirst on that hot day.

33. Col. William C. Oates, "Gettysburg—The Battle on the Right," *SHSP*, VI, 174–175; *OR*, XXVII, pt. 1, pp. 518–519.

34. *Ibid.*, pt. 2, p. 392.

35. Oates, "Gettysburg—The Battle on the Right," *SHSP*, VI, 175–176. In another version of his account Oates said that Law ordered him with his regiment and seven companies of the 47th Ala. to "pass up between the Round Tops, find the Union left, turn it and capture Little Round [Top]." Oates to Hon. Elihu Root, Sec. of War, June 2, 1903, Typed copy, Joshua L. Chamberlain Papers, LC.

36. *OR*, XXVII, pt. 1, p. 623.

37. Oates, "Gettysburg—The Battle on the Right," *SHSP*, VI, 176.

38. Bachelder, "Gettysburg Campaign," III, 114–115, MS, Bachelder Papers.

39. *OR*, XXVII, pt. 2, p. 392.

40. Oates to Bachelder, Mar. 29, 1876, Bachelder Papers.

41. Oates, "Gettysburg—The Battle on the Right," *SHSP*, VI, 176.

42. These figures give the numbers of men in the 15th and 47th Ala. and the 20th Maine regiments who were available for front-line duty, but do not make allowances for detachments. Oates thought that straggling and detachments reduced his forces to fewer than 400 officers and men. The size of the 47th Ala. is an educated guess. The number of officers who went into battle was twenty-one, and the ratio on the average of officers to men in infantry regiments was from 7:1 to 10:1. Therefore the number of men ranged roughly from 210 to 290. Chamberlain said he had 358 guns for his line before he sent out Co. B under Capt. Morrill as skirmishers to protect his left flank. Later he revised the figure slightly upward. *Ibid.*, 178; Oates, *War between the Union and the Confederacy*, 221–222; *OR*, XXVII, pt. 1, p. 626; pt. 2, p. 395; Chamberlain to Barnes, Apr. 6, 1864, Manuscripts of General James Barnes, NYHS.

43. *OR*, XXVII, pt. 1, p. 623; Bachelder, "Gettysburg Campaign," III, 113 note, MS, Bachelder Papers. For map of terrain and action at Little Round Top see Col. James C. Rice's report in *OR*, XXVII, pt. 1, p. 619.

44. J. L. Chamberlain to Bachelder, [no date], Bachelder Papers. In his battle report Chamberlain complimented Capt. Orpheus S. Woodward, commanding the 83rd Pa., for his "hearty co-operation" in making "his movements conform to my necessities, so that my right was at no time exposed to a flank attack." *OR*, XXVII, pt. 1, p. 624.

45. *Ibid.*, pp. 623–624.

46. Oates to Bachelder, Mar. 29, 1876, Bachelder Papers; Oates, "Gettysburg—The Battle on the Right," *SHSP*, VI, 176–178. Chamberlain, who is partly borne out by Oates, placed the time of his charge near sunset. Chamberlain to Bachelder, Jan. 25, 1884, Bachelder Papers.

47. *OR*, XXVII, pt. 1, p. 624.

48. *Ibid.*, pp. 624–625. In case of retreat Oates had arranged that once he gave the sign everyone was to run up the north slope of Big Round Top. He said he saw long blue lines of Federal infantry coming down on his right and threatening his rear, while some dismounted cavalry were blocking his only avenue of escape on his left. Therefore he gave the signal, and his men ran "like a herd of wild cattle right through the line of dismounted cavalrymen. . . ." Oates, "Gettysburg—The Battle on the Right," *SHSP*, VI, 176–178. Bachelder suggested a solution to Oates's puzzling reference to Union cavalry. He said a cavalry vidette, which had been on duty as a provost guard near the Wheatfield, had fallen back to a position in the rear of Little Round Top. He thought too that Union infantry moving rapidly upon Oates's rear constituted the advance of Col. Joseph W. Fisher's Third Brigade sent by Gen. Crawford to reinforce Vincent's brigade. The reports of Crawford and Fisher support this explanation, though Chamberlain heatedly refused to accept it. He said that it was almost dark and the charge had already been made when Fisher came up and reported to Col. Rice, who had replaced the wounded Vincent. Rice then

massed Fisher's brigade in Chamberlain's rear. Bachelder, "Gettysburg Campaign," III, 114–115, MS; Chamberlain to Bachelder, Jan. 25, 1884, Bachelder Papers; *OR*, XXVII, pt. 1, pp. 625, 653–654, 658.

49. *Ibid.*, p. 625. Chamberlain claimed to have captured 400 prisoners, including two field and several line officers. They were mainly from the 15th and 47th Ala. regiments with some from the 4th and 5th Texas.

50. *Ibid.*, pt. 2, pp. 391–396, 404–405, 410–413. The order in line of Confederate forces attacking Little Round Top from right to left was as follows: 15th Ala., 47th Ala., 4th Ala., 5th Texas, 4th Texas, 48th Ala., and 44th Ala.

51. Welch reported that he had only 150 muskets in line, while Chamberlain claimed the records showed that 250 riflemen were there. Regardless of who was right, the regiment was considerably smaller than any of the others in the brigade. *Ibid.*, pt. 1, p. 628; Chamberlain to Barnes, Apr. 6, 1864, Manuscripts of General James Barnes, NYHS.

52. Norton, *Strong Vincent*, 52–55; Norton, *Little Round Top*, 271; *OR*, XXVII, pt. 1, pp. 619–620, 628.

53. [Maj.] William H. Lamont to Capt. C. B. Mervine, Sept. 2, 1863, Manuscripts of General James Barnes, NYHS.

54. Warren to Porter Farley, July 13, July 24, 1872, in Norton, *Little Round Top*, 309–312; *OR*, XXVII, pt. 1, p. 659. Bachelder gave Capt. A. P. Martin, commanding the Artillery Brigade of the Fifth Corps, credit for ordering Hazlett to occupy Little Round Top with his battery. See Bachelder, "Gettysburg Campaign," III, 115, MS, Bachelder Papers. Warren said there was not room for more than two cannon on the crest of the hill; the rest of the battery was apparently placed lower down on the northern slope. See Warren to Porter Farley, July 24, 1872, in Norton, *Little Round Top*, 311–312. Hazlett had six 10-pounder Parrotts in his battery. Because of the rocky character of the ground it evidently took him considerable time to get all of his guns into position. Though Warren was quite sure that Hazlett arrived before O'Rorke, he thought he brought at first only a section of the battery into action. Capt. Porter Farley of the 140th N.Y. recalled how some of the guns of Hazlett's battery broke through the regiment's files before they reached the top. See *OR*, XXVII, pt. 1, p. 236; Warren to Porter Farley, July 13, 24, 1872, in Norton, *Little Round Top*, 310–312; Fox, ed., *New York at Gettysburg*, III, 956.

55. Lt. E. Bennett of the 44th New York to Editor, *National Tribune*, Feb. 7, 1888, Frost Family Collection, 1886–1889, YU; Norton, *Little Round Top*, 332.

56. Warren to Porter Farley, July 13, 1872; W. A. Roebling to *id.*, Dec. 13, 1877, in Norton, *Little Round Top*, 310–311, 330.

57. *OR*, XXVII, pt. 1, p. 593.

58. Edgar Warren to Bachelder, Nov. 15, 1877, Typescript, Bachelder Papers; G. K. Warren to Porter Farley, Nov. 17, 1877, in Norton, *Little Round Top*, 318.

59. [Capt.] A. S. Marvin to Bachelder, Oct. 29, 1877, [quoting from his journal]; Edgar Warren to *id.*, Nov. 15, 1877, Typescript, Bachelder Papers. There was a dispute over whether O'Rorke's regiment led the brigade or

brought up the rear. In spite of Warren's statement to the contrary, Bachelder, who made a careful study of the matter, came to the conclusion that the 140th N.Y. regiment was in the rear when it was "broken off" to the left and taken up Little Round Top. See Bachelder, "Gettysburg Campaign," III, 115A, MS, Bachelder Papers; Warren to Bachelder, Oct. 26, 1876, Bachelder Papers in possession of Francis C. Carleton, Belmont, Mass., Microfilm, MHS.

60. Fox, ed., *New York at Gettysburg*, III, 951.

61. *Ibid.*, 956–957; Statement of Capt. Joseph M. Leeper of the 140th New York, [no date], Typescript, Bachelder Papers. Leeper was walking beside O'Rorke when Warren intercepted the regiment and ordered it to Little Round Top. Apparently Leeper remained close to O'Rorke until his death.

62. *OR*, XXVII, pt. 1, p. 593; [Capt.] A. S. Marvin to Bachelder, Oct. 29, 1877, [quoting from his journal]; Edgar Warren to *id.*, Nov. 15, 1877, Typescripts, Bachelder Papers.

63. *OR*, XXVII, pt. 2, pp. 405, 410–414; Mary Lasswell, ed., *Rags and Hope, The Recollections of Val C. Giles, Four Years with Hood's Brigade, Fourth Texas Infantry* (New York, 1961), 179–181; Fletcher, *Rebel Private*, 59–61. Despite contrary claims of participants in the 146th N.Y., one of the regiments in Weed's brigade, the evidence gathered from casualty figures for the brigade and the battle report of Col. Kenner Garrard, who succeeded the fallen Weed, indicate that there was little fighting after the rest of the brigade arrived. For claims of heavy fighting see Fox, ed., *New York at Gettysburg*, III, 966, 970–971; Col. David T. Jenkins of the 146th New York to Bachelder, Jan. 7, 1864, Bachelder Papers. For casualty figures and Garrard's report see *OR*, XXVII, pt. 1, pp. 180, 651–652.

64. [Capt.] A. S. Marvin to Bachelder, Oct. 29, 1877, [quoting from his journal], Typescript, Bachelder Papers; Warren to Porter Farley, July 13, 1872, in Norton, *Little Round Top*, 311. Warren was wounded in the neck.

65. *Ibid.*

66. Bachelder, Map of the Battlefield of Gettysburg, Second Day; De Trobriand, *Four Years with the Army of the Potomac*, 493–501.

67. *Ibid.*; *OR*, XXVII, pt. 1, pp. 235, 585–586, 885–888. The units were Capt. A. Judson Clark's Battery B, 1st N.J., six 10-pounders; Capt. Charles A. Phillips' Battery E, 5th Mass., six 3-inch; Capt. John Bigelow's 9th Battery, Mass. Light, four 12-pounders; Capt. Patrick Hart's 15th Battery, N.Y. Light, four 12-pounders.

68. *OR*, XXVII, pt. 1, pp. 160, 520. According to the returns for June 30, 1863, De Trobriand had 1,790 officers and men present for duty. Selected Pages from Historical and Statistical Record of the Principal Military Commands in the Union and Confederate Armies, IV, 80, Entry 161, Record Group 94, NA.

69. The June 30, 1863, returns credited Ward's brigade with 2,597 officers and men present for duty. *Ibid.* Ward in his report said that the "number of effective men in the brigade when they engaged the enemy was not 1,500. . . ." *OR*, XXVII, pt. 1, p. 494. Apparently he included officers in this figure. See *ibid.*, p. 495. Both estimates seem to be wrong, although Ward's appears

closer to the truth. Two of his regiments, the 3rd Maine and Berdan's U.S. Sharpshooters numbering around 460 officers and men, cooperated with Graham's brigade at the Peach Orchard, leaving him, according to the June 30 returns, with a little over 2,100 officers and men in six regiments. According to other records the total for four of his regiments amounted to only 1,115. As for the other two, since they were veteran regiments, very likely neither mustered more than about 350 officers and men. If so, Ward probably had a total of around 1,800 officers and men. *Ibid.*, pp. 508, 511, 516; Fox, ed., *New York at Gettysburg*, II, 862; [Anon.], *Pennsylvania at Gettysburg* (Harrisburg, 1904), I, 173.

70. Selected Papers from Historical and Statistical Record of the Principal Military Commands in the Union and Confederate Armies, IV, 80, Entry 161, Record Group 94, NA. Other records substantiate pretty well the figures for Graham's brigade on the returns for June 30. See *Pennsylvania at Gettysburg*, I, 172–173.

71. *OR*, XXVII, pt. 1, pp. 532, 534, 570. Burling's brigade took its first position in the woods northwest of the famous Wheatfield and the Fairfield crossroad. George C. Burling to Batchelder [Bachelder], Feb. 8, 1884, with accompanying map, Bachelder Papers.

72. The June 30 returns put the figure at 1,606 officers and men present for duty. Other records place the figure at 1,532. Selected Pages from Historical and Statistical Record of the Principal Military Commands in the Union and Confederate Armies, IV, 80, Entry 161, Record Group 94, NA; Samuel Toombs, *New Jersey Troops in the Gettysburg Campaign from June 5 to July 31, 1863* (Newark, 1887), 10; *Pennsylvania at Gettysburg*, I, 173; *OR*, XXVII, pt. 1, p. 573.

73. The two regiments remaining with De Trobriand were the 5th Mich. and the 110th Pa. The latter mustered only 152 officers and men. Two fairly large regiments, the 17th Maine and the 40th N.Y., moved to the left to help Ward. The 3rd Mich. operated in or near the Peach Orchard. As for Burling's brigade, the 5th N.J. went back to Humphreys, the 7th N.J. and the 2nd N.H. joined Graham, and the 6th and 8th N.J. and the 115th Pa. fought on Ward's front. *Ibid.*, pp. 483, 494, 520–529, 569–579; *Pennsylvania at Gettysburg*, I, 173; Col. T. W. Egan to Bachelder, Mar. 25, 1864; Capt. G. W. Verrill to *id.*, Feb. 11, 1884, Bachelder Papers.

74. John Haley to Bachelder, Feb. 8, 1884, *ibid.*

75. De Trobriand mentioned sending the 17th Maine, as well as the 40th N.Y. to Ward; yet neither he nor Birney acknowledged the presence of the 17th Maine. Lt. Col. Charles B. Merrill of that regiment gave the impression in his report that he was running affairs his own way until Gen. Birney appeared on the field to lead a counterattack. *OR*, XXVII, pt. 1, pp. 483–484, 494, 520, 522; De Trobriand, *Four Years with the Army of the Potomac*, 493–501. The experiences of the 115th Pa. and 8th N.J. of Burling's brigade and the 17th Maine of De Trobriand's exemplified the confusion, the lack of coordination, and frequent failures to close gaps in the line. Proponents of the 115th Pa. and 17th Maine argued for years after the battle about who held the stone wall on

the south end of the Wheatfield and for how long. Lt. Col. John P. Dunne to Bachelder, June 30, 1884; Capt. G. W. Verrill to *id.*, Feb. 11, 27, Aug. 15, 22, 1884; Bachelder, "Gettysburg Campaign," III, 126–127, MS, Bachelder Papers.

76. *OR*, XXVII, pt. 1, p. 571.

77. Humphreys to his wife, July 4, 1863, A. A. Humphreys Papers, HSP. In addition to losing the services of Burling's brigade Humphreys had to send the 93rd N.Y. to the aid of Graham. Humphreys to Bachelder, Nov. 14, 1863, Bachelder Papers.

78. *OR*, XXVII, pt. 1, pp. 483, 532, 592. Birney thought Sykes had been ordered originally to send a division, not just a brigade, to his aid.

79. *Ibid.*, p. 592. Sykes, who was regular army, said that every soldier understood that Meade's order to move all of the Fifth Corps to the left "annulled any previous one contemplating support of Sickles with a brigade." Sykes to Editor of the *Chronicle* [Washington, D. C.], Dec. 9, 1865, in Gross, *Battlefield of Gettysburg,* 26–27.

80. *OR*, XXVII, pt. 1, p. 592.

81. *Ibid.*, pp. 116, 592; CCW, *Report,* I, 331.

82. *OR*, XXVII, pt. 1, pp. 235, 593, 660. Sickles said that he sent Capt. Alexander Moore, one of his aides, to order Sykes to bring up his command. Meade, he asserted, had authorized him to call upon Sykes and Hancock to aid him. Sickles to Bachelder, Nov. 25, 1892, Typescript, Bachelder Papers.

83. *OR*, XXVII, pt. 1, pp. 592–593; Sykes to Editor of the *Chronicle* [Washington, D. C.], Dec. 9, 1865, in Gross, *Battlefield of Gettysburg,* 26–27.

84. *OR*, XXVII, pt. 1, p. 483.

85. CCW, *Report,* I, 367. The same charge was repeated with embellishments by "Historicus" on Mar. 12, 1864, in the *New York Herald* five days after Birney testified before the Committee on the Conduct of the War. "Historicus" said bluntly that the Third Corps fought the Confederates for nearly an hour before the Fifth Corps arrived, while Birney only implied that was the case. Sickles in his testimony claimed the Fifth Corps came up "somewhat tardily, to be sure." *Ibid.*, 299. In view of the publication by N. Y. papers of some of Birney's and Pleasonton's testimony before the committee, Meade asked them to give him a summary of what they said. They referred the matter to the chairman, Sen. B. F. Wade, who said unctuously that all testimony before the committee was confidential. Apparently Birney's reticence in revealing any of his testimony to Meade did not prevent him from supplying information to Sickles. *OR*, XXVII, pt. 1, pp. 122, 125–126, 132, 136–137. Sykes in flatly denying the story said that when Meade at the meeting of the corps commanders at three o'clock directed him to throw his whole corps upon the left of the Union line, he immediately sent a staff officer to put the troops in motion. At that time Sykes's troops were about two miles from the front, and Barnes's division thus made good time to get near the Wheatfield in less than an hour. Circumstantial evidence and the testimony of Col. Tilton corroborate Sykes's denial of procrastination. Tilton stoutly asserted that his and Sweitzer's brigades were in position before any rifle shots were fired, although there was

some shelling. William S. Tilton to Barnes, Mar. 14, 1864, Copy, Manuscripts of General James Barnes, NYHS; Sykes to Editor of the *Chronicle* [Washington, D. C.], Dec. 9, 1865, in Gross, *Battlefield of Gettysburg*, 26–27.

86. *OR*, XXVII, pt. 1, p. 601.

87. *Ibid.*, pp. 593, 601.

88. Bachelder, "Gettysburg Campaign," III, 133A–134A, MS; R. G. Carter [of 22nd Mass.] to Bachelder, Nov. 6, 1889; C. W. Prescott to *id.*, Sept. 27, 1894, Bachelder Papers; *OR*, XXVII, pt. 1, pp. 483, 601, 607, 610–611.

89. R. G. Carter to Bachelder, Nov. 6, 1889, Bachelder Papers. To this positive statement about their ignorance of De Trobriand's location can be added the argument of silence. None of the official reports revealed that De Trobriand was aware of the presence of Barnes's brigades, or that Sweitzer and Tilton knew of his location. *OR*, XXVII, pt. 1, pp. 520, 525, 601, 607, 610–611.

90. *Ibid.*, pp. 235, 593–594, 660. The batteries were Lt. Aaron F. Walcott's 3rd Battery (C), Mass. Light, six 12-pounders, and Lt. Malbone B. Watson's 5th U. S. Battery I, four 3-inch. Hunt charged that there was no need for this highhanded action, because the Artillery Reserve had been able to take care of all the demands of the Third Corps. "The effect," he said, "was to deprive the Fifth Corps of its batteries, without the knowledge and to the inconvenience of the commander of the corps." *Ibid.*, p. 235.

91. *Ibid.*, pp. 369, 379.

92. CCW, *Report*, I, 406.

93. *OR*, XXVII, pt. 1, p. 379.

94. *Ibid.*, pp. 494, 520. The statements of Birney in both his report and his testimony before the Committee on the Conduct of the War are very misleading. They give the impression, as do the claims by "Historicus," that Third Corps troops were supported, not relieved, by brigades from the Fifth and Second Corps. See *ibid.*, pp. 132, 133, 483–484; CCW, *Report*, I, 367. The testimony of "Historicus" is so unreliable, if not downright mendacious, that it would be unworthy of attention if certain recent accounts of the battle did not depend upon it as a source of information.

95. *OR*, XXVII, pt. 1, pp. 593–594; F. T. Locke to J. S. Chamberlain, July 5, 1886, Frost Family Collection, YU.

96. CCW, *Report*, I, 367; *OR*, XXVII, pt. 1, p. 483; Tremain, *Two Days of War*, 81–85. Tremain told a neat little story of how he saw what turned out to be Gen. Samuel K. Zook's brigade of Caldwell's division moving in a direction away from De Trobriand's line, where it was needed. He could not find Caldwell but prevailed upon Zook to turn his troops, without orders from his superior, and help De Trobriand. Zook's troops arrived in the "nick of time" and thus relieved a critical situation. Later, Tremain said, he "happily" introduced Zook to Birney. If so, it must have been Zook's ghost, for Lt. Col. John Fraser of the 140th Pa. reported Zook had been mortally wounded when leading his brigade into the action Tremain mentioned. *OR*, XXVII, pt. 1, p. 395.

97. Maj. Gen. St. Clair A. Mulholland, "The Gettysburg Campaign," *Philadelphia Weekly Times*, Feb. 14, 1880.

98. *OR*, XXVII, pt. 1, pp. 370–371; CCW, *Report*, I, 407. With this

change Birney resumed his role as commander of the Third Corps and Gibbon took charge again of the Second Corps. Hancock said he directed operations along the "left centre" of the Union line, a vague phrase which presumably did not include the area of the Round Tops.

99. *OR*, XXVII, pt. 1, pp. 696–697.

100. *Cf. ante*, XV, 386. In his report Robertson said that to keep the right of his brigade in touch with Law's left he could not rest his own left on the Emmitsburg road, as he had been instructed to do, and so he pulled away from it toward the east. *OR*, XXVII, pt. 2, p. 404.

101. According to some fairly reliable accounts Hood received his wound very early in the engagement, before Benning's and Anderson's brigades came into action. *OR*, XXVII, pt. 1, p. 405; *The Times* [London], Aug. 18, 1863; Gen. George T. Anderson to Bachelder, Mar. 15, 1876, Bachelder Papers.

102. *OR*, XXVII, pt. 2, p. 405. Benning made no mention of having received a dispatch from Robertson, whereas Anderson did. *Ibid.*, pp. 414–415; Gen. George T. Anderson to Bachelder, Mar. 15, 1876, Bachelder Papers. Anderson said he did not see Law during the fight. *Ibid.* If Law did all he claimed for himself in directing operations of Anderson's and Benning's brigades in support of Robertson, it is peculiar that none of these generals mentioned having received orders from him. As a matter of fact, Benning claimed he went into action on his own initiative when he saw Robertson could not carry the heights above Devil's Den without help. See Law, "The Struggle for 'Round Top,' " *B&L*, III, pt. 1, p. 324; *OR*, XXVII, pt. 2, pp. 407–409, 415.

103. *Ibid.*, pt. 1, pp. 379–382, 386, 393–395, 400–401, 493–494, 520–521, 601–602, 611, 634, 645; pt. 2, pp. 397, 399–402, 415, 420–422, 424–426.

104. McLaws to his wife, July 7, 1863, Lafayette McLaws Papers, UNC; Alexander, *Military Memoirs*, 395; *OR*, XXVII, pt. 2, pp. 397, 399, 404–405. Alexander claimed McLaws' division was held back an hour, while Capt. George Hillyer of the 9th Ga. put the time the division advanced an hour and a half after Anderson's brigade went into action. Both estimates seem excessive.

105. Ross, *Cities and Camps*, 56; *The Times* [London], Aug. 18, 1863.

106. *The Times, ibid.* Fremantle presented a slightly different version of this incident when he wrote that Longstreet led a Ga. regiment in a charge against a battery, "hat in hand, and in front of everybody." *Three Months in the Southern States*, 261. Wofford's brigade was composed entirely of Ga. regiments.

107. Fremantle wrote: "Everyone deplores that Longstreet *will* expose himself in such a reckless manner." *Ibid.*

108. Ross, *Cities and Camps*, 52.

109. McLaws to his wife, July 7, 1863, Lafayette McLaws Papers, UNC.

110. Notes on Gettysburg, [no date], Lafayette McLaws Papers, DU. Robertson, feeling pressure on his left before Benning and Anderson arrived, sent word to Hood asking that he request McLaws to advance. *OR*, XXVII, pt. 1, pp. 404–405. Law recalled how, on becoming aware of no activity from McLaws, he had halted his line, put it in a defensive position, and then ridden

to the Emmitsburg road to get help from McLaws. He found Kershaw, who said he had no orders to move but would do so if Law would show where he could be of most help. A likely story, but it has at least two things wrong with it. No one except Law vouches for it, and it is doubtful whether Kershaw would have moved without orders from McLaws or Longstreet. See Law, "The Struggle for 'Round Top,' " *B&L*, III, pt. 1, p. 325.

111. *OR*, XXVII, pt. 1, pp. 607, 611; pt. 2, pp. 397, 399; R. G. Carter [22nd Mass.] to Bachelder, Nov. 6, 1889, Bachelder Papers. Anderson recalled that someone ordered the 15th S. C. under Col. W. D. De Saussure from Kershaw's brigade to cover his left. Gen. George T. Anderson to Bachelder, Mar. 15, 1876, Dec. 4, 1894, Bachelder Papers. That may be, but by then Kershaw's brigade, followed soon by Semmes's, had entered the fray farther to the left. See Kershaw's report in *OR*, XXVII, pt. 2, pp. 368–369. This sequence of events suggests that McLaws' division moved sooner than his critics said.

112. *Ibid.*, pt. 1, p. 607; pt. 2, p. 368; Oral Statements of Confederate Wounded, in Bachelder, "Gettysburg Campaign," III, 150, MS, Bachelder Papers.

113. According to Bachelder the "stony hill covered with timber" mentioned in Kershaw's report was the same as that occupied by Barnes's two brigades. Except for the fact that Tilton's flank was in the air Bachelder considered it a "peculiarly strong military position." *Ibid.*, 137–138; R. G. Carter to Bachelder, Nov. 6, 1889, Bachelder Papers; *OR*, XXVII, pt. 1, pp. 607–608.

114. Account of [Col.] J. B. Sweitzer, [no date], Joshua L. Chamberlain Papers, LC; *OR*, XXVII, pt. 1, p. 611.

115. Bachelder, "Gettysburg Campaign," III, 138, MS, Bachelder Papers.

116. *Ibid.*, 150; *OR*, XXVII, pt. 1, pp. 379, 386, 393–395; pt. 2, p. 368; Warner, *Generals in Gray*, 171, 272.

117. Alexander, *Military Memoirs*, 395. Alexander said they moved twenty minutes later but did not indicate how he arrived at that figure. Kershaw in his battle report clearly implied that Barksdale came into action soon after his brigade had begun to fight. In a much later account he claimed that Barksdale's brigade was not even lined up for an immediate advance when his own brigade had already moved some distance toward the enemy, and that not until he got to the Emmitsburg road did Barksdale's drums beat the assembly. As a result he claimed to have had no support on his left for a considerable time. *OR*, XXVII, pt. 2, p. 368; J. B. Kershaw, "Kershaw's Brigade at Gettysburg," *B&L*, III, pt. 1, p. 334. More convincing evidence suggested just the contrary; Barksdale could hardly wait for the order to advance.

118. Ross, *Cities and Camps*, 52–53; B. G. Humphreys, "Gov. Wm. Barksdale and Barksdale's Brigade," MS, [no date], J. F. H. Claiborne Papers, UNC; Bachelder, "Gettysburg Campaign," III, 175, MS; B. G. Humphreys to Bachelder, May 1, 1876, Bachelder Papers.

119. *Ibid.*; Bachelder, "Gettysburg Campaign," III, 175, MS, Bachelder Papers; *OR*, XXVII, pt. 1, pp. 177–178; pt. 2, pp. 369, 429–430.

120. *Ibid.*, pp. 429–430; "Colonel E. P. Alexander's Report of the Battle of

Gettysburg," *SHSP*, IV, 235–236. Alexander wrote this report in his capacity as acting chief of Longstreet's artillery. It was not published in the *OR*.

121. "The Campaign of Gettysburg (as I Saw It)," Frederick M. Colston Book and Clippings, UNC. At Gettysburg Colston was a 2nd Lt. of artillery ordnance assigned to Alexander's Battalion of Artillery. This account appeared in the *Confederate Veteran* sometime after 1897.

122. "Colonel E. P. Alexander's Report of the Battle of Gettysburg," *SHSP*, IV, 235–236.

123. Longstreet's immediate presence undoubtedly contributed to his success on this part of the field. In his report Kershaw very clearly stated that he kept in touch with McLaws and Longstreet by means of messages or personal conferences, and that he made his advance according to their instructions. *OR*, XXVII, pt. 2, pp. 367–368.

124. *OR*, XXVII, pt. 1, p. 379; Bachelder, Map of the Battlefield of Gettysburg, Second Day.

125. R. G. Carter to Bachelder, Nov. 6, 1889, Bachelder Papers.

126. *OR*, XXVII, pt. 1, p. 379.

127. *Ibid.*, p. 611.

128. *Ibid.*, pp. 379, 634, 645.

129. Birney said he assumed command of the corps at 6:00 P.M. when he found Sickles near Trostle's farm, seriously wounded. He then rode to Humphreys' part of the front and stayed there some time. "Historicus" put the time of Sickles' wound near 7:00 P.M. *Ibid.*, pp. 133, 483. For information about the location of Sykes, Zook, and Barnes see *ibid.*, pp. 380, 395, 593, 612; Account of J. B. Sweitzer, [no date], Joshua L. Chamberlain Papers, LC; Barnes to Gen. Birney, Aug. 22, 1863, Copy, Manuscripts of General James Barnes, NYHS.

130. *OR*, XXVII, pt. 1, pp. 611–612. For accounts of other units in the Caldwell counterattack see *ibid.*, pp. 379–380, 382, 386, 389–390, 394, 396–398, 401, 634–635, 639, 645–650.

131. Oral Statement of Gen. Wofford in Bachelder, "Gettysburg Campaign," III, 175A, MS, Bachelder Papers.

132. *OR*, XXVII, pt. 1, p. 612.

133. *Ibid.*, pp. 175, 177–179, 380, 382, 386, 394, 401, 483–484, 494, 497–499, 501, 520–521, 593, 602, 608, 612, 635.

134. Lt. Col. C. H. Morgan's Account, Typescript, Bachelder Papers. Hancock was right, for as far as can be determined the men fought splendidly. Whether the disaster to Caldwell's division on July 2 was considered a reflection on his generalship is not known, but in the reorganization of the Army of the Potomac in Mar., 1864, he was relieved of his command. See Webb to his wife, Mar. 26, 1864, Webb Collection. Webb wrote: "Caldwell leaves in [?]. He feels very badly. I am very fond of him, and am sorry to see him owsted [sic]."

135. *OR*, pt. 1, p. 483. Although Birney did not say so, he was probably referring to the withdrawal of Barnes's brigades to avoid a flanking attack on his right by Kershaw's men coming from the direction of the Rose house. See

ibid., pp. 601, 607–608, 611. Because of his wound Barnes left the Army of the Potomac right after the battle, never to return. Some good friend in the army, however, tipped him off about Birney's adverse comments in his report, which was written on Aug. 7, 1863, but not published until later. *Ibid.,* pp. 482, 605. Barnes was completely surprised to hear of Birney's complaint about the want of proper support given him by his division, and he wrote Birney about it. Barnes recalled that he had met Birney on the field several times and at Birney's request had changed the position of one of his brigades. He did not remember him evincing any dissatisfaction with his conduct. Birney stiffly refused to enlighten Barnes and gave as his excuse army orders regulating the publication of official reports. Barnes to Gen. Birney, Aug. 22, 23, 1863, Copies, Manuscripts of General James Barnes, NYHS.

136. *OR,* XXVII, pt. 1, pp. 132–133. See also a version of the same story in De Trobriand, *Four Years with the Army of the Potomac,* 498. The weight of evidence favors Barnes's indignant denunciation of the story as an outright fabrication. His reply and that of a staff officer in the Fifth Corps to "Historicus" appeared in the *New York Herald* on Mar. 18 and 21, 1864. Quoted in Meade, *Life and Letters,* II, 331–335. Col. Tilton, thoroughly outraged, wrote: "The idea of our division lying down to let other troops pass over them to the front! This is too much and I must ask you to recall . . . that the first two brigades of your division . . . did not budge until the troops of the Third Corps on their right and left had broken and were routed." William S. Tilton to Barnes, Mar. 14, 1864, Copy, Manuscripts of General James Barnes, NYHS. "Historicus" in his answer to Barnes on Apr. 4, 1864, in the *Herald* said that Birney had made the charge of Barnes's misconduct in a letter to him. In this communication Birney said he had complained about Barnes to Sedgwick and Sykes in the council meeting in Meade's headquarters on the night of July 2. According to this account Sykes had told Birney that Sweitzer had made the same allegation. Quoted in Meade, *Life and Letters,* II, 337–340. Barnes then wrote to Sweitzer and Sedgwick to verify Birney's accusation. Both denied any knowledge of Birney's dissatisfaction with Barnes. Barnes to J. B. Sweitzer, Apr. 6, 1864; Sweitzer to Barnes, Apr. 8, 1864; Barnes to John Sedgwick, Apr. 8, 1864; Sedgwick to Barnes, Apr. 10, 1864, Manuscripts of General James Barnes, NYHS.

137. William S. Tilton to Bachelder, Feb. 8, 1875, Bachelder Papers. Ironically Barnes in his own report mentioned passing over troops of a Third Corps brigade who were lying down, apparently refusing to move. See *OR,* XXVII, pt. 1, p. 601.

138. *Ibid.,* pt. 2, pp. 399–400.

139. *Ibid.,* p. 402.

140. *Ibid.,* pt. 1, p. 653; Bachelder, "Gettysburg Campaign," III, 160, MS, Bachelder Papers.

141. Adam Torrance to his wife, July 5–6, 1863, Torrance Collection, PDPR; *OR,* XXVII, pt. 1, p. 653; Crawford to Prof. Jacobs, Dec. [no date], 1863, S. W. Crawford Papers, LC.

142. E. M. Woodward to S. P. Bates, Feb. 7, 1876, Bates Collection.

143. Crawford to Prof. Jacobs, Dec. [no date], 1863, S. W. Crawford Papers, LC.

144. Crawford said the cheers of his men exceeded anything he ever heard. *Ibid.*; Crawford to Rothermel, Mar. 8, 1871, Peter F. Rothermel Collection, PDPR. For a confirmation of Crawford's account see Robert A. McCoy to Rothermel, June 20, 1871, *ibid.*; J. R. Sypher, *History of the Pennsylvania Reserve Corps* (Lancaster, 1865), 460–461.

145. *OR*, XXVII, pt. 1, pp. 653–654. Crawford said he met the enemy just after crossing Plum Run. Crawford to Rothermel, Mar. 8, 1871, Peter F. Rothermel Collection, PDPR.

146. Col. G. M. Jackson to Rothermel, July 5, 1871, *ibid.* For claims of similar nature see Robert A. McCoy to *id.*, June 20, 1871, *ibid.*; E. M. Woodward to S. P. Bates, Feb. 7, 1876, Bates Collection; Jacobs, *Rebel Invasion*, 32–34. Jacobs said the Reserves saved the Union left. Of Jacobs' account Edward Everett remarked sceptically: "I am inclined to think, however, that it claims too much credit for the 'Reserves.'" Everett to Lyman, Dec. 4, 1863, Theodore Lyman Papers, MHS.

147. *OR*, XXVII, pt. 1, pp. 663, 665, 671, 684–685. About the role of Nevin's brigade see also Bachelder, "Gettysburg Campaign," III, 162 note, MS, Bachelder Papers.

148. Alexander later wrote: "And when I got to take in all the topography I was very much disappointed. It was not the enemy's main line we had broken." "Battle of Gettysburg," MS, E. P. Alexander Papers, UNC. In describing the battle at the time Alexander reported that the enemy retreated about three-fourths of a mile, to a "high ridge & very strong position where they were reinforced & stood, repulsing our infantry line. . . ." Alexander to his father, July 17, 1863, Alexander-Hillhouse Papers, UNC.

149. *OR*, XXVII, pt. 2, p. 359; Notes on Gettysburg, [no date], Lafayette McLaws Papers, DU. Both Sykes and Crawford agreed that it was almost dark when the Reserves gained possession of the stone wall. *OR*, XXVII, pt. 1, pp. 593, 654.

NOTES TO CHAPTER XVI

1. *OR*, XXVII, pt. 1, p. 370; Bachelder, Map of the Battlefield of Gettysburg, Second Day.

2. *OR*, XXVII, pt. 1, p. 533.

3. CCW, *Report*, I, 393.

4. *OR*, XXVII, pt. 1, pp. 532–533.

5. *Ibid.*, p. 533. Humphreys said he had no intention of moving his division back until Birney ordered him to do so. He had just carried out the order when Birney reached the division. Humphreys to Birney, Oct. 4, 1863, A. A. Humphreys Papers, HSP. In a letter written on Oct. 2 Humphreys objected to a statement in Birney's original battle report, which he thought did him a "great injustice." Birney said that after he assumed command of the corps he rode

over to the Second Division, and finding it in " 'some confusion,' " he " 'aided its officers in rallying it.' " The officers and men responded, Birney said, with " 'great alacrity' " and changed front. Humphreys, denying that he had ever lost control of his division so as to need Birney's assistance, asked him to delete or modify the offensive passage, and Birney did so. See Birney to Humphreys, Oct. 4, 1863, *ibid*.

6. Humphreys to Archibald Campbell, Aug. 6, 1863, *ibid*.

7. Bachelder, "Gettysburg Campaign," III, 195, MS, Bachelder Papers.

8. Humphreys to his wife July 4, 1863, A. A. Humphreys Papers, HSP.

9. *OR*, XXVII, pt. 1, pp. 370, 416, 419, 423, 426; Bachelder, Notes relating to the services of troops at Gettysburg, 1863, MS, Huntington Library.

10. *OR*, XXVII, pt. 1, p. 533; Gibbon, *Recollections*, 137–138.

11. *OR*, XXVII, pt. 1, pp. 370, 416.

12. Humphreys to Archibald Campbell, Aug. 6, 1863, A. A. Humphreys Papers, HSP.

13. Humphreys said he brought but 5,000 officers and men into action on July 2. Col. William R. Brewster, commander of the Second Brigade, reported 1,837 officers and men on hand the same day. The official count for June 30, 1863, reported 6,120 present for duty in Humphreys' division, and 2,269 in Brewster's brigade. In comparing these figures with those reported by Humphreys and Brewster, there is the suggestion that in each brigade the official count was inflated by 350 to 450 officers and men. If so, Brigadier General Joseph B. Carr, commander of the First Brigade, who is credited with 2,241 officers and men, had actually about 1,800 on duty. Therefore Humphreys probably had on his line 1,800 officers and men in the First Brigade, 1,837 in the Second, and 221 in Sewell's regiment of Burling's brigade, for a total of 3,858. *OR*, XXVII, pt. 1, pp. 534, 560; Selected Pages from Historical and Statistical Record of the Principal Military Commands in the Union and Confederate Armies, IV, 143–144, Entry 161, Record Group 94, NA; Toombs, *New Jersey Troops*, 10.

14. The batteries were Lt. Francis W. Seeley's Battery K, 4th U.S., of six 12-pounders, and Lt. John G. Turnbull's Batteries F and K, 3rd U.S., also six 12-pounders. *OR*, XXVII, pt. 1, pp. 161, 167, 235, 533.

15. Humphreys to Archibald Campbell, Aug. 6, 1863, A. A. Humphreys Papers, HSP.

16. *OR*, XXVII, pt. 1, p. 873. Humphreys said the men dragged the guns back until they came to some rough ground. He gave orders to abandon them when too many men pulling on them were killed. Later on Union infantry recovered them. Humphreys to Hancock, Oct. 2, 1863, A. A. Humphreys Papers, HSP.

17. *OR*, XXVII, pt. 1, p. 533.

18. Humphreys to his wife, July 4, 1863, A. A. Humphreys Papers, HSP.

19. *Id*. to Archibald Campbell, Aug. 6, 1863, *ibid*.

20. CCW, *Report*, I, 392.

21. Young, *What a Boy Saw in the Army*, 303, 307, 309; Humphreys to Gen. Hammond, Surgeon General, U. S. Army, Aug. 5, 1863, A. A. Humphreys

Papers, HSP. Humphreys wrote to inquire whether his orderly, James F. Dimond, 6th U.S. Cavalry, missing since Gettysburg, might be lying in some army hospital. Humphreys last saw him during the retreat of his division on July 2. Dimond, though wounded in the right arm, insisted upon turning his horse over to Humphreys, who had been forced to dismount when his own horse was killed.

22. Humphreys to his wife, July 4, 1863, *ibid.* See also *id.* to Hancock, Oct. 2, 1863, *ibid.*, in which he said that it took his division more than half an hour to retreat from its battle line to the ridge.

23. W. R. Brewster to Humphreys, Oct. 4, 1863, *ibid.* See similar expressions in Gen. Carr's report in *OR*, XXVII, pt. 1, p. 544.

24. Gibbon, *Recollections*, 137–138; *OR*, XXVII, pt. 1, pp. 370, 442–443, 451.

25. Hancock to Humphreys, Oct. 10, 1863, A. A. Humphreys Papers, HSP; *OR*, XXVII, pt. 1, pp. 371, 533.

26. *Ibid.*, p. 178. Maj. John F. Langley of the 12th N.H. regiment testified that the enemy kept crowding them closely and grabbed several of his men as prisoners. Langley to Bachelder, Mar. 24, 1864, Typescript, Bachelder Papers.

27. *OR*, XXVII, pt. 1, pp. 497–505; John Bigelow, Jr., *The Peach Orchard, Gettysburg, July 2, 1863* (Minneapolis, 1910), 12. Between 5:00 and 6:00 P.M. shot and shell coming from Confederate artillery centered more and more on the Trostle farm buildings, so that the place became too "hot" for a corps headquarters. Sickles decided to move to the rear, and while on the way he was hit by round shot just below the knee. Seeing the break in his line at the Peach Orchard and the rapid retreat of his infantry and artillery, Sickles worried about being captured. G. E. Randolph to Bachelder, Mar. 4, 1866, Bachelder Papers.

28. Report of Henry J. Hunt to Gen. William T. Sherman, Feb. 1, 1882, Copy, *ibid.*

29. *OR*, XXVII, pt. 1, pp. 167, 235, 872, 881. See map in Naisawald, *Grape and Canister*, 369. Bigelow had six 12-pounders instead of the four Hunt reported.

30. *OR*, XXVII, pt. 1, pp. 167, 499, 601, 607–608, 872, 881–882, 885–890; Bigelow, *The Peach Orchard*, 17. Bigelow explained what it meant to "retire by prolonge." The prolonges or ropes were attached, he said, at one end to the pintles or hooks of the limbers, and at the other end to the gun trails. After the gun was fired it was pulled back a safe distance by horses hitched to the limber.

31. This number is a calculated guess based upon approximate figures furnished by Col. Humphreys for the size of the brigade. Unfortunately he was not consistent in his approximations. See *OR*, XXVII, pt. 2, pp. 338, 363; "Gov. William Barksdale and Barksdale's Brigade," by B. G. Humphreys, MS, J.F.H. Claiborne Papers, UNC; B. G. Humphreys to Bachelder, May 1, 1876, Bachelder Papers. Wofford's brigade immediately followed Barksdale's and went in the direction taken by the 21st Miss. Undoubtedly some of Wofford's men aided them in their exploits.

32. "Gov. William Barksdale and Barksdale's Brigade," by B. G. Humphreys, MS, J. F.H. Claiborne Papers, UNC; B. G. Humphreys to Bachelder, May 1, 1876; Bachelder, "Gettysburg Campaign," III, 167, 175, 187–188, MS, Bachelder Papers. Humphreys threatened Phillips' and overran Bigelow's and Watson's batteries, temporarily capturing at least eight guns.

33. *OR*, XXVII, pt. 1, p. 882.

34. Capt. [John] Bigelow's Letter, [no date], Typescript, Bachelder Papers.

35. *OR*, XXVII, pt. 1, pp. 501, 505; Survivors' Association, *History of the 118th Pennsylvania Volunteers*, 247–251; Toombs, *New Jersey Troops*, 222–223.

36. Naisawald, *Grape and Canister*, 390, 392; Bigelow's Letter, [no date], Typescript, Bachelder Papers.

37. *Ibid.* According to Bigelow, McGilvery's horse was "riddled" with bullets during the ride.

38. *OR*, XXVII, pt. 1, p. 882.

39. *Ibid.*, pp. 608, 886; Survivors' Association, *118th Pennsylvania Volunteers*, 244–245; William S. Tilton to Barnes, Mar. 14, 1864, Copy, Manuscripts of General James Barnes, NYHS. Tilton complained: "I had men injured . . . by being jumped upon by fleeing Third Corps men as we lay behind a stone wall after our change of front."

40. Naisawald, *Grape and Canister*, 394; *OR*, XXVII, pt. 1, pp. 882, 886; John Bigelow to Bachelder, Apr. 10, 1885, in possession of Francis C. Carleton, Belmont, Mass. Bigelow recalled that he held back most of the 21st Miss. with his frontal fire, but a part of the regiment came down Trostle's lane on his right to outflank him. Before making his stand near Trostle's lane Bigelow sent his two left pieces to the rear because he could not find enough room to work them among the boulders strewn over that part of the field. Bigelow, *The Peach Orchard*, 18.

41. *OR*, XXVII, pt. 1, pp. 159, 162, 167–168, 235–236, 882–883. McGilvery collected the following batteries: Lt. M. F. Watson's Battery I, 4th U.S. of the Fifth Corps Artillery Brigade, four 3-inch; a volunteer battery, identity and number of guns unknown; Phillips' 5th Mass. of the Artillery Reserve, three 3-inch; Thompson's Pa. Battery of the Artillery Reserve, two 3-inch; Lt. Edwin B. Dow's Battery F, 6th Maine of the Artillery Reserve, Capt. R. H. Fitzhugh's brigade, four 12-pounders; Capt. James McKay Rorty's Battery B, 1st N.Y. of Second Corps Artillery Brigade, four 10-pounders.

42. *Ibid.*, p. 883; Capt. C. A. Phillips to Bachelder, [no date], Typescript; Bachelder, "Gettysburg Campaign," III, 175, MS, Bachelder Papers. The 21st Miss. captured Watson's guns; the volunteer battery was driven off by the fire of the enemy artillery; Rorty's battery apparently suffered the same fate; and Thompson's guns ran out of ammunition. McGilvery did not say what happened to one of Phillips' pieces.

43. *OR*, XXVII, pt. 1, pp. 882–883, 897. It was Lt. Dow who concluded that by creating a bold front McGilvery completely fooled the enemy about the strength of the Union forces on that part of Cemetery Ridge.

44. For praise by his subordinates of McGilvery's inspiring leadership see

ibid., p. 898; Capt. J. H. Huntington to Bachelder, June 6, 1878, Bachelder Papers.

45. *OR*, XXVII, pt. 1, pp. 370, 472, 474–475, 483–484; Bachelder to John Bigelow, Mar. 23, 1885, Press Letter Book, Bachelder Papers. Birney said he assigned Willard's brigade to its position. There is no corroborating evidence to support this statement. To the contrary, Hancock reported that Birney stayed with troops of the Third Corps who were retreating to the rear. *OR*, XXVII, pt. 1, pp. 371, 483–484; CCW, *Report*, I, 407. Bigelow claimed that after his battery had been overrun, McGilvery with his guns filled the gap in the Union lines from 6:30 to 7:15 P.M., at which time Willard's brigade was brought to his support. Bigelow, *The Peach Orchard*, 23, 32.

46. Capt. C. A. Richardson to Bachelder, Aug. 18, 1869, Bachelder Papers.

47. *OR*, XXVII, pt. 1, pp. 472–473, 477.

48. *Ibid.* pp. 472, 660; Bachelder, "Gettysburg Campaign," III, 187–188, MS, Bachelder Papers. Information is based upon official reports and oral statements of Capt. J. B. Fassett of Birney's staff and Col. Humphreys.

49. Slocum had turned command of his corps over to Williams twice during the battle, on the afternoon of the 1st and the morning of the 2nd. In the second instance Meade, expecting to take the offensive on the right, had made Slocum commander of a wing consisting of two other corps besides his own. When Meade transferred the Fifth and Sixth Corps to bolster his sagging left flank, he thought Slocum had automatically assumed he was no longer wing commander. But Slocum still considered himself in charge of the right wing. Perhaps he thought the Eleventh Corps had been continued under him after the first day. In any event Slocum kept Williams on as commander of the Twelfth Corps, and as such he appeared at the council of war that night, much to the surprise of Meade, who nevertheless was too polite to say anything about it. *OR*, XXVII, pt. 1, pp. 765, 768–770. Williams had a very high opinion of Ruger as a soldier and a man. Williams to his daughters, Aug. 6, 1863, in *Alpheus Williams Letters*, 252.

50. *OR*, XXVII, pt. 1, pp. 766, 773–774.

51. Williams to Bachelder, Nov. 10, 1865, Bachelder Papers; Williams to his daughters, July 6, 1863, in *Alpheus Williams Letters*, 228. Williams said that an officer of Gen. Slocum's staff started with him but was of little help, for he did not know just where the reinforcements were needed. Fortunately Col. William P. Maulsby, a resident of Westminster, Md., who was familiar with the country around Gettysburg, commanded the lead regiment in the column. Though Williams made no mention of this coincidence, Maulsby's immediate superior, Gen. Lockwood, cited the usefulness to operations of the Marylander's knowledge of local geography. Klein, ed., *Just South of Gettysburg*, 222; *OR*, XXVII, pt. 1, p. 804.

52. *Alpheus Williams Letters*, 228.

53. Williams to Bachelder, Nov. 10, 1865, Bachelder Papers.

54. *Id.* to *id.*, Apr. 21, 1864, Nov. 10, 1865, *ibid.*; *Alpheus Williams Letters*, 228; *OR*, XXVII, pt. 1, pp. 766, 774, 778, 780, 783, 789, 793, 800, 803, 804–806, 809; Bachelder, Map of the Battlefield of Gettysburg, Second Day. The

time of Williams' arrival is uncertain; though there is conflicting evidence, most likely he arrived after Willard's brigade had engaged and driven back the enemy. All Twelfth Corps accounts agree that the fighting had pretty well subsided and the enemy was retreating when Williams and his men got to the left.

55. *Alpheus Williams Letters*, 228. If the First Division advanced at all beyond Cemetery Ridge it did not go very far, or get into action. With respect to Lockwood's advance none of the accounts are clear.

56. *Ibid.*; Williams to Bachelder, Apr. 21, 1864, Nov. 10, 1865, Bachelder Papers. Williams said he did not know whose guns Lockwood's men had captured. Bachelder after a careful study of battle reports and interviews with participants concluded that they helped Lt. Dow bring off three of Bigelow's guns. The Pa. Reserves, he asserted, brought off the fourth one in the morning of July 3, together with five caissons. *Id.* to *id.*, Apr. 21, 1864; Bachelder to John Bigelow, Mar. 23, 1885, Press Letter Book, *ibid.*

57. *Alpheus Williams Letters*, 228; Williams to Bachelder, Apr. 21, 1864, Bachelder Papers. A tradition of the battle based upon a statement in Hancock's battle report had Meade himself leading Lockwood's brigade into action. Williams, however, very definitely said that he met only one general officer (and it was not Meade) before his men charged the enemy. He mentioned seeing Meade in connection with his march back to Culp's Hill. Though Hancock knew both generals, in the heat and smoke of battle he or someone on his staff might have mistaken Williams for Meade. Both were middle-aged and both sported large bushy beards.

58. Wilcox, Wright, and Col. David Lang who commanded Perry's brigade understood that they were to move forward together. Instead of one signal being given for all to go forward in a solid line, the brigade on the left would wait until the one on the right started out. Obviously each brigadier was to have his men in formation ready to go on an instant's notice. Depending upon the efficiency of the brigadier, there would be intervals of varying lengths of time between the movement of the right and the departure of the left brigades. The effect was to move *en echelon* as Hill reported, but not nearly to the extent he indicated. *OR*, XXVII, pt. 1, pp. 608, 614, 618, 622, 631, 633.

59. *Ibid.*, pp. 618, 623; A. R. Wright to Mrs. Wright, July 7, 1863, quoted in Freeman, *Lee's Lieutenants*, III, 125–126. Gens. Humphreys and Wilcox agreed almost to the minute about when Barksdale's, Wilcox', and Lang's brigades hit the Union line. A. A. Humphreys to Wilcox, Nov. 30, 1877, quoted in "General C. M. Wilcox on the Battle of Gettysburg," *SHSP*, VI, 99. The sequence of events strongly substantiates the correctness of this hour.

60. Humphreys was positive that the attack on his front and right occurred "nearly simultaneous" with that on his left. He identified the attacking units as Barksdale's, Wilcox', Perry's, and Wright's brigades. See *ibid.* If their attack had been truly *en echelon* they would not have hit his line at almost the same time.

61. *OR*, XXVII, pt. 1, pp. 159, 167, 371, 419, 423, 426, 478, 880; Bachelder, Map of the Battlefield of Gettysburg, Second Day.

62. *Ibid.; OR*, XXVII, pt. 2, pp. 633–634. If Posey had advanced to attack the Union main line, he would have hit the section held by Gen. Alexander Hays's division of the Second Corps. Union reports for July 2 from that division say nothing of a real threat on that front. The only references to fighting there are to skirmishes which occurred around the Bliss buildings. See *ibid.*, pt. 1, pp. 453, 457, 464–465, 470.

63. *Ibid.*, pt. 2, p. 621; Addendum to Copy of Report of Brig. Gen. Cadmus M. Wilcox . . . , July 17, 1863, quoted in Freeman, *R. E. Lee*, III, 555. Wright maintained that in response to a call for supports, Anderson sent a message saying that both Posey and Mahone had been ordered in and he would repeat the order. Wright to Mrs. Wright, July 7, 1863, quoted in Freeman, *Lee's Lieutenants*, III, 126.

64. See Alexander, *Military Memoirs*, 403–404.

65. *OR*, XXVII, pt. 2, pp. 618, 620, 623, 631. Humphreys vehemently denounced as false Confederate reports of breaking successive lines of his infantry and compelling him to abandon much of his artillery. Humphreys, "The Fight for Round Top," *Philadelphia Weekly Times*, Feb. 2, 1878.

66. Bachelder, Map of the Battlefield of Gettysburg, Second Day.

67. Wright described how his men climbed up the "side of the mountain" which in one place was "so precipitous," he said, that they could with "difficulty climb it." Wright to Mrs. Wright, July 7, 1863, quoted in Freeman, *Lee's Lieutenants*, III, 126. If he thought the western slope of Cemetery Ridge was steep, he should have tried the western face of Little Round Top!

68. *OR*, XXVII, pt. 2, pp. 623–624. There is no rocky gorge on that part of the east slope of Cemetery Ridge.

69. Alexander, *Military Memoirs*, 421–422.

70. The few extant regimental reports in Wright's brigade do not substantiate his claims of a successful penetration of the enemy's lines. *OR*, XXVII, pt. 2, pp. 628–630. Just as misleading as Wright's account of his advance were the claims of the number of guns captured by Anderson's men. No more than four Union batteries with a total of twenty-four guns had positions on or close to the Emmitsburg road where they might be exposed to capture. The batteries were Weir's Battery C, 5th U.S.; Turnbull's Batteries F and K, 3rd U.S.; Seeley's Battery K, 4th U.S.; and Brown's Battery B, 1st R. I. Without question Weir lost three, Turnbull four, and Brown from one to six guns. Seeley got all his guns safely off the field, but on the way to join McGilvery's line he might have taken a temporary position to fire away at Wilcox' men and lost his six guns for his pains. However, he made no mention of this happening, but Wilcox reported the capture of six unidentified guns in the Plum Run Valley. The Confederates claimed to have overrun and temporarily seized from thirty-five to thirty-seven guns. Even assuming they captured all the guns of the four batteries, which they did not, their calculations lead to the supposition that two, or possibly three phantom batteries were wandering about somewhere in the fields west of Cemetery Ridge.

71. *Ibid.*, pt. 1, p. 417.

72. *Ibid.*, pp. 371, 425; pt. 2, pp. 618, 631. Wilcox' and Lang's brigades worked closely together under the supervision of Wilcox because he outranked Lang.

73. Col. [William] Colvill, Jr., to Bachelder, June 9, 1866, Typescript, Bachelder Papers.

74. Diary of P. H. Taylor, Entry for July 2, 1863, Copy; Bachelder to Hancock, Nov. 13, 1885, Press Letter Book, *ibid.*; OR, XXVII, pt. 1, pp. 176, 425. The 1st Minn. lost 224 officers and men, over two-thirds of the number which went into action.

75. Colvill to Bachelder, June 9, 1866, Typescript, Bachelder Papers.

76. Bachelder to Hancock, Nov. 13, 1885, Press Letter Book, *ibid.* For a warm tribute to Lt. Thomas, whose courage and skill as an artillerist contributed greatly to checking and repulsing the enemy, see Gen. William Harrow's report. *OR*, XXVII, pt. 1, p. 420. Harrow was temporarily in command of Gibbon's division.

77. *Ibid.*, pp. 258, 261, 349, 371.

78. *Ibid.*, pp. 351–352. For an account of Stannard's activities which temporarily separated him from his command, see General Stannard's Diary, Entry for July 2, 1863, Typescript, Bachelder Papers.

79. Humphreys to Hancock, Oct. 2, 1863; *id.* to Mrs. Humphreys, July 4, 1863; *id.* to Archibald Campbell, Aug. 6, 1863, A. A. Humphreys Papers, HSP. Humphreys said he saw his men drag off two of the pieces "under his own eyes." See also *OR*, XXVII, pt. 1, pp. 533, 559.

80. The regiments were the 19th Maine, First Brigade; 69th Pa., Second Brigade; and 7th Mich., Third Brigade. The 69th Pa. held a line behind the stone wall immediately in front of the famous Clump of Trees. The 7th Mich. after a considerable gap held a position in line with the stone wall to the south of the 69th Pa. The 19th Maine stood way to the left and front of the 7th Mich. The 20th Mass. in the Third Brigade never got into action, for it was kept in reserve in the second line. The men in the 7th Mich. apparently fired from a prone position. *Ibid.*, pp. 419–420, 422, 425, 427, 430–431, 436, 447.

81. Webb to his wife, July 6, 1863, Typescript, Bachelder Papers; *OR*, XXVII, pt. 1, p. 427.

82. A. R. Wright to Mrs. Wright, July 7, 1863, in Freeman, *Lee's Lieutenants*, III, 126. Wright or someone on his staff took back his harsh words about Perry's brigade by saying that it acted well and fell back only in obedience to orders despite the pressure of overwhelming numbers of the enemy. See Letter to Editor of *Georgia Constitutionalist*, author unknown, Hdqrs. Wright's Brigade, Aug. 5, 1863, in Moore, ed., *Rebellion Record, Rumors and Incidents*, VII, 45.

83. *OR*, XXVII, pt. 2, p. 624.

84. Wilcox' and Wright's brigades had about 1,800 men each and Perry's nearly 700. Wilcox said he had about 1,200 officers and men on July 3 and had lost 577 the day before. Anderson therefore used about 4,300 officers and men in the assault. The numbers for Mahone's and Posey's brigades are not available, but a correspondent of the *Richmond Enquirer* referred to them as "*two*

of his [Anderson's] strongest brigades." It is fair to assume then that they had around 2,000 officers and men each. *Ibid.*, pp. 620, 633; Alexander, *Military Memoirs*, 402; Special Correspondent, Hagerstown, July 8, in *Richmond Enquirer* (Semi-weekly Edition), July 24, 1863.

85. *OR*, XXVII, pt. 2, p. 618. For criticism of Anderson's tactics see Alexander, *Military Memoirs*, 403–404.

86. Gen. J. J. Pettigrew to [Gov.] Vance, July 9, 1863, Zebulon B. Vance Papers, North Carolina State Department of Archives and History.

87. Two contemporary accounts pictured Hill as watching the battle from a distance in company with Lee and Heth. A postwar but pretty reliable account told how he rode with his staff over to McLaws' division to see how affairs were going, just after it had launched its offensive. This writer mentioned the work of Hill's staff in rallying some of the Confederates who were falling back in groups of two or three. Fremantle, *Three Months in the Southern States*, 259–260; John Richardson Porter Diary, DU; W. W. Chamberlaine, *Memoirs of the Civil War* (Washington, D. C., 1912), 70–71.

88. Wilcox said he came near preferring charges against Anderson. Addendum to Copy of Report of Brig. Gen. Cadmus M. Wilcox . . . , July 17, 1863, quoted in Freeman, *R. E. Lee,* III, 555–556. In Wilcox' and Wright's reports references were made to messages flying back and forth between the brigadiers and Anderson. None of the reports even hinted that Anderson was near the battle line. *OR*, XXVII, pt. 2, pp. 618, 623.

89. The total of Wilcox' losses for two days of fighting was 777, and of this number 257 were captured or missing. He incurred most of his casualties on July 2. The losses for Perry's brigade were 455, of which 205 were captured or missing, most as a result of the action on July 2. All of Wright's losses resulted from the attack on July 2. His total casualties were 668, of which 333 were captured or missing. The number of troops captured or missing in Hood's entire division was 442 and in McLaws' 327. *OR*, XXVII, pt. 2, pp. 388–340, 343, 619, 631–632.

90. Alexander, *Military Memoirs*, 393.

91. *OR*, XXVII, pt. 1, pp. 371–372, 417, 453, 457, 706.

92. In a letter sent to the Editors of the *Cincinnati Commercial Gazette* and the *Washington Chronicle*, Mar. 27, 1864, Howard wrote: "For fearlessness and energetic action, Col. Carroll has not a superior." Howard Papers.

93. [Lyman to his wife], June 2, 1864, in Agassiz, ed., *Meade's Headquarters*, 139.

94. Quoted in Young, *What a Boy Saw in the Army*, 327.

95. *OR*, XXVII, pt. 1, pp. 372, 417, 427–428, 432, 434, 706, 826–827, 856. The two regiments were the 71st Pa., Col. R. Penn Smith commanding, and the 106th Pa. under Lt. Col. William L. Curry. Despite Hancock's intentions Gibbon, Webb, and the regimental commanders understood that these two units were to reinforce the Eleventh Corps. The 71st Pa., however, ended up on Culp's Hill and was placed on the right of Gen. George S. Greene's brigade.

96. *Ibid.*, pp. 233–234, 358, 365, 870; pt. 2, pp. 446, 470, 504, 543. Fourteen of the sixteen Confederate guns fired from Benner's Hill; the remaining

two, which were 20-pounder Parrotts, had a longer range and so took a position to the rear on a high point just off the Hanover road. See *ibid.*, p. 543. In addition to the help Wainwright received from eight cannon of the Twelfth Corps to the southeast of his position, he was reinforced by two 20-pounder Parrotts. See *ibid.*, pt. 1, p. 870; *Wainwright Journals*, 243.

97. *Ibid.*, 244.

98. *OR*, XXVII, pt. 2, p. 446.

99. *Ibid.*, pp. 470, 543; Wise, *Long Arm of Lee*, 637, 652.

100. *OR*, XXVII, pt. 2, pp. 470, 504, 543; pt. 3, p. 487. The statement about Ewell's foreknowledge of the time of Longstreet's attack is based not upon what Ewell said, but upon an inference from Early's report. Early said he had been informed that the attack would begin at 4:00 P.M. If he knew, it is fair to infer that Ewell was equally well informed.

101. Johnson's skirmishers might have noticed a considerable lessening of resistance along a part of their front and reported it to their respective command posts. Whether such information affected Ewell's thinking would depend upon the time he received it and the importance he attached to it. Nowhere is there the suggestion that Ewell knew about the movements of the Twelfth Corps. If aware of Longstreet's successes, he might have guessed shrewdly that Meade was weakening parts of his line to strengthen the threatened sectors. He could also hope that troops were being drawn from the front he faced, but it is doubtful that he was certain of it.

102. *Ibid.*, pt. 2, p. 447. If Ewell had thought of working with Pender's division early in the afternoon his messenger would have seen Pender, not Lane, for Pender was wounded no earlier than 6:00 P.M. Lane said he received word of it about sunset. *Ibid.*, pp. 658, 665.

103. *Ibid.*, pp. 659, 666.

104. *Ibid.*, pp. 447, 470, 555–556, 580, 582, 587–588; Bachelder, Map of the Battlefield of Gettysburg, Second Day. Early gave the impression in his report that Ewell had told him the attack would involve everyone, Hill's divisions as well as Rodes's.

105. *OR*, XXVII, pt. 2, pp. 446–447, 470, 504. According to Bachelder's Map of the Battlefield of Gettysburg, Second Day, Johnson had lined up his division in the triangular shaped area between the York and Hanover roads and about a mile from Culp's Hill. Jones's brigade moved forward about half a mile when it was detached to support the artillery.

106. *OR*, XXVII, pt. 1, p. 956; pt. 2, pp. 504, 518–519. In Johnson's advance Jones led the way followed by Nicholls and then Steuart.

107. *Ibid.*, pp. 447, 504; pt. 1, pp. 862–863. Ewell said the creek had steep banks and was only passable here and there. To overcome this obstacle the brigades had to break battle formation, form columns to wade across, and then re-form on the other side. These evolutions all took time. According to Johnson, it was dark when the attack was finally made; Ewell said it was dusk, and other accounts mention an earlier hour. See Greene's report in *ibid.*, pt. 1, p. 856. He set the time of the first charge at a few minutes before 7:00 P.M., which seems too early.

108. *Ibid.*, pp. 261, 266–267, 427, 432, 705, 731, 856; pt. 2, pp. 447, 513, 532–533, 537–539; *Wainwright Journals*, 244–245; Oral Statement of Col. E. B. Fowler of 84th N.Y., in Bachelder, "Gettysburg Campaign," III, 244–245, MS; E. B. Fowler to Bachelder, May 8, 1878; R. R. Dawes to *id.*, Mar. 18, 1868, Bachelder Papers; Dawes, "With the Sixth Wisconsin at Gettysburg," *Sketches of War History*, Ohio Commandery, MOLLUS, III, 386–387. There is a question about the identity of a N.Y. regiment sent to Greene, whether it was the 147th or the 157th. The former came from Wadsworth's division and the latter from Schurz's. Neither regiment had a battle report. Greene reported that the 147th came to his aid, whereas Schurz said it was the 157th. After the war Adjt. Henry H. Lyman in a "Historical Sketch" of the 147th claimed that it reinforced Greene on the night of July 2. See Fox, ed., *New York at Gettysburg*, III, 1002–1003.

109. *OR*, XXVII, pt. 1, pp. 857, 865–868; pt. 2, pp. 447, 504, 509–510; Oral Statement of Col. E. B. Fowler in Bachelder, "Gettysburg Campaign," III, 244–245, MS; E. B. Fowler to Bachelder, May 8, 1878; R. R. Dawes to *id.*, Mar. 18, 1868; C. P. Horton to *id.*, Jan. 23, 1867, Bachelder Papers; E. B. Fowler's Account as Told to Webb, Mar., 1894, Typescript, 1895, Webb Collection. Confederate accounts were reluctant to admit that Steuart's gains consisted mainly of empty trenches. Where reinforcing units were extending Greene's lines, Steuart did take some breastworks they were trying to occupy. As a result he inflicted casualties and took some prisoners, how many is impossible to determine. See Johnson's and Steuart's battle reports, *OR*, XXVII, pt. 2, pp. 504. 509–510; William P. Zollinger, Lamar Hollyday, and D. R. Howard, "General George H. Steuart's Brigade at the Battle of Gettysburg," *SHSP*, II, 105–107; Clark, ed., *North Carolina Regiments*, I, 148–149. Alexander accepted the Union version without question and said the trenches seized by Steuart were empty. See *Military Memoirs*, 409–410.

110. None of the Confederate battle reports mentioned the advance of their skirmishers from the empty trenches to near the pike, a distance of approximately 1,500 feet, but a few Union accounts did. See C. P. Horton to Bachelder, Jan. 23, 1867; Surgeon H. N. Howard [10th Maine] to *id.*, Mar. 23, 1882, Bachelder Papers; *OR*, XXVII, pt. 1, pp. 780, 783, 793, 800, 817. Dr. Howard told Bachelder that before Williams and Geary returned with their divisions, nothing but the 250 men in the 10th Maine battalion who were on provost guard duty along the pike stood between the enemy and the Union ordnance train a little more than a mile away.

111. This attitude is well displayed in Henry Kyd Douglas, *I Rode with Stonewall* (Chapel Hill, N. C., 1940), 249.

112. For the importance the Confederates attached to Culp's Hill see Ewell's report, *OR*, XXVII, pt. 2, p. 446; Campbell Brown, Memoranda on Gettysburg, July 2 and 3, 1878, Polk-Brown-Ewell Collection, UNC; McKim, *A Soldier's Recollections*, 195. For preoccupation of Confederates with their fight against Greene see C. P. Horton to Bachelder, Jan. 23, 1867, Bachelder Papers.

113. *OR*, XXVII, pt. 1, p. 680. Neill's was the Third Brigade of Gen. Albion

P. Howe's Second Division. Neill reported his arrival on the battlefield at 6:00 P.M. Meade detached his brigade and placed it apparently on Power's Hill in support of a battery with orders to hold the height. Subsequently Slocum ordered it to Culp's Hill less than a mile away to back up Wadsworth and Greene. Neill did not give the hour of this move, but did say Meade ordered him back to his original position at midnight. Neill probably had 1,700 men in his command. *Ibid.*, pp. 153, 163.

114. Williams to his daughters, July 6, 1863, in *Alpheus Williams Letters*, 229.

115. A. S. Williams to Bachelder, Nov. 10, 1865, Bachelder Papers. Capt. C. P. Horton, Greene's asst. adj. gen., said Greene's brigade was ordered to accompany the rest of Geary's division, but before it could evacuate its lines the Confederate attack began. Horton to Bachelder, Jan. 23, 1867, *ibid*. Slocum had a different version which suggested that Meade's order was framed in such a way as to give him no discretion and no alternative but to send the entire Twelfth Corps. At the same time he had Col. Rodgers, his asst. adj. gen., ride ahead to advise Meade that with the enemy on his front Slocum "deemed it very hazardous" to leave the entrenchments entirely undefended and asked permission to keep a division. Rodgers returned, saying that Meade regarded the left as the "point of real danger," but if Slocum thought it "absolutely essential" he could retain a brigade. It proved to be Greene's, since it was in the rear of the column and had not as yet left its position. Gen. H. W. Slocum to Messrs. Davis & Co., Sept. 8, 1875, Bates Collection. Slocum put the burden of the responsibility for virtually stripping Culp's Hill of defenders on Meade, while Williams pointed the finger at Slocum. It does not seem possible that Meade ordered the entire Twelfth Corps to evacuate its entrenchments before getting an opinion from Slocum about the advisability of such a move, especially as by 5:30 that afternoon he knew of a heavy concentration of the enemy on Slocum's front and warned him of it. *OR*, XXVII, pt. 3, p. 489.

116. *Ibid.*, pt. 1, p. 826.

117. A. S. Williams to Bachelder, Nov. 10, 1865, Bachelder Papers.

118. *Ibid.*; C. P. Horton to Bachelder, Jan. 23, 1867, *ibid.*; *OR*, XXVII, pt. 1, p. 833. Geary said he received an order at 7:30 P.M. to hold his position down to the creek "at all hazards." In view of developments at that hour, this message makes no sense unless the sender assumed Geary was still occupying the entrenchments on Culp's Hill. See *ibid.*, p. 826.

119. *Ibid.*, pp. 780, 783–784, 793, 813, 816–818, 820. For an account more complete than any of the battle reports including his own see Lt. Col. Charles F. Morse, *Letters Written during the Civil War, 1861–1865* (Boston, 1898), 144–145. Morse told how the skirmish line of the 2nd Mass. skillfully effected its reconnaissance and located the enemy's position.

120. Williams to his daughters, July 6, 1863, in *Alpheus Williams Letters*, 229. Williams said though there was moonlight, it was quite hazy and things were very indistinct. Williams to Bachelder, Nov. 10, 1865, Bachelder Papers. In the same letter he said that he had reached the Baltimore Pike when a staff officer told him he was wanted in Meade's headquarters. It was near midnight

when he got back to his troops and learned for the first time that the enemy was in his entrenchments. He made the same statement in his battle report. *OR*, XXVII, pt. 1, p. 775.

121. *Ibid.*, pp. 827–828, 836, 840, 842, 847, 849, 851–852, 854. Kane apparently returned just before Ruger and Lockwood arrived. The battle reports of Kane's brigade and regiments seem almost purposely vague in this respect. They and Geary's are beyond doubt very misleading. Though the time of his arrival is uncertain, Ruger categorically stated that Geary had not returned with his division before he got back. Greene said positively that he heard about 10:00 P.M. that Kane was on the way. If Ruger started back from the Union left just at dark, 8:30, he could have completed the mile and a half march easily before 10:00 P.M. Some of his regimental reports put their arrival at this hour. Since there is nowhere a suggestion that Ruger's and Kane's columns met on the pike which both used, and accepting the reliability of his evidence, Kane probably reached Greene around 10:30. As for Candy's brigade, Greene said it came to his support at 1:30 A.M., July 3. Other reports set the time no earlier than midnight.

122. *Ibid.*, pp. 358, 361, 705; pt. 2, pp. 447, 470, 480, 484–487; Bachelder, Map of the Battlefield of Gettysburg, Second Day; Bvt. Capt. Edward N. Whittier, "The Left Attack (Ewell's), Gettysburg," *Campaigns in Virginia, Maryland and Pennsylvania*, 327–330; *Wainwright Journals*, 245. Because a sniper had wounded Stevens in the morning of July 2, Whittier commanded the battery for the remainder of the battle.

123. *Ibid;* Whittier, "The Left Attack," *Campaigns in Virginia, Maryland and Pennsylvania*, 328; *OR*, XXVII, pt. 2, p. 480. Hays stressed the protection the smoke and fading light gave his men.

124. *Wainwright Journals*, 245; [Capt.] R. Bruce Ricketts to Bachelder, Mar. 2, 1866, Bachelder Papers; Lt. C. B. Brockway, Battery F, 1st Pa. Light, to D. McConaughy, Mar. 5, 1864, Peter F. Rothermel Collection, PDPR. Ricketts said Ames's men fired hardly a shot; Brockway said they fired a volley. Ames's division numbered about 1,150 muskets. See *OR*, XXVII, pt. 3, p. 485.

125. Ricketts to Bachelder, Mar. 2, 1866, Bachelder Papers.

126. *Wainwright Journals*, 245. Although regimental accounts gave the impression that Ames's men put up a good fight, which was perhaps true of some units, there was almost universal agreement among eyewitnesses in the Eleventh Corps that the enemy broke through his line very quickly. *OR*, XXVII, pt. 1, pp. 706, 715, 718, 720, 731, 743; B. F. Young to Bachelder, Aug. 12, 1867; Col. Andrew L. Harris to *id.*, Mar. 14, 1881, Typescript; A. J. Rider to *id.*, Aug. 20, Oct. 3, 1885; Michael Wiedrich to *id.*, Jan. 20, 1886; J. Clyde Millar to *id.*, Mar. 2, 1886, Bachelder Papers; Schurz, *Reminiscences*, III, 24–25; Schurz to Frank Moore, June 6, 1865, Andre de Coppet Collection, PU; Howard, *Autobiography*, 429. Compared to the heavy losses incurred, for instance, by Wright's brigade in making an assault against the Second Corps, the casualties of Early's brigades under similar circumstances were very light. *OR*, XXVII, pt. 2, pp. 340, 343.

127. *Wainwright Journals*, 245–246; Michael Wiedrich to Bachelder, Jan.

20, 1886; J. Clyde Millar to *id.*, Mar. 2, 1886, Bachelder Papers; *OR*, XXVII, pt. 1, p. 706; William Simmers and Paul Bachschmid, *The Volunteer's Manual; or, Ten Months with the 153d Penn'a Volunteers, Being a Concise Narrative of the Most Important Events of the History of the Said Regiment* (Easton, Pa., 1863), 29–30.

128. R. Bruce Ricketts to Bachelder, Mar. 2, 1866, Typescript, Bachelder Papers.

129. Schurz, *Reminiscences*, III, 24–25; Schurz to Frank Moore, June 6, 1865, Andre de Coppet Collection, PU; Howard, *Autobiography*, 429; *OR*, XXVII, pt. 1, pp. 706, 722, 731. Schurz's division had an effective force of about 1,500 men. *Ibid.*, pt. 3, p. 486.

130. According to Ricketts, in several conversations with Col. Morgan, Hancock's chief of staff, he learned that as soon as the Confederate attack started, Howard asked for help on the grounds that he had "no confidence in his own men." R. Bruce Ricketts to Bachelder, Mar. 2, 1866, Bachelder Papers.

131. Capt. J. F. Huntingdon to Gibbon, Mar. 26, 1864, Copy; S. S. Carroll to Hancock, July 23, 1876, Copy, Bates Collection. Carroll said a staff officer guided him, but it was Huntingdon who gave him precise information about the situation.

132. Browne, *Dunn Browne in the Army*, 195.

133. S. S. Carroll to Hancock, July 23, 1876, Copy, Bates Collection; C. B. Brockway to D. McConaughy, Mar. 5, 1864, Peter F. Rothermel Collection, PDPR. In Naisawald's *Grape and Canister*, 406, there is a dramatic but highly improbable account of how the guns in Lt. James Stewart's Battery B, 4th U.S., which were pointed down the pike toward town, were pulled around to blast the Confederates charging Wiedrich's and Ricketts' commands. There are several things wrong with the story. It was based upon the recollections of one Augustus Buell, who in his book, *The Cannoneer* (Washington, D.C., 1890), wrote what was purported to be a firsthand account of the Gettysburg campaign. It became suspect, to say the least, when a careful check by a historian showed that Buell enlisted in the army Aug. 21, 1863. See Milton W. Hamilton, "Augustus C. Buell, Fraudulent Historian," *PMHB*, LXXX, 478–492. Furthermore, Stewart's battery had a position to the rear of Ricketts. It can be well imagined what would have happened to both Wiedrich's and Ricketts' gunners if Stewart from this position had fired on the charging Confederates. Finally, Wainwright made no mention of the purported incident. Wainwright had five batteries, including Stevens', with twenty-seven guns in all under his command. All except four of Stewart's pointed toward the north and northeast. At the height of the action Wainwright said that with seventeen guns on the hill firing furiously he had no fears of the enemy getting up that front. Consequently he rode forward toward town to see whether the enemy was up to anything from that direction. All was quiet, but Stewart was keeping a sharp lookout. *Wainwright Journals*, 238, 245.

134. *OR*, XXVII, pt. 2, p. 481.

135. S. S. Carroll to Hancock, July 23, 1876, Copy, Bates Collection; *OR*, XXVII, pt. 1, p. 457; pt. 2, p. 481.

136. *Ibid.*, pt. 1, p. 706; *Pennsylvania at Gettysburg,* I, 173. The 106th Pa. brought 335 officers and men into the battle.

137. *OR,* XXVII, pt. 1, p. 358.

138. *Ibid.*, pt. 2, p. 480.

139. *Ibid.*, pp. 484–486; pt. 1, p. 358. See also J. W. [Jackson] to Lt. R. S. Jackson, July 20, 1863, Merl E. Reed Typescript; Samuel W. Eaton Diary [Eaton was in Co. B, 57th N.C. regiment], UNC. Jackson said some of the men in Hays's brigade went on up to the battery. Eaton noted that since they were "under a desperate fire, only a few [of the men] got to the batteries and could not hold them."

140. *OR,* XXVII, pt. 2, p. 484; pt. 1, p. 358.

141. *Ibid.*, pp. 470, 481.

142. *Ibid.*, pp. 556, 587–588.

143. D. F. Boyd to Early, Jan. 1, 1891, Jubal A. Early Papers, LC. Boyd said he heard the story from Gen. Hays, who claimed that Lee made the statement in his presence at Culpeper in Oct., 1863.

144. *OR,* XXVII, pt. 1, pp. 261, 290, 294, 296, 298, 301–302, 305, 308, 680.

145. *Ibid.*, pp. 604, 618, 625, 653–654, 658; Joshua Chamberlain to Bachelder, Jan. 25, 1884, Bachelder Papers. Having just fought Confederates who had attacked Little Round Top by way of Big Round Top, Rice obviously was well aware of the need to take it and secure the Union flank. Apparently he thought Fisher's men had been sent to him for that purpose and were subject to his orders. At least that is the way Chamberlain remembered it.

146. *Ibid.* In this letter to Bachelder Chamberlain recalled that Fisher "emphatically declined; and I remember his saying that his men were armed with some inefficient rifle—'smooth bores' it seems to me he said—& especially that the ground was difficult & unknown to his men. He & his men also were much agitated." The softer and vaguer version of this incident in his battle report substantiates the harsher one in the Bachelder letter. *OR,* XXVII, pt. 1, p. 625.

147. In his battle report Fisher made no mention of Rice and said that it was he who perceived the need to occupy Big Round Top. Crawford admitted that Rice had also pointed out to him the importance of occupying it. *Ibid.*, pp. 654, 658; [Crawford] to Rice, Dec. 23, 1863, S. W. Crawford Papers, LC; CCW, *Report,* I, 470.

148. *OR,* XXVII, pt. 1, pp. 604, 618, 625, 654, 658; Sykes to Crawford, Dec. 17, 1863, Copy, Joshua L. Chamberlain Papers, LC; [Crawford] to Prof. Jacobs, Dec., 1863, S. W. Crawford Papers, LC; Chamberlain to Bachelder, Jan. 25, 1884, Bachelder Papers. Fisher's report gave the impression that he led Chamberlain's 20th Maine, as well as two of his own regiments, up the hill. All other accounts, even Crawford's, agreed that the 20th Maine took the lead and the others followed. The question was: When? Chamberlain swore supports did not reach him until he had been on the hill at least three hours. Also he made no mention of Fisher being with them.

149. The Confederates greeted the 20th Maine with a scattered and uncer-

tain fire as it reached the top, mortally wounding one of Chamberlain's favorite lieutenants. The 20th Maine in return captured twenty-five prisoners. *OR,* XXVII, pt. 1, p. 625.

150. *Ibid.,* pp. 625–626. Two of Fisher's regiments, perhaps the same ones that had been there before, came up the hill again and took position considerably to Chamberlain's left, where they were not needed.

NOTES TO CHAPTER XVII

1. J. B. Clifton Diary, North Carolina State Department of Archives and History.

2. Crounse's dispatch, July 3, in the *New York Times,* July 4, 1863.

3. Coffin, *Boys of '61,* 289; Howard, *Autobiography,* 431.

4. A reasonable estimate places the Union losses at approximately 10,000 officers and men, of which a little over 1,200 were taken prisoner. The figures for the First, Second, Eleventh, and Twelfth Corps are rough estimates based upon the total number of casualties for the three days of fighting and information about the extent to which each brigade in the corps became involved on July 2. There was no problem in the case of the Third and Fifth Corps because they incurred practically all their casualties on July 2. The same thing was true of McLaws' and Hood's divisions of Longstreet's corps, Wright's brigade of Anderson's division, and Hoke's and Hays's brigades of Early's division. Confederate casualties were about 6,800 officers and men, of which almost 1,400 were listed as missing. Most of the missing were probably captured. *OR,* XXVII, pt. 1, pp. 173–187; pt. 2, pp. 338–341, 343, 475, 619, 624, 632.

5. Meade to Mrs. Meade, Gettysburg, 8:45 [A.M.], July 3, 1863, George Gordon Meade Papers, HSP.

6. Jacobs, *Rebel Invasion,* 38; *OR,* XXVII, pt. 1, p. 272. Col. Henry A. Morrow of the 24th Mich., though held captive in Gettysburg, had freedom of movement and many opportunities to converse with Confederate soldiers and officers and get their reactions to developments.

7. *Ibid.,* pt. 2, pp. 308, 320.

8. "Historicus" used this word to describe the importance of the heights. *Ibid.,* pt. 1, p. 130.

9. CCW, *Report,* I, 298.

10. Alexander, "Battle of Gettysburg," MS, E. P. Alexander Papers, UNC.

11. *OR,* XXVII, pt. 2, p. 320; Douglas, *I Rode with Stonewall,* 249. Douglas wrote that after the battle he had occasion to go to the headquarters of both Gens. Lee and Ewell, and he was not encouraged by any "appearance of cheerfulness at either place." Gen. Lee, he said, was not in "good humor over the miscarriage of his plans and his orders." At that time Douglas was on Gen. Edward Johnson's staff. *Ibid.,* 247–248, 352.

12. Pettit to his wife, July 8, 1863, W. B. Pettit Paper, UNC; Memorandum Book, Entry for July 2, 1863, Jedediah Hotchkiss Papers, LC; Special Cor-

respondent, Hagerstown, July 8, in the *Richmond Enquirer* (Semi-weekly Edition), July 24, 1863; Special Correspondent, Hagerstown, July 8, in the *Times* [London], Aug. 18, 1863.

13. Ross, *Cities and Camps*, 55.

14. Special Correspondent, Hagerstown, July 8, in the *Times* [London], Aug. 18, 1863; Special Correspondent, Hagerstown, July 8, in the *Richmond Enquirer* (Semi-weekly Edition), July 24, 1863. Although he did not get the story completely straight, Doubleday was right when he said the Confederates were critical of Anderson's generalship on July 2. Doubleday to Bates, Apr. 5, 1874, Bates Collection.

15. McLaws to his wife, July 7, 1863, Lafayette McLaws Papers, UNC.

16. Alexander, *Military Memoirs*, 393.

17. *Ibid.*, 408–409.

18. *Ibid.*, 397. For instance, Alexander cited Kershaw's misleading account in *B&L* to the effect that the delay in Barksdale's attack exposed Kershaw's left to heavy artillery fire, causing unnecessary casualties. It is questionable whether Barksdale's brigade was slow in coming into action, and furthermore Kershaw's real difficulties were on his right when Caldwell's division pushed many of his and Semmes's men back toward the Rose house. *OR*, XXVII, pt. 2, pp. 368–369, 372; Kershaw, "Kershaw's Brigade at Gettysburg," *B&L*, III, pt. 1, pp. 334–335.

19. Alexander, *Military Memoirs*, 395, 397, 405.

20. Fremantle, *Three Months in the Southern States*, 259–260; Morrison, ed., "Heth Memoirs," *CWH*, VIII, 306.

21. John Richardson Porter Diary, Entry for July 2, 1863, DU.

22. *Ibid.*; Fremantle, *Three Months in the Southern States*, 260. It is amazing how the Porter and Fremantle diaries agree even in particulars. Porter was an artilleryman in Longstreet's corps, whose unit was kept in reserve, while Fremantle was a British officer on a visit to the Confederacy. Though very likely strangers to each other, both were in positions to observe Lee. They referred to a message coming from Longstreet around 6:00 P.M. (they did not agree exactly on the time), and another at 7:00 P.M. announcing the capture of the enemy strong point.

23. *Ibid.*

24. John Richardson Porter Diary, Entry for July 2, 1863, DU.

25. Kershaw, "Kershaw's Brigade at Gettysburg," *B&L*, III, pt. 1, pp. 334, 337; Fremantle, *Three Months in the Southern States*, 261; Special Correspondent, Hagerstown, July 8, the *Times* [London], Aug. 18, 1863.

26. *Cf. ante*, XIV, 369–377.

27. For instance, the losses for Ward's brigade in Birney's division were 60 percent. *OR*, XXVII, pt. 1, pp. 175–180, 395, 494, 534, 601, 605, 613, 616; Selected Pages from the Historical and Statistical Record of the Principal Military Commands in the Union and Confederate Armies, IV, 80, 143–144, Entry 161, Record Group 94, NA; J. L. Chamberlain to Barnes, Apr. 6, 1864, Manuscripts of General James Barnes, NYHS; Toombs, *New Jersey Troops*, 10; De Trobriand, *Four Years with the Army of the Potomac*, 506; Richard Rob-

bins, "The Regular Troops at Gettysburg," *Philadelphia Weekly Times*, Jan. 4, 1879; G. B. Dandy to Bachelder, Jan. 3, 1890, Bachelder Papers. Robbins said the two regular army brigades (First and Second Brigades) in Ayres's division went into action with about 2,125 officers and men in all; Dandy gave a figure of almost 3,000. Their casualties were 829 officers and men.

28. When Hancock said that Caldwell's division lost nearly half its numbers, he was probably referring to its condition immediately after it had retired from the battlefield on July 2. The losses as finally computed were between 30 and 35 percent. The difference in the percentage of losses could probably be explained by the large number of men temporarily separated from their commands. Caldwell's division regrouped during the night and came back to the left of Doubleday's division on Cemetery Ridge. *OR*, XXVII, pt. 1, pp. 175, 369, 380; Selected Pages from the Historical and Statistical Record of the Principal Military Commands in the Union and Confederate Armies, IV, 143–144, Entry 161, Record Group 94, NA. For more evidence of straggling and the need for reorganization see *OR*, XXVII, pt. 1, pp. 536, 571, 635, 645; Patrick Journal, Entry for July 2, 1863, LC; CCW, *Report*, I, 407; Ford, ed., *Adams Letters*, II, 56; A. S. Williams to Bachelder, Nov. 10, 1865, Bachelder Papers. Williams said that when he found Meade and quite a crowd of general and staff officers in an open field, he also saw bodies of troops re-forming. Officers and men were busily calling out for members of particular regiments and brigades.

29. P. R. Guiney to General [Chamberlain], Oct. 26, 1865, Joshua L. Chamberlain Papers, LC. For the condition of Ayres's regular army brigade see *OR*, XXVII, pt. 1, p. 179; Robbins, "Regular Troops at Gettysburg," *Philadelphia Weekly Times*, Jan. 4, 1879.

30. John Haley to Bachelder, Feb. 2, 1884, Bachelder Papers. See also Young, *Battle of Gettysburg*, 226.

31. Battine, *Crisis of the Confederacy*, 216. See also Chamberlaine, *Memoirs of the Civil War*, 77.

32. Battine, *Crisis of the Confederacy*, 215; "Historicus," "Battle of Gettysburg," *OR*, XXVII, pt. 1, pp. 130–133; Sickles to H. P. Smith, Aug. 11, 1911, D. E. Sickles Press Letter Book, DU; Pamphlet published by Sickles, New York, May 5, 1911, Gen. Daniel E. Sickles Correspondence, NYHS; "The Third Corps and Sickles at Gettysburg, [Address] Delivered before the 'Third Army Corps Union' . . . on Wednesday, 5th May, 1886 . . . ," Pamphlets, Gettysburg, A. A. Humphreys Papers, HSP.

33. CCW, *Report*, I, 331–332; *OR*, XXVII, pt. 1, pp. 116, 138, 592.

34. For information on his orders to various commanders during the fighting see *ibid.*, pp. 369–371; Gen. H. W. Slocum to Messrs. Davis & Co., Sept. 8, 1875, Bates Collection; Meade, *Life and Letters*, II, 89, 93, 125.

35. *Ibid.*, 125.

36. *Ibid.*, 89.

37. *Ibid.*, 103.

38. *OR*, XXVII, pt. 1, p. 72.

39. CCW, *Report*, I, 350–351; *cf. ante*, IX, 235–236.

40. John Gibbon, "The Council of War on the Second Day," *B&L*, III, pt. 1,

p. 313. Hunt and Tyler were also invited to attend the meeting, but by the time they had finished their preparations for the next day's encounter, the gathering had disbanded. CCW, *Report*, I, 452.

41. Gibbon, "Council of War," *B&L*, III, pt. 1, p. 313. This version of Gibbon's recollections of the meeting appeared in his own book, *Recollections of the Civil War* and in the *Biographical Memorial of Butterfield*. He wrote a shorter account as early as Mar. 4, 1864, in response to a request from Gen. Meade for his recollections of the meeting. A little over two weeks later he gave substantially the same account in testifying before the Committee on the Conduct of the War. See *OR*, XXVII, pt. 1, pp. 123–124, 126–127; CCW, *Report*, I, 441–442.

42. Since the council met very soon after the fighting had ceased along Sykes's, Hancock's, and Howard's fronts, they had no opportunity to get even the roughest kind of returns from their regiments, especially those which had been in action. In the tabulation Butterfield did not indicate which figures belonged to which corps. Minutes of Council, July 2, [18]63, MS, [Back of p. 2], George Gordon Meade Papers, HSP. The minutes were kept on what seems to be ordinary tablet paper and consist of three pages, each about five by eight inches in size. Butterfield used both sides of the paper and on the back of p. 3 wrote: "Minutes of Council held Thursday P.M. July 2/63. DB/MG C of St." [Daniel Butterfield, Major General, Chief of Staff]. For printed copies of the document, see *OR*, XXVII, pt. 1, p. 74; Gibbon, "Council of War," *B&L*, III, pt. 1, p. 314.

43. Butterfield noted on the back of p. 3 of the minutes some off-the-record remarks of several officers. The recommendation to stay and fight was made by Slocum. Minutes of Council, July 2, [18]63, MS, George Gordon Meade Papers, HSP. In his testimony before the Committee on the Conduct of the War Birney said that the council was divided and that he was among those who voted to continue fighting at Gettysburg. CCW, *Report*, I, 368. According to one story, while Birney was watching the small number of survivors of the day's battle gathering about him in the twilight, he whispered to one of his lieutenants, "I wish I were already dead." Whittier, "The Left Attack, Gettysburg," *Campaigns in Virginia, Maryland and Pennsylvania*, 340.

44. *OR*, XXVII, pt. 1, p. 74. For Howard's poor opinion of the morale of the Eleventh Corps see *Wainwright Journals*, 247.

45. Williams to his daughters, July 6, 1863, *Alpheus Williams Letters*, 229. On July 1 Gen. Rufus Ingalls, chief quartermaster, informed Quartermaster General M. C. Meigs that he *thought* the army had enough supplies to last it during a battle. Early in the morning two days later he sent Meigs another message saying that supplies from Westminster must come up the next day if the army was to remain near Gettysburg. *OR*, XXVII, pt. 3, pp. 472, 503.

46. Gibbon, "Council of War," *B&L*, III, pt. 1, p. 313.

47. Newton et al., "Further Recollections of Gettysburg," *North American Review*, CLII, 276.

48. Newton to Gibbon, Jan. 5, 1876, in Gibbon, *Recollections*, 197.

49. *Wainwright Journals*, 246.

50. Williams to Bachelder, Nov. 10, 1865, Bachelder Papers.

51. Gibbon, "Council of War," B&L, III, pt. 1, p. 313; CCW, Report, I, 350–351. Warren also considered these meetings informal affairs rather than councils of war. Ibid., 378.

52. Minutes of Council, July 2, [18]63, MS, pp. 1–3, George Gordon Meade Papers, HSP. All voted except Warren, Butterfield, and Meade. Warren was apparently still snoozing comfortably when the vote was taken.

53. CCW, Report, I, 442. Gibbon gave virtually the same version in his article, "Council of War," B&L, III, pt. 1, p. 314, as in his testimony before the committee.

54. CCW, Report, I, 368, 425.

55. Ibid., 425; OR, XXVII, pt. 1, pp. 138–139. Gibbon said that in 1881 Meade's son, Col. George Meade, showed him the Minutes of Council, July 2, 1863. Gibbon, "Council of War," B&L, III, pt. 1, p. 414.

56. OR, XXVII, pt. 1, pp. 123–127, 139. Meade's inquiry was in the form of a circular sent out on Mar. 10, 1864. Since Warren had slept through the proceedings and Birney and Butterfield were unfriendly to Meade, it is apparent why it was not sent to them. But why were Howard and Hancock overlooked? Hancock's testimony given to the committee about two weeks later in no way supported Butterfield's and Birney's charges. CCW, Report, I, 407. Years later Col. George Meade in seeking to defend his father's reputation asked Howard for his recollections of the meeting. Howard wrote on June 9, 1883, that he did not hear the general utter a word in favor of retreat or express dissatisfaction with the results of the vote. Meade, Life and Letters, II, 418–419.

57. George Meade said that Slocum never received the circular because he was "at that time in the West, under General Sherman." Ibid., 413. This explanation is unsatisfactory for several reasons. Both Alpheus Williams and Slocum were together at Tullahoma, Tenn., and it seems strange that one of them got the circular and the other did not. But more important, at that time Slocum was thoroughly annoyed with authorities in Washington and his former commander, and very likely he chose not to respond to Meade's request for information. When his corps was transferred to the West in September, he was forced to serve again under General Hooker, in whom he had no confidence. Unhappy about this arrangement, Slocum offered to resign but Lincoln would not let him. Late in November while still disgruntled with his lot he read Meade's battle report of Gettysburg. He immediately saw red and rightly so, for the report left much to be desired, and unfortunately Meade had made the greatest number of errors when describing operations of the Twelfth Corps. Slocum and his lieutenant, Alpheus Williams, took these mistakes as personal affronts, for they considered them the result of a deliberate attempt on the part of Meade to belittle their services, of which they were justly proud. Slocum wrote Meade a long letter pointing out his errors. In his reply, which was delayed because of illness, Meade accepted most of Slocum's corrections and expressed profound regrets for any "injustice" his report might have done to the Twelfth Corps or its officers. The mistakes had been entirely accidental, he

said. The letter mollified Williams but left Slocum cold. Previously he had praised Meade for his generalship in the campaign, but now he turned against his former commander and in a private letter to his brother-in-law made the same damning indictment of Meade's conduct that Butterfield was to present to the Committee on the Conduct of the War. Butterfield was serving in Tenn. with Slocum, and they must have discussed their recollections of the meeting on July 2. Obviously Butterfield must have convinced Slocum that his good impressions of Meade were erroneous. Slocum, *Life of Slocum*, 135–136, 139–140, 182–186; Basler, ed., *Collected Works of Lincoln*, VI, 486; *OR*, XXVII, pt. 1, pp. 116–117, 120–121, 763–770; Slocum to Howland, July 17, 1863, Miscellaneous Manuscripts of [Col.] Joseph Howland, NYHS; Williams to his daughters, Nov. 20, 1863, in *Alpheus Williams Letters*, 272; Slocum to Le Roy H. Morgan, Jan. 2, 1864, in *ibid.*, 286.

58. *OR*, XXVII, pt. 1, pp. 124–127, 139.

59. *Ibid.*, p. 125.

60. *Ibid.*, p. 139; Williams to his daughters, July 6, 1863, in *Alpheus Williams Letters*, 222–230. Whereas Meade's Northern critics said he did not retreat on the night of July 2 on the recommendation of his lieutenants, the Southerners offered an explanation based upon fact, fancy, and fiction which is a perfect example of history by innuendo. The hero of the story was Capt. Ulric Dahlgren, son of a well-known admiral, who in scouting with his men back of the Confederate lines captured a courier at Greencastle carrying messages to Lee from Gen. Cooper and President Davis. These letters told Lee that his idea of creating even a phantom army under Beauregard at Culpeper to threaten Washington from another direction was impracticable and could not be carried out. Dahlgren perceived the importance of the messages, and he brought them to Meade as soon as possible, arriving at headquarters shortly after midnight. According to the story, when Meade learned that he did not have to worry about Lee receiving more reinforcements from Virginia, he immediately cancelled his orders to retreat and ordered the artillery back into line. As proof, those who told the yarn cited reports by Confederate pickets along Ewell's front that around midnight they had heard the rumble of heavy wheels, which suggested the withdrawal of Union artillery to the rear. Suddenly the sounds of a retrograde movement stopped, and the guns could be heard rolling back to their former positions. Then the narrators offered what they considered even more convincing evidence that Dahlgren had prevented Meade from making a serious blunder. Several months later he received his reward by being jumped in rank from captain to colonel, an unheard-of procedure, they said. There are several things they did not know which discredit this story. Spectacular promotions, especially in the cavalry, though rare did occur at this time more frequently than is realized. A few days before the battle, for example, Capts. Farnsworth, Merritt, and Custer became brigadier generals at one stroke of the pen. Dahlgren's promotion was overdue, for he had been cited several times by superiors for his efficiency and bravery. More important, Dahlgren in his diary mentioned his exploit of capturing the papers and bringing them to Meade but said nothing about their effect upon Meade's actions. As for the sounds of turn-

ing wheels during the night, Ewell's pickets probably heard Hunt getting his artillery ready for tomorrow's work by replenishing ammunition chests, reducing and reorganizing batteries, and posting two of them opposite the center of the Twelfth Corps line so as to dominate Rock Creek ravine. Alexander, "Battle of Gettysburg," MS, E. P. Alexander Papers, UNC; W. J. Seymour, "Some of the Secret History of Gettysburg," *SHSP*, VIII, 521–526; Copies of Ulric Dahlgren's diary found in Letters of John A. Dahlgren and his Son Ulric, 1854–1864, LC; *OR*, XXVII, pt. 1, pp. 237, 995, 1046; pt. 3, pp. 25, 28, 30, 86, 172.

61. *Ibid.*, pt. 1, p. 72.

62. Williams to his daughters, July 6, 1863, in *Alpheus Williams Letters*, 228.

63. Alpheus Williams said: "There were those who doubted our ability to hold where we were—though in the end, there was an unanimity for making the trial." Williams to Bachelder, Nov. 10, 1865, Bachelder Papers. In testifying under oath to the committee Meade asserted that "the opinion of the council was unanimous, which agreed fully with my own views. . . ." CCW. *Report*, I, 350.

64. Meade, *Life and Letters*, II, 103.

65. Minutes of Council, July 2, [18]63, MS, pp. 1–3, George Gordon Meade Papers, HSP.

66. A. S. Williams to Bachelder, Nov. 10, 1865, Bachelder Papers; Williams to his daughters, July 6, 1863, in *Alpheus Williams Letters*, 230.

67. *OR*, XXVII, pt. 1, p. 770.

68. Williams to his daughters, July 6, 1863, in *Alpheus Williams Letters*, 230. Thought not particularly accurate, the map in Ruger's battle report shows the relative positions of the opposing forces and makes clear why Williams chose to attack the Confederates on their right. *OR*, XXVII, pt. 1, p. 779.

69. Long, *Memoirs of Lee*, 287.

70. *OR*, XXVII, pt. 2, pp. 556, 568, 593.

71. *Ibid.*, p. 471.

72. *Ibid.*, p. 544; pt. 3, p. 498.

73. *Ibid.*, pt. 2, p. 320.

74. *Ibid.*, p. 447.

75. *Ibid.*, p. 320.

76. *Ibid.*, p. 447. With respect to the hour of the attack, the Confederate reports are noticeably vague. The Union reports place the hour of the opening of the cannonade by Federal artillery from dawn, which was about 3:25 A.M., to 4:30 A.M. The fire continued about fifteen minutes, and before Geary could move his infantry the Confederates attacked. Half an hour later Lee's message reached Ewell. Both Ruger, who wrote the most satisfactory report, and Lt. Edward D. Muhlenberg, chief of artillery, Twelfth Corps, agreed that the time of the cannonade was 4:30 A.M. *Ibid.*, pt. 1, pp. 761, 775, 780, 828, 836, 857, 870.

77. *Ibid.*, pt. 2, p. 320.

78. Gen. Alexander Shaler's brigade from the Sixth Corps and two regiments

from Wadsworth's division of the First Corps went into action on Geary's part of the line. Slocum sent Neill's brigade to Wolf's Hill, across Rock Creek, to protect the extreme right flank of the Twelfth Corps. It did not engage the enemy along the main battle line. The two brigades totalled approximately 3,100 officers and men. *Ibid.*, pt. 1, pp. 153, 678, 681, 761.

79. Longstreet, *Memoirs*, 385. Longstreet established his headquarters at Pitzer's School House, which was about three miles from the place where Lee was staying on Seminary Ridge.

80. *OR*, XXVII, pt. 2, p. 320.

81. Longstreet's account of the order changed drastically over the years. In his battle report he hinted that he had received an order to renew the attack, but it gave no indication of the direction he was to take. Sixteen years later he implied just the opposite when he wrote: "Fearing that . . . [Lee] was still in his disposition to attack, I tried to anticipate him, by saying: 'General, I have had my scouts out all night, and I find that you still have an excellent opportunity to move around to the right of Meade's army, and maneuvre him into attacking us.' " Several years later he used different language to tell substantially the same story, but in his reminiscences, published in 1896 after he had become thoroughly embittered, he flatly denied having received any orders from Lee for the morning of the third day. *Ibid.*, p. 359; Longstreet, "Lee in Pennsylvania," *Annals*, 429; Longstreet, "Lee's Right Wing at Gettysburg," *B&L*, III, pt. 1, p. 342; Longstreet, *Memoirs*, 385.

82. Alexander, "Battle of Gettysburg," MS, E. P. Alexander Papers, UNC. Italics are mine.

83. *OR*, XXVII, pt. 2, p. 359; Longstreet, *Memoirs*, 385.

84. *OR*, XXVII, pt. 1, p. 678.

85. *Ibid.*, pt. 2, p. 359. In discussing the plan he had in mind for an attack Longstreet again gave different versions. In his battle report he referred obviously to an envelopment or flanking attack. Later in recalling his conversation with Lee on the morning of July 3, he talked about the possibility of making a turning movement, which was quite different from an envelopment. Longstreet, "Lee in Pennsylvania," *Annals*, 429.

86. *OR*, XXVII, pt. 1, pp. 663, 665, 674, 678.

87. *Ibid.*, pt. 3, p. 490.

88. Longstreet, *Memoirs*, 385.

89. Longstreet, "Lee's Right Wing at Gettysburg," *B&L*, III, pt. 1, p. 342.

90. Longstreet, "Lee in Pennsylvania," *Annals*, 430.

91. Newton et al., "Further Recollections of Gettysburg," *North American Review*, CLII, 276.

92. In his report Longstreet said that a few moments after he had given orders for the execution of his plan, Lee appeared at his headquarters. In his memoirs Longstreet recalled that Lee rode up after sunrise. *OR*, XXVII, pt. 2, p. 359; Longstreet, *Memoirs*, 385–386. Various accounts have Pickett's division arriving at Longstreet's part of the battle line no earlier than 8:00 A.M. and no later than 11:00 A.M. *OR*, XXVII, pt. 2, p. 385; Report of Col. Joseph Mayo, Jr., July 25, 1863, MS; Report of Capt. R. W. Douthat, July 3, 1863,

MS, George E. Pickett Papers, DU; William N. Wood, *Reminiscences of Big I,* Bell I. Wiley, ed. (Jackson, Tenn., 1956), 43; John T. James to his father, July 9, 1863, quoted in Thomas D. Houston, "Storming Cemetery Hill," *Philadelphia Weekly Times,* Oct. 21, 1882.

93. *OR,* XXVII, pt. 2, p. 320.

94. *Ibid.;* Harrison, *Pickett's Men,* 88, 90; W. W. Wood, "Pickett's Charge at Gettysburg," *Philadelphia Weekly Times,* Aug. 11, 1877; Durkin, ed., *John Dooley War Journal,* 101; Hamilton, ed., *Shotwell Papers,* I, 499–501. Partly because of the length of the column of almost 5,000 men the time of its arrival varied according to different witnesses from 2:00 to almost 6:00 P.M. Assuming that the latter time is correct, Pickett's men would still have had three hours rest if they had moved again around 9:00 P.M. All accounts agreed that the division resumed its march about 3:30 the next morning.

95. *OR,* XXVII, pt. 2, p. 320.

96. Long, *Memoirs of Lee,* 287–288.

97. Alexander, *Military Memoirs,* 421–422.

98. Long, *Memoirs of Lee,* 288.

99. *Ibid.*

100. Taylor, *Four Years with General Lee,* 103.

101. Longstreet, "Lee's Right Wing at Gettysburg," *B&L,* III, pt. 1, p. 343. Longstreet revealed his dislike for the plan in his report when he stressed the difficulties of making a successful attack in open country "in plain view" of the enemy's batteries. *OR,* XXVII, pt. 2, p. 353. The number of Longstreet's objections to Lee's plan and the intensity of his feelings toward it seemed to increase over the years. In his memoirs they are more in the nature of afterthoughts. Longstreet, *Memoirs,* 385–391.

102. *Ibid.,* 386; Longstreet, "Lee's Right Wing at Gettysburg," *B&L,* III, pt. 1, p. 343. For Longstreet's insistence that he and Lee had the best of personal relations see *ibid.,* p. 628.

103. *OR,* XXVII, pt. 2, pp. 320, 620, 632.

104. Long, *Memoirs of Lee,* 288; Taylor, *Four Years with General Lee,* 103–104, 106–108. Taylor quoted Venable's views in his footnotes.

105. *Ibid.,* 103.

106. *Ibid.,* 107–109.

107. Longstreet, *Memoirs,* 393.

108. *OR,* XXVII, pt. 2, p. 320.

109. Taylor, *Four Years with General Lee,* 103; Longstreet to [Heth], Feb. 14, 1897, in Morrison, ed., "Heth Memoirs," *CWH,* VIII, 306; Freeman, *Lee's Lieutenants,* III, 181.

110. *OR,* XXVII, pt. 2, pp. 320, 344–345, 645, 656–658, 661–663, 667–673.

111. *Ibid.,* pp. 289, 658; Freeman, *Lee's Lieutenants,* III, 146, 151, 182, 193–194. When Trimble heard that Heth and Pender had been wounded, he asked Lee to put him in command of one of Hill's divisions. "The Civil War Diary of General Isaac Ridgeway Trimble," *Maryland Historical Magazine,* XVII, 12.

112. *OR*, XXVII, pt. 2, pp. 614–615, 621, 634.

113. *Ibid.*, p. 320.

114. The size of Pickett's division was variously estimated to be 4,500, 4,700, 5,400. The middle figure seems the most realistic estimate, even though not enough allowance has been made for a normal complement of officers. Pickett therefore had about 5,000 in all. Pettigrew's (Heth's) division had between 4,850 and 5,250 officers and men; the two brigades of Pender's division totalled about 1,900 in all. Wilcox and Perry were assigned to supporting roles with about 1,600 troops. *Ibid.*, pp. 620, 632–633, 647, 667, 671; Battle Report of R. M. Mayo, Aug. 13, 1863, Henry Heth Collection, Confederate Museum; Louis G. Young to Early, Mar. 14, 1878, Jubal A. Early Papers, LC; Love, "Mississippi at Gettysburg," *Publications of the Mississippi Historical Society*, IX, 44; Harrison, *Pickett's Men*, 90–91; Longstreet, "The Mistakes of Gettysburg," *Annals*, 632; Longstreet, "Lee's Right Wing at Gettysburg," *B&L*, III, pt. 1, p. 345; *cf. ante*, XI, 80 note; Robert A. Bright, "Pickett's Charge," *SHSP*, XXXI, 228.

115. *OR*, XXVII, pt. 2, p. 320.

116. *Ibid.* Hill said he was directed to hold his line with Anderson's division and half of Pender's. Anderson, he added, had been ordered, presumably by him in accordance with Lee's instructions, to hold his division "ready to take advantage of any success which might be gained by the assaulting column, or to support it, if necessary." *Ibid.*, p. 608.

117. *Ibid.*, pp. 320, 359; Alexander, *Military Memoirs*, 418–419.

118. *Ibid.*, 418. Long did not refer to the Clump of Trees but mentioned a weak point in the Union line in the general location of that memorable landmark toward which Lee directed the attack to be made. Long, *Memoirs of Lee*, 287–288.

119. Longstreet, *Memoirs*, 386.

120. *Ibid.*, 388.

121. This is the opinion of Freeman, who said: "Lee, with Jackson dead, had no other subordinate of the same experience or military grasp as Longstreet." *Lee's Lieutenants*, III, 146.

122. The accounts do not tell how long Lee's reconnaissance of the enemy's position and conference with his generals lasted, but it is safe to assume that they started around 5:00 A.M. and were completed by the time Pickett's division came up between 7:00 and 9:00 A.M.

NOTES TO CHAPTER XVIII

1. Samuel Wilkeson, "Battle of Gettysburg," in Frank Moore, ed., *Anecdotes, Poetry and Incidents of the War: North and South, 1860–1865* (New York, 1866), 333.

2. Dispatch from Headquarters, Army of the Potomac, July 3, 9:40 A.M., in the *New York Times*, July 6, 1863.

3. One way of making a comparison of the size of the opposing forces is to count the number of brigades engaged. At Culp's Hill fifteen brigades, eight Union and seven Confederate, fought each other.

4. Williams to Bachelder, Nov. 10, 1865, Bachelder Papers.

5. Column by Agate [Whitelaw Reid], Near Gettysburg, July 4, in *Cincinnati Daily Gazette*, July 8, 1863; *OR*, XXVII, pt. 1, p. 770; pt. 3, pp. 498–500; Slocum to Morgan, Jan. 2, 1864, in *Alpheus Williams Letters*, 285.

6. *OR*, XXVII, pt. 1, pp. 761, 775, 827–828. In his report Geary gave the impression that he did most of the planning for the attack. However, Williams had already worked out his plan of operations, probably in consultation with Slocum, by the time Geary returned from his wanderings, which was around midnight. See Williams to Bachelder, Nov. 10, 1865, Bachelder Papers. In writing to a correspondent after the war Williams warned him to accept the reliability of Geary's reports with caution. Williams to General E. A. Carman, Aug. 13, 1876, Carman Correspondence, 1859–1897, E. A. Carman Papers, New York Public Library.

7. Williams to Bachelder, Nov. 10, 1865, Bachelder Papers.

8. *Ibid.* The two batteries near Williams' headquarters were Lt. S. T. Rugg's Battery F, 4th U. S., six 12-pounders, and Lt. David H. Kinzie's Battery K, 5th U. S., four 12-pounders. On Power's Hill were Lt. Charles A. Atwell's Battery E, Pa. Light, six 10-pounder Parrotts, and Capt. James H. Rigby's Battery A, Md. Light, six 3-inch rifles. On McAllister's Hill there was Lt. Charles E. Winegar's Battery M, 1st N. Y. Light, four 10-pounder Parrotts. *OR*, XXVII, pt. 1, pp. 166, 237, 870, 899.

9. Williams to Bachelder, Nov. 10, 1865, Bachelder Papers; *OR*, XXVII, pt. 1, pp. 780, 784, 793, 820; Bachelder, Map of the Battlefield of Gettysburg, Third Day. The extreme right of the Third Brigade, First Division was held by the 13th N. J. To its left were the 27th Ind., 2nd Mass., and 3rd Wis. See Lt. Col. John Grimes to Bachelder, Apr. 2, 1864, Bachelder Papers.

10. *OR*, XXVII, pt. 1, p. 793; William B. Wooster to Bachelder, Dec. 19, 1886, Bachelder Papers; John W. Storrs, *The Twentieth Connecticut, A Regimental History* (Ansonia, Conn., 1886), 92.

11. Williams to Bachelder, Apr. 7, 1864, Nov. 10, 1865, Bachelder Papers. The third regiment of Lockwood's brigade, the First Eastern Shore Maryland Regiment, arrived at the battlefield around 8:00 A.M. on July 3. *OR*, XXVII, pt. 1, p. 808. Rugg's battery was commonly known as Muhlenberg's. Lt. Edward D. Muhlenberg during the battle commanded the Twelfth Corps Artillery Brigade. *Ibid.*, p. 166.

12. *Ibid.*, pp. 780–781; pt. 2, pp. 471, 489–490, 504–505, 511, 513, 519, 521–523, 526, 528, 530, 532–533, 535–539, 568–569, 572–578, 593–595, 601.

13. *Ibid.*, pt. 1, pp. 761, 775, 780, 791, 793, 800, 803, 813, 817–818, 824, 828, 836, 839, 842, 847, 849, 852–853, 855, 857, 861. Of the general officers, Geary said the cannonade opened at 3:30 A.M., Candy 3:45 A.M., Greene and Slocum 4:00 A.M., Ruger 4:30 A.M., and Williams "daylight," a rather vague word. Lt. Muhlenberg gave the time as 4:30 A.M. It would appear that he was

in a better position to know the time than anyone else. However, since Greene and Slocum, who were generally reliable witnesses, put the hour at 4:00 A.M., it is possible the guns opened then. Also Williams' word "daylight" could mean around 4:00 A.M., certainly not dawn which was about 3:25 A.M. Muhlenberg's report made no mention of Rigby's battery which apparently took part in the opening cannonade. *Ibid.*, p. 899.

14. *Ibid.*, p. 828.

15. *Ibid.*, pt. 2, p. 447. Johnson mentioned a Union attack which took place after he had made his first one. He may have been referring to a charge made by a regiment in Lockwood's brigade, followed by the 147th Pa. in Candy's brigade, to a stone wall, probably the one on the northeast side of Pardee field. *Ibid.*, p. 504; pt. 1, pp. 804–806, 836, 846.

16. *Ibid.*, pp. 184–185, 833. The losses for Kane's brigade, incurred almost entirely during long hours of fighting on July 3, were 98 officers and men out of 700. Greene's brigade fought bitterly in the evening and night of July 2 as well as the morning of July 3. It suffered the loss of 303 officers and men out of 1,424.

17. *Ibid.*, p. 775. See also Williams to Bachelder, Nov. 10, 1865, Bachelder Papers. Williams wrote that the Union artillery fire seemed to be the signal for the rebel infantry to start the attack.

18. *OR*, XXVII, pt. 1, p. 828.

19. *Ibid.*, pt. 2, p. 504.

20. *Ibid.*, pp. 519, 523, 526, 528, 530.

21. *Ibid.*, pp. 504, 593. Geary made specific reference to this charge. The time of its occurrence according to his report was almost exactly the same as that given in O'Neal's account. Geary also said that the strength of the assault made him so fearful of the outcome that he asked for reinforcements. As a result, he claimed, Shaler's brigade of the Sixth Corps came to his relief at 8:45 A.M. Now for Geary to see the need for reinforcements around 8:00 A.M., clear the request through channels, and receive them approximately forty-five minutes later from their bivouac near Little Round Top almost two miles away was mighty good time—suspiciously good. Shaler said he reported to Geary at 8:00 A.M., not 8:45 A.M. See *ibid.*, pt. 1, pp. 681, 829. These circumstances lead to the conclusion that somebody else besides Geary knew a thing or two about how to fight a battle and had anticipated his need for reinforcements.

22. *Ibid.*, pt. 2, p. 519.

23. *Ibid.*, pp. 504, 511, 568–569, 572–575, 577; pt. 1, pp. 831, 847, 849; Civil War Diary of S. Thomas McCullough, Entry for July 3, 1863, UV.

24. McKim quoting from his diary in *A Soldier's Recollections*, 188. Years later Col. James Wallace of the First Eastern Shore Maryland Regiment wrote a poignant account of this charge: "The 1st Maryland Confederate Regiment met us & were cut to pieces. We sorrowfully gathered up many of our old friends & acquaintances & had them carefully & tenderly cared for." Wallace to Bachelder, July 4, 1878, Bachelder Papers.

25. This statement as well as the previous one that Daniel's brigade lined up to the right of Steuart's is an inference based upon a close examination of battle

reports. McKim's claim that Daniel's brigade never made the charge brought forth a challenge from Maj. (later Col.) John R. Winston of the 45th N. C. See Winston, "A Correction of Dr. McKim's Paper," *SHSP*, VII, 94; R. H. McKim, "Colonel Winston's Correction Corrected," *SHSP*, VII, 315. Battle reports clearly show that Daniel's brigade did participate in the charge, but the manner and extent were not shown. *OR*, XXVII, pt. 2, pp. 568–569, 572–575, 577.

26. Wainwright on Cemetery Hill listening to the fight recorded: "Such a feu d'enfer I never heard. . . . I hear that some of Geary's division fired forty rounds per man." [In some cases it was a lot more.] *Wainwright Journals*, 248. Meade at first also thought Geary's men were wasting ammunition, but he revised his opinion when he got the whole story of the engagement. *OR*, XXVII, pt. 1, p. 770.

27. *Ibid.*, pp. 681–683, 775, 804–805, 830, 836–837, 857.

28. *Ibid.*, pp. 681–683, 805, 807–810, 837, 841–843, 845, 849, 852–855, 857; Bachelder, "Gettysburg Campaign," IV, 42–43, MS, Bachelder Papers.

29. *Wainwright Journals*, 248. Later Wainwright visited the scene of the battle, and although observing evidences of much wild shooting he noted from the number of Confederate dead that many bullets had found their marks. *Ibid.*, 251.

30. *OR*, XXVII, pt. 1, pp. 810, 855.

31. *Ibid.*, p. 839.

32. *Ibid.*, pp. 828, 836, 846.

33. *Ibid.*, pp. 804–806.

34. *Ibid.*, pp. 828–829, 837, 844; pt. 2, p. 533; [Gen.] Eugene Powell to Bachelder, Mar. 23, 1886, Bachelder Papers. In his report Powell said the left of his line rested on Greene's entrenchments and the right down the hill. In this instance he must have confused his right with his left, for otherwise his regiment would have been shooting toward Cemetery Hill.

35. *OR*, XXVII, pt. 1, pp. 784, 793–794.

36. *Ibid.*, pp. 781, 784–785, 798, 800–801, 803; Williams to Bachelder, Apr. 7, 1864, Bachelder Papers. Stray shots and premature explosion of shells probably caused in all a dozen casualties in four or five regiments.

37. Gen. T. H. Ruger to Bachelder, Aug. 12, 1869, Bachelder Papers.

38. *OR*, XXVII, pt. 1, pp. 781, 813. Ruger said either the messenger made a mistake or Colgrove misunderstood the order. Colgrove categorically denied any misunderstanding on his part and claimed the messenger said, " 'The general directs that you advance your line immediately.' " *Ibid.*, p. 813. The strength of the 2nd Mass. was 320 officers and men, and of the 27th Ind. 339. *Ibid.*, p. 815. They formed a line about 525 feet long. John Bresno Han to Bachelder, Sept. 27, 1890, Bachelder Papers. One startling and puzzling feature in the story of this affair is the five hours difference in the time given for the charge in the regimental reports and that mentioned by Ruger and Colgrove. Commanders of the regiments claimed to have received the order early in the morning; one said 5:30, while the other put it between 5:00 and 6:00 A.M. Ruger set the hour he received the order as around 10:00 A.M. The cir-

cumstances under which he got it suggest that he was probably more accurate than his subordinates. By implication Colgrove corroborated Ruger. *OR*, XXVII, pt. 1, pp. 781, 813, 815–817. If the charge did take place around 5:30 A.M., then it was a more senseless move than later. Furthermore, Colgrove in claiming that he could not send skirmishers to test the strength of the enemy lines overlooked the fact that one company of the 2nd Mass. had maintained a skirmish line in front of the regiment from the beginning of the fighting. [Morse], *Civil War Letters*, 146.

39. *OR*, XXVII, pt. 2, pp. 489, 505, 521–522. The regiments were the 2nd Va., Stonewall Brigade, and the 31st, 49th, and 52nd Va. of Smith's brigade.

40. Quote from a paper written by Col. Charles F. Morse of the 2nd Mass. and delivered May 10, 1878, in Whittier, "The Left Attack, Gettysburg," *Campaigns in Virginia, Maryland and Pennsylvania*, 347. John A. Fox, who was Mudge's adjutant, substantiates this story of Mudge's amazement and his demand that the messenger repeat the order. Fox to Gen. Carman, Apr. 4, 1877, E. A. Carman Papers, New York Public Library.

41. *OR*, XXVII, pt. 1, pp. 184, 813–815, 817.

42. Williams to Bachelder, Apr. 7, 1864, Bachelder Papers.

43. Quoted from a paper written by Col. Morse, in Whittier, "The Left Attack, Gettysburg," *Campaigns in Virginia, Maryland and Pennsylvania*, 348.

44. Fox to Carman, Apr. 4, 1877, E. A. Carman Papers, New York Public Library.

45. *OR*, XXVII, pt. 1, pp. 761, 775, 781, 794, 814, 824, 830, 847, 849, 852, 871; pt. 2, pp. 511, 526, 528, 577.

46. Union reports placed the climax of the engagement between 10:00 and 11:00 A.M., when the enemy made his final charge, followed by the Union counterattack. All heavy firing probably ceased before twelve o'clock. *Ibid.*, pt. 1, pp. 761, 775, 794, 806, 824, 830, 839, 841, 847, 849, 852, 867, 870. Maj. Philo B. Buckingham of the 20th Conn., who served as asst. inspector general of the Twelfth Corps during the battle, said the fight for Culp's Hill lasted till twelve o'clock noon. *Ibid.*, p. 776; Buckingham to his wife, July 18, 1863, Civil War Letters of Lt. Col. Philo B. Buckingham, American Antiquarian Society. Ewell indicated in oblique fashion that the fight was over at 1:00 P.M. when Johnson evacuated the entrenchments. He did not give Union infantry attacks credit for this development, but claimed that Johnson had reports, which later proved groundless, that Union cavalry was threatening his rear. *OR*, XXVII, pt. 2, p. 448. None of the other Confederate reports mentioned the hour of their evacuation or when the engagement for all practical purposes was over. *Ibid.*, pp. 489–490, 505, 511, 519, 522, 526.

47. Williams to Bachelder, Apr. 7, 1864, Bachelder Papers.

48. *Wainwright Journals*, 251.

49. Frank A. Haskell, *The Battle of Gettysburg* (Wisconsin History Commission, 1908), 83–84 [Collated with the original MS in PDPR]. Haskell said his line was about 3,000 feet in length. It was actually a third less. He also estimated the strength of the two divisions to be fewer than 6,000 men. Hays had

only two brigades in position on the ridge and the 8th Ohio of Carroll's brigade on the skirmish line. *OR*, XXVII, pt. 1, pp. 457, 461–462.

50. *Ibid.*, pp. 261–262, 663; Tyler, *Recollections of the Civil War*, 108–109; Meade, *Life and Letters*, II, 110–111; A. A. Humphreys to Bachelder, Feb. 13, 1864, Bachelder Papers.

51. *OR*, XXVII, pt. 1, pp. 593, 604, 618, 654, 657, 663, 665, 671, 674, 678, 685; A. P. Morrison to his brother Will, July 21, 1863, Torrance Collection, PDPR; David T. Jenkins to Bachelder, Jan. 7, 1864, Bachelder Papers.

52. *OR*, XXVII, pt. 1, p. 238. Lt. T. Fred Brown's 1st R. I. Light, Battery B, had been reduced from six to four guns as a result of the action on July 2. *Ibid.*, p. 478. McGilvery had thirty-nine guns in his command on July 3. Thomas' 4th U.S., Battery C, had a position between McGilvery's and Hazard's artillery. *Ibid.*, p. 238.

53. *Ibid.*, pp. 237, 238, 373, 873, 878–879. Hancock admitted that only half of his corps ammunition train got to Gettysburg but did not explain why. He said his batteries received a supply from the Artillery Reserve "though not to the full extent required." *Ibid.*, p. 372. Knowing how meticulous Hunt was about such matters, it does not seem possible that he would deliberately short-change Hancock. Only the Third Corps received slightly more rounds from the reserve than the Second Corps. *Ibid.*, p. 879.

54. *Ibid.*, p. 238; Hunt, "Third Day at Gettysburg," *B&L*, III, pt. 2, p. 371; CCW, *Report*, I, 451; Hunt to Bachelder, Jan. 6, 1866, Bachelder Papers.

55. Alexander, *Military Memoirs*, 418.

56. Alexander, "Battle of Gettysburg," MS, E. P. Alexander Papers.

57. Hunt, "Second Day at Gettysburg," *B&L*, III, pt. 1, p. 300.

58. Hunt, "Third Day at Gettysburg," *B&L*, III, pt. 2, p. 372. Hunt later gave a fuller explanation for his orders, saying that the Federals occupied the "chord of the arc" on which the enemy assembled his batteries. As a result Hunt could bring fewer guns into action than the Confederates. Furthermore, part of his line was so broken by woods and rocks that only a portion of it was suitable for artillery, and he had to offset the enemy's advantage by superior effectiveness of fire "through close observation, deliberate, slow and sure practice, aiming *low*. . . ." By making every shot count he hoped that when the enemy artillery fire ceased the Federals would have enough ammunition in their chests to sustain a rapid and effective fire from all Union batteries on the infantry the minute it advanced from the woods. Hunt to Bachelder, Jan. 6, 1866, Bachelder Papers.

59. Haskell, *Gettysburg*, 81.

60. Lt. Col. C. H. Morgan's Account, Typescript, Bachelder Papers.

61. *OR*, XXVII, pt. 1, pp. 663, 665, 668–669, 671, 674, 678, 680, 681–683, 688–690, 692–693, 695; E. D. Halsey to Bachelder, Mar. 24, 1864; J. R. Lewis to *id.*, Mar. 24, 1864; Bachelder, "Gettysburg Campaign," IV, 116A, MS, Bachelder Papers.

62. *OR*, XXVII, pt. 1, p. 151.

63. R. F. Halsted to Miss [Emily] Sedgwick, July 17, 1863, Sedgwick Com-

missions, etc., Cornwall Historical Collection, No. 400, Cornwall, Conn., Library.

64. *OR*, XXVII, pt. 1, pp. 261–262, 485, 536, 593, 663; A. A. Humphreys to Bachelder, Feb. 13, 1864; D. B. Birney to *id.*, Mar. 22, 1864, Bachelder Papers.

65. At times in the Chancellorsville campaign he had commanded besides his own large corps two others and a division from a third one. *OR*, XXV, pt. 1, pp. 557–559.

66. Boatner, *Civil War Dictionary*, 413, 730, 765.

67. CCW, *Report*, I, 407; Hancock to Rothermel, Dec. 31, 1868, Peter F. Rothermel Collection, PDPR. Hancock wrote: "I had . . . general command of the whole line, from Cemetery Hill to Round Top on that day, consisting of the 1st, 2nd and 3d Corps, styled the Left Centre. . . ."

68. Gibbon said that Hancock resumed command of the Second Corps at one o'clock, and he returned to his division.

69. *OR*, XXVII, pt. 1, pp. 374–375; Hunt to Bachelder, Jan. 6, 1866, Jan. 20, 1875, June 18, 1879, May 8, 1881, Bachelder Papers. Hunt maintained that the only basis for Hancock's claim was Meade's reference in his report to Hancock's command of the left center and Gibbon's command of the Second Corps. Meade, Hunt said, did not define left center and was in error about Gibbon. On the other hand, Hunt added, Hancock made no claim in his report to a command of more than his own corps on July 3. See copy of Report of General H. J. Hunt to General Sherman, Feb., 1882, Bachelder Papers.

70. Haskell, *Gettysburg*, 68; Hunt to Bachelder, Jan. 20, 1875, Bachelder Papers.

71. CCW, *Report*, I, 452; *OR*, XXVII, pt. 1, p. 878.

72. Slocum to Morgan, Jan. 2, 1864, in *Alpheus Williams Letters*, 285.

73. *OR*, XXVII, pt. 3, p. 502.

74. *Ibid.*, pp. 499, 501–502. The message to French was sent at 7:30 A.M. and to Couch an hour later.

75. Meade to Mrs. Meade, 8:45 A.M., July 3, 1863, in Meade, *Life and Letters*, II, 103.

76. Column by Agate [Whitelaw Reid], July 4, in *Cincinnati Daily Gazette*, July 8, 1863.

77. *OR*, XXVII, pt. 3, p. 502; Meade, *Life and Letters*, II, 103.

78. Haskell, *Gettysburg*, 85.

79. *Ibid.*, 86, 92–93; Meade, *Life and Letters*, 104; CCW, *Report*, I, 408; Gibbon, *Recollections*, 145; Newton et al., "Further Recollections of Gettysburg," *North American Review*, CLII, 276–277; *OR*, LI, pt. 1, p. 1068. Meade called the sector held by Howard, which was Cemetery Hill, the center of his line. See CCW, *Report*, I, 334.

80. Haskell, *Gettysburg*, 92. Gibbon's account of the incident varies considerably from Haskell's, but both agreed that Meade did have a noon meal with them. Gibbon, *Recollections*, 146.

81. Haskell, *Gettysburg*, 93–94.

82. Meade, *Life and Letters,* II, 105.

83. *OR,* XXVII, pt. 1, pp. 372, 454, 465, 476, 478; Haskell, *Gettysburg,* 88.

84. Bachelder, Maps of the Battlefield of Gettysburg, Second and Third Days. Description of the barn is based upon general knowledge of such buildings on farms in eastern Pa. and upon a statement of a participant who recalled that rebel sharpshooters fired with "impunity" on Union lines from "loop-holed windows." C. A. Richardson to Bachelder, Aug. 18, 1869, Bachelder Papers.

85. *OR,* XXVII, pt. 1, pp. 454, 464–465, 467, 469–471; Depositions signed by Sergt. Major William B. Hinchs and others of the 14th Conn. Sept. 19–24, 1870; C. A. Richardson to Bachelder, Aug. 18, 1869; Theodore G. Ellis to *id.,* Oct. 31, Nov. 3, 1870; Copy of letter of Gen. Hays to [Gov.] Horatio Seymour, Aug. 15, 1863, in C. D. MacDougall to *id.,* Jan. 11, 1886; John L. Brady to *id.,* May 24, 1886; Charles A. Hitchcock to *id.,* Jan. 28, 1886, Typescript, Bachelder Papers. Sergt. Hitchcock of the 111th N. Y. at considerable personal risk volunteered to carry the order to set the buildings on fire to Col. Theodore G. Ellis of the 14th Conn. Apparently just as Ellis had his men apply matches to the hay and straw in the barn, a shell from an enemy battery exploded and started a fire on the roof. See John L. Brady to Bachelder, May 24, 1886, *ibid.* Fremantle confirmed the version that an exploding shell set the barn ablaze. Fremantle, *Three Months in the Southern States,* 262.

86. Fremantle was riding along in the company of Lee's and Longstreet's staffs and his fellow foreign visitors when he saw the barn burn. He noticed the exchange of only a few shots. *Ibid.* There is the suspicion that Alexander exaggerated the importance of the affair. He was the only witness to call the fusillade a cannonade, which he said lasted for fully half an hour. *Military Memoirs,* 420. In another account he said the duel occurred between eleven and twelve o'clock and finally involved at least 120 guns on the two sides. Alexander, "Battle of Gettysburg," MS, E. P. Alexander Papers, UNC. No Union report mentioned a duel of that magnitude and certainly not at that hour. Capt. John G. Hazard, chief of the Artillery Brigade, Second Corps, did mention heavy fire on his position which caused three limbers of Cushing's battery to explode. He placed the time, however, at eight o'clock. *OR,* XXVII, pt. 1, p. 478.

87. Alexander, "Battle of Gettysburg," MS, E. P. Alexander Papers, UNC; *OR,* XXVII, pt. 2, pp. 351–352. For reference to the change of position of his guns to avoid an enfilading fire see Maj. B. F. Eshleman's report in *ibid.,* p. 434.

88. Alexander, *Military Memoirs,* 418. In an earlier account he implied that his orders came directly from Gen. Lee. See Alexander, "The Great Charge and Artillery Fighting at Gettysburg," *B&L,* III, pt. 1, p. 361.

89. Alexander, "Battle of Gettysburg," MS, E. P. Alexander Papers, UNC.

90. "Colonel E. P. Alexander's Report of the Battle of Gettysburg," *SHSP,* IV, 235.

91. Alexander, *Military Memoirs,* 418–419. Alexander said that a Maj. Richardson had command of the nine howitzers. The only Confederate artilleryman of that name with the rank of major at Gettysburg was Charles Rich-

ardson who served in Lt. Col. John J. Garnett's Artillery Battalion of Hill's Corps. Garnett said Richardson commanded nine rifled pieces of the battalion and that late on July 3 Longstreet ordered him to a position to the right of Maj. W. J. Pegram. The report made no mention of Richardson commanding 12-pounder howitzers, which are smoothbore cannon. *OR*, XXVII, pt. 2, pp. 652–653. Garnett could have been mistaken about the nine rifled pieces. His battalion had only six rifled guns, two of which were Parrotts. However, Hill's corps carried fifteen 12-pounder howitzers into battle, and Maj. Richardson, who apparently had no regular command, might have been temporarily assigned to the howitzers by Pendleton. See *ibid.*, pp. 289, 356.

92. *Ibid.*, pp. 352, 356, 610, 635, 652–653, 673–675, 678. There is some question whether nine rifled guns under Maj. Charles Richardson, assuming that these were the guns he commanded, saw any action during the cannonade. The reports are far from clear in this respect. Walker implied that they saw action and Garnett indicated the opposite. If the latter is correct, then Walker employed only fifty-one guns. *Ibid.*, 610, 652–653. The range of the howitzers at five-degree elevation was 1,072 yards and of the Napoleons 1,619. Federal artillery was at least 1,400 yards away from Walker's line. See Jack Coggins, *Arms and Equipment of the Civil War* (New York, 1962), 66.

93. *OR*, XXVII, pt. 2, pp. 352, 355–356, 456, 458–459, 495, 544, 603–606.

94. These figures include eight guns of Henry's battalion on Alexander's extreme right. The uncertainty about the nine pieces purported to be under Maj. Richardson accounts for the two totals. Alexander said that the Confederates finally used 172 guns in the cannonade, but he did not explain how he arrived at that number. *Military Memoirs*, 419. Alexander never did seem certain about the number of guns Walker had used in the cannonade. At one time he estimated it to be from fifty to sixty; at another he set the figure at sixty-five, then sixty-three, and finally sixty. Alexander to his father, July 17, 1863, Alexander-Hillhouse Papers, UNC; "Colonel Alexander's Report of the Battle of Gettysburg," *SHSP*, IV, 236–238; Alexander, "Artillery Fighting at Gettysburg," *B&L*, III, pt. 1, p. 362; Alexander, *Military Memoirs*, 419.

95. Alexander to Bachelder, May 3, 1876, Bachelder Papers.

96. *Id.* to *id.*, *ibid.*; Alexander to his father, July 17, 1863, Alexander-Hillhouse Papers, UNC.

97. Longstreet to Alexander, July 3, 1863, E. P. Alexander Papers, UNC. [Notation on message.] This note was received from Longstreet on the battlefield about 11:45 A.M., July 3.

98. Alexander, *Military Memoirs*, 421.

99. Alexander to Longstreet, Near Gettysburg, July 3, 1863, E. P. Alexander Papers, UNC.

100. Longstreet to Alexander, Hdqrs., July 3, 1863, with notation, "Received about 12:15 P.M. in reply to mine." *Ibid.*

101. Alexander, *Military Memoirs*, 421–422.

102. Alexander to Longstreet, Near Gettysburg, July 3, 1863, about 12:30 P.M., E. P. Alexander Papers, UNC. In another version of his account of this

exchange of notes Alexander used the word "order" instead of "advise" when referring to Pickett's charge. Obviously this was a mistake, for even Longstreet did not try to give Alexander authority to *order* Pickett. See Alexander, "Artillery Fighting at Gettysburg," *B&L*, III, pt. 1, p. 363. In his memoirs Alexander used the verb "advise." *Military Memoirs*, 422.

103. Fremantle, *Three Months in the Southern States*, 262–263. Longstreet stated he rode into a "woodland" nearby to lie down and seek for some "new thought that might aid the assaulting column." He did this, he claimed, right after his first note to Alexander. Longstreet, *Memoirs*, 390–391. If Longstreet did catch a few minutes of sleep, as Fremantle suggested, he would have had enough time between the dispatch of his second message to Alexander around noon and the firing of the signal shot at 1:00 P.M.

104. *OR*, XXVII, pt. 2, pp. 385, 650, 671; Harrison, *Pickett's Men*, 90–91.

105. Longstreet, "Lee's Right Wing at Gettysburg," *B&L*, III, pt. 1, p. 343; *OR*, XXVII, pt. 2, pp. 359, 614–615, 619, 632, 999; Harrison, *Pickett's Men*, 90–91. Just how Armistead's brigade lined up with reference to the right and left flanks of the first line is uncertain. One writer said his brigade was to the rear of the center of the first line, covering the space between Kemper's left and Garnett's right flanks. He supposed this position was assigned to Armistead so that he might at the critical moment rush to the assistance of the two leading brigades and if possible put the capstone upon their work. "Colonel Rawley Martin's Account," *SHSP*, XXXII, 185.

106. *OR*, XXVII, pt. 2, p. 359. Lee reported the same deployment for Heth's division. *Ibid.*, 320. Lee's statement about the arrangement of Heth's men is not necessarily a corroboration of Longstreet's report. On the contrary, it could be a mere echo, for a commanding officer's report depended largely upon information coming from his subordinates. However, all other accounts which referred to this matter agreed that the four brigades in the division fronted on the same line. That being the case, the division could be divided into two lines by placing approximately half of the men in each brigade in the first line and the rest in the second. According to George R. Stewart, a student of the battle, this arrangement was made in the following manner: "The division was in line of regiments, with each regiment having half its companies in the first line and half in the second." Stewart, *Pickett's Charge* (Boston, 1959), 87. Unfortunately none of the accounts by officers who would have been aware of it mentioned this unusual formation. Also none of them except Lee and Longstreet referred to the "lines" of Heth's division, but to the "line." *OR*, XXVII, pt. 2, pp. 644, 647, 650–651, 659, 671; Battle Report of R. M. Mayo, Col. 47th Va. Reg. of Brockenbrough's Brig., Aug. 13, 1863, MS, Henry Heth Collection, Confederate Museum; Gen. James H. Lane to Messrs. Editors [Raleigh *Observer*], Sept. 7, 1877, Typescript; Lt. W. B. Shepard to *id.*, Sept. 18, 1877, Typescript; Louis G. Young to Maj. W. J. Baker, Feb. 10, 1864, Typescript, Bryan Grimes Papers, UNC.

107. In this deployment the four brigades from right to left in the front line would have been Kemper's, Garnett's, Fry's (Archer's), Marshall's (Pettigrew's); second line, Armistead's, Davis', Mayo's (Brockenbrough's); third

line, Lowrance's (Scales's), Lane's. In addition in the third line possibly Wilcox' and Perry's brigades were on the far right.

108. *Id.* to *id., ibid.*

109. *Ibid.; OR,* XXVII, pt. 2, pp. 646, 650. Col. J. Jones, who assumed command of the brigade after Pettigrew's death, wrote that his brigade, not Fry's, was on the right of Heth's division during the charge, but other reliable participants stated just the opposite. For Jones's account see Jones to Col. H. K. Burgwyn, July 30, 1863, Typed Copy, Bryan Grimes Papers, UNC.

110. Freeman, *Lee's Lieutenants,* III, 185–186; *OR,* XXVII, pt. 2, p. 650; Battle Report of R. M. Mayo, Aug. 13, 1863, Henry Heth Collection, Confederate Museum. The 11th Miss., which up to July 3 had been guarding the wagon train for Heth's division, rejoined Davis' brigade and added from 300 to 400 fresh men to its strength. *OR,* XXVII, pt. 2, p. 649; Love, "Mississippi at Gettysburg," *Mississippi Historical Society Publications,* IX, 44.

111. *OR,* XXVII, pt. 2, p. 666. Maj. C. S. Venable of Lee's staff later told Maj. T. M. R. Talcott, an aide of the general, that Pettigrew had understood that Pender's two brigades under Trimble were to "advance in echelon on his left, and when his left was threatened he sent an aide to Trimble urging him to push ahead." Not receiving the support he expected, he had to change the front of Davis' brigade under fire with disastrous results. Talcott, "The Third Day at Gettysburg," *SHSP,* XLI, 44.

112. B. D. Fry to Bachelder, Dec. 27, 1877, Bachelder Papers. Apparently Longstreet was unaware of this arrangement, for in his report he said Gen. Pickett's line was to guide Pettigrew's. *OR,* XXVII, pt. 2, p. 359.

113. John T. James to his father, July 9, 1863, in Houston, "Storming Cemetery Hill," *Philadelphia Weekly Times,* Oct. 21, 1882; Wood, *Reminiscences of Big I,* 43–44; Harrison, *Pickett's Men,* 91–92; Fremantle, *Three Months in the Southern States,* 210–211. In his article, "Lee in Pennsylvania," *Annals,* 431–432, Longstreet said that Lee rode with him twice over the lines to see that everything was arranged according to his wishes, and then leaving Longstreet, he rode over the field once more for a final inspection. But a good many years later Longstreet changed his story completely and claimed Lee had given him no assistance whatever in preparations for the attack. See *Memoirs,* 388.

114. Longstreet, "Lee in Pennsylvania," *Annals,* 432.

NOTES TO CHAPTER XIX

1. Longstreet, "Lee in Pennsylvania," *Annals,* 430; Alexander, "Artillery Fighting at Gettysburg," *B&L,* III, pt. 1, p. 362, note. Two guns in Capt. M. B. Miller's battery of the Washington, La., Artillery fired the signal shots in quick succession. *OR,* XXVII, pt. 2, p. 434; LI, pt. 2, p. 733.

2. Alexander, *Military Memoirs,* 422; Alexander to his father, July 17, 1863, Alexander-Hillhouse Papers, UNC. A vast majority of the reports on both sides, including those of Lee, Hill, Pendleton, Walker, Meade, Hunt, Newton, Hancock, Gibbon, Harrow, Webb, Hall, and Hazard agreed that the signal guns

went off at or about 1:00 P.M. *OR*, XXVII, pt. 1, pp. 117, 239, 262, 372, 417, 420, 428, 437, 448, 454, 464, 478, 874, 883; pt. 2, pp. 320, 352, 359, 376, 385, 434, 608, 610, 614, 631, 643, 650, 678. On the other hand Walton noted that he had received Longstreet's order to fire at 1:30 P.M. Maj. B. F. Eshleman, commanding the Washington Artillery, was less definite and said he received his order from Walton between one and two o'clock. *Ibid.*, p. 434; LI, pt. 2, p. 733. It is impossible to reconcile this evidence with Alexander's statement, which is substantiated by an overwhelming majority of reliable witnesses.

3. Haskell, *Gettysburg*, 94–95.

4. Gibbon, *Recollections*, 147–148; Haskell, *Gettysburg*, 105; *OR*, XXVII, pt. 1, p. 445.

5. *Ibid.*, p. 372.

6. Gibbon, *Recollections*, 149–150.

7. *Wainwright Journals*, 249.

8. Gibbon, *Recollections*, 148–150; Haskell, *Gettysburg*, 98, 101–102, 109; *OR*, XXVII, pt. 1, pp. 445, 448, 476; Benedict, *Vermont at Gettysburgh*, 14.

9. Letter of a soldier in the 108th N. Y. to his father, July 4, 1863, quoted in George T. Fleming, *Life and Letters of General Alexander Hays* (Pittsburgh, 1919), 442–443.

10. Carl Schurz to Frank Moore, June 6, 1865, Andre de Coppet Collection, PU; Coffin, *Boys of '61*, 294; Haskell, *Gettysburg*, 105–109; *OR*, XXVII, pt. 1, pp. 262, 373, 706; Schurz, *Reminiscences*, III, 29–30; Benedict, *Vermont at Gettysburgh*, 13–15.

11. Gibbon, *Recollections*, 147–148; Browne, *Dunn Browne in the Army*, 202–203; Benedict, *Vermont at Gettysburgh*, 15; *OR*, XXVII, pt. 1, pp. 239, 428, 437, 467, 480–481.

12. Webb to his wife, July 6, 1863, Typescript, Bachelder Papers.

13. Alexander, "Battle of Gettysburg," MS, E. P. Alexander Papers, UNC; Alexander, *Military Memoirs*, 427.

14. *OR*, XXVII, pt. 1, p. 706.

15. Thomas W. Osborn, "The Artillery at Gettysburg," *Philadelphia Weekly Times*, May 31, 1879. Osborn's battle report was much less dramatic than his later account and gave no detailed information about the effects of Confederate fire. *OR*, XXVII, pt. 1, p. 750.

16. *Ibid.*, pp. 706, 750, 752, 755–757, 891, 894.

17. *Ibid.*, p. 358; see also *Wainwright Journals*, 249.

18. *OR*, XXVII, pt. 1, p. 814; see also *ibid.*, pp. 801, 820.

19. Samuel Wilkeson, "Battle of Gettysburg," in Moore, ed., *Anecdotes of the War*, 333–334.

20. Meade to M. [J.] B. Batchelder [Bachelder], Dec. 4, 1869, MS Copy, Peter F. Rothermel Collection, PDPR. A printed copy of the letter can be found in Bachelder, *The Story of the Battle of Gettysburg and Description of the Painting of the Repulse of Longstreet's Assault* (Boston, 1904), 34.

21. *OR*, XXVII, pt. 1, pp. 874, 879, 902; Hunt, "The Third Day at Gettysburg," *B&L*, III, pt. 2, p. 373; Wilkeson, "Battle of Gettysburg," in Moore, ed., *Anecdotes of the War*, 333–334. Lt. C. Gillett, ordnance officer of the Artillery

Reserve, reported that the ammunition was moved to a field about 3,000 feet to the rear. Maj. Ewing reported that his regiment stopped and reorganized between 400 and 500 men.

22. After the surrender at Appomattox Court House, Hunt had a visit with his friend and former pupil, Gen. A. L. Long, who had served as colonel on Lee's staff at Gettysburg. Amused by Hunt's sharp comments about the poor marksmanship of Confederate batteries on July 3, Long said that at the time he had wondered what his former teacher would think about it. Hunt, "Third Day at Gettysburg," *B&L*, III, pt. 2, pp. 373–374.

23. *Ibid.*, p. 372; *OR*, XXVII, pt. 1, pp. 238–239.

24. It is very difficult to get an accurate count of the number of Union guns in position to answer Confederate batteries on Seminary Ridge. The number changed during the cannonade. Also some batteries which Hunt mentioned as being on Cemetery Hill were kept in reserve and did not get into action. Many reports were vague and incomplete. *Ibid.*, pp. 238, 358, 690, 748–750, 753, 755–757, 883, 891, 893–895, 1022–1023. Osborn, whose batteries had positions on Cemetery Hill south of the Baltimore Pike, probably had thirty-one guns to bear on the assaulting infantry. To the right of McGilvery's line of guns were Capt. Andrew Cowan's 1st N.Y. Independent Battery of six 3-inchers. Capt. Jabez J. Daniel's 9th Mich. Battery, Horse Artillery, and Thomas' 4th U.S., Battery C, to support Gen. Newton's troops. Wainwright on the north side of the pike said he could get only six of his guns to bear upon Seminary Ridge. *Wainwright Journals*, 249.

25. *OR*, XXVII, pt. 1, p. 239; Hunt, "Third Day at Gettysburg," *B&L*, III, pt. 2, pp. 373–374.

26. *Ibid.*, p. 375; Francis A. Walker, "General Hancock and the Artillery at Gettysburg," *B&L*, III, pt. 2, pp. 385–387; *OR*, XXVII, pt. 1, pp. 884–885, 888–889; Hunt to Bachelder, Jan. 6, 1866, June 18, 1879, May 8, 1881; Copy of a Statement by Henry J. Hunt sent to Bachelder, Jan. 20, 1875, Bachelder Papers. This conflict in authority over the proper use of artillery started a rather acrimonious dispute between two fine generals, which persisted for years after the war and colored their interpretations of the battle.

27. Hunt, "Third Day at Gettysburg," *B&L*, III, pt. 2, pp. 373–374; *OR*, XXVII, pt. 1, p. 239; Hunt to Bachelder, Jan. 6, 1866; Copy of a Statement by Henry J. Hunt sent to Bachelder, Jan. 20, 1875, Bachelder Papers. Hunt said that after inspecting McGilvery's chests, which were getting low in ammunition, he thought it time to induce the Confederates to make their assault. He decided to go to Meade's headquarters directly without stopping to observe Hazard's batteries because he felt confident that Hazard had obeyed his orders.

28. *OR*, XXVII, pt. 1, p. 750. Osborn claimed that it was he who suggested the cease fire order to encourage the enemy to make an infantry attack while the Union artillery was still in good condition. It is one of those claims that is difficult to pin down, but the question is immaterial since Meade issued the same order about the same time. Osborn, "Artillery at Gettysburg," *Philadelphia Weekly Times*, May 31, 1879.

29. Hunt, "Third Day at Gettysburg," *B&L*, III, pt. 2, p. 374; Copy of a Statement by Henry J. Hunt sent to Bachelder, Jan. 20, 1875, Bachelder Papers; *OR*, XXVII, pt. 1, p. 117.

30. Bachelder to Gen. A. M. Scales, Oct. 29, 1877, Typescript, Bryan Grimes Papers, UNC. The same letter was printed in the *Philadelphia Weekly Times*, Dec. 15, 1877.

31. Reports of Col. Joseph Mayo, Jr., July 25, 1863; Capt. William W. Bentley, July 9, 1863, George E. Pickett Papers, DU; Durkin, ed., *John Dooley's War Journal*, 103–104; Westwood A. Todd, "Reminiscences of the War between the States," Typescript, I, 131, UNC; B. D. Fry to Bachelder, Dec. 27, 1877, Bachelder Papers; "Capt. John H. Smith's Account [of Pickett's Charge]," *SHSP*, XXXII, 190; Charles T. Loehr, "The 'Old First' Virginia at Gettysburg," *SHSP*, XXXIV, 34; Col. Joseph Mayo, Jr., "Pickett's Charge at Gettysburg," *SHSP*, XXXIV, 329–330; Wood, *Reminiscences of Big I*, 44; *OR*, XXVII, pt. 2, p. 385.

32. *Ibid.*, pp. 379, 430, 435, 611, 635–636.

33. *Ibid.*, p. 352; Alexander, *Military Memoirs*, 424.

34. Alexander to his father, July 17, 1863, Alexander-Hillhouse Papers, UNC; Alexander to Bachelder, May 3, 1876, Bachelder Papers; *OR*, XXVII, pt. 2, pp. 381, 382, 389.

35. Alexander to his father, July 17, 1863, Alexander-Hillhouse Papers, UNC; Alexander to Bachelder, May 3, 1876, Bachelder Papers; Alexander, *Military Memoirs*, 423. Alexander's accounts had a tendency to change somewhat with the passage of time. In his letter to his father he said he watched forty minutes before sending his first message to Pickett. In later accounts he shortened the waiting period to twenty-five or thirty minutes. In view of the number of guns engaged in the duel, the first figure seems more realistic, for he could hardly have expected to get results in much shorter time. Alexander quoted his message in his memoirs.

36. Alexander to his father, July 17, 1863, Alexander-Hillhouse Papers, UNC. These words were an unconscious tribute to the three batteries on which the Confederates concentrated their fire. In his later accounts he referred to them as the eighteen guns on Cemetery Hill, confusing it with the Clump of Trees. The ones which pulled out were Capt. William A. Arnold's Battery A, 1st R. I. Light, on Cushing's right, and Lt. T. Fred Brown's Battery B, 1st R. I. Light, on his left. *OR*, XXVII, pt. 1, pp. 159, 239, 428, 467, 478–480; Hunt, "Third Day at Gettysburg," *B&L*, III, pt. 2, p. 374.

37. Alexander, *Military Memoirs*, 423.

38. *Ibid.*

39. Alexander to Bachelder, May 3, 1876, Bachelder Papers.

40. Longstreet, "Lee in Pennsylvania," *Annals*, 430–431. A shorter version of this episode is found in Alexander, *Military Memoirs*, 423–424. Pendleton offered Alexander the use of nine guns, not seven as Longstreet said. *Ibid.*, 418–419.

41. Alexander to Bachelder, May 3, 1876, Bachelder Papers. Alexander had put the guns in the hollow near Pitzer's house, and as he expected to accom-

pany them himself in the advance, he gave Maj. Richardson "most positive orders to wait there until I sent for him." After writing his last note to Longstreet just before the cannonade, Alexander sent a courier named Catlett, who had been with him when he posted Richardson, to move him up. When Catlett could not find Richardson, Alexander thought he had made a mistake in directions and sent him back again with careful instructions. Catlett was gone for half an hour and returned after the cannonade had opened, saying he had looked everywhere and could not find the guns. *Id.* to *id.*, May 3, 1876, *ibid.* Years later Alexander discovered what had happened to them. Pendleton had taken away four, and Richardson with the remaining five, finding himself in the line of Federal fire during the brief artillery duel late in the morning, had moved off to find cover. Alexander, *Military Memoirs,* 420.

42. *Ibid.*, 424; Longstreet, "Lee in Pennsylvania," *Annals,* 431; Alexander, "Artillery Fighting at Gettysburg," *B&L,* III, pt. 1, p. 365. By the time Pickett's lines moved, Alexander had only from five to fifteen rounds of ammunition per gun. Alexander to his father, July 17, 1863, Alexander-Hillhouse Papers, UNC.

43. *OR,* XXVII, pt. 2, p. 360. Freeman makes the point that Alexander's first note to Longstreet warned him of the shortage of ammunition, but because the message was badly written "the fact had not impressed itself on the General's mind." *Lee's Lieutenants,* III, 156.

44. Hunt, "Second Day at Gettysburg," *B&L,* III, pt. 1, pp. 297–300.

45. Alexander, "Battle of Gettysburg," MS, E. P. Alexander Papers, UNC; Alexander, *Military Memoirs,* 420.

46. *OR,* XXVII, pt. 2, p. 321. Alexander made an estimate of the number of rounds of ammunition per gun which were carried to Pa. and the rate of consumption. The average gun, he said, carried about 125 rounds in its limber and caisson, which included canister. To the best of his recollection the ordnance reserve wagons carried in the campaign a good many fewer than 100 extra rounds per gun. He guessed that maybe the army had in all an average of about 200 rounds per gun. A gun in action would easily fire from thirty carefully aimed shots an hour to 100 hurriedly aimed ones. On July 2 the First Corps, he reported, had had sixty-two guns in action from one to four hours. They had refilled their chests from the trains. He figured that the reserve wagons were very nearly empty of all but canister, presumably at the end of the cannonade, although he did not say so. Alexander, "Battle of Gettysburg," MS, E. P. Alexander Papers, UNC. Maj. James Dearing, commander of Pickett's artillery battalion, made an even more pessimistic report of the situation after the cannonade. He wrote: "Every round of ammunition was fired out & no more could be obtained. We did not have a third enough in all of the trains combined to refill the chests. The supply was completely exhausted. When we started we had only fifty some odd rounds extra to each gun in the ordnance wagons, and there was no rifle ammunition in Richmond when we left and it is sent to us now as fast as it is prepared." [Punctuation mine.] [Dearing] to his mother, Near Culpeper C. H., July 26, 1863, James Dearing Letters, UV.

47. Alexander, *Military Memoirs,* 424. Longstreet wrote frankly in his battle report that "the order for this attack, which I could not favor under better aus-

pices, would have been revoked had I felt that I had that privilege." *OR*, XXVII, pt. 2, p. 360.

48. Alexander, *Military Memoirs*, 424.

49. Longstreet, "Lee's Right Wing at Gettysburg," *B&L*, III, pt. 1, p. 345.

50. Hamilton, ed., *Shotwell Papers*, II, 4.

51. "Colonel Rawley Martin's Account [of Pickett's Charge]," *SHSP*, XXXII, 186–187; James Hodges Walker, "The Charge of Pickett's Division by a Participant," MS, Virginia State Library. The story of the band playing may be apocryphal, for Walker's account is the only one to be seen which mentioned it. He may have confused the events of July 3 with those of July 2 when a band did play, according to Fremantle, as the battle raged along the Emmitsburg road. *Three Months in the Southern States*, 260. At "quick time" the men marched 110 steps a minute in order to cover 86 yards. See Coggins, *Arms and Equipment*, 23. It is doubtful whether they could have maintained this pace for long because of the fences along the way.

52. "Col. E. P. Alexander's Report of the Battle of Gettysburg," *SHSP*, IV, 235–238; Alexander, "Artillery Fighting at Gettysburg," *B&L*, III, pt. 1, p. 365. Certain students of the battle have worried over the question of how many Confederate officers rode in the charge. Of one there is no doubt, General Garnett. He had been totally incapacitated by a kick from a horse but recovered sufficiently to ride to his death. His body was never found. Two letters signed "R. B. G." contain the information about his physical condition. Their tenor indicates clearly that Garnett wrote them. R. B. G[arnett] to Mrs. Serena Catherine [Pendleton] Dandridge, June 21, 25, 1863, Danske Dandridge MSS, DU. For information about his death see Col. Winfield Peters, "The Lost Sword of General R. B. Garnett . . . ," *SHSP*, XXXIII, 28–29. More officers in Pickett's division rode into battle than has been generally supposed. The following list of riders is probably not complete: Gen. Garnett; Gen. Kemper and two members of his staff; Col. Lewis B. Williams of the 1st Va.; Col. Eppa Hunton of the 8th Va.; Gen. Pickett and at least five members of his staff. Mayo, "Pickett's Charge at Gettysburg," *SHSP*, XXXIV, 329; Eppa Hunton, "C. S. A., Gettysburg," MS, John Warwick Daniel Papers, DU; W. Stuart Symington to Charles Pickett, Oct. 17, 1892; Thomas R. Friend to *id.*, Dec. 10, 1894, Charles Pickett Papers, VHS. The information about the number of mounted officers in Pettigrew's and Trimble's commands is not so complete. Both of these officers led their troops on horseback and so did Lane. I. R. Trimble to Daniel, Nov. 24, 1875, John Warwick Daniel Papers, DU; Gen. James H. Lane to Messrs. Editors [Raleigh *Observer*], Sept. 7, 1877; Lt. W. B. Shepard to *id.*, Sept. 18, 1877, Typescripts, Bryan Grimes Papers, UNC.

53. Alexander, "Battle of Gettysburg," MS, E. P. Alexander Papers, UNC; Poague, *Gunner with Stonewall*, 75.

54. *OR*, XXVII, pt. 1, pp. 373, 428, 437; Walker, "Charge of Pickett's Division by a Participant," MS, Virginia State Library; Haskell, *Gettysburg*, 111–112.

55. Hamilton, ed., *Shotwell Papers*, II, 11.

56. I. R. Trimble to Bachelder, Feb. 28, 1883, Bachelder Papers.

57. Bachelder, Map of the Battlefield of Gettysburg, Third Day; Bachelder to Gen. A. M. Scales, Oct. 29, 1877, Typescript, Bryan Grimes Papers, UNC; Loehr, "The 'Old First' Virginia at Gettysburg," *SHSP*, XXXII, 34–35; "Colonel Rawley Martin's Account [of Pickett's Charge]," *SHSP*, XXXII, 186–187; Mayo, "Pickett's Charge at Gettysburg," *SHSP*, XXXIV, 331–334; John T. James to his father, July 9, 1863, quoted in Houston, "Storming Cemetery Hill," *Philadelphia Weekly Times*, Oct. 21, 1882; *OR*, XXVII, pt. 2, p. 647.

58. *OR*, XXVII, pt. 2, pp. 386, 647; [Walter Harrison] to Kemper, Oct. 2, 1869, James L. Kemper Correspondence, UV; "Colonel Rawley Martin's Account," *SHSP*, XXXII, 188.

59. Bachelder, Map of the Battlefield of Gettysburg, Third Day; Bachelder to Gen. A. M. Scales, Oct. 29, 1877; Joseph H. Saunders to Messrs. Editors [Raleigh *Observer*], Sept. 22, 1877, Typescripts, Bryan Grimes Papers, UNC; Loehr, "The 'Old First' Virginia at Gettysburg," *SHSP*, XXXII, 34–35; Mayo, "Pickett's Charge at Gettysburg," *SHSP*, XXXIV, 331.

60. *OR*, XXVII, pt. 2, pp. 360, 647; "Colonel Rawley Martin's Account," *SHSP*, XXXII, 188. Although the accounts do not say so, the topography of the field, the location of the Emmitsburg road, and documentary evidence strongly suggest that all or at least most of Pickett's men were east of the road and Pettigrew's troops had yet to cross it when the two lines converged and dressed ranks.

61. Fry to Bachelder, Dec. 27, 1877, Bachelder Papers; Joseph H. Saunders to Messrs. Editors [Raleigh *Observer*], Sept 22, 1877; Lt. W. B. Shepard to *id.*, Sept. 18, 1877, Typescripts, Bryan Grimes Papers, UNC.

62. Hamilton, ed., *Shotwell Papers*, II, 10–15.

63. Sorrel, *Recollections*, 173.

64. *Ibid.;* Lane to Messrs. Editors [Raleigh *Observer*], Sept. 7, 1877, Typescript, Bryan Grimes Papers, UNC.

65. Sorrel, *Recollections*, 173.

66. Longstreet, "Lee's Right Wing at Gettysburg," *B&L*, III, pt. 1, p. 345; Mayo, "Pickett's Charge at Gettysburg," *SHSP*, XXXIV, 331–334; Harrison, *Pickett's Men*, 97; Durkin, ed., *John Dooley's War Journal*, 106; Wood, *Reminiscences of Big I*, 47; Poague, *Gunner with Stonewall*, 75; Loehr, "The 'Old First' Virginia at Gettysburg," *SHSP*, XXXII, 35; Frank E. Moran, "A New View of Gettysburg," *Philadelphia Weekly Times*, Apr. 22, 1882.

67. See Monroe F. Cockrell, "Where Was Pickett at Gettysburg?", Typescript presented to University of Virginia, Oct. 1, 1949. See also A. S. Perham to [Webb], Feb. 5, 1903, Typescript; "Battle of Gettysburg and Personal Recollections of That Battle by Col. Fred. Fuger," Typescript, Webb Collection; Haskell, *Memoirs*, 51–52; A. S. Perham to Chamberlain, July 22, Dec. 29, 1903, Typescripts, Joshua L. Chamberlain Papers, LC.

68. Charles Pickett, who was major and asst. adj. gen. on his brother's staff, said unequivocally that the general commanded all the troops in the advance. Charles Pickett to Editor, *Richmond Times*, Nov. 11, 1894, Charles Pickett Papers, VHS. In refutation of this claim made by a proud relative thirty-one years later, there is the evidence of Lee's report in which he specifically stated

that the attack had been made under Longstreet's direction. *OR*, XXVII, pt. 2, p. 320. Nowhere in his report or in later accounts did Longstreet say anything about making Pickett director of operations. More convincing, the latest editor of Pickett's letters has concluded that Pickett did not consider himself in command of more than his own division. He cited excerpts from two of the general's letters written on July 3 and one on July 4 to the future Mrs. Pickett. Arthur Crew Inman, ed., *Soldier of the South, General Pickett's War Letters to His Wife* (Boston, 1928), 54, 57, 60.

69. Robert A. Bright to Charles Pickett, Oct. 15, 1892; W. Stuart Symington to *id.*, Oct. 17, 1892; Thomas R. Friend to *id.*, Dec. 10, 1894; Charles Pickett to Editor, *Richmond Times*, Nov. 11, 1894, Charles Pickett Papers, VHS; W. Stuart Symington to "My dear Gen'l." [Longstreet], Oct. 26, 1892, James Longstreet Letters, Microfilm, DU; "Colonel Rawley Martin's Account," *SHSP*, XXXII, 187; R. A. Bright to J. H. Stine, June 8, 1891, quoted in Cockrell, "Where Was Pickett at Gettysburg?", Typescript, UV; Mayo, "Pickett's Charge at Gettysburg," *SHSP*, XXXIV, 331–334; Ross, *Cities and Camps*, 58. Not one of Pickett's staff claimed that he had gone to the stone wall on Webb's front, but a participant in the charge implied that he had. See Durkin, ed., *John Dooley's War Journal*, 106. In contrast J. Walter Coleman, former superintendent of the Gettysburg National Military Park and careful student of the battle, made this comment on Aug. 29, 1949: "There are no official records in this, but tradition has it that he [Pickett] advanced as far as the orchard on the north side of the Codori house on the Emmitsburg road. Charles Cobean, who was on duty at the Cyclorama for quite a number of years, has also stated that when Mrs. Pickett saw the painting and where the artist had placed the General, she said that the spot was correct from the accounts of the battle her husband had given her." Quoted in Cockrell, "Where Was Pickett at Gettysburg?", Typescript, UV.

70. Thomas R. Friend to Charles Pickett, Dec. 10, 1894, Charles Pickett Papers, VHS.

71. Longstreet, *Memoirs*, 394. For the accusation of Pickett's cowardice see Haskell, *Memoirs*, 51–52.

72. Report of Col. Joseph Mayo, Jr., July 25, 1863, George E. Pickett Papers, DU; Mayo, "Pickett's Charge at Gettysburg," *SHSP*, XXXIV, 331–334; "Colonel Rawley Martin's Account," *SHSP*, XXXII, 186–187; Loehr, "The 'Old First' Virginia at Gettysburg," *SHSP*, XXXII, 34–35; Hamilton, ed., *Shotwell Papers*, II, 10–15; *OR*, XXVII, pt. 2, pp. 386, 999.

73. *Ibid.*, p. 386.

74. *Ibid.*, pt. 1, p. 239.

75. *Ibid.*, pt. 2, p. 386.

76. Battle Report of Col. R. M. Mayo, Aug. 13, 1863, Henry Heth Collection, Confederate Museum. Freeman states there is nothing in the Confederate records to indicate why Mayo was in command on July 3. *Lee's Lieutenants*, III, 185.

77. Taylor, "Campaign in Pennsylvania," *Annals*, 315.

78. *OR*, XXVII, pt. 1, p. 750; Alexander, *Military Memoirs*, 431.

79. *OR*, XXVII, pt. 1, p. 457.

80. *Ibid.*, pp. 457, 461–462; *cf. ante*, XVI, 438.

81. Carroll's brigade of four regiments was a small one. On June 30 it mustered present for duty 1,081 officers and men. The 4th Ohio brought into the battle 299 officers and men, and probably the 8th Ohio had about the same number for duty on July 2. *OR*, XXVII, pt. 1, pp. 460–461, 463; Selected Pages from the Historical and Statistical Record of the Principal Military Commands in the Union and Confederate Armies, IV, 143–144, Entry 161, Record Group 94, NA. Lt. Thomas F. Galwey of the 8th Ohio kept a diary during the war, from which he wrote a narrative of his experiences. He said his regiment went into battle with 216 men. W. S. Nye, ed., *The Valiant Hours: An Irishman in the Civil War* (Harrisburg, Pa., 1961), 119.

82. *OR*, XXVII, pt. 1, p. 462; pt. 2, p. 651; Lt. W. B. Shepard to Messrs. Editors [Raleigh *Observer*], Sept. 18, 1877; Lt. Col. W. G. Morris to *id.*, Oct. 1, 1877, Typescripts, Bryan Grimes Papers, UNC. Davis never admitted the effectiveness of the flanking attack on his left; for that matter, neither did Mayo acknowledge the devastation caused by Sawyer's and Osborn's fire. Mayo merely said he held Sawyer off, which of course was misleading since Sawyer did not attempt to advance. Mayo's Report, Henry Heth Collection, Confederate Museum. Gen. Edward L. Thomas, whose men occupied the sunken road, told Lane the next day that Mayo with Brockenbrough's brigade did not advance beyond the road. He also said that Davis' brigade pushed forward in advance of the general line with "too much impetuosity" and was driven back. Gen. James H. Lane to Messrs. Editors [Raleigh *Observer*], Sept. 7, 1877, Typescript, Bryan Grimes Papers, UNC.

83. *Ibid.; OR*, XXVII, pt. 2, pp. 660, 671–672; Louis G. Young to Maj. W. J. Baker, Feb. 10, 1864; James H. Lane to Messrs. Editors [Raleigh *Observer*], Sept. 7, 1877; Joseph H. Saunders to *id.*, Sept. 22, 1877, Typescripts, Bryan Grimes Papers, UNC; I. R. Trimble to Bachelder, Feb. 8, 1883, Bachelder Papers. In his diary Trimble said his men got only as far as a point some 200 yards from the Yankee "breastworks." See "Trimble Diary," *Maryland Historical Magazine*, XVII, 12. Other accounts by Northerners and Southerners, including his own later ones, describe how some troops in Trimble's command reached the main Union line.

84. Recollections of Shields, in Fleming, *Life and Letters of Hays*, 457; I. R. Trimble to Bachelder, Feb. 8, 1883, Bachelder Papers; Hamilton, ed., *Shotwell Papers*, II, 18–21; Lt. Daniel F. Kinney to Messrs. Editors [Raleigh *Observer*] Oct. 23, 1877; Lt. Col. W. G. Morris to *id.*, Oct. 1, 1877; Bachelder to Scales, Oct. 29, 1877, Typescripts, Bryan Grimes Papers, UNC.

85. *OR*, XXVII, pt. 2, p. 671; Fremantle, *Three Months in the Southern States*, 265; W. R. Bond, "Longstreet's Assault at Gettysburg," 38, Article printed in 1904, Bryan Grimes Papers, UNC. The name of the periodical is missing.

86. Fleming, *Life and Letters of Hays*, 424, 436.

87. Hays to his wife, July 11, 1863; *id.* to [John B. McFadden], July 18, 1863, in Fleming, *Life and Letters of Hays*, 409, 419. The insignia of the Second

Corps was the trefoil or clover-leaf, the color of which was different for each division. The Third Division's color was blue.

88. *Id.* to [Mrs. John B. McFadden], July 27, 1863, in *ibid.*, 421.

89. Ezra J. Warner, *Generals in Blue, Lives of Union Commanders* (Baton Rouge, La., 1964), 223.

90. David Shields to Bachelder, Aug. 27, 1884, Bachelder Papers. Shields at the time of the battle was a lieutenant and aide on Hays's staff.

91. Account of Lt. L. E. Bicknell in 1883, quoted in Fleming, *Life and Letters of Hays*, 439.

92. Letter of a member of the 108th N.Y. to his father, July 4, 1863, quoted in *ibid.*, 442–443. The writer said Hays cheered Union skirmishers who were driving the vanguard of the enemy main line. Very likely he meant the 8th Ohio and two companies of the 4th Ohio. *Ibid.*, 452–453.

93. On June 30 the Second Brigade had 1,522 officers and men present for duty, and the Third had 1,779. The losses for the Third totalled 714, of which the vast majority occurred on the 2nd. Perhaps a third of all the casualties of the Second Brigade, amounting to 366 for the battle, occurred also on the 2nd. *OR*, XXVII, pt. 1, pp. 176–177; Selected Pages from the Historical and Statistical Record of the Principal Military Commands in the Union and Confederate Armies, IV, 143–144, Entry 161, Record Group 94, NA. In the opinion of C. D. MacDougall, who was colonel of the 111th N.Y. at the battle, all commands of the division were small on July 3, having been decimated by casualties and skirmish details, so much so that the line of battle at times was reduced to a heavy skirmish line. [Gen.] C. D. MacDougall to Gettysburg Memorial Association, Aug. 27, 1890, Bachelder Papers.

94. Recollections of Capt. David Shields, quoted in Fleming, *Life and Letters of Hays*, 450–453; Letter of member of 108th N.Y. to his father, July 4, 1863, quoted in *ibid.*, 443; Shields to Bachelder, Aug. 27, 1884; *id.* to C. D. MacDougall, Aug. 26, 1890, Copy; A. P. Seeley to *id.*, June 25, 1890, Copy; Theo. G. Ellis to Bachelder, Sept. 27, Nov. 3, 1870; C. A. Richardson to *id.*, Aug. 18, 1869, Bachelder Papers; *OR*, XXVII, pt. 1, pp. 158–159, 465–467. Col. Thomas A. Smyth of the 1st Del., who commanded the Second Brigade, received a wound during the cannonade. The next officer in rank was Lt. Col. Francis E. Pierce, but since his regiment was way to the right in the grove and he could not take over quickly, Maj. Ellis commanded the brigade during the assault. The line of the 111th N.Y. apparently ran between the Bryan house and barn. The barn was on its front and the house to its rear.

95. Account of Lt. E. L. Bicknell, quoted in Fleming, *Life and Letters of Hays*, 438–439.

96. Recollections of Shields, quoted in Fleming, *Life and Letters of Hays*, 457–458; Toombs, *New Jersey Troops*, 293–294.

97. *OR*, XXVII, pt. 1, pp. 239, 373, 417, 428, 437, 454, 467, 480. Apparently Capt. J. M. Rorty's Battery B, 1st N.Y. Artillery, of four 10-pounder Parrotts could no longer fire. Arnold's Battery A, 1st R. I., of six 3-inchers had withdrawn. See *ibid.*, pp. 238, 478, 480–481. The number of guns Cushing could work against the enemy infantry has been a subject of dispute. Bachelder

said Cushing pushed three of his guns down to the wall; Cowan referred to both Cushing's "gun" and "guns"; Sgt. Fred Fuger, who was cited by Hazard for his bravery that day, insisted that all six of Cushing's guns were finally placed behind the wall to stop Pickett's charge. However, Webb and Col. Norman J. Hall, commander of the brigade next to Webb's, in their battle reports very definitely said Cushing could fire only one gun. Webb said elsewhere that three of Cushing's guns were pushed to the wall carrying their canister with them. His statements can be reconciled if it is assumed that Cushing had only enough shot and shell on hand to work one gun, but sufficient canister for three. See Bachelder, Notes Relating to the Services of Troops at Gettysburg, 1863, MS, Huntington Library; Cowan to Webb, Nov. 6, 1885; Cowan, "The First New York Independent Battery at Gettysburg," MS; "Battle of Gettysburg and Personal Recollections of That Battle by Col. Fred. Fuger," Typescript, Webb Collection; OR, XXVII, pt. 1, pp. 428, 437.

98. Andrew Cowan to Bachelder, Aug. 26, 1866; Statement of Col. Charles Banes, Apr. 24, 1890, Bachelder Papers; OR, XXVII, pt. 1, p. 690.

99. Ibid., p. 366; Hancock to Rothermel, Dec. 31, 1868, Peter F. Rothermel Collection, PDPR.

100. [R. Penn] Smith to Rothermel, Nov. 25, 1867, ibid.; OR, XXVII, pt. 1, pp. 428–429, 431–435.

101. Ibid., pp. 443, 445, 448; Diagram showing position of regiments near Clump of Trees, July 3, Bachelder to New York Gettysburg Commission, July 12, 1888, Press Letter Book, 632–633; George N. Macy to Bachelder, May 12, 1866, Bachelder Papers.

102. OR, XXVII, pt. 1, pp. 420, 422–426. Battle reports of the First Brigade indicate that regimental positions were very different from their locations on Bachelder's map. See Map of Battlefield of Gettysburg, Third Day.

103. OR, XXVII, pt. 1, pp. 258, 318, 321–322, 349, 352–353. Benedict, Vermont at Gettysburgh, 10–11; Benedict to Bachelder, Dec. 24, 1863, Mar. 16, 1864, Bachelder Papers. Benedict felt that Doubleday's and Newton's distrust of the ability of the Vt. nine-month men to withstand a charge was an additional reason for the arrangement of the troops. That might have been true, but it should be noted that the colonels of both the 13th and 14th regiments asked permission to advance their men considerably beyond the main line so as to place them in better defensive positions. See Benedict, Vermont at Gettysburgh, 10; OR, XXVII, pt. 1, p. 352.

104. Ibid., p. 366; Hancock to Rothermel, Dec. 31, 1868, Peter F. Rothermel Collection, PDPR.

105. General Stannard's Diary, Entry for July 3, 1863, Typescript, Bachelder Papers; OR, XXVII, pt. 1, pp. 349, 439. Col. Hall remarked that there was "a disposition in the men to reserve their fire for close quarters. . . ." However, Hall ordered two of his regiments, the 7th Mich. and the 20th Mass., to open fire at a range of about 600 feet to disrupt an enemy maneuver. Ibid., pp. 438–439.

106. Benedict, Vermont at Gettysburgh, 16–17; Durkin, ed., John Dooley's War Journal, 106; Hamilton, ed., Shotwell Papers, II, 10–15; Report of Col.

Joseph Mayo, Jr., July 25, 1863, George E. Pickett Papers, DU. Lt. Shields, who watched the rebels come on from Hays's front, recalled no rebel yell, which he thought was unusual. See Recollections of Shields, quoted in Fleming, *Life and Letters of Hays*, 458.

107. *Ibid.; OR*, XXVII, pt. 1, pp. 373, 439, 445, 447, 454.

108. *Ibid.*, p. 349; Hunt, "Third Day at Gettysburg," *B&L*, III, pt. 2, p. 375.

109. *OR*, XXVII, pt. 2, pp. 659–660, 666–667, 671–672; I. R. Trimble to Bachelder, Feb. 8, 1883, Bachelder Papers; Trimble to Daniel, Nov. 24, 1875, John Warwick Daniel Papers, UV; Lane to Messrs. Editors [Raleigh *Observer*], Sept. 7, 1877; Joseph H. Saunders to *id.*, Sept. 22, 1877, Typescripts, Bryan Grimes Papers, UNC.

110. *OR*, XXVII, pt. 1, p. 454. After the war Hays's aide, Lt. Shields, questioned the wording in Hays's published report. He said he had had access to two copies of the report in Mrs. Hays's possession, and though each was written in a different handwriting, they agreed in the text. Instead of stating, as did the report, that "four lines arose," each of these copies said " 'our lines.' " David Shields to Bachelder, Aug. 27, 1884, Bachelder Papers. Shields has a point, for as far as can be determined Hays had only two lines along the wall.

111. Ellis to Bachelder, Nov. 3, 1870, *ibid.*

112. Lane to Messrs. Editors [Raleigh *Observer*], Sept. 7, 1877; Joseph H. Saunders to *id.*, Sept. 22, 1877; P. C. Carlton to *id.*, Sept. 26, 1877, Typescripts, Bryan Grimes Papers, UNC.

113. A. P. Seeley to C. D. MacDougall, June 25, 1890, Copy; Samuel Roberts to Webb, Aug. 18, 1883, Copy, Bachelder Papers. One Union officer who distinguished himself that day wrote: "I could not but admire the pluck of the enemy especially when after the fight I saw many of them who had rushed ahead of their fellows, lying dead, a few paces from our breastworks, mostly North Carolinians, lean lank fellows in rusty old suits, but heroes." Capt. S. C. Armstrong to Bachelder, Feb. 6, 1884, *ibid.* For Southern accounts of the extent of Lane's advance see P. C. Carlton to Messrs. Editors [Raleigh *Observer*], Sept. 26, 1877; Joseph H. Saunders to *id.*, Sept. 22, 1877; J. G. Harris to *id.*, Nov. 28, 1877, Typescripts; E. B. Cope, A Map showing scene of Longstreet's Final Assault . . . July 3, 1863, Bryan Grimes Papers, UNC.

114. Account by L. E. Bicknell, quoted in Fleming, *Life and Letters of Hays*, 439; Bicknell to Bachelder, Aug. 6, 1883, Bachelder Papers.

115. C. A. Richardson to Bachelder, Aug. 18, 1869; S. C. Armstrong to *id.*, Feb. 6, 1884, *ibid.* Armstrong estimated that he had about 200 men with him in the flanking attack.

116. *Ibid.*

117. Bicknell to Bachelder, Jan. 8, 14, 1884, *ibid.*

118. Hays estimated that he captured no less than 1,500 prisoners. In addition his command gathered up 2,500 stand of arms, leaving he guessed another 1,000 on the ground. As highly esteemed trophies of their victory his men, he said, picked up twenty-two enemy standards. *OR*, XXVII, pt. 1, p. 454; Hays to [John B. McFadden], July 13, 1863, in Fleming, *Life and Letters of Hays*,

409–410. Fleming said the men acquired twenty-one standards, fifteen of which went to army headquarters and six to Webb, presumably because they were found after the battle along his front. *Ibid.*, 409, 467–469.

119. William E. Barrows to Hall, Aug. 12, 1866; Gibbon to Ned [Edward Moale], June 17, 1866; Moale to General [Gibbon], June 25, 1866, Bachelder Papers; Hancock to Rothermel, Dec. 31, 1868, Peter F. Rothermel Collection, PDPR; Benedict, *Vermont at Gettysburgh*, 17, 21.

120. On June 20 the strength of the Vt. regiments which fought at Gettysburg was as follows: 13th Vt., 719 officers and men; 14th Vt., 729; and 16th Vt., 735. General Stannard's Diary, Entry for June 20, 1863, Typescript, Bachelder Papers. Webb had 953 officers and men of his brigade with him at the time of Pickett's charge. Webb to his wife, Aug. 8, 1863, Webb Collection.

121. *OR*, XXVII, pt. 1, pp. 352–353.

122. *Ibid.*, p. 350.

123. *Ibid.*, pp. 350, 353, 1042; Benedict, *Vermont at Gettysburgh*, 17–18; Hancock to Rothermel, Dec. 31, 1868, Peter F. Rothermel Collection, PDPR; Statement of Henry H. Bingham to Hancock, Jan. 5, 1869, copied Mar. 16, 1869, Bachelder Papers. Randall made no reference to having received an order from anyone to make the attack. Implying perhaps it was his own idea, he said Doubleday rode up and assured him the movement would be a success. *OR*, XXVII, pt. 1, p. 353. Stannard said he received no orders or suggestions from any officer of the Second Corps except Hancock, who rode down to him when the movement was nearly completed. Apparently Hancock did not like the way Stannard was doing it, for when the Vermonter told him about it, Hancock remarked that Stannard had "gone to H--l." The response was, "To Hell it was then, as it was the only thing that could possibly save the day." Immediately after this exchange Hancock was wounded. Stannard to Doubleday, Sept. 3, 1865, Abner Doubleday Papers, Baseball Hall of Fame, Cooperstown, N.Y.

124. *OR*, XXVII, pt. 2, p. 435; Haskell, *Memoirs*, 50–51. Benedict admitted Haskell's fire caused the only casualties among the Vermonters, but vehemently denied that it threw them into disorder or confusion. Benedict to Bachelder, Dec. 24, 1863, Bachelder Papers.

125. *OR*, XXVII, pt. 1, pp. 350, 353, 1042. Randall said he took more prisoners than there were men in his regiment. For Confederate accounts see Reports of Col. Joseph Mayo, Jr., July 25, 1863; Capt. R. W. Douthat, [no date]; Capt. William W. Bentley, July 9, 1863, George E. Pickett Papers, DU; Hamilton, ed., *Shotwell Papers*, II, 13–15; Loehr, "The 'Old First' Virginia at Gettysburg," *SHSP*, XXXII, 34–35.

126. Hamilton, ed., *Shotwell Papers*, II, 14; "Colonel Rawley Martin's Account," *SHSP*, XXXII, 186–187; Loehr, "The 'Old First' Virginia at Gettysburg," *SHSP*, XXXII, 34–35; W. B. Shepard to Messrs. Editors [Raleigh *Observer*], Sept. 18, 1877; Gaston Broughton to *id.*, Oct. 15, 1877; H. C. Moore to *id.*, Nov. 6, 1877; J. Jones to Col. H. K. Burgwyn, July 30, 1863; Louis G. Young to Maj. W. J. Baker, Feb. 10, 1864; John B. Bachelder to Gen. A. M. Scales, Oct. 29, 1877, Typescripts, Bryan Grimes Papers, UNC; *OR*, XXVII,

pt. 1, pp. 373–374; pt. 2, pp. 671–672. In the final drive for the Clump of Trees and the Angle, troops from Archer's, Pettigrew's, and Scales's brigades crowded in with Pickett's men.

127. Account of Col. W. W. Wood, quoted in J. Bryan Grimes, "Gettysburg," Typescript, 1911, Bryan Grimes Papers, UNC; Webb to his wife, July 6, 1863, Copy, Bachelder Papers.

128. *Ibid.;* Charles H. Banes to Webb, Aug. 9, 1887, Webb Collection; Testimony of Col. [C. H.] Banes, Apr. 24, 1890; A. W. McDermott to Bachelder, Oct. 21, 1889, Bachelder Papers; R. P. Smith to Rothermel, Nov. 25, 1867, Peter F. Rothermel Collection, PDPR; *OR,* XXVII, pt. 1, p. 437.

129. Cowan, "The First New York Independent Battery at Gettysburg," MS; Remarks by Andrew Cowan, Webb Collection; Cowan to Bachelder, Aug. 26, 1866, Dec. 2, 1885, Bachelder Papers.

130. Webb to Rothermel, Jan. [?], [1868 or 1869], Peter F. Rothermel Collection, PDPR.

131. *OR,* XXVII, pt. 1, pp. 321, 440, 446.

132. Account of J. C. Timberlake, Sept. 24, 1877; Louis G. Young to Maj. W. J. Baker, Feb. 10, 1864, Typescripts, Bryan Grimes Papers, UNC; Kemper to W. H. Swallow, Feb. 4, 1886, James Lawson Kemper Papers, UV; [Dearing] to his mother, July 26, 1863, James Dearing Letters, UV; Loehr, "The 'Old First' Virginia at Gettysburg," *SHSP,* XXXII, 34–35; John T. James to his father, July 9, 1863, in Houston, "Storming Cemetery Hill," *Philadelphia Weekly Times,* Oct. 21, 1882; M. A. Cogbill to E. Scott [Gibbs], Sept. 28, 1894, Charles Pickett Papers, VHS; Scheibert, *Seven Months in the Rebel States,* Hoole, ed., 114–115.

133. "Colonel Rawley Martin's Account," *SHSP,* XXXII, 186–187. Webb said Armistead led about 150 men over the wall. He and forty-two of the men were wounded or killed. Webb to his father, July 17, 1863, Webb Collection.

134. Account of J. C. Timberlake, Sept. 24, 1877; Bachelder to Gen. A. M. Scales, Oct. 29, 1877, Typescripts, Bryan Grimes Papers, UNC.

135. Webb to his wife, July 6, 1863, Copy; A. W. McDermott to Bachelder, Sept. 17, Oct. 21, 1889; A. F. Devereux to *id.,* July 22, 1889; Webb to *id.,* Nov. 25, 1869, June 16, 1888; Testimony of Col. Charles H. Banes, Taken before the Commissioners at the Office of W. W. Ker, April 24, 1890, Philadelphia, Copy, Bachelder Papers; Charles H. Banes to Webb, Sept. 30, Oct. 1, 2, 10, 1889; Typed Copy of Synopsis of Testimony and Examples of Testimony given before the Pennsylvania Supreme Court, May 1, 1891, presented to House Military Affairs Committee; Webb to his father, July 17, 1863; *id.* to his wife, July 27, 1863, Webb Collection; Webb's Testimony in Appeal of the Gettysburg Battlefield Memorial Association from the Decree of the Court of Common Pleas of Adams County, Supreme Court of Pennsylvania, Middle District, May Term, 1891, No's. 20 and 30; Charles H. Banes, *History of the Philadelphia Brigade* (Philadelphia, 1876), 173.

136. Webb to his wife, July 6, 1863, Copy, Bachelder Papers. Though Col. Hall made a point of citing Lt. Haskell for gallantry in leading regiments into action, he did not substantiate Haskell's statement that he had gone and asked

Hall to assist Webb. Instead Hall reported that he himself had seen a portion of Webb's line give way and immediately began to bring up reinforcements. Haskell, *Gettysburg*, 123–124; *OR*, XXVII, pt. 1, pp. 439–440.

137. *Ibid.*, pp. 373–374, 417–418, 420, 423, 425, 426, 428, 431, 439–440, 443–446, 448–451; George N. Macy to Bachelder, May 12, 1866; A. W. McDermott to *id.*, Oct. 10, 1889, Bachelder Papers; Devereux to Maj. Samuel Roberts, Nov. 11, 1883, Copy; E. Wise to Webb, Aug. 1, 1887, Webb Collection.

138. *OR*, XXVII, pt. 1, pp. 318–319, 321–322; Gates, *The "Ulster Guard,"* 466–467, 471–472.

139. Benedict, *Vermont at Gettysburgh*, 21; Gibbon, *Recollections*, 153.

140. *OR*, XXVII, pt. 1, pp. 374, 439–440, 443–446; W. Raymond Lee to Webb, Apr. 22, 1864 [?], Webb Collection; A. C. Plaisted to Bachelder, June 11, 1870, Bachelder Papers; Loehr, "The 'Old First' Virginia at Gettysburg," *SHSP*, XXXII, 34–35.

141. Alexander, *Military Memoirs*, 425; Bachelder to Gen. A. M. Scales, Oct. 29, 1877, Typescript, Bryan Grimes Papers, UNC. One of Pickett's aides asserted that Wilcox did not follow Pickett's instructions. W. Stuart Symington to Charles Pickett, Oct. 17, 1892, Charles Pickett Papers, VHS.

142. Criticism of John Esten Cooke's *Life of Lee*, contributed to Southern Historical Society, MS, no date, Cadmus M. Wilcox Papers, LC.

143. *OR*, XXVII, pt. 1, pp. 350, 1042; pt. 2, p. 632; Bachelder to Scales, Oct. 29, 1877, Typescript, Bryan Grimes Papers, UNC.

144. Criticism of Cooke's *Life of Lee*, contributed to Southern Historical Society, MS, no date, Cadmus M. Wilcox Papers, LC; *OR*, XXVII, pt. 2, p. 633.

145. *Ibid.*, p. 615. For Longstreet's version see *ibid.*, p. 360.

146. *Ibid.*, pp. 697, 699. See maps in William E. Miller, "The Cavalry Battle near Gettysburg," *B&L*, III, pt. 2, p. 400.

147. *OR*, XXVII, pt. 2, p. 699.

148. *Ibid.*, p. 697.

149. *Ibid.*, pt. 1, p. 956; Bachelder, "Battle of Gettysburg," MS, IV, 160, Bachelder Papers.

150. McClellan, *Campaigns of Stuart*, 338.

151. *Ibid.*, 338–339.

152. David McM. Gregg, *The Second Cavalry Division of the Army of the Potomac in the Gettysburg Campaign* (Philadelphia, 1907), 11; *OR*, XXVII, pt. 1, p. 956. Gregg said the fight began almost immediately after his arrival on the field. Gregg to Nicholson, Oct. 16, 1908, John Page Nicholson Collection, Huntington Library.

153. Miller, "Cavalry Battle," *B&L*, III, pt. 2, p. 401; *OR*, XXVII, pt. 1, p. 956. Gregg said he learned from Confederate sources that Stuart had between 6,000 and 7,000 mounted men. It was a force considerably larger than his. Gen. D. McM. Gregg to Maj. J. E. Carpenter, Dec. 27, 1877, Copy, William Brooke Rawle Papers, HSP. McClellan gave no overall figures for Stuart's forces but claimed that the hardships of the campaign had drastically cut down their strength. *Campaigns of Stuart*, 346–347. According to the returns for June 30,

McIntosh's brigade had 1,393 officers and men present for duty, J. I. Gregg's 1,477, and Custer's 2,345. These figures seem inflated. For instance, Custer probably had no more than 2,100 officers and men ready for action on July 3. See Selected Pages from the Historical and Statistical Record of the Principal Military Commands in the Union and Confederate Armies, IV, 80, Entry 161, Record Group 94, NA; *OR*, XXVII, pt. 1, p. 991.

154. *Ibid.*, pt. 2, pp. 697–698; Report of Jenkins' Brigade, no date, John Warwick Daniel Papers, DU. Some of Jenkins' men got to Gettysburg on the 1st. The next day the brigade was held in reserve and guarded prisoners. Jenkins was wounded while coming from Gen. Lee's headquarters, where he had gone to receive orders. E. E. Bouldin to Bachelder, July 29, 1886, Bachelder Papers.

155. *OR*, XXVII, pt. 1, p. 957. Capt. A. M. Randol and Lt. A. C. M. Pennington, Jr., were commanders of the batteries.

156. McClellan, *Campaigns of Stuart*, 339, 341; McClellan to Bachelder, Apr. 12, 1886, Bachelder Papers. The 5th Mich. and a few companies in other Mich. regiments were equipped with Spencer rifles. The effect of these lethal weapons on the outcome of the engagement cannot be determined. The men in the 5th Mich. used their rifles until they exhausted their ammunition. Notes of a Conversation with Major Trowbridge, no date, Typescript, Bachelder Papers; *cf. ante*, X, 255–259.

157. Rawle to Gen. D. McM. Gregg, May 29, 1879; *id.* to [W. E.] Miller, June 12, 1878; W. E. Miller to his brother, July 7, 1863, Copy, William Brooke Rawle Papers, HSP; "George W. Beale to His Mother, July 13, 1863," *SHSP*, XI, 324–325; Baker to his parents, July 5, 1863, William B. Baker Papers, UNC.

158. The literature of the engagement is quite voluminous, especially on who defeated whom. Neither side would give an inch, with H. B. McClellan acting as the spokesman for the Confederates and William Brooke Rawle for the Federals. For examples of the arguments and testimony to substantiate the conflicting claims, as well as information on the course of events in the battle, see W. E. Miller to his brother, July 7, 1863, Copy; Gregg to Maj. J. E. Carpenter, Dec. 27, 1877, Copy; Rawle to Gregg, May 29, 1879, William Brooke Rawle Papers, HSP; Gregg to McClellan, Oct. 26, Nov. 5, 1877, Jan. 21, 1878, Henry B. McClellan Papers, VHS; McClellan to Bachelder, Dec. 28, 1885; Col. A. M. Randol to Bachelder, Mar. 24, 1886, Typescript; Col. Carey Breckinridge to Gen. T. T. Munford, July 14, 1885, Typescript; Fragment of a letter from H. B. McClellan to [Bachelder], no date, found in folder next to letter from McClellan to *id.*, Apr. 12, 1886; *id.* to *id.*, Apr. 14, 1886; Hampton S. Thomas to *id.*, July 1, 1886; V. A. Witcher to Hon. Secy. of War, Mar. 27, 1887, forwarded to Bachelder, Bachelder Papers; McClellan, *Campaigns of Stuart*, 341–345; *OR*, XXVII, pt. 1, pp. 916, 956–957, 977, 998–1000, 1050–1051; pt. 2, pp. 697–699, 724–725.

159. W. E. Miller to his brother, July 7, 1863, Copy, William Brooke Rawle Papers, HSP.

160. Stuart's three brigades lost 181 officers and men. There was no report

for Jenkins' brigade. Gregg's losses were 254 officers and men. *OR*, XXVII, pt. 1, p. 958; pt. 2, p. 714. Pleasonton of course claimed that Stuart suffered "heavy loss." *Ibid.*, pt. 1, p. 916.

161. E. G. Fishburne to McClellan, no date, Typescript, Bachelder Papers.

162. McClellan, *Campaigns of Stuart*, 341.

163. *Ibid.*

164. *OR*, XXVII, pt. 1, pp. 943, 948; pt. 2, pp. 752, 756, 760.

165. *Ibid.*, pt. 1, pp. 914–916, 943, 956, 992–993.

166. E. M. Law to Bachelder, June 13, 1876, Bachelder Papers.

167. Law, "The Struggle for 'Round Top,'" *B&L*, III, pt. 1, pp. 327–328; *OR*, XXVII, pt. 1, p. 943; pt. 2, pp. 397, 400, 402–403; Law to Bachelder, June 13, 1876, Apr. 22, 1886, Bachelder Papers. Semmes's brigade relieved Anderson's brigade in the main Confederate battle line. *OR*, XXVII, pt. 2, p. 403.

168. H. C. Parsons, "Farnsworth's Charge and Death," *B&L*, III, pt. 2, p. 394; Law, "Struggle for 'Round Top,'" *ibid.*, pt. 1, pp. 328–330; Law to Bachelder, June 11, 13, 1876, Apr. 22, 1886, Bachelder Papers; Notes for Gen. Alexander by Gen. Benning, [1866?], Henry L. Benning Papers, UNC; George M. Neese Diary, Virginia State Library. The 1st Texas, the 4th Ala., and the 15th Ala. also got into the act to stop Farnsworth.

169. *OR*, XXVII, pt. 1, pp. 993, 1011–1012, 1018–1019; Parsons, "Farnsworth's Charge and Death," *B&L*, III, pt. 2, pp. 393–396.

170. *OR*, XXVII, pt. 1, pp. 916, 993.

171. *Ibid.*, p. 993.

172. Judge James F. Crocker, "Colonel James Gregory Hodges," *SHSP*, XXXVII, 193; Harrison, *Pickett's Men*, 101–102; [Uriah Parmelee] to Sam [Parmelee], July 21, 1863, Samuel Spencer and U. N. Parmelee Letters, DU; Owen to his wife, Dec. 21, 1863, Capt. Henry T. Owen Letters, Virginia State Library; Thompson to his mother and sister, July 20, 1863, W. G. Thompson Papers, NYHS. Pickett's division made the assault with about 4,900 officers and men and incurred 2,888 casualties, of which 1,499 were listed as captured or missing. *OR*, XXVII, pt. 2, p. 339.

173. Fremantle, *Three Months in the Southern States*, 266–270.

174. *OR*, XXVII, pt. 2, pp. 360, 615, 625; Alexander, *Military Memoirs*, 433; Longstreet, *Memoirs*, 395. Gen. Law recalled that the order to withdraw came soon after Farnsworth's charge. E. M. Law to Bachelder, June 13, 1876, Bachelder Papers.

175. Poague, *Gunner with Stonewall*, 75–76; Alexander, *Military Memoirs*, 425–426.

176. Fremantle, *Three Months in the Southern States*, 267–269. See also Special Correspondent, July 8, in the *Times* [London], Aug. 18, 1863; E. M. Hays to Bachelder, Oct. 15, 1890, Bachelder Papers.

177. H. T. Owen, "Pickett at Gettysburg," *Philadelphia Weekly Times*, Mar. 26, 1881.

178. Fremantle, *Three Months in the Southern States*, 269; Hamilton, ed., *Shotwell Papers*, II, 26; Wood, *Reminiscences of Big I*, 47; Joseph A. Engel-

hard to Messrs. Editors [Raleigh *Observer*], Aug. 29, 1877, Typescript, Bryan Grimes Papers, UNC.

179. *OR*, XXVII, pt. 1, p. 366. In the report he said that he had to break the right end of his formation in order to attack the enemy's flank. For circumstances of Hancock's wound and writing of his report see Hancock to Rothermel, Dec. 31, 1868, Peter F. Rothermel Collection, PDPR.

180. C. A. Richardson to Bachelder, May 8, 1868, Bachelder Papers.

181. *OR*, XXVII, pt. 1, pp. 376, 418, 421, 440. Strangely enough, Webb made no mention of Frank Haskell.

182. Webb to his father, undated; S. P. Chase to J. W. Webb, Nov. 7, 1863, Webb Collection.

183. Warner, *Generals in Blue*, 545.

184. Webb to Rothermel, Jan. [?], [1868 or 1869], Peter F. Rothermel Collection, PDPR.

185. Account of J. C. Timberlake, Sept. 24, 1877, Typescript, Bryan Grimes Papers, UNC. For a description of Pickett as he returned from the front see Frank E. Moran, "A New View of Gettysburg," *Philadelphia Weekly Times*, Apr. 22, 1882.

186. Webb to his father, July 17, 1863, Webb Collection. See also S. B. McIntyre to C. D. MacDougall, June 27, 1890, Copy, Bachelder Papers.

187. As an example of a tendency to overemphasize the weakness of their lines see C. D. MacDougall to Bachelder, Aug. 27, 1890, Copy, *ibid.*

188. For examples of this complaint see Harrison, *Pickett's Men*, 98–99; Pickett to Mrs. Pickett, July [?], 1863, in Inman, ed., *Soldier of the South*, 70; Allan, "The Strategy of the Gettysburg Campaign," *Campaigns in Virginia, Maryland and Pennsylvania*, 443; H. C. Moore to Messrs. Editors [Raleigh *Observer*], Nov. 6, 1877; Account of J. C. Timberlake, Sept. 24, 1877, Typescripts, Bryan Grimes Papers, UNC; *OR*, XXVII, pt. 2, p. 1000.

189. Report of Col. Joseph Mayo, Jr., July 25, 1863, George E. Pickett Papers, DU.

190. Report of Capt. A[rthur] N. Jones, July 5, 1863, *ibid.*

191. *OR*, XXVII, pt. 2, p. 386.

192. *Ibid.*, p. 615.

193. *Ibid.*, pt. 1, pp. 238–239, 241, 753, 880, 896, 899–900; Alexander, *Military Memoirs*, 434. Hunt was near Cowan's battery and in the center of the storm around the Clump of Trees. Mounted on his black horse, he kept firing at the rebels with his revolver until his horse was shot from under him. Cowan to Bachelder, Aug. 26, 1866, Bachelder Papers. The batteries were Capt. Robert H. Fitzhugh's K, 1st N. Y. Light, six 3-inchers; Lt. Augustin N. Parson's A, 1st N. J. Light, six 10-pounders; Lt. Gulian V. Weir's C, 5th U. S., six 12-pounders.

194. *OR*, XXVII, pt. 1, p. 263.

195. Col. Thomas W. Osborn, "The Artillery at Gettysburg," *Philadelphia Weekly Times*, May 3, 1879.

196. *OR*, XXVII, pt. 1, pp. 262, 290, 294, 296, 298, 308, 485, 488, 501, 503, 521–522, 525, 536, 544, 549, 551, 559, 563, 571, 578, 665–669, 674, 681, 683–684, 761, 775, 781, 785, 795, 798, 801, 805; Col. Nelson Cross to

Bachelder, Mar. 24, 1864; A. A. Humphreys to *id.*, Feb. 13, 1864; D. B. Birney to *id.*, Mar. 22, 1864, Bachelder Papers; Tyler, *Recollections of the Civil War*, 108–109; Haskell, *Gettysburg*, 116. Gen. Hays also sent word to Meade about the advance of enemy infantry. Meade, *Life and Letters*, II, 107, 109. Newton ordered Birney to send three regiments to reinforce Webb and to mass the rest of the Third Corps behind the left of Gibbon's position in readiness to fall upon enemy forces should they succeed in piercing the line. At approximately the same time Newton moved Robinson's division of his corps from behind Cemetery Hill to protect the right flank of Hays's division. Robinson got there just as Trimble's men were turning back. Meade intervened when he learned that Gen. Shaler, who had been with the Twelfth Corps in the morning, was on his way to report to Newton. He ordered Shaler to take a position behind the Third Corps.

197. This estimate is based upon the returns for the Army of the Potomac on July 4, 1863. *OR*, XXVII, pt. 1, p. 153.

198. *Ibid.*, p. 785; George Meade to Bachelder, May 6, 1882, Bachelder Papers; Meade, *Life and Letters*, II, 109.

199. George Meade to Bachelder, May 6, 1882, Bachelder Papers.

200. [Lt. John] Egan to George Meade, Feb. 8, 1870, Copy, Peter F. Rothermel Collection, PDPR.

201. George Meade to Bachelder, May 6, 1882, Bachelder Papers.

202. W. G. Mitchell to General [Hancock], Jan. 10, 1866, Copy; Hancock to Rothermel, Dec. 31, 1868, Peter F. Rothermel Collection, PDPR. Hancock and Mitchell insisted that Meade had not visited the Second Corps lines before Mitchell brought the message, implying therefore that he was the first person to give Meade news of the victory. Ironically in the excitement of the moment Meade remembered seeing Haskell but neither Mitchell nor Egan. Hancock to Rothermel, Dec. 13, 1870; Mitchell to *id.*, Dec. 19, 1870; Gen. Meade to M. [J.] B. Batchelder [Bachelder], Dec. 4, 1869, Copy, *ibid.* If George Meade was correct in his recollections, which were partly borne out by Egan and Haskell, then Mitchell met Meade after he had returned from a visit with Howard. Mitchell said he came up to Meade not far from army headquarters. Since the house was near Cemetery Hill, there is no reason why Meade could not have gone there and picked up his staff before proceeding along the Second Corps lines. For Haskell's account of his meeting with Meade see *Gettysburg*, 136–138.

203. George Meade to Bachelder, May 6, 1882, Bachelder Papers; Meade, *Life and Letters*, II, 109–110. Gen. Crawford said that Gens. Warren, Sykes, and Pleasonton were among the officers with Meade on Little Round Top. Crawford to Prof. Jacobs, Dec. [no date], 1863, S. W. Crawford Papers, LC.

204. CCW, *Report*, I, 333–334. Meade did not say when he got to Little Round Top. Fremantle said the Confederates heard and saw a general officer ride along the line with a retinue of about thirty horsemen. He set the time at 6:00 P.M. See *Three Months in the Southern States*, 270. If this hour is correct, Meade then arrived on the extreme left after six o'clock. There is strong evidence that the advance, the fighting around the Clump of Trees, and the with-

drawal of Pickett's men all took place within an hour. Within the next hour Wilcox' advance followed Pickett's charge, Union troops made sorties from their lines to pick up prisoners, and Union leaders figuratively felt themselves all over to see how badly they were hurt. Consequently Meade might not have left Cemetery Hill until after 5:00 P.M., and the next hour might have been taken up with getting to Little Round Top. See *ibid.*, 270; William Brooke Rawle to Webb, Feb. 14, 1910, Webb Collection.

205. Meade to Mrs. Meade, Dec. 3, 1864, in Meade, *Life and Letters*, II, 249.

206. Meade's friends were not critical of him, but some of them brought out evidence that others would interpret in a way damaging to his reputation. See CCW, *Report*, I, 311, 314, 360, 378, 394, 408–409, 426, 454–455, 460–462, 471–472. Many Confederates felt Meade was wise in not attempting a counterattack. Longstreet's opinions, however, had a weathervane quality; they seemed to change with his mood. For Confederate opinion see *Philadelphia Inquirer*, May 1, 1893, clipping in Webb Collection; Long, *Memoirs of Lee*, 291; Gordon, *Reminiscences of the Civil War*, 174; McLaws, Notes on Gettysburg, MS, Lafayette McLaws Papers, DU; Alexander, *Military Memoirs*, 432; Ross, *Cities and Camps*, 59–60; Allan, "Strategy of the Gettysburg Campaign," *Campaigns in Virginia, Maryland and Pennsylvania*, 444–445.

207. CCW, *Report*, I, 408.

208. *Ibid.*, 408–409.

209. The First and Third Brigades lost a total of 1,145 officers and men July 2 and 3. It is safe to assume that at least a third of these casualties occurred July 3. Webb said that out of the 953 officers and men he brought into action on July 3, 494 of them were casualties. *OR*, XXVII, pt. 1, p. 176; Webb to his wife, Aug. 8, 1863, Webb Collection.

210. Col. W. G. Veasey to Bachelder, no date, Typescript; General Stannard's Diary, Entry for July 3, 1863, Typescript, Bachelder Papers.

211. In the First Division the First and Third Brigades were supporting the First and Second Corps; in the Second Division the Third Brigade held a position on the extreme right; in the Third Division the First and Second Brigades were supporting the Second Corps. *OR*, XXVII, pt. 1, pp. 665, 668, 674–675, 681; Tyler, *Recollections of the Civil War*, 108–109.

212. CCW, *Report*, I, 409.

213. McLaws stressed the dangers to the flanks of the Union force should it attempt to move on the same ground over which Pickett had just advanced. Also if the Fifth and Sixth Corps made up the force their forward movement would expose the Round Tops to capture. See McLaws, Notes on Gettysburg, MS, Lafayette McLaws Papers, DU.

214. Sykes to the Editor of the *Chronicle* [Washington, D.C.], Dec. 9, 1865, in Gross, *The Battlefield of Gettysburg*, 27; CCW, *Report*, I, 461.

215. *Ibid.*, 461–462. Sedgwick said he was with Sykes when he got the order for a reconnaissance and thought it might have been four o'clock, or perhaps a little later. *Ibid.*, 462. Crawford said he received orders at five o'clock from Sykes to drive the enemy out of the woods southwest of the Wheatfield.

OR, XXVII, pt. 1, p. 654. Later Crawford changed his account somewhat when he said his orders had instructed him to "clear the woods if possible," but in case the enemy was found in force to retire slowly and reoccupy his position. Crawford to Prof. Jacobs, Dec. [no date], 1863, S. W. Crawford Papers, LC.

216. *OR,* XXVII, pt. 1, pp. 654–655, 657–658, 671, 685; pt. 2, pp. 397, 402–403, 416–417, 423–424; E. M. Law to Bachelder, June 13, 1876, Bachelder Papers. Anderson's brigade was nowhere near this part of the field.

217. *OR,* XXVII, pt. 1, p. 75. The reports of the brigade commanders were more complete and accurate than Crawford's. Indulging in a little horn-tooting, Crawford in his report and in his testimony before the Committee on the Conduct of the War ignored the help given his men by Nevin's brigade and said that McCandless drove all of Hood's division back to where they had started on July 2. CCW, *Report,* I, 471. Meade was not misled by the false picture Crawford had drawn of his operations.

218. Gordon, *Reminiscences of the Civil War,* 174.

NOTES TO CHAPTER XX

1. Dispatch from Carleton [C. C. Coffin], near Gettysburg, July 3 [?], in *Boston Morning Journal,* July 7, 1863.

2. *OR,* XXVII, pt. 1, p. 74.

3. Fremantle, *Three Months in the Southern States,* 271.

4. In a report to Davis on July 7, 1863, Lee stressed the difficulties in collecting supplies, with "local and other troops" watching the passes, as the big reason for retreating. At this time he said nothing about the shortage of ammunition, but mentioned it in his battle reports. *OR,* XXVII, pt. 2, pp. 299, 309, 322. Although the Confederates had not exhausted their supplies of small arms and artillery ammunition, they considered them too low for safety. For further information about ammunition supplies see Ross, *Cities and Camps,* 78; Fremantle, *Three Months in the Southern States,* 273; Pendleton to Cols. Walton, Walker, and Brown, July 10, 1863, William N. Pendleton Press Letter Book, Confederate Museum; Early to I. F. Richard, May 7, 1886, Jubal A. Early Correspondence, NYHS; Joseph C. Haskell to his mother, July 8, 1863, Rachel Susan (Bee) Cheves Papers, DU. For the poor condition of the horses see Halsey [Wigfall] to Louly [sister], July 18, 1863, Wigfall Family Papers, LC; E. P. Alexander to his brother, July 26, 1863, Alexander-Hillhouse Papers, UNC; *OR,* XXVII, pt. 2, p. 322.

5. Ross, *Cities and Camps,* 80.

6. *Ibid.;* Dispatch from Chambersburg, July 7, signed by "Franklin," in *New York Tribune,* July 10, 1863; De Peyster, *The Decisive Conflicts of the Late Civil War,* 101; CCW, *Report,* I, 300, 316, 360.

7. Scheibert, *Seven Months in the Rebel States,* Hoole, ed., 119. For further information on the good state of Confederate morale see Joseph H. Trundle to his sister, July 7, 1863, in "Gettysburg as Described in Two Letters from a

Maryland Confederate," *Maryland Historical Magazine*, June, 1959, pp. 211–212; J. W. [Jackson] to Lt. R. S. Jackson, July 20, 1863, Typescript of Prof. Merl E. Reed; Fremantle, *Three Months in the Southern States*, 270–271, 274; Dispatch from Washington, D.C., July 12, in *New York Tribune*, July 13, 1863; McKim to his mother, July 7, 15, 1863, in McKim, *A Soldier's Recollections*, 181; James B. Sheeran, *Confederate Chaplain, A War Journal*, Joseph T. Durkin, ed. (Milwaukee, 1960), 49–50.

8. *OR*, XXVII, pt. 2, pp. 338, 346. Strong evidence indicates that the figure for Confederate losses as officially tabulated is too low. In Heth's division, for instance, Pettigrew's brigade according to Louis G. Young suffered 1,100 casualities on July 1; yet losses for the entire battle are given in the *OR* as 1,105. Casualties in Brockenbrough's brigade are noted in the *OR* as 148, while Col. R. M. Mayo reported a loss of 300 riflemen on July 1 alone. It is well known that a good number of Davis' men were captured on July 1, but the *OR* have none listed. Louis G. Young to Early, Mar. 14, 1878, Jubal A. Early Papers, LC; Battle Report of R. M. Mayo, Aug. 13, 1863, Henry Heth Collection, Confederate Museum. The number of ablebodied Confederates captured during the battle was about 15 percent greater than the total given in a table in the *OR*. See *OR*, XXVII, pt. 2, p. 346, note. The Confederates also used a different standard in determining their casualties. Even though wounded, unless a soldier was declared unfit for duty by a doctor, he was not included in the casualty lists. *Ibid.*, XXV, pt. 2, p. 798.

9. Pickett's division apparently was so badly cut up that Lee sent it to the rear and assigned it the onerous duty of herding Union prisoners to Virginia. *Ibid.*, XXVII, pt. 3, pp. 983, 986–987; Owen to Harriet, July 18, 1863, Capt. Henry T. Owen Letters, Virginia State Library. For the condition of Heth's division see Moore, *A Life for the Confederacy*, 153–156.

10. The Confederates lost none of their usable pieces through capture during the battle. Pendleton reported that the enemy got three of his disabled guns. The Confederates abandoned two of them as worthless and lost the third one to Union cavalry as they were carrying it to the rear. As compensation for these losses he pointed to the capture of three 10-pounder Parrotts, one 3-inch rifle, and three Napoleons, all in good shape. *OR*, XXVII, pt. 2, pp. 354–356.

11. Alexander, *Military Memoirs*, 435. Col. William Allan stated that after the battle, ordnance officers found that the army had expended about half of its artillery ammunition, but it still had plenty for "defensive operations." "Reminiscences of Field Ordnance Service," *SHSP*, XIV, 142–143.

12. Figures for the size of Lee's mounted forces, which included Jenkins' and Imboden's brigades and Stuart's division, are very elusive. On May 31 the returns for Stuart's division of five brigades reported 10,292 officers and men. The strength of Jenkins' brigade at the beginning of the campaign was variously estimated to have been between 1,600 and 3,800 officers and men. On July 3 Imboden reported with 2,100 men. For the campaign therefore Lee had between 14,000 and 16,100 mounted men. The losses from combat in Stuart's division were negligible, and those in the other units for which there were no

reports are presumed to be proportionately the same. However, the hardships of the campaign wore out many mounts, thus reducing the strength and effectiveness of these forces perhaps to about half of what they had been. Therefore after the battle probably from 7,000 to 8,000 mounted Confederates were available to fight against about 11,000 Union cavalrymen. *OR*, XXV, pt. 2, p. 846; XXVII, pt. 1, p. 152; pt. 2, pp. 346, 547; McClellan, *Campaigns of Stuart*, 319, 346–347; "Extracts from the Diary of Lieut. Hermann Schuricht," *SHSP*, XXIV, 340; John D. Imboden, "The Confederate Retreat from Gettysburg," *B&L*, III, pt. 2, p. 422.

13. Hotchkiss to his wife, July 5, 1863, Jedediah Hotchkiss Papers, LC.

14. M. Jacobs, "Later Rambles over the Field of Gettysburg," *United States Service Magazine*, I, 75; Ropes to Gray, Oct. 22, 1863, in Gray and Ropes, *War Letters*, 249–250.

15. Meade to Mrs. Meade, July 5, 1863, in Meade, *Life and Letters*, II, 125. Whatever Lee might have felt about a Federal attack on his position on July 4, there is evidence that his soldiers were disappointed when it did not occur. See S. Thomas McCullough Diary, UV; Pettit to his wife, July 8, 1863, W. B. Pettit Papers, UNC; Sheeran, *Confederate Chaplain*, 48–49. In contrast Col. Wainwright expressed pleasure over Meade's wisdom in not attacking the Confederates. Both armies he felt had suffered equally heavy losses and were so well matched that the "assaulting party" was sure to fail if the other had time to "post itself and do anything at entrenching." He estimated Lee's position to have been as strong, if not stronger than Meade's. He also shrewdly guessed that Lee was "probably somewhat short of artillery ammunition, but not of small arm or canister." *Wainwright Journals*, 253.

16. Alexander, *Military Memoirs*, 435.

17. Fremantle, *Three Months in the Southern States*, 276.

18. *OR*, XXVII, pt. 2, pp. 326–327, 346, 557; Hood, *Advance and Retreat*, 60; Imboden, "Confederate Retreat," *B&L*, III, pt. 2, p. 424; J. B. Walton to Alexander, July 3, 1863, 3:00 A.M. [Notation at top: "This date should be July 4th. E. P. A."], E. P. Alexander Papers, UNC. The Confederates left as many members of their medical staff as they could spare to attend to their wounded, but they were not enough. Fortunately Dr. Jonathon Letterman, medical director of the Army of the Potomac, felt just as responsible for the treatment of Confederate wounded as Union. The United States Sanitary Commission and other charitable organizations and people rushed supplies to Gettysburg for the relief of soldiers in both armies. For further information on the Confederate wounded see *OR*, XXVII, pt. 1, p. 198; pt. 2, p. 557; "Report of Dr. Douglas," Moore, ed., *Rebellion Record, Documents*, VII, 127–128; Anna M. Holstein, *Three Years in Field Hospitals of the Army of the Potomac* (Philadelphia, 1867), 42–50; L. P. Brockett and Mary C. Vaughan, *Woman's Work in the Civil War . . .* (Boston, 1867), 136–137; William Q. Maxwell, *Lincoln's Fifth Wheel; The Political History of the United States Sanitary Commission* (New York, 1956), 211–213; Dr. J. E. Green Diary, North Carolina State Department of Archives and History; [Anon.], *Three Weeks at Gettysburg* (New York, 1863), 3–24.

19. Humphreys said the passes near Fairfield were midway between Get-

tysburg and Hagerstown, being about fifteen miles from each. A. A. Humphreys, *From Gettysburg to the Rapidan, The Army of the Potomac, July, 1863 to April, 1864* (New York, 1883), 2–8.

20. *OR*, XXVII, pt. 1, pp. 943, 948; pt. 2, pp. 752, 756, 760.

21. *Ibid.*, pp. 326–327, 699; Imboden, "Confederate Retreat," *B&L*, III, pt. 2, p. 422.

22. Lee, Stuart, and other Confederates had a poor opinion of Imboden and his command. See *OR*, XXVII, pt. 2, pp. 654–656, 703; pt. 3, pp. 985–986; Charles S. Venable to Early, Apr. 10, 1871, Jubal A. Early Papers, LC.

23. *OR*, XXVII, pt. 2, pp. 353, 436, 610, 654, 699; pt. 3, pp. 966–967; Imboden, "Confederate Retreat," *B&L*, III, pt. 2, pp. 422–423. Imboden said that including his battery of six guns he had altogether twenty-three pieces at his disposal. *Ibid.*, p. 423. For unfavorable comments about Imboden's account of his role in the retreat, which was described as overly dramatic and not too accurate, see Charles S. Venable to Early, Apr. 10, 1871, Jubal A. Early Papers, LC.

24. *OR*, XXVII, pt. 2, pp. 557–558, 699.

25. *Ibid.*, pp. 322, 361, 448, 699. It began raining heavily at 1:00 P.M. Saturday afternoon, July 4, let up around 2:00, and then poured shortly after 9:00 that night. Fremantle, *Three Months in the Southern States*, 274, 276. The care with which the Confederates planned the order of march was illustrated by detailed orders sent from Longstreet's headquarters at 5:30 A.M., July 6, to Col. Alexander. E. P. Alexander Papers, UNC. For information on the unhurried pace of Lee's retreat see Long, *Memoirs of Lee*, 295–297. More contemporary is the comment by a soldier of Ewell's corps who said they started the retreat at 2:00 A.M., July 5, and marched along in a leisurely way, bringing up the rear. J. W. [Jackson] to Lt. R. S. Jackson, July 20, 1863, Typescript of Prof. Merl E. Reed. See also Blackford to his wife, July 6, 1863, in Blackford, *Letters from Lee's Army*, 188. He said the retreat was so orderly that he would call it a "counter-march."

26. Humphreys, *From Gettysburg to the Rapidan*, 4–5.

27. By taking the shortest route Lee lost the advantage in wet weather of a macadamized road such as the Chambersburg Pike. The wagons and artillery using the Fairfield road cut it up badly and made it almost impassable. Welch to his wife, Aug. 2, 1863, in Welch, *Letters to His Wife*, 69. The weather was so bad that for awhile Lee wondered whether he should countermand his retreat, which he would not have started if he had anticipated the heavy rain. However, with the trains well on their way he had to follow with his army in order to protect them. Ross, *Cities and Camps*, 65–66. Campbell Brown, a member of Ewell's staff, reflected the critical attitude of a Jackson man toward a rival corps when he said that Longstreet, "notorious for moving slowly," kept the Second Corps from going at a good pace. In making this comment Brown completely and unfairly ignored the effect of the weather in slowing down the rate of the march. Brown, "Reminiscences," MS, Campbell Brown Books, UNC.

28. In a late dispatch to Couch on the night of July 3 Meade clearly summed

up his difficulties. He indicated a desire to attack Lee, but did not say how he would go about it. Above all he wished to avoid frontal assaults. *OR*, XXVII, pt. 3, p. 499; Meade to Mrs. Meade, July 5, 1863, in Meade, *Life and Letters*, II, 125.

29. This interpretation is based upon a statement made by Warren about the dangers of a premature movement of the army. CCW, *Report*, I, 379.

30. *OR*, XXVII, pt. 3, p. 499. Couch agreed with Meade about the passes and said that "unquestionably" the rebels had fortified them. *Ibid.*, p. 515.

31. CCW, *Report*, I, 334.

32. *Ibid.*

33. *OR*, XXVII, pt. 1, p. 78. Meade made this announcement in a dispatch sent to Halleck at noon, July 4. As for rain on July 4, although it came down heavily in the afternoon, it had already begun to fall in the morning. See Fremantle, *Three Months in the Southern States*, 274, 276; Testimony of Butterfield, CCW, *Report*, I, 426; William Byrnes Diary, 1863, DU.

34. *OR*, XXVII, pt. 1, p. 78.

35. *Ibid.*, pt. 3, pp. 502–503, 511–512, 520–524; Herman Haupt, *Reminiscences* (Milwaukee, 1901), 216, 220–222. The messages reproduced in Haupt's account do not always agree in time and content with the same ones published in the *OR*. Haupt, who was critical of Meade for waiting to bring up supplies from Westminster, obviously had no idea of the condition of the army. Ingalls had told Meigs on July 3 that he had to bring supplies up the next day if the army was to remain at Gettysburg. Patrick noted in his diary that on Saturday morning, July 4, everybody was without anything to eat and was waiting for subsistence. *OR*, XXVII, pt. 3, p. 503; Patrick Journal, Entry for July 6, 1863, LC.

36. *OR*, XXVII, pt. 1, p. 187; pt. 3, pp. 514, 516, 519–520; Patrick Journal, Entry for July 6, 1863, LC.

37. *OR*, XXVII, pt. 1, p. 299; pt. 2, p. 225; pt. 3, pp. 515, 518, 549, 983, 986–987; Patrick Journal, Entry for July 6, 1863, LC. Lee said he paroled 1,500 prisoners, but Couch said 2,000 were turned over to Gen. W. F. Smith near Mount Holly. Later he reduced the number to 1,300. Smith on the other hand reported that the Confederate escort turned over to him 2,000 paroled prisoners captured on July 1. Lee mentioned paroling some Union wounded as well. Who they were and where they were he did not say.

38. *OR*, XXVII, pt. 3, pp. 507, 517–518, 524, 538, 548; LI, pt. 1, p. 1069.

39. *Ibid.*, XXVII, pt. 3, pp. 446, 448, 509.

40. *Ibid.*, p. 502.

41. *Ibid.*, p. 507.

42. *Ibid.*, pt. 2, pp. 221, 225; pt. 3, pp. 507–509, 514–515, 517, 525, 539. Meade also said he hesitated to strip Couch of all his forces and leave the fords of the Susquehanna undefended. *Ibid.*, p. 539.

43. *Ibid.*, p. 506.

44. *Ibid.*, p. 549.

45. *Ibid.*, pp. 507–508, 549.

46. CCW, *Report*, I, 334, 360.

47. *OR*, XXVII, pt. 1, p. 916.

48. *Ibid.*, pp. 916–917, 928, 939, 943, 958–959, 967, 970, 977, 993–994; Boatner, *Civil War Dictionary*, 97, 216, 357, 459, 544.

49. *OR*, XXVII, pt. 3, p. 516.

50. *Ibid.*, pt. 1, pp. 79, 153.

51. CCW, *Report*, I, 350–351, 426–427.

52. *Ibid.*, 334; *OR*, XXVII, pt. 1, p. 79; pt. 3, pp. 499, 517, 540.

53. *Ibid.*, p. 78; CCW, *Report*, I, 379.

54. *OR*, XXVII, pt. 3, p. 517; CCW, *Report*, I, 379.

55. *OR*, XXVII, pt. 1, p. 79; pt. 3, pp. 532–533; CCW, *Report*, I, 334. In his first meeting with the Committee on the Conduct of the War Meade testified without benefit of any written records. In this instance he made a mistake in saying that he had directed the orders for the movement to be prepared on July 6 instead of July 5. Meade's testimony could thus be used against him by his enemies to prove that he frittered away at least two precious days in Gettysburg while Lee continued his retreat comparatively free of any harassment from Union forces.

56. Haupt, *Reminiscences*, XIV–XV, 220–229. There is one positive error of fact in Haupt's story and another probable one. Haupt stated that Lee left Gettysburg Saturday morning, July 4, in retreat, whereas that day he only withdrew Ewell's corps to a new position west of the town. The retreat of the army started Saturday night, but Ewell's corps did not take up its march until almost Sunday noon. It was still in the vicinity of Gettysburg when Haupt left Meade at noon. As for the other questionable statement made by Haupt, it is doubtful whether Meade said then that the rising waters of the Potomac had cut Lee off. Very likely Meade knew nothing about the condition of the river until he received word from Couch at three o'clock that afternoon. *Ibid.*, 221, 224, 227–228; *OR*, XXVII, pt. 2, p. 448; pt. 3, p. 548. French reported to Halleck early on Monday morning, July 6, that the river was not only rising, but it could not be forded at Shepherdstown or Williamsport. *Ibid.*, p. 564.

57. *Ibid.*, 567; Haupt, *Reminiscenes*, 224.

58. Lincoln to Howard, July 21, 1863, quoted in Basler, ed., *Collected Works of Lincoln*, VI, 341.

59. *Ibid.* See also a letter dated July 14, 1863, in *ibid.*, 327–328, which Lincoln never sent to Meade.

60. Haupt very likely saw Lincoln sometime during the day on July 6. Haupt, *Reminiscences*, 227. At seven o'clock that night Lincoln, evidently in gloomy and captious mood, complained to Halleck about the tenor of Meade's congratulatory order to his troops, a dispatch from Pleasonton to French explaining why the army was not moving, and one from French to Halleck saying that the enemy was sending his wounded across the river in flatboats. He felt these statements revealed a lack of aggressiveness on the part of the three generals. *OR*, XXVII, pt. 3, p. 567.

61. *Ibid.*, p. 519.

62. *Ibid.*

63. *Ibid.*, p. 567.

64. *Ibid.*, pt. 1, pp. 78–80.

65. In a dispatch to Halleck on July 6 he spoke of his "great difficulty in getting reliable information." *Ibid.*, p. 80. For other examples of his uncertainty and desire for precise information see *ibid.*, pt. 3, pp. 531, 535, 540, 630–631.

66. Meade to Mrs. Meade, July 8, 1863, in Meade, *Life and Letters*, II, 132.

67. *OR*, XXVII, pt. 1, p. 79.

68. *Ibid.*, pt. 3, p. 537. The famous newspaper correspondent, L. L. Crounse, said the order to move was issued sometime between 10:00 A.M. and 6:00 P.M. See Crounse, "The Escape of Lee's Army," Moore, ed., *Rebellion Record, Documents*, VII, 345–346. What evidently happened was that orders to move went out to various corps at different times during the day. *OR*, XXVII, pt. 1, pp. 386, 401, 429, 455, 708, 786, 832. For reports Meade received of enemy movements see *ibid.*, pt. 3, pp. 532–537. One puzzle in the accounts of events of this day was Meade's statement to the Committee on the Conduct of the War that Butterfield had without his knowledge put the marching schedule into effect. CCW, *Report*, I, 334. Yet Meade at 7:30 P.M. on July 5 sent Sedgwick a message saying positively that he had authorized the "issue of the order of march." *OR*, XXVII, pt. 3, p. 537.

69. *Ibid.*, pt. 1, pp. 971, 988.

70. *Ibid.*, pp. 971, 993–994, 998, 1006; pt. 2, pp. 471–472, 700–701, 752–753, 764; McClellan, *Campaigns of Stuart*, 352–355. The quote came from McClellan, *ibid.*, 352.

71. Kilpatrick reduced the number of prisoners from 1,500 to 1,360. *OR*, XXVII, pt. 1, p. 994. Huey, whose brigade accompanied Kilpatrick's division, reported the capture of 150 wagons, but he said nothing about destroying any. *Ibid.*, p. 970. Ewell kept silent about the attack on his trains. Lee said that although a number of wagons and ambulances were taken, the loss was not serious. Stuart set the figure at not more than forty wagons. *Ibid.*, pt. 2, pp. 309, 322, 448, 700–701. Jedediah Hotchkiss, Ewell's engineer, stated that most of the train got through and reached Williamsport safely. Memorandum Book, Entry for July 5, 1863, Jedediah Hotchkiss Papers, LC. Another account said the Union cavalry turned over about twenty wagons and hurled them down the mountainside. Casler, *Four Years in the Stonewall Brigade*, 177–178. Fremantle put the loss at thirty-eight wagons. *Three Months in the Southern States*, 276.

72. *OR*, XXVII, pt. 2, pp. 326–327.

73. *Ibid.*, pt. 1, pp. 663, 666, 669–670, 672, 692–693; pt. 2, pp. 448, 471–472, 493; pt. 3, pp. 530–531. In his dispatches Meade referred to Sedgwick's movement as a reconnaissance, but in his report as a pursuit. *Ibid.*, pt. 1, p. 117.

74. *Ibid.*, pp. 145, 386, 401, 429, 455, 708, 761, 786, 832; pt. 3, pp. 531, 533, 537, 539, 540–541, 554–555; CCW, *Report*, I, 334.

75. *OR*, XXVII, pt. 3, pp. 554–555, 558. Col. J. Irvin Gregg's brigade of Gen. Gregg's division clashed with the enemy near Greenwood on the Chambersburg Pike late in the day on July 5. On the 6th it pushed on to Marion and

found the road filled with broken-down wagons, abandoned limbers, and caissons carrying ammunition. See Col. Gregg's report in *ibid.*, pt. 1, pp. 977–978.

76. *Ibid.*, p. 80.

77. *Ibid.*, pt. 3, pp. 556, 559–561.

78. *Ibid.*, pp. 561–562.

79. *Ibid.*, pt. 1, pp. 917, 967; pt. 3, pp. 530–531.

80. *Ibid.*, p. 535.

81. *Ibid.*, pt. 1, pp. 663, 666, 669–670, 672, 679, 691–693, 695; pt. 2, pp. 448, 471–472, 493, 558; pt. 3, pp. 537, 554, 558, 561–562.

82. Memorandum Book, Entry for July 6, 1863, Jedediah Hotchkiss Papers, LC.

83. Ropes to Gray, Apr. 16, 1864, in Gray and Ropes, *War Letters*, 319.

84. *OR*, XXVII, pt. 1, pp. 145–146.

85. Stuart admitted the loss of sixty wagons but made no mention of the cannon or prisoners, while Couch in his report reduced the size of the losses in materiel Pierce claimed to have inflicted, and increased the number of prisoners that were taken. There was no report on the outcome of Stuart's request for a court of inquiry. *Ibid.*, pt. 2, pp. 214, 280, 703.

86. The total number of officers and men present for duty on June 30 was 4,752. The casualties of the division in the battle were 614. *Ibid.*, pt. 1, p. 919; Selected Pages from the Historical and Statistical Record of the Principal Military Commands in the Union and Confederate Armies, IV, 60, Entry 161, Record Group 94, NA.

87. *OR*, XXVII, pt. 1, p. 928; pt. 3, p. 564.

88. *Ibid.*, pt. 1, pp. 994–995, 998–1000, 1006; pt. 2, pp. 322, 361, 370, 558, 581, 701–703; Longstreet, *Memoirs*, 428; McClellan, *Campaigns of Stuart*, 359.

89. *OR*, XXVII, pt. 1, pp. 928, 935, 939–940, 943, 971, 995, 1006–1007.

90. By deducting casualties incurred at Gettysburg but making no allowances for straggling and the breaking down of horses, Buford and Kilpatrick had about 7,800 cavalrymen. This number is obtained by using the official figures of June 30, 1863, as a base, though they are by no means reliable. The debilitating effects of hard campaigning are shown in the case of Huey's brigade. On June 30 it had on its muster rolls 1,323 officers and men; yet on July 6, according to one report, it could mount only 200 men. *Ibid.*, pp. 919, 991, 1031; Selected Pages from the Historical and Statistical Record of the Principal Military Commands in the Union and Confederate Armies, IV, 60, Entry 161, Record Group 94, NA; Imboden, "Confederate Retreat," *B&L*, III, pt. 2, p. 426. Imboden guessed the Union force to be about 7,000 men. It was he who said it had eighteen guns.

91. *Ibid.*, pp. 422–423, 426–428.

92. Three of Early's regiments did not accompany his division into Pa. They had a combined strength of 936 officers and men, so it is safe to assume that each had between 250 and 350 muskets. The regiments which joined Imboden were the 54th N.C. and the 58th Va. Early, *War Memoirs*, 282; Early to the Count of Paris, Oct. [no date], 1877, Jubal A. Early Papers, LC. Imboden

made no mention of these reinforcements but Lee did. *OR*, XXVII, pt. 2, p. 322.

93. Imboden said the two brigades under Fitz Lee numbered 3,000 cavalrymen. There is good reason to believe that the remainder of Stuart's force numbered no less than 2,000 men. Gen. Birney received reports from civilians that Jenkins' brigade, which they had seen at Mechanicsburg and Cavetown, had 2,000 men. Imboden, "Confederate Retreat," *B&L*, III, pt. 2, p. 427; *OR*, XXVII, pt. 3, p. 586. For the strength of Iverson's brigade and the arrival of the Army of Northern Virginia in Hagerstown see *ibid.*, pt. 2, pp. 309, 361, 562. For Buford's tactics see *ibid.*, pt. 1, pp. 928, 935, 939–940.

94. *Ibid.*, pt. 2, pp. 702–703; Imboden, "Confederate Retreat," *B&L*, III, pt. 2, pp. 425–429. For other Confederate accounts of the action at Williamsport see *OR*, XXVII, pt. 2, pp. 436–438, 655.

95. *Ibid.*, pt. 1, pp. 82, 925–926, 928–929, 935–936, 940–942, 944, 971, 996, 998–1001, 1010, 1020, 1033, 1036; pt. 3, p. 585.

96. *Ibid.*, pt. 1, pp. 81–82, 145–146, 404, 408, 429, 536, 544, 556, 595, 621, 627, 633, 636, 666–667, 670, 693–694, 708, 733, 736, 741, 761, 771, 834, 838, 850, 859, 876; pt. 3, pp. 580–581, 587.

97. *Ibid.*, pt. 1, pp. 82–84, 86–87, 146; pt. 3, pp. 577, 611.

98. *Ibid.*, pt. 1, pp. 84–86, 536, 708; pt. 3, pp. 593, 601, 606, 615; *Wainwright Journals*, 237.

99. *OR*, XXVII, pt. 3, pp. 543–544, 568–569, 591–593, 608–609, 625–626; CCW, *Report*, I, 379. J. W. Garrett, president of the Baltimore and Ohio, said French held up ten trains on the night of July 6 and had not released them by 9:55 the next morning. Subsequently French must have detained more trains, because Haupt reported on July 8 that twenty trains were standing by at Frederick. *OR*, XXVII, pt. 3, pp. 592, 609.

100. Ingalls' dispatches from Frederick do not fully substantiate the statement in his report that "ample supplies of forage, clothing, and subsistence were received and issued to fill every necessary want without in any instance retarding military movements." *Ibid.*, pt. 1, p. 222. Haupt undoubtedly had this report in mind when he denied the truth of Meade's assertion on the 8th that his army, though short of rations and barefooted, had been making forced marches. Both Howard and Slocum in reporting the condition of their corps supported Meade's report. There is evidence also that the Third Corps was without rations from July 7 to July 9. Haupt could not understand how, with the vast accumulation of stores he had built up in Westminster, the army could be without shoes and provisions, but in his anxiety to indict Meade's generalship he conveniently overlooked the problem of transporting these supplies by wagon over bad roads. Then when the troops got near Frederick, they did not find adequate supplies awaiting them because of the temporary snarl in railroad transportation. Incidentally the Twelfth Corps, which had been at Littlestown, left there poorly equipped with shoes. Littlestown was on the Baltimore Pike and only fifteen miles from Westminster. *Ibid.*, pp. 85, 566, 761; pt. 3, p. 601; Haupt, *Reminiscences*, 238–239.

101. *OR*, XXVII, pt. 1, p. 86; pt. 3, pp. 543–544, 568–569, 601, 608, 615;

Reed to his mother, July 11, 1863, Charles W. Reed Letters, Typescript, PU.

102. Meade to Mrs. Meade, July 18, 1863, in Meade, *Life and Letters*, II, 136.

103. Patrick Journal, Entry for July 10, 1863, LC. Reasons for Butterfield's departure are also found in a letter from Meade to him, July 14, 1863, in CCW, *Report*, I, 429.

104. Patrick Journal, Entry for July 10, 1863, LC; Meade, *Life and Letters*, II, 125–126. Special orders announcing Humphreys' appointment were dated July 8, but probably he did not assume his duties until the next day. *OR*, XXVII, pt. 3, pp. 600, 606. For an appreciation of Humphreys see [Lyman to his wife], Nov. 27, 1864, Mar. 3, 1865, in Agassiz, ed., *Meade's Headquarters*, 279, 307; Warner, *Generals in Blue*, 241.

105. *OR*, XXVII, pt. 1, pp. 488, 537; pt. 3, pp. 265, 395; Warner, *Generals in Blue*, 162.

106. *OR*, XXVII, pt. 3, p. 503.

107. *Wainwright Journals*, 268.

108. Hays rejoined the army in Feb., 1865, as commander of the Second Division of the Second Corps. Three days before Appomattox Humphreys, who then commanded the Second Corps, furious at finding Hays and all his staff asleep at 6:30 A.M., summarily relieved him of his duties. Warner, *Generals in Blue*, 225.

109. *OR*, XXVII, pt. 3, pp. 795–803. For reasons unknown the 12th N.H. regiment was not included in the roster of the army on July 31. In addition to the Vt. regiments two other nine-month units were mustered out, the 153rd and 151st Pa., on July 14 and 19 respectively. About the same time the last two companies of the 27th Conn. left the Second Corps, as well as the entire 2nd N.H. which went home to get new recruits. Samuel P. Bates, *History of the Pennsylvania Volunteers, 1861–1865* (Harrisburg, 1870), IV, 681, 776; Walker, *History of the Second Corps*, 311.

110. *OR*, XXVII, pt. 3, p. 649.

111. *Ibid.*, pt. 1, pp. 488–489; pt. 3, pp. 444–445, 597–598, 796, 798–799; Statement of Reinforcements which joined Army of the Potomac between 7th & 14th July, 1863, George Gordon Meade Papers, HSP. In addition to these reinforcements 1,500 cavalrymen of the Army of the Potomac rejoined their outfits after having received fresh mounts in Washington. *OR*, XXVII, pt. 1, p. 81. Gen. Bartlett undoubtedly reflected the feelings of many in the army toward their reinforcements when he wrote that they "amount to nothing as far as fighting is concerned. . . ." Joseph J. Bartlett to Howland, July 16, 1863, Miscellaneous Manuscripts of [Col.] Joseph Howland, NYHS.

112. *OR*, XVIII, pp. 652, 736–737; XXVII, pt. 3, pp. 438, 442, 450–451, 547, 570, 600, 617–618, 639, 703, 711, 795; Statement of Reinforcements which joined Army of the Potomac between 7th & 14th July, 1863, George Gordon Meade Papers, HSP.

113. *OR*, XXVII, pt. 3, pp. 662, 711; CCW, *Report*, I, 338.

114. These regiments were the 8th and 46th Mass. which went to the First Corps, and the 168th N.Y., the 169th Pa., and the 172nd Pa. which went to the

Eleventh Corps. Statement of Reinforcements which joined Army of the Potomac between 7th & 14th July, 1863, George Gordon Meade Papers, HSP.

115. *OR*, XXVII, pt. 1, pp. 79–80; pt. 3, pp. 528, 549–550, 575–576, 617–618, 625, 634, 644, 652, 680–681, 698–699.

116. *Ibid.*, p. 700.

117. *Ibid.*, p. 611.

118. *Ibid.*, p. 651.

119. *Ibid.*, pt. 2, p. 223; pt. 3, pp. 677, 700. There is an error in Ingalls' dispatch. Either he made a mistake and wrote Cashtown for Cavetown, or the printer of the *OR* did.

120. *Ibid.*, pt. 1, pp. 79–80; pt. 3, pp. 577–579. On June 28 Halleck had placed Couch himself under Meade's authority. *Ibid.*, pt. 1, p. 62. The wire of July 5 gave Meade control over Couch's troops in the field without having to go through Couch.

121. *Ibid.*, pt. 3, p. 585. Somebody in the War Dept. also had little faith in the ability of Smith's command to accomplish much. Gen. Lorenzo Thomas, the Adjutant General of the Armies who was at Harrisburg, sent a cyphered dispatch on July 6 saying that Smith was moving toward Cashtown Pass to place himself on one of the enemy's lines of retreat. Someone made the following notation on the message: "Thundering humbug." See L. Thomas to Bishop Henrietta, [July 6], Dispatches, PDMA, PDPR.

122. *OR*, XXVII, pt. 1, p. 996; pt. 2, pp. 223, 226–227; pt. 3, pp. 697, 704. In their accounts of their conference on July 12 Smith and Meade do not agree. Contrary to Smith's statement, Meade in recollecting their meeting before the Committee on the Conduct of the War said Smith had advised him not to attach his new and undisciplined force to one of the old divisions of the army. CCW, *Report*, I, 338. Contemporary dispatches indicate that Meade was wrong.

123. *OR*, XXVII, pt. 3, pp. 697–698.

124. *Ibid.*, p. 704.

125. *Ibid.*, p. 550. Stanton sent this message to Kelley on July 5.

126. *Ibid.*, p. 612. Lincoln sent this message to Gen. Lorenzo Thomas on July 8.

127. *Ibid.*, pt. 1, p. 80. Meade used these words in a message to Halleck on July 6.

128. *Ibid.*, pt. 3, p. 568. They were the words used in a message from Ingalls to Meigs, July 6. Pleasonton also referred to the enemy as "very much crippled" in a dispatch to French on July 6. However, that part of the telegram did not appear in the copy received at the War Dept.

129. Basler, ed., *Collected Works of Lincoln*, VI, 314; *OR*, XXVII, pt. 1, pp. 79–83.

130. *Ibid.*, p. 83.

131. *Ibid.*, pp. 84–86, 89.

132. *Ibid.*, pp. 86, 89–91.

133. *Ibid.*, pt. 3, pp. 521–523, 633, 678.

134. *Ibid.*, p. 621; Patrick Journal, Entry for July 10, 1863, LC; [Uriah

Parmelee] to his mother, Smoketown, July 13, [1863], Samuel S. & Uriah N. Parmelee Letters, DU. In referring to his position on July 12 and 13 Gen. Slocum said Marsh Run extended along the line held by the enemy and was passable only at the bridges, the heavy rains having raised the water much beyond its usual depths and caused it to overrun the low land in front of the Twelfth Corps position. OR, XXVII, pt. 1, p. 762. For the difficulties Meade had in maneuvering in rough country see editorial in the *New York Times*, July 8, 1863.

135. *Cf. ante*, XX, 553.

136. *OR*, XXVII, pt. 3, p. 588.

137. *Ibid.*, pt. 1, p. 91; Humphreys, *From Gettysburg to the Rapidan*, 4–5; Memorandum Book, Entries for July 8, 9, 10, 1863, Jedediah Hotchkiss Papers, LC.

138. *Wainwright Journals*, 261–262. Humphreys also pronounced the Confederate position as exceedingly strong. Its flanks he thought could "not be turned." *From Gettysburg to the Rapidan*, 6.

139. Memorandum Book, Entries for July 11, 12, 1863, Jedediah Hotchkiss Papers, LC; Humphreys, *From Gettysburg to the Rapidan*, 4–5. For this criticism of the length of the line see Scheibert, *Seven Months in the Rebel States*, Hoole, ed., 121. See also Crounse, "Escape of Lee's Army," Moore, ed., *Rebellion Record, Documents*, VII, 346.

140. *OR*, XXVII, pt. 1, pp. 86, 91, 928–929, 935–936, 940–942, 971, 996, 1007; pt. 2, pp. 299–302, 704. Scheibert, *Seven Months in the Rebel States*, Hoole, ed., 120. Scheibert referred to two old ferries. *Ibid.*, 122. Sufficient artillery and presumably rifle ammunition arrived from Va. on July 10. Pendleton to Cols. Walton, Walker, and Brown, July 10, 1863, William N. Pendleton Letter Book, Confederate Museum.

141. *OR*, XXVII, pt. 2, pp. 361, 448, 704–705; pt. 3, p. 998.

142. J. W. [Jackson] to Lt. R. S. Jackson, July 20, 1863, Typescript of Prof. Merl E. Reed. According to a Union clergyman who was behind Confederate lines near Falling Waters, the rebels hoped fervently that Meade would attack them but thought he was too smart to do so. See Rev. Dr. Falk to [Sypher, no date], quoted in Sypher, *History of the Pennsylvania Reserves*, 485–486.

143. *OR*, XXVII, pt. 1, p. 91.

144. Testimonies of Meade, Pleasonton, Warren, Humphreys, Wadsworth, and Sedgwick, CCW, *Report*, I, 336, 360, 379–381, 396–397, 415–416, 462–463. Humphreys said he did not consider Pleasonton a member of the council, although he was there, nor for that matter Warren and himself. *Ibid.*, 396–397.

145. *Ibid.*, 397.

146. *OR*, XXVII, pt. 1, p. 92.

147. F. L. Olmsted to [E. L.] Godkin, July 15, 1863, in Evelyn Page, "After Gettysburg," *PMHB*, LXXV, 437. On July 12, 1863, Meade complained to Mrs. Meade that because of his inability to get reliable information of the enemy he had to grope his way in the dark. "It is wonderful," he said, "the difficulty I have in obtaining correct information." George Gordon Meade Papers,

HSP. After Slocum turned on Meade he accused Meade of having framed questions in the council of war so his corps commanders would vote against an attack, while he himself could go publicly on record as being in favor of it, although secretly agreeing with their decision. Slocum to Morgan, Jan. 2, 1864, in *Alpheus Williams Letters*, 286–287.

148. CCW, *Report*, I, 336, 462; H. J. Hunt to Webb, Jan. 19, 1888, Webb Collection; *Wainwright Journals*, 360, 362–363. See also Gray to Ropes, July 28, 1863, in Gray and Ropes, *War Letters*, 161–162.

149. CCW, *Report*, I, 397–398.

150. Wadsworth stressed this point in arguing for an attack. *Ibid.*, 416. Humphreys also said that as one of the preparations for the attack some entrenchments were dug in the event of a repulse and heavy losses. *From Gettysburg to the Rapidan*, 6. For further information about Union entrenchments see *Wainwright Journals*, 258; Olmsted to Godkin, July 15, 1863, in Page, "After Gettysburg," *PMHB*, LXXV, 438.

151. CCW, *Report*, I, 398.

152. *Ibid.*

153. Meade revealed his lack of confidence in his chief subordinates when he wrote to Mrs. Meade on July 12, 1863: "*I want Corps Commanders.*" [Italics are his.] George Gordon Meade Papers, HSP.

154. *OR*, XXVII, pt. 1, p. 152; Long, *Memoirs of Lee*, 295. Olmsted reported that Gen. Ingalls said to him: " 'I dare not say how weak we are.' " Olmsted to Godkin, July 19, 1863, in Page, "After Gettysburg," *PMHB*, LXXV, 445. Scheibert gave the figure of 70,000 men for the size of Lee's army on July 11. *Seven Months in the Rebel States*, Hoole, ed., 121. How Scheibert arrived at these figures and what they included are not known. Usually the Confederates put only the number of their combat troops in their returns. For another source giving the same estimate for the size of Lee's army see Falk to [Sypher, no date], quoted in Sypher, *History of the Pennsylvania Reserves*, 486. Since Sypher's book was published in 1865, the letter was fairly contemporary.

155. Memorandum Book, Entry for July 13, 1863, Jedediah Hotchkiss Papers, LC.

156. Scheibert, *Seven Months in the Rebel States*, Hoole, ed., 121–122.

157. *Ibid.*, 122; Long, *Memoirs of Lee*, 300; *OR*, XXVII, pt. 2, pp. 323, 361–362, 448–449, 640, 705. Ewell's corps had the advantage of the turnpike and marched with less difficulty.

158. *Ibid.*, pt. 3, p. 675. The corps apparently involved in the movement were from left to right the Twelfth, Second, Fifth, and Sixth. The reconnoitering force from each corps was to include at least a division and the necessary artillery. The cavalry on both flanks of the army received orders to cooperate with the reconnoitering forces, while all the remaining infantry stood under arms ready for a general engagement.

159. *Ibid.*, pt. 1, p. 667; pt. 3, pp. 683, 686.

160. *Ibid.*, pt. 1, pp. 93–94.

161. *Ibid.*, pt. 2, pp. 303–304.

162. *Ibid.*, pt. 1, pp. 929, 936–937, 942, 990; pt. 2, pp. 639–642, 648, 667,

672; Battle Report of R. M. Mayo, Aug. 13, 1863, MS, Henry Heth Collection, Confederate Museum; [Major J.] Jones to his father, July 17, 1863, Edmund Walter Jones Papers, UNC; Henry C. Albright War Diary, Entry for July 14, [1863], North Carolina State Department of Archives and History; Welch to his wife, Aug. 2, 1863, in Welch, *Letters to His Wife*, 71; Capt. L. F. Lyttle to Capt. H. B. Todd, July 17, 1863, Office of Provost Marshal General, [Army of the Potomac], Special Orders, No. 101, July 17, 1863, Vol. 67, p. 101, Vol. 72, p. 151, Record Group 98, NA.

163. Buford sent word to Kilpatrick that he would put his whole force on Heth's flank and rear for the purpose of seizing the road and bridge over which the enemy was to retreat. Col. William Gamble, commander of Buford's First Brigade, sourly observed that while Buford was carrying out his move, Kilpatrick permitted the two small squadrons to make their ill-advised attack. Also the prisoners Buford took were turned over by mistake to Kilpatrick's men, who then claimed the credit of the capture for his command. Kilpatrick in his report barely acknowledged that Buford was even around to take part in the action. *OR*, XXVII, pt. 1, pp. 929, 936–937, 990.

164. Welch said the surprise attack at Falling Waters was "disgraceful either to General Hill or General Heth." Welch to his wife, Aug. 2, 1863, in Welch, *Letters to His Wife*, 71.

165. John Hay Diary, Entry for July 14, 1863, Typescript, Brown University Library.

166. *Ibid.*

167. *Ibid.*, Entry for July 19, 1863.

168. On July 14 Kelley was perfectly willing to advance on Williamsport until he heard that Longstreet's corps was within supporting distance of it. Then he nervously suggested he might do something else. *OR*, XXVII, pt. 3, p. 698.

169. *Ibid.*, pt. 1, p. 105. Humphreys pointed out that Lee could have retreated up the river. Evidently he considered Kelley's force of little account. CCW, *Report*, I, 398.

170. For instance, on July 19 Meade wanted to promote Warren to major general and put him in command of the Second Corps, but Halleck replied it was impossible because there were no vacancies. He had tried to get rid of useless major generals but so far had not succeeded. *OR*, XXVII, pt. 1, pp. 96–97, 100–101.

171. Editorial in *New York Tribune*, July 15, 1863.

172. Endorsement on back of letter of July 17, 1863, from Gen. Alexander S. Webb to his father, Gen. James Watson Webb, U. S. Minister to Brazil, reads as follows: "Chase, Seward and others write me that Lee really won that Battle!" Webb Collection.

173. Hays to [John B. McFadden], July 18, 1863, in Fleming, *Life and Letters of Hays*, 418.

174. Slocum to Howland, July 17, 1863, Miscellaneous Manuscripts of [Col.] Joseph Howland, NYHS.

175. Weld, *War Diaries and Letters*, 242.

176. *Ibid.*; Crounse, "Escape of Lee's Army," Moore, ed., *Rebellion Record*,

Documents, VII, 347; Blake, *Three Years in the Army of the Potomac,* 226–227; Young, *What a Boy Saw in the Army,* 365–367; Brooks, *Washington in Lincoln's Time,* 81; James to his mother, July 19, 1863, E. C. James Collection, YU; Connor to his father, July 17, 1863, Selden Connor Correspondence, Brown University Library; De Trobriand, *Four Years with the Army of the Potomac,* 520.

    177. *OR,* XXVII, pt. 3, p. 691.

Bibliography

MANUSCRIPTS

Charles Francis Adams Diary, Jan. 1, 1862–Apr. 30, 1864, MHS
Charles Francis Adams, 2nd, Diary, 1863, MHS
Henry C. Albright War Diary, North Carolina State Department of Archives and History
Diary of John W. Alloway, HSP
Edward Porter Alexander Papers, LC
Alexander-Hillhouse Papers, UNC
Edward P. Alexander Papers, UNC
John B. Bachelder Papers, NHHS
John B. Bachelder Papers, in possession of Francis C. Carleton, Belmont, Mass.; microfilm in MHS.
John B. Bachelder, Notes relating to the services of troops at Gettysburg, Huntington Library
William B. Baker Papers, UNC
Francis C. Barlow Papers, MHS
S. L. M. Barlow Collection, June and July, 1863, Huntington Library
Manuscripts of General James Barnes, NYHS
Samuel P. Bates Collection, PDPR
Henry L. Benning Papers, UNC
Berry G. Benson Papers, UNC
Henry Robinson Berkeley Diary, VHS
Letter of H. H. Bingham, Gettysburg National Military Park
Thomas F. Boatwright Papers, UNC
Diary of Sarah M. Broadhead, Gettysburg National Military Park
Campbell Brown Books, UNC
Philo B. Buckingham Civil War Letters, American Antiquarian Society
W. H. S. Burgwyn Diary, North Carolina State Department of Archives and History
William Byrnes Diary, 1863, DU
Patrick H. Cain Letters, DU
William Calder Papers, UNC
Seth C. Carey Scrapbooks, Brown University
Ezra A. Carman Papers, New York Public Library
Joshua L. Chamberlain Papers, LC
John J. Chandler Letters, Virginia State Library
Horatio Dana Chapman Diary, Connecticut State Library
Rachel Susan (Bee) Cheves Papers, DU
J. F. H. Claiborne Papers, UNC
Charles H. Clark Letters, Connecticut State Library
Walter Clark Papers, North Carolina State Department of Archives and History
James Freeman Clarke Papers, DU
John Cleek Papers, DU

BIBLIOGRAPHY

Jacob B. Click Papers, DU
J. B. Clifton Diary, North Carolina State Department of Archives and History
Monroe F. Cockrell, "Where Was Pickett at Gettysburg?", UV
B. B. Coiner Report, UV
The Coles Collection, UV
Frederick M. Colston Book and Clippings, UNC
Henry N. Comey Letters, in possession of Morton C. Jaquith, Worcester, Mass.
A Confederate Soldier's Letter, Virginia State Library
Confederate States of America—Army Prisons, Army Experience of Major Morton
    Tower from 1861 to 1864, Typescript, VHS
Selden Connor Correspondence, Brown University
Papers of Samuel W. Crawford, LC
[Samuel W. Crawford], Notes on Route to Gettysburg, Huntington Library
John A. Dahlgren Papers, LC
Danske Dandridge Manuscripts, DU
John W. Daniel Papers, UV
John W. Daniel Papers, DU
James Dearing Letters, UV
Abner Doubleday Papers, National Baseball Hall of Fame and Museum
Adam L. and Daniel R. Dunlop Papers, DU
Jubal A. Early Correspondence, NYHS
Jubal A. Early Papers, LC
Samuel W. Eaton Diary, UNC
George P. Erwin Papers, UNC
Edward Everett Papers, MHS
Richard S. Ewell Papers, LC
Charles Fairchild Letters, Typescript in possession of Miss Lee Bacon, Milwaukee,
    Wis.
Lucius Fairchild Letters, Typescript in possession of Miss Lee Bacon, Milwaukee,
    Wis.
Federal Civil War Records: Records of the Adjutant General's Office, No. 94; Records
    of the United States Army Commands, No. 98; War Department Collection Con-
    federate Records, No. 109; Records of the Office of the Judge Advocate General
    (Army), No. 153; Records of the Office of the Chief of Ordnance, No. 156, NA.
War Diary of Samuel Angus Firebaugh, UNC
Louis R. Fortescue Diary, UNC
Frost Family Collection, YU
Diary of Joseph D. Galloway, New York Public Library
Miscellaneous [Papers] of Theodore Burr Gates, NYHS
Sydney Howard Gay Collection, Columbia University
J. E. Green Diary, North Carolina State Department of Archives and History
J. Bryan Grimes Papers, UNC
Bryan Grimes Papers, North Carolina State Department of Archives and History
Book of E. C. Haas, Virginia State Library
Wade Hampton Papers, UNC
Charles Alexander Harrison Diary, PU
Haskell Family Collection, 1863–1907, PDPR
Jasper [Hawse] Diary, UV
John Hay Diary, Brown University
Henry Heth Collection, Confederate Museum
Turner W. Holley Letters, DU
Hooker Papers, Huntington Library
Hooker Letters, NYHS
Jedediah Hotchkiss Papers, LC
Oliver O. Howard Papers, Bowdoin College
Miscellaneous Manuscripts of Joseph Howland, NYHS

BIBLIOGRAPHY

A. A. Humphreys Papers, HSP
Diary of John Irvin, HSP
Edward C. James Collection, YU
Bradley T. Johnson Papers, UV
Edmund Walter Jones Papers, UNC
James L. Kemper Papers, VHS
James L. Kemper Correspondence, UV
Henry L. Kendrick Papers, NYHS
Francis M. Kennedy Diary, UNC
John Knight Papers, DU
Robert E. Lee Papers, DU
Claude G. Leland Papers, NYHS
J. O. M. Lemon Correspondence in William Todd Collection, UV
Armistead L. Long Papers, UNC
Longstreet Papers, UNC
James Longstreet Papers, DU
Edwin Baker Loving Diary, Virginia State Library
Theodore Lyman Diary and Papers, MHS
Jacob Lyons Diary, UNC
Henry B. McClellan Papers, VHS
Civil War Diary of S. T. McCullough, UV
John Baillie McIntosh Correspondence, Brown University
Lafayette McLaws Papers, UNC
Lafayette McLaws Papers, DU
Hugh MacRae Papers, DU
George Gordon Meade Papers, HSP
John S. Mosby Papers, DU
Munford-Ellis Family Papers, DU
Diary of John I. Murray, NYHS
George M. Neese Diary, Virginia State Library
John Page Nicholson Collection, Huntington Library
William Norris Papers, UV
Henry T. Owen Letters, Virginia State Library
Warren W. Packer Diary and Memoranda, Connecticut State Library
Samuel S. and Uriah N. Parmelee Letters, DU
Marsena R. Patrick Journal, LC
William H. Payne Papers, Virginia State Library
William D. Pender Papers, UNC
William N. Pendleton Papers, UNC
William N. Pendleton Press Letter Book, Confederate Museum
William B. Pettit Papers, UNC
Letter of H. E. Peyton, Virginia State Library
Charles R. Phelps Letters, UV
Charles Pickett Papers, VHS
George E. Pickett Papers, DU
Polk-Brown-Ewell Collection, UNC
John R. Porter Diary, DU
Samuel M. Quincy Papers, MHS
Stephen D. Ramseur Papers, UNC
William Brooke Rawle Papers, HSP
Diary of William M. Read, in private possession
Pennsylvania Department of Military Affairs, Record Group 19, PDPR
Pennsylvania Auditor General, Papers of Board of Claims under Act of 16 April 1862,
    Border Claims, Adjudicated under Act of May 22, 1871, PDPR
Charles W. Reed Letters, PU
Isaac V. Reynolds Papers, DU

BIBLIOGRAPHY

John Fulton Reynolds Family Papers, Franklin and Marshall College
Thomas L. Rosser Papers, UV
Peter F. Rothermel Papers, PDPR
Harlan P. Rugg Diary and Memorandum, Connecticut State Library
John F. Sale Letters, Virginia State Library
Carl Schurz Papers, LC
James A. Seddon Papers, DU
John Sedgwick Collection, Cornwall, Conn., Library
Daniel E. Sickles Correspondence, NYHS
Daniel E. Sickles Letter Book, DU
Daniel E. Sickles Papers, LC
William D. Simpson Papers, DU
Diary of William Stackhouse, HSP
Stuart Collection, Huntington Library
W. B. Sturtevant Letter, Confederate Museum
W. H. Taylor Letter, VHS
W. G. Thompson Papers, NYHS
William U. Tillinghast Papers, DU
Westwood A. Todd Reminiscence, Typescript, UNC
Adam Torrance Collection, PDPR
Papers of Casper Trepp, NYHS
Mrs. George A. Trumbull Correspondence, Brown University
Zebulon B. Vance Papers, North Carolina State Department of Archives and History
Paul T. Vaughan Diary and Papers, DU
James W. Wadsworth, Jr., Family Papers, LC
Charles S. Wainwright Journal, Huntington Library
James H. Walker Manuscript, Virginia State Library
John H. H. Ward Papers, New York Public Library
Thomas L. Ware Diary, UNC
Letters and Miscellaneous Manuscripts of Gouverneur K. Warren, Sylvanus Warren,
    William Warren, and others, New York State Library
William H. Warren Civil War Diaries, YU
Alexander Stewart Webb Collection, YU
James Watson Webb Papers, YU
Wigfall Family Papers, LC
Cadmus M. Wilcox Papers, LC
John and Philip J. Winn Letters, DU
Francis D. Winston Papers, North Carolina State Department of Archives and History
E. M. Woodward Diary, Huntington Library

NEWSPAPERS

Boston Morning Journal, July, 1863
Cincinnati Daily Gazette, July, 1863
New York Herald, July, 1863
New York Times, June–July, 1863
New York Daily Tribune, June–July, 1863
Philadelphia Weekly Times, Mar. 3, 1877–Feb. 17, 1883
Richmond Enquirer (Semi-weekly edition), July 21, 24, 1863
Scrapbook of newspaper clippings, Gettysburg National Military Park
The Times [London], July–Aug., 1863
Washington Daily Morning Chronicle, June–July, 1863
Washington National Intelligencer, June–July, 1863

PRINTED PRIMARY SOURCES

LETTERS, DIARIES, MEMOIRS

Agassiz, George R., ed., *Meade's Headquarters, 1863–1865, Letters of Colonel Theodore Lyman from the Wilderness to Appomattox.* Boston, 1922.

Alexander, E. P., *Military Memoirs of a Confederate.* . . . New York, 1907.

Anderson, James S., "The March of the Sixth Corps to Gettysburg," *War Papers,* IV, 77–84. (Commandery of the State of Wisconsin, MOLLUS.) Milwaukee, 1914.

The Annals of the War, Written by Leading Participants, North and South. Philadelphia, 1879.

[Anon.], *Three Weeks at Gettysburg.* New York, 1863.

Applegate, John S., *Reminiscences and Letters of George Arrowsmith of New Jersey.* Red Bank, N.J., 1893.

Bancroft, Frederic, ed., *Speeches, Correspondence and Political Papers of Carl Schurz.* New York, 1913.

Bandy, William T., trans., "Civil War Notes of a French Volunteer," *Wisconsin Magazine of History,* XIV, No. 4 (Summer, 1962), 239–250.

Barziza, Decimus et Ultimus, *The Adventures of a Prisoner of War, 1863–1864,* ed. Henderson Shuffler. Austin, Texas, 1964.

Basler, Roy P., ed., *The Collected Works of Abraham Lincoln.* 8 vols. and index. New Brunswick, N.J., 1953.

Battles and Leaders of the Civil War, eds. Robert U. Johnson and Clarence C. Buel. 4 vols. New York, 1884–1888.

Beale, Howard K., ed., *The Diary of Edward Bates, 1859–1866. (Annual Report of the American Historical Association for the Year 1930, IV.)* Washington, 1933.

Beale, Howard K., and Alan W. Brownsword, eds., *Diary of Gideon Welles.* New York, 1960.

Bigelow, John, Jr., *The Peach Orchard, Gettysburg, July 2, 1863.* Minneapolis, 1910.

Blackford, Charles Minor, III, ed., *Letters from Lee's Army.* . . . New York, 1947.

Blackford, W. W., *War Years with Jeb Stuart.* New York, 1945.

Blake, Henry N., *Three Years in the Army of the Potomac.* Boston, 1865.

Bonham, Milledge Louis, ed., "A Little More Light on Gettysburg," (Letter of Abner Perrin to Governor Milledge Luke Bonham, July 29, 1863), *Mississippi Valley Historical Review,* XXIV (Mar., 1938), 519–525.

Brooks, Noah, *Washington in Lincoln's Time,* ed. Herbert Mitgang. New York, 1958.

Brown, Varina D., ed., *A Colonel at Gettysburg and Spotsylvania.* Columbia, S.C., 1931.

Browne, Dunn [Fiske, Samuel W.], *Mr. Dunn Browne's Experiences in the Army.* Boston, 1866.

Buell, Augustus, *The Cannoneer, Recollections of Service in the Army of the Potomac.* Washington, 1890.

Cary, Catherine S., ed., *Dear Belle, Letters from a Cadet and Officer to His Sweetheart, 1858–1865.* Middletown, Conn., 1965.

Casler, John O., *Four Years in the Stonewall Brigade.* Marietta, Ga., 1951.

Chamberlaine, William W., *Memoirs of the Civil War.* Washington, 1912.

Coffin, Chárles Carleton, *The Boys of '61; or, Four Years of Fighting.* Boston, 1883.

Commager, Henry Steele, ed., *The Blue and the Gray.* 2 vols. Indianapolis, 1950.

Confederate Veteran. 40 vols. Nashville, Tenn., 1893–1932.

Cooke, John Esten, *Wearing of the Gray, Being Personal Portraits, Scenes and Adventures of the War,* ed. Philip Van Doren Stern. Bloomington, Ind., 1959.

Croffut, W. A., ed., *Fifty Years in Camp and Field, Diary of Major-General Ethan Allen Hitchcock, U.S.A.* New York, 1909.

BIBLIOGRAPHY

Crotty, D. G., *Four Years Campaigning in the Army of the Potomac.* Grand Rapids, Mich., 1874.

Dana, Charles A., *Recollections of the Civil War, with the Leaders at Washington and in the Field in the Sixties.* New York, 1913.

Dawes, Rufus R., "With the Sixth Wisconsin at Gettysburg," *Sketches of War History, 1861–1865.* (Commandery of the State of Ohio, MOLLUS.) Cincinnati, 1890.

De Forest, John W., *A Volunteer's Adventures, A Union Captain's Record of the Civil War,* ed. James H. Croushore. New Haven, 1946.

De Trobriand, Regis, *Four Years with the Army of the Potomac.* Boston, 1889.

Devereux, Arthur F., "Some Account of Pickett's Charge at Gettysburg," *Magazine of American History,* XVIII (July, 1887), 13–19.

Douglas, Henry Kyd, *I Rode with Stonewall.* Chapel Hill, N.C., 1940.

Dowdey, Clifford, and Louis H. Manarin, eds., *The Wartime Papers of R. E. Lee.* New York, 1961.

Durkin, Joseph T. S. J., ed., *John Dooley, Confederate Soldier, His War Journal.* Washington, 1945.

———, *Confederate Chaplain, A War Journal of Rev. James B. Sheeran, C. s s. r., 14th Louisiana, C.S.A.* Milwaukee, 1960.

Early, Jubal A., *Autobiographical Sketch and Narrative of the War Between the States.* Philadelphia, 1912.

Eggleston, George Cary, *A Rebel's Recollections.* (Introduction by David Donald. Civil War Centennial Series.) Bloomington, Ind., 1959.

Fatout, Paul, ed., *Letters of a Civil War Surgeon.* West Lafayette, Ind., 1961.

Fletcher, William Andrew, *Rebel Private, Front and Rear.* (Preface by Bell I. Wiley.) Austin, Texas, 1954.

Ford, Worthington C., ed., *A Cycle of Adams Letters.* 2 vols. Boston, 1920.

Freeman, Douglas S., and Grady McWhiney, eds., *Lee's Dispatches. . . .* New York, 1957.

Fremantle, James A. L., *Three Months in the Southern States: April–June, 1863.* New York, 1864.

Gibbon, John, *Personal Recollections of the Civil War.* New York, 1928.

Gordon, John B., *Reminiscences of the Civil War.* New York, 1903.

Graham, Ziba B., *On to Gettysburg: Ten Days from My Diary of 1863.* Detroit, 1889.

Gray, John C., and John C. Ropes, *War Letters, 1862–1865.* Boston, 1927.

Hamilton, J. G. de Roulhac, ed., *The Papers of Randolph Abbott Shotwell.* 3 vols. Raleigh, N.C., 1929.

Hancock, Winfield Scott, "Gettysburg, Reply to General Howard," *The Galaxy,* XXII (Dec., 1876), 821–831.

[Hancock, Mrs. W. S., ed.], *Reminiscences of Winfield Scott Hancock.* New York, 1887.

Haskell, Frank A., *The Battle of Gettysburg.* Madison, Wis., 1908.

Haskell, John C., *The Haskell Memoirs,* eds. Gilbert E. Govan and James W. Livingood. New York, 1960.

Haupt, Herman, *Reminiscences of General Herman Haupt.* Milwaukee, 1901.

Hincks, Elizabeth E., *Undismayed, The Story of a Yankee Chaplain's Family in the Civil War.* Privately Printed, 1952.

Hinkley, Julian W., *A Narrative of Service with the Third Wisconsin Infantry.* Madison, Wis., 1912.

Holstein, Anna M. (Ellis), *Three Years in Field Hospitals of the Army of the Potomac.* Philadelphia, 1867.

Hood, John B., *Advance and Retreat, Personal Experiences in the United States and Confederate States Armies.* New Orleans, 1880.

Hopkins, C. A. Porter, ed., "The James J. Archer Letters," *Maryland Historical Magazine,* LVI (Mar. and June, 1961).

Howard, Charles H., "First Day at Gettysburg," *Military Essays and Recollections,*

BIBLIOGRAPHY

IV, 238–264. (Commandery of the State of Illinois, MOLLUS.) Chicago, 1907.

Howard, O. O., *Autobiography of Oliver Otis Howard.* 2 vols. New York, 1908.

———, "Campaign and Battle of Gettysburg, June and July, 1863," *The Atlantic Monthly,* XXXVIII (1876), 48–71.

Hyde, T. W., *Following the Greek Cross or Memories of the Sixth Army Corps.* Boston, 1894.

Inman, Arthur Crew, ed., *Soldier of the South, General Pickett's War Letters to His Wife.* New York, 1928.

Jaquette, Henrietta Stratton, ed., *South after Gettysburg, Letters of Cornelia Hancock from the Army of the Potomac, 1863–1865.* Philadelphia, 1937.

Jones, J. B., *A Rebel War Clerk's Diary,* ed. Howard Swiggett. New York, 1935.

Lasswell, Mary, ed., *Rags and Hope: The Recollections of Val C. Giles, Four Years with Hood's Brigade, Fourth Texas Infantry.* New York, 1961.

Lee, Robert E., *Recollections and Letters of General Robert E. Lee.* New York, 1904.

Livermore, Thomas L., *Days and Events, 1860–1866.* Boston, 1920.

Long, Armistead L., *Memoirs of Robert E. Lee.* New York, 1886.

Longstreet, James, *From Manassas to Appomattox, Memoirs of the Civil War in America.* Philadelphia, 1896.

McClure, A. K., *Abraham Lincoln and Men of War Times.* Philadelphia, 1892.

McCreary, Albertus, "Gettysburg: A Boy's Experience of the Battle," *McClure's Magazine,* XXXIII (July, 1909), 243–253.

Mackey, T. J., "An Incident of Gettsyburg," *McClure's Magazine,* III (June, 1894), 68–70.

McKim, Randolph H., *A Soldier's Recollections, Leaves from the Diary of a Young Confederate.* London, 1910.

Malone, Bartlett Y., *Diary of Bartlett Y. Malone,* ed. W. W. Pierson. Chapel Hill, N.C., 1919.

Maurice, Sir Frederick, ed., *An Aide-de-Camp of Lee, Being the Papers of Colonel Charles Marshall. . . .* Boston, 1927.

Miers, Earl S., and Richard A. Brown, eds., *Gettysburg.* New Brunswick, N.J., 1948.

Monroe, Haskell, ed., " 'The Road to Gettysburg'—The Diary and Letters of Leonidas Torrence of the Gaston Guards," *North Carolina Historical Review,* XXXVI (Oct., 1959), 476–517.

Moore, Frank, ed., *Rebellion Record: A Diary of American Events with Documents, Narratives, Illustrative Incidents, Poetry, etc.* 11 vols. and supplement. New York, 1861–1868.

Morrison, James L. ed., "The Memoirs of Henry Heth," *Civil War History,* VIII (Mar., 1962), 5–24; (Sept., 1962), 300–326.

[Morse, Charles Fessenden], *Letters Written during the Civil War.* Boston, 1898.

Murray, Robert K., and Warren W. Hassler, Jr., "Gettysburg Farmer," *Civil War History,* III (June, 1957), 179–187.

Nevins, Allan, ed., *A Diary of Battle: The Personal Journals of Colonel Charles S. Wainwright, 1861–1865.* New York, 1962.

Nichols, G. W., *A Soldier's Story of His Regiment (61st Georgia).* Kennesaw, Ga., 1961.

Nickerson, A. H., "Personal Recollections of Two Visits to Gettysburg," *Scribner's Magazine,* XIV (July, 1893), 19–28.

Norton, Oliver Willcox, *Army Letters, 1861–1865.* Chicago, 1903.

Nye, W. S., ed., *The Valiant Hours: An Irishman in the Civil War.* Harrisburg, 1961.

Page, Evelyn, ed., "After Gettysburg, Frederick Law Olmsted on the Escape of Lee," *Pennsylvania Magazine of History and Biography,* LXXV (Oct., 1951), 436–446.

Pennypacker, S. W., "Six Weeks in Uniform . . . Gettysburg Campaign, 1863," *Historical and Biographical Sketches.* Philadelphia, 1883.

Philadelphia Brigade Association, *Reply . . . to the Foolish and Absurd Narrative of Lieutenant Frank A. Haskell. . . .* Philadelphia, 1910.

Poague, William T., *Gunner with Stonewall, Reminiscences,* ed. Monroe F. Cockrell. Jackson, Tenn., 1957.

Polley, J. B., *A Soldier's Letters to Charming Nellie.* New York, 1908.

Quaife, Milo M., ed., *From the Cannon's Mouth, The Civil War Letters of General Alpheus S. Williams.* Detroit, 1959.

Reagan, John H., *Memoirs, with Special Reference to Secession and the Civil War.* New York, 1906.

Ross, Fitzgerald, *Cities and Camps of the Confederate States,* ed. Richard B. Harwell. Urbana, Ill., 1958.

Runge, William H., ed., *Four Years in the Confederate Artillery, The Diary of Private Henry Robinson Berkeley.* Chapel Hill, N.C., 1961.

Russell, Charles Wells, ed., *The Memoirs of Colonel John S. Mosby.* Boston, 1917.

Schaff, Philip, "The Gettysburg Week," *Scribner's Magazine,* XVI (July, 1894), 21–30.

Scheibert, Justus, *Seven Months in the Rebel States during the North American War, 1863,* trans. Joseph C. Hayes, ed. William Stanley Hoole. Tuscaloosa, Ala., 1958.

Schurz, Carl, *The Reminiscences of Carl Schurz.* 3 vols. New York, 1907–08.

———, "The Battle of Gettysburg," *McClure's Magazine,* XXVIX (July, 1907), 272–285.

Sedgwick, John, *Correspondence of Major-General John Sedgwick.* 2 vols. New York, 1902–03.

Sickles, Daniel E., D. McM. Gregg, John Newton, and Daniel Butterfield, "Further Recollections of Gettysburg," *North American Review,* CLII (Mar., 1891), 257–286.

Silver, James W., ed., *A Life for the Confederacy: As Recorded in the Pocket Diaries of Pvt. Robert A. Moore. . . .* Jackson, Tenn., 1959.

Simmers, William, and Paul Bachschmid, *The Volunteer's Manual; or, Ten Months with the 153d Penn'a Volunteers. . . .* Easton, Pa., 1863.

Skelly, Daniel A., *A Boy's Experiences during the Battles of Gettysburg.* Gettysburg, 1932.

Small, Harold A., ed., *The Road to Richmond, The Civil War Memoirs of Major Abner R. Small of the Sixteenth Maine Volunteers. . . .* Berkeley, Calif., 1939.

Sorrel, G. Moxley, *Recollections of a Confederate Staff Officer.* New York, 1917.

Southern Historical Society Papers. 50 vols. Richmond, 1876–1953.

Stevens, George T., *Three Years in the Sixth Corps.* New York, 1870.

Strong, George T., *The Diary of George Templeton Strong,* eds. Allan Nevins and M. H. Thomas. 3 vols. New York, 1953.

Taylor, Walter H., *Four Years with General Lee.* New York, 1877.

Tremain, Henry Edwin, *Two Days of War, A Gettysburg Narrative and Other Excursions.* New York, 1905.

Trimble, I. R., "The Campaign and Battle of Gettysburg," *Confederate Veteran,* XXV (May, 1917), 209–213.

[———], "The Civil War Diary of General Isaac Ridgeway Trimble," *Maryland Historical Magazine,* XVII (Mar., 1922), 1–20.

Trowbridge, John T., *The Desolate South, 1865–1866: A Picture of the Battlefields and of the Devastated Confederacy.* New York, 1956.

[———], "The Field of Gettysburg," *The Atlantic Monthly,* XVI (Nov., 1865), 616–624.

[Trundle, Joseph H.], "Gettysburg As Described in Two Letters from a Maryland Confederate," *Maryland Historical Magazine,* LIV (June, 1959), 210–212.

Truxall, Aida Craig, ed., *"Respects to All," Letters of Two Pennsylvania Boys. . . .* Pittsburgh, 1962.

Tyler, Mason Whiting, *Recollections of the Civil War,* ed. William S. Tyler. New York, 1912.

Vandiver, Frank E., ed., *The Civil War Diary of General Josiah Gorgas.* University, Ala., 1947.

BIBLIOGRAPHY

Wallber, Albert, "From Gettysburg to Libby Prison," *War Papers*, IV, 191–200. (Commandery of the State of Wisconsin, MOLLUS.) Milwaukee, 1914.

Welch, Spencer Glasgow, *A Confederate Surgeon's Letters to His Wife*. Marietta, Ga., 1954.

Weld, Stephen Minot, *War Diary and Letters*. Boston, 1912.

Wheeler, Cornelius, "Reminiscences of the Battle of Gettysburg," *War Papers*, II, 207–220. (Commandery of the State of Wisconsin, MOLLUS.) Milwaukee, 1896.

Wilkeson, Samuel, "Battle of Gettysburg," Frank Moore, ed., *Anecdotes, Poetry and Incidents of the War: North and South, 1860–1865*. New York, 1866.

Wood, William N., *Reminiscences of Big I*, ed. Bell I. Wiley. Jackson, Tenn., 1956.

Young, Jesse Bowman, *What a Boy Saw in the Army*. New York, 1894.

Younger, Edward, ed., *Inside the Confederate Government, The Diary of Robert Garlick Kean*. New York, 1957.

PUBLIC DOCUMENTS

Eighth Census of the United States, 1860, Population. Washington, 1864.

State of Pennsylvania, *Report of the Auditor General on the Finances of the Commonwealth of Pennsylvania for the Year Ending November 30, 1880*. Harrisburg, 1881.

Supreme Court of Pennsylvania. May Term, 1891. No's. 20, 30. Middle District. *Appeal of the Gettysburg Battlefield Memorial Association from the Decree of the Court of Common Pleas of Adams Co., Paper Book of Appellants*.

U.S. Congress, *Report of the Joint Committee on the Conduct of the War at the Second Session, Thirty-Eighth Congress*. Vol. I. Washington, 1865. *Supplemental Report*, Part 2. Washington, 1866.

U.S. Department of War, *Official Army Register of the Volunteer Force of the United States Army for the Years 1861, '62, '63, '64, '65*. Washington, 1865.

U.S. Department of War, *The War of the Rebellion: A Compilation of the Official Records of the Union and Confederate Armies*. 128 vols. and index. Washington, 1880–1901.

SECONDARY SOURCES

GENERAL WORKS AND ARTICLES

Adams, George W., *Doctors in Blue: The Medical History of the Union Army in the Civil War*. New York, 1952.

Andrews, J. Cutler, *The North Reports the Civil War*. Pittsburgh, 1955.

Bates, Samuel P., *Martial Deeds of Pennsylvania*. Philadelphia, 1875.

Boatner, Mark M., III, *The Civil War Dictionary*. New York, 1959.

Brockett, L. P., and Mary C. Vaughan, *Woman's Work in the Civil War: A Record of Heroism, Patriotism and Patience*. Philadelphia, 1867.

Bruce, Robert V., *Lincoln and the Tools of War*. New York, 1956.

Buckeridge, J. O., *Lincoln's Choice*. Harrisburg, 1956.

Buechler, John, " 'Give 'Em the Bayonet'—A Note on Civil War Mythology," *Civil War History*, VII (June, 1961), 128–132.

Coggins, Jack, *Arms and Equipment in the Civil War*. New York, 1962.

Croffut, W. A., and John M. Morris, *The Military and Civil History of Connecticut during the War of 1861–65*. New York, 1868.

Cunningham, H. H., *Doctors in Gray, The Confederate Medical Service*. Baton Rouge, La., 1958.

Dawson, W. F., ed., *A Civil War Artist at the Front. Edwin Forbes' Life Studies of the Great Army*. New York, 1957.

De Peyster, J. W., *The Decisive Conflicts of the Late Civil War*. New York, 1867.

Donald, David, ed., *Divided We Fought: A Pictorial History of the War, 1861–1865.* New York, 1952.

Dyer, Frederick H., ed., *A Compendium of the War of the Rebellion.* . . . Des Moines, 1908.

Fox, William F., *Regimental Losses in the American Civil War, 1861–1865.* Albany, 1898.

Freeman, Douglas S., *Lee's Lieutenants, A Study in Command.* 3 vols. New York, 1943.

Gardner, Alexander, *Gardner's Photographic Sketch Book of the Civil War.* New York, 1959.

Gold, Theodore S., *Historical Records of the Town of Cornwall, Litchfield County, Connecticut.* Hartford, 1904.

Halleck, H. Wager, *Elements of Military Art and Science.* . . . New York, 1846.

Hamilton, Milton W., "Augustus C. Buell, Fraudulent Historian," *Pennsylvania Magazine of History and Biography,* LXXX (Oct., 1956), 478–492.

Hancock, Harold Bell, *Delaware during the Civil War, A Political History.* Wilmington, Del., 1961.

Heitman, Francis B., *Historical Register and Dictionary of the United States Army.* . . . 2 vols. Washington, 1903.

Hesseltine, William B., *Lincoln and the War Governors.* New York, 1948.

Huston, James A., "Logistical Support of Federal Armies in the Field," *Civil War History,* VII (Mar., 1961), 36–47.

Johnston, Angus J., II, *Virginia Railroads in the Civil War.* Chapel Hill, N.C., 1961.

Jones, Archer, *Confederate Strategy from Shiloh to Vicksburg.* Baton Rouge, La., 1961.

Klein, Frederic Shriver, *Lancaster County, 1841–1941.* Lancaster, Pa., 1941.

Livermore, Thomas L., *Numbers and Losses in the Civil War in America, 1861–65.* Boston, 1900.

Lonn, Ella, *Foreigners in the Union Army and Navy.* Baton Rouge, La., 1952.

Lord, Francis A., *They Fought for the Union.* Harrisburg, 1960.

Lossing, Benson J., *Pictorial History of the Civil War.* Hartford, 1874.

———, *Field Book of the Civil War.* 3 vols. New Haven, 1878.

Luvaas, Jay, *The Military Legacy of the Civil War, The European Inheritance.* Chicago, 1959.

———, ed., *The Civil War: A Soldier's View, A Collection of Civil War Writings by Col. G. F. R. Henderson.* Chicago, 1958.

MacKay, Winnifred H., "Philadelphia during the Civil War," *Pennsylvania Magazine of History and Biography,* LXX (Jan., 1946), 3–51.

Manakee, Harold R., *Maryland in the Civil War.* Baltimore, 1961.

Mauncy, Albert, *Artillery through the Ages.* (National Park Service Interpretive Series. History. No. 3.) Washington, 1949.

Maxwell, William Q., *Lincoln's Fifth Wheel, The Political History of the U.S. Sanitary Commission.* New York, 1956.

Miller, Francis T., ed., *Photographic History of the Civil War.* 10 vols. New York, 1911.

Moore, Albert B., *Conscription and Conflict in the Confederacy.* New York, 1924.

Moore, Frank, ed., *Women of the War; Their Heroism and Self-sacrifice.* Hartford, 1866.

Munden, Kenneth W., and Henry P. Beers, *Guide to Federal Archives Relating to the Civil War.* Washington, 1962.

Nevins, Allan, *The War for the Union.* 2 vols. New York, 1959.

Patrick, Rembert W., *Jefferson Davis and His Cabinet.* Baton Rouge, La., 1944.

Pennypacker, Isaac R., "Civil War Historians and History," *Pennsylvania Magazine of History and Biography,* LI (No. 3, 1927), 330–350.

———, "Military Historians and History," *Pennsylvania Magazine of History and Biography,* LIII (No. 1, 1929), 28–50.

BIBLIOGRAPHY

Peterson, Harold L., *Notes on Ordnance of the American Civil War, 1861–1865.* New York, 1959.

Phisterer, Frederick, *The Army in the Civil War, Statistical Record of the Armies of the United States.* New York, 1882, 1885.

Pierson, William W., Jr., "The Committee on the Conduct of the War," *American Historical Review,* XXIII (Apr., 1918), 550–576.

Quiner, E. B., *The Military History of Wisconsin: A Record of the Civil and Military Patriotism of the States in the War for the Union.* . . . Chicago, 1866.

Ramsdell, Charles W., "General Robert E. Lee's Horse Supply, 1862–1865," *American Historical Review,* XXXV (July, 1930), 758–777.

Randall, James G., "The Newspaper Problem in Its Bearing upon Military Secrecy during the Civil War," *American Historical Review,* XXIII (Jan., 1918), 308–323.

Ropes, John C., and W. R. Livermore, *The Story of the Civil War.* . . . 4 vols. New York, 1933.

Shannon, Fred A., *The Organization and Administration of the Union Army, 1861–1865.* Glendale, Calif., 1928.

Starr, Louis M., *Bohemian Brigade: Civil War Newsmen in Action.* New York, 1954.

Vandiver, F. E., *Rebel Brass; The Confederate Command System.* Baton Rouge, La., 1957.

Weber, Thomas, *The Northern Railroads in the Civil War, 1861–1865.* New York, 1952.

Weisberger, Bernard A., *Reporters for the Union.* Boston, 1953.

Weller, Jac, "The Confederate Use of British Cannon," *Civil War History,* III (June, 1957), 135–152.

Wiley, Bell I., and Hirst D. Milhollen, *They Who Fought Here.* New York, 1959.

Williams, Kenneth P., *Lincoln Finds a General: A Military Study of the Civil War.* 5 vols. New York, 1949–1959.

Williams, T. Harry, *Lincoln and His Generals.* New York, 1952.

BIOGRAPHIES

Allen, Louis F., *Memorial of the Late Gen. James S. Wadsworth.* . . . Buffalo, 1864.

Ambrose, Stephen E., *Halleck: Lincoln's Chief of Staff.* Baton Rouge, La., 1962.

[Anonymous], *Life of David Bell Birney.* . . . Philadelphia and New York, 1867.

Appleton's Cyclopaedia of American Biography, eds. James Grant Wilson and John Fiske. 6 vols. New York, 1888.

Bache, Richard M., *Life of General George Gordon Meade.* Philadelphia, 1897.

Bridges, Hal, *Lee's Maverick General, Daniel Harvey Hill.* New York, 1961.

Butterfield, Julia L. S., ed., *A Biographical Memorial of General Daniel Butterfield.* New York, 1904.

Carpenter, John A., *Sword and Olive Branch, Oliver Otis Howard.* Pittsburgh, 1964.

Cleaves, Freeman, *Meade of Gettysburg.* Norman, Okla., 1960.

Current, Richard N., *Old Thad Stevens, A Story of Ambition.* Madison, Wis., 1942.

Daly, Louise Haskell, *Alexander Cheves Haskell, The Portrait of a Man.* Norwood, Mass., 1934.

Dyer, J. P., *The Gallant Hood.* Indianapolis, 1950.

Fairmount Park Art Association, *Unveiling of the Equestrian Statue of Major-General George Gordon Meade.* Philadelphia, 1887.

Fleming, George T., *Life and Letters of Alexander Hays.* Pittsburgh, 1919.

Freeman, Douglas S., *R. E. Lee, A Biography.* 4 vols. New York, 1935.

Gorham, George C., *Life and Public Services of Edwin M. Stanton.* 2 vols. Boston, 1899.

Haight, Theron W., *Three Wisconsin Cushings.* [No place], 1910.

Hassler, William W., *A. P. Hill, Lee's Forgotten General.* Richmond, 1957.

Hebert, Walter H., *Fighting Joe Hooker.* Indianapolis, 1944.

BIBLIOGRAPHY

Humphreys, Henry H., *Andrew Atkinson Humphreys: A Biography.* Philadelphia, 1924.

Jones, Virgil Carrington, *Ranger Mosby.* Chapel Hill, N.C., 1944.

Kamm, Samuel R., *The Civil War Career of Thomas A. Scott.* University of Pennsylvania Press, 1940.

McClellan, H. B., *The Life and Campaigns of Major-General J. E. B. Stuart.* . . . New York, 1885.

Meade, George, *The Life and Letters of George Gordon Meade,* ed. G. G. Meade [grandson]. 2 vols. New York, 1913.

The New York Monuments Commission, *Webb and His Brigade at the Angle, Gettysburg, In Memoriam, Alexander Stewart Webb, 1835–1911.* Albany, 1916.

Nichols, Edward J., *Toward Gettysburg: A Biography of General John F. Reynolds.* University Park, Pa., 1958.

Nicolay, John G., and John Hay, *Abraham Lincoln: A History.* 10 vols. New York, 1890.

[Obituary of General John Buford], *Harper's Weekly,* Jan. 2, 1864.

O'Connor, Richard, *Hood: Cavalier General.* New York, 1949.

Pennypacker, Isaac R., *General Meade.* New York, 1901.

Pinchon, Edgcumb, *Dan Sickles: Hero of Gettysburg and "Yankee King of Spain."* New York, 1945.

Proceedings at Dedication of Statue of Maj. Gen. John Sedgwick at Gettysburg. Hartford, 1913.

Rosengarten, J. G., *Reynolds Memorial Address, March 8th, 1880.* [Pamphlet printed by Historical Society of Penna.]

Sanger, Donald B., and Thomas R. Hay, *James Longstreet.* Baton Rouge, La., 1952.

Sedgwick Memorial Association, VIth Army Corps, Spotsylvania Court House, Va., May 11, 12 and 13, 1887. [No place or date.]

Slocum, C. E., *Life and Services of Major-General Henry Warner Slocum.* Toledo, Ohio, 1913.

Swanberg, W. A., *Sickles, The Incredible.* New York, 1956.

Taylor, Emerson G., *Gouverneur Kemble Warren, The Life and Letters of an American Soldier, 1830–1882.* Boston, 1932.

Thomas, Benjamin P., and Harold M. Hyman, *Stanton, The Life and Times of Lincoln's Secretary of War.* New York, 1962.

Thomason, John W., Jr., *Jeb Stuart.* New York, 1930.

Tucker, Glenn, *Hancock, The Superb.* Indianapolis, 1960.

Vandiver, Frank E., *Ploughshares into Swords, Josiah Gorgas and Confederate Ordnance.* Austin, Texas, 1952.

Walker, Francis A., *General Hancock.* New York, 1894.

Wallace, Willard M., *Soul of the Lion, A Biography of General Joshua L. Chamberlain.* New York, 1960.

Warner, Ezra J., *Generals in Gray, Lives of Confederate Commanders.* Baton Rouge, La., 1959.

———, *Generals in Blue, Lives of Union Commanders.* Baton Rouge, La., 1964.

Weigley, Russell F., *Quartermaster General of the Union Army, A Biography of M. C. Meigs.* New York, 1959.

Welch, Mrs. Emily (Sedgwick), *John Sedgwick, Major-General.* Printed by Private Circulation, 1899.

Wellman, Manly W., *Giant in Gray, A Biography of Wade Hampton of South Carolina.* New York, 1949.

Williams, T. Harry, *P. G. T. Beauregard, Napoleon in Gray.* Baton Rouge, La., 1955.

HISTORIES OF MILITARY UNITS

An Address Delivered at Gettysburg, August 27, 1883, by Gen. Alexander S. Webb at the Dedication of the 72d Pa. Vols. Monument. Also, An Historical Sketch of the 72d Regiment, by Charles H. Banes. . . . Philadelphia, 1883.

BIBLIOGRAPHY

Banes, Charles H., *History of the Philadelphia Brigade.* . . . Philadelphia, 1876.
Bates, Samuel P., *History of the Pennsylvania Volunteers, 1861–1865.* 5 vols. Harrisburg, 1869–1871.
Benedict, G. G., *Vermont at Gettysburgh.* Burlington, Vt., 1870.
Boyle, John R., *Soldiers True, The Story of the One Hundred and Eleventh Regiment Pennsylvania. . .Volunteers.* . . . New York, 1903.
Brewer, A. T., *History, Sixty-first Regiment, Pennsylvania Volunteers, 1861–1865.* Pittsburgh, 1911.
Brown, Edmund R., *The 27th Indiana Volunteer Infantry in the War of the Rebellion.* [No place], 1899.
Caldwell, J. F. F., *The History of a Brigade of South Carolinians Known First As "Gregg's" and Subsequently as "McGowan's Brigade"* . . . . Philadelphia, 1866, and Marietta, Ga., 1951.
Chamberlin, Thomas, *History of the One Hundred and Fiftieth Regiment Pennsylvania Volunteers.* . . . Philadelphia, 1905.
Clark, Walter, ed., *Histories of the Several Regiments and Battalions from North Carolina in the Great War, 1861–65.* 5 vols. Raleigh, N.C., 1901.
Clark, William, ed., *History of Hampton Battery F, Independent Pennsylvania Light Artillery.* Pittsburgh, 1909.
Cudworth, Warren H., *History of the First Regiment Massachusetts Infantry.* Boston, 1866.
Fox, William F., ed., *New York at Gettysburg.* 3 vols. Albany, 1900.
Gates, Theodore B., *The "Ulster Guard" [20th N.Y. State Militia] and the War of the Rebellion.* New York, 1879.
Glover, Edwin A., *Bucktailed Wildcats, A Regiment of Civil War Volunteers.* New York, 1960.
Gregg, David McM., *The Second Cavalry Division of the Army of the Potomac in the Gettysburg Campaign.* Philadelphia, 1907.
Haines, Alanson A., *History of the Fifteenth Regiment New Jersey Volunteers.* New York, 1883.
Harrison, Walter, *Pickett's Men, A Fragment of War History.* New York, 1870.
Hays, Gilbert A., and William H. Morrow, *Under the Red Patch, Story of the Sixty-third Regiment, Pennsylvania Volunteers, 1861–1864.* Pittsburgh, 1908.
Kiefer, William R., *History of the 153d Regiment, Pennsylvania Volunteers. . . , 1862–1863.* Easton, Pa., 1909.
Marvin, Edwin E., *The Fifth Regiment Connecticut Volunteers, A History.* . . . Hartford, 1889.
Moyer, H. P., *History of the Seventeenth Regiment Pennsylvania Volunteer Cavalry.* Lebanon, Pa., 1911.
Muffly, J. W., ed., . . . *A History of the 148th Pennsylvania Vols.* Des Moines, Ia., 1904.
Mulholland, St. Clair A., *The Story of the 116th Regiment Pennsylvania Volunteers.* . . . Philadelphia, 1903.
Naisawald, L. Van Loan, *Grape and Canister, The Story of the Field Artillery in the Army of the Potomac, 1861–1865.* New York, 1960.
Nicholson, John P., and Lewis E. Beitler, eds., *Pennsylvania at Gettysburg.* 3 vols. Harrisburg, 1914.
Nolan, Alan T., *The Iron Brigade: A Military History.* New York, 1961.
Norton, Oliver W., *Strong Vincent and His Brigade at Gettysburg, July 2, 1863.* Chicago, 1909.
Oates, William C., *The War between the Union and the Confederacy and Its Lost Opportunities, with a History of the 15th Alabama Regiment.* . . . New York, 1905.
Page, Charles, *History of the Fourteenth Regiment, Connecticut Volunteer Infantry.* Meriden, Conn., 1906.
Pickett, La Salle Corbell, *Pickett and His Men.* Atlanta, 1899.

BIBLIOGRAPHY

Porter, John T., ed., *Under the Maltese Cross. . . , Campaigns 155th Pennsylvania Regiment. . . .* Pittsburgh, 1910.
Publication Committee of the Regimental Association, *History of the Eighteenth Regiment of Cavalry Pennsylvania Volunteers.* New York, 1909.
Pullen, John J., *The Twentieth Maine. . . .* Philadelphia and New York, 1957.
Pyne, Henry R., *Ride to War: The History of the First New Jersey Cavalry,* ed. Earl S. Miers. New Brunswick, N.J., 1961.
Quint, Alonzo H., *The Record of the Second Massachusetts Infantry, 1861-65.* Boston, 1867.
Rauscher, Frank, *Music on the March, 1862-65. . . . 114th Reg't P. V., Collis' Zouaves.* Philadelphia, 1892.
Regimental History Committee, *History of the Third Pennsylvania Cavalry . . . in the American Civil War, 1861-1865.* Philadelphia, 1905.
Robertson, James I., Jr., *The Stonewall Brigade.* Baton Rouge, La., 1963.
Schenck, Martin, *Up Came Hill, The Story of the Light Division and Its Leaders.* Harrisburg, 1958.
Smith, Donald L., *The Twenty-fourth Michigan of the Iron Brigade.* Harrisburg, 1962.
Stevens, C. A., *Berdan's United States Sharpshooters in the Army of the Potomac, 1861-1865.* St. Paul, Minn., 1892.
Stevenson, David, *Indiana's Roll of Honor.* Indianapolis, 1864.
Stewart, Robert L., *History of the One Hundred and Fortieth Regiment Pennsylvania Volunteers.* [No place], 1912.
Storrs, John W., *The Twentieth Connecticut, A Regimental History.* Ansonia, Conn., 1886.
Survivors' Association, *History of the 121st Regiment Pennsylvania Volunteers. . . .* Philadelphia, 1906.
Survivors' Association, *History of the Corn Exchange Regiment, 118th Pennsylvania Volunteers.* Philadelphia, 1888.
Swinton, William, *Campaigns of the Army of the Potomac.* New York, 1866.
Sypher, J. R., *History of the Pennsylvania Reserve Corps.* Lancaster, Pa., 1865.
Thomson, O. R. Howard, and William H. Rauch, *History of the "Bucktails". . . .* Philadelphia, 1906.
Toombs, Samuel, *New Jersey Troops in the Gettysburg Campaign. . . .* Orange, N.J., 1888.
Vautier, John D., *History of the 88th Pennsylvania Volunteers in the War for the Union, 1861-1865.* Philadelphia, 1894.
Walker, Francis A., *History of the Second Corps in the Army of the Potomac.* New York, 1886.
Ward, Joseph R. C., *History of the One Hundred and Sixth Regiment Pennsylvania Volunteers. . . .* Philadelphia, 1906.
Williamson, James J., *Mosby's Rangers. . . .* New York, 1909.
Wise, George, *Campaigns and Battles of the Army of Northern Virginia.* New York, 1906.
Wise, Jennings C., *The Long Arm of Lee, The History of the Artillery of the Army of Northern Virginia.* New York, 1959.

BOOKS ABOUT THE CAMPAIGN AND BATTLE

Bachelder, John B., *Bachelder's New Historical Guide Book: Gettysburg, What to See and How to See It.* Boston, 1889.
————, *Descriptive Key to the Painting of the Repulse of Longstreet's Assault at the Battle of Gettysburg.* New York, 1870.
Battine, Cecil, *The Crisis of the Confederacy, A History of Gettysburg and the Wilderness.* London, 1905.

Beecham, Robert K., *Gettysburg, The Pivotal Battle of the Civil War.* Chicago, 1911.

Bellah, James W., *Soldier's Battle, Gettysburg.* New York, 1962.

Bigelow, John, Jr., *The Campaign of Chancellorsville.* New Haven, 1912.

Brown, Andrew, *Geology of the Gettysburg Campaign.* (Educational Series No. 5, Bureau of Topographic and Geologic Survey, Pennsylvania Department of Internal Affairs.) Harrisburg, [no date].

Catton, Bruce, *Glory Road: The Bloody Route from Fredericksburg to Gettysburg.* New York, 1952.

———, *Never Call Retreat.* (Centennial History of the Civil War, III.) New York, 1965.

Dalbiac, P. H., *American War of Secession, 1863: Chancellorsville and Gettysburg.* London and New York, 1911.

De Peyster, John Watts, *Before, At, and After Gettysburg.* New York, 1887.

Ditterline, T., *Sketch of the Battles of Gettysburg, July 1st, 2nd, and 3d, 1863. . . .* New York, 1864.

Doubleday, Abner, *Chancellorsville and Gettysburg.* New York, 1882.

———, *Gettysburg Made Plain.* New York, 1888.

Dowdey, Clifford, *Death of a Nation: The Story of Lee and His Men at Gettysburg.* New York, 1958.

Downey, Fairfax, *The Guns at Gettysburg.* New York, 1958.

———, *Clash of Cavalry; The Battle of Brandy Station, June 9, 1863.* New York, 1959.

Drake, Samuel Adams, *The Battle of Gettysburg, 1863.* Boston, 1892.

Everett, Edward, *Address of Edward Everett at the National Cemetery, Gettysburg, November 19, 1863.* Boston, 1864.

Gross, George J., *The Battlefield of Gettysburg.* Philadelphia, 1866.

Hoke, Jacob, *The Great Invasion of 1863. . . .* New York, 1959.

Humphreys, A. A., *Gettysburg to the Rapidan, The Army of the Potomac, July, 1863, to April, 1864.* New York, 1883.

Jacobs, M., *Notes on the Rebel Invasion of Maryland and Pennsylvania and the Battle of Gettysburg, July 1st, 2nd and 3d, 1863.* Philadelphia, 1864.

Klein, Frederic S., ed., *Just South of Gettysburg.* Westminster, Md., 1963.

Longstreet, Helen Dortsch, *Lee and Longstreet at High Tide; Gettysburg in the Light of the Official Records.* Gainesville, Ga., 1905.

Meligakes, N. A., *The Spirit of Gettysburg.* Gettysburg, 1950.

Montgomery, J. S., *The Shaping of a Battle: Gettysburg.* Philadelphia and New York, 1959.

Mosby, John S., *Stuart's Cavalry in the Gettysburg Campaign.* New York, 1908.

Nelson, A. H., *The Battles of Chancellorsville and Gettysburg.* Minneapolis, 1899.

Norton, Oliver W., *The Attack and Defense of Little Round Top, Gettysburg, July 2, 1863.* New York, 1913.

Nye, Wilbur S., *Here Come the Rebels!* Baton Rouge, La., 1965.

Paris, Louis Philippe Albert d'Orleans, Comte de, *The Battle of Gettysburg.* Philadelphia, 1907.

Spear, William E., *The North and the South at Antietam and Gettysburg.* Boston, 1908.

Stackpole, Edward J., *They Met at Gettysburg.* Harrisburg, 1957.

Stewart, George R., *Pickett's Charge.* Boston, 1959.

Storrick, W. C., *Gettysburg: The Place, the Battles, the Outcome.* Harrisburg, 1932.

Tucker, Glenn, *High Tide at Gettysburg: The Campaign in Pennsylvania.* Indianapolis, 1958.

Young, Jesse Bowman, *The Battle of Gettysburg: A Comprehensive Narrative.* New York, 1913.

BIBLIOGRAPHY

ARTICLES ABOUT THE CAMPAIGN AND BATTLE

(The numerous articles published in the *Annals of War,* the *Philadelphia Weekly Times,* and the *Southern Historical Society Papers* are not included in this list.)

Allan, William, "The Strategy of the Gettysburg Campaign. Objects, Progress, Results," *Campaigns in Virginia, Maryland and Pennsylvania, 1862–1863.* (Papers of the Military Historical Society of Massachusetts, III, 415–448.) Boston, 1903.

Ambrose, Stephen E., "A Theorist Fights: Emory Upton in the Civil War," *Civil War History,* IX (Dec., 1963), 341–364.

"Banquet Given by the Historical Society of Pennsylvania, To Celebrate the Ninety-fifth Anniversary of the Birth of Major General George Gordon Meade, December 31, 1910," *Pennsylvania Magazine of History and Biography,* XXXV (No. 1, 1911), 1–40.

Bryant, Edwin E., "The Battle of Gettysburg," *War Papers,* II, 230–275. (Commandery of the State of Wisconsin, MOLLUS.) Milwaukee, 1896.

Carpenter, John A., "General O. O. Howard at Gettysburg," *Civil War History,* IX (Sept., 1963), 261–276.

Coddington, Edwin B., "The Strange Reputation of General George G. Meade: A Lesson in Historiography," *The Historian,* XXIII (No. 2, 1962), 145–166.

Coulter, Victor A., "Smoke at Gettysburg," *Infantry Journal,* XLIV (Jan.–Dec., 1937), 159–160.

Crist, Robert G., "Highwater, 1963: The Confederate Approach to Harrisburg," *Pennsylvania History,* XXX (Apr., 1963), 158–183.

Curtis, Greely S., "Gettysburg (Report of Committee)," *Campaigns in Virginia, Maryland and Pennsylvania, 1862–1863.* (Papers of the Military Historical Society of Massachusetts, III, 357–365.) Boston, 1903.

———, "The Cause of the Confederate Failure at Gettysburg," *Campaigns in Virginia, Maryland and Pennsylvania, 1862–1863.* (Papers of the Military Historical Society of Massachusetts, III, 366–375.) Boston, 1903.

Davis, George B., "From Gettysburg to Williamsport," *Campaigns in Virginia, Maryland and Pennsylvania, 1862–1863.* (Papers of the Military Historical Society of Massachusetts, III, 449–469.) Boston, 1903.

———, "The Operations of the Cavalry in the Gettysburg Campaign," *Cavalry Studies from Two Great Wars.* (International Series, No. 2, Arthur L. Wagner, ed.) Kansas City, Mo., 1896.

———, "The Strategy of the Gettysburg Campaign," *Campaigns in Virginia, Maryland and Pennsylvania, 1862–1863.* (Papers of the Military Historical Society of Massachusetts, III, 376–414.) Boston, 1903.

Driver, William R., "Pickett's Charge at Gettysburg," *Campaigns in Virginia, Maryland and Pennsylvania, 1862–1863.* (Papers of the Military Historical Society of Massachusetts, III, 351–356.) Boston, 1903.

[Foster, J. Y.], "Four Days at Gettysburg," *Harper's New Monthly Magazine,* XXVIII (Feb., 1864), 381–388.

Gibbon, John, "Another View of Gettysburg," *North American Review,* CLII (June, 1891), 704–713.

G[odkin], E. L., "The Gettysburg Celebration," *The Nation,* XLVII (July 12, 1888), 27.

Goodnow, Harold B., "The Battle of Gettysburg," *Annual Report of the American Historical Association for the Year 1895,* 413–432.

Gordon, John B., "Gettysburg," *Scribner's Magazine,* XXXIV (July, 1903), 2–24.

Hardin, Martin D., "Gettysburg Not a Surprise to the Union Commander," *Military Essays and Recollections,* IV, 265–275. (Commandery of the State of Illinois, MOLLUS.) Chicago, 1907.

Hassler, Warren W., Jr., "The First Day's Battle of Gettysburg," *Civil War History,* VI (Sept., 1960), 259–276.

BIBLIOGRAPHY

Jacobs, M., "Later Rambles over the Field of Gettysburg," *United States Service Magazine,* I (1864), 66–76, 158–168.

Johnston, Mary, "Gettysburg," *The Atlantic Monthly,* CX (July, 1912), 1–9.

Kempster, Dr. Walter, "The Cavalry at Gettysburg," *War Papers,* IV, 397–429. (Commandery of the State of Wisconsin, MOLLUS.) Milwaukee, 1914.

Love, William A., "Mississippi at Gettysburg," *Mississippi Historical Society Publications,* IX (1906), 25–51.

Paris, Count of, O. O. Howard, Henry W. Slocum, and Abner Doubleday, "Gettysburg Thirty Years After," *North American Review,* CLII (Feb., 1891), 129–147.

"Presentation of Portrait of Colonel William Brooke Rawle, and an Address on His Military Record," *Pennsylvania Magazine of History and Biography,* XLI (No. 1, 1917), 126–146.

[Review], *The Battle of Gettysburg.* By the Comte de Paris. *The Nation,* XLIII (Oct. 21, 1886), 334–335.

[Review], *The Battle of Gettysburg.* From the *History of the Civil War in America.* By the Comte de Paris. *The Atlantic Monthly,* LVIII (Dec., 1886), 852–856.

Rhodes, James Ford, "The Battle of Gettysburg," *American Historical Review,* IV (July, 1899), 665–677.

Sanger, D. B., "Was Longstreet a Scapegoat?", *Infantry Journal,* XLIII (Jan.–Feb., 1936), 39–45.

Singmaster, Elsie, "Mary Bowman of Gettysburg," *Harper's Monthly Magazine,* CXXV (Oct., 1912), 707–715.

———, "The Battle of Gettysburg, July 1–3, 1863," *The Outlook,* CIV (June 21, 1913), 372–376.

Smith, James Power, "General Lee at Gettysburg," *Petersburg, Chancellorsville, Gettysburg.* (Papers of the Military Historical Society of Massachusetts, V, 377–410.) Boston, 1906.

Weigley, Russell F., "The Emergency Troops in the Gettysburg Campaign," *Pennsylvania History,* XXV (Jan., 1958), 39–57.

W[hite], H., "Gettysburg Thirty Years After," *The Nation,* LVI (May 4, 1893), 326–327.

Whittier, Edward N., "The Left Attack (Ewell's), Gettysburg," *Campaigns in Virginia, Maryland and Pennsylvania, 1862–1863.* (Papers of the Military Historical Society of Massachusetts, III, 315–350.) Boston, 1903.

Young, Jesse B., "Gettysburg," *The Nation,* LXXXIX (Nov. 18, 1909), 483–484.

Index

NOTE: All military units which took part in the battle of Gettysburg are listed under Army of Northern Virginia and Army of the Potomac. Page references include their activity preceding and following the battle. See also, in the general alphabetical list, the names of individuals, e.g., Longstreet; Sickles. Units which were not involved in the Gettysburg battle may be found in the general listing, e.g., Eighteenth Corps.

Hancock, Maj. Gen. Winfield S. (*cont.*)
terattack, 533; loss of his services distresses Meade, 558; claims to have been offered command of Union army, 611n
Hanover, 200, 205, 206, 230, 237, 238, 249, 334, 335, 545
Hanover Court House, 248
Hanover Junction, 51, 53, 68, 102, 115, 117, 168, 170, 225, 545, 565
Hanover road, 314, 334, 337, 430, 482, 486, 521, 522
Hardie, Col. James A., 209, 217, 218, 664n, 665n
Hargbroad, Jacob, 175
Harpers Ferry, 74, 75, 80, 86, 87, 89, 90, 92-95, 97, 121, 122, 129, 130, 132, 185, 204-5, 216, 217, 222-24, 482, 554, 557, 560, 625nn, 653n
Harrisburg, 8, 107, 127, 140, 142, 143, 148, 149, 150, 165, 169, 170, 187, 188, 192, 197, 205, 230, 235, 236, 483, 565, 653n; headquarters of Department of the Susquehanna, 136, 140; Confederate threats to, 144-47
Harrisburg-Carlisle Turnpike, 188
Harrisburg road, 172
Harrisburg Street (Gettysburg), 304
Harrison, James, 180-81, 188-89, 651n
Harrow, Brig. Gen. William, 512, 518
Hart, Capt. J. F., 56, 525
Hart, Capt. Patrick, 745n
Haskell, Lieut. Frank, 528, 531, 800-1n
Haskell, Maj. J. C., 515
Haupt, Brig. Gen. Herman, 541, 545-46, 557, 811n, 812n, 815n
Hayden, Lieut. Col. Julius, 328-29
Hay Market, 112
Hays, Brig. Gen. Alexander, 98, 508-9, 527, 531, 558; leads detachment against Confederates, 514; describes effects of volley on Pickett's forces, 514; comments on Meade, 573
Hays, Brig. Gen. William, 816n; replaces Hancock, 558
Hazard, Capt. John G., 477, 497, 510, 784n
Hazlett, Lieut. Charles E., 392, 478; killed, 396
Heidlersburg, 189, 190, 191, 192, 193, 195, 200, 206, 282
Heidlersburg road, 281, 287, 290, 291, 292
Heintzelman, Maj. Gen. Samuel P., 95, 96-97, 99, 221, 223
Heiser, Lieut. Col. Theodore, 517

Henry repeating rifles, 254-55, 257
Herr Ridge, 266, 271, 378, 379
Herr's Tavern, 380
Heth, Maj. Gen. Henry, 197, 263-64, 267, 272-75, 280, 309-10, 444, 459, 570-72, 605n
High Knob Pass, 555
High Water Mark of the Confederacy, 517
Hill, Lieut. Gen. Ambrose Powell, 172, 193-95, 263-64, 274, 280, 293, 309-10, 318, 444-45 459; temporary commander of Second Corps, 11; commander of Third Corps, 12; left in charge at Fredericksburg, 52; objects to Lee's plan to attack, 371; criticized for Anderson's mode of attack, 425-26; relations with Longstreet, 489
Hill, Maj. Gen. D. H., 15-16, 67, 68, 117, 604n; difficulties with Lee, 18-21; comments on Dix's threat to Richmond, 102
Hilltown, 166
"Historicus," 348, 408, 721-22n, 747n, 748n
Hitchcock, Sgt., 784n
Hitchcock, Gen. Ethan Allen, 215
Hofmann, Col. J. William, 269
Hollidaysburg, 140
Hood, Maj. Gen. John B., 537; rejoins First Corps, 18; comments on Lee, 197; Longstreet denies permission to change line of attack, 382; wounded, 402, 749n
Hood's Mill, 199
Hooker, Maj. Gen. Joseph, 181, 219, 222, 260; prepares to advance on Richmond, 4; defeated at Chancellorsville, 4; comments on Confederate fighting, 24-25; reorganization of Army of the Potomac, 26-31, 40-42; demotes Hunt, 30-31; mistakes at Chancellorsville, 33-34; rationalizations, 34, 609n; Union army's lack of confidence in, after Chancellorsville, 35-38, 45-46; difficulties with Halleck, 42-44; appoints Pleasonton as cavalry chief, 43; and infantry corps commanders, 44-45; preparations to protect Washington and Harpers Ferry, 49-53; uncertainty concerning Lee's plans, 52, 623n; preparations for Battle of Brandy Station, 54-56; proposes strategy after Brandy Station, 66-67, 70-71; prepares to meet possible threats by Lee, 69-71; loses initiative to Lee, 71; indecisive-

Newton, Maj. Gen. John, 326, 333, 342-
43, 449-50, 452, 477, 690n, 805n; re-
places Reynolds, 275, 558; command
on July 3, 481
New Windsor, 229, 231
New York Herald, 243, 348
New York militia, 137; thirty-day regt.,
560
New York Monuments Commission for
the Battlefields of Gettysburg and
Chattanooga: report, 340-41
Nicholls, Brig. Gen. Francis R. T., 91
Nine-month men, 98, 560, 797n, 816n
Norfolk, 51, 100, 101
North Anna River, 101
North Carolina: Union forces transferred
to Maryland Heights, 560
Northern Central Railroad, 165, 168, 170

Oak Hill, 278, 286, 288, 289, 462, 486
Oak Ridge, 251, 266, 267, 278, 282, 286,
287, 288, 289, 295, 537
Oates, Col. William C., 391-94, 742nn
Occoquan River, 113
Officers, shortage of, in Army of North-
ern Virginia, 11-12
*Official Records of the Union and Con-
federate Armies*, 248
Olmsted, Frederick Law: comments on
Meade, 210-11
O'Neal, Col. E. A., 289
168th New York regt., 816n
169th Pennsylvania regt., 816n
172d Pennsylvania regt., 816n
Orange and Alexandria Railroad, 54, 69,
71, 75; bridge, 48, 55
Orange and Fredericksburg Railroad, 81
Ordnance, 90, 253-58, 251
O'Rorke, Col. Patrick H., 334, 395, 743-
44n; killed, 396
Osborn, Maj. Thomas W., 279, 298,
789n; comments on Confederate cannonade, 495; advises cessation of
Union fire during Confederate cannonade, 498; comments on damage to
Brockenbrough's Brigade, 506; comments on Meade's manner on July 3,
530

Paine, Capt. W. W., 330
Pardee, Col. Ario, Jr., 472
Pardee (Ario) Field, 467
Parker, Capt. I. B., 324
Parker, Joel, 139
Parr Ridge, 239
Parrotts (10-pounder) cannon, 251

Parsons, Lieut. Augustin N., 804n
Patrick, Col. John H., 473, 735n
Patrick, Brig. Gen. Marsena R., 219,
226-27, 332, 496, 541; comments on
Hooker, 84; criticizes Hooker for confusion at Potomac crossing, 125-26;
comments on Butterfield, 219, 558;
confirms Buford's report on engagement at Falling Waters, 571
Paul, Brig. Gen. Gabriel R., 287
Peace sentiment, in Pennsylvania, 141
Peach Orchard, 336, 344, 345, 353, 372,
373, 377, 378, 380, 381, 382, 383, 395,
397, 400, 404, 405, 407, 412, 414, 415,
417, 419, 462, 477, 478, 485; salient,
353, 355, 385, 386, 397, 405, 412,
725n
Pemberton, Lt. Gen. John C., 7
Pender, Maj. Gen. William D., 316, 537,
605n; comments on marching, 23; comments on Lee, 105; comments on Pennsylvania and Pennsylvanians, 156; comments on Confederate depredations in
Pennsylvania, 177; wounded, 429
Pendleton, Brig. Gen. W. N.: chief of artillery and headquarters liaison officer,
13; comment on hour of attack, 370;
reconnaissance, 372; places howitzers
at Alexander's disposal, 485, takes
back four, 791n; lack of authority over
batteries, 499
Peninsular campaign, 213
Pennington, Lieut. A. C. M., Jr., 522,
802n
Pennsylvania and Pennsylvanians: Con-
federate impressions of, 156-58
Pennsylvania Canal, 147, 641n
Pennsylvania Central Railroad, 139, 168
Pennsylvania Dutch (Germans), 141
Pennsylvania General Assembly, 141
Pennsylvania Reserve Corps, 96, 97, 98;
2d brigade, 96, 97, 626n
Pennsylvanians: reluctance to join fed-
eral militia, 135-37; apathy when faced
with invasion, 140-42; reactions to ar-
rival of Confederates, 149-52
Perrin, Col. Abner, 293, 294; criticizes
Lee and Anderson, 316
Petersburg, 101, 158, 190, 191
Pettigrew, Brig. Gen. J. J., 181, 197, 232,
263, 425, 461, 489-90, 772n; killed,
571
Philadelphia, 8, 9, 144, 147, 148, 150,
236
Philadelphia, Wilmington and Baltimore
Railroad, 150